Labour Law

Labour Law offers a comprehensive and critical account of the subject by a team of prominent labour lawyers, and includes both collective labour rights and individual employment rights. As the book places the law in its social, economic and political contexts, and shows how the law works in practice through case-studies, students will acquire not only a good knowledge of the law but also an appreciation of its importance and the complexity of the issues. Fully updated with recent developments in the field, the text's clear structure, logical chapter organisation, and uncluttered text design combine to make it a truly accessible way into the subject.

Suitable for undergraduates and postgraduates studying British labour and employment law, this book is a must-read for those wishing to excel in the field.

Hugh Collins is Vinerian Professor of English Law at the University of Oxford.

K. D. Ewing is Professor of Public Law at King's College London.

Aileen McColgan is a barrister at 11 KBW and Professor of Law and Social Justice at the University of Leeds.

The Law in Context Series

Editors: William Twining (University College London),
Maksymilian Del Mar (Queen Mary, University of London) and
Bronwen Morgan (University of New South Wales).

Since 1970 the Law in Context series has been at the forefront of the movement to broaden the study of law. It has been a vehicle for the publication of innovative scholarly books that treat law and legal phenomena critically in their social, political and economic contexts from a variety of perspectives. The series particularly aims to publish scholarly legal writing that brings fresh perspectives to bear on new and existing areas of law taught in universities. A contextual approach involves treating legal subjects broadly, using materials from other social sciences and from any other discipline that helps to explain the operation in practice of the subject under discussion. It is hoped that this orientation is at once more stimulating and more realistic than the bare exposition of legal rules. The series includes original books that have a different emphasis from traditional legal textbooks, while maintaining the same high standards of scholarship. They are written primarily for undergraduate and graduate students of law and of other disciplines, but will also appeal to a wider readership. In the past, most books in the series have focused on English law, but recent publications include books on European law, globalisation, transnational legal processes and comparative law.

Roberts & Palmer: *Dispute Processes: ADR and the Primary Forms of Decision-Making*
Rowbottom: *Democracy Distorted: Wealth, Influence and Democratic Politics*
Sauter: *Public Services in EU Law*
Scott & Black: *Cranston's Consumers and the Law*
Seneviratne: *Ombudsmen: Public Services and Administrative Justice*
Seppänen: *Ideological Conflict and the Rule of Law in Contemporary China*
Siems: *Comparative Law, 2nd Edition*
Stapleton: *Product Liability*
Stewart: *Gender, Law and Justice in a Global Market*
Tamanaha: *Law as a Means to an End: Threat to the Rule of Law*
Turpin & Tomkins: *British Government and the Constitution: Text and Materials*
Twining: *Globalisation and Legal Theory*
Twining: *Rethinking Evidence: Exploratory Essays*
Twining: *General Jurisprudence: Understanding Law from a Global Perspective*
Twining: *Human Rights, Southern Voices: Francis Deng, Abdullahi An-Na'im, Yash Ghai and Upendra Baxi*
Twining: *Jurist in Context*
Twining & Miers: *How to Do Things with Rules*
Ward: *A Critical Introduction to European Law*
Ward: *Law, Text, Terror*
Ward: *Shakespeare and Legal Imagination*
Wells & Quick: *Lacey, Wells and Quick: Reconstructing Criminal Law*
Zander: *Cases and Materials on the English Legal System*
Zander: *The Law-Making Process*

International Journal of Law in Context: A Global Forum for Interdisciplinary Legal Studies

The *International Journal of Law in Context* is the companion journal to the Law in Context book series; it provides a forum for interdisciplinary legal studies and offers intellectual space for ground-breaking critical research. It publishes contextual work about law and its relationship with other disciplines including but not limited to science, literature, humanities, philosophy, sociology, psychology, ethics, history and geography. More information about the journal and how to submit an article can be found at http://journals .cambridge.org/ijc.

Labour Law

Second Edition

HUGH COLLINS
University of Oxford

K. D. EWING
King's College, London

AILEEN MCCOLGAN
University of Leeds

CAMBRIDGE
UNIVERSITY PRESS

CAMBRIDGE
UNIVERSITY PRESS

University Printing House, Cambridge CB2 8BS, United Kingdom

One Liberty Plaza, 20th Floor, New York, NY 10006, USA

477 Williamstown Road, Port Melbourne, VIC 3207, Australia

314–321, 3rd Floor, Plot 3, Splendor Forum, Jasola District Centre, New Delhi – 110025, India

79 Anson Road, #06–04/06, Singapore 079906

Cambridge University Press is part of the University of Cambridge.

It furthers the University's mission by disseminating knowledge in the pursuit of education, learning, and research at the highest international levels of excellence.

www.cambridge.org
Information on this title: www.cambridge.org/9781316515747
DOI: 10.1017/9781108617758

First edition 2012
Second edition 2019

Printed in Printed in the United Kingdom by TJ International Ltd. Padstow Cornwall

A catalogue record for this publication is available from the British Library.

Library of Congress Cataloging-in-Publication Data
Names: Collins, Hugh, 1953– author. | Ewing, K. D. (Keith D.), author. | McColgan, Aileen, author.
Title: Labour law / Hugh Collins, University of Oxford; K. D. Ewing, King's College, London; Aileen McColgan, University of Leeds.
Description: Cambridge, United Kingdom ; New York, NY : Cambridge University Press, 2019. | Series: The law in context series | Includes bibliographical references and index.
Identifiers: LCCN 2019003352 | ISBN 9781316515747 (hardback : alk. paper) | ISBN 9781108462211 (pbk. : alk. paper)
Subjects: LCSH: Labor laws and legislation–Great Britain.
Classification: LCC KD3009 .C649 2019 | DDC 344.4101–dc23
LC record available at https://lccn.loc.gov/2019003352

ISBN 978-1-316-51574-7 Hardback
ISBN 978-1-108-46221-1 Paperback

Contents

Preface

This textbook aims to provide a comprehensive study guide for students on labour law or employment law courses. It is divided into twenty chapters, corresponding approximately to a full-year university course. It includes both a comprehensive discussion of collective labour law issues as well as individual employment law disputes. For shorter or more focused courses, teachers may prefer to concentrate on some of the chapters or parts of the book and will find that each chapter is largely self-contained. As well as providing a description and analysis of the law in Great Britain, in the spirit of the *Law in Context* series, the textbook offers criticisms of the law drawn from different perspectives and disciplines. Most chapters also include brief vignettes, often based on examples drawn from the news, which should provide a stimulus to classroom discussion.

The second edition of this book has retained the same organisation of chapters as the first. As before, responsibility for the different chapters has been divided unevenly: Collins: Chapters 1, 3–7, 10, 11 and 18–20; Ewing: Chapters 2, 8 and 12–17; and McColgan: Chapter 9. The second edition examines recent legislation including notably the Children and Families Act 2014, the Modern Slavery Act 2015, the Trade Union Act 2016, the National Minimum Wage Regulations 2015, and the Shared Parental Leave Regulations 2014. There is extensive discussion of recent cases in the courts including controversial decisions about employment status in the Supreme Court, such as *Pimlico Plumbers Ltd* v. *Smith*, and innovative decisions of the European Court of Human Rights regarding the right to privacy, such as *Bărbulescu* v. *Romania*. At the time of writing, other important appeals are pending, notably in *Uber* v. *Aslam*.

In the years since the first edition, perhaps the most significant legal development in practice was the introduction by the Coalition government of substantial fees in employment tribunals. This had the predictable effect of reducing sharply the number of tribunal applications, as the cost of enforcing many of the legal rights described in this book was rendered prohibitive for most workers. In *R (Unison)* v. *Lord Chancellor*, however, the Supreme Court ruled that the tribunal fees were unlawful because they violated the rule of law and disproportionately obstructed the constitutional right to access to justice.

Lord Reed reminded governments that 'When Parliament passes laws creating employment rights ... it does so not merely in order to confer benefits on individual employees, but because it has decided that it is in the public interest that those rights should be given effect.'

But although fees have been removed, access to justice continues to be a concern, as does the evidence of non-compliance with workers' rights by employers, whether it be the statutory minimum wage or maternity rights. There is also concern about the emergence of a new 'precariat', and the development of new precarious forms of employment, often beyond any significant regulatory protection. More alarming still, however, has been the evidence of new forms of exploitation, whether they be trafficking, forced labour, or modern slavery, and with them the need for legal responses to behaviour that we thought had long been eradicated from modern civilisation.

This edition will be published in the centenary year of the International Labour Organization (ILO), the work of which is referred to in the pages that follow. Now an agency of the United Nations, the ILO is one of the oldest international organisations in existence, having operated continuously ever since 1919. Much of the Organization's work continues to be highly relevant, not least its commitment to the principle that 'labour is not a commodity', all the more relevant today as workers are constantly degraded as objects in 'labour markets'. But although we can celebrate the ILO's institutional survival as the conscience of the international community, we have a long way to go before we can celebrate its unequivocal institutional success. If anything, labour law is experiencing an era of sustained regression after long periods of progress. A matter of real anxiety in particular is the rapid decline in collective bargaining coverage in many countries, putting at risk the very principle of tripartism by which the ILO is sustained.

As we reflect on these matters of great importance to workers everywhere, we take this opportunity to renew our thanks to those already acknowledged in the preface to the first edition. On this occasion, we would like to record our debts specifically to Daniel Blackburn (ICTUR), Alan Bogg (Bristol), Nicola Countouris (UCL), Ruth Dukes (Glasgow), Kate Ewing, Michael Ford (Bristol), Mark Freedland (Oxford), John Hendy QC, Carolyn Jones (Institute of Employment Rights), Ewan McGaughey (KCL), Virginia Mantouvalou (UCL), Tonia Novitz (Bristol), Keith Puttick (Staffordshire), Hannah Reed (formerly TUC, now RCN), Joo-Cheong Tham (Melbourne), and Jeff Vogt (Solidarity Center, formerly International Trade Union Confederation). We are grateful to the editors of this series and the publishers at Cambridge University Press for their encouragement for revising the book and their patience in awaiting its delivery.

We have endeavoured to state the law up to 1 January 2019. At the time of writing, the issue of whether, when, and on what terms the United Kingdom would leave the European Union was unresolved. We have assumed, however, that whatever happens, in the short term there will be no significant changes to the substantive law described in this work.

HC
KDE
AMcC
10 May 2019

Acknowledgements

Every attempt has been made to secure permission to reproduce copyright material in this title and grateful acknowledgement is made to the authors and publishers of all reproduced material. In particular, the publishers would like to acknowledge the following for granting permission to reproduce material from the following publications: Trades Union Congress, *Hard Work, Hidden Lives* (2007); and UNISON, Rules: Schedule D (2011).

Table of Cases

Table of Statutes

Table of Statutory Instruments

Table of European Union Instruments

Table of ILO Instruments

Table of Other International Instruments

Abbreviations

AC	Appeal Cases
ACAS	Advisory, Conciliation and Arbitration Service
ACTTS	Association of Cinematograph, Television and Allied Technicians
AEEU	Amalgamated Engineering and Electrical Union
All ER	All England Law Reports
ALR	American Law Reports
AML	additional maternity leave
APEX	Association of Professional, Executive, Clerical and Computer Staff
ASLEF	Associated Society of Locomotive Engineers and Firemen
ASTMS	Association of Scientific, Technical and Managerial Staffs
AUEFW	Amalgamated Union of Engineering and Foundry Workers
AUEW	Amalgamated Union of Engineering Workers
BALPA	British Airline Pilots' Association
BECTU	Broadcasting Entertainment Cinematograph and Theatre Union
BEIS	Department for Business, Energy and Industrial Strategy
BIS	Department for Business, Innovation and Skills
BNP	British National Party
BRB	British Railways Board
BT	British Telecommunications plc
CA	Court of Appeal
CAC	Central Arbitration Committee
CBI	Confederation of British Industry
CEEP	European Centre for Employers and Enterprises Providing Public Services
CFA	ILO Freedom of Association Committee
ChD	Chancery Division

CJEU	Court of Justice of the European Union
CMLR	Common Market Law Reports
CPS	Crown Prosecution Service
CWU	Communication Workers Union
DDA 1995	Disability Discrimination Act 1995
DG	Directorate General
DR	Decisions and Reports of the European Commission of Human Rights
DTI	Department of Trade and Industry
EAT	Employment Appeal Tribunal
EC	European Community/European Communities
ECHR	European Convention on Human Rights
ECJ	European Court of Justice
ECommHR	European Commission on Human Rights
ECR	European Court Reports
ECtHR	European Court of Human Rights
EDT	effective date of termination
EEA	European Economic Area
EEC	European Economic Community
EEPTU	Electrical Electronic Telecommunications and Plumbing Union
EHRR	European Human Rights Reports
EMLR	Entertainment and Media Law Reports
EqA 2010	Equality Act 2010
EqPA 1970	Equal Pay Act 1970
ERA 1996	Employment Rights Act 1996
ET	employment tribunal
ETI	Ethical Trade Initiative
ETOR	economic, technical or organisational reason
ETUC	European Trade Union Confederation
EU	European Union
EWC	European Works Council
EWC	expected week of confinement
EWCA	England and Wales Court of Appeal
EWHC	England and Wales High Court
FBU	Fire Brigades Union
FSR	Fleet Street Reports
GCHQ	Government Communications Headquarters
GDPR	General Data Protection Regulation
GLA	Gangmasters Licensing Authority
GLAA	Gangmasters and Labour Abuse Authority
GMB	General Municipal and Boilermakers Union
GOR	genuine occupational requirement

GPMU	Graphical, Paper and Media Union
GSP	Generalised System of Preferences
GUF	Global Union Federation
HC	House of Commons
HL	House of Lords
HMRC	Her Majesty's Revenue and Customs
HMSO	Her Majesty's Stationery Office
HRA 1998	Human Rights Act 1998
HRM	Human Resources Management
HSE	Health and Safety Executive
ICCPR	International Covenant on Civil and Political Rights 1966
ICE Regulations	Information and Consultation of Employees Regulations 2004
ICFTU	International Confederation of Free Trade Unions
ICO	Information Commissioner's Office
ICR	Industrial Cases Reports
ICTU	Irish Congress of Trade Unions
ILO	International Labour Organization
IRLR	Industrial Relations Law Reports
ITF	International Transport Workers' Federation
ITUC	International Trade Union Confederation
IUF	International Union of Foodworkers
KB	King's Bench
MP	Member of Parliament
MR	Master of the Rolls
MSF	Manufacturing, Science and Finance Union
NAECI	National Agreement for the Electrical Contracting Industry
NALGO	National and Local Government Officers' Association
NAS/UWT	National Association of Schoolmasters/Union of Women Teachers
NATSOPA	National Society of Operative Printers, Graphical and Media Personnel
NCP	National Contact Point
NGA	National Graphical Association
NGH	National Group on Homeworking
NGO	Non-Governmental Organisation
NHS	National Health Service
NICA	Northern Ireland Court of Appeal
NIRC	National Industrial Relations Court
NISA	News International Staff Association
NMW	National Minimum Wage

NMWA 1998	National Minimum Wage Act 1998
NMWR 2015	National Minimum Wage Regulations 2015
NUGSAT	National Union of Gold, Silver and Allied Trades
NUJ	National Union of Journalists
NUM	National Union of Mineworkers
NUPE	National Union of Public Employees
NUR	National Union of Railwaymen
NUT	National Union of Teachers
ODW	overseas domestic worker
OECD	Organization of Economic Co-operation and Development
OFSTED	Office for Standards in Education, Children's Services and Skills
OJ	Official Journal of the European Communities/Union
OML	ordinary maternity leave
PCP	provision, criterion or practice
PCS	Public and Commercial Services Union
POA	Prison Officers' Association
POEU	Post Office Engineering Union
QB	Queen's Bench
QBD	Queen's Bench Division
RMT	National Union of Rail, Maritime and Transport Workers
RORR	range of reasonable responses
RRA 1976	Race Relations Act 1976
SBWU	Swedish Building Workers' Union
SC	Supreme Court
SCC	Supreme Court of Canada
SCR	Supreme Court Reports
SDA 1975	Sex Discrimination Act 1975
ShPP	shared parental pay
SI	Statutory Instrument
SLT	Scots Law Times
SNB	Special Negotiating Body
SOGAT	Society of Graphical and Allied Trades
SPL	shared parental leave
TEU	Treaty on European Union
TFEU	Treaty on the Functioning of the European Union
TGWU	Transport and General Workers Union
TICE Regulations	Transnational Information and Consultation of Employees Regulations 1999
TLR	Times Law Reports
TNCs	transnational corporations

TPP	Trans-Pacific Partnership
TSSA	Transport Salaried Staffs' Association
TTIP	Transatlantic Trade and Investment Partnership
TUC	Trades Union Congress
TULRCA 1992	Trade Union and Labour Relations (Consolidation) Act 1992
TUPE 2006	Transfer of Undertakings (Protection of Employment) Regulations 2006
UCATT	Union of Construction and Allied Trades and Technicians
UCTA	Unfair Contract Terms Act 1977
UEAPME	European Association of Craft, Small and Medium-sized Enterprises
UKHL	United Kingdom House of Lords
UKSC	United Kingdom Supreme Court
UNI	UNI Global Union (representing service-sector workers)
UNISON	Public Services Union
USDAW	Union of Shop, Distributive and Allied Workers
WLR	Weekly Law Reports
WTD	Working Time Directive
WTO	World Trade Organization

Part I
Introduction

1

Nature and Sources of Labour Law

Contents

What is Labour Law?

What are the aims of labour law? Why is it regarded as a distinct and important field of study? One place to start thinking about these questions is the Universal Declaration of Human Rights, adopted by the United Nations in 1948.

Universal Declaration of Human Rights, Article 23

(1) Everyone has the right to work, to free choice of employment, to just and favourable conditions of work and to protection against unemployment.
(2) Everyone, without any discrimination, has the right to equal pay for equal work.
(3) Everyone who works has the right to just and favourable remuneration ensuring for himself and his family an existence worthy of human dignity, and supplemented, if necessary, by other means of social protection.
(4) Everyone has the right to form and to join trade unions for the protection of his interests.

Article 23 identifies many of the characteristic aims of labour law:

- to secure fair access to labour markets under conditions of equal opportunity;
- to ensure that the conditions under which people work are just, safe, healthy and respectful of human dignity;
- to require pay to be fair and sufficient for a decent standard of living;
- to protect job security and fair treatment at work;
- to permit workers to form trade unions and other representative organisations to protect their interests at work.

The case for studying this subject rests in part on the crucial economic, social and political significance of paid work in a market economy,[1] and in part on the distinctive characteristics and problems that labour law must address.

Significance of Labour Law

For most people, employment provides the principal source of income and wealth. The legal institutions that constitute and govern the relations of production between workers and their employers provide one of the corner-stones of market economies. From a social perspective, work not only occupies a large proportion of most people's days but also provides one of the principal

---

[1] H. Collins, 'Labour Law as a Vocation' (1989) 105 *Law Quarterly Review* 468; K. Klare, 'The Horizons of Transformative Labour Law and Employment Law', in J. Conaghan, R. M. Fischl and K. Klare (eds.), *Labour Law in an Era of Globalization: Transformative Practices and Possibilities* (Oxford University Press, 2002), p. 3.

sites where we can construct social relationships and seek meaning for our lives. The consequence of unemployment is often described as 'social exclusion', which means both that the ensuing poverty prevents individuals from enjoying the benefits of society and that the unemployed are likely to experience less productive and meaningful lives.

From a political perspective the employment relation lies at the centre of a fundamental conflict of interest that is intrinsic to capitalist societies. The conflict lies between the owners of capital, who invest in productive activities, and the workers, who supply the necessary labour. Employers seek to maximise the return on their investments, whereas the workers seek the highest price available for their labour, which digs into the employer's profits. As in other contractual relations, however, the parties ultimately share a common interest in the successful achievement of production and profits through the combination of capital and labour. The balance of strength between the competing interests of capital and labour always constitutes a key issue in politics because it contributes a vital element in the patterns of the distribution of wealth and power to which a society aspires. The law plays a pivotal role in both constituting and restricting the power of both capital and labour. Labour law is assuredly never far from the centre of political debate and controversy.

To examine labour law thoroughly, therefore, it is important to study the legal rules in their economic, social and political context. The details of the legal rules have a profound influence on the efficiency of the economic system, the life-chances of individuals and the type of social justice achieved in society. For example, the rules that prohibit discrimination in access to employment on grounds such as sex, race and disability are intended to ensure that all people can contribute to the generation of wealth, to promote the possibility of equality of opportunity for all citizens and to help to combat patterns of persistent social disadvantage and exclusion for particular groups. Similarly, the legal rules that permit workers to take collective industrial action in order to support their claims for increases in pay and improvements in other terms and conditions have a significant influence on the distribution of wealth and power both within the firm and within society more broadly. The importance of legal rules should not be unduly exaggerated, for broader economic, social and political forces will ultimately shape a society and the experience of its citizens. For example, levels of unemployment, which depend heavily these days on global economic trends and monetary policies, have a profound influence on levels of wages, the bargaining power of workers and, more diffusely, on perceptions of social justice. Nevertheless, the rules of labour law shape how these global economic and social forces become translated into the experiences of workers.

The appreciation of labour law as a fundamental constitutive element in modern societies implies the need to study a vast range of legal rules and institutions. We might study the rules governing access to labour markets, the regulation of any type of transaction involving work, the rules governing organisations of capital and labour, social-welfare systems for handling unemployment, the supply of training and education to workers and the links between workplace relations and broader political institutions. This large terrain trespasses over many fields that have traditionally been studied independently, such as immigration law, social security law, company law and constitutional law. At the same time, labour law requires consideration of a wide range of conceptually distinct categories of law such as contract, tort, public law, social security law and company law. The challenge we face in this book is to provide a selective study of the key legal rules and institutions at the heart of the discipline which forms a coherent whole and which is also of a manageable size. When making this selection, we need to strike a balance also between, on the one hand, a consideration of those legal rules which have a profound influence in shaping the economic and social system and, on the other hand, an examination of laws which have greater daily significance for lawyers. For example, the rules governing trade union organisation and industrial action configure the bargaining power of many workers in the labour market, but in practice most lawyers are far more likely to encounter the rules relating to claims for missing wages, unfair dismissal and discrimination brought by individual workers. Our approach to the scope of labour law is guided by the goal of examining every aspect of the legal regulation of the employment relation, without paying heed to limits set by legal classifications and concepts. Our emphasis upon particular topics, however, depends upon a pragmatic compromise between the need to analyse the fundamental structures supported by the law while providing a full explanation of the rules governing common problems and disputes arising between employers and workers.

The Employment Relation

At the core of the subject, however, we must consider the principal legal relation through which work is performed in a market economy: the contract of employment. This contract resembles other contractual relations in many respects. It is formed by an agreement between two parties: the employer and the employee. It comprises an exchange: the employee promises to perform work in return for a promise by the employer to pay wages and other types of remuneration. Like other contracts, it is legally enforceable in the courts and the parties can claim compensation for breach of its terms. Yet the contract of employment is also distinctive in many respects. These distinctive attributes of the employment relation provide the second principal reason for a separate study of the field of labour law.

A contract of employment is typically a long-term contract for an indefinite period. The agreement is unlikely to be static but rather will be subject to modifications such as alterations in working methods and increases in pay. The contract of employment is also likely to be less specific than other types of contract about the details of the performance required from the worker. The terms are likely to avoid precise specification of the work to be performed, but instead to grant to the employer the right to fix the details of the required performance through subsequent instructions. As a consequence, the contract of employment creates a relation of power in which the employer has the discretion, within limits, to direct labour and the employee has the duty to obey lawful instructions. Surrounding this relation of power, both parties are likely to develop implicit and mutual expectations of fair treatment, trustworthy conduct and co-operation in good faith. These distinctive features of the contract of employment – its indeterminate duration, its variability, its incompleteness and its construction of a relation of subordination surrounded by implicit mutual expectations of trustworthy behaviour – create the need for special regulation beyond the ordinary rules of the law of contract.

Today, this special regulation is generally found in legislation. These laws modify, supplement or replace the terms of the contract of employment. Legislation also regulates the operation of the labour market both to ensure fair access to jobs and to address problems arising from unemployment. The appropriate aims and details of this legislation are often deeply contested political issues. For instance, should workers be guaranteed a minimum wage (and if so how much should it be) or should such a measure be rejected because it may cause higher levels of unemployment among poorly skilled workers, thereby hurting those whom the law is supposed to help the most? To some extent, proposals for labour legislation pose technical questions about the likely costs and benefits of legislation, which can be measured and predicted, although rarely with great precision. We will refer to many such assessments in the course of this book in order to illustrate the effects of the law and a recurrent theme of how difficult it is in a market economy to ensure that desired outcomes are achieved. As well as the special legal regulation of the contract of employment and the labour market, it is also vital to appreciate the significant impact of collective organisations of workers.

The Universal Declaration of Human Rights upholds the right of workers to form trade unions for the purpose of protecting their interests. Trade unions can play many roles in the workplace: conduct collective bargaining with the employer with a view to securing better terms and conditions for the workforce; represent individual workers who are in dispute with their employer; give voice to the concerns of employees about other aspects of their jobs, such as security of employment, their hours of work and their work/life balance and health and safety issues in the workplace. Trade unions can also monitor the employer's compliance with labour legislation and either report breaches of the rules to a regulator or inspector or press for compliance themselves. Although the impact of trade unions on workplaces has declined in recent decades in the United Kingdom (UK) and many other countries, trade unions still retain an important influence in many sectors of the economy, and for many workers they provide more effective protection of their interests than the formal legal mechanisms. For a proper understanding of labour law in practice, it is therefore vital to understand the complementary role played by trade unions in securing the aims of labour law and how the legal framework both supports and controls their activities.

Because work is central to people's lives, both in terms of its provision of material well-being and as a source of meaning and social integration, the idea that employment relations should be regarded merely as an economic transaction has always been contested in labour law. The economist's analysis of labour as a 'factor of production' to be bought or sold like other commodities and machines is challenged by a rival perception that maintains that 'labour is not a commodity'. This slogan insists that, although the market economy drives employers to purchase labour like any other commodity used in production of goods and services, the human beings who provide labour should not be treated like commodities to be bought at the cheapest price possible and discarded when no longer needed. Workers should be accorded the dignity of human beings and should be treated fairly. One important way of expressing this idea is to say that human rights are not discarded at the factory gate or the office reception when the employee comes to work. Labour law must ensure the observance of those fundamental rights by employers.

In particular, the relation of subordination created by the contract of employment grants the employer considerable discretionary power over employees, which creates the risk of the abuse of power, interference with the values represented by human rights law and the danger of unfair treatment. The key power of the employer in this respect is the power of dismissal or termination of the contract of employment. The ever-present threat of dismissal functions to coerce employees to comply with the orders of the employer for fear of losing their jobs and all the associated benefits of social integration. Control over the employer's power of termination of contracts of employment is therefore a key issue in labour law: it protects the right to work, protects the dignity of workers, ensures fair treatment, prevents serious abuses of power and, above all, prevents employers from treating their employees like a commodity that can be discarded at will.

This brief description of the subject of labour law explains the outline of this book. After two introductory chapters that explain the sources of labour law and the issues that confront it in today's world, Part II examines the law governing the contract of employment, Part III considers the principal statutory measures that regulate the employment relationship, Part IV explores the aspect of trade unions and collective labour rights and Part V analyses the law protecting employees against unjust discipline and dismissal. A proper understanding of these topics requires an appreciation of how they are interrelated and why the laws are often interdependent. There are also many cross-cutting themes, such as the protection of human rights at national and international levels in a variety of contexts from the hiring to the firing of employees.

United Kingdom Labour Law

Like most branches of legal studies today, the sources of labour law in the UK combine the common law created by judicial precedent and parliamentary primary and secondary legislation. Apart from shaping the contract of employment, however, the common law plays a diminishing role. As this field of study is deeply contested between the political parties, on being elected each is likely to enact a political programme involving the dismantling and replacement of many aspects of the legislation. Although the UK lacks a labour code, it does have three substantial consolidation statutes. The Trade Union and Labour Relations (Consolidation) Act 1992 (TULRCA 1992) provides the rules regulating trade unions and their members, collective bargaining and the use of industrial action. The Employment Rights Act 1996 (ERA 1996) contains most of the rights granted to individual employees in connection with their employment, such as family-friendly rights and protection against unfair dismissal. The Equality Act (EqA) 2010 consolidates all the laws regarding discrimination in employment. Many new pieces of legislation take the form of amendments to these consolidating statutes. Nevertheless, several other statutes such as the National Minimum Wage Act (NMWA) 1998 and statutory instruments such as the Working Time Regulations 1998 play an important role in the regulation of employment relations. A complete collection of all this labour legislation occupies many thousands of pages.

The history of this legislation will be explained, where appropriate, in the course of the book. But it is worth pointing out at the beginning that most legislation is of fairly recent origin. By the early decades of the twentieth century, the framework of rules governing trade unions, collective bargaining and industrial action was established by the Trade Union Act 1871, the Trade Disputes Act 1906 and the Trade Union Act 1913. These statutes served to confirm collective bargaining between trade unions and employers as the principal legitimate mechanism for determining the terms and conditions of employment. Until the 1960s, apart from wartime measures, Parliament had rarely sought to intervene in the details of contracts of employment directly. Otto Kahn-Freund, who may be described as the founder of studies of labour law in the UK, described this system of labour law as 'collective *laissez faire*',[2] by which he meant that the principal role of labour law was to establish the mechanisms of collective bargaining, but not to regulate such matters as wages and hours directly. While most other industrialised countries introduced mandatory legislation on such matters as maximum hours or minimum wages, the UK followed a distinctive pattern of minimal direct statutory regulation of contracts of employment. For example, unlike in other industrialised countries, until 1998 there was no regulation of maximum hours of

---

[2] O. Kahn-Freund, 'Labour Law', in O. Kahn-Freund, *Selected Writings* (London: Stevens, 1978), pp. 1, 8.

work or minimum wages that applied to all workers, although particular industrial sectors such as mines were closely regulated. This pattern, sometimes dubbed 'legal abstentionism',[3] has now been reversed.

Since the 1960s, Parliament has increasingly intervened to fix mandatory terms of employment or grant statutory rights to employees. Key moments in these interventions were the law of unfair dismissal in 1971, the Sex Discrimination Act (SDA) 1975 (and the Equal Pay Act 1970, which came into effect in 1975) and the National Minimum Wage and Working Time Regulations of 1998. There were many reasons for this increase in the volume of legislation that addresses individual employment relations.[4] As in the case of the anti-discrimination laws, to some extent the legislation responded to a wider concern to protect the rights of individuals through the law. The need for legislative minimum standards became more compelling as the power of trade unions and the effectiveness of collective bargaining to secure good working conditions began to wane in the 1980s. A crucial consideration was always a concern that small disputes should not erupt into strikes and other forms of industrial action because that was harmful to everyone's economic prosperity. Governments were also concerned to help the labour market to work efficiently, both by creating fair equality of opportunity and by removing rigidities and restrictions on the efficient use of labour. Finally, as we shall see shortly, the European Union (EU) pressed for harmonisation of employment laws in many fields.

Nevertheless, it would certainly be incorrect to see in the history of UK labour law a steady rise in employment protection rights during the last fifty years. There was an important resurgence of *laissez-faire* political ideas in the 1980s and early 1990s, under which governments stressed the importance of permitting free markets to work without restrictions either from legislation or from powerful trade unions. That neo-liberal perspective persists to this day in many respects, but it has been qualified by the recognition that, first, some minimum standards are required to protect workers against the worst forms of abuse and exploitation and, secondly, that employment protection laws can actually assist in making the labour market more efficient and business more competitive.[5] For instance, the right of women to return to their job after a period of maternity leave protects them against the unfairness of automatically losing their jobs on having a family; but it also helps to ensure that women are put to their best productive use in the labour market by enabling them to use their skills and experience in a job for which they have been trained, rather than forcing them to start afresh. Although labour laws are always hotly contested in politics owing to their role in shaping the distribution of wealth

---

[3] H. Collins, 'Against Abstentionism in Labour Law', in J. Eekelaar and J. Bell (eds.), *Oxford Essays in Jurisprudence Third Series* (Oxford: Clarendon Press, 1987), p. 79.

[4] P. Davis and M. Freedland, *Labour Legislation and Public Policy* (Oxford University Press, 1993).

[5] H. Collins, 'Regulating the Employment Relation for Competitiveness' (2001) 30 *Industrial Law Journal* 15.

and power in society, the disagreements today mostly revolve around three criteria that are considered important across the political spectrum: the benefits for employers and the wealth of the nation in keeping labour costs down; the importance of protecting workers against unfair treatment and exploitation by setting mandatory minimum standards; and the importance of promoting competitiveness in business by regulatory support for the most productive uses of labour.

European Union Employment Law

Most of the legal materials considered in this book originate from the common law or UK legislation. In recent decades, however, the EU has increasingly exerted an influence on this legislation. As well as the binding Treaty on European Union (2009) (TEU) and the Treaty on the Functioning of the European Union (2009) (TFEU), numerous European Directives require the UK to ensure that its laws conform to harmonised European minimum standards. Following the projected withdrawal of the UK from the EU, although these Treaties will no longer be binding, existing laws based upon EU standards will be retained as binding law in the UK. Subsequently, Parliament may choose to amend those laws, but for the time being the substance of EU employment law remains binding as re-enacted UK law. UK courts can have regard to interpretations placed upon EU Directives and the implementing UK law by the Court of Justice of the EU (CJEU), before 2010 known as the European Court of Justice (ECJ), but the UK courts will no longer be absolutely bound to follow those decisions.[6]

In this introduction, we explain briefly how the power to legislate in the field of labour law has been shared between the EU and its Member States and the complexities of the legal effectiveness of EU legal instruments; we then consider in general the aims and purposes of EU regulation of the labour market and employment relations. More detailed consideration of particular aspects of EU labour law will be found in the relevant chapters.

Competence

In the section of the TFEU headed 'Social Policy', there is, first, in Article 151, a general statement of the aims of the EU, which includes the promotion of employment, the improvement of living and working conditions, the promotion of dialogue in the workplace and the combating of social exclusion. Article 153 then provides that the EU should complement the activities of Member States in certain fields, which includes the power to legislate on certain topics and under certain conditions. Unpacking this carefully

---

[6] European Union (Withdrawal) Act 2018, s. 6.

negotiated allocation of powers with respect to labour law, we can divide labour law issues into three categories:

(1) those fields that are outside the competence of the EU: pay (except discrimination in pay), freedom of association for workers and trade unions and the right to strike or the right to impose lock-outs;

(2) those fields that are within the competence of the EU, but where legislation is only permitted after a unanimous vote of Member States: social security law, dismissal, collective representation for workers and the right of non-EU nationals to work. To this list is added anti-discrimination law under TFEU, Article 19;

(3) those fields which are within the competence of the EU, where legislation can be approved by a majority vote of Member States (under the weighted voting system that grants bigger countries more votes): health and safety, working conditions, information and consultation of workers, equal opportunity of men and women and combating social exclusion.

The TFEU, Article 153, also makes clear that any Directives agreed at the EU level should set only minimum standards, leaving Member States to retain or introduce superior national protections for workers.

An additional procedure for making rules in labour law, known as the Social Dialogue, has been developed under the TFEU, Article 155. Under this procedure, representatives of employers' associations and trade union organisations at a European level may negotiate collective agreements that fix minimum standards in the areas of EU competence. If the 'social partners' agree upon a standard, they may then ask the Council of Ministers to enact it as a Directive. The Council of Ministers still has the power to reject the proposed Directive, but so far it has been unwilling to do so, given that in effect the employers' associations are asking, albeit reluctantly and in fear of worse measures (from their point of view), for the legislation. This procedure has resulted in Directives on parental leave,[7] part-time work[8] and fixed-term work,[9] and it has laid the groundwork for one on agency work.[10]

A further complexity of European law concerns the lack of direct effect of most legislation. Unlike national legislation which grants individuals legal rights that may be claimed directly in courts, EU employment law usually takes the form of a Directive, which is an instruction to Member States to enact legislation[11] in conformity with the principles laid down in the Directive. In the UK, the European Communities Act 1972 enabled Parliament to implement Directives by means of statutory instruments. Unless the Directive has been so implemented, however, it does not usually afford individuals any

---

[7] Directive 96/34; Directive 97/75.   [8] Directive 97/81.   [9] Directive 99/70.
[10] Directive 2008/104.
[11] Or, as occurs in some Member States, legally binding collective agreements: TFEU, Art. 153(3).

legal rights against their employer. It is said that Directives do not have 'direct horizontal effect'.

A Directive that has not been implemented, or not properly implemented, by national legislation does, however, have two significant legal effects:

(1) *Vertical direct effect*: where Directives envisage the granting of legal rights to workers, even though those rights have not been enacted in national law, a worker may be able to claim the promised right against the government or an 'emanation of the State' at least to the extent of obtaining compensation for the failure to enact the right under national law.[12]

(2) *Interpretation or indirect horizontal effect*: the national courts are under a legal obligation to interpret national law in a manner that brings its meaning into conformity with European law. Notice that this obligation applies to all UK law, including legislation that preceded EU law.

The ECJ has insisted that this interpretative obligation is extremely strong:

> When hearing a case between individuals, a national court is required, when applying the provisions of domestic law adopted for the purpose of transposing obligations laid down by a directive, to consider the whole body of rules of national law and to interpret them, so far as possible, in the light of the wording and purpose of the directive in order to achieve an outcome consistent with the objective pursued by the directive.[13]

The ECJ is sending a clear message to national courts that they should interpret national laws in a way that conforms to an EU Directive, even if that means completely distorting the literal meaning of the national law. Even that process of interpretation is not sufficient where a Directive is implementing a 'fundamental principle of EU law'. Although the CJEU has yet to explain the source and scope of these fundamental principles, it is evident that they include a general prohibition on invidious forms of discrimination. In the field of anti-discrimination laws, therefore, a national court is expected to 'disapply' national law if it does not conform to a relevant Directive:

> The need to ensure the full effectiveness of the principle of non-discrimination on grounds of age, as given expression in Directive 2000/78, means that the national court, faced with a national provision falling within the scope of European Union law which it considers to be incompatible with that principle, and which cannot be interpreted in conformity with that principle, must decline to apply that provision, without being either compelled to make or prevented from making a reference to the Court for a preliminary ruling before doing so.[14]

---

[12] Cases C-6/90 and C-9/90, *Francovich and Bonifaci* v. *Italy* [1992] IRLR 161 (ECJ).
[13] Cases C-397/01–C-403/01, *Pfeiffer* v. *Deutsches Rotes Kreuz, Kreisverband Waldshut eV* [2005] IRLR 137 (ECJ).
[14] Case C-555/07, *Kücükdeveci* v. *Swedex GmbH & Co. KG* [2010] IRLR 346 (CJEU).

Although Directives are the main legislative instruments of the EU in labour law, two other types of directly effective EU law should be mentioned. First, the Council of Ministers has the power to make Regulations, which usually grant individuals the right to enforce the applicable rules. Regulations have been made in limited fields relevant to labour law concerned with the free movement of workers throughout the Single Market of the EU, the conflict of laws concerning contracts of employment and with data protection. Secondly, the European treaties can themselves be the source of legal rights between individuals, provided that their provisions are clear and can be interpreted to confer rights on individuals. In the field of labour law, the most significant of such treaty provisions is the one that grants equal pay for male and female workers for equal work or work of equal value.[15]

Effects

Membership of the EU requires acceptance of the principle in the TFEU, Article 45, of free movement of workers throughout the economic area of the Single Market, without discrimination on grounds of nationality. The effect of Article 45, combined with detailed regulations, and read in the light of the establishment of citizenship of the EU by the TEU, Article 20, is that it is possible for workers with EU nationalities to take up jobs, reside with their families and take advantage of the local social security system in any Member State. In particular, EU nationals seeking work in another Member State cannot be denied jobseeker's allowance or its equivalent simply on the ground that they have not been habitually resident in the country in which the social security claim is made; rather, such benefits have to be granted to any EU national who has been genuinely seeking employment for a reasonable period in that state.[16] The law therefore expands the potential size of the labour market enormously.

It was correctly predicted that the treaty provisions for free movement of establishment (capital) and services together with free trade without tariffs within the EU would tend to intensify competition. The consequence would be that Member States would be unable to protect domestic industries from foreign competition, which for inefficient industries would compel major reorganisations, mergers or closure. The foreseeable adverse effect on employment security was not, however, regarded initially as a problem that the EU should address through legislation, because in the long run the benefits of a more competitive market and pressures towards higher productivity and

---

[15] TFEU, Art. 157; Case 43/75, *Defrenne* v. *Sabena* [1976] ECR 455 (ECJ).
[16] Case C-138/02, *Collins* v. *Secretary of State for Work and Pensions* [2005] ICR 37 (ECJ).

innovation would improve the wealth of all the citizens of the EU.[17] Instead, the Social Fund was created to grant regeneration aid to areas affected by high levels of unemployment.[18] Nevertheless, some Directives have introduced common standards for business reorganisations, in particular those concerned with sales of businesses, mass redundancies, consultation and information rights of employees in those contexts and the protection of wages in the event of insolvency. These Directives, which are examined in Chapters 15 and 20, provide workers with some substantive rights aimed at protecting employment security, but their principal objective is to harmonise the required procedures for these types of business reorganisations throughout the EU with a view to subjecting all businesses to roughly equivalent costs.

As the market of the EU has become more integrated through cross-border trade, there have been increasing calls for the introduction of a 'social dimension' to EU law.[19] The call is in effect for the adoption of transnational labour standards, which would establish minimum labour standards across all Member States. This movement received its formal expression in the Community Charter of the Fundamental Social Rights of Workers (10 December 1989), a document that is not legally binding, but which may influence the interpretation of EU law. These social and economic rights have been reasserted in the Charter of Fundamental Rights of the European Union 2007, which was given legal force in the TEU. In the 1990s, the EU passed many Directives that aimed at fixing minimum standards in order to protect employees against the potential adverse effects of the intensification of competition on their working conditions and legal protections. It was feared that national governments would succumb to pressures from business to weaken labour protections in order to make their national economies appear more attractive to inward investment and reduce the cost of labour to employers. This fear of 'social dumping' arising from a competition between Member States to reduce their standards of legal protection for employees provided the EU institutions with a justification to seek to extend their field of action to all aspects of labour law. Perhaps the most significant development from the EU as an aspect of its social dimension was the enactment of comprehensive anti-discrimination laws, which extended beyond sex and race to include religion or belief, disability, age and sexual orientation.[20] Two other key innovations of EU social policy have been the Directives on Working Time[21] and on

---

[17] S. Deakin, 'Labour Law as Market Regulation: The Economic Foundations of European Social Policy', in P. Davies, A. Lyon-Caen, S. Sciarra and S. Simitis (eds.), *European Community Labour Law: Principles and Perspectives* (Oxford University Press, 1996), p. 63.

[18] TFEU, Art. 162.

[19] C. Barnard, 'EU Employment Law and the European Social Model: The Past, the Present and the Future' (2014) 67 *Current Legal Problems* 199.

[20] TFEU, Art. 19; Directive 2000/78 establishing a general framework for equal treatment in employment and occupation.

[21] Directive 2003/88.

Information and Consultation with employee representatives ('works coun-cils').[22] During the last decade or so, opposition to further EU employment law measures led by the UK has prevented any major initiatives in this field.

The vote in the UK referendum to leave the EU was no doubt fuelled at least in part by the consequences of participation in the Single Market and, in particular, free movement of workers. Outside the EU, the UK will be able to control better the migration of workers and flows of capital investment, although the usual aggregate welfare benefits of freedom of movement are likely to lead governments not to erect inconvenient obstructions at the borders. The UK government has promised to keep all workers' rights based on EU law for the time being, but in the longer term there is likely to be divergence from EU standards in cases where a government regards the original EU legislation as unsatisfactory. Furthermore, it is clear that the economically powerful countries that participate in the single currency of the euro have ambitions to achieve deeper and fairer institutions for monetary union by harmonising their taxes, social welfare systems and employment laws. With support from the EU Council and Parliament, the EU Commis-sion's policy is to promote twenty principles of social policy, including employment law measures such as fair wages and protection against unfair dismissal, under the banner of the European Pillar of Social Rights.[23] Even were the UK to remain in the Single Market or to continue to align its employment laws with EU laws, it seems unlikely that it would choose to conform to all of these proposed new employment law rights in the future.

Compliance

Having considered briefly the principal sources of labour law in the common law of the contract of employment, UK legislation and transnational EU employment law, we should examine the perennial problem of securing compliance with labour laws. Labour law uses a wide range of techniques for tackling its objectives. Indeed, one of the distinctive characteristics of this regulation has been the subtlety and variety of its methods for channelling labour markets in ways that are consistent with social and political aims. The most innovative method of regulation has been the use of collective bargaining as a source of rules to govern employment relationships. But labour law also uses private-law techniques such as implied terms in contracts, mandatory standards backed up by criminal penalties, and occasionally public-law prin-ciples, to achieve its ends. The variety of techniques is partly explained by the complexity of the subject matter: not only are there many different kinds of

---

[22] Directive 2002/14.

[23] *European Pillar of Social Rights*, November 2017, https://ec.europa.eu/commission/publications/european-pillar-social-rights-booklet_en.

jobs but employment relations also take many different forms, from the casual hourly paid manual worker to the permanently employed, salaried and bonus-rich managing director of a large multinational enterprise. The variety of legal techniques is, however, more directly driven by considerations of effectiveness and efficiency.

Effectiveness of regulation requires employers and workers to conform to the relevant standards. But effectiveness is constantly undermined by economic incentives for evasion and avoidance. Regulation may impose additional costs upon employers, such as the cost of paying a minimum wage or adopting safety measures; so employers, ever with an eye to profitability, may be reluctant to comply with the law or at least seek to minimise their costs in so doing. At the same time, employees may be reluctant to insist upon any legal rights they may be given for fear of losing their jobs to others who may be prepared to work for wages below the minimum or in unsafe conditions. It is also possible that employees will be unaware of their legal rights derived from contracts or statute. The perennial difficulty that confronts labour law is to render its standards effective.

The efficiency of regulation raises a further set of problems. A government must weigh the costs of regulation against its prospective benefits. Those costs comprise not only the expense to government of administering the system, such as the costs of courts and inspectors, but also the costs imposed upon businesses, often described as 'red tape', which, if significant, may reduce their competitiveness. The task for labour law is to find techniques of regulation that minimise those costs while at the same time achieving as many of the intended benefits of the regulation as possible.

With these perennial problems of effectiveness and efficiency in mind, we can briefly consider the principal regulatory techniques used by labour law.

Regulatory Standards with Criminal Sanctions

Early labour legislation in the nineteenth century typically set standards which were enforceable in the magistrates' courts by criminal penalties. The tasks of monitoring and enforcement of the standards were often given to factory inspectors, who could prosecute an employer for breach of the statutory rules. This criminal law technique of regulation survives to this day primarily in relation to health and safety legislation, but many other statutes such as the NMWA 1998, the Data Protection Act 2018 and the Working Time Regulations 1998 include the possibility of criminal prosecutions. The typical model for this legislation is that the inspector issues an enforcement notice requiring the employer to comply with the law. If the employer fails to comply with that order, then, subject to any appeal by the employer against the order, the inspector will issue a final warning and then bring a prosecution. Conviction of the employer will lead to the imposition on the employer of a fine or even imprisonment.

The strength of this method of regulation lies in its nicely calibrated enforcement pyramid, in which the threats slowly escalate, with the ultimate threat of large fines. Its principal weakness concerns the resources of the inspectorate, which may lack the time and personnel to police compliance with the regulation effectively. In connection with the National Minimum Wage (NMW), for instance, it is claimed that on current resources it will take 350 years for every business to be inspected. In the UK, there are fewer than 600 successful prosecutions of employers for health and safety violations each year, although close to 10,000 enforcement notices are issued.[24] Many employers appear to make the calculation that the costs of extra safety precautions far exceed the risk of incurring the rare costs of complying with an enforcement notice or paying a fine. To some extent this calculation that leads to 'efficient breach of regulation' can be affected by raising the level of fines, but the underlying problem of detection of breaches of the regulations cannot be solved without greatly increasing the costs of inspection.

Individual Civil Claims

In the late twentieth century in the UK, the predominant regulatory technique was to grant individual workers legal rights to seek compensation from the employer for breach of statutory standards. Some of the most important legislation that broadly follows this pattern is the law relating to unfair dismissal and redundancy, discrimination and equal pay. This technique was also developed by the courts much earlier in relation to safety legislation, where the Factories Acts, precursors to the Health and Safety at Work Act 1974, were interpreted to grant an individual worker who was injured as a result of breach of the regulations the right to claim compensation in tort. The same technique of granting individuals rights to claim compensation also comprises part of the enforcement mechanism for the NMWA 1998 and the Working Time Regulations 1998.

The strength of this legislation is that it grants clear legally enforceable rights to workers and gives them an incentive to enforce those rights by bringing claims for compensation. But the effectiveness of the regulation to secure compliance by employers with these standards depends crucially on workers' awareness of their legal rights and their willingness to enforce their rights. Most will be reluctant to do so, for fear of retaliatory actions by their employer, at least until the termination of the employment relation. The daunting and expensive task of going to court to enforce claims for compensation will also detract from the effectiveness of the regulation, although this problem can be reduced, as we shall see below, by the creation of inexpensive and informal specialist tribunals. A further weakness of this regulatory

---

[24] Health and Safety Executive, *Annual Statistics 2016–17*.

technique is that it is designed not to prevent breaches of standards but rather to compensate for losses incurred by workers as a result of those breaches. The potential cost to employers of paying compensation no doubt encourages their compliance with the standard, but often employers may make the assessment that it is cheaper to risk the uncertain costs of potential claims than to incur the clear and immediate expense of compliance. The attraction to governments of this technique of regulation is that it avoids the cost of expensive administrative machinery such as inspectors, which perhaps explains its prevalence. In recent years all governments have fretted about the number and cost of claims before tribunals, even though they are proportionately fewer than in other EU countries.[25] If we view tribunal claims as the only way to combat widespread perceptions of unfairness at work,[26] following Linda Dickens, we could plausibly argue that there are too few cases.[27]

The effectiveness of individual civil law rights can be strengthened, however, by techniques of collective representation. Trade unions offer valuable assistance to their members in pursuing their statutory rights, and they sometimes fund litigation of a test case brought by an individual member to challenge a management decision. A trade union can also co-ordinate multiple claims brought by many workers in a similar position, as in the frequent occurrence of mass claims for equal pay for women. In the context of anti-discrimination legislation, the statutory body, the Equality and Human Rights Commission, helps to police compliance with the legislation and sometimes assists individual litigants on questions of principle.

Collective Bargaining

As we have already noted, for most of the twentieth century the principal regulatory technique for employment was the facilitation of collective bargaining between employers and trade unions.[28] Collective self-regulation could be achieved through collective agreements, which would set standards and fix the terms and conditions for individual contracts of employment. Collective bargaining could also establish mechanisms involving the trade union for monitoring compliance with those standards, procedures for varying the standards and methods for resolving disputes. A collective agreement might

[25] M. Gibbons, *Better Dispute Resolution: A Review of Employment Dispute Resolution in Great Britain* (London: Department of Trade and Industry (DTI), 2007), p. 15.

[26] R. Fevre, T. Nichols, G. Prior and I. Rutherford, *Fair Treatment at Work Report: Findings of the 2008 Survey* (London: Department for Business, Innovation and Skills (BIS), 2009).

[27] L. Dickens, 'Introduction – Making Employment Rights Effective: Issues of Enforcement and Compliance', in L. Dickens (ed.), *Making Employment Rights Effective* (Oxford: Hart, 2012) pp. 1, 3.

[28] K. Klare, 'Countervailing Workers' Power as a Regulatory Strategy', in H. Collins, P. Davies and R. Rideout (eds.), *Legal Regulation of the Employment Relation* (London: Kluwer Law International, 2000), p. 63.

be made either at the level of an industrial sector, thus applying to all employers in that sector a minimum level of terms and conditions or, more commonly from the 1960s onwards, at the level of a single employer or workplace.

The strategy of supporting the method of collective bargaining to set standards, although avoiding direct regulation of the employment relation, still required considerable intervention by the state. The first step was to remove the legal obstacles to the establishment of collective bargaining relationships. The law needed to protect the workers' right to join a trade union that would engage in collective bargaining on their behalf. The law also needed to protect the right of workers to take industrial action in order to back up their demands for satisfactory terms and conditions of employment, for otherwise the employer would be inclined to ignore them. The essential elements of this system of collective self-regulation in the UK were established by the Trade Disputes Act 1906, but only after protracted political and social struggles. The common law created by the judges in the nineteenth century, often supplemented by legislation, regarded trade unions as criminal and civil conspiracies, so legislation was required to grant immunity to trade unions in order to permit their lawful existence. Similarly, the law regarded industrial action as both a criminal and a civil wrong. It was a crime under the Master and Servant Acts for a servant to leave employment without permission, and in the middle of the nineteenth century there were thousands of prosecutions a year before the magistrates. Again, Parliament needed to abolish these offences (largely achieved by 1875) and to grant immunities to trade unions against civil actions (in 1906). This legislation was not without its loopholes, which were exploited from time to time by employers to fight trade unions and strikes, but for much of the twentieth century the legal system achieved the goal of permitting the development of collective bargaining for the purpose of setting terms and conditions of employment.

But the state also took a second step, which was not merely to permit collective bargaining to take place, but to promote it.[29] After the First World War, the new Ministry of Labour encouraged industrial sectors to create Joint Industrial Councils, following the recommendation of a sub-committee of the Committee of Reconstruction chaired by J. H. Whitley. Where no voluntary collective bargaining arrangements were in place, if employers failed to establish a Joint Industrial Council, the government took powers under the Trade Boards Act 1918 to impose a form of collective regulation with the addition of independent members. Although the pressure from the Ministry of Labour to establish industrial sector bargaining was not always sustained, at its peak this strategy achieved coverage through collective agreements or decisions of trade

---

[29] K. D. Ewing, 'The State and Industrial Relations: "Collective Laissez-Faire" Revisited' (1998) 5 *Historical Studies in Industrial Relations* 1; A. Bogg, *The Democratic Aspects of Trade Union Recognition* (Oxford: Hart, 2009).

boards (or Wages Councils as they were called later in the comprehensive Wages Councils Act 1945) of about 85 per cent of the British workforce. These industrial sector agreements set wages and hours not only for employers in the relevant association and members of the relevant union, but also for any employers in the industrial sector or trade and any workers employed by them.

The methods by which the state promoted the development of collective bargaining or self-regulation shifted decisively after the Report of the Royal Commission on Trade Unions and Employers' Associations (the Donovan Commission),[30] when it became public policy to promote enterprise- (single-employer) or plant-level bargaining. To develop this form of collective bargaining, legislation created procedures by which trade unions might compel an employer to recognise the union and to bargain with it over terms and conditions of employment. Subsequently, the legal mechanisms for promoting industrial-sector bargaining (Wages Councils) and for extending the effects of sector-level agreements to all workers have been dismantled. Instead, there is now a statutory procedure to help trade unions to gain recognition by a single employer for the purposes of collective bargaining.[31] Governments have not continuously pursued a policy of promoting collective bargaining but, when they have, this support has often seemed crucial to its success in achieving coverage of the workforce and in setting high standards. Certainly, the state has never been neutral about the development of collective bargaining, either promoting and channelling it or, in some periods, seeking to confine it.

Of course, the effectiveness of collective bargaining, particularly when conducted at the enterprise level, also depends crucially on high levels of union membership among the workforce together with effective organisation and representation by officials of the union. When these conditions are satisfied, collective bargaining, viewed as a system of regulation of the employment relation, proves an effective and efficient system of regulation of the employment relation. Collective bargaining is likely to be effective where a strong union can both demand good terms and conditions and then monitor and enforce those terms subsequently. It is also efficient in the sense that the costs to the state are minimal, and the employer is permitted to use its bargaining power to insist upon terms under which the business can remain competitive. Enterprise-level bargaining also has the potential advantage that the terms and conditions can be tailored more precisely than general legislative standards to the particular conditions of the business. Unlike in other countries, collective agreements at the level of either the industrial sector or the enterprise were not legally enforceable in themselves in the UK, but they did set legally enforceable standards indirectly by often fixing the binding terms of individual contracts of employment. This enforcement mechanism provided little security against the revocation of collective agreements by employers, but

[30] Cmnd 3623 (1968).   [31] TULRCA 1992, Sched. A1; see Chapter 14.

in practice the standards were normally observed because they were supported by the effective social sanction of the threat of industrial action. In this way, with the support and encouragement of the state, employers and trade unions can operate their own procedures for the regulation of terms and conditions of employment.

Effectiveness of Labour Law

In this brief survey, we have distinguished between three paradigms of regulation in labour law: mandatory standards backed by a criminal process, civil law rights supported by individual claims for compensation and collective self-regulation. These techniques represent the major types of regulation in labour law. Nevertheless, other methods are frequently used. Codes of practice provide guidance to employers, workers and courts about what is regarded as reasonable behaviour in contexts such as picketing and disciplinary procedures. Although such codes are not directly legally binding, courts and tribunals use them to interpret discretionary standards, so that a breach of the code of practice is normally also a breach of the legal standard. Licensing schemes operate in some sectors, such as agency work and agricultural gang labour, under which the employer must have a licence issued by a statutory body in order to operate the business. The conditions of the licence will include requirements to treat these workers fairly.[32]

In many instances, such as health and safety laws, all three main types of regulation are used in order to maximise the chances of compliance. As well as the system of criminal penalties enforced by inspectors, the individual employee has various civil claims, including the claim for compensation for injuries. In addition, the legislation requires employers to appoint health and safety representatives, who may ask for the formation of a committee in order to formulate and monitor health and safety policies within the workplace. Although these committees do not bargain about terms and conditions of employment, they share the feature with collective agreements that they create a collective mechanism for self-regulation and monitoring, in the hope of achieving higher levels of compliance with health and safety standards.

Yet the law of health and safety at work teaches us a salutory lesson. Despite the use of the most sophisticated and expensive regulatory techniques in labour law, it fails to meet the aspirations of the regulators. In the UK, there has been a steady decline in deaths in the workplace but there were 144 fatalities in 2015–16.[33] Employers report about 72,000 significant workplace

---

[32] On the variety of modern techniques of regulation, see A. Ogus, 'New Techniques for Social Regulation: Decentralisation and Diversity', in H. Collins, P. Davies and R. Rideout (eds.), *Legal Regulation of the Employment Relation* (London: Kluwer Law International, 2000), p. 83.

[33] Health and Safety Executive, *Annual Report and Accounts 2016–17*.

injuries annually,[34] but the broader Labour Force Survey estimates that about 600,000 workers experience some minor or major injury at work each year. To those numbers should be added occupational diseases, such as cancers like mesothelioma caused by working with asbestos and pulmonary diseases like emphysema linked to occupations with exposure to fumes, dust and chemicals. Office workers are exposed to risks such as musculoskeletal disorders and stress, which can also be severely incapacitating. It is estimated from a variety of surveys that more than 500,000 workers take time off work each year as a result of stress, anxiety and depression.

The important point to bear in mind always in the study of labour law is that legal regulation has to overcome substantial obstacles to achieve its goals and that rarely will legal regulation prove completely efficacious. Employers may resist or try to avoid regulation of every kind because it is perceived to impose extra costs on the business. Workers may be ignorant of their legal rights or may be reluctant to seek to enforce standards owing to the fear of victimisation. Given the number and variety of workplaces, the government does not have the capacity to monitor and enforce all the standards that it seeks to promote. What we need to consider always in connection with labour law is whether changes in the design and techniques of legal regulation might serve its objectives better.[35]

Sources of Workplace Conflict

As well as seeking to establish fair and effective standards for working conditions, labour law is centrally concerned with the resolution of conflict in the workplace. Disputes between employers and workers often prove intractable. The most obvious symptom of the problem is the employees' recourse to industrial action, either in support of a claim or as a defence against a decision made by management. Less visible, although far more numerous, are the cases where the employer disciplines or dismisses a worker, or the worker decides to quit the job because of some disagreement. In some instances, the employer's grievance procedure or disciplinary procedure may sort out the problem. Alternatively, where the employer has recognised a trade union, it may have created a procedure for resolving disputes through negotiation or private arbitration. Yet many disputes end up either in open industrial conflict or in acerbic litigation before the courts. The special difficulty presented to the legal system by labour disputes will be examined before we consider how the legal system can develop adequate and effective institutions for dispute settlement

---

[34] Employers have to report serious injuries under the Reporting of Injuries, Diseases and Dangerous Occurrences Regulations 2013, SI 2013 No. 1471.

[35] H. Collins, 'Justifications and Techniques of Legal Regulation of the Employment Relation', in H. Collins, P. Davies and R. Rideout (eds.), *Legal Regulation of the Employment Relation* (London: Kluwer Law International, 2000), p. 3.

in this context. Three principal sources of conflict in the workplace can be identified.

First, structural features of employment relations create the risk of special tensions arising between employer and employee. The employer's general power to direct the workforce according to the needs of production inevitably creates the risk of the abuse of that discretionary power and the exploitation of the employee's position of subordination to disciplinary action. Furthermore, an employer needs to adapt to changing market conditions and innovations, so that there is constant pressure to vary settled arrangements. Employees will naturally resist and challenge harsh and unreasonable management decisions and try to preserve or enhance their existing working conditions. These structural features of the employment relation are the principal explanation of why contracts of employment provoke more disputes and litigation than most other contractual arrangements.

A second major source of conflict in employment relations concerns the allocation of power in the workplace. By virtue of ownership of the business, the employer claims the right to control everything that happens in the organisation. While employers and managers frequently argue that everyone should work together as a team that is loyal to the goals of the organisation, workers' representatives insist that, although co-operation is certainly necessary, it is important to recognise that employees have interests that conflict with the employer with respect to wages, working conditions and job security, and that it is therefore appropriate for this divergence of interests to shape the governance of the organisation.[36] Accordingly, workers seek opportunities to participate in the running of the organisation, and to use their voice, often collectively, to challenge managerial decisions. At the very least, workers expect to be informed and consulted about changes that are likely to affect their working conditions and job security. Trade unions are often committed to having an even greater say in the running of the enterprise, which can amount to joint regulation of the workplace with management, or, as it is sometimes called, 'industrial democracy'. In light of these considerations, industrial conflict such as strikes should be understood not merely as a conflict of interest between the owners of capital and labour over levels of pay and working conditions but also as a dispute about the allocation of power to determine how the organisation is managed.

A third source of conflict in the workplace arises from conflicts of interest between different groups of workers within the workforce. The conflict may arise, for instance, over differentials in pay, the arrangement of hierarchies or selection for redundancy. The rival groups may comprise workers

---

[36] A. Fox, *Industrial Sociology and Industrial Relations*, Research Paper 3, Royal Commission on Trade Unions and Employers' Associations (London: HMSO, 1966). See also C. Crouch, *Class Conflict and the Industrial Relations Crisis: Compromise and Corporatism in the Politics of the British State* (London: Heinemann, 1977).

differentiated by skills or members of rival unions or men and women. An employer is likely to side with one group, so the conflict takes on the appearance of a dispute between employer and worker or employer and union, but at root it concerns a clash of interests between categories of workers or their representative unions. For example, an employer may agree with a union to select for redundancy agency workers rather than full-time workers, or the employer may strike a wage bargain with the union that improves the terms and conditions of the majority of workers, but involves a disadvantage to a few. How should such conflicts be resolved? Should the law uphold the collective interest or subvert that interest by protecting the rights or expectations of the minority? We shall see in the course of the book that the law, in pursuing the general approach of protecting the legal rights of individuals at the expense of collective interests, does not always appreciate the damage this may cause to the fragile solutions agreed through collective bargaining to the first and second sources of conflict described above.[37] But, on the other hand, legal support for collective self-regulation rather than the protection of individual rights can be criticised on the ground that it thereby ignores the interests of minorities, disadvantaged groups and women:

Feminism and Labour Law

Many of the fundamental features of collective *laissez faire* ideology express a largely hidden gendered content. The dominant assumption, for example, that voluntary collective bargaining is the most effective means of safeguarding workers' interests problematically presupposes that all workers are, or can be, effectively represented by collective bargaining and that workers' interests largely coincide. Yet the history of the trade union movement graphically reveals their persistent failure to embrace certain categories of workers (largely populated by women) or advance their interests. The pluralist reliance upon a bifurcated model of class conflict, with its implicit conception of homogeneous labour, has obscured both the complexity of conflicting interests characterising workplace relations and the hierarchical context within which such conflicts of interests are routinely played out.

Equally problematic is the pluralist view of law as a largely inappropriate mechanism for the regulation of industrial relations. 'Legal abstentionism' not only fundamentally misconceived the role of the state, it also operated to distort and diminish the significance of legal regulation in the workplace with, *inter alia*, gender implications. Protective legislation, for example, governing the hours of women's work in factories, was traditionally designated as external to the system of collective bargaining and, consequently, never accorded the same legitimacy by pluralist ideology. Yet for women workers, it was clearly of considerable practical and economic significance . . .

---

[37] S. Leader, 'Review of Labour Law and Freedom by Lord Wedderburn' (1996) 25 *Industrial Law Journal* 83.

> A final flaw in collective *laissez faire* ideology lies in its representation of the workplace as a largely autonomous, self-governing entity with relatively fixed and uncontested boundaries. In so doing, it presupposes a conceptual and practical separation of the realms of work and family life which is both artificial and misleading. In fact the spheres of production and reproduction are neither fixed nor separate but constantly changing and interacting.[38]

Labour Courts and Dispute Resolution

The discussion above explains why labour disputes present complex and sensitive problems. If the issue comes before a court for a legal determination of the rights and obligations of the parties, the court is likely to become involved in complex issues of fairness and the breakdown of informal and implicit understandings in working relations. Its intervention in the dispute can easily become portrayed as a political issue, where the court has the unappealing role of siding with either 'the bosses' or 'the workers'. To be sure, some disputes can be resolved according to the more traditional role of courts, such as the interpretation of a written contract of employment, the award of compensation for personal injury or the interpretation of a regulatory statute. But many disputes pose far more multifaceted and controversial issues. Did the employer act fairly in dismissing the worker? Do the workers have a valid reason for going on strike? Is the payment system used by the employer justifiable, even though one of its effects is that female employees receive on average lower wages because of the types of jobs they perform?

Most legal systems take steps to avoid allocating disputes arising in the context of employment to the ordinary courts. Legislation either creates special labour courts, such as the employment tribunals (ETs) in the UK, or attempts to divert these issues into systems of alternative dispute resolution such as arbitration. This strategy is justified in part as providing a forum for dispute resolution where the adjudicator or mediator has the necessary expertise in industrial relations and employment issues to provide a constructive and acceptable solution to the parties. The strategy is also influenced by the view that the legitimacy and authority of ordinary courts might be undermined if they were given the task of adjudicating such contentious issues that often have political undercurrents. There may also be the hope that the use of alternative dispute resolution may prevent any escalation of the dispute by avoiding the zero-sum game for high stakes that typifies the litigation process before ordinary courts. Alternative dispute resolution employs many techniques, including conciliation, arbitration and informal tribunals that provide a context-sensitive method of adjudication. Having examined the use of these

---

[38] J. Conaghan, 'Feminism and Labour Law: Contesting the Terrain', in A. Morris and T. O'Donnell (eds.), *Feminist Perspectives on Employment Law* (London: Cavendish, 1999), p. 13, pp. 23–5 (footnotes omitted).

techniques in labour law, we will finally consider the contribution of the ordinary courts to the resolution of labour disputes.

Internal Dispute Resolution Procedures

Most people agree that it would be best if disputes and grievances could be resolved quickly and informally in the workplace. Although there is no explicit legal requirement for employers to operate formal disciplinary and grievance procedures, in practice larger employers invariably do so. The purpose of these procedures is not only to head off potential disputes at an early stage and certainly before a legal claim is launched, but also to try to establish a reputation for fair treatment of the workforce. Smaller employers that often lack their own dispute resolution procedures make up a disproportionate percentage of employers facing legal claims. The Advisory, Conciliation and Arbitration Service, known as ACAS, publishes a Code of Practice that provides useful guidance on the steps involved in a good dispute resolution procedure, such as the need for a meeting with the employee to discuss allegations of misconduct or performance issues.[39] Legislation provides an incentive for both employers and employees to conform to the Code. In the event of a subsequent claim before an employment tribunal, if the tribunal issues an award of compensation, it can be increased by 25 per cent if the employer unreasonably failed to follow the Code of Practice, but also diminished by 25 per cent if the employee unreasonably failed to comply with the Code of Practice such as by a failure to attend a meeting.[40] As well as offering advice on the telephone and publishing helpful leaflets offering guidance to employers and employees, ACAS also offers employers a mediation service under which their staff visit a workplace with a view to promoting discussions that may resolve the issue.

Conciliation

The conciliation of disputes in the workplace requires an independent third person to explore the possibility of finding a consensual resolution of the conflict. In the UK, ACAS provides parties to a collective industrial dispute with an optional conciliation service.[41] In 2016/17, ACAS helped the parties to move to a resolution of the collective dispute in about 90 per cent of its cases.[42] In carrying out this conciliation service, ACAS can provide expert advice on improvements in industrial relations, such as proposals with respect to how organisational change might be handled and how communication and

---

[39] ACAS Code of Practice 1, Code of Practice on Disciplinary and Grievance Procedures (March 2015).
[40] TULRCA 1992, s. 207A.   [41] TULRCA 1992, s. 210.
[42] ACAS, *Annual Report and Accounts 2016–17*.

consultation may be improved. The Trades Union Congress (TUC) Disputes Committee can assist this work when there is a need to resolve inter-union disputes, a problem that may arise when rival unions are both trying to recruit members in a particular enterprise for the purpose of establishing collective bargaining. For internal union disputes, the government-appointed Certification Officer can often help to resolve issues by hearing complaints by individual union members about the administration of the trade union,[43] by investigating the financial affairs of trade unions,[44] by hearing complaints about breaches of the requirements for election of officials[45] and by adjudicating on many potential disputes between a union and its members.[46]

ACAS also has a compulsory conciliation role in connection with most individual disputes, such as those on unfair dismissal, discrimination, equal pay, protection of wages, breach of contract, minimum wage and working time.[47] Since 2014,[48] before a claim can be filed with a tribunal, the claimant has to seek early conciliation through ACAS. The process normally lasts up to one month, although it can be extended by agreement. The job of ACAS conciliation officers is to endeavour to promote a settlement between the persons who would be the parties to the legal proceedings. After the prescribed period has elapsed without a settlement, the ACAS officer provides a certificate to a prospective claimant, who may then launch proceedings before a tribunal. Even after proceedings have been instituted, the parties can return to ACAS for further attempts at conciliation.[49] ACAS reports that in 38 per cent of cases where people took part in ACAS conciliation the issue was resolved before an ET claim was lodged; and 55 per cent of cases which went on to become tribunal claims were settled through the assistance of ACAS conciliators.[50]

Arbitration

Private arbitration provides an independent person, selected by the parties, to adjudicate on the merits of a dispute, though without the formality and delay of the ordinary courts. It may be hoped that an arbitrator will understand better the industrial relations issues and the 'law of the workplace', in order to find a solution acceptable to both parties. Although many countries use arbitration as the dominant method for resolving collective industrial disputes, and some make it compulsory, in the UK this method is less common. ACAS is charged with the obligation to make a public arbitration service available to the parties,[51] but there is no compulsion for the parties to use it. In the year 2016/17, ACAS dealt with only seventeen cases.[52]

---

[43] TULRCA 1992, ss. 25 and 31.   [44] TULRCA 1992, s. 37B.   [45] TULRCA 1992, s. 55.
[46] TULRCA 1992, s. 108A.   [47] Employment Tribunals Act 1996, s. 18A.
[48] Enterprise and Regulatory Reform Act 2013, s. 7.
[49] Employment Tribunals Act 1996, s. 18C.   [50] ACAS, *Annual Report and Accounts 2016–17*.
[51] TULRCA 1992, s. 212.   [52] ACAS, *Annual Report and Accounts 2016–17*, p. 27.

Insofar as UK legislation imposes compulsory arbitration on the parties to a collective dispute, this task is given to another statutory body, called (since 1975) the Central Arbitration Committee (CAC).[53] The CAC tends, however, to try to induce a negotiated settlement between the parties rather than to impose a judgment on the merits. The CAC plays a pivotal role in resolving disputes in connection with the statutory recognition procedure for trade unions which are seeking to be recognised by an employer for the purposes of collective bargaining. In addition, the CAC arbitrates disputes concerning the requirement for the employer to disclose information for the purposes of collective bargaining and in connection with complaints that the employer is not complying with a legal duty to inform and consult representatives of the workforce about the probable developments of the business and employment prospects in it.[54]

In relation to individual disputes, again there is no tradition of using arbitrators. Employers may agree to the use of arbitration as part of a grievance procedure or a disciplinary procedure, but an employee cannot in general agree to forfeit a right to make a claim for statutory rights, even if the arbitration result is favourable. An exception that is rarely used is the possibility for the parties to a claim for unfair dismissal to agree in writing that their claim shall be resolved in a legally binding manner by an arbitrator appointed by ACAS.[55] That jurisdiction has been extended to a parent's statutory right to ask for flexible working.

Employment Tribunals

Most claims brought by individuals against their employers for breach of statutory rights and standards fall within the jurisdiction of ETs, formerly known as industrial tribunals. Since their creation in 1964, the jurisdiction of these tribunals has been gradually expanded, so that now they can hear in addition to claims for numerous statutory rights some common law contract claims, such as claims for shortfalls in wages and wrongful dismissal up to claims for £25,000. The principal exclusions from their jurisdiction are claims for compensation for personal injuries, claims for injunctions against collective industrial action and any legal process contemplating the application of a criminal penalty. In 2016/17, out of the total of 88,922 claims accepted by ETs, the statutory rights that received in excess of about a thousand claims were:

---

[53] TULRCA 1992, s. 259.
[54] Transnational Information and Consultation of Employees (TICE) Regulations 1999, SI 1999 No. 3323; Information and Consultation of Employees Regulations 2004, SI 2004 No. 3426.
[55] ACAS Arbitration Scheme (Great Britain) Order 2004, SI 2004 No. 753.

Age discrimination	7,628
Breach of contract	7,934
Disability discrimination	3,794
Equal pay	10,467
Public interest disclosures	1,497
Race discrimination	2,240
Failure to consult before redundancy	2,410
Redundancy pay	2,317
Sex discrimination	8,841
Unauthorised deductions	9,152
Unfair dismissal	12,038
Working time	30,313[56]

This particular year is not a good guide to future levels of claims, because at that time tribunal fees, which we discuss below, deterred a large number of low-value claims. Following the abolition of fees, the number of claims has more than doubled and is returning to previous levels. Small claims in categories such as unauthorised deductions of sums from wages (which may include claims for the minimum wage or holiday pay) are likely to increase even more.

In newspapers, ETs are sometimes presented as upholding unfounded or even ridiculous claims by employees, but a brief look at the statistics suggests that in fact there are slim chances of success for claimants. In 2016/17, out of a total of 88,922 accepted claims, the results were:

ACAS conciliated settlements	26%
Withdrawn	19%
Successful at hearing	6%
Unsuccessful at hearing	5%
Dismissed at a preliminary hearing	1%
Struck out (not at a hearing)	11%
Default judgment	4%
Dismissed upon withdrawal	24%

Claimants' overall success rate of approximately 36 per cent is ascertainable by adding together ACAS settlements (assuming employees won something in the settlement) 26 per cent, successful at hearing 6 per cent, and default judgments 4 per cent.

In the past, ETs sat with three adjudicators: an employment judge, who was a qualified barrister or solicitor, and two other members, one appointed from each of two panels proposed by employers' organisations and organisations representative of employees. An ET thus represented a hybrid system of dispute resolution: it was partly a court, since it provided adjudication in a

---

[56] Source: Ministry of Justice, Tribunals and gender recognition certificate statistics quarterly, Main Tables: ET1 (8 March 2018).

public forum using legal standards, but also partly deliberately not a court, with its majority of lay members, who brought knowledge of the practices and standards of industrial relations, and with its informal rules of evidence and procedures. An industrial tribunal was likened to an industrial jury.[57] Today, in order to expedite proceedings, save on costs and facilitate the determination of complex points of law, normally an employment judge sits alone.[58] All the potential advantages of having disputes resolved by persons with expertise, especially in cases of unfair dismissal where the standard of reasonableness must depend on conventional understandings of acceptable standards, have been forgone.

ETs are expected, like other tribunals, to act less formally than an ordinary court, without a requirement for legal representation, with a view to settling the dispute expeditiously. Final decisions of the tribunal may be enforced in the ordinary way like a judgment of a court through the county court system. Unfortunately, research has revealed that only about half of those county court orders are paid by employers in full and one-third are never paid at all.[59] The legislative response so far has been to empower ETs to order an employer to pay a financial penalty for failure to pay a tribunal compensation order or an agreed settlement.[60] In a period of about three years, 483 warning notices have been issued to employers that failed to pay an ET award or ACAS-conciliated settlement by the due date, and as a result ninety-two tribunal awards have been paid with a total value of £829,343: £363,361 in 2016/17 and £465,982 in 2017/18. Has this measure helped to secure compliance with tribunal orders? Perhaps a little, but there is no evidence of any financial penalties having been issued. The government is now considering proposals to digitise and stream-line enforcement mechanisms.[61]

Like that of a court, the procedure of an ET is adversarial, but the members of the tribunal are required to avoid formality, to ask questions of witnesses in order to clarify issues and to avoid strict adherence to the legal rules of evidence. Tribunals have been accused of 'legalism': in their approach to claims, they tend to analyse the issues exclusively within a legal framework and by reference to legal criteria, rather than appreciating and giving weight to the industrial relations context of the dispute. Yet it is hard to see how ETs can operate in any other way, for they are required to reach decisions in accord-ance with legal standards, which, as we will see, are often complex and

---

[57] *Williams* v. *Compair Maxam Ltd* [1982] ICR 156 (EAT), *per* Browne-Wilkinson J.

[58] Employment Tribunals Act 1996, s. 4.

[59] BIS, 'The Payment of Tribunal Awards: 2013 Study' (London, 2014).

[60] Employment Tribunals Act 1996, ss. 37A–Q.

[61] Department for Business, Energy & Industrial Strategy (BEIS) and Ministry of Justice, *Good Work: The Taylor Review of Modern Working Practices: Consultation on Enforcement of Employment Rights Recommendations* (February 2018).

technical.[62] If an ET makes an 'error of law', a litigant can bring an appeal to the Employment Appeal Tribunal (EAT), where a judge of a status equivalent to the High Court will subject the decision to forensic examination and point out the tribunal's mistakes of law, sometimes with withering comments. Furthermore, legalism has the virtue that it pays strict attention to the rights of individuals, not permitting them to be sacrificed for collective benefits, such as efficient production or harmonious industrial relations. The legalism of tribunals indirectly compels employers and representatives of the workforce to pay close attention to the rights and interests of individual workers, which promotes one dimension of fairness in the workplace.

Behind the criticism of legalism in tribunals, however, there lurks a more serious concern about access to justice. One potential advantage of tribunals over ordinary courts is that individual employees may be able to bring their claims without the need for incurring the expense of lawyers. Although it is permissible for an individual to present a claim without legal representation, this approach is probably not advisable. The legal issues are often sufficiently complex for legal advice, from either a lawyer or an experienced trade union representative, to become essential, but there is no legal aid for claims before tribunals (except in Scotland). The preparation of the case in order to be able to establish the facts and to present its strengths also benefits significantly from legal advice. In addition, the employer is likely to be represented either by a lawyer or by an experienced personnel manager, which will give the employer a comparative advantage against an unrepresented claimant. For example, in a sample of cases before tribunals, unrepresented claimants against employers with legal representation won in only 10 per cent of cases, but, when the positions were reversed, the claimants with legal representation won in 48 per cent of cases.[63] Although many factors may explain such outcomes, it is likely that the complexity of the legal issues addressed by ETs renders it impossible for the tribunal to discuss the claim in simple, lay terms, which leads inexorably to the relative advantage of those parties who benefit from legal advice and representation.

In sharp opposition to this concern about access to justice for workers, in recent years governments have expressed the view that access to tribunals is too easy and too cheap. It is claimed that workers are encouraged to bring frivolous or hopeless cases.[64] Since employers defend themselves by using either managerial time or expensive lawyers, the cost of the legal proceedings may induce them to agree to pay a sum in settlement of the claim even, it is alleged, in completely hopeless cases. In addition, on this view, if employers

---

[62] R. Munday, 'Tribunal Lore: Legalism and the Industrial Tribunals' (1981) 10 *Industrial Law Journal* 146.

[63] H. Genn and Y. Genn, *The Effectiveness of Representation at Tribunals* (London: Faculty of Law, Queen Mary and Westfield College, University of London, 1989), p. 99.

[64] A. Beecroft, *Report on Employment Law* (London: BIS, 2011); BIS, *Resolving Workplace Disputes: A Consultation – Response Form* (London, 2011).

refuse to pay up, the tribunals will become swamped with frivolous cases at great expense to the taxpayer. The evidence to support this concern is anecdotal; nevertheless, it is a firmly held belief of employers' organisations. To discourage such supposed frivolous claims, the rules of tribunal procedure have gradually been tightened up.[65] The application form has become much more elaborate. Administrators can reject the form if there is any minor error in its completion. An employment judge inspects the completed application and can reject the application in whole or in part if the judge considers either that the ET has no jurisdiction to consider the claim or that the claim has no reasonable prospect of success. An employment judge can also require a deposit of up to £1,000 for the claim to proceed.[66] In addition, although tribunals do not usually require the losing party to pay the costs of the other side, the tribunal has the power to order costs if it believes that the claimant is acting 'vexatiously, abusively, disruptively or otherwise unreasonably', or if one party has caused postponements or if the claim or the employer's response had no reasonable prospect of success.[67] For example, an employee was made to pay costs of £5,000 when, in the view of the tribunal, the claimant acted unreasonably in rejecting an offer of settlement of £5,700 and in persisting in some 'ludicrous' aspects of the claim in which the employer was accused of torture and slavery.[68]

Although all these measures gradually reduced the number of tribunal applications and hearings, it was only when fees were introduced on 29 July 2013 that access to tribunals was barred for most claimants. The main reason for the introduction of fees was to address a budgetary cut of 23 per cent for the Ministry of Justice, but the official reason given was to reduce frivolous claims by charging workers the cost of the service. The official statistics show a fall of at least two-thirds for applications from individual complainants. In 2012/13 the total number of claims was 191,541; but in 2014/15 the total was just 61,308. The level of fees set by the government was high. For straightforward and low-value claims, such as a claim for an unauthorised deduction of £100 from wages, the application fee and the hearing fee amounted to £390. For a more complex claim such as unfair dismissal, the fees totalled £1,200. Since there was no guarantee or established practice of successful claimants recovering these fees from the employer, for those with low-value claims it was irrational to bring a claim.[69] The legislation failed to weed out unmeritorious claims, as those headstrong claimants persisted notwithstanding the change in

---

[65] The Employment Tribunals (Constitution and Rules of Procedure) Regulations 2013, Sched. 1, SI 2013 No. 1237.
[66] Employment Tribunals Act 1996, s. 9.
[67] Employment Tribunals Act 1996, s. 13; The Employment Tribunals (Constitution and Rules of Procedure) Regulations 2013, Sched. 1, para. 76, SI 2013 No. 1237.
[68] *Kopel* v. *Safeway Stores plc* [2003] IRLR 753 (EAT).
[69] A. Adams and J. Prassl, 'Vexatious Claims: Challenging the Case for Employment Tribunal Fees' (2017) 80(3) *Modern Law Review* 412.

costs. Instead, it was low-value claims and impoverished claimants that the fees order excluded from the tribunal system. As a result, most employees lacked an effective way to vindicate most of their employment law rights. Ironically, the radical decline in the number of claims significantly reduced the expected revenue from fees for the government; fees probably covered less than 10 per cent of the costs of the ETs.[70]

In an application for judicial review of the ET fees, the Supreme Court in *R (Unison)* v. *Lord Chancellor*[71] declared them unlawful under the common law and invalid. The Court held that the fees undermined the rule of law, because rights that had been conferred on workers by Parliament in legislation were systematically blocked, creating a real risk that employees would be prevented from having access to justice and therefore removing much of the incentive for employers to comply with the laws. Furthermore, insofar as fees served a legitimate purpose and had a rational basis, a matter that was open to doubt, the level of fees was disproportionate and therefore represented an unlawful unjustified interference with Article 6 of the ECHR and Article 47 of the Charter of Fundamental Rights of the EU (the right to a fair trial). The government now has to refund all fees paid by claimants.[72] Possibly some claimants may launch new claims arguing that, although they have exceeded the limitation period, usually set at three months, the prohibitive cost of the fees had rendered the claim not 'reasonably practicable' until the fees order was abolished.[73]

The Employment Appeal Tribunal and the Courts

Ordinary courts are often regarded as unsuitable for handling labour disputes. The historical source of the problem for ordinary courts perhaps lies in their key jurisdiction in collective labour disputes of being empowered to issue 'labour injunctions'. These interim injunctions consist of orders to trade union officials or trade unions to withdraw calls for industrial action, backed up with the potential sanctions of fines, the sequestration of the assets of the union and possibly imprisonment of union officials for contempt of court. The common law, as developed by the judges, emphasises the importance of individual freedom of contract, the freedom of markets and the protection of individual property rights. According to those values, it is hard to comprehend the possibility that collective industrial action that interferes with these freedoms

---

[70] *R(Unison)* v. *Lord Chancellor (Equality and Human Rights Commission Intervening)* [2017] UKSC 51, [2017] ICR 1037 [56].

[71] *R(Unison)* v. *Lord Chancellor (Equality and Human Rights Commission Intervening)* [2017] UKSC 51, [2017] ICR 1037

[72] Since the introduction of the scheme, a total of 9,472 applications for refunds have been received and 7,733 payments have been made, with a total value of £6,555,595 as at 31 March 2018.

[73] M. Ford, 'Employment Tribunal Fees and the Rule of Law: *R(Unison)* v. *Lord Chancellor in the Supreme Court*' (2018) 47 *Industrial Law Journal* 1, at 38.

and individual rights might ever be legitimate. To the extent that courts issue such injunctions, they can be presented as invariably intervening on the side of the employers in order to break strikes and damage the interests of workers. These values embedded in the common law may also affect their approach to claims brought by individual employees, where by culture and training the judges may not be sympathetic to their interests. As Lady Hale once observed in the Supreme Court:

> I should perhaps declare an interest, as the only member of this court to have spent a substantial proportion of her working life as an employee rather than as a self-employed barrister or tenured office holder.[74]

Despite these reservations about the capacity of the courts to understand the issues posed by labour disputes in ways that coincide with general perceptions of the public interest, the ordinary courts continue to occupy a commanding role in labour law. As well as their continuing jurisdiction to issue labour injunctions in collective industrial disputes, the ordinary courts provide the ultimate appeal courts in decisions taken by ETs. Parties to proceedings in ETs can appeal against their decisions on the ground that the tribunal committed an 'error of law'. The appeal goes first to the EAT, and then to the Court of Appeal and finally to the Supreme Court. At all stages of these proceedings, references can also be made to the CJEU for determinations of the meaning of EU law.

The EAT, which replaced the National Industrial Relations Court in 1975, has the exclusive jurisdiction to hear appeals from ETs on points of law. Like employment tribunals, the EAT was traditionally a tripartite body, but since 2013 it has been composed of a judge alone (unless a judge otherwise directs).[75] The EAT must consider only points of law and not permit an appeal on all the merits of the case. The normal way in which a decision of an ET can be challenged is to assert that the tribunal asked itself the wrong legal question, which depends upon an interpretation of the relevant statute and the precedents set by the courts. In addition, it can be asserted that no reasonable tribunal could have reached the decision that it did by applying the correct legal test to the facts of the case, that is, a claim of irrationality or perversity, which is also an error of law. These grounds for review permit the EAT to intervene quite broadly, should it so wish, but it can also prevent a flood of appeals by a restrictive definition of points of law. When an appeal is successful, the EAT will normally remit the case to an ET, sometimes with a different membership, to reconsider the facts in the light of the correct legal test.

---

[74] *Edwards* v. *Chesterfield Royal Hospital* [2011] UKSC 58 (SC), para. 110.
[75] Employment Tribunals Act 1996, s. 28.

The EAT itself is subject to appeals on points of law to the Court of Appeal and then the Supreme Court. These higher courts can thus control the extent to which the EAT can expand its jurisdiction by discovering points of law. The appeal courts also police the interpretations placed upon the legislation by the EAT, and can substitute their own binding interpretations of the legislation, without the benefit of advice from lay members on the industrial relations context.

Prospects for Labour Law

To conclude this introduction to the subject of labour law, we outline some of the principal themes and challenges that inform contemporary debates about the subject.

Flexibility and Security

In the twentieth century, business organisation tended towards large, vertically integrated systems of production, which produced goods and services for mass markets. In these large firms, such as car manufacturers and banks, the business operated through a bureaucratic organisation. This organisation linked together and co-ordinated numerous jobs by means of managerial hierarchies. Employees typically joined these companies in entry positions, received training in the necessary skills for their jobs and then, subject to good performance, remained in those jobs or received promotion and training to other jobs for much of their working careers. The jobs were usually full time, of indefinite duration and were expected to last until retirement, at which point most employees of these large organisations would benefit from the employer's occupational pension scheme.

Although this kind of job has certainly not disappeared, there are many signs of significant changes occurring in working relations which signal the decline of this standard pattern to about 60 per cent of the workforce in the UK. People move jobs more frequently, often taking fixed-term appointments, temporary jobs, agency work and casual jobs. About 15 per cent of the workforce are self-employed in the sense that they sell their services as if they represented a separate business. Training is more often provided outside the workplace through educational institutions. Hours of work have become subject to greater variability: the nine-to-five workday is disappearing; services often have to be delivered by a business 24/7. The type of work to be performed in any given job has often become diversified, so that workers are expected to perform a wider range of tasks. With this expectation also comes more responsibility and discretion, so that workers often have to decide what will be the most efficient and productive use of their time. Finally, wages are no longer always paid at a fixed rate per hour or by the month, but are frequently linked in a variety of ways to individual performance, the achievement of targets and business profits.[76]

Behind these changes in the form of work, which are sometimes described as 'flexibilisation', are some powerful economic forces that give reason to think that the changes are both permanent and evolving. Intensification of competition as a result of globalisation of capital and product markets forces employers to experiment with systems of ever more efficient use of labour. These systems often require all kinds of flexibility from employees, including variations in hours of work and job tasks. One of the principal sources of competitive advantage for businesses stems from technological innovations, which depend upon research and rapid adaptations to new types of production systems. In this 'knowledge-based' economy, employers need to reorganise their businesses in order to tap into the knowledge and innovative capacity of their employees, so that the old bureaucratic top-down command systems are no longer always the most efficient. It is also suggested that consumers now expect products and services that meet their desires more precisely, having ceased to be content with mass production goods of moderate quality. In order to meet this demand, employers have to be able to respond rapidly to changes in taste, to be able to customise their products and services and to create organisations that achieve constant improvements in design and quality. There is little room in such production systems for the permanent lifetime job with unchanging content and moderate skills requirements.

Under the pattern of a job for life or for a long-term indefinite duration, many legal rights were designed to protect expectations of job security, such as the statutory rights to claim unfair dismissal and redundancy payments, and the common law protected many express contractual undertakings of job continuity. Under modern patterns of more precarious jobs, as exemplified by fixed-term contracts, agency work, zero-hours contracts, consultancies and rapid variations in job content in order to adapt to changing production requirements, neither party to the employment relation has the same expectations of job security and constant employment in the same job. The question arises whether the law should continue its policy of protecting job security, or whether this policy will come to be perceived as inappropriate and be replaced by notions of protecting income security and employability.[77]

The tension between the policy of protecting job security and the need for reasons of efficiency to enhance the flexible use of labour are illustrated by the

---

[76] B. Kersley, C. Alpin, A. Bryson, H. Bewley, G. Dix and S. Oxenbridge, *Inside the Workplace: Findings from the 2004 Workplace Employment Relations Survey* (London: Routledge, 2006), pp. 190–3.

[77] A. Supiot, *Beyond Employment* (Oxford University Press, 2001); P. Davies and M. Freedland, *Towards a Flexible Labour Market: Labour Legislation and Regulation since the 1990s* (Oxford University Press, 2007).

European Employment Strategy.[78] Here, the key policy that affects labour law is described as 'flexicurity'.[79] The main aim behind this policy of 'flexicurity' is to address problems of competitiveness of Europe in comparison to other parts of the world for the sake of raising levels of employment and increasing or at least maintaining standards of living. On the one hand, it is said that labour markets must become less rigid and jobs more varied, so that employers can employ workers in the most efficient way. On the other hand, workers need to be protected by measures that provide economic security. Legal regulation of the employment relation might assist employers to establish workplace relations which achieve the level of co-operation and flexibility that is efficient, while at the same time providing adequate assurances and safeguards for the workforce that they will be treated fairly and have a reasonable degree of income security. The problem is, of course, to reconcile these competing policies, especially when the state suffers from depleted resources or for other reasons is unwilling to support unemployed workers and their dependants. Under this policy of 'flexicurity', for instance, the European Commission urges employers to offer permanent jobs to provide security, but also exhorts them to adjust working time (and therefore wages paid) to vary labour input according to need. Governments are advised to improve the skills of the workforce, which will make them more employable (security) but also more adaptable to change (flexible). Security becomes employability, not a steady job.

Vulnerable Workers

Flexibility brings with it a large pool of vulnerable workers. These are workers whose skills and bargaining power are weak, so that they are forced to take jobs that are insecure, low paid and perhaps unsafe. Examples are casual workers or zero-hours employees, who are only given work and pay when they are required, temporary workers on short-term contracts, agency workers who earn a living from short-term placements with the customers of the agency and workers who take on particular jobs on a short-term, self-employed basis, as in the case often of couriers and taxi-drivers. These workers can be described as vulnerable both because their income from work is always precarious and because they have no power to resist unfair and oppressive treatment by employers, since grievances and disagreements are likely to be met by instant dismissal. Those who end up in the category of vulnerable workers, which is sometimes described as the secondary labour market, are

---

[78] Council Decision of 21 October 2010 on guidelines for the employment policies of the Member States (2010/707/EU), OJ 2010 L308/46.

[79] Council Conclusions on 'Towards Common Principles of Flexicurity' of 5/6 December 2007 (Doc. 16,201/07); European Commission, An Agenda for New Skills and Jobs, COM (2010) 682 final.

most likely to be poorly educated or drawn from minority groups, immigrants or mothers with young children.

Vulnerable workers present two key challenges to labour law. The first is to broadly frame employment protection rights so that the legislation includes these vulnerable groups where appropriate. Employers can devise contractual arrangements that appear to take these vulnerable workers outside the scope of the protective legislation, as for example in the case of labelling workers 'self-employed' when in reality they are performing a job under the supervision and instruction of an employer. Nor is it easy to define laws so that they apply straightforwardly to the wide variety of employment relations. For example, the idea that there should be a maximum number of hours in a working week in order to protect the health of workers can be applied fairly simply to the traditional form of full-time employment, but how should it apply, if at all, to workers hired for a particular task, people who work from home or casual workers whose hours vary dramatically from day to day? Similarly, it may be asked how a minimum wage per hour might be applied to workers who are paid exclusively by commissions on sales or tips or by a fixed fee for a particular piece of work. As more and more work is performed outside conventional employment relationships, the analytical foundation of the subject of labour law in full-time contracts of employment of indefinite duration ceases to provide a useful guide to the field of study.[80] The Taylor Review,[81] commissioned by the government, displayed a reluctance to redraw regulation to protect vulnerable workers, in order to protect their freedom of choice in selecting suitable work,[82] but it did accept that the scope of the current protections for the various categories of vulnerable workers needs to be further clarified in legislation.

The second challenge presented by vulnerable workers is to ensure that the applicable legal protections are enforced. Typically, these groups are unlikely either to be organised by a trade union or to know their legal rights and to be able to enforce them in practice. For instance, many of these vulnerable workers believe incorrectly that they can forgo payment of the national living wage by agreement.

---

[80] P. Davies and M. Freedland, 'Employees, Workers, and the Autonomy of Labour Law', in H. Collins, P. Davies and R. Rideout (eds.), *Legal Regulation of the Employment Relation* (London: Kluwer Law International, 2000), p. 267; M. Freedland, *The Personal Employment Contract* (Oxford University Press, 2003); S. Deakin, 'Does the Personal Employment Contract Provide a Basis for the Reunification of Employment Law?' (2007) 36 *Industrial Law Journal* 68.

[81] *Good Work: The Taylor Review of Modern Working Practices* (BEIS, 2017), available at https://www.gov.uk/government/publications/good-work-the-taylor-review-of-modern-working-practices.

[82] As highlighted and criticised in K. Bales, A. Bogg and T. Novitz, '"Voice" and "Choice" in Modern Working Practices: Problems with the Taylor Review' (2018) 47 *Industrial Law Journal* 46.

Social Exclusion

Social exclusion refers to the predicament of many groups in society who are unable to participate in its benefits and material wealth. An inability to obtain a job is one of the prime sources of social exclusion. This inability may stem from many causes, including inadequate education and training, membership of a group against which there is discrimination and incompatible family responsibilities. Tackling social exclusion requires governments to support many social programmes, not least education and training. These programmes can intersect with regulation of the labour market, as for example where the government subsidises the wages of young workers in their first job in order to assist them in obtaining some training and work experience by exercising a right to take time off work;[83] or where the government supports employers' schemes for encouraging young workers to continue their education and training part time after the school-leaving age.[84] The most important role of government in addressing social exclusion is to raise levels of employment through its macroeconomic policies.

In relation to combating social exclusion caused by the operation of the labour market, a key principle is the idea of equality of opportunity, which states a principle of social justice that insists that jobs should be allocated on the basis of merit in the sense of ability to perform the job. The challenge for legal regulation is both to remove obstacles to equal opportunity and to assist people to take up opportunities by, for example, helping with education and training. To achieve effective equality of opportunity is, however, a complex and multifaceted task. To achieve equality of opportunity for women in the labour market, for instance, it is not sufficient merely to declare deliberate discrimination against women to be unlawful. The law needs to tackle also 'institutional discrimination', which comprises rules and practices of organisations, which, although neutral on their face, have the effect of preventing or discouraging women from taking up jobs with that organisation. Such a rule might be one that requires employees to be willing to accept work in the evenings, a rule that many women may be reluctant to accept if they have other compelling family responsibilities. Tackling the problem of institutional discrimination requires the law to question many assumptions of the labour market, such as the view that employers rather than employees should unilaterally determine hours and location of work.

Regulatory Strategies

The changing nature of jobs and the shifting focus of the aims of labour law require a rethinking of techniques of regulation. For the purpose of trying to set minimum standards below which no one should fall, such as an NMW, the

---

[83] ERA 1996, s. 63A.   [84] Learning and Skills Act 2000.

established techniques of mandatory rules and criminal and civil penalties will still prove essential tools. But when a government wants to encourage flexibility, adaptation to innovation and competitiveness in business by using labour laws, the old command-and-control strategy of regulation may prove inappropriate and dysfunctional. Such policy goals require regulatory techniques that do not simply focus on prohibiting unacceptable conduct but also provide routes and incentives to restructure businesses and working practices with a view to helping businesses and employing organisations to achieve better productivity and international competitiveness. Many of the aims of labour law can be supported, for instance, by tax incentives to employers and workers, as in the cases of occupational pensions, employee share-ownership schemes and temporary subsidies to encourage businesses to hire additional workers from the pool of long-term unemployed youth. Other kinds of regulation and government intervention can assist in helping the labour market to function more effectively, by matching workers to jobs, reducing the cost of searching for jobs, assisting in mobility and by improving the skills and education of workers. The European Commission also calls for 'smarter regulation' which is less rigid and can be adapted to the needs of business, even perhaps abandoning formal laws in favour of 'soft law' or instruments that do not provide legal rights. Working out practical legal measures that can be rolled out throughout the EU to implement the policy of 'flexicurity' is a central preoccupation of European social policy.

Underneath the debates about appropriate regulatory strategies, there lurks a persistent controversy regarding the economic effects of the traditional forms of mandatory labour regulation on levels of employment and efficiency. Employment protection laws certainly impose some costs on businesses, even if they are only administrative costs and the costs of defending cases in tribunals. But the costs of compliance may prove greater than merely depressing the profits of business. For example, it is sometimes argued that minimum wage legislation, by artificially increasing labour costs, will cause employers to reduce the number of employees or even go out of business altogether, with the undesirable effect of increasing levels of unemployment. Similarly, it is suggested that compulsory laws against unfair dismissal impose costs upon employers, which lead employers either to reduce the number of employees (an unemployment effect) or to retain unproductive workers (a productive inefficiency effect) or to lower wages in order to keep labour costs constant (an inefficient transaction, if most workers would prefer higher wages to protection of job security). On this view, therefore, mandatory labour standards both tend to backfire on the workers they are designed to help and to create inefficiencies in production. These economic arguments for deregulation of the labour market and contracts of employment became extremely influential in the 1980s. They remain at the heart of political disputes regarding labour legislation. In the course of the book, however, we will discover that these economic arguments for deregulation are far too crude, that the labour market is more complex than this simple model describes and that legal regulation such as the law of unfair dismissal and the minimum wage can be effective in achieving its goals without imposing undesirable side-effects such as weakening efficiency or increasing levels of unemployment. Indeed, legal regulation, by raising the cost of labour, may have the beneficial effect of forcing employers to consider capital investment in new technologies in order to improve productivity in order to be able to afford the higher labour costs.[85] Nevertheless, considerations of costs must always influence the framework of legal regulation.

When calculating those costs, however, it is always important to include 'social costs' in the assessment. For example, a firm may decide that it can improve its profitability by reducing the size of its workforce. These redundancies may be an efficient outcome for the firm, but, when we take into account the costs of supporting unemployed workers and their dependants, we may discover that these 'social costs' far exceed the benefits to the business. Legal regulation can force employers to include some of these social costs in their calculations of efficient decisions, that is, to internalise the costs of externalities, with a view to minimising social cost that will have to be picked up by the taxpayer. As well as reducing the cost to the public purse, labour regulation may also help to combat social exclusion.

Voice at Work

As we have already noted, one unique characteristic of labour law is the regulation of employment achieved by collective bargaining. As well as setting standards for the workplace, such as hours of work, working conditions and wages, collective bargaining may also negotiate change and restructuring. But collective bargaining is not the only route to enabling workers to have a voice in the workplace. It is possible to have other institutions such as works councils and staff committees that share information about production plans, discuss innovations and plan restructuring. In a world where all jobs undergo a degree of flexibilisation, the potential advantages of information and consultation mechanisms are that it may prove possible to increase workers' sense of security while at the same time facilitating, without industrial conflict, the necessary changes to productive arrangements. Giving workers a voice in all these matters, not only working conditions but the long-term plans for the business, requires employers and managers to share information and decision-making procedures, a concession that they may not be willing to make. Legal regulation may assist in promoting these types of 'partnerships' between employers and representatives of the workforce, by providing both a workable

---

[85] S. Deakin and F. Wilkinson, 'Labour Law and Economic Theory: A Reappraisal', in H. Collins, P. Davies and R. Rideout (eds.), *Legal Regulation of the Employment Relation* (London: Kluwer Law International, 2000), p. 29.

institutional framework and incentives for using it. Achieving an effective voice for workers in their organisations, not just token consultation, remains a key ambition of labour law, not only because it signals a democratisation of the workplace but also because it is a key regulatory strategy in achieving the elusive balance between flexibility and security.[86]

Work/Life Balance

Legal regulation designed to help people achieve a practical balance between work and their other responsibilities, as well as the need for leisure time, initiates a broad agenda. It implies that jobs must pay sufficiently well to achieve a decent standard of living without requiring excessive hours of work. To achieve this goal, the regulation needs to address both minimum wages and maximum working hours. Furthermore, a practical balance between work and other responsibilities requires a rejection of an employer's unfettered right to insist upon strict performance of the terms of the contract of employment where those other responsibilities represent a compelling need for a worker to take time-off. Employers have to adjust their demands to the needs of workers, rather than the other way round. Examples of such regulation include parental leave and the right to request more flexible working hours. More generally, a right to flexibility or a right of workers to ask for changes in their hours, duration and location of work appears to be emerging as a key element in the statutory framework governing employment.[87]

The vesting of greater discretion and responsibility further down the organisation has the effect that work is not so easily separated from the rest of social life, because the responsibilities will be carried home. Indeed, owing to the ease of communications, working from home for part of the time has become more common. Working time has also become a less distinct sphere of social life, so that many people work longer, although more flexible, hours. Helping people to achieve a satisfactory work/life balance becomes even more fraught when work is demarcated by neither time nor place. Constant availability by mobile phone and email is a recipe for greater stress and a risk of unfair exploitation. In the future, we are likely to see demands from workers, as has happened in France, for a legal right to be left alone and a right to turn off email and messaging systems outside working hours.

---

[86] A. Bogg and T. Novitz (eds.), *Voices at Work: Continuity and Change in the Common Law World* (Oxford University Press, 2014); K. D. Ewing, J. Hendy and C. Jones (eds.), *A Manifesto for Labour Law: Towards a Comprehensive Revision of Workers' Rights* (London: Institute of Employment Rights, 2016).

[87] H. Collins, 'The Right to Flexibility', in J. Conaghan and K. Rittich (eds.), *Labour Law, Work, and Family: Critical and Comparative Perspectives* (Oxford University Press, 2005), p. 99.

Human Rights

In recent decades, the human rights movement has increasingly framed labour law issues. Many labour standards can be described as individual rights – the right to work, the right to fair wages, the right to equal treatment. The Human Rights Act (HRA) 1998 added impetus to this movement by enabling individuals to rely upon the rights protected in the European Convention on Human Rights (ECHR) before national courts and tribunals. Convention rights are primarily concerned with political freedom and civil liberties, but these rights can have relevance in the workplace where, for instance, an employer uses intensive electronic surveillance which deprives employees of their right to privacy. One civil liberty, the right to freedom of association, has become a vital bastion in supporting workers' voices and protecting the activities of trade unions.

As well as endorsing those civil liberties, the Charter of the Fundamental Rights of the European Union, which has the status of a legally binding treaty, also protects a wide range of social and economic rights such as rights to information and consultation, to collective bargaining and industrial action, to protection against unjustified dismissal and to fair and just working conditions. Although the Charter should not create directly enforceable rights for individuals, courts are expected to interpret EU law in the light of Charter rights. Many of these rights may contain fundamental principles that require national courts to ensure that national laws are disapplied in the event of a conflict with EU Directives that articulate those rights in greater detail. Following the UK's withdrawal from the EU, these Charter Rights will no longer be binding, but it seems likely that the rights and principles the Charter contains will continue to be taken into account in the interpretation by UK courts of EU law.

There is a danger that this new emphasis on individual rights in labour law will obscure the importance of collective solidarity among workers in securing effective protection of labour standards. Nevertheless, the legal protection of a broader range of social and economic rights, either directly or through interpretive techniques, should compel governments to take the legitimate claims of workers much more seriously.[88]

Globalisation

In Chapter 2, we bring together many of these themes in connection with the challenges posed by globalisation. Simply put, national economies are increasingly connected by a web of finance, communications, transport and productive links. A product like a mobile phone may be conceived in a scientific laboratory or workshop, designed by a business organisation somewhere else,

---

[88] S. Fredman, *Human Rights Transformed* (Oxford University Press, 2008).

then assembled where factory labour is cheap from components sourced from a variety of locations and finally marketed on a global basis. The capital for these activities may be organised locally, within a multinational enterprise or by global banking institutions. The location of all these activities will be governed primarily by considerations of cost, taking into account the availability of a workforce with the necessary skills and access to global markets and facilities. A consequence of globalisation is that most businesses are subject to global competitive pressures. Governments have to respond to such pressures by avoiding costly regulation, high levels of corporate taxation and other disincentives to investment and the creation of jobs.

Globalisation is likely to have many effects on workers. It creates competitive pressures on their employers to improve productivity and reduce labour costs. The need for innovation, adaptation and flexibility becomes intensified. Businesses may rise and fall more rapidly, sucking in workers, both local and migrants, and then making them redundant as the business fails. The migration of workers looking for jobs, taking advantage of better transport links, becomes more frequent. There are risks that these workers will be exploited both by the traffickers who assist their travel and by the new employers in a foreign country. Globalisation also offers opportunities and benefits, both to workers in developing countries where industrialisation promises higher standards of living, and to workers in advanced economies, most of whom may have more interesting jobs in the knowledge economy.

Globalisation has also generated increasing intergovernmental co-operation and integration through the dismantling of trade barriers and the creation of international bodies to manage the intense economic and social relations being forged across borders. Although regional associations like the EU can help to protect workers against the pressures of globalisation by, for instance, fixing minimum labour standards at a transnational level within the Single Market, as we shall see in Chapter 2, there are no effective international standards that guarantee minimum standards across the world.[89] Another possible response to globalisation is to invoke human rights which, as universal standards, do not respect national boundaries, although again it is hard to find effective mechanisms to enforce those rights against unreceptive nation states. Although these developments in transnational and international labour law are to be welcomed, the task of disciplining the activities of private capital that operates at a global level by means of political institutions that still primarily focus on the territory of a nation state is plainly fraught with difficulties.

Of all the challenges facing labour law at present, perhaps globalisation is at once the greatest and the most intractable.[90] It creates the severest risks of

---

[89] B. Hepple, *Labour Laws and Global Trade* (Oxford: Hart, 2005); A. Supiot, *The Spirit of Philadelphia: Social Justice vs. the Total Market* (London: Verso, 2012).

[90] J. E. Stiglitz, *Globalization and Its Discontents Revised: Anti-Globalization in the Era of Trump* (London: Penguin Books, 2017).

exploitation, forcing workers into positions that are tantamount to slavery, and yet the transnational economic forces too often prove able to elude effective national labour laws. At the same time, globalisation tends to render most job precarious and places a constant downward pressure on pay in order for employers to remain competitive. Responses to these adverse consequences have included the election of or support for populist leaders who promise to hold back the tide of globalisation, and perhaps most significantly for the prospects for UK labour law, to include votes to support the exit of the UK from the EU. Since that withdrawal will take some time and there will be a transition period, EU employment law is likely to remain highly relevant for another four or five years, but after that the UK government may have the opportunity to strike out in its own direction to develop labour laws that address the problems caused by globalisation for ordinary workers.

2

Globalisation and Labour Law

Contents

Introduction

We begin this chapter with a child's school blazer. In a study on the role of trade unions in small businesses by one of the authors of this book, an interview was conducted with an employer in a town in the north-west of England. The business in question had previously manufactured school blazers, but now imported them to sell on to retail stores. In as good an illustration of the process of globalisation as any, the businessman explained that:

> [T]he actual yarn starts in Kilkenny in southern Ireland, produced by a company ... which is American. And it's then shipped to Ashton-under-Lyne where it's woven by a company who are Japanese. Once it's woven, it then goes back to Mansfield to the finishing and dyeing plant where they finish and dye it and ship it to Burma for us ... They make it there and it's made by Burmese workers. The factory is owned by the Chinese and it's over-managed by the Koreans and then it comes back to us as a finished garment.[1]

This simple garment thus has the input of the capital and labour of at least seven different countries. Even then, before it comes back to 'us', it will of course have to be shipped, and that again could involve the input of several shipping companies, with owners in yet other countries, the ships registered in other countries still, with crews recruited from yet others. And we have not started to work out the source of the buttons and labels.

There is nothing more basic than a school blazer. Yet this simple product brings home the opportunities and challenges of globalisation for workers everywhere, these opportunities and challenges arising principally as a result of the relaxation of controls on the free movement of capital and labour. It reveals the globalisation of capital, with the Irish production process owned by an American company, the British production process owned by Japanese capital and the Burmese factory owned by what is likely to be the Chinese government, though managed by a Korean contractor. And just as importantly, it reveals the globalisation of labour, with work previously undertaken for a consumer market in this country now being undertaken by workers in Burma, a country which at the time was something of a pariah state, not least because of the use of forced labour.[2] Yet while the parable of the school blazer provides us with a poignant insight into the process of globalisation, it cannot tell the whole story of a process that is leading to the relocation of business in search of cheaper labour, the cavalier conduct of foreign capital as it acquires,

---

[1] K. D. Ewing and A. Hock, *Partnership Working between Trade Unions and Small Businesses* (London: AMICUS-GPM and Community, 2005), para. 4.1.

[2] See ILO, *Report of the Commission of Inquiry Appointed under Article 26 of the ILO Constitution to Examine the Observance by Myanmar of the Forced Labour Convention, 1930* (No. 29) (GB 267/16/2, GB 268/14/8, GB 268/15/1): 'There is abundant evidence before the Commission showing the pervasive use of forced labour imposed on the civilian population throughout Myanmar by the authorities and the military [for a wide range of activities]' (para. 528).

restructures and discards businesses, and the capacity of workers to move freely across borders. While some have benefited greatly from globalisation and open markets, others face a reality of falling standards and long-term unemployment. So whatever the opportunities there may have been for Burmese workers in the example above, deskilled British manufacturing workers were having to adapt to a new life in storage and distribution.

Trying to deal with all this by regulation is very daunting, and indeed the idea of regulating for globalisation may seem to many to be implausible. Partly this is because globalisation creates competition between states, and there is little evidence yet that all governments see that their self-interest would be served by co-operation on labour standards. Partly it is because globalisation has transferred power from the nation state to the transnational corporation, and there is little evidence of any capacity to bring the transnational corporation within some kind of effective global regulation. And partly it is because of competition between workers' groups, with trade unions in the South, and in Asia in particular, anxious about protectionism in the North and West, and their exclusion from the markets of the developed world by high entry barriers. This last problem raises another, which is that regulatory objectives are not always expressed with conspicuous clarity, with a false competition being created between complementary objectives. Globalisation presents a need to (1) eschew protectionism so that all can enjoy the fruits of progress; (2) prevent a drift (if not a race) to the bottom and growing inequality within states (including the UK and the United States) as well as between states; and (3) above all prevent the exploitation of workers in both the developing and the developed worlds, who should be participants rather than spectators in the process. As already suggested, it is a daunting challenge, for although there may be an emerging consensus as to will,[3] as already suggested there may not yet be enough commitment as to means.

International Standards

It is perhaps paradoxical that there should be any problem with labour standards in the global economy, given that the International Labour Organization (ILO) has been in place since 1919 with a mandate to promote such standards.[4] Now an agency of the United Nations, the ILO was founded in the wake of the Russian Revolution and in the aftermath of the First World War,[5] for reasons made very clear in the preamble to the ILO Constitution.

---

[3] See pp. 92–5.

[4] On the origins and history of the ILO, see A. Alcock, *The International Labour Organization* (London: Macmillan, 1971).

[5] Indeed, it was said by one of the influential British representatives at the Versailles peace conference that the ILO was designed as an 'international Soviet of an evolutionary and constructive kind': G. N. Barnes, *The Industrial Section of the League of Nations* (London: Barnett House Papers No. 5, 1920), p. 16.

ILO Constitution, Preamble

Whereas universal and lasting peace can be established only if it is based upon social justice;

And whereas conditions of labour exist involving such injustice hardship and privation to large numbers of people as to produce unrest so great that the peace and harmony of the world are imperilled; and an improvement of those conditions is urgently required; as, for example, by the regulation of the hours of work including the establishment of a maximum working day and week, the regulation of the labour supply, the prevention of unemployment, the provision of an adequate living wage, the protection of the worker against sickness, disease and injury arising out of his employment, the protection of children, young persons and women, provision for old age and injury, protection of the interests of workers when employed in countries other than their own, recognition of the principle of equal remuneration for work of equal value, recognition of the principle of freedom of association, the organization of vocational and technical education and other measures;

Whereas also the failure of any nation to adopt humane conditions of labour is an obstacle in the way of other nations which desire to improve the conditions in their own countries.[6]

The ILO survived the traumatic events of the 1930s and was renewed towards the end of the Second World War, the ILO Declaration of Philadelphia of 1944 reaffirming a number of fundamental principles on which the ILO is constructed, including the principle that 'labour is not a commodity'.[7]

ILO Conventions

The ILO is a tripartite body, with its annual conference consisting of representatives of governments, business and labour from each of its 186 Member States.[8] Representatives from each constituent part are expected to operate independently: workers' representatives are delegates of workers' organisations not representatives of their government.[9] Under the ILO Constitution, the conference has responsibility to approve conventions and recommendations,[10] the former having the status of treaties in international law when they come into effect, creating binding obligations on those countries that ratify the convention in question. As at the end of 2017, there were no fewer than 189 international labour conventions (although not all of these are now in

---

[6] See www.ilo.org/ilolex/english/constq.htm.

[7] This is reaffirmed in the ILO Declaration on Social Justice for a Fair Globalisation (2008), which is considered at pp. 93–4. On the principle that 'labour is not a commodity', see P. O'Higgins, '"Labour Is Not a Commodity": An Irish Contribution to International Labour Law' (1997) 26 *Industrial Law Journal* 225. On a related theme, see E. McGaughey, 'A Human is Not a Resource', KCL Law School Research Paper, 2018–08.

[8] Only 6 of the 193 UN Member States are not also members of the ILO, the notable exception being North Korea.

[9] ILO Constitution, Art. 4(1).   [10] *Ibid.*, Art. 19.

force), with the first (in 1919) dealing with hours of work and the eight-hour day, and the most recent dealing with the rights of domestic workers. ILO conventions cover a vast territory, including freedom of association, forced labour, child labour and discrimination.[11] Although these four might be seen to be the core areas of ILO activity, other conventions deal with particular aspects of the employment relationship, such as wage-setting, health and safety at work and the termination of employment, as well as particular forms of employment.[12] Most recently, the ILO undertook a major revision and consolidation of labour standards for seafarers.[13] But there is also special protection for workers engaged in agriculture, fishing, hotels and restaurants and nursing, as well as for those engaged in particular forms of work such as part-time work.

The UK has ratified sixty-nine ILO conventions, but only fifty-two are now in force.[14] Those ratified include the eight core conventions dealing with freedom of association, forced labour, child labour and discrimination. Indeed, so far as freedom of association is concerned, the UK has ratified a number of important instruments in addition to the standard Conventions 87 and 98,[15] these including the Workers' Representatives Convention, 1971 and the Labour Relations (Public Service) Convention, 1978. Although the number of conventions in force in the UK is high compared to that in other common law jurisdictions (such as the United States, with only twelve in force), it is at the low end of EU Member States, with Spain (eighty-six), France (seventy-nine), Italy (seventy-five), Belgium (seventy-four), Finland (seventy-two), Netherlands (seventy), Luxembourg (sixty-eight), Sweden (sixty-six), Portugal (sixty-three), Germany (fifty-nine), and Denmark (fifty-three) applying more, and only Greece (fifty-one), Ireland (forty-six) and Austria (forty-three) of the original EU15 having ratified fewer. So far as the denounced conventions are concerned, many of these denunciations took place in the 1980s when the

[11] See ILO Convention 87 (Freedom of Association and Protection of the Right to Organise Convention, 1948); ILO Convention 98 (Right to Organise and Collective Bargaining Convention, 1949); ILO Convention 29 (Forced Labour Convention, 1930); ILO Convention 105 (Abolition of Forced Labour Convention, 1957); ILO Convention 138 (Minimum Age Convention, 1973); ILO Convention 182 (Worst Forms of Child Labour Convention, 1999); ILO Convention 100 (Equal Remuneration Convention, 1951); and ILO Convention 111 (Discrimination (Employment and Occupation) Convention, 1958). All eight have been ratified by the UK, which in 2016 also ratified the Protocol to Convention 29, which came into force in the same year.

[12] Important conventions include ILO Convention 26 (Minimum Wage-Fixing Machinery Convention, 1928); ILO Convention 155 (Occupational Safety and Health Convention, 1981); and ILO Convention 158 (Termination of Employment Convention, 1982). The first was denounced by the UK in 1985 and the other two have never been ratified by the UK.

[13] ILO Maritime Labour Convention, 2006, which revises and updates a number of maritime conventions.

[14] Conventions in force are not the same as conventions ratified. The UK has ratified eighty-seven conventions, but twenty-seven have been denounced over the years and another eight abrogated.

[15] See note 11.

then-government was engaged in a process of active labour law deregulation that ran against the grain of existing ILO obligations.[16] Major denunciations at this time included the Minimum Wage-Fixing Machinery Convention, 1928, the Labour Clauses (Public Contracts) Convention, 1949 and the Protection of Wages Convention, 1949. Denunciation is in effect a process of deratification, which must take place in accordance with a procedure in the relevant convention, and has the effect that the state ceases to be bound by the obligation in question.

ILO Supervision

The ILO Constitution provides that members must make 'an annual report to the International Labour Office on the measures which it has taken to give effect to the provisions of Conventions to which it is a party'.[17] As we have seen, there are currently 189 conventions and 186 Member States, suggesting a potential 24,487 reports annually.[18] It is true that no state has ratified all conventions and that the level of ratification stands at less than 8,000. But even so, annual reporting in relation to *all* ratified conventions would impose a heavy burden on both the Member States and the ILO Governing Body which is primarily responsible for supervising compliance with these conventions, at least in the first instance. As a result, reporting takes place on a less frequent schedule, with reporting of core conventions taking place every two years and for the other conventions much less often.[19] Reports submitted by governments to the International Labour Office about national law and practice in relation to a ratified convention are sent for comment to the national business and trade union organisations. In the case of the UK, this means that the TUC will submit observations on the government's report, to counteract inevitable government claims that national law meets international standards. Since 1926, these reports have been examined by the Committee of Experts on the Application of Standards, a body of eminent independent jurists appointed by the Governing Body,[20] whose conclusions are widely regarded as containing authoritative interpretations of ILO instruments, creating a substantial body of jurisprudence on which other bodies now rely.[21]

---

[16] On denunciation, see K. Widdows, 'The Denunciation of International Labour Conventions' (1984) 33 *International and Comparative Law Quarterly* 1052.

[17] ILO Constitution, Art. 22.

[18] Actually it would be fewer, given that some conventions are no longer in force and others have not yet been brought into force.

[19] See B. A. Hepple, *Labour Laws and Global Trade* (Oxford: Hart, 2005), Ch. 2.

[20] Members of the Committee in the past have included Earl Warren (later to be Chief Justice of the US Supreme Court) and Archibald Cox (Richard Nixon's nemesis).

[21] Notably the European Court of Human Rights (ECHR). See *Demir and Baycara* v. *Turkey* [2008] ECHR 1345, (2009) 48 EHRR 54. But see now the discussion relating to ILO jurisprudence in *RMT* v. *United Kingdom* [2014] ECHR 366, paras. 96–8.

Although some countries do what is required, a study by Ewing and Sibley found that others tended to report late, a number of others had not submitted reports for several years, while others had been told repeatedly by the Committee of Experts that their domestic law failed to meet ILO standards.[22] The last of these problems can be illustrated by the experience of the UK (though many other countries could also be selected). In 1989, the Committee of Experts undertook a comprehensive review of the anti-union legislation passed since 1980, and concluded that UK law breached ILO Conventions 87 and 98 for several reasons, relating mainly to the restrictions on the right to strike.[23] These conclusions have been repeated regularly ever since, with a number of additional concerns being picked up on the way. Many of these repeats were on display during the period from 1997 to 2010, despite the fact that the Labour government had made some significant changes to domestic law, which nonetheless retained the bulk of the restrictions inherited from previous administrations.[24] In a particularly important report in 2010, the Committee had an opportunity to review the impact on national law of the controversial decisions of the ECJ in the *Viking* and *Laval* cases of 2007.[25] The Committee found that the restrictions in UK law as a result of these decisions (and the national law of other EU Member States) were incompatible with the obligations of ILO Member States under ILO Convention 87.[26]

The ILO and Freedom of Association

It is to be noted that, although ILO conventions are binding only on those countries that have ratified them, all ILO Member States are required by virtue of membership of the organisation to comply with freedom of association principles. The ILO Freedom of Association Committee (CFA) (a tripartite body) was established to hear complaints from trade unions alleging that national governments are in breach of these principles, a procedure that may be used whether or not the government in question has ratified the freedom of association

---

[22] K. D. Ewing and T. Sibley, *International Trade Union Rights for the New Millennium* (London: International Centre for Trade Union Rights, 2000), pp. 34–8.

[23] ILO Committee of Experts, Observation Concerning Convention 87 (United Kingdom) (1989). Much of the concern related also to the ban on trade unions at the UK's Government Communications Headquarters (GCHQ), imposed in 1984 and not removed until 1997. See Chapter 12.

[24] It is also the case that some of the measures of the new government (such as the trade union recognition procedure in the Employment Relations Act 1999) did not go as far as ILO standards require. See pp. 631–2.

[25] Case C-438/05, *International Transport Workers' Federation* v. *Viking Line ABP* [2007] ECR I-10779, [2008] IRLR 143 (ECJ) and Case C-341/05, *Laval un Partneri Ltd* v. *Svenska Byggnadsarbetareförbundet* [2007] ECR I-11767, [2008] IRLR 160 (ECJ) respectively. See pp. 88–9 and 65–7.

[26] ILO Committee of Experts, Observation Concerning Convention 87 (United Kingdom) (2010). Also 2011.

conventions. Countries that have ratified these conventions are – of course – also subject to the ongoing scrutiny of the Committee of Experts (discussed above), whereas those countries that have not ratified these conventions are not subject to such scrutiny. In these latter cases, a freedom of association complaint is the only effective way of bringing matters to the attention of the supervisory bodies. Both US and Canadian trade unions have been frequent applicants to the CFA, with outcomes which in the case of Canada have been valuable in domestic litigation. As already mentioned, the United States has ratified neither Convention 87 nor Convention 98, and while Canada has ratified Convention 87 it has only recently ratified Convention 98.

Global Trade

In recent years, a number of other means have been proposed as a way to address the responsibility of states. These include using trade as a coercive device or as an incentive to encourage states to comply with international labour standards. In the 1990s, there was much talk – to which the ILO contributed – about a social clause in trade agreements whereby access to international markets would be made to depend in part on a country's compliance with core ILO conventions. The idea is by no means new, and indeed we can see its genesis in ILO Convention 94,[27] which provides for the economic power of the state to be used to ensure that public service contractors observe fair labour standards.[28] The social clause transfers from the national to the international level the idea that economic power can be used to encourage compliance with fair standards, both to respect the individual worker and to ensure fair competition between countries.

The Social Clause

The real prize for many was the introduction of a social clause into the proceedings of the World Trade Organization (WTO), seen by the ILO and others as a potentially effective way of promoting compliance with ILO standards.[29] The idea here is that a country that failed to comply with certain core ILO conventions would be subject to a process of scrutiny by the ILO with a view to ultimately being denied certain trade benefits or being excluded from certain markets altogether. Just as sanctions are imposed on some regimes on human rights and governance grounds, so trade penalties or

---

[27] Labour Clauses (Public Contracts) Convention, 1949 (previously ratified but since denounced by the UK).

[28] In domestic law, it is to be seen in the now-revoked Fair Wages Resolution of 1946, a resolution of the House of Commons whereby government contractors were required to observe fair wages and to respect their workers' right to freedom of association.

[29] For a full discussion, see B. A. Hepple, *Labour Laws and Global Trade* (Oxford: Hart, 2005) especially Ch. 6.

sanctions would be imposed on those countries that were seen to compete unfairly or to operate exploitative labour practices. But although this idea gained ground in the 1990s,[30] it was struck a fatal blow by the first Ministerial Conference of the WTO, when it was resolved in Singapore that:

> We renew our commitment to the observance of internationally recognized core labour standards. The International Labour Organization (ILO) is the competent body to set and deal with these standards, and we affirm our support for its work in promoting them. We believe that economic growth and development fostered by increased trade and further trade liberalization contribute to the promotion of these standards. We reject the use of labour standards for protectionist purposes, and agree that the comparative advantage of countries, particularly low-wage developing countries, must in no way be put into question. In this regard, we note that the WTO and ILO Secretariats will continue their existing collaboration.[31]

This statement concealed a wide range of differences between the different Member States of the WTO, between those in the developed world (such as the United States and France), which were pressing for a social clause for what were thought to be protectionist reasons, and those in the developing world, which opposed it because it would be detrimental to their national interests.[32] It also concealed differences between trade unionists in the prosperous North and the less prosperous South, it being claimed that trade unionists in the United States in particular saw the social clause as a way of protecting workers in manufacturing jobs from being displaced by cheap imports of manufactured goods. The aim of the social clause would be to lift working conditions in the developing world to reverse the gradual erosion of standards and loss of jobs in the developed world. It now appears to be accepted that the 'comparative advantage of any country should not be called into question'. By this is meant 'the comparative advantage that some countries enjoy by virtue of a relative abundance of lower-cost labour', which 'has been affirmed as a legitimate advantage in trade, as it was historically for today's industrialized countries'.[33]

Legacy of the Social Clause

If the Ministerial Statement of 1996 concealed differences about the linking of trade and labour standards, it also made explicit a desire to confine labour standards to the jurisdiction of the ILO. One consequence of this was the ILO

---

[30] For a particularly helpful contribution, see D. Chin, *A Labour Clause for Labour's Cause: Global Trade and Labour Standards* (London: Institute of Employment Rights, 1998).

[31] Singapore Ministerial Declaration, adopted on 13 December 1996, para. 4.

[32] See V. Leary, 'The WTO and the Social Clause: Post-Singapore' (1997) 1 *European Journal of International Law* 118, at 119.

[33] ILO, *Reducing the Decent Work Deficit: A Global Challenge* (Geneva: ILO, 2001), p. 54.

Declaration of Fundamental Principles and Rights at Work of 1998, reflecting a need to concentrate on a few core themes and to ensure more widespread respect for certain core standards relating to freedom of association, the elimination of forced or compulsory labour, the effective abolition of the worst forms of child labour, and the elimination of discrimination in respect of employment and occupation. All Member States of the ILO have signed the Declaration which boldly declares that all members, 'even if they have not ratified the Convention in question,[34] have an obligation arising from the very fact of membership in the Organisation, to respect, to promote and to realize, in good faith and in accordance with the Constitution, the principles concerning the fundamental rights which are the subject of those Conventions'.[35] The follow-up procedure established under the Declaration suggests that, although progress was being made in some areas, it remained very slow. For example:

> So far as freedom of association is concerned, it was reported in 2004 that '213 trade unionists were killed worldwide, some 1,000 were injured or subjected to violence, 2,562 were arrested and detained, and 89 were sentenced to prison terms'. This was said not to 'include many more who were dismissed or harassed on account of their membership of a trade union', while the murder of 184 trade unionists in Colombia alone was said to threaten the very survival of trade unionism in that country.[36]
>
> So far as child labour is concerned, although very significant improvements were reported in 2006, it remained the case that 218 million children were said to have been trapped in child labour in 2004, of whom 126 million were engaged in what is described as 'hazardous work'. In the 5–14 age group it was estimated that 166 million children were involved in child labour, accounting for about 14% of all the children in the age group.[37]

As predicted by the Director General of the ILO in 1996, the social-clause debate has had another legacy, namely the use of labour standards in bilateral trade agreements. There has been a notable increase in the negotiation of such agreements, led initially by the USA and now by the EU. Indeed, the current preference is for multilateral agreements such as (1) the Trans-Pacific Partnership (TPP), from which the USA withdrew at a late stage,[38] and (2) the aborted

---

[34] The conventions referred to here are those referred to in note 11.

[35] For critical analysis, see P. Alston, 'Core Labour Standards and the Transformation of the International Labour Regime' (2004) 15 *European Journal of International Law* 457, and P. Alston, 'Facing up to the Complexities of ILO's Core Labour Standards Agenda' (2005) 16 *European Journal of International Law* 467.

[36] ILO, *Organising for Social Justice* (Geneva: ILO, 2004).

[37] ILO, *The End of Child Labour* (Geneva: ILO, 2006).

[38] See J.-C. Tham and K. D. Ewing, 'Trade Agreements and Australian Labour Law: Implications of the Death of the Transatlantic Partnership Agreement', in J. Howe, A. Chapman and I. Landau (eds.), *The Evolving Project of Labour Law* (Annandale, NSW: Federation Press, 2017). On outstanding issues post-US withdrawal, see J.-C. Tham and K. D. Ewing, Submission to the inquiry of the Senate Foreign Affairs, Defence and Trade References Committee into the proposed Comprehensive Progressive Trans-Pacific Partnership, 22 May 2018.

Transatlantic Trade and Investment Partnership (TTIP) between the EU and the USA.[39] Important recent agreements to which the EU (and the UK) are a party include those concluded with Canada and Korea, under the terms of which the parties reaffirm their obligations as members of the ILO and the commitments made to the ILO's Declaration of Fundamental Principles and Rights at Work. The parties also undertake to strive to ensure that these principles and other internationally recognised labour rights are recognised and protected by domestic labour law. But there are serious doubts about how far these obligations are effectively enforced, (1) with all countries typically in breach of at least some of the obligations at the point of ratification,[40] (2) with no intention it seems of ever fully complying, and (3) with no procedure in the agreements to compel them to do so.[41] One of the possible implications of Brexit is that existing EU free trade agreements (to which the UK is a party along with the other twenty-seven Member States) will roll over as bilateral agreements between the UK and the third country, though presumably this will require the consent of each of the third parties concerned.[42] The UK's obligations in respect of labour rights will thus continue, and may indeed be reaffirmed by other agreements concluded after departure from the EU.

Trade Incentives to Improve Labour Standards

An important initiative within the EU uses trade as an incentive to raise standards. The Generalised System of Preferences (GSP) is an arrangement that provides preferential access to the EU for developing countries. The obligations on beneficiaries are much more demanding than the obligations on third countries arising under free trade agreements, even though not all free trade agreements are with countries with admirable records on labour rights. The EU–Korea agreement is a case in point, Korea not having ratified all eight core conventions and with the CFA exposing its egregious record on freedom of association.[43] Nevertheless, the GSP arrangements – currently set out in Council Regulation (EC) No. 978/2012 – are very different, and apply to all three categories of tariff preference: the general arrangement, the special incentive arrangement for sustainable development and good

---

[39] For a brief review of some of the issues relating to TTIP, see K. D. Ewing and J. Hendy QC, 'TTIP and the Rule of Law', *Left Futures*, 11 June 2015.

[40] See K. D. Ewing and J. Hendy QC, 'The Eclipse of the Rule of Law: Trade Union Rights and the EU' (2015) 4 *Revista Derecho Social y Empresa* 80.

[41] Some of the problems are discussed in K. D. Ewing, 'International Standards: The ILO and Other Agencies', in C. Frege and J. Kelly (eds.), *Comparative Employment Relations in the Global Economy* (London: Routledge, 2013), Ch. 23 and J.-C. Tham and K. D. Ewing, 'Labour Clauses in the TPP and TTIP: A Comparison without a Difference?' (2016) 17 *Melbourne Journal of International Law* 369.

[42] Trade Bill 2017–19, cl. 2.

[43] See K. D. Ewing, 'International Standards: The ILO and Other Agencies', in C. Frege and J. Kelly (eds.), *Comparative Employment Relations in the Global Economy* (London: Routledge, 2013).

governance (GSP+) and 'a special arrangement for the least-developed countries'. Different countries at different stages of development fall into different categories, although in all cases trading preferences can be suspended where there is a 'serious and systematic violation of principles laid down in the fifteen "conventions" listed in Annex VIII'.[44] These include not only the International Covenant on Civil and Political Rights (ICCPR) and the International Covenant on Economic, Social and Cultural Rights but also the eight core ILO conventions dealing with child labour, forced labour, the elimination of discrimination, and freedom of association. European Commission reports suggest that suspension of trading preferences arises typically in relation to the second and third categories of preference referred to above.[45]

In addition to the foregoing, there are separate provisions that apply exclusively to countries falling within the second category (GSP+), which are required not only to comply with the principles, but also to have ratified all the fifteen conventions referred to above as well as another twelve dealing with environmental issues and corruption. In addition, GSP+ countries must be able to show that the most recently available conclusions of the monitoring bodies under those conventions 'do not identify a serious failure to effectively implement any of those conventions'.[46] Moreover, GSP+ countries must give 'a binding undertaking to maintain ratification of the relevant conventions and to ensure the effective implementation thereof', and accept without reservation 'the reporting requirements imposed by each convention and [give] a binding undertaking to accept regular monitoring and review of its implementation record in accordance with the provisions of the relevant conventions' (Article 9(1)(d)–(f)). The European Commission is required to report to the European Parliament and to the Council every two years 'on the status of ratification of the relevant conventions, the compliance of the GSP+ beneficiary countries with any reporting obligations under those conventions and the status of the effective implementation thereof'.[47] GSP+ countries are thus subject to regular monitoring by the European Commission, which engages with the countries in question to identify shortcomings and provide technical assistance for remedial action.[48] Preferences may be withdrawn in the event of a failure to comply with the provisions of Article 9(1)(d)–(f), above, in addition to any failure already referred to.

Working Abroad

Globalisation provides new opportunities for workers. It is true that British people have occasionally worked abroad for many centuries. In the Imperial past, however, a posting to a job in a colony did not affect the legal position: English law would apply, as illustrated by *Addis* v. *Gramophone Co. Ltd*,[49] a leading decision on the law of wrongful dismissal arising from employment in

---

[44] Council Regulation (EC) No. 978/2012, Art. 19(1)(a).   [45] *Ibid.*   [46] *Ibid.*, Art. 9(1)(b).
[47] *Ibid.*, Art. 14.
[48] European Commission, Report on the Generalised Scheme of Preferences covering the period 2016–2017, COM(2018) 36 final (20 January 2018).
[49] [1909] AC 488 (HL).

Calcutta. In recent decades, however, with the opening up of the Single Market in Europe, the advent of multinational enterprises and the operation of global markets, UK workers travelling abroad have become much more common. It is common, for instance, for large London firms of solicitors to send their employees to their branches in foreign cities. For those working abroad, in most cases the local foreign law will apply to disputes arising with their foreign employer and rights will have to be vindicated in local courts. In some cases, however, such as when a UK worker is posted abroad to work for a foreign subsidiary of a UK company, it may be possible to argue that English law should apply to the dispute. The law that determines which system of employment should apply is a European Regulation, either 'Rome I' concerning contractual disputes,[50] or 'Rome II' concerning claims in tort.[51] The CJEU provides the authoritative interpretation of their application. Following the UK's withdrawal from the EU, these Regulations will become UK domestic law and UK courts will be empowered to place their own interpretations on them, 'having regard to' any relevant decisions of the CJEU.

Rome I Regulation and Contract

The general framework of the Rome I Regulation provides that the parties to a contract of employment are free to choose the applicable law. Nevertheless, this 'subjectively applicable' choice cannot deprive an employee of the protection of mandatory provisions of the law applicable in the absence of an explicit choice of law – the 'objectively applicable law'. If the parties do not specify an applicable law, the contract of employment is governed by the law of the country of the habitual place of work or, in the absence of a habitual place of work, by the law of the country of the business engaging the employee – the 'objectively applicable law'. Where it appears from the circumstances as a whole, however, that the contract is more closely connected with another country than the objectively applicable law based on the habitual place of work, that other country's law applies. The meaning of a contract of employment in the EU Regulations imitates the meaning of 'worker' in EU law.[52] Under these rules of the Rome I Regulation, for instance, a person from the UK who takes a job in France would normally have a contract of employment governed by French law (the habitual place of work), but English law would probably apply either if the contract actually specified that English law should be applicable or if the employer was a company based in the UK.

In such a case, however, the choice for English law could not deprive the worker of non-derogable workers' rights that arise in the place of performance

---

[50] Regulation 593/2008 of 17 June 2008 on the law applicable to contractual obligations.
[51] Regulation 864/2007 of 11 July 2007 on the law applicable to non-contractual obligations.
[52] Case C-47/14, *Holterman Ferho Exploitatie BV* v. *Spies von Büllesheim* [2016] ICR 90; for the EU concept of 'worker' see Chapter 6.

of work – the 'objectively applicable law' – which in this example would comprise French mandatory employment rights. Confusion about the application of these principles has been sown by the decision of the House of Lords in a group of cases known as *Lawson* v. *Serco Ltd*.[53] This decision was based on an earlier treaty between the Members of the EU, the Rome Convention,[54] though the wording of the treaty was broadly the same as the current Rome I Regulation. In *Lawson* v. *Serco Ltd*, the House of Lords insisted that although for ordinary contractual disputes the principles described in the previous paragraph would apply, for the purpose of statutory claims under UK law, such as claims for unfair dismissal, the minimum wage or for discrimination, the application of English law depended on Parliament's intention with respect to the territorial scope of application of the statute.[55] While some statutes specify where they apply, such as the NMWA which applies to a worker who 'is working, or ordinarily works, in the United Kingdom',[56] unfortunately many statutes are virtually silent on the matter, including the law with respect to unfair dismissal and discrimination.

Rome I Regulation and Statute

The ERA 1996, section 204 (applicable to unfair dismissal) states that: 'For the purposes of this Act, it is immaterial whether the law which … governs any person's employment is the law of the UK, or of a part of the UK, or not'. That phrase seems to mean that the choice of law rules of the Rome I Regulation are inapplicable to claims for unfair dismissal, but no light is shed on how to determine whether the statutory claims of the ERA 1996 apply. In *Lawson* v. *Serco Ltd*, the House of Lords held that statutory claims for unfair dismissal could be brought by employees working in the UK and also in three additional cases: where the employee was based in the UK, although working peripatetically (such as airline pilots and international salesmen and women);[57] an employee posted abroad for the purpose of a business carried on in the UK (such as a foreign correspondent of a newspaper); and an employee posted to a territorial UK enclave located abroad (such as working at an army base).[58] Subsequently, in *Ravat* v. *Halliburton Manufacturing and Services Ltd*,[59] the

---

[53] *Lawson* v. *Serco Ltd*; *Botham* v. *Ministry of Defence*; *Crofts* v. *Veta Ltd* [2006] UKHL 3, [2006] ICR 250 (HL).

[54] Rome Convention on the law applicable to contractual obligations (1980) [1980] OJ L266/1, implemented by the Contracts (Applicable Law) Act 1990.

[55] L. Merrett, *Employment Contracts in Private International Law* (Oxford University Press, 2011); U. Grusic, *The European Private International Law of Employment* (Cambridge University Press, 2015).

[56] NMWA 1998, s. 1(2)(b).   [57] *Crofts* v. *Veta Ltd* [2006] UKHL 3, [2006] ICR 250 (HL).

[58] *Lawson* v. *Serco Ltd*; *Botham* v. *Ministry of Defence* [2006] UKHL 3, [2006] ICR 250 (HL); *Duncombe* v. *Secretary of State for Children, Schools and Families (No. 2)* [2011] UKSC 36, [2011] ICR 1312 (HL).

[59] [2012] UKSC 1.

Supreme Court held that these three categories were not exhaustive and applied English law to a UK resident, employed by a UK company, but who worked in Libya for fixed periods of a month at a time for an affiliated German company.[60]

By not applying the Rome I Regulation and the predecessor Convention in these ways, the courts in the UK have provoked considerable litigation, but oddly they have been reaching conclusions that appear to duplicate the results that would have been reached under the Regulation. In *Ravat*, for instance, the Supreme Court applied an approach that was almost identical to the proviso applicable to the 'objectively applicable' law that prescribes that, even if the place of work and the place of business of the employer is not the UK, English law can be applied if in the circumstances it appears to be the most closely connected law,[61] by stating that there must be a 'sufficiently close connection' to English law to displace the foreign jurisdiction based on the place of performance. The main problem now thus concerns the 'subjectively applicable law' where the parties have expressly stated that English law should apply, even though the employee would be working abroad in circumstances that do not fall within the exceptions specified in *Lawson* v. *Serco Ltd* and *Ravat* v. *Halliburton*.

Under the Rome I Regulation, such an express choice of law should be effective unless and to the extent that it removes beneficial employment rights arising under the objectively applicable law. But ERA 1996 section 204 has been interpreted to mean that an express choice of law is irrelevant, because the territorial scope of statutory employment rights depends on the intention of Parliament, not the choice of the parties.[62] Nevertheless the Supreme Court observed in *Duncombe* v. *Secretary of State for Children, Schools and Families (No. 2)* that the fact that English law was chosen by the parties 'must be relevant to the expectation of each party as to the protection which the employee would enjoy'. This distinction drawn between contractual claims and statutory claims makes no sense from a civil law perspective, where all claims are based on the relevant civil code. The CJEU approaches questions about the choice of law in employment from the civil law perspective. Following withdrawal from the EU, courts in the UK will be able to reassert the traditional common law view that statutes determine their field of application. Given how vague most statutes are on this issue, that approach will surely prove unsatisfactory.

---

[60] A similar approach seems likely to apply to the EqA 2010 with respect to claims for discrimination, because that statute, unlike the earlier legislation in that field, does not specify its territorial scope.

[61] Cf. Case C-64/12 *Schlecker* v. *Boedeker* [2013] ICR 1274.

[62] *Bleuse* v. *MBT Transport Ltd* [2008] ICR 488 (EAT).

Working Abroad: Two Further Considerations

When considering cases concerning jobs that involve working abroad, two further matters need to be borne in mind. First, as an exception to the rules outlined above the Rome I Regulation permits courts to apply the overriding mandatory provisions of their own jurisdiction that safeguard 'its public interests, such as its political, social or economic organisations'.

While ordinary employment law rights probably do not qualify as an overriding mandatory provision of public policy, it seems likely that the requirement to conform to ECHR rights under the HRA 1998 would suffice. In *Netjets Management Ltd* v. *Central Arbitration Committee*,[63] the High Court preferred an interpretation of the territorial application of the statutory recognition procedure for trade unions that both relied upon the approach in *Ravat* v. *Halliburton* that there was a sufficiently close connection between the airline pilots and English law, despite the fact that they were peripatetic workers, and upon the point that only this interpretation protected the freedom of association rights of the pilots under Article 11 ECHR.

The second point to remember is that as well as determining the applicable law, it is also necessary to consider whether or not a court or tribunal in the UK has jurisdiction to hear a case with foreign elements. Here again EU law provides the mandatory rules under the Brussels I Regulation.[64] In general terms, under the Brussels I Regulation, an employee may bring a claim in the country of the employer's domicile or where the employee habitually works. In the case of internationally peripatetic workers, the claim can also be brought in the courts for the place of engagement. The employer must bring a claim against an employee in the country where the latter is domiciled (even if that allocation of jurisdiction is disadvantageous for the employee)[65]. The aim of the Regulation is to protect employees by permitting them to bring a claim in the most convenient jurisdiction for them, but the rules do not straightforwardly achieve that goal in the case of peripatetic workers, because those employees may prefer to bring a claim in their home state rather than the one where the employer is based or where they habitually work in practice.

For this reason, the ECJ has permitted claims to be brought by peripatetic workers where they can establish an effective centre of their working activities, regarding that place as where they habitually work even if they spend more time working in other countries.[66] The aim of enabling an employee to enjoy a more advantageous choice of jurisdiction in comparison to other parties is not always achieved, however, as in the case of a succession of employments with affiliated employers domiciled in different countries, where it was not possible to join them as co-defendants before a single court.[67]

---

[63] *Netjets Management Ltd* v. *Central Arbitration Committee* [2012] EWHC 2685 (Admin).
[64] Regulation 44/2001.
[65] *Yukos International UK BV* v. *Merinson* [2018] EWHC 335 (Comm), [2018] ICR 1165.
[66] Case C-125/92, *Mulox IBC Ltd* v. *Geels* [1993] ECR I-4075 (ECJ); Case C-383/95, *Rutten* v. *Cross Medical Ltd* [1997] ICR 715 (ECJ); Case C-37/00, *Weber* v. *Universal Ogden Services Ltd* [2002] ECR I-2013 (ECJ).
[67] Case C-462/06, *GlaxoSmithKline* v. *Rouard* [2008] ECR I-3965 (ECJ).

Posted Workers and Working Conditions

Although labour mobility provides opportunities for many workers, it also generates a number of serious problems for labour law. An illustration of these problems arose in relation to the posting of workers, a matter regulated by the Posted Workers Directive of 1996,[68] an instrument that deals with the position where workers are posted by their employer or by an agency in their home state to work in another EU Member State (the host state). To take two simple examples of what are often complex employment relationships, this could arise where:

- a company in country A wins a service or construction contract in country B, and rather than employ people in country B, recruits and sends staff from country A;
- a company in country A needs workers to perform certain tasks (such as pick vegetables) and engages workers through a labour supply company in country B.

Country B in these examples may be a relatively poor country with low wages, and it is necessary to ensure that the posted workers are paid the wages of the host state not the home state, in order not only to prevent exploitation but also undercutting. The European Commission estimates that there are approximately two million workers posted in the EU as a whole, representing less than 1 per cent of total employment, with over a third being in the construction sector.[69] It was thought that in 2015 there were just over 50,000 posted workers in the UK, an increase from about 30,000 in 2010.[70] Most EU workers who come to the UK thus do so by virtue of freedom of movement under the TFEU: they are directly employed by employers and are not as such posted workers. The posting of workers has nevertheless given rise to acute political controversy.

Core Standards

A posted worker is defined by the Directive to mean a 'worker who, for a limited period, carries out [his or her] work in the territory of a Member State other than the state in which [he or she] normally works'.[71] Member States must ensure that certain minimum terms and conditions of employment applicable to workers in the host state are also applicable to posted workers where contracts made in their home state are inferior. For this purpose, the

---

[68] Directive 96/71/EC. See P. L. Davies, 'The Posted Workers Directive and the EC Treaty' (2002) 31 *Industrial Law Journal* 298.

[69] European Commission, *Posted Workers in the EU* (n.d.).

[70] *Ibid.* There are thought to be about 30,000 workers posted from the UK to other EU states (*ibid.*).

[71] Posted Workers Directive, Art. 2(1).

Directive applies to terms and conditions of employment laid down by law, regulation or administrative provision, and in some cases by collective agreements.[72] The core questions to which the Directive applies are set out in Article 3(1) of the Directive:

(a) maximum work periods and minimum rest periods;
(b) minimum paid annual holidays;
(c) the minimum rates of pay, including overtime rates; this point does not apply to supplementary occupational retirement pension schemes;
(d) the conditions of hiring-out of workers, in particular the supply of workers by temporary employment undertakings;
(e) health, safety and hygiene at work;
(f) protective measures with regard to the terms and conditions of employment of pregnant women or women who have recently given birth, of children and of young people;
(g) equality of treatment between men and women and other provisions on non-discrimination.

Article 3(10) of the Directive permits additions to be made to this list, by providing that 'terms and conditions of employment on matters other than those referred to in the first subparagraph of paragraph 1 in the case of public policy provisions'.

For workers posted to the UK, this list may provide rather thin pickings at least in relation to pay, given that all that is guaranteed is the minimum rate of pay laid down by law, rather than the prevailing rate of pay that may be laid down in the contracts of the workers alongside whom posted workers may be engaged. It is true that under the Directive posted workers in some cases may be entitled to the minimum terms set out in collective agreements. But this applies only where the latter 'have been declared universally applicable within the meaning of [Article 3], paragraph 8', and only 'insofar as they concern the activities referred to in the Annex'. Collective agreements for these purposes are 'universally applicable' only if they 'must be observed by all undertakings in the geographical area and in the profession or industry concerned'. There is no procedure in UK law for declaring collective agreements universally applicable (which means that this will not be an issue for workers posted to the UK), though this is not the case in other jurisdictions (which means that this may be an issue for UK workers posted to other EU Member States). The Annex refers mainly to the construction industry and building maintenance and services, though Article 3(10) permits Member States to extend the application of universally applicable collective agreements to activities other than those in

---

[72] *Ibid.*, Art. 3(1). See Case C-396/13, *Sähköalojen ammattiliitto ry* v. *Elektrobudowa Spółka Akcyjna*, 12 February 2015, on calculating the 'minimum', notable also for holding that posted Polish workers could not be prevented by Polish law from assigning a claim to a Finnish union to pursue a claim on their behalf for unpaid wages relating to work done in Finland.

the Annex. So, while the terms of universally applicable collective agreements (where they exist) *must* be applied in construction, they *may* be applied in other sectors at the discretion of the state in question.[73]

The Posted Workers Directive and the East Lindsey Dispute

The Posted Workers Directive was thrust into the limelight as a result of a bitter dispute at East Lindsey Oil Refinery in 2009, partly as a result of concern about non-compliance by Italian sub-contractors with a national agreement for the electrical contracting industry (NAECI). Although the public face of the dispute was the slogan 'British jobs for British workers',[74] an underlying concern was that the terms of the national agreement were in danger of being undercut by the use of sub-contractors supplying workers recruited overseas. The dispute revealed the dangers of the Posted Workers Directive, whereby Article 3(1) workers were entitled to the minimum terms laid down by statute, and the more favourable terms of collective agreements but only if the latter had been declared universally applicable in accordance with Article 3(8). Because there is no procedure for declaring collective agreements universally applicable, the industrial action at East Lindsey designed to uphold the NAECI agreement would have fallen foul of EU law as discussed later in the text. The dispute was resolved by the constructive intervention of ACAS and the negotiation of a new agreement making it clear that all contractors and sub-contractors are required to comply with its terms.[75] The agreement also contained better inspection procedures to ensure full compliance.[76]

Raising Standards

Although the Posted Workers Directive is perhaps the first attempt to regulate the working conditions of transnational workers, its operation has not been without difficulty. Some of these difficulties were exposed in the *Laval* case,[77]

---

[73] Though, following the decision in Case C-319/06, *Commission* v. *Luxembourg* [2008] ECR I-4323, it may be very difficult in practice for Member States to rely on Art. 3(10). But see pp. 66–7 below.

[74] See C. Barnard, '"British Jobs for British Workers": The Lindsey Oil Refinery Dispute and the Future of Local Labour Clauses in an Integrated EU Market' (2009) 38 *Industrial Law Journal* 245.

[75] See ACAS, *Report of an Inquiry into the Circumstances Surrounding the Lindsey Oil Refinery Dispute* (London, 2009). See further, p. 807.

[76] The full agreement and its most recent supplements may be found on the Electrical Construction Industry Association website.

[77] Case C-341/05, *Laval un Partneri Ltd* v. *Svenska Byggnadsarbetareförbundet* [2007] ECR I-11767, [2008] IRLR 160. See also Case 346/06, *Rüffert* v. *Land Niedersachsen* [2008] ECR I-1989 and Case C-319/06, *Commission* v. *Luxembourg* [2008] ECR I-4323. Some commentators detect a softening of the approach of the CJEU in Case 115/14, *RegioPost GmbH* v. *Stadt Landau in der Pflaz*, 17 November 2015, though it is difficult to see why. See also Case C-549/13, *Bundesdruckerei GmbH* v. *Stadt Dortmund*, 18 September 2014, which reveals another limitation of the Posted Workers Directive: contractor in country A elects to have the work done in country B where wages are low. The Posted Workers Directive applies only if workers

where a Latvian company secured a building contract in Sweden. It appears that Laval did not pay its workers posted from Latvia in accordance with the applicable collective agreements operating in Sweden. Although these agreements were not declared universally applicable, the Swedish unions nevertheless took industrial action to compel Laval to observe the agreements. According to the ECJ, however,

> the level of protection which must be guaranteed to workers posted to the territory of the host Member State is limited, in principle, to that provided for in Article 3(1), first subparagraph, (a) to (g) of Directive 96/71, unless, pursuant to the law or collective agreements in the Member State of origin, those workers already enjoy more favourable terms and conditions of employment as regards the matters referred to in that provision.[78]

Because the relevant collective agreements were not universally applicable, the Latvian workers were thus not entitled to the rate for the job in the jurisdiction where the work was performed, and the Latvian employer was permitted – in the exercise of its freedom to provide services – to undercut Swedish companies and to undermine Swedish collective agreements. This seemed to many like unfair competition and led to claims that posted workers were being used to undercut terms and conditions of employment.

The *Laval* decision and its progeny also led to steps being taken to strengthen the Posted Workers Directive, these steps being designed initially to secure the 'better and more uniform implementation, application and enforcement in practice of Directive 96/71/EC'.[79] The most eye-catching feature of the regulations implementing the so-called Enforcement Directive of 2014 in the UK is the provision enabling a posted worker to sue for unpaid wages a contractor who has hired a sub-contractor by whom the applicant was engaged.[80] However, it was not until 2018 that a significant revision of the substantive provisions of the Directive was concluded.[81] The new Directive – which is scheduled to come into force in 2020 – replaces the requirement to observe minimum standards with the equality of treatment principle for posted workers in relation to the items in Article 3(1) set out above, so that in principle posted workers are to enjoy the going rate rather than the minimum rate for the job. It also purports to strengthen the position in relation to temporary agency workers who have an employment relationship with the posting temporary work agency, to ensure equal treatment with agency workers of the

---

are posted to the work, but not where the work is posted to the workers. In both cases it is the law of the country where the work is performed that would govern.

[78] Case C-341/05, *Laval un Partneri Ltd* v. *Svenska Byggnadsarbetareförbundet* [2007] ECR I-11767, [2008] IRLR 160, para. 81.

[79] Directive 2014/67/EU on the enforcement of Directive 96/71/EC concerning the posting of workers in the framework of the provision of services.

[80] SI 2016 No. 539, Regulation 5.

[81] Directive (EU) 2018/957 of 28 June 2018 amending Directive 96/71/EC concerning the posting of workers.

employer in the host state. Other changes will enable Article 3(8) to apply to collective agreements in all sectors rather than the construction and related sectors only, although this will be of little British interest in view of the absence of universally applicable collective agreements in any sector.[82]

Globalisation and Exploitation

The Rome Regulation and the Posted Workers Directive deal with one aspect of labour mobility in the global economy. This is the aspect that relates to what might be described as the formal economy and the movement of skilled workers from one country to another. But there is another aspect of labour mobility that relates to the informal economy, with globalisation having contributed to the emergence of new forms of exploitation, as developed countries import workers to do work that cannot be exported.[83] There is no definition of exploitation, and it may be argued that in a febrile global economy all employment is now exploitative. Such arguments may be made with particular force in relation to the UK where, in an important but neglected report of the House of Commons Trade and Industry Committee in 2005, it was said that 'the United Kingdom still has a more lightly regulated labour market than most comparable economies'.[84] That remains the case today. But although there may be an element of truth in the exploitative nature of all employment, such claims nevertheless tend to diminish and make light of the very real problems faced by people who are trafficked, who are held in domestic servitude or who are engaged in modern slavery.

Morecambe Bay

On 5 February 2004, it is believed that twenty-three Chinese nationals were killed by the incoming tide while collecting shellfish in Morecambe Bay. It appears that most of the victims had been trafficked by so-called snakehead gangs from villages in China and were working in this country in breach of immigration rules. All but one were from Fujian Province in south-east China, the other from Liaoning Province in north-east China.[85] According to press

---

[82] Moreover, where the posting applies for more than a year (which may be extended to eighteen months), the principle of equal treatment is to apply to *all* but a few terms and conditions of employment. Member states have until 20 July 2020 to comply with the new Directive.

[83] We remain grateful to Klara Boonstra for this very important insight.

[84] House of Commons Trade and Industry Committee, *UK Employment Regulation*, HC 90 (2004–5), para. 20. See also TUC, *Hard Work, Hidden Lives: Report of the TUC Commission on Vulnerable Employment* (London, 2007), pp. 19–20, where it is reported that 'the OECD's employment protection index ranks the UK as the second least protected of all developed nations', a point highlighted by a very sobering chart.

[85] CPS, Press Release 117/2006.

reports, the deceased had been engaged by a man called Lin Liang Ren, who had been resident in the UK since 2000,[86] it also being reported that:

> As gangmaster, he provided food and accommodation for the workers, plus tools and waterproof clothing. They were paid £5 for each bag of cockles which they picked; Lin Liang Ren received £15 a bag. [Lin] rented various properties in which to house the workers, greatly overcrowded with many persons sharing each room and he employed someone to cook meals for them. He bought cheap vans and minibuses to transport the workers to the beaches.[87]

It appears that there had been 'a combination of factors' in Morecambe Bay on the night the workers died, including a 'high tide and bad weather'. Indeed, conditions were so bad that local cockle-pickers 'did not go out at all or were on the sands for a short time'.[88]

Apart from shedding light on the darkest corners of working life in the UK, the case of the cockle-pickers is significant also for the response of the state authorities. The gangmaster was caught by the police and prosecuted for manslaughter and for perverting the course of justice. According to the prosecution, it was 'the fact that he was the boss, effectively the employer of the cockle-pickers who drowned, which lies at the heart of the charges of manslaughter against him'.[89] Lin was found guilty (along with two others) and sentenced to fourteen years' imprisonment following his conviction for the manslaughter of twenty-one victims.[90] In a complex case that took the Crown eighteen months to prepare,[91] the Crown Prosecution Service (CPS) called nearly 150 witnesses in a six-month trial, including survivors, eye-witnesses and emergency service personnel, as well as a number of experts.[92] Taking the unusual step at the end of the trial, the CPS issued a statement condemning the 'exploitation' of the victims, who had 'died because their lives were considered less important than the pursuit of profit'.[93] Continuing in this vein, the CPS pointed out that the case was about:

> workers who have no employment rights, no choice about the work they do, no rights to contact the authorities to complain about working conditions – indeed the need to avoid the attention of the authorities because of why they came to be in this country – who can be forced into carrying out hazardous work that nobody else wants to do.[94]

Gangmasters (Licensing) Act 2004

If the prosecution and conviction of Lin was unusual, it also highlighted an urgent need to address the problem of the conditions of those working beyond

---

[86] *Guardian*, 20 September 2005.   [87] *Ibid.*   [88] *Ibid.*   [89] *Ibid.*
[90] *Guardian*, 28 March 2006. No charges were brought following the discovery of the remains of a twenty-second victim: *BBC News*, 26 October 2010.
[91] CPS, Press Release 117/2006.   [92] *Ibid.*   [93] *Ibid.*   [94] *Ibid.*

the pale. Quite fortuitously, Labour backbencher Jim Sheridan MP had already identified the need for better regulation of the activities of people like Lin and had prepared a private member's bill to that effect. The Morecambe Bay tragedy played a large part in neutralising opposition to Mr Sheridan's measure, which was enacted as the Gangmasters (Licensing) Act 2004. The Act requires gangmasters to be licensed by what is now the Gangmasters Labour and Abuse Authority (GLAA),[95] the responsibilities and powers of which were expanded by the Immigration Act 2016.[96] A gangmaster for these purposes is defined to mean someone who 'supplies a worker to do work to which this Act applies for another person'.[97] One problem with the Act, however, is that it is limited in scope, applying only to gangmasters supplying workers for the purpose of harvesting or otherwise gathering agricultural produce, gathering shellfish or processing or packaging agricultural produce.[98] Nevertheless, it is a criminal offence for anyone to act as a gangmaster except under the authority of a licence issued by the GLAA.[99] Summary conviction may lead to a fine, while a conviction on indictment may lead to imprisonment, with a maximum sentence being ten years. It is also an offence to enter into an arrangement with a gangmaster for the supply of workers to undertake unlicensed activities.

The benefit of these arrangements is that they bring this type of employment practice into public view, with the Act also requiring a register of gangmasters to be kept by the GLAA. The Act is important for labour lawyers because of its definition of a worker, a term which means 'an individual who does work to which this Act applies'.[100] That in itself is wide and way beyond the normal requirement that the Act applies to those engaged under a 'contract of employment', then defined to mean a 'contract of service'.[101] Even more interesting is the subsequent provision that 'a person is not prevented from being a worker for the purposes of this Act by reason of the fact that he has no right to be, or to work, in the United Kingdom'.[102] More importantly still, however, the licence conditions under the Act impose duties on the gangmaster in relation to labour standards. Detailed provision to this end is

---

[95] Immigration Act 2016, s. 10 renamed what was until then the Gangmasters Licensing Authority.

[96] These new responsibilities (Immigration Act 2016, s. 11 and Sched. 2) potentially include National Minimum Wage enforcement and enforcement of the Modern Slavery Act 2015. According to to the Gangmasters Licensing Authority (GLA) (before it became the GLAA), the amendments would give it responsibility for about 10 million workers: GLA, *Annual Report and Accounts 2016–17* (2017). The new powers (Immigration Act 2016, ss. 14–24) include seeking labour market enforcement undertakings from employers, and applying for labour market enforcement orders to be imposed by a court. These are powers shared with other agencies.

[97] Gangmasters (Licensing) Act 2004, s. 4.   [98] *Ibid.*, s. 4(5).   [99] *Ibid.*, s. 12.

[100] *Ibid.*, s. 26(1).   [101] ERA 1996, s. 230. See Chapter 6.

[102] Gangmasters (Licensing) Act 2004, s. 26(2). Although the protection of the most vulnerable is to be applauded, this may be a double-edged sword in the sense that more transparency will lead to more exposure, and to the application of other areas of the law to the detriment of those people the Gangmasters (Licensing) Act 2004 is designed to protect.

made in the Gangmasters (Licensing Conditions) Rules 2009,[103] which provide for the imposition of licence requirements designed to ensure that any placement of a worker is voluntary, that terms and conditions of employment are agreed in advance of a placement, that pay due to a worker is not improperly withheld by the gangmaster, that proper records are kept and that (where relevant) suitable accommodation is made available for workers.[104]

GLAA Revokes Cornish Gangmasters' Licence

A Cornish gangmaster has been shut down by the Gangmasters and Labour Abuse Authority (GLAA).

Neringa Butkeviciute, owner of DNK Recruitment, systematically exploited her workers through skimming off their pay, sending them to work double shifts with insufficient breaks and charging them to live in unhygienic and unsafe caravans.

Butkeviciute operated her business out of the Bosparva Caravan Park in Leedstown, Hayle, where she provided workers for various roles in the GLAA regulated sector.

But an inspection was carried out to check on how the licence holder was running her business after DNK was reported to the GLAA.

The GLAA found Butkeviciute sent her workers out with insufficient breaks to boost her own profits, failed to pay them all they were due and also charged for accommodation in caravans that were deemed both unsanitary and unsafe.

Her company failed eight of the authority's Licensing Standards – four of them 'critical' – racking up a total of 144 penalty points. (A licence can be revoked after the discovery of one critical failure, which carries 30 points.)

In one example, one worker started work at 17:47 at a fish-processing factory, finished at 04:17 the next day, and then was supplied by DNK to work at another site from 06:00 to 18:30. Over a two-day period the employee worked 24 hours and 43mins, with a break of only 1hr 43min.

The GLAA's head of licensing Charlotte Woodliffe said: 'The GLAA licensing scheme exists to protect vulnerable workers. In cases like this, where the bottom line appears to be the only thing that matters at the cost of the health & safety of its employees, then we have no hesitation in taking away a gangmaster's licence.'

Enquiries found that the 29-year-old businesswoman from Camborne had been providing workers to harvest and process crops at a nearby vegetable producer, as well as a seafood processing factory in the South-West.[105]

---

[103] SI 2009 No. 307. The licence conditions are set out in some detail in the Schedule.
[104] See *Galdikas* v. *DJ Houghton Catching Services Ltd* [2016] EWHC 1376 (QB). Annual reports of what was then the GLA reveal that between 2008 and 2016, there were 118 prosecutions involving 75 offenders for offences under the 2004 Act.
[105] *The Recruiter*, 29 January 2018.

Forced Labour, Modern Slavery and Human Rights

The Gangmasters (Licensing) Act 2004 is one approach to dealing with the worst forms of exploitation of workers in the global economy. But, although there has been a campaign to extend it to other sectors (such as construction),[106] it clearly would not be appropriate for all forms of exploitation. A different approach is needed to deal – for example – with the problems encountered by the growing army of migrant domestic workers engaged in employment in private homes to provide a variety of services such as cleaning, cooking and child-care. There are estimated to be 67 million domestic workers worldwide,[107] an unknown number of whom are migrant workers. According to the *Guardian* blog of 18 October 2011, there is a 'hidden world of workers who are brought to this country and end up living like virtual slaves', many of them being trafficked to work here. As the blog continues, 'often they come from impoverished backgrounds with little education, may not speak English, and don't have a support network in the UK'. According to the TUC in 2007:

> [O]f 687 migrant domestic workers registered with [the welfare group] Kalayaan between 2006 and Spring 2008 (sic) 22.5 per cent stated they had experienced physical assault. A commonly reported physical abuse was that of employers burning workers' hands on stoves as punishments for cooking 'mistakes'. 66 per cent stated psychological abuse including racist abuse and threats to harm themselves or their families. 60 per cent reported they were not allowed to leave their employers' house and 66 per cent were not allowed any time off. 51 per cent of workers did not have their own room to live in, but were expected to live in a corridor, kitchen with children or other communal space, and over a third (36 per cent) did not even have their own bed to themselves. 84 per cent earned less than £500 per month, and nine workers said they did not receive any wages at all.[108]

Convention Rights

These reports give rise to a number of concerns, the most obvious being that migrant domestic workers appear to be the victims of crime, from assault (kicking, spitting, slapping) to sexual assault (said to be under-reported).[109]

---

[106] See HL Paper 153/HC 443 (2016–17), paras. 128–9 (Joint Committee on Human Rights).

[107] See ILO, *Migrant Domestic Workers Across the World: Global and Regional Estimates* (2016); 11.5 million are thought to be migrant domestic workers. There is now an ILO Convention (Convention 189 (Domestic Workers Convention, 2011)), but it has not been ratified by the UK. See E. Albin and V. Mantouvalou, 'The ILO Convention on Domestic Workers: From the Shadows to the Light' (2012) 47 *Industrial Law Journal* 47.

[108] TUC, *Hard Work, Hidden Lives: Report of the TUC Commission on Vulnerable Employment* (London, 2007), p. 203. Kalayaan is a non-governmental organisation (NGO) that exists to assist migrant domestic workers.

[109] Kalayaan, *Annual Report and Financial Statements 2016–17* (London, 2017), p. 6.

They also appear to be the victims of human rights abuse, generating a human rights response to the problems encountered. In *Siliadin* v. *France* (this is by no means a uniquely UK problem),[110] the question was whether (1) the treatment of a young Togolese national as a chattel by a French family, in circumstances where (2) there was no effective legislation to prosecute the perpetrators of such mistreatment, (3) amounted to a breach of the ECHR, Article 4. The latter provides that 'no one shall be held in slavery or servitude', and that 'no one shall be required to perform forced or compulsory labour'. In this case, the applicant had been sent to France to work with Mrs D who then 'lent' her to Mrs B, who 'decided to keep her'. According to the report of the case:

> The applicant subsequently became a general housemaid for Mr and Mrs B. She worked seven days a week, without a day off, and was occasionally and exceptionally authorised to go out on Sundays to attend mass. Her working day began at 7.30 am, when she had to get up and prepare breakfast, dress the children, take them to nursery school or their recreational activities, look after the baby, do the housework and wash and iron clothes. In the evening she prepared dinner, looked after the older children, did the washing up and went to bed at about 10.30 pm. In addition, she had to clean a studio flat, in the same building, which Mr B. had made into an office. The applicant slept on a mattress on the floor in the baby's room; she had to look after him if he woke up.[111]

The applicant – who was never paid – claimed after unsuccessful attempts to prosecute the employers that there was a breach of Article 4 because of a failure by the state to comply with its duty 'to put in place adequate criminal law provisions to prevent and effectively punish the perpetrators of [the offending conduct]'. The ECHR agreed, and also held that the situation of the applicant fell within Article 4 on the ground that her treatment amounted to forced labour. Relying on ILO Convention 29 (Forced Labour Convention, 1930), which is 'binding on almost all the Council of Europe Member States', the Court held that the two key ingredients of forced labour had been met, in the sense that the work had been performed against the will of the person concerned and had not been performed voluntarily. The Court also considered whether the treatment of the applicant amounted to servitude, noting that this was a 'particularly serious form of denial of freedom', said to be 'an obligation to provide one's services that is imposed by the use of coercion'.[112] The Court continued:

> She had been brought to France by a relative of her father's, and had not chosen to work for Mr and Mrs B. As a minor, she had no resources and was vulnerable

---

[110] [2005] ECHR 545. See V. Mantouvalou, 'Modern Slavery: The UK Response' (2010) 39 *Industrial Law Journal* 425; and V. Mantouvalou, 'Servitude and Forced Labour in the 21st Century: The Human Rights of Domestic Workers' (2006) 35 *Industrial Law Journal* 395.

[111] [2005] ECHR 545, para. 14.   [112] *Ibid.*, para. 124.

and isolated, and had no means of living elsewhere than in the home of Mr and Mrs B, where she shared the children's bedroom as no other accommodation had been offered. She was entirely at Mr and Mrs B's mercy, since her papers had been confiscated and she had been promised that her immigration status would be regularised, which had never occurred.

In addition, the applicant, who was afraid of being arrested by the police, was not in any event permitted to leave the house, except to take the children to their classes and various activities. Thus, she had no freedom of movement and no free time.

As she had not been sent to school, despite the promises made to her father, the applicant could not hope that her situation would improve and was completely dependent on Mr and Mrs B.

In those circumstances, the Court concludes that the applicant, a minor at the relevant time, was held in servitude within the meaning of Article 4 of the Convention.[113]

British Law

The Coroners and Justice Act 2009 included provisions designed to give effect to this remarkable decision (even if the Court did hold that the conditions experienced by the applicant did not constitute slavery).[114] These are now to be found in the Modern Slavery Act 2015 which repealed, replaced and strengthened the provisions of the 2009 Act relating to slavery and servitude, while adding new offences relating to trafficking for a wide range of purposes. Both the 2009 and 2015 iterations expressly provided that 'the references to holding a person in slavery or servitude or requiring a person to perform forced or compulsory labour are to be construed in accordance with Article 4 of the [ECHR]', thereby incorporating not only the *Siliadin* decision into domestic law but also subsequent jurisprudence that develops the principles established therein.[115] A person guilty of an offence under the Modern Slavery Act 2015 is liable (1) on summary conviction, to imprisonment of up to twelve months or a fine, or both; and (2) on conviction on indictment to imprisonment for life or a fine, or both. Also as a result of the Modern Slavery Act 2015,[116] the immigration rules have been changed '[automatically to extend] the leave, and the permission to work, of a person admitted as an overseas domestic worker in a private

---

[113] *Ibid.*, paras. 126–9.   [114] Coroners and Justice Act 2009, s. 71.

[115] See *Rantsev* v. *Cyprus and Russia* [2010] ECHR 22, which involved sex trafficking and the engagement of Article 2 in a case where a young woman trafficked from Russia to Cyprus died in what appeared either to be an unsuccessful escape attempt from or unlawful homicide at the hands of her captors.

[116] Modern Slavery Act 2015, s. 53.

household if, before their original grant of leave expires' there has been a determination that the person in question has been a victim of slavery or human trafficking.[117]

These statutory developments have taken place at a time when the courts are also beginning to remove barriers to migrant domestic workers enforcing employment rights, these workers often facing claims that the employer (a foreign diplomat) is protected by diplomatic immunity,[118] or that any statutory rights are unenforceable by virtue of the illegality of the working relationship (on account of the worker having an irregular immigration status).[119] But for all that, there is a sense that the position has got worse as a result of the changes to the visa rules for migrant domestic workers announced on 29 February 2012:

> ODWs [overseas domestic workers] in private households will only be permitted to accompany and work for visitors. They must leave the UK with the visitor, after a maximum of six months. They may not extend their stay, switch employer, sponsor dependants or settle here. ODWs in diplomatic households will be able to remain for the diplomat's duration of stay, up to a maximum of five years. They may not switch employer or settle but may be accompanied by their dependants.[120]

This gave rise to concern that, being tied to one employer, migrant domestic workers who experience abuse and exploitation would face the choice of continuing to suffer or fleeing and becoming illegal. These concerns have been vindicated, with Kalayaan reporting that those who were tied to their employer by the post-2012 visas were more likely to suffer physical abuse, not to be permitted to leave their employer's house unsupervised, not to have their own room or private space, to be on call any time of day or night, to have their passports withheld, to receive low pay (£50 a week or less) or no pay at all and to have been trafficked.[121]

---

[117] Home Office, *Domestic Workers in Private Households* (London, 2017).

[118] *Reyes* v. *Al-Malki* [2017] UKSC 61, [2017] 3 WLR 923.

[119] *Hounga* v. *Allen* [2014] UKSC 47, [2014] ICR 847. See also *Patel* v. *Mirza* [2016] UKSC 42, [2017] AC 467 (on which see A. Bogg, 'Illegality in Labour Law after Patel v. Mirza: Retrenchment and Restraint', in A. Bogg and S. Green (eds.), *Illegality after Patel v. Mirza* (2018)). But no one has yet successfully brought a claim for non-payment of wages or holiday pay. Note now the new offences for illegal working and for employing illegal workers introduced by the Immigration Act 2016, ss. 34 and 35, the implications of which for *Hounga* must be uncertain.

[120] HC Debs., 29 February 2012, cols. 34–6 WS (Theresa May).

[121] See further, V. Mantouvalou, 'Am I Free Now?' Overseas Domestic Workers in Slavery' (2015) 42 *Journal of Law and Society* 329.

Modern Slavery Act 2015

As we have seen in the text, the Modern Slavery Act 2015 addresses questions of slavery, servitude and forced labour (section 1). It also deals with human trafficking, which is defined to mean arranging or facilitating the travel of a person for the purposes of exploitation (section 2). That exploitation may be for a number of purposes set in the Act, including trafficking for the purposes of slavery, servitude or forced labour and trafficking for the purposes of sexual exploitation (section 3). The Act also increases the penalties for those convicted of modern slavery (section 5), and makes provision for the confiscation of the assets of those convicted (section 7), as well the compensation of victims from confiscated assets by way of a slavery and trafficking reparation order (section 8). In addition to a number of other protections for the victims of modern slavery, the Act provides for the appointment of an Independent Anti-Slavery Commissioner to 'encourage good practice' in the 'prevention, detection, investigation and prosecution of slavery and human trafficking offences' (section 41). However, the Commissioner has few powers with which to promote this duty, and the first incumbent resigned citing concerns about Home Office interference.[122]

Otherwise, the most eye-catching feature of the Act is the duty on the part of commercial organisations with a total turnover of at least £36 million annually, to prepare each year a slavery and human trafficking statement (section 54). Designed to promote supply chain transparency, this should set out 'the steps the organisation has taken during the financial year to ensure that slavery and human trafficking is not taking place (i) in any of its supply chains, and (ii) in any part of its own business'. This applies not only to domestic employment practices but to employment practices in other parts of the world where goods are sourced. Yet although it is mandatory to provide a statement, those to whom the duty applies are free to say that they have taken no such steps, if they are prepared to risk the potential adverse publicity in doing so. Where, however, steps have been taken, the Act provides non-binding guidance by section 54(5) about what the statement might contain:

(a) the organisation's structure, its business and its supply chains;

(b) its policies in relation to slavery and human trafficking;

(c) its due diligence processes in relation to slavery and human trafficking in its business and supply chains;

(d) the parts of its business and supply chains where there is a risk of slavery and human trafficking taking place, and the steps it has taken to assess and manage that risk;

(e) its effectiveness in ensuring that slavery and human trafficking is not taking place in its business or supply chains, measured against such performance indicators as it considers appropriate; and

(f) the training about slavery and human trafficking available to its staff.

---

[122] *Independent*, 17 May 2018. For full analysis of the Modern Slavery Act 2015, see J. Fudge, 'Why Labour Lawyers Should Care About the Modern Slavery Act 2015' (2018) 29 *King's Law Journal* 377; V. Mantouvalou, 'The Modern Slavery Act 2015 Three Years On' (2018) 81 *Modern Law Review* 1017.

An organisation's slavery and human trafficking statement must be approved by the board of directors (or similar in the case of non-corporate commercial bodies) and be published on its website. The foregoing obligations are enforceable only by a government minister bringing proceedings for a mandatory injunction in the High Court (or in Scotland specific performance in the Court of Session). Although the Act was said shortly after its introduction to have 'some beneficial effects', concerns have been expressed already about its shortcomings.[123] These include the poor quality of many of the slavery and human trafficking statements, partly as a result of the directory rather than mandatory nature of the statute and the lack of effective guidance from the government. Concern has also been expressed about the lack of a central repository for the many thousands of statements now produced, which makes it difficult to monitor compliance.[124] There are also doubts about the exclusion of public bodies from the reporting obligation, as well as the civil enforcement of statutory obligations exclusively by a government minister, rather than by shareholders or other interested parties, no doubt to protect companies from unwelcome litigation.[125]

Global Corporations

The second and third sections of this chapter were concerned with the responsibility of states to ensure fair labour standards. But, although ultimately a matter of state responsibility, this is not to overlook the corresponding obligation of transnational corporations to comply with these standards. Transnational companies are major national players and often dominate national economies, able to extract concessions from national governments. Many large companies have been embarrassed by the employment practices in their supply chain, as workers in developing countries are paid comparatively

---

[123] HL Paper 153/HC 443 (2016–17) (Joint Committee on Human Rights), paras. 92–7.

[124] *Ibid.*, paras. 98–100. The issue has also been raised about whether a strengthened s. 54 could be a template for other reporting obligations, including compliance with freedom of association principles and collective bargaining practices throughout the supply chain: *ibid.*, para. 102. Additional human rights reporting obligations by companies to shareholders are to be found in SI 2016 No. 1245, which is designed to implement Directive 2014/95/EU as regards disclosure of non-financial and diversity information by certain large undertakings and groups. It is, however, a feeble implementation, with a reference to human rights generally but no reference to labour standards, despite the following statement in recital 7 of the Directive's preamble: 'As regards social and employee-related matters, the information provided in the statement may concern the actions taken to ensure gender equality, implementation of fundamental conventions of the International Labour Organisation, working conditions, social dialogue, respect for the right of workers to be informed and consulted, respect for trade union rights, health and safety at work and the dialogue with local communities, and/or the actions taken to ensure the protection and the development of those communities'.

[125] For all its weaknesses and limitations, the Modern Slavery Act 2015 is being adopted in Australia, but with modifications. See Commonwealth Parliament, Joint Standing Committee on Foreign Affairs, Defence and Trade, *Hidden in Plain Sight: An Inquiry into Establishing a Modern Slavery Act in Australia* (December 2017). In recommending the adoption of a Modern Slavery Act in Australia, the latter report also provides a good critique of the UK legislation.

low wages and often work in poor (if not squalid) conditions to feed the hunger of consumers in the developed world.

- At the time of writing the first edition of this book, the Apple Corporation was the latest in a long line of such companies to be discomfited by allegations about employment practices, with one British newspaper reporting that 'around 150 Chinese workers at Foxconn, the world's largest electronics manufacturer, threatened to commit suicide by leaping from their factory roof in protest at their working conditions'. Foxconn, which was said to '[manufacture] gadgets for the likes of Apple, Sony, Nintendo and HP, among many others', was also said to have had 'a grim history of suicides' and to have 'installed safety nets in some of its factories'.[126]
- At the time of writing the second edition, memories of the Rana Plaza factory collapse in Bangladesh in 2013 are still vivid. As a result of the collapse, more than 1,200 workers were killed, and thousands more were injured, in what was an industrial disaster on a shocking scale. The disaster is one in which a number of British companies (and indeed numerous global companies) were implicated in an industrial landscape that was notoriously violent, repressive, authoritarian, exploitative, unsafe, ramshackle and rife with danger. UK multinationals knew about – or should have known about – these conditions and yet tolerated them and allowed them to continue for years.[127]

Codes of Conduct

Many companies now accept that they have responsibilities that arise independently of legal obligations. These responsibilities are often expressed in codes of conduct that are now widely used by corporations, though the content of these codes varies from company to company. In the case of G4S (the UK's largest private sector employer, and thought to be the second or third largest private sector employer in the world), the Business Ethics Policy commits the company to being 'a good corporate citizen, taking account of the economic, social and environmental impact of our business and aiming to maximise the benefits and minimise any negative impact of our global operations'. This means 'fulfilling its responsibilities on human rights around the

---

[126] *Daily Telegraph*, 11 January 2012. Apple nevertheless had a detailed Code of Practice for Suppliers, which covered a wide range of issues. The immediate problem was a working hours regime in a supplier company where it was alleged that workers were working for fifteen hours a day, seven days a week. The Code of Practice provided that: 'Except in Emergency or Unusual Situations, a work-week shall be restricted to 60 hours, including overtime, workers shall be allowed at least one day off every seven-days, and overtime shall be voluntary.' The more recent version of the Code is similar, providing in addition for a regular working week of 48 hours (Apple, *Supplier Code of Conduct* (2015), p. 3).

[127] This is drawn from D. Blackburn and K. D. Ewing, Written Evidence to Joint Committee on Human Rights (HRB0042), HL Paper 153, HC 443 (2016–17), paras. 17–28.

world by applying the United Nations Guiding Principles on Business and Human Rights (2011)' (on which see below). The G4S Business Ethics Policy covers a range of issues, from the environment, to forms of political engagement, to the rights of employees. In the case of the last, the company undertakes to 'act in compliance with national regulatory requirements', and accepts that 'employers' obligations to employees under labour or social security laws and regulations must be respected'. Perhaps more importantly, in a paragraph headed ILO Declaration on Fundamental Principles and Rights at Work, it is stated that 'G4S supports the four fundamental principles in the ILO Declaration'. Thus, 'in accordance with local legislation and practice', the company undertakes 'to respect freedom of association and the right to collective bargaining', while 'employment will be freely chosen with no use of forced or child labour'.[128]

This is an impressive document, which also covers matters such as harassment, equal opportunity, health and safety, and terms of employment. However, self-regulation is generally not a solution to the problem of corporate power, and even in the case of G4S there has been strong involvement by trade unions and others to promote compliance with the foregoing principles. As a matter of general principle, Hepple points out that:

> The weakness of such codes is that the norms which they uphold are not always consistent with ILO core standards (e.g. many do not include the right to collective bargaining), and they usually rely on self-enforcement, although some now permit independent social audits.[129]

Even where it fully subscribes to ILO standards, it does not follow that the company in question will be thought by all to have warmly adopted the principles these standards embrace. For example, General Electric has a Human Rights Statement of Principles in which it is committed to uphold 'the human rights of our employees as established in the International Labour Organization's (ILO's) Declaration on Fundamental Principles and Rights at Work', including freedom of association and the right to engage in collective bargaining.[130] But this has not prevented those using the company name from ensuring that collective bargaining will take place only where legally required, there being several decisions of the CAC in this country in which UK-based GE companies at least give the impression of not being enthusiastic about the idea of trade union recognition. There is also the question of how far down the supply chain obligations of this kind go: do they apply only to employment by the company or do they oblige the company's suppliers and customers to subscribe to similar principles?

---

[128] G4S, *Business Ethics Policy* (2017).

[129] B. A. Hepple, 'New Approaches to International Regulation' (1997) 25 *Industrial Law Journal* 353, at 364.

[130] General Electric, *Human Rights Statement of Principles* (2016).

Global Framework Agreements

An alternative to the unilateral corporate code is the bilateral global framework agreement, usually negotiated between the transnational corporation and a global union federation.[131] As will be discussed more fully below, the latter are sector-based federations of national trade unions, including the International Union of Foodworkers (IUF), IndustriALL (representing mining, energy and manufacturing workers) and UNI (representing service sector workers). The global framework agreements started in part as a response to the growing scepticism about company codes of conduct, the agreements typically embracing a commitment by the company to observe core labour standards throughout the company's operations, including freedom of association, the abolition of child labour, the elimination of discrimination and the abolition of forced labour. In some cases, these commitments are embellished beyond the core ILO conventions. For example, the commitment to freedom of association sometimes includes a commitment to protect workers' representatives, often with an express reference to ILO Convention 135. In many cases there is also a commitment to fair labour standards on matters such as pay, working time, and health and safety.[132] As a number of unions have made clear, however, international framework agreements may have a purpose beyond compliance with core labour standards. There is evidence that they provide national trade unions in the developed world with organising and bargaining opportunities at local level.[133] Indeed, this is thought to be a key motivation in the negotiation of at least some of these agreements.[134]

But although global framework agreements are an important initiative, there are many obstacles to be overcome. First, not all employers are enthusiastic, partly because of concern about the legal status of such agreements.[135] Secondly, there is the question of capacity on the trade union side: there are many more transnational companies than there are global union federations. Nevertheless, an important recent development has been the Bangladesh Accord, which takes global framework agreements in a qualitatively different direction. Unlike the typical agreement, the accord moves the process to a

---

[131] See K. D. Ewing, 'International Regulation of the Global Economy: The Role of Trade Unions', in B. Bercusson and C. Estlund (eds.), *Regulating Labour in the Wake of Globalisation: New Challenges, New Institutions* (Oxford: Hart, 2007), Ch. 10.

[132] For a review of some of these agreements, see *ibid.*

[133] See J. Wills, 'Bargaining for the Space to Organize in the Global Economy: A Review of the Accor-IUF Trade Union Rights Agreement' (2002) 9 *Review of International Political Economy* 675.

[134] P. Rossman, 'The IUF, Chiquita and Union Rights' (2001) 8(3) *International Union Rights* 13.

[135] See K. D. Ewing, 'International Regulation of the Global Economy – The Role of Trade Unions', in B. Bercusson and C. Estlund (eds.), *Regulating Labour in the Wake of Globalisation: New Challenges, New Institutions* (2007), p. 223. For the possible enforceability of these agreements in US courts, see S. Coleman, 'Enforcing International Framework Agreements in US Courts: A Contract Analysis' (2010) 41 *Columbia Human Rights Law Review* 60.

sectoral level dragging multiple global companies into a single net. Promoted by UNI and IndustriALL, the accord is a direct response to the Rana Plaza disaster of 2013 referred to above. Under the terms of the accord companies enter into a legally binding agreement which is designed to force them to take responsibility for working conditions in their supply chains. The accord is designed to promote health and safety in the Bangladeshi garment sector, and in particular to ensure that buildings where work is carried out are safe and that there are effective measures to deal with the risk of fire. The operation of the accord is overseen by a steering committee with equal representation of trade union and employer signatories, with an independent chair appointed by the ILO. The accord has been signed by over 180 brands, retailers and importers from twenty countries, including twenty-one British companies. This is a significant if belated achievement, the progeny of wretched circumstances.[136]

Ethical Trading Initiative

The Ethical Trading Initiative (ETI), set up in 1998, seeks to bring together companies, trade unions and NGOs to encourage companies to promote ethical trade practices when dealing with suppliers in developing countries. The ETI receives financial support from the British government and is otherwise sustained by the membership fees of its corporate members. In what is said to be a unique alliance, there are now almost a hundred companies in membership, many in the clothing and food sectors, along with the International Trade Union Confederation (ITUC), the TUC and global union federations, as well as a number of prominent NGOs. Corporate members have a combined turnover of £166 billion.

The ETI Base Code embraces a number of familiar principles, though it goes beyond the four ILO core principles. The principles in question are as follows: employment must be freely chosen, respect for freedom of association and the right to collective bargaining, safe and hygienic working conditions, no recruitment of child labour, the payment of a living wage, working hours which are not excessive (forty-eight-hour week, one day off in seven and voluntary overtime), no discrimination on a wide range of protected grounds, the provision of regular employment, and no harsh or inhumane treatment of workers to be allowed.

Corporate members are required to accept the ETI's Principles of Implementation, setting out the approaches to ethical trade that the companies are expected to follow. Thus companies must 'demonstrate a clear commitment to ethical trade; integrate ethical trade into their core business practices; drive year-on-year improvements to working conditions; support suppliers to improve working conditions, for example through advice and training; and report openly and accurately about their activities'. Member companies are required to report annually on progress, and a system of inspection is in place. Failure to comply can lead to membership being terminated.[137]

---

[136] Full details are available on the accord's website.   [137] For details, see the ETI website.

OECD Guidelines for Multinational Enterprises

While voluntary initiatives of these latter kinds are clearly important, so too are intergovernmental measures that are addressed to transnational corporations. The most important of these measures are the OECD Guidelines for Multinational Enterprises, most recently revised in 2011.[138] Before examining the latter, reference should also be made to the ILO Tripartite Declaration on Multinational Enterprises, first produced in 1977 and most recently revised in 2017: this is addressed to governments, employers' and workers' organisations, and to multinational corporations as well.[139] Yet there is no formal complaints mechanism whereby concerns can be raised about the breach of the principles contained in the Declaration, though the Declaration does contain measures whereby the International Labour Office will facilitate dialogue between a company and trade unions, and provision is also made for requests about the interpretation of the Declaration to be made to the International Labour Office. Otherwise, disputes can be addressed through the normal procedures of the ILO, with the conduct of multinationals often forming the basis of complaints to the CFA.[140]

OECD Guidelines in Outline

The OECD Guidelines for Multinational Enterprises ('the Guidelines') were first agreed in 1976, following public concern that multinational enterprises were becoming too powerful and unaccountable. The Guidelines may not be binding in a legal sense at the international level, but they are not optional for corporations. Governments have committed themselves to respecting the principles and have established complaints mechanisms and supervisory procedures to this end. The Guidelines cover a wide range of corporate activity. But so far as Chapter V (Employment and Industrial Relations) is concerned, they (1) explicitly adopt all four of the core ILO principles recognised in the ILO Declaration on Fundamental Principles and Rights at Work (1998), as well as (2) embrace standards on matters which have been excluded from the ILO Declaration (such as minimum conditions of employment and health and safety at work). On freedom of association, the Guidelines require enterprises 'within the framework of applicable law, regulations and prevailing labour relations and employment practices' to:

---

[138] See J. Murray, 'A New Phase in the Regulation of Multinational Enterprises: The Role of the OECD' (2001) 30 *Industrial Law Journal* 255, for an earlier revision.

[139] ILO Tripartite Declaration on Multinational Enterprises (Revised) (2017), the preamble to which 'invites' multinationals to 'observe' the principles embodied therein.

[140] See K. D. Ewing, 'International Regulation of the Global Economy: The Role of Trade Unions', in B. Bercusson and C. Estlund (eds.), *Regulating Labour in the Wake of Globalisation: New Challenges, New Institutions* (Oxford: Hart, 2007).

[r]espect the right of workers employed by the multinational enterprise to have trade unions and representative organisations of their own choosing recognised for the purpose of collective bargaining, and engage in constructive negotiations, either individually or through employers' associations, with such representatives with a view to reaching agreements on terms and conditions of employment.

Enterprises are also expected to 'provide facilities to employee representatives as may be necessary to assist in the development of effective collective agreements', and 'provide information to employee representatives which is needed for meaningful negotiations on conditions of employment'. There are also important duties of consultation on matters of mutual concern, and to give reasonable notice of collective redundancies.

Since the 2000 revision of the Guidelines, governments have been expected to establish National Contact Points (NCPs). The NCPs have a twofold mandate: to promote the Guidelines and to facilitate the making of complaints from a variety of stakeholders – notably trade unions and NGOs – about alleged non-compliance by companies registered in or operating from the territory of the relevant NCP. Located in the Department for International Trade but partly funded by the Department for International Development, the work of the UK NCP is overseen by a steering board which includes a trade union representative, along with representatives of business and NGOs.[141] This reflects concerns by the OECD's Trade Union Advisory Committee, which has consistently noted that 'tripartite NCPs have generally been more effective than others',[142] referring specifically to the need for trade union involvement in the supervisory process. But despite these procedural changes, the Joint Committee on Human Rights of the UK Parliament has nevertheless been critical of the operation of the OECD Guidelines in the UK in two separate inquiries, though it is not clear that these criticisms are entirely fair in relation to the labour cases discussed below. Nevertheless, in its most recent report the Committee said that:

> The UK National Contact Point for the OECD Guidelines has the potential to provide meaningful non-judicial access to justice, alongside the more traditional routes of civil and criminal law. Findings of the NCP also have the potential to feed into judicial cases. In its current form, however, the NCP is largely invisible, and lacks the resources and essential human rights expertise necessary to undertake such a role.[143]

In addition, the report of the UN's Special Representative on Human Rights and Transnational Corporations specifically endorsed the OECD Guidelines as

---

[141] For details, see HM Government, *The UK National Contact Point for the OECD Guidelines for Multinational Enterprises* (2018).

[142] D. Blackburn and K. D. Ewing, Memorandum to Joint Committee on Human Rights, HL Paper 5-II, HC 64-II (2009–10), para. 3.3.

[143] HL Paper 154, HC 433 (2016–17), para. 216.

a useful mechanism for addressing the business and human rights agenda. But the Special Representative also noted that the Guidelines have 'too often failed' to meet their potential.[144]

OECD Procedures in Operation

It is a striking feature of the OECD Guidelines in the UK that after a steady stream of labour references from 2007 to 2012, these have now all but dried up, with only one trade union application since, on which at the time of writing no final statement has been made. Eight notable complaints between 2007 and 2012 were brought against Peugeot (in relation to failures to inform and consult about its relocation from the UK to the Czech Republic),[145] G4S (in relation to alleged wages and hours violations in Nepal, Mozambique, Malawi and the Democratic Republic of Congo),[146] Unilever (in relation to claims relating to anti-union discrimination in Pakistan),[147] Unilever (in relation to the closure of a factory in alleged breach of Indian law),[148] Unilever (in relation to the denial of collective bargaining rights to temporary workers in Pakistan),[149] Unilever (in relation to an alleged denial of the right of workers to join the trade union of their choice at one of its establishments in India),[150] British American Tobacco (in relation to changes to working practices without consulting employee representatives in Malaysia),[151] and

---

[144] According to the Special Representative, 'The housing of some NCPs primarily or wholly within government departments tasked with promoting business, trade and investment raises questions about conflicts of interest. NCPs often lack the resources to undertake adequate investigation of complaints and the training to provide effective mediation. There are typically no time frames for the commencement or completion of the process, and outcomes are often not publicly reported. In sum, many NCP processes appear to come up short': Report of the UN Special Representative of the Secretary-General on the Issue of Human Rights and Transnational Corporations and other Business Enterprises – John Ruggie, 'Protect Respect and Remedy: A Framework for Business and Human Rights', UN Doc. A/HRC/8/5J, 7 (2008), paras. 98–9.

[145] NCP Final Statement, Complaint from Amicus and T&G against PSA Peugeot Citroen (February 2008),

[146] NCP Final Statement, Complaint from UNI against G4S (12 December 2008).

[147] NCP Final Statement, Complaint from the International Union of Food, Agricultural, Hotel, Restaurant, Catering, Tobacco and Allied Workers' Associations against Unilever plc on Pakistan's Rahim Yar Khan Factory (13 August 2009).

[148] NCP Final Statement, Complaint from the International Union of Food, Agricultural, Hotel, Restaurant, Catering, Tobacco and Allied Workers' Associations against Unilever plc on India's Sewri Factory (9 November 2009).

[149] NCP Final Statement, Complaint from the International Union of Food, Agricultural, Hotel, Restaurant, Catering, Tobacco and Allied Workers' Associations against Unilever plc on Pakistan's Khanewal Factory (20 November 2009).

[150] NCP Final Statement, Complaint from the International Union of Food, Agricultural, Hotel, Restaurant, Catering, Tobacco and Allied Workers' Associations against Unilever plc (Doom Dooma factory – Assam – India) (18 October 2010).

[151] NCP Final Statement, Complaint from the Malaysian Trade Union Congress against British American Tobacco Malaysia Berhad (Malaysia) (4 March 2011).

Compass Group in relation to trade union rights in Algeria.[152] The complaints
have been brought variously by UK trade unions (Peugeot, G4S), national
trade unions from other jurisdictions (BAT) and global union federations
(G4S and Unilever). On receipt of a complaint, the UK NCP has adopted a
fairly sophisticated process of conciliation to resolve matters without the need
for a formal determination, leading to an agreement being concluded between
the parties in all but two of the complaints.[153] In the case of the G4S
complaint, the NCP helped in the negotiation of an impressive global framework agreement between the company, UNI and the British trade union
GMB.[154]

It is not known why the spate has been followed by a drought, for it is
notable that in these labour complaints the NCP has been willing to read the
obligations under the Guidelines widely.[155] It is true that in the Peugeot case
the NCP said that:

> Obeying domestic law is the first obligation of business. The Guidelines are not a
> substitute for nor should they be considered to override national law and
> regulation. They represent supplementary principles and standards of behaviour
> of a non-legal character, particularly concerning the international operations of
> these enterprises. While the Guidelines extend beyond the law in many cases,
> they should not and are not intended to place an enterprise in situation (sic)
> where it faces conflicting requirements.[156]

However, in a case which involved an earlier version of the Guidelines, it was
also said that 'it is reasonable to conclude that the Guidelines would expect a
meaningful consultation',[157] and to this end the NCP introduced into the very
general obligation to consult a requirement that it must at least meet the
standard set in British law by the decision in *R* v. *British Coal, ex parte*

---

[152] NCP Final Statement, Complaint from the International Union of Food, Agricultural, Hotel,
Restaurant, Catering, Tobacco and Allied Workers' Associations (IUF) against Compass
Group plc on Eurest Algerie Spa (Algeria) (1 February 2012).

[153] The exceptions being the Peugeot and British American Tobacco Malaysia cases.

[154] For an account of the background to this agreement and an analysis of its content and
significance, see D. Blackburn and K. D. Ewing, Memorandum to Joint Committee on Human
Rights, HL Paper 5-II, HC 64-II (2009–10); and K. D. Ewing, 'Global Framework Agreements
in Context' (2011) (2) *International Union Rights* 10. The OECD process and the global
framework agreement was the end-point in what had been in effect a global dispute, contested
in several jurisdictions and using several forums. Apart from the OECD, see ILO, CFA, Case
2494 (Indonesia) (Complaint by ASPEK Indonesia about alleged acts of anti-union
discrimination).

[155] We recognise that this may not be the case in relation to other human rights complaints in
relation to which NGOs were especially critical in evidence to the Joint Committee on Human
Rights: HL Paper 154, HC 433 (2016–17).

[156] NCP Final Statement, Complaint from Amicus and T&G against PSA Peugeot Citroen, note
145, para. 59.

[157] *Ibid.*, para. 49. The relevant passage of the new Guidelines is unchanged: see Chapter V,
para. 3.

Vardy,[158] and thus indirectly the relatively high standards of EU law.[159] The NCP concluded that Peugeot had breached the Guidelines: 'the Company should have engaged with the Unions when the decision to make the closure was at a formative stage, providing sufficient information to allow the Union to understand the reasoning for the decision and to contribute appropriately'. The NCP recommended that, when in future Peugeot considers closures of its premises, 'it should engage the unions at the appropriate time and provide adequate information for meaningful discussions to take place'.[160]

Global Unions

In the context of globalisation, what do trade unions do? There is a clear understanding that power in the global economy is moving from states to companies, and that trade unions must adopt new strategies in what continue to be largely hostile legal conditions to deal with the global companies. It was recognised at an early stage in the development of trade unionism that workers also needed to have an international voice, pioneering spokesmen railing against the 'misuse of the foreign workman', in 'cases of strikes and lock-outs'.[161] Indeed the question was raised at the first meeting of the TUC in 1868, where it was resolved that:

> As local organisations of labour have almost disappeared before organisations of a national character, so we believe the extension of the principle of free trade, which induces between nations such a competition that the interest of the workman is liable to be lost sight of and sacrificed in the fierce international race between capitalists, demands that such organisations should be still further extended and made international.[162]

As recorded by Rojot, moves to establish an international trade union federation began over the last quarter of the nineteenth century and in the early part of the twentieth century.[163] But progress was impeded by two world wars and the ideological splits in the international labour movements following the Russian Revolution of 1917, Lenin famously 'credited with the dictum that workers must choose between Moscow and Geneva'.[164] These problems

---

[158] [1993] ICR 720 (DC). See pp. 655–6.

[159] It does not follow that a similar approach will be adopted by NCPs in other countries.

[160] NCP Final Statement, Complaint from Amicus and T&G against PSA Peugeot Citroen, note 145, para. 62.

[161] K. Marx, 'Instructions for Delegates to the Geneva Congress', in K. Marx, *The First International and After* (ed. D. Fernbach, Harmondsworth: Pelican Marx Library, 1974), p. 86.

[162] As quoted by K. Marx, 'Report to the Basle Congress (1869)', in K. Marx, *The First International and After* (ed. D. Fernbach, 1974), p. 91.

[163] J. Rojot, 'International Collective Bargaining', in M. Morley, P. Gunnigle and D. G. Collings (eds.), *Global Industrial Relations* (London: Routledge, 2006), Ch. 12.

[164] E. J. Phelan, *Yes and Albert Thomas* (London: Cresset Press, 1936), p. 184. Albert Thomas was the first Director General of the ILO.

appear to have been overcome, though predictably there are other tensions in the international trade union movement, but now between North and South as well as between East and West.

Global Union Organisation

As explained by Rojot, workers' organisations have developed both horizontal and vertical structures at global level.[165] So far as horizontal structures are concerned, here we are concerned with forms of representation bringing together the representative bodies of national trade unions. Representation at this level has gradually evolved over many years, with the most important example of such organisation at the present time being the ITUC, to which national trade union confederations affiliate, including the TUC from the UK and the Irish Congress of Trades Unions (ICTU) from Ireland. The ITUC was formed in 2006 following a merger between the International Confederation of Free Trade Unions (ICFTU) and the World Confederation of Labour. The ITUC has a constitutional mandate to 'strive for the universal respect of fundamental rights at work, until child labour and forced labour in all their forms are abolished, discrimination at work eliminated and the trade union rights of all workers observed fully and everywhere'.[166] To this end, it works closely with international agencies (including the ILO), it works to build trade union capacity and representation throughout the world, and it works closely with regional confederations (such as the European Trade Union Confeder-ation (ETUC), with which it shares premises).[167] Claiming to represent 175 million workers in 156 countries, the ITUC works 'to strengthen the role of the ILO, and for the setting and universal application of international labour standards'.[168]

So far as vertical structures are concerned, perhaps the most important is what are now the 'global union federations' (GUFs), many of which trace their origins to the International Trade Secretariats which were established in the late nineteenth century. The International Transport Workers' Federation (ITF) – for example – was formed in 1896, its campaign against flags of convenience in the interests of seafarers being perhaps the most highly visible example of GUF activity, at least for the lawyer well versed in the case-law.[169] The GUFs are vertically based structures in the sense that they are sector specific, and represent national affiliates from all over the world in the sectors

---

[165] J. Rojot, 'International Collective Bargaining', in M. Morley, P. Gunnigle and D. G. Collings (eds.), *Global Industrial Relations* (2006), pp. 258–9.

[166] ITUC, Constitution (2014), p. 7.

[167] See J. Rojot, 'International Collective Bargaining', in M. Morley, P. Gunnigle and D. G. Collings (eds.), *Global Industrial Relations* (2006), p. 259.

[168] ITUC, Constitution (2014), p. 8.

[169] See N. Lillie, 'Global Collective Bargaining on Flag of Convenience Shipping' (2004) 42 *British Journal of Industrial Relations* 47.

in question. In countries such as the UK where general unions operate across sectors, some unions may affiliate to more than one GUF, a good example of this being Unite, which is affiliated to six. Working 'to coordinate international standards within their industries and to represent their members globally',[170] there are today nine GUFs, which help national affiliates with representations to international bodies and national governments, negotiate global framework agreements with transnational corporations and co-ordinate action and campaigns against such corporations. They also work closely with the ITUC, one of whose founding bodies (the ICFTU) the International Trade Secretariats helped to create,[171] with the ITUC now having a constitutional mandate to 'promote and support the coordination of international trade union policies and activities on multinational enterprises', in co-operation with the GUFs.[172]

Global Union Action

Although the ITUC and the GUFs (at least in the form of their predecessor bodies) have been around a long time, their visibility and activities appear to have increased in recent years. There is, however, a problem in the sense that, while national governments may tolerate the loose international organisation of workers, they are likely to be much less tolerant of effective international activity by the same workers. Not least of the problems encountered here is thus the extent to which transnational trade unionism in an era of globalisation is undermined paradoxically by national legal sovereignty and the continuing importance of national labour laws. A good example of this is provided by the flag-of-convenience campaign of the ITF to which reference has already been made. Shipping companies will often seek to register their vessels in countries that offer various financial advantages and low labour costs. By registering in these countries, the employer need only pay wages and observe other terms and conditions of employment in accordance with the law of the country of the flag where the vessel is registered, rather than the law of the country of the owner of the vessel. This gives rise to exploitative working conditions for groups of workers who are captive on the high seas, being poorly paid to work in dangerous conditions and in unpleasant circumstances. The flag campaign led to action by the ITF – working with national affiliates – to blockade vessels in port until the owners agreed to observe minimum terms and conditions of employment demanded by the federation.[173]

---

[170] International Centre for Trade Union Rights, *The Global Workplace* (2001), p. 30.
[171] See J. Rojot, 'International Collective Bargaining', in M. Morley, P. Gunnigle and D. G. Collings (eds.), *Global Industrial Relations* (2006), p. 259.
[172] ITUC, Constitution (2014), p. 8.
[173] See J. Atleson, 'The Voyage of the Neptune Jade: The Perils and Promises of Transnational Labor Solidarity' (2004) 52 *Buffalo Law Review* 85.

This was perhaps the most effective form of global action ever undertaken by the international trade union movement. It has predictably led to tight controls. In the UK, such action would almost certainly be tortious, but in the late 1970s the courts accepted that it was protected in domestic law as being done in contemplation or furtherance of a trade dispute, most notably by the House of Lords in *The Nawala*.[174] After lobbying by the UK shipping industry, however, the law was changed in 1982,[175] so that the protection from tortious liability would apply only where the dispute was between workers and their own employer.[176] This would generally exclude action by the ITF, which would be a party to a dispute with the owner in its own right, and may not have been acting at the direct request of the crew. The change in the law in 1984 requiring mandatory pre-strike ballots would settle any doubts about the legality of the ITF campaign in the UK, simply because it would be impossible for the ITF to organise a ballot of a crew on board a ship to which its officials had no right of access.[177] The last reported case in an English court relating to the ITF campaign at a British port was thus in 1985. But because the ITF is based in London, there have been other cases in which the English courts have been asked to restrain ITF action in other countries, most notably in the *Viking* case.[178]

The *Viking* Case and Flags of Convenience

In the *Viking Line* case, the owner of a ferry (the *Rosella*) based in Finland proposed to re-flag it in Estonia, where wages are lower. The Finnish Seamen's Union and the ITF instructed their members to boycott the *Rosella* to prevent what they saw as social dumping. The Finnish owners of the *Rosella* brought proceedings in the English Commercial Court to have the action restrained on the ground that it violated their freedom of establishment under what was then EC Treaty, Article 43 (now TFEU, Article 49). An injunction was granted by Mrs Justice Gloster,[179] but a sceptical Court of Appeal decided to make a reference to the ECJ to determine how the balance is to be struck between the so-called economic freedoms in the treaty and

---

[174] *NWL Ltd* v. *Woods* [1979] ICR 867 (HL).

[175] See Official Report, Standing Committee G, 29th Sitting, cols. 1312–14 (19 April 1982). The legality of such action had in any event already been called into question by the restrictions on secondary action introduced in 1980: see *Merkur Island Shipping Corporation* v. *Laughton* [1983] 2 AC 570 (HL). See now TULRCA 1992, s. 224.

[176] Employment Act 1982, s. 18; see now TULRCA 1992, ss. 219 and 244.

[177] See *Shipping Co. Uniform Inc.* v. *ITF* [1985] IRLR 71 (QB): the ballot obligation is one that the ITF could not comply with, being a trade union of affiliated but not individual members. It was held that it was not exempt from the duty to ballot.

[178] *International Transport Workers' Federation* v. *Viking Line ABP* [2005] EWCA Civ 1299, [2006] 1 Lloyd's LR 303 (CA). See also *Patrick Stevedores* v. *ITF* [1998] 2 Lloyd's LR 523 (QB), [1998] 2 Lloyd's LR 523 (CA) and *White Sea and Omega Shipping Co. Ltd* v. *ITF* [2001] 1 Lloyd's LR 421 (QB).

[179] [2005] EWHC 1222, [2005] 3 CMLR 29 (Comm).

the fundamental social rights of workers, to which reference was freely made in the EU Treaty (to say nothing of the EU Charter of Fundamental Rights).[180]

To the surprise of many people, the ECJ took a very conservative approach to fundamental social rights. Although acknowledging ILO Convention 87 and accepting that the right to strike was part of the fundamental principles of EU law, the ECJ also held that EU Treaty, Article 49, had horizontal direct effect and that industrial action to secure a collective agreement was a restriction on the employer's freedom of establishment.[181] These restrictions could be permitted only in highly controlled circumstances which were unlikely ever to arise, the Court holding that restrictions could in principle be justified only 'by an overriding reason of public interest, such as the protection of workers, provided that it is established that the restriction is suitable for ensuring the attainment of the legitimate objective pursued and does not go beyond what is necessary to achieve that objective'.[182] The case was settled without the matter having to be reconsidered by the domestic court.

Although the terms of the settlement are confidential, the decision of the ECJ was seen as a major defeat for trade unions generally and the ITF in particular.

Global Labour Law

The question for trade unions is the extent to which their global ambitions are underpinned by a system of global labour law. As we saw in the second section of this chapter, there is a body of international labour law addressed to national governments, designed to ensure that they comply with minimum standards set down in ILO conventions, which ILO Member States may choose whether or not to ratify. But do these conventions anticipate the possibility that trade unions may operate across frontiers to protect their members' interests? These issues are most likely to arise in relation to the freedom of association conventions, namely, Conventions 87 and 98, which together (and in different ways) protect the three core trade union rights: the right to organise, the right to bargain, and the right to strike. Although not designed with transnational activity in mind, here we find in embryo the makings of a system of protection and support for co-ordinated trade union activity to underpin some, though not all, of the developments traced in the previous section of this chapter. This is most visible in relation to the right to organise at transnational level, with ILO Convention 87 providing by Article 5 that:

Workers' and employers' organisations shall have the right to establish and join federations and confederations and any such organisation, federation or

---

[180] [2005] EWCA Civ 1299, [2006] 1 Lloyd's LR 303 (CA).

[181] Case C-438/05, *International Transport Workers' Federation* v. *Viking Line ABP* [2007] ECR I-10779, [2008] IRLR 143. See A. Davies, 'One Step Forward, Two Steps Back? The *Viking* and *Laval* cases in the ECJ' (2008) 37 *Industrial Law Journal* 126.

[182] Case C-438/05, *International Transport Workers' Federation* v. *Viking Line ABP* [2007] ECR I-10779, [2008] IRLR 143, para. 90.

confederation shall have the right to affiliate with international organisations of workers and employers.

But what about the right to bargain and the right to strike at a transnational level?

Right to Bargain Collectively

So far as the right to bargain collectively is concerned, there is nothing in the relevant ILO conventions that relates directly to collective bargaining that crosses national boundaries. ILO Convention 98 provides, by Article 4, that:

> Measures appropriate to national conditions shall be taken, where necessary, to encourage and promote the full development and utilisation of machinery for voluntary negotiation between employers or employers' organisations and workers' organisations, with a view to the regulation of terms and conditions of employment by means of collective agreement.

This would appear to be addressed to national governments with a view to establishing collective bargaining structures within their own national systems. There is no equivalent in Convention 98 to Article 5 in Convention 87, despite the fact that Conventions 87 and 98 are very close siblings. So to the extent that global framework agreements are being concluded between global corporations and global union federations, this would appear to be beyond any obligation on any nation state to promote. The promotion of such agreements by governments may of course be one of the ways by which a state could comply with its obligations under the convention (particularly where the employer undertakes to comply with Convention 98 in all of its global operations). But although there is evidence of some government involvement in supporting such agreements,[183] there is no evidence of any formal legal support for such agreements under national law.

This is by no means the end of the matter, for at least at EU level there is some support for the development of co-ordinated transnational action by trade unions in their dealings with transnational corporations in the form of the European Works Council Directive,[184] which was recast and strengthened in 2009. This is a development which is considered in some detail in Chapter 15, but for present purposes it is sufficient to note that the Directive provides a framework of minimum standards for information and consultation in which workers' representatives (who will usually be trade unionists) will come together to deal with company management on a regular basis. This process

---

[183] See Ewing, 'International Regulation' (Oxford: Hart, 2007), p. 224 (role of New Zealand government in agreement between Fonterra and the IUF).

[184] Directive 2009/38/EC on the establishment of a European works council or a procedure in Community-scale undertakings and Community-scale groups of undertakings for the purposes of informing and consulting employees (Recast). See pp. 646–51 below.

of information and consultation may lead to agreements on matters of mutual interest, and indeed some of the international framework agreements concluded by employers and trade unions are agreements to which European works councils (EWCs) are a party.[185] It is also the case that, although there are reports that EWCs fail to meet workers' expectations, they have also been the catalyst in some cases for the development of global works councils in the case of companies such as DaimlerChrysler and Orange, again without legal obligation on the part of the corporations in question.[186] This is not to deny, however, that the European Works Council Directive (even as recast) is an adequate substitute for an amended ILO Convention 98, which would require governments to promote collective bargaining at a national *and* transnational level on the part of companies based in their territory.[187]

Right to Collective Action

So far as collective action is concerned, the right to strike is not formally recognised by any ILO instrument. However, it has been read into ILO Convention 87, Article 3, by the supervisory bodies responsible for applying the Convention. Article 3(1) provides that:

> Workers' and employers' organisations shall have the right to draw up their constitutions and rules, to elect their representatives in full freedom, to organise their administration and activities and to formulate their programmes.

For the purposes of international law, the right to strike thus hangs by a slender thread on the words 'to organise their administration and activities and to formulate their programmes'. Although thus implied, the right is nevertheless widely construed so that collective action taken by workers in one country in support of workers in another country will be protected. This is illustrated by conclusions of the Committee of Experts in 1989 in relation to the UK, the Committee criticising the removal of legal protection 'for industrial action which was intended to protect or to improve the terms and conditions of employment of workers outside the United Kingdom, or to register disapproval of the social or racial policies of a government with whom the United Kingdom has trading or economic links'.[188] This would allow workers in one country to take international solidarity action in support of

---

[185] See K. D. Ewing, 'International Regulation of the Global Economy – The Role of Trade Unions', in B. Bercusson and C. Estlund (eds.), *Regulating Labour in the Wake of Globalisation: New Challenges, New Institutions* (2007), Ch. 10.

[186] Details of the Orange Global Works Council are on the corporation's website. Strikingly, Orange for a long time resisted trade union recognition in the UK.

[187] For a discussion of this issue, see K. D. Ewing and T. Sibley, *International Trade Union Rights for the New Millennium* (London: International Centre for Trade Union Rights, 2000), pp. 27–33.

[188] ILO Committee of Experts, Observation Concerning Convention 87 (United Kingdom) (1989).

other workers in dispute with their employers in another country, though such action has always been extremely rare, at least in the UK.[189]

This, however, is slightly different from co-ordinated collective action where a group of workers act together against the same global employer. So far as international labour law is concerned, such action ought to be permitted. But ILO Convention 87 provides by Article 6 that the provisions of Article 3 of the convention apply to the 'federations and confederations of workers' and employers' organisations', which are recognised by Article 5. Noticeably, however, they do not apply to 'international organizations of workers' to which reference is also made in Article 5. The problem of co-ordinated industrial action against a transnational company is that it is thus likely to stumble at the hurdles erected by national labour laws, which various temporal and procedural restraints would make it very difficult if not impossible to organise. In some countries, the action would not be possible until the expiry of a collective agreement (and expiry dates may be different in different countries). In the UK, it will be necessary to engage in a lengthy process of balloting the workforce, and a very technical process requiring notice to be given to the employer. There are few, if any, countries that dispense with national rules to facilitate transnational action, and there is little likelihood of any now doing so. So, although we may have international standards protecting trade union freedom in individual states, there is little obligation on Member States to facilitate co-ordinated transnational action by trade unions. In other words, 'international' standards addressed to nation states do not necessarily facilitate 'global' action.

Conclusion

In this chapter, we have considered some of the consequences of the globalisation of trade, finance and labour supply. Globalisation is taking place within the framework of international labour standards, and within a context in which many would like to see trade sanctions or privileges being tied more closely to the observance of these standards. As we have also seen, globalisation provides opportunities for workers to move from this country to other countries and from other countries to this country, in both cases subject to certain minimum standards being observed (as a result of the Posted Workers Directive) in some circumstances. But globalisation has also exposed serious problems for other workers, and the emergence of different systems of labour law within the same jurisdictions. At a time when bankers in London were contesting contractual bonus claims of £51.8 million (plus interest) in the High Court,[190] other workers were being trafficked to work in circumstances

---

[189] But see K. W. Wedderburn, 'Multinational Enterprises and National Law' (1972) 1 *Industrial Law Journal* 16.

[190] *Attrill* v. *Dresdner Kleinwort Ltd* [2011] EWCA Civ 229, [2011] IRLR 613 (CA). See also *Société Générale, London Branch* v. *Geys* [2012] UK 63, [2013] ICR 117.

which required the law to be changed to make modern slavery a criminal offence. Questions have also been asked about the way in which transnational corporations make use of the opportunities that globalisation has provided for them, with the loss of jobs in the developed world being accompanied by concerns about labour conditions in the developing world and in the supply chains of businesses that supply Western consumers in particular. Responding to these developments presents a formidable challenge for the international trade union movement, inadequately supported by an embryonic global labour law and constrained by a variety of national legal restrictions.

These are aspects of globalisation that are by no means unique to the UK. They have elicited a response from the ILO, which unanimously adopted the ILO Declaration on Social Justice for a Fair Globalisation on 10 June 2008. This is an historic event, not least for the fact that it is only the third major statement of principles since the ILO was founded in 1919, the other two being the Declaration of Philadelphia of 1944, and the Declaration on Fundamental Principles and Rights at Work of 1998. The 2008 Declaration acknowledges that a number of countries have benefited from high rates of economic growth and employment creation, but recognises too that many others face challenges of income inequality and high levels of unemployment.[191] In the face of these and other concerns, the International Labour Conference committed itself to promote four strategic objectives of equal importance, namely: (1) promoting employment by creating a sustainable institutional and economic environment; (2) developing and enhancing measures of social security and labour protection, where these are sustainable and adapted to national circumstances; (3) promoting social dialogue and tripartism; and (4) respecting, promoting and realising the fundamental principles and rights at work, including freedom of association and the effective recognition of the right to collective bargaining. So far as the last principle is concerned, it was also agreed that the 'violation of fundamental principles and rights at work cannot be invoked or otherwise used as a legitimate comparative advantage and that labour standards should not be used for protectionist trade purposes'.[192]

Governments throughout the world have been reluctant to honour these pledges, which were made on the eve of the global financial collapse in September 2008. The latter has been met with austerity and the erosion of standards rather than growth and the raising of standards. It has also been met by a sustained attack on the ILO itself by employers' organisations, focused initially on the Committee of Experts whose authority was called into question, particularly in relation to its longstanding jurisprudence that the right to freedom of association included the right to strike. It is not clear what provoked this onslaught, though it may have been the gradual erosion of the barrier between international and domestic law, which has seen human rights and

---

[191] ILO Declaration on Social Justice for a Fair Globalisation (Geneva: ILO, 2008), p. 5.
[192] *Ibid.*, pp. 9–11.

constitutional courts taking into consideration ILO instruments in the interpretation of human rights instruments, deferring to the ILO Committee of
Experts in the process.[193] The stand-off was resolved by a truce concluded in
2014 in which the employers – faced with the prospect of a reference to the
International Court of Justice – accepted both the authority of the Committee of
Experts and the existence of the right to strike as a feature of the principle of
freedom of association.[194] But in truth this has been an uneasy truce, and there
is a sense that employers empowered by the current state of the global economy
are in a position at the moment to throw their weight around at the ILO.[195]

As a result the balance on which tripartism relies is now under severe strain,
as may be the capacity of the ILO to fulfil a mission as necessary in 2019 as it
was in 1919.

UN Guiding Principles

The ILO Declaration on Social Justice for a Fair Globalisation is not the only recent international
initiative to address matters considered in this chapter. In 2005, the business and human
rights agenda re-surfaced in the United Nations in a different form. Professor John Ruggie was
appointed to lead a project that would map existing human rights obligations of corporate
actors and assess the way forward. The ideas developed during the first phase were worked
up into the now widely recognised 'Protect, Respect, Remedy' framework, which involves:

- the state's duty to protect against human rights abuses by third parties, including business;
- the corporate responsibility to respect human rights; and
- the need for more effective access to remedies.[196]

---

[193] See note 21. UK employers were heavily involved in this process, concerned about the
implications of *Demir and Baycara* v. *Turkey*, above, for the controversial anti-union labour
laws introduced in the UK since 1980. Much of that legislation breached ILO Conventions
87 and 98, and employers feared that the ECtHR would transmit ILO jurisprudence into
convention case-law. These fears were allayed, however, when the Strasbourg court beat a
retreat in *RMT* v. *United Kingdom* [2014] ECHR 366. See A. Bogg and K. D. Ewing, 'The
Implications of the *RMT* Case' (2014) 43 *Industrial Law Journal* 221, and K. D. Ewing and J.
Hendy QC, 'Article 11(3) of the European Convention on Human Rights' [2017] *European
Human Rights Law Review* 356.
[194] The trade union case for the ICJ is to be found in ITUC, *The Right to Strike and the ILO: the
Legal Foundations* (Brussels, 2014).
[195] For four different accounts of this crisis, which has generated a large body of literature, see J.
Bellace, 'The ILO and the Right to Strike' (2014) 153 *International Labour Review* 29; K. D.
Ewing, '"The Lady Doth Protest Too Much, Methinks": The Right to Strike, International
Standards and the Supreme Court of Canada' (2014–15) 18 *Canadian Labour and
Employment Law Journal* 197; C. La Hovary, 'Showdown at the ILO? A Historical Perspective
on the Employers' Group's 2012 Challenge to the Right to Strike' (2013) 42 *Industrial Law
Journal* 338 and J. Vogt, 'The Right to Strike and the International Labour Organisation'
(2016) 27 *King's Law Journal* 110.
[196] Report of the UN Special Representative of the Secretary-General on the Issue of Human
Rights and Transnational Corporations and other Business Enterprises – J. Ruggie, 'Protect,

The UK Parliament's Joint Committee on Human Rights expressed concern about the framework: '[I]n circumstances where states were unwilling or unable to fulfil their duty to protect, the responsibility on companies operating in those countries should be more onerous.'[197] There are fresh concerns that the weaknesses of the framework have not been addressed by the subsequent Guiding Principles,[198] which have now been adopted by the UN Human Rights Council.

The most interesting features of the UN Guiding Principles are those relating specifically to corporations, the obligation to respect human rights to apply – at a minimum – to the 'International Bill of Rights', which means the UN Declaration of Human Rights, the ICCPR and the International Covenant on Economic, Social and Cultural Rights, as well as the rights set out in the ILO Declaration on Fundamental Principles and Rights at Work. From this flows a number of secondary obligations, such as a duty to seek to prevent or mitigate adverse human rights impacts directly linked to the operations of a company's business relationships, which might suggest some responsibility for the supply chain, as well as a duty to have in place a policy commitment to meet these responsibilities and a due diligence process to identify, prevent and mitigate human rights impacts. Other obligations on businesses create expectations about (1) accountability through reporting about how they deal with potential human rights impacts, as well as (2) remediation where their activities have caused adverse human rights effects.

One problem with the foregoing provisions is that they are guiding principles rather than mandatory obligations, and they have no legal effect in international law or domestic law. As always, only states can impose obligations on companies, these principles being designed along with others to encourage companies to behave in circumstances where because of the imbalance of power they are clearly beyond the ability of nation states to confront. It has been suggested that the next step should be an international treaty to give legal effects to something like the United Nations Guiding Principles, a suggestion that has only superficial attraction. Even if agreement between states could be secured, it is hard to believe that there would be a rush to ratification, and harder also to believe that states would introduce and enforce legislation to address corporate impunity. As it is, an indication of the problem of government is revealed by the JCHR, which revisited this matter in 2016. Although it applauded the UK government for being the first in the world to produce a National Action Plan on the implementation of the Guiding Principles, the Joint Committee on Human Rights was critical of the Plan's modesty of scope and the failure to incorporate best practice in relation to measurable objectives.[199]

Respect and Remedy: A Framework for Business and Human Rights', UN Doc. A/HRC/8/5 (2008), para. 17.

[197] HL Paper 5-I, HC 64-I (2009–10), para. 94.

[198] Human Rights Council, Report of the Special Representative of the Secretary-General on the Issue of Human Rights and Transnational Corporations and other Business Enterprises – J. Ruggie, Guiding Principles on Business and Human Rights: Implementing the United Nations 'Protect, Respect and Remedy' Framework, UN Doc. A/HRC/17/31 (2011).

[199] HL Paper 154, HC 433 (2016–17).

Part II
The Contract of Employment

3

Terms of the Contract of Employment

Contents

The Contract of Service

People work under many different institutional arrangements. In the past, slavery, forced labour, household servants and feudal serfdom were recognised legal frameworks for work. During the nineteenth century, as industrialisation spread in Europe, the predominant legal framework for paid work was located in the law of contract. The legal analysis used the law of contract to express the idea that, in an economic system where the relations of production were co-ordinated through market transactions, the hire of workers to perform work was like other market transactions – a freely undertaken exchange of goods or services in return for payment. On analogy with the contract for the hire of a thing, the relation between employer and labourer was analysed by lawyers as a contract for the hire of services.

Lawyers drew a further distinction within the category of contracts for the provision of services. Where suppliers of services such as craftsmen and artisans acted independently, managing their own work, the agreements they made with other businesses were labelled 'contracts for services'. In contrast, where the hirer managed, supervised and controlled the work performed by the labourer, this arrangement was classified as a 'contract of service' or, in modern times, a contract of employment.

Like other contracts governed by the common law of England and Wales, a legally enforceable contract of service or employment requires an agreement between the parties and consideration. The agreement may be express or inferred from conduct. The consideration in a contract of service consists in the employer's promise of a wage or other remuneration in return for a promise by the employee that he or she will personally perform work under the employer's control and direction.

Freedom of Contract

This contractual analysis invoked and applied the general principles of contract law to contracts of service. These principles respect the freedom to enter into contracts. Older legal regulations compelled labourers to stay in their communities, imposed compulsory status obligations towards their superiors in a social hierarchy and prevented free movement of labour and freedom to contract. These regulations were gradually dismantled during the nineteenth century, leaving workers free to choose their jobs.

The parties were also free to choose the terms of their bargain. The common law of contract developed by the judges accorded almost complete flexibility to the parties to devise their legal relation, subject only to the restraint-of-trade doctrine and general rules against enforcement of illegal contracts.[1] The express terms of the contractual agreement shape the whole design of the economic relation: the type of work, the conditions under which work has to be performed, the duration of the relation, the allocation of risks and the remuneration to be paid. This flexibility of the contractual framework permits considerable diversity in the terms under which people work. Constraints on freedom of contract arise almost entirely from statute. Legislation sometimes prohibits certain kinds of work relation such as the employment of children, but more commonly legislation places additional obligations or confers additional statutory rights on the parties to contracts of employment.

---

[1] See Chapter 4.

This respect accorded by the common law to freedom of contract has the consequence that the starting-point for the analysis of legal obligations arising in the context of working relations must always be the terms of any contractual arrangement between employer and worker. The contract of employment provides the scaffolding for the construction of the legal relation for the performance of work. Express and implied terms of the contract are legally enforceable obligations which establish the basic rights and obligations of the employer and the worker or supplier of services. Statutory regulation often supplements, qualifies and occasionally replaces those rights and obligations. But that statutory regulation normally presupposes and depends on the existence of a contract of employment. Thus, a thorough legal analysis of the law of employment relations should always commence by ascertaining the content of the contractual framework.

Implied Terms and the Standard Model of Employment

Until the middle of the twentieth century, working arrangements were usually formed by oral contracts, so that only some key points such as wages and hours were expressly agreed, leaving many crucial details unspecified. To resolve many of the disputes that arose between employers and their workers, the courts needed to flesh out the detail of the contractual arrangements. As in other contractual arrangements, the courts construed the express terms of the agreement and then supplemented those terms with implied obligations. These judicial decisions in effect created the legal institution of the contract of employment, which became the standard model for personal work arrangements.

The courts' model of the contract of employment viewed the central obligations of the parties as the exchange of work for wages. Yet most contracts of employment were incomplete in the specification of the work to be provided under the contract. The express terms describing the job on offer might be one of 'labourer', 'mechanic', 'machine operator' or 'clerk', labels which merely indicate in general terms the type of work expected. This uncertainty in job specification was resolved by creating a standard default rule for contracts of service that the employer has the implied power to direct labour and that the employee is under a correlative obligation to comply with all lawful instructions of the employer. Employers exercise this contractual power to direct labour not only through explicit instructions issued by managers, but also through standing orders contained in notices in the workplace or staff handbooks. This legal solution to the problem of incompleteness in contracts of employment thus creates a power relation or, more precisely, a legal relation of practical authority of the employer over the employee.[2]

---

[2] H. Collins, 'Is the Contract of Employment Illiberal?', in H. Collins, G. Lester and V. Mantouvalou (eds.), *Philosophical Foundations of Labour Law* (Oxford University Press, 2018).

The subordination of the worker to the management of the employer became the central characteristic of this model contract of employment. The relation of practical authority was confirmed by the development of further implied obligations designed to put flesh on the transaction placing upon the employee duties of loyalty and co-operation.

In the common law's terminology, this standard model of the employment relation was articulated as a set of implied terms.[3] These terms were presumed to form part of every contract of employment, unless there were express contradictory terms agreed between the parties. Some of these terms might perhaps be justified as resting on the actual, though unexpressed, intentions of the parties. Their insertion might therefore be warranted on the traditional legal test that they were necessary to give 'business efficacy' to the contract.[4] In the past, terms could also be implied into the contract of employment by virtue of custom in the trade or locality,[5] although today any custom would only assist in the interpretation of the express terms of the contract. These days it is openly acknowledged by the courts that in fact they use a standard model of the employment relation that imposes many obligations on the parties without detailed examination of their possible intentions. These terms are sometimes described as terms 'implied by law', terminology which captures the point that these terms comprise the standard legal incidents of employment relations.[6] As general implied terms or default rules, these terms implied by law express judicial preconceptions about the essential obligations arising in the context of work relations.[7] These preconceptions both steer the interpretation of the express terms of the contract and supplement and qualify those terms.

These implied terms or default rules governing contracts of employment are constantly evolving and being refined by the courts. Some statutory rights, such as the right to a minimum wage,[8] are also regarded as imposing terms implied by law into contracts. It is therefore difficult at any one time to give a precise and uncontroversial account of their content. Nevertheless, it is helpful to provide as an introduction a rough and incomplete summary of terms implied by law, divided with respect to the obligations of the employer and the employee. All of these implied terms will be examined in greater detail in subsequent chapters according to their appropriate context.

---

[3] H. Collins, 'Implied Terms in the Contract of Employment', in M. Freedland (gen. ed.), *The Contract of Employment* (Oxford University Press, 2016), p. 471.

[4] E.g. *Devonald* v. *Rosser & Sons* [1906] 2 KB 728 (CA).

[5] E.g. *Sagar* v. *Ridehalgh & Sons Ltd* [1931] 1 Ch 310 (CA).

[6] E.g. *Mahmoud* v. *Bank of Credit and Commerce International SA* [1998] AC 20 (HL).

[7] B. Napier, 'Judicial Attitudes to the Employment Relationship' (1977) 6 *Industrial Law Journal* 1.

[8] *Mruke* v. *Khan* [2018] EWCA Civ 280, [2018] ICR 1146.

Implied terms of the contract of employment

An employer's implied obligations include obligations:

- to take reasonable care of the health and safety of employees;
- not, without reasonable cause, to act in a manner likely to destroy mutual trust and confidence;
- not to treat an employee arbitrarily, capriciously or irrationally in matters of remuneration; and
- to give reasonable notice of termination of the contract.

An employee's implied obligations include obligations:

- to obey lawful orders of the employer;
- to take reasonable care in the performance of the contract;
- to act loyally towards the interests of the employer;
- to serve the employer faithfully within the requirements of the contract; and
- to give reasonable notice of termination of the contract.

Each of these implied terms may be formulated by different judges in slightly varying terminology. For example, the implied term that the employer should not, without reasonable cause, act in a manner likely to destroy mutual trust and confidence has sometimes been described as a duty to act responsibly and in good faith or as a duty to act fairly:

> The trust and confidence implied term means, in short, that an employer must treat his employees fairly. In his conduct of his business, and in his treatment of his employees, an employer must act responsibly and in good faith.[9]

Since these implied terms describe what were called above judicial preconceptions about the structure and content of the contract employment, the nuances of various formulations may prove significant in the construction of a particular contract. Professor Mark Freedland has further suggested that, underlying these general principles governing the construction of contracts of employment, it is useful to identify 'an overarching principle of fair management and performance'.[10] This overarching principle, he argues, both links together the strands in the judicial preconceptions about the content of the employment relation and serves to provide a bridge to principles underlying legislative interventions that replace or qualify the contractual framework for employment.

This standard model of the contract of employment, comprised of express and implied terms, provides the legal institution at the heart of work relations.

---

[9] *Eastwood* v. *Magnox Electric plc* [2004] UKHL 35, [2004] ICR 1064, para. 11, *per* Lord Nicholls.
[10] M. Freedland, *The Personal Employment Contract* (Oxford University Press, 2003), pp. 186–95.

Labour legislation usually modifies, supplements or controls the standard model. For example, minimum wage legislation uses as one of its enforcement mechanisms the possibility that a worker can enforce the entitlement to a minimum wage rather than the contract terms.[11] The legal concept of the contract of employment played a central role in the development not only of labour law, but also tort law, tax law and social security law. In the law of tort, the contract of employment was used to fix the scope of the vicarious liability of employers for the negligence of agents who had caused loss to third parties. The Workmen's Compensation Acts 1897 and 1906 used the contract of service to set the outer boundaries of the scheme for compensation for workplace injuries. In taxation of personal income, the contract of employment was used to draw the line between wage-earners, for whom tax should be deducted by the employer, and the self-employed, who would be responsible for their own tax obligations and who could take advantage of a broader range of deductions to reduce their tax liability.[12] In the social security system, the contract of employment or contract of service was used in the National Insurance Act 1911 to establish the boundaries of the new provisions regarding pensions and compulsory health insurance. The use of the contract of employment as the legal institution that determined the legal incidents of work and the scope of the social security system was confirmed by the Beveridge Report that established the general principles of what became known as the welfare state.[13]

Criticisms of the Contractual Model

Over the centuries of its existence, the contract of employment has proved to be a flexible tool for governing the legal relationship between employer and worker. At the outset of our examination of its features it is, however, worth highlighting the key criticisms that have been voiced against this legal institution.

The first point is that, although the law presents the contract of employment as a bargain between equals in the marketplace, in practice the employer's bargaining power is normally stronger. The principal bargaining weakness of a jobseeker lies in the importance of employment for securing an income. In the absence of substantial personal wealth, most workers accept the first job that appears more or less satisfactory, even though, if they had been able to hold out for longer, it might have been possible to find a job with better conditions and higher wages. For much the same reason, in fear of becoming unemployed

---

[11] NMWA 1998, s. 17.   [12] Finance Act 1922 and Income Tax (Employments) Act 1943.
[13] *Social Insurance and Allied Services*, Cmd 6405 (1942); see S. Deakin, 'The Evolution of the Contract of Employment, 1900–1950: The Influence of the Welfare State', in N. Whiteside and R. Salais (eds.), *Governance, Industry and Labour Markets in Britain and France* (London: Routledge, 1998), p. 212.

and impoverished, a typical worker will be reluctant to quit a job, even if the employer makes increasing demands for harder work and imposes tougher conditions. The employer usually operates without such pressures because in general workers can easily be replaced. The presentation in law of the employment relation as a contract that is freely entered into on the basis of consensual terms belies the reality in many instances of a contract reluctantly undertaken by the employee as a matter of necessity without any real choice about the terms.

Building on that point, the employer's superior bargaining power permits it to impose a standard-form contract on the employee. Today, an employer typically requires an employee to agree to a standard-form contract on a take-it-or-leave-it basis.[14] The printed contract supplied by the employer may provide some entitlements for employees, but it also contains an extensive list of requirements. In short, the employer typically dictates all the rules that govern the workplace and the employment relation. These rules not only specify the content of the job to be performed, but also insert the contract into the organisational framework of larger employers. For instance, the rules may specify the clothing to be worn at work, how employees should conduct themselves towards co-workers and customers, how they should perform within the bureaucratic organisation, how they might make complaints and how discipline will be exercised. Some employers' rules go further and seek to dictate an employee's lifestyle outside of the workplace. The rules constitute not just a contract, but a code to govern the worker and the workplace. The employer's unilateral power to legislate this code is heavily disguised by the legal image of the consensual agreement of a contract.

A third important criticism of the contractual model of employment concerns the manner in which the focus on the express terms of the contract tends to ignore or downplay the significance of the implicit expectations of the parties. When the contract of employment is formed, both parties frequently hope and expect that it will continue for a considerable period of time. Over the years, there will no doubt have to be adjustments to the agreement. Employees will hope for wage increases, promotions, training, fair treatment, job security and other kinds of rewards for long service. While also desiring such a long-term co-operative and profitable relationship, employers will be reluctant to include in the express terms of the contract any hard promises about the long-term future. Instead, the contract will remain tied to the present, flexibility left to the employer's discretion and mutual expectations of good faith in performance left unsaid. The formal contract tends to specify the wage/work bargain and the duties of the employee, but to abstain from articulating in detail the relational aspects of the contract such as expectations of fair treatment and rewards for good performance. The contract of

---

[14] H. Collins, 'Legal Responses to the Standard Form Contract of Employment' (2007) 36 *Industrial Law Journal* 2.

employment normally specifies that it can be terminated on fairly short notice by either party, while the implicit expectations of both employer and employee are that a contract of indefinite duration will last for a considerable period of time, perhaps for an entire career.

The lack of fit between the express terms of the contract, which emphasise the wage/work bargain, and the implicit expectations of the parties about a broader, ongoing relationship, places the traditional legal model of the contract of employment under strain.[15] That pressure can be relieved by the development of implied terms that try to express those implicit expectations. Statutory measures also adjust the express terms to meet the social expectations. For instance, the statutory law of unfair dismissal requires an employer to have a substantial reason for dismissal; it is not sufficient for the employer merely to say that it is exercising a power conferred by a term of the contract to terminate the contract. The tension between the express commitments and the implicit expectations creates an unstable model of the contract of employment. Legal reasoning constantly oscillates between an emphasis on the explicit exchange of work for wages and on the relational qualities and implicit expectations of the parties. Judgments and legal rules may always be criticised for paying too much or too little attention to one dimension of the contract of employment:[16]

> [T]here is a state of structural uncertainty which characterizes the law concerning the content of personal employment contracts. At the heart of this structural uncertainty lies the dichotomy between exchange transactions and relational contracts. Most of the problems about the content and internal structure of personal employment contracts result from doubt and ambiguity as to whether and when those contracts are to be regarded more as exchange transactions than as relational contracts . . . . The two ideas coexist as competing paradigms which exert pressures towards different approaches or solutions to issues of the construction or regulation of personal employment contracts.[17]

A particular instance of this gap between express commitments and implicit expectations concerns the adaptation of the contract of employment to new circumstances. The common law of the formation of contracts assumes that the initial agreement fixes the rights and obligations of the parties. This assumption runs directly contrary to the expectations of the parties to many employment relations, which, in the context of a long-term relation, envisage a constant process of adjustment. These adjustments may occur in practice through the exercise of managerial discretion to direct the workforce, or

---

[15] D. Brodie, 'Relational Contracts', in M. Freedland (gen. ed.), *The Contract of Employment* (Oxford, 2017), p. 145.

[16] H. Collins, 'The Contract of Employment in 3D', in D. Campbell, L. Mulcahy and S. Wheeler (eds.), *Changing Concepts of Contract: Essays in Honour of Ian Macneil* (Basingstoke: Palgrave Macmillan, 2013), p. 65.

[17] M. Freedland, *The Personal Employment Contract* (Oxford University Press, 2003), pp. 88 and 92.

agreement between the parties including through a collective agreement or simply by the gradual variation of conduct in the performance of the contract. There is a stark 'contrast between the lawyer's static model of the formation of terms and the evolutionary character of actual practice'.[18]

Finally, but most importantly, the traditional contractual analysis tends to overlook the significance of the terms that create a relation of subordination. Unlike most contracts, a crucial purpose of the agreement is to put one party, the worker, under the control of the other, a manager, at least as regards performance of work. The terms and organisational rules that construct this authority relation inevitably create the risk of abuse or misuse of authority by managers.[19] The law imposes liability on the employer for a manager's misconduct either on the ground of the responsibility of a principal for the acts of its agent or on the ground of vicarious liability in tort.[20] Far from constituting a relation between equals, the contract of employment is designed to construct a relation of subordination.

The Psychological Contract

The gap between the express terms of the contract and the implicit (and sometimes explicit) promises and expectations of the parties to the contract of employment has been described in various ways. Following Macneil,[21] the contract of employment can be termed a relational contract rather than a discrete contract, because there are usually (though not invariably) implicit expectations of co-operation, fair dealing and long-term commitment.[22] In the literature of human resources management (HRM), it is more common to describe the implicit expectations of the parties as 'the psychological contract'[23] and this idea has sometimes been adopted for the analysis of legal issues.[24] A term of this non-legal

---

[18] P. Davies and M. Freedland, *Labour Law* (2nd edn, London: Weidenfeld & Nicolson, 1984), p. 299.

[19] H. Collins, 'Market Power, Bureaucratic Power and the Contract of Employment' (1986) 15 *Industrial Law Journal* 1.

[20] P. Davies and M. Freedland, 'The Complexities of the Employing Enterprise', in G. Davidov and B. Langille (eds.), *Boundaries and Frontiers of Labour Law* (Oxford: Hart, 2006), p. 273.

[21] I. R. Macneil, 'Contracts: Adjustment of Long-Term Economic Relations under Classical, Neoclassical, and Relational Contract Law' (1978) 72 *Northwestern University Law Review* 854; D. Campbell (ed.), *Ian Macneil, The Relational Theory of Contract: Selected Works of Ian Macneil* (London: Sweet & Maxwell, 2001).

[22] D. Brodie, 'How Relational Is the Employment Contract?' (2011) 40 *Industrial Law Journal* 232; M. Boyle, 'The Relational Principle of Trust and Confidence' (2007) 27 *Oxford Journal of Legal Studies* 633; R. C. Bird, 'Employment as a Relational Contract' (2005) 8 *University of Pennsylvania Journal of Labor and Employment Law* 149.

[23] For an overview, see D. E. Guest, 'The Psychology of the Employment Relationship: An Analysis Based on the Psychological Contract' (2004) 53 *Applied Psychology: An International Review* 541.

[24] K. V. W. Stone, 'The New Psychological Contract: Implications of the Changing Workplace for Labor and Employment Law' (2001) 48 *UCLA Law Review* 519.

psychological contract might be a belief on the part of employees that by working hard they will keep their jobs indefinitely. This belief is more than just a subjective opinion, because the employee is likely to believe, in addition, that the employer is under a reciprocal obligation to comply with a principle that hard work will be rewarded by job security.[25]

The psychological contract, defined as 'individual beliefs, shaped by the organization, regarding terms of an exchange agreement between individuals and their organization',[26] has been shown to affect key organisational outcomes. Employee perceptions that the organisation is providing what it promised, referred to as psychological contract fulfilment (PC fulfilment), have been related to job satisfaction, in-role performance and organisational citizenship behaviours. On the other hand, employee perceptions of the extent to which the organisation has failed to fulfil its obligations, referred to as psychological contract breach (PC breach), have been related to lowered job satisfaction and commitment and increased turnover intentions.[27]

HRM understands that the psychological contract can be shaped by the organisation. Managers can induce workers to believe in a reciprocal obligation, such as the idea that hard work will be rewarded by job security, by various practices such as vague assurances and policy statements, appeals to the ethos of the corporation and organisational structures and processes (such as bonuses based on performance) that appear to endorse the existence of the reciprocal obligations of the psychological contract. While the benefits to the employer of increased commitment and low turnover of staff are plain, for employees the value of the vague promises of the psychological contract remain uncertain without formal legal guarantees. Breach of the psychological contract by the employer is likely to be regarded as more than non-compliance with a contract; it will be regarded by employees as signalling a betrayal of the employment relationship,[28] a breakdown in mutual trust and confidence. When thinking about the psychological contract in comparison to the binding legal agreement, employees should be advised to 'mind the gap'.

Indeterminacy and Plurality of Sources of Rules Governing Employment

What are the terms of my employment? A simple answer might be expected to this straightforward question posed by an employee. A fairly precise answer could normally be given to an analogous question in the context of a commercial contract between two businesses. Yet, in employment, rarely can anyone describe the terms and rules governing an employment relation with similar assurance. There may be a written contract between employer and

---

[25] D. M. Rousseau, 'Psychological and Implied Contracts in Organisations' (1989) 2 *Employee Responsibilities and Rights Journal* 121.

[26] D. M. Rousseau, *Psychological Contracts in Organizations: Understanding Written and Unwritten Agreements* (Thousand Oaks, CA: Sage, 1995), p. 9.

[27] A. Chaudry *et al.*, 'A Sensemaking Model of Employee Evaluation of Psychological Contract Fulfillment' (2009) 45 *Journal of Applied Behavioral Science* 498 (notes omitted).

[28] E. W. Morrison and S. Robinson, 'When Employees Feel Betrayed: A Model of How Psychological Contract Violation Develops' (1997) 22 *Academy of Management Review* 226.

employee that supplies many of the terms of the contract, but it is unlikely to provide a comprehensive account.

In the wings of the stage set by the contract of employment often stands a trade union, which may negotiate many of the vital elements of the contract yet appear to have no legal status at all with respect to the contract of employment. The union is not usually the agent of the employee for the purpose of negotiating terms of employment. Nevertheless, any collective agreement reached between the union and the employer may have legal effects on the contract of employment. When there is a strong recognised union in the workplace, the legal emphasis upon individual consent by an employee to the contractual agreement may only remotely correspond with the perceptions of the participants in the organisation, who may turn to the collective agreement as the primary source of terms of employment. If the union succeeds in bargaining for a pay rise for the employees, everyone expects the new pay rates to replace the existing terms of employment, even though an individual employee may not have agreed to or even be aware of the new deal.

Most employers also supplement any written contract of employment with further rules to govern the organisation. These rules comprise a mixture of descriptions of how the organisation should function, what procedures should be followed and how work should be performed. These rules serve the managerial function of directing the workforce, although they also construct and articulate many of the relational aspects of employment contracts. Yet there is often considerable uncertainty about whether all or part of these rule-books establish contractual entitlements.

The surprising result of this multiplicity of potential sources of terms of the contract is that, in this central economic relation in a market society, there is often considerable uncertainty about the content of the contract of employment. Legal regulation only makes ineffectual attempts to reduce this level of uncertainty. The remainder of this chapter considers the written contract, the rule-book and the collective agreement in turn. It is important to appreciate, however, that each workplace is likely to produce its own mix of rules governing employment relations, which combine contractual terms, customs, codes of practice, rule-books, collective agreements, as well as the applicable statutory labour legislation, other regulatory requirements and fundamental rights protected in the constitution.

Harry Arthurs on Legal Pluralism

Put briefly, the argument is that each workplace is its own legal system, different from any other, and different as well from the legal system of the state. Whether we look at the content of the rules governing workplace behaviour, the source of those rules, the processes by which they are generated, enforced or modified – even the value system or ideology in which they are embedded – the predominant impression is the same: deed determines word, context dominates text, specific trumps general, and 'law' – as we lawyers know it – is seen, if at all, 'through a glass, darkly'. A worker arrives for work at a stipulated hour, enters the premises by a designated door, records his arrival in the prescribed manner, dons work clothes, takes tools in his hand, goes to an assigned work station, and in accordance with minutely-detailed procedures, addresses a narrow range of tasks. Virtually his every move is bounded by rules. So too his relations with fellow workers, management representatives and third persons, such as customers, which are neither wholly spontaneous nor random: they are rule bound. His remuneration and his exposure to discipline and redundancy, his enjoyment of amenities and his exposure to hardship at work, are all carefully defined by rules.

There is no point in dismissive rhetoric whose general purport is that such trivial rules do not rise to the dignity of 'law'. It matters profoundly to the worker (and his employer) whether his tea break is ten minutes or only five; whether his production quota is 110 per cent. or only 90 per cent. of what he feels capable of; whether he must silently bear his foreman's abuse or can give as good as he gets without fear of being sacked. These are 'legal' questions with an immediacy that, for the worker, far exceeds that of the law of assault or the European Convention on Human Rights. And they are often 'legal' questions of considerable complexity: whether or to what extent plant practise tolerates blunt speech demands no less careful a balancing of interests than the limits of fair comment in the law of defamation; the complex reciprocal claims of worker and employer for pay and performance are sometimes more exquisitely arcane than feudal tenures.[29]

Regulating Express Terms

In the past, most workers were hired by an oral contract but today, except in small businesses, it is normal for employees to be issued with a written contract, which the employer is likely to invite the new recruit to sign.[30] The document is typically a standard-form contract that deals fairly comprehensively with the terms and conditions of employment. The personal details of the recruit – name, address, salary – can be entered into the spaces provided by the printed document. Under the general principles of the law of contract, the express terms of the agreement between the employer and employee provide the principal guide to their respective rights and obligations. As in other contracts, these terms occasionally provoke problems of interpretation and disputed applications to changed circumstances. Here we focus on the question of the extent to which employment law attempts to control the misuse of the power to issue one-sided standard-form contracts. Two topics will be

---

[29] H. Arthurs, 'Understanding Labour Law: The Debate over "Industrial Pluralism"' (1985) *Current Legal Problems* 83 (notes omitted).

[30] W. Brown, S. Deakin, M. Hudson, C. Pratten and O. Ryan, *The Individualisation of Employment Contracts in Britain* (London: DTI, Employment Relations Research Series, URN 98/943, 1998), para. 6.2.7.

considered: duties to provide details of the terms of employment in a transparent manner and controls over unfair terms.

First, though, it is helpful to look at a typical standard-form contract of employment. This hypothetical, though fairly representative, example of a contemporary contract of employment is shorter than a typical standard form used by employers and does not include relevant appendices etc. The drafting is also more internally consistent and grammatical than a typical contract, which usually suffers from *ad hoc* amendments introduced from time to time into the word-processing file without checking consistency with other terms and revising section numbers. Antique legal jargon has also been omitted for the most part, though some is so common (e.g. clause 12.3) it has to be retained for reasons of authenticity.

Statement of Terms and Conditions of Employment

Job title: _____ [e.g. clerk grade 6; sales assistant; operative grade 1]

This document along with your letter of appointment sets out the terms and conditions of employment which are required to be given to an employee under section 1 of the Employment Rights Act 1996.

1. **Parties' details**
   1.1. Name of employee: _____
   1.2. Name of employer: _____ ('the Company')
2. **Date of continuous service (and termination of employment)**
   2.1. Your date of continuous service with the Company began on _____. No employment with a previous employer counts as part of a period of continuous service unless stated below.
   2.2. (Fixed term only) Your employment will terminate on _____ unless your contract is terminated earlier in accordance with clause 10.
3. **Job title**
   3.1. You shall be employed as a _____ [e.g. clerk grade 6; sales assistant; operative grade 1].
   3.2. You are required to undertake the duties in the attached document, which is your job description. Please be advised that your job description does not form part of your terms of employment.
   3.3. You may be required to perform such other duties as the Company may reasonably require.
   3.4. You will be responsible to _____ (Manager) and _____ (Assistant Manager).
4. **Place of employment**
   4.1. Your place of employment shall be at any of the Company's premises or those of its customers.
   4.2. You may be required to travel to other locations, as appropriate.

4.3. You are required to reside within reasonable travelling time of the main premises of the Company that you operate from.

5. **Remuneration and benefits**

   5.1. Your basic pay is equivalent to £250 per week. (This is calculated by reference to the guaranteed minimum hours.) Your actual rate of pay, overtime rates, and other benefits are set out in Appendix 1. Any overtime should be authorised in advance by the appropriate Manager.

   5.2. Payment will be made weekly on Fridays in arrears by BACS into a bank account nominated by you.

   5.3. On termination of employment, any monies owing to the Company will be deducted from your final payment.

   5.4. Pay reviews are conducted in April each year, though an increase is not guaranteed.

   5.5. You authorise the company to deduct from your wages any sums which you owe to the Company including the value of any property belonging to the Company which you have lost, damaged or failed to return.

6. **Hours of work and flexibility**

   6.1. A working week is defined as Monday through Sunday. You are guaranteed at least 35 hours per week.

   6.2. The Company reserves the right to average these hours out over a calendar month, so you will receive typically 150 hours of work per month.

   6.3. These guaranteed hours can be worked at any time, including bank holidays.

   6.4. You are required to work such hours as are required to complete your duties, including overtime if necessary.

   6.5. You are required to make yourself available for all work as required. Failure to be available will be regarded as a serious breach of contract and will result in disciplinary action.

   6.6. During your employment you will be required to co-operate in the development of new working practices.

   6.7. As a term of your employment, you can be required to undertake such other duties or hours of work, temporarily or on a continuing basis, as may be reasonably required of you.

   6.8. As a term of your contract, you agree that the Company may require you to work in excess of 48 hours in a working week.

7. **Commitment to work**

   7.1. Persistent lateness or failure to turn up for work without good reason will render you liable to disciplinary action which may lead to dismissal.

   7.2. The Company may lay you off without pay or put you on short-time working with reduced pay, if for any reason outside of the Company's control there is a shortage of work.

8. **Holidays**

   8.1. Your paid holidays will be at the rate of 28 days per calendar year, inclusive of bank holidays. Your holiday accrues on a weekly basis.

8.2. Holidays may only be taken at times convenient to the Company, as previously arranged by notice to the Company as far in advance as possible, and as approved by the Manager.

8.3. On termination of employment, if you have taken more holidays than your accrued entitlement, these monies will be deducted from your final pay.

9. **Pension**

9.1. The Company operates a Stakeholder Pension scheme, but does not make any contribution to it.

10. **Absence due to sickness or injury**

10.1. If you cannot attend work through sickness or injury you must, unless there is some good reason to the contrary, advise your Manager of the reason for non-attendance on the first working day of absence no later than 30 minutes after your booked shift starting time. Failure to do so may result in sickness pay not being paid.

10.2. Immediately on your return to work you must obtain, complete and return to your Manager before the end of the day of your return to work a self-certification form, or for periods of absence of more than 7 days a doctor's certificate/fit note.

10.3. You must report any accident at work to your Manager and complete an Accident Report form.

10.4. If you are absent from work by reason of injuries sustained wholly or partly as a result of the actionable negligence or breach of statutory duty on the part of any third party or the Company, all sickness payments made to you shall, to the extent that compensation is recoverable from the third party, constitute loans by the company to you, which shall be repaid when and to the extent that you recover compensation for loss of earnings from that third party or the Company by action or otherwise.

10.5. Appointment is subject to passing a medical examination, and passing a 'clean' drugs and alcohol test.

10.6. It is a condition of employment that during the course of it, you must disclose to the Company any medical treatment or condition that you may have diagnosed that will or may have an effect on your ability to carry out your duties.

10.7. You will provide on request by an authorised person of the Company's Occupational Health a specimen of breath and/or urine for the purpose of screening for alcohol and prohibited drugs. Any refusal will normally result in dismissal.

11. **Probation period**

11.1. There is a probation period of 6 months for new employees, during which time you shall be entitled to 1 day's notice up to four weeks and thereafter one week's notice. The Company's disciplinary scheme, sick pay and pension provisions shall not apply. The Company reserves the right to extend this period, as appropriate.

12. **Notice to terminate**

12.1. Save in cases of gross misconduct, the Company's notice to employees with continuous service from four weeks to two years will be one week, and thereafter one additional week's notice for each year of continuous employment, up to a maximum of 12 weeks' notice.

12.2. An employee's notice to the Company shall be one week after the completion of the probationary period, and after two years' continuous service, 2 weeks' notice.

12.3. The Company reserves the right to waive notice periods and make payment in lieu of notice.

12.4. If you terminate your employment without giving your contractual period of notice, the Company reserves the right to make a deduction from your final pay equal to the amount that would have been paid in salary during the appropriate notice period, including any amount due from accrued holiday pay not yet taken.

12.5. When your employment is under notice to terminate, it is hereby agreed that the Company shall be entitled to require you not to attend the Company's premises and you will not be permitted to work for any other person or on your own behalf without the Company's permission.

12.6. Gross misconduct consists of dishonesty, gross incompetence, wilful neglect of duty, persistent breach of your employment conditions, and acting in any manner which is likely to bring the Company into disrepute.

13. **Collective agreements**

13.1. There are no collective agreements governing your terms and conditions of employment.

14. **Disciplinary and grievance procedures**

14.1. The disciplinary and grievance procedures applicable to your appointment are contained in the staff handbook. They are for guidance only and do not form part of your contract of employment.

15. **Other employment**

15.1. Work for any other company or client is forbidden without prior consent from the Company.

15.2. During your employment by the Company and at all times thereafter you shall not, other than in the proper course of your duties, directly or indirectly use, disclose or publish to any person any information of a confidential or secret nature which you may acquire in the course of your employment by the Company concerning the business or products or services of the Company or of any third party to whom the Company is under an obligation of confidence such as suppliers and customers.

16. **General**

16.1. This Agreement will be subject to the laws of England and Wales and shall be subject to the exclusive jurisdiction of the English courts.

16.2. The Company reserves the right to vary these terms and conditions for operational, commercial or financial reasons according to the needs of the business. Any changes will be notified in writing.

When reading this contract, it is worth reflecting in particular on the implications of that final clause 16.2.[31] In the light of this term, how binding is the remainder of the contract on the employer? Here, the focus will be on two particular problems presented by the express terms of the contract of employment, as found in printed contracts of this kind. The first issue concerns

---

[31] See Chapter 5.

transparency: providing information to the employee about the terms of the agreement. The second problem concerns the employer's use of small print in standard-form contracts.

Disclosure of Terms of Employment

The three most important statutory provisions regarding the disclosure of information about the terms of a contract of employment require:

- a written statement of the principal terms and conditions of employment (ERA 1996, section 1);
- an itemised pay statement explaining how wages have been calculated (ERA 1996, section 8); and
- a written notification of terms of the contract that permit an employer to make deductions from wages (ERA 1996, section 13).[32]

Written Statement of Particulars

The duty to supply a written statement of the particulars of the principal terms of employment to a new employee preceded but now implements the requirements of EC Directive 91/533.[33] The stated objectives of this Directive are to clarify the contractual rights of employees, in order to avoid confusion and disputes, and to create greater transparency and competitiveness in the labour market. Until a recent reform the law provided a weak and ineffective instrument for achieving these objectives. Because the written documents did not have to be provided by the employer until two months after the commencement of the employment, the legislation failed to tackle the problem of helping the potential employee to make an informed choice about whether or not to accept an appointment. As a result of the Employment Rights (Employment Particulars and Paid Annual Leave) (Amendment) Regulations 2018 SI 1378, from April 2020, the duty to supply written particulars will arise on the first day of employment.

Nor does the legislation require that the information supplied by the employer should provide a complete description of the terms of employment. The Directive only requires the statement to include the 'essential aspects' of the terms of the contract.[34] It remains open to the parties to claim that some additional terms were included in their contractual agreement, even though they were not reported in the written particulars. Nevertheless, as a result of many amendments to the national legislation, nearly all the key items of an

---

[32] For analysis of the second and third items, see Chapter 7.
[33] Directive 91/533 on an employer's obligation to inform employees of the conditions applicable to the contract of employment relationship, OJ 1991 L288.
[34] Directive 91/533, Art. 2.

employment relationship must now be mentioned by the employer in the written statement of the particulars of employment issued within eight weeks of the commencement of employment.

Employment Rights Act 1996, Section 1

. . .

(3) The statement shall contain particulars of –
   (a) the names of the employer and employee,
   (b) the date when the employment began, and
   (c) the date on which the employee's period of continuous employment began . . .
(4) The statement shall also contain particulars, as at a specified date not more than seven days before the statement (or the instalment containing them) is given, of –
   (a) the scale or rate of remuneration or the method of calculating remuneration,
   (b) the intervals at which remuneration is paid (that is, weekly, monthly or other specified intervals),
   (c) any terms and conditions relating to hours of work (including any terms and conditions relating to normal working hours),
   (d) any terms and conditions relating to any of the following –
      (i) entitlement to holidays, including public holidays, and holiday pay (the particulars given being sufficient to enable the employee's entitlement, including any entitlement to accrued holiday pay on the termination of employment, to be precisely calculated),
      (ii) incapacity for work due to sickness or injury, including any provision for sick pay, and
      (iii) pensions and pension schemes,
   (e) the length of notice which the employee is obliged to give and entitled to receive to terminate his contract of employment,
   (f) the title of the job which the employee is employed to do or a brief description of the work for which he is employed,
   (g) where the employment is not intended to be permanent, the period for which it is expected to continue or, if it is for a fixed term, the date when it is to end,
   (h) either the place of work or, where the employee is required or permitted to work at various places, an indication of that and of the address of the employer,
   (j) any collective agreements which directly affect the terms and conditions of the employment including, where the employer is not a party, the persons by whom they were made, and
   (k) where the employee is required to work outside the United Kingdom for a period of more than one month –
      (i) the period for which he is to work outside the United Kingdom,
      (ii) the currency in which remuneration is to be paid while he is working outside the United Kingdom

(iii) any additional remuneration payable to him, and any benefits to be provided to or in respect of him, by reason of his being required to work outside the United Kingdom, and

(iv) any terms and conditions relating to his return to the United Kingdom.[35]

In addition, ERA 1996, section 3, requires the employer to provide information about any applicable disciplinary or grievance procedure. The separation of these procedures from the rest of the written statement reflects the possibility that the employer may not intend them to be legally binding,[36] although normally courts will infer that such procedures are apt to create at least some contractual entitlements.[37]

Although this statutory list of items to be recorded in the written statement is extensive and implements the specific requirements of EC Directive 91/533, it omits many potentially important pieces of information, not least issues concerning the precariousness of the job. The 2018 amending regulations will require from April 2020 written particulars about how long a job is expected to last, how much notice of termination will be given, the days and time of work, and fuller details about remuneration and leave. The Directive has been interpreted to include a general principle requiring disclosure of essential elements of the contract, even if that information is not included in the list above.[38] Even if it is not practicable to require employers to supply a comprehensive account of all the important terms of employment, perhaps they should not be permitted to rely on alleged essential terms of employment that have not been supplied in the written particulars. The EU has proposed a reformed Directive that requires employers to give more complete information, not only to employees but also to a 'worker',[39] and requires that the written statement should be issued at the latest on the first day on the job (rather than up to two months afterwards).[40] From April 2020, the 2018 amending regulations anticipate those proposed changes about the statutory statement, and the Employment Rights (Miscellaneous Amendments) Regulations 2019 SI 731 extend the requirement to supply written particulars to the statutory concept of worker.

Confusion surrounding the terms of employment often stems from the use of incorporated documents to provide details of the terms. These documents may be collective agreements, staff handbooks, occupational pension schemes

---

[35] Note that s. 1(4) does not contain a para (i) in the Queen's Printer's copy of this Act.

[36] As was held to be the case in *Johnson* v. *Unisys Ltd* [2001] UKHL 13, [2001] ICR 480 (HL).

[37] *Edwards* v. *Chesterfield Royal Hospital NHS Foundation Trust* [2011] UKSC 58, [2012] 2 AC 22 [28].

[38] Case C-350/99, *Lange* v. *Georg Schunemann GmbH* [2001] IRLR 244 (ECJ).   [39] See p. 220.

[40] Proposal for a Directive on transparent and predictable working conditions in the European Union, Brussels, 21 December 2017, COM(2017) 797 final. This initiative is one of Commission's key actions to follow up on the European Pillar of Social Rights: http://data.consilium.europa.eu/doc/document/ST-13129–2017-INIT/en/pdf.

and similar statements of obligations and entitlements. The legislation does not require the employer to give new employees copies of these documents, but places two constraints on satisfying the duty to supply written information about the terms by merely referring to such documents. The written statement of terms can only be achieved by reference to other documents produced by the employer in respect of information about rights in relation to sickness or injury, occupational pension rights, training entitlements, and disciplinary and grievance procedures.[41] Where notification is attempted by reference to other documents, the employee must have a reasonable opportunity of reading these documents in the course of employment or the documents must be made reasonably accessible in some other way.[42] The employer is also permitted to refer employees to relevant collective agreements to satisfy the requirement of written notification of any terms of employment, although again the document must be made reasonably accessible.[43] Apart from these exceptions, the employer should provide the main written particulars in one document.[44]

It must be questioned whether these rules on supplying information by reference to accessible documents adequately serve the purpose of clarifying for employees the terms of their engagement, although it should be appreciated that more stringent requirements might force employers to incur considerable expense in producing elaborate documentation for each new recruit. The legal requirement of reasonable access to documents is surely too vague to guide employers about what is required. Examples of where employers claim compliance with this requirement by holding one copy of the document in the head office or making it available only on written request to a senior manager cast doubt on the extent to which the requirement achieves the delivery of information to employees.[45] Perhaps modern electronic storage of information together with computer terminal access could reduce the cost to employers and make all the documents properly accessible to new employees. Nevertheless, we should acknowledge that substantial compliance with most of the legal requirements for written particulars is now achieved by most employers. Analysis of the Workplace Employment Relations Survey of 1998 revealed that, in about 93 per cent of establishments with ten or more employees, the employer does provide written details of the principal ingredients of the wage/work bargain as required by the legislation on appointment or shortly afterwards.[46]

It is also not at all clear that the supply of written particulars really assists the parties to resolve disputes about the terms of employment. The information that must be supplied by the employer in the written particulars has an

---

[41] ERA 1996, ss. 2(2) and 3(1).   [42] ERA 1996, s. 6.   [43] ERA 1996, s. 6.

[44] ERA 1996, s. 1(2), as amended.

[45] P. E. Leighton and S. L. Dumville, 'From Statement to Contract: Some Effects of the Contracts of Employment Act 1972' (1977) 6 *Industrial Law Journal* 133, at 147.

[46] W. Brown, S. Deakin, D. Nash and S. Oxenbridge, *The Employment Contract: From Collective Procedures to Individual Rights* (Cambridge: ESRC Centre for Business Research, Working Paper 171, 2000).

unreliable status: it is the employer's view of the governing terms of employment. But it is always possible that the true terms reached by agreement between the parties were different or that the employer's view of what counts or does not count as a term of the contract is incorrect. In *System Floors (UK) Ltd* v. *Daniel*,[47] as a preliminary point in defence to a claim for unfair dismissal, the employer argued that the employee lacked the necessary qualifying period of employment to bring a claim. As a result of a mix-up, however, the employee's original statement of written particulars issued by the employer had declared that his employment had commenced a week earlier than it had in reality, with the possible effect that he satisfied the statutory qualifying period. The industrial tribunal held that the employer was bound by the statement, but the EAT allowed the employer's appeal and found that the applicant failed to satisfy the necessary qualifying period. The written particulars of the essential terms of the contract is neither itself a contract nor conclusive evidence of the terms of the contract and nor does it bind the employer in some other way. As the EAT observed, the written statement 'provides very strong *prima facie* evidence of what were the terms of the contract between the parties, but does not constitute a written contract between the parties. Nor are the statements of the terms finally conclusive: at most, they place a heavy burden on the employer to show that the actual terms of contract are different from those which he has set out in the statutory statement.'[48]

Many employers now seek to satisfy the statutory requirement of supplying written particulars at the same time as establishing a written contract of employment by requiring the employee to sign a document that serves both purposes.[49] Although this side-effect of the legislation was probably not intended, the practice has the merit that it brings forward the time when written details are supplied and gives the employee the opportunity to discover and negotiate about particular aspects of the offer at the time of the formation of the contract. Employers are also induced to provide a written contract for other compliance reasons, for example to ensure the lawfulness of deductions from pay,[50] and to overcome any problems presented by the common-law rule in relation to standard-form contracts that the employer should take reasonable steps to notify the employee of any unusual and onerous terms.[51] To this extent, the legislation does indirectly serve the purpose of enhancing

[47] [1982] ICR 54 (EAT).

[48] *Per* Browne-Wilkinson J. This approach to treating the employer's statement as merely evidence of the terms of the contract has been approved by the Court of Appeal (*Robertson* v. *British Gas Corporation* [1983] ICR 351), and it also applies under the European Directive: Cases C-253/96 to 258/96, *Kampelmann* v. *Landschaftsverband Westfalen-Lippe* [1998] IRLR 333 (ECJ).

[49] ERA 1996, s. 7B, provides that a written contract of employment or letter of engagement containing the particulars of employment given before the employee's job commences will be regarded as satisfying the duty to supply a written statement of those particulars.

[50] ERA 1996, s. 13; see Chapter 7.

[51] E.g. *Peninsula Business Services Ltd* v. *Sweeney* [2004] IRLR 49 (EAT).

transparency and competitiveness in labour markets by inducing employers to make written offers of employment.

The national legislation applies only to employees, not the broader category of worker, though, as is common with European Directives, the scope is defined to include 'every paid employee having a contract or employment relationship'.[52] The right does not apply to an employee if his or her employment continues for less than a month.[53] Thus for temporary workers, casual workers and freelance workers, there is a risk that the legislation may not apply,[54] unless they can establish continuity of employment for more than a month through a succession of short-term contracts of employment. This exception for short-term employees is presumably designed to reduce costs for employers, but again it undermines the effect of the regulation to promote transparency in the labour market. If the outcome of national legislation is to exclude some employees who in fact work more or less continuously for longer than a month, it may not satisfy the principle established in the Directive of requiring an objective justification for exclusions.[55]

The accuracy or adequacy of any statement of written particulars issued by an employer can be questioned in an ET by the employer or employee making a reference.[56] The tribunal may then issue the correct particulars or particulars that ought to have been given.[57] The same provisions apply to the requirement to give itemised pay statements. The job of the tribunal is not to create terms for the parties, but merely to discover what terms had been agreed expressly or by implication, if any, and to ensure their accurate transposition into the statutory statement.[58] Oddly, the tribunal has no jurisdiction to interpret the statutory statement of written particulars in order to resolve ambiguities in it.[59] The absence of any monetary sanction in general reduces the effectiveness of this legislation to promote disclosure of information about the terms of the contract, although we have noted that larger employers routinely comply with its provisions by adopting written contracts of employment.

Implied Duty of Disclosure

The obligation to supply information about the principal terms of employment is a continuing one during the lifetime of the employment relation.[60] The mere issuing of new written particulars does not, of course, effect a change in the terms of the contract of employment unless they have been agreed by the employee.[61] The common law may provide compensation for breach of contract in some circumstances where the employee can demonstrate

---

[52] Directive 91/533, Art. 1(1); see Chapter 6.   [53] ERA 1996, s. 198.
[54] E.g. *Carmichael* v. *National Power plc* [1999] ICR 1226 (HL).   [55] Art. 1(2).
[56] ERA 1996, s. 11.   [57] ERA 1996, s. 12.
[58] *Eagland* v. *British Telecommunications plc* [1992] IRLR 323 (CA).
[59] *Southern Cross Healthcare Co. Ltd* v. *Perkins* [2011] ICR 285 (CA).   [60] ERA 1996, s. 4(1).
[61] *Jones* v. *Associated Tunnelling Co. Ltd* [1981] IRLR 477 (EAT).

economic loss resulting from the failure to supply information about a variation in the terms of employment. In *Scally* v. *Southern Health and Social Services Board*,[62] junior hospital doctors missed an opportunity to enhance their occupational pensions owing to a failure by their employer to notify them of a change in the pension scheme and the employer's subsequent refusal to waive the deadline to apply for the additional benefit. The doctors successfully claimed compensation for the loss of this potential benefit by alleging a breach of an implied term in their contracts of employment for the employer to take reasonable steps to bring the existence of the contingent right to the notice of employees in circumstances where they would not otherwise learn about it.

This continuing implied legal obligation of disclosure of information about the terms of employment appears to be limited to supplying information about the terms of the contract where the employee could not otherwise become aware of those terms. It has not been extended to a duty to give advice about how best to exercise rights under the contract of employment, although, if the employer voluntarily assumes the responsibility to give advice and to help the employee, the employer will be liable for negligence in providing that advice and assistance inadequately.[63] It may seem fair that an employee should seek his or her own advice about the contractual position rather than relying upon an employer which may have a conflict of interest. But in relation to complex terms such as the occupational pension scheme established by the employer, the case for imposing a duty to give advice has seemed more compelling, although this argument has ultimately been rejected by the courts.[64] In *Crossley* v. *Faithful & Gould Holdings Ltd*,[65] the claimant suffered a nervous breakdown and after a period of sick leave agreed to take early retirement. Under the terms of the employer's long-term disability insurance scheme, the claimant was entitled to benefits provided he remained in employment. His entitlement therefore ceased on taking retirement. Mr Crossley claimed that, by failing to alert him to this consequence of taking early retirement, the employer had breached an implied term of the contract of employment. The Court of Appeal rejected the claim, holding that there is no standard implied term in all contracts of employment that an employer will take reasonable care of an employee's well-being, nor an implied duty for an employer to give an employee financial advice in relation to benefits accruing from his employment. This case was distinguished from *Scally* v. *Southern Health and Social Services Board*, because, as a senior manager, the employee could reasonably have been expected to be aware of the relevant provisions of the insurance

[62] [1992] 1 AC 294 (HL).
[63] *Lennon* v. *Commissioner of Police of the Metropolis* [2004] EWCA Civ 130, [2004] IRLR 385 (CA).
[64] E.g. *University of Nottingham* v. *Eyett* [1999] ICR 721 (ChD).
[65] [2004] EWCA Civ 293, [2004] ICR 1615 (CA).

scheme and the employee also had access to advice from the insurance company.

Unfair Terms

A standard-form contract issued by an employer may contain considerable detail and complexity. Some of the small print in these documents may not be easily comprehensible and may contain unexpected exceptions and qualifications to the apparent undertakings of the employer. Under the normal principles of the law of contract, these terms will be binding on the employee, whether read and understood or not, especially if the employee signed the contract. It is possible that, in rare instances, an employee may be able to benefit from the common-law doctrine that the person issuing a standard-form contract must take reasonable steps to draw the attention of the other party to unusual or onerous terms.[66] Apart from that control over the inclusion of unconscionable terms in the small print, what legal controls exist over unfair terms buried in the contract?[67]

The Unfair Contract Terms Act 1977 (UCTA) invalidates exclusion clauses that purport to limit or exclude liability for negligently caused personal injuries.[68] That provision should protect employees against contractual restrictions on the employer's duty to ensure health and safety in the workplace.[69] Section 3 UCTA also provides controls over unfair exclusion clauses in standard-form contracts by invalidating unreasonable clauses. Under the second limb of section 3, however, the control over the reasonableness of the terms only applies if the employer is using its 'standard terms of business'. The Court of Appeal in *Keen* v. *Commerzbank AG*[70] held that section 3 UCTA could not apply to a contract of employment, because an employee was not contracting on the employer's standard terms of business. The Court drew a distinction between a standard-form contract and standard terms of business: 'A bank's business is not entering into contracts of employment with its employees.'[71] This decision creates an unfortunate loophole in the legislation. Although employees need protection against unfair small print just as much as consumers (who are protected by the Consumer Rights Act 2015) and independent contractors, they fall through the gap. To plug this lacuna in the statutory protection against unfair terms in the small print of standard-form contracts of employment, the Law Commission has recommended the inclusion of a specific provision for judicial review of the fairness of exclusion

---

[66] *Interfoto Picture Library Ltd* v. *Stiletto Visual Programmes Ltd* [1989] QB 433 (CA).
[67] H. Collins, 'Legal Responses to the Standard Form Contract of Employment' (2007) 36 *Industrial Law Journal* 2.
[68] UCTA 1977, s. 2. [69] *Johnstone* v. *Bloomsbury Health Authority* [1992] QB 333 (CA).
[70] [2006] EWCA Civ 1536, [2007] ICR 623. [71] Moses LJ, para. 115.

clauses in contracts of employment.[72] This protection would need to include not only unfair exclusion clauses but also terms that provide confusing descriptions of an employee's entitlements and permit the employer to render performance that is substantially different from what was expected.[73]

In the absence of protection under UCTA, the small print in the contract of employment, no matter how unfair and unreasonable, is likely to bind employees. Although statutory rights such as the minimum wage and unfair dismissal cannot be excluded by contrary agreement in a contract of employment,[74] the other benefits conferred by the terms of the contract can be qualified and excluded in a variety of unexpected ways in the details of the standard terms. As a consequence, the written contract may deviate substantially from the reasonable expectations of an employee.

Organisational Rules

We have already noted that contracts of employment typically provide vague or incomplete descriptions of the work to be performed by the employee. Being unsure in advance exactly what work needs to be done, the employer bargains for the right to direct labour and to monitor performance of the job. In a small workshop, the employer can issue oral instructions and supervise performance in person. Once the business becomes larger, however, with many employees and with the employment of managers or supervisors to give instructions and to monitor the performance of work, the employment relation becomes embedded in an organisational framework. The organisational rules establish hierarchies between employees, allocate responsibility and authority and create a set of standing orders for the direction and monitoring of work.

The most visible aspect of this construction of rules is known as the 'works rules' or 'staff handbook'. These are booklets issued to workers, or documents that can be accessed through the firm's computer network. These documents contain a mixture of statements about the employer's policies, the employer's expectations from employees, explanations of procedures and the authority structure of the firm, and may describe further obligations and entitlements of employees. The form of the rule-book is not usually a written contract, but rather a document containing instructions and information. In a large organisation, these rules may cover a wide range of matters, including:

- facilitation of production: rules which specify procedures to be followed, forms to be used, feed-back mechanisms and quality assurance procedures;

---

[72] Law Commission, *Unfair Terms in Contracts* (Law Com No. 292, 2005), cl. 12 of the Draft Bill, 154.
[73] E.g. *Peninsula Business Services Ltd* v. *Sweeney* [2004] IRLR 49 (EAT).   [74] ERA 1996, s. 230.

- co-ordination: a framework for interaction and co-ordination between employees within the workplace. In large undertakings, the purpose of these rules is to permit senior management to direct and shape the organisation. They comprise a set of standing orders to middle management and employees about how the business should be operated and how employees should be managed;
- detailed job descriptions of the different grades;
- disciplinary codes: describing unwanted behaviour, specifying disciplinary procedures, grievance procedures and possible sanctions;
- payment system: rules governing grading of jobs, rates of pay for jobs, methods for calculating pay and bonuses and the availability of and entitlements to fringe benefits, such as sick pay, occupational pensions and sports facilities.

What is the legal status of the rule-book? Is the rule-book part of the express terms of the contract of employment? Or is the rule-book merely a formal expression of the power of management to issue directions to the workforce? In principle, the answer to those questions depends upon the intention of the parties to the contract of employment. The courts approach the discovery of intention in two stages. First, the courts enquire whether the parties intended the rule-book in general to be legally enforceable. Second, the courts then consider whether the particular term at issue is suitable or apt for legal enforcement.

The handbook itself or the terms of the contract state may state expressly that the handbook provides further terms of employment, in which case a court is likely to regard much of the handbook as conferring contractual rights on the employee. A court may infer the intention to include all or part of the handbook in the terms of the contract of employment from the language of the contract and the surrounding circumstances. References to the handbook in the required statutory statement of the written particulars under ERA 1996 section 1 may well encourage the view that all or part of the handbook has been expressly or by implication incorporated as terms of the contract.[75] This process of implied incorporation of provisions in the handbook should be distinguished from the device of implying terms into the contract of employment. Implied incorporation depends upon whether or not the parties intended to incorporate a document that contains rules applicable to their relationship; the implication of terms relies upon a court to formulate new terms in accordance with a test of commercial necessity or precedent. The essential question to be considered in most cases of implied incorporation is 'whether, by its conduct ... in the context of all the surrounding

---

[75] A. Sanders, 'The Content of Contracts of Employment: Terms Incorporated from Collective Agreements or From Other Sources' in M. Freedland (gen. ed.), *The Contract of Employment* (Oxford University Press, 2016), pp. 449, 452.

circumstances, the employer has evinced to the relevant employees an intention that they should enjoy that benefit [described in the handbook] as of
right'.[76] References to 'custom and practice' in the case-law are misleading, for
they appear to suggest that past practice can bind the employer to a contractual term, whereas the correct question in accordance with orthodox contract
law must be whether the employee reasonably understood the employer to be
making a binding commitment through its words and conduct.[77] Of course, if
the employer has in the past publicised the rule or practice, such as the
payment of redundancy payments above the statutory minimum, and in fact
has invariably paid the additional amount to redundant employees, it would
be reasonable for employees to infer an intention on the part of the employer
to be bound by the rule or practice, and therefore the court should hold that
the rule or practice is a binding contractual term.

Commonly, however, employers expressly state that the handbook merely
provides a set of standing orders and policies issued by management.[78] That
stance suits the interests of employers because, as a policy document or set of
instructions, the handbook is unlikely to confer legally enforceable rights on
employees, whereas the implied duty to obey lawful instructions requires
employees to obey any rules or instructions in the handbook. Having its cake
and eating it, the employer can rely upon the rules as imposing effective legal
obligations on employees but at the same time insist that the rules confer no
legal rights on employees because they are not express terms of the contract of
employment. In the absence of explicit guidance in the express terms of the
contract as to the legal status of a particular rule in the staff handbook, the
courts have to decide whether the parties intended that any particular rule was
incorporated as a binding term of the contract.

Whatever the conclusion on whether the handbook contains legally
enforceable terms, a court will proceed to examine the language of particular
provisions in the handbook to determine whether or not they are 'apt' to be
incorporated as a legally enforceable term of the contract. If the contract or
employer's handbook appears to make its provisions part of the contract, a
court may decide that some but not all of its provisions confer legal rights on
employees according to what is regarded as apt for inclusion as a term. In
contrast, if the contract or an employer's handbook makes it clear that the
document is purely a policy statement that confers no legal rights, it is
nevertheless possible that a court will decide that the nature of a particular
provision suggests that it should be regarded as a binding contractual term: as
Auld LJ remarked in *Keeley* v. *Fosroc International Ltd*:[79]

---

[76] Underhill LJ, *Park Cakes Ltd* v. *Shumba* [2013] EWCA Civ 974, [2013] IRLR 800 [35],
following *Garratt* v. *Mirror Group Newspapers Ltd* [2011] EWCA Civ 425, [2011] ICR 880.
[77] *Smith* v. *Hughes* (1871) LR 6 QB 597.   [78] E.g. cl. 14.1 in the specimen contract above.
[79] *Keeley* v. *Fosroc International Ltd* [2006] EWCA Civ 1277, [2006] IRLR 961 (CA) [33].

the fact that the Staff Handbook was presented as a collection of 'policies' does not preclude their having contractual effect if, by their nature and language they are apt to be contractual terms, as clearly many were in the 'Employee benefits and rights' Part of the Handbook, incorporating in that way by reference what was not expressly referred to or detailed in the Statement of Employment Terms.

Provisions in the rule-book that determine or give greater specificity to core obligations and entitlements in the wage/work bargain, such as the method for calculating wages and other benefits, hours of work, the place of work and the tasks to be performed, are more likely to be regarded by a court as apt for inclusion as additional express terms of the contract of employment, provided that this inference is not countered by express agreement. The rule-book may also be apt for inclusion as a term of the contract because it provides a crucial aid to the construction of the express terms of the contract of employment. For example, the contract may appoint an employee to a position of 'administrator grade 3'; the rule-book can be used to explain the meaning of that technical terminology. This aspect of the rule-book may also provide the necessary information about pay grades and scales by which an employee may determine what salary is properly due.

The results of disputes about whether a provision in the handbook is 'apt' for inclusion as a term of the contract are not entirely predictable. A provision that refers to pay or remuneration is likely to be regarded as apt for inclusion. Examples may include enhanced redundancy payments,[80] fringe benefits attached to the job such as a profit-sharing scheme[81] and 'check-off' arrangements under which employers agree, subject to the consent of the employee, to deduct union membership fees from wages and transfer them directly to the union.[82] In contrast, the provisions in the handbook by which an employer determines what procedures should be followed with respect to sick leave and other personnel issues are usually regarded as falling within the employer's discretion.[83] Nevertheless, if those procedures include disciplinary procedures or rules governing termination of employment for long-term sickness, those rules, like other disciplinary procedures,[84] are likely to be regarded as conferring contractual rights.[85] Although presented as an enquiry into the intention of the parties, these judicial decisions reveal implicit judgements about the

---

[80] *Keeley v. Fosroc International Ltd* [2006] EWCA Civ 1277, [2006] IRLR 961 (CA); *Park Cakes Ltd v. Shumba* [2013] EWCA Civ 974, [2013] IRLR 800.

[81] *Financial Techniques Ltd v. Hughes* [1981] IRLR 32 (CA).

[82] *Cavanagh v. Secretary of State for Work and Pensions* [2016] EWHC 1136, [2016] ICR 826 (QB); similarly, for collective agreements *Hickey v. Secretary of State for Communities and Local Government* [2013] EWHC 3163, [2014] IRLR 22 (QB).

[83] *Wandsworth London Borough Council v. D'Silva* [1998] IRLR 193 (CA).

[84] *Edwards v. Chesterfield Royal Hospital NHS Foundation Trust* [2011] UKSC 58, [2012] 2 AC 22 [28].

[85] *Sparks v. Department for Transport* [2016] EWCA Civ 360, [2016] ICR 695; *Hussain v. Surrey and Sussex Healthcare NHS Trust* [2011] EWHC 1670, [2012] Med LR 163 (QB).

proper boundary to draw in contracts of employment between the protection of express contractual rights for employees and the need for management to preserve its discretionary powers to direct the workforce and to use disciplinary sanctions including dismissal.

There is a further reason why employers typically prefer the view that the rule-book comprises an exercise of managerial discretion. This interpretation of the legal status of the company handbook entitles the employer to vary the rules at its discretion, without the need for the consent of the employee. But this power to vary the rule-book is not unfettered. An employer is subject to implied terms that may affect the proper exercise of this power. Courts may conclude that a variation of the rule-book broke various implied terms: a duty not to act capriciously or arbitrarily, a duty not to act in a manner calculated to destroy mutual trust and confidence or a duty to give reasonable notice of a change so that an employee can have the necessary time to adjust to new working conditions.[86] To avoid the conclusion that in changing the rule-book the employer breached an implied term, an employer would be well advised to present a good reason for the change, give adequate notice of the change, consult relevant employees or their representatives about the change and respond to the concerns of staff. An employer who followed this advice when introducing a no-smoking policy in a hospital and its surrounds succeeded in rebutting any claim for breach of an implied term, even though the nursing auxiliary concerned, who was a smoker, felt that she had been left no option by the no-smoking policy but to resign her job.[87] *French* v. *Barclays Bank plc*[88] illustrates a situation where the employer failed to take such care. A manager was required under the terms of his contract to relocate from Oxfordshire to Essex, for which purpose he needed to sell his family home and purchase another. Under the rules of the bank in the staff manual, Mr French was offered a discretionary interest-free bridging loan to enable him to complete the purchase of a new house before selling the old one. Following a collapse in the housing market, which made it difficult for Mr French to sell his former home, the bank changed the policy stated in the staff manual, withdrew the loan and required him to enter into a new scheme that left him worse off. One question on appeal was whether the bank was in breach of contract. Although the loan scheme was regarded as a non-contractual discretionary scheme, the bank was held liable in damages for breach of the implied term to refrain from conduct which would be likely to destroy trust and confidence.

In summary, rule-books and company handbooks may sometimes confer contractual rights upon employees through a process of express or implied incorporation, especially if the rules provide greater specificity to some of the core elements of the wage/work bargain. But it is more usual for courts to

---

[86] *United Bank Ltd* v. *Akhtar* [1989] IRLR 507 (EAT).
[87] *Dryden* v. *Greater Glasgow Health Board* [1992] IRLR 469 (EAT).
[88] [1998] IRLR 646 (CA).

classify rule-books as an exercise of managerial discretion that does not confer any contractual rights. The latter interpretation permits employers to vary the rules unilaterally, without the consent of the employees. Nevertheless, the policies may have significant indirect legal effects through the implied terms of the contract. An employee must conform to the rules in good faith in order to avoid being in breach of the implied terms of the contract of employment. Furthermore, in the striking development in the *French* case, the employer who varies the rule-book hastily without consultation, or unnecessarily, or for an illegitimate purpose or in a way that imposes harsh consequences on the employee, may be found to have broken an implied obligation not to vary the rules in a way which destroys mutual trust and confidence.

Collective Agreements

A collective agreement is a bargain reached between a trade union and an employer (or sometimes a group of employers). The content of a collective agreement is likely to comprise three elements. First, it usually determines for the group of employees covered by the agreement (the bargaining unit) the core aspects of their wage/work bargain, such as wage rates and normal hours of work. Secondly, the collective agreement may determine aspects of the rule-book, thus fixing how the employer should regulate the business within the scope of management's discretion. Thirdly, it is likely to contain rules about how future collective labour relations should be conducted, such as how and when bargaining should occur between the union and the employer. These three elements may be described briefly as fixing the market price of labour, joint regulation of the workplace and procedural self-regulation of collective relations in the workplace.

Legal Enforceability

A collective agreement is unlikely to be a legally enforceable contract itself. This absence of legal sanctions for collective agreements is due in part to statute.

Trade Union and Labour Relations (Consolidation) Act 1992, Section 179

(1) A collective agreement shall be conclusively presumed not to have been intended by the parties to be a legally enforceable contract unless the agreement –
   (a) is in writing, and
   (b) contains a provision which (however expressed) states that the parties intend that the agreement shall be a legally enforceable contract.

This provision leaves open the possibility that a legally enforceable agreement might be reached, but in practice the parties to a collective agreement are unlikely to wish to use legal remedies in order to enforce the agreement. The trade union and the employer have powerful non-legal sanctions to support compliance with the terms of a collective agreement: the union can threaten industrial action and the employer can exclude the employees from the workplace (a lock-out) or threaten deductions from pay for any refusal to work in accordance with the agreement. In addition, the use of legal sanctions such as an injunction against breach of the agreement is as likely to exacerbate and prolong conflict as to help the parties to resolve their differences with the minimum disruption to production and income. For these reasons, neither party to a collective agreement normally seeks the option of legal enforceability, so the statutory presumption merely emphasises what is likely to be the case in fact.

Incorporation

The absence of legal enforceability of collective agreements does not prevent them from having legal effects. A collective agreement typically creates a written document setting out the terms of the agreement. This document, like any other document, can be incorporated into a legally enforceable contract of employment by express or implied agreement between the employer and the employee. In workplaces where collective agreements have been reached, the contract of employment often incorporates the relevant collective agreement into its terms by stating expressly that the wages, hours and other conditions of employment will be set by a particular collective agreement and subsequent revisions of it. The effect of this express incorporation is that aspects of legally unenforceable collective agreements become part of the legally enforceable express terms of the individual contract of employment.

In the absence of such a term in the contract of employment providing expressly for incorporation of a relevant collective agreement, however, the precise legal effects of collective agreements become harder to determine and to explain. English law has never taken the step of insisting that the implied incorporation of relevant collective agreements should be done automatically as a matter of law, as one of the standard incidents of all contracts of employment. The courts must therefore try to identify the implied intentions of the parties from the words, conduct and the surrounding circumstances. Writing at a time when it was unusual for the terms of individual contracts of employment to be written down and when collective bargaining took place at the level of an industrial sector or district rather than with a particular employer, Kahn-Freund suggested that incorporation of collective agreements took place by 'custom'.[89] Another possible explanation for the incorporation of collective agreements is based on a course of dealing between the parties over a period of time in which the collective agreement is treated as providing essential terms of the contract. In principle, however, this contractual issue turns on the joint intention of the parties to the contract of employment: did the employer and individual employee intend to incorporate relevant parts of the collective agreement into the contract of employment?[90] Custom and a course of prior dealing may throw some light on the answer to that question, but cannot provide an answer in itself. Any statements in the collective agreement to the effect that particular provisions should or should not be enforceable via incorporation into individual contracts of employment should not govern this issue, because it is the intention of the employee and employer that is vital, not the intention of the union representatives. Nevertheless, in most instances a court will readily infer that the parties to the contract of employment do not intend that terms should be incorporated from the collective agreement where the collective parties take the view that they should not be.[91]

Despite these conceptual problems, the courts nowadays usually accept without argument that a relevant collective agreement has been incorporated into a contract of employment, provided that there has been some reference to it as forming part of the contract in either the contract of employment or any documents issued by the employer to the employee such as a rule-book or written statement about the principal terms of employment. Alternatively, if in consequence of a new collective agreement an employer introduces new terms and conditions, the employees will be regarded as having consented to the change by continuing to work normally.[92]

A more vexing question for the court is to determine which provisions within the collective agreement have become incorporated into contracts of employment. As with employers' handbooks, not all the provisions in the collective agreement will be regarded as suitable or 'apt' for incorporation. It is helpful to divide the discussion of which terms in the collective agreement are apt for inclusion according to which party is seeking to enforce the term via the contract of employment.

Enforcement by Employees

This view that some provisions of collective agreements are unsuitable for incorporation into contracts of employment depends in part on the language

---

[89] O. Kahn-Freund, 'Legal Framework', in A. Flanders and H. Clegg (eds.), *System of Industrial Relations in Great Britain* (Oxford: Blackwell, 1954), p. 58.

[90] *Alexander v. Standard Telephones & Cables Ltd (No. 2); Wall v. Standard Telephones & Cables Ltd (No. 2)* [1991] IRLR 287 (QB).

[91] *Martland v. Co-operative Insurance Society Ltd* [2008] UKEAT 0220_07_1004 (10 April 2008).

[92] *Henry v. London General Transport Services Ltd* [2002] EWCA Civ 488, [2002] ICR 910 (CA).

used in the collective agreement and in part on the context of the whole document. It is usually accepted that terms of the collective agreement that set the core obligations of the wage/work bargain such as wages and hours have been incorporated into the contract of employment. We have also noted that enhanced redundancy payments and disciplinary and grievance procedures are apt for incorporation. In contrast, terms in the collective agreement that are designed to regulate the procedures of the collective bargaining relationship itself, such as a provision for conciliation over disagreements about its meaning, will not be regarded as apt for incorporation.[93] Similarly, statements in collective agreements that represent mere aspirations or hopes for the future will not be regarded as apt for incorporation. Outside these fairly settled areas, however, there are many instances of contested provisions of collective agreements that may or may not have been incorporated into individual contracts of employment.

Much of the litigation about the appropriateness of the incorporation of terms in collective agreements has concerned redundancy procedures. These collective agreements try to determine in advance how the employer should handle the need to dismiss workers for economic reasons. The agreement may establish procedures for negotiation and consultation with the union and determine the criteria for selection for compulsory redundancy. Often, the unions bargain for a seniority principle known as LIFO (last in, first out) to regulate selection for compulsory redundancy. The legal issue that arises is whether an employee can compel the employer to comply with the collective agreement by enforcing its provisions through the contract of employment. Employees with considerable seniority will be particularly concerned that the employer should comply with the LIFO principle. Occasionally, employees have succeeded in enforcing the LIFO principle through their contracts of employment.[94] But courts have not readily accepted that collective agreements can confer individual contractual rights regarding procedures governing dismissals for redundancy.

In *Kaur* v. *MG Rover Group Ltd*,[95] in a doomed attempt to ensure the company's survival, the employer entered into a succession of collective agreements, beginning with 'Rover Tomorrow – The New Deal', each described as partnership agreements, in which, in return for promises by the union to secure greater flexibility and co-operation on the part of the workforce, the employer agreed to protect employees' job security. The conditions of Mrs Kaur's employment included the following term: 'Employment with the company is in accordance with and, where appropriate, subject to ... collective agreements made from time to time with the recognised trade unions representing employees within the company.' She claimed a

[93] *National Coal Board* v. *National Union of Mineworkers* [1986] ICR 736.
[94] *Anderson* v. *Pringle of Scotland Ltd* [1998] IRLR 64 (Court of Session, Outer House).
[95] [2004] EWCA Civ 1507, [2005] ICR 625 (CA).

declaration that her terms of employment precluded compulsory redundancy dismissal in accordance with a collective agreement made at her plant in Longbridge called 'The Way Ahead Partnership Agreement', which included the following provision:

Job Security

2.1. It will be our objective to ensure that the application of the 'Partnership Principles' will enable employees who want to work for Rover to stay with Rover. As with the successful introduction of 'Rover Tomorrow – The New Deal', THERE WILL BE NO COMPULSORY REDUNDANCY.

2.2. The company recognises that its employees are the company's most valuable asset.

2.3. Any necessary reductions in manpower will be achieved in future, with the cooperation of all employees, through natural wastage, voluntary severance and early retirement, after consultation with trade unions.

The Court of Appeal refused to grant the declaration that the applicant had a contractual right not to be made compulsorily redundant. Even where there was express incorporation of the collective agreement into the individual contract of employment, according to the court the question was whether the content and the character of the relevant parts of the collective agreement were such as to make them apt to be a term of the individual contract of employment. In this case, the Court of Appeal regarded paragraph 2, viewed as a whole, as aspirational rather than a binding promise. The Court emphasised that in paragraph 2.1 job security was described as an 'objective' rather than a binding commitment. In paragraph 2.3, the need for co-operation of the workforce as a whole revealed that job security was regarded as a collective matter, and so was unsuitable as a basis for individual contractual rights. The Court concluded that the promise of no compulsory redundancies was not intended to be incorporated into the contracts of employment of individual employees and was not apt for such incorporation.

Another issue that poses the question of the appropriateness of the incorporation of terms of a collective agreement into contracts of employment concerns controls over management discretion to determine staffing levels and the deployment of staff. The dispute in *Malone v. British Airways plc*[96] concerned the enforceability of a term in a collective agreement that specified the minimum number of cabin staff for each type of plane. This term formed part of a collective agreement that limited monthly hours of work, established procedures for rosters for working, reporting processes and lateness for work, and set out what would happen if flights were cancelled or delayed. The union and the airline had failed to agree on new proposals for reduced staffing levels

---

[96] [2010] EWCA Civ 1225, [2011] ICR 125 (CA).

on planes. Managers then introduced these changes unilaterally. The Court of Appeal accepted that some terms in the collective agreement were apt for incorporation, such as the rules on maximum working hours, but the provisions regarding cabin crew staffing levels were not regarded as appropriate for incorporation. The Court justified this conclusion on the ground that there might be disastrous consequences for the employer if this term were enforceable, because employees would become contractually entitled to refuse to fly on a plane without a full complement of staff. Unfortunately, this conclusion resulted in the necessity for the union to call for industrial action to enforce the collective agreement, an even worse outcome for the employer. Moreover, it is hard to see why the potential adverse consequences for the employer might be relevant to the key legal question, which concerns the intentions of the parties to the contract of employment. Taken to its logical conclusion, any term in a collective agreement that restricts the scope of management discretion might have adverse consequences on the profitability of the employer, so on this reasoning few terms could ever be suitable for incorporation.

As these decisions demonstrate, even if employees establish that the collective agreement has been expressly incorporated into the contract of employment, many provisions that it contains will still be regarded as inappropriate for transfer to the individual contract as legal entitlements. What is the basis for this judgment about whether a provision is apt for incorporation? Does the judgment turn on whether or not the provision concerns the core elements of the wage/work bargain? Or does the decision turn on whether the provision of the collective agreement is expressed in a particular way, that is, with precision and in a form that describes individual entitlements? Or perhaps these determinations rest ultimately on judicial perceptions of the extent to which employers are likely to give up powers to manage the business unilaterally by conferring contractual rights? The effect of these decisions about aptness for incorporation is not only to generate uncertainty and unpredictability regarding the content of the terms of contracts of employment, but also to remove the legal process from providing assistance for the resolution of disputes arising from the application of collective agreements to contracts of employment.

Enforcement by Employers

The same issue of whether or not provisions in a collective agreement are appropriate for incorporation into a contract of employment can also apply to terms that impose obligations or restrictions on employees. For the most part, collective agreements confer benefits on employees, so the employer has little reason to seek enforcement of its terms. Yet it is certainly possible, by using suitable language that is precise and can be translated simply into individual obligations, for a collective agreement to place significant obligations upon employees via the individual contract of employment, such as express requirements to work at different tasks flexibly and to accept variable hours of work.

Collective agreements often contain a 'peace obligation', which is a promise not to take any form of industrial action for the period of the agreement. This agreement is usually supplemented by a procedural agreement for the resolution of disputes through further negotiations or in some instances arbitration. The question arises whether the peace obligation or the procedural agreement may be legally enforceable against individual employees.

It is arguable that a peace obligation is directed solely to the collective relationship and represents a procedural undertaking at a collective level that is not suitable or apt for incorporation into the individual contract of employment. Yet this view has not always been accepted by the courts. In *Camden Exhibition &Display Ltd* v. *Lynott*,[97] one question was whether the defendant employee was entitled to refuse to perform overtime work. Unless a contract of employment expressly provides for the employee to work for longer than the regular hours of employment at the request of the employer, an employee is legally entitled to refuse the extra work. In this case, the relevant collective agreement stated: 'Overtime required to ensure the due and proper performance of contracts shall not be subject to restriction, but may be worked by mutual agreement and direct arrangement between the employer and the operatives concerned.' The majority of the Court of Appeal interpreted this clause to mean that there was a term in the contract of employment that the employees would not collectively impose a ban on overtime work, although any particular duties had to be arranged by mutual agreement. Russell LJ, dissenting, argued persuasively, however, that the collective agreement had merely refrained from setting a ceiling or restriction on overtime, leaving the matter to individual negotiation, so that, even if a group of employees refused to work overtime, this action would not amount to a breach of contract.

In 1974, legislation introduced a procedural obstacle to the enforcement of peace obligations and collective dispute procedures via the individual contract of employment:

Trade Union and Labour Relations (Consolidation) Act 1992, Section 180

(1) Any terms of a collective agreement which prohibit or restrict the right of workers to engage in a strike or other industrial action, or have the effect of prohibiting or restricting that right, shall not form part of any contract between a worker and the person for whom he works unless the following conditions are met.

---

[97] [1966] 1 QB 555 (CA).

> (2) The conditions are that the collective agreement –
>   (a) is in writing,
>   (b) contains a provision expressly stating that those terms shall or may be incorporated in such a contract,
>   (c) is reasonably accessible at his place of work to the worker to whom it applies and is available for him to consult during working hours, and
>   (d) is one where each trade union which is a party to the agreement is an independent trade union;
>   and that the contract with the worker expressly or impliedly incorporates those terms in the contract.

This section appears to block an employer's attempt to enforce a peace obligation or a dispute resolution procedure through the individual contract of employment without an express written agreement with the union to that effect. Even if such an agreement were concluded, it is unclear what benefit might accrue to an employer. A court would certainly not grant an injunction against an individual employee for refusing to work, if that would amount to an order to force the employee to resume work. Such an order would be tantamount to an order for specific performance of a contract of employment, which is both contrary to the equitable principles governing such orders, and in any case, is prohibited by statute.[98] The strike action itself would almost certainly constitute a breach of contract that would entitle the employer at common law to claim damages or to dismiss the employee, even without the additional breach of contract constituted by breach of any express peace obligation. Therefore, it seems unlikely that employers would ever wish to enforce this aspect of any collective agreement.

The Binding Force of Collective Agreements

Unlike most other legal systems, collective agreements in the UK are not usually legally enforceable by the parties. The aim is to keep the courts out of the task of adjudication over claims based upon collective agreements, especially those brought by employers seeking to enforce a peace obligation. But this legal abstention leaves uncertainty about the precise significance of collective agreements for the individual contracts of employment. Whether or not a term of a collective agreement becomes incorporated into a contract depends partly on whether it has been expressly or impliedly incorporated and partly on whether the term is apt for incorporation. As for implied incorporation, at one time most lawyers seem to have accepted Kahn-Freund's

---

[98] TULRCA 1992, s. 236.

unorthodox suggestion that a special labour law rule applied to collective agreements by which custom would nearly always point towards incorporation,[99] but today the courts seem to apply the classic test of general contract law to ask, from an objective point of view, whether the parties reasonably understood each other to be making binding promises. As for the question of whether a term of the collective agreement is apt for incorporation, this test grants the courts considerable discretion on a fundamental question of industrial relations, that is, whether or not the employer is legally bound by promises made in collective agreements to the workforce. Neither employers nor unions seem interested in seeking to resolve these ambiguities about the legal effects of collective agreements. In the context of antagonistic relationships between the union and the employer, the collective agreement is treated like a ceasefire or temporary truce rather than a permanent peace treaty.

The Autonomy of Labour Law

Different theories have been advanced about the distinctive characteristics of labour law as a subject, what lies at its core and how its limits should be set. When Otto Kahn-Freund presented his views on these matters in the middle of the twentieth century, he regarded the system of collective bargaining as lying at the core because of its practical importance and its normative function of challenging inequality of bargaining power. From his perspective, the contract of employment was of marginal significance, although it served the purpose of providing a mechanism for the enforcement of collective agreements and some statutory rights.[100]

Today, it is possible to argue the opposite: it is the contract of employment that holds the subject of labour law together and provides its core ingredient. The contract of employment not only provides a mechanism for enforcing the rights of both parties but also provides the legal framework for the enforcement of regulations designed as individual employment rights. When there is no legally enforceable contract, those rights tend to melt away. Yet it is not straightforward to claim that the contract of employment provides the paradigm for labour law for two main reasons.[101] First, the law of the contract of employment continues to draw on the general law of contract for its norms,

---

[99] Described as 'in the realms of legal fiction' in D. Brodie, 'The Autonomy of the Common Law of the Contract of Employment From the General Law of Contract' in M. Freedland (gen. ed.), *The Contract of Employment* (Oxford University Press, 2016), pp. 124, 129.

[100] M. Freedland, 'Otto Kahn-Freund, the Contract of Employment and the Autonomy of Labour Law', in A. Bogg, C. Costello, A.C.L. Davies and J. Prassl (eds.), *The Autonomy of Labour Law* (Oxford: Hart, 2015), p. 29.

[101] H. Collins, 'Contractual Autonomy', in A. Bogg, C. Costello, A. C. L. Davies and J. Prassl (eds.), *The Autonomy of Labour Law* (Oxford: Hart, 2015), p. 45.

which risks diminishing its separate and distinctive qualities and its need for special regulation.[102] Second, the emphasis on employment as a contractual relation tends to emphasise its material and exchange aspects at the expense of overlooking its relational aspects and the need to protect the fundamental rights of workers.

---

[102] M. Freedland and N. Kountouris, *The Legal Construction of Personal Work Relations* (Oxford University Press, 2011).

4

Authority and Co-operation

The Legal Construction of Hierarchy

The legal model of the employment relation presents a structure of authority. From the terms of the contract of employment, the employer obtains the legal authority to direct work and the employee assumes an implied obligation to obey lawful orders. In the words of Kahn-Freund, the contract of employment typically involves submission to a condition of 'subordination':

> But the relation between an employer and an isolated employee or worker is typically a relation between a bearer of power and one who is not a bearer of power. In its inception it is an act of submission, in its operation it is a condition of subordination, however much the submission and the subordination may be concealed by that indispensable figment of the legal mind known as the 'contract of employment'. The main object of labour law has always been, and we venture to say will always be, to be a countervailing force to counteract the inequality of bargaining power which is inherent and must be inherent in the employment

relationship. Most of what we call protective legislation – legislation on the employment of women, children and young persons, on safety in mines, factories and offices, on payment of wages in cash, on guarantee payments, on race and sex discrimination, on unfair dismissal, and indeed most labour legislation altogether – must be seen in this context. It is an attempt to infuse law into a relation of command and subordination.[1]

This construction of managerial authority over the workforce serves a valuable economic purpose. Some kind of governance structure is certainly required to achieve efficient production. The employer needs to adjust the details of work according to ever-changing requirements. Owing to unforeseen eventualities and the constant need to adapt to changing circumstances in a long-term contract, these detailed adjustments cannot be specified in advance by the express terms of the contract. Minor changes need to be handled by a management structure that has the capacity to fill in the details of the contract of employment by further directions. To facilitate efficient management, the common law presumed that the governance structure implicit in the contract of employment should be one that accorded to the employer a general discretionary power or 'prerogative' to direct labour unilaterally.

To buttress this managerial framework, disobedience to the instructions of the employer was regarded under the common law as potentially a fundamental breach of contract, which would entitle the employer to dismiss the employee summarily without compensation. Not every act of disobedience to instructions will be regarded these days as a fundamental breach of contract. What is required is that the nature of the employee's conduct should be such as to demonstrate an intention to repudiate the contract.[2] Minor acts of disobedience falling short of repudiation may, however, justify lesser disciplinary sanctions such as demotion and deductions from pay. This implied duty to obey the orders of the employer is subject to two important limitations. First, the task must fall within the scope of the job as described in the terms of the contract of employment. Secondly, the employer's order must be lawful in the sense that it must not require the employee to engage in criminal conduct or other actions prohibited by law, such as unlawful discrimination.

The alternative to this structure of unilateral authority would have been one of requiring agreement between employer and employee on every detail of work. Such a requirement would clearly raise transaction costs considerably and render production inefficient and prone to hold-ups caused by workers haggling over minor details of work assignments. Accordingly, apart from the core terms of the wage/work bargain, the legal model of the contract of employment did not require joint decisions by the employer and employee or even prior consultation about change. Instead, the implied terms of the

---

[1] P. Davies and M. Freedland, *Kahn-Freund's Labour and the Law* (3rd edn, London: Stevens, 1983), p. 18.
[2] *Laws v. London Chronicle (Indicator Newspapers) Ltd* [1959] 1 WLR 698 (CA); see Chapter 18.

contract conferred unilateral discretion upon management to direct production within the loose parameters set by the express terms of the contract.

In practice, however, where a strong union is recognised by the employer, it will be necessary for the employer to negotiate significant changes in working practices through collective procedures. The union provides a 'countervailing force' to the employer's contractual power to direct the workforce. A strong union can engage in joint regulation of the workplace with management.

While it is apparent that these hierarchical features of the contract of employment were necessitated by considerations of efficiency, workers and their spokespersons always challenged the degree and intensity of the authoritarian structure of managerial control:

> The capitalist is very fond of declaring that labour is a commodity, and the wage contract a bargain of purchase and sale like any other. But he instinctively expects his wage-earners to render him, not only obedience, but also personal deference. If the wage contract is a bargain of purchase and sale like any other, why is the workman expected to doff his hat to his employer, and to say 'sir' to him without reciprocity ... ?[3]

The combination of the legal structure of authority with the economic need of the worker to hold on to a job created the conditions for subordination, for the treatment of workers in a demeaning manner and the potential for a whole variety of abuses of power.

In the twentieth century, as the size of firms grew, the power of the employer was exercised through the ranks of managers. Management became a distinct function within the enterprise. With the objective of maximising the productive capacity of the business, including labour productivity, managers developed their own 'science' of how best to improve efficiency. They held themselves out as experts in organising production, for which purpose they required the power to command and control the workforce. The most developed version of this management science in the early part of the twentieth century was a movement named Taylorism or scientific management,[4] which involved the centralised, detailed control over every aspect of factory production. This method justified hierarchies, the minimisation of worker discretion and the subordination of the worker in every detail of work to the authority of management. The method of scientific management increased the division of labour by breaking down each job into simple tasks that could be performed by cheap, unskilled labour, and with the work co-ordinated and designed by management, using techniques such as 'time and motion' studies, in order to achieve the best use of labour power. The efficiency of production was measured by a cost-accounting system, which was also used to fix

---

[3] S. Webb and B. Webb, *Industrial Democracy* (London: Longmans, 1902) (first published 1897), p. 842, footnote.
[4] F. W. Taylor, *Scientific Management* (New York: Harper and Row, 1947).

standard times for work to be performed. For many employees, the effect of scientific management on the experience of work was a deskilling of tasks to be performed, the removal of any discretion in performance of work, the intensification of work effort and systematic, detailed surveillance of the worker.

Yet a strict and unforgiving hierarchical authority structure rarely achieves the greatest measure of productivity from the workforce. Fear of disciplinary sanctions provides some motivation to work hard, but better productivity can often be achieved through more active co-operation among the workforce and a psychological attitude of identification with the goals of the enterprise. In order to achieve more active co-operation and commitment to the goals of the organisation, standard techniques of management during the twentieth century became more sophisticated than the mechanistic techniques adopted under the influence of Taylorism. These new methods of management are often referred to as HRM.

The Hawthorne Experiment and Human Resources Management

Many of the seeds of the ideas of HRM can be discovered in conclusions drawn from an American study at the Hawthorne plant of the Western Electric Company.[5] In one of the assembly rooms at this manufacturer of electrical components, the experimenters agreed a programme of changes in working conditions with the workers with a view to determining which conditions would produce greater productivity. Various changes in working conditions were introduced, one at a time: rest periods of different numbers and length, changes in the length of the working day and the week, variations in lighting, the provision of food and refreshments. Slowly, but steadily, the output of the group of workers in the test room increased. What was striking was the increase in productivity whatever changes were made, including a reversion to the original working conditions. Even stranger, the workers concerned reported that they felt less tired and that they were not working harder. A plausible explanation of this remarkable result is that the crucial dimension of the experiment was that the group of workers was consulted closely on all the changes in working conditions, many of which they suggested themselves.

The central problem addressed by HRM is that hierarchical and authoritarian work relations are unlikely to achieve the highest possible work effort from employees, because workers will resent their position of subordination and tend to suspect, perhaps correctly, that additional effort will not be rewarded in the long term by higher pay. The implication of the Hawthorne experiment (described in the box) and many other studies is that greater productivity can

---

[5] The experiment was written up in: F. J. Roethlisberger and W. J. Dickson, *Management and the Worker* (Cambridge, MA: Harvard University Press, 1939), but has been examined subsequently by many management theorists: e.g. E. Mayo, *The Social Problems of Industrial Civilization* (London: Routledge, 1949), Ch. 4.

often be achieved by treating workers with respect, consulting them about work, granting them some autonomy to determine working methods and encouraging a sense of team-work. Modern management techniques use command and control less, and instead emphasise inducements for workers to co-operate in ways that go beyond strict requirements under the contract of employment. Employers emphasise the 'mutual gains' to be achieved through 'partnership' between management and the workforce.[6] HRM seeks to improve the commitment of employees to the aims of the organisation. Payment systems link wages to performance targets through bonuses, share schemes and promotion ladders. Employers demonstrate concern for the interests of their employees by becoming 'investors in people', equal opportunity employers and by offering a variety of possibilities for dialogue and consultation. Work tasks and methods can be allocated by mechanisms of consultation with the workforce or their representatives. Hierarchies can be softened and legitimated by the creation of an impersonal system of rules in a bureaucratic organisation that applies to everyone. The subordination entailed by hierarchies can be significantly softened by delegating responsibility for the achievement of efficient production to the work groups themselves. Above all, employers promise to manage the workforce fairly, treating individuals with personal care and respect. All these methods and others are commonplace in modern managerial techniques designed to secure the active co-operation of the workforce, including engagement in innovative and spontaneous activity that goes beyond formal job descriptions or 'beyond contract'.[7]

Of course, not all employers live up to these high standards all of the time. Nor should one forget that the underlying aim of this better treatment of the workforce is to maximise productivity. Many employees may like to exercise some discretion in their work, to be permitted to make decisions and to work as part of a team. Yet they can also appreciate that these advantages of empowerment and an element of self-realisation through work can bring with them the burden of greater responsibilities, an intensification of work effort and greater stress in the performance of work.[8] Although the removal of the dictatorial management style is welcome to most people, its replacement by HRM techniques can be experienced as a more subtle and intensive form of subordination and exploitation. The employer is not merely seeking to govern workers' physical activities but also to control minds, attitudes and commitments.

---

[6] D. Guest and R. Peccei, 'Partnership at Work: Mutuality and the Balance of Advantage' (2001) 39 *British Journal of Industrial Relations* 207.

[7] D. Katz, 'The Motivational Basis of Organisational Behavior' (1964) 9 *Behavioural Science* 131; C. A. Smith, D. W. Organ and J. P. Near, 'Organisational Citizenship Behaviour: Its Nature and Antecedents' (1983) 68 *Journal of Applied Psychology* 653.

[8] P. Rosenthal, S. Hill and R. Peccei, 'Checking Out Service: Evaluating Excellence, HRM and TQM in Retailing' (1997) 11 *Work, Employment and Society* 481.

These widespread HRM techniques in the management of businesses have almost certainly influenced legal perceptions of the employment relation. The legal response is to be discovered in part in modern legislation, such as the law of unfair dismissal, which requires managers to act fairly when disciplining employees. Another important ingredient in the legal response has been the subtle transformation of the implied terms of the contract of employment by the judges. By developing these implied terms in the contract of employment, the courts have given legal expression to the new expectations of both employers and employees. The employer expects performance of the job that goes 'beyond contract' to amount to a commitment to the aims of the enterprise. The employee has the expectation of being treated with respect, with trust and confidence, with dignity and fairly. These expectations, which were described in the previous chapter as a 'psychological contract', can be protected through the law by constructing implied terms of the contract of employment. In other words, the implied terms can give some legal force to the expectations generated within the psychological contract. Serious violations of these implied terms can be sanctioned as breaches of contract. This chapter explores the development and reach of these implied terms of the contract of employment.

Mutual Trust and Confidence

The implied term in the contract of employment that protects an employee's expectations is usually described as the implied term of mutual trust and confidence. The authoritative formulation of the term takes the following complex form:

> the employer shall not, without reasonable and proper cause, conduct itself in a manner calculated as likely to destroy or seriously damage the relationship of confidence and trust between employer and employee.[9]

This formulation deliberately avoids more colloquial expressions such as a duty to act reasonably or fairly. It aims to set a minimum standard of conduct below which the employer should not fall. A similar duty probably applies to employees, but in practice it is rarely invoked because the law already sets the higher standard of requiring employees to comply with all lawful instructions of the employer. In a rare example of breach of this implied term by an employee, *Williams* v. *Leeds United*,[10] the employer sought to justify the summary dismissal of the employee for gross or repudiatory breach of contract, but could not refer to the disciplinary code in the express terms of the

---

[9] *Woods* v. *W. M. Car Services (Peterborough) Ltd* [1981] ICR 666, at 670 (*per* Browne-Wilkinson J), approved in *Lewis* v. *Motorworld Garages Ltd* [1986] ICR 157 (CA), and *Mahmoud* v. *Bank of Credit and Commerce International SA* [1998] AC 20 (HL).

[10] *Williams* v. *Leeds United Football Club* [2015] EWHC 376, [2015] IRLR 383.

contract because that had not been communicated to the employee. The employer was able to justify summary dismissal instead on a breach by the employee of the implied term of mutual trust and confidence, which consisted in forwarding a pornographic email to a female colleague five years previously. In general, though, the significance of the implied term has been that for the first time the courts have acknowledged a general legal obligation requiring fair management behaviour. Previously, although courts urged employers to be 'good and considerate', failure by employers to behave in such a manner rarely involved any breach of contract. The implied term forms a cornerstone of the legal construction of the contract of employment and assumes 'a central position in the law of the contract of employment'.[11] Mark Freedland aptly describes it as being 'undoubtedly the most powerful engine of movement in the modern law of employment contracts',[12] although it should be added that movement has occurred at a snail's pace.

The existence of the implied term of mutual trust and confidence was confirmed by the House of Lords in *Mahmoud and Malik* v. *Bank of Credit and Commerce International S. A.*[13] The appellants were dismissed for redundancy following the collapse of the employing bank amid allegations that the bank's business had been conducted fraudulently. Although innocent of any personal wrongdoing, the appellants claimed that they were unable to obtain any further employment in the banking sector due to a stigma of fraudulent conduct being attached to them. They sought a claim in damages against the liquidator of the bank for this loss, which is known as 'stigma damages'. The possibility of such a claim was confirmed by the House of Lords. Breach of the implied term of mutual trust and confidence could result in a claim for compensatory damages for any provable material losses, including damage to the success of job applications.

The implied term of mutual trust and confidence is a standardised term implied by law into all contracts of employment. As an implied term, it operates as a default rule, so the parties are free to exclude or modify the term. It provides a general instrument by which the courts can strike a balance between the employer's interest in managing the business as it sees fit and the employee's interest in not being unfairly and improperly exploited. Although many of the instances when the implied term is invoked concern harsh treatment of an employee, it can also apply more generally to the way in which the business is conducted by the employer and may concern matters unknown to the employee at the time, as in the *Mahmoud* and *Malik* case itself. Nor does the employer's conduct have to be intended to have a

---

[11] D. Brodie, 'Mutual Trust and the Values of the Employment Contract' (2001) 30 *Industrial Law Journal* 84, at 86. See also D. Brodie, 'The Heart of the Matter: Mutual Trust and Confidence' (1996) 25 *Industrial Law Journal* 121; D. Brodie, 'Beyond Exchange: The New Contract of Employment' (1998) 27 *Industrial Law Journal* 79.

[12] M. Freedland, *The Personal Employment Contract* (Oxford University Press, 2003), p. 166.

[13] [1998] AC 20 (HL).

detrimental impact on the employee; what matters is not the motive or aim of the employer but the effect on the employee of having grounds for believing that the relationship of mutual trust and confidence has been seriously damaged. In response to a breach of the implied term, the employee is entitled to bring a claim for damages under the common law of contract to compensate for the loss resulting from the breach of contract.

In practice, employees usually raise such a claim of breach of the implied term after they have terminated the employment relation in response to a perceived abuse of discretionary power by management. A breach of the implied term of mutual trust and confidence justifies a termination of the contract because the breach counts as a fundamental or repudiatory breach of contract by the employer. In these circumstances, in law, the employee's resignation is regarded as a constructive dismissal. The employee may then advance a statutory claim for (constructive) unfair dismissal or a common-law claim for (constructive) wrongful dismissal.

The large number of cases that have invoked the implied term of mutual trust and confidence range over the whole gamut of abuses of managerial power: victimisation, inequitable treatment, unnecessary rigidity, harassment, bullying, oppressive demands, disrespectful treatment, harsh and foul language, deceit, scapegoating and cover-ups. The task of the courts and tribunals is to unpick the details of the events that occurred, in order to assess whether, looked at objectively, the employer's conduct was so serious as to destroy the relationship of trust and confidence, while bearing in mind that the employer's conduct may have had 'reasonable and proper cause' in the circumstances, thereby avoiding breach of the implied term. In reaching such judgments, the courts determine the proper standards of behaviour of management, not by imposing general rules, but by making contextual assessments in each case. Some cases illustrate the variety of situations where an employer's conduct, viewed objectively by a court or tribunal, is regarded as having destroyed mutual trust and confidence.

Post Office v. *Roberts*:[14] a junior clerical assistant was refused a transfer to a different area. She discovered that the reason for the refusal of the transfer was that Mr O'Keefe, a senior manager, had written on her personnel record that she was unlikely to qualify for promotion, and that she was irresponsible and lacked industry and comprehension. The senior manager had no grounds for this opinion, since her immediate supervisor had indicated that she was fully acceptable in her present junior grade. The senior manager had made the mistake carelessly, not deliberately or in bad faith. Subsequently, instead of disclosing the real reason for the refusal of the transfer, the manager had falsely claimed that there were no vacancies. The employee resigned and

---

[14] [1980] IRLR 347 (EAT).

brought a claim for unfair dismissal. The EAT upheld the claim that the employer had broken the implied term of mutual trust and confidence.

Isle of Wight Tourist Board v. *Coombes*:[15] the claimant was the personal secretary to a director of the company. In the course of an argument, the director had spoken to another employee about her, saying that she was an 'intolerable bitch on a Monday morning'. Stressing the need for complete confidence in the relationship between a director and his personal secretary, the EAT found a breach of the implied term.

Courtaulds Northern Textiles Ltd v. *Andrew*:[16] during a heated argument, the manager said to the employee: 'You can't do the bloody job anyway.' In fact, the manager did not hold that view. If he had had grounds for that view, the statement might have been made with reasonable and proper cause. In the absence of such grounds, the manager had broken the implied term.

Transco plc v. *O'Brien*:[17] the employer awarded its permanent workforce a new contract on better terms. By mistake, the employer failed to offer the claimant the enhanced contract, believing erroneously that he was not on a permanent contract. Although there was no bad faith on the part of the employer, the exclusion of the employee by error was a breach of the implied term of mutual trust and confidence. For this breach of contract, the employee was entitled to be put in as good a financial position as if the mistake had not been made.

Visa International Service Association v. *Paul*:[18] while the applicant was on maternity leave, the employer advertised a position for which the applicant regarded herself as suited and for which she would have applied, but the employer had not notified the applicant of the vacancy. The tribunal upheld the claim that the failure to notify her of the vacancy was a breach of the implied term of mutual trust and confidence, even though the tribunal also accepted the employer's contention that she was not qualified for the position and would not have been appointed.

Bournemouth University Higher Education Corporation v. *Buckland*:[19] a professor and his co-examiner failed a high number of students in the end of year examinations. Worried about the adequacy of the second marking and fearing appeals against the results on the part of the students, the programme director and a colleague re-marked the papers and raised some marks. The chair of the exam board confirmed these higher marks, without consulting the professor. A subsequent official inquiry criticised the conduct of the university for going behind the professor's back in changing the exam marks. Not mollified by the inquiry's report, the professor resigned and successfully claimed constructive unfair dismissal. The tribunal held that the employer had committed a fundamental breach of the implied term of mutual trust and

---

[15] [1976] IRLR 413 (EAT).　　[16] [1979] IRLR 84.
[17] [2002] EWCA Civ 379, [2002] ICR 721 (CA).　　[18] [2004] IRLR 42 (EAT).
[19] [2010] EWCA Civ 121, [2010] ICR 908 (CA).

confidence by changing the professor's marks without consulting him, because that conduct had impugned his integrity as an examiner. Endorsing this decision, the Court of Appeal also confirmed that the university's subsequent attempt to make amends through the official enquiry could not cure the original breach of the implied term.

Stevens v. *Birmingham University:*[20] in the course of a disciplinary investigation into alleged irregularities in Professor Stevens' clinical trials, the university proposed a meeting at which the professor was entitled under collectively agreed disciplinary rules to be accompanied by either a trade union official or a colleague. Relying on those rules and not wishing to make any exceptions, the university refused to admit to the proposed meeting a suitably qualified representative from the Medical Protection Society, a leading medical defence organisation of which Professor Stevens was a member, although it is not a trade union. The court held that the express terms of the contract had to be interpreted in a way that was consistent with the 'overriding obligation of trust and confidence', which in this case required the university to permit the professor to be accompanied by this suitable person, for otherwise the investigatory process would be 'patently unfair'.

Good Faith

We will encounter many other examples of the application of the implied term of mutual trust and confidence in other chapters. The terminology has sometimes been modified. In a pair of cases in the House of Lords concerning the outrageous abuse of disciplinary powers by the employer, Lord Nicholls invoked the language of good faith:

> The trust and confidence implied term means, in short, that an employer must treat his employees fairly. In his conduct of his business, and in his treatment of his employees, an employer must act responsibly and in good faith.[21]

In the same cases, Lord Steyn suggested that it might be more conducive to clarity if the courts used the terminology of an implied obligation of good faith.[22]

The terminology of good faith may be a useful tool by which to stress the special obligations arising in the contract of employment. It reflects the idea that an employer has broken the psychological contract under which the employee believed he or she worked. Such a breach amounts to more than non-compliance with the terms of the contract. The employee is likely to experience a sense of betrayal which goes to the root of the trust and confidence that lies at the heart of the contract of employment.

---

[20] *Stevens* v. *University of Birmingham* [2015] EWHC 2300, [2017] ICR 96 (QB).
[21] *Eastwood* v. *Magnox Electric plc* [2004] UKHL 35, [2004] IRLR 732, para. 11.   [22] Para. 50.

But, when using the terminology of good faith, it should be remembered that deliberate misconduct is not necessary for a breach of the implied term of good faith; an honest, if careless, mistake was sufficient for liability for breach of the implied term in *Transco plc* v. *O'Brien* and *Post Office* v. *Roberts*. If the terminology of good faith is used, it should not be understood in the sense of deliberate bad faith. Nor is bad faith on its own sufficient for a breach of the implied term. It is necessary to examine the likely effect of the employer's conduct on the perceptions of a reasonable employee. One instance of lying or duplicity on the part of the employer may not, in the circumstances, be regarded objectively as amounting to serious betrayal of trust.

Arbitrariness and Irrationality in Discretionary Decisions

In the context of disputes about the proper exercise of managerial discretion, which may be in relation to bonuses, fringe benefits and other types of remuneration, the description of the relevant implied term is commonly framed in terms of an obligation not to act arbitrarily, capriciously or irrationally. In *Mallone* v. *BPB Industries plc*,[23] the claimant sought compensation for the withdrawal of all his share-option entitlements as a result of a directors' resolution under a rule of the share-option scheme that permitted the directors to award share options to employees whose employment had been terminated in an 'appropriate proportion' 'as the directors in their absolute discretion shall determine'. The Court of Appeal found that the way that the directors had exercised their discretion constituted a breach of contract. Even with regard to such an unfettered discretion, the directors were bound by the purposes of the scheme to provide incentives for good performance to executives to the extent that decisions about the exercise of the discretion should not be made dishonestly, for an improper motive, capriciously or arbitrarily. The exercise of discretion would be invalid if the directors reached a decision that no reasonable employer could have reached on analogy with the test in *Associated Provincial Picture House Ltd* v. *Wednesbury Corporation*.[24] The judge at first instance had been correct to find that the directors' decision was one that no reasonable employer could have reached, even though, of course, the decision was expected to save the employer more than £100,000.

More recently, in *Braganza* v. *BP Shipping Ltd*,[25] the Supreme Court extended the review of contractual discretion to replicate the whole of the public law *Wednesbury* review standard in the context of an employer's discretionary decision. A chief engineer who disappeared without trace on a voyage benefited from a contractual entitlement to a death-in-service payment, save where, in the opinion of the company, death had resulted from the employee's wilful act. Although there was a paucity of evidence about what

---

[23] [2002] EWCA Civ 126, [2002] IRLR 452 (CA).   [24] [1948] 1 KB 223 (CA).
[25] *Braganza* v. *BP Shipping Ltd* [2015] UKSC 17, [2015] ICR 449.

had happened, the employer decided that in its opinion the death had been caused by suicide, thereby depriving the widow of about £230,000. Holding the employer to be in breach of contract and awarding the death-in-service benefit, a majority of the Supreme Court held that to ensure that a contractual power was not abused in circumstances where there was a potential conflict of interest, there was an implied term that the power should be exercised not only in good faith but also without being arbitrary, capricious or irrational. An employer's discretionary decision could be impugned not only where no reasonable decision-maker could have reached it, but also where the process had failed to exclude irrelevant considerations or had failed to take into account relevant considerations. A discretionary decision must therefore be made rationally, in good faith, consistently with its contractual purpose and in general in accordance with the implied term of mutual trust and confidence. In this case, the employer had failed to take into account the extreme unlikelihood of anyone committing suicide, an improbability that had not been countered by any cogent evidence.

This use of a public-law standard of review in a contractual context seems to be a response to the presence of a discretionary power in the express terms of the contract, which is a power that resembles the powers often conferred on public authorities. How far that analogy can be taken will be a matter of debate.[26] Although these rationality criteria imitate the judicial review of public authorities in their exercise of discretion, the remedy differs: in public law the decision is quashed and has to be taken again properly; in contract of employment cases, if successful, the employee obtains the expected discretionary contractual benefit. Moreover, although a public authority is normally required to act in the public interest, there is nothing wrong in principle in most contractual contexts in a party acting in its own interests. In a contractual context, the rationality requirement appears to reach the odd result that a court concludes that it was irrational for the employer to save itself a large sum of money by exercising a discretionary power for its own benefit.[27] That oddity may perhaps be explained by the argument that the contractual power was conferred for a particular purpose, so that its use for an ulterior purpose is a breach of contract,[28] although it is unclear how that conduct can be described as irrational. In the context of employment relations, the test of irrationality seems to be targeting once again a mismatch between the express terms of the contract and the expectations of the psychological contract which provide the essential dynamic of the employment relationship. The standard of rationality confines the exercise of discretion to factors that accord with this implicit

---

[26] D. Brodie, 'Legal Coherence and the Employment Revolution' (2001) 117 *Law Quarterly Review* 604.

[27] H. Collins, 'Discretionary Power in Contracts', in D. Campbell, H. Collins and J. Wightman (eds.), *Implicit Dimensions of Contract* (Oxford: Hart, 2003), p. 219.

[28] E.g. *Horkulak* v. *Cantor Fitzgerald International* [2004] EWCA Civ 1287, [2005] ICR 402 (CA).

expectation, despite any broader wording of the express contractual agreement.

A final puzzle posed by this use of the language of arbitrariness and irrationality is whether this term that is implied with respect to issues of remuneration is merely part of the implied term of mutual trust and confidence or another separate implied term. No legal consequences appear to attach to this issue: whichever implied term is used, breach by the employer will be regarded as a serious breach of contract giving rise to damages and will enable the employee to claim constructive dismissal. Perhaps the best view is that the implied term of mutual trust and confidence supplies the most general and abstract version of the implied obligation of the employer, which can be expressed in relation to particular sorts of issues in slightly different language as seems appropriate in that context.

An Essential Foundation of the Contract?

The invention of the implied term of mutual trust and confidence (and other associated formulations of the implied term) has been one of the most remarkable and significant developments of the common law of the contract of employment in recent decades. It brings the common law closer into line with modern views about fairness in employment relations by controlling the abuse of managerial power in the workplace. Despite its archaic legal terminology, the implied term expresses modern views about the need to treat employees fairly and with respect. These views stem in part from management policies concerning productivity, as outlined earlier in the chapter and elsewhere. Employers can manipulate the psychological contract that describes an employee's expectation by vague promises and holding out the organisation as one that treats its employees fairly. Although the express terms of the contract are unlikely to protect all these expectations, the implied term of mutual trust and confidence can prevent excessive abuse of these techniques of manipulation.

Yet the implied term of mutual trust and confidence also corresponds to broader social and political values, which reject hierarchical class structures and require equal concern and respect for all persons. Instead of the image of master and faithful servant that informed the earlier legal construction of the contract of employment, modern law tries to present the employment relationship as one between equals, where both parties need to co-operate, to assist each other in good faith, to use the powers and responsibilities conferred by the contract for proper purposes and to treat each other with dignity and respect. Of course, the implied term does not alter one wit the basic structure of the employment contract, in which the employer has the discretionary power to direct and manage the workforce. Nevertheless, the implied term sets minimum legal standards of fair treatment and respect for employees according to which the employer's discretionary power must be exercised.

The source of the implied term of mutual trust and confidence in management techniques and broader social attitudes towards authority relations provokes a further question. Should it be possible any longer for employers to insist upon the older command and obedience model of the authority relation in the workplace? As a matter of conventional legal doctrine, it should nearly always be possible for employers, through suitably worded express terms of the contract of employment, to oust implied legal constraints on the exercise of their powers to direct and control the workforce. Of course, there remains the mandatory limitation on express terms that an employer can only validly give lawful orders to employees. In addition, for some employees, especially those in the public sector, it may be possible to rely upon the HRA 1998 to insist that limits should be placed upon the express terms of the contract. But none of these constraints goes so far as to prohibit an employer from expressly excluding the implied obligation not to act in a way that is likely to destroy mutual trust and confidence.

It is tempting to accept the suggestions of Douglas Brodie and Mark Freedland that the implied term of mutual trust is so fundamental to the modern contract of employment that it should not be possible to exclude it by express terms.[29] It seems unlikely that an employer would have the temerity to put an express term in the contract entitling it to behave arbitrarily, extremely unfairly or in bad faith. But an employer might try to achieve a similar result by stating vaguely that the contract excludes additional implied terms or that the express agreement is the 'entire agreement'. An exclusion of the implied term was apparently achieved in *Johnson* v. *Unisys Ltd*;[30] a majority of the House of Lords held that the implied term was excluded in relation to dismissal by a rather general clause that permitted the employer to terminate the contract of employment on giving four weeks' notice. In dissent, Lord Steyn argued that such a term implied by law would require express words to cut down its scope. As a matter of legal doctrine, to insist that such an exclusion clause should be invalid because it destroys the foundation or a necessary incident of the employment relation might be thought to be an attempt to revive a discredited notion in the general law of contract that contracts possess fundamental terms that cannot be excluded even by express terms.[31] Nevertheless, it is an attractive idea that, alongside mandatory statutory provisions such as the law of unfair dismissal that protect expectations of employees within the psychological contract, the common law might abandon the legal orthodoxy that always protects freedom of contract and the superiority of express terms over implied terms. Courts should at least be reluctant in

---

[29] M. Freedland, *The Personal Employment Contract* (Oxford University Press, 2003), pp. 164–6; D. Brodie, 'Beyond Exchange: The New Contract of Employment' (1998) 27 *Industrial Law Journal* 79.

[30] [2001] UKHL 13, [2003] 1 AC 518.

[31] *Suisse Atlantique Société d'Armement Maritime SA* v. *Rotterdamsche Kolen Centrale NV* [1967] 1 AC 361 (HL).

their interpretations of contracts of employment, which are after all much like standard-form contracts imposed on a take-it-or-leave-it basis, to permit express exclusions of all aspects of the obligation to perform in good faith as opposed to some of its more detailed applications. For example, an employer might be permitted to limit any obligations of disclosure of information based on the implied term of mutual trust and confidence, but not be allowed to exclude the implied term altogether.[32]

Performance in Good Faith

Looking now on the other side of the employment relationship, at the employee's implied duty of co-operation under the contract, the implied term has evolved beyond a duty to obey lawful instructions. The employer can enforce an expectation that the employee will do more than perform the tasks listed in the express terms of the contract of employment or laid down in the employer's rule-book. The employee's obligation is sometimes described as a duty to co-operate. But how far this implied duty extends is hard to pin down. Although the duty applies to the whole workforce, the expectation of co-operation is probably greater for more senior staff, managers and professionals than for other employees.

Many of the examples of the application of the duty concern a deliberate and concerted withdrawal of co-operation in the context of industrial action. In these cases, the language of 'fidelity' or good faith is invoked, because it is clear that the employees concerned are not trying to do their jobs to the best of their abilities, but rather to perform them in a manner calculated to disrupt the purposes of the employer.

In *Secretary of State for Employment* v. *ASLEF (No. 2)*,[33] the union, ASLEF (Associated Society of Locomotive Engineers and Firemen), instructed its members, who were railway workers, to work to rule, that is, to comply strictly with the rule-book of the employers, the British Railways Board (BRB), with the objective of disrupting the railways. Under statutory powers contained at that time in the Industrial Relations Act 1971, the Secretary of State intervened to ask the court to order a ballot of the workforce. The union contended that the necessary statutory condition for the court to order a ballot, namely, 'irregular industrial action short of a strike', was not satisfied, because the workers were not in breach of their contracts of employment. The Court of Appeal held that the 'work to rule' constituted breaches of contracts of employment and ordered a ballot to be held. Although the rule-book was not itself a contractual document, but merely comprised instructions issued by the employer, the employees were in breach of an implied term of the contract.

---

[32] H. Collins, 'Implied Terms in the Contract of Employment', in M. Freedland (gen. ed.), *The Contract of Employment* (Oxford University Press, 2016), pp. 471, 483.

[33] [1972] ICR 19 (CA).

Lord Denning MR held that it was an implied term of the contract of employment that an employee must not wilfully obstruct his employer's business. Buckley LJ said that it was an implied term of the contract to serve the employer faithfully within the requirements of the contract. Roskill LJ described the implied term as a duty not to seek to obey lawful instructions so wholly unreasonably as to disrupt the efficient running of the system in which they were employed. This decision reveals how the implied duty of co-operation or performance in good faith requires the employee not merely to comply with the rule-book, but in addition to interpret and apply the rules in ways which promote the objectives of the employer's business. Employers can therefore demand compliance with the rule-book, not only in its letter but in its spirit, without the rule-book itself comprising express terms of the contract.

The formulation of the implied term as a duty to serve the employer faithfully within the requirements of the contract was subsequently approved by the Court of Appeal in *British Telecommunications plc* v. *Ticehurst*.[34] Mrs Ticehurst was a manager in charge of forty staff. Her union, the Society of Telecommunications Executives (STE), was conducting a campaign of industrial action in support of a pay claim. The union instructed its 30,000 members to take action falling short of a strike, including a withdrawal of goodwill, working strictly according to contractual hours and generally not taking on tasks outside of their normal duties without written instructions. The industrial action escalated into a series of one-day strikes. The employers then sent a letter to all employees declaring that those employees who were not prepared to honour fully the terms of their contract and to perform all the requirements of their jobs would be sent home without pay until they were prepared to work normally. Mrs Ticehurst refused to sign an undertaking to work 'normally in accordance with the terms of my contract . . . and to take no further industrial action', although she did state in writing that she was prepared to work normally in accordance with the contract. She was sent home without pay until the trade dispute was settled about two weeks later. The legal action was for the pay withheld by the employer. The claim was rejected by the Court of Appeal on the ground that Mrs Ticehurst had been in breach of contract by withdrawing goodwill and that the employers were entitled to refuse to accept part performance of the contract. The withdrawal of goodwill was described as a refusal to serve the employer faithfully within the requirements of the contract. The Court stressed that Mrs Ticehurst's position as a manager meant that her employer was entitled to trust her to exercise her judgement and discretion in the interests of the employer. It was not necessary for the employer to demonstrate any particular harm caused to its interests. The implied term is breached:

---

[34] [1992] ICR 383 (CA).

when the employee does an act, or omits to do an act, which it would be within her contract and the discretion allowed to her not to do, or to do, as the case may be, and the employee so acts or omits to do the act, not in honest exercise of choice or discretion for the faithful performance of her work but in order to disrupt the employer's business or to cause the most inconvenience that can be caused. . .[35]

In these decisions, the courts favour a description of the implied term in the antique language of the faithful servant. They emphasise the bad faith of the employee's conduct. Employees who are doing their best for the business, however incompetent their best may be, will not be in breach of this implied term. The courts have not described the duty in such terms as a duty to use 'best endeavours', which is a common way to describe a positive duty to co-operate in the performance of a contract. It may be wrong, therefore, to describe this obligation as a positive duty to co-operate. In the cases, the obligation placed on the employee seems narrower: a duty not to perform the contract in a manner deliberately calculated to cause inconvenience and disruption to the employer's business or organisation. In short, we might say that it is a duty not to perform the contract in bad faith.

Other implied terms, however, may buttress the employer's position in seeking to ensure co-operation from the workforce. An employee is under a duty to take reasonable care of the employer's property.[36] There is also an independent duty of loyalty, to be considered below. The courts can also interpret the express terms of the contract in expansive ways that require employees to adapt to new working conditions and tasks, such as the use of new technologies.[37] In most instances, however, the employer can require full co-operation from an employee either by issuing express instructions or by issuing a comprehensive rule-book, for then the employee falls under an implied legal duty to obey these instructions in accordance with the best interests of the employer.

Loyalty and Confidentiality

Traditional statements of the implied terms of the contract of employment also include an implied obligation of loyalty or fidelity. This duty has been applied to employees, but not to employers, although it is likely that the implied term of mutual trust and confidence could apply in analogous situations to require disclosure of information to employees.[38] Employers will also

---

[35] [1992] ICR 383, *per* Ralf Gibson LJ giving the judgment of the court.
[36] *Lister* v. *Romford Ice & Cold Storage Co.* [1957] AC 555 (HL).
[37] *Cresswell* v. *Board of Inland Revenue* [1984] ICR 508 (QB).
[38] E.g. *Mahmoud and Malik* v. *BCCI* [1998] AC 20 (HL).

be liable in tort for negligent misstatements about an employee.[39] An employee's duty also extends to respecting the confidentiality of information obtained in the course of employment. Employers have to respect confidential information under data protection legislation and it seems likely that they also must respect information provided in confidence under the common law of implied terms or tort law.

Duty of Loyalty

An employee's duty of loyalty concerns conduct by employees that might damage the economic interests of the employer. For example, such conduct might include disclosing information that harms the employer's business reputation or gives aid to a competitor of the employer.[40] This duty of loyalty seems to have been shaped by the notion that during the course of employment an employee acts as an agent for the employer.[41] Under general legal principles, an agent should act in the interests of the principal; similarly, an employee should be loyal to the interests of the employer. But unlike formal agents, employees are not regarded as being bound by a strict fiduciary duty under which they must always place the interests of the employer ahead of their own. The contractual duty of loyalty occupies an intermediate position between a full equitable fiduciary duty and the freedom of most contracting parties to act in their own best interests. The duty exemplifies the way contracts of employment are relational contracts: an employee must be loyal to the purpose of the contract by not undermining it, but can otherwise have regard to his or her own interests.

This contrast between a duty of loyalty and a fiduciary duty is illustrated in cases concerning the failure of employees to disclose their own misconduct. The venerable authority of Lord Atkin in *Bell* v. *Lever Bros Ltd*[42] stands in the way of a duty to disclose misconduct as part of the duty of loyalty:

> The servant owes a duty not to steal, but, having stolen, is there superadded a duty to confess that he has stolen? I am satisfied that to imply such a duty would be a departure from the well established usage of mankind and would be to create obligations entirely outside the normal contemplation of the parties concerned.

But the courts have developed ways by which to circumvent that *dictum*. If the employee lies to the employer as part of a cover-up, that fraudulent concealment will amount to a breach of the duty of fidelity. It has also been held that a

---

[39] E.g. *Spring* v. *Guardian Assurance plc* [1995] 2 AC 296 (HL); *TSB Bank plc* v. *Harris* [2000] IRLR 157 (EAT).

[40] *Hivac Ltd* v. *Park Royal Scientific Instruments Ltd* [1946] Ch 169 (CA).

[41] R. Flannigan, 'The [fiduciary] Duty of Fidelity' (2008) 124 *Law Quarterly Review* 274; A. Frazer, 'The Employee's Contractual Duty of Fidelity' (2015) 131 *Law Quarterly Review* 53.

[42] [1932] AC 161 (HL).

manager may be required to disclose information about misconduct by sub-ordinates.[43] Where the nature of the employee's tasks requires the employee to disclose all relevant information to the employer, a failure to disclose information may also amount to a breach of the obligation of fidelity.

Directors of companies are bound by fiduciary duties owed to the company. Many of these directors will also be employees, so they will be bound by enhanced duties of loyalty. Senior managers may also fall under enhanced duties of loyalty. For instance, where the employer makes a disadvantageous business decision as a result of a manager's failure to disclose information, knowing that the omission would cause the employer loss, it seems possible that the senior manager, like a director of the company, would be found to be in breach of the duty of loyalty.[44] In the unusual case where the employee is under a fiduciary duty (as in the case of a director/employee), there is also a duty to disclose any conflict of interest.[45] The existence of a legal duty of the employee to disclose information to the employer may also determine criminal liability. Under the Fraud Act 2006, section 3, an employee who dishonestly fails to disclose to an employer information that he is under a legal duty to disclose with the intention of making a gain or causing a loss may have committed a serious criminal offence.

In cases of breach of the contractual duty of loyalty, as well as or in the alternative to the ordinary remedy of damages for breach of contract, courts may award remedies that imitate those for fiduciary duties in order to ensure that the duty of loyalty is observed.[46] For instance, where an employee receives money as an agent for the employer, there is a duty to account for the money. If the money goes missing, in principle the employee will be under a duty to reimburse the employer. Equally, if an employee receives a secret commission or a bribe from a customer or supplier of the employer, the employee will be liable to account to the employer for the sum (as well as facing criminal prosecution for corruption). Similarly, the employee may be held accountable for any profits made from the unauthorised use of the employer's property, including the case of the misuse of trade secrets. The use of the equitable remedies does not mean that employees are fiduciaries. Instead these remedies are used to ensure compliance with the contractual duty of loyalty.

Nottingham University v. *Fishel*[47] illustrates this contrast between fiduciary duties and the contractual duty of loyalty. Dr Fishel was the scientific director of a clinic that provided *in vitro* fertilisation to patients. As well as running the clinic successfully, he undertook work privately abroad at other clinics and

---

[43] *Sybron Corp.* v. *Rochem Ltd* [1983] ICR 801 (CA).

[44] This duty has been applied to a company director, who is under a fiduciary duty: *Item Software (UK) Ltd* v. *Fassihi* [2004] EWCA Civ 1244, [2005] ICR 450 (CA).

[45] *Tesco Stores Ltd* v. *Pook* [2003] EWHC 823, [2004] IRLR 618 (ChD).

[46] M. Conaglen, *Fiduciary Loyalty: Protecting the Due Performance of Non-Fiduciary Duties* (London: Hart, 2010).

[47] [2000] IRLR 471 (QB).

occasionally he sent his junior staff to perform such work. After termination of the employment, the university claimed compensation for the value of this private work, arguing that it was performed in breach of contract in that Dr Fishel had not sought prior permission, as required under his contract of employment. Elias J held that, although Dr Fishel had broken his contract by failing to obtain prior permission, the university could only claim damages for losses caused by breach of contract, since there was no fiduciary duty to account for that income either under the standard incidents of the contract of employment or under the express terms of this particular contractual arrangement. The university had in fact suffered no loss, because the patients would not have come to the clinic in the UK, and in fact the university may have benefited from Dr Fishel's opportunity both to improve his expertise and to publicise the reputation of the university. However, Dr Fishel was in breach of a duty of loyalty by directing junior staff to take outside work, because this step created a potential conflict between his duty to the university to direct those employees to work for the university and his personal interest in profiting from their work. For that breach of duty of loyalty, Dr Fishel was liable to account for the profits that he made from his staff's outside work. On this view, the misuse of the time of junior staff was analogous to the use of the employer's property to make a personal profit, so a restitutionary remedy was appropriate.

Confidential Information

The employee's implied obligation of loyalty also requires employees to use information that is confidential to the employer solely for the purposes of the employment relationship and not for any other purpose. The implied contractual obligation appears to run parallel to the tort of breach of confidence under which the law imposes a duty not to disclose information 'whenever a person receives information that he knows or ought to know is fairly and reasonably to be regarded as confidential'.[48] The duty of confidence is typically breached by an employee taking files containing confidential information with a view to setting up a rival business or to providing it to third parties such as rival businesses. The duty only applies to confidential information as opposed to information that is generally known or easily obtainable without cost. Nor does the implied obligation extend to the use of information after the employment relation has ended that an employee acquired while performing work and was merely kept in an employee's head, so that it became part of the employee's general skill, experience and knowledge, such as information or 'know-how' about the marketing of products. An employee can, for instance, use his or her experience of a particular line of business to set up a rival

---

[48] *Campbell* v. *MGN Ltd* [2004] 2 AC 457 [14] Lord Nicholls.

company and to contact customers, including customers of his former employer, using knowledge about the preferences of those customers and the prices that they might be willing to pay.[49]

An employer's remedy for breach of an employee's obligation not to divulge confidential information may include an order to return the files or documents that were taken, an injunction to prevent use of the confidential information for commercial purposes (known as a springboard injunction),[50] compensatory damages for any actual loss caused by misuse of the information or, if justice so requires, the amount of a charge that the employer would have made to license use of that information[51] and, as an exceptional remedy, an accounting of any profits made from misuse of the confidential information.[52] In a case where the files and documents are not used, however, the absence of loss to the employer or gain to the former employee should result in an award of only nominal damages.[53]

Many employers try to extend the protection of confidential information by including a broadly drafted express term in the contract of employment that forbids retention or divulgence of confidential information before or after termination of the contract of employment. Subject to any mandatory limit protecting the right to work such as the restraint of trade doctrine (discussed below), an express term may also define what counts as confidential information broadly to include every piece of stored information on the employer's computer data files. A dramatic illustration of the use of an express term occurred in *Attorney-General* v. *Blake*.[54] Blake had been a member of the UK intelligence service, but had acted also as a spy for the Soviet Union, for which he was convicted. He escaped from prison, wrote his memoirs and sold them to a publisher. The Attorney-General sought to prevent the payment of royalties to Blake, who had agreed to an express confidentiality clause that applied after the termination of employment. The Attorney-General claimed damages for breach of contract assessed by reference to the amount of royalties. Such a claim would have fallen within the existing remedies for breach of confidence if the information had still been confidential, but since the information was about fifty years old and already public knowledge, it was no longer confidential and nor was there any damage or loss to the public interest. Nevertheless, the House of Lords, by a majority, permitted, exceptionally, a remedy of 'disgorgement of profits' as the measure of damages for breach of contract. A distinguishing feature of this case was thought to be the breadth of the contractual undertaking that Blake was not to divulge any information, confidential or otherwise, obtained during his service in the

---

[49] *Faccenda Chicken Ltd* v. *Fowler* [1986] ICR 297, [1987] Ch 117 (CA).
[50] *Roger Bullivant Ltd* v. *Ellis* [1987] ICR 464 (CA).
[51] *Morris-Garner* v. *One Step (Support) Ltd* [2018] UKSC 20, [2018] 2 WLR 1353.
[52] *Attorney-General* v. *Blake* [2001] 1 AC 268 (HL).
[53] *Marathon Asset Management LLP* v. *Seddon* [2017] EWHC 300 (Comm), [2017] ICR 791.
[54] [2001] 1 AC 268 (HL).

intelligence service, for his lifetime, and that, of course, Blake was hoping to obtain the royalties by doing the very thing that he had promised not to do. Lord Hobhouse, dissenting, asserted the orthodox view that a claim for accounting for profits could be successful only if the defendant had used the employer's proprietary rights (e.g. trade secrets) or commercial information still protected by the duty of confidence or fidelity.

The majority decision demonstrates how an express term of confidentiality can provide an effective supplement to the implied term after the termination of the employment to protect against the use of information that may not strictly speaking be confidential any longer. This express term may be effective even if the contract of employment was terminated by a repudiatory breach committed by the employer.[55] This issue has not been finally determined, however, because, in other contexts, such as restraint-of-trade clauses,[56] the courts have been reluctant to grant injunctions to employers to restrain employees when it was the employer that initially repudiated the contract.

In principle, unlike the duty of loyalty, the duty of confidentiality is mutual, so that it applies also to the employer. Employers collect personal information about workers for many legitimate purposes, such as the payment of taxation, conformity to health and safety regulations and compliance with discrimination laws. In practice, most of the confidential information held by an employer about an employee is protected by the EU General Data Protection Regulation.[57] The implied term requiring the employer to keep personal information about employees confidential may apply, however, outside the protections afforded by the statute. This argument was accepted in principle in pre-trial proceedings, in order to prevent an employer from disclosing information about the names and addresses of employees to a local authority, which had sought the information for the purpose of checking whether or not the employees had paid a local tax.[58]

Lawfulness

The implied term that an employee must obey the orders of the employer is subject to the restriction that the order must be lawful. What happens if an employee refuses to obey an instruction to commit an unlawful act? In many cases, the employer is likely to dismiss the employee for disobedience. Such a dismissal will almost certainly be an unfair dismissal. Where a manager repeatedly instructed a driver to falsify records regarding fuel usage in order to cover up a shortfall and the driver refused to connive in this falsification, the

---

[55] *Campbell* v. *Frisbee* [2002] EWCA Civ 1374, [2003] ICR 141 (CA).
[56] *General Billposting Ltd* v. *Atkinson* [1909] AC 118 (HL).
[57] General Data Protection Regulation, 2016/679 OJ L119, 4 May 2016, p. 1. See Chapter 11.
[58] *Dalgleish* v. *Lothian and Borders Police Board* [1991] IRLR 422 (Court of Session, Outer House).

dismissal of the driver for disobedience was an unfair dismissal; nor could the employer succeed in the argument that the amount of compensation should be reduced for the employee's disobedience on the ground of contributory fault.[59] In principle, it should also be possible for an employee to seek a declaration from a court that the instruction was unlawful and an injunction against issuing such an order,[60] although this expensive and complex course of action will be unrealistic in many situations.

Health and Safety Risks

In the context of health and safety, an important practical question for many workers is whether they can refuse to obey instructions when they perceive a threat to their health and safety. Where the employer issues an instruction that necessarily involves a breach of a specific health and safety regulation, such as a requirement for fencing of machinery or the wearing of protective clothing, the employee should be entitled to disobey the instruction and be protected against retaliation by the law of unfair dismissal. In *Barber* v. *RJB Mining Ltd*,[61] for instance, the employee obtained a declaration that the employer was not entitled to instruct him to work more than forty-eight hours per week in contravention of the Working Time Regulations 1998.

The law of unfair dismissal also protects an employee 'in circumstances of danger which the employee reasonably believed to be serious and imminent', but only if the employee took appropriate steps to protect himself in light of his knowledge and the facilities and advice available to him at the time.[62] Such appropriate steps might include a refusal to work according to instructions. In those circumstances, if the employee is dismissed for disobedience to instructions, the dismissal is automatically unfair.

The employer's general duty of care also places a limit on the scope of lawful instructions. In *Johnstone* v. *Bloomsbury Health Authority*,[63] the Court of Appeal granted a declaration that the employer could not lawfully require junior hospital doctors to work such long hours as would foreseeably damage their health, even though the express terms of the contract permitted the employer to require the doctors to work up to eighty-eight hours per week.

Tax Evasion

A frequent problem that arises in the context of contracts of employment is the use of schemes for tax evasion, such as the payment of workers in cash,

[59] *Morrish* v. *Henlys (Folkestone) Ltd* [1973] ICR 482 (NIRC).
[60] *Hughes* v. *Southwark London Borough Council* [1988] IRLR 56.
[61] [1999] IRLR 308; A. Edwards, 'Barber v. RJB Mining in the Wider Context of Health and Safety' (2000) 29 *Industrial Law Journal* 280.
[62] ERA 1996, s. 100(1)(e).   [63] [1992] QB 333 (CA).

without any formal records or tax being deducted. In these cases, employees are in principle entitled to refuse to participate in tax evasion, but are often reluctant to do so both because they may reasonably fear that they will lose the job and because the proposed scheme may work to their financial benefit as well as saving the employer money. But the risks of participation in tax evasion or some other breach of statute are considerable.

Workers who participate or collaborate with this kind of unlawful conduct risk the possibility that their contracts of employment will be unenforceable on the ground of illegality. Such employees will not even be able to claim arrears of wages. Under the general principles of the law of contract, a contract of employment is unenforceable if it is entered into for an illegal purpose, if it is directly prohibited by statute or if the party seeking to enforce the contract participated knowingly in illegality during performance of the contract. The source of the illegality may be found in legislation or general principles of public policy.

What counts as participation by an employee in a scheme to evade taxes such as to render the contract of employment unenforceable? The test proposed in *Hall* v. *Woolston Hall Leisure Ltd*[64] is whether the employee has actively participated in the illegality, rather than having merely acquiesced to the employer's unlawful conduct. The mere knowledge that an employer is not paying the tax due is not sufficient to render the contract unenforceable by the employee. In this 'shadow economy', workers will normally be aware that they are participating in illegal conduct, but at the same time feel that they have no option but to go along with it in order to keep their jobs. This awareness of the illegality should not in itself prevent the employee from enforcing the contract. But where the employee suggests the scheme of tax evasion, that conduct will render the contract unenforceable.[65] Nevertheless, the contract will be enforceable in the common situation where the employee agrees to self-employed status for the purpose of reducing taxes and the tax authorities accept that status on the basis of the correct information, but then subsequently it is determined by a tribunal that the worker should have been properly classified as an employee for the purpose of employment law.[66]

A more complex issue is whether an employee loses all statutory employment rights, such as claims for unfair dismissal and discrimination, if the contract is potentially unenforceable owing to illegality. It is argued, on the one hand, that, if the contract of employment is unenforceable, the statutory rights which presuppose the existence of a contractual relation should also be unenforceable; but on the other hand, it can be asserted that statutory rights should not depend upon the enforceability of common law claims under the contract of employment and should be enforced subject to any explicit

---

[64] [2001] ICR 99 (CA).   [65] *Salvesen* v. *Simons* [1994] ICR 409 (EAT).

[66] *Enfield Technical Services Ltd* v. *Payne; Grace* v. *BF Components Ltd* [2008] EWCA Civ 393, [2008] ICR 1423.

exclusions within the statutory scheme. In connection with claims for unfair dismissal, this distinction between contractual and statutory rights has not been accepted, and so many employees have had their claims excluded owing to their participation in tax evasion.[67] But the exclusion is not automatic. It depends on the extent of the applicant's knowledge and participation in the tax evasion. A claim was permitted in the case of a cook employed in a Thai restaurant, who spoke little English and who was paid in cash, usually without being given a written pay slip.[68] A statutory claim for unfair dismissal may also be permitted where the legal responsibility to give correct tax returns is imposed primarily on the employer (e.g. VAT), where the employee's participation in the fraudulent scheme was not essential or significant and where the denial of a claim for compensation for unfair dismissal could well discourage the disclosure of the fraud.[69]

In contrast, where the statutory claims are perceived as more analogous to tort, as in the case of claims against discrimination, a court may permit a statutory claim if the court can be persuaded that it is unnecessary for the claimant to rely on the facts constituting illegality in order to bring a claim and that the balance of public policy considerations favours permitting such a claim.[70] Insofar as a balancing test is applied to such cases, however, it will be hard to predict whether the court will regard the public policy that supports collection of taxes for the general welfare as outweighed by the importance of protecting workers against discrimination.

Immigration

Another major source of illegality in relation to contracts of employment is breach of immigration laws. In such cases of 'irregular' migrants, both employer and employee may be committing criminal offences, and of course the migrant risks deportation. Although the wrongdoing may look equivalent between the parties and therefore apparently justify the refusal to enforce any employment rights,[71] in practice employers may select migrant workers who lack the correct paperwork, for they can offer them poor or exploitative terms and conditions that the workers may feel they have little choice but to accept. Many such cases involve labour trafficking and modern slavery. Although the general principles of the law of illegal contracts, as set out above in connection with taxation, are likely to render an irregular migrant's contract of employment and its associated statutory rights unenforceable, it may be possible to

---

[67] E.g. *Newland* v. *Simons & Willer (Hairdressers) Ltd* [1981] ICR 521; *Salvensen* v. *Simons* [1994] ICR 409 (EAT).

[68] *Wheeler* v. *Quality Deep Ltd* [2004] EWCA Civ 1085, [2005] ICR 265 (CA).

[69] *Hewcastle Catering Ltd* v. *Ahmed* [1992] ICR 626 (CA).

[70] *Hall* v. *Woolston Hall Leisure Ltd* [2001] ICR 99 (CA), which seems to be consistent with *Patel* v. *Misra* [2016] UKSC 42, [2017] AC 467.

[71] E.g. *Vacante* v. *Addey and Stanhope School* [2004] EWCA Civ 1065, [2005] ICR 231 (CA).

persuade a court that public policy considerations point in favour of at least the enforcement of some rights that protect vulnerable irregular migrant workers.[72]

In *Hounga* v. *Allen*,[73] the claimant had been trafficked illegally as a minor to perform domestic work. She was exploited and treated extremely poorly by her employer in breach of various statutory rights such as the NMW. Having been denied all her legal claims on the ground that she was an irregular migrant, in the Supreme Court it was successfully argued that at least she should be protected against discrimination. The public policy that requires upholding immigration laws in order to deter irregular migration was thought to be outweighed in this case by the importance of upholding laws against discrimination and especially human trafficking. That argument in favour of protection of the victim's rights may have been assisted by the point that a claim for discrimination is to some extent independent of the contract and rather like a statutory tort.[74] It may also help that discrimination law is derived from EU law, where it is regarded as a fundamental principle that can be directly effective,[75] whereas immigration laws are national arrangements without constitutional status. But other cases have made it clear that ultimately the judicial decision to prevent enforcement of rights under the contract of employment or associated statutory rights is a matter of policy, so that a court must balance the purposes of the legislation that renders the conduct unlawful against the purpose of the protective legislation for workers in that particular context, making sure that the protections are proportionate to the harm.[76] Most labour lawyers would regard the importance of protecting the employment rights of vulnerable workers as normally outweighing the legitimate objectives of laws against irregular migration.[77] If that view is accepted more widely, vulnerable irregular migrants may receive protections against violations of employment rights.

Restraint of Trade

The implied duty of loyalty only lasts during the employment relationship. Afterwards, the employee is in general free to use knowledge and skills acquired during employment in a new job. The common law recognises two

---

[72] C. Costello and M. Freedland (eds.), *Migrants at Work: Immigration and Vulnerability in Labour Law* (Oxford University Press, 2014).

[73] *Hounga* v. *Allen* [2014] UKSC 47, [2014] 1 WLR 2889.

[74] *Leighton* v. *Michael* [1995] ICR 1091 (EAT).

[75] Case C-144/04, *Mangold* v. *Helm* [2005] ECR I-9981 (ECJ); Case C-555/07, *Kücükdeveci* v. *Swedex GmbH & Co. KG* [2010] ECR I-00365 (ECJ).

[76] *Patel* v. *Mirza* [2016] UKSC 42, [2017] AC 467.

[77] C. Costello, 'Migrants and Forced Labour: A Labour Law Response', in A. Bogg, C. Costello, A.C.L. Davies and J. Prassl (eds.), *The Autonomy of Labour Law* (Oxford: Hart, 2015), p. 189.

exceptions to that freedom to use knowledge. First, as we noted above, some information is regarded as confidential, because it was imparted to the employee in confidence, and should not be disclosed to others without the consent of the employer. Second, certain types of information are regarded as proprietary interests of the employer in 'trade secrets'. Examples of trade secrets could be a closely guarded secret chemical formula or a special manufacturing technique. Courts will issue injunctions to restrain the use of trade secrets or the disclosure of confidential information, but otherwise will not prevent employees from setting up in business for themselves or joining a rival employer.

Yet many employers do not regard these protections against unfair competition from former employees as sufficient. They fear that, having taught the employee skills and provided the employee with a network of contacts, the employee will leave and work for a competitor, taking advantage of that experience and knowledge. For example, a solicitor working in a small town who takes on a trainee may be concerned that once fully qualified and experienced the recruit will set up in business in a rival establishment next door and effectively take away the employer's business. Although the former employee cannot use confidential information about clients, he or she can use general skills, know-how and familiarity with the locality and customers to create a rival business. In order to address this concern, many employers include a term in the contract of employment that restricts the right of the former employee to enter into competition subsequent to the termination of the contract of employment. The term creates a covenant not to compete in a particular locality for a period of time.

Such covenants not to compete interfere with former employees' rights to work and to pursue their trade or occupation. In response to these concerns about the impact of such restrictive covenants, the common-law courts developed the restraint-of-trade doctrine that seeks to balance the former employer's interest in protecting itself against competition with the employee's right to work. Under the restraint-of-trade doctrine, a covenant will only be enforceable if it is reasonable as between the parties and in the public interest. In practice, a court is only likely to uphold a non-compete clause if it is aimed at protecting the former employer's client or customer connections against poaching for a limited period of time.[78] A clause that seeks to protect an employer against competition arising simply from general knowledge of the business will be regarded as void for unreasonable restraint of trade. It is also possible that a clause that prohibits an employee from enticing other employees to leave with him or her and set up a rival venture will also be permitted as a reasonable restraint of trade, because an employer has an interest in maintaining a stable trained workforce.[79] It seems likely that such covenants against

[78] *Faccenda Chicken Ltd* v. *Fowler* [1986] ICR 297 (CA).
[79] *Dawnay, Day & Co. Ltd* v. *De Braconier d'Alpen* [1998] ICR 1068 (CA).

poaching of staff will only be upheld in the context of highly skilled, knowledge-based industries, where there is intensive competition for key workers as in, for example, the investment banking sector.

Even where a covenant not to compete is potentially valid because it protects a genuine economic interest of the employer, the courts will scrutinise it to check that it does not interfere with the former employee's right to work to a greater extent than is reasonably necessary. The length of time the covenant lasts and the geographical scope of the restriction are examined closely to determine whether or not the covenant is excessive. If the covenant is too broad, it will be declared void. For example, when some employees left a temporary employment agency to set up their own rival business, the former employer tried to restrain them from contacting that employer's clients and agency workers on the basis of a clause that forbade the former employees of the agency from setting up a rival business within one kilometre of their former office for a period of six months. This clause was held to be invalid and unenforceable because it provided the former employer with more protection than necessary.[80] A different clause that prevented the former employees from contacting clients of the employer for a shorter period of time would, however, have been regarded as reasonable and valid.

The degree of discretion involved in a court's assessment of the reasonableness of a restraint-of-trade clause makes such terms inherently unreliable. Employers have therefore often sought other contractual mechanisms by which to protect themselves against competition from former employees. One such technique is a 'garden leave' clause under which, when a contract of employment is terminated by giving notice, the employee is required to stay at home and not work for another business during the period of notice. Alternatively, the employee may be required to continue to work for the employer throughout the period of notice.[81] If the period of notice is lengthy, this term of the contract, if enforceable by an injunction, has the effect of preventing the employee from engaging in competition.[82] If the employee refuses to work normally during his notice period, as requested by the employer, the employer will not even incur liability to pay wages.[83] Such garden-leave clauses or their equivalent may be challenged by asking a court to decline to issue an injunction to enforce them. When granting injunctions, the court always deploys principles of equitable discretion that occasionally permit exceptions to be made, as in cases of exceptional financial hardship. Furthermore, the considerations that arise with respect to the reasonableness of restraint-of-trade clauses also apply to the exercise of the discretion to issue

---

[80] *Office Angels Ltd* v. *Rainer-Thomas and O'Connor* [1991] IRLR 214 (CA).
[81] *Evening Standard Co. Ltd* v. *Henderson* [1978] ICR 588 (CA).
[82] *Euro Brokers Ltd* v. *Rabey* [1995] IRLR 206; *GFI Group Inc.* v. *Eaglestone* [1994] IRLR 119.
[83] *Sunrise Brokers LLP* v. *Rodgers* [2014] EWCA Civ 1373, [2015] ICR 272.

an injunction.[84] 'A court should be careful not to grant interlocutory relief to enforce a garden leave clause to any greater extent than would be covered by a justifiable covenant in restraint of trade previously entered into by an employee.'[85]

The courts have also recognised one further anomalous restriction on the enforceability of restraint-of-trade clauses in contracts. In *General Billposting Ltd* v. *Atkinson*,[86] the House of Lords refused to enforce what was otherwise a valid non-compete clause against a former employee on the ground that the employer had repudiated the contract by wrongful dismissal. The court was keen to protect the employee's right to work when the employer had unjustifiably summarily dismissed the employee. The principle applied seems to have been that the employer's repudiatory breach of contract meant that no part of the contract, including the restraint, survived the wrongful dismissal. Under English law, however, termination of performance of a contract, whether or not permitted under the contract, does not usually prevent the survival of terms that were clearly intended to regulate the relationship of the parties once performance of the primary obligations has ended.[87] Arbitration clauses, limitation-of-damages clauses, indemnities and vested occupational pension rights clearly fit into this category and should be enforceable. It therefore seems unlikely that a suitably worded restraint will become unenforceable in every case of wrongful dismissal. In a comparable situation concerning the enforcement of a confidentiality clause after an alleged repudiation by the employer, the Court of Appeal hinted strongly that the term would remain enforceable.[88] As Lord Phillips has observed:

> Employees who have been unfairly dismissed are entitled to statutory compensation. It does not seem to me necessarily fair or reasonable that an employer who is held liable to pay such compensation should also be at risk of losing the protection that is reasonably necessary to safeguard his confidential information or goodwill.[89]

The underlying aim of the doctrine of restraint of trade can be understood as an attempt to draw a distinction between, on the one hand, protecting the employee's right to use his human capital (skills, knowledge, know-how) to earn a living and, on the other hand, protecting the assets, advantages and goodwill of the employer's business, which can be regarded as a form of property belonging to the employer that a former employee should not be

---

[84] *Provident Financial Group plc* v. *Hayward* [1989] ICR 160 (CA).
[85] *William Hill Organisation Ltd* v. *Tucker* [1999] ICR 291 (CA), *per* Morritt LJ.
[86] [1909] AC 118 (HL).
[87] S. Honeyball and D. Pearce, 'Contract, Employment and the Contract of Employment' (2006) 35 *Industrial Law Journal* 30, at 39–53; M. Freedland, *The Personal Employment Contract* (Oxford University Press, 2003), pp. 391–2.
[88] *Campbell* v. *Frisbee* [2002] EWCA Civ 1374, [2003] ICR 141 (CA).
[89] *Rock Refrigeration Ltd* v. *Jones* [1997] ICR 938 (CA).

permitted to appropriate for his or her own purposes. But drawing this distinction in practice proves extremely difficult, especially in the service sector of the economy where knowledge of the identity and requirements of the customers of the business is a vital ingredient in the success of the business but at the same time can be regarded as part of the human capital of former employees. In order to promote competition in markets and the dispersal of skills, knowledge and know-how among all businesses, some economic analysis suggests that all restraints on trade should be invalid.[90] Where employers are concerned that, if they train staff and enable them to learn the business, these employees will then leave and set up in competition, they can protect themselves by other means. For instance, the employer can remove the incentive to set up in competition by paying more to reflect the true market value of the services provided by the experienced and knowledgeable employee. This economic analysis may receive some support from the success of software businesses in Silicon Valley in California, where non-compete clauses are generally invalid. It can be suggested that the ability of employees to flit from one company to another without restraint offers the competitive advantage to this region that knowledge can be swiftly disseminated and the human capital of employees can be recombined swiftly in innovative ways.

---

[90] P. H. Rubin and P. Shedd, 'Human Capital and Covenants Not to Compete' (1981) 10 *Journal of Legal Studies* 93.

5

Flexibility and Precarious Work

Contents

Under the general law of contract, employer and employee are bound by the terms of their initial agreement. Unless otherwise provided in the terms of the contract, the law assumes that these terms will last indefinitely until the contract is terminated. In theory, the constancy and rigidity of the legal rights conferred by the contract of employment protect both employer and employee against opportunism and unfair conduct. The employee can, in principle, reject demands for changes made by the employer and instead can insist upon the pay, the hours of work and the type of work laid down in the contract. Equally, the employer can refuse to accept unliteral attempts by employees to avoid aspects of the job or to shorten their hours of work. Despite these benefits provided by the common law of contract, this static legal framework fits uncomfortably with the real needs and expectations of both employer and employee for flexibility and variation in the functioning of this contract in the longer term. In practice, however, the static protection afforded by the contract of employment tends in many instances to prove illusory or at least unenforceable. Having considered briefly why the contract of employment must address employers' need for flexibility, the chapter considers the legal controls over both variations in the wage/work bargain and attempts to devise contracts for the personal performance of work that confer great flexibility for employers but precarious job security for workers.

The Need for Flexibility

To remain a profitable and effective organisation, an employer needs to be able to adapt to changing market conditions and new technologies. Innovation in products and services is often the key to long-term success in business, and these developments may require significant alterations in the type of work performed by employees. New methods of work, often using information technology, may produce vital savings and a more effective service to customers. In times of economic recession, employers will often intensify their search for avenues to reduce labour costs by, for example, cuts in wages, removal of bonuses, closure of pension schemes and reduced working hours. To maintain and improve efficiency and productivity, an employer therefore usually requires various types of flexibility from its employees. Studies of managerial practice often distinguish between three types of flexibility sought by employers: functional, numerical and wage flexibility.[1]

- *Functional flexibility* requires the workforce to operate new technologies, work variable hours, take on new duties, and transfer to new locations. Functional flexibility was a key management strategy for the improvement of productivity in manufacturing in the 1980s and led to attacks on traditional craft demarcations between jobs and an insistence upon workers agreeing to be flexible in the work that they performed. This continuing trend towards task enlargement and intensification of work effort can achieve significant productivity gains for employers.[2]
- *Numerical flexibility* aims to permit the employer to decrease labour costs by reducing the size of the workforce or the number of hours worked in response to changes in demand. The employer may achieve that goal by dismissing some of the workforce, but such dismissals for redundancy tend to be a last resort where the employees have skills and experience. The employer can instead reduce the hours of work by using temporary short-time working or part-time work. Alternatively, the employer may hire skilled and low-skilled workers on a casual or temporary basis, as required.
- *Wage flexibility* varies rates of pay through mechanisms such as bonuses and performance-related pay, in order to reflect market conditions, profitability and levels of productivity. Similarly, by altering the shift system, the

[1] J. Atkinson, 'Flexibility or Fragmentation? The UK Labour Market in the Eighties' (1987) 12 *Labour and Society* 87; L. Hunter, A. McGregor, J. MacInnes and A. Sproul, 'The "Flexible Firm": Strategy and Segmentation' (1993) 31 *British Journal of Industrial Relations* 385.
[2] See T. Elger, 'Task Flexibility and the Intensification of Labour in UK Manufacturing in the 1980s', in A. Pollert (ed.), *Farewell to Flexibility?* (Oxford: Blackwell, 1991).

employer may avoid higher wage costs associated with overtime or night work.

The labour market has always been replete with contractual arrangements that permit employers considerable variety and flexibility. It was only in the first half of the twentieth century that the model of the full-time indefinite contract of employment performed in a separate workplace became the dominant practice. This prevalence coincided with an industrialised economy, using mass production techniques. Now, with the relative importance of the service sector in the UK economy, combined with pressures from increasing global competition in markets, that dominant model of the full-time, contract of indefinite duration has declined. Only about half of workers have a full-time permanent contract of employment. Employers have sought flexibility in their contracts for the supply of labour by reference to hours, location, payment systems, legal incidents of the relation and so forth. A particular worker may fall outside the standard model of indefinite full-time employment in several respects: by working part time, working at home, being paid for tasks completed rather than regular hours or working on a freelance basis. While it is true that sometimes these alternatives to full-time employment suit the needs of workers by permitting them to care for dependants by working part time or by permitting students to take temporary jobs in their vacations, most people take non-standard jobs because they are the only type of work available.[3] Workers with poor skills, training and experience, or those who often suffer from adverse discrimination in the labour market, may have little option but to take short-term jobs, part-time work or temporary work through an agency.

In Chapter 6, we examine the legal consequences for workers who accept non-standard jobs that may not even amount to contracts of employment. In this chapter the focus is on, first, the legal consequences of the kind of dynamic flexibility that can be obtained by the employer's power to change the terms of the contract of employment or the content of the job. The key question is to what extent can and should the law try to protect employees from unwelcome changes to their contracts or their jobs. The second part of the chapter considers the regulation of employers' strategies for achieving numerical flexibility by offering various kinds of precarious work packages such as casual work and temporary, fixed-term contracts. Here the key question is to what extent legal regulation should prevent the use of precarious work packages that provide employees with intermittent wages and tenuous job security. Consideration of the important topic of dismissals for economic reasons, which may also be motivated by the need for flexibility, is reserved for a separate chapter.[4] Chapter 10 provides an examination of the statutory measures that address an

---

[3] B. Burchell, S. Deakin and S. Honey, *The Employment Status of Individuals in Non-Standard Employment* (London: DTI, Employment Relations Research Series No. 6, URN/99/770, 1999), para. 7.5.

[4] See Chapter 20.

employee's need for flexibility as a contribution to an acceptable work/life balance.

Unilateral Variation of Terms

From a legal perspective, a crucial distinction between the different types of flexibility sought by management concerns the question of whether the proposed measure requires alterations in the terms of the contract of employment. The general contractual principle is that the parties are entitled to insist upon their original agreement made at the formation of a contract of employment until such time as, by agreement, the parties substitute a new contract or vary the terms of the contract for consideration. An employer cannot simply vary the terms of employment unilaterally, no matter how much notice is given. In contrast, if the change does not require any alteration in the terms of the contract, as for example where the contract confers a discretionary power on the employer to make the change in the job or the remuneration, an employee must rely upon implied terms or statute for protection.

Faced with an employer's announcement of a unilateral variation such as a wage cut or an increase in hours of work, an employee is entitled to treat it as a serious breach of contract. An employee then has a choice: the employee may disregard the proposed variation, protest against the change and affirm and enforce the existing contract; or the employee may resign and claim compensation for dismissal.

Enforcement of the Contract

If an employee continues to work normally despite a unilateral variation of the contract by the employer, there is a risk that this behaviour may be regarded as acceptance by conduct of the new terms offered by the employer. To avoid that risk, the employee needs to make it clear that he or she continues to work normally only under protest and still expects the employer to honour the original agreement. To clarify the legal position, the employee may seek a judicial declaration that the original agreement is still binding,[5] and also claim any shortfall in wages or other benefits resulting from the unilateral variation by the employer. The House of Lords confirmed these principles in *Rigby v. Ferodo Ltd.*[6] The plaintiff was a lathe operator who had worked for the employer for twenty years, giving him a statutory entitlement to twelve weeks' notice of dismissal. Owing to severe financial pressures on the business, the employer decided that it had no option but to reduce wages by 5 per cent in order to remain in business. The management sought to reach agreement with the unions for this reduction, but the plaintiff's union made no agreement

[5] E.g. *Burdett Coutts* v. *Hertfordshire County Council* [1984] IRLR 92 (HC).
[6] [1988] ICR 29 (HL).

other than to refrain from strike action. The employer then imposed the wage reduction on the workforce. The plaintiff continued to work, but by his conduct indicated that he did not accept the reduction in wages. After more than a year, the plaintiff successfully claimed the difference in wages on the basis of a breach of contract. The employer's reduction of wages was a fundamental breach of contract, but this action would not bring the contract to an end unless the employee had accepted the repudiation of the contract. Nor had the employer terminated the contract by notice. Nor indeed had the employee accepted any variation of the contract by his conduct, because he had clearly objected to the variation. The contract had persisted on its original terms, but the employer had withheld part of the wages. That shortfall of wages could be claimed. The same principles based upon the general law of contract should apply to any other kind of unilateral variation by the employer, such as changes to the hours of work or the location of work. It is much harder, however, for an employee to avoid the trap of appearing to acquiesce in the change when the variation consists in a change of duties, for as soon as the employee performs new duties, albeit under protest, that conduct appears to amount to an acceptance of the variation.[7]

In response to unilateral wage cuts and other imposed variations, a worker can bring an ordinary common law claim for breach of contract and compensation. In the case of wage cuts, there is also the possibility of using the relatively straightforward statutory protection against deductions from wages in ERA 1996, section 13.[8] This measure provides a simplified mechanism through an ET to claim missing wages. Unless the employer negotiates a new written contract of employment containing the wage reduction, the payment of a lesser sum will be regarded as a 'deduction' from wages that the employee can recover. For example, in Bruce v. Wiggins Teape (Stationery) Ltd,[9] employees successfully challenged the employer's unilateral withdrawal of a shift bonus as a deduction from wages.

Where a wage cut results from a reduction of the number of normal working days, there may be no 'deduction' because the employee is not entitled under the contract to full payment in the event of a three- or four-day week. An employee may claim some of the shortfall by claiming a statutory guarantee payment from the employer.[10] A guarantee payment consists of minimum remuneration during days of lay-off. The entitlement is, however, extremely meagre, for it applies only to a maximum of five workless days in a period of three months,[11] and the maximum payment in respect of any one day is £23.50, a figure which is well below the minimum wage. The employer may be able to avoid paying guarantee pay entirely by

---

[7] R. White, 'Working under Protest and Variation of Employment Terms' (2008) 37 *Industrial Law Journal* 365.
[8] See Chapter 7.   [9] [1994] IRLR 536 (EAT).   [10] ERA 1996, s. 28.
[11] ERA 1996, s. 31(2) and (3).

negotiating a contract that has no fixed hours, such as casual work by the day as required.[12]

Claim for Unfair Dismissal

A refusal by an employee to agree to a wage cut, increased hours and other proposed changes to the terms of the contract of employment may lead eventually to a termination of the contract. The employer may dismiss the employee for a refusal to agree to the new contract. Alternatively, the employee may resign rather than put up with the changes. In either case, the employee may be able to bring a claim for compensation for unfair dismissal.[13] By insisting on a unilateral variation of the contract, the employer has committed a significant breach of contract. Yet the employee's prospects for a successful claim are slim.

For claims for unfair dismissal in these circumstances, there are two crucial questions that must be considered by the tribunal. The first is whether the employer has established a 'substantial reason of a kind such as to justify the dismissal of an employee holding the position which the employee held'.[14] Since the employer cannot rely upon the normal reasons for dismissal that relate to the personal conduct of the employee such as lack of capability or misconduct, the employer must point to the business need for the variation in the contract combined with the employee's refusal to accept the variation. This combination was accepted in *Hollister* v. *National Farmers' Union*[15] as sufficient to count as a substantial reason for dismissal. The applicant was dismissed when he had refused to accept a new contract of employment, which offered improved remuneration in some respects but less advantageous pension arrangements. Lord Denning MR held that, provided the employer had a sound, good business reason for the reorganisation and variation, an employee's refusal to agree to the variation could amount to a substantial reason for dismissal. He rejected the view that the business reason for the variation must satisfy a test of necessity in the sense that, without the change, the business would fail or be brought to a standstill.

The second issue that must be addressed in a claim for unfair dismissal is whether it was reasonable for the employer to dismiss the employee for this substantial reason in all the circumstances.[16] The issue here is not whether it was reasonable for the employee to object to the change in the terms of the contract, but rather whether it was reasonable for the employer to insist on the change even to the extent of dismissing the employee. For instance, in *Richmond Precision Engineering Ltd* v. *Pearce*,[17] following the sale of a business and its relocation to the purchaser's premises, an employee was offered a

---

[12] E.g. *Mailway (Southern) Ltd* v. *Willsher* [1978] ICR 511 (EAT).   [13] See Chapter 19.
[14] ERA 1996, s. 98(1).   [15] [1979] ICR 542 (CA).   [16] ERA 1996, s. 98(4).
[17] [1985] IRLR 179 (EAT).

new contract of employment on the same terms as those enjoyed by the existing employees of the purchasing company. The employee rejected the offer on the grounds that it involved a slight reduction in his rate of pay, an increase in hours, a reduction in annual holiday entitlement and loss of an occupational pension scheme and other fringe benefits. The EAT stressed that the mere fact that the employee would be worse off under the new contract was not a sufficient reason for a finding of unfairness. Where the employer had good reasons for making the variation, as in this case when the employer sought to harmonise the terms and conditions of all employees, a reasonable employer could insist upon the change and fairly dismiss employees who rejected the variation. The tribunals have indicated that, as part of the test of reasonableness, a balance should be struck between the employer's reasons for the variation against the degree of detriment to the employee.[18] But this balance seems strongly tilted in favour of the employer, because the employer is unlikely to be insisting on a change in the terms of the contract to the extent of dismissing an employee without a good business reason, and that purpose will almost invariably outweigh the employee's concern about personal detriment. This weighting in favour of the employer is evident in the observation of Balcombe J that:

> It may be perfectly reasonable for an employee to decline to work extra overtime, having regard to his family commitments. Yet, from the employment point of view, having regard to his business commitments, it may be perfectly reasonable to require an employee to work overtime.[19]

Notice how, in the reference to overtime, in this balancing exercise, the courts place little weight on the employee's interest in preserving an acceptable work/life balance.

In principle, we have seen that an employee can reject an employer's unilateral variation of the terms of the contract of employment. In practice, however, the employer can insist upon the change by threatening to dismiss the employee fairly unless he or she accedes to the variation. The terms of the contract of employment therefore provide scant protection against demands from the employer for flexibility on the part of the workforce. In a case concerning an employee who had resigned in the face of the employer's proposals for a pay cut, longer working hours and additional duties, the policy aim of the courts was candidly summed up by Watkins LJ:

> The obdurate refusal of the employee to accept conditions very properly and sensibly being sought to be imposed upon her was unreasonable. Employers must not, in my opinion, be put in a position where, through wrongful refusal of their employees to accept change, they are prevented from introducing

---

[18] *St John of God (Care Services) Ltd* v. *Brooks* [1992] ICR 715 (EAT); *Chubb Fire Security Ltd* v. *Harper* [1983] IRLR 311 (EAT); *Catamaran Cruisers Ltd* v. *Williams* [1994] IRLR 384 (EAT).
[19] *Chubb Fire Security Ltd* v. *Harper* [1983] IRLR 311, at 313 (EAT).

improved business methods in furtherance of seeking success for their enterprise.[20]

In short, the predominant view of the courts is that it is unreasonable for employees to expect the law to uphold their terms of employment if the employer has a sound business reason for changing them. By a sleight of hand, an employer's repudiatory breach of contract becomes a substantial reason for a fair dismissal.

Variation by Collective Agreement

If the employer recognises a trade union and a collective agreement determines the content of the terms and conditions of individual contracts of employment,[21] the employer will almost certainly have to attempt to vary contracts of employment through negotiations with the union. If the employer simply terminates the collective agreement without agreeing a variation with the union, the existing collective agreement should continue to provide the terms of employment until such time as individual employees consent to a variation.[22] In many countries, the law ensures that revised collective agreements are always effective to achieve variations, so that 'concession bargaining', as it is sometimes called, will automatically vary the terms of individual contracts of employment, whether or not individual workers approve of the change. In the UK, however, there is no legally binding process of automatic variation. Instead, the effect of variations in collective agreements that have been expressly incorporated into contracts of employment depends upon the precise terms of the incorporation as set out in the contract of employment. In order to achieve automatic incorporation and variation, it is vital that the way in which the collective agreement is incorporated into the contract of employment overcomes the basic principle of the common law that the individual employee must always consent to a variation of the terms of the contract of employment.

If the contract of employment incorporates the relevant collective agreement in terms which expressly envisage that any alterations in the collective agreement will automatically vary the terms of the contract of employment, the variation of the collective agreement should be effective to vary the terms of the contract of employment. Here is an example of an effective clause, which in this instance appears to create an agency relation between the union and individual employees:

> The Company recognises the [Union] as having sole Bargaining rights for you under this Contract of Employment. [The Union] is your agent and is empowered to negotiate variations to your terms and conditions of employment

---

[20] *Woods* v. *WM Car Services (Peterborough) Ltd* [1982] ICR 693 (CA).   [21] See Chapter 3.
[22] *Robertson* v. *British Gas Corporation* [1983] ICR 351 (CA).

(including diminution of terms and conditions) on your behalf ... The instrument through which the Company and [Union] establish all your terms and conditions of employment is the Collective Agreement ... This Collective Agreement is hereby expressly and specifically incorporated into your Contract of Employment ... If the Collective Agreement ... is at any time replaced by a subsequent Collective Agreement between the Company and the [Union] your terms and conditions of employment shall be determined under that subsequent Agreement.[23]

But it is unnecessary to create an agency relationship in order to achieve automatic variations. It should be sufficient for the contract of employment to make it clear that the terms and conditions are determined by the relevant collective agreement for the time being whenever it is renegotiated and replaced.[24]

In the absence of an express automatic variation clause in the contract of employment, a revised collective agreement may only affect the terms of the contract of employment if either the individual employee consented, either expressly or by implication, to the change personally or if it can be held that the revised collective agreement became incorporated into the contract of employment by means of an implied term.

In practice, consent by employees to variations in the terms of the contract of employment created by collective agreements is usually inferred from the conduct of an employee in continuing to work normally after a pay increase or variation of hours or duties. If the employee protests against the change, however, a refusal to accept the variation negotiated by the union prevents the employer from implementing it unilaterally. This legal position protects the employee against the union representatives negotiating unwelcome variations in the terms of employment, but it also undermines attempts by unions and management to engage in concession bargaining or productivity agreements because, in the absence of automatic incorporation of variations, individual employees are entitled to reject the outcome, or part of the outcome, of such collective agreements. In *Lee* v. *GEC Plessey Telecommunications Ltd*,[25] a collective agreement awarded a pay increase but also withdrew a generous severance or redundancy scheme, leaving any new scheme to be devised by further collective agreement. The employee obtained a declaration that the terms of the earlier agreement regarding a severance payment remained in force in the contract of employment. The result might have been different if the employer had bargained in the collective agreement for a provision that withdrawal of the severance-pay scheme was a condition of the pay increase,

---

[23] W. Brown, S. Deakin, M. Hudson, C. Pratten and P. Ryan, *The Individualisation of Employment Contracts in Britain* (London: DTI, Employment Relations Research Series No. 4, 1998), p. 47.
[24] E.g. *Alemo-Herron* v. *Parkwood Leisure Limited* [2011] UKSC 26, [2011] ICR 920.
[25] [1993] IRLR 383 (QB).

so that the employee could not have accepted the pay increase without by implication also accepting the abolition of the redundancy scheme.

An alternative argument for holding an employee to terms created by a revised collective agreement is to argue that the terms of an applicable collective agreement have become an implied term of contracts of employment in that workplace. A court may be able to infer that the employer and employee intended that the collective agreement should be automatically applicable because presumed incorporation had been the long-standing practice and expectation in a particular workplace. In *Henry* v. *London General Transport Services Ltd*,[26] a trade union had negotiated with prospective owners of the business (a management buy-out by share transfer) a collective agreement that would impose reduced pay and less favourable conditions on its members. While the vast majority of employees signed statements agreeing to changed terms and conditions, a minority of the workforce, including the sixty-one applicants in this case, wrote to the employer saying that they would continue to work only under protest about the new terms. Their legal claims were for unlawful deductions from wages contrary to ERA 1996, section 13.[27] Even though there was no express incorporation clause in the contracts of employment, the Court of Appeal remitted the case to a tribunal for failure to consider the possibility that the collective agreement might have been incorporated without individual consent as a result of a well-established custom in the workplace. This case demonstrates that concession bargaining may be effective to change the terms of employment, even in the absence of a provision in the contract of employment for automatic incorporation of the terms negotiated from time to time in collective agreements, provided that there is a well-established customary practice evidencing an intention that the collective agreement should determine terms and conditions of employment at a particular workplace.

Changing the Job

Without altering the terms of employment, however, the employer may be able to achieve considerable flexibility. One technique is to avoid much detail in the terms about the description of the work to be performed, the hours of work and other important conditions, leaving these matters to be determined by managerial discretion or the promulgation of works rules and staff handbooks to which the employee must conform under the general implied obligation of obedience. Provided the variation in the job falls within the powers of the employer conferred by the contract, the fact that it has adverse consequences for the employee in terms of pay or hours will not provide the basis for a claim for breach of contract. In *Hussman Manufacturing Ltd* v. *Weir*,[28] the employer exercised a power under the contract of employment to change

---

[26] [2002] EWCA Civ 488, [2002] ICR 910 (CA).   [27] See Chapter 7.
[28] [1998] IRLR 288 (EAT).

the shift system, with the consequence that the claimant was transferred to a shift that attracted a lower rate of pay. The EAT rejected the argument that the reduction in pay amounted to a deduction contrary to ERA 1996, section 13, because the wages, although lower, were those properly payable for the shift to which the employee had been transferred. There was therefore no unauthorised deduction from wages in this case of unilateral wage reduction because the contract indirectly conferred this power on the employer.

By describing a job in the contract in general terms, employers can insist upon the introduction of new working methods and technologies without breaching the terms of the contract. For example, in *Cresswell v. Board of Inland Revenue*,[29] in place of the traditional methods of paper files and writing on documents used by tax officers, the employer proposed to introduce a computerised system for records, for the calculation of taxes owed and for sending out letters. The employees refused to co-operate with the introduction of the new technology in the absence of a guarantee that its introduction would not result in redundancies. The employers declined to give such a guarantee or to pay the employees unless they used the new technology. The employees brought a test case seeking a declaration that the Revenue was in breach of contract. The terms of the contracts of employment did not specify the work to be performed except in the general terms of an obligation to perform the general duties appropriate to the particular grade of tax officer. The employees argued that the changes in working methods amounted to a change in the nature of the job, which necessarily involved a wholly new contract. The declaration was refused on the ground that the direction to adopt the new technology was not a breach of contract. On the contrary, Walton J suggested that an employee 'is expected to adapt himself to new methods and techniques introduced in the course of his employment' though 'in a proper case the employer must provide any necessary training or re-training'. The jobs were defined in the contracts as 'clerical assistants' and the role of the staff would remain the same, namely, keeping records, albeit now on a computer instead of paper files. This decision, like many others, confirms that courts view the contract of employment as containing a broad residual discretion for management to direct the workforce to undertake new working methods subject only to express limits in the contract.

Nevertheless, it may be possible to discover further constraints upon managerial discretion derived from implied terms of the contract of employment. These may be terms to be implied in fact, on the basis of the presumed agreement between the parties based upon their joint intentions. In *Cresswell v. Board of Inland Revenue*, the court found such an implied term, namely, the duty of the employer to provide instruction in how to use the new computers. To establish such an implied term, the court must be persuaded that it

---

[29] [1984] ICR 508 (QB).

conforms to the joint intentions of the parties and satisfies a test of business necessity. In *Jones* v. *Associated Tunnelling Co. Ltd*,[30] the EAT agreed with the employee that there must be a term implied into the contract that fixed his place of work, thereby placing a limit on employer's apparent contractual power to direct him to other distant locations, but agreed with the employer's contention that, at the very least, the joint intention of the parties was to permit the employer to move Mr Jones to other collieries within reasonable daily reach of his home.

As well as terms implied in fact on the basis of the presumed intentions of the parties, it is also possible, as we have seen, to invoke the implied term of mutual trust and confidence as a ground for restricting the employer's exercise of a discretionary power conferred by the contract.[31] Recall, for instance, how the employer in *French* v. *Barclays Bank plc*[32] was entitled in principle to vary or eliminate a discretionary low-cost mortgage scheme for employees, because it was not a contractual entitlement but merely a policy stated in the staff handbook. In withdrawing the scheme peremptorily without reasonable notice, thereby causing the employee considerable loss, the employer was held to have broken the implied term to refrain from conduct which would be likely to destroy mutual trust and confidence.

Flexibility and Variation Clauses

Instead of relying upon the general residual discretionary power to direct labour contained in the contract of employment, the employer may alternatively bargain more explicitly for a contractual obligation to be flexible. The contract of employment may contain a 'flexibility clause' that gives the employer the express contractual right to vary the content of the job unilaterally. Such terms became increasingly common in contracts of employment during the 1980s and 1990s. These flexibility clauses may provide that the employer has the right to vary job duties, the place of work, the hours of work and the allocation of shifts, and to require overtime without receiving higher rates of pay. Here is an example of such a sweeping flexibility clause:[33]

> During your employment with the Company, you will be required to co-operate in the development of new working arrangements as necessary, including participating in training in order to improve both individual skills and the profitability of the Company. This will include being flexible in regard to the duties undertaken and mobile within the Company's establishment in which you are employed.

---

[30] [1981] IRLR 477 (EAT).   [31] See Chapter 4.   [32] [1998] IRLR 646 (CA).
[33] W. Brown, S. Deakin, M. Hudson, C. Pratten and P. Ryan, *The Individualisation of Employment Contracts in Britain* (London: DTI, Employment Relations Research Series No. 4, 1998), pp. 45–6.

In *Haden Ltd* v. *Cowen*,[34] the contract contained a clause that required the employee to 'undertake . . . any and all duties which reasonably fall within the scope of his capabilities'. The Court of Appeal interpreted that clause narrowly, however, by denying that it entitled the employer to require the employee to change his role from divisional contracts surveyor to the more junior position of a quantity surveyor even though he had the capability to perform the other work. The flexibility clause was restricted by its context in the contract under the heading of 'job title', which stated that the position was for a divisional contracts surveyor.

As well as a flexibility clause, a contract of employment may include a term that permits the employer to vary the terms of the contract unilaterally:

> The Company may make reasonable additions and/or changes to any of your terms of employment from time to time. Such addition and/or changes may be made by way of a general notice applicable to all employees or by way of specific notice to you.[35]

> It may, at some future date, be necessary to add to, delete or change any general condition of employment; if so, due notice will be given of such changes by announcements on company notice boards or by individual notice to the employee.[36]

It is worth reconsidering the specimen contract set out in Chapter 4,[37] to identify all the various flexibility clauses there, which include applications to hours and duties of the job (paragraph 6.7) and place of work (paragraph 4.2). The contract culminates in the final term (clause 16.2) that provides the employer with an apparent power to vary any term of the contract unilaterally for business reasons. Such sweeping provisions appear to grant the employer a discretionary power to vary the content of the job and to rewrite the terms of the contract at will. Even the ostensible guarantee of a minimum weekly amount of pay is effectively contradicted by clause 7.2 that permits lay-offs without pay and shorter hours with lower remuneration. These flexibility clauses and unilateral variation clauses apparently remove any vestige of legal protection that the contract affords to employees against adverse changes in their terms of employment. Provided the employer notifies employees of the proposed variation in the terms of employment, a sufficiently broad unilateral variation clause should be effective to alter the terms of employment and avoid any breach of contract by the employer.

Nevertheless, the employer will have to operate the discretionary powers conferred by flexibility clauses and variation clauses within some loose legal constraints. When interpreting the contract of employment, a court is likely to

---

[34] [1983] ICR 1 (CA).

[35] This term appeared in the relevant contracts of employment that were the subject of litigation in the High Court in *Malone* v. *British Airways* [2011] IRLR 32 (CA).

[36] Another term of the contract in *Haden Ltd* v. *Cowen* [1983] ICR 1 (CA).　　　[37] See p. 111.

insist that a sweeping flexibility clause or variation clause must clearly indicate the scope of the powers it confers on the employer. In the absence of such transparency, the scope of the clause should be construed narrowly. As well as making this point about transparency in *Wandsworth London Borough Council* v. *D'Silva*,[38] Lord Woolf also invoked the general principle of interpretation of terms of contracts that the more unreasonable the result of a proposed interpretation, the less likely it is that the parties to the contract intended it. Lord Woolf also observed that a 'court is unlikely to favour an interpretation which does more than enable a party to vary contractual provisions with which that party is required to comply'. In other words, if the flexibility clause is ambiguous about the extent of the changes that it permits, a court is more likely to interpret it as enabling the employer to vary its own obligations than to impose additional or more onerous duties on employees. This remark was made in the context of an employer's revision of the rules governing the procedures for the award of sickness benefit and the period before long-term sickness might trigger a dismissal procedure. The employer was permitted to make the variation on the ground that the procedure was part of the staff handbook rather than a term of the contract, but, even if it were a term, a suitably worded flexibility clause could have conferred the right to impose a variation. It is unclear whether Lord Woolf also had in mind a variation of the employer's principal obligation under the contract of employment to pay wages.

That issue arose in *Bateman* v. *ASDA Stores Ltd.*[39] The employer wanted to put all staff on the same pay scales and terms and conditions known as 'Top Rate'. About 16,000 employees under an older scheme were required to accept the new pay scales. While 9,330 employees agreed, the remainder did not, including the claimants, who argued that the variation in the pay scheme was detrimental and unacceptable. They brought claims for declaratory relief and under ERA 1996 section 13 for deductions from wages resulting from the application of the new pay scale. The company's rule-book (the 'Colleague Handbook') stated that ASDA 'reserved the right to review, revise, amend or replace the contents of this handbook, and introduce new policies from time to time reflecting the changing needs of the business'. The handbook also provided details of pay and other conditions of employment. The company argued successfully that the clause in the handbook that permitted the company to replace the contents of the handbook was a term of the contract of employment that entitled the company to revise and replace the pay scales. The EAT concluded that the clause was wide enough and sufficiently transparent or unambiguous for the company to be entitled to introduce these changes to wages without the further consent of the workforce.

One further principle of interpretation may be applicable to flexibility and variation clauses. In many instances, the discretion conferred on the employer

---

[38] [1998] IRLR 193 (CA).   [39] [2010] IRLR 370 (EAT).

is stated to be conferred for a particular purpose. In the *Bateman* v. *ASDA* case, the power of variation refers to changes that reflect the 'changing needs of the business'. In the specimen contract, the variation is linked to 'operational, commercial or financial reasons according to the needs of the business'. A court is likely to regard such phrases as placing limits on the discretionary power. If challenged, an employer would need to be able to demonstrate that the power to vary the contract had been used for the purpose specified in the term, such as 'changing needs of the business'. While it is true that such phrases are often broadly drawn, it may sometimes be possible for employees to argue that the proposed variation is not being introduced for the purpose of responding to a changing need of the business or similar limiting clause, but that it has some other inappropriate purpose.

As well as confining the scope of flexibility clauses by techniques of interpretation, the courts may also insert an implied term that creates limits on the discretion conferred on the employer. Here, the implied term of mutual trust and confidence provides the underlying principle for placing constraints on the exercise of managerial power. In *United Bank Ltd* v. *Akhtar*,[40] a junior employee working in a branch of the bank was subject to an express mobility clause that enabled the bank to transfer employees to other branches. The bank purported to transfer the employee from Leeds to Birmingham on a few days' notice; and it failed to respond to his requests for the transfer to be postponed so that he could move house or for information about any assistance that the bank might be able to give him in moving. The employee succeeded in a claim for unfair dismissal by establishing that the bank had committed a repudiatory breach of contract. The employer had broken an implied term that it would give reasonable notice of transfers and an implied term that the discretion would not be exercised in such a way as to render it impossible for the employee to comply with the contractual obligation to move. These implied obligations were founded ultimately on the employer's duty not to destroy the trust and confidence on which the employment relation is based.

In *Bateman* v. *ASDA*, prior to making the change in the pay scales to 'Top Rate', the company had consulted widely with the workforce. This process of consultation and of giving notice seems to have been regarded by the ET as sufficient to comply with the employer's obligation under the implied term of mutual trust and confidence or the version of the implied term that prohibits arbitrary, capricious or irrational conduct with respect to remuneration. The outcome of the case was, therefore, that the employer had the legal right unilaterally to vary the payment system (and other terms contained in the handbook) simply by inserting this revise-and-replace clause in the terms of the contract. Provided the term was clear enough about the powers it

---

[40] [1989] IRLR 507 (EAT).

conferred on the employer, it would be effective to justify the imposition of changes in terms and conditions subject only to procedural requirements of consultation and a test of whether the employer's aim was rational.

We should note finally that to use an implied term to restrict the scope of an express term may run up against the principle that implied terms cannot be used to contradict express terms of the contract. If the flexibility clause is sufficiently explicit, it will be hard to read into it some implied condition. For example, if the mobility clause states that employees can be instructed to move their place of work without notice, it will probably be impossible to insert an implied term requiring reasonable notice of a transfer. This problem of using implied terms to override express terms was addressed in different ways in *Johnstone* v. *Bloomsbury Health Authority*.[41] A hospital doctor was employed under a contract which provided for a standard forty-hour week, but also required the doctor to be available on call for, on average, an additional forty-eight hours per week. The doctor claimed that the employer's requirement for long hours was damaging his health, and he sought (1) a declaration that the employer could not lawfully require such long hours as would foreseeably damage his health, and (2) damages for breach of contract. The employing hospital moved to strike out the action, so for the purpose of the hearing the court assumed that the doctor had established that his long hours of work were causing damage to his health. A majority of the Court of Appeal awarded the declaration in the terms sought. The difficulty confronting the court was that there was an apparent contradiction between, on the one hand, the proposed implied term that the employer should take reasonable care of the health and safety of the employee and, on the other, the express term that gave the hospital the right to require up to forty-eight hours of overtime per week on average. Stuart Smith LJ insisted, however, that, as the implied term was one implied by law, rather than one implied in fact, the court must interpret the contract in a manner that reconciled the two obligations. Here, the employer could require the forty-eight hours of overtime work, but only if that could be done in a manner consistent with the employer's duty of care. In particular, if the employer was aware or should have been aware that the long hours were damaging the doctor's health, the employer should not insist on the maximum hours of work. Browne-Wilkinson VC interpreted the clause regarding overtime not as conferring an entitlement on the employer to forty-eight hours of overtime, but merely a power to ask for that amount. That power or discretion had to be exercised in accordance with implied terms in the contract, including the duty to take reasonable care of the health and safety of employees. Leggatt LJ, dissenting, insisted that the implied term could not be used to restrict the hospital's express contractual entitlement to overtime, to which the junior doctor had agreed: 'Those who cannot stand the heat should stay out of

---

[41] [1992] QB 333 (CA).

the kitchen.' All the members of the court agreed, however, that, if the contract had been interpreted to include a term that excluded the employer's liability to take reasonable care of the health and safety of employees, such an express term of the contract would be invalid by virtue of section 2(1) of the Unfair Contract Terms Act 1977, which prohibits terms that exclude liability for negligently causing personal injuries.

The differences between these judgments may be crucial in determining the extent to which an employer's power to govern the workplace can be achieved through flexibility clauses. On the view of Stuart Smith LJ, no matter how specific the power to direct labour conferred by a flexibility clause, the exercise of the power is always subject to implied limitations based upon the implied terms inserted into contracts of employment by the common law. On the view of Browne-Wilkinson VC, the employer's rights under a flexibility clause of this type can be limited by conflicting implied legal duties placed upon the employer only when the terms confer a discretion or option upon the employer, not when the terms give the employer a right and the employee a correlative obligation. The difference between these approaches may, however, be less significant in the context of most flexibility clauses, for the terms usually describe the power to redirect labour as conferring a discretion upon the employer.

Temporary and Casual Employment

At the beginning of this chapter we noted that employers often need some degree of flexibility with regard to the number of staff they employ (numerical flexibility). In the UK, about 6 per cent of employees work under temporary contracts. Although some workers may seek temporary employment, about 30 per cent of those in temporary work would prefer a permanent job.[42] Seasonal factors may dictate peaks of demand for labour followed by relatively quiet periods. These fluctuations may be found, for instance, in hotels in seaside resorts, farms and producers of Christmas decorations. For other jobs, an employer's need for staff may vary not only by the season but also by the day. A hotel may earn most of its income from hosting business conferences, banquets and big social events such as weddings. The hotel's need for catering staff will fluctuate considerably according to the bookings. It is common in the hospitality sector of the economy for employers to offer casual work, calling on staff to work as and when required. Similarly, dock-workers will only be required when a ship is berthed, so their work may only be intermittent.

One way to achieve flexibility in the numbers of staff employed is for an employer simply to hire workers when they are needed and then dismiss them when the demand diminishes. In the nineteenth century, industrial workers

---

[42] Office for National Statistics 'Full-time, part-time and temporary workers', Table EMP01 (2018).

were frequently employed by the day, the hour or even the minute.[43] Today, the statutory minimum notice period of a week's notice usually prevents such extreme flexibility in hiring and firing.[44] Instead, the preferred way in which to achieve numerical flexibility is to hire workers on short fixed-term contracts rather than contracts of indefinite duration. On the expiration of those fixed-term contracts, at common law an employee has no claim for wrongful dismissal because in effect the contract has been terminated by notice given at the commencement of the contract. In many instances the use of fixed-term contracts may be justified, as for example where an external body has granted funds for a limited period to employ someone to perform a particular task or there is a need to fill a temporary vacancy caused by maternity leave. There is clearly a danger, however, that fixed-term contracts may be disguised permanent employment, although constituted in a legal form that seeks to avoid or minimise protections for job security and compensation for dismissal. To prevent this misuse of fixed-term contracts, the statutory definition of dismissal deems the termination of such 'limited-term' contracts to count as a dismissal for the purposes of claims for unfair dismissal or redundancy (but not the common law).[45] With regard to the statutory entitlement to a minimum notice period, in principle fixed-term employees should receive the same entitlement as those with contracts of an indefinite duration in order to avoid discrimination against them.[46] In practice, however, provided an employer gives notice of a date of termination of the fixed-term contract at the commencement of the contract, that process satisfies the statutory minimum entitlement, no further notice period of wages should be required. With respect to claims for dismissal on termination of limited-term contracts, an EU Directive against discrimination in employment conditions between permanent and fixed-term employees extends to compensation for dismissal.[47] Compensation must be the same unless the difference in compensation can be justified in accordance with a test of proportionality on 'objective grounds.'[48]

Another common method by which employers can handle fluctuations in their demand for labour is to use agency workers. Under this arrangement, the

---

[43] N. Countouris, 'The Contract of Employment as an Expression of Continuing Obligations' in M. Freedland (gen. ed.), *The Contract of Employment* (Oxford University Press, 2016), pp. 362, 367.

[44] ERA 1996, s. 86; see Chapter 18.

[45] ERA 1996, ss. 95(1)(b), 136(1)(b) and 235(2A) and (2B); see Chapter 19. D. Cabrelli, 'Duration, Lawful Termination, and Frustration of the Employment Contract' in M. Freedland (gen. ed.), *The Contract of Employment* (Oxford University Press, 2016), pp. 515, 533.

[46] Fixed-Term Employees (Prevention of Less Favourable Treatment) Regulations 2002, SI 2002 No. 2024.

[47] The UK Regulations only refer to terms of the contract (Fixed Term Employees (Prevention of Less Favourable Treatment) Regulations 2002, reg. 3), but the laws on dismissal make no discrimination with respect to compensation.

[48] Directive 1997/70, Annex, cl. 4; C-596/14 *De Diego* v. *Ministerio de Defensa* [2016] ICR 1184.

employer becomes a customer of an agency, which supplies the employer with staff to meet its needs on a temporary basis. The employer pays the agency a fee for this service and the agency pays the workers their wages. These workers are not usually directly employed by the customer-employer. In the absence of any contractual relation between the customer-employer and the workers, the customer-employer incurs no legal obligations with respect to dismissals, thereby achieving maximum flexibility. The legal rights, if any, of agency workers are considered in the next chapter.

Here, we focus on the legal position of temporary and casual workers. The problem that they face is that the intermittent nature of their employment means that not only is their income from work unpredictable and precarious, but also that they may be disqualified from nearly all the statutory protections for employees owing to the lack of continuity of employment. Even if they work for a particular employer over a number of years, there is a danger that they will not satisfy the necessary qualifying period for statutory rights, because they have only worked intermittently with gaps in between the jobs. A waiter for a banqueting hall may only be required on average two or three evenings a week over several years, with no work being offered in some weeks and much more in others. It is arguable in such circumstances that the waiter has not been permanently employed during these years of service for the banqueting hall, but instead has only been employed on a casual and temporary basis for each evening when he has worked. As a result, the waiter may never build up the necessary continuity of service to qualify for statutory rights. A new kind of extremely precarious casual worker has emerged in recent years through what is known as the gig economy.

The Gig Economy

Many people today have jobs in the gig economy. Drawing a misleading analogy with musicians who perform for a single night in return for a fee, workers in the modern smartphone economy appear similarly to provide a service for a short period and then move on. The gig economy involves the exchange of work performed personally in return for payment through a digital internet mechanism that facilitates matching between workers and customers on a short-term, payment by the task, basis. Courier and package delivery services are the most common kind of work, but other well-known examples are taxi services provided through Uber, food delivery services provided by Deliveroo and freelancing work through PeoplePerHour. All of these kinds of service jobs have long existed; what is different today is the way a business can use the internet and smartphones to roll out these service mechanisms globally and in huge numbers. The smartphone apps provide extraordinarily efficient tools for matching workers with customers.

A government-funded on-line survey of 2,184 individuals in 2017 suggested that in fact only about 4.4 per cent of the population had worked in the gig economy in the previous year.[49] The workers tended to be younger and most commonly lived in the London area. Most had only recently started participating in the gig economy. Most worked in the gig economy only intermittently and for about two-thirds of workers it represented only 5 per cent of their annual income. It was less than 10 per cent of those involved who earned their total income through the gig economy, with most using it to top up their regular income from other jobs.

From an employment law perspective, there is a valid concern that this highly precarious form of work slips under the radar of employment rights.[50] This exclusion may occur because the work is too transitory to acquire legal rights; or, as we shall discover in Chapter 6, some of the operators of these apps such as Uber deny that they are employers at all and try (unsuccessfully) to insist that their workers are independent contractors who are excluded from most statutory entitlements.[51] About a quarter of respondents to the above survey reported that they earned an hourly income of less than the NMW. The internet platform may enable these firms to secure an oversupply of workers, which will not only keep wages down but will also tend to undercut any competitor employers. Although the flexibility to top up regular income or for students to make some pocket money as and when they have a bit of spare time can be an attractive option, workers in the gig economy only ever have short-term jobs, with no income security. The mechanisms of the gig economy come extremely close to treating labour as a commodity.

The legal position of such temporary and casual employees who routinely but intermittently work for the same employer has generated some confusion and complexity in the law. Two separate questions must be considered. The first is whether a contract of employment exists throughout the period of intermittent employment, even though the employee has not been doing regular hours of work. This is the question of whether there is an 'umbrella contract of employment' or a 'contract for intermittent employment'.[52] If such a binding contract can be found, provided that it has lasted the requisite period, the employee should be able to satisfy the necessary qualifying period for a statutory right and have a contract of employment for the purpose of bringing a statutory claim, even if the alleged breach of a statutory right by the employer occurs at a time when the employee is not actually working. The answer to the question of the existence of an umbrella contract depends on the common law of the contract of employment. The second question is whether, notwithstanding the absence of a permanent or an umbrella contract,

---

[49] BEIS, *The Characteristics of Those in the Gig Economy Final Report* (February 2018).

[50] J. Prassl, *Humans as a Service: The Promise and Perils of Work in the Gig Economy* (Oxford University Press, 2018).

[51] *Uber BV* v. *Aslam* [2018] EWCA Civ 2748.

[52] M. Freedland, *The Personal Employment Contract* (Oxford University Press, 2003), p. 110; A. C. L. Davies, 'The Contract for Intermittent Employment' (2007) 36 *Industrial Law Journal* 102.

the employee can claim statutory rights because of provisions in the ERA 1996 that deem certain instances of intermittent employment to count as continuous periods of employment. The answer to that question turns on the interpretation of complex statutory provisions concerning continuity of employment.

Umbrella Contracts

In its essentials, the question posed under the terminology of the umbrella contract, the framework contract or the global contract is whether the parties were bound by some kind of contract both during and in between intermittent periods of work. On days when a casual worker is actually working, there is evidently a contractual relation involving the performance of work in return for remuneration. The question here is whether these short contracts are joined up by a continuous umbrella contract. In this context, the courts have focused on the question of whether or not there was 'mutuality of obligation'. Under this test, the question is whether or not there was an agreement by the employer to provide work on an ongoing basis and a promise by the employee to take work if it were offered. The terminology of 'mutuality of obligation' tends to lead to confusion, for it elides two separate questions.[53] The first issue is whether the intermittent instances of casual work were bound together by a long-term contract. The second issue is whether, if such an umbrella contract exists in the particular circumstances, the contract is properly characterised as a contract of employment or some other kind of contract. The first issue turns on an application of the ordinary principles of the law of contract concerning agreement and consideration. The second issue, which will be considered more broadly in Chapter 6, is whether the obligations of the parties under an umbrella contract are such as to qualify the agreement as a contract of employment as opposed to some other kind of contract.

Some agreements regarding a long-term arrangement for casual work lack consideration (or 'mutuality of obligation' in the former sense). The employer does not promise to offer work; nor does the worker promise to undertake work if requested to do so. The express agreement between the parties may spell out the lack of commitment on either side: in the agreement the employer merely states the terms on which it is prepared to offer work, if work is required and offered to this particular individual worker, and the worker agrees that, if work is offered, accepted and performed, the remuneration and duties will be on the stated terms. In itself, however, this umbrella agreement is not a binding contract, for the employer has not promised any work and nor has the employee promised to perform any work. The agreement is merely a framework that fixes the express terms if the parties do in fact

---

[53] As pointed out by Elias J in *Stephenson v. Delphi Diesel Systems Ltd* [2003] ICR 477 (EAT).

enter into a contract for the performance of work. A similar problem of consideration probably prevents many so-called 'zero-hours' agreements from being a long-term binding contract. Although the content of this category of agreements is unclear,[54] in these agreements an employee promises to work if called upon by the employer, but the employer does not promise to offer a minimum number of hours of work, there is no consideration. Again such a 'zero-hours' agreement is merely setting a framework for the terms when casual work is actually performed. The introduction of the now prohibited term that forbids such zero-hours workers from offering their services to other employers does not alter that legal analysis,[55] for though the exclusive-dealing clause certainly qualifies as consideration provided by the employee, the absence of a promise to offer any hours of work still removes any consideration on the part of the employer. The only way in which such zero-hours contracts or casual work contracts can become legally binding is to find further express or implied promises by the employer to provide regular remunerated work.

In practice, of course, the expectation of both parties is usually that work will in fact be offered and that the worker will normally perform any work offered. In the absence of express promises to provide and perform work, however, such expectations will probably not be regarded by the courts as binding legal commitments. In *Carmichael* v. *National Power plc*,[56] the question was whether tour guides at a nuclear power station had an umbrella contract of employment. It was determined that the formal agreement was merely a framework under which the employer was not committed to offer work and nor were the tour guides committed to accept it if it was offered. In practice, however, the tour guides worked for up to twenty-five hours nearly every week and seldom declined the offer of work. On this basis, the Court of Appeal found that the real agreement did have mutuality of obligation or an ongoing commitment, because a term could be implied in fact that bound both parties to offer and perform work on a regular basis. But the House of Lords disagreed: it held that the correct construction of the agreement was that neither party was committed either to offer work or to perform work. In other words, there was no long-term contract of any kind owing to the absence of consideration. In a commercial law context, this type of agreement would be called a requirements contract or a framework agreement which, though not legally binding in itself, fixes the terms applicable to any contracts that the parties enter into in the future.[57]

---

[54] A. Adams, M. Freedland and J. Prassl, 'The "Zero-Hours Contract": Regulating Casual Work, or Legitimating Precarity?' University of Oxford Legal Research Paper Series paper, February 2015, http://ssrn.com/abstract= 2507693.

[55] ERA 1996, s. 27B(1) and (5) and 209(1); The Exclusivity Terms in Zero Hours Contracts (Redress) Regulations 2015, SI 2015 No. 2021.

[56] [1999] ICR 1226 (HL).

[57] H. Collins, 'Employment Rights of Casual Workers' (2000) 29 *Industrial Law Journal* 73.

An objection to the decision of the House of Lords in *Carmichael* is that it pays too much attention to the formal terms of the agreement and gives insufficient attention to the real nexus of the bargain that the parties had struck. Although the tour guides may have been free in principle to decline to take a particular assignment on a particular day, in practice that was unlikely to happen for a number of reasons. This work was their principal source of income, so normally they would have been keen to accept any work offered. Although they might decline a job for reasons of illness or some other pressing need, their willingness to work was surely no different from that of ordinary employees who would also be absent in equivalent circumstances. Similarly, although the employer was uncertain about the quantity of work available to tour guides, it was certain that tour guides would be needed and the employer had selected and trained a number of them accordingly with the clear intention of offering them regular, although intermittent, employment. In line with that expectation, the employer would not look outside this pool of trained workers for people to fill the job of being a guide. Furthermore, we can be reasonably sure that, if any tour guide had started to reject assignments frequently, he or she would have been dropped from the list of potential guides. One could say that, looking at the substantive expectations of the parties and their economic needs rather than merely the formal agreement, this arrangement was a contract with a term that allocated the risk of the absence of work to be performed on to the worker rather than, as is normal, on to the employer. By accepting that risk of the precariousness of the work, the tour guides had possibly deprived themselves of the statutory protections owing to their lack of continuity of employment. By discovering mutuality of obligation or an ongoing commitment between the parties, the Court of Appeal in *Carmichael* may have misinterpreted the formal contractual arrangement, but they may have grasped more accurately than the House of Lords the economic reality of the relation of mutual economic dependence of the tour guides and the employer, and the expectations of trust that made up the psychological contract.[58]

Looking at the economic reality and actual practice and expectations of the parties led the Court of Appeal to find an umbrella contract of employment in *Nethermere (St Neots) Ltd* v. *Gardiner*.[59] The applicants had worked for several years, although not every week, at home sewing boys' trousers for the company. There were no fixed hours of work, payment was by reference to the piece and the applicants were not obliged to accept any fixed amount of work. They claimed unfair dismissal when the company dispensed with their services following a dispute. The industrial tribunal decided that the applicants were employees for the purpose of bringing a claim for unfair

---

[58] H. Collins, 'The Contract of Employment in 3D', in D. Campbell, L. Mulcahy and S. Wheeler (eds.), *Changing Concepts of Contract* (Basingstoke: Palgrave Macmillan, 2013), pp. 65, 84.

[59] [1984] ICR 612 (CA).

dismissal. The Court of Appeal, by a majority, upheld this decision, finding that the tribunal had not misdirected itself in law. The Court approved of the tribunal's finding of an 'umbrella contract' of employment, because there was evidence from the dealings between the company and the workers that there was in fact a mutual obligation to offer work and to accept it, although the quantities and timing were flexible. For example, employees who were unable to undertake work in a particular week would notify the company in advance, and the company ensured that the work was evenly distributed among their eleven home-workers unless they requested otherwise. But this is an unusual decision in finding the existence of an umbrella contract. The House of Lords in *Carmichael* subsequently set the tone of looking at the express agreement rather than the implicit expectations, treating the contract of employment like a commercial deal rather than a relational contract, and as a consequence preventing the finding of an umbrella contract by giving determinative importance to express terms that stress the casual or intermittent nature of the job.

The second question that arises in connection with an umbrella contract, assuming one can be found, is whether it qualifies as a contract of employment or instead is some other kind of contract, In *O'Kelly* v. *Trusthouse Forte*, the Court of Appeal held that, even if there was an umbrella contract that created a permanent relation despite the intermittent nature of the performance of work, that umbrella contract was not itself a contract of employment. The umbrella contract, if it existed, would be a kind of option contract: 'an umbrella or master contract for, not of, employment'.[60] The question is whether the contract includes promises to provide remunerated work and for the worker to perform it in accordance with instructions. This umbrella contract might be more limited: a promise by the employer to call the worker each week to fix a schedule of work according to what is available. In *Stringfellow Restaurants Ltd* v. *Quashie*,[61] the Court of Appeal concluded that the umbrella contract between a lap dancer and a nightclub, under which she was permitted to perform dances at the club in return for payments by customers, was a binding contract, but one which concerned intermittent independent contracting. The Court approved the reasoning of the tribunal that the presence of an employment relation was negatived by the absence of a promise to pay wages on the part of the club, and the evidence that the dancer negotiated her own fees with the clients, took the risk that on any particular night she would be out of pocket and received back from the employer only monies received from clients after deductions. In Chapter 6 we consider in detail the criteria for employment status.

---

[60] *Per* Sir John Donaldson MR.   [61] [2012] EWCA Civ 1735, [2013] IRLR 99.

Continuity of Employment

Fortunately this judicial opposition to the finding of an umbrella contract of employment matters less as a result of reforms to the statutory definition of a period of continuous employment that in some instances permits intermittent work to be deemed to be a continuous period of employment. The general rule is that, if there is a week in which continuity of employment is broken by a termination of the contract, the calculation of the time necessary to qualify for a statutory right must be reset to start again. Interrupting continuity of employment by only one workless week is likely to cause difficulties for many intermittent workers, particularly for those whose work is partly seasonal. The government's Taylor Review recommended that the period of a gap between work should be increased to one month before continuity would be broken.[62]

Fortunately it is not strictly necessary in every case for an employee actually to work all the week or indeed to perform any work during a week that establishes continuity of employment.

Employment Rights Act 1996 s. 212(1).

Any week during the whole or part of which an employee's relations with his employer governed by a contract of employment counts in computing the employee's period of employment.

Under this provision, a week can count towards the computation of the qualifying period of employment provided that during at least some of the week there was a contract of employment without the need for any work to be performed. Equally, casual workers who have no regular hours, but who are employed as required by the employer and subject to their own availability, may establish that a particular week counts for the purpose of preserving continuity of employment, provided that at some point during the week they worked under a contract of employment. Assuming, as seems likely,[63] that the tour guides in *Carmichael* worked under a contract of employment when they were actually conducting tours, this statutory provision would mean that, provided the guides took at least one tour each week, today they would establish continuity of employment despite the intermittent nature of their job.

---

[62] *Good Work: The Taylor Review of Modern Working Practices* (July 2017), p. 45. The government announced its intention to legislate for the possibility of a four-week break in work in HM Government, *Good Work Plan* (December 2018), p. 14.

[63] Although unnecessary for the decision in that case, Lord Hoffmann suggested that probably the casual 'as required' tour guides worked under short-term contracts of employment when they actually performed the service.

In addition, the statutory definition of continuous employment creates four significant instances where continuity of employment is not broken, even though the employee is performing no work. The first is when an employee takes strike action: the strike action does not break the period of continuous service, but even a short strike of an hour prevents the whole week from contributing to the length of service.[64] The second protection of continuity is where the employee is incapable of work in consequence of sickness or injury and as a result has no contract of employment. During the first twenty-six weeks of this sickness leave, there is no break in the continuity of employment.[65] The third instance of the preservation of continuity of employment concerns the case where the employee is absent from work on account of a 'temporary cessation of work' and has no contract of employment.[66] The fourth instance is where the employee is 'absent from work in circumstances such, by arrangement or custom, he is regarded as continuing in the employment of his employer for any purpose' even though there is no contract of employment.[67] One example of such an arrangement is where an employee is reinstated after successfully appealing to the employer after a dismissal. Despite the period of absence of work, pay and a binding contract following the dismissal, the reinstatement is likely to be regarded as restoring continuity of employment.[68] In a decision that is hard to reconcile with the statute, the right type of custom or arrangement was said by the Court of Appeal not to be established in a case where an employee took advantage of an employer's career break scheme to take four years of absence, with a right to return to a job at the end of the period, even though the scheme required the employee to work at least two weeks a year.[69]

The importance of these provisions for the protection of statutory employment rights of precarious workers was illustrated in *Cornwall County Council* v. *Prater*.[70] The claimant worked as a home tutor for a local authority for ten years. Her job involved visiting a number of pupils in their homes for the purpose of giving tuition. Although she was not obliged to take on any particular pupil, once she had accepted an assignment, she was obliged to continue the work. She taught several pupils each week, visiting usually once a day. The length of the assignments varied from a few months to as long as five years. In some periods, especially during the school holidays in August, the tutor was doing no work at all for the local authority. Because she was not obliged to accept work and nor was the council obliged to offer work,

---

[64] ERA 1996, s. 216.   [65] ERA 1996, s. 212(3)(a) and (4).   [66] ERA 1996, s. 212(3)(b).

[67] ERA 1996, s. 212(3)(c).

[68] *Ingram* v. *Foxon* [1984] ICR 685 (EAT); *London Probation Board* v. *Kirkpatrick* [2005] ICR 965 (EAT). If an ET reinstates an employee after dismissal, continuity of employment is also protected: Employment Protection (Continuity of Employment) Regulations 1996, SI 1996 No. 3147.

[69] *Curr* v. *Marks & Spencer plc* [2002] EWCA Civ 1852, [2003] ICR 443.

[70] [2006] EWCA Civ 102, [2006] ICR 731.

following *Carmichael* v. *National Power plc*, there could be no successful argument that there was an umbrella contract throughout this period. But the Court of Appeal held that for each assignment the home tutor provided her services under a contract of employment. Furthermore, there was continuity of service because there had only been 'temporary cessations of work' between assignments. She had therefore been continuously employed for the whole period of ten years for the purpose of claiming statutory rights, even though she might be described as working on a 'casual as required' basis. If these statutory provisions had been applicable at the time when *Carmichael* was decided,[71] notwithstanding the absence of an umbrella contract of employment, the tour guides might have been able to establish the necessary continuity of employment even though during some weeks there had been no work available for them, because those weeks could be regarded as merely 'temporary cessations of work'.

How long a period is a 'temporary cessation of work'? The House of Lords decided in *Fitzgerald* v. *Hall Russell & Co. Ltd*[72] that breaks between periods of employment could be examined with the benefit of hindsight in order to determine whether or not they were merely 'temporary'. Even though the employer cannot be sure whether or not it will require the services of a dismissed temporary worker or a casual worker again in the near future, if the break between periods of work can be described with the benefit of hindsight as 'temporary', the periods of employment (and unemployment) can be added together to constitute the necessary qualifying period. This reasoning was applied to a succession of fixed-term contracts in *Ford* v. *Warwickshire County Council*.[73] A teacher was employed for eight successive academic years on fixed-term contracts from September to July with a break during the annual summer holidays. The question was whether, for the purpose of establishing continuity of employment for eight years, the annual summer holidays could be regarded as 'temporary cessations of work'. The House of Lords allowed the employee's appeal, holding that continuity of employment was established. The test of whether the break in employment is temporary, as proposed by Lord Diplock, is to assess from the viewpoint of the end of the second period of employment whether the break was short in comparison to the combined duration of the two periods of employment. In this case, the gap of about a month in a combined period of twenty-two months was short enough to be described as a temporary cessation of work. It is a question of fact and degree whether the gap in employment was sufficiently short, which should be left to an assessment by an ET.

---

[71] The provisions were amended by the Employment Relations Act 1999, ss. 9 and 44 and Sched. 4, Part III to make it easier to add together short periods of intermittent employment to establish continuity.
[72] [1970] AC 984 (HL).   [73] [1983] ICR 273 (HL).

Conversion of Fixed-term Contracts into Permanent Contracts

We now return to consider the protections afforded to workers who accept a succession of fixed-term contracts rather than being provided with a contract of indefinite duration. These jobs are apparently precarious because at the end of the fixed term there is no certainty that the employee will be offered a new job and, at common law, the expiry of a fixed term is treated as termination by notice, not any kind of dismissal that might provide the basis for compensation. But the precarious nature of fixed-term contracts is modified in two ways by legislation. First, we noted above that the expiry of a fixed term is deemed to be a dismissal for the purposes of the statutory claims for unfair dismissal and redundancy payments (although not the common law). If the period of employment has been continuous and has lasted for the qualifying period of two years, the employees may claim compensation for dismissal. Secondly, in compliance with an EU Directive,[74] the Fixed-Term Employees (Prevention of Less Favourable Treatment) Regulations 2002[75] provide in regulation 8 that the term of a contract that limits its duration shall be of no effect once the total period of employment exceeds four years. The employee will be regarded as a permanent employee, unless the employer can justify the use of fixed-term contracts on 'objective grounds'.

These 'objective grounds' are not defined, but it seems likely that the employer would have to demonstrate that in each instance a fixed-term contract had been offered because it seemed unlikely at the time of the offer that work would be available beyond the date of termination. That approach was satisfied, for instance, in *Kücük* v. *Land Nordrhein-Westfalen*,[76] where the worker was given a succession of fixed-term contracts during which she provided cover for the temporary leave of other employees. Interpreting the concept of 'objective grounds' in the Directive, the CJEU held that in these circumstances the use of fixed-term contracts was justified, even though she had been employed in total for more than eleven years on thirteen fixed-term contracts. In contrast, in cases such as *Ford* v. *Warwickshire County Council*,[77] if the continuation of the college's need for teachers was likely from one year to the next, almost certainly under the 2002 Regulations employees in a similar position to Mrs Ford with eight years of teaching would be regarded in law as permanent staff. In *Secretary of State for Children, Schools and Families* v. *Fletcher*,[78] Baroness Hale, speaking for the Supreme Court, stressed that the concept of objective grounds should be understood in the light of the mischief tackled by the Directive, which was permitting employers to manipulate contractual arrangements to avoid the legal obligations arising in

---

[74] Directive 99/70 concerning the framework agreement on fixed-term work, OJ 1999 L175/43.

[75] SI 2002 No. 2024.   [76] [2012] ICR 682.

[77] [1983] ICR 273 (HL); e.g. C-16/15, *Pérez Lopéz* v. *Servicio Madrileno de Salud (Comunidad de Madrid)* [2016] ICR 1168.

[78] [2011] UKSC 14, [2011] ICR 495 (SC).

permanent contracts. If the particular case did not amount to disguised permanent employment, but in fact corresponded to necessary limits on the period of employment, the use of a fixed term was justified.

Whether or not employees in the UK would actually benefit from the conversion of a fixed-term contract into one of indefinite duration is rather dubious. Assuming that employees have the requisite continuity of service for the statutory qualifying period, the rights of employees under fixed-term contracts and permanent contracts would be the same with respect to claims for unfair dismissal and redundancy payment. It is even possible that a conversion might place employees in a worse position, because a contract of indefinite duration can nearly always be terminated by reasonable notice, whereas the fixed term might be binding for its whole duration.[79]

Precarious Work

At the beginning of this chapter we asked two key questions: (1) to what extent can and should the law try to protect employees from unwelcome changes to their contracts or their jobs? And (2) to what extent should legal regulation prevent the use of precarious work packages that provide employees with little income and job security? The response to the first question in broad terms is that although in principle employees can insist on and enforce their existing terms of employment, in practice there is very little to stop an employer from driving through changes to terms of employment and the content of jobs. The response to the second question is that there is little to prevent employers from constructing highly transitory employment relations. Modern regulation tends to ensure that if these precarious arrangements persist more or less continuously for a period of time, the employees become entitled to the same statutory rights such as protection against unfair dismissal as permanent employees. Yet there has been no attempt to prevent employers from using highly precarious forms of work in the first place even though these devices present employees with high levels of income insecurity.

Many workers therefore experience such high levels of insecurity. Not only may the content of their jobs radically change with little warning but their work and pay may also be intermittent, with no guarantees of the continuation of a job at all. Many employers claim that their business need for flexibility requires them only to offer temporary, casual or zero-hours contracts. But there is no legal constraint on adopting such contracts even where there is no business imperative. To provide an incentive for employers to consider offering better conditions, the Taylor report commissioned by the government suggested that the NMW might be raised for various kinds of precarious work,[80] thereby forcing employers to think twice about a decision to offer

---

[79] M. Freedland, *The Personal Employment Contract* (Oxford University Press, 2003), p. 317.
[80] *Good Work: The Taylor Review of Modern Working Practices* (July 2017), p. 44.

insecure working conditions. In addition, the report proposes that those on zero-hours contracts should be entitled after a year's service to a contract with minimum hours that correspond to those actually worked.[81] The government's proposal is to give all workers after twenty-six weeks of service a right to request a contract with predictable and stable hours of employment.[82] Of course, that request might be rejected by the employer or, if accepted, the minimum hours set, though predictable, might be minimal. While such measures might reduce the level of exploitation of these kinds of precarious employees, they may provoke employers to adopt a strategy that is even more detrimental for workers, which is for employers to insist that their workers are all independent contractors and therefore that their contracts are not governed by labour law at all.

[81] *Ibid.*, p. 48.   [82] HM Government, *Good Work Plan* (December 2018), p. 13.

6

The Personal Scope of Labour Law

Contents

The Challenge of Employment Status

Labour legislation must target particular kinds of work relations. Regulation needs to distinguish, for instance, employment relations from business relations. For the former, labour law provides statutory rights for workers and employees such as a statutory minimum wage or protection from unfair dismissal. In commercial and business relations, however, such as a solicitor's provision of professional services to a client or a hairdresser's grooming for a customer, these statutory rights will not be applicable: the solicitor and the hairdresser cannot insist on being paid a minimum wage by a client nor complain of unfair dismissal if the customer chooses to go elsewhere for these services. This focus of the statutory protections on employment can be explained by their purpose. Most of this legislation aims to protect employees against the misuse of managerial power and instances of exploitation such as low pay. These problems arise typically in contracts of employment where, as we have seen, workers are vulnerable to exploitation of their weak bargaining position and harsh and unfair exercises of managerial power. Labour laws are therefore directed at contracts of employment as the paradigm that merits regulation. The problem addressed in this chapter is whether these laws should also apply to other kinds of contract involving the performance of services when the contracts at issue closely resemble contracts of employment.

This topic is conventionally described as the personal scope of labour law or employment status because it is concerned with identifying the types of persons who are covered by the legislation. These include employees but may also include other types of workers or suppliers of services who may not have a contract of employment. Strictly speaking, the scope of labour law does not depend on types of person or the law of persons but rather on types of contractual relationship for the provision of work and services. The practice of speaking of the personal scope of labour law has, perhaps unfortunately, been transplanted from civil-law systems into the common law in recent decades. Legislation in the UK encourages this practice by defining its scope by reference to categories of worker, such as 'employee' or 'worker', although these terms are defined in the legislation by reference to the type of contractual relations made with the employer of the services.

Why does this topic of the personal scope of labour law cause difficulty? The underlying problem confronted by the law concerns the interaction of two variables. The first variable concerns the purposes of the different pieces of legislation. The intended coverage of labour laws may differ in light of the social problems they address. Compare, for instance, the law of unfair dismissal and the law regarding health and safety. The law of unfair dismissal is concerned with the abuse of managerial disciplinary power and so it should apply only to those types of contract where the terms of the contract create an authority relation and the associated risk of an abuse of power. This kind of contract is associated primarily with contracts of employment, although other 'employment-like' contracts may create similar relations of subordination. In contrast, accidents causing personal injuries in the workplace may happen to anyone present, including visiting contractors and professionals, so the scope of the legislation can be expected to be far broader. In particular, section 3(1) of the Health and Safety at Work Act 1974 requires an employer to 'conduct his undertaking in such a way as to ensure, so far as is reasonably practicable, that persons not in his employment . . . are not exposed to risks to health and safety'. This provision imposes a duty of care towards independent contractors and their employees, provided that the work of the contractor can be regarded as the employer's method for the 'conduct of the undertaking'.[1] Each piece of labour legislation therefore has to define its particular scope and there is no uniformity in the definitions of coverage. As well as often being vague and

---

[1] E.g. *R* v. *Associated Octel Ltd* [1996] 1 WLR 1543 (HL).

imprecise about its intended scope, it is debatable whether legislation always contains a carefully considered scope of application, as opposed to an incoherent and erratic use of the terminology of employee status according to historical accident.

The second variable concerns the terms of contracts under which people work. As we have noted, a central principle of the common law grants freedom to the parties to shape their contractual relations. In practice, an employer who is seeking the use of services of another such as a carpenter can devise a wide variety of contractual arrangements: the employer may decide to hire a carpenter as an employee or may choose to create a contract that describes the carpenter supplying the work as an independent business supplying a service. In either case there is a contract for the supply of work in return for payment, but in the former the employer will typically demand the right to direct how and when the work is performed by the employee, whereas in the latter arrangement the carpenter, as an independent contractor, will organise his or her own performance of the service in order to produce an agreed result. This simple contrast between an employee and an independent contractor masks what in practice is a spectrum of types of work relations, in which the terms of contracts delineate a wide variety of contractual relations. The common law does not supply a finite range of contractual possibilities; instead, there is a plethora of contractual options. Each contractual relation has to be analysed to identify its characteristics with a view to determining whether or not it fits within the coverage of the legal regulation. This legislation often presupposes sharp and standardised conceptual contrasts between contractual types that do not exist in practice: each contractual relation can be idiosyncratic in its allocation of risks, with the inevitable consequence that classification is a complex and indeterminate process.

Moreover, it has proved impossible to devise simple tests to distinguish between the varieties of contract for the purpose of determining the application of this legislation. Even the most established and common legal category of the contract of employment cannot be identified easily. There is no convenient formula for distinguishing this economic relation from other kinds of contract through which services are supplied. Two contracts for the provision of a particular service such as carpentry may appear very similar, but the eventual legal classification may vary according to relatively minor differences, such as whether the worker is paid by the day or by the job and whether the worker supplies his or her own tools. By reference to these minor differences the worker may be classified in law as an employee or self-employed (an independent contractor), with the consequence that regulation designed to protect the interests of employees but not contractors, such as the law of unfair dismissal, will have no application to those workers classified as self-employed.

Either of these two variables in the personal scope of labour law would create some complexity in the application of the law, but in many cases that reach the courts the two variables are combined. These cases concern people who are performing work in return for payment, but where it may be unclear whether or not they fall within the purpose of the legislative protection, and where part of this uncertainty stems from the difficulty of classifying the contractual relation under which the work is performed. In other words, we are unsure about the precise purpose of the legislation and its application in this particular context, and to compound the difficulty we are equally uncertain about the appropriate classification of this particular work relation. It may be agreed, for instance, that the law of unfair dismissal should apply to employees working under a contract of employment. But should the law also apply to a person providing professional services such as a lawyer, or a skilled carpenter contracted to perform a particular job or the franchisee of a distribution outlet? It seems to make sense to exclude these types of worker from the scope of unfair dismissal legislation, because they appear to be running independent businesses and under the terms of their contracts they are not subject to the direction and disciplinary powers of an employer. But this legal form of the contract may conceal the kind of economic dependence and authority structure that is typical of employment relations and that the law of unfair dismissal was expected to regulate. A carpenter who appears at first sight to be an independent contractor hired to perform a particular task for a fee may in practice perform services solely for one business, be subject to detailed instructions and control from that business, and termination of the contract for some unfounded or irrelevant reason may be as offensive and economically damaging to the carpenter as the dismissal of an employee. Reliance upon the express contractual form of the relation between the parties therefore may not correlate with the social issue that the regulatory legislation is designed to address.

Although the combination of these two variables of the intended scope of the legislation and the variety of forms of contract used for the performance of work for another explains the source of much of the complexity in this aspect of labour law, there are many other sources of confusion and difficulty. Of these, it is worth highlighting four at the outset:

- UK legislation uses different statutory terms to describe the scope of application of labour rights. In some instances, rights are confined to contracts of employment; in other instances, there is a broader scope of application to 'workers', which includes an ill-defined group of persons who are contracted to perform work personally but who do not have a contract of employment. Each statutory right has to be examined independently in order to discover its scope.
- Secondly, the legal concepts used to define the scope of labour law, such as 'employee' and 'worker', may have different meanings according to whether the statutory right derives from national law or EU law.
- Thirdly, the law has to grapple with divisions within the employing entity. For instance, the employee may have a contract of employment with one

company, yet in practice be directed by managers of a different, although associated, company. Similarly, temporary agency workers may receive their wages from the agency although they work under the direction of the managers of a company that is a client of the agency. The difficulty arises in these instances of determining which legal entity should count as the employer for the purpose of enforcement of labour rights.

- Finally, the law has to address the problem of avoidance of regulation by employers. The question is whether an employer, by altering the terms on which it acquires the services of another, can change the legal classification of the work relationship in order to avoid the application of statutory protections for those workers. Should the employer of the carpenter in our earlier example be permitted to avoid the law of unfair dismissal by merely rewriting the contract to make the carpenter an independent contractor rather than an employee? By tying mandatory social legislation to particular contractual forms, an invitation is presented to employers to avoid the legislation by selecting a different contractual form. The questions posed by such a practice are whether this avoidance is undesirable, and also whether anything can be done to prevent it. It may seem undesirable to exclude workers from protections provided by labour law, but defenders of these practices insist that the 'flexibility' enables many people to find work who otherwise might be excluded from the labour market altogether because of their lack of skills or vulnerable legal status, such as undocumented migrants.

Contracts of Employment and Contracts for Services

Nearly all labour laws apply to contracts of employment, although some legislation applies to broader categories or specified groups in addition. Legislation in the twentieth century adopted the concept of a contract of employment to provide a unifying legal label for contracts of service, thereby avoiding former distinctions drawn between such groups as workmen, artisans and domestic servants.[2]

Employment Rights Act, 1996, section 230(1) and (2)

(1) In this Act 'employee' means an individual who has entered into or works under (or, where the employment has ceased, worked under) a contract of employment.
(2) In this Act 'contract of employment' means a contract of service or apprenticeship, whether express or implied, and (if it is express) whether oral or in writing.

---

[2] M. Freedland, *The Personal Employment Contract* (Oxford University Press, 2003), pp. 15–22.

Notice that the statute makes no serious attempt to define a contract of employment. A contract of employment, we are told, is a contract of service, but we need to remember that a contract of service is exactly the same as a contract of employment. In short, employment means employment. The concept of a contract of employment must therefore be derived from the common law. The common law has traditional drawn a binary division between employees and independent contractors, or between contracts of service and contracts for services. To understand the scope of application of modern employment-protection laws, therefore, it is necessary to understand how the common law contrasted employment from contracts for services.

The problem of determining the application of legal obligations by reference to the concept of a contract of employment is not unique to modern employment law. Under the master and servant laws of the eighteenth and nineteenth centuries it was a criminal offence for a servant to leave his job or not complete it, whereas an independent provider of a service was outside the scope of the legislation. Magistrates had to distinguish between 'servants', who could be imprisoned for leaving work without permission, and independent contractors, who could work for a number of masters on a footing of equality and leave work incomplete without criminal penalty (albeit in breach of contract). If a magistrate made a mistake in the classification and imprisoned an independent contractor, the magistrate could be sued for false imprisonment and trespass to the person.[3]

In the common law of tort, the liability of employers to compensate workers who have been injured has turned traditionally on the question of whether or not the worker was an employee. If the worker was an employee or working under a 'contract of service', the employer invariably owed the employee an extensive duty of care; if the worker was an independent contractor or working under a 'contract for services', the employer was unlikely to owe a common law duty of care in respect of the performance of work. The independent contractor, as a separate business, was supposed to take the risk of health and safety issues itself. Claims for personal injuries therefore often turned on whether the worker was an employee or independent contractor. The predominant test used for this purpose concerned the degree of control of the employer.

The 'Control Test'

The 'control test' asks: '[W]ho lays down what is to be done, the way in which it is to be done, the means by which it is to be done, and the time when it is done? Who provides

---

[3] *Hardy* v. *Ryle* (1829) 9 B&C 611; C. Frank, *Master and Servant Law* (Farnham: Ashgate, 2010), Ch. 1.

(i.e. hires and fires) the team by which it is done, and who provides the material, plant and machinery and tools used?'[4] If the employer decides these matters, or at least has the right to decide them, it is a contract of employment; and vice versa.

Only a contract of service automatically creates a relation of authority and control: the employer instructs the employee to perform tasks and is entitled to impose disciplinary sanctions for any dereliction of duty. In contrast, independent contractors working under a contract for services retain their own autonomous discretion to determine how the contract should be performed, subject to any terms of the contract. The independent contractor is not a servant but another master. An independent contractor, but never an employee, can perform work for two customers at the same time.

The binary distinction between employees and independent contractors has also been crucial in connection with the scope of the vicarious liability of employers. If an employee causes loss to another person by a tortious act committed in the course of employment, the employer is normally vicariously liable for that tort provided that there was a 'sufficient connection' to the employee's duties under the contract of employment.[5] In contrast, this 'enterprise liability' is not usually attached to torts committed by independent contractors working under contracts for services with the core business. For this purpose, the control test was used to assess whether the employer would be vicariously liable. Under the control test, however, highly skilled workers and senior managers who enjoy considerable autonomy in determining what tasks need to be done and how they should be performed arguably fail to qualify as employees, even though for most other purposes, such as the allocation of the risk of profit and loss, they could be regarded as employees. Similarly, pay incentive systems such as commissions on sales could turn some groups of workers into individual profit centres, making them appear like independent contractors even though ultimately the employer was the residual profit-taker. To include such workers within the duty of care and vicarious liability, the courts sometimes referred to an organisation test.

The 'Organisation Test'

The 'organisation test' asks whether the workers are members of the employer's organisation, taking into account such factors as the application of dress and grooming codes, supply of infrastructure such as office accommodation and communications facilities and the application of the employer's rule-book or staff handbook. Even a senior manager with considerable

---

[4] *Lane v. Shire Roofing Company (Oxford) Ltd* [1995] IRLR 493 (CA), *per* Henry LJ.
[5] *Mohamud v. Wm Morrison Supermarkets plc* [2016] UKSC 11, [2016] ICR 485.

autonomy and paid exclusively by profit-sharing could be regarded as an employee by reference to the organisation test, because it only requires formal legal subordination to the employing entity rather than actual subordination to a managerial hierarchy.

Although the common law still uses the distinction between 'contracts of service' and 'contracts for services' in setting the boundaries of the vicarious liability of employers in tort, its significance has been reduced by the modern test of whether the imposition of vicarious liability would be 'fair, just and reasonable', taking into account factors such as whether the employer created the risk of the tort being committed by entering into the contract for services as an integrated part of its business.[6]

A similar distinction between employees and independent contractors is a key ingredient of income tax and social security laws. One important practical difference arising from the classification for tax purposes is that employers under a contract of employment are required to deduct income tax and national insurance payments before payment of wages, whereas employers under other contracts for services incur no such obligation. Independent contractors may claim more deductions against income tax and pay reduced national insurance contributions and their 'employer' avoids national insurance altogether. In the UK there is a total workforce of about 32 million, of whom 27 million are usually classified as employees in the official statistics, leaving about 5 million who are self-employed and working under contracts for services. In order to assess tax and national insurance liabilities, while also using the control test, the courts have tended to emphasise the question of whether a person is in business on his own account. An independent contractor is in business on his own account, taking the risk of profit or loss on the contract he entered into, whereas a worker under a contract of service is simply paid a wage.

The 'Business Risk' or 'Economic Reality' Test

The 'business risk' or 'economic reality'[7] test asks: '[I]s the person who has engaged himself to perform these services performing them as a person in business on his own account? . . . [F]actors, which may be of importance, are such matters as whether the man performing the services provides his own equipment, whether he hires his own helpers, what degree of financial risk he takes, what degree of responsibility for investment and management he has,

---

[6] *Cox* v. *Ministry of Justice* [2016] UKSC 10, [2016] ICR 470.
[7] *United States* v. *Silk*, 331 US 704 (1946) (US Supreme Court).

and whether and how far he has an opportunity for profiting from sound management in the performance of his task.'[8] If the worker assumes these risks, it is likely to be a contract for services; and vice versa.

For the purposes of interpreting the application of employment law statutes, all these various tests have been used. It is unclear, however, whether these tests tend to support the purposes of protecting employment rights where they are needed and appropriate. In particular, although a worker may accept many risks linked to the business, such as the risk of the absence of work, by agreeing to be a casual worker, instead of being an indication that the worker should be regarded as an independent contractor, the acceptance of this risk may be a sign of a vulnerable worker who especially needs the protection of employment rights. Similarly, if a worker's remuneration depends entirely on tips or other payments by customers rather than any wage paid directly by the employer, that additional risk of irregular payments will also tend to exclude the worker from the legal category of a contract of employment, even though this worker may need the protections afforded by employment law more than most.[9]

Moreover, the binary division between contracts of service and contracts for services does not serve the purposes of labour regulation satisfactorily: many types of jobs fall on the boundary between the legal categories. As a result, the issue is hotly contested by employers, who appreciate that they may be able to avoid the requirements of employment law by having their workers classified as independent contractors. To address the problem of borderline cases, legislation sometimes extends a particular employment right to identifiable groups of workers such as agency workers. In other instances, legislation extends the employment law right beyond employees to a broader class of workers, including some independent contractors who are in practice economically dependent on a core business. This broader class is usually termed 'workers' to distinguish them from 'employees', although the terminology is unfortunately inconsistent.

Despite these criticisms of the relevance and application of the distinction between contracts of employment and contracts for services, UK legislation still defines the scope of many labour law rights by reference to the presence of a contract of employment. Among these statutory rights are the right to minimum periods of notice prior to termination of employment; the right to claim unfair dismissal; the right to claim a redundancy payment; and the right

---

[8] *Market Investigations* v. *Minister of Social Security* [1969] 2 QB 173, *per* Cooke J.
[9] E. Albin, 'A Worker-Employer-Customer Triangle: The Case of Tips' (2011) 40 *Industrial Law Journal* 181.

to a written statement of the particulars of employment, maternity leave and pay and parental leave. In determining the application of these rights, drawing on the traditional tests, a court will typically apply a list of factors that are regarded as important indications of the presence of a contract of employment. The opposite of these factors points towards a finding of a contract for services. While no single factor should be determinative, the absence of one or two of these factors is often sufficient for a legal conclusion that the contract is not a contract of employment.

The Multifactor Approach

Indicative factors favouring the finding of a contract of employment:

- the employer's control over the content of the work and the manner in which it is done;
- the employer agreeing to pay wages and accepting the business risk of profit and loss;
- the worker being integrated into the organisation;
- the employer supplying capital, raw materials, tools and equipment;
- the worker usually being required to perform work personally rather than using substitutes;
- the business accepting the allocation of other risks such as sickness and health and safety responsibility.

As we shall see below, these factors are also relevant to a finding of the statutory concept of worker. The difference between a worker and an employee is a matter of degree. It is possible to be a worker while not meeting many of these factors in full. For instance, some workers who are classed as independent contractors because they take on the business risk of profit and loss to a considerable extent may be classified as workers (but not employees) under the statutory concept if some of the other factors such as control and integration within the business are met.

It is often said that 'mutuality of obligations' is a factor that helps to determine whether a contract should be classified as creating employee status or worker status. It is true that an agreement to provide work in return for remuneration is necessary for some kind of contract to exist. But the requirement of mutuality of obligations is unhelpful in distinguishing between different kinds of employment status, because for all these types of contract – employment, worker and independent contractor – the agreement on mutuality of obligation is the same: an exchange of work for another in return for payment. As we noted in Chapter 5, sometimes the phrase 'mutuality of obligations' is taken to mean a long-term commitment by the employer to provide work and remuneration, but such a long-term arrangement has never been a necessary feature of contracts of employment: hirings by the day, the hour and even the minute have been permitted.

Bogus and Sham Contracts

The tensions and difficulties surrounding the determination of employment status become even more acute once it is recalled that the employer normally fixes the terms of the contract on a take-it-or-leave-it basis. The employer or its lawyers can devise terms for the contracts with its workers that apparently prevent them from acquiring the relevant employment status, whether as employee or worker. The principal device for ensuring that exclusion from statutory protection is to use terms of the contract to transfer some risks on to the employee. If the employee has to accept the risk of the absence or shortage of work, if the employee's remuneration depends on an incentive payment system, if the worker is told that he or she is responsible for paying taxes, supplying equipment and ensuring continuity of production or service even when ill, the employee takes on the appearance of an independent contractor in business on his or her own account. In an attempt to exclude workers from statutory protections, the employer imposes terms that appear to cast doubt on the presence of any of the factors that normally indicate the presence of a contract of employment. As Elias J perspicaciously remarked:

> [t]he concern to which tribunals must be alive is that armies of lawyers will simply place substitution clauses, or clauses denying any obligation to accept or provide work in employment contracts, as a matter of form, even where such terms do not begin to reflect the real relationship.[10]

It is not always true, however, that the main object of the employer's adoption of such terms is to avoid the application of employment-protection rules. Measures designed to increase efficiency and work effort can have that side-effect. The use of outsourcing from independent contractors responds to the need to be able to increase or reduce production capacity quickly, but might also be a way of acquiring specialist skills and permitting management to concentrate its attention on the core business. For example, in a survey asking why fourteen publishers had changed from employing editorial assistants under contracts of employment to the use of 'freelance', independent, self-employed contractors to perform the same task, the most common reason for the change was to match the availability of workers with demand more precisely (numerical flexibility) or, to put the point another way, to transfer the risk of unemployment due to lack of demand for copy-editing on to the provider of the service rather than the publisher.[11] Avoidance of social regulation does not appear to have been a significant consideration in determining this shift to contracts for services from direct employment, but its effect of depriving the editorial assistants of the benefits of many employment

---

[10] *Consistent Group Ltd* v. *Kalwak* [2007] IRLR 560 (EAT).

[11] C. Stanworth and J. Stanworth, 'Managing an Externalised Workforce: Freelance Labour-Use in the UK Book Publishing Industry' (1997) 28 *Industrial Relations Journal* 43.

protection laws was nonetheless virtually inevitable. Broader surveys confirm that the use of sub-contracting, temporary agency workers and casual workers is usually a response to weak and uncertain product demand rather than firms using these arrangements to avoid the application of statutory protections such as the law of unfair dismissal.[12]

Nevertheless, it is apparent that many employers try to disguise the contract as one for an independent contractor although in substance it is really some kind of an employment relation for the purpose of avoiding the obligations of employment law. The contract at issue in *Pimlico Plumbers Ltd* v. *Smith*[13] is an example of a bogus independent contractor. The employer's business plan was that qualified plumbers received assignments through the company; they attended customers' premises allocated to them wearing a uniform and driving a van with the company insignia. The plumbers received about half the fee for labour charged by the company to the customers, plus the costs of materials with a mark-up, but only if the customer actually paid the invoice. To avoid employment law and national insurance contributions, the employer drafted a contract that, while keeping tight control over the work of the plumbers, tried to present them as independent contractors. The contract included these terms:

(c) You shall provide the Services for such periods as may be agreed with the Company from time to time. The actual days on which you will provide the Services will be agreed between you and the Company from time to time. For the avoidance of doubt, the Company shall be under no obligation to offer you work and you shall be under no obligation to accept such work from the Company. However, you agree to notify the Company in good time of days on which you will be unavailable for work . . .

(e) If you are unable to work due to illness or injury on any day on which it was agreed that you would provide the Services, you shall notify the Company . . .

(f) You . . . will represent the Company in the provision of the Services and that a high standard of conduct and appearance is required at all times. While providing the Services, you also agree to comply with all reasonable rules and policies of the Company from time to time and as notified to you, including those contained in the Company Manual . . .

(i) You will account for your income tax, value added tax and social security contributions to the appropriate authorities.

(j) You will provide all your own tools, equipment, materials and other items as shall be required for the performance of the Services . . .

(k) You will have personal liability for the consequences of your services to the Company. . .

---

[12] S. Evans, J. Goodman and L. Hargreave, *Unfair Dismissal Law and Employment Practice in the 1980s* (London: Department of Employment, Research Paper No. 53, 1985), p. 24.

[13] [2018] UKSC 29, [2018] ICR 1511.

(l)   You shall at all times keep the Company informed of your other activities
      which could give rise to a direct or indirect conflict of interest with the
      interests of the Company, provided that ... you shall not be permitted at
      any time to provide services to any Customer ... other than under this
      Agreement...

(n)   You are an independent contractor of the Company, in business on your
      own account. Nothing in this Agreement shall render you an employee,
      agent or partner of the Company and the termination of this Agreement ...
      shall not constitute a dismissal for any purpose.

Many of these clauses try to eliminate a factor that might suggest there is a
contract of employment or the statutory status of being a worker while at the
same time maintaining detailed control over the worker. Clause (c) attempts to
deny any mutuality of obligation in the mistaken belief that this is relevant,
though clause (e) immediately contradicts the assertion that the plumber does
not have to accept work by requiring notice of illness or any deviation from a
normal working week. While insisting in clause (f) on the kind of obedience
and subordination characteristic of contracts of employment, since that control was essential to the business operation, the next three clauses specify that
the plumber assumes the normal risks and obligations of an independent
contractor. In practice, however, arrangements for the payment of tax appear
to carry little weight when the courts are determining the nature of the
contract for the purposes of employment-protection legislation.[14] Clause (l)
protects the company's interest in a duty of loyalty that one would normally
associate with an employee. Clause (n) sums things up by an explicit assertion
that the plumber is an independent contractor. It is well established, however,
that the courts will not be much influenced by an explicit statement that the
contract is one of employment or a contract for services.[15] Clause (n) may also
be invalid as it purports in effect to exclude the law of unfair dismissal contrary
to ERA 1996, section 203.

Attempts to draft contracts in such a way that an employer has all the
benefits of being an employer, including complete control over the operation,
while avoiding onerous commitments and statutory employment rights can be
challenged in three ways. The first approach applies the multifactor test and
concludes that even if the terms of the contract can be taken at face value,
there are still sufficient indications of employment or worker status to justify
the application of statutory rights. The second approach involves construction
of the contract, taking into account all of its terms. This approach will reveal
internal contradictions in the contract that reveal its duplicitous nature. In the
contract of the Pimlico Plumbers, for instance, the terms imposed the normal

---

[14] *Young & Woods Ltd* v. *West* [1980] IRLR 201 (CA).

[15] *McMeechan* v. *Secretary of State for Employment* [1997] ICR 549 (CA), although older cases
appear to have placed greater weight on explicit statements: *Massey* v. *Crown Life Insurance Co.*
[1978] ICR 590 (CA).

implied obligations of employment such as obedience and loyalty, while at the same time asserting that the plumbers were in business in their own account and therefore would not normally owe such obligations. A court can then attempt to reconcile the internal contradictions in the terms of the contract by holding that its key ingredients should lead to a particular employment status. The third approach is to hold that the contract or some of its terms are a sham.

In general contract law, a sham contract is one where the formal written terms of the agreement do not correspond to the real agreement and intentions of the parties. In commercial contracts lawyers may concoct a misleading transaction in order to avoid tax liabilities or restrict the rights of third parties. In such commercial cases, the finding of a sham transaction requires convincing evidence that both parties really intended a rather different contractual arrangement from that contained in the written agreement. Applying that test of the joint intentions of the parties to an employment context would, however, rarely assist workers in obtaining protection from labour laws, for typically an employer would intend that the formal agreement that presents the worker as an independent contractor should accurately state the rights and obligations of the parties. In *Autoclenz Ltd* v. *Belcher*,[16] the Supreme Court decided on a different, employment-specific, approach to sham contracts.

In *Autoclenz Ltd* v. *Belcher* the workers were car cleaners or valeters, who worked full time for a company that arranged for cars to be cleaned prior to sale at auction. These workers claimed rights under the NMWA 1998 and the Working Time Regulations 1998. One preliminary issue was whether or not their employment status was that of employee or worker, as opposed to being independent contractors without those rights. The contract stated explicitly that the valeters were independent sub-contractors, responsible for their own taxes and by a subsequent amendment the contract also stated (for the avoidance of doubt, it said) that the work was casual, as required, that suitably qualified substitutes were permitted and that the valeters would supply their own cleaning equipment. In practice, however, the valeters worked as full-time employees, using the firm's uniform and equipment and obeyed the instructions of the manager. Working in teams of four people, they were paid on a piecework basis, in accordance with records (called invoices) kept and processed by the employer. Further evidence before the tribunal revealed that the employer did not expect in practice that any substitutes would be offered work. While not ignoring the written terms of the contract as a principal source for characterising the legal relationship between employer and worker, the Supreme Court stated that: 'the relative bargaining power of the parties must be taken into account in deciding whether the terms of any written agreement in truth represent what was agreed and the true agreement will

---

[16] [2011] UKSC 41, [2011] ICR 1157 (SC).

often have to be gleaned from all the circumstances of the case, of which the written agreement is only a part'.[17] The Supreme Court agreed with the tribunal that these legal efforts to disguise the relationship were a sham and that by taking into account actual practice and expectations of the parties the tribunal had correctly identified the legal status of the car valeters as employees. This decision will make it much harder in future for employers to avoid the application of labour rights by drafting a contract that creates the appearance of a contract for services when in practice the parties expect the transaction to function as a contract of employment.

Unfortunately, as illustrated by *Pimlico Plumbers Ltd* v. *Smith*, lawyers still include terms that purport to negative the status of employment or worker. In that case, the contract included a substitution clause, permitting a plumber to find another Pimlico Plumber to perform an assignment. That substitution might happen if the plumber was unwell, unable to do that particular type of work or if he or she had the chance to perform a more lucrative assignment. Personal performance of the contract is a normal feature of contracts of employment and is part of the statutory definition of worker, as we shall see below. Independent contractors sometimes offer a personal service, but often the identity of the worker is not material to the contract. Some courts have treated substitution clauses as breaching an essential condition for a finding of employment status. In connection with employment status, this approach erroneously treats one of the factors as a necessary condition, so that any right to provide a substitute prevents a finding of a contract of employment, whereas under the multifactor analysis, this right to use a substitute only points against a finding of employment. It is correct, however, as we shall see below, that the statutory concept of worker speaks of a requirement of personal performance, so that a right to provide a substitute makes it difficult to qualify as a worker. Second, it is correct that unfettered rights to provide a substitute worker have been treated as a strong indication of independent-contractor status. For instance, a practice of undertaking to provide a substitute worker is common among lorry-drivers; as a consequence of assuming the business risk of illness or absence, the drivers are usually classified as independent contractors.[18] In contrast, significant restrictions on the right to provide a substitute to perform the work will often lead to the conclusion that the arrangement is consistent with the employment status of employee or worker.[19] In *Pimlico Plumbers* v. *Smith*, the restriction on substitutions to other Pimlico Plumbers was sufficient to permit the conclusion that the tribunal had not been in error in classifying the plumber as a worker under

---

[17] Para. 35, *per* Lord Clarke.
[18] *Express & Echo Publications Ltd* v. *Tanton* [1999] ICR 693 (CA); *Ready Mixed Concrete (South East) Ltd* v. *Minister of Pensions and National Insurance* [1968] 2 QB 49 (QB).
[19] *Byrne Bros (Formwork) Ltd* v. *Baird* [2002] ICR 667 (EAT).

the statute. The Supreme Court held that the dominant feature of the contract was for personal performance by the plumber, notwithstanding occasional substitutions in practice under the contract.

Workers and Dependent Contractors

Despite their flexibility, the various tests and factors considered in the distinction drawn between contracts of service and contracts for services may not precisely identify some of the crucial issues from the perspective of labour legislation. Many labour laws seek to address the economic dependence of the worker on the employer in the sense that the worker relies heavily upon the job as the principal source of income. Economic dependence arises because the worker may feel tied to the job owing to a lack of alternatives or at least a lack of jobs where the employee, with his or her particular set of skills and experiences, could earn an equivalent income. This economic dependence usually occurs in contracts of employment but it is not necessarily confined to such contracts.

Consider the position of a van driver who owns the van and earns a living by delivering goods from a logistics company to customers in return for a fee paid by the company for each delivery. Although the contract does not guarantee that any packages will need to be delivered, the driver is contractually bound to make herself available for twenty-eight days a month (or find a substitute) in case the company needs her services. In practice, she is expected to work nearly every day except Sundays, and this is her only job. She does not have to display the company's logo on her van or clothing, but must obtain a signature from customers on a mobile device supplied by the company. According to the multifactor test for employment, it is unlikely that the driver will be classified as an employee. She may be in business on her own account, because her income is determined in part by how many packages she chooses to deliver, although of course the company determines how many packages are allocated and the payment for each delivery. She is not integrated into the organisation in many respects and has considerable freedom in how she performs the service, although the company's computer proposes a fastest route and can monitor her progress and inform customers of when packages are likely to arrive. She is also permitted to use substitutes from among her colleagues, which is essential if she is to have any days-off or holidays. What this classification of the driver being an independent contractor misses, however, is that in reality the driver is economically dependent on the company for work and must comply with its instructions or fail to obtain an income. A dependent contractor of this kind may be as vulnerable to abuse of managerial power and exploitation as an ordinary employee, but as a result of the application of the control test and the business-risk test is likely to be classified in law as an independent contractor who enters into contracts for services and is excluded from employment protection legislation.

Dependent Contractors

An instructive example of how dependent contractors may effectively be as economically dependent as employees, if not more so, is provided by a study of doorstep milk deliveries.[20] In the context of intensified competition from supermarkets, the dairies decided to replace employed milkmen with franchisees. The job of delivering milk early in the morning to a neighbourhood and collecting payments from customers remained the same, but under the franchise contract the milkmen had to purchase the milk from the dairy, pay for the right to operate the franchise and manage their own tax affairs as independent contractors. From the dairy's point of view, the arrangement was more efficient because the franchisee milkmen rarely called in sick, unlike before on cold rainy mornings, the milkmen bore the risk of customers not paying or deciding not to take the service any longer and there were few administrative overheads. Crucially, the dairy determined the price of the milk sold to the milkmen, thereby controlling the income of the milkmen derived from their profit margin. While forbidding the milkmen to purchase products from other dairies, the dairy continued to sell milk at a lower price to supermarkets and even to non-franchised independent milkmen. In their legal form, these franchise contracts appeared to be contracts between two businesses, but in substance little had changed from the prior contracts of employment except that the workers now bore most of the risks of the business as well. As one franchisee observed: 'I think they introduced franchising because the whole depot was carrying too much debt ... there was thousands of pounds on the books that wasn't collected or could not be collected in ... They're passing on the risk with franchising, it ain't their problem any more.'

O'Kelly v. *Trusthouse Forte*[21] is a leading example of such a dependent contractor being classified as an independent contractor rather than an employee. Some casual waiters at a hotel, who were also stewards of their union, claimed unfair dismissal and interim relief against dismissal,[22] on the ground that the reason for dismissal was their membership of a trade union. This claim for unfair dismissal was dependent on the finding that the waiters had contracts of employment. We have already considered one claim of these casual waiters that they had a continuous contract of employment (an 'umbrella contract')[23] that lasted between the days when they were required to serve at banquets at the hotel. A second issue in the case was whether, on those evenings when they did perform work, they were properly classified as employees or independent contractors. Due to the fluctuating demand for banquets and private functions, the employer had a small number of permanent staff plus a pool of casual waiters, who regularly supplied services when called upon and who were paid at a set rate for each job. Some of these 'regulars', including the applicants, worked for no other employer, and in

---

[20] J. O'Connell Davidson, 'What Do Franchisors Do? Control and Commercialisation in Milk Distribution' (1984) 8 *Work, Employment and Society* 23.

[21] [1984] QB 90 (CA).   [22] ERA 1996, s. 128.   [23] See Chapter 6.

practice served almost every week of the year for between thirty and forty hours per week on average. The waiters worked under the supervision of the hotel's management, were paid weekly on the company's computer payroll and had tax and social security deducted as employees. Although the casual waiters were not legally obliged to perform any particular job, if they refused they would be dropped or suspended from the list of those regularly asked to work. The letters of alleged 'dismissal' were statements made by the employer that the applicants would not be asked to work again. A tribunal rejected the waiters' claim that they worked under contracts of employment either in the form of an 'umbrella contract' which persisted all the time, or under separate contracts of employment each time that they worked at a function. The EAT reversed the second aspect of the decision on the ground that the waiters were not in business on their own account:

> Standing back and looking at the matter in the round, what we have to ask is whether these applicants can be said to have been carrying on business on their own account. We can well understand that casuals who have their services to sell, and sell them in the market to whoever needs them for the time being, can be said to be in business on their own account in the marketing or selling of their services; but we find it difficult to reach that conclusion in a situation where the services are, in fact, being offered to one person only against a background arrangement (albeit not contractual) which requires the services to be offered to one person only and which involves a repetition of those contracts (albeit under no obligation to do so) as is shown by the weekly pay packet, the holiday pay and other matters of that kind. In our judgment, each of these individual contracts is a contract of employment, not a contract for services.

In the course of this reasoning, the EAT uses the fact that the waiters were in practice wholly economically dependent on the hotel for work to justify in part the conclusion that they were employees. The Court of Appeal sharply disagreed: 'This must involve a misdirection on a question of law or every independent contractor who is content or able only to attract one client would be held to work under a contract of employment.'[24] The Court of Appeal concluded that the industrial tribunal had posed the correct legal question and examined the facts carefully before reaching its conclusion that the waiters were at all times independent contractors, and so there was no error of law in their initial decision.

This rejection of economic dependence on a single employer as a relevant criterion for the classification of workers as employees must be questioned in the context of determining the proper scope of employment laws. This factor may be irrelevant to issues of tort liability or taxation, but it surely goes to the core of issues of employment law. In this particular case, for instance, the waiters lost their jobs almost certainly because they were involved in attempts

---

[24] *Per* Sir John Donaldson MR.

at union organisation and efforts to obtain payment for notice periods prior to dismissal. These are precisely the sorts of entitlements that economically dependent workers need for their protection. By offering the waiters only casual work, rather than a regular job, and treating them as independent contractors, the employer not only succeeded in transferring the risk of the absence of work on to the waiters, but also managed to rely upon this transfer of risk as a ground for avoiding the application of vital labour rights. The Court of Appeal's error was to ignore the point that the waiters were completely integrated into the employer's business, so that their self-employment was largely bogus.

In order to provide some employment protection rights to dependent contractors and others whose personal work contracts are closely akin to contracts of employment, many statutory employment rights apply to the statutory employment status of a 'worker'. The most important of these rights include the National Minimum Wage Act 1998,[25] the Working Time Regulations 1998,[26] unauthorised deductions from wages,[27] protections for whistle-blowers,[28] rights in connection with trade unions, collective bargaining and industrial action,[29] and from April 2020 the written particulars required under ERA 1996 s.1.

Employment Rights Act 1996, Section 230(3)

(3) In this Act 'worker' means an individual who has entered into or works under (or, where the employment has ceased, worked under) –

(a) a contract of employment; or

(b) any other contract, whether express or implied and (if it is express) whether oral or in writing, whereby the individual undertakes to do or perform personally any work or services for another party to the contract whose status is not by virtue of the contract that of a client or customer of any profession or business undertaking carried on by the individual ...

The main aim of using this definition of qualifying employment status is to include within the scope of the protective legislation some independent contractors of the kind that were described above as dependent contractors.[30] This statutory definition of workers covers independent contractors who provide services personally that are integrated into another business undertaking, as in the Pimlico Plumbers. It can also include other groups such as equity partners in a limited-liability-partnership law firm.[31] It has been estimated that the

---

[25] National Minimum Wage Act 1998, s. 54.   [26] Working Time Regulations 1998, reg. 2
[27] ERA 1996, s. 13.   [28] ERA 1996, s. 47(B)(1).
[29] Trade Union and Labour Relations (Consolidation) Act 1992, s. 296(1).
[30] G. Davidov, 'Who Is a Worker?' (2005) 34 *Industrial Law Journal* 57.
[31] *Bates van Winkelhof* v. *Clyde & Co LLP* [2014] UKSC 32, [2014] ICR 730.

definition of worker extends the selected employment protection laws beyond employees to a further 5 per cent of the workforce.[32] The breadth of application may in practice be greater in relation to the NMWA 1998, where there is a reversal of the burden of proof, so that an employer is required to prove that the self-employed individual is not a worker but an independent business.[33]

The type of independent contractors to be included as 'workers' should be self-employed individuals who for the most part only enter into contracts to perform work personally for a single employer, and whose degree of dependence or subordination is broadly similar to that of an employee.[34] The concept of worker was held in *Redrow Homes (Yorkshire) Ltd* v. *Wright* to include bricklayers contracted personally to perform particular jobs on building sites although clearly in the capacity of independent contractors rather than employees.[35] It was also agreed, *obiter*, that the car valeters in *Autoclenz Ltd* v. *Belcher* were certainly workers, even if they had not also qualified as employees. There would be a good chance that casual workers such as the waiters in *O'Kelly* v. *Trusthouse Forte* would today be classified as 'workers' during their particular engagements at banquets.

The statutory definition of a worker includes two key elements. First, the concept of worker requires the personal performance of work, so that, as soon as a person manages and pays others to perform the work rather than performing it in person, this managerial role is likely to take the person outside the statutory concept of a worker. Equally, an unfettered contractual right to use substitutes instead of performing the work personally should normally exclude a person from the statutory category of worker. A sub-postmaster who provides his own premises and can employ staff to perform the work has been held to be carrying on a business undertaking and therefore not a worker.[36] Where the right to provide a substitute is restricted, however, it is possible that a court will conclude that, in accordance with the test proposed in *Pimlico Plumbers Ltd* v. *Smith*,[37] the 'dominant feature' of the contract is nevertheless personal performance. In *James* v. *Redcats (Brands) Ltd*,[38] the contract provided that a courier had the right to find an alternative courier if she was 'unable to work'. Elias J held that, since the right to provide a substitute only arose when she was unable to work, perhaps through sickness, rather than leaving the matter to her discretion according to whether or not she wished to

---

[32] B. Burchell, S. Deakin and S. Honey, *The Employment Status of Individuals in Non-Standard Employment* (London: DTI, Employment Relations Research Series No. 6, URN/99/770, 1999), para. 8.2.

[33] NMWA 1998, s. 28.   [34] *Byrne Bros (Formwork) Ltd* v. *Baird* [2002] ICR 667 (EAT).

[35] [2004] EWCA Civ 469, [2004] IRLR 720 (CA).

[36] *Commissioners of Inland Revenue* v. *Post Office Ltd* [2003] IRLR 199 (EAT).

[37] [2018] UKSC 29, [2018] ICR 15 11. M. Ford, 'Pimlico Plumbers: Cutting the Gordian Knot of Substitution Clauses?', UK Labour Law Blog, 19 July 2018, available at https://wordpress.com/view/uklabourlawblog.com.

[38] [2007] ICR 1006 (EAT).

do the job personally, this arrangement meant that the claimant was obliged to do the work personally. Similarly, in *Pimlico Plumbers Ltd* v. *Smith*, because the right to substitute other workers was limited to other Pimlico Plumbers, the dominant feature of the contract was personal performance, so that the plumber could be classified as a worker.

The second key element of the statutory definition of worker is the exclusion of contracts where the business is a client or customer of the person performing the service. If the person performing work has a variety of clients and customers, or at least has a realistic option of working for other clients and markets the business in that way, the contract will be characterised as one of independent contracting rather than satisfying the statutory definition of a worker. In contrast, if the worker has been recruited by the core business to work for it as an integral part of its operations, this case is likely to be classified as a worker.[39] To identify cases where the independent contractor is performing the work for the other business, a number of terms of the contract are likely to be important. For instance, if the contract prohibits working for other clients, or requires full-time work or requires the contractor to comply with a wide range of organisational rules and accounting practices, it is likely that the contractor will be classified as a worker. In *Pimlico Plumbers Ltd* v. *Smith*, for instance, the plumber had to wear the company's uniform, hire a van with logos from the business, work for about forty hours each week and comply with a restrictive covenant preventing work as a plumber in London on termination of the contract. These contractual requirements were sufficient to indicate that the core business was not a customer or client of the plumber but rather his or her employer.

This statutory definition of worker also defines the scope of many collective labour law rights.[40] A trade union is defined as an association of workers, the statutory procedure to claim recognition for the purpose of collective bargaining is granted to workers and the protection for industrial action in a trade dispute is confined to workers. In this context, employers may argue that the persons providing work personally are professionals supplying their services to clients and therefore fall outside the protections for the establishment of collective bargaining relationships and strike action. The questionable assumption here is that professional independent contractors may have no need to form trade unions for the purpose of collective bargaining. That restriction on collective bargaining rights was applied to a claim brought by freelance wildlife cameramen and women under the statutory trade-union recognition procedure.[41] It was also applied to exclude Deliveroo riders from that procedure on the dubious ground that because they had an unrestricted

---

[39] *Cotswold Developments Construction Ltd* v. *Williams* [2006] IRLR 181 (EAT); *Hospital Medical Group Ltd* v. *Westwood* [2012] EWCA Civ 1005, [2013] ICR 415.
[40] TULRCA 1992, s. 296(1).
[41] *R* v. *Central Arbitration Committee* [2003] EWHC 1375 Admin, [2003] IRLR 460 (QB).

right to use substitutes they did not have to perform work personally and therefore were not workers within the statutory definition.[42] EU law may not be so restrictive when determining the scope of collective bargaining that is exempt from competition law, for it has been applied to freelance musicians, who substitute for other musicians in orchestras, even though they are largely in business on their own account.[43]

EU law has used another concept of employment status to extend the application of rights beyond employees. Some EU Directives and the UK legislation that implements it defines its scope of application with the phrase 'contract of employment or employment relationship'. An example is Article 1 of Directive 91/533 on the employer's obligation to inform employees of the conditions applicable to the contract of employment.[44] The reason for adopting this extended definition of protected contracts seems likely to be that some national systems of law in Europe have applied labour regulation to 'employment and employment-like' contracts, an extension that serves the same purpose as the UK statutory concept of worker. Instead of always adopting the term worker,[45] however, some UK implementing legislation refers to an 'employment relationship'. Since the EU Directives typically insist that its meaning should depend upon national law,[46] the scope of application of these Directives turns on the meaning of the concept of 'employment relationship' in UK law, though no such concept has hitherto existed in domestic law. The meaning of the concept is therefore open to considerable speculation. It may mean exactly the same as contract of employment, or it may be equivalent to the statutory concept of worker. It seems possible that persons holding a 'public office', such as judges, who would not be regarded as working under a contract of employment under UK law, might be classified as having an 'employment relationship' suitable for the acquisition of rights under European law.[47] It also seems possible that an 'employment relationship' may not require the existence of a contractual relation, as in the case of volunteers who, as unpaid workers, may not have any contractual relation owing to the absence of consideration. Yet in a case of dismissal involving a teacher who had a contract of employment with a local authority, but who was managed and in effect dismissed by the governing body of the school where he worked, a majority of the Court of Appeal preferred the view that this

---

[42] *Independent Workers' Union of Great Britain (IWGB)* v. *RooFoods Limited T/A Deliveroo* TUR1/985(2016), 14 November 2017.

[43] *FNV Kunsten Informatie en Media* v. *Staat der Nederlanden* (Case C-413/13) [2015] All ER (EC) 387.

[44] See Chapter 4. The employment relationship also defines the scope of Framework Directive 96/34 on parental leave, Framework Directive 97/81 on part-time work, and Framework Directive 99/70 on fixed-term work.

[45] E.g. Agency Worker Regulations 2010, SI 2010 No. 93, reg. 3.

[46] Acquired Rights Directive 77/187, Art. 2.2, as amended.

[47] *Percival-Price* v. *Department of Economic Development* [2000] IRLR 380 (NICA).

non-contractual relation with the governing body could not count as an 'employment relationship'.[48]

EU Worker

As well as this UK statutory definition of 'worker', the scope of some EU law applies also to the concept of a 'worker'.[49] Confusingly, this EU concept of a worker has its own independent meaning and may not defer to national interpretations of the concept. This independent meaning of the EU concept of a worker was confirmed in the application of the European Treaty provisions on equal pay by the ECJ in *Allonby* v. *Accrington and Rossendale College*.[50] The college had failed to renew the contracts of fixed-term part-time lecturers, most of whom were women, and instead engaged them through an employment agency with which the lecturers were registered as self-employed independent contractors. Under these new arrangements, the lecturers' income fell and they lost some fringe benefits, including an occupational pension scheme. In a claim for equal pay in comparison with a retained full-time permanent male employee, the Court of Appeal referred certain questions to the ECJ regarding the scope of European equal pay law.[51] The ECJ held that the Treaty provisions on equal pay applied to 'workers', which had an independent meaning under Community law. A worker was defined as: 'a person who, for a certain period of time, performs services for and under the direction of another person in return for remuneration'.

This definition emphasises three features of the relationship: personal performance of work, subordination or control by the employer and persistence over a period of time rather than a one-off transaction. These features are similar to the requirements under the common law for a finding of a contract of employment, although the long-term character of the relation may differ. It is also possible that some who are classified as workers under the UK statutory concept, such as the Pimlico Plumbers, might also qualify as 'workers' under this EU autonomous concept. Thus a person who may be classified as self-employed or an independent contractor under national law could be a 'worker' within the EU law governing equal pay, if her independence disguised the reality of a relation of subordination. Notice that the ECJ does not refer to a requirement of a direct contractual relation between employer and worker, which made it possible for the agency workers in this case to bring a claim for equal pay against the client of the agency. The ECJ ultimately decided, however, that the comparison with a full-time male employee of the college

---

[48] *Governing Body of Clifton Middle School* v. *Askew* [2000] ICR 286 (CA).
[49] N. Kountouris, 'The Concept of "Worker" in European Labour Law: Fragmentation, Autonomy and Scope' (2018) 47 *Industrial Law Journal* 192.
[50] Case C-256/01, *Allonby* v. *Accrington and Rossendale College* [2004] ICR 1328 (ECJ).
[51] TFEU, Art. 157 (formerly Art. 141 of the EC Treaty).

could not be made for the purposes of equal-pay law, because the part-time lecturers were now paid by a different 'employer', the employment agency.

The term 'worker' is also used elsewhere in the EU treaties. In particular, it applies to the treaty provisions on free movement of workers.[52] It also applies to the duty to notify public authorities and representatives of workers of collective redundancies, where the concept of a worker has been applied to a remunerated director of a company and a trainee or apprentice who was funded by a public jobseekers' centre.[53] Although the ECJ has warned that the term 'worker' may not always have the same meaning when it is used in the treaties,[54] the same elements of performance remunerated work under the direction of another have been used in these different contexts.[55]

A Contract Personally to Do Work

For the purposes of discrimination law, the Equality Act 2010 defines its scope as employment and a contract personally to do work.

Equality Act 2010, Section 83(2)

(2) Employment means –
   (a) employment under a contract of employment, a contract of apprenticeship or a contract personally to do work . . .

This provision uses the common-law definition of employment but differs from the statutory definition of 'worker' because it drops the explicit exclusion of professionals and independent businesses. It also appears broader than the EU concept of worker discussed above, because there is no explicit requirement that work should be performed under the direction of the employer. Unfortunately, this definition is seriously ambiguous. On the one hand, the word employment is used as a preliminary condition for the whole definition, as in 'employment under . . . a contract personally to do work', so that it is arguable that only employees or 'employees in an extended sense'[56] are covered by discrimination laws. On the other hand, because it differs from the statutory definition of employment (and worker), the statutory formulation appears to have the purpose of extending coverage beyond contracts of employment to any persons who have a contract personally to do work, which

---

[52] TFEU, Art. 45.
[53] Case C-229/14, *Balkaya v. Kiesel Abbruch- und Recycling Technik GmbH* EU:C:2015:455.
[54] Case C-85/96, *Martinez Sala v. Freistaat Bayer* [1998] ECR I-2691, para. 31 (ECJ).
[55] Case C-66/85, *Lawrie-Blum v. Land Baden-Wurttemberg* [1987] ICR 483 (ECJ).
[56] Underhill LJ, *Windle v. Secretary of State for Justice* [2016] EWCA Civ 459, [2016] ICR 721 [10].

might include independent contractors, including professionals, provided that the contract required the individual to perform the work personally rather than manage a business that provided the service. The exact scope and meaning of this statutory concept and therefore the scope of application of laws against discrimination is contested. A number of controversial points should be highlighted.

First, the concept of a contract personally to do work requires there to be a contract, or the potential offer of a contract, in the case of discrimination in recruitment. This requirement is likely to exclude unpaid internships and voluntary work.[57] Leaving such volunteers and interns outside the scope of the EqA 2010 renders this unpaid sector vulnerable to discriminatory practices and cronyism. At best, it can be argued that, by permitting this regulatory-free zone, employers, including small charities and NGOs, may be more willing to take a chance on giving some valuable work experience to individuals who would otherwise find it much harder to break into the world of work. The requirement of a contract also creates difficulties in some kinds of triangular arrangements where the functions of management are divided between two or more employing entities.[58] Insofar as the domestic legislation seeks to implement EU equal-pay law, this requirement of a contract seems inconsistent with *Allonby* v. *Accrington and Rossendale College.*

Secondly, the contract must be of a kind that contains an obligation to perform work. This element excludes an umbrella or framework agreement where there is no promise on either side to offer or perform work, but merely an agreement that, if work is offered by the employer and if the offer is accepted, the job will be governed by the terms of the umbrella agreement.[59] It is possible, therefore, that offers of umbrella contracts or framework agreements may fall outside the UK laws against discrimination.

Thirdly, the concept of a personal work contract cannot apply where the individual who is party to the contract is not obliged to perform the work personally but may employ others to do the job. The interpretation placed upon this requirement of personal work is likely to be the same as the test in *Pimlico Plumbers* v. *Smith*, which is that, notwithstanding some restricted possibilities of using substitutes, the dominant feature of the contract is that it requires personal performance by the worker. The contrast is with a contract where the promise is merely to ensure that the work is performed by managing the performance of the service by others. In *Mirror Group Newspapers* v. *Gunning*,[60] the applicant's father had held a distributorship for newspapers, which involved the purchase of newspapers in bulk, and then the resale and

---

[57] *X* v. *Mid Sussex Citizens Advice Bureau* [2012] UKSC 59, [2013] ICR 249.   [58] See p. 229.
[59] *Mingely* v. *Pennock and Ivory (trading as Amber Cars)* [2004] EWCA Civ 328, [2004] ICR 727 (CA), decided under an earlier version of EqA 2010, s. 83(2).
[60] [1986] ICR 145 (CA), applying the same definition of employment in Sex Discrimination Act 1975, s. 82(1).

delivery of newspapers to about ninety retail outlets by means of employing about eight people using rented vans. The father's work involved direct supervision of the collection of the newspapers and their loading on to the vans. On her father's retirement, the applicant applied for the distributorship, but the defendant refused the application and instead gave the work to two other businesses in the area. The applicant brought a claim for sex discrimination. As the dominant purpose was not the personal performance of work by the owner of the distributorship, but rather the supply of a service through managing a team of workers, the claim was excluded from the scope of discrimination laws.

Fourthly, there is a question whether the element of control or subordination that is characteristic of a contract of employment must be present in a contract personally to do work. In a controversial decision in *Jivraj* v. *Hashwani*,[61] the Supreme Court inserted this requirement of subordination into the meaning of EqA 2010, section 83(2). In a commercial contract, a term provided that any dispute arising should be resolved by arbitration before three arbitrators, each of whom was required to be a respected member of the Ismaili community. The Ismaili community comprises Shia Iambi Ismaili Muslims and is led by the Aga Khan. The main question before the court was whether this contractual requirement became void on the ground that it was contrary to the Employment Equality (Religion or Belief) Regulations 2003, now consolidated in the EqA 2010. The Supreme Court held that the Regulations (and therefore now the Act) did not apply to the appointment of an arbitrator. Although a contract with an arbitrator is clearly a contract to perform work personally, the Supreme Court insisted that the correct statutory phrase to be construed was 'employment . . . under a contract to perform work personally'. By adding the term 'employment' in front of the phrase, the Supreme Court used the reference to employment to insist that the relationship should be one of subordination, as in a contract of employment. An arbitrator was described as an independent provider of services who was not in a relationship of subordination with the person who received the services. In effect, by introducing the requirement of subordination implied by the term 'employment', the Supreme Court narrowed the scope of equality laws to the same range as that described by the European concept of 'worker', as described above.

The Supreme Court expressed the view that it was appropriate for the law governing equal pay and discrimination to have the same scope. In UK law, the EqA 2010 had used section 83(2) to define the scope of both equal pay law and anti-discrimination law. As UK equality laws are now governed by EU law, it was believed that their scope should be harmonised by reference to the European concept of worker, as set out by the ECJ in *Allonby* v. *Accrington*

---

[61] [2011] UKSC 40, [2011] ICR 1004.

and Rossendale College.[62] As we have seen, that concept of worker includes as an essential element the criterion of subordination or direction by the employer, which would exclude an arbitrator. That view can be challenged, however, because the EU equal-pay laws refer to the concept of 'worker' to define their scope, whereas the EU Framework Directive on equality that determines the scope of the remainder of anti-discrimination laws applies in Article 3 to 'conditions for access to employment, to self-employment or to occupation', and to 'employment and working conditions, including dismissals and pay', without referring to the concept of worker. In response to that point, the Supreme Court suggested that Article 3 only refers to the processes of qualifying and setting up in business as an arbitrator (or a plumber or a lawyer) and not to the application of discriminatory choices by customers of those self-employed professionals. On this view, which was strongly endorsed by the Supreme Court, if a customer declines to hire a solicitor, a plumber, a gardener, a painter or some other self-employed person on one of the grounds prohibited by the EqA 2010, such as race, sex or religion, there will be no remedy available.

This restrictive decision on the scope of discrimination laws may perhaps be explained in this particular case by reference to a policy of supporting private arbitration in civil matters by minority groups with a view to enabling the law to accommodate religious difference (although it was possible to achieve a similar goal by declaring the religious affiliation of the arbitrator to be a justifiable occupational requirement, an argument that the Supreme Court also approved).[63] Yet the decision in *Jivraj* v. *Hashwani* seems to diminish considerably the field of application of anti-discrimination laws. Crucially, it seems to exclude virtually all self-employed persons from their scope. In that respect, it is hard to reconcile with the earlier decision of the House of Lords in *Kelly* v. *Northern Ireland Housing Executive*, where, in this instance of a solicitor applying for work, it was said to be 'clear that the definition of employment is wide enough to include work done by an independent contractor'.[64] Similarly, the Court of Appeal suggested in *Mirror Group Newspapers* v. *Gunning*,[65] that a contract with a plumber to perform work would be included within the scope of discrimination law, even though the plumber was always accompanied and assisted by his or her mate or apprentice, because the dominant purpose in the contract was the performance of work personally by the plumber. It is true that in those earlier decisions, the rulings of the ECJ regarding the scope of application of equal-pay laws were not cited or available. But it is unclear that those rulings should be determinative for two reasons. First, it needs to be explained why equal-pay laws should have the

---

[62] Case C-256/01, *Allonby* v. *Accrington and Rossendale College* [2004] ICR 1328 (ECJ).
[63] See Chapter 10.   [64] [1998] ICR 828, at 833, *per* Lord Slynn.
[65] [1986] ICR 145 (CA), applying the same definition of employment in Sex Discrimination Act 1975, s. 82(1).

same scope as anti-discrimination law. In the case of equal-pay law, clearly it should be a defence for the employer that the worker is an independent contractor who sets his or her own wages. In contrast, a self-employed person seems to be equally vulnerable to invidious types of discrimination when seeking access to work as a person seeking employment. If the aim of the law is to cleanse the labour market from discriminatory preferences of employers, it surely should make no difference whether the contract for the personal performance of work falls one side or the other of the boundary between employment and self-employment. Second, it should be remembered that EU law sets minimum standards, so there is no reason why the UK should not provide wider protection for workers against discrimination than EU Directives.

Fifthly, we need to ask whether there is a requirement of continuous employment or mutuality of obligation. If the work is intermittent with no ongoing commitment on either side, the Court of Appeal has indicated that this feature is relevant and likely to count against a finding that the contractor qualifies as an employee,[66] or under EqA 2010, section 83(2) as 'employment under ... a contract personally to do work'.[67] The reason given for this exclusion is that the worker's right to refuse work on any occasion tends to prevent a relation of subordination, which is necessary for both a contract of employment and a contract personally to do work, from arising. For instance, in *Windle* v. *Secretary of State for Justice*,[68] which concerned allegations of discrimination brought by translators who worked as independent contractors on a casual basis in courts and the criminal justice system, their right to refuse a particular job was used as a reason to classify them as genuine independent contractors even though when working on a particular job they had to comply with detailed court and police regulations. This argument that casual workers without a binding permanent contract are less likely to be in a relation of subordination and therefore less likely to be in employment in an extended sense seems dubious. It appears to suggest that precarious workers are less subordinated than those who have permanent jobs, whereas in practice they may be especially vulnerable to the imposition of exploitative conditions of employment. The argument also confuses the issue of the impermanence of the contract with the presence of control exercised by the employer.

Towards a Unified Concept of Employment Status?

The above description of the personal scope of different employment protection statutes, though complex, still remains broad brush and necessarily simplifies the statutory provisions. Many statutes contain additional rules that explicitly include or exclude other types of work relationships within their scope. For example, the NMWA 1998 explicitly includes agency workers and

---

[66] *Quashie* v. *Stringfellow Restaurants Ltd* [2012] EWCA Civ 1735, [2013] IRLR 99 [12].
[67] *Windle* v. *Secretary of State for Justice* [2016] EWCA Civ 459, [2016] ICR 721.   [68] *Ibid.*

home-workers, even if they may not be 'workers' under the general provision governing the scope of the legislation.[69] Although most civil servants and public-sector workers are now regarded as working under an ordinary contract of employment governed by the ordinary law of contract,[70] special rules and exclusions sometimes apply to certain categories of public-sector jobs such as the police, the armed services, workers in the Houses of Parliament, judges and 'office-holders'. As office-holders, most judges do not have a contractual relation with the Ministry of Justice, which apparently excludes them from UK legislation apart from the HRA 1998,[71] although judges can rely upon directly effective EU legislation such as equal pay.[72] Ministers of religion may also be excluded from employment law protections on the ground that they are appointed or elected office-holders rather than working under a contract,[73] or if they have a contract, that it is not one of employment.[74] Domestic workers such as maids working in private households are excluded from working-time regulation,[75] work outside health and safety supervision,[76] and, if treated as family members, are excluded from the NMW.[77] These exclusions for domestic workers seem to recall their historical role as part of the household of an unconstrained master.[78]

It should be noted here as well that for cases that involve an interference with rights protected by the HRA 1998, any statutory limitations on the personal scope of enjoyment of those rights may be regarded as incompatible with the state's obligation to protect human rights, so they may either be avoided by interpretation or declared incompatible with the protection of convention rights under the Act. In *Bates van Winkelhof* v. *Clyde & Co LLP*,[79] although the partner of the LLP was found to be a worker within the statutory definition, since the claim concerned the exercise of the right to freedom of expression protected under Article 10 of the ECHR, the Supreme Court indicated that, if necessary, it would have had a duty under HRA 1998, section 3 to interpret the statutory concept of worker to ensure effective protection of the convention right. In *Vining* v. *London Borough of Wandsworth*,[80] the claimants worked for the council's parks police service. As members of a police service, they were prevented from bringing a claim for protective awards in the context of dismissals for redundancy by a statutory

---

[69] Ss. 34 and 35.

[70] *R* v. *East Berkshire Health Authority, ex parte Walsh* [1984] ICR 743 (CA); *McClaren* v. *Home Office* [1990] IRLR 338 (CA).

[71] *Gilham* v. *Ministry of Justice* [2017] EWCA Civ 2220, [2018] ICR 827.

[72] Case C-393/10, *O'Brien* v. *Ministry of Justice* EU:C:2012:110, [2012] ICR 955.

[73] *Sharpe* v. *Worcester Diocesan Board of Finance Ltd* [2015] EWCA Civ 399, [2015] ICR 1241.

[74] *Preston* v. *President of the Methodist Conference* [2013] UKSC 29, [2013] ICR 833.

[75] Working Time Regulations 1999, reg. 19   [76] Health and Safety at Work Act 1974, s. 51.

[77] National Minimum Wage Regulations 2015, reg. 57.

[78] E. Albin and J. Prassl, 'Fragmenting Work, Fragmented Regulation', in M. Freedland (gen. ed.), *The Contract of Employment* (Oxford University Press, 2016), pp. 209, 226.

[79] [2014] UKSC 32, [2014] ICR 730 [41]–[45].   [80] [2017] EWCA Civ 1092, [2018] ICR 499.

exclusion of the police service.[81] Absent this exclusion, the protective awards were payable for the employer's failure to consult the trade union. This exclusion was regarded as an unjustified interference with the rights of workers to be represented by a union, contrary to Article 11 ECHR. The Court of Appeal held that, under the interpretive obligation of the HRA 1998, section 3, it was possible to construe the statutory exclusion of the police service from rights to consultation not to apply to parks police even though they were properly regarded as police and therefore excluded for other purposes. In effect, HRA 1998, section 3 was used to circumvent the statutory limitation on one aspect of coverage of employment rights.

Two final questions should be asked about this tangle of provisions regarding the personal scope of labour law. The first question is: do the circles describing the scope of the protections construct an intelligible pattern? Even though the pattern is complex, are there underlying principles, perhaps based on the purposes of the legislation? It may be possible to argue that, when the legal regulation is primarily directed at the possible misuse of managerial authority, the legislation is confined to contracts of employment, because those contracts contain the implied terms of the requirement of obedience and performance in good faith. When the legislation is directed primarily at the operation of the labour market, however, as in the case of wages and hours regulation and laws against discrimination, the scope is broader because it is recognised that the market for performance of work extends beyond traditional contracts of employment to all contracts for the personal performance of work. But this pattern behind the legislation is certainly not followed consistently. For example, the rule in ERA 1996, section 1 which requires employers to provide a written statement of the principal terms of the contract is confined to contracts of employment, even though one of its apparent purposes is to improve transparency in labour markets by compelling employers to disclose the terms of a job in writing. In contrast, the prohibition on unauthorised deductions from pay in ERA 1996, section 13 applies to workers, not just employees, even though the problem of unauthorised deductions might be described as a misuse of managerial power. Furthermore, we must doubt whether the singling out of the contract of employment as the unique site where the risk of abuse of managerial power is present relies upon a satisfactory analysis of the construction of power relations in the labour market. We have noted how some dependent contractors (such as the milkmen or deliverers of packages for logistics companies), although formally classified as independent contractors and not under the direct control of the employer's managers, nevertheless are as subordinate as employees owing to their economic dependence on the employer as their sole customer. As a result, these dependent contractors are as vulnerable to the misuse of

---

[81] TULRCA 1992, s. 280; *London Borough of Redbridge* v. *Dhinsa and McKinnon* [2014] EWCA Civ 178, [2014] ICR 834.

managerial power as employees. It is therefore hard to detect any coherent pattern in the use of the two main definitions of personal scope – employee and worker. Insofar as there may be an explanation, it seems to turn on the historical antecedents of the legislation: prior to the 1960s and, after 1997, the term worker predominated in labour legislation, but in that middle period, with the exception of the anti-discrimination legislation, personal scope was determined by the presence of a contract of employment.

The second question that may be posed about the personal scope of labour law is whether it might be simplified around a single concept of employment status.[82] Plainly, the common law's concept of the contract of employment is too narrow for this purpose, but can the law be unified around the statutory concept of a 'worker' or perhaps 'a contract to perform work personally'? Baroness Hale in *Bates van Winkelhof* v. *Clyde & Co LLP* argued cogently that a pattern was emerging from the statutes that extended protection beyond employees to a worker who was integrated into the main business in the sense that the worker was recruited to perform an integral part of its operations. The combination of contracts of employment and the concept of a worker could supply a unified rule for the personal scope of employment-protection legislation.[83] It would have to be supplemented with a suitable protection against sham clauses in contracts and other disguised employment relations.[84] In order to ensure that the worker concept functioned appropriately, the law would have to offer further guidance than exists at present. The use of the factor of control would need to be clarified to indicate that it is more about integration into the core employer's business than detailed instructions about the performance of work. Economic dependence on the main employer, although a factor that is relevant to the question of integration, should not be determinative, for many genuinely independent small businesses are nevertheless dependent on a major client for a substantial proportion of their work. Contrary to *Windle* v. *Secretary of State for Justice*, there is no reason to exclude intermittent workers and casual workers from the scope of the concept of worker, for they may be integrated into the employer's business as in the case of the waiters in *O'Kelly* v. *Trusthouse Forte*, while being particularly vulnerable to exploitative treatment. Although this interpretation of the concept of worker in UK legislation would address many of the difficulties of the personal scope of employment protection laws, the scope perhaps seems too narrow for anti-discrimination laws. Contrary to the decision of the Supreme

---

[82] M. Freedland, 'From the Contract of Employment to the Personal Work Nexus' (2006) 35 *Industrial Law Journal* 1; S. Deakin, 'Does the "Personal Employment Contract" Provide a Basis for the Reunification of Employment Law?' (2007) 36 *Industrial Law Journal* 68.

[83] H. Collins, 'A Missed Opportunity of a Unified Test of Employment Status', UK Labour Law Blog https://uklabourlawblog.com/2018/07/31.

[84] P. Davies and M. Freedland, 'Employees, Workers, and the Autonomy of Labour Law', in H. Collins, P. Davies and R. Rideout (eds.), *Legal Regulation of the Employment Relation* (London: Kluwer, 2000), p. 267, pp. 282–4.

Court in *Jivraj* v. *Hashwani*, the aim of eliminating discrimination in labour markets can only be achieved by a broad inclusion of self-employed workers, including professionals who are not controlled or integrated into an organisation, as well as employees and anyone seeking to perform work personally with or without remuneration.

Part of the uncertainty surrounding the personal scope of employment protection laws stems from the paucity of statutory guidance. An independent report commissioned by the government entitled *Good Work: The Taylor Review of Working Practices* proposed that more detailed legislation is needed to guide employers and tribunals about the proper classification of workers.[85] Accepting that recommendation, in 2018 the government commenced a consultation exercise regarding the detailed shape of a reform of the law governing employment status.[86] There is no proposal, however, to apply the same personal scope to all statutory employment rights.

Employers' Responsibility in Triangular Relations

The discussion of the personal scope of labour law has so far focused on the legal character of the worker, but we must now turn to the identity of the employer or duty-bearer. In general, the legislation only holds the employer who is in a contractual relation with the employee or worker responsible for the performance of regulatory and contractual obligations. The one important exception to that principle concerns health and safety in the workplace, where the controller of the premises and systems of work will be liable for injuries to a worker in addition to the direct employer. Although it is usually possible to identify the relevant employer by examination of the contractual arrangements, there are several types of situation where confusion arises. In these cases, several employers or employing entities may be involved and it may be difficult to identify which, if any, of the employers should be held responsible for breach of the statutory obligations. It is evident in these triangular relations that the many functions of an employer can be split between two or more legal entities.[87] Hiring and firing and day-to-day management of activities may be separated from the payment of wages and responsibility for compliance with tax law and other regulations.[88]

---

[85] (11 July 2017) www.gov.uk/government/publications/good-work-the-taylor-review-of-modern-working-practices.

[86] BEIS, HM Treasury, HMRC, *Employment Status Consultation* (February 2018). The government has announced that further research is needed before bringing forward legislative proposals: HM Government, *Good Work Plan* (December 2018), p. 29.

[87] J. Prassl, *The Concept of the Employer* (Oxford University Press, 2015), p. 32.

[88] M. Freedland, *The Personal Employment Contract* (Oxford University Press, 2003), pp. 40–5.

Associated Employers

One occasion where a multi-employer pattern may arise is within a group of companies that is controlled centrally by a parent or holding company. The different companies may have been formed to perform different functions or they may exist simply to minimise taxation. A worker may have a contract of employment with one of these companies in the group but in practice work for another company within the group. Although the statutory written statement of particulars requires notification of the identity of the employer,[89] this statement may be inaccurate or be overtaken by changes in the group of companies. Under normal legal principles only one company in the group can be the employer, and in particular an employment relation with a subsidiary company does not imply any contract of employment with the parent company; the law does not generally 'pierce the corporate veil'. The precise identity of the employer can be important not only for the obvious purpose of ensuring that any legal claims are directed against the correct entity but also in the establishment of legal rights in many circumstances. A transfer of the employee from one company in a group to another, although it may appear insignificant if the work remains exactly the same, does technically require at common law a dismissal followed by the issue of a fresh contract of employment by the new subsidiary company.[90]

The UK legislation introduces the concept of an 'associated employer' for the purpose of combating disadvantages to employees arising from their employment within a group of companies.

Employment Rights Act 1996, Section 231; Trade Union and Labour Relations (Consolidation) Act 1992, Section 297

For the purposes of this Act any two employers shall be treated as associated if –

(a) one is a company of which the other (directly or indirectly) has control, or
(b) both are companies of which a third person (directly or indirectly) has control;

and 'associated employer' shall be construed accordingly.

Using the concept of associated employer, for example, an employee retains continuity of employment for the purpose of qualifying for employment rights despite transfers between associated employers within a group of companies.[91] Similarly, in calculating the total number of employees for the purpose of

---

[89] ERA 1996, s. 1.
[90] The common law position is now subject to the EU Acquired Rights Directive 2001/23; see Chapter 20.
[91] ERA 1996, s. 218(6); *Da Silva* v. *Composite Mouldings & Design Ltd* [2009] ICR 416 (EAT).

determining whether certain statutory requirements apply or fall within an exclusion for small businesses, it is usual to include associated employers in the count of employees.

The courts have interpreted the statutory concept of control to refer to ownership of shares rather than some other source of power and influence. For two companies to count as associated employers, either a single legal entity has to own more than 50 per cent of the shares in both companies, or a group of persons, which always acts in concert, has similar voting control by virtue of share ownership in two companies. It follows that neither common ownership by a single individual of 50 per cent of the shares in two companies nor actual practical day-to-day control of two companies by the same minority share-holder suffices to satisfy the test of control.[92]

Service Companies

Another example of a multi-employer pattern concerns instances where the employee forms a company and provides work through that service company by a contract with the principal employer. Formerly, there were some tax advantages for employees to constitute this kind of service company.[93] The potential disadvantage to the employee of this arrangement is that, when the main employer terminates the contract with the service company, it is hard to classify this termination as a dismissal from a contract of employment because, first, the contract between the main employer and the service company is in appearance a commercial contract between two businesses to supply a service, not a contract of employment, and, secondly, if the individual has a contract of employment at all it should be with his own service company, not the main employer.

In *Catamaran Cruisers Ltd* v. *Williams*,[94] a preliminary issue in the context of a claim for unfair dismissal was whether Mr Williams was an employee of Catamaran Cruisers. At the suggestion of Catamaran Cruisers, in the course of a restructuring of the business, Mr Williams had formed a limited company (Unicorn Enterprises) with his mother through which he provided his personal services to the employer instead of being directly employed by them. The employer paid Unicorn Enterprises a fee and did not deduct income tax or national insurance contributions, although at one point it offered Mr Williams 'holiday pay' and 'sick pay'. Under the normal principles of company law, Unicorn Enterprises represented a separate legal entity. Mr Williams, if he was

---

[92] *Poparm Ltd* v. *Weekes* [1984] IRLR 388 (EAT); *South West Launderettes Ltd* v. *Laidler* [1986] ICR 455 (EAT).

[93] The use of such personal service companies for the purpose of obtaining the more favourable tax position accorded to independent businesses was discouraged for 'disguised employees' by the Finance Act 2000, s. 60, and the Social Security Contributions (Intermediaries) Regulations 2000, SI 2000 No. 727.

[94] [1994] IRLR 386 (EAT).

the employee of any company, should have been the employee of Unicorn Enterprises (as well as a director and major shareholder).[95] Any contract entered into by Catamaran Cruisers was plainly with Unicorn Enterprises, not directly with Mr Williams, so logically not only did Mr Williams not have a contract of employment with Catamaran Cruisers, he probably had no contractual relation with them at all. Notwithstanding this logical problem, the tribunal, whose decision was upheld by the EAT, found that Mr Williams had, on the special facts of this case, a contract of employment with Catamaran Cruisers. In effect, the tribunal 'pierced the corporate veil' and found a direct contract of employment. Though difficult to reconcile with established legal principles, the decision might be justified on the ground that in a sense the creation of the service company was a sham transaction, forced on the employee by the employer as part of a restructuring plan, while the intentions of the parties were plainly to continue the employment relationship much as before.

Agency Workers

Perhaps the most troublesome instance of multi-employer arrangements for the application of labour regulation concerns temporary agency workers. It is estimated that between 1.1 and 1.5 million people find work in the UK through agencies.[96] Although typically these jobs last less than three months, there is no formal limit on how long they may last. In this triangular relation, the worker enters into a contract with an agency to find temporary work with its clients or end-users for the worker, on terms as illustrated below. If the agency finds such a placement, it enters into a contract with the client or end-user for fees for its service. If the worker accepts an assignment with a client, the agency pays the worker an agreed rate of pay and, in return, the worker undertakes to comply with the rules of the agency. These rules are likely to include a requirement to serve the agency's client faithfully, as if the worker were an employee of the client. There is, however, no express contractual relation between the worker and client, even though while on an assignment the worker will be performing work personally for and under the control of the client. It is common for the terms of the contract between the worker and the agency to state expressly that the worker is not an employee of the agency, but an independent contractor. The question that arises in connection with agency workers is: do they qualify as 'employees' or 'workers' or parties to a contract

---

[95] *Bottrill v. Secretary of State for Trade and Industry* [1999] IRLR 326 (CA).

[96] *Agency Working in the UK: A Review of the Evidence* (London: Department for Business Enterprise and Regulatory Reform, Employment Relations Research Series No. 93, October 2008), www.bis.gov.uk/files/file48720.pdf. About 1.5 million identify themselves as temporary workers, not all of whom will be supplied through agencies.

to perform work personally, and, if so, whether the employer or duty-bearer is the client, the agency or perhaps even both?[97]

Conditions of Service (Temporary Self-employed Workers)

(1) You will provide your services to the contractor as a self-employed worker and not under a contract of service.

(2) You will provide your services commencing on the date shown on the timesheet until the end of the same week or such earlier date as the hirer (referred to below as 'the client') may determine.

(3) The contractor agrees to offer you the opportunity to work on a self-employed basis where there is a suitable assignment with a client but the contractor reserves the right to offer each assignment to such temporary worker ('temporary') as it may elect in cases where that stated above assignment is suitable for one of several temporaries.

(4) The contractor shall pay your wages calculated at the rate stated above payable weekly in arrears subject to deductions for the purposes of National Insurance, PAYE or any other purpose required by law. An overtime premium will be paid provided this is agreed in writing by the client.

(5) You are under no obligation to accept any offer made under paragraph (3) but if you do so you are required to fulfil the normal common law duties which an employee would owe to an employer as far as they are applicable. In addition, you will at all times when services are to be performed for a client comply with the following conditions. You will:

(a) not engage in any conduct detrimental to the interests of the contractor;

(b) upon being supplied to the client by the contractor not contract with any other contractor, consultant or agency for the purpose of the supply of your temporary services of what ever nature to the client unless a period of 13 weeks has elapsed since the time that you ceased to be supplied to the client by the contractor;

(c) be present during the times, or for the total number of hours, during each day and/ or seek as are required by the contractor or the client;

(d) provide to the client faithful service of a standard such as would be required under a contract of employment;

(e) take all reasonable steps to safeguard your own safety and the safety of any other person who may be affected by your actions at work;

(f) comply with any disciplinary rules or obligations in force at the premises where services are performed to the extent that they are reasonably applicable;

---

[97] Liability for both employers is possible for vicarious liability in tort: *Viasystems (Tyneside) Ltd v. Thermal Transfer (Northern) Ltd* [2005] EWCA Civ 1151, [2006] ICR 327.

(g) comply with all reasonable instructions and requests within the scope of the agreed services made either by the contractor or the client; and

(h) keep confidential all information which may come to your notice whilst working for the client and keep secret all and any of the client's affairs of which you may gain knowledge.

(6) The contractor is not obliged to provide and you are not required to serve any particular number of hours during any day or week. In the event of your declining to accept any offer of work or failing to attend work for any reason for any period, this contract shall terminate.

(7) You are not entitled to payment from the contractor for holidays (including statutory holidays) or absence due to sickness or injury. The contractor provides no pension rights.

(8) The contractor shall be responsible for making all statutory deductions relating to earnings-related insurance and income tax under Schedule E in accordance with the Finance (No. 2) Act 1975 and transmitting these to the Inland Revenue.

(9) You acknowledge and confirm that the nature of temporary work is such that there may be periods between assignments when no work is available.

(10) The contractor may instruct you to end an assignment with a client at any time on summary notice to that effect, without specifying any reasons.

(11) Following a decision by the contractor that your services are no longer required on a self-employed basis you shall have the right to request a review of the decision by the relevant branch manager.

(12) If you have any grievance connected with the offered assignment or relations with the client or any employee of the client, you shall have the right to present the grievance to the manager of the branch of the contractor through which you are offered work. If no conclusion satisfactory to you is reached at this stage you may present the grievance for ultimate decision to the area manager.

(13) The qualifying days for statutory sick pay shall be Monday to Friday or the days in the week when you would be available for work and when a suitable assignment had been offered but in any event shall not exceed Monday to Friday inclusive.

(14) You are required to inform the contractor by no later than 10 am on the first qualifying day of sickness so that the contractor can make arrangements to provide alternative workers to the client.[98]

From the decided cases, the most likely answer to that question regarding the identity of the employer seems to be that only the agency can be the employer, although it is uncertain whether even the agency is bound by the legal obligations of an employer. The problem with bringing any kind of claim

---

[98] Quoted in *McMeechan* v. *Secretary of State for Employment* [1997] ICR 549 (CA).

against the client is that apparently there is no contractual arrangement at all between the client and the worker. Without a contract, it is not possible to satisfy the UK statutory definitions of employment status. The courts have considered whether it may be possible to imply a contract between the client and the worker, since the statutory definitions of employee and worker include both express and implied contracts. Out of respect for freedom of contract, however, the common law has always been extremely reluctant to imply a contract in the absence of a clear indication by the parties that they were through their conduct indicating an intention to undertake obligations towards each other.

This orthodox view of implied contracts was applied in *James* v. *Greenwich London Borough Council*.[99] Ms James worked for the council as a housing support worker, but she had obtained the engagement through an employment agency that paid her. The council, not the agency, arranged all her instructions, orders and working conditions, and provided the materials used in her work, including a staff badge. The council's disciplinary and grievance procedure did not apply to agency workers and nor did they benefit from the council's sick-pay and holiday-pay provisions applicable to employees. At one point, Ms James changed the agency that supplied her services because it offered a higher rate of pay, but in other respects she continued in the same job for the council. The terms of her contract with the agency described her as self-employed and not under a contract of employment with the agency. After about three years working under these arrangements, Ms James was absent from work through ill health. At the council's request, the agency replaced her with another worker and so, on her return, she discovered that she had no job. She brought a claim for unfair dismissal against the council, which the council resisted on the ground that she was not an employee of the council, and indeed that she had no contractual relation whatsoever with the council and so had not been dismissed by the council. The ET rejected the existence of an implied contract of employment between the claimant and the client, and this decision was upheld on appeal. The Court of Appeal stressed that an implied contract could only be discovered where it was necessary in order to give business efficacy to a transaction in circumstances where the parties are dealing with one another with the expectation that enforceable obligations exist. But it was unnecessary to imply such a contract between the claimant and the client in these circumstances, because the other contractual arrangements between client and agency and between agency and worker fully met those expectations. It was unnecessary to imply such a contract in order to explain why the worker was supplying services to the client and why the agency paid the worker.

---

[99] [2008] EWCA Civ 35, [2008] ICR 545 (CA).

This rejection of any contract between the client and the worker must also prevent the application of other kinds of employment-protection duties to the client, even if the scope of application of those rights is not employment but a different kind of contract such as a personal work contract. This barrier prevented the application of anti-discrimination laws in the relation between client and agency worker in *Muschett* v. *HM Prison Service*.[100] The claimant was supplied by an agency to work in the prison laundry. Following termination of this position after four months, he brought various claims against the prison service including race discrimination and harassment. Although this discrimination claim benefited from the looser definition of personal scope that refers to a personal work contract, the claim was dismissed on the ground that there was no express or implied contract of any kind between the claimant and the prison service.

In some instances, the anti-discrimination legislation may address this gap in its coverage with respect to agency workers in its provision concerning 'contract workers' in the EqA 2010, section 41. The purpose of this provision is to prevent discrimination by the main employer against a worker who is employed by a sub-contractor. It was applied, for instance, to an employee of a contractor operating a concession within a department store who complained of race discrimination by the store.[101] It may be applicable to agency workers, but only if they satisfy the requirement that they are employed by the agency.[102] Claims by agency workers for a right to return to their job with a client after maternity leave have been successful, but only on the basis that the worker was employed by the agency.[103] This special provision concerning contract workers may also overcome the problem described above for workers who supply their services through a service company.[104]

In contrast, in the interpretation of the EU concept of 'worker', the ECJ has not limited its scope to direct contractual relations, and this relaxation permits its application to the non-contractual relation between client and agency worker. In *Allonby* v. *Accrington and Rossendale College*,[105] as we have seen, a 'worker' was defined for the purpose of the EU Treaty provisions on equal pay as a person who, for a certain period of time, performs services for and under the direction of another person in return for remuneration. This definition permitted the part-time lecturers supplied by an employment agency to bring a claim for equal pay against the college, even in the absence of a direct contractual relation. The claim failed, however, on the different though related point that the college no longer determined the wages of the lecturers so that, in the absence of a 'single source' or employing entity to

---

[100] [2010] EWCA Civ 25, [2010] IRLR 451 (CA).
[101] *Harrods Ltd* v. *Remick* [1998] ICR 156 (CA).   [102] Employment Act 2010, s. 41(5).
[103] *BP Chemicals Ltd* v. *Gillick* [1995] IRLR 128 (EAT); *Patefield* v. *Belfast City Council* [2000] IRLR 664 (NICA).
[104] *MHC Consulting Services Ltd* v. *Tansell* [2000] ICR 789 (CA).
[105] Case C-256/01, *Allonby* v. *Accrington and Rossendale College* [2004] ICR 1328 (ECJ).

determine both sets of wages, no comparison could be drawn for the purposes of equal pay.

Although it seems that, in general, agency workers cannot bring a successful claim against the client in the absence of a contract, is it possible for them to bring a claim against the employment agency itself? The first hurdle for such a claim is that the contract between the worker and the agency will often describe itself as one of a contract for services and expressly state that the worker is an independent contractor. It is true that the agency is not promising to provide work or a job but merely to try to locate opportunities for suitable work with its clients. It is also true that the worker is not bound to accept any assignment produced by the agency. At the search for work stage of the relationship, the normal elements of a contract of employment of a promise to work in return for remuneration are absent. Nevertheless, once a position has been found and the worker has accepted the placement, the relation takes on many of the features of a contract of employment, such as payment of a wage by the agency in return for the performance of work personally by the worker. The Court of Appeal in *McMeechan* v. *Secretary of State for Employment*[106] distinguished between the general framework arrangement or umbrella contract between the agency and the worker, which might be a contract for services, and the arrangement during a particular assignment, when an employment relation might be established. Similarly, some agency workers have been found to qualify under the scope set for equality laws concerning employment under a contract to perform work personally.[107]

A second hurdle is that it is the client who directs work, not the agency, so the normal element of control or subordination in employment relations is not readily apparent. But this division of the tasks of management does not exclude the possibility of the agency being the employer, for the agency could be regarded as having delegated day-to-day management of the worker to the client. If the complaint of the worker is about unfair treatment such as discrimination by the client or unfair termination of the assignment, a third hurdle is that it will be difficult to fit such a complaint into the framework of the law of unfair dismissal. The reason given by the agency for termination of the employment is likely to be that the client is no longer willing to pay for the services of that particular worker, so that the agency will not be reimbursed for any wages paid to the worker. It is hard to view that reason as anything other than a fair substantial reason for the termination of the posting to that client. Where the complaint is about the conduct of the agency, however, there is a better chance of success. In *McMeechan* v. *Secretary of State for Employment*,[108] the complaint was that the agency had failed to pay the wages due to a worker owing to the insolvency of the agency. Under the legislation

---

[106] [1997] ICR 549 (CA).
[107] *London Borough of Camden* v. *Pegg* [2012] UKEAT 0590_11_1304.
[108] [1997] ICR 549 (CA).

governing insolvency, now contained in ERA 1996, section 182, an employee of a company that goes into insolvent liquidation may claim unpaid wages from the Secretary of State for Employment.[109] The Secretary of State disputed the claim for unpaid wages on the ground that Mr McMeechan was not an employee of the agency. The Court of Appeal upheld the claim for wages on the ground that, during the four days of the assignment, the claimant was an employee of the employment agency.

It is apparent from these decisions that not only do the client employers obtain the benefits of numerical flexibility from hiring temporary agency workers, but they may also obtain exemption from most employment protection rights such as unfair dismissal and anti-discrimination laws. The growth of long-term agency work suggests that employers have been using this device systematically to avoid the application of employment-protection laws. On the other hand, if the reasoning in *McMeechan* is followed, while the worker is carrying out work on an assignment, the worker may be either an employee or perhaps within the statutory concept of worker with regard to the agency. If it is correct that agency workers on assignment qualify as workers with respect to the agency, they should be entitled to the paid holiday, rest-breaks and limits on working time of the Working Time Regulations, protection from unlawful deductions and protection against discrimination on the part of the agency.

Regulation of the employment agencies themselves (described in law as 'employment businesses') has been directed at their misconduct with respect to workers.[110] This UK regulation primarily addresses the major abuses of 'labour trafficking', such as a requirement for workers to pay a proportion of their income to the person who arranges a job for them, though undoubtedly this indentured labour still happens to migrant workers, including those trapped into prostitution. There is power to make delegated legislation on the way in which and the terms on which services may be provided by persons carrying on such agencies and businesses.[111] This power has been used primarily to require employment businesses and agencies to be transparent in the terms on which they deal with workers. It also prohibits the charging of fees upfront to agency workers with the partial exception of those seeking work as photographic models or entertainers. The regulations do not restrict the freedom of the employment business to determine that the worker will be regarded as an independent contractor. The tax legislation, however, requires these workers to be treated as employees.[112] Agency workers are also covered

---

[109] See Chapter 20.

[110] Employment Agencies Act 1973, as amended by Employment Relations Act 1999, s. 31; Conduct of Employment Agencies and Employment Businesses Regulations 2003, SI 2003 No. 3319.

[111] Employment Agencies Act 1973, s. 5(1)(eb).

[112] Income and Corporation Taxes Act 1988, s. 134; Social Security (Categorisation of Earners) Regulations 1978, SI 1978 No. 1689.

by the NMW regardless of the precise contractual arrangements.[113] The policing and enforcement of these regulations governing agency workers is carried out by the Employment Agency Standards Inspectorate. Breaches of the regulations can be prosecuted and may result in a fine and a disqualification of the directors of the agency. In the case of agricultural workers and gatherers of shellfish, however, there is a separate authority, the Gangmasters and Labour Abuse Authority, which requires organisers of this kind of work to obtain a licence under stringent conditions.[114]

Legislation on agency workers, the Agency Workers Regulations 2010,[115] based on an EU Directive,[116] does not address most of the problems considered in this chapter regarding the personal scope of labour law. The general aim of the legislation is to ensure that, after twelve weeks of work for a particular client, the agency worker should receive the same pay and basic conditions as those enjoyed by comparable employees of the client. The basic conditions include the duration of working time, rest periods, holidays and antenatal care.[117] But they do not include many other possible contractual benefits, such as occupational pensions, maternity leave and pay, and sick pay provided by the employer. The agency is liable to the worker for default, unless it can show that it was misled by the client, in which case the client is liable.[118] The legislation is designed to tackle the problem that temporary agency workers may be used as a source of cheap labour, because they work longer hours than regular employees at a lower rate of pay. Survey evidence, however, tends to demonstrate that the rates of pay of temporary agency workers, taking into account experience, approximate to the amounts of direct pay received by regular employees.[119] The new legislation is not designed to combat the disadvantage of temporary agency workers with regard to other significant fringe benefits, such as the occupational pensions at stake in *Allonby* v. *Accrington and Rossendale College*. Nor does this legislation address the issue regarding personal scope so that, in the absence of a contract with the client, it seems unlikely that the agency worker can claim any employment protection and anti-discrimination rights against the client. Instead, any rights must be claimed against the agency, and for that purpose it will be necessary to overcome both the hurdle that the contract with the agency may not have a character that qualifies for protection under labour law and the problem of attributing responsibility to the agency for the misconduct or failings of its client. It has been suggested that agency workers must be recognised as falling within the statutory concept of workers, for otherwise the effectiveness of the

---

[113] NMWA 1998, s. 34.
[114] Gangmasters (Licensing) Act 2004 as amended; The Gangmasters (Licensing Authority) Regulations 2015, SI 2015 No. 805.
[115] SI 2010 No. 93.   [116] Directive 2008/104.   [117] Reg. 5.   [118] Reg. 14.
[119] *Agency Working in the UK: A Review of the Evidence* (London: Department for Business Enterprise and Regulatory Reform, Employment Relations Research Series No. 93, October 2008), www.bis.gov.uk/files/file48720.pdf.

EU requirement of equal treatment in basic working conditions with regular staff would be frustrated.[120]

It is worth noting, however, that one side-effect of the legislation is that it may encourage agencies to take on agency workers as direct permanent employees, because in that way they are likely to be able to avoid the application of the requirement that after twelve weeks those workers should receive the same basic conditions as the employees of the client. To meet the requirements of that exemption, the agency must offer permanent employment, with a guaranteed minimum amount of weekly pay, and expressly state in the contract of employment that comparisons with rates of pay of employees of clients are not permitted.[121]

Platforms

A final scheme that obstructs any clear view of which business entity should be regarded as responsible for employment law rights concerns platforms. A platform is a device for putting workers in touch with customers. The platform charges for its services either by taking a fee or a percentage of the income of the worker or charging a supplement to the customer or both. Platforms with a physical presence have existed for centuries. Barristers' chambers provide an example: solicitors acquire the services of barristers through negotiations with clerks of chambers, and the barristers pay a fee for participating in the chambers' services, including the provision of office space. A minicab firm charges drivers a weekly fee for which the drivers obtain access to the telephone bookings from customers received by the firm, and the drivers receive the whole fare paid by the customer.[122] Golf caddies may be permitted to offer their services to players at a golf club, with the tips or fees being charged by the club to its members and the caddie receiving payment from the club.[123] Similarly, the lap dancing club in *Stringfellow Restaurants Ltd* v. *Quashie*[124] provided a venue for the dancers to negotiate fees for their dances with the customers, with the club charging various fees and commissions as its remuneration. In the contemporary world, many platforms are constructed on the internet. The platform for taxi services provided by Uber is a well-known example: customers are connected to taxi-drivers through a smartphone app, and the fare is paid through charges set and organised by the

---

[120] A. Davies, 'The Implementation of the Directive on Temporary Agency Work in the UK: A Missed Opportunity' (2010) 1 *European Labour Law Journal* 307, 312–13.

[121] Reg. 10. The government has proposed to abolish this opt-out on the ground that it has been abused by employment agencies by using the required contractual form but in practice treating workers as still being on a zero-hours arrangement. HM Government, *Good Work Plan* (December 2018), pp. 15–16.

[122] *Mingeley* v. *Pinnock (Trading as Amber Cars)* [2004] ICR 727 (CA).

[123] *Cheng Yuen* v. *Royal Hong Kong Golf Club* [1998] ICR 131 (PC).

[124] [2012] EWCA Civ 1735, [2013] IRLR 99.

platform on the customers' credit cards. The convenience and efficiency of internet platforms permits workers in the gig economy such as the taxi-drivers of Uber to have a succession of one-off jobs, with no guarantee of future work at all. Many other businesses seek to present themselves as merely providing a platform rather than acting as an employer. Platforms typically rely to some extent on customers to provide some typical managerial functions,[125] such as determining hours of work as in the case of care workers,[126] or assessing the quality of the services and engaging in performance management through reporting mechanisms on the platform's smartphone app.

Platforms present employment law with two main challenges. First, the workers providing their services possess many of the typical features of genuine independent contractors, such as being in business on their own account and determining their own hours of work, so they appear likely to be excluded from most employment law protection. Nevertheless, as in the case of the drivers in *Uber BV* v. *Aslam*,[127] these contractors may well fall within the statutory concept of 'worker', because their contract is to perform work personally under the direction of the platform business and the references to self-employment in public statements and contractual terms will often be regarded by courts as bogus and sham. Managers in platform businesses go to great lengths to avoid suggestions of an employment relation. For instance, in a handbook issued to managers in Deliveroo, they are told to say 'Under the hourly fees system we offer riders hours of work and they choose how many to accept based on their availability and the area(s) they want to work in' and not to say 'Under the hourly pay system we assign drivers set shifts in the zones where we need them.'[128] Similarly, the contract for a cycle courier tried unsuccessfully to prevent her raising the question of her employment status by means of a contractual term: 'The Contractor agrees and warrants that he is a self-employed contractor and is neither an employee nor a worker and City Sprint enters into this agreement on that basis.'[129]

Second, even if these workers can be classified as employees in the extended sense of 'workers', the platform will contest whether it can be regarded as an employer. The platform presents itself as a neutral go-between, putting customers in touch with suppliers, acting merely as an agent for the workers or customers or both. This argument was rejected as a sham by the ET (quoted and largely approved by the CA) for the arrangements under consideration in *Uber BV* v. *Aslam*.[130] Uber had argued that the only contract for performance

---

[125] E. Albin, 'Labour Law in a Service World' (2010) 73 *Modern Law Review* 959.
[126] *Walton* v. *Independent Living Organization* [2003] EWCA Civ 199, [2003] ICR 688 (CA).
[127] *Uber BV* v. *Aslam* [2018] EWCA Civ 2748.
[128] House of Commons Work and Pensions Committee, *Self-employment and the Gig Economy*, Thirteenth Report of Session 2016–17, 1 May 2017, HC 847, 10.
[129] *Dewhurst* v. *City Sprint Ltd*, Case No. 2202512/2016 (ET).
[130] *Uber BV* v. *Aslam* [2018] EWCA Civ 2748, [90]–[97].

of a service personally was between the driver and a customer, and that there was no contract for the performance of work with Uber. Yet that analysis would mean that a driver would enter a contract with a customer, neither party ever knowing each other's identity, to undertake a journey to a destination not told to the driver until the journey began, by a route prescribed by Uber at a price prescribed by Uber, which also took a substantial commission. On the analysis proposed by Uber, if there was any 'employer', it was the customer. The ET concluded: 'The absurdity of these propositions speaks for itself.'

Vulnerable Workers

From this study of the personal scope of labour law, several conclusions may be drawn. The first is that a number of categories of people who perform personal services for others fall outside the scope of protection of labour laws. While many of these people are genuinely self-employed and running their own business such as lawyers, plumbers, gardeners and decorators, others are in practice economically dependent on a core business and are vulnerable to exploitation. Typically, these vulnerable people work under contracts that put most of the economic risks on to their shoulders, such as risks of the absence of work or the need to work flexibly though possibly long hours on short notice. People accept such jobs because they need employment desperately and, owing to their lack of skills, work experience and other capabilities such as fluency in the English language or physical strength, together with perhaps time constraints on their availability for work owing to caring responsibilities, they find that they have no option but to take any work on offer. These economically vulnerable groups may then discover that, as a result of the contractual arrangements that render them bogus self-employed or precarious casual workers, they have also been excluded from all or part of the normal protections afforded to workers by labour laws and anti-discrimination laws. They are both economically and legally vulnerable workers.

A second conclusion is that the greater use of the statutory concept of 'worker', which applies to any contract to perform work personally other than in the case of professionals and genuine independent businesses, has reduced the size of the excluded group of vulnerable workers. That classification, however, requires a difficult boundary line to be drawn between a self-employed but dependent worker and a genuinely independent entrepreneur. In drawing that boundary, the requirement of personal performance of work is clearly important, but perhaps economic dependence in the sense of the employer being the principal source of a worker's income should also be regarded as critical. The question that now arises is whether all employment protection laws, including in particular the law of unfair dismissal, should be extended to workers in this sense, thereby abandoning the concept of employee as a suitable definition for the proper scope of labour laws. A parliamentary committee has recommended that there should be a presumption in favour of 'worker' status that could only be rebutted by an employer putting forward a compelling case.[131]

As that report recognises, at the root of the problem of the personal scope of labour law lies the freedom granted to employers to determine the character and details of the terms of the contracts under which they acquire labour power. The flexibility accorded to employers by the underlying principle of freedom of contract ensures that, whatever boundary is selected by regulation, it will always be possible to find instances of contracts that may fall outside the scope of the protection yet are arguably within the intended purpose of the legislation. It is possible for a minister, by statutory instrument, to make *ad hoc* inclusions of particular categories of workers within the scope of protective legislation,[132] although this power has never been used. The courts have not used the general prohibitions against contracting out of the statutory rights such as that contained in ERA 1996, section 203, to challenge the employer's use of non-standard forms of employment. These various statutory provisions, although potentially helpful to legally vulnerable workers, never address the fundamental problem that employers may avoid the application of aspects of labour law by devising idiosyncratic contractual arrangements.

In some European countries the problem of personal scope is addressed by a radically different approach. In these jurisdictions, employers are denied freedom of contract and instead are forced to use a limited number of approved types of contract. Once the number of permissible contractual forms of work relations is limited, it becomes possible to determine the scope of regulation with precision. Such interference with freedom of contract carries its own dangers. By reducing the flexibility accorded to employers to devise efficient methods for the acquisition of labour power, employers may decide that they can no longer offer work of any kind (an unemployment effect), or that they should cut wage costs to compensate for the inflexibility that reduces the competitiveness of business (a low-wage effect). In the example of casual workers, if an employer were forced to offer contracts of employment guaranteeing a minimum number of hours of work, these fixed overheads might force the employer to reduce staff, reduce wages, or increase its prices and lose business. These possible outcomes are, of course, based upon theoretical models informed by economics, but they illustrate the potential dangers of prohibitions against certain contractual forms of work relationship. Nor should we ignore the possibility that some workers may have a strong preference for certain types of work relations. A worker who places a strong value on independence and the chance to earn a higher income may prefer the risks

---

[131] House of Commons Work and Pensions Committee, *Self-employment and the Gig Economy,* Thirteenth Report of Session 2016–17, 1 May 2017, HC 847.

[132] Employment Relations Act 1999, s. 23. A similar power can be found in other statutes, for example in the NMWA 1998, s. 41.

associated with self-employment, whereas another worker may prefer employment because it offers relative security of earnings and work.

With regard to the problem of triangular relations and the uncertainty
about the allocation of the employer's legal responsibility between different
legal entities, it has been suggested that the solution lies in holding all the
entities concerned in management functions jointly responsible for breach of
employment-protection laws.[133] This proposal, although tempting, has a
degree of artificiality or fiction, because in effect it tries to invent a single
business organisation or quasi-partnership when the business reality is rather
a heterarchical network between autonomous businesses such as the employment agency and its clients. The joint-employer notion fits even less satisfactorily on the commercial reality when some functions of an employer in the
service sector are performed by customers as in the case of some platforms and
waiters in restaurants.

In these triangular relations the network provides managerial functions not
through a single entity but rather through contracts in which the businesses
deal at arm's length with a view to maximising their own interests, not the
common interest. This intensification of the division of labour with respect to
management functions, although serving the goal of efficiency, creates the risk
that a member of the network may opportunistically or collusively take
advantage of the network structure to evade legal liabilities. On this view, in
the absence of explicit contractual allocation of risks of liability between
members of the network, such as the agency and its client, it should be the
client that retains legal responsibility for conforming to labour law, for the
purpose of creating the network should be confined to the efficiency gains in
performance of aspects of the managerial function and not be permitted to
serve as a device for the evasion of employees' rights.[134] Employer members of
the network should be held responsible for breaches of their own obligations
constructed in the contracts, such as the agency's obligation to pay wages and
the client's obligation to ensure health and safety in the workplace. In the
absence of such a clear allocation of responsibility, despite the legal difficulties
involved and rather than imagining a fictitious entity, it would be better for the
law to complete the framework of the contractual network by attributing
responsibilities for legal compliance to those members of the network in the
best position to fulfil the relevant legal duties.[135] This would work better than
the suggestion that the duty-bearers should be those actually performing the
regulated task,[136] because in some cases the problem will be precisely that no

[133] G. Davidov, 'Joint Employer Status in Triangular Employment Relationships' (2004) 42 *British Journal of Industrial Relations* 727.
[134] H. Collins, 'Introduction', in G. Teubner, *Networks as Connected Contracts* (ed. H. Collins, Oxford: Hart, 2011), pp. 59–62.
[135] H. Collins, 'Ascription of Legal Responsibility to Groups in Complex Patterns of Economic Integration' (1990) 53 *Modern Law Review* 731.
[136] J. Prassl, *Humans as a Service* (Oxford University Press, 2018), p. 101.

one is performing the managerial function. This allocation of responsibility to various employers is done, for instance, in the Agency Workers Regulations 2010, where regulation 14 holds both the agency and client liable to the extent that it is responsible for the breach of the regulations. The allocation of responsibility between the employing entities may not always prove straightforward,[137] but during this process it should be borne in mind that the purpose of the legal regulation should not be thwarted by elaborate constructions of management networks that appear to be designed to achieve organised irresponsibility.

---

[137] E.g. *Amissah* v. *Trainpeople.co.uk Ltd* [2017] ICR 581 (EAT).

Part III
Statutory Regulation of the Employment Relationship

7

Wages

Contents

The Wage/Work Bargain

The legal construction of the core bargain of the contract of employment comprises the promise to perform work in return for a promise to pay wages. The terms of this agreement that fix the nature of the work to be performed and the required payment become the legally enforceable obligations. In the absence of such express mutual undertakings, there may be no contract at all for want of consideration. It is therefore sometimes said that the mutuality of obligation, namely the promise to perform work in return for a promise to pay wages, is an essential element of the contract of employment.

Using its freedom of contract, an employer can construct complex systems of payment for work. As well as a regular weekly or monthly salary, to attract staff the employer may add fringe benefits, incentive payments such as bonuses and commissions and then add longer-term deferred payments such as pensions to encourage loyalty and discourage labour turnover. The amount payable may be varied according to the hours worked, such as shift systems designed to provide 24/7 services involving unsocial hours. In the illustrative specimen contract given in Chapter 3, the contract purports to provide a guaranteed minimum number of hours, which will lead to a basic weekly pay, but the calculation of the wages due each week depends on further details in an appendix (not supplied) about the shift system and overtime payments, and the guarantee of minimum hours is not absolute. The complexity of these payment systems may often give rise to difficult questions about the interpretation of the small print in the contract and its appendixes.

During recent decades, perhaps the most significant change in relation to wages has been a decline in the use of structured payment systems in large organisations. Under these payment systems, each job is allocated a wage by reference to a system of job evaluation, taking into account such matters as the skills and responsibilities required by the job. Incentives for employees to acquire skills, to work hard and to stay with a firm derive from the possibility of promotion to higher grades. Economists describe these payment systems as 'internal labour markets',[1] in order to distinguish how pay is set independently within the system rather than by reference to the broader labour market external to the firm. A 'manager, grade 2' is paid according to the firm's established scales, which might rank everyone from the bottom to the top of the organisation on a comprehensive grading system; that salary could easily deviate from the level that this manager might obtain in the open market, because it is determined by relativities within the structured payment system not by reference to market rates.

The widespread use by employers of internal labour markets was criticised in the 1980s because these payment structures prevent employers from adjusting wages quickly to changing external labour market conditions (e.g. high levels of unemployment) and because they obstruct individualised performance-related payment systems from being used by employers to acquire higher levels of co-operation from the workforce.[2] In the public sector, the government sought to dismantle internal labour markets within

---

[1] P. B. Doeringer and M. J. Piore, *Internal Labour Markets and Manpower Analysis* (Lexington, MA: Lexington Books, D. C. Heath, 1971); O. E. Williamson, M. L. Wachter and J. E. Harris, 'Understanding the Employment Relation: The Analysis of Idiosyncratic Exchange' (1975) 6 *Bell Journal of Economics and Management Science* 250.

[2] Department of Employment, *Employment for the 1990s*, Cm 540 (1988).

government services by such measures as contracting out work to private companies that typically paid the lower external market rates.[3] The government also encouraged the 'derigidification' of the labour market in the private sector.[4] For example, it provided tax incentives for performance-related pay in the form of employee share ownership schemes.[5] Although the use of internal labour markets, at least in their most rigid form, has declined, their existence and operation is often of the utmost practical significance to the workforce. The organisational framework creates an expectation that in return for hard work an employee can expect to reap the rewards of promotion to grades commanding higher wages and a high degree of employment security. Yet this aspect of the psychological contract of employment, which the employer certainly encourages, is rarely protected by equivalent legal obligations.

Occupational Pensions

In order to promote commitment to the goals of the organisation, employers frequently offer, in addition to a salary or wages, various kinds of deferred pay, such as occupational pensions (to which the employer may contribute) and share-ownership schemes. These occupational pension schemes have typically provided that on retirement the employee will receive either a lump sum that is used to purchase an annuity or an annuity calculated as a proportion of the final salary or the career-average salary. Although a valuable contribution to economic security in old age, this contractual arrangement of a contributory pension scheme creates many risks for the employee. For example, the employer may fail to make its promised contribution or decide to alter the benefits of the scheme or in some other way reduce the value of this deferred remuneration at a time when it is too late for the employee to make adequate alternative provision for income during retirement.

Following various abuses of occupational pension schemes by employers, these are now heavily regulated. The Pensions Act 2004 created a Pensions Regulator, who must supervise a scheme's investment policy and ability to meet its commitments, with residual powers to compel contributions to avoid deficits. The Act also created a Protection Fund, supported by levies on all occupational pensions, in order to provide compensation to members of schemes that nevertheless fail by reason of the insolvency of the employer. A third of the trustees of the scheme must be nominated by its members, so that they may be fully informed about their pension prospects. In addition, a Pensions Ombudsman has extensive powers to investigate complaints about maladministration of an occupational pension scheme that

[3] E.g. Local Government Act 1988.

[4] P. Davies and M. Freedland, *Labour Legislation and Public Policy* (Oxford University Press, 1993), Ch. 10.

[5] Finance (No. 2) Act 1987. Various tax efficient share and share option schemes are now set out in Income Tax (Earnings and Pensions) Act 2003, Part 7.

has caused injustice to its members and then make a legally binding instruction to the trustees to rectify a valid complaint.[6] Nevertheless, it remains true that the terms of the occupation scheme are usually set by the employer, and the scheme often contains within it the flexibility to increase contributions payable by employees and to reduce the benefits received by pensioners, with the consequence that employees always need to be wary about the reliability of the promise of a pension. With increasing longevity and the additional costs imposed by changes in taxation and regulation, most private-sector employers have terminated their pensions for new employees or have seriously eroded their value.

The Pensions Act 2008 introduced a scheme requiring all employers to offer a pension scheme to their employees and to make contributions to it. The aim of the legislation is to encourage all workers to save for their retirement through tax-efficient and relatively secure pension schemes. The government has established a low-cost scheme for employers to use: the National Employment Savings Trust (NEST). The private sector also offers multi-employer pension schemes, known as master trusts, that have to be authorised by the Pensions Regulator.[7] Employees earning more than a prescribed sum currently set at £10,000 are automatically enrolled in the employer's scheme. The Pensions Regulator reports that by the end of March 2017 more than 7 million workers had been successfully automatically enrolled into a workplace pension, so that about 78 per cent of the workforce now have an occupational pension.[8]

Under the general principles of the law of contract, if the employee performs the assigned work, but the employer fails to pay the agreed wages, the employee can bring a claim for the missing wages, subject, of course, to any general defences against claims for breach of contract such as the invalidity of the contract for fraud or its illegality. Equally, if the employee fails to perform the specified work, the employer does not have to pay the wages. This general principle of 'no work, no pay' encounters many complexities, however, when applied to particular disputes arising from the course of employment. Difficult questions include: what payment falls due if the work is not completed or if the work is defective or if there is no work to be done or if the employer forbids the employee to perform any more work?

One broad distinction between forms of employment relation provides a starting-point for answers to those questions. We can distinguish loosely between 'time-service' contracts and systems of 'performance-related pay'. The former contracts offer remuneration on condition that the employee is available and willing to perform the allotted work at the time prescribed by the employer, and payment is calculated by reference to the amount of time that labour power is made available. Performance-related payment systems, such as

---

[6] Pension Schemes Act 1993, ss. 145–51A (as amended by the Pensions Act 1995).
[7] Pension Schemes Act 2017.
[8] The Pensions Regulator, *Automatic Enrolment: Commentary and Analysis* (July 2017).

piecework, commissions and bonuses, are expressed to be contingent upon satisfactory completion of particular tasks or the achievement of particular goals. This broad distinction provides a rough answer to many questions about the allocation of risk between the parties. Under a time-service contract, subject to the express terms of the contract the employer normally bears the risk that the work is not completed, that the work is defective or that there is no work to be done, but the employer is entitled to insist that the employee should remain available for work during the working time fixed by the contract. These allocations of risks are typically reversed in contracts based upon performance-related payment systems. In such contracts, the worker will only be paid when the work is completed, if it is of satisfactory quality and if there was a job to be done. But these presumptions about the intentions of the parties are no more than starting-points for the legal analysis, which becomes more refined by an examination of the express and implied terms of the contract.

In this chapter, we consider how the courts have construed contractual arrangements in order to allocate some of these standard risks associated with the wage/work bargain. We may ask whether the judges, when using the common law to interpret the variety of contracts of employment and how they allocate risks and liabilities, seek to establish some element of fairness of exchange or equilibrium in the wage/work bargain and some element of stability in the relation that avoids unforeseen deprivations of work or income.[9] In pursuit of that enquiry, we initially ask when an employer may withhold payment of wages on the ground that the employee has not done the requisite work, and then examine the mirror-image issue of when and how an employee may seek wages that the employer has failed to pay. We then consider the circumstances, if any, when an employer is required to provide work to be performed. The chapter concludes by examining why and the extent to which legislation overrides the contractual allocation of risks in the wage/work bargain and, in particular focuses on the justification for replacement of the contractual term governing payment by the NMW.

Deductions for Incomplete and Unsatisfactory Work

An employer's power to withhold wages is a powerful self-help remedy in response to perceived failures by the employee to perform the contractual undertaking to work. By reducing or eliminating payment, the employer forces the worker to commence a legal claim for the missing wages, an action which the employee will be reluctant to take against his or her current employer. The employer's entitlement to withhold wages depends upon the terms of the contract and their implications, as determined by the common law of contract.

---

[9] M. Freedland and S. Deakin, 'The Exchange Principle and the Wage-Work Bargain', in M. Freedland *et al.* (eds.), *The Contract of Employment* (Oxford University Press, 2016), pp. 52, 55.

Equity may invalidate some express terms on the ground that they constitute penalty clauses. The question is whether the impugned financial charge for the employee's breach of contract imposes a detriment on the employee out of all proportion to any legitimate interest of the employer in the enforcement of the term that the first party has broken.[10] Statute provides workers with a simplified mechanism for recovering unlawful 'deductions' from pay, but provides only a marginal deterrent against misuse of the power to withhold wages. We will consider first the extent to which the common law buttresses the employer's power to use the reduction of wages in order to discipline the workforce, and then examine the extent of the statutory protection for workers against unlawful deductions.

Withholding Pay at Common Law

The express and implied terms of the contract determine the employer's power at common law to reduce wages. Under a performance-related payment system in the contract, such as piecework, the employer is only obliged to pay wages when the task has been completed satisfactorily. The sanction for failure to work hard is simply the refusal to pay wages on the ground that a contractual condition for payment has not been satisfied. Under time-service contracts, however, the position is more complex, for the core of the wage/work bargain is that the employee promises to be available and willing to work according to the employer's instructions for the hours prescribed in the contract. Nevertheless, if the employer can point to a failure to work the agreed hours or to perform the agreed tasks, the employer may also withhold a proportionate amount of the wages. For instance, if employees take strike action for one day, subject to any relevant express terms of the contract, the employer can withhold pay for that day or in the case of an annual salary for 1/365 of the salary under the Apportionment Act 1870, section 2.[11] In addition, in any case of breach of contract by the employee, the employer might also seek to claim compensatory damages for losses resulting from the breach. This claim for damages might be set off against wages owed, again resulting in a reduction in payment.

Under a time-service contract, if the employee attends work, but not for all the hours prescribed in the contract, the employer has an option: either to refuse any of the work offered and thereby avoid any payment or to accept the work offered and reduce pay on a pro rata basis. In *Miles* v. *Wakefield Metropolitan Borough Council*,[12] a registrar of births, deaths and marriages refused to work normally on Saturday mornings, which amounted to a

---

[10] *Cavendish Square Holding BV* v. *Talal El Makdessi*; *ParkingEye Limited* v. *Beavis* [2015] UKSC 67, [2016] AC 1172.

[11] *Hartley* v. *King Edward VI College* [2017] UKSC 39, [2017] ICR 774.

[12] [1987] AC 539 (HL).

reduction of three hours from his normal working week of thirty-seven hours. The House of Lords held that the employer was entitled to deduct 3/37ths of his salary. But the House of Lords also pointed out that an employer might have an option to refuse to pay any wages at all. Lord Bridge stated:

> If an employee refused to perform the full duties which can be required of him under this contract of service the employer is entitled to refuse to accept any partial performance. The position then resulting, during any relevant period while these conditions obtain, is exactly as if the employee were refusing to work at all.

Lord Brightman stated:

> If an employee offers partial performance, as he does in some types of industrial conflict falling short of a strike, the employer has a choice. He may decline to accept the partial performance that is offered, in which case the employee is entitled to no remuneration for his unwanted services, even if they are performed.

If the employee is available for work during the prescribed hours, but is unwilling to perform some aspect of the job which is required by the employer, the employer has the same option to pay a proportion of wages or refuse to accept the services rendered as performance of the contract at all. Wages do not fall due unless the employee is 'ready and willing' to perform work as directed; mere attendance at the prescribed time is insufficient. This power to withhold all payment of wages for partial defective performance is especially significant in cases of industrial action falling short of a strike, such as 'working to rule', the withdrawal of co-operation in good faith or the elimination of any additional voluntary activities. In *Wiluszynski* v. *Tower Hamlets London Borough Council*,[13] a local government officer participated in industrial action organised by his union that involved a refusal to answer enquiries from councillors. This refusal was a breach of contract, although it amounted only to a very small proportion of his duties. The three hours of work missed was made up after the five weeks of industrial action. The employer had warned its employees that, unless they fulfilled their full range of contractual duties, they would not be paid at all for any work performed. The plaintiff worked normally during the industrial action apart from the refusal to answer enquiries from councillors, but received no pay for that period. At first instance, the plaintiff's claim for the full salary succeeded on the ground that there had been substantial performance of the job and management had acquiesced in the variation by permitting the employee to attend work. The Court of Appeal allowed the employer's appeal and held that no payment was due. The applicable principles of the common law were stated by Nicholls LJ:

---

[13] [1989] ICR 493 (CA).

In my view the defendant was entitled to adopt the stance that, so long as the plaintiff continued to refuse to carry out part of his contractual duties, the defendant would not accept his services and the plaintiff would not be paid. Replying to enquiries from councillors was a material part of the duties of estate officers such as the plaintiff. The plaintiff's considered statement that he would not discharge this part of his duties was, in law, a repudiatory breach of his contract. Subject to any provision to the contrary in his contract of employment, such conduct entitled the defendant to treat the contract as terminated and to dismiss the plaintiff. The contrary conclusion would mean that the defendant would be obliged to continue to employ and pay the plaintiff even though part of the work required of him and others in his position would not be done. That cannot be right.

In my view, however, termination of the contract is not the only remedy available to an employer in such circumstances. A buyer of goods is entitled to decline to accept goods tendered to him which do not conform to a condition in the contract, without necessarily terminating the contract altogether. So with services. If an employee states that for the indefinite future he will not be performing a material part of his contractual services, the employer is entitled in response, and in advance of the services being undertaken, to decline to accept the proffered partial performance. He can hold himself out as continuing to be ready and willing to carry out the contract of employment, and to accept from the employee work as agreed and to pay him for that work as agreed, while declining to accept or pay for part only of the agreed work.

The effect of this decision is to permit employers to withhold all payment under the contract, even if the employee is working almost normally, provided that the employer makes it clear to the employee in advance that the refusal to perform some aspect of the job as directed is regarded by the employer as a fundamental breach of contract.

The employer's implied right to withhold pay for incomplete performance of the contract by the employee raises the issue of the exact scope of the duties of the employee. The express terms and the rule-book will provide some guidance. The duty to obey the lawful orders of the employer may resolve any further doubt. In addition, the implied term requiring an employee to serve the employer faithfully applies to expand the duties arising under the contract of employment. In Chapter 4, we noted the existence of this term which appears to require from the employee a duty to perform in good faith. The implied term was formulated by Buckley LJ in *Secretary of State for Employment* v. *ASLEF (No. 2)*[14] in these terms:

> within the terms of the contract the employee must serve the employer faithfully with a view to promoting those commercial interests for which he is employed.

---

[14] [1972] ICR 19 (CA).

Agreeing with the formulation that there is an implied term to serve the employer 'faithfully within the requirements of the contract', Ralph Gibson LJ in *British Telecommunications plc* v. *Ticehurst*,[15] added:

> The term is breached, in my judgment, when the employee does an act, or omits to do an act, which it would be within her contract and the discretion allowed to her not to do, or to do, as the case may be, and the employee so acts or omits to do the act, not in honest exercise of choice or discretion for the faithful performance of her work but in order to disrupt the employer's business or to cause the most inconvenience that can be caused.

Using this formulation of the implied term requiring good faith in performance, industrial action short of a strike, such as the 'work-to-rule' in the *ASLEF* case or the 'withdrawal of goodwill' in *Ticehurst*, will invariably result in a breach of contract. The employer is then entitled to respond by a refusal to pay any wages as long as the industrial action continues.

A power to withhold wages may also apply to an employee's breach of an implied term regarding the quality of performance of the contract. The relevant implied term may be based upon the custom of the trade, provided that the custom is 'notorious, certain, and reasonable', or one of the general implied terms that courts insert into contracts of employment, such as the duty to perform work with reasonable care. By virtue of these implied terms, an employer may be able to insist upon a reasonable quality of work and failure to conform to this standard can be regarded as a breach of contract. Unless the terms of the contract, including custom, make express provision for a deduction from wages in these circumstances, the remedy for such a breach of contract probably lies in a claim for damages against the employee. But that claim for damages may be set off against the payment of wages, thereby producing a deduction in the payment.

In *Sagar* v. *Ridehalgh & Son Ltd*,[16] a weaver claimed pay that had been deducted from wages on the ground of poor workmanship. The contract of employment was an oral agreement, but the rates of pay were fixed by collective agreement. Most mills in the locality had the custom of making deductions for work that had been performed in the view of management without reasonable care and skill, and the custom had prevailed at the defendant employer's mill for more than thirty years. There was no reference to the practice in either the oral agreement or the collective agreement. It was held, among other points, that the evidence established an implied term, based upon custom, that the employer could make reasonable deductions for bad work. That decision involved an interpretation of a typical contract in the manufacturing sector that used a performance-related payment mechanism of piecework. To justify the deductions from pay, the employer could point to

---

[15] [1992] ICR 383 (CA).   [16] [1931] 1 Ch 310 (CA).

defects in the pieces produced and, for those defective pieces that had been rejected, no payment fell due.

In the case of a time-service contract, the terms of the contract may not specify in any detail the expectation of quality in performance, but the employer can rely upon the general implied terms of the obligation to take reasonable care in the performance of work and the duty to perform in good faith. In *Lister* v. *Romford Ice and Cold Storage Co. Ltd*,[17] a lorry-driver injured another employee when backing the lorry while performing his job. The injured employee successfully claimed damages against his employer. The employer (or rather its insurance company) then claimed damages against the negligent driver on the ground of breach of an implied term in the contract of employment. The House of Lords held that contracts of employment contain an implied term that an employee owes a duty to take reasonable care of his employer's property entrusted to him and generally in the performance of his duties. There was no implied term, however, that the employee was entitled to be indemnified by his employer from the employer's insurance. In principle, therefore, the employer could claim compensatory damages against the lorry-driver, and those damages might be set off against any wages due. Such a claim for damages against an employee is rare, because in practice the case will usually be a dispute between insurance companies about which one should bear the loss, and insurance companies have agreed not to pursue such actions against employees. Nevertheless, the decision does give employers a powerful right against employees which may affect the level of compensation in cases of dismissal for negligent damage to the employer's property or form the basis of a set-off against wages.

The judicial elaborations of an employee's implied obligations indicate that employers will often be in a strong position to insist that the employee has broken the wage/work bargain when unsatisfactory performance is offered under a time-service contract. The implied obligation amounts to a duty placed on the employee to perform the contract in good faith or a duty to co-operate in the performance of work in order to further the employer's business objective. The principle of 'no work, no pay' becomes 'work that does not further the employer's business objective in good faith, no pay'. These interpretations of the express and implied terms of the contract of employment plainly reinforce the managerial power to direct labour and to require co-operation from the workforce by giving management the powerful self-help sanction of the lawful refusal to pay wages. It seems possible that the duty may be more onerous for managerial employees, although this outcome may simply result from the fact that senior employees are likely to enjoy greater discretion in the determination of the tasks to be performed under their contract. This power to refuse to pay full wages in response to

---

[17] [1956] AC 583 (HL).

the implied term to perform the contract in good faith will, except in the case of industrial action, usually be subject to statutory controls over unlawful deductions.

Statutory Protection against Deductions

Regulation might endeavour to control the common law power of the employer to withhold wages for a number of purposes:

- transparency: clear information to workers in advance about when wages may be reduced and by how much;
- deterrence against misuse of the power: a sanction against the employer's misuse of the disciplinary power contained in the contract to impose cuts in wages, where, for instance, the power is not used in good faith;
- fairness of the power: control over the terms of the contract to prevent it conferring the power to make either disproportionate deductions or deductions for trivial breaches of the employee's performance obligations.

In support of any of the above purposes, legal regulation might also create a simple, inexpensive mechanism through which an employee can challenge an unlawful deduction from wages and recover any money due.

For nearly a century, the Truck Act 1896 achieved all three of the above purposes for workmen (not white-collar workers) and shop assistants. The enforcement mechanism was a prosecution brought by inspectors before a magistrates' court, together with the possibility for the workman to recover any excess deduction. Though not without defects, until its abolition and replacement by the Wages Act 1986, the Truck Act 1896 provided almost comprehensive regulatory protection for many workers against abuse of the employer's power to enforce discipline by withholding wages. With one exception, the revised law confines its regulation to the first purpose, transparency, and even that objective is qualified. ERA 1996, section 8, gives an employee the right to a written itemised pay statement at the time of the payment of wages. In the absence of such a statement, any unnotified deductions made by the employer have to be repaid to the employee.[18] The replacement law for the Truck Act 1896, which is consolidated in ERA 1996, Part II, essentially only requires prior consent from the employee or worker to the grounds on which the employer has made the deduction from wages. That prior consent can be obtained in the contract of employment or contract for personal performance of work, provided the employer has given the employee or worker a written copy of the contract.

---

[18] ERA 1996, s. 12(4).

Employment Rights Act 1996, Section 13

(1) An employer shall not make a deduction from wages of a worker employed by him unless –
  (a) the deduction is required or authorised to be made by virtue of a statutory provision or a relevant provision of the worker's contract, or
  (b) the worker has previously signified in writing his agreement or consent to the making of the deduction.

(2) In this section 'relevant provision', in relation to a worker's contract, means a provision of the contract comprised –
  (a) in one or more written terms of the contract of which the employer has given the worker a copy on an occasion prior to the employer making the deduction in question, or
  (b) in one or more terms of the contract (whether express or implied and, if express, whether oral or in writing) the existence and effect, or combined effect, of which in relation to the worker the employer has notified to the worker in writing on such an occasion.

The exception to this limited control for the purpose of transparency concerns deductions made for stock shortages in the retail trade. At the time of the passage of the legislation, studies[19] and cases[20] revealed how some retail workers, such as attendants at self-service petrol stations, worked under contracts of employment that permitted the employer to deduct the value of stock that went missing during the worker's shift, even without the attendant's fault, as in the case of a motorist driving away without paying for petrol. As a limited exception to the general scheme of permitting freedom of contract with respect to deductions, sections 17–22 ERA 1996 in effect restrict deductions for cash shortages and stock deficiencies to 10 per cent of wages on any pay day, except for the final payment of wages when the employer can demand full reimbursement.

The requirement of transparency in all other cases imposes upon employers that wish to exercise their common-law disciplinary power to make deductions from pay the need to comply with the statutory requirements. The expectation of the transparency requirement is that employers will have difficulty in relying upon obscure or implied terms like the one advanced in *Sagar* v. *Ridehalgh*, or express terms that have not been expressly agreed in writing and adequately notified, in order to justify the withholding of pay. The EAT has required strict conformity to section 13, which in effect demands

---

[19] T. Goriely, 'Arbitrary Deductions from Pay and the Proposed Repeal of the Truck Acts' (1983) 12 *Industrial Law Journal* 236.
[20] *Bristow* v. *City Petroleum Ltd* [1988] ICR 165 (HL).

both that the deductions rule should be a provision of the worker's contract and that the worker should have been adequately notified of its content. Tribunals can prevent deduction rules from being inserted into contracts without the express consent of the worker. For example, in *Pename Ltd v. Paterson*,[21] it was held that an employer had not been entitled, on the strength of a statement made in the letter confirming the applicant's employment, to deduct a week's wages from his final salary when he failed to give notice of his leaving. The employee had not put his name to the employer's declaration, and the rule could not be regarded as a contractual term so as to satisfy section 13(1)(a). Even if the rule has become a term of the contract, it may still not justify the deduction if the notification requirement in section 13(2) has not been satisfied. In *Kerr v. The Sweater Shop (Scotland) Ltd*,[22] a general display within the workplace of a term, incorporated into the worker's contract, which purported to authorise the disputed deduction, was not sufficient notification. According to the EAT, section 13(2)(b) required personal, rather than general, notification of the employees affected. The requirement of transparency is also supported by strict construction of deduction rules in the contract, so that permission must be granted expressly and clearly. For example, it was held in *Potter v. Hunt Contracts Ltd*[23] that an agreement made by an employee to repay the costs of training if his employment was terminated prior to a particular date did not amount to an agreement on his part that the sums could be deducted from his wages in that event. Despite these robust interpretations of the transparency requirement, it should be observed that employers can operate a sweeping and oppressive policy of making deductions provided they ensure that express rules are contained in a written contract of employment that the worker is required to sign.

An important subsidiary question is whether the ERA 1996 provisions construct an effective means of enforcement. Unlike under the former Truck Acts, there is no system of inspectors to uphold the legislation. Instead, as under the common law, workers must bring a claim in person to recover pay that has been withheld. The provisions were intended to assist enforcement by permitting claims for deductions to be brought inexpensively and expeditiously before an ET rather than an ordinary court. The requirement to pay tribunal fees temporarily made the tribunals more expensive than ordinary courts, thereby significantly reducing the statutory protection against deductions. For instance the fees in a county court to recover a sum of £300 were £50, but in an ET they were £390. When fees were introduced, the number of claims for deduction from wages dropped by about 75 per cent.[24] If it finds an unlawful deduction to have been made, the remedy awarded by an ET under ERA 1996, section 24 is a declaration to that effect and an order requiring the

---

[21] [1989] IRLR 19 (EAT).   [22] [1996] IRLR 425 (EAT).   [23] [1992] IRLR 108 (EAT).
[24] Ministry of Justice, Tribunal and Gender Recognition Statistics Quarterly, July to September 2016.

employer to pay the worker the amount of any unlawful deduction subject to a limitation period of two years prior to the presentation of the complaint.[25] Before the introduction of tribunal fees, the median award for deductions from pay was about £900, with 25 per cent of claimants seeking less than £500. Given other expenses involved in making a claim and the risk that the employer would never pay, it was hardly surprising that in the face of tribunal fees the majority of claimants decided not to bother making a claim.

Following the abolition of tribunal fees, however, one should expect this statutory remedy of compensation for deductions from pay to resume its role as the standard method by which employees claim any money owing from the employer, thereby avoiding claims in the ordinary courts for breach of contract. This result has been achieved by a combination of the broad definition of wages contained in the statute and the wide definition given to the concept of a 'deduction' from wages by the courts. The concept of wages has a broad statutory definition.

Employment Rights Act 1996, Section 27(1)

In this Part 'wages', in relation to a worker, means any sums payable to the worker in connection with his employment, including –

(a) any fee, bonus, commission, holiday pay[26] or other emolument referable to his employment, whether payable under his contract or otherwise,

(b) statutory sick pay . . .

(c) statutory maternity pay . . .

(d) statutory paternity pay . . .

(e) statutory adoption pay . . .

(f) a guarantee payment . . .

(g) any payment for time off . . . for carrying out trade union duties . . .

(h) remuneration on suspension on medical grounds . . . and on suspension on maternity grounds,

(i) any sum payable in pursuance of an order for reinstatement or re-engagement,

(j) any sum payable in pursuance of an order for the continuation of a contract of employment,

(k) remuneration under a protective award.

---

[25] ERA 1996, s. 23(4A), inserted by The Deduction from Wages (Limitation) Regulations 2014, SI 2014 No. 3322.

[26] This includes claims for payment in respect of periods of annual leave under Working Time Regulations 1998, reg. 16: *HM Revenue and Customs Commissioners* v. *Stringer* [2009] UKHL 31, [2009] ICR 985 (HL).

Any failure to pay all or part of these sums regarded as wages could be regarded as a 'deduction', even if the employer had not intended to impose a disciplinary sanction. Once judicial supervision of the fairness of the deduction or fine was removed as a purpose of the legislation, the narrow conception of the word 'deduction' as a disciplinary penalty became inappropriate; the courts were prepared to enforce the limited transparency requirement of the ERA 1996 with respect to any disputes over wages. Thus, as a practical matter, most workers are likely to use this jurisdiction in any dispute with an employer over wages and other sums due, whether the issue is related to unauthorised disciplinary penalties, failure to pay a sum owed or a deliberate unilateral reduction of pay by the employer.

The two principal exceptions to the coverage of claims for money brought by workers against their employer under this jurisdiction for deductions concern claims in the context of industrial action and claims on termination of employment for payments in lieu of notice (sometimes referred to as PILON). The statutory claim for deductions from pay does not apply to a deduction from a worker's wage made by his employer where the worker has taken part in a strike or other industrial action and the deduction is made by the employer on account of the worker's having taken part in that strike or other action.[27] Thus the common-law principles that were described above concerning the employer's power to refuse to pay any wages in response to industrial action remain untouched by the legislation. With respect to claims for pay or damages in the event of termination of contract by the employer, the House of Lords, in *Delaney* v. *Staples*,[28] has drawn a distinction between claims for wages or agreed sums, for which the statutory procedure for deductions is available, and claims for damages for breach of contract, where the procedure is unavailable; instead the employee should bring a claim for damages for wrongful dismissal (or seek compensation through the statutory claim for unfair dismissal). In respect of a claim for an annual bonus payment, for instance, if the precise amount of the bonus has not been declared,[29] and there is no formula by which it may be calculated, this discretionary bonus will not be recoverable under the statutory regime for deductions, but must be claimed in the ordinary courts by way of a claim for damages for breach of contract.[30] Where an employer dismisses an employee summarily and unjustifiably without notice, an employee may bring a claim for damages for wrongful dismissal. Unfortunately an employer's promise of a PILON is ambiguous: in some instances, it seems to represent an acknowledgement by the employer that wages were due under the contract, so the deductions procedure will be available; in other cases, it may represent a sum paid to the employee in anticipation of the claim for damages. A claim for damages for wrongful

---

[27] ERA 1996, s. 14(5).   [28] [1992] ICR 483 (HL).
[29] Declared bonus recoverable in *Farrell Matthews & Weir* v. *Hansen* [2005] ICR 509 (EAT).
[30] *Coors Brewers Ltd* v. *Adcock* [2007] EWCA Civ 19, [2007] ICR 983 (CA).

dismissal for sums of less than £25,000 can also be brought before an ET,[31] although the process is likely to be more complex in order to address such matters as counterclaims by the employer and mitigation of loss.

A Duty to Provide Work?

In the wage/work bargain of the contract of employment, does the employer promise to provide work and does the employee have a right to work? Does an employer have a duty to provide work or at least does an employee have the right to be paid even though the employer has no work to be done? In Chapter 3 it was suggested that the consideration to support a contract of employment is usually found in the employee's promise to perform work in return for the employer's promise to pay for the work done. The normal interpretation placed on contracts of employment by the courts is that the employer does not promise to provide work to be done, but merely promises to pay wages.[32] Yet it is possible that a court may infer a duty to provide work as an incident or an implied term of a particular contract of employment. Breach of that term would give rise to compensatory damages for the loss of wages that would have been earned.

Shortage of Work

In time-service contracts, although typically there is no duty to provide work to be done, the employee is entitled to wages provided the employee is ready and willing to work, even if the employer does not direct the employee to perform any work. The employer bears the risk of a shortfall in work to be done. Using the express terms of the contract, however, the employer may shift the risk back on to the employee by inserting a condition that the employee will be paid only when required, not for a regular number of hours. Such contracts can take the form of 'zero-hours' contracts or casual-work contracts. Under the express terms of such contracts, the employee is paid only for those hours that are actually worked and the employer determines unilaterally when work is required. Under a zero-hours contract, the employee promises to be ready and available for work, but the employer merely promises to pay for time actually worked according to the requirements of the employer. These contracts may lead to the abuse that workers can be kept hanging around at their place of work waiting for work, but not actually working and therefore earning no money. Under arrangements for casual work, again the employer does not promise to offer any work, but equally in this case the employee does not promise to be available when required. Such

---

[31] Employment Tribunals Extension of Jurisdiction (England and Wales) Order 1994, SI 1994 No. 1623.

[32] *Turner* v. *Sawdon & Co* [1901] 2 KB 653 (CA).

arrangements may not amount to binding contracts at all; rather they comprise 'umbrella agreements' about the terms of employment when and if the employee is called upon and agrees to perform work.[33] These forms of employment secure to the employer the advantage of allocating the risk of the lack of work to be performed on to the employee, thereby permitting the employer to adjust labour costs precisely to its needs at any particular time. For these workers, their income is precarious and they risk exclusion from employment-protection rights on the grounds of lack of continuous employment.[34]

In contracts of employment under which payment is contingent upon the completion of a task, as in the case of piecework and commissions on sales, at first sight this arrangement permits the employer to decline to pay any wages when no work is available. But *Devonald* v. *Rosser & Sons*[35] illustrates the reluctance of courts to interpret contracts of employment in a way that imposes all risks of the absence of work on the employee. The plaintiff worked as a rollerman in the defendant's tinplate factory. Under the express terms of his contract, the employee was required to perform those tasks directed by the employer and both parties were entitled to twenty-eight days' notice of termination of employment. The employer used a piece-rate payment system for each completed box of 112 tin plates, though this payment mechanism was not specified in the written contract of employment. Following a decline in demand for its product, the employer closed the plant and two weeks later gave the employee notice of dismissal. The question before the court was what payment, if any, fell due during the six-week period between the plant closure and the expiration of the notice period, during which time the employer had not provided the employee with any work to perform. The Court of Appeal awarded the employee a sum equivalent to his average earnings prior to the plant closure for a period of six weeks. This result was achieved in part by regarding the contract of employment as a time-service contract, despite the payment mechanism of piece-rates, by referring to the term specifying a contractual notice period. The court distinguished between the continuing existence of the contract, which was determined by the operation of its notice provision, and its mechanism for calculating the amount of pay due. According to the court, as long as the contract persists and the employee is able and willing to work, the employer must either provide a reasonable amount of work to be performed, so that the employee may complete the required pieces, or pay compensation instead. Another line of argument endorsed by the court was that, on a proper construction of the contract and giving it business efficacy, although the employee bore the risk of lack of work as a result of some contingencies such as breakdown of the machinery, an employee did not bear the risk of absence of work due to plant closure. The

---

[33] See Chapter 6.   [34] See Chapter 6.   [35] [1906] 2 KB 728 (CA).

decision in *Devonald* v. *Rosser & Sons* therefore provides support for the idea that there may be a duty to pay wages when the payment mechanism adopted is based upon performance and there is no work to be done, provided that the employee is also under an obligation to be ready and willing to work and both parties are under duty to give notice of unavailability or termination of the contract. Nevertheless, express terms of the contract may always negative any such implication.

If the employer has work to be done, does the employee have a right to insist upon being able to work rather than be idle? Is there, in this narrow sense, a 'right to work'? In general, there is no obligation on the employer to direct an employee to perform work. The employer's obligation is to pay wages, not to provide work to be done. Three exceptions qualify this general presumption.

Suspension

As a disciplinary measure, an employer may decide to suspend an employee. During a suspension, the employer requires the employee not to attend the workplace on a temporary basis, usually pending the outcome of disciplinary proceedings. Suspension is usually made on full pay, although the employer may also decide not to pay wages. The contract of employment has not been interpreted to grant an employer an inherent power to suspend an employee. Unless the employer benefits from a term in the contract of employment that expressly confers the power to make suspensions, such a disciplinary measure, which involves a refusal to give the employee work, should be regarded as a breach of contract.[36] Similarly, without an express power in the contract to suspend an employee from work on medical grounds, an employee who is ready and able to work, perhaps having recovered from an illness, should be entitled to wages.[37] Any wages that have been withheld during suspension without express contractual provision will normally be recoverable as 'deductions' from wages under ERA 1996, section 13. The exercise of an express disciplinary power to suspend the employee has to be exercised in good faith and on reasonable grounds, for otherwise the employer may be found liable for breach of the implied duty not to act in a way calculated to destroy mutual trust and confidence.[38]

Garden Leave

An employer's refusal to provide work may be based on a 'garden leave' provision under the express terms of the contract. Under such a provision, the employer inserts a term in the contract stating that, following notice of

[36] *Hanley* v. *Pease & Partners Ltd* [1915] 1 KB 698.
[37] *Beveridge* v. *KLM UK Ltd* [2000] IRLR 765 (EAT).
[38] *Gogay* v. *Hertfordshire County Council* [2000] IRLR 703 (CA).

termination of the contract, the employee will not be permitted to work for another employer until the expiration of the notice period. The objective of such a clause is to prevent an employee from working for a competitor. If the employer permits the employee to work out his notice, a court will issue an injunction to prevent the employee from leaving earlier to work for a competitor.[39] If the employer refuses to permit the employee to work and insists that the employee should stay at home during the notice period on full pay ('garden leave'), some courts have issued injunctions to prevent the employee from working for a competitor during a notice period.[40] But if the contractually specified period of idleness is regarded by the court as unreasonable in length or unnecessary to protect the employer from unfair competition, a long period of garden leave during notice of dismissal can be challenged as a violation of the restraint of trade doctrine.[41] Alternatively, the court may uphold the validity of the garden-leave clause, but decline to enforce it by way of an injunction, if the court in exercising its discretion to award that equitable remedy believes that the employer does not need such protection from competition.[42]

Reputation and Employability

The third exception is where the employee claims that the refusal to supply work causes the loss of an opportunity to enhance his reputation or employability. If a court finds that, in the particular circumstances of the case, the employee suffers such losses, subject to a proper construction of the terms of the contract, the employer's refusal to supply work may be regarded as a breach of contract. In the case of theatrical engagements, the courts have been ready to find an obligation on the part of the employer to afford the opportunity to the employee to perform the part for which he was engaged.[43] Similarly, an engagement for a specific project, such as participation in a specific voyage,[44] or employment in a specific and unique post such as the chief sub-editor of a newspaper,[45] have been treated by the courts as giving rise to an obligation on the part of the employer not to do anything that puts the promised employment out of the employee's reach. In *William Hill Organisation Ltd* v. *Tucker*,[46] a senior dealer in a betting business resigned in order to take a job with a competitor. His work involved the complex calculation of the

---

[39] *Evening Standard Co. Ltd* v. *Henderson* [1987] ICR 588 (CA).
[40] *Euro Brokers Ltd* v. *Rabey* [1995] IRLR 206; *GFI Group Inc.* v. *Eaglestone* [1994] IRLR 119.
[41] *William Hill Organisation Ltd* v. *Tucker* [1999] ICR 291 (CA); for restraint of trade, see Chapter 4.
[42] *Provident Financial Group plc* v. *Hayward* [1989] ICR 160 (CA).
[43] *Fechter* v. *Montgomery* (1863) 33 Beav 22; *Marbe* v. *George Edwardes (Daly's Theatre) Ltd* [1928] 1 KB 269; *Herbert Clayton and Jack Waller Ltd* v. *Oliver* [1930] AC 209.
[44] *Driscoll* v. *Australian RMSN Co.* [1859] 1 F & F 458.
[45] *Collier* v. *Sunday Referee Publishing Co. Ltd* [1940] 2 KB 647.   [46] [1999] ICR 291 (CA).

determination of betting odds in a new market known as 'spread betting'. Under the terms of his contract, he was required to give six months' notice of termination. Although the contract did not contain a garden-leave clause, the employer insisted that the employee should not work for a competitor during that period, but instead remain at home and continue to receive his wages. The employer sought an injunction to restrain the employee from working for a competitor, but the injunction was refused. The Court of Appeal construed the contract to provide that, if the job is there to be done and the employee was appointed to do it and is ready and willing, then the employer must permit him to do the job. The employee needed to be able to exercise his skills and keep abreast of this rapidly developing specialist market. If the employer failed to provide suitable work during a lengthy notice period, the employee should be free to exercise his skills and maintain his employability by working for another employer. There may be other situations where, in view of the terms and circumstances of the particular contract of employment, a court may imply a term that the employer should provide suitable work for an employee or permit the employee to perform professional work without impediment[47] or, alternatively, a failure to do so might be regarded as a breach of the implied term of mutual trust and confidence.[48]

The Principle of Mutuality

The cases in this and the previous section illustrate how the risks of the wage/work bargain can be allocated according to methods of interpretation of the express terms of the contract and the insertion of implied terms that purport to represent the implicit intentions of the parties. The construction placed by a court on the terms of the contract determines the allocation of such risks as the unavailability of work, the need to exercise skills and the failure to perform work tasks as directed. The respect afforded to freedom of contract both leads to the conclusion that the express contractual agreement should govern the wage/work bargain and also requires that, as a matter of legal technique, disputes about the content of the wage/work bargain should be resolved exclusively by reference to the apparent or presumed intentions of the parties as evidenced by the terms of the contract. The statutory protection against deductions from pay reinforces this contractual analysis by insisting, with few exceptions, that the express terms should also govern the employer's use of the power to withhold wages. In carrying out the task of construing the contract by inserting conditions and implied obligations, the courts appear to articulate a view of the mutual and reciprocal obligations of the contract which, at its heart, embraces the idea that normally the reasonable expectations of the

---

[47] H. Collins, 'Progress towards the Right to Work in the United Kingdom', in V. Mantouvalou (ed.), *The Right to Work: Legal and Philosophical Perspectives* (Oxford: Hart, 2015).
[48] M. Freedland, *The Personal Employment Contract* (Oxford University Press, 2003), p. 489.

parties that should be protected are that the employer will provide work to be done, the employee will perform the work or be ready and willing to do so and that the employer will pay the agreed remuneration or an appropriate proportion of the wages in view of the performance of the contract. This guiding principle of mutuality or reciprocity is, however, always subject to express terms of the contract, which can permit the employer to provide wages but no work, as in the example of garden leave, or even permit the employer to provide no work and no pay at all, as in the case of zero-hours contracts. Insofar as the express terms of the contract confer a discretionary power on the employer to withdraw benefits or deny bonuses and other kinds of remuneration, as we have seen, the employer will not be permitted to exercise this power arbitrarily, capriciously or irrationally.[49]

National Minimum Wage

The European Social Charter 1961 provides a right for workers to 'remuneration such as will give them and their families a decent standard of living',[50] a level which has been set by the Committee of Social Rights at 60 per cent of the national average wage in the relevant country.[51] Before the implementation of the NMWA 1998, the UK was virtually isolated among Western economies in lacking a comprehensive protection for a minimum wage. Nevertheless, the evil of wages below the poverty level had long been recognised.

Winston Churchill MP

It is a national evil that any class of Her Majesty's subjects should receive less than a living wage in return for their utmost exertions ... [W]here you have what we call sweated trades, you have no organisation, no parity of bargaining, the good employer is undercut by the bad and the bad by the worst; the worker, whose whole livelihood depends upon the industry, is undersold by the worker who only takes up the trade as a second string ... [W]here these conditions prevail you have not a condition of progress, but a condition of progressive degeneration.[52]

Churchill was speaking during the debates on the Trade Boards Act 1909, which established wage-fixing mechanisms for the 'sweated industries', defined as those providing wages 'barely sufficient to sustain existence ... hours of labour ... such as to make the lives of the worker periods of almost ceaseless toil ... sanitary conditions ... injurious to the health of the persons

[49] P. 148, *Braganza* v. *BP Shipping Ltd* [2015] UKSC 17, [2015] ICR 449.   [50] Art. 4.
[51] K. D. Ewing, 'Social Rights and Human Rights: Britain and the Social Charter: The Conservative Legacy' [2000] *European Human Rights Law Review* 91, at 98.
[52] 155 HC Debs. (24 April 1906), col. 1888.

employed and . . . dangerous to the public'.[53] The Trade Boards, later renamed Wages Councils,[54] established tripartite mechanisms involving negotiations between employers, unions and independent members for setting minimum rates of pay for particular economic sectors, often on a regional basis. It was hoped that the Wages Councils would stimulate proper collective bargaining in the sweated industries,[55] but that hope was never realised. In sectors such as agriculture and hotels and catering, unions were rarely able to achieve effective collective bargaining arrangements for a variety of reasons such as the geographical dispersal of workers. It became evident that Wages Councils were focused on what was termed by economists a 'secondary labour market', where the jobs available were predominantly temporary or casual, part time, requiring low skills and little training, involving unsocial hours and often filled by women and migrant workers.

Low Pay Commission (June 1998)

Some groups of workers are more likely to be low paid than others. These include . . . women, young people, ethnic minorities, people with disabilities, part-time workers, lone parents, temporary and seasonal workers and home-workers . . . Many sectors in which low pay prevails – such as cleaning, hospitality and social care – are those where female workers have traditionally been in the majority. In the social care sector, for example . . . 90 per cent of staff in residential and nursing homes are women. But . . . certain types of working patterns in which female workers predominate – such as part-time work and homeworking – can significantly influence the level of pay. Many jobs with those working patterns exist in the lowest-paying sectors, which creates further downward pressure on women's pay.[56]

These structural features of the labour market in these economic sectors with low pay blocked union organisation and the growth of effective collective bargaining. Those structural features also led to the Wages Councils setting low minimum rates of pay, typically between 34 per cent and 43 per cent of the full-time male average hourly rate.

Statutory regulation of minimum wages has attracted fierce political controversy in the past. Although the idea of setting a floor on wages can be defended either in terms of a fair distribution of wealth in society or on the ground of protecting individual rights, including a basic right to dignity,[57] there are justifiable concerns about its economic effects and practicability.

---

[53] Select Committee on the Sweating System, Fifth Report (1890).
[54] Wages Councils Act 1945.   [55] The aim of reforms in the Wages Councils Act 1979.
[56] *The National Minimum Wage*, First Report of the Low Pay Commission (June 1998), paras. 3.7–3.10.
[57] G. Davidov, 'A Purposive Approach to the National Minimum Wage Act' (2009) 72 *Modern Law Review* 581.

From a neoclassical economic perspective, there is a risk that, if the government artificially raises wages above market rates, this will reduce the demand for labour, thereby provoking higher levels of unemployment, fuelling inflationary pressures and reducing the competitiveness of business. Trade unions were also hesitant about statutory wage fixing, because they feared that it would make it even more difficult to recruit members from the secondary labour market and to establish effective collective bargaining arrangements. Against these considerations, it was argued that, in the absence of the setting of a floor on wages, there were the dangers of the progressive impoverishment of workers as a result of competition between employers. Therefore, to avoid widespread poverty, and in particular child poverty, the government would have to subsidise the low paid by paying them working tax credits and abolishing tax for the lower paid. In effect, without a minimum wage set at a high level, taxpayers would end up subsidising employers who paid wages that were below the poverty level. The unemployment and anti-competitive effects of a minimum wage were also doubted, at least if the minimum was set at a sensible level. Wilkinson and Deakin argued further that the absence of protection from low wages tended to damage productivity, at least in some sectors, which in turn weakened the competitiveness of the economy as a whole:

> The availability of under-valued labour has important negative influences on productive efficiency by providing a means by which firms can compensate for organisational and other managerial inefficiencies, delay the scrapping of obsolete capital equipment and engage in destructive price competition. The absence of wage discipline means that technologically and managerially backward firms can survive and this helps prevent more progressive firms from expanding their share of the market. The overall effect is a lower average level of productivity and the slow rate of introduction of new techniques and products.[58]

In pursuance of the neoclassical economic arguments and the assertion that high levels of unemployment were caused by workers 'pricing themselves out of jobs', a Conservative government finally abolished Wages Councils in 1993 (with the exception of the Agricultural Wages Board which was abolished only in 2013). Following the election of a Labour government in 1997, however, the NMWA 1998 and the accompanying statutory instrument, now revised as the National Minimum Wage Regulations 2015 (NMWR 2015),[59] established for the first time a comprehensive statutory floor on wages. After an examination of the framework of the legislation, we can assess its impact on wages, unemployment and other social considerations. The NMWA 1998 also provides an interesting example of the difficulties of regulating effectively the wide

---

[58] F. Wilkinson and S. Deakin, *Labour Standards: Essential to Economic and Social Progress* (London: Institute of Employment Rights, 1996).
[59] SI 2015 No. 621.

range of types of paid employment through the imposition of a single formula of an hourly rate of pay. This is command-and-control regulation, with detailed rules and penal sanctions, without much scope for flexibility and adaptation to context.

Scope of Application

The NMWA 1998, section 1(2), provides that it applies in respect of any 'worker' in the UK. It applies the broad statutory definition of worker,[60] which includes not only employees and apprentices, but also the group described earlier as 'dependent contractors' who are self-employed but supply their services exclusively to a particular employer.[61] Section 34 expressly applies the NMW to 'agency workers' 'as if there were a worker's contract . . . between the agency worker' and whichever of the agent or the principal either (a) is responsible for paying the worker or (b) actually does so. Section 35 applies the NMW to home-workers, and section 41 permits the Secretary of State to designate others as 'workers'. Members of the armed forces are excluded from the NMW by section 37, and share fishermen, unpaid volunteers, residential members of religious communities (except independent schools and providers of further and higher education) and prisoners are excluded by sections 43–5. There is also an exclusion for work by family members for a family business, and for live-in nannies or *au pairs* who are treated like a member of the family, an exclusion that risks permitting the exploitation of domestic workers.[62] The NMWA 1998 also excludes workers within the compulsory school age (sixteen), so it does not apply to teenagers who take casual work such as babysitting or newspaper deliveries.

Although the Act is broad in scope, it will exclude workers where there is no expectation of payment at all and young people on publicly funded training and work experience schemes.[63] In *Edmonds* v. *Lawson*,[64] a pupil barrister attempted to claim the NMW on the ground that she was either a worker or an apprentice. The Court of Appeal decided that she was not a worker, because a pupil does not undertake to perform work or services for her pupil master but rather seeks training and development with a view to obtaining a practising certificate. Nor was she an apprentice, because she was under no obligation to perform work and had no expectation of payment during her training. This ruling may suggest that interns, who work for no pay or merely expenses in order to obtain work experience, do not qualify for the NMW. But not all interns will be excluded. Where the intern is simply supplying unpaid labour, in the view of some tribunals he or she may well qualify as a 'worker'. The intern is certainly undertaking to perform work personally, but in the absence of consideration in the form of a promise to pay wages or some other benefit

---

[60] NMWA 1998, s. 54.   [61] See Chapter 6.   [62] NMWR 2015, reg. 57.
[63] NMWR 2015, regs. 51–6.   [64] [2000] ICR 567 (CA).

there must be a doubt whether the intern satisfies the element of the statutory definition of a worker that requires a contract,

Unpaid Website Intern Celebrates Court Victory

Keri Hudson should be happy about her recent victory. She is one of the first interns in the UK to take on their employer and win the right to be recognised as a paid worker. In January, after six weeks of interning without pay for the on-line review site My Village, Hudson, 21, resigned in disgust. 'I'd done ridiculous amounts of work for them,' she says. 'I'd practically run the site.' And yet, to her employers, 'all the work I'd done equalled zero pounds. I knew that was unfair, that it wasn't right. And as soon as I walked out, I knew I wanted to do something about it.'

Hudson's stint at My Village began in December when she responded to an advert on Gumtree for an unpaid intern. There was no training and no induction, and promised pay repeatedly failed to materialise, she says. Instead she found herself working free from 10am until 6pm editing and uploading content, and eventually managing six other unpaid interns who were all crammed on to a desk meant for two in the company's offices. While she survived by maxing out her credit card and taking handouts from her parents, Hudson says, her boss was off holidaying in Morocco.

With the help of the NUJ's Cashback for Interns campaign, Hudson took TPG Web Publishing, owner of My Village, to a tribunal, and earlier this month she was awarded £1,025 for five weeks' work at the National Minimum Wage rate, plus pro rata holiday pay.

Roy Mincoff, the NUJ's legal officer, believes this should send a shiver down the spines of many media employers. 'This judgment says that if someone is taken on as intern, and is doing a proper job rather than just being trained, then they will be regarded as a worker for the purposes of the National Minimum Wage.'[65]

Setting the National Minimum Wage

In view of the risk of adverse effects on levels of employment and productivity, the precise hourly rate of pay for the NMW raises both difficult technical economic questions and also political dilemmas. Under the legislation, the Secretary of State sets the NMW. Technical evaluation and advice is provided by the Low Pay Commission, which consists of three representatives of employers, three trade unionists and two academic economists and experts on employment relations, and an independent chair. A description of the process of setting the NMW by one member reveals how the commissioners realised that unanimity was essential for their proposals to be accepted by the Secretary of State so, after some hard bargaining, eventually a compromise was

---

[65] S. Malik, *Guardian*, 23 May 2011.

always reached.[66] After a few years, much better statistical information on average earnings, on the location of low-paid workers in the economy and on the measurable effects of the NMW became available, which greatly facilitated agreement. So far, the advice of the Commission on the rate for the NMW has been followed by the Secretary of State.

On its introduction in April 1999, the NMW was set at £3.60 per hour, with a lower rate of £3.00 per hour for those aged 18–21. There is no automatic process of raising the NMW in line with inflation or earnings. Nevertheless, the NMW has increased annually, so that in its first decade the rate exceeded average increases in earnings. In 2016 the conservative government introduced a new higher rate for workers aged twenty-five or over, which was called the National Living Wage. In making recommendations for the other rates, the Low Pay Commission is instructed to recommend a rate that should not have negative impacts on levels of employment, which in practice is achieved by rates that represent about 50 per cent of median earnings. But for the National Living Wage, the Commission is required to recommend a rate that will achieve a level of 60 per cent of median earnings by 2020, even though it may have negative effects on levels of employment.

National Minimum Wage, April 2019

- £8.21 per hour for workers aged twenty-five or over (the National Living Wage);
- £7.70 per hour for workers aged twenty-one to twenty-four years old;
- £6.15 per hour for workers aged eighteen to twenty years old;
- £4.35 per hour for workers above school leaving age but under eighteen years old;
- £3.90 for apprentices under the age of nineteen, or aged nineteen years old or over and in the first year of their apprenticeship

The risks posed by the new policy behind the National Living Wage to levels of employment and of compliance were noted by the Chair of the Low Pay Commission, Sir David Norgrove, in his letter to the Secretary of State recommending the current rates:

Around 1.6 million workers aged 25 and over – 6.7 per cent of the cohort – were covered by the introductory rate, with the large increase in April 2016 rippling some way up the pay distribution. This is reflected in hourly pay growth of nearly 6 per cent for the bottom quarter of workers, with women and part-timers particularly benefiting, and many workers aged under-25 also receiving the NLW rate. Low inflation meant real gains in pay were almost as large as nominal increases. Pay increases were in some cases

---

[66] W. Brown, 'The Process of Fixing the British National Minimum Wage 1997–2007' (2009) 47 *British Journal of Industrial Relations* 429.

offset by reductions in benefits and premium pay as well as squeezing of differentials. Gains may also have been reduced by an increase in non-compliance, with recorded underpayment appearing to rise sharply, although this could be partly measuring higher non-compliance at the beginning of the NLW year. But it may also be a more sustained increase, and makes it more important to recognize that the demands on HMRC enforcement will rise in line with the NLW.[67]

The rapidly rising National Living Wage also has the effect that whereas the former minimum rates only applied to about 1 million workers, they are likely to apply to about 2 million workers by 2018 and 3 million workers (or about 10 per cent of the workforce) by 2020. The government appears to be willing to risk unemployment effects in order to save large sums of social security expenditure on working tax credits or universal benefits that are paid to those on low pay who cannot live on their wages alone. Although early labour market data could not identify negative effects on levels of employment that might be caused by the National Living Wage, there were strong indications that non-compliance levels had doubled.[68]

Case Study: Farm in Herefordshire

A farm in Herefordshire employing 22 permanent staff and 1,000 seasonal workers told us that the NLW had affected the differential in pay between skilled and supervisory staff. 70 per cent of its production cost is labour so the business is sensitive to changes in wage rates.

In 2015 the differential was 11 per cent, but a 9 per cent increase in labour costs for NLW workers since October last year, once increased National Insurance payments, holiday pay and pension contributions were taken into account, meant that it had had to reduce the maximum differential to 5.5 per cent.

It had also reviewed jobs and downgraded some to lower pay scales. Some benefits had been reduced, for example the number of free bus trips available to staff.[69]

Assessing Whether the Minimum Wage is Paid

The general formula for determining whether or not a worker has received the statutory minimum wage is:

the 'total amount of remuneration' for the 'reference period' minus the total of 'reductions' to be made, and then divide this sum by the 'total hours' worked in that period.

---

[67] https://www.gov.uk/government/uploads/system/uploads/attachment_data/file/571777/Letter_from_LPC_Chair_2017_NLW_NMW_rates.pdf.

[68] Low Pay Commission Report Autumn 2016 (November 2016) Cm 9272, paras. 2.125 *et seq.*

[69] *Ibid.*, para. 2.33.

The 'reference period' of time is a month or, in the case of workers paid by reference to a shorter period, such as weekly payments, that period.[70] The general formula takes as its starting-point the model of workers being paid by the hour, so that the assessment of whether the minimum wage has been paid is basically to divide the amount of pay by the number of hours worked. In practice, however, contractual arrangements deviate significantly from the model of regular hours of work with payment by the hour. Consider, for instance, the difficulty of working out the hourly pay of a home-worker who is paid by the piece and has no fixed hours of work. Even major employers with sophisticated management and IT systems can make mistakes in the complex and detailed calculations required to ensure compliance with the statutory minimum wage.

Calculating Working Hours

The legislation addresses the complexity of assessing working time by dividing workers into four groups. In brief these categories are:

- salaried hours work: a person who is paid for a basic number of hours in a year and is paid an annual salary by weekly or monthly instalments;[71]
- time work: work that is paid for by reference to the time for which a worker works under a contract of employment (other than salaried hours work), including cases where the amount of pay per hour is calculated by reference to output;[72]
- output work: a person who is paid by the number of pieces made or processed, or wholly by reference to some other measure of output such as the number or value of sales made;[73]
- unmeasured work: this is the residual category, which includes work where there are no specified hours, as in the case of casual workers.

Detailed regulations try to specify what should count as working time within each of these categories for the purpose of calculating the hours worked during the pay reference period. In most cases, time work is fixed by the terms of the contract: the hours of work are those specified in the contract, and those duties may be performed anywhere including the home and may consist of trivial or only irregular matters. For instance, in *British Nursing Association* v. *Inland Revenue (National Minimum Wage Compliance Team)*,[74] the job involved manning a telephone line overnight in order to answer queries from customers. Apart from when speaking on the phone, the worker was free to perform other activities such as reading or watching television. The Court of Appeal ruled that the night work counted in its

---

[70] NMWR 2015, reg. 16.   [71] NMWR 2015, reg. 21.   [72] NMWR 2015, reg. 30.
[73] NMWR 2015, reg. 36.   [74] [2002] IRLR 480 (CA).

entirety as working time for the purposes of entitlement to the NMW. The Court took the view that it would make a 'mockery' of the NMW if it were to find that workers were only working when they were actually dealing with phone calls. Similarly a security guard who is required by the terms of the contract to be present at the workplace for a fixed number of hours per day will be regarded for all of that time as being at work, even if the guard is permitted to watch television or have a nap. Unfortunately, some contracts of employment do not make it clear what are the contracted working hours and therefore create uncertainty.

Some contracts of employment specify that workers will be 'on call' overnight and offer a small sum in compensation for any possible inconvenience. The worker may be permitted to stay at home by the phone or to sleep at the employer's premises, which is often done in care homes to meet a legal requirement. The small payment would be wholly inadequate if the overnight period were treated as working hours for the purpose of assessing compliance with the minimum wage. In such cases, in a rather misleading provision, the Regulations specify that work time also includes hours when a worker is required to be available at or near a place of work for the purposes of working, but not when the worker is at home.[75] Such a worker at the workplace will only be entitled to claim the minimum wage for those hours when the worker is awake for the purpose of working and not when the worker is by arrangement asleep but on call.[76] Although that rule makes sense in many cases, in some caring jobs the worker will have to keep an ear open at all times, even when dozing, in which case payment of the minimum wage may be deserved. It should be noted, however, that this provision only applies in the absence of a clear contractual term specifying the hours of work. The confusion that this provision generates could be resolved easily by imposing a legal requirement on employers to state explicitly in contracts of employment the remunerated hours of work and prohibiting the option of a token sum for being 'on call'.

Time spent on rest-breaks also does not count towards working hours.[77] Bob Simpson has described this as 'an astonishing provision which is arguably inconsistent with the health and safety underpinning of the Working Time Regulations',[78] under which there is a statutory entitlement to twenty-minute rest-breaks for health and safety reasons.[79]

---

[75] NMWR 2015, reg. 32. Similar provisions apply to salaried work: NMWR 2015, reg. 27.

[76] E.g. *South Manchester Abbeyfield Society Ltd* v. *Hopkins* [2011] ICR 254 (EAT); *Royal Mencap Society* v. *Tomlinson-Blake* [2018] EWCA Civ 1641.

[77] NMWR 2015, reg. 35(3).

[78] B. Simpson, 'A Milestone in the Legal Regulation of Pay: The National Minimum Wage Act 1998' (1999) 28 *Industrial Law Journal* 1, at 18.

[79] Working Time Regulations 1998, SI 1998 No. 1833, reg. 12.

Case Study: 'I Cannot Teleport Myself'

Another controversial field of application for the minimum wage concerns travelling time between periods of work. Home-care workers, for instance, spend a large portion of their day travelling between the homes of clients. It is clear that they must be paid for the time spent on visits to each client, but should the minimum wage also be paid for the journeys between clients? Regulation 34 NMWR 2015 states that time work should include 'hours when the worker is travelling for the purpose of carrying out assignments to be carried out at different places between which the worker is obliged to travel, and which are not places occupied by the employer'. Although that provision (as did its predecessor) appears to require payment for travel time between clients, it appears to be widely ignored in practice.

"I have been a care worker for five months. I can make up to 15 visits a day, sometimes seeing the same client several times a day. I am on a zero-hours contract but generally get seven shifts a week, from 6am to 2pm or 2pm to 11pm. I work 56 hours but only get paid for 27 hours. I am only paid for the length of time I am with the client. I don't get travel time. Mileage is covered at 20p per mile but not if there is more than an hour between appointments. I don't understand this as it's not like we cannot teleport ourselves to the next client. I get paid between £7 and £8.40 an hour. If I were paid for the average 56 hours I am out for, I would earn £1,680 every four weeks, instead I am earning £810. My friend and I worked out that we are basically earning about £3 an hour. I enjoy my job and I like face time with my clients. It is not just this company, it's all companies. They don't have the funding to be able to pay us properly.' **Anonymous, 23, from Wakefield.**[80]

With regard to output work, where there are no fixed hours of work, the Regulations provide two options for calculating working hours. Either the hours must be assessed by reference to the hours actually worked or by reference to 'rated output work'.[81] The 'rated output work' is based on an employer's notice of a calculation of the 'average hourly output rate'.[82] The latter option provides the employer with an incentive to make an assessment of the normal output rate, based upon a representative test of how long it takes to produce a piece of work, in order to demonstrate compliance with the NMW. Using this measure of average output per hour, the calculation of working hours is treated as being 120 per cent of the number of hours that a worker producing the pieces actually delivered in the reference period would have taken according to the employer's average hourly output rate.[83] This uplift of the number of hours deemed to have been worked was necessary in order to counter the employers' tendency to overestimate how many pieces could be produced in an hour (or under-estimate how long it took to complete

---

[80] BBC news report, citing a study by the Resolution Foundation: www.bbc.co.uk/news/uk-31258205.
[81] NMWR 2015, reg. 37.   [82] NMWR 2015, regs. 41–2.   [83] NMWR 2015, reg. 43.

a piece), which resulted in many home-workers receiving less than the NMW in practice.

Home-working

Julie's main home-working job was making crackers. This involved lots of paper, card and glue and having to store boxes before collection, which, Julie reports, left the house in a near constant mess. Although the glue and 'snaps' were a health and safety risk, there was no health and safety information or training. Pay was a cash-in-hand piece-rate of £35–40 per cracker 'kit'. Kits contained 1,800 crackers and each took around 40 hours to make, giving a pay rate of under £1 per hour. A system of 'quality controls' also meant a kit could be rejected with no pay: 'If you don't get it perfect you don't get your pay.' There was no sick pay, holiday pay, maternity pay or pension contribution; there were no pay slips or written contract. The work was also insecure and irregular: 'You never knew if you would have work in every week. You could have rush orders. They could turn up and say, "can you do these and we'll pick them up in the morning?", and the following week you'd have no work … You couldn't plan anything.'

Julie says the job put her under significant strain and pressure. Kits had to be made by the time the van came round every week or you did not get paid and Julie constantly had to juggle her other commitments in order to get the work done in time. She says that she often ended up working until 2 or 3 in the morning the night before and conscripting her husband and daughter to help her; she also worked through illness. She told us: 'I am so annoyed they are ripping the homeworkers off. They work harder than in a factory. When you work in a factory you clock off and come home and forget about it. A home-worker can't. You have to carry on.'

Julie was entirely unaware of her employment rights until she saw a piece in a newspaper on the National Minimum Wage (NMW). This prompted her to contact the National Minimum Wage enforcement body and, through it, the National Group on Homeworking (NGH). With NGH's support Julie reported her case and confronted her manager. Under pressure, the employer brought in a 'fair estimate agreement'. However, the 12½ hours per kit stated was so far off a fair estimate that Julie refused to sign. Julie is disappointed that nothing came of her reporting the company to the Minimum Wage Enforcement Unit: 'I put my head on the block for these people and the minimum wage people let me down badly.' However, with the support of NGH she also put forward a tribunal claim and, after a year, was finally given a hearing. The firm settled out of court.[84]

With respect to the residual category of unmeasured work, again there is an option of either counting the total number of hours actually worked, or for the employer and employee to agree in writing a determination of the average

[84] TUC, *Hard Work, Hidden Lives: Full Report of the TUC Commission on Vulnerable Workers*, p. 10, available at www.vulnerableworkers.org.uk/files/CoVE_full_report.pdf.

daily number of hours likely to be worked.[85] In *Walton* v. *Independent Living Organisation Ltd*,[86] a care worker attended in the client's home for three whole days a week. With the care worker's agreement, her employing agency had estimated that the tasks she completed for her client absorbed on average about 6 hours 50 minutes each day. The remainder of the time the client was asleep or not otherwise requiring assistance. The question was whether the working hours should be based on the estimate for three days (about twenty-one hours) or the full twenty-four hours each day (seventy-two hours) when the care worker was required to be available in the home. The first question was whether this was time work or unmeasured work. The Court of Appeal held that the tribunal had been entitled to find that it was not time work, despite the fact that the contract specified that the care worker was required to be on the premises for three whole days each week. For the purpose of assessing the working time for unmeasured work, the agreed estimate of hours applied. The claim for the NMW therefore failed because the total wages divided by twenty-one surpassed the minimum amount.

Calculating Total Remuneration Minus Reductions

Having assessed the correct working hours, it is then necessary to work out the pay received by the worker during the reference period. The amount is the gross pay before any deductions are made.[87] The wages paid are assessed as far as possible by the standard or basic rate of pay, so that, for instance, premium rates of pay that reflect particular duties such as overtime rates will be ignored to the extent that they exceed the basic pay. This gross pay does not include, however, any benefit in kind, such as a car or vouchers, with the exception of accommodation.[88] For free living accommodation attached to the job, the employer is entitled to deduct a maximum of £6.40 per day even if its value is greater. For the purpose of calculating the minimum wage, any lawful deductions under the terms of the contract made by the employer in respect of the conduct of the employee, such as a reduction of pay for lateness or as a disciplinary measure, should be ignored.[89] The Regulations provide other detailed instructions on deductions that should either be counted or ignored including the obscure regulation 10(k) that excludes 'payments paid by the employer to the worker attributable to a particular aspect of the working arrangements or to working or personal circumstances that are not consolidated into the worker's standard pay unless the payments are attributable to the performance of the worker in carrying out the work'. The point of this

---

[85] NMWR 2015, reg. 45.   [86] [2003] ICR 688 (CA).   [87] NMWR 2015, regs. 8–9.
[88] NMWR 2015, regs. 10, 14.
[89] NMWR 2015, reg. 12. E.g. *Revenue and Customs Commissioners* v. *Lorne Stewart plc* [2015] ICR 708 (EAT) (repayment of an agreed part of cost of training by a deduction from wages).

provision appears to be to exclude special payments or allowances that are not regarded by the parties as simply part of the wage for the job.

Deductions from the gross pay are also permitted with respect to periods when the worker was absent from work but nevertheless received payments such as sick pay or holiday pay. Those times of absence are equally excluded from the calculation of total working time within a reference period. As Bob Simpson comments on this provision:

> It reflects an important general principle underlying the NMW legislation. This is that the law seeks to guarantee a minimum level of pay for workers only in respect of times when they are working ... For those workers who qualify, statutory sick pay provides a minimum guarantee of income during sickness – at well below the NMW rate in most cases. While Regulation 13 of the Working Time Regulations provides an entitlement to [four] weeks paid holiday ... the failure to provide any link between this and the NMW has resulted in an apparent lacuna in the government's social policy. While it can be readily appreciated that the NMW legislation is primarily concerned with the reward workers receive for work actually done, it is generally accepted that paid holiday is earned over the working year. To the extent that this is so, a provision that holiday pay for the period of the statutory minimum entitlement should be at least equivalent to the worker's NMW entitlement for normal working would appear to be both appropriate and desirable.[90]

The handling of tips paid by customers for services such as meals in restaurants presents a conundrum for the NMW. In the past, waiters relied exclusively on tips for their income.[91] The law now requires employers to pay their workers at least the relevant minimum wage. Hospitality workers would no doubt like to receive the minimum wage from the employer plus their share of any tips given by customers. Employers in these establishments, in contrast, would prefer to use the tips as a source of funds to pay the wage bill, although it is plainly in their interest as well to provide some incentive for staff to provide good service by giving them a share in the bonuses represented by tips. The practice of restaurants imposing 'service charges', so that tips become part of the bill, appears to be motivated primarily by tax avoidance, but it also enables employers to use those charges to pay the minimum wage. Unlike cash tips,[92] credit-card payments by customers entail that any tips included in the payment are credited to the employer's account. It follows that any redistribution of those tips to the workers is apparently a payment by the employer out of its own funds, not those of the workers,[93] and therefore could be set off

[90] B. Simpson, 'A Milestone in the Legal Regulation of Pay: The National Minimum Wage Act 1998' (1999) 28 *Industrial Law Journal* 1, at 14–15.

[91] E. Albin, 'A Worker–Employer–Customer Triangle: The Case of Tips' (2011) 40 *Industrial Law Journal* 181, at 190–6.

[92] *Wrottesley* v. *Regent Street Florida Restaurant* [1951] 1 All ER 566 (KB).

[93] *Nerva* v. *RL&G Ltd* [1996] IRLR 461 (CA); *Nerva* v. *United Kingdom* (2003) 36 EHRR 4 (ECtHR).

against the amount due under the living wage. To prevent that result and to try ensure that waiters and waitresses receive both the minimum wage and their share of tips, regulation 10(m) now excludes from the calculation of wages paid 'payments paid by the employer to the worker representing amounts paid by customers by way of service charge, tip, gratuity or cover charge'. The law does not address the risk that the employer will decide to keep all or most of the tips paid by credit card for itself and simply pay the workers the minimum wage, although the government has promised fresh legislation to prevent that practice. [94] Nor does the law prevent employers from instructing their staff, on threat of dismissal for disobedience, not to enable customers to override the gratuity option on the card machine and pay a cash tip instead, or indeed not to tell customers that the staff do not receive all or most of the tips paid by card.

Enforcement of the National Minimum Wage

The NMW may be enforced both individually and administratively. NMWA 1998, section 17, provides workers with a contractual right to any shortfall between their wages and the NMW. This right may be enforced in an ET either by way of a contractual claim or by way of a claim under ERA 1996, section 13, in respect of an unauthorised deduction from wages. The NMWA 1998, section 18, permits such claims for deductions even by those (such as 'workers' but not 'employees') who are not generally entitled to protection under ERA 1996, section 13. In either case, NMWA 1998, section 28, imposes on the employer the burden of proving that the worker does not qualify for the NMW or that the appropriate NMW rate was paid. The NMWA 1998 also provides protection against victimisation of employees who bring such a claim or provoke administrative enforcement.[95]

If the worker succeeds in a claim because the employer is unable to demonstrate compliance with the minimum wage, the worker is entitled to arrears of pay.[96] These arrears are calculated by reference to the level of the NMW at the time that the tribunal determines the case, not at the time when the payments should have been made.[97] Although contracting out of the statute is not permitted, a dispute can be settled by a written settlement agreement after the worker has received independent advice.[98]

Turning to the administrative enforcement of the NMW, HMRC officers are empowered to inspect, examine and copy employers' records and to

---

[94] HM Government, *Good Work Plan* (December 2018), p. 20.
[95] NMWA 1998, ss. 23–4 (detriment); ERA 1996, s. 104A (unfair dismissal, confined to employees).
[96] NMWA 1998, s. 17(1).   [97] NMWA 1998, s. 17(4).   [98] NMWA 1998, s. 49.

compel evidence from individuals.[99] The NMWA 1998 requires employers to keep records that are sufficient to demonstrate compliance (or otherwise) with the NMW.[100] If compliance officers find a failure to comply with the NMW for one or more workers, they may serve an enforcement notice requiring the employer thereafter to comply with the NMW and to make retrospective payments of arrears.[101] The notice of underpayment must also contain a requirement for an employer to pay a financial penalty (on top of payment of arrears), which comprises twice the total amount of the arrears, subject to a maximum of £20,000.[102] The employer can reduce the amount of the penalty by paying arrears and half of the penalty within fourteen days. Such notices may be appealed to an employment tribunal within four weeks of service, the tribunal having powers of amendment or rescission. In addition, compliance officers are given the power to complain, on behalf of any workers in respect of whom an enforcement notice is not complied with, of an unlawful deduction from wages under the ERA 1996, or to commence proceedings for breach of contract.[103]

In addition to that administrative inspection and enforcement scheme, an employer who refuses or wilfully neglects to pay the minimum wage or who fails to keep adequate records or who falsifies records may be charged with a criminal offence.[104] An employer may be prosecuted before a magistrates' court, and, if found guilty, will be subject to a fine.

Finally, the government seeks to enhance compliance by placing the reputation of firms at risk. It publishes a list of employers who have been found not to have paid the NMW, whether deliberately or as a result of accident. Retail (including major chain stores), hospitality and hairdressers appear to be the most prolific offenders. Larger employers do not always seem to appreciate that such matters as compulsory staff meetings, video screenings, health and safety tests, security checks and other periods when staff are not actually working at their jobs will nevertheless count as working time for the purpose of the NMW. The naming and shaming list of 233 employers published in August 2017 starts at the largest amount with the retailer Argos, which owed £1,461,881.78 to 12,176 workers, down to Mr Dilwar Singh trading as Golden Fry, County Durham, who failed to pay £101.35 to one worker. In the previous year's naming and shaming list, John Lewis plc had failed to appreciate that its sophisticated system for averaging monthly pay according to annual hours would in some instances come into conflict with the rigid pay reference period of one month. The error cost the chairman his bonus, although his remuneration was still about a hundred times the NMW per hour.

---

[99] NMWA 1998, s. 14.   [100] NMWA 1998, s. 9.   [101] NMWA 1998, s. 19.
[102] NMWA 1998, s. 19A.   [103] NMWA 1998, s. 19D.   [104] NMWA 1998, s. 31.

John Lewis Profits Suffer £36m Dent from Minimum Wage Error

The retailer . . . said it was working with HMRC to examine its practice of pay averaging, which aims to smooth out monthly pay over the year. The error affects all staff paid by the hour over the past six years . . . The John Lewis chairman, Charlie Mayfield, said arrangements had already been made to contact those affected and make payments . . . John Lewis said employees received the correct pay over the year, but in months where those on hourly rates worked more than average pay fell below the national minimum rate required by law because of the pay averaging system . . . John Lewis has to compensate employees for any breach, even on such a technical basis, and so has now revised down its 2016–17 pre-tax profits before partner bonus to £541m, from £577m.

'This arrangement was implemented to support [staff] with a steady and reliable monthly income, but we now believe this arrangement may not meet the strict timing requirements for calculating compliance with the national minimum wage regulations,' John Lewis said.

The pay error comes less than four years after John Lewis was forced to pay employees an extra £40m when it realised it had been miscalculating holiday pay for seven years . . .

The annual report also reveals that Mayfield has waived his annual bonus following a tough year for the company. The chairman's total pay fell 7.4% last year to £1.41m according to the report. His basic salary rose nearly 5% to £1.13m but Mayfield requested not to receive his annual bonus, which amounted to £105,000 the year before, and also took a reduced pension supplement.[105]

From this outline description of the enforcement mechanisms for the NMW, it is evident that the legislation deploys all available enforcement techniques, from private claims brought by individual workers to collective claims managed by compliance officers to the possibility of criminal conviction. The government has committed £25.3 million for minimum wage enforcement in 2017 to 2018, as well as a £1.7 million awareness campaign. Furthermore, the Immigration Act 2016 provided for the appointment of a Director of Labour Market Enforcement to bring together a coherent assessment of the extent of labour-market exploitation, identifying routes to tackle exploitation and harnessing the strength of the three main enforcement bodies, including the enforcement of the NMW by the HMRC. No other labour law in the UK has such a complete ordnance of enforcement measures. But does it work? Is there full compliance with the law? As ever, resources may prove to be the Achilles' heel of the enforcement mechanisms. As the top rate or National Living Wage moves upwards to encompass about three million workers or 10 per cent of the workforce, it will place severe strains on the official system of compliance. Will the

---

[105] Extract from the *Guardian*, 9 May 2017.

compliance officers have the resources to visit on a regular basis all the hairdressers and the chip shops in town, let alone the agricultural workers in far-flung villages?

Impact of the National Minimum Wage

There is little doubt that in general the NMW has been successful in its aim of increasing the wages of the lowest paid without reducing levels of employment in the economy as a whole. When the NMW was first introduced it gave about 1 million workers an average pay rise of 10–15 per cent, which has reversed some aspects of the trend towards greater wage inequality and has also narrowed the pay gap in average hourly wages between men and women from about 17.4 per cent to about 13 per cent.[106] But have these benefits for the low paid been obtained at the price of higher levels of unemployment? In view of the constant upward trend of aggregate employment and the constant proportion of employment accounted for by the low-paying sectors such as retail, hospitality, cleaning, agriculture, security, textiles, clothing and hairdressing, Metcalf confidently answers no.[107] Metcalf explains the lack of effect on levels of employment and jobs by reference to four factors:

- The employer has much more discretion in setting the wage than orthodox economic theory admits. In particular, where firms were making good profits from paying low wages prior to the minimum wage, now these excess profits are moderated and channelled back to low-paid workers. In such firms, profits rather than jobs took the strain.
- Although the studies I have surveyed show no employment effects, there is some suggestion of modest cuts in hours.
- There is evidence of illegal collusion between some employers and workers so that both gain at the expense of the state. The employer pays below the minimum wage but understates true hours. This permits the worker to get a larger tax credit, the top-up payment designed to 'make work pay'. There is evidence of this in some Bangladeshi restaurants and Indian clothing manufacturers.
- Incomplete compliance with the minimum wage, particularly among the immigrant communities. My own research on the Chinese labour market in London covering restaurants, health shops, food manufacture and distribution and clothing, concluded that not a single worker below the level of chef or shop manager was receiving the minimum wage.

---

[106] D. Metcalf, 'Britain's Minimum Wage: What Impact on Pay and Jobs?' *CentrePiece*, Winter 2006/07, p. 10.

[107] D. Metcalf, 'Why Has the British National Minimum Wage Had Little or No Impact on Employment?' (2008) 50(3) *Journal of Industrial Relations* 489.

The Low Pay Commission confirms the point that employers may have responded to the minimum wage not by reducing the number of jobs, but by other measures designed to reduce wage costs:

> Our own analysis, commissioned research, evidence submitted in our consultation and anecdotal evidence from visits and meetings have found that some employers have responded to the change in earnings (and consequent increase in labour costs) by adjusting non-wage costs and changing pay structures. Overtime and unsocial hours premia may have been reduced; pensions and annual leave entitlement made less generous; pay zones (geographic and hierarchical) merged; or differentials may have been squeezed. Further, there is also evidence to suggest that some firms may have coped with minimum wage increases by reducing hours, raising prices, or by accepting lower profits. However, the evidence available to date suggests that minimum wages do not appear to have cut employment to any significant degree. Further, the reduced hours do not appear to have reduced weekly earnings and the lower profits have not led to business closures.[108]

In general, therefore, the NMW has had the positive effect of reducing low pay that was hoped for, while avoiding significant damage to levels of employment. The big question is now whether the rapidly rising National Living Wage will not have a significant effect on levels of unemployment. Evidence gathered by the Low Pay Commission about small businesses gives worrying signals about rising prices and redundancies.

Case Study: Baker in Essex

In our Spring 2016 Report, the owner of a small family-owned bakery in Essex told us that the NLW was a threat to the viability of his business. The business was made up of three bread and cake shops employing 23 workers, including 18 shop staff (all but one of whom were paid the minimum wage), 2 bakers and a delivery driver. Under pressure from large chains competing locally and with an artisanal product range that is expensive to produce, the firm had generally been under financial pressure.

The owner had predicted a 9.2 per cent rise in labour costs as a combined result of the October 2015 NMW uprating and the NLW, and an additional 7.2 per cent each year until 2020. Returning to the business following the implementation of the NLW, the owner told us that he was now going to close a bakery and a retail shop from which the firm had traded since 1952. This will mean that 6 of its 23 staff will be made redundant, including one of its two skilled bakers.

The closures will centralise production to one site and reduce the company's overheads, but the anticipated £23,000 cost of the redundancies will damage its position to the extent that

---

[108] Low Pay Commission Report 2011, *National Minimum Wage*, Cm 8023 (April 2011), p. ix.

the rest of the business is in the balance. Commodity prices have risen recently, having been falling in recent years, adding to pressures on the firm.

To mitigate these costs the owner estimates that prices will have to rise by at least 3 per cent or 6 per cent to maintain its profit margin. The owner does not consider this sustainable beyond the short term and anticipates the closure of the business in approximately 4 years.[109]

The remaining concerns about the Act are principally directed at problems of effective enforcement. Although greater resources for the compliance officers might help in this respect, it is clear that some groups of vulnerable workers prefer to collude with employers in receiving low pay in order to avoid other more alarming prospects, including deportation of migrant workers, liability for tax and, of course, retaliatory dismissal. The details of the case-law also reveal the complexity of trying to impose a uniform body of regulations on the wide diversity of jobs carried out. We illustrated this problem primarily by reference to tips in restaurants, but of equal difficulty are those cases of workers in residential 'on-call' jobs, where minor differences in the contractual arrangements can determine whether that time is regarded as working time and whether any payment made in respect of that time is treated as part of wages or an exempted allowance.

Fair Wages

In the nineteenth century, Friedrich Engels was critical of the motto 'A Fair Day's Wages for a Fair Day's Work', on the ground that it appeared to justify and permit the existing situation under which employers set the lowest wages possible to obtain sufficient workers for the needs of their businesses.[110] Engels' proposed alternative of workers seizing control of the means of production did not happen, but instead, for most of the twentieth century, the principal mechanism for ensuring fair pay for the majority of workers was collective bargaining. The benefits of collective bargaining were extended by regulation to other workers by such mechanisms as Wages Councils, although pockets of low-paid workers still remained. In the twenty-first century, however, while reverting to and reinforcing the idea that wages rates should be determined in general by markets and individual bargaining between employer and employee, governments have sought to regulate the labour market in four principal ways. First, regulation requires integrity in the labour market. In accordance with the principle of mutuality, both employers and

[109] Low Pay Commission Report Autumn 2016 (November 2016) Cm 9272, para. 2.63.
[110] F. Engels, *The Labour Standard*, No. 1, 7 May 1881. As an alternative to the pricing of labour according to supply and demand, Engels urged workers to seize ownership of the means of production and set their own wages.

employees can be required to stick to their explicit and implicit undertakings. Moreover, an employer is required to be transparent in all its dealings regarding pay. Second, equal pay laws (to be considered below)[111] attempt to eliminate sex discrimination in pay. Third, regulation prohibits discrimination in pay against part-time workers in comparison to full-time workers.[112] Finally, but perhaps most significant of all in the quest for fair wages, for the first time in the UK there is a plan to implement a National Living Wage, which can be understood as a level of pay that is sufficient for a person working forty hours a week, with no additional income or in-work social security benefits, to afford a decent quality of life, including food, shelter, utilities, transport, health care and some recreational activities. As we have seen, even in the context of a healthy growing economy, the implementation and enforcement of a genuine National Living Wage is extremely ambitious and fraught with difficulty and risks including raising levels of unemployment. This regulatory scheme, although perhaps not achieving fair wages for all and probably not providing sufficient income for a living wage for all families, is beginning to construct a legal framework that may ensure that everyone will receive at least enough to pay for a dignified life.

---

[111] Chapter 9.
[112] Chapter 10. Discrimination is also forbidden with respect to agency workers: see Chapter 6, p. 239.

8

Working Time

Contents

Introduction

Until the Working Time Regulations 1998,[1] there was no general framework
of legislation in the UK dealing with working time. But this does not mean that
there is no tradition of statutory regulation. For many years, we had legislation
setting limits on the hours of work for those engaged in certain occupations,
such as coal-mining and road transport.[2] We also had legislation regulating
the working time of women and young people in factories,[3] with the (now
repealed) Factories Act 1961 making fairly detailed provision for a maximum
nine-hour day, a maximum forty-eight-hour week, and rest-breaks of at least
half an hour after a maximum of four-and-a-half hours work.[4] And we further
had legislation authorising Trade Boards (subsequently renamed as Wages
Councils) to regulate working time in the different industries in which they
were established. Otherwise, working time would be governed by collective
agreements negotiated between employers and trade unions, with collective
agreements having very high levels of coverage in the period between 1946 and
1979 in particular.

The Working Time Directive 93/104 (WTD) and the Working Time Regulations 1998 (WTR) are, however, now the focus of attention. But before
examining aspects of these instruments, we should not overlook that the law
of working time contains many other dimensions discussed in other chapters of
this book. Thus, by virtue of the 'statement of written particulars' issued under
ERA 1996,[5] employees have a right to be informed about the hours they are

---

[1] SI 1998 No. 1833, implementing Council Directive 93/104/EC of 23 November 1993 concerning
certain aspects of the organisation of working time. The Directive has since been repealed and
replaced with Directive 2003/88/EC of the European Parliament and of the Council of
4 November 2003 concerning certain aspects of the organisation of working time. The Working
Time Regulations 1998 have been amended as a result. The Regulations also take in some of the
provisions of Council Directive 94/33/EC of 22 June 1994 on the protection of young people
at work.

[2] See K. D. Ewing, 'The State and Industrial Relations: Collective Laissez-Faire Revisited' (1998) 5
Historical Studies in Industrial Relations 1. On the campaign for working time regulation in coal-
mining (an industry which employed about 1 million workers at the time) culminating in the
Coal Mines Act 1908, see R. Page Arnot, *The Miners: A History of the Miners' Federation of
Great Britain 1889–1910* (London: Lawrence and Wishart, 1949), a superb account.

[3] One of the best accounts of the emergence of this legislation is still F. Engels, *The Condition of
the Working Class in England* (Moscow: Progress Publishers, 1844), pp. 207–10, tracing the
origins of the Factory Act 1833, forbidding the employment of children under nine years of age.
It also limited the working hours of children aged between nine and thirteen to forty-eight hours
per week (with a nine-hour daily maximum), and the working hours of young persons from
fourteen to eighteen years to sixty-nine hours per week (with a twelve-hour daily maximum).
Provision was made for meals and breaks and night work banned for those under eighteen (*ibid.*,
p. 209). The Act was important also for providing for the appointment of inspectors to enforce
the law. Another good source is J. Rae, *Eight Hours for Work* (London: Macmillan, 1894).

[4] Factories Act 1961, s. 86. See also s. 94 (bank holidays).

[5] ERA 1996, s. 1(4)(c) and (d). See pp. 115–20.

required to work under their contract. Secondly, employees will have rights relating to working time under the terms of their contract (relating to hours, overtime, shifts and holidays), which admittedly may be difficult to enforce, but which nevertheless may have implications for the law relating to redundancy and unfair dismissal.[6] And thirdly, employees may have statutory rights affecting working time other than those provided in the WTD and the WTR. These include rights under the Posted Workers Directive,[7] as well as rights to maternity, paternity and parental leave; time-off for trade union activities and trade union duties, and time-off for union learning representatives.[8] These various provisions relating to working time should be kept in mind in order to capture a full picture of working time regulation. Indeed, the WTR do not stand isolated from these other provisions, with the WTD jurisprudence being relevant in other areas of the law.[9]

Quite apart from thus being a jigsaw puzzle with many pieces, the area of working time regulation generally is especially interesting as a crossroads on which many of the important themes and concerns of contemporary labour law now converge. This is an area with detailed coverage by international labour conventions, the latter having a growing influence on the jurisprudence of the ECJ/CJEU, by which working time regulation is seen in terms of a fundamental social right. This is also an area where there has been a dynamic interplay between EU social law and UK domestic law, as fundamental social rights come into conflict with freedom of contract, revealing very different approaches to worker protection by the ECJ/CJEU and the domestic legislature and domestic courts.[10] The Directive was introduced against the wishes of the UK government (which was deftly outmanoeuvred politically), and the standard of domestic law has gradually had to rise as a result of the intervention of the ECJ/CJEU. Looking forward, uncertainty is created by Brexit, once the legal demands of EU membership have disappeared. But quite apart from the links between international law and EU law on the one hand and between EU law and domestic law on the other, the Directive is important also for the potential links that it created between individual and collective labour law.[11] It is a remarkable legal instrument.

---

[6] See, for example, *Gascol Conversions Ltd* v. *Mercer* [1974] ICR 420 and *Lesney Products & Co.* v. *Nolan* [1977] ICR 235.

[7] See Case C-396/13, *Sähköalojen ammattiliitto ry* v. *Elektrobudowa Spółka Akcyjna*, 12 February 2015.

[8] See, respectively, Chapters 10 and 14.

[9] See Case C-396/13, *Sähköalojen ammattiliitto ry* v. *Elektrobudowa Spółka Akcyjna*, 12 February 2015.

[10] For vivid examples of different styles, compare Case C-214/16, *King* v. *Sash Window Workshop Ltd*, 29 November 2017, with *Grange* v. *Abellio London Ltd* [2017] IRLR 108, and the latter with *Thera East* v. *Valentine* [2017] IRLR 878.

[11] A point first identified by B. Bercusson, *Working Time in Britain: Towards a European Model, Parts I and II* (London: Institute of Employment Rights, 1993).

International Standards

The establishment of an eight-hour day has long been a demand of the international labour movement.[12] Indeed, it was the subject of the very first ILO convention (Hours of Work Convention, 1919),[13] which was initially supported by the UK, but which the UK ultimately refused to ratify.[14] Thirty-four of the 189 ILO conventions now deal directly with hours at work, holidays or night work,[15] while several others – such as ILO Convention 189 (Domestic Workers Convention, 2011) – deal with one or more of these matters as a part of their general treatment of the working conditions of the workers addressed by the convention in question. It is also the case that many of the thirty-four conventions deal with groups of workers who are excluded from the Directive, such as seafarers.[16] These conventions are unusually important in the context of EU law relating to working time, not only because ILO Convention 89 (Night Work Convention (Revised), 1948) was in direct conflict with EU equality law, but also because recital 6 in the preamble to the WTD now provides expressly that 'account should be taken of the principles of the International Labour Organization with regard to the organisation of working time, including those relating to night work'. These ILO principles are expressed in the ILO conventions and recommendations that deal with hours of work and holidays, and it is interesting to reflect that, while account should be taken of these instruments, none of these instruments has been ratified by all EU Member States.[17]

ILO Conventions on Working Time

The main ILO Conventions on working time are as follows:

- ILO Convention 1 (Hours of Work (Industry) Convention, 1919)
- ILO Convention 30 (Hours of Work (Commerce and Offices) Convention, 1930)

---

[12] Indeed, May Day as the Festival of Labour has its origins in the international demonstrations for the eight-hour day held on 1 May 1890. See H. Pelling, *A History of British Trade Unionism* (3rd edn, Harmondsworth: Penguin, 1976), p. 119.

[13] 'The regulation of the hours of work including the establishment of a maximum working day and week' is also one of the objectives of the ILO set out in the preamble to the ILO Constitution. See also ILO, Declaration of Philadelphia, 1944 Part III(d).

[14] See K. D. Ewing, *Britain and the ILO* (2nd edn, London: Institute of Employment Rights, 1994), p. 16.

[15] Although not all are now in force, some having been revised. The core working time conventions are set out in the box on p. 293.

[16] It is also to be noted that ILO Convention 189 (Domestic Workers Convention, 2011) deals with working time, although such workers are excluded from the Directive and the Regulations.

[17] Indeed, the seminal ILO Convention 1 has been ratified by only fourteen of the twenty-eight (and is in force in only eleven) Member States, with those not having ratified including Germany, Netherlands, Poland and Sweden, as well as the UK.

- ILO Convention 14 (Weekly Rest (Industry) Convention, 1921)
- ILO Convention 106 (Weekly Rest (Commerce and Offices) Convention, 1957)
- ILO Convention 132 (Holidays with Pay Convention (Revised), 1970)
- ILO Convention 171 (Night Work Convention, 1990).

The UK has not ratified any of the above. It did ratify ILO Convention 4 (Night Work (Women) Convention, 1919). This convention was replaced by ILO Convention 41 (Night Work (Women) Convention (Revised), 1934), ratified by the UK but then denounced in 1947. The UK did not ratify the replacement ILO Convention 89 (Night Work (Women) Convention (Revised), 1948), which has caused difficulty for some EU Member States.

From Conflict ...

The relationship between the EU and ILO standards on working time is thus complex. The earliest conflict between the two arose in Case C-345/89, *Alfred Stoeckel*,[18] which concerned the prosecution of a French employer for engaging women to work at night in breach of the French Labour Code. Such work was permitted in exceptional circumstances, and in this case night shifts were introduced for economic reasons, following a collective agreement with a trade union and the subsequent agreement of a majority of the women voting in a ballot. In holding that the provisions of the Labour Code prohibiting night work by women were in breach of the Equal Treatment Directive,[19] the ECJ held that Article 5 of the latter was 'sufficiently precise' to impose on the Member States the obligation not to prohibit night work by women in circumstances where night work by men is not also prohibited. This is despite the fact that France had ratified the ILO Convention 89 (Night Work (Women) Convention (Revised), 1948), which provides by Article 3 that:

> Women without distinction of age shall not be employed during the night in any public or private industrial undertaking, or in any branch thereof, other than an undertaking in which only members of the same family are employed.

As a result of this decision, France denounced ILO Convention 89 on 26 February 1992, and fourteen other Member States have also denounced it.[20] (In some cases, however, it was denounced in the early 1980s, perhaps in anticipation of problems under the Equal Treatment Directive, which had been due for implementation by late 1978.) ILO Convention 89 was never ratified by the United Kingdom, though its predecessor, ILO Convention 41 (Night Work (Women) Convention (Revised), 1934), had been until it was

---

[18] [1991] ECR I-4047.
[19] Council Directive 76/207/EEC of 9 February 1976 on the implementation of the principle of equal treatment for men and women as regards access to employment, vocational training and promotion and working conditions.
[20] ILO Convention 89 is ratified by only one EU Member State (Romania).

replaced in 1948 by ILO Convention 89. Returning to the *Stoeckel* decision, although France denounced ILO Convention 89 in 1992, it failed to introduce any legislation to amend the Labour Code, leading to enforcement proceedings being initiated by the Commission against the French government. In Case C-197/96, *Commission* v. *France*, France argued that because of the denunciation of ILO Convention 89 and the direct effect of the Directive, it was not necessary to amend the Labour Code and that France was no longer in breach of the Directive. According to the ECJ, however, in the interests of legal certainty, it was necessary to change the law. Given the association of night work with various illnesses (including breast cancer and type 2 diabetes), not everyone will be convinced that the removal of health and safety restrictions is the most propitious use of equality law.

... to Co-operation

By virtue of recital 6 of the WTD's preamble, the relationship between EU law and the ILO conventions is now very different. The latter appears to impose a duty on the part of the legislature to take ILO conventions into account when implementing EU instruments, the role of the ECJ being to ensure that this obligation is complied with fully.[21] It is, however, a formidable commitment, given that – as already explained – there are at present thirty-four conventions dealing directly with working time, along with several others that also address the question incidentally. Nevertheless, in Joined Cases C-350/06 and C-520/06, *Schultz-Hoff* v. *Deutsche Rentenversicherung;* and *Stringer* v. *HM Revenue and Customs,*[22] the ECJ referred to ILO Convention 132, Article 5(4), which provides that 'absence from work for such reasons beyond the control of the employed person concerned as illness, injury or maternity shall be counted as part of the period of service'.[23] Notably, ILO Convention 132 has been ratified by only fifteen of the twenty-eight Member States, and not by the UK. Nevertheless, it also played a crucial role in Case C-214/10, *KHS AG* v. *Schulte,*[24] in determining for how long after the year in which it was due to be taken a worker can carry over his or her annual leave in the event of illness.

In *Schulte,* the worker in question had his employment terminated on 31 August 2008, after having been in receipt of an invalidity pension since 2003. Having brought legal proceedings to recover allowances in lieu of paid annual leave for 2006, 2007 and 2008, he was confronted by a provision in a

---

[21] Case C-214/10, *KHS AG* v. *Schulte* [2012] IRLR 156.   [22] [2009] ECR I-179.

[23] See also the detailed consideration of ILO Convention 132 in the Opinion of Advocate General Trstenak, in Joined Cases C-350/06 and C-520/06, *Schultz-Hoff* v. *Deutsche Rentenversicherung Bund; Stringer* v. *HM Revenue and Customs,* 24 January 2008.

[24] [2012] IRLR 156 (CJEU). See also Case C-214/16, *King* v. *The Sash Window Workshop Ltd* [2018] IRLR 142. For domestic law, see especially *Plumb* v. *Duncan Print Group Ltd* [2015] IRLR 711. See also *Dudley MBC* v. *Willett* [2017] IRLR 870.

collective agreement that said that, where leave could not be taken due to illness, it could be carried forward into the next year but would lapse after fifteen months. In holding that a carry-over period of fifteen months was consistent with the requirements of the Directive, the Court of First Instance said that there comes a point when the carried-over leave 'ceases to have its positive effect for the worker as a rest period and is merely a period of relaxation and leisure'.[25] In the view of the Court, 'a worker who is unfit for work for several consecutive years and who is prevented by national law from taking his paid annual leave during that period cannot have the right to accumulate, without any limit, entitlements to paid annual leave acquired during that period'.[26] In reaching this conclusion, the Court took fully into account the provisions of ILO Convention 132, Article 9(1), which provides that:

> The uninterrupted part of the annual holiday with pay referred to in Article 8, paragraph 2, of this Convention shall be granted and taken no later than one year, and the remainder of the annual holiday with pay no later than eighteen months, from the end of the year in respect of which the holiday entitlement has arisen.[27]

Perhaps inevitably, ILO principles were thus used in *Schulte* ironically to justify a restriction rather than an expansion of the scope of the Directive. But that is not likely always to be the case.

European Social Charter of 1961

In addition to the ILO conventions, provision relating to working time is to be found in the European Social Charter of 1961. Under the rubric, 'the right to just conditions of work' (there is separate provision made for health and safety at work), Article 2 provides that:

> With a view to ensuring the effective exercise of the right to just conditions of work, the Contracting Parties undertake:
> (1) to provide for reasonable daily and weekly working hours, the working week to be progressively reduced to the extent that the increase of productivity and other relevant factors permit;
> (2) to provide for public holidays with pay;
> (3) to provide for a minimum of two weeks annual holiday with pay;

---

[25] Case C-214/10, *KHS AG* v. *Schulte*, above, para. 33.   [26] *Ibid.*, para. 34.

[27] The reference to the 'uninterrupted part of the annual holiday with pay' is a reference to the provisions of Art. 8(2) that, '[u]nless otherwise provided in an agreement applicable to the employer and the employed person concerned, and on condition that the length of service of the person concerned entitles him to such a period, one of the parts shall consist of at least two uninterrupted working weeks'. This is an issue that arises also in relation to the conditions under which annual leave may be taken. See pp. 311–13.

(4) to provide for additional paid holidays or reduced working hours for workers engaged in dangerous or unhealthy occupations as prescribed;

(5) to ensure a weekly rest period which shall, as far as possible, coincide with the day recognised by tradition or custom in the country or region concerned as a day of rest.

The UK has accepted Article 2(2)–(5), but not Article 2(1).

According to the most recent report on Article 2 by the Social Rights Committee which supervises compliance with the Charter, the UK is in breach of all four accepted obligations. This is despite the WTD and the WTR. It was found that the UK was in breach of:

- Article 2(2) because 'the right of all workers to public holidays with pay is not guaranteed': 'there is no specific entitlement to take leave on bank and public holidays in the United Kingdom';
- Article 2(4) because it had not been established that adequate provision was made to reduce working hours or provide additional holidays for workers exposed to occupational health risks; and
- Article 2(5) because there are inadequate safeguards to prevent workers working for more than twelve consecutive days without a rest period. It was also noted that in 2012 some 17.2 per cent of all persons in employment and in 2009 some 16 per cent of all persons in employment worked regularly on a Sunday.[28]

But it was also found that the UK was no longer in breach of Article 2(3) as a result of the decisions in *NHS Leeds* v. *Larner*,[29] and *Sood Enterprises Ltd* v. *Healy*,[30] under the Working Time Regulations. These decisions, which are considered more fully below, were construed to mean that 'if a worker is unable to take any of their four-week annual leave entitlement due to sickness, he can choose to take it at a later date, including, if necessary, in the next leave year'.[31]

Working Time Directive

The WTD was enacted under procedures of the then EC Treaty, introduced by the Single European Act of 1986. This amended the then EC Treaty by inserting a new Article 118a, enabling social policy issues to be introduced by qualified majority voting in limited circumstances:

Member States shall pay particular attention to encouraging improvements, especially in the working environment, as regards the health and safety of

---

[28] European Committee of Social Rights, Conclusions XX-3 (2014) (United Kingdom).
[29] [2012] EWCA Civ 1034, [2012] ICR 1389. See pp. 177–8.
[30] [2013] ICR 1361. See pp. 299, 319.
[31] European Committee of Social Rights, Conclusions XX-3 (2014) (United Kingdom).

workers, and shall set as their objective the harmonization of conditions in this area, while maintaining the improvements made.

A commitment to regulate working time was expressed in the Community Charter of the Fundamental Social Rights of Workers of 1989. Under the rubric of improvement of living and working conditions, Article 8 provides that:

> Every worker of the European Community shall have a right to a weekly rest period and to annual paid leave, the duration of which must be harmonised in accordance with national practices while the improvement is being maintained.

The Action Programme accompanying the 1989 Charter clearly indicated an intention to legislate at the Community level for working time,[32] and relying on powers under Article 118a to this end the WTD was approved in 1993, with a major revision in 2003.[33] Although not referred to in the latter, the other major development in the trajectory of EU law on working time is the EU Charter of Fundamental Rights of 2000, which under the rubric 'fair and just working conditions' provides by Article 31(2) that 'Every worker has the right to limitation of maximum working hours, to daily and weekly rest periods and to an annual period of paid leave.'[34] Two major questions of EU law have arisen in relation to the Directive: first, was it a lawful exercise of power by the Community institutions? And, secondly, does it have direct effect so that it can be enforced in domestic courts against public authorities?

Challenging the Legality of the Directive

The UK government opposed the WTD, and brought proceedings in the ECJ contending that it was an improper exercise of Article 118a,[35] the challenge advancing on four fronts: that the legal base of the Directive was defective, that there was a breach of the principle of proportionality, that it was a misuse of power, and that there had been an infringement of essential procedural requirements. All four arguments were rejected (although the Court did

---

[32] European Commission, Communication from the Commission concerning its Action Programme relating to the implementation of the Community Charter of Basic Social Rights for Workers, COM (89) 568, p. 16.

[33] Respectively, Council Directive 93/104/EC concerning certain aspects of the organisation of working time, and Directive 2003/88/EC of the European Parliament and of the Council of 4 November 2003 concerning certain aspects of the organisation of working time.

[34] The Charter is now frequently cited in jurisprudence. See especially Case C-282/10, *Dominguez* v. *Centre informatique du Centre Ouest Atlantique* [2015] IRLR 321, and see *R(URTU)* v. *Secretary of State for Transport* [2013] EWCA Civ 962. Also important in working time cases is Article 47 which deals with the right to an effective remedy, on which see Case C-214/16, *King* v. *The Sash Window Workshop Ltd*, above. For a valuable account of Article 31 in particular, see A. Bogg, 'Article 31: Fair and Just Working Conditions', in S. Peers *et al.*, *The EU Charter of Fundamental Rights: A Commentary* (Oxford: Hart, 2014).

[35] Case C-84/94, *United Kingdom* v. *Council* [1996] ECR I-5755.

uphold the challenge to a provision in the Directive as introduced that the minimum rest period should in principle include Sunday).[36] The government argued that the Directive was 'in reality a measure concerned with the overall improvement of the living and working conditions of employees and with their general protection, and is so broad in its scope and coverage as to be capable of classification as a social policy measure, for the adoption of which other legal bases exist'.[37] These other bases at the time would, however, require unanimity before they could be used, thereby permitting the UK government effectively to exercise a veto on working time regulation. Although this would deny the protection of the kind in the Directive to all workers in all Member States, there would be nothing to stop those governments supporting such measures to do so by using powers in national law. The UK government appeared to feel that it was being stitched up, by being bound to implement working time obligations under the cover of treaty powers to regulate health and safety by qualified majority voting.[38]

In a bullish decision taking a wide approach to 'health and safety', the ECJ dismissed the challenge, in what was the first of several working time defeats for the UK before that court. In the view of the ECJ, 'it does not follow from the fact that the directive falls within the scope of Community social policy that it cannot properly be based on Article 118a, so long as it contributes to encouraging improvements as regards the health and safety of workers'.[39] Moreover, while it could not 'be excluded that the directive may affect employment', according to the Court that was 'clearly not its essential object-ive',[40] the evidence for this to be found in the preamble to the Directive, suggesting that superficially felicitous drafting may be enough to head off potential legal challenges to other instruments. Nor was the Court convinced by the argument that:

> no adequate scientific evidence exists to justify the imposition of a general requirement to provide for breaks where the working day is longer than six hours (Article 4), a general requirement to provide for a minimum uninter-rupted weekly rest period of twenty-four hours in addition to the usual eleven hours' daily rest (Article 5, first sentence), a requirement that the minimum rest period must, in principle, include Sunday (Article 5, second sentence), a general requirement to ensure that the average working time for each seven-day period, including overtime, does not exceed forty-eight hours (Article 6(2)), and a general requirement that every worker is to have a minimum of four weeks' paid annual leave (Article 7).[41]

So far as the Court was concerned, 'legislative action by the Community, particularly in the field of social policy, cannot be limited exclusively to

---

[36] *Ibid.*, para. 37.   [37] *Ibid.*, para. 26.   [38] See now TFEU, Art. 153(1)(a).
[39] Case C-84/94, *United Kingdom* v. *Council* [1996] ECR I-5755, para. 27.   [40] *Ibid.*, para. 30.
[41] *Ibid.*, para. 32.

circumstances where the justification for such action is scientifically demonstrated'.[42]

Extending the Reach of the Directive

Having established the WTD's legal base, the ECJ has since been called on to consider its legal effects. The question of direct effect arose in Case C-397/01, *Pfeiffer* v. *Deutsches Rotes Kreuz*,[43] which raised a number of important legal questions about the construction of the Directive, to which we return below. The case was concerned with the provisions of what was then Article 6(2) of the Directive (the maximum forty-eight-hour week), which according to the CJEU is 'a rule of Community social law of particular importance from which every worker must benefit since it is a minimum requirement necessary to ensure protection of his safety and health'.[44] It was held that German domestic law was not compatible with the Directive and that what was then Article 6(2) satisfied the settled criteria for the direct effect of EU law, namely, that it was 'unconditional and sufficiently precise' to enable an individual to rely on it in legal proceedings against public authorities in the national courts of the state in question. Article 6(2) was said to meet this requirement because it:

> imposes on Member States in unequivocal terms a precise obligation as to the result to be achieved, which is not coupled with any condition regarding application of the rule laid down by it, which provides for a 48-hour maximum, including overtime, as regards average weekly working time.[45]

This position was adopted despite the fact that the Directive gives Member States 'a degree of latitude' in the implementation of Article 6.[46] This latitude relates to both the 'reference period to be fixed for the purposes of applying Article 6',[47] and (perhaps more importantly) the right not to apply Article 6 at all by means of an opt-out.

It has since been held that Article 7 (paid annual leave) also has vertical direct effect, though this seems to be more obvious and straightforward. In Case C-282/10, *Dominguez* v. *Centre informatique du Centre Ouest Atlantique*,[48] the issue was again whether the applicant was entitled to carry over annual leave from one leave year to another, and the conditions that could be

---

[42] *Ibid.*, para. 39. It is to be noted, however, that the reason why the challenge to Sunday as the rest day succeeded was because the Council had 'failed to explain why Sunday, as a weekly rest day, is more closely connected with the health and safety of workers than any other day of the week' (*ibid.*, para. 37).

[43] Case C-397/01, *Pfeiffer* v. *Deutsches Rotes Kreuz* [2004] ECR I-08835.   [44] *Ibid.*, para. 100.

[45] *Ibid.*, para. 104.   [46] *Ibid.*, para. 105.   [47] *Ibid.*

[48] [2012] IRLR 321. See also *NHS Leeds* v. *Larner* [2012] EWCA Civ 1034, [2012] ICR 1389, *Sood Enterprises Ltd* v. *Healy* [2013] ICR 1361, and *Dudley MBC* v. *Willett* [2017] IRLR 870. Compare *Gibson* v. *East Riding Council* [2000] EWCA Civ 199, [2000] ICR 890 (CA) (an action to recover holiday pay for the period in which the government had failed to implement the Directive).

imposed on the exercise of any such entitlement. In the course of the decision, the Grand Chamber provided a textbook analysis of the role of domestic courts in the implementation of EU law. The first duty of national courts when applying domestic law is that 'they are bound to interpret it, so far as possible, in the light of the wording and the purpose of the directive concerned in order to achieve the result sought by the directive'.[49] To this end, the national court must take 'the whole body of domestic law into consideration' and apply 'the interpretative methods recognised by domestic law with a view to ensuring that Directive 2003/88 is fully effective'.[50] If this is not possible, it is then necessary to consider whether Article 7 had direct effect and if so whether the respondent was a party against which the Article could be enforced. Here the Court was uncompromising in its view that Article 7 'imposes on Member States, in unequivocal terms, a precise obligation as to the result to be achieved that is not coupled with any condition regarding application of the rule laid down by it, which gives every worker entitlement to at least four weeks' paid annual leave'.[51] Even though Member States had a 'degree of latitude when they adopt the conditions for entitlement to, and granting of, the paid annual leave which it provides for, that does not alter the precise and unconditional nature of the obligation'.[52]

Questions of Scope

By Article 1(3), the Directive states that it applies to 'all sectors of activity', both public and private, within the meaning of Directive 89/391 (the framework on safety and health at work).[53] By virtue of Article 2(1), the latter applies to 'all sectors of activity, both public and private (industrial, agricultural, commercial, administrative, service, educational, cultural, leisure, etc.)'. By virtue of Article 2(2), however, Directive 89/391 'shall not be applicable where characteristics peculiar to certain specific public service activities, such as the armed forces or the police, or to certain specific activities in the civil protection services inevitably conflict with it'.[54] The leading case on the scope of the Directive (and by extension the Regulations) is Case C-397/01, *Pfeiffer*

---

[49] Case C-282/10, *Dominguez* v. *Centre informatique du Centre Ouest Atlantique*, above, para. 24.
[50] See also Case C-397/01, *Pfeiffer* v. *Deutsches Rotes Kreuz* [2004] ECR I-08835, para. 118.
[51] Case C-282/10, *Dominguez* v. *Centre informatique du Centre Ouest Atlantique*, above, para. 34.
[52] In the event of domestic law being incapable of interpretation consistently with the Directive and in the absence of direct effect, the 'party injured as a result . . . can none the less rely on the judgment in Joined Cases C-6/90 and C-9/90 *Francovich and Others* [1991] ECR I-5357 in order to obtain, if appropriate, compensation for the loss sustained' (*ibid.*, para. 43).
[53] A point emphasised in Case C-337/10, *Neidel* v. *Stadt Frankfurt am Main* [2012] IRLR 607. There are, however, certain exceptions to the scope of the Directive set out in Arts. 14 and 17–19, and there is also an express exception for seafarers. See pp. 323–36.
[54] Where Art. 2(2) applies, 'the safety and health of workers must be ensured as far as possible in the light of the objectives of this Directive'.

v. *Deutsches Rotes Kreuz*,[55] to which we have just referred. Here, the Court rejected the argument of the German government that the Directive did not apply to ambulance-drivers on the ground that they were covered by the exception for workers engaged in civil protection services. According to the Court, this exception:

> was adopted purely for the purpose of ensuring the proper operation of services essential for the protection of public health, safety and order in cases, such as a catastrophe, the gravity and scale of which are exceptional and a characteristic of which is the fact that, by their nature, they do not lend themselves to planning as regards the working time of teams of emergency workers.[56]

Although the employer in this case dealt with events that were unforeseeable, they were nevertheless capable of being organised in advance.[57]

'Worker'

Apart from questions about the range of application of the Directive, there are two crucial questions of definition. Throughout the Directive (and the Regulations), there is a reference to 'workers'. But we find that there is no definition of a 'worker' in the Directive, as noted by the ECJ in Case C-428/09, *Union Syndicale Solidaires Isère* v. *Premier Ministre*.[58] In some cases, EU social policy Directives leave the scope of application to be determined by the Member States.[59] In this case, however, there is no definition at all, and no reference to the Framework Directive on health and safety which applies also to workers, but defines a worker to mean 'any person employed by an employer, including trainees and apprentices but excluding domestic servants'.[60] In the absence of any definition in the Directive, the ECJ has held that, 'for the purposes of applying Directive 2003/88, [the] concept [of worker] may not be interpreted differently according to the law of Member States but has an autonomous meaning specific to European Union law'.[61] In an important passage, the Court went on to say that a worker 'must be defined in accordance with objective criteria which distinguish the employment relationship by reference to the rights and duties of the persons concerned'.[62] The Court concluded that:

---

[55] [2004] ECR I-08835.   [56] *Ibid.*, para. 55.   [57] *Ibid.*, para. 57.

[58] [2010] ECR I-09961, para. 27.

[59] See, for example, Council Directive 2001/23/EC of 12 March 2001 on the approximation of the laws of the Member States relating to the safeguarding of employees' rights in the event of transfers of undertakings, businesses or parts of undertakings or businesses, Art. 2(1)(d): '"employee" shall mean any person who, in the Member State concerned, is protected as an employee under national employment law.'

[60] Council Directive 89/391/EEC, Art. 3(a).

[61] Case C-428/09, *Union Syndicale Solidaires Isère* v. *Premier Ministre* [2010] ECR I-09961, para. 28.

[62] *Ibid.*, para. 29.

[t]he essential feature of an employment relationship, however, is that for a certain period of time a person performs services for and under the direction of another person in return for which he receives remuneration.[63]

In contrast, the term 'worker' is defined in the Working Time Regulations, to mean 'an individual who has entered into or works under (or, where the employment has ceased, worked under)' either (a) a contract of employment; or (b) any other contract, 'whereby the individual undertakes to do or perform personally any work or services for another party to the contract whose status is not by virtue of the contract that of a client or customer of any profession or business undertaking carried on by the individual'.[64] This would appear to be consistent with the test articulated by the ECJ in Case C-428/09, *Union Syndicale Solidaires Isère* v. *Premier Ministre* above[65] In light of the directions of the latter, however, the domestic courts are obliged to take steps to ensure that the concept of a 'worker' in domestic law is applied consistently with its autonomous meaning under EU law. As pointed out in Chapter 6, many of the recent cases on employment status have been concerned with holiday pay under the Working Time Regulations, with workers as disparate as car valeters, contract plumbers and Uber drivers wrongly classified by their employers as self-employed,[66] rather than workers within limb (b) of the foregoing statutory definition. The decisions in these cases are consistent with the purposive approach of the CJEU, concerned to ensure that the WTD has the widest possible application. Consistently with this approach, earlier decisions of the EAT and the Court of Appeal had taken a robust view of contracts involving building workers, looking at what the parties really intended regardless of the formal terms of their written agreements.[67]

'Working Time'

In addition to 'worker', the other key term of the Directive and the Regulations is 'working time', defined in the Directive to mean 'any period during which the worker is working, at the employer's disposal and carrying out his activity

---

[63] *Ibid.*, para. 32. In this case, it was held that casual and seasonal staff, 'completing a maximum of 80 working days per annum in holiday and leisure centres', came within the definition of 'worker' within para. 28 of the decision. See also Case C-337/10, *Neidel* v. *Stadt Frankfurt am Main* [2012] IRLR 607.

[64] Working Time Regulations 1998, reg. 2(1). And for the broader context, see N. Kountouris, 'The Concept of 'Worker' in European Labour Law: Fragmentation, Autonomy and Scope' (2018) 47 *Industrial Law Journal* 192.

[65] [2010] ECR I-09661, para. 28.

[66] See respectively *Autoclenz Ltd* v. *Belcher* [2011] UKSC 41, [2011] ICR 1157; *Pimlico Plumbers Ltd* v. *Smith* [2018] UKSC 29, [2018] ICR 1511; and *Uber BV* v. *Aslam* [2018] EWCA Civ 2748. See also the *Independent*, 6 April 2018 (CitySprint workers wrongly classified as self-employed).

[67] *Redrow Homes* v. *Buckborough* [2009] IRLR 34 (EAT). See also *Redrow Homes (Yorkshire) Ltd* v. *Wright* [2004] EWCA Civ 469, [2004] ICR 1126 (CA). Contrast *Bacica* v. *Muir* [2006] IRLR 35.

or duties in accordance with national laws and/or practice'.[68] This definition which applies only for the purposes of WTR benefits, but not also for calculating working time for the purposes of pay has been written into the Regulations almost word for word, with working time defined also to mean not only any period during which the worker is receiving relevant training, but also 'any additional period which is to be treated as working time for the purpose of these Regulations under a relevant agreement'.[69] A difficult problem which has occupied a great deal of time in the ECJ/CJEU relates to 'on-call' time, when workers are not necessarily working but may be required to be at the disposal of their employer and to undertake duties if required.

- In the *SIMAP* case,[70] the ECJ held that time spent on call when the worker is required to be on the employer's premises (as in the case of a doctor required to be at a medical centre) counts as working time for the entirety of the period when the worker is required to be present. The Court appeared to accept that to 'exclude on call duty from working time if physical presence is required would seriously undermine [the] objective [of the Directive]'.[71] Where, however, the worker is merely required to be contactable when on call, 'only time linked to the provision of primary care services must be regarded as working time'.[72] While it is true in the latter case that doctors must still be at the disposal of their employer, 'they manage their time with fewer constraints and pursue their own interests'.[73] That said, it has been held that stand-by at home constituted working time in the case of a firefighter under a duty to respond to calls from his employer within eight minutes, as this significantly restricted his opportunity to do other things.[74]
- Case C-151/02, *Landeshauptstadt Kiel* v. *Jaeger*,[75] concerned a doctor who was required to be on call on the employer's premises, but was provided with sleeping accommodation when not actually working. It appears that the doctor in question performed duties for less than half of the time he was required to be on the employer's premises. In confirming that the 'downtime' (during which the doctor may have been sleeping) was 'working time', the ECJ held that 'the periods during which their services are not required in order to cope with emergencies may, depending on the case, be of short

---

[68] WTD, Art. 2(1).

[69] Working Time Regulations 1998, reg. 2(1). According to the EAT, the need to be at the employer's disposal means being required by the employer 'to be in a specific place and ... ready to work to the employer's benefit'; while carrying out the employer's activity means 'engaged in activities that are (at least in part) for the employer's benefit and done with the employer's knowledge and (however broadly) in the manner and at the time of the employer's approval'. Applying these principles, attending meetings as a trade union or health and safety representative was done in working time: *Edwards* v. *Encirc* [2015] IRLR 528.

[70] Case C-303/98, *Sindicato de Médicos de Asistencia Pública (Simap)* v. *Conselleria de Sanidad y Consumo de la Generalidad Valenciana* [2000] ECR I-7963.

[71] *Ibid.*, para. 49.   [72] *Ibid.*, para. 50.   [73] *Ibid.*

[74] Case C-518/15, *Ville de Nivelles* v. *Matzak* [2018] IRLR 457.   [75] [2003] ECR I-8389.

duration and/or subject to frequent interruptions', while 'it cannot be ruled out that the persons concerned may be prompted to intervene, apart from in emergencies, to monitor the condition of patients placed under their care or to perform tasks of an administrative nature'.[76] In so holding, the Court strongly reaffirmed the principle that – like the concept of worker – the concept of working time and rest period are concepts of Community law which must be applied 'uniformly' throughout Member States.[77]

A different issue relates to travelling time, many workers required to travel in the course of their work from one client or location to another. The worker will not normally be able to count as working time the time spent travelling to the same base before starting work. But what happens if the worker is not required to start from the employer's premises and is required to travel to the first client directly from home? This was the issue in Case C-266/14, *Federación de Servicios Privados del sindicato Comisiones obreras* v. *Tyco Integrated Security SL*,[78] where there was evidence that workers could be expected to travel significant distances to their first job of the day, with the example being given of 'a case in which, because of the volume of traffic, the time spent travelling between home and customers was three hours'.[79] In holding that the travelling time was working time, the CJEU held that 'the journeys of the workers, who are employed in a job such as that at issue in the main proceedings, to go to the customers designated by their employer, is a necessary means of providing those workers' technical services to those customers'.[80] Failing to take this time into account would 'distort that concept and jeopardise the objective of protecting the safety and health of workers'.[81] It is true that much was made in this case of the fact that the employer had previously had a central location to which workers reported each day before being dispatched to their jobs, and that the time spent travelling from the depot to the first job had always been counted as working time. But this does not seem to be material to the principle expressed by the court, though it is important to emphasise that what constitutes working time for the WTR may not constitute working time for the payment of wages.[82]

---

[76] *Ibid.*, para. 70.

[77] *Ibid.*, para. 58. In the same vein, see Case C-14/04, *Dellas* v. *Premier Ministre* [2005] ECR I-10253. See also Case C-437/05, *Vorel* v. *Nemocnice Český Krumlov* [2007] ECR I-331. The principle that 'on-call' time should be treated as working time is recognised in ILO Convention 189 (Domestic Workers Convention, 2011), which provides by Art. 10 that '[p]eriods during which domestic workers are not free to dispose of their time as they please and remain at the disposal of the household in order to respond to possible calls shall be regarded as hours of work to the extent determined by national laws, regulations or collective agreements, or any other means consistent with national practice'.

[78] [2015] ICR 1159.   [79] *Ibid.*, para. 12.   [80] *Ibid.*, para. 32.   [81] *Ibid.*

[82] Thus, while travelling time was held in *Tyco* to constitute working time (despite the objections of the UK government which had intervened in the case), the CJEU said that 'even if, in the specific circumstances of the case at issue in the main proceedings, travelling time must be regarded as working time, *Tyco* remains free to determine the remuneration for the time spent

Limits and Entitlements

The Working Time Regulations deal fairly comprehensively with a range of matters relating to working time. Although the classification is controversial, the Regulations may be seen to impose limits on employers and confer entitlements on workers.[83] Not only is this division reflected in the language of the Regulations, but it is also reflected in the enforcement machinery, with the limits generally enforced by the criminal law, and the entitlements by way of a complaint to an ET. Before considering what is in effect the core of the Directive and the Regulations, it is to be recalled that, in recital 6 of the former, 'account should be taken of the principles of the ILO with regard to the organisation of working time, including those relating to night work'. As already pointed out there are as many as thirty-four ILO conventions dealing with working time, though the most important in terms of general application are those set out in the box on pages 292–3. It is worth noting that, although the Directive and the Regulations represent progress, the standard set does not always reflect the ILO principles to which recital 6 refers.[84] In particular, the Directive and the Regulations provide for an average forty-eight-hour week over a seventeen-week reference period. Although ILO Convention 1 (Hours of Work (Industry) Convention, 1919) provides for flexibility in the operation of the eight-hour day, it also provides that in no case 'shall the daily limit of eight hours be exceeded by more than one hour'.[85]

Limits

In the first place, regulation 4(1) deals with the length of the working week by providing that 'a worker's working time, including overtime, in any reference period which is applicable in his case shall not exceed an average of 48 hours for each seven days'.[86] In the absence of a collective or workforce agreement under regulation 23,[87] the reference period for this purpose is seventeen weeks,[88] meaning that working hours are subject to an average of forty-eight

---

travelling between home and customers' (*ibid.*, para. 47). See subsequently *Thera East v. Valentine* [2017] IRLR 878. On working time and the NMW, see esp. pp 276–7 above.

[83] See C. Barnard, *EC Employment Law* (4th edn, Oxford University Press, 2012).

[84] Nor does it necessarily reflect the standard previously embodied in domestic law. For example, compare Factories Act 1961, s. 86. See the box on p. 309.

[85] Art. 2(b). Similarly, Art. 2(c) provides that 'where persons are employed in shifts it shall be permissible to employ persons in excess of eight hours in any one day and forty-eight hours in any one week, if the average number of hours over a period of three weeks or less does not exceed eight per day and forty-eight per week'.

[86] The employer must 'take all reasonable steps, in keeping with the need to protect the health and safety of workers, to ensure that the limit in paragraph (1) is complied with': Working Time Regulations 1998, reg. 4(2). The 'average' is computed by means of a formula in reg. 4(6).

[87] On which, see pp. 328–9.

[88] Working Time Regulations 1998, reg. 4(3). On the meaning of a workforce agreement, see pp. 327–8. Note also that, in some cases, the reference period is twenty-six rather than seventeen weeks: *ibid.*, regs. 4(5) (workers excluded from other provisions of the Regulations by reg. 21) and 25A (doctors in training). See, respectively, pp. 324 and 321.

hours weekly over a period of seventeen weeks. In some weeks, working hours may thus lawfully exceed forty-eight hours. In addition, regulation 5 gives effect to the opt-out negotiated by the UK government (but now made use of by other Member States), the effect of which is that workers may agree in writing not to be bound by the forty-eight-hour limit.[89] However, the agreement must be in writing, and the worker may terminate it at any time by giving a minimum of seven days' notice (though a longer notice period of up to three months may be agreed with the employer).[90] As pointed out by the British government, the opt-out agreement can be cancelled in this way at any time 'even if it is part of [the worker's] contract of employment'.[91] And, as the government also points out, a worker 'can't be sacked or treated unfairly for refusing to [agree to a request to opt out]'.[92] There is no opt-out for young workers (under eighteen years of age), whose working time limit is set at eight hours a day and forty hours a week.[93]

The other major limit applies to night work. By virtue of regulation 6(1), a night worker's normal hours of work in any reference period applicable in his or her case shall not exceed an average of eight hours in each period of twenty-four hours.[94] As with regulation 4, the reference period for the purposes of regulation 7 is seventeen weeks.[95] Night work is defined to mean work during night-time, defined in turn to mean a period of not less than seven hours that includes the period between midnight and 5 am.[96] In the absence of an agreement (which may be a collective or workforce agreement,[97] or a

---

[89] On the operation of the opt-out, see C. Barnard, S. Deakin and R. Hobbs, 'Opting Out of the 48-Hour Week: Employer Necessity or Individual Choice? An Empirical Study of the Operation of Article 18(1)(b) of the Working Time Directive in the UK' (2003) *Industrial Law Journal* 223.

[90] The employer must keep records relating to each of the workers who has opted out: Working Time Regulations 1998, reg. 4(2).

[91] UK Government, *Maximum Weekly Working Hours* (n.d.), where it is also made clear that 'your employer can't force you to cancel your opt-out agreement'.

[92] *Ibid*. See Employment Rights Act 1996, ss. 45A (detriment) and 101A (unfair dismissal).

[93] Working Time Regulations 1998, reg. 5A(1). Note also reg. 5A(2), which provides that, where 'on any day, or, as the case may be, during any week, a young worker is employed by more than one employer, his working time shall be determined for the purpose of paragraph (1) by aggregating the number of hours worked by him for each employer'. Note also that the employer must 'take all reasonable steps, in keeping with the need to protect the health and safety of workers, to ensure that the limits in paragraph (1) are complied with': reg. 5A(4).

[94] The employer must 'take all reasonable steps, in keeping with the need to protect the health and safety of workers, to ensure that the limit in paragraph (1) is complied with': reg. 6(3). The 'average' is computed by means of a formula in reg. 6(5).

[95] Working Time Regulations 1998, reg. 6(2).

[96] *Ibid*., reg. 2(1). See also ILO Convention 171 (Night Work Convention, 1990), Art. 1, for a similar definition of night work. The definition of night worker in the latter is different from the Directive: 'an employed person whose work requires performance of a substantial number of hours of night work which exceeds a specified limit. This limit shall be fixed by the competent authority after consulting the most representative organisations of employers and workers or by collective agreements.' Only six Member States (which do not include the UK) have ratified ILO Convention 171.

[97] On the meaning of workforce agreement, see pp. 327–8.

contractual provision), the default seven hours are those between 11 pm and 6 am.[98] A night worker is then defined to mean a worker 'who, as a normal course, works at least three hours of [his or her] daily working time during night time'.[99] A 'normal course' for these purposes means the working of such hours on the majority of the worker's working days.[100] In other words, someone is a night worker if, on a majority of days in the reference period in which he or she works, he or she works at least three hours between 11 pm and 6 am. Also important is regulation 6(7), which provides that a night worker should not be employed on work that involves special hazards or heavy physical or mental strain 'for more than eight hours in any 24-hour period during which the night worker performs night work'. Young workers may not be employed at night time,[101] and adult workers should not be assigned to night work without first undergoing a (free) medical assessment.[102]

Working Hours in the United Kingdom

In its annual survey of working time, Eurofound (an EU agency which conducts research on working conditions) reported that in the year 2015-16 UK workers worked longer hours than their European counterparts:

> In the EU, full-time employees in the UK report the longest usual weekly working hours in their main jobs in 2016 – 42.3 hours, 0.1 hours less than in 2014 and 2015. They are followed by employees in Cyprus (41.7 hours), Austria (41.4 hours), Greece (41.2 hours), Poland and Portugal (41.1 hours). Employees in Denmark report the shortest weekly hours (37.8 hours). This is 4.5 hours less per week than their counterparts in the UK – the equivalent of more than five working weeks per year (p. 22).

The EU average was 40.3 hours, higher in the EU15 than in the New Member State 13 (p. 23).

At 28 days annually, UK workers have among the lowest number of statutory holidays in the EU: 'The combined total of agreed annual leave and public holidays in the EU varies greatly. In 2016, it ranged from 28 days in Estonia, Hungary, and Ireland, to 39 days in Denmark and 41 days in Croatia, representing a difference of more than two working weeks. Other notably high-leave countries in 2016 were Slovakia and Germany, with 37 leave days in total. Other, notably low-leave countries included Poland with 29 days and Belgium, Latvia, Lithuania, Romania and Slovenia with 30 days. The average figure for the EU28 was 33.8 days – 34.7 days in the EU15 and 31.3 days in the [New Member State] 13'.[103]

---

[98] Working Time Regulations 1998, reg. 2(1).   [99] *Ibid.*   [100] *Ibid.*   [101] *Ibid.*, reg. 6A.
[102] *Ibid.*, reg. 7.   [103] J. Cabrita, *Developments in Working Time 2015–2016* (Eurofound, 2017).

Entitlements

Turning to 'entitlements', there are two different types of right set out in the Directive and the Regulations: those relating to working hours, and those relating to annual leave. So far as the former are concerned, provision of three different kinds is made. By virtue of regulation 10(1), an adult worker is entitled to a daily rest of not less than eleven consecutive hours in each twenty-four hour period during which he or she works for his or her employer. (A young worker is generally entitled to a rest period of not less than twelve consecutive hours in each twenty-four hour period.)[104] In addition, regulation 11(1) provides that an adult worker is entitled to weekly rest, that is to say, 'an uninterrupted rest period of not less than twenty-four hours in each seven-day period during which [he or she] works for [his or her] employer'.[105] As an alternative, the employer may decide instead to have a working time regime in which an adult worker is entitled to either (a) two uninterrupted rest periods of at least twenty-four hours each in each fourteen-day period; or (b) one uninterrupted rest period of not less than forty-eight hours in each such fourteen-day period.[106] (A young worker is generally entitled to a rest period of not less than forty-eight hours in each seven-day period.)[107]

Regulation 12(1) provides that, where an adult worker's daily working time is more than six hours, he or she is entitled to a rest-break.[108] Following the language of the Directive, the regulation provides that the details of the rest-break are to be in accordance with any provisions in a collective agreement or a workforce agreement.[109] Subject to the provisions of any applicable agreement, the rest-break should be 'an uninterrupted period of not less than 20 minutes, and the worker is entitled to spend it away from his workstation if he

---

[104] Working Time Regulations 1998, reg. 10(2). By virtue of reg. 10(3), however, the minimum rest period provided for in reg. 10(2) may be 'interrupted in the case of activities involving periods of work that are split up over the day or of short duration'.

[105] See also ILO Convention 106 (Weekly Rest (Commerce and Offices) Convention, 1957), Art. 6: a general entitlement to 'an uninterrupted weekly rest period comprising not less than 24 hours in the course of each period of seven days'. ILO Convention 106 has been ratified by thirteen EU Member States (but not by the UK).

[106] Working Time Regulations 1998, reg. 11(2). See also Case 306/16, *Da Rosa* v. *Varzim Sol*, 9 November 2017.

[107] Working Time Regulations 1998, reg. 11(3).

[108] It appears that the entitlement is to only one break, regardless of the time worked: see *Corps of Commissionaires* v. *Hughes (No. 1)* [2009] IRLR 122 (EAT). Note, however, reg. 8, which provides that, 'where the pattern according to which an employer organizes work is such as to put the health and safety of a worker employed by him at risk, in particular because the work is monotonous or the work-rate is predetermined, the employer shall ensure that the worker is given adequate rest breaks'. But under the Regulations, the latter is not enforceable by the worker. See pp. 229–30.

[109] Working Time Regulations 1998, reg. 12(2).

has one'.[110] That said, the CJEU has made it clear that the WTD does not require Member States to ensure that workers are paid during rest-breaks,[111] and there is no such right in the Working Time Regulations.[112] Modest though it may be, this provision has nevertheless given rise to a surprising amount of litigation, in the course of which the Court of Appeal has held that 'a rest break is an uninterrupted period of at least 20 minutes which is neither a rest period nor working time and which the worker can use as he pleases'.[113] It is not acceptable to permit a worker to leave half an hour early after an eight-hour shift in lieu of a break.[114]

Raising Standards?

As already explained, the working time standards do not fully meet the international labour principles by which they are informed. It is also the case that modern standards are in some respects less demanding than the legislation which previously operated in this field. A good example of this relates to the now contentious question of rest-breaks. Under the Factories Act 1961, section 86(c), a woman or young person was not to be employed continuously for a spell of more than four-and-a-half hours without an interval of at least half an hour for a meal or rest. By contrast, under the Directive and Regulations, the comparable period for all adults is six hours (though it is still four-and-a-half hours for under-eighteens). Moreover, under the 1961 Act, the period of the break was thirty rather than twenty minutes, and there was an entitlement to a break after every period of four-and-a-half hours worked.

Annual Leave

Article 7(1) of the Directive provides that workers are entitled to at least four weeks' annual leave, it also being expressly provided by Article 7(2) that this minimum period of paid annual leave 'may not be replaced by an allowance in lieu, except where the employment relationship is terminated'. These provisions are to be found in regulation 13 of the Working Time Regulations 1998, which also addresses the provisions of Article 7(1) of the Directive to the effect that 'the conditions for entitlement to, and granting of, such leave laid down

---

[110] *Ibid.*, reg. 12(3). In the case of a young worker, where daily working time is more than four-and-a-half hours, he or she is entitled to a rest-break of at least thirty minutes, which shall be consecutive if possible, and he or she is entitled to spend it away from his or her workstation if he or she has one (reg. 12(4)). Note also reg. 12(5): 'If, on any day, a young worker is employed by more than one employer, his daily working time shall be determined for the purpose of [reg. 5](4) by aggregating the number of hours worked by him for each employer.'

[111] Case C-518/15, *Ville de Nivelles* v. *Matzak* [2018] IRLR 457.

[112] Many workers will, however, have a contractual right to be paid during breaks.

[113] *Gallagher* v. *Alpha Catering Services Ltd* [2004] EWCA Civ 1559, [2005] ICR 673 (CA), para. 50 (Peter Gibson LJ).

[114] *Grange* v. *Abellio London Ltd* [2017] IRLR 108.

by national legislation and/or practice'. As originally enacted, regulation 13 provided that a worker had to be employed for thirteen weeks in order to enjoy the benefit of paid annual leave. In the ground-breaking decision of the ECJ in the *BECTU* case (a second major blow to the UK on working time),[115] however, it was held that such a restriction 'not only negates an individual right expressly granted by Directive 93/104 but is also contrary to its object-ive'.[116] In a decision with wider implications than the exclusion of workers on short-term contracts, the ECJ noted that Article 7 of the Directive 'is not one of the provisions from which Directive 93/104 expressly allows deroga-tions'.[117] The Court concluded that:

> the entitlement of every worker to paid annual leave must be regarded as a particularly important principle of Community social law from which there can be no derogations and whose implementation by the competent national authorities must be confined within the limits expressly laid down by Directive 93/104.[118]

Nature of the Right to Annual Leave

Regulation 13(1) provides that workers are entitled to four weeks' annual leave in each leave year. Unless governed by a collective or workforce agreement, the leave year will vary according to when the worker was first engaged: if before 1 October 1998, then the leave year will run from 1 October each year; if after 1 October, the leave year will begin from the date of appointment.[119] The leave may be taken in instalments, but must be taken in the year in which it is due.[120] As we will see, however, the ECJ has held that in some circumstances annual leave may be carried over from one year to the next (and perhaps even beyond).[121] By virtue of regulation 13A, additional provision is made so that, as from 1 April 2009,[122] workers are entitled to 'additional annual leave' of 1.6 weeks. It is expressly provided that this is subject to a maximum under regulations 13 and 13A of twenty-eight days. Like basic annual leave, add-itional annual leave may be taken in instalments (indeed, it was designed in part to ensure entitlement to paid bank holidays), although unlike basic annual leave, additional annual leave may be carried forward into the next leave year, only where a collective agreement, workforce agreement or con-tractual provision so provides.[123]

So far as part-time workers are concerned, the principle of *pro rata temporis* appears to be widely applied. According to the government's website:

---

[115] Case C-173/99, *R* v. *Secretary of State, ex parte BECTU* [2001] ECR I-04881.
[116] *Ibid.*, para. 48.   [117] *Ibid.*, para. 41.   [118] *Ibid.*, para. 43.
[119] Working Time Regulations 1998, reg. 13(3).   [120] *Ibid.*, reg. 13(9).   [121] See pp. 316–20.
[122] SI 2007 No. 2079.
[123] Working Time Regulations 1998, reg. 13A(7). For a 'workforce agreement', see pp. 327–8 below.

Part-time workers get less paid holiday than full-time workers. They're entitled to at least 5.6 weeks of paid holiday but this amounts to fewer than 28 days because they work fewer hours per week.[124]

The right of part-time workers to annual leave on a pro rata basis arises by virtue of the fact that the entitlement in the Regulations is to annual leave expressed in four (regulation 13) and 1.6 (regulation 13A) weeks. A part-time worker will be entitled to 5.6 part-time weeks as annual leave, just as a full-time worker will be entitled to 5.6 full-time weeks as annual leave. One final point to note at this stage is that neither the right to annual leave in regulation 13 nor the right to additional annual leave in regulation 13A may be bought out by wages in lieu, reflecting the importance of annual leave in EU social law.[125] Where, however, the worker's contract is terminated, regulation 14 enables the worker to recover compensation for any leave due but not taken at the date of termination. As explained clearly by Lord Rodger in *HM Revenue and Customs* v. *Stringer*:

> in effect, the worker receives a proportion of the total amount of pay relating to his annual leave that corresponds to the proportion of the leave year for which the worker has been employed at the time his employment comes to an end. So, if he has worked for three months without taking leave, he gets a quarter of the total pay relating to his annual leave; if he has worked for six months, he gets half etc. Where the worker has already taken some leave, the payment in lieu is reduced accordingly.[126]

Exercising the Right to Annual Leave

Regulation 15(1) provides that a worker may take the leave to which he or she is entitled by giving notice to the employer. However, this is subject to regulation 15(2), which provides that the employer may give counter-notice to require the worker to take leave or not to take leave on particular days.[127] But what if the employer refuses a worker's request and requires the worker to take annual leave in circumstances the worker considers to be unreasonable? In *Sumsion* v. *BBC*,[128] a carpenter was engaged on a twenty-four-week contract, on a salary of £1,200 per week for a six-day week. He was entitled to six days' paid leave, which he was required to take on a 'non-scheduled production day', that is to say, 'a day when he would not otherwise be required to work or attend for the purposes of work'. He was told that he could not take his leave in a single block as he requested, but must take it only on every

---

[124] UK Government, *Holiday Entitlement* (n.d.).
[125] Working Time Regulations 1998, regs. 13(9) and 13A(6).
[126] [2009] UKHL 31, [2009] ICR 985 (HL), para. 13 (Lord Rodger).
[127] On the length of notice to be given, see reg. 15(4).   [128] [2008] IRLR 678 (EAT).

second Saturday. In robustly holding that the employer's practice was consistent with the Regulations, the EAT said that:

> It is plain that it is open to an employer, if so advised, to give notice that specified single days will be leave days. Indeed, such has long been the practice, we understand, at certain factories in respect of Monday holidays. There is, further, nothing in the regulations to restrict the days which an employer can nominate as leave days.[129]

There are, however, two overlapping issues here. The first is the right of the employer to insist that leave be taken at a time to suit its needs rather than the welfare of the worker. While the possibility that schoolteachers might want to take leave in term time may well be an 'unbelievable consequence' of the arguments advanced in *Sumsion*,[130] their situation is distinguishable from that of Mr Sumsion in the sense that they are able to enjoy the benefits of uninterrupted periods of leave under current arrangements.[131] The point is that the practice endorsed by the EAT appears to deny workers the right to uninterrupted leave, a principle recognised by ILO Convention 132 (Holidays with Pay Convention (Revised), 1970) to which the domestic courts ought to have regard. The second issue relates to the power of the employer to specify that single days could be leave days. Does this mean that an employer of a full-time worker on a 'typical' contract of service could require leave to be taken on every second Friday over the course of the year? Following *Sumsion*, why not? It has been suggested that 'any unreasonable response [by an employer to a request for leave] would lead to grievances and even possible claims for constructive dismissal'.[132] But if this is all that stands between a worker and the right to an uninterrupted period of annual leave, does it not suggest that *Sumsion* needs to be reconsidered?[133] As acknowledged by the EAT, 'if a train

---

[129] *Ibid.*, para. 30. The EAT appears to have been greatly concerned about the implications for other sectors – citing education as an example. Thus, if an employer could not insist on workers taking leave when they were not required to be at work, schoolteachers would be able to take their annual leave in term time rather than in the school holidays.

[130] *Ibid.*, para. 29. Here, the EAT recalled the *dictum* of Lord Steyn in *Malik* v. *BCCI* [1998] AC 20, para. 48, that '[i]f a train of reasoning leads to an unbelievable consequence, it is in need of re-examination'.

[131] The same is true of the oil-rig workers who work several weeks on and an equivalent number of weeks off the rigs, and were told that they must take their leave during their period on-shore, a practice upheld in what seems another harsh decision: *Russell* v. *Transocean International Resources Ltd* [2011] UKSC 57. Special provision is made for oil-rig workers in relation to the forty-eight-hour week (reg. 25B), but not in relation to annual leave.

[132] *Lyons* v. *Mitie Security* [2010] IRLR 288 (EAT), para. 33.

[133] An elegant solution to this was suggested *obiter* by Lord Hope in *Russell* v. *Transocean International Resources Ltd* [2011] UKSC 57, para. 41: acknowledging the possibility of abuse, he said that there seemed to be much to be said for the view that 'the entitlement is to periods of annual leave measured in weeks, not days. The worker can opt to take all or part of it in days, if he chooses to do so. But the employer cannot force him to do so.' However, Lord Hope made it clear that this was not his concluded view on the matter.

of reasoning leads to an unbelievable consequence, it is in need of re-examination'.[134]

Payment during Annual Leave

Regulation 16 provides that a worker is 'entitled to be paid in respect of any period of annual leave to which he is entitled under Regulation 13 and Regulation 13A, at the rate of a week's pay in respect of each week of leave'. For this purpose, a week's pay is to be determined in accordance with the provisions of ERA 1996, sections 221–4.[135] These provisions deal respectively with both (a) workers who have normal working hours,[136] and with (b) workers who have no normal working hours.[137] As to the former,

- These provisions deal with workers whose wages are not determined by the amount of work they do, as well as with workers whose wages are so determined (such as pieceworkers).[138]
- They also deal with workers whose wages vary according to the time when they work (such as shift-workers)[139]
  - where there are normal working hours and no fluctuations, a week's pay is 'the amount which is payable by the employer under the contract of employment'.[140]
  - where there are normal working hours but fluctuations based on the amount or time of the work, a week's pay is to be calculated based on the average weekly pay in the previous twelve weeks.[141]

So far as workers who have no normal working hours are concerned, an average is taken of the last twelve weeks to determine the amount of a week's pay.[142] By a shockingly incomprehensible statutory provision, in both cases voluntary overtime is treated as excluded in calculating normal working hours.[143]

What is Pay?

The question of what constitutes pay has given rise to some difficulty, the domestic courts having initially taken a very narrow approach, in a world in which workers' remuneration packages are often quite complex. In *Williams*

---

[134] *Malik* v. *BCCI* [1998] AC 20, para. 48.
[135] Working Time Regulations 1998, reg. 16(2). This does not affect any contractual entitlement which makes more favourable provision: reg. 16(4).
[136] ERA 1996, ss. 221–3.   [137] *Ibid.*, s. 224.   [138] *Ibid.*, s. 221(2) and (3).   [139] *Ibid.*, s. 222.
[140] *Ibid.*, s. 221(2).
[141] *Ibid.*, ss. 221(3) and 222. Special provision is made in the case of weeks in which no wages are paid, in which case the week is disregarded and an earlier week brought in to make up the twelve weeks for the purpose of averaging (*ibid.*, s. 223).
[142] *Ibid.*, s. 224.   [143] *Ibid.*, s. 234.

v. *British Airways plc*,[144] the Court of Appeal was concerned with the salary of airline pilots, whose pay consisted of three parts: a fixed annual sum, a supplementary amount based on flying hours (treated as remuneration and fully taxable) and another supplementary amount based mainly on expenses (with only 18 per cent treated as taxable).[145] The Court of Appeal held that, in determining a week's pay for holiday pay purposes, only the fixed annual sum was to be taken into account, resisting the pilots' argument that paid annual leave should be based on the total payment package. In a reference to the CJEU by the Supreme Court,[146] however, it was held that the worker has a right to 'enjoy, during his period of rest and relaxation, economic conditions which are comparable to those relating to the exercise of his employment'.[147] As a result, it was held by the CJEU that

> any payment which is linked intrinsically to the performance of the tasks which the worker is required to carry out under his contract of employment and in respect of which a monetary amount is provided which is included in the calculation of the worker's total remuneration, such as, in the case of airline pilots, the time spent flying, must necessarily be taken into account for the purposes of the amount to which the worker is entitled during his annual leave.[148]

On return of the case to the Supreme Court, the matter was remitted to the employment tribunal for assessment.[149]

The *Williams* decision of the CJEU was followed by *Lock*, in which it was held that commission was to be taken into account in determining holiday pay.[150] But what about overtime payments? As pointed out above, the right to holiday pay under the Working Time Regulations is (a) based on the statutory definition of a week's pay, which in turn is (b) based on normal working hours, which in turn (c) includes compulsory, but not voluntary overtime.[151] In *Dudley MBC* v. *Willett*,[152] however, it was acknowledged that this statutory restriction was inconsistent with *Williams* and the subsequent decision in

[144] [2009] EWCA Civ 281, [2009] ICR 906 (CA).

[145] Strictly, the case was concerned with a separate body of law governing the working time of airline pilots, based on Council Directive 2000/79/EC (the Aviation Directive). However, the terms of the latter were similar in terms to the WTD, Art. 7, and the reference to the CJEU addressed the question of obligations arising under both the instruments.

[146] [2010] UKSC 16.

[147] Case C-155/10, *Williams* v. *British Airways plc* [2011] IRLR 948 , para. 23.

[148] *Ibid.*, para. 24. In contrast, any part of the remuneration designed to cover costs arising from the performance of the worker's duties – such as time spent away from home – need not be taken into account (para. 25).

[149] *Williams* v. *British Airways plc (No. 2)* [2012] UKSC 43, [2012] ICR 1375.

[150] Case C-539/12, *Lock* v. *British Gas Trading Ltd* [2014] ICR 813; *British Gas Trading Ltd* v. *Lock* [2017] ICR 1.

[151] *Bamsey* v. *Albon Engineering Ltd* [2004] EWCA Civ 359, [2004] ICR 1083 (CA); *British Airways plc* v. *Noble* [2006] EWCA Civ 537, [2006] ICR 1227 (CA); *Bear Scotland Ltd* v. *Fulton* [2015] IRLR 15.

[152] [2017] IRLR 870.

Lock.[153] In *Willetts*, WTD, Article 7 had direct effect (the employer being a public authority), although it was accepted by both parties that domestic law could be interpreted in a manner consistently with the Directive, without explaining how this might be done. The EAT nevertheless effectively endorsed the 'overarching principle' advanced by Michael Ford QC for the applicant that the legislation was to ensure that 'workers benefit from remuneration comparable to that paid in respect of periods of work; or to put it another way, do not suffer any financial disadvantage as a result of taking annual leave'. Without referring to Court of Appeal authority to the contrary decided pre–*Williams* and *Lock* respectively,[154] the EAT held in *Willetts* that voluntary overtime payments and other allowances were to be taken into account in determining holiday pay. That said, this well-received decision applies only in respect of holiday pay due under regulation 13 (four weeks' leave), leaving open the question whether voluntary overtime payments count in determining pay for the purposes of regulation 13A (additional annual leave).[155]

Timing of Payment

Apart from the question of what constitutes pay for the purposes of annual leave, there is also the question of when the payment must be made. Neither the Directive nor the Regulations says that holiday pay must be paid at the same time as the holiday. As a result, the practice of 'rolled-up holiday pay' emerged, whereby the employer would not make a discrete payment for the period of leave, on the ground that the weekly wage or monthly salary already included a component for holiday pay. The worker would be expected to put a portion of the weekly wage or monthly salary aside to cover for a period of leave later in the year. In *Clarke* v. *Frank Staddon Ltd;* and *Caulfield* v. *Marshalls Clay Products Ltd*,[156] the Court of Appeal thought the practice compatible with the Regulations, expressing the view that 'there is no reason why workers generally should not manage rolled-up holiday pay perfectly sensibly'.[157] The Court of Appeal was reinforced in its view by the fact that the practice at least in *Caulfield* was incorporated in a collective agreement, in the negotiation of which a trade union will be 'astute to protect its members' proper interests'.[158] According to Laws LJ, 'a failure to accord great weight to the collective agreement would, in the absence of special circumstances, betray a bureaucratic centralism wholly unjustified by the legislation'.[159] However,

---

[153] Case C-539/12, *Lock* v. *British Gas Trading Ltd* [2014] ICR 813; *British Gas Trading Ltd* v. *Lock* [2017] ICR 1

[154] *Bamsey* v. *Albon Engineering Ltd* [2004] EWCA Civ 359, [2004] ICR 1083 (CA); *British Airways plc* v. *Noble* [2006] EWCA Civ 537, [2006] ICR 1227 (CA).

[155] *Bamsey* v. *Albon Engineering Ltd*, above, may thus still be relevant here.

[156] [2004] EWCA Civ 422, [2004] ICR 1502 (CA).   [157] *Ibid.*, para. 47.   [158] *Ibid.*, para. 49.

[159] *Ibid.*

the Inner House of the Court of Session had come to a different conclusion[160] and it was necessary for the difference to be resolved by a reference to the ECJ.

In addressing this question,[161] the ECJ acknowledged that no provision is made in the Directive as to when the payment for annual leave is to be made.[162] However, the Court took the view that the 'purpose of the requirement of payment for that leave is to put the worker, during such leave, in a position which is, as regards remuneration, comparable to periods of work'.[163] It also held that the right to leave and the right to be paid were two aspects of the same right, emphasising that 'a worker is normally entitled to actual rest, with a view to ensuring effective protection of his health and safety'.[164] Apparently concerned that the practice of rolled-up holiday pay could lead to situations in which workers did not take their leave, the ECJ concluded that:

> Article 7 of the directive precludes the payment for minimum annual leave within the meaning of that provision from being made in the form of part payments staggered over the corresponding annual period of work and paid together with the remuneration for work done, rather than in the form of a payment in respect of a specific period during which the worker actually takes leave.[165]

However, the Court permitted the implications of the decision to be phased in, so that where a rolled-up holiday pay scheme was in force, employers could set off against holiday pay any payments already made under the existing arrangements, provided the latter were transparent and comprehensible.[166] This was a third major defeat for the UK government in the ECJ in relation to working time. It was not the last.

The Question of Deferred Pay

One final question is whether the worker can carry over holiday pay from one year to the next. The matter does not appear to be addressed directly in the Directive, which, by Article 7(2), provides that 'the conditions for entitlement to and granting of such leave [is] to be laid down in national law and/or practice'. As already pointed out:

> WTR, Regulation 13 provides expressly that the basic four weeks' annual leave under Regulation 7 must be taken in the leave year in respect of which it falls

---

[160] *MPB Structures Ltd* v. *Munro* [2003] IRLR 350.

[161] Joined Cases C-131/04 and C-257/04, *Robinson-Steele* v. *R. D. Retail Services Ltd; Clarke* v. *Frank Staddon Ltd; Caulfield* v. *Hanson Clay Products Ltd (formerly Marshalls Clay Products Ltd)* [2006] ECR I-0253 (ECJ). See A. L. Bogg, 'The Right to Paid Annual Leave in the Court of Justice: The Eclipse of Functionalism' (2006) 31 *European Law Review* 892.

[162] Joined Cases C-131/04 and C-257/04, *Robinson-Steele* v. *R. D. Retail Services Ltd; Clarke* v. *Frank Staddon Ltd; Caulfield* v. *Hanson Clay Products Ltd (formerly Marshalls Clay Products Ltd)* [2006] ECR I-0253, para. 54.

[163] *Ibid.*, para. 58.   [164] *Ibid.*, para. 60.   [165] *Ibid.*, para. 63.   [166] *Ibid.*, para. 66.

due;[167] while WTR, Regulation 13A in contrast provides that additional annual leave may be carried forward into the leave year immediately following the leave year in respect of which it is due, with the agreement of the employer.[168]

In both cases it is expressly provided that the leave may not be replaced by a payment in lieu, except on termination of the contract, in which case accumulated leave will have to be paid for by the employer. Regulations 13(9) and 13A(7) give rise to problems in two situations, the first being where the worker is unable to take annual leave because he or she may be on leave for other reasons (such as ill health) during the leave year, and the second being where the worker works throughout the year without requesting the full amount of annual leave to which he or she may be due.

Holiday Pay and Sickness Absence

The issue here is that while some employers would not permit their workers to take annual leave and hence holiday pay during periods of illness, others appeared to do so. Some workers of course will not want to take annual leave during periods of ill health, but others might in order to top up income with holiday pay in periods of extended illness. Some employers may take the view that it is bad luck if annual leave coincides with periods of ill health, but also take the view that annual leave not taken is annual leave that is lost, with holiday pay forfeited as a result. Workers on the other hand may argue that annual leave with pay is an accrued right so that if unused in one year, it should be possible to carry it over to future years and to use it then. But if annual leave and holiday pay are to be carried over in this way, employers may argue that it should be possible to do so only if tight conditions are met, such as (a) a duty on the worker's part to give notice of intent to carry over annual leave, and (b) temporal limits on the period in which any unused leave must be taken so that it is not possible to carry over multiple years worth of unused leave for an indefinite period.

This has become a heavily litigated issue, which has vexed both the ECJ/CJEU and the domestic courts in an expanding body of jurisprudence. The essence of that jurisprudence at the time of writing can be boiled down into the following simple propositions:

- An employer may refuse to permit annual leave and holiday pay to be taken during a period of sick leave, in which case the right to annual leave must be carried over, thereby qualifying the express term of regulation 13(9) to the contrary.[169]

---

[167] Working Time Regulations 1998, reg. 13(9).   [168] *Ibid.*, reg. 13A(7).

[169] Joined Cases C-350/06 and C-520/06, *Schultz-Hoff* v. *Deutsch Rentenversicherung Bund; Stringer* v. *HM Revenue and Customs* [2009] ECR I-179. For the decision of the Court of Appeal in this case, see *Inland Revenue Commissioners* v. *Ainsworth* [2005] EWCA Civ 441,

- A worker on sick leave may claim holiday pay in the period of sick leave if the contract of employment so permits. But he or she is not required to do so, and may instead carry the annual leave period into the following year.[170]
- Where a worker is absent from work because of sickness leave and does not choose to take annual leave during the period of sickness, he or she is not required to demonstrate that he or she is unable to take annual leave because of his or her medical condition.[171]
- A worker who becomes ill during annual leave must have the opportunity, 'after his recovery, to take his annual leave at a time other than that originally scheduled'.[172] The same applies in the case of a worker who becomes ill shortly before a period of annual leave begins.[173]
- Where a worker is on sick leave, it cannot be a precondition of carrying over the annual leave that the worker has formally requested that this should be done. The worker on sick leave will be treated by virtue of the sick leave as not having an opportunity to make a request.[174]
- The right to carry over annual leave is not unlimited: 'The Directive, at most, only requires that employees on sick leave are able to take annual leave within a period of 18 months of the end of the leave year in respect of which the annual leave arises'.[175] In one case fifteen months was deemed long enough.[176]
- A worker who is absent from work because of sickness is still a worker and will continue to accumulate holiday entitlement during the period in which any earlier annual leave must be taken.[177] A worker may thus be entitled to three periods of annual leave in one leave period.[178]
- Where annual leave carried over for reasons of sickness has not been taken before the contract is terminated, the worker is entitled to receive holiday

---

[2005] ICR 1149. For the subsequent disposal of the case, see *HM Revenue and Customs* v. *Stringer* [2009] UKHL 31, [2009] ICR 985 (HL). See A. L. Bogg, 'Of Holidays, Work and Humanisation: A Missed Opportunity?' (2009) 34 *European Law Review* 738.

[170] *NHS Leeds* v. *Larner* [2012] EWCA Civ 1034, [2012] IRLR 825.

[171] *Plumb* v. *Duncan Print Group Ltd* [2015] IRLR 711.

[172] Case C-277/08, *Pereda* v. *Madrid Movilidad SA* [2009] ECR I-8405. One commentator has questioned whether this decision is a 'chancer's charter': D. Cabrelli, 'Dreaming of My Holidays', Edinburgh Centre for Commercial Law blog, 12 October 2009.

[173] Case C-78/11, *Asociación Nacional de Grandes Empresas de Distribución* v. *Federación de Asociaciones Sindicales (FASGA)* [2012] IRLR 779.

[174] *NHS Leeds* v. *Larner* [2012] EWCA Civ 1034, [2012] IRLR 825.

[175] *Plumb* v. *Duncan Print Group Ltd* [2015] IRLR 711. This is the ILO standard which curiously the EAT overcame its reluctance to apply because the relevant treaty had not been ratified by the UK.

[176] Case C-214/10, *KHS AG* v. *Schulte* [2012] IRLR 156 (CJEU). But see Case C-337/10, *Neidel* v. *Stadt Frankfurt am Main* [2012] IRLR 607, where nine months was not long enough.

[177] *NHS Leeds* v. *Larner* [2012] EWCA Civ 1034, [2012] IRLR 825.

[178] This is because it will be possible to take annual leave due in the current year (1), annual leave due in the previous twelve months (2), and following *Plumb* or *Schulte* annual leave due in the year before that (3).

pay in lieu of the carried over annual leave on termination. A new regulation 14(5) has been read into the Working Time Regulations for this purpose.[179]

- The foregoing applies only in relation to annual leave in regulation 13, the Court of Appeal refusing to be drawn on whether the same principles apply in regulation 13A,[180] which unlike regulation 13 states expressly that additional leave can be carried over with the consent of the employer.[181]

Holiday Pay and Unused Leave

Apart from the implausibly complicated position relating to illness, the general principle in the WTD is that paid annual leave cannot be carried over from one year to the next. As we have seen, regulation 13 thus provides expressly that paid annual leave must be taken in the year in which it falls. The position is different in relation to additional paid annual leave under Working Time Regulations, regulation 13A, which provides expressly that additional paid annual leave may be carried over with the agreement of the employer. The basic rule of the WTR, regulation 13, is thus 'use it or lose it', subject to the sickness cases discussed above, a point acknowledged by Bean J in the EAT in *NHS Leeds* v. *Larner*, when he said that:

> The position might be different in the case of a fit employee who fails to make any request for leave during the whole of a pay year. He or she might then lose the right to take annual leave, certainly if the contract so provides, because that worker, unlike Mrs Larner, has in the words of the Court in *Pereda* 'had the opportunity' to exercise the right to leave.[182]

There are, however, circumstances where 'the conditions for entitlement to, and granting of, such leave laid down by national legislation' could make it difficult for workers to exercise their right to leave. It will be recalled that under regulation 15 workers must give notice of their intention to take leave and that minimum notice periods may be required, which may be extended by contract. Although these mechanisms 'must not be operated by an employer in an unreasonable, arbitrary or capricious way so as to deny any entitlement lawfully requested', equally even 'if operated correctly by both employee and employer', any such mechanism 'could result, as was envisaged in the *Stringer* case, in the loss of the right at the end of the leave year in respect of leave not taken'.[183]

In such circumstances both the WTD and the Regulations make it clear that the worker is not entitled to holiday pay in lieu of the time lost, nor is it likely

---

[179] *NHS Leeds* v. *Larner* [2012] EWCA Civ 1034, [2012] IRLR 825.   [180] *Ibid.*

[181] The proposition is supported by Case C-337/10, *Neidel* v. *Stadt Frankfurt am Main* [2012] IRLR 607, where the CJEU accepted that any provision beyond the minimum requirements of the Directive would not be bound by obligations arising thereunder. See also *Sood* v. *Healy* [2013] IRLR 865.

[182] [2011] IRLR 895, para. 18.   [183] *Lyons* v. *Mitie Security* [2010] IRLR 288 (EAT).

that a claim could be brought for compensation under the Regulations, regulation 30 (unless it could be shown that the employer has acted unlawfully: non-payment of holiday pay where the conditions had not been met would not be unlawful, unless the employer behaved unreasonably, arbitrarily or capriciously). Nor would there be a right to recover the holiday pay for the annual leave never taken at the point of termination, again except that due in the leave year in question. An unusual example where liability might arise was revealed in Case C-214/16, *King v. Sash Window Workshop Ltd*,[184] where the worker had been engaged by the employer for thirteen years, in which he had not taken leave because it would have been unpaid. Although it appears to have been possible for Mr King to have challenged the employer under regulation 30, the CJEU nevertheless ruled that a worker can carry over and accumulate 'paid annual leave rights not exercised in respect of several consecutive reference periods because his employer refused to remunerate that leave'. These rights can be redeemed on termination, as in the illness cases discussed above. In so holding, the CJEU denied that this would be unfair to employers, claiming on the contrary that 'if the worker's acquired entitlement to paid annual leave could be extinguished, that would amount to validating conduct by which an employer was unjustly enriched to the detriment of the very purpose of that directive, which is that there should be due regard for workers' health'.

Exclusions

Consistently with the provisions of the Directive, the Regulations include a number of categories of worker who are either excluded or for whom specific provision is made. Some of the exclusions apply vertically to particular economic sectors, while others apply horizontally depending on the nature of the work. As amended, regulation 18(1) excludes seafarers, workers engaged on fishing vessels and certain workers engaged in inland waterways, for all of whom separate provision is made in other instruments.[185] Apart from the total exclusion of the latter sectors, regulation 18(2) also excludes the operation of certain provisions of the Regulations to certain activities of the armed forces, the police and civil protection services,[186] as well as mobile staff in civil

---

[184] [2018] IRLR 142.

[185] See, for example, the European Agreement on the Organisation of Working Time of Seafarers, 30 September 1998, put into effect by Council Directive 1999/63/EC of 21 June 1999.

[186] The exclusion applies where 'characteristics peculiar to certain specific services such as the armed forces or the police, or to certain specific activities in the civil protection services, inevitably conflict with the provisions of these Regulations': reg. 18(2)(a). Remarkably, the Regulations otherwise apply to the armed forces (reg. 38, though subject also to reg. 25) and the police (reg. 41), with some modifications. The effect of reg. 18(2)(a) is that the Regulations will not apply on the battlefield. The Regulations also apply to civil servants and parliamentary staff (regs. 37, 39 and 40).

aviation,[187] though the exclusion of doctors in training has been revoked. These latter exclusions apply to regulations 4(1) and (2) (maximum working week), 6(1), (2) and (7) (night work), 7(1) and (6) (health assessment), 8 (additional rest-breaks where there is a monotonous work pattern), 10(1) (daily rest), 11(1) and (2) (weekly rest), 12(1) (rest periods), and 13, 13A and 16 (annual leave and payments relating to annual leave). A further exclusion is made for workers performing mobile road transport activities. This exclusion applies in relation to regulations 4(1) and (2) (maximum working week), 6(1), (2) and (7) (night work), 8 (additional rest-breaks where there is a monotonous work pattern), 10(1) (daily rest), 11(1) and (2) (weekly rest) and 12(1) (rest-breaks).[188] The mobile road transport exclusion is narrower than the original, which applied to all workers in road transport, regardless of whether they were mobile or office based.[189] By virtue of regulation 19, domestic servants in a private household are excluded from the forty-eight hour week, the restrictions on night work and additional rest-breaks for monotonous work.[190] But they are not excluded from the right to paid annual leave.

Doctors in Training

The removal of the exclusion of junior doctors from the Regulations has been particularly controversial, especially when combined with the decisions of the ECJ relating to on-call time (to be treated as working time when the doctor is required to be on the employer's premises, even though not working).[191] The forty-eight-hour week for junior doctors was phased in

---

[187] This exclusion applies to workers covered by the European Agreement on the Organisation of Working Time of Mobile Staff in Civil Aviation, 22 March 2000, implemented by Council Directive 2000/79/EC of 27 November 2000. See Case C-155/10, *Williams* v. *British Airways plc* [2011] IRLR 948 and *Williams* v. *British Airways plc (No. 2)* [2012] UKSC 43, [2012] ICR 1375.

[188] Working Time Regulations 1998, reg. 18(4). These provisions do not apply to workers covered by Directive 2002/15/EC of the European Parliament and of the Council on the Organisation of the Working Time of Persons Performing Mobile Road Transport Activities, dated 11 March 2002 (the 'Drivers' Hours Directive). See *R(URTU)* v. *Secretary of State for Transport* [2013] EWCA Civ 962, which highlights the lack of an individual remedy in the Drivers' Hours Directive, which the Court of Appeal was not prepared to read to give effect to the EU Charter, Article 47 (right to effective remedy). Enforcement is by way of criminal proceedings, in contrast to not only the WTD/Regulations, but also Council Directive 2000/79/EC of 27 November 2000, above.

[189] Case C-133/00, *Bowden* v. *Tuffnells Parcels Express Ltd* [2001] ECR I-7031.

[190] That is to say, regs. 4(1) and (2), 5A(1) and (4), 6(1), (2) and (7), [6A], 7(1), (2) and (6), and 8. It is not clear what reason there is for this exclusion. Compare ILO Convention 189 (Domestic Workers Convention, 2011), Art. 10(1): 'Each Member shall take measures towards ensuring equal treatment between domestic workers and workers generally in relation to normal hours of work, overtime compensation, periods of daily and weekly rest and paid annual leave in accordance with national laws, regulations or collective agreements, taking into account the special characteristics of domestic work'.

[191] On these cases, see pp. 303–4.

gradually from 2004 and took full effect on 1 August 2011.[192] The reference period for a doctor in training is twenty-six weeks (regulation 25A(3)) rather than the seventeen weeks for other workers (regulation 4(3)).

NHS Employers (the organisation representing NHS employers) accept that the Directive is an important safeguard protecting patients from sub-standard care from tired doctors (it being reported that, in the past, 120-hour weeks by junior doctors were not unknown), but argues that there is a need for 'greater flexibility' than that which the Directive currently provides. Although individual junior doctors can opt out of the forty-eight-hour week, it has been pointed out that 'entire departments or groups of staff cannot opt out collectively'. As NHS Employers also recognise, 'deciding to opt out is an individual and voluntary decision', and it is therefore 'not sensible to plan doctors' rotas on the assumption that every single member of the rota, now and in future, will make that choice'.[193]

NHS employers argue that the 'current rules have a negative impact on running costs', with some hospitals having to employ additional workers to cover shift patterns, and that shorter working hours and compensatory rest periods mean that doctors in training get less time with supervisors and less experience of performing clinical procedures. They called for greater flexibility in the timing of compensatory rest, the important consideration being whether the health care worker is fit to work; and also that 'any inactive on-call time should count as rest and that time spent on standby – where the employee is not working, should also count as rest'. Predictably, the NHS Employers supported the forty-eight-hour week opt-out, which should be 'maintained'.[194]

Unmeasured Working Time

Apart from the foregoing largely sectoral exclusions, regulation 20 excludes some workers from various provisions of the Regulations largely because of the nature of the work performed. The exclusions apply to regulations 4(1) and (2) (maximum working week), 6(1), (2) and (7) (night work), 10(1) (daily rest), 11(1) and (2) (weekly rest) and 12(1) (rest-breaks). These latter provisions 'do not apply in relation to a worker where, on account of the specific characteristics of the activity in which he is engaged, the duration of his working time is not measured or predetermined or can be determined by the worker himself'. This is provided to apply expressly where appropriate in the case of managing executives or other persons with autonomous decision-making powers, family workers and workers officiating at religious ceremonies in churches and religious communities. As the Regulations were originally

---

[192] SI 2003 No. 1684, SI 2009 No. 1567.
[193] NHS Employers, European Working Time Directive, 10 March 2011.
[194] NHS Employers, Working Time Directive (2017).

enacted, regulation 20(2) made provision for workers whose work was partially not measured, or predetermined, or capable of being determined by workers themselves. In these cases, regulations 4, 6, 10, 11 and 12 applied to the extent that the work was not measured or predetermined or capable of being determined by the worker himself or herself. However, regulation 20(2) has been revoked, being found by the ECJ to be inconsistent with Article 17 of the Directive, which applies only to workers whose working time as a whole is not measured or predetermined or can be determined by the workers themselves.[195]

The provisions of regulation 20 are far from clear as to their scope, and there is little case-law on the point. The matter was raised as one of several questions in *Sayers* v. *Cambridgeshire County Council*,[196] where the employee left work in August 2003 on account of psychiatric illness. She brought a number of claims against her employer, alleging liability in tort for breach of the duty of care, liability in contract for breach of the duty of mutual trust and confidence, and liability for breach of various statutory duties. There were also claims under the Directive. The application failed, though one of the employer's defences was rejected by the High Court, this being the defence that the Directive did not apply because the claimant was covered by regulation 20. According to Ramsey J, the question in this case was whether the claimant was a 'managing executive or other person with autonomous decision-taking powers'. In holding that she was not, the court noted that the claimant had a contract of employment that regulated her hours, that there were 'not any specific characteristics of the activity in which she was engaged which meant that the duration of her working time was not measured or predetermined or could not be determined by her'.[197] Moreover, although she occupied a high-level post as an operations manager, she reported to a deputy director, while the council itself had indicated in documents relating to working time that only 'chief officers', 'the Chief Executive' and 'Directors' were to be regarded as falling within the scope of regulation 20.

'Other Special Cases'

Under the heading 'Other special cases', regulation 21 (which is based on WTD, Article 17) provides that regulations 6(1), (2) and (7) (relating to night work), 10(1) (daily rest), 11(1) and (2) (weekly rest), and 12(1) (rest-breaks) do not apply:[198]

---

[195] Case C-484/04, *Commission* v. *United Kingdom* [2006] ECR I-7471.
[196] [2006] EWHC 2029, [2007] IRLR 29 (QB).   [197] *Ibid.*, para. 259.
[198] It is also the case that the reference period for the purposes of reg. 4 is twenty-six rather than seventeen weeks in the case of workers to whom reg. 21 applies: see reg. 4(5).

Working Time Regulations, Regulation 21

(a) where the worker's activities are such that his place of work and place of residence are distant from one another, including cases where the worker is employed in offshore work, or his different places of work are distant from one another;

(b) where the worker is engaged in security and surveillance activities requiring a permanent presence in order to protect property and persons, as may be the case for security guards and caretakers or security firms;

(c) where the worker's activities involve the need for continuity of service or production, as may be the case in relation to –

  (i) services relating to the reception, treatment or care provided by hospitals (including the activities of doctors in training) or similar establishments, residential institutions and prisons;

  (ii) work at docks or airports;

  (iii) press, radio, television, cinematographic production, postal and telecommunications services and civil protection services;[199]

  (iv) gas, water and electricity production, transmission and distribution, household refuse collection and incineration;

  (v) industries in which work cannot be interrupted on technical grounds;

  (vi) research and development activities;

  (vii) agriculture;

  (viii) the carriage of passengers on regular urban transport services;

(d) where there is a foreseeable surge of activity, as may be the case in relation to –

  (i) agriculture;

  (ii) tourism; and

  (iii) postal services;

(e) where the worker's activities are affected by –

  (i) an occurrence due to unusual and unforeseeable circumstances, beyond the control of the worker's employer;

  (ii) exceptional events, the consequences of which could not have been avoided despite the exercise of all due care by the employer; or

  (iii) an accident or the imminent risk of an accident;

(f) where the worker works in railway transport and –

  (i) his activities are intermittent;

  (ii) he spends his working time on board trains; or

  (iii) his activities are linked to transport timetables and to ensuring the continuity and regularity of traffic.

---

[199] In Case C-518/15, *Ville de Nivelles* v. *Matzak* [2018] IRLR 457, it was held that under the corresponding provisions of the WTD, it is not possible to derogate in the case of firefighters from the definition of working time in Art. 2.

Various provisions of these 'special cases' have featured prominently in a number of important cases. In relation to regulation 21(c), it was held in *Gallagher* v. *Alpha Catering*[200] (a case relating to workers employed by a company supplying catering to airlines) that there was insufficient evidence to 'support the view that the activities of the employees, as distinct from their employer, involve the need for continuity of service or production'.[201] Nor was it explained why the employees could not have their working time organised in such a way as to have rest-breaks within each six-hour period of working time. In taking this view, Sir Peter Gibson rebuffed arguments that 'the economic consequences' to the employer 'would be devastating':

> That assertion is not backed by a finding of the [ET], and I am not persuaded that so apocalyptic a consequence would flow if the employees are right. No doubt health and safety requirements do add to the economic burdens of an employer, but that fact cannot justify an interpretation which the Directive and the Regulations would otherwise not allow.[202]

So far as regulation 21(d) is concerned, the 'relatively modest fluctuations which [the employer] experienced within the working day and working week' did not amount to a 'surge'. In the view of the Court of Appeal, this 'derogation' was to be construed restrictively, endorsing the view that 'a surge only occurred when there is an exceptional level of activity, beyond the fluctuations experienced within the working day and working week'.[203]

A rather different approach may be detected in *Hughes* v. *Corps of Commissionaires Management (No. 2)*,[204] where security guards working twelve-hour shifts were given a twenty-minute break but were required during that break to be available for duty. If, however, the break was interrupted, they were entitled to start another break of twenty minutes. It was held that the guards were covered by regulation 21(b), and that the dispute fell to be determined by regulation 24. The latter provides that, when regulation 21 is engaged, the worker must be allowed an equivalent period of compensatory rest;[205] where exceptionally this is not possible, the employer must afford the worker 'such protection as may be appropriate in order to safeguard the worker's health and safety'.[206] In *Hughes*, it was held that 'the period which is free from work is at least 20 minutes. If the break does not display those characteristics then we do not think it would meet the criteria of equivalence and compensation.'[207] In this case, the arrangements were found to meet those criteria, the Court of Appeal noting that, 'since the rest break begins again following any

---

[200] [2004] EWCA Civ 1559, [2005] ICR 673 (CA).   [201] *Ibid.*, para. 33.   [202] *Ibid.*, para. 38.
[203] *Ibid.*, para. 45.   [204] [2011] EWCA Civ 1061, [2011] IRLR 915 (CA).
[205] Working Time Regulations 1998, reg. 24(a). Reg. 24 applies also in relation to reg. 22 (which modifies the application of regs. 10 (daily rest), 11 (weekly rest) to shift workers) and reg. 23 (which allows for the modification or exclusion of various provisions by collective or workforce agreement). On the latter, see pp. 327–8.
[206] *Ibid.*, reg. 24(b).   [207] [2011] EWCA Civ 1061, [2011] IRLR 915 (CA), para. 54.

interruption, many would say that this was more beneficial than a Regulation 12 ... break would be'.[208] That said, the decisions make it clear that if working arrangements can be made to enable the worker to carry out his or her duties without his or her permanent presence being required, regulation 21(b) is not engaged and the matter ought not to be considered under regulation 24.[209]

Negotiated Flexibility and the Role of Collective Agreements

There are many fascinating aspects of the Directive, yet another of which is that – as suggested in the introduction to this chapter – it is a potentially important bridge between collective and individual labour law. It is true that the Directive confers a range of rights for individuals and imposes duties on employers in relation to individuals. The interest here, however, is the way in which trade unions can be integrated into the process of determining the scope and content of these rights and duties. At first blush, this may seem strange in light of what has been said above about collective bargaining and collective agreements. As we saw in the *Pfeiffer* case,[210] the ECJ held clearly that trade unions cannot by collective bargaining extend the length of the working week. And, as we saw in the *Robinson-Steele* case,[211] the ECJ held that trade unions could not agree with the employer that workers' holiday pay could be rolled up with wages paid during the year. It is true, however, that in Case C-214/10, *KHS AG* v. *Schulte*,[212] it was held that a collective agreement could impose a limit of fifteen months on the amount of time a worker could accumulate entitlement to paid annual leave which the worker had been unable to take because of illness in previous leave years.[213]

The Directive and Collective Agreements

In light of *Pfeiffer* in particular, it is paradoxical that the Directive gives to trade unions a potentially important regulatory role in the operation of

---

[208] *Ibid.*

[209] See also *Associated British Ports* v. *Bridgeman* [2012] IRLR 639, where *Gallacher* and *Hughes* were considered in some detail in a case about harbour pilots covered by reg. 21(c)(ii). The issue there was whether the need for continuity of service provided a blanket exemption from all the entitlements to which the derogation related, or whether it had to be made out in relation to each of them. This would mean that although the derogation could be made out in relation to reg. 10 (rest-breaks), it would not follow that it would be made out in relation to reg. 12 (rest-breaks). The EAT referred to the ECJ the question whether 'the requirement of continuity of service has to be established separately as regards each right under the Directive from which derogation is made or whether continuity of service should be addressed generally without consideration of the specific rights from which derogation has been made'.

[210] Case C-397/01, *Pfeiffer* v. *Deutsches Rotes Kreuz* [2004] ECR I-08835.

[211] Case C-131/04, *C. D. Robinson-Steele* v. *R. D. Retail Services Ltd* [2006] ECR 1–0253 (ECJ).

[212] [2012] IRLR 156 (CJEU).

[213] See also Case C-78/11, *Asociación Nacional de Grandes Empresas de Distribución* v. *Federación de Asociaciones Sindicales (FASGA)* [2012] IRLR 779, on the scope of a collective agreement.

working time, and a potentially important incentive to employers to engage with trade unions to make the law work. This arises in three ways, the first being in relation to the substance of the obligations in the Directive, most obvious in relation to Article 4. The latter deals with the entitlement to rest-breaks, 'the details of which, including duration and terms on which it is granted', are to be 'laid down in collective agreements or agreements between the two sides of industry'. Only failing such agreements is the matter to be dealt with by national legislation. Collective bargaining is thus not only a source of the scope of the obligation under the Directive, but potentially the primary source.[214] Secondly, the Directive provides for the possibility that the rights and limits which it introduces may be implemented by collective agreements, a good example of this being Article 6, which provides that Member States must take measures to ensure that 'the period of weekly working time is limited by means of laws, regulations or administrative provisions or by collective agreements or agreements between the two sides of industry'. On this occasion, it will be noted that collective agreements have equal status but are not a primary source in the hierarchy of permissible means of implementation.

The third role of collective bargaining in the operation of the Directive is in relation to derogation. Thus, Article 18 provides that certain derogations may be made from Articles 3 (daily rest), 4 (rest-breaks), 5 (weekly rest period), 8 (length of night work) and 16 (reference periods) 'by means of collective agreements or agreements concluded between the two sides of industry at national or regional level or, in conformity with the rules laid down by them, by means of collective agreements or agreements concluded between the two sides of industry at a lower level'. This formulation would provide a problem for countries like the UK where there are many sectors where collective agreements are not now concluded at national or regional level. In these cases, Article 18 provides that derogations from the aforementioned paragraphs may be made 'by way of collective agreements or agreements concluded between the two sides of industry at an appropriate collective level'. Again emphasising the regulatory importance of collective agreements, it is also provided that Member States may lay down rules for 'the extension of the provisions of collective agreements or agreements concluded in conformity with this Article to other workers in accordance with national legislation and/or practice'. Where such derogations are made, equivalent compensating rest periods 'must be granted to the workers concerned or, in exceptional cases where it is not possible for objective reasons to grant such periods, the workers concerned are afforded appropriate protection'.

---

[214] See also Art. 16(c): Member States may lay down 'for the application of Article 8 (length of night work), a reference period defined after consultation of the two sides of industry or by collective agreements or agreements concluded between the two sides of industry at national or regional level'.

The Regulations and Collective Agreements

These provisions presented something of a challenge for the UK. There is no longer national or sector-wide collective bargaining on a universal scale,[215] and while collective bargaining has moved or is moving from sector to enterprise, most employers do not recognise a trade union for the purposes of collective bargaining. Rather than use the Directive as an incentive to employers to recognise a trade union in order to secure the flexibility that the Directive permits, the government chose instead to accommodate non-union forms of worker representation so that employers could satisfy the provisions of the Directive by making agreements with workers' representatives who would not necessarily be trade union representatives, and whose role would not necessarily be consistent with the freedom of association principles promoted by the ILO.[216] So rather than being a vehicle indirectly to promote collective bargaining as the Directive appeared to anticipate, the Regulations have become a means that enables employers to entrench non-union forms of workplace representation. For this purpose the concept of the 'workforce agreement' has been created, a 'workforce agreement' being defined to mean 'an agreement between an employer and workers employed by him or their representatives in respect of which the conditions set out in Schedule 1 to these Regulations are satisfied'.[217] No provision is made for the legal status of such agreements (which may not fall within the legal definition of a collective agreement and so the statutory presumption against legal enforceability may not apply (although this is not to say that the agreements will be legally binding)).[218]

The Role of Collective Agreements and Workforce Agreements

As we have seen, the details relating to rest-breaks may be determined by a collective or workforce agreement (regulation 12(2)). By virtue of regulation 23, a collective agreement or a workforce agreement may modify or exclude the application of regulations 6(1) to (3) (night work maximum, and seventeen-week reference period) and (7) (determining what is a special hazard for the purposes of night work), 10(1) (daily rest period), 11(1) and (2) (weekly rest period) and 12(1) (rest-break after six hours' work). Regulation 23 also provides that a collective agreement or a workforce agreement 'for objective or technical reasons or reasons concerning the organization of work' may modify the seventeen-week reference period in regulation 4, substituting a different period not to exceed fifty-two weeks, in relation to particular workers or groups of workers.

---

[215] See Chapter 14.

[216] Unfortunately, recital 6 in the preamble to the Directive refers only to the principles of the ILO relating to working time, including night work, but not also freedom of association, on which see Chapter 12.

[217] Working Time Regulations 1998, reg. 2(1).

[218] The statutory presumption is to be found in TULRCA 1992, s. 179. See p. 128.

For the purposes of the Regulations, a workforce agreement is an agreement which is in writing, has an effect for a specified period not exceeding five years and applies either to (a) all of the relevant members of the workforce, or (b) all of the relevant members of the workforce who belong to a particular group. The agreement must also be signed by a workers' representative, or by the majority of the workers employed by the employer in the case of businesses with twenty or fewer workers.[219] A workers' representative must be elected in accordance with the provisions of paragraph 3 of Schedule 1, which provides that it is for the employer to determine the number of representatives to be elected, the candidates to be relevant members of the workforce to which the agreement will relate. It is also provided that a worker eligible to be a candidate may not be unreasonably excluded from standing for election, and that all the relevant members of the workforce are entitled to vote in the election. Further provision requires the election to be conducted to secure that, so far as is reasonably practicable, those voting do so in secret, and that the votes cast at the election are fairly and accurately counted. No provision is made to challenge any election where there are concerns that these procedures have not been complied with. In the absence of authority, we can only speculate that the courts will give such agreements legal effects in the sense that their terms will be incorporated into individual contracts of employment (including those who voted against the agreement?).

Enforcement and Remedies

The final question for consideration relates to enforcement of the foregoing provisions and remedies for their breach. Here we find that there is a role for both the criminal law and the civil law.[220] In common with other health and safety provisions, enforcement is carried out principally by the Health and Safety Executive (HSE). Except to the extent that other agencies have enforcement obligations,[221] the HSE has the responsibility to make 'adequate arrangements' for the enforcement of regulations 4(2) (weekly limit), 5A(4) (young worker weekly limit), 6(2) and (7) (night work), 6A (young worker night work), 7(1), (2) and (6) (health assessment and transfer of night workers to day work), 8 (additional rest-breaks where there is a monotonous pattern of work), and 9 (maintaining adequate records) and 27A(4)(a) (protection for young workers).[222] HSE inspectors have wide powers to enter employers' premises, to question individuals and to require the production of records for

---

[219] In this case, before the agreement is made available for signature, the employer must provide all the workers to whom it was intended to apply with copies of the text of the agreement and such guidance as those workers might reasonably require in order to understand it fully.

[220] But note the absence of any right of individual enforcement under the Drivers' Hours Hours Directive, note 188. See *R(URTU)* v. *Secretary of State for Transport* [2013] EWCA Civ 962.

[221] Notably local authorities, the Civil Aviation Authority (CAA), and the Vehicle and Operator Services Agency (VOSA): Working Time Regulations 1998, reg. 28.

[222] Working Time Regulations 1998, reg. 28(2).

inspection.[223] Where the inspector finds evidence of a breach of the foregoing provisions, he or she may issue an improvement notice requiring the contravention to be remedied within a specified period, or a prohibition notice to stop the activities of the employer being carried on until certain improvements have been made.[224] An appeal may be made to an ET against either an improvement notice or a prohibition notice, and the tribunal may either cancel or affirm (with or without modifications) the notice.[225] Failure to comply with regulations 4(2) (weekly limit), 5A(4) (young worker weekly limit), 6(2) and (7) (night work), 6A (young worker night work), 7(1), (2), and (6) (health assessment and transfer of night workers to day work), 8 (additional rest-breaks where there is a monotonous pattern of work), 9 (maintaining adequate records), and 27A(4)(a) (protection for young workers) is an offence, punishable by a fine.[226] Failure to comply with an improvement or prohibition notice is also an offence, which in this case may lead to a fine or imprisonment.[227] There is also a range of offences relating to the obstruction of inspectors.[228]

Problems of Enforcement

Although inspection and enforcement by the HSE is said to be 'the most effective way the official safety watchdog can ensure compliance with workplace health and safety', concern has been expressed about enforcement of the working time limits.

According to the health and safety journal, *Hazards*,[229] by 2009 there had been 'just two HSE working time-related prosecutions since 2001'. In that time, 'the HSE had issued 38 improvement notices relating to the Working Time Regulations', though there had not been more than two notices issued in any year since 2003. Between 2004/5 and 2007/8, the HSE 'took just 16 prosecutions on *any* work-related health issues, compared to over 4,700 prosecutions for safety offences'.

Hazards called for more HSE resources to be targeted at workers on atypical hours, rigorous enforcement of working time law, and an end to the UK opt-out from the WTD's forty-eight-hour working week limit. Better enforcement of working time seems unlikely in the present climate of public spending cuts. Concerns about enforcement of health and safety law was expressed in strong terms by the House of Commons Work and Pensions Committee in 2008,[230] and by others.[231]

---

[223] *Ibid.*, reg. 28(7) and Sched. 3, para. 2. Employers are required to keep 'adequate records' to show whether the limits in regs. 4(1), 5A(1), and 6(1) and (7), and the requirements in regs. 6A and 7 are being complied with: *ibid.*, reg. 9.

[224] *Ibid.*, Sched. 3, paras. 3–5.   [225] *Ibid.*, Sched. 3, para. 6.   [226] *Ibid.*, reg. 29(1) and (3).

[227] *Ibid.*, reg. 29(3) and (7).   [228] *Ibid.*, reg. 29(3), (5), (6) and (8).

[229] Hazards, 'Safety Watchdog Goes Missing on the Night Shift', 30 May 2009.

[230] HC 246 (2007–8).

[231] S. Tombs and D. Whyte, *Regulatory Surrender: Death, Injury and Non-Enforcement of Law* (London: Institute of Employment Rights, 2010), pp. 59–64.

Individual Remedies

In other cases, enforcement is by way of a complaint by an individual to an ET. This applies principally where the worker complains that the employer has refused to permit him or her to exercise any right under regulations 10(1) or (2) (daily rest), 11(1), (2) or (3) (weekly rest), 12(1) or (4) (rest-breaks), 13 (annual leave) or 13A (additional annual leave). It also applies where the worker claims that the employer has failed to make payments in breach of the right to paid annual leave.[232] The application should normally be made within three months of the denial of the entitlement concerned.[233] If a complaint relating to regulations 10(1) or (2), 11(1), (2) or (3), 12(1) or (4), or 13(1) is upheld, the tribunal may make a declaration and may make an award of compensation to be paid by the employer to the worker.[234] But having made a declaration, there is no duty to make an award of compensation, a position which the EAT clearly thought unusual.[235] Where, however, the tribunal decides that an award of compensation is to be made, the Regulations provide in standard form that the amount of the compensation shall be such 'as the tribunal considers just and equitable in all the circumstances', having regard to the employer's default, and any loss sustained by the worker as a result.[236] If a complaint relating to holiday pay is upheld, the tribunal must order the employer to pay to the worker the amount that it finds to be due to him or her.[237] There is no compensation for injury to feelings as a result of a breach of the Working Time Regulations.[238]

Informing Workers of Their Working Time Rights

A notable omission from the WTD and the Regulations is the absence of an obligation on the employer to bring working time rights to the attention of workers.[239] Under the Factories Act 1961, section 88(1)(b), the employer was required to post a notice in the factory which

---

[232] Working Time Regulations 1998, reg. 30.   [233] *Ibid.*, reg. 30(2).   [234] *Ibid.*, reg. 30(3).

[235] *Miles* v. *Linkage Community* [2008] IRLR 602. No compensation was paid in that case, in which there was a breach of the daily rest provisions.

[236] Working Time Regulations 1998, reg. 30(4). Compensation may thus be recoverable even in the case of entitlements to leave in respect of which there is no right to be paid, as in the case of daily rest-breaks. See, for example, *Associated British Ports* v. *Bridgeman* [2012] IRLR 639.

[237] *Ibid.*, reg. 30(5).

[238] *Gomes* v. *Higher Level Care Ltd* [2018] EWCA Civ 418, [2018] ICR 1571.

[239] See *Fraser* v. *South West London St George's Trust* [2012] IRLR 100: 'there can, absent particular circumstances, be no duty on an employer to advise his employees of their rights as a matter of general law', EAT dismissing a claim based on *Scally* v. *Southern Health and Social Services Board* [1991] ICR 771 that the employer had an obligation arising under an implied term of the contract of the right to carry over annual leave, so that the worker could inform the employer of her intention to exercise this right. It has since been held that there is no duty to give such notice: *NHS Leeds* v. *Larner* [2012] EWCA Civ 1034, [2012] ICR 1389.

would include details of working hours as well as 'the intervals allowed for meals or rest to those women and young persons [employed in the factory]'.

It is true that the employer is now required to provide a statement of particulars that ought to include details of working time.[240] But this applies only to employees rather than workers, and relates only to contractual rather than statutory rights of the kind found in the Regulations. Information is, however, provided on various government and public body websites (such as those of BEIS, ACAS and the HSE).

The information provided on the government's website in relation to daily and weekly rest periods stated that 'employers must make sure that workers can take their rest, but are not required to make sure they do take their rest'.[241] In enforcement proceedings brought by the European Commission, it was held that the provision of information of this kind violated the government's obligations under the Directive.

According to the Court:

the guidelines are clearly liable to render the rights enshrined in Articles 3 and 5 of that directive meaningless and are incompatible with the objective of that directive, in which minimum rest periods are considered to be essential for the protection of workers' health and safety (see, to that effect, *BECTU*, paragraph 49).[242]

In so holding, the Court reinforced its view that, in line with 'the essential purpose' of the Directive, each worker must 'enjoy adequate rest periods, which must not only be effective in enabling the persons concerned to recover from the fatigue engendered by their work, but also preventive in nature, so as to reduce as much as possible the risk of affecting the safety or health of employees which successive periods of work without the necessary rest are likely to produce'.[243]

Claims for unpaid holiday pay can also be brought under ERA 1996, section 23, as an unauthorised deduction from wages. The benefit to the worker, however, is that the time limits under the latter are potentially more generous than under regulation 30. In *HM Revenue and Customs* v. *Stringer*,[244] it was held that although payments under regulation 16 (holiday pay) were clearly wages for the purposes of the 1996 Act, payments under regulation 14 (payments in lieu of annual leave on termination) were more difficult in light

---

[240] ERA 1996, s. 1. See pp. 115–20.

[241] Case C-484/04, *Commission* v. *United Kingdom* [2006] ECR I-7471. If, however, the employer has taken active steps to ensure working arrangements that enable the worker to take the requisite rest-break, it will have met the obligation upon it: workers cannot be forced to take the rest-breaks but they are to be positively enabled to do so: *Grange* v. *Abellio London Ltd* [2017] IRLR 108.

[242] Case C-484/04, *Commission* v. *United Kingdom* [2006] ECR I-747, para. 44.

[243] *Ibid.*, para. 41.

[244] [2009] UKHL 31, [2009] ICR 985 (HL). The Court of Appeal had reached a different conclusion on this point: *Inland Revenue Commissioners* v. *Ainsworth* [2005] EWCA Civ 441, [2005] ICR 1149 (CA).

of the earlier decision of the House of Lords in *Delaney* v. *Staples*,[245] where it had been held that payments in lieu of notice were not wages. However, the latter was distinguished, Lord Rodger expressing the view that:

> the payment in lieu of leave is one which the worker has earned by working for the relevant proportion of the leave year. So, even though he receives it only when his employment has been terminated, just like any other final payment of wages, it is part of the consideration for the services which he has previously performed under his contract of employment.

The right to recover holiday pay under ERA 1996, section 23 is limited to sums due within the two years before the claim was presented to the employment tribunal.[246] But this may have to be reviewed in light of Case C-214/16, *King* v. *Sash Window Workshop Ltd*,[247] where the worker was entitled to recover the full amount of holiday pay withheld by the employer, even though this stretched back over many years.[248]

Individual Remedies and Regulation 4

A striking omission from the right of individual enforcement is the right of the worker to enforce the restriction on the forty-eight hour week.[249] Two attempts have been made to address this gap. In *Barber* v. *RJB Mining Ltd*,[250] a group of pit deputies challenged their employer's insistence that they work in excess of forty-eight hours a week, having refused to opt out of the Regulations. Having been required to work for more than forty-eight hours in the previous seventeen weeks, the pit deputies sought a declaration of their rights under regulation 4 of the Regulations and an injunction to enforce these rights, arguing that the Regulations incorporated into their contracts of employment an enforceable right to work no more than forty-eight hours a week. Gage J agreed that 'Parliament intended that all contracts of employment should be read so as to provide that an employee should work no more than an average of 48 hours in any week during the reference period.'[251]

---

[245] [1992] 1 AC 687. See p. 263, above.   [246] SI 2014 No. 3322, amending ERA 1996, s. 23.

[247] [2018] IRLR 142 (distinguishing *Schultz-Hoff*, above, and *KHS*, above).

[248] This calls into question the restrictions introduced in 2014 insofar as they apply to the core annual leave derived from WTD, Art. 7, and contained in reg. 13 (but not additional annual leave in reg. 13A).

[249] This is perhaps all the more striking in view of the decision of the ECJ that Art. 6 of the Directive has direct effect: Case C-397/01, *Pfeiffer* v. *Deutsches Rotes Kreuz* [2004] ECR I-08835.

[250] [1999] ICR 679 (QB).

[251] *Ibid.*, p. 690. Parliament has expressly provided in contrast that the right to holiday pay arises by virtue of statute only and does not give rise to contractual remedies, in a measure designed to restrict enforcement options: SI 2014 No. 3323, reg. 3. Were the 'contractual' right in the Regulations, reg. 4 to have produced a meaningful contractual remedy, we could expect the same to have happened in relation to it as well.

He also held that the claimants' rights under regulation 4 had been breached, this having the effect that they could 'if they so choose ... refuse to continue working until the average working hours come within the specified limit'.[252] But although a declaration was thus granted, the application for an injunction to prevent the employer from requiring the claimants to work in breach of the Regulations was refused. Nevertheless, the finding that breach of the forty-eight-hour limit is a breach of contract is an important one, even if it may be a term that the High Court has made very difficult to enforce in practice.

In *Sayers* v. *Cambridgeshire County Council*,[253] doubt was cast on the decision in *Barber*. It was said by counsel for the employer to conflict with the decision of the Court of Appeal in *Inland Revenue Commissioners* v. *Ainsworth*,[254] which 'appeared to proceed on the assumption that [*Barber*] is wrongly decided'.[255] To add further to the confusion, however, the Court of Appeal decision in *Ainsworth* appears to be of little authority following the decision of the ECJ in *Stringer*, and the subsequent decision of the House of Lords in the same case.[256] But even so, the decision in *Barber* leaves workers in practice without the means to take legal action to enforce their right to work no more than forty-eight hours a week. The best option would appear to be to adopt the advice of Gage J and refuse to work for more than the law permits. But this will almost inevitably lead to some form of retribution from the employer, though workers do have a right not to suffer a detriment and employees have a right not to be dismissed because they 'refused (or proposed to refuse) to comply with a requirement which the employer imposed (or proposed to impose) in contravention of the [Regulations]'.[257] Whether empowering individual workers to sue to enforce the forty-eight-hour limit would make much difference is unclear. But it certainly cannot help that, at a time when the HSE is under pressure, the High Court should hold that breach of regulation 4 does not give rise to an action in tort for breach of a statutory duty,[258] thereby denying workers the right even to recover losses (such as damage to health) arising from the employer's breach.[259]

---

[252] [1999] ICR 679 (QB), p. 692.   [253] [2006] EWHC 2029, [2007] IRLR 29 (QB), para. 282.

[254] [2005] EWCA Civ 441, [2005] ICR 1149 (CA).

[255] [2006] EWHC 2029, [2007] IRLR 29 (QB), para. 263.

[256] Joined Cases C-350/06 and C-520/06, *Schultz-Hoff* v. *Deutsch Rentenversicherung Bund*; *Stringer* v. *HM Revenue and Customs* [2009] ECR I-179; *HM Revenue and Customs* v. *Stringer* [2009] UKHL 31, [2009] ICR 985 (HL).

[257] ERA 1996, ss. 45 A(1)(b) and 101A(1)(b).

[258] *Sayers* v. *Cambridgeshire County Council* [2006] EWHC 2029, [2007] IRLR 29 (QB). Having regard to the enforcement procedure in the Regulations and the opt-out provisions in reg. 5, Ramsey J thought that it was not intended that there should be a cause of action for breach of statutory duty. Note that the Enterprise and Regulatory Reform Act 2013, s. 69 (removal of civil liability for breach of health and safety duties) does not apply to the Working Time Regulations.

[259] Nor can it help that a worker who has been required to work in excess of the maximum (as in the case of a worker required to be on call) has no right under the Directive (or the

Conclusion

We conclude this chapter with three questions. The first is what will happen to working time rights after Brexit? This is one of the areas where domestic law has been most heavily influenced by EU obligations. It is not, however, only the protection of the legislation that is a matter of concern,[260] with the loss of access to the CJEU also significant. This is because the CJEU has had an important role not only in ensuring that the UK complied with its core obligations under the Directive, but also in expanding the reach of these obligations with a purposive approach to interpretation that sometimes leaves domestic judges bemused. Post-Brexit this will all become EU-derived UK law, save for the EU Charter of Fundamental Rights which will cease to have any effect in the UK, despite being an important source of inspiration of the CJEU's largely progressive jurisprudence. It is true that the European Union (Withdrawal) Act 2018 provides for the continued binding effect of pre-Brexit CJEU jurisprudence.[261] But it also provides that the latter decisions may be overruled by the UK Supreme Court,[262] making clear that while post-Brexit jurisprudence may be taken into account by the domestic courts, it will not have binding effect.[263] Quite apart from the risk that the Working Time Regulations may now be amended if not revoked, there is a danger of an interpretive gap opening up between EU law and EU-derived law as a result of the different traditions of the different courts.

The second question is whether the current limits on working time are sufficient. The main problem is the opt-out, which gives scope to the argument that there is no limit on working time at all. Although negotiated by the UK government, it is not only the UK that makes use of the opt-out, the Commission claiming that it is now used by other Member States (although some permit it only in sectors or activities which make heavy use of on-call time).[264] According to the Commission, political consensus on ending the opt-out is unachievable, so that 'it makes more sense to reduce the need for using the opt-out in the long term, by providing more targeted forms of flexibility'.[265] In countries where the opt-out is used, however, this would appear to be the worst of both worlds: no regulation for many (by reason of the opt-out), plus inadequate regulation for all (by reason of greater flexibility). In truth, the end

---

Regulations) to claim remuneration for the excessive hours: Case C-437/05, *Vorel* v. *Nemocnice Český Krumlov* [2007] ECR I-331.

[260] See K. D. Ewing, 'Implications of the Post-Brexit Architecture for Labour Law' (2017) 28 *King's Law Journal* 403. The concern is not so much that the Working Time Regulations will be revoked but that they will be amended to regain some of the ground lost in litigation, and to respond to employer concerns for greater flexibility around breaks, rest periods, the definition of working time, and holiday pay.

[261] European Union (Withdrawal) Act 2018, s. 6(3).   [262] *Ibid.*, s. 6(4).

[263] *Ibid.*, s. 6(1)–(2).

[264] European Commission, Reviewing the Working Time Directive, COM (2010) 810 final, p. 14.

[265] *Ibid.*

of the opt-out and the introduction of effective limits on working time cannot be dealt with in isolation from other aspects of working conditions, particularly those relating to pay. One reason why some people work long hours is because of low pay, and it is implausible to suggest that working time could be reduced by law without at the same time raising wages. Workers who most need to reduce their hours in order to protect their health are the same workers who most need to increase their hours in order to maintain their income.

The third question is whether there is a need not only to limit maximum working hours, but also now to guarantee minimum working hours. The question is prompted by the proliferation of part-time work, and the growth in the use of zero-hours contracts in particular, with many workers now unable to secure enough working time to make decent life sustainable.[266] The latter has seen the introduction of working time proposals in the European Commission's otherwise lamentable Social Pillar initiative.[267] It has also led to several private member's bills, though little by way of government awareness or concern.[268] This in turn nevertheless prompts wider questions relating to the shortage of work to meet the needs of all, concerns once reflected in ILO Convention 47 (Forty Hour Week Convention, 1935). Here, a forty-hour rather than a forty-eight-hour week was proposed to deal with the shortage of work, which at the time was causing 'hardship and privation' among workers, for 'which they are not themselves responsible and from which they are justly entitled to be relieved'.[269] If we see work as a resource, is there a case for saying that it needs to be allocated or shared on a more equitable basis than is currently the case? Alongside the traditional concern of labour law for legally mandated minimum wages and maximum hours, is there now also a case for maximum wages and minimum hours?

---

[266] See A. Adams and J. Prassl, *Zero-Hours Work in the United Kingdom* (Geneva: ILO, 2018).

[267] On the Social Pillar, see European Commission, European Pillar of Social Rights (2017). For comment, see A. Bogg and K. D. Ewing, 'A Tale of Two Documents: The Eclipse of the Social Democratic Constitution', in E. Nanopoulos and F. Vergis (eds.), *The Crisis Behind the Euro-Crisis: The Euro-Crisis as a Multi-Dimensional Systematic Crisis of the EU* (forthcoming).

[268] Zero Hours Contracts Bill 2014 (sponsored by Ian Mearns MP, Labour Party), and Workers (Definition and Rights) Bill 2018 (sponsored by Chris Stephens MP, SNP). These were both drafted by the second-named author. Both bills are available on the Parliament website.

[269] ILO Convention 47 (Forty-Hour-Week Convention, 1935), preamble. The forty-hour week was also designed to enable workers 'to share in the benefits of the rapid technical progress which is a characteristic of modern industry'. ILO Convention 47 has been ratified by only fifteen countries, including only three EU Member States.

9

Equality

Contents

Introduction

This chapter is concerned with anti-discrimination law, namely, the EqA 2010 which replaced its many predecessor provisions governing discrimination.[1] The only major discrimination legislation which survives the implementation of the EqA 2010 in Great Britain is the Equality Act 2006 insofar as it establishes the Equality and Human Rights Commission.

The EqA 2010 extends well beyond the area of employment (broadly understood) to regulate discrimination in housing, in access to goods, facilities and services and in the exercise by public authorities of their functions. It protects against discrimination connected with 'protected characteristics' (age, disability, gender reassignment, marriage and civil partnership, race, religion or belief, sex and sexual orientation). It also imposes positive obligations on public authorities to pay 'due regard' to the need to eliminate discrimination and promote equality related to the 'protected characteristics'. Like its predecessor provisions, it operates by defining various types of discrimination, then prohibiting such discrimination across a range of areas (most importantly, for our purposes, in relation to employment, broadly defined).

The EqA 2010 cannot be considered in isolation from underlying EU provisions,[2] although for the most part the Act appears to implement EU law without obvious gaps or flaws. Where there are questions over compatibility, with the result that the Act may be interpreted or require amendment so as to comply with the underlying EU provisions, this will be mentioned in the text, although this is an issue the practical significance of which is likely to change in light of the UK's likely withdrawal from the EU.

The Act's prohibitions on discrimination apply in relation to employment, broadly defined to include a personal work contract.[3] The protection extends to contract workers, police officers, business partners, barristers and (in Scotland) advocates, office holders (sections 49 and 50), but 'employment' is defined as 'employment under a contract of service or of apprenticeship' or a contract 'personally to do work' (section 83). Neither the EqA 2010 nor its predecessor provisions extends to volunteers although they do apply to protect applicants for work.[4]

Qualifications bodies, providers of employment services and 'trade organisations' (unions and employers' organisations) are covered by the prohibitions on discrimination.[5] The prohibitions on discrimination in relation to all the protected characteristics apply to local authorities *vis-à-vis* members of the

---

[1] The EqA 2010 does not apply in Northern Ireland which has yet to adopt a comprehensive equality Act.

[2] In particular, Art. 157 of the Treaty on the Functioning of the EU (previously Art. 141 EC and Council Directives 2000/43, 2000/78 and 2006/54 (respectively the race, employment equality and 'recast' gender Directives)).

[3] *Hashwani* v. *Jivraj* [2011] ICR 87. See Chapter 6.   [4] *Ibid.*

[5] Respectively, ss. 53–4, 55–6 and 58.

authority who are carrying out official business.[6] The detail of the EqA 2010's material scope is dealt with further below, after we consider some of the major issues of principle that arise under the EqA 2010, namely, on what grounds is discrimination regulated and what is meant by 'discrimination'.

'Protected Characteristics'

EqA 2010, section 4, lists as 'protected characteristics', discrimination relating to which is regulated, 'age; disability; gender reassignment;[7] marriage and civil partnership; pregnancy and maternity; race; religion or belief; sex [and] sexual orientation'.[8] These concepts will be briefly introduced here and, where necessary, considered in more detail just below:

- 'Age' is not defined by the EqA 2010 which, however, makes it clear (section 5) that a person may complain about being discriminated against because she is a member of a particular age group (the explanatory notes point out that this could be '"over fifties" or twenty-one year olds' and that, while a person of twenty-one is not in the same age group as 'people in their forties', they are all in the 'under fifty' age group).[9] A claim could also be based on having been 'too old' or 'too young' for the job.
- A person ('P') is generally defined as having a 'disability' for the purposes of the EqA 2010 if (section 6) he or she 'has a physical or mental impairment' which 'has a substantial and long-term adverse effect on P's ability to carry out normal day-to-day activities'. The Act protects those who have had a disability, as well as those who are currently disabled.[10] The concept of disability is discussed further below.
- 'Gender reassignment' is defined as 'a process which is undertaken under medical supervision for the purpose of reassigning a person's sex by changing physiological or other characteristics of sex, and includes any part of such a process'.[11] The Act protects anyone who 'is proposing to undergo, is undergoing or has undergone a process (or part of a process) for the purpose of reassigning the person's sex by changing physiological or other attributes of sex', no requirement being imposed for medical involvement in the actual or planned process of reassignment.
- The Act protects those who are married or in civil partnerships from discrimination connected with that status in the context of employment

---

[6] Ss. 58 and 9.

[7] Discrimination connected with gender reassignment was recognised as a species of gender discrimination by the ECJ in Case 13/94, *P* v. *S and Cornwall County Council* [1996] ECR I-2143.

[8] Discrimination connected with sexual orientation was not accepted as amounting to a form of gender discrimination by the High Court in *R* v. *Ministry of Defence, ex parte Smith and Others* [1996] QB 517 or by the ECJ in Case 249/96, *Grant* v. *South West Trains* [1998] ECR I-0621 but was subsequently regulated by Council Directive 2000/78 and, from 2003, by domestic law.

[9] Para. 37.   [10] S. 6(4).   [11] S. 82(1).

(but not otherwise). In common with disability discrimination, but by contrast with discrimination related to most of the protected characteristics, protection from discrimination related to married or civilly partnered status is asymmetrical in the sense that the protection applies only to those who are, and not to those who are not, married or civilly partnered.

- Also asymmetrical is the protection provided by the EqA 2010 in relation to pregnancy and maternity, section 18 providing that 'A person (A) discriminates against a woman if [while she is pregnant or on maternity leave] ... A treats her unfavourably – (a) because of the pregnancy, or (b) because of illness suffered by her as a result of it', or because she is on maternity leave or is attempting to exercise maternity rights or to return from maternity leave.[12] The term 'unfavourably' is used, rather than 'less favourably', because ECJ case-law makes it clear that no comparator is needed to establish pregnancy discrimination.
- 'Race' is defined (section 9) to include 'colour; nationality; [and] ethnic or national origins'. Discrimination against (say) Irish people would be caught within the prohibition on nationality discrimination, and the prohibition on discrimination on grounds of national origin is breached by discrimination as between English and Scottish people (equally between Northern Irish and Welsh).[13]
- 'Religion' is defined to mean 'any religion' and 'a lack of religion', while '[b]elief means any religious or philosophical belief ... [or] a lack of belief' (section 10). Religion and belief are discussed further below.

Disability

The definition of 'disability' is set out above. It is largely a medical and functional test, rather than one which regards disability as being a product of the environment (this is called the 'social model' of disability and highlights the fact that a wheelchair user is not 'disabled' in terms of her functioning in an environment which is designed for wheelchair users). It is for a claimant to establish that he or she is (or has been) disabled in a claim under the EqA 2010, this generally requiring medical evidence.

EqA 2010, Schedule 1, Part 1 provides that some conditions (cancer, HIV infection and multiple sclerosis (MS)) qualify as disabilities without more.[14] So too do severe disfigurements[15] while anyone who is certified as 'blind, severely sight impaired, sight impaired or partially sighted by a consultant ophthalmologist' is deemed to be disabled for the purposes of the Act.[16] Progressive

---

[12] S. 18(5) provides that 'if the treatment of a woman is in implementation of a decision taken [while she was pregnant or on leave] ... the treatment is to be regarded as occurring in that period (even if the implementation is not until after the end of that period)'.

[13] *Northern Joint Police Board* v. *Power* [1997] IRLR 610 (EAT) and *BBC Scotland* v. *Souster* [2001] IRLR 150 (CS).

[14] Para. 5.   [15] Para. 3.   [16] Equality Act 2010 (Disability) Regulations 2010, reg. 7.

conditions other than cancer, HIV and MS which will probably result in substantial impairment of a person's ability to carry out normal day-to-day activities will be regarded as disabilities from the point at which they have some such effect.[17]

In other cases, 'disability' requires (1) 'physical or mental impairment' with a (2) 'substantial' and (3) 'long-term adverse effect' on a person's ability to carry out normal day-to-day activities.

As to (1), the Equality Act 2010 (Disability) Regulations 2010, Part 2, provide that 'impairments' do not include, for the purposes of the EqA 2010, addictions to alcohol, nicotine or any substance other than prescribed drugs.[18] 2011 'Guidance on Matters to be Taken into Account in Determining Questions Relating to the Definition of Disability', which must be followed by tribunals, points out that conditions produced by or associated with impairments (such as liver disease or depression) may well amount to disabilities.[19] Exhibitionism, voyeurism and the tendency to set fires, to steal or to engage in physical or sexual abuse of others are also excluded from recognition as 'impairments' as is hay fever, except in cases where it aggravates the effect of another condition,[20] while tattoos (except where they have been removed) and non-medical piercings are not to be regarded as having a substantial adverse effect on the ability to carry out normal day-to-day activities.[21]

As to (2), '"substantial" means more than minor or trivial'.[22] 'An impairment is to be treated as having a substantial adverse effect on the ability of the person concerned to carry out normal day-to-day activities if (a) measures are being taken to treat or correct it, and (b) but for that, it would be likely to have that effect',[23] 'measures' being defined to include 'the use of a prosthesis or other aid' but not the wearing of spectacles or contact lenses.

If such 'measures' have produced a permanent improvement (as might be the case with drug or counselling treatment of depression), the level of the adverse effect on the ability to carry out normal day-to-day activities should be judged by reference to the (permanently) improved state. Where, by contrast, the improvement is dependent on the ongoing treatment (as might be the case with a steel rod inserted into a person's body), the person's level of functioning is to be judged as if the treatment had been withdrawn.[24] This is so even where (as may be the case with diabetes or epilepsy, for example) ongoing treatment has the effect of completely controlling the symptoms of a condition such that the person does not appear to be impaired in any way.

---

[17] Para. 8.   [18] Reg. 3.
[19] Para. A7. The Guidance is issued under EqA 2010, s. 6(5). EqA 2010, Sched. 1, para. 12, states that the guidance must be taken into account by any adjudicating body determining whether someone is disabled for the purposes of the Act.
[20] Reg. 4.   [21] Reg. 5.   [22] S. 212.   [23] Para. 5.
[24] *Abadeh* v. *British Telecommunications* [2001] IRLR 23; *Carden* v. *Pickerings Europe Ltd* [2005] IRLR 720.

As to (3), a condition will be regarded as 'long term' if 'it has lasted for at least 12 months, it is likely to last for at least 12 months, or it is likely to last for the rest of the life of the person affected'.[25] Further, if an impairment has had, and is likely again to have, a substantial adverse effect on a person's ability to carry out normal day-to-day activities, it is to be treated as continuing to have that effect.[26]

Perhaps optimistically, the 2011 Guidance suggests (paragraph 3) that '[i]n the vast majority of cases there is unlikely to be any doubt whether or not a person has or has had a disability, but this guidance should prove helpful where the matter is not entirely clear'.

In *Goodwin* v. *Patent Office*,[27] a case decided under the Disability Discrimination Act (DDA) 1995 but still good law, the EAT ruled (*per* Morison J) that a tribunal faced with a claim of disability should ask itself the following four questions:

> [1] Does the applicant have an impairment which is either mental or physical? ... [2] Does the impairment affect the applicant's ability to carry out normal day-to-day activities ... and does it have an adverse effect? ... [3] Is the adverse condition (upon the applicant's ability) substantial? ... [4] Is the adverse condition (upon the applicant's ability) long-term?

There would, he said, often be a 'complete overlap between conditions (3) and (4), but it will be as well to bear all four of them in mind'. It was also important to note that disabled people often made adjustments to their lives by reason of their disabilities ('a person whose capacity to communicate through normal speech was obviously impaired might well choose, more or less voluntarily, to live on their own'). Such adjustments might allow the disabled person to get on with daily life without undue difficulty but the person's 'ability to lead a "normal" life' would still have been impaired.

Morison J's third question (whether an impairment has a 'substantial' effect) is one for the tribunal, rather than a medical expert, and should be determined in marginal cases having regard to the Secretary of State's Guidance.[28] In *Vicary* v. *British Telecommunications plc*,[29] a tribunal had ruled that a woman who was unable to prepare vegetables, cut meat or roast potatoes or carry a meal on a tray did not suffer from any impairment which substantially impaired her ability to carry out her normal day-to-day activities. The EAT allowed the claimant's appeal, emphasising that 'substantial' meant

---

[25] Para. 2.

[26] Para. 2. Note that the likelihood of recurrence is to be judged at the time of the alleged discrimination rather than with the benefit of hindsight (*Richmond Adult Community College* v. *McDougall* [2008] IRLR 227).

[27] [1999] ICR 302 (EAT).

[28] The predecessor guidance to the 2011 Guidance considered above, which was in materially similar terms.

[29] [1999] IRLR 680 (EAT).

no more than 'more than ... minor or trivial' and that it should have been clear to a tribunal, even without reference to the guidance, that the claimant met the test. And in *Leonard* v. *Southern Derbyshire Chamber of Commerce*[30] the EAT emphasised that tribunals ought not to balance what a claimant could do against what she could not do for the purposes of determining whether her condition substantially impaired her ability to carry out normal day-to-day activities. In that case the claimant, who was clinically depressed, was able to eat and drink and catch a ball but could not negotiate pavement edges safely. The EAT ruled that the tribunal had erred in balancing the former abilities against the latter disability, as her ability to catch a ball did not assist the claimant in negotiating pavements. The tribunal ought to have concentrated on what a claimant could not do or could do only with difficulty.[31]

Race

One of the major questions which arose in the past in relation to definitions of the various protected grounds concerned the boundaries of 'race'. This was highly significant when there was no or limited protection from discrimination connected with religion and belief (as was the case prior to 2006). Thus the decision of the House of Lords in *Mandla and Another* v. *Dowell Lee and Another* was very important in its articulation of the meaning of 'ethnic origins'.[32]

The particular question their Lordships there addressed concerned whether the less favourable treatment of the claimant as a Sikh was race discrimination in the sense of being discrimination on grounds of ethnicity (there being no argument that it was discrimination related to nationality, colour or national origin). Lord Fraser stated that '"ethnic" is used nowadays in an extended sense to include other characteristics which may be commonly thought of as being associated with common racial origin', and laid emphasis on factors such as history, cultural tradition, common geography or descent, common language, literature and religion rendering the group distinct from the minority and 'being a minority or being an oppressed or a dominant group within a larger community, for example a conquered people'. Lord Templeman suggested that 'a group of persons defined by reference to ethnic origins must possess some of the characteristics of a race, namely group descent, a group of geographical origin and a group history'.

The decision in *Mandla* allowed some, but not all, religious/cultural discrimination to be caught by the Race Relations Act (RRA) 1976. It had already been accepted by the EAT that Jews could be defined as a racial group by reference to race or ethnic origin and that 'gypsies', as distinct from 'travellers',

---

[30] [2001] IRLR 19 (EAT).
[31] See also *Chief Constable of Lothian and Borders Police* v. *Cumming* [2010] IRLR 109.
[32] [1983] 2 AC 548.

also qualified.[33] Rastafarians were (in 1993) denied protection against race discrimination on the ground that they lacked a sufficiently long 'shared history' to satisfy the test set out by Lord Fraser in *Mandla*.[34] And discrimination against Muslims proved particularly difficult to bring within the framework of the RRA 1976 while Islam, being (like Christianity) a world religion, lacked sufficient connection with 'race' to qualify under the *Mandla* test.[35]

The overlap between 'race' and 'religion' fell to be considered by the Supreme Court in *E* v. *JFS*,[36] which concerned the ability of a Jewish school to select on grounds of maternal descent, this being a standard test for Jewishness. The particular treatment challenged in the *JFS* case would have been lawful if it was determined to amount only to religious, rather than race, discrimination. In the context of work, however, the differences in the protections afforded against discrimination connected with race and religion are limited, and the questions of whether and to what extent the less favourable treatment of particular religious/cultural groups also amounts to race discrimination is not one which is likely to generate much litigation.

Section 9(5) of the EqA 2010 has, since 2013, required that a 'minister of the Crown must by order amend this section so as to provide for caste to be an aspect of race'.[37] First plans to put this into effect were shelved following the decision of the EAT in *Chandhok & Anor* v. *Tirkey* that caste discrimination is capable of being unlawful under current law,[38] but following threatened legal action a public consultation was held in 2017 on 'whether caste is required to be an aspect of race in the Equality Act', and legislation has yet to be adopted at the time of writing.[39]

The 2017 Consultation Paper indicated concern about possible unintended consequences of including caste within race either by the evolution of case-law, the likely effect of which would be to apply exactly the same rules to caste as to other aspects of race/ethnicity, or by legislation, which would allow for

---

[33] Respectively, *Seide* v. *Gillette* [1980] IRLR 427 and *Commission for Racial Equality* v. *Dutton* [1989] QB 783. Irish travellers were accepted as an ethnic group by the County Court in *O'Leary* v. *Allied Domecq* (unreported, 2000) and by the Race Relations (Northern Ireland) Order 1997.

[34] *Dawkins* v. *Department of the Environment* [1993] ICR 517 (CA).

[35] See, for example, B. Hepple and T. Choudhury, *Tackling Religious Discrimination: Practical Implications for Policy-Makers and Legislators* (Home Office Research Study 221, London: Home Office, 2001), p. 12.

[36] [2010] 2 AC 728.

[37] As amended by the Enterprise and Regulatory Reform Act 2013, s. 97. For discussion of caste discrimination in Great Britain see the House of Commons Briefing Paper (2015, http://researchbriefings.parliament.uk/ResearchBriefing/Summary/SN06862).

[38] [2015] IRLR 195. The question of caste had also been considered by ETs in *Naveed* v. *Aslam* (ET/1603968/2011, 26 November 2012), in which the tribunal did not accept that it could be seen as an aspect of race discrimination, and *Begraj* v. *Heer Manak Solicitors*, in which the hearing was aborted for reasons unconnected with the merits of the case after thirty days of evidence (see the EAT's decision at [2014] IRLR 689).

[39] See 'Caste in Great Britain and Equality Law: A Public Consultation', available at www.gov.uk/government/consultations/caste-in-great-britain-and-equality-law-a-public-consulation (accessed 2 March 2018).

the particular treatment of caste as regards (for example) the scope of any prohibition on discrimination and the provision of exceptions thereto. According to the Consultation Paper, 'caste is a controversial and sensitive issue' of which there is 'very little knowledge and understanding . . . in Great Britain and no universally accepted functional definition of caste which can be relied on. . . There remains the danger of stereotyping caste as a discriminatory practice of certain ethnic groups creating potential problems in the harmony of the social fabric of modern British society.'[40] The paper noted that 'People who identify, or are regarded by others, as Dalits are considered to be the main victims of caste discrimination, and proposals to prohibit caste discrimination are normally associated with a desire to protect them', but that 'the inclusion of caste as an aspect of race within the Equality Act could potentially have unintended implications for members of those communities which are most naturally associated with issues of caste more generally'.[41]

Religion/Belief

The EqA 2010 does not define 'religion or belief' other than to state that 'belief means any religious or philosophical belief' and that lack of religion and lack of belief are included within the terms. The explanatory notes to the Act state that the Act's approach is 'broad' and 'is in line with the freedom of thought, conscience and religion guaranteed by Article 9 of the European Convention on Human Rights'.[42] The notes go on to state that '[t]he main limitation for the purposes of Article 9 is that the religion must have a clear structure and belief system. Denominations or sects within a religion can be considered to be a religion or belief, such as Protestants and Catholics within Christianity.'[43]

The explanatory notes and the Code of Practice on Employment produced by the Equality and Human Rights Commission suggest that, in order to qualify for protection under the Act, a 'philosophical belief' must be (1) 'genuinely held', (2) 'a belief and not an opinion or viewpoint based on the present state of information available',[44] (3) 'a belief as to a weighty and substantial aspect of human life and behaviour', which (4) must 'attain a certain level of cogency, seriousness, cohesion and importance'; and (5) 'be worthy of respect in a democratic society, not incompatible with human dignity and not conflict with the fundamental rights of others'.[45] This 'checklist' is based on the decision of the EAT in *Grainger plc* v. *Nicholson*.[46]

One difficulty with it is that it is capable of accommodating almost any respectable belief. Thus, in *Grainger plc* v. *Nicholson*, the EAT accepted that the 'beliefs' protected by the EqA 2010 in a similar fashion to ethnicity, sexual orientation and gender etc. included a belief that climate change is the result of

---

[40] Para. 1.8   [41] Para. 2.3.   [42] Para. 51.   [43] *Ibid.*
[44] Cf. *McClintock* v. *Department for Constitutional Affairs* [2008] IRLR 29.
[45] Paras. 52 and 2.59, respectively.   [46] [2010] IRLR 4 (EAT).

human behaviour. ETs have also accepted as 'protected characteristics' under the Act the 'belief that public service broadcasting has the higher purpose of promoting cultural interchange and social cohesion' and a 'fervent anti fox-hunting belief (and also anti hare coursing belief)'.[47] These decisions were given implicit support by *Harron* v. *CC Devon Police* in which the EAT remitted to a tribunal the question whether the claimant's view that public service was improperly wasteful of money amounted to a protected belief.[48] The tribunal had ruled that, while genuinely held, the claimant's belief did not satisfy elements 2–4 of the *Grainger*/Code of Practice test:

> it is not on the particular facts of this case, a belief as to weighty and substantial aspects of human life and behaviour and its level of cogency, seriousness or cohesion importance is entirely confined to the workplace rather than human life and behaviour in general [sic]... [it] is not so much a belief but a set of values which manifest themselves as an objective or goal principally operating in the work place. The fact that the belief is worthy of respect in a democratic society is not challenged...

The EAT ruled that the tribunal's decision was inadequately reasoned and remitted the question for reconsideration.

Whether the *Grainger* approach amounts to an over-extension of the protection of the EqA 2010 is an important question. The final criterion imposed by that decision attempts to avoid a situation in which protection can be demanded under the EqA 2010 from discrimination because of a person's beliefs, for example, in white supremacy. Attractive as this attempt may be, however, the inclusion of the final criterion within the *Grainger* list appears to result from a misunderstanding on the part of the courts[49] as to the Article 9 jurisprudence. Article 9 protects all beliefs, however unattractive, insofar as it provides an absolute right to hold religious and other beliefs, although the right to manifest beliefs is subject to qualifications, and justifications for its limitation may turn in part on the nature of the belief (at least where its manifestation is incompatible with the convention rights of others).[50] The rubric about 'convictions ... worthy of respect in a "democratic society" [which] are not incompatible with human dignity',[51] is in fact taken

---

[47] See, respectively, *Maistry* v. *BBC*, ET Case No. 1313142/2010 (the ET's conclusion on this was not questioned by the Court of Appeal which refused the claimant permission to appeal on another aspect of the case: [2014] EWCA Civ 1116), and *Hashman* v. *Milton Park*, ET Case No. 3105555/2009. Cf. *R (Brown)* v. *Canal River Trust* [2012] EWHC 3133 (Admin) in which the High Court ruled that a choice to live on a boat did not meet the threshold.

[48] [2016] IRLR 481.

[49] Including by the House of Lords in *Williamson* v. *Secretary of State for Education and Employment* [2005] 2 AC 246.

[50] ECHR, Art. 17, prohibiting reliance on Convention rights to defeat the rights of others.

[51] Applied by the House of Lords in *Williamson* v. *Secretary of State for Education and Employment* [2005] 2 AC 246 as a criteria of 'beliefs' protected by Art. 9, and subsequently adopted in *Grainger*.

from a decision of the ECtHR in a case concerned with the application of a wholly different provision, namely, Article 1 of Protocol 1, which provides that 'the State shall respect the right of parents to ensure ... education and teaching in conformity with their own religious and philosophical convictions'.[52] The ECtHR ruled, in relation to Article 1 of Protocol 1, that, '[h]aving regard to the Convention as a whole, including Article 17, the expression "philosophical convictions" in the present context' was limited to those 'worthy of respect in a democratic society' etc. This approach has limited application to Article 9, however, whose protection for the right to hold beliefs (although not to manifest them) is, as was mentioned above, absolute.

The importance of this point is that the parameters of 'religion or belief' under the EqA 2010 and its predecessor legislation are intended, and taken, to reflect those imposed by Article 9. This being the case, it is only a question of time before the point is taken that the Act protects all beliefs which satisfy the first four of the *Grainger* requirements, with the fourth being interpreted so as not to require a value judgement on the content of the belief in question. Protected beliefs might then be understood to include, for example, beliefs in white supremacy, female subordination and/or the evils of homosexuality. Certainly, these beliefs form part, or have previously formed part, of many mainstream religious views.

Gender Identity

The EqA protects from discrimination because of 'sex' (being a man or a woman) and 'gender reassigment' (proposing to undergo, undergoing or having undergone a process (or part of a process) for the purpose of reassigning the person's sex by changing physiological or other attributes of sex). The House of Commons Women and Equalities Committee (WEC) recommended in 2016 that the Act should be amended to protect against discrimination because of 'gender identity',[53] defined by the Yogyakarta Principles[54] as an individual's 'deeply felt internal and individual experience of gender, which may or may not correspond with the sex assigned at birth, including the personal sense of the body (which may involve, if freely chosen, modification of bodily appearance or function by medical, surgical or other means) and other expressions of gender, including dress, speech and mannerism'.

The WEC's report pointed out that 'Trans people "have a gender identity which differs from that of their (assigned) birth sex"' with trans identities

---

[52] *Campbell and Cosans* v. *UK* (1982) 4 EHRR 293.
[53] First Report of Session 2015–16, *Transgender Equality*, HC 390 (January 2016).
[54] The Yogyakarta Principles on the Application of International Human Rights Law in relation to Sexual Orientation and Gender Identity, adopted by the International Commission of Jurists in 2007.

taking a 'wide variety of forms' including '"non-binary"... located at a (fixed or variable) point along a continuum between male and female; or "non-gendered", i.e. involving identification as neither male nor female'. It also referred to the difficulties faced by intersex people, although it pointed out that not all such people identify as transgender. The model adopted by the EqA is to presuppose that trans people can be defined by reference to a process of transition which, as the WEC pointed out, tends not to reflect people's lived experiences. The Committee recommended that the EqA 2010 be amended to protect from discrimination because of 'gender identity', which would apply on the basis of self-identification. It also recommended that the genuine occupational requirement (GOR) exemptions in the EqA 2010 (see further below) be amended so as not to apply to anyone whose acquired gender has been recognised under the Gender Recognition Act 2004. Coupled with the WEC's recommendation that the 2004 Act be amended 'in line with the principles of gender self-declaration that have been developed in other juris-dictions', this would have significant implications for the continued existence of women-only spaces or services.

In its response to the WEC report the government undertook to review the 2004 Act 'to determine whether changes can be made to improve it in order to streamline and de-medicalise the gender recognition process', and to 'keep under review' the EqA 2010. Maria Miller, chair of the WEC, introduced the Gender Identity (Protected Characteristic) Bill 2016–17, which had its first reading in the Commons in December 2016. The Bill, which would have replaced 'gender reassignment' as a protected characteristic with 'gender identity', was expected to have a second reading in May 2017, but fell with the dissolution of Parliament on 3 May 2017. In August 2017 it was announced that there would be a consultation in autumn 2017 in England and Wales on replacing the scheme in the 2004 Act with a self-identification approach to gender reassignment (a similar consultation closed in Scotland on 1 March 2018). In December 2017 it was announced that the consultation would be delayed to take account of the 100,000 responses to an LGBT survey just then carried out by the government. A subsequent consultation closed in October 2018 but government proposals have yet to be finalised, most likely because of concerns about threats to women-only spaces.

'Discrimination': An Introduction

The types of discrimination (broadly understood) that are regulated by the EqA 2010 are as follows: direct discrimination, indirect discrimination, vic-timisation, harassment,[55] failure to make a reasonable adjustment and

---

[55] Harassment is not strictly a form of discrimination but operates in the same way in that it is prohibited insofar as it relates to particular protected characteristics and takes place in a particular context.

discrimination arising from disability. These definitions are discussed below. It should be recognised that the dividing line between direct and indirect discrimination, in particular, is not entirely clear. Philosophers may argue about the moral distinctions between the concepts of direct and indirect discrimination, and the relationship between them and different notions of justice.[56] The most significant distinction from the point of view of employment lawyers is that, except in the case of age, direct discrimination is not capable of justification, whereas indirect discrimination is.[57]

Direct Discrimination

The definition of direct discrimination is set out in EqA 2010, section 13.

Equality Act 2010, Section 13(1)

A person (A) discriminates against another (B) if, because of a protected characteristic, A treats B less favourably than A treats or would treat others.

Comparison is required for a finding of less favourable treatment (as distinct from unfavourable treatment such as is sufficient to establish pregnancy discrimination, or discrimination arising from disability).[58] It is clear from section 13, however, that B can challenge her treatment by reference to that which was or would have been received by another person. In other words, a hypothetical comparator suffices.

EqA 2010, section 23 then provides that, for the purposes of making a comparison as required in cases of direct (and indirect) discrimination, 'there must be no material difference between the circumstances relating to each case'.[59] Section 23's predecessor provisions have caused difficulties in the past.[60] In *Shamoon* v. *Chief Constable of the RUC* the House of Lords

---

[56] See, for example, A. Morris, 'On the Normative Foundations of Indirect Discrimination Law: Understanding the Competing Models of Discrimination Law as Aristotelian Forms of Justice' (1995) 15 *Oxford Journal of Legal Studies* 199; and J. Gardner, 'Discrimination as Injustice' (1996) 16 *Oxford Journal of Legal Studies* 353. See also the recent decision of the Supreme Court in *Bull* v. *Hall* [2013] UKSC 73, [2014] 1 All ER 919 in which the Court was split 3:2 as to whether the discrimination there at issue was direct or indirect.

[57] Direct discrimination on grounds other than age is lawful only if a specific defence applies.

[58] See below.

[59] S. 23(2) provides that, where the protected characteristic is disability, '[t]he circumstances relating to a case include a person's abilities'. And s. 23(3) provides that, '[i]f the protected characteristic is sexual orientation, the fact that one person (whether or not the person referred to as B) is a civil partner while another is married is not a material difference between the circumstances relating to each case'.

[60] See the discussion of pregnancy discrimination below.

attempted to defuse these problems by placing emphasis on the reason for the treatment complained of.[61] This has been largely successful in preventing a situation in which meritorious claims are defeated by arguments relating to comparators.

Comparators are returned to below. It is worth stating that the prohibition on direct discrimination is generally symmetrical in the sense that the less favourable treatment of men than of women because of sex is prohibited in precisely similar terms to the less favourable treatment, because of sex, of women than of men. The same is true in relation to race, religion and belief, sexual orientation and age, although as we discuss below some 'positive action' is permitted by the Act. In the case of disability, however, section 13(3) provides that, where 'the protected characteristic is disability, and B is not a disabled person, A does not discriminate against B only because A treats or would treat disabled persons more favourably than A treats B'. In other words, and subject to what is said below about discrimination on the basis of association and perceived status, protection against disability discrimination applies only to disabled people.[62] Section 13(4) similarly provides that, '[i]f the protected characteristic is marriage and civil partnership', the prohibition on discrimination (which applies in the context of work alone) 'applies . . . only if the treatment is because it is B who is married or a civil partner',[63] while sections 7 and 18 make it clear that the protections against discrimination in connection with gender reassignment and pregnancy/maternity protect only those having the protected characteristics of gender reassignment and pregnancy/maternity. Section 13(6) further provides that, '[i]f the protected characteristic is sex . . . in a case where B is a man, no account is to be taken of special treatment afforded to a woman in connection with pregnancy or childbirth'.[64]

Direct discrimination because of age (alone of all the protected characteristics) is capable of justification where the discriminator can show that the less favourable treatment was 'a proportionate means of achieving a legitimate aim'.[65]

Intention, Motivation and Discrimination

Direct discrimination is defined in terms of less favourable treatment because of a protected characteristic. This change of wording was not intended to alter

---

[61] [2003] ICR 337 (HL).   [62] Except as regards victimisation: see pp. 373–5.

[63] Note that this appears to exclude claims on the basis of association with a person who is married/civilly partnered.

[64] Though note the decision in *Eversheds Legal Services Ltd* v. *DeBelin* [2011] IRLR 448 in which the EAT ruled that the selection of the claimant for redundancy was discriminatory because the person who was not selected had been unduly advantaged by the employers in connection with her maternity leave.

[65] EqA 2010, s. 13(2).

the approach taken by the courts from that established in relation to the previous legislative provisions' prohibitions on discrimination on grounds of the protected characteristics. Some of that case-law is, accordingly, set out here.

In a number of early cases under the Sex Discrimination Act (SDA) 1975, respondents attempted to argue that treatment which, although less favourable in respect of one group than another, was benignly motivated, did not amount to unlawful discrimination. In other cases, respondents sought to argue that the disputed treatment, although different, was no less favourable to one group than another. Both of these arguments were unsuccessfully deployed by the respondents in *Equal Opportunities Commission* v. *Birmingham City Council*, which remains good law.[66] There, the House of Lords ruled that the denial of an opportunity was sufficient to amount to 'less favourable treatment' and that there was no requirement for the discriminator to be malignly motivated in order for direct discrimination to be established. In *James* v. *Eastleigh Borough Council*, the House of Lords established the 'but for' test for direct discrimination under which, as long as it could be said that 'but for' his or her sex the claimant would have been treated more favourably, direct discrimination was established without reference to the motivation of the discriminator (even in a case in which the discriminator was motivated by the desire to redress perceived disadvantage).[67]

A similar approach was taken more recently by the Supreme Court in *R (Coll)* v. *Secretary of State for Justice*, a challenge by a woman former prisoner to the provision of 'approved premises' in which various categories of prisoner are required to live post-discharge from prison while still on licence.[68] Such premises are invariably single-sex. At the material time there were ninety-four in England and Wales which accommodated men and only six for women of which none were in London or in Wales. The claimant argued that, although the 112 beds in the six female approved premises were sufficient to meet demand, the lack of provision in London (where she came from) amounted to direct and/or indirect discrimination. That claim failed at first instance and the Court of Appeal dismissed the claimant's appeal. The Supreme Court, however, ruled that she had been subject to direct sex discrimination in being required to live in approved premises in Bedford, away from her home and children, in circumstances in which, had she been a man, she would have been accommodated in London. Women who were required to live in approved premises were placed at a much higher risk of being required to live far from home and family by reason of the combination of the much smaller number of women who had to be catered for by the system and the policy decision that all approved premises should be single sex

---

[66] [1989] AC 1155.
[67] [1990] 2 AC 751. See also *R (European Roma Rights Centre and Others)* v. *Immigration Officer at Prague Airport and Others* [2005] 2 WLR 1.
[68] [2017] 1 WLR 2093.

(the latter in order to protect vulnerable women on release). That amounted to less favourable treatment of women than of men, and the fact that not all women were placed at a disadvantage by the nature of the provision did not mean that those who were so placed had not been subject to direct discrimination. It did not matter that the Secretary of State had no desire to treat women less favourably than men.

Comparators were mentioned above. The Secretary of State in *Coll* sought to argue that there was a material difference between the circumstances of the male and female offenders so that their cases were not comparable for the purpose of section 23 EqA 2010. This was accepted by the High Court, which ruled that comparing the women prisoners with the men prisoners was not comparing like with like because fewer women prisoners on release were categorised as high or very high risk, and the criteria for admitting them to approved premises were different.[69] The Court of Appeal rejected the comparator-based defence, ruling that those differences were not material to the distance between women's accommodation and their homes.[70] The Supreme Court agreed, Lady Hale (with whom the rest of the Court agreed) stating that 'The question of comparing like with like must always be treated with great care', that the relevant circumstances for the purposes of section 23 would usually be something extrinsic rather than intrinsic to claimants and their comparators, and that here 'the material circumstances are that they are offenders being released on licence on condition that they live in [Approved Premises]. Those circumstances are the same for men and women. But the risk of being placed far from home is much greater for the women than for the men.'[71]

Another very significant recent decision on direct discrimination is that of the Court of Appeal in *R (Al-Hidraj)* v. *Ofsted*.[72] This case concerned a challenge by the school to a critical Ofsted report which, *inter alia*, concluded that the school had acted unlawfully in imposing strict gender segregation of its pupils from age nine. Ofsted had not found that the education provided by the schools to girls was of lower quality than that provided to boys, or vice versa (this despite some material in its report on which it could have so concluded).[73] It had, however, concluded that the very fact of sex segregation absent any educational purpose amounted to less favourable treatment because of sex of both boys and girls.

The High Court (Jay J) ruled that Ofsted had erred in its approach; the symmetrical treatment of both girls and boys, even if disadvantageous to both, entailed 'detriment' to boys and girls but did not amount to or involve 'less

---

[69] [2013] EWHC 4077 (Admin), §54.   [70] [2015] 1 WLR 3781, §44.   [71] Para. 32.

[72] [2017] EWCA Civ 1426, [2017] IRLR 30.

[73] Specifically the existence of library books supporting men's right to inflict violence on their wives, evidence that teachers were encouraging the view that women's place was in the home and the fact that girls invariably had to wait for boys to finish their break periods before girls were allowed to enjoy theirs.

favourable treatment' of either, since boys and girls were equally disadvantaged by not being permitted to mix with children of the other sex.[74] The Court of Appeal disagreed, ruling that Jay J had erred in his approach by comparing boys and girls as collectives rather than individuals. The correct view was that a girl pupil who wished to mix or socialise with a boy pupil was prevented from so doing because of her sex, in circumstances in which, had she been a boy, she would have been allowed to mix or socialise with other boys. Equally, a boy pupil who was prevented from mixing or socialising with a girl pupil in circumstances in which a girl pupil would have been allowed to so mix or socialise was precluded from doing so because of his sex. That, the Court of Appeal ruled, amounted to sex discrimination against girls and boys, contrary to the EqA 2010.

One of the interesting elements of the Court of Appeal's decision in *Al-Hidraj* is the dissenting judgment of the sole woman on the Court, Gloster LJ. She did not disagree with that part of the decision set out above. She did, however, go considerably further than the two men on the Court. It had been argued on behalf of Ofsted, and by two minority women's NGOs which intervened, that sex segregation within a mixed-sex school was (in addition) discriminatory because it inevitably involved less favourable treatment of girls (taken collectively as well as individually) than of boys. The argument rested on the disadvantage suffered by women in society and within conservative Islam in particular. The majority did not accept this position but Gloster J, in a powerful dissent on this aspect of the judgment, pointed to the fact that girls were in fact disadvantaged more than were boys by the education provided at the school.[75] Further, and importantly, she accepted that socialising children to regard girls and women as:

> relevantly different in contexts where gender should be treated as irrelevant ... creates a particular detriment for females as neither male nor female pupils are socialised to regard women as normal working and social companions for men, or 'like them', in a society in which men still hold the significant majority of power. If men and women find it more natural and comfortable to form exclusive and different social networks around working life only with those of their own sex, women lose out more than men, because women are disproportionately excluded from networks of power and influence in later life. . .

> [O]nce the principle is accepted, as it was by the Judge (and the majority in this court), that, as a generality, men exercise more influence and power in society than women, and that persistent gender inequalities remain in the employment market, evidence is not required to establish that an educational system, which promotes segregation in a situation where girls are not allowed to mix with boys or to be educated alongside them, notwithstanding they are studying the same curriculum and spending their days on the same single school site, is bound to endorse traditional gender stereotypes that preserve male power, influence and

---

[74] [2016] EWHC 2004 (Admin).   [75] See §§140–142 of the Court of Appeal decision.

economic dominance. And the impact of that is inevitably greater on women than on men. One does not need to have been educated at a women's college at a co-educational university, at a time when women were still prohibited from being members of all-male colleges, to take judicial notice of the career opportunities which women are even today denied, simply because they are prevented from participating in hierarchical male networking groups, whether in the social, educational or employment environment.

Gloster LJ's judgment is a rare example of overtly feminist law. The decision in *Al-Hidraj* is also noteworthy for its approach to comparators. Jay J's approach appeared to have its roots in *Macdonald* v. *Ministry of Defence, Pearce* v. *Governing Body of Mayfield Secondary School*, in which the House of Lords rejected arguments that a gay man and a lesbian had been subject to sex discrimination in circumstances in which they had been treated less favourably, respectively, than a straight man and woman would have been.[76] The claimants had sought to argue in each case that they had been less favourably treated (as a man and a woman who were sexually attracted to men and women respectively) than they would have been if they were a woman and a man who were sexually attracted to men and women respectively. This on the face of it was the same argument accepted by the Court of Appeal in *Al-Hidraj* (i.e. that the sex of the chosen companions of the notional claimant and her comparator should remain the same, rather than being defined by reference to the sex of the claimant and comparator). But in *Macdonald* the House of Lords had ruled that the comparator for each claimant was a person of the opposite sex who was orientated towards individuals of the same sex as the claimant.

The decisions in *Macdonald* and in *Al-Hidraj* are reconcilable in view of the focus of the House of Lords in the earlier case on the reason for the treatment in issue. In that case there was no dispute that it was the sexual orientation of the claimants (this at a time when there was no legislative prohibition on sexual orientation discrimination). Viewed in this way, the decision in *Al-Hidraj* is perhaps best seen (in relation to the comparator question) as an application of the approach in *Shamoon* in which the House of Lords treated the comparator as a secondary question and refused to allow it to 'wag the dog' of determining the reason for less favourable treatment.

'Less Favourable Treatment': Appearance Rules

The courts have struggled to apply the prohibition on 'less favourable treatment' 'on grounds' of (now 'because of') sex to clothing and appearance rules. We saw above the robust approach taken by the House of Lords in *Equal Opportunities Commission* v. *Birmingham City Council* to the respondent's claim that, although different, the treatment it accorded to female pupils was

---

[76] [2003] UKHL 34, [2003] ICR 937.

no less favourable than that afforded to boys: their Lordships ruled that the denial of a choice sufficed to establish less favourable treatment. By contrast, it is characteristic of sex discrimination challenges to clothing and appearance rules that this argument has succeeded. Such rules are common, and frequently apply different restrictions to male and female employees. The approach of the courts was established in *Schmidt* v. *Austicks Bookshops*, in which the EAT ruled that a requirement that women staff wear overalls, and that they not wear trousers, whereas male employees were prohibited only from wearing tee-shirts, did not involve 'discrimination'.[77] According to Phillips J, employers were entitled to impose sex-specific dress codes as long as some restrictions were imposed on both men and women, referring to the 'large measure of discretion' to which an employer was entitled 'in controlling the image of his establishment'.

The *Schmidt* approach entails (1) accepting that a 'sex-appropriate dress code' can be a 'relevant circumstance' within (now) EqA 2010, section 23, and (2) finding discrimination only if the terms of the code, as they govern employees of the claimant's sex, are significantly less favourable than those which govern employees of the opposite sex. This approach is problematic for a number of reasons, not least because the courts appear blind to the social significance of dress. In *Schmidt*, the EAT took the view that requiring women, but not men, to wear overalls could not be regarded as detrimental to women, despite the messages about women's hierarchical position within the organisation that this must have conveyed.[78] The *Schmidt* approach was applied by the Court of Appeal in *Smith* v. *Safeway plc*, a case in which a male delicatessen assistant challenged a rule that men had to have short hair, women being allowed to wear long hair tied off their faces.[79] The EAT had, by a majority, distinguished *Schmidt* on the basis that the appearance rule, unlike the uniform rule in *Schmidt*, affected on employees outside as well as inside the workplace. The Court of Appeal did not agree, and dismissed an argument that dress codes designed to mirror 'conventional' differences between the sexes were difficult to reconcile with the underlying rationale of the sex-discrimination legislation, which was to challenge traditional assumptions about sexes, by demanding, rhetorically, whether there could 'be any doubt that a code which required all employees to have 18-inch hair, earrings and lipstick would treat men unfavourably by requiring them to adopt an appearance at odds with conventional standards?'

---

[77] [1978] ICR 85.

[78] See also *Burrett* v. *West Birmingham Health Authority* (3 March 1994, unreported), in which the Court of Appeal agreed with the EAT ([1994] IRLR 7) that a uniform code which required female (but not male) nurses to wear starched linen caps which served no practical purpose and which were regarded by nurses as demeaning did not amount to or involve sex discrimination since male nurses had to wear uniforms too.

[79] [1996] ICR 868. The EAT judgment is at [1995] IRLR 132.

In *Al-Hidraj* counsel for the school sought to rely on *Smith* v. *Safeway* as 'clear and binding authority that different but equal treatment for reasons of sex cannot constitute unlawful discrimination unless those of one sex are treated less favourably than the other sex, and so the same is necessarily true where they are treated similarly' (as in *Al-Hidraj* itself). The Court declined to follow the case on the basis that its facts were 'very different from those of the present case.'[80] The fact is, however, that the decision in *Al-Hidraj* does threaten the sustainability of the line of authority on clothing and appearance rules which is inconsistent with principle, focused as it is on permitting employers to insist on the maintenance of 'gender-appropriate' behaviour. The cases on dress codes are also increasingly anachronistic given that the protection from discrimination in connection with gender reassignment applies from the point of a decision to reassign gender, an early manifestation of which is likely to involve appearance.

Other challenges are posed to appearance and dress codes by the prohibitions on discrimination because of race, ethnicity and religion/belief. The general approach of the courts in the UK is to allow individuals broad freedom to manifest their religious views through their appearance regardless of dress/uniform codes,[81] although some limits are permitted in the interests of health and safety[82] and the rights and freedoms of others.[83]

A number of other European states are much less accommodating of religious dress, as is the ECtHR which until recently took the view that such dress does not attract protection under Article 9 as a manifestation of religion. In *Sahin* v. *Turkey* the Court recognised that a ban on the wearing of hijab in Turkish universities did amount to a restriction on the manifestation of religion, although it ruled that the interference had been justified.[84] Similar approaches were taken to challenges before the ECtHR to bans in France and Belgium on the wearing of full-face coverings in public.[85] And in *Achbita & Anor* v. *G4S Secure Solutions* the CJEU ruled that an employer could prohibit the wearing of visible signs of employees' political, philosophical or religious

---

[80] Para. 76.

[81] See e.g. *Mandla* v. *Dowell Lee* (Sikh turban), *R (Watkins-Singh)* v. *Governing Body of Aberdare Girls' High School* [2008] EWHC 1865 (Admin), [2008] ELR 561 (Sikh kara), *G* v. *St Gregory's Catholic Science College* [2011] EWHC 1452 (Admin) [2011] ELR 446 (corn rows).

[82] See the Chaplin applicant in *Eweida & Ors* v. *United Kingdom* [2013] ECHR 48420/10 (2013) 34 BHRC 519.

[83] *Azmi* v. *Kirklees Metropolitan Borough Council* [2007] ICR 1154 (niqab) and see the dissent of Lady Hale in *R (B)* v. *Governing Body of Denbigh School* [2006] UKHL 15, [2007] 1 AC 100 in which she expressed concern for the interests of other pupils in a case in which the claimant (a schoolgirl) wished to wear the jilbab to school.

[84] App. No. 44774/98, (2005) 19 BHRC 590. See, similarly, *Dogru* v. *France*, App. No. 27058/05 [2008] ECHR 27058/05.

[85] *SAS* v. *France* [2014] ECHR 43835/11, (2014) 36 BHRC 617, *Case of Belcacemi and Oussar* v. *Belgium*, App. No. 37798/13.

beliefs in the workplace, including in the form of hijab, in order to maintain a corporate position of neutrality.[86]

Discrimination on the Basis of Association or Perception

Questions have arisen as to whether the prohibition on direct discrimination prohibits less favourable treatment which results from a protected characteristic related not to the claimant but rather to someone with whom that person is associated, and whether it regulates less favourable treatment resulting from the discriminator's mistaken belief as to the sex, race or other protected characteristic of the victim. The answer under the EqA 2010's predecessor provisions was complicated by reason of the variety of different definitions of direct discrimination they included, but the decision of the ECJ in *Coleman* v. *Attridge Law* made it clear that Directive 2000/78/EC prohibited discrimination against a woman because of her son's disability.[87] While the facts concerned disability discrimination by association, the tone of the Advocate General's opinion and the judgment of the ECJ indicated strongly that discrimination on the basis of perceived status would also be unlawful, and that the same approach would be taken to other protected characteristics as to disability.

The definition of direct discrimination as less favourable treatment 'because of' a protected characteristic is intended to apply to discrimination on the basis of association and perceived status.'[88] The issue of discrimination because of perceived disability gives rise to particular questions in light of the fact that – uniquely – the EqA provides protection from disability discrimination only to those who meet the statutory definition of disability (the other protected characteristics being protected asymmetrically). In *J* v. *DLA Piper UK plc* Underhill P, as he then was, pointed out the difficulties to which this gives rise, in particular, that in circumstances in which the definition of disability is a legal one it may be unclear whether that which the alleged discriminator perceives would amount to a disability:

---

[86] C-157/15, [2017] IRLR 466. Cf. the discussion of C-188/15 *Bougnaoui and Another* v. *Micropole SA* [2017] IRLR 447, below.

[87] C-03/06, *Coleman* v. *Attridge Law* [2008] ECR I-5603. The EAT subsequently confirmed in *EBR Attridge LLP and Another* v. *Coleman* [2010] ICR 242 that the DDA 1995 was capable, post the decision of the ECJ, of interpretation to cover the facts alleged in that case but it was clear that legislative change was needed.

[88] See Explanatory Notes to the Act, paras. 59–61. The Notes expressly state that the use of the words 'because of' in place of the previous 'on grounds of '(which had been held in *Weathersfield Ltd t/a Van & Truck Rentals* v. *Sargent* [1999] IRLR 9 (CA) to cover discrimination on grounds of someone else's race, as well as the race of the person discriminated against: see also *Showboat Entertainment Centre Ltd* v. *Owens* [1984] ICR 65) does not change the legal meaning of the definition, but rather is designed to make it more accessible to the ordinary user of the Bill'.

If the perceived disability is, say, blindness, there may be no problem: a blind person is necessarily disabled. But … [i]f a manager discriminates against an employee because he believes her to have a broken leg, or because he believes her to be 'depressed', the question whether the effects of the perceived injury, or of the perceived depression, are likely to last more or less than twelve months may never enter his thinking, consciously or unconsciously (nor indeed, in the case of perceived 'depression', may it be clear what he understands by the term). In such a case, on what basis can he be said to be discriminating 'on the ground of' the employee's – perceived – disability?[89]

Indirect Discrimination

'Indirect discrimination' is concerned with the application of apparently neutral rules, practices etc., which serve in practice to disadvantage groups of people defined by reference to a protected characteristic such as race, religion or belief etc.

Equality Act 2010, Section 19

(1) A person (A) discriminates against another (B) if A applies to B a provision, criterion or practice which is discriminatory in relation to a relevant protected characteristic of B's.

(2) For the purposes of subsection (1), a provision, criterion or practice is discriminatory in relation to a relevant protected characteristic of B's if –

    (a) A applies, or would apply, it to persons with whom B does not share the characteristic,

    (b) it puts, or would put, persons with whom B shares the characteristic at a particular disadvantage when compared with persons with whom B does not share it,

    (c) it puts, or would put, B at that disadvantage, and

    (d) A cannot show it to be a proportionate means of achieving a legitimate aim.

Section 19(3) provides that all the protected characteristics (with the exception of pregnancy and maternity) are 'relevant'. The reason for the exclusion of pregnancy and maternity from this form of protection is unclear but indirect discrimination connected with pregnancy or maternity may well in any event amount to indirect sex discrimination.

The Supreme Court applied *Bilka-Kaufhaus* in considering the justification of indirect age discrimination in *Homer* v. *Chief Constable of West Yorkshire Police*.[90] The claimant, who was sixty-two, challenged the application to him of a requirement that, in order to achieve promotion beyond a certain grade, he

---

[89] [2010] IRLR 93 and see *Peninsula Business Service Ltd* v. *Baker* [2017] IRLR 394, [2017] ICR 714.

[90] [2012] UKSC 15, [2012] IRLR 601.

had to have a law degree or equivalent. The employer operated a retirement age of sixty-five, extendable by one year at the employer's discretion. The claimant argued that the provision, criterion or practice (PCP) indirectly discriminated against workers aged sixty to sixty-five. A tribunal upheld his claim but the EAT and the Court of Appeal ruled that the employer had not applied any PCP which disparately affected him as an older worker, any disadvantage the claimant experienced resulting from his proximity to leaving the respondent's employment (albeit because of the respondent's mandatory age-related termination policy) rather than from the respondent's rule about qualifications.

Lady Hale was highly critical of the rigid and unhelpful approach to the identification of indirect discrimination that characterised much of the domestic jurisprudence since the early days of the SDA 1975. She suggested that the approach of the lower courts would

> have alarming consequences for the law of discrimination generally. Take, for example, a requirement that employees in a particular job must have a beard. . . the argument leaves sex out of account and says that it is the inability to grow a beard which puts women at a particular disadvantage and so they must be compared with other people who for whatever reason, whether it be illness or immaturity, are unable to grow a beard.[91]

Having pointed out that successive reformulations of the test for indirect discrimination had been intended to make it easier rather than more difficult to establish her ladyship referred back to the Tribunal the question of justification which required consideration of appropriateness and necessity, including proportionality.

An important element of establishing indirect discrimination is demonstrating that the claimant, and his or her 'group',[92] are disadvantaged by the provision or criterion at issue. A relatively small discrepancy might, on the facts, be sufficient to demonstrate 'particular disadvantage'. Thus, for example, in *London Underground Ltd* v. *Edwards (No. 2)*, the Court of Appeal accepted that a 'considerably smaller proportion' of women than of men[93] could comply with a requirement, imposed on London Underground drivers, to move to a flexible shift system. The claimant, a single mother, was the only one of twenty-one women tube drivers who could not comply with the requirement. All of the 2,023 male drivers could comply. The tribunal concluded, in these circumstances, that the 95.2 per cent of women who could comply was a considerably smaller proportion of women than the 100 per cent of men who

---

[91] Para. 13.

[92] This may be women, Muslims, older or younger people etc.: people inhabit many groups but the indirect discrimination claim needs to identify of which 'group' it is that the claimant is (in relation to the particular provision, criterion or practice under challenge) disadvantaged by her membership.

[93] [1999] ICR 494, this being the relevant statutory test at the time.

could comply, 'taking into account the number of male train operators as compared to the very few female train operators . . . and also added to the fact that it is common knowledge that females are more likely to be single parents and caring for a child than males'. The EAT rejected the employer's appeal, ruling that the tribunal had been entitled to take into account the absolute numbers involved. The Court of Appeal agreed, stressing (*per* Potter LJ) the 'high preponderance' of female single parents and the fact that '[n]ot one of the male component of just over 2,000 men was unable to comply with the rostering arrangements. On the other hand, one woman could not comply out of the female component of only 21.'[94]

The test for indirect discrimination considered by the Court of Appeal in the *London Underground* case was by its nature less flexible than that now found in section 19(2)(b), and the contextualised approach would appear to have more, rather than less, statutory support under the EqA 2010. The approach in section 19 is designed to reflect the EU definition of indirect discrimination which, as the European Commission made clear in the Explanatory Memorandum to the Racial Equality Directive,[95] was intentionally chosen to avoid the need for statistical proof. And, in the absence of any such need, it is difficult to ascertain the purpose of any comparative pool (as distinct from evidence of some sort about actual or expected disparate impact).

In *London Borough of Islington* v. *Ladele*, the EAT accepted that a requirement to be involved in civil partnerships placed persons of the same religion or belief as the claimant, an evangelical Christian registrar, 'at a particular disadvantage when compared with other persons, namely those who did not share her religious beliefs about same sex relationships', such that the defendant was required to justify the requirement (which it did).[96] In *Eweida* v. *British Airways*, however, the Court of Appeal ruled that a devout Christian who challenged her employer's refusal (subsequently abandoned) to allow her to wear a visible crucifix had failed to establish a *prima facie* case that the uniform policy put Christians at a particular disadvantage.[97] The Court ruled that neither domestic legislation nor EU law required that 'solitary disadvantage' should be sufficient to establish indirect discrimination.[98] In *Eweida* v. *UK* the EctHR ruled that her Article 9 (freedom of religion) rights had been violated when she was subject to detriment by reason of her insistence on wearing the crucifix in breach of her employer's uniform policy.[99] In *Mba* v. *Mayor and Burgesses of the London Borough of Merton*[100] the Court of Appeal ruled that the domestic test for indirect discrimination could not be read to exclude a requirement of group disadvantage.

---

[94] *Ibid.*, paras. 25–6.   [95] Council Directive 2000/78.   [96] [2009] ICR 387. See further below.
[97] [2010] ICR 890.   [98] [2009] IRLR 78 (EAT), [2010] IRLR 322 (CA).
[99] [2013] IRLR 231.   [100] [2013] EWCA Civ 1562, [2014] ICR 357.

In *Essop & Ors* v. *Home Office (UK Border Agency)* and *Naeem* v. *Secretary of State for Justice* the respondents sought to argue that, in order to establish indirect discrimination, a claimant had to prove why a PCP impacted disproportionately on the affected group, and also that the reason was peculiar to the relevant group.[101] The claimants in the joined cases were, respectively, older and/or black and minority ethnic (BME) civil servants who sought to challenge the application to them of a test in respect of which older and BME candidates had a significantly lower pass rate, and a Muslim prison chaplain who sought to challenge a pay system which linked pay to length of service in circumstances in which Muslim chaplains had only been relatively recently recruited to the prison service, and so had less service and correspondingly lower pay than Christian chaplains.

The respondents' argument had found favour with the Court of Appeal[102] but the Supreme Court gave it short shrift. Lady Hale, with whom the rest of the Court agreed, reviewed the various definitions of indirect discrimination over time and set out six 'salient features' of indirect discrimination, among them that none of the definitions of indirect discrimination in domestic or EU law had ever included any express requirement such as that which the respondents advanced, and that, whereas direct discrimination required a causal link between the less favourable treatment and the protected characteristic, indirect discrimination required a causal link between the PCP and the particular disadvantage suffered by the group and the individual. Further, it was commonplace for the disparate impact, or particular disadvantage, to be established on the basis of statistical evidence, which could point only to correlations rather than causal links, and it was always open to the respondent to show that the PCP was justified. In Lady Hale's view, all six factors pointed against the respondents' argument that the claimant had to establish the reason for the disparate impact of the PCP on the relevant group, although a claimant would have to establish the causal link between the PCP and the disadvantage (i.e. that an older or BME candidate failed the test despite sitting it, rather than because she had failed to turn up).

Justification

Indirect discrimination is always capable of justification, as is direct age discrimination (but not direct discrimination because of the other 'protected characteristics'). The test, of justification, for present purposes, is set out in EqA 2010, section 19(2)(d) which provides that, the other criteria being satisfied, indirect discrimination will occur where the alleged discriminator 'cannot show [the provision, criterion or practice] to be a proportionate means of achieving a legitimate aim'. This test has not materially changed

---

[101] [2017] UKSC 27, [2017] ICR 640.   [102] [2015] ICR 1063 and [2016] ICR 289 respectively.

from that which applied in the employment context prior to the implementation of the EqA 2010.

The leading case on justification is the decision of the ECJ (now CJEU) in *Bilka-Kaufhaus GmbH* v. *Weber von Hartz* in which that Court ruled that the disparately impacting practice in question would have to be necessary and proportionate to objective economic grounds pursued by the relating to the management of its undertaking.[103] *Bilka* was cited with approval by the Supreme Court in *Homer* v. *Chief Constable of West Yorkshire Police and West Yorkshire Police Authority* in which Lady Hale, with whom the rest of the Court agreed, stated that:

> The approach to justification of what would otherwise be indirect discrimination is well settled. A provision criterion or practice is justified if the employer can show that it is a proportionate means of achieving a legitimate aim. The range of aims which can justify indirect discrimination on any ground is wider than the aims which can, in the case of age discrimination, justify direct discrimination ... [and] can encompass a real need on the part of the employer's business.[104]

The legitimate aim must in fact be pursued by the PCP in dispute, although this need not have been its rationale on adoption; in other words, *ex post facto* rationalisations are permissible.[105]

As we have seen above, age is unique in permitting the justification of direct as well as indirect discrimination. In *Seldon* v. *Clarkson Wright and Jakes* the Supreme Court considered whether a law firm's imposition on a partner of a mandatory retirement age of sixty-five was justifiable.[106] The question for the Court was whether the imposition of a mandatory retirement age by an employer could be justified by reason of Article 6(1) of Directive 2000/78 which provides that:

> Member States may provide that differences of treatment on grounds of age shall not constitute discrimination, if, within the context of national law, they are objectively and reasonably justified by a legitimate aim, including legitimate employment policy, labour market and vocational training objectives, and if the means of achieving that aim are appropriate and necessary.[107]

Lady Hale, who delivered the judgment of the Court, suggested that the reason why factors which were concerned with broader social and economic

---

[103] C-170/84, [1986] IRLR 317, [1987] ICR 110.   [104] [2012] UKSC 15, [2012] IRLR 601 §19.

[105] *Seldon* v. *Clarkson Wright and Jakes* [2012] UKSC 16, [2012] IRLR 590, *Cadman* v. *Health and Safety Executive* [2004] IRLR 971, [2005] ICR 1546.

[106] *Ibid.* At the time, domestic law provided a default retirement age of sixty-five, subsequently abolished. The default retirement age was not applicable to the claimant in *Seldon*, however, given that he was a partner in a law firm.

[107] In *Homer*, which was decided on the same day as *Seldon*, the Supreme Court ruled that the legitimate aims capable of justifying indirect discrimination were much more extensive than the social policy aims required to seek to justify direct age discrimination.

policy and had nothing to do with the characteristics of the individual could justify direct discrimination on the ground of age alone was because:

> age is different . . . not 'binary' in nature (man or woman, black or white, gay or straight) but a continuum which changes over time . . . younger people will eventually benefit from a provision which favours older employees, such as an incremental pay scale; but older employees will already have benefitted from a provision which favours younger people, such as a mandatory retirement age.

Having reviewed the authorities at domestic and CJEU level, she concluded that: (1) direct age discrimination could be justified only by reference to social policy objectives of a public interest nature; (2) the tests for justification of indirect and direct (age) discrimination were not identical; (3) it was for Member States rather than individual employers to establish the legitimacy of the aim pursued; (4) flexibility for employers was not itself a legitimate aim, although 'a certain degree of flexibility may be permitted to employers in the pursuit of legitimate social policy objectives'; (5) legitimate aims recognised to date in this context included those concerned, broadly, with 'inter-generational fairness' and 'dignity';[108] and (6) in all cases 'the measure in question must be both appropriate to achieve its legitimate aim or aims and necessary in order to do so', the gravity of the effect on the employees discriminated against being weighed in the balance against the importance of the legitimate aims pursued.

One of the big questions which has arisen in recent years has been whether and to what extent considerations of cost can establish justification. In *Cross* v. *British Airways plc* the EAT drew on CJEU jurisprudence in deciding that cost alone could not justify indirect sex discrimination, although it could be taken into account together with other justifications, if there were such.[109] In *Woodcock* v. *Cumbria PCT* a tribunal rejected an age discrimination claim by a man who had been dismissed for redundancy, the precise timing of the dismissal having been chosen to avoid the fact that the employer would otherwise have incurred huge financial liabilities towards him had he turned fifty while still in employment.[110] On the fact of it this looked like a case in which cost alone was in play. On the other hand the very reason why delayed dismissal would have been so advantageous to the claimant was precisely because of his age, which would have triggered the application to him of early retirement benefits. Further, the case was an unusual one in that the claimant had been under informal notice of dismissal for some time and the haste with

---

[108] As to the latter, Lady Hale expressed 'some sympathy' with the view that arguments linking age to incapacity, which lay at the root of the 'dignity'-based justifications for age discrimination, 'look suspiciously like stereotyping' but accepted that the CJEU had held that the 'avoidance of unseemly debates about capacity is capable of being a legitimate aim'.

[109] [2005] IRLR 423. See, similarly, *Redcar & Cleveland BC* v. *Bainbridge* [2007] IRLR 91, [2008] ICR 249.

[110] The decision of the Court of Appeal is at [2012] EWCA Civ 330, [2012] ICR 1126.

which his notice of dismissal was finally given was the result of delays in the process which were found to have been no one's fault.

The Court of Appeal in *Woodcock* accepted that the *Cross* approach 'represent[ed] the current orthodoxy' although the Court did 'not find it convincing'. Having declared that 'considerations of cost must be admissible in considering whether a provision, criterion or practice which has a discriminatory impact may nevertheless be justified' the Court suggested that it found 'it hard to see the principled basis for a rule that such considerations can never *by themselves* constitute sufficient justification or why they need the admixture of some other element in order to be legitimised. The adoption of such a rule, it seems to us, tends to involve parties and tribunals in artificial game-playing – "find the other factor" – of a kind which is likely to produce arbitrary and complicated reasoning' (emphasis added). Had the Court been free to do so it would have accepted that disproportionate cost could justify discrimination. It was not so free, however, and in any event it accepted that the tribunal had adopted the 'costs plus' approach in the instant case in which the primary reason for the claimant's dismissal was the fact that he had become redundant.[111] That being the case, the appeal failed.

In the *O'Brien* v. *Ministry of Justice* case, which concerned discrimination against part-time judges in relation to pension arrangements, the CJEU ruled that 'budgetary considerations cannot justify discrimination'.[112] On its return to the Supreme Court the UK government accepted that cost alone could not justify discrimination, although it argued that 'cost plus' other factors may do so. Lord Hope and Lady Hale, who delivered the judgment of the Court, characterised this as 'a subtle point which is not without difficulty', stated that it was '[n]o doubt ... because the Court of Justice foresaw that the ministry would seek to rely upon considerations of cost when the case returned to the national courts that it took care to reiterate that "budgetary considerations cannot justify discrimination"' and stated that it was 'unnecessary for us to express a view upon whether *Woodcock*'s case was rightly decided'.[113]

The requirement for proportionality demands that a balance be struck between the discriminatory effect of the measure and the reasonable needs of the undertaking. The test to be applied is an objective one, rather than a 'band of reasonable responses' approach.[114] The more severe the disparate impact of a PCP on a group defined by reference to one or more protected characteristics the more will be demanded by way of justification for it, though it is clear from the dicta of Lady Hale in *Homer* that the test of proportionality requires only that the PCP is reasonably (rather than absolutely) necessary to

[111] This might also explain the outcome in *HM Land Registry* v. *Benson* [2012] IRLR 373.

[112] C-393/10, [2012] IRLR 421.   [113] [2013] UKSC 6, [2013] 1 WLR 522, §§63, 69 & 70.

[114] See the decision of the Court of Appeal in *Hardy & Hansons plc* v. *Lax* [2005] EWCA Civ 846, [2005] ICR 1565.

achieve the legitimate aim pursued.[115] One of the factors to be taken into account in assessing proportionality is whether non-discriminatory alternatives were available to the employer,[116] although the existence of such an alternative by which a legitimate aim could have been pursued will not necessarily mean that a disparately impacting PCP is disproportionate (and therefore unlawful).[117]

In *Seldon* v. *Clarkson Wright and Jakes* the Supreme Court accepted, in a case involving a challenge to a mandatory retirement rule, that what fell to be justified was the general rule rather than its application in the particular case.[118] In *G* v. *St Gregory's Catholic Science College*, on the other hand, the Administrative Court ruled that a school uniform policy which prohibited boys from wearing their hair in cornrows, which was intended to discourage gang culture, impacted disproportionately on racial grounds because it failed to provide for exceptions to accommodate genuine cultural or family practices.[119] The cases may be reconcilable on the basis that, whereas Seldon was concerned with direct (age) discrimination, *G* concerned indirect discrimination. This being the case, the policy pursued in *G* could be achieved without discriminatory impact if exceptions to it were allowed, while that pursued in *Seldon* could not, and so it had to stand or fall on its own terms.[120]

Recent decisions on justification include *R (C)* v. *Secretary of State for Pensions* in which a woman who had undergone gender reassignment complained that the information held on her in the Department for Work and Pensions' database included the fact that she was previously recorded as having a different sex, as well as her former name. She also complained that the special customer records (SCR) policy, which applied, *inter alia*, to transgender customers, and which limited Department of Work and Pensions staff from accessing their sensitive details, alerted such staff to the fact that the customer was subject to the SCR policy from which they might readily infer the probable reason for the restricted access. The claimant put her claim on a number of grounds, one of which was that the retention and SCR policies discriminated against her indirectly. The judge at first instance granted a declaration that the retention policy breached Article 8 ECHR because it lacked clarity and precision and was not readily accessible and thus was not in accordance with the law, but otherwise dismissed the claim. After the judgment and following

---

[115] §§22 and 24 and see the decision of Slade J in *Kapenova* v. *Department of Health* [2014] ICR 884, [2014] EqLR 501.

[116] *Homer*, [2012] UKSC 15, [2012] IRLR 601 §25.   [117] *Kapenova, ibid.*   [118] *Ibid.*

[119] *Ibid.*

[120] And see *Buchanan* v. *Commissioner of Police of the Metropolis* [2016] IRLR 918 in which the EAT drew a distinction between cases such as *Seldon* in which A's treatment of B is the direct result of applying a general rule or policy, and those in which a policy would permit of a number of responses to an individual's particular circumstances. In the former the question will be whether the general rule or policy is justified whereas in the latter it will be whether the particular treatment of the individual is.

discussions with the claimant the retention policy was clarified and reference to the gender recognition field on the database was masked, so that nothing was visible to frontline users which stated in terms that the person whose records were under consideration had reassigned gender, but the policies were otherwise unaltered. The claimant appealed, seeking further modifications and pursuing her claim of indirect discrimination. The Court of Appeal and Supreme Court upheld the judge's decision, the latter ruling that, although gender reassignment changed a person's identity at a much deeper level than getting married, divorced, being bereaved, adopting a new name or any other reason why a change of name or title might be recorded, the PCP adopted by the SCR policy was a proportionate means of achieving a legitimate aim.

In *Mba* v. *Mayor and Burgesses of the London Borough of Merton*[121] the claimant, a care assistant in a children's home, argued that she had been subject to unlawful discrimination because of her Christian faith when she was required to work Sunday shifts. She lost her claim in part because an ET found that her belief that no paid work should be done on a Sunday was not a core component of Christian faith. The Court of Appeal ruled that this approach was inconsistent with the claimant's Article 9 rights, but that the tribunal had been 'plainly and unarguably right' in finding that the PCP imposed on the claimant was proportionate. The tribunal had taken into account the fact that the respondent had sought to accommodate the claimant for two years and that it was prepared to organise her shifts to allow her to attend church on Sundays. According to Elias LJ, with whom Vos LJ agreed, these factors were not relevant to the proportionality analysis; they did 'show that the council was acting in good faith and had travelled some way towards meeting her concerns; but the issue is whether the council had gone far enough, and these factors do not help at all in answering that question'.[122] As to the question whether or not the claimant's belief concerned 'a core component of the Christian faith', Elias LJ ruled that, while domestic justification analysis would conventionally require greater justification for PCPs which disproportionately affected large groups, the fact that Article 9 protected individual views regardless of whether they reflected those of large proportions of the relevant group meant that the obverse would be true here: 'paradoxically, if a belief is not widely shared, which is more likely to be the case where it is not a core belief of a particular religion, that is a factor which under art 9 is likely to work in favour of the employee rather than against' (this because it would be easier to accommodate). This approach should and could be taken under domestic law by reason of the interpretive obligation imposed by the Human Rights Act, although in this case none of the errors made by the tribunal altered the fact that its conclusion, that the respondent was entitled to require the claimant to work on Sundays, was 'clearly and unarguably right'.

---

[121] *Ibid.*   [122] §29.

The expansion of the 'protected characteristics', in particular the prohibition of discrimination on grounds of religion, has resulted in a number of cases involving apparent conflicts between the rights of the parties not to be discriminated against. In *Ladele* v. *Islington London Borough Council*,[123] the Court of Appeal ruled that the employer was entitled to insist that the claimant perform her functions as a registrar in relation to civil partnerships, despite her religious objections (and the *prima facie* indirect discrimination on grounds of religion entailed) because to accommodate her beliefs would have been incompatible with its purpose of providing a non-discriminatory registration service. This was the case whether or not the council could have accommodated her refusal to be involved in civil partnerships in a practical way. The importance of this case is that it establishes the proposition that A's right not to be indirectly discriminated against by reference to a protected characteristic does not entitle A to discriminate directly on a protected ground (at least in the absence of a specific provision allowing A to discriminate).

'Multiple Discrimination'

Those who practise in and comment on discrimination law have called for many years for legislative accommodation of 'multiple discrimination' claims, that is, claims of discrimination arising from the combination of, or the intersection between, protected characteristics. EqA 2010, section 14, was introduced in partial recognition of these calls. It provided for the recognition of 'dual discrimination' (less favourable treatment 'because of a combination of two relevant protected characteristics').[124] In March 2011 the coalition government announced that the provision would not be implemented. Meanwhile, however, the decision of Cox J in *Ministry of Defence* v. *DeBique* may have rendered less significant the provision which does not in any event apply to indirect discrimination.[125] There, the EAT accepted that the claimant, a soldier who had been recruited from St Vincent and the Grenadines, was subject to unlawful indirect discrimination as a woman of Vincentian national origin by the combined effect of a requirement to work 24/7 and an immigration rule which prevented her from securing family assistance with her childcare needs.

Positive Action

Of considerable potential significance are EqA 2010, sections 158 and 159, found in Part 11 of the Act, which is entitled 'Advancement of Equality'.

---

[123] [2010] ICR 532 (CA).
[124] These characteristics, which are listed in s. 14(2), do not include pregnancy or married/civilly partnered status.
[125] [2010] IRLR 471.

Equality Act 2010, Section 158

(1) This section applies if a person (P) reasonably thinks that –

    (a) persons who share a protected characteristic suffer a disadvantage connected to the characteristic,

    (b) persons who share a protected characteristic have needs that are different from the needs of persons who do not share it, or

    (c) participation in an activity by persons who share a protected characteristic is disproportionately low.

(2) This Act does not prohibit P from taking any action which is a proportionate means of achieving the aim of –

    (a) enabling or encouraging persons who share the protected characteristic to overcome or minimise that disadvantage,

    (b) meeting those needs, or

    (c) enabling or encouraging persons who share the protected characteristic to participate in that activity.

Section 158 allows any proportionate action to overcome or minimise disadvantages or meet needs connected with protected grounds, and/or to encourage or enable participation by persons sharing a protected characteristic where that participation in an activity is disproportionately low. It does not allow more favourable treatment, because of a protected characteristic, in connection with recruitment or promotion, this being dealt with by section 159, which provides that such treatment is permissible (only) where one ('as qualified') candidate is treated more favourably than another candidate as a proportionate means to overcome or minimise disadvantage connected to a protected characteristic or to encourage participation in an activity by persons sharing a protected characteristic whose participation in that activity is disproportionately low. Section 159(4)(b) provides, somewhat delphically, that the provision applies only where the person relying on it 'does not have a policy of treating persons who share the protected characteristic more favourably in connection with recruitment or promotion than persons who do not share it'.

Section 158 is to be welcomed as a clear recognition that symmetry of approach is not an absolute. (It is useful to note here that neither provision has any application to disability, the prohibition on this form of discrimination protecting only disabled people, with the effect that positive action does not amount, *prima facie*, to prohibited discrimination. Further, and given that age discrimination is subject to a general justification defence, it is to be expected that positive action with respect to age would fall to be justified under the general approach rather than by resort to section 158 or 159.)

The Explanatory Notes to the EqA 2010 state that the provision 'will, for example, allow [proportionate] measures to be targeted to particular groups, including training to enable them to gain employment, or health services to address their needs', and '[t]he extent to which it is proportionate to take positive action measures which may result in people not having the relevant characteristic being treated less favourably ... depend[ing], among other things, on the seriousness of the relevant disadvantage, the extremity of need or under-representation and the availability of other means of countering them'.[126] The Notes are silent as to the application of section 158 to those in employment, the examples provided dealing with education and health. A 'Quick Start Guide to Using Positive Action When Making Appointments', released by the Government Equalities Office in 2011, states that section 158 'replicate[s] provisions in earlier legislation and allow[s] employers to target measures such as dedicated training to groups, such as women or people from ethnic minorities, who are under-represented or disadvantaged in the work-place, or to meet their particular needs'. The guide provides, by way of an example of the operation of section 158, a scenario in which an employer with 'very few women in its senior management team ... offers a development programme which is only open to women to help female staff compete for management positions', stating that 'This is not unlawful discrimination against male staff, because it is allowed by the positive action provisions.'

The Equality and Human Rights Commission's Code of Practice on Employment gives a number of similar examples of potentially lawful positive action measures.[127] The Code suggests that 'some indication or evidence will be required' to show that persons sharing the relevant characteristic are at a particular disadvantage, share particular needs or under-participate, but that no 'sophisticated statistical data or research' is required and the requirement may be satisfied by:

> an employer looking at the profiles of their workforce and/or making enquiries of other comparable employers in the area or sector.[128] Additionally, it could involve looking at national data such as labour force surveys for a national or local picture of the work situation for particular groups who share a protected characteristic [or a] decision could be based on qualitative evidence, such as consultation with workers and trade unions.

The Quick Start Guide and Code of Practice both stress that positive action is entirely voluntary, although the Code of Practice also states that 'as a matter of good business practice, public and private sector employers may wish to take positive action measures', and that such measures may result in benefits to the employer including 'a wider pool of talented, skilled and experienced people from which to recruit; a dynamic and challenging workforce able to respond to changes; a better understanding of foreign/global markets; [and] a

---

[126] Paras. 511–12.   [127] See paras. 12.6–12.24.   [128] See para. 12.4.

better understanding of the needs of a more diverse range of customers – both nationally and internationally'.[129] It might have added to this list the development of employment practices which avoid unlawful indirect discrimination against those in disadvantaged or under-represented groups.

EqA 2010, section 159, permits what might be regarded as 'harder-edged' positive action measures, and is subject to more onerous restrictions than section 158. The Quick Start Guide suggests that it would permit the selection of a Muslim over a non-Muslim candidate, where both were equally qualified, to a counselling service for teenagers in an area of high Muslim population which has no Muslim staff,[130] or the selection of a BME over an equally qualified non-BME candidate for the final place on a shortlist of twenty for an accountancy firm's graduate training scheme, where BME people were under-represented in the firm. The interesting question which arises, of course, is what is meant by 'as qualified as' in section 159(4)(a). The Code of Practice is silent on section 159, which was not in force at the relevant time (having been implemented only in April 2011). The Quick Start Guide suggests that: 'Employers must consider whether candidates are of equal merit in relation to the specific job or position they are applying for. While two candidates may be considered to be of equal merit for one particular post, the same two candidates might not be equally suitable for another job.' The guide goes on to emphasise (under the heading 'Artificially low thresholds') that, '[i]f one candidate is superior to another the position should be offered to that candidate. If the pass mark in an assessment is set at 70% and one candidate scores 71% and another scores 91%, it would generally be wrong to consider that just because both passed the minimum success threshold the two candidates are of equal merit', and that 'employers must not adopt policies or practices designed to routinely favour candidates with a certain protected characteristic, even where there is evidence of under-representation or disadvantage' with all 'suitably qualified candidates [being] considered on their individual merits for the post' and that '[w]here one candidate is clearly superior or better qualified for the job than the others, then an employer should offer the position to that candidate'.

There are real difficulties in a situation in which the parameters of lawful positive action are unclear, and such action is voluntary. Most employers, faced with uncertainties as to whether their perception of disadvantage, need or under-representation is reasonable, whether a given action will be regarded as proportionate to such disadvantage, need or under-representation, whether two candidates are 'as qualified as' each other such as to permit 'tie-break' discrimination, and whether such discrimination will be regarded as proportionate, will choose to avoid the risk of a claim, whether ultimately successful or not, by a disgruntled person disadvantaged as a result of positive action.

---

[129] See paras. 12.9–12.10.   [130] See p. 5.

Only those employers most committed to such action will brave the uncertain waters of this area of the law.

Harassment

Equality Act 2010, Section 26(1)

A person (A) harasses another (B) if –

(a) A engages in unwanted conduct related to a relevant protected characteristic,[131] and
(b) the conduct has the purpose or effect of –
  (i) violating B's dignity, or
  (ii) creating an intimidating, hostile, degrading, humiliating or offensive environment for B.

Section 29(4) provides that the perception of B, 'the other circumstances of the case' and 'whether it is reasonable for the conduct to have that effect' must be taken into account '[i]n deciding whether conduct has the effect referred to in subsection (1)(b)'. Section 29(2) defines sexual harassment as 'unwanted conduct *of a sexual nature*', the definition otherwise being on all fours with that in section 29(1); and section 29(3) further defines *quid pro quo* harassment (i.e. less favourable treatment because a person has submitted to, or refused to submit to, 'conduct of a sexual nature or that is related to gender reassignment or sex').[132]

Note that there is no requirement for a comparator in a claim of harassment (section 26(1)) or sexual harassment (section 26(2) or (3)). The approach taken in domestic law is somewhat broader than the definitions of harassment/ sexual harassment in the race, employment equality and recast gender Directives in that it provides the violation of dignity and the creation of an intimidating etc. environment as alternative rather than cumulative requirements. The inclusion of the objective test for harassment in the EqA 2010's predecessor legislation generated criticism as it had the potential to invite conclusions (for example) that a women working in a male environment would be unreasonable to take objection to sexualised comments or behaviour. Such an approach would undermine the very purpose of a prohibition on sexual harassment.

---

[131] Listed in s. 29(5) as age, disability, gender reassignment, race, religion or belief, sex, and sexual orientation.
[132] Note, therefore, that s. 29 prohibits both harassment related to sex and sexual harassment.

In *Richmond Pharmacology* v. *Dhaliwal*,[133] Underhill P stated that the purpose of the objective test was (in the context of a racial harassment claim) to avoid a finding of harassment where 'the tribunal believes that the claimant was unreasonably prone to take offence' and to avoid 'a culture of hypersensitivity or the imposition of legal liability in respect of every unfortunate phrase'. Despite fears that the inclusion of an express objective test would invite arguments that claimants should 'in Rome, do as the Romans', or at least put up with what Romans do, there is no evidence that the test was used in this way, and the inclusion of an objective element in the assessment of harassment is perhaps both necessary and inevitable to avoid a situation in which wholly unreasonable offence is taken.[134] In *Richmond Pharmacology* the EAT accepted that an ET had been entitled (just) to find racial harassment where a British woman of Indian ethnicity was told, in the context of a heated discussion with her manager, that '[w]e will probably bump into each other in future, unless you are married off in India', although Underhill P went out of his way to stress that 'not every racially slanted adverse comment or conduct may constitute the violation of a person's dignity. Dignity is not necessarily violated by things said or done which are trivial or transitory, particularly if it should have been clear that any offence was unintended.'[135]

The Court of Appeal accepted, in *English* v. *Thomas Sanderson*,[136] that a man could be harassed on grounds of sexual orientation when his colleagues made repeated references to his being gay and subjected him to 'homophobic banter', even though it was accepted that all concerned knew that he was not. Collins LJ stated in terms that repeatedly calling someone 'Paki' or 'Jew-boy' could amount to racial harassment whether or not the person was, or was believed to be, Asian or Jewish. The decision was reached under the predecessor provisions of the EqA 2010 but would be the same today.

Section 40 EqA 2010, in its original form, provided that employers could be liable for acts of harassment by third parties in some circumstances. This provision was repealed in 2013, as part of the-then government's 'burdens on business'-reducing agenda. Without it, workers will generally be unable to challenge harassment by clients, customers and/or workers who are self-employed, or who are employed by individuals or organisations who occupy the same premises (or whose staff occupy the same premises) as the

---

[133] [2009] ICR 724, paras. 33 and 34.

[134] See *Grant* v. *HM Land Registry* [2011] IRLR 748 in which the Court of Appeal ruled that the claimant had not been subjected to harassment despite his subjective perception to the contrary.

[135] *Ibid.*, para. 22. And see *Quality Solicitors CMTH* v. *Tunstall* [2014] EqLR 679 in which the EAT ruled that an overheard remark that the claimant was 'Polish [as she was] but very nice' (emphasis added) was not capable of amounting to harassment.

[136] [2009] IRLR 206.

person harassed.[137] Vulnerability to these types of harassment has become increasingly common with the atomisation of working relationships, while recent coverage of matters such as the 'President's Club' dinner in 2018, and the '#MeToo' movement illustrates the endemic nature sexual harassment, much of it beyond the reach of the EqA 2010 in its present form.

Victimisation

Equality Act 2010, Section 27

(1) A person (A) victimises another person (B) if A subjects B to a detriment because –
 (a) B does a protected act, or
 (b) A believes that B has done, or may do, a protected act.

(2) Each of the following is a protected act –
 (a) bringing proceedings under this Act;
 (b) giving evidence or information in connection with proceedings under this Act;
 (c) doing any other thing for the purposes of or in connection with this Act;
 (d) making an allegation (whether or not express) that A or another person has contravened this Act.

(3) Giving false evidence or information, or making a false allegation, is not a protected act if the evidence or information is given, or the allegation is made, in bad faith.

The victimisation provisions in all of the EqA 2010's predecessor legislation required claimants to establish that they had been subject to 'less favourable treatment' by reason of having done a 'protected act'. Section 27 does away with the need for a comparator. It is necessary,[138] though not sufficient, for the claimant to establish a causal link between protected act and detriment complained of; the protected act has to be the reason for the detriment in order for victimisation to be established.[139]

---

[137] The suggestion in *Burton* v. *De Vere* [1996] IRLR 596 that a worker could make a discrimination claim against his or her own employer if he or she could establish that the employer could have controlled the events was disapproved of by the House of Lords in *Pearce* v. *Governing Body of Mayfield Secondary School* [2003] UKHL 34, [2003] ICR 937. An attempt to revive *Burton* failed in *Conteh* v. *Parking Partners Ltd* [2011] ICR 341.

[138] See for example *Cousins* v. *Forum@Greenwich* 1 February 2016, Appeal No. UKEAT/0183/15/DM, unreported, in which the tribunal found as a fact that attempts to influence a board to victimise the claimant had been unsuccessful, and that her dismissal had been for a different reason.

[139] *Chief Constable of Greater Manchester* v. *Bailey* [2017] EWCA Civ 425. There the Court of Appeal ruled that the claimant had not been victimised when the secondment which had been put in place as part of a settlement of his race-discrimination complaint came to an end in accordance with the settlement agreement.

One difficulty which can arise in this context is illustrated by the decision in *HM Prison Service and Others v. Ibimidun*.[140] The claimant had brought multiple race discrimination claims against the employer all of which had been rejected, on five occasions with costs awarded against him, and with the tribunal ruling on one occasion that his motive in litigating had not been to seek just compensation but, rather, to harass the employer into settlement by a sustained campaign of litigation. He was eventually dismissed for the express reason that he had harassed his employer and the members of staff against whom he had made unreasonable allegations, causing the latter staff stress and anxiety and putting a huge strain on financial and personnel resources. Section 27(3) provides that false complaints made in bad faith do not amount to unprotected acts. In the *Ibimidun* case the EAT did not consider whether this provision applied. Rather, it accepted that the act of bringing the discrimination proceedings had been protected by section 27, but ruled that the reason for the claimant's dismissal was not simply that he had brought the claim, but that he had brought it to harass the Prison Service and its other employees. In those circumstances, the claim failed without any need to consider section 27(3). This outcome may have been all but inevitable on the facts of the case, but care should be taken to avoid a situation in which this reasoning is not over-extended (for example to a case in which the employer argued that a claimant was not dismissed because she alleged sex discrimination, rather because of the manner of the allegation (loudly, or other than by using the appropriate procedure, or otherwise to the wrong person, for example)).

Difficulties have also arisen in relation to the scope of action which employers might take to safeguard their positions in relation to legal action taken against them by current employers. In *Chief Constable of West Yorkshire Police v. Khan*,[141] the House of Lords ruled that the employer's refusal to provide a reference to a police officer who was in the throes of a race-discrimination claim did not amount to victimisation. Had the employer provided a favourable reference, this fact could have been used against it in the claim, which concerned a failure to promote. If it had provided an unfavourable reference, this could have been regarded as a further act of discrimination. Lord Nicholls, with whom the majority agreed, suggested that employers who acted 'honestly and reasonably' in taking 'steps to preserve their position in pending discrimination proceedings' would 'not [be] doing so because of the fact that the complainant has brought discrimination proceedings [but] ... because, currently and temporarily; [they] need ... to take steps to preserve [their] position[s] in the outstanding proceedings'.

The scope of the room left to employers to 'safeguard their positions' in the context of litigation fell to be considered by the House of Lords in *St Helens Metropolitan Borough Council v. Derbyshire and Others*.[142] The background to

---

[140] [2008] IRLR 940.   [141] [2001] ICR 1065.   [142] [2007] ICR 841.

the case was an equal pay claim brought by women employees of the council. Many of the women, but not the claimants in this case, had settled their claims. Two months before the equal pay claims were due to be heard by tribunal, the employers wrote to a large number of employees, including the claimants, stating that 'the continuance of the current claims and a ruling against the council will have a severe impact on *all* staff', and explaining in some detail why this would be so. A further letter was sent to the remaining claimants alone, renewing an offer to settle proceedings and stating that the writer was 'greatly concerned about the likely outcome of this matter as stated in the letter to all catering staff'. Lord Neuberger, who delivered the leading speech in the House of Lords, suggested that the question whether those claiming victimisation had been subject to 'detriment' was to be determined by reference to the view of a 'reasonable worker'. While '[d]istress and worry which may be induced by the employer's honest and reasonable conduct in the course of his defence or in the conduct of any settlement negotiations, cannot (save, possibly, in the most unusual circumstances) constitute "detriment"',[143] the tribunal was entitled to conclude from the circumstances in this case (which included the fact that the letters had been sent to the individual litigants, rather than their legal representatives, that they were designed to get the claimants to settle against the view of their union and that they were sent simultaneously with letters to other claimants who had settled), that the letters had been intimidatory.

Disability

Duty of Reasonable Accommodation

In addition to the generally applicable prohibitions on direct and indirect discrimination, harassment and victimisation, the EqA 2010 sets out two forms of discrimination which are applicable only in connection with disability. These consist of (1) the failure to make a reasonable adjustment (a type of discrimination first established in domestic law by the DDA 1995) and, (2) 'discrimination arising from disability'.

Taking first the duty to make reasonable adjustments, EqA 2010, section 20 (2)–(4), provides that the employer is under a duty 'to take such steps as it is reasonable to have to take to avoid' a disadvantage which arises from 'a provision, criterion or practice' applied by or on behalf of the employer or 'a physical feature' of premises occupied by the employer which 'puts a disabled person at a substantial disadvantage in relation to a relevant matter in comparison with persons who are not disabled'.[144] Section 20(5) provides that an

---

[143] *Ibid.*, para. 68.
[144] The extract above reads s. 20 with Sched. 8, which applies the duty of reasonable adjustment in the context of work.

employer is under a duty 'to take such steps as it is reasonable to have to take to provide' an auxiliary aid or service the absence of which would put the disabled person 'at a substantial disadvantage in relation to a relevant matter in comparison with persons who are not disabled'. Section 20(7) provides that '[a] person (A) who is subject to a duty to make reasonable adjustments is not (subject to express provision to the contrary) entitled to require a disabled person, in relation to whom A is required to comply with the duty, to pay to any extent A's costs of complying with the duty'.

The application of the duty to make reasonable adjustments in the context of employment (broadly defined) is further defined in Schedule 8 to the Act which provides, so far as relevant, that references in section 20(3), (4) or (5) to a disabled person are to a potential job applicant, where the alleged discrimination is connected with job offers, and an applicant or employee of A's, where the alleged discrimination is connected with employment by A. The 'relevant matters' in relation to section 20(3), (4) and (5) concern appointment and employment.[145]

With section 20 and Schedule 8 having set out the parameters of the duty to make reasonable adjustments as it applies to 'work', broadly defined, section 21 states that a failure to comply with the duty amounts to discrimination for the purposes of the EqA 2010. Schedule 8, paragraph 20, goes on to provide that the duty does not arise if the person to whom it would apply 'does not know, and could not reasonably be expected to know' that a relevant person has a disability. The Code of Practice states that an 'employer must ... do all they can reasonably be expected to do to find out whether' a relevant person (an employee, for example, or a candidate) has a disability and is likely to be placed at a substantial disadvantage by a PCP etc. and that, '[w]hen making enquiries about disability, employers should consider issues of dignity and privacy and ensure that personal information is dealt with confidentially'.[146] It provides an example of a call-centre worker who cries at work and 'has difficulty dealing with customer enquiries when the symptoms of her depression are severe', suggesting that '[i]t is likely to be reasonable for the employer to discuss with the worker whether her crying is connected to a disability and whether a reasonable adjustment could be made to her working arrangements'.

EqA 2010, section 60, prohibits pre-employment health questions from being asked of applicants except, under section 60(6), in order to comply with any duty to make reasonable adjustment, to 'establish ... whether [they] will be able to carry out a function that is intrinsic to the work concerned', or for

---

[145] Particular provision is made by Sched. 8 in relation to contract workers, partners, barristers, office holders etc., the duty to make adjustments in each case being imposed on the person who is in a position to make such adjustments and the 'interested disabled person' being defined as the person in a position to benefit from the adjustment.

[146] Para. 6.19.

monitoring or positive action purposes. The purpose of this provision is to protect applicants with disabilities from being discriminated against when they disclose their disability, although there is a certain tension, notwithstanding the inclusion of section 60(6), because it is regarded as good practice for employers to invite disclosure of disabilities where such conditions might, in the absence of reasonable adjustment, affect a candidate's performance in the application process.[147] The Code of Practice provides, as examples of lawful pre-employment questions related to health: application forms inviting disabled candidates to contact the employer concerning interview-related adjustments and questions designed to ensure that candidates for jobs as scaffolders have the ability 'to climb ladders and scaffolding to a significant height', such ability being 'intrinsic to the job'.[148] Employers are warned, however, to tread carefully in response to any disclosure by a candidate of a disability not directly relevant to his or her ability to perform the intrinsic functions of the job.

In determining whether an employer has failed to comply with a duty to make reasonable adjustments a tribunal should proceed by identifying:

(a) the provision, criterion or practice applied by or on behalf of an employer, or;
(b) the physical feature of premises occupied by the employer;
(c) the identity of non-disabled comparators (where appropriate); and
(d) the nature and extent of the substantial disadvantage suffered by the claimant.[149]

These steps are required before a tribunal can determine whether any particular adjustment would be reasonable.

The precedessor to the EqA, the DDA 1995, section 18B, set out factors to which tribunals were required to have regard in determining whether any particular step would have been reasonable for an employer to take. These included, *inter alia*, 'the extent to which taking the step would prevent the effect in relation to which the duty is imposed', questions of practicability, costs and disruption, and the availability to the employer of resources and outside assistance. Among the examples of the steps provided by section 18B(2) were the making of adjustments to premises, transfer of the disabled employee and/or reallocation of some of his or her duties, changes to hours or place of work, the provision of time off, mentoring, special equipment and assistance from (for example) a reader or interpreter etc. Section 18B did not find its way into

---

[147] S. 60(6)(a) states that the prohibition does not apply to a question asked in order to 'establish ... whether B [the disabled person] will be able to comply with a requirement to undergo an assessment or establishing whether a duty to make reasonable adjustments is or will be imposed on A in relation to B in connection with a requirement to undergo an assessment'.

[148] Paras. 10.30–10.36.

[149] *Environment Agency* v. *Rowan* [2008] IRLR 20, [2008] ICR 218, approved post EqA 2010 in *Newham Sixth Form College* v. *Sanders* [2014] EWCA Civ 734.

the EqA 2010 but paragraph 6.28 of the Code, which suggests 'some of the factors which might be taken into account when deciding what is a reasonable step for an employer to have to take', has its origin in DDA 1995, section 18B, as do the examples provided at paragraph 6.33 of the 'steps it might be reasonable for employers to have to take'. Paragraph 6.29 of the Code goes on to state that: 'Ultimately the test of the "reasonableness" of any step an employer may have to take is an objective one and will depend on the circumstances of the case.'[150]

Discrimination Arising from Disability

Equality Act 2010, Section 15

(1) A person (A) discriminates against a disabled person (B) if –
  (a) A treats B unfavourably because of something arising in consequence of B's disability, and
  (b) A cannot show that the treatment is a proportionate means of achieving a legitimate aim.
(2) Subsection (1) does not apply if A shows that A did not know, and could not reasonably have been expected to know, that B had the disability.

An employer who dismisses a disabled worker in connection with sickness absence will be caught by section 15, but will be able to justify the dismissal if it was 'a proportionate means of achieving a legitimate aim'. Direct discrimination against a disabled person (such as might result from the application, for example, of a blanket policy on refusing to employ anyone who is HIV+ or who has a history of mental illness) is incapable of justification. A refusal to employ someone who is HIV+ will not amount to direct discrimination, however, if the refusal is based not on the fact of the diagnosis but rather because the person poses a risk to others by virtue of the nature of the job or the circumstances in which it is carried out. Thus, for example, the dismissal of a residential support worker, because he was HIV+, did not amount to direct disability discrimination because the employer would have dismissed anyone who posed the same level of risk, because of a serious communicable disease other than HIV, to residents with severely challenging behaviour who sometimes scratched and bit support workers.[151]

---

[150] See the decision of the Supreme Court in *Paulley* v. *FirstGroup plc* [2017] UKSC 4, [2017] 2 All ER 1 for a recent example, albeit in the context of transport rather than employment, of the highest judicial authority on the application of the duty to make reasonable adjustments. The question there concerned the extent of the obligation placed on bus operators (and therefore drivers) to require fellow passengers to make space for wheelchair users.

[151] *High Quality Lifestyles* v. *Watts* [2006] IRLR 850 (EAT).

It follows that the concept of direct disability discrimination is very narrow, and most of the work will be done by the combination of the requirement to make reasonable adjustments (which might entail adjustments to the job such that a HIV+ person could do it safely) and the prohibition (subject to the possibility of justification) of discrimination arising from disability. The dismissal of the HIV+ support worker in *Watts* (above) would fall within section 15 and the question would be whether that dismissal was a proportionate means of achieving a legitimate aim. In *Watts*, the EAT went on to accept that the claimant's treatment (which at the time was understood to amount to 'disability-related discrimination') was not justified because the employers had failed to carry out a proper investigation or adequate risk assessment of the situation created by the claimant's condition. In addition, the employers had discriminated against him by failing to make reasonable adjustments, no proper consideration having been given to how his condition might have been accommodated.

Prohibited Discrimination

The EqA 2010 does not prohibit all discrimination related to the 'protected characteristics', although its material scope does extend beyond the employment context to regulate discrimination in the provision of goods, services etc. This is beyond the scope of this chapter. As far as employment-related discrimination is concerned, the position is governed by Part 5 of the Act, entitled 'Work', which itself consists of four chapters: 'Employment etc.' (sections 39–60); 'Occupational pension schemes' (sections 61–3); 'Equality of terms' (sections 64–80); and 'Supplementary' (sections 81–3). Here, we consider Chapter 1 in particular and Chapter 2 in passing, returning to deal with Chapter 3 below. Of central significance to this chapter is section 39, which prohibits discrimination and victimisation by employers in relation to access to jobs and the terms on which work is offered (section 39(1) and (3)), the terms of employment, access to promotion, training etc., dismissal and subjection to 'any other detriment' (section 39(2) and (4)), and imposes a duty of reasonable adjustment on employers (section 39(5)).

Most incidents of discrimination in employment will come within the relevant legislative provisions. It is clear, for example, that discriminatory dismissals (actual or constructive) will be covered (these may, in addition, also be challenged under the ERA 1996). So, too, will discriminatory refusals to employ, discriminatory interviewing and other recruitment arrangements. The House of Lords ruled in *Shamoon*, also considered above, that 'detriment' under section 39(2)(b)'s materially identical predecessor provisions is to be interpreted broadly: such 'detriment' would be established in relation to employment if a reasonable worker would or might take the view that she had been disadvantaged in the circumstances in which she had thereafter to work. An unjustified sense of grievance cannot amount to 'detriment', but it was not necessary for the claimant to establish that she had suffered some physical or economic consequence. Further protection is afforded by section 108 which prohibits discrimination and harassment 'aris[ing] out of and ... closely connected to a relationship which used to exist between' the parties, and in which that discrimination or harassment would have been prohibited. Duties of reasonable adjustment are imposed in this context by section 108(4).

Sections 53–9 provide that the prohibitions on discrimination, harassment and victimisation apply to:

- 'qualifications bodies' (authorities or bodies which can confer 'relevant qualification') in relation to the conferring of 'relevant qualifications' ('authorisation[s], qualification[s], recognition[s], registration[s], enrol-ment[s], approval[s] or certification which [are] needed for, or facilitate ... engagement in, a particular trade or profession');
- 'employment service providers' in relation to their provision of employment services (vocational training or guidance or arrangements relating to the provision thereof, finding jobs for people and people for jobs, careers services etc.);
- 'trade organisations' (trade unions and employers' organisations); and
- local authorities in relation to their members (who are not 'employed' by the authority, however broadly the term 'employed' is interpreted).

In its application to trade unions and employers' organisations *vis-à-vis* their members (as distinct from in their activities as employers), the EqA 2010, section 57 prohibits discrimination, harassment and victimisation in relation to admission to and membership of such organisations, section 57(8) impos-ing duties of reasonable adjustment on trade organisations, defined by section 57(9) as 'organisation[s] of workers ... [or] of employers' and 'any other organisation whose members carry on a particular trade or profession for the purposes of which the organisation exists'. Chapter 2 of Part 5 then provides that those who run occupational pension schemes must not discriminate, harass or victimise members, subject to exceptions relating primarily to age discrimination.

'General Occupational Requirement' and Other Exceptions to the Prohibitions on Discrimination

The exceptions to the prohibitions on discrimination in the context of work are found in Part 14 of and Schedule 22 to the EqA 2010, which set out general exceptions to the prohibitions, and in Schedule 9 which deals specifically with exceptions to the prohibition on work-related discrimination. Dealing first (and very briefly) with the general exceptions, section 192 provides that: 'A person does not contravene this Act only by doing, for the purpose of safeguarding national security, anything it is proportionate to do for that purpose.' Schedule 22, insofar as it applies to work, provides in paragraph

1 fairly broad exceptions in the case of age, disability and religion/belief where the discriminator is required to act as he or she did by statute. Sex discrimination under statutory authority is lawful only where it is necessary to comply with specific provisions concerning the protection of women in connection with pregnancy, maternity or other risks 'specifically affecting women' (paragraph 2).

Provision is made by paragraph 3 of Schedule 22 for educational establishments whose founding instruments require particular members of academic staff to be from a particular religious order, or to be women and (more controversially) by paragraph 4 for schools governed by the School Standards and Framework Act 1998 which allows religious schools to discriminate on grounds of religion as regards staff. Finally, exceptions are provided by paragraph 5 in relation to 'rules restricting to persons of particular birth, nationality, descent or residence (a) employment in the service of the Crown; (b) employment by a prescribed public body; (c) holding a public office'.

EqA 2010, Schedule 23, also permits nationality discrimination and discrimination relating to place of residence where (paragraph 1) it is required (broadly) by statutory provision or ministerial arrangements. Paragraph 4 allows the provision of training specifically to non-EEA residents not expected to work thereafter in the UK.

The exceptions in Schedule 9 relate particularly to the context of work. Paragraph 4 provides that the prohibitions on disability and age discrimination do not apply to service in the armed forces, and further permits discrimination against women and transgendered people 'in relation to service in the armed forces ... if the person shows that [it] ... is a proportionate means of ensuring the combat effectiveness of the armed forces'.

Further exceptions are provided in Part 2 of Schedule 9 to the prohibition on age discrimination in employment. Part 1 of Schedule 9 also sets out the GOR defence, which is based on Article 4 of Council Directive 2000/78/EC.

Council Directive 2000/78/EC, Article 4

1 ... Member States may provide that a difference of treatment which is based on a characteristic related to any of the grounds referred to in Article 1 shall not constitute discrimination where, by reason of the nature of the particular occupational activities concerned or of the context in which they are carried out, such a characteristic constitutes a genuine and determining occupational requirement, provided that the objective is legitimate and the requirement is proportionate.[152]

---

[152] Art. 4 of Council Directive 2000/43/EC is in materially similar terms to Art. 1 of Council Directive 2000/78/EC, as is Art. 14.2 of Council Directive 2006/54/EC, neither having any equivalent to Art. 4.2 above.

2. Member States may maintain national legislation in force at the date of adoption of this Directive or provide for future legislation incorporating national practices existing at the date of adoption of this Directive pursuant to which, in the case of occupational activities within churches and other public or private organisations the ethos of which is based on religion or belief, a difference of treatment based on a person's religion or belief shall not constitute discrimination where, by reason of the nature of these activities or of the context in which they are carried out, a person's religion or belief constitute a genuine, legitimate and justified occupational requirement, having regard to the organisation's ethos. This difference of treatment shall be implemented taking account of Member States' constitutional provisions and principles, as well as the general principles of Community law, and should not justify discrimination on another ground.

Provided that its provisions are otherwise complied with, this Directive shall thus not prejudice the right of churches and other public or private organisations, the ethos of which is based on religion or belief, acting in conformity with national constitutions and laws, to require individuals working for them to act in good faith and with loyalty to the organisation's ethos.

The domestic transposition of Article 4 is in EqA 2010.

Equality Act 2010, Schedule 9, Paragraphs 1–3

1. (1) A person (A) does not contravene a [prohibition on work-related discrimination] . . . by applying in relation to work a requirement to have a particular protected characteristic, if A shows that, having regard to the nature or context of the work –
   (a) it is an occupational requirement,
   (b) the application of the requirement is a proportionate means of achieving a legitimate aim, and
   (c) the person to whom A applies the requirement does not meet it (or A has reasonable grounds for not being satisfied that the person meets it) . . .
   . . .

2. (1) A person (A) does not contravene a [prohibition on work-related discrimination] . . . by applying in relation to employment a requirement to which sub-paragraph (4) applies if A shows that –
   (a) the employment is for the purposes of an organised religion,
   (b) the application of the requirement engages the compliance or non-conflict principle, and
   (c) the person to whom A applies the requirement does not meet it (or A has reasonable grounds for not being satisfied that the person meets it).
   . . .

(3) A person does not contravene section 53(1) or (2)(a) or (b) by applying in relation to a relevant qualification (within the meaning of that section) a requirement to which sub-paragraph (4) applies if the person shows that –

(a) the qualification is for the purposes of employment mentioned in sub-paragraph (1)(a), and

(b) the application of the requirement engages the compliance or non-conflict principle.

(4) This sub-paragraph applies to –

(a) a requirement to be of a particular sex;

(b) a requirement not to be a transsexual person;

(c) a requirement not to be married or a civil partner;

(d) a requirement not to be married to, or the civil partner of, a person who has a living former spouse or civil partner;

(e) a requirement relating to circumstances in which a marriage or civil partnership came to an end;

(f) a requirement related to sexual orientation.

(5) The application of a requirement engages the compliance principle if the requirement is applied so as to comply with the doctrines of the religion.

(6) The application of a requirement engages the non-conflict principle if, because of the nature or context of the employment, the requirement is applied so as to avoid conflicting with the strongly held religious convictions of a significant number of the religion's followers . . .

3. A person (A) with an ethos based on religion or belief does not contravene a provision mentioned in paragraph 1(2) by applying in relation to work a requirement to be of a particular religion or belief if A shows that, having regard to that ethos and to the nature or context of the work –

(a) it is an occupational requirement,

(b) the application of the requirement is a proportionate means of achieving a legitimate aim, and

(c) the person to whom A applies the requirement does not meet it (or A has reasonable grounds for not being satisfied that the person meets it).

The decision of the ECJ in *Wolf* v. *Stadt Frankfurt am Main*[153] suggests a relatively relaxed approach to the GOR defence but this may be particular to the context: age discrimination which is subject (by contrast to all the other protected characteristics) to a general justification defence applicable to direct as well as indirect discrimination. In *Wolf* the ECJ accepted that an age limit of thirty for joining the fire service was a GOR to ensure the fitness of recruits notwithstanding the fact that recruits were also subjected to rigorous fitness

---

[153] C-229/08, *Wolf* v. *Stadt Frankfurt am Main* [2010] IRLR 244.

testing, because very few officers aged over forty-five, and none aged over fifty, had the physical capacity to engage in fire-fighting. While it may be the case, notwithstanding the ability to pass a fitness test at (say) forty, that the improbability (or even impossibility) of remaining fit for active service at forty-five or fifty would have the effect of making 'being under forty' a GOR for the job, it seems that allowing a cut-off point of fifteen or twenty years before likely or certain unfitness is stretching the notion of the GOR very thin indeed.[154]

Leaving aside the decision in *Wolf*, paragraph 1 is relatively uncontroversial because it will permit only those instances of discrimination which are necessary and proportionate. Among these may be the requirement that counselling staff at rape crisis centres or domestic violence refuges catering to women are women,[155] and that those providing similar services primarily to women of particular minority ethnic groups also share the ethnicity of the client base. Similarly, being a gay man (even a young gay man) might be a GOR for an outreach job in sexual health working with young male sex workers, while being a Catholic priest or a rabbi might well be a GOR for appointment to a particular chaplaincy in a hospital trust or a university, although being a Catholic will not be a GOR in relation to a position as head teacher of a local-authority-controlled Catholic school.[156]

Most of the CJEU case-law on article 4(1) concerns age limits. One which did not was *Bougnaoui and another* v. *Micropole SA* in which an employer sought to rely on the provision to justify the dismissal of a design engineer who wore hijab, and who had refused to remove her headscarf in line with instructions from the customer at whose site she was working.[157] The CJEU ruled that the concept of a 'genuine and determining occupational requirement' within Article 4(1) 'refers to a requirement that is objectively dictated by the nature of the occupational activities concerned or of the context in which they are carried out' and could not 'cover subjective considerations, such as the willingness of the employer to take account of the particular wishes of the customer'.[158]

More problematic than Article 4(1) is Article 4(2) and its domestic implementation in Schedule 9 paragraph 2, extracted above. That paragraph is not significantly changed from its predecessor provisions, the application of which had been considered in *R(Amicus and Others)* v. *Secretary of State for Trade and Industry and Others*.[159] There the High Court rejected the argument put

---

[154] See C-416/13 *Vital Pérez* v. *Ayuntamiento de Oviedo* [2015] IRLR 158 in which the CJEU rejected a thirty-year age limit for police officers, and C-258/15 *Salaberria Sorondo* v. *Academia Vasca de Policía y Emergencias* [2017] IRLR 162 in which it permitted a thirty-five-year age limit.

[155] Some discrimination against non-natal women is also likely to be lawful in this context.

[156] *Glasgow City Council* v. *McNab* [2007] IRLR 476.   [157] Case C-188/15 [2017] IRLR 447.

[158] §40. Note the decision in *Achbita*, discussed at pp. 355–6, in which an employer was permitted to prohibit religious/political insignia in pursuit of a 'secular' workplace without reliance on Art. 4.

[159] [2004] IRLR 430.

for the applicants that a church could refuse to employ a gay cleaner 'in a building in which he is liable to handle religious artefacts, to avoid offending the strongly-held religious convictions of a significant number of adherents', that a Catholic order could dismiss a science teacher for having a lesbian relationship and that an Islamic institute could refuse 'to employ as a librarian a man appearing to the employer to be homosexual, reasoning that his sexual orientation will conflict with the strongly held religious convictions of a significant number of Muslims'.[160] Richards J (as he then was) ruled that:

> the exception was intended to be very narrow; and in my view it is, on its proper construction, very narrow. It has to be construed strictly since it is a derogation from the principle of equal treatment; and it has to be construed purposively so as to ensure, so far as possible, compatibility with the Directive. When its terms are considered in the light of those interpretative principles, they can be seen to afford an exception only in very limited circumstances.[161]

Notwithstanding the decision of the High Court in *Amicus*, a leaked reasoned opinion of the European Commission in infringement No. 2006/2450 (such documents generally being confidential) disclosed the Commission's view that the predecessor provision to paragraph 2 was not compatible with EU law,[162] primarily because of the absence of any proportionality requirement. The Equality Bill in its original form included a proportionality requirement in paragraph 2 but this did not survive the legislative process.[163]

In *Pemberton* v. *Inwood* the EAT considered the respondent bishop's refusal to provide the claimant, a Church of England priest, with an extra parochial ministry licence 'EPML' after the claimant announced his intention to marry his same-sex partner.[164] The EPML was required as a condition of the claimant's appointment as chaplain and bereavement manager at an NHS trust. The claimant brought proceedings complaining of unlawful direct discrimination because of sexual orientation and/or marital status and/or of unlawful harassment related to sexual orientation. The tribunal having found that the EPML authorisation was a 'relevant qualification' as defined in section 54 EqA 2010 (see p. 380), ruled that the bishop could rely on the GOR defence in Schedule 9 paragraph 2(3); the employment would have been for the purposes of an organised religion, and the bishop's actions were necessary because to be in a same-sex marriage was incompatible with the doctrine of the Church of England in relation to marriage. The claim of

---

[160] *Ibid.*   [161] §115.

[162] European Commission, reasoned opinion infringement No. 2006/2450, 20 November 2009.

[163] Nor did the proviso that employment would only be classified as being for the purposes of an organised religion if it 'wholly or mainly involves (a) leading or assisting in the observation of liturgical or ritualistic practices of the religion, or (b) promoting or explaining the doctrine of the religion (whether to followers of the religion or to others)'.

[164] [2017] IRLR 211, [2017] ICR 929.

harassment was dismissed because the only actions of which the claimant complained were those permitted by paragraph 2(3), which the tribunal ruled could not, absent any aggravating features, amount to unlawful harassment even though they were humiliating and degrading for the claimant.

The discussion above relates to paragraph 2 of Schedule 9. Paragraph 3 imposes a proportionality requirement in relation to discrimination by employers 'with an ethos based on religion or belief', but the potential for overlap between paragraphs 2 and 3 is clear from an advertisement which was placed in the *Sunday Times* in June 2011. The advertisement, which invited applications for the post of Communications Director for the Church of England, stipulated (relying on EqA 2010, Schedule 9, Part 1, without specifying paragraph 1, 2 or 3) that the successful appointee would be 'somebody who will share our values and whilst not necessarily an Anglican; [will be] a practising Christian ... because of [the post holder's] representational role and ... responsibility for maintaining a Christian ethos within the national Church, as one of its senior officers'.[165] As interesting as what this advertisement stipulates was what it did not state in so many words. At the Public Bill Committee hearing of 10 June 2009 into the Equality Bill, William Fittall, secretary general of the General Synod of the Church of England, stated that: 'The director of communications for the Church of England has a representational role, and it would not be credible for him to do his job if he had been married three times and caused a scandal, or if he were a campaigning member for gay rights in a sexually active relationship.'[166]

The decision of an employment tribunal in *Saini* v. *National Offender Management Services [NOMS] and Others* illustrates an additional hurdle likely to be faced by those in respect of whom the paragraph 9(3) defence might be pleaded.[167] The claimant was a Sikh prison chaplain whose services were dispensed with as a result of a dispute which arose between him and the Director of NOMS' Sikh Chaplaincy Service as to a question of Sikh doctrine. The tribunal struck out his claim of religious discrimination because its determination would have required the tribunal to decide whether or not the views that he had been advocating were or were not contrary to the Sikh religion. It had long been established that this kind of decision is beyond the competence of the secular courts and so the claim was non-justiciable.[168]

In addition to the GORs set out above, particular age-related exceptions are provided by Part 2 of Schedule 9. These include provisions permitting (without the requirement to consider proportionality) benefits related to length of service (paragraph 9); allowing age-related payment reflective of the National Minimum Wage (paragraphs 10 and 11) and differential redundancy payments

---

[165] http://appointments.thesundaytimes.co.uk/job/409478/communications-director.
[166] www.publications.parliament.uk/pa/cm200809/cmpublic/equality/090609/am/90609s03.htm.
[167] Case No 2200542/2015, 25 November 2015, available as Westlaw 2015 WL 12591127.
[168] See for example *R* v. *Chief Rabbi ex parte Wachmann* [1992] 1 WLR 1036.

depending on age (paragraph 13), also the provision of insurance only to employees who are under the age of sixty-five or the state pensionable age (whichever is the greater) and the making of age-related payments into personal pension schemes (paragraphs 14 and 16).

Equal Pay

EqA 2010, Part 5, Chapter 3, regulates sex equality in pay and pensions. The central provision dealing with 'equality of terms' is section 66(1), which provides that: 'If the terms of A's work do not (by whatever means) include a sex equality clause, they are to be treated as including one.' A sex-equality clause is one which modifies any relevant term of A's contract to be no less favourable than that of a suitable comparator (B), or includes a comparable term to one which B enjoys if A's contract does not include such a term. By section 64, the Act expressly applies to those holding personal or private offices, as well as to employees,[169] and provides that the claimant and her comparator need not be contemporaneously employed, with the effect that a claimant should be able to rely on successors as well as predecessors in employment.[170] Section 67 makes similar provision in relation to pensions as that made by section 66 in relation to pay, by providing that pension schemes will be treated as including a 'sex equality rule' requiring non-discriminatory treatment on grounds of sex as regards the operation of the scheme.

   Section 64 provides that the sex-equality clause/rule applies (only) where A and B perform 'work that is equal', as defined by section 65.

Equality Act 2010, Section 65

(1) For the purposes of this Chapter, A's work is equal to that of B if it is –
   (a) like B's work,
   (b) rated as equivalent to B's work, or
   (c) of equal value to B's work.
(2) A's work is like B's work if –
   (a) A's work and B's work are the same or broadly similar, and
   (b) such differences as there are between their work are not of practical importance in relation to the terms of their work.
(3) So on a comparison of one person's work with another's for the purposes of subsection (2), it is necessary to have regard to –
   (a) the frequency with which differences between their work occur in practice, and
   (b) the nature and extent of the differences.

[169] In which case, the required comparator is adjusted (s. 79).   [170] S. 64(2).

(4) A's work is rated as equivalent to B's work if a job evaluation study –
  (a) gives an equal value to A's job and B's job in terms of the demands made on a worker, or
  (b) would give an equal value to A's job and B's job in those terms where the evaluation is not made on a sex-specific system.
(5) A system is sex-specific if, for the purposes of one or more of the demands made on a worker, it sets values for men different from those it sets for women.
(6) A's work is of equal value to B's work if it is –
  (a) neither like B's work nor rated as equivalent to B's work, but
  (b) nevertheless equal to B's work in terms of the demands made on A by reference to factors such as effort, skill and decision-making.

Section 79 further provides that A and B must be employed by the same or associated employers, and must work at the same establishment or at establishments at which 'common terms apply at the establishments (either generally or as between A and B)'. Section 79(9) provides that 'employers are associated if (a) one is a company of which the other (directly or indirectly) has control, or (b) both are companies of which a third person (directly or indirectly) has control'. If the claimant and her comparator hold personal or public offices, the same person must be responsible for paying both.

The requirement (other than in the case of office holders) that the claimant and her comparator must be employed by the same or associated employers was a feature of the Equal Pay Act 1970 and was challenged on a number of occasions as inconsistent with the directly effective Article 141 EC (formerly Article 119, now 157 TFEU). *Lawrence* v. *Regent Office Care Ltd*[171] was a claim brought by women who had been employed by North Yorkshire County Council as 'dinner ladies', but whose employment had been contracted out to private-sector employers and whose terms and conditions had fallen behind those of the men still working for the council, to whom the women had had comparable terms prior to contracting out.[172] It was accepted that they were employed on 'work rated as equivalent' to the men. The question was whether Article 141 allowed them to bring a claim by reference to the men notwithstanding the fact that they were no longer employed 'by the same employer'. The matter eventually reached the ECJ which ruled that, although the scope of Article 141 was not limited to cases in which men and women worked for the same employer, it could not be relied upon to challenge pay differences in a case such as this in which the pay differences at issue could not be attributed to a single source, since there was no body which was responsible for the inequality and which could restore equal treatment.

[171] C-320/00 [2002] ECR I-7325.   [172] [2000] IRLR 608.

The ECJ was again asked to consider the scope of Article 141 in *Allonby* v. *Accrington and Rossendale College*,[173] a claim brought by a part-time hourly lecturer whose job had been contracted out by her employers who wished to avoid the implications of the Part-Time Workers (Prevention of Less Favourable Treatment) Regulations 2000. She, with all her part-time colleagues, was made redundant and advised to supply her services on a self-employed basis through an agency called Education Learning Services. This had the effect of reducing her hourly income and various benefits including sick pay and career structure, and of denying her access to her former employer's pension scheme which was open only to employees of the college. The claimant cited as her comparator a male full-time lecturer at the college. The Court of Appeal referred to the ECJ the questions (1) whether, under Article 141, she could compare herself with an employee of the college in the circumstances and (2) whether Article 141 (now Article 157 TFEU) had direct effect so as to entitle her to claim access to the pension scheme either (a) by comparing herself with a man still employed by the college or (b) by showing statistically that a considerably smaller proportion of female than of male teachers who were otherwise eligible to join the scheme could comply with the requirement of being employed under a contract of employment.[174] The ECJ ruled, on the same basis as it had in *Lawrence*, that she could not make an equal pay claim using the comparator employed by the college. But it went on to rule that a comparator was not always necessary to establish a breach of Article 141 where, for example, legislation indirectly discriminated (as was here alleged) against women as a group. Such claims are now also possible under the EqA 2010 by reason of section 71, though only, as we saw where (unlike the case in *Allonby* itself) direct discrimination is claimed. Thus, for as long as the UK remains bound by EU law, there remains some scope for claims under Article 157 TFEU.[175]

The EqA 2010 restricts comparators not only to those men employed 'by the same employer' but also to those 'in the same employment' as the claimant or at an establishment at which 'common terms apply at the establishments (either generally or as between A and B)'. This criteria featured also in the Equal Pay Act (EqPA) 1970 and gave rise to a number of decisions over the years. In *British Coal Corporation* v. *Smith and Others*,[176] the House of Lords ruled that a broad approach should be taken, with coverage by the same (national) collective agreement being a paradigmatic example of 'common terms and conditions' notwithstanding the existence of local collective agreements on relatively minor matters. In *North* v. *Dumfries and Galloway Council*

---

[173] C-256/01 [2004] ECR I-873.   [174] [2001] IRLR 364.

[175] Note also that, in *North Cumbria Acute Hospitals NHS Trust* v. *Potter* [2009] IRLR 176, the EAT confirmed that the 'single-source' rule did not apply to the Equal Pay Act 1970, whose terms were materially similar.

[176] [1996] ICR 515. See, for recent applications of this principle, *City of Edinburgh Council* v. *Wilkinson* [2010] IRLR 756.

the Supreme Court reiterated this position in a case in which female support staff employed by the local authority in schools and nurseries challenged a decision by the Court of Session that they were not entitled to compare themselves with males employed by the local authority as groundsmen, road-workers, refuse collectors and a leisure attendant.[177] The women were employed under the 'Blue Book' collective agreement, the men under the 'Green Book'. The tribunal decided that, had the comparators been employed at the establishments in which the women worked, they would have been employed under broadly similar terms to those that they currently enjoyed. The Court of Session had reversed that finding on the basis that the evidence did not show a 'real possibility' that the comparators could be transferred to the claimants' workplaces. The Supreme Court ruled that the Court of Session had erred in introducing this 'gloss' on the *BCC* v. *Smith* case, further that this additional test would defeat the object of the 'common-terms' test which was to extend the range of comparators in an equal-pay claim.

In *Asda Stores Ltd* v. *Brierley*, notable for being the first mass equal-pay claim by private sector employees, the EAT considered an appeal from Asda against a finding that predominantly female supermarket workers could compare themselves with male distribution workers based at separate depots.[178] One significant feature which differentiated this case from many of the big public-sector cases was that, whereas the predominantly male distribution workforce was unionised, and its terms and conditions collectively agreed, the predominantly female shop-workers were not. Asda argued that Article 157 did not have direct effect in equal value claims, alternatively that (if it did) it was insufficient for terms and conditions of claimants and comparators to have a 'single souce', and that there had to be, in addition, a single establishment, collective agreement or statutory framework applicable to them. The EAT (Kerr J presiding) ruled that Article 157 was directly effective in equal-value claims and that it was sufficient for the purposes of a claim that a 'single source' of pay and conditions existed for claimant and comparator. Here, in a case in which no comparators were employed at the establishments in which the claimants worked, the tribunal had correctly asked itself whether, if distribution staff did their jobs at store locations, broadly similar terms would apply, such that it could be said that common terms were observed at both types of establishment. He had been entitled on the evidence to conclude that this was the case.

The decisions of the tribunal and EAT in *Asda*, like those of the trbunal and Supreme Court in *North*, involve the entirely orthodox application of a principle established by the House of Lords in *BCC* v. *Smith*. It is testament to the ecomomic impact of potential equal-pay claims on this scale that Asda has nevertheless appealed, the Court of Appeal having recently rejected that appeal.

---

[177] [2013] UKSC 45, [2013] 4 All ER 413.
[178] [2017] IRLR 1058 and see [2019] EWCA Civ 44, [2019] IRLR 335.

Section 70 provides that, where an equal-pay claim can be brought within section 66 or 67 (subject to any section 69 defence: see immediately below), the claimant cannot choose instead to proceed by way of a sex-discrimination claim under section 39.[179] Where, however, no such claim is available (where there is no suitable comparator), section 71 allows a claim to be brought under section 39 as long as the discrimination complained of is direct. So, for example, if an employer has a policy of paying women 20 per cent less as a matter of course because they are women than he would pay them if they were men, then a claim can be brought under section 39 if the absence of a suitable comparator means that one cannot be brought under section 66. If, on the other hand, the policy is that part-timers are paid 20 per cent less, in terms of the hourly rate, than those who work full time, this indirect sex discrimination can only be challenged if a suitable comparator can be found. Section 71 may also facilitate claims by reference to comparators where disproportionately large pay differences can be established notwithstanding acknowledged differences in value between the jobs done by claimants and (actual) comparators. It is perhaps difficult to envisage cases in which direct discrimination regarding pay could be established, as a matter of evidence, in the absence of an actual comparator save in the (unlikely) event that an employer has declared that the claimant would have been paid more if she was a man. However welcome a step, then, section 69 is likely to have very limited practical effect in view of its application only to direct discrimination. The majority of equal pay challenges concern indirect discrimination in the form of disparately impacting pay practices, rather than deliberate differential payment of men and women because they are men and women. Further, and in particular, challenges to disparately impacting pay practices lend themselves more readily to a non-comparator-based conceptual approach than do full-frontal complaints of direct sex discrimination.

Returning to equal pay claims brought under sections 66 (or, insofar as they relate to pensions, section 67), section 69 provides the employer with a defence to an equal pay claim.

Equality Act 2010, Section 69

(1) The sex equality clause in A's terms has no effect in relation to a difference between A's terms and B's terms if the responsible person shows that the difference is because of a material factor reliance on which –

   (a) does not involve treating A less favourably because of A's sex than the responsible person treats B, and

---

[179] Or, where the claimant is a personal or a public office-holder, ss. 49 or 50 EqA 2010. The EAT ruled in *BMC Software Ltd* v. *Shaikh* [2017] IRLR 1074 that the effect of s. 70 was that the claimant could not rely on a failure to comply with the obligation of equal pay to claim constructive dismissal.

> (2) A factor is within this subsection if A shows that, as a result of the factor, A and persons of the same sex doing work equal to A's are put at a particular disadvantage when compared with persons of the opposite sex doing work equal to A's.
>
> (3) For the purposes of subsection (1), the long-term objective of reducing inequality between men's and women's terms of work is always to be regarded as a legitimate aim...
>
> (6) For the purposes of this section, a factor is not material unless it is a material difference between A's case and B's.

One example of section 69 in practice is provided by the decision of the EAT in *Cooksey (GMB Claimants)* v. *Trafford Borough Council.*[180] Most of the claimants were care workers, cooks, school meal, teaching and passenger assistants, school-crossing patrol workers and school technicians who worked part time, largely to accommodate child-care needs. They were employed by the same council as their comparators, who were manual workers in parks and countryside, cemeteries and crematoria, street cleaning and lighting and highways. These claimants were paid about two-thirds of their comparators' wages and, in particular, did not receive bonus payments, attendance allowance or on-call allowance. A tribunal concluded that the respondent had failed to establish that the payment of bonuses and attendance allowance was untainted by sex where they derived from nationally agreed schemes which reflected the attitude prevalent in the 1960s and 1970s that women worked part time for 'pin money' while men were 'breadwinners'. It accepted that payment of the on-call allowance, by contrast, was genuinely for a material reason not tainted by sex, namely, that the employer needed to have qualified staff available on stand-by for the various duties, but ruled that the employer had failed to establish that this aim could not have been achieved by a less discriminatory means, such as imposing contractual call-out requirements without additional pay. The EAT rejected the employer's appeal in relation to bonus payments and attendance allowance but ruled that the tribunal had erred in relation to on-call allowances. The legitimate aim for which these payments were made having been identified as being to pay extra in order to encourage people to be available on-call, it was an error of law for the tribunal to consider an alternative means by which the Council could have achieved a different legitimate aim (that of encouraging people to be available on-call without making additional payment).

Also of interest are sections 77 and 78, which, respectively, provide protection against victimisation in relation to 'discussions about pay' for the purposes of ascertaining whether pay disparities exist between persons classified according to different 'protected characteristics', and permit regulations to be

---

[180] [2012] EqLR 744.

drawn up requiring the disclosure of various types of pay-related information by employers. The Equality Act 2010 (Gender Pay Gap Information) Regulations 2017 require that employers with at least 250 employees will by April 2018 have to publish information relating to the differences in the average and median hourly rates of, and bonus payments made to, male and female employees, together with the proportions of male and female employees who were paid bonus pay who were, respectively, in the lower, lower-middle, upper-middle and upper quartile pay band. Information published by virtue of the Regulations has caused significant public interest and a gender-pay row at the BBC which resulted in the resignation of Carrie Gracie as China editor over gender pay inequality and in the initiation by the EHRC of a formal investigation into the BBC's pay practices.

Establishing a Claim

Much discrimination and harassment occurs not because of the actions of the employer itself, but rather because of the actions of managers and – particularly where the complaint is one of harassment – other staff. EqA 2010, section 109, which is materially similar to the various provisions in the predecessor legislation, provides that employers are liable for the actions of their employees 'in the course of employment', and principals for the acts of their agents, subject to a defence where B (the employer or principal) shows that it 'took all reasonable steps to prevent A [the discriminator] (a) from doing that thing, or (b) from doing anything of that description'.[181] The scope of vicarious liability was considered by the Court of Appeal in *Tower Boot Co. Ltd* v. *Jones*, in which it gave a very wide reading to 'course of employment' in order to avoid the situation in which 'the more heinous the act of discrimination, the less likely it will be that the employer would be liable'.[182] The EAT had found that the employer was not liable in a case in which the claimant, who was of mixed ethnic origin, had been branded with a hot screwdriver, whipped, had metal bolts thrown at his head, had a notice stuck on his back which read 'Chipmunks are go' and been the victim of repeated racist name-calling.

EqA 2010, section 110, goes on to provide that the employees or agents who perform the acts of discrimination, harassment etc. for which their employers may be held responsible will also themselves be liable, regardless of whether or not the employer or principal has a defence under section 108(4). A defence is provided by section 109(3) to the employee/agent if he or she 'relies on a

---

[181] Note this changes the previous position whereby there was no defence for discrimination by agents, as distinct from employees: *Lana* v. *Positive Action Training in London* [2001] IRLR 501. See *Reynolds* v. *CLFIS (UK) Ltd* [2015] EWCA Civ 439, [2015] ICR 1010 for a case in which an employer escaped liability for an age discrimination claim because the individual employee who had done the act complained of was not motivated by age, even though others who had provided information on which that decision was partly based may have been.

[182] [1997] ICR 254, *per* Waite LJ.

statement by the employer or principal that doing that thing is not a contravention of this Act, and it is reasonable for A to do so', section 109(4) making it an offence for the employer or principal 'knowingly or recklessly' to make a false or misleading statement in this context.[183] Section 111 prohibits A from instructing, inducing or causing B to discriminate against or harass C in a way which breaches the EqA 2010, where A is a person who could him- or herself discriminate against B contrary to the Act. In other words, so far as it is relevant to this chapter, it is a breach of the Act for someone who is an employer, a service provider or a public authority etc., to encourage or require its staff, clients or customers, to discriminate against or harass its workers. Section 112 then provides that it is a breach of the EqA 2010 for A knowingly to help B to discriminate or harass contrary to the Act, again subject (as in section 110) to a defence where A reasonably relies on B's statement that the act which is assisted does not contravene the Act, section 112(3) making it an offence for the employer or principal 'knowingly or recklessly' to make a false or misleading statement in this context.[184]

Burden of Proof

Recognition of the particular difficulties of proving discrimination resulted in the adoption of legislation at the EU level which had the effect of shifting the burden of proof in such claims. This is now captured by EqA 2010, section 136.

Equality Act 2010, Section 136

. . .

(2) If there are facts from which the court could decide, in the absence of any other explanation, that a person (A) contravened the provision concerned, the court must hold that the contravention occurred.
(3) But subsection (2) does not apply if A shows that A did not contravene the provision.

There were materially identical provisions in the predecessor legislation, the leading decision on their implementation being that of the Court of Appeal in *Igen Ltd* v. *Wong*, which established a two-stage approach to the drawing of inferences.[185] The first, as the Court of Appeal made clear in *Madarassy* v. *Nomura International plc*, will be satisfied only if 'a reasonable tribunal could properly conclude' from the evidence before it that discrimination had occurred.[186] If, and only if, this stage is satisfied does the alleged discriminator

---

[183] Such an offence is punishable by a fine not exceeding level 5 on the standard scale.
[184] Such an offence is punishable by a fine not exceeding level 5 on the standard scale.
[185] [2005] ICR 931.   [186] [2007] ICR 867.

have to prove that he or she did not commit the act which is complained of. There will be cases, however, as Elias J recognised in *Laing* v. *Manchester City Council*,[187] where the facts do not require a rigid application of the two-stage approach. This will be the case where facts which could provide an explanation from the employer at the second stage will, if taken into account at the first stage, mean that the claimant will fail to establish facts from which an inference of discrimination could (properly) be drawn. To use the example he there provided, 'it may be legitimate to infer that a black person may have been discriminated on grounds of race if he is equally qualified for a post which is given to a white person and there are only two candidates, but not necessarily legitimate to do so if there are many candidates and a substantial number of other white persons are also rejected'.[188]

Discrimination claims in employment-related cases are heard by ETs. Time limits, other than for equal-pay cases, are set out in EqA 2010, section 123, which provides a three-month time limit subject to extension 'as the employment tribunal thinks just and equitable'. Section 129 then provides that proceedings in equal-pay claims must be brought within a 'qualifying period' which, other than in cases concerning the armed forces, is generally six months 'beginning with the last day of the employment or appointment', with special provision being made for cases in which the facts were concealed from the claimant or he or she was incapacitated. Otherwise, in equal-pay cases, unlike other cases brought under the EqA 2010, there is no provision for the extension of time limits on a 'just and equitable' basis or otherwise, though an equal pay claim can be brought as a breach of contract claim in the ordinary courts subject to the normal limitation period (six years in England and Wales) which there apply.

Remedies

Remedies in discrimination, harassment and victimisation cases are governed by EqA 2010, section 124, which permits tribunals to issue declarations and 'appropriate recommendations' and order compensation, including compensation for injury to feelings. Section 124(3) provides that '[a]n appropriate recommendation is a recommendation that within a specified period the respondent takes specified steps for the purpose of obviating or reducing the adverse effect of any matter to which the proceedings relate on the complainant'. Section 124(3) in its original form had allowed recommendations to be made for the purpose of obviating or reducing the adverse effect of any matter to which the proceedings relate 'on any other person' but this useful provision was removed in an act of legislative vandalism in 2015.

---

[187] [2006] ICR 1519.
[188] *Ibid.*, referring to his judgment in *Network Rail Infrastructure* v. *Griffiths-Henry* [2006] IRLR 865, para. 17.

The availability of compensation in respect of injury to feelings, coupled with the absence of any cap on the damages which may be recovered in discrimination claims, means that damages can be significant. Guidance issued in September 2017 by the Presidents of the ETs in England and Wales and Scotland suggests that £800 to £8,400 would be appropriate for injury to feelings awards in less serious cases, £8,400 to £25,200 in more serious cases which do not merit an award in the upper band, and £25,200 to £42,000 in the most serious cases, with the most exceptional cases capable of exceeding £42,000.[189]

In *Chagger* v. *Abbey National plc*,[190] for example, the Court of Appeal upheld an award of £1,325,322 in respect of future loss to a claimant whose career in the financial services industry had been destroyed by the stigma resulting from his having sued his employers for race discrimination. The Court of Appeal ruled that 'the original employer must remain liable for so-called stigma loss', even where the actions of the third-party employers in victimising the employee were unlawful. In *Bullmore* v. *Pothecary Witham Weld and Another (No. 2)*,[191] too, the EAT confirmed that damages could be recovered by a claimant against a former employer in respect of loss of earnings resulting from victimisation even though the losses had resulted in part from the unlawful conduct of a third party (there, a prospective employer which had withdrawn a job offer on being made aware by the former employer of the claim previously brought against it by the claimant). Aggravated and exemplary damages may also be awarded in discrimination cases, although the award of the latter is rare.[192]

In equality-clause cases, EqA 2010, section 132, provides that the court or tribunal may make a declaration and make an award 'by way of arrears of pay or damages in relation to the complainant', the award generally being limited in time to six (in Scotland five) years before the date of the claim.[193]

---

[189] These bands have been uprated from those established in In *Vento* v. *Chief Constable of West Yorkshire Police (No. 2)* [2002] EWCA Civ 1871, [2003] ICR 318.
[190] [2010] ICR 397.   [191] [2011] IRLR 18.
[192] See *Ministry of Defence* v. *Fletcher* [2010] IRLR 25.
[193] Or, in a concealment or incapacity case, the date when the breach of the equality clause first occurred.

10

Work/Life Balance

Contents

Statutory Entitlements to Leave and Flexible Working

Most people need to work to earn an income on which to live. For most of us, the bulk of the day will be occupied by work and commuting to work. At the same time, most people have a biologically fuelled desire to start a family, which requires time each day to care for children. Within families we also incur moral caring responsibilities towards other members of the family, such as elderly parents or dependent siblings. These family responsibilities often add up in terms of time to the equivalent of a full-time job or more. Furthermore, these family responsibilities, such as the care of babies, are usually regarded as our most compelling moral duties to which all other interests, including earning a living through work, will have to be sacrificed if necessary. The combination of demanding work and caring responsibilities often places extreme time pressure on workers. Although other demands on our time affect the division between work and other aspects of living, the key issue for most people with regard to the work/life balance is the difficulty of managing the demands of work and family.

In the past, individuals with family responsibilities had to bear the entire burden of providing and caring for them. A common response was the 'male breadwinner' model of the family, in which the male partner continued in full-time work while the female partner reduced working hours or gave up work entirely in order to care for their children. Women often had to take jobs that could be synchronised with school times and holidays. Such jobs, like being a 'dinner lady' or a cleaner, were usually not well paid and offered few career prospects. The alternative for a woman of taking a long-term break from work during the early years of child-care would probably damage her career prospects and certainly reduce her lifetime earnings and probably adversely affect any pension entitlement. Sometimes a man took on the home-carer role, but the adverse economic effects were equally applicable. As women increasingly entered the labour market with a view to pursuing a career, using their qualifications obtained from the opening up of higher education and the dismantling of discriminatory barriers to the better jobs resulting from the SDA 1975, the 'male-breadwinner' model became discredited as both wrong in principle in a society committed to equal opportunities and as impractical since most families needed two sources of income to achieve a satisfactory standard of living. The legal requirement of equal pay for women also reduced the likelihood that it would be the man rather than the woman who was taking home the bigger income, thereby removing the economic case for the male-breadwinner model in many homes.

Modern legislation tries to establish a better distribution of the costs of child-care and other family responsibilities, sharing them between the government (the taxpayer), the employer and the employee. A wide range of measures are possible, not all of which directly affect labour law. For instance, the government or employers can supply child-care nurseries and crèches for pre-school-age children or, alternatively, financial support can be provided to parents for child-care. We focus here on the legislation that directly controls the employment relationship, although it is clear from successful Nordic models of establishing better work/life balances that what is needed is a combination of assistance from the state plus regulation of employment relations. The key early measures of the legislation focused on the protection of women against disadvantages in their employment relation caused by pregnancy or maternity leave. These measures are reflected in Article 33(2) of the EU Charter of Fundamental Rights, which states: 'To reconcile family and professional life, everyone shall have the right to protection from dismissal for a reason connected with maternity and the right to paid maternity leave and to parental leave following the birth or adoption of a child.' Although the UK legislation conferred welcome rights to protection for job security and paid leave for women, there was an obvious danger that the additional costs associated with employing women of child-bearing age might, even if only unconsciously, deter employers from hiring women or giving them positions of responsibility.[1] Recent legislation, in particular the Children and Families Act 2014 Part 7, prefers as far as possible a gender-neutral approach, by introducing shared parental leave and pay for both parents (while retaining maternity rights), and expanding rights for all employees to negotiate flexible working arrangements in order to suit their particular family needs.

Although these statutory rights differ in their details, the broad outline of the protections shows a similar pattern. The various legal rights to take paid or unpaid leave in respect of family responsibilities, or to ask for an adjustment of working hours, are enforceable through complaints to ETs. If an employer victimises an employee in response to such a request to take a statutory entitlement to leave, there is legal protection against both dismissal by the employer[2] and the imposition of any other kind of detriment to the employee.[3] What counts as a detriment is not defined except to specify that it may include omissions as well as acts. The requirement was satisfied where the employer held a disciplinary hearing and the employee was given a written warning for his absence from work while taking leave.[4] Although many of these statutory rights to take leave or to request flexible working require a qualifying period of employment before the entitlement accrues, the protections against victimisation are 'day one' rights.[5] In addition, some adverse actions by employers will constitute unlawful discrimination under the EqA 2010 or breach the special protection for part-time workers against discriminatory treatment. While taking statutory leave, an employee should not suffer any disadvantage. For example, an employee should continue to qualify for any seniority rights, for general pay increases and to accrue holiday entitlements. Some contracts of employment, particularly those covered by collective bargaining, may contain superior entitlements to leave and pay, which should be enforceable as ordinary contractual rights.

In this chapter, we examine the principal statutory entitlements to leave and flexible working with a view to assessing the extent to which individual employees can obtain, if not a satisfactory, then at least a feasible, balance between the demands of work and family and caring responsibilities. The principal measures that need to be considered concern maternity leave and pay (including pregnancy), shared parental care and pay, unpaid parental and emergency leave, the right to request flexible working and protection for part-time workers against discrimination.

---

[1] W. Chan, 'Mothers, Equality and Labour Market Opportunities' (2013) 42 *Industrial Law Journal* 224; C. Hakim, 'Is Gender Equality Legislation becoming Counterproductive?' (2008) 15 *Public Policy Research* 133.

[2] ERA 1996, s. 99.   [3] ERA 1996, s. 47C.

[4] *New Southern Railway Ltd* v. *Rodway* [2005] EWCA Civ 443, [2005] ICR 1162 (CA).

[5] ERA 1996, s. 108(3).

Right to Paid Leave on Birth of a Child

A woman's right to paid maternity leave is based upon the Pregnant Workers Directive,[6] which also requires employers to comply with health and safety measures such as risk assessments that are particular to pregnancy. In national law, the basic right to maternity leave is established in ERA 1996, sections 71–3, but the detail is set out in the Maternity and Parental Leave Regulations 1999 (as amended). These rules set out the entitlement of employees to maternity leave, the rights enjoyed while on leave, the right to statutory maternity pay and the right to return to work. In practice, many employees enjoy more favourable contractual terms, particularly with respect to the continuation of wages during leave. Where this is the case, they are entitled to enjoy whichever of the contractual or statutory provisions is more favourable in any given respect, although not to exercise them cumulatively.[7] The right to take leave when adopting a child mirrors the equivalent statutory provisions for maternity leave and pay, with minor adjustments.[8]

Statutory Maternity Leave

All women employees are now entitled to twenty-six weeks of 'ordinary maternity leave' (OML) and to twenty-six weeks of 'additional maternity leave' (AML), making a year in total. These two periods of leave originally differed considerably in their legal incidents, but now their only distinction is with respect to notice of return to work, so it is more convenient to discuss the two periods together as statutory maternity leave. Although the statutory entitlement to leave provides for fifty-two weeks, in practice the majority of women return to work after thirty-nine weeks when the entitlement to statutory maternity pay expires.[9] Women may choose the date on which maternity leave begins, although this date may not be more than eleven weeks prior to the beginning of the expected week of childbirth (EWC). Maternity leave will also be triggered automatically by absence from work 'wholly or partly because of pregnancy' in the four weeks prior to the beginning of the EWC.[10] Maternity leave is compulsory for two weeks after the birth and this period is extended to four weeks for factory workers and even longer where statutorily required.[11]

---

[6] Directive 92/85/EC.   [7] Maternity and Parental Leave Regulations 1999, reg. 21.

[8] ERA 1996, ss. 75A and 75B; Paternity and Adoption Leave Regulations 2002, SI 2002 No. 2788, as amended. The Children and Families Act 2014 extends maternity rights to surrogate parents.

[9] J. Chanfreau, S. Gowland, Z. Lancaster, E. Poole, S. Tipping and M. Toomse, *Maternity and Paternity Rights Survey and Women Returners Survey 2009/10* (Department for Work and Pensions Research Report No. 777, 2011), p. 2.

[10] Maternity and Parental Leave Regulations 1999, reg. 6.

[11] ERA 1996, s. 72; and Maternity and Parental Leave Regulations 1999, reg. 8.

Pregnant employees are also entitled, on production of appropriate evidence, to reasonable paid time-off for antenatal care.[12] According to the government's official advice, antenatal care may include relaxation classes and parent-craft classes as long as these are advised by a registered medical practitioner, midwife or registered health visitor. Expectant fathers now also have the right to time-off to accompany a partner to an antenatal appointment on two occasions.[13]

In order to qualify for maternity leave, the employee must notify the employer of her pregnancy, the EWC and the date on which she intends her maternity leave to begin 'no later than the end of the fifteenth week before her expected week of childbirth, or, if that is not reasonably practicable, as soon as is reasonably practicable'.[14] This notice requirement does not apply in a case where maternity leave is triggered by the birth itself, in which case notice must be given 'as soon as is reasonably practicable'. If the employer so requests, notice must be given in writing and medical evidence of the pregnancy supplied. The notice of the intention to take maternity leave starting on a certain date can be varied, but only by giving twenty-eight days' warning of the change prior to the date varied unless that is 'not reasonably practicable'. The aim of these provisions is to try to give employers as much notice as possible of maternity leave, so that they can make the necessary adjustments in staffing. The criticism often made of the notice provisions is that they create the risk that a woman will lose her right to leave by failing to give the requisite notice and then be vulnerable to disciplinary proceedings for absence from work.[15] ERA 1996, section 99, makes dismissal for taking maternity leave automatically unfair only when the woman is taking leave that satisfies these notice provisions but not if she has failed to comply with the notice provisions.

Rights during Maternity Leave and Pregnancy

During the period of statutory maternity leave, employees are entitled to retain many of their terms and conditions of employment. Essentially, the idea is that, apart from pay, employees should retain or accrue all their benefits as if they had been working.[16] Equally, the employee remains bound by her obligations under the contract of employment, apart from the requirement to perform work. For instance, during maternity leave, where holiday entitlement would normally accrue if the employee had been at work, it should continue to accrue while she is on maternity leave. Other examples might include participation in share schemes, reimbursement of professional subscriptions and the use of a company car or mobile phone (unless provided for

---

[12] ERA 1996, ss. 55 and 56.   [13] ERA 1996 ss. 57ZE, 57ZF.
[14] Maternity and Parental Leave Regulations 1999, reg. 4.
[15] J. Mair, 'Maternity Leave: Improved and Simplified?' (2000) 63 *Modern Law Review* 877.
[16] ERA 1996, s. 71(4).

business use only). If the employer awards a pay rise to the employee's pay grade while she is on leave, she will be entitled to that improvement in her remuneration, either on her return to work or during her leave if the employer provides contractual paid maternity leave. The ECJ has held that the deprivation of the right to an annual performance assessment as a result of absence on maternity leave amounted to unfavourable treatment.[17] Statutory maternity leave counts towards the period of continuous employment for the purpose of qualifying for other statutory entitlements. If the employer contributes to a pension scheme, it must keep up the contributions during the period of leave.

The laws against sex discrimination in the EU were interpreted to rule out adverse treatment for women on pregnancy-related grounds,[18] but now specific legislation protects women during pregnancy and maternity leave. National law must conform to the requirement of prohibition of dismissals contained in the European Pregnant Workers Directive.[19] Dismissal on grounds related to pregnancy, maternity or maternity leave will be regarded as automatically unfair under ERA 1996, section 99. Dismissals that are 'related to' pregnancy or maternity do not have to occur during pregnancy or maternity leave. For example, an employer who decides to replace a woman while she is on maternity leave, but only carries out the dismissal once she has returned from leave, may be regarded as having dismissed her for the reason of her maternity leave.[20] There is also protection against detrimental actions taken by the employer for the same reasons.[21]

Furthermore, the Equal Treatment Directive and implementing national legislation were amended to create an independent ground of liability for pregnancy discrimination.[22]

Equality Act 2010, Section 18(2)

(2) A person (A) discriminates against a woman if, in the protected period in relation to a pregnancy of hers, A treats her unfavourably –
   (a) because of the pregnancy, or
   (b) because of illness suffered by her as a result of it.

---

[17] Case C-136/95, *Thibault* v. *Caisse Nationale d'Assurance Vieillesse des Travailleurs Salariés* [1999] ICR 160 (ECJ).

[18] Case C-177/88, *Dekker* v. *VJV-Centrum* [1991] IRLR 27 (ECJ); Case C-32/93, *Webb* v. *EMO Air Cargo Ltd* [1994] IRLR 482 (ECJ); Case C-394/96, *Brown* v. *Rentokil Ltd* [1998] IRLR 445.

[19] Directive 92/85, Art. 10.

[20] Case C-460/06, *Paquay* v. *Société d'Architectes Hoet et Minne SPRL* [2008] ICR 420 (ECJ).

[21] ERA 1996, s. 47C and Maternity and Parental Leave Regulations 1999, reg. 19.

[22] Directive 2006/54 on the implementation of the principle of equal opportunities and equal treatment of men and women in matters of employment and occupation (recast).

This legislation removes the need to find a male comparator. The prohibition also applies to a woman who takes maternity leave or who is seeking to exercise a right to maternity leave.[23] The protection only applies from the beginning of the pregnancy until the end of the period of maternity leave.[24] Unlike the protection in the law of unfair dismissal, discrimination law does not apply to unfavourable treatment after that period, even though the reason for detriment or dismissal may be connected to childbirth as in the case of maternal illness.[25] This discrimination claim is limited to direct discrimination.[26] Men cannot make a complaint about sex discrimination if a female employee receives more favourable treatment on the ground of pregnancy or childbirth.[27] Detrimental treatment of women during maternity leave and pregnancy may sometimes amount to indirect sex discrimination, where the employer operates an unjustifiable policy that disproportionately adversely affects women in comparison to men. In *Commissioner of Police of the Metropolis* v. *Keohane*,[28] the police operated a policy that removed dogs from their handlers where a handler was likely to be non-operational for a while. This policy was both a case of direct discrimination, because the dog might never be returned to the handler, thereby causing a loss of income and a detriment, and also possibly an instance of indirect sex discrimination if the policy disproportionately affected women and could not be justified.

Dismissal of the employee on a ground related to pregnancy or while she is taking statutory maternity leave is therefore likely to be both automatically unfair and suitable for a claim for greater compensation to redress direct discrimination. It is possible, however, that an employer may be able to justify such a dismissal on a ground unrelated to pregnancy or maternity leave. For instance, an employer may be able to demonstrate that a redundancy situation had genuinely arisen, as where part of the business in which the employee worked had shut down. In such a case, there would be no claim for discrimination or unfair dismissal unless it could be shown that the reason why the woman was selected instead of other employees was that she was pregnant or on maternity leave. Because that claim is hard to prove and since there are widespread reports of women being dismissed on spurious grounds of redundancy when they are maternity leave, regulation 10 of the Maternity and Parental Leave etc. Regulations 1999 makes the special protective provision that women who are made redundant while they are taking statutory maternity leave benefit from an additional entitlement to be offered suitable alternative employment, ahead of all other dismissed employees, if it becomes available at her employer's undertaking or its successor or an associated employer. Failure to offer available suitable alternative employment results

---

[23] EqA 2010, s. 18(2) and (3).   [24] EqA 2010, s. 18(6).
[25] Case 179/88, *Hertz* [1992] ICR 332 (ECJ); *Lyonds* v. *DWP Jobcentre Plus* [2014] ICR 668 (EAT).
[26] EqA 2010, s. 19(3).   [27] EqA 2010, s. 13(6).
[28] *Commissioner of Police of the Metropolis* v. *Keohane* UKEAT/463/12 [2014] ICR 1073.

in a finding of automatic dismissal.[29] For instance, where two jobs were amalgamated into one as part of a restructuring exercise, the holder of one of those jobs who was on maternity leave was entitled to the amalgamated position even though the other employee being made redundant may have been better suited to the new role.[30] The employer's duty to offer the job to the employee on maternity leave does not arise if the restructuring does not result in the creation of a suitable alternative vacancy because the new jobs are, for instance, in a different location, with more flexibility in the hours and at lower pay.[31]

The combination of the protection of automatically unfair dismissal and the protection against discrimination that may give rise to unlimited compensation might lead one to expect that dismissals of pregnant workers and women taking maternity have now been eliminated. But there is much evidence that discrimination persists more surreptitiously, some of which is recounted anecdotally on the website: pregnantthenscrewed.com/. A detailed investigation commissioned by the Equality and Human Rights Commission tended to confirm the suspicion that women continue to suffer pregnancy and maternity-related disadvantages.[32] The research demonstrated that while employers accept that there are benefits to their organisations from protections in connection with maternity, in practice employers are reluctant to employ women giving birth on the ground of the cost and harm to their work performance. Women taking maternity leave confirm that in practice they experience hostility and disadvantage.

The key findings included:

- Overall, three in four mothers (77 per cent) said they had a negative or possibly discriminatory experience during pregnancy, maternity leave and/or on return from maternity leave.
- Around one in nine mothers (11 per cent) reported they felt forced to leave their job. This included those being dismissed (1 per cent); made compulsorily redundant, where others in their workplace were not (1 per cent); or feeling treated so poorly they felt they had to leave their job (9 per cent).
- One in ten (10 per cent) mothers were discouraged from attending antenatal appointments.
- Over two-thirds of mothers (68 per cent) submitted a flexible working request and around three in four of these mothers reported that their flexible working request was approved. Around half of mothers (51 per cent) who had their flexible working request approved said that they felt it resulted in negative consequences.

---

[29] Maternity and Parental Leave Regulations 1999, regs. 10 and 20.
[30] *Sefton Borough Council* v. *Wainwright* UKEAT/164/14, [2015] ICR 652.
[31] *Simpson* v. *Endsleigh Insurance Services* [2011] ICR 75 (EAT).
[32] Equality and Human Rights Commission, *Pregnancy and Maternity Related Discrimination and Disadvantage* (2016).

- The majority of employers (84 per cent) reported that it was in their interests to support pregnant women and those on maternity leave. The main reasons for this were because it increased staff retention (58 per cent) and created better morale among employees (20 per cent).
- Most employers (70 per cent) said they felt women should declare upfront during recruitment if they were pregnant. A quarter of employers felt it was reasonable during recruitment to ask women about their plans to have children.
- 27 per cent felt pregnancy put an unreasonable cost burden on the workplace.
- 17 per cent believed that pregnant women and mothers were less interested in career progression and promotion than other employees.
- 7 per cent did not think mothers returning from maternity leave were as committed as other members of their team.

Despite this strong evidence of discrimination against pregnant workers and mothers taking maternity leave, few legal claims are brought before tribunals, perhaps as little as 1 per cent of possible claims.[33] As well as the normal difficulties presented to any employee seeking to claim employment rights against their employer, new mothers no doubt will have to overcome other preoccupying serious financial and possibly emotional issues.[34]

Maternity Pay

Women may be entitled to maternity pay under the terms of their contract or by virtue of a statutory entitlement. About one-third of mothers in employment benefit from maternity pay included as a term of the contract of employment.[35] As a result of the meagre level of the statutory entitlement, employees on maternity leave are usually much better off if they receive such a top-up contractual payment from their employer, even if it is not their full salary or not for the full extent of the maternity leave. The minimum standard for statutory entitlement is fixed by the Pregnant Workers Directive.[36] Article 11 of the Directive requires the allowance to be 'adequate', but deems the allowance to be adequate if it is 'equivalent to that which the worker concerned would receive in the event of a break in her activities on grounds connected with her state of health, subject to any ceiling laid down under national legislation'. The Directive thus draws a comparison with sick pay that must

---

[33] G. James, 'Family-friendly Employment Law (Re)assessed: The Potential of Care Ethics' (2016) 45 *Industrial Law Journal* 477.

[34] A. Gentleman, 'Pregnant? Wait Till the Boss Hears', *Guardian*, 23 June 2011.

[35] J. Chanfreau, S. Gowland, Z. Lancaster, E. Poole, S. Tipping and M. Toomse, *Maternity and Paternity Rights Survey and Women Returners Survey 2009/10* (Department for Work and Pensions Research Report No. 777, 2011), p. 2.

[36] Directive 92/85.

be paid by employers when employees are unable to work through illness, and states that a statutory entitlement to maternity pay must be at least equivalent to sick pay, although it can be subject to 'conditions of eligibility' such as a qualifying period of continuous employment for the right to statutory maternity pay to arise.

In accordance with this European requirement, employees on maternity leave may claim statutory maternity pay if they satisfy two conditions.[37] First, it is necessary to have been employed by the employer for a continuous period of at least twenty-six weeks prior to the fifteenth week before the EWC.[38] Secondly, to qualify for statutory maternity pay, an employee must have earned in gross wages at least the lower earnings limit under which national insurance contributions are payable, which was £116 per week in the 2018/19 tax year. These conditions are likely to exclude women who are working part time and so earning low pay, or who have temporary employment, casual work and other kinds of precarious employment, including agency workers. For women who do not qualify for the statutory maternity pay (and for whom there is no contractual maternity pay), there is the possibility of claiming a maternity allowance from the social security system if they have been working either on low pay or as a self-employed worker and, failing that, they may be able to claim the most basic level of income provided by the employment and support allowance.

Statutory maternity pay is paid for the first six weeks of leave at 90 per cent of the employee's average gross weekly earnings, and for a further thirty-three weeks at the lower of either 90 per cent of average gross weekly earnings or the standard rate of £140.98 per week (2017/18). Statutory maternity pay counts as earnings, so that normal taxes, national insurance and other deductions such as pension contributions must be made by the employer. The employer is entitled to a rebate of 92 per cent from the national insurance fund for these payments (or 104 per cent for very small employers).[39]

The low level set for statutory maternity pay has been challenged unsuccessfully before the ECJ. The central argument has been that any reduction in normal pay amounts to subjecting women to a detriment, contrary to discrimination and equal-pay laws. But this view has been rejected on the ground that the Pregnant Workers Directive in effect derogates from the general rules against sex discrimination by permitting Member States to fix

---

[37] The rules are set out in the Social Security Contributions and Benefits Act 1992, ss. 164–71, and in more detailed statutory instruments, including the Statutory Maternity Pay (General) Regulations 1986, SI 1986 No. 1960.

[38] In social security law, EWC refers to 'expected week of confinement'. The rules governing periods of continuous employment are explained in Chapter 5.

[39] Social Security Contributions and Benefits Act 1992, s. 167; Statutory Maternity Pay (Compensation of Employers) and Miscellaneous Amendments Regulations 1994, SI 1994 No. 1882.

an allowance in comparison with sick-pay entitlements.[40] The comparison with a sick male, which was rejected for pregnancy discrimination, is therefore reinstated for the purposes of determining the amount of statutory maternity pay.[41] Furthermore, in *Boyle* v. *Equal Opportunities Commission*[42] it was argued unsuccessfully that, in order to determine the adequacy of the payment, as required by Article 11 of the Directive, the correct comparison should have been not the level of statutory sick pay but the employer's higher rate of contractual sick pay. Maternity pay can be supplemented during a woman's ten 'keep in touch days' taken during maternity leave, but only if the employer agrees to pay for them at the normal rate under her contract of employment. The low level of statutory maternity pay has also been criticised for its unfairness to low-paid women.[43] Whereas most women from professional backgrounds stay on maternity leave for more than twenty-six weeks, only a third at the bottom of the income scale do. This difference arises almost certainly because low-paid women without savings cannot afford to live on the statutory minimum for maternity pay for very long.

Return from Maternity Leave

About three-quarters of women return to work after maternity leave. About 90 per cent of women who receive generous maternity pay from their employer return, whereas only about 38 per cent of those confined to statutory maternity pay (or maternity allowance) return to work.[44] A woman does not have to give notice that she plans to return to work at the expiration of the statutory maternity-leave period of fifty-two weeks. If she wishes to return earlier, for instance at the time when the statutory maternity pay expires at thirty-nine weeks, she must give eight weeks' notice. Failure to give such notice entitles the employer, if it wishes, to insist on a delay of eight weeks before the return to work. A woman who decides not to return to work at all must give notice of termination of contract in the normal way.

Failure to comply with a woman's right to return to work after maternity leave amounts to an automatically unfair dismissal. This prohibition on dismissal is required by the Equal Treatment Directive.

---

[40] Case C-342/93, *Gillespie* v. *Northern Health and Social Services Board* [1996] ECR I-047 (ECJ).
[41] M. Wynn, 'Pregnancy Discrimination: Equality, Protection or Reconciliation?' (1999) 62 *Modern Law Review* 435, at 442–4.
[42] Case C-411/96, *Boyle* v. *Equal Opportunities Commission* [1998] ECR I-6401 (ECJ).
[43] R. Shorthouse, *Guardian*, 16 May 2011.
[44] J. Chanfreau, S. Gowland, Z. Lancaster, E. Poole, S. Tipping and M. Toomse, *Maternity and Paternity Rights Survey and Women Returners Survey 2009/10* (Department for Work and Pensions Research Report No. 777, 2011), p. 3.

Equal Treatment Directive 2006/54, Article 15

A woman on maternity leave shall be entitled, after the end of her period of maternity leave, to return to her job or to an equivalent post on terms and conditions which are not less favourable to her and to benefit from any improvement in working conditions to which she would have been entitled during her absence.

The ECJ has held that Article 15 is directly effective against a Member State and that national courts are under a duty to give full effect to the provision, if necessary refusing of its own motion to apply any conflicting provision of national legislation.[45] Under the UK legislation, the Maternity and Parental Leave Regulations 1999 regulation 18, when returning to work after the first twenty-six weeks of the statutory maternity leave (the OML period), a woman has the right to the same job and the same terms and conditions as if she had not been absent. In particular, she is entitled to return with her seniority, pension rights and similar rights being the same as if she had not been absent.[46] When returning to work after or during the second period of twenty-six weeks (the AML period), a woman has the same right, but the employer can refuse to give the original job back if the employer shows it is not reasonably practicable for her to return to the same job (for example, because the job no longer exists or has been given to someone else). In that case, the woman must be offered alternative work which is suitable and appropriate, with the benefit of the same terms and conditions.[47] Disputes may arise as to whether or not the employer has offered the same job on the return from maternity leave. The definition in the Maternity and Parental Leave Regulations 1999 provides: '"job", in relation to an employee returning after maternity leave or parental leave, means the nature of the work she is employed to do in accordance with her contract and capacity and place in which she is so employed'.[48] In a case where a schoolteacher, on her return to work, was not given the role of class teacher for the reception class that she had previously performed but the role of teacher for a different class, it was held that she had been given the same job back because, under the terms of her contract, it was the head teacher who decided on the allocation of classes to staff.[49] The head teacher had, however, treated her less favourably on account of her maternity leave, because she had failed to consult the claimant about her preferences for class allocation, as she would have done had the claimant not been on leave.

Having returned to work without taking the full entitlement to maternity leave, some women may want a further period of leave, which may be possible

---

[45] Case C-595/12, *Napoli v. Ministerio della Giustizia* [2014] ICR 486.
[46] Maternity and Parental Leave Regulations 1999, reg. 18A.   [47] *Ibid.*, reg. 20(7).
[48] *Ibid.*, reg. 2.   [49] *Blundell v. St Andrew's Catholic Primary School* [2007] ICR 1451 (EAT).

if taken as statutory parental leave during the first year after the child's birth. A woman may also take her paid-holiday entitlement, even if by collective agreement the employer had fixed the period of annual leave for employees to occur during the period of the woman's maternity leave.[50] About two-fifths of women want to reduce their hours of work,[51] and for that purpose they may invoke the right to ask for a change of terms and conditions and go part time. These rights are considered below.

Paid Paternity or Partner Leave at the Time of Birth

Fathers also have the statutory right to paid leave on the birth of a child or an adoption under similar conditions to those for maternity leave.[52] The period is restricted to one or two weeks within fifty-six days of the birth (or adoption). On the birth of a child, the vast majority of fathers do take a short period of leave, either as paternity leave or annual holiday.[53] To qualify for paternity leave and payment, there is a qualifying period of twenty-six weeks prior to the EWC. The father must give notice to the employer of the intention to take paternity leave at the same time as the mother. To qualify for paternity leave, it is necessary to be either the biological father of the child, the mother's husband or partner or the child's adopter or husband or partner of the adopter. The right applies equally to same-sex relationships. The leave can start at any time after the birth of the child, but has to finish within fifty-six days of the birth. The statutory right to paternity pay is not to the regular contractual level of remuneration but to a statutory rate that is the same as statutory maternity pay. This short period of paid leave for fathers on the birth of a child, although a welcome innovation in 2002, could be criticised for its inflexibility and its endorsement of the stereotype that the mother will always take care of the baby or adopted child. Since 2011, legislation has been challenging that stereotype by gradually introducing the option of shared parental leave (SPL) and shared parental pay (ShPP).[54]

Shared Parental Leave and Shared Parental Pay

The central goal of SPL and ShPP is to make it possible for partners to share the entitlement to maternity leave and maternity pay between them. The

---

[50] Case C-342/01, *Merino Gómez* v. *Continental Industrias del Caucho SA* [2005] ICR 1040 (ECJ).

[51] J. Chanfreau, S. Gowland, Z. Lancaster, E. Poole, S. Tipping and M. Toomse, *Maternity and Paternity Rights Survey and Women Returners Survey 2009/10* (Department for Work and Pensions Research Report No. 777, 2011), p. 4.

[52] ERA 1996, s. 80A; Paternity and Adoption Leave Regulations 2002, SI 2002 No. 2788, as amended.

[53] J. Chanfreau, S. Gowland, Z. Lancaster, E. Poole, S. Tipping and M. Toomse, *Maternity and Paternity Rights Survey and Women Returners Survey 2009/10* (Department for Work and Pensions Research Report No. 777, 2011), p. 6.

[54] Additional Paternity Leave and Pay Regulations 2010, SI 2010 No. 1055.

legislation permits the parents to divide the fifty-two weeks of maternity leave between them in various ways, and to transfer the right to the thirty-nine weeks of maternity pay between them at the time that the father takes parental leave and the mother returns to work.[55] For instance, assuming that both the mother and her partner satisfy the eligibility conditions for SPL and ShPP, the mother might end her maternity leave after twelve weeks, leaving the parents free to choose how to split the remaining forty weeks of SPL and twenty-seven weeks of ShPP between themselves. Unlike maternity leave, which terminates completely on a return to work, SPL creates the possibility of taking leave in up to three blocks. For instance, the parents may split the remaining forty weeks of SPL so that the father takes fifteen weeks of leave and then the mother takes SPL for the remaining twenty-five weeks. The parents can both take SPL at the same time, though only one would be eligible for the ShPP. The amount of the ShPP is the same as ordinary maternity pay and paternity pay.

Assuming that the mother meets the eligibility criteria for maternity leave and maternity pay described above, and has given notice to her employer that she will curtail those arrangements, the question is what the key criteria for eligibility by her partner for shared leave and pay are. There is a broad definition of a 'partner', which includes the biological father, husband, a civil partner and more broadly a person of the same or a different sex who lives in an enduring family relationship with the mother (except for close relatives).[56] Similar rules apply to parents adopting a child. To be entitled to SPL, the partner must have been employed continuously by the same employer for at least twenty-six weeks by the end of the fifteenth week before the due date and stay with the same employer throughout the period of the SPL. In addition, the child's mother must have satisfied a minimum earnings requirement: during the sixty-six weeks before the week the baby's due, the mother must have worked as an employee or as self-employed for at least twenty-six weeks in total and have earned at least £390 in total in thirteen of the sixty-six weeks.[57] This requirement tends to exclude fathers from taking SPL if the mother has not been working to any great extent and had therefore not been contributing to the national insurance system, though leave can still be taken if the mother ceased work long before the EWC provided those criteria about minimum earnings are met. To be eligible for the ShPP, normally the eligibility requirement for the partner is the same as for statutory paternity pay, namely twenty-six weeks of continuous employment prior to the birth, plus the requirement that the mother meets the eligibility requirement for maternity pay.[58]

[55] ERA 1996, ss. 75E–75K, inserted by the Children and Families Act 2014 s. 117(1); Shared Parental Leave Regulations 2014, SI 2014 No. 3050.

[56] Shared Parental Leave Regulations 2014, SI 2014 No. 3050, reg. 2; Statutory Shared Parental Pay (General) Regulations 2014, SI 2014 No. 3051, reg. 2.

[57] Statutory Shared Parental Pay (General) Regulations 2014, SI 2014 No. 3051, reg. 5.

[58] *Ibid.*, SI, regs. 29–30.

The implementation of the provision for sharing maternity leave and pay with the father is likely to cause employers practical difficulties. It may become less frequent that women take a year's maternity leave, so employers may find it harder to arrange suitable temporary cover. As mother and father are likely to work for different employers, it may prove complicated to police the sharing of the maternity leave and pay without a great deal of 'red tape'. In addition, men may be adversely affected for the first time by the possible chilling effect on employers when considering the recruitment of younger staff who may be planning to start a family.

It is too early to know whether fathers and partners will take advantage of these rights to take leave and receive pay during the first year of their child's life. The experience of other countries that have introduced the option for fathers to take paid leave has been that fathers overwhelmingly choose not to take time off work. If governments want to promote ideas of parents sharing child-care responsibilities, the legislation may have to move towards a compulsory division of leave on the birth of a child. Parents may resist such measures on the ground that they would be excessively paternalistic and also cause economic loss where the father earns substantially more than the mother.

Imposing Parental Leave on Fathers

The Norwegian government argues that there needs to be a quota for fathers, because otherwise they wouldn't bother taking the time off. It cites the dramatic drop in participation by fathers in Denmark after it removed its quota in 2002 as proof there needs to be a political solution. According to Norway's equality and anti-discrimination ombudsman, only 25% of Danish fathers now use their quota compared to 60% in Norway, putting the Danes bottom in the Nordic region.

Norway is proposing an even higher quota for fathers from this November, under a three-way split with 12 weeks for the father, 12 weeks for the mother, and 20 for 'family negotiations'. The total period of leave would be extended by a week to 47 weeks at 100% covered earnings up to the 6G level, three weeks of which are reserved for the mother before the birth, or 57 weeks at 80%.

By comparison, Iceland reserves three months each for fathers and mothers, and three months to be decided between them. Sweden offers 13 months at 80% covered earnings, which is split between the parents – two months of which are earmarked for each parent. Much like Norway, fathers in these countries make use of their paternity quota, and women take out the rest of the maternity leave, according to the Norwegian government. Swedish fathers on average take more than their quota.

Henriette Westhrin, Norway's deputy minister of children, equality and social inclusion, says one of the main ideas behind the proposed system is to provide a political solution for the differences in income between the sexes. The wage gap increases when women have children, and the more children they have, the more the difference becomes. In addition, there is a need for women to keep up the birth rate and still get back to work to help pay for the welfare costs associated with the country's ageing population. 'We think it makes for a more equal society', Westhrin says. 'We see in Norway people get more children than most European countries and there are more women in the employment market. But we also have to make sure they are not just part-time jobs. We have to push women into work and have to pull men back into the family.'[59]

Unpaid Parental Leave and Emergency Leave

Although the rights discussed above help parents with a new child, none addresses the long-term problem that parents have of reconciling their need to work with the provision of satisfactory child-care arrangements. The European Parental Leave Framework Directive was adopted under the 'social dialogue' procedures.[60] It was implemented by the Maternity and Parental Leave Regulations 1999. The Directive was subsequently replaced in 2010 by a slightly more comprehensive measure, once again produced by a social dialogue.[61] The Directive sets out minimum standards that are exceeded by the amended UK Regulations.

Maternity and Parental Leave Regulations 1999, Regulations 13(1) and 14(1)

13 (1) An employee who –
   (a) has been continuously employed for a period of not less than a year; and
   (b) has, or expects to have, responsibility for a child, is entitled, in accordance with these Regulations, to be absent from work on parental leave for the purpose of caring for that child.

   . . .

14 (1) An employee is entitled to eighteen weeks' leave in respect of any individual child.[62]

   . . .

15 An employee may not exercise any entitlement to parental leave in respect of a child after the date of the child's 18th birthday.[63]

---

[59] V. Criscione, *Guardian*, 19 March 2011.   [60] Directive 96/34.

[61] Directive 2010/18/EU of 8 March 2010 implementing the revised Framework Agreement on parental leave concluded by BUSINESSEUROPE, UEAPME (the employers' organisation representing SMEs), CEEP (the Centre européen de l'entreprise publique) and ETUC.

[62] The period was increased from thirteen to eighteen weeks by the Parental Leave (EU Directive) Regulations 2013, SI 2013 No. 283, reg. 3(1) (2)(a).

[63] As amended by the Maternity and Parental Leave etc. (Amendment) Regulations 2014, SI 2014 No. 3221, before which the leave only applied to children aged five or under except for children with disabilities.

The Regulations reflect the 'social dialogue' approach of the EU Parental Leave Directive inasmuch as their detailed provisions on parental leave are by way of a default position. The primary method by which the Regulations are intended to be implemented is through collective agreements or 'workforce agreements'. The provisions concerning the definition of such agreements, and the mechanisms for electing workforce representatives, are materially identical to those applicable under the Working Time Regulations 1998, as discussed in Chapter 8. Where workforce or collective agreements on parental leave are in place, they will provide the detail concerning notice requirements, timing and duration of parental leave. Schedule 2 to the Regulations provides the default provisions applicable to any employee whose contract does not confer an entitlement to absence from work for the purpose of caring for a child or does not incorporate such a term from a collective agreement or a workforce agreement.[64]

Schedule 2 imposes requirements in terms of evidence of parenthood and normally a notice period of at least twenty-one days.[65] It also provides that leave may be taken in blocks of no less than one week at a time,[66] except in the case of children in receipt of disability living allowance, and that no more than four weeks may be taken 'in respect of any individual child during a particular year'.[67] An employer may postpone leave, save at the time of birth or adoption, if he or she 'considers that the operation of his business would be unduly disrupted if the employee took leave during the period identified in his notice' and providing that he or she offers alternative leave within six months, at a date 'determined by the employer after consulting the employee'.[68] Notice of postponement must be in writing and with reasons and be given within seven days. Although there is no duty to pay wages or to work during the period of parental leave, the Regulations provide that other terms of the contract subsist.

Maternity and Parental Leave Regulations 1999, Regulation 17

An employee who takes parental leave –

(a) is entitled, during the period of leave, to the benefit of her employer's implied obligation to her of trust and confidence and any terms and conditions of her employment relating to –

(i) notice of the termination of the employment contract by her employer;

(ii) compensation in the event of redundancy; or

(iii) disciplinary or grievance procedures;

---

[64] Maternity and Parental Leave Regulations 1999, reg. 16.   [65] *Ibid.*, Sched. 2, paras. 1–5.

[66] *Ibid.*, para. 7; *New Southern Railway Ltd* v. *Rodway* [2005] EWCA Civ 443; [2005] ICR 1162 (CA).

[67] Maternity and Parental Leave Regulations 1999, Sched. 2, para. 8.   [68] *Ibid.*, para. 6.

(b) is bound, during that period, by her implied obligation to her employer of good faith and any terms and conditions of her employment relating to –
  (i) notice of the termination of the employment contract by her;
  (ii) the disclosure of confidential information;
  (iii) the acceptance of gifts or other benefits; or
  (iv) the employee's participation in any other business.

Those who take parental leave in a block no longer than four weeks are entitled to return to the same job in much the same way as employees returning from maternity leave.[69] Those who take longer leave are entitled to return to the same job 'or, if it is not reasonably practicable for the employer to permit … return to that job, to another job which is both suitable for [the employee] and appropriate for her to do in the circumstances'.[70] Terms and conditions on return must be no less favourable than they would have been had the employee not been absent.[71] Employees who take parental leave are similarly protected against detriment and unfair dismissal.[72]

The parental-leave provisions, although copying the other family-leave provisions in most respects, lack any right to payment, which will inevitably deter parents from exercising the right to parental leave. In particular, it is likely to deter low-income parents who lack any resources to tide them over during a week without pay. In other EU countries where payments are made, such as Germany, the take-up by women is much higher, but the take-up by men remains low.[73] It seems likely that men might be more interested in taking parental leave if it could be taken more flexibly, for periods of less than a week, or for reduced hours of work for a limited period of time. These options are only available under the 'right to ask for flexible working' (see below), but not as a statutory entitlement.

Until 1999, workers had no statutory entitlement to take time off work in an emergency to deal with illness suffered by children or other dependants. This left many – particularly the mothers of dependent children – forced to resort to subterfuge when their presence was required at home. If their deceit was discovered, the employer was in a strong position to carry out a fair dismissal. The dilemma facing parents and other workers was recognised by a provision in the original Parental Leave Directive, which is now re-enacted in a revised Framework Directive and is implemented by the ERA 1996.

---

[69] Maternity and Parental Leave Regulations 1999, reg. 18(1).   [70] *Ibid.*, reg. 18(2).
[71] *Ibid.*, reg. 18A.   [72] *Ibid.*, regs. 19 and 20.
[73] A. McColgan, 'Family Friendly Frolics: The Maternity and Parental Leave, Etc. Regulations 1999' (2000) *Industrial Law Journal* 125, at 139–42.

Parental Leave Directive 2010, Clause 7

Member States and/or social partners shall take the necessary measures to entitle workers to time off from work, in accordance with national legislation, collective agreements and/or practice, on grounds of force majeure for urgent family reasons in cases of sickness or accident making the immediate presence of the worker indispensable.[74]

Employment Rights Act 1996, Section 57A

(1) An employee is entitled to be permitted by his employer to take a reasonable amount of time off during the employee's working hours in order to take action which is necessary –

   (a) to provide assistance on an occasion when a dependant falls ill, gives birth or is injured or assaulted,

   (b) to make arrangements for the provision of care for a dependant who is ill or injured,

   (c) in consequence of the death of a dependant,

   (d) because of the unexpected disruption or termination of arrangements for the care of a dependant, or

   (e) to deal with an incident which involves a child of the employee and which occurs unexpectedly in a period during which an educational establishment which the child attends is responsible for him.

(2) Subsection (1) does not apply unless the employee –

   (a) tells his employer the reason for his absence as soon as reasonably practicable, and

   (b) except where paragraph (a) cannot be complied with until after the employee has returned to work, tells his employer for how long he expects to be absent.

'Emergency leave' is available only to 'employees', but no qualifying period of employment is imposed. The concept of a dependant is defined to include a spouse, partner, child, parent or a person living in the same house other than a lodger, or any other person who reasonably relies upon the employee in an emergency.[75] If an employer refuses the emergency leave, an employee can present a claim to a tribunal which can make a declaration that the right has been violated and award compensation that is just and equitable taking into account any loss suffered by the employee.[76] A dismissal in response to a valid exercise of the right is automatically unfair.[77]

No absolute limits are imposed on the amount of time-off permitted annually or in relation to a single emergency, but it is clearly envisaged that

---

[74] Directive 2010/18/EU of 8 March 2010 implementing the revised Framework Agreement on parental leave concluded by BUSINESSEUROPE, UEAPME, CEEP and ETUC Sched. 1, cl. 7.
[75] ERA 1996, s. 57A(3) and (4).   [76] ERA 1996, s. 57B.   [77] ERA 1996, s. 99(3)(d).

only short periods of leave will be permitted and that longer periods may have to be taken as parental leave. The thinking behind section 57A was explained by Lord Sainsbury for the government in the House of Lords debates on the legislation:

> We have not set a limit on the amount of time which employees can take off. This right is to help people deal with emergencies. A limit would not make sense and could be seen as a minimum, which employees might well consider an entitlement to be added to their annual leave. In all cases, the right will be limited to the amount of time which is reasonable in the circumstances of a particular case. For example, if a child falls ill with chickenpox the leave must be sufficient to enable the employee to cope with the crisis – to deal with the immediate care of the child and to make alternative longer-term care arrangements. The right will not enable a mother to take a fortnight off while her child is in quarantine. In most cases, whatever the problem, one or two days will be the most that are needed to deal with the immediate issues and sort out longer-term arrangements if necessary.[78]

The extent of the period of emergency leave was considered in *Qua* v. *John Ford Morrison Solicitors*,[79] where the claimant had taken seventeen days' absence on grounds connected with her young son's medical problems. Recorder Cox observed that:

> Whilst we recognise that no limit has been set on the number of times when an employee can exercise this right, an employee is not in our view entitled to unlimited amounts of time off work under this section even if in each case s/he complies with the notice requirements in s. 57A(2) and takes a reasonable amount of time off on each occasion. Logically this could result in an employee being entitled, regularly, to take a day or more off each week whenever the medical condition causes the child to become unwell; and we do not regard this as being what the legislation is intended to provide. The legislation contemplates a reasonable period of time off to enable an employee to deal with a child who has fallen ill unexpectedly and thus the section is dealing with something unforeseen. Once it is known that the particular child is suffering from an underlying medical condition, which is likely to cause him to suffer regular relapses, such a situation no longer falls within the scope of subsection (1)(a) or indeed within s. 57A at all. An employee would, in such circumstances, be permitted to reasonable time off work in order to make longer-term arrangements for care, as is provided by subsection (1)(b). Where the line is to be drawn seems to us to be a matter which will always fall to be decided on the facts of each case. A parent who has been permitted time off to deal with a child who has fallen ill with chickenpox might, for example, subsequently be permitted to further time off if unexpected complications arise requiring immediate action. The key to this is in our view, foreseeability and it will inevitably be a question of fact and degree in each situation.

---

[78] HL Debs., 8 July 1999, cols. 1084–5.   [79] [2003] ICR 482 (EAT).

Under section 57A(2), an employee must tell her employer as soon as reasonably practicable for how long she expects to be absent. In emergencies, of course, it may not be practicable to give much advance notice or to be sure how long the absence will last. In *Qua* v. *John Ford Morrison Solicitors*, the tribunal had held that the claimant had failed to give the proper notice to the employer of how long she expected to be absent, so she had not been unfairly dismissed, but the EAT allowed her appeal, ruling that section 57A does not require the employee to provide the employer with daily updates on her likely return to work but, rather, to tell her employer about the reason for her absence and, except where she was unable to do so before she returned to work, how long she expected to be absent. The provision did not impose a continuing obligation on the employee to update the employer as to her situation. Similarly, in *Truelove* v. *Safeway Stores plc*,[80] the claimant had told his employers that he might need the following day off to care for his daughter, but did not explain that the alternative child-care arrangements he had made with his sister to cover for his partner's unavailability had unexpectedly fallen through. The tribunal held that he had not been unfairly disciplined because he had not disclosed the full reasons for his absence, so the employers could not appreciate that his position fitted within the emergency-leave provision. The EAT allowed the appeal, holding that the employee had done enough to communicate to the employer that something had unexpectedly happened to cause a breakdown in the child-care arrangements, making it necessary, urgently, for the employee to take time-off.

If the emergency leave is refused, an employee can bring a claim under ERA 1996 section 57B that the employer has 'unreasonably refused' a request for emergency leave. The question arises what factors are relevant to the reasonableness of the employer's response. In *Truelove* v. *Safeway Stores plc*, the EAT suggested that relevant factors were how often requests for emergency leave had been made before; whether or not there was another way of solving the problem; and the business needs of the employer. Following a successful complaint, the tribunal may make a declaration and make an award of compensation that is just and equitable in all the circumstances. If the employer dismisses an employee for taking emergency leave, the dismissal will be automatically unfair,[81] unless the employer can successfully persuade the tribunal that the amount of time taken off work was unreasonable and therefore outside the protected right in ERA 1996, section 57A. The EAT in *Qua* v. *John Ford Morrison Solicitors*, suggested that the tribunal should not take into account the disruption or inconvenience caused to the employer's business by the employee's absence in determining what amount of absence was 'reasonable' under section 57A.

---

[80] [2005] ICR 589 (EAT).   [81] ERA 1996, s. 99.

Right to Request 'Flexible Working'

Employees with continuous service of at least twenty-six weeks have a right to apply to their employer for a change in their terms and conditions of work concerning the hours of work, the times that they are required to work, and where they are required to work.[82] The employer must deal with such a request in a reasonable manner and only reject it on a prescribed ground.

Employment Rights Act 1996, Section 80G(1)

(1) An employer to whom an application under section 80F is made –

. . .

(b) shall only refuse the application because he considers that one or more of the following grounds applies –

(i) the burden of additional costs,

(ii) detrimental effect on ability to meet customer demand,

(iii) inability to re-organise work among existing staff,

(iv) inability to recruit additional staff,

(v) detrimental impact on quality,

(vi) detrimental impact on performance,

(vii) insufficiency of work during the periods the employee proposes to work,

(viii) planned structural changes, and

(ix) such other grounds as the Secretary of State may specify by regulations.

If the employer denies the request for flexible working, the employee may make a complaint to an ET that the employer has not followed the correct procedure or has not complied with the grounds set out in ERA 1996 section 80G(1). If the ET finds the complaint well founded, it may make a declaration and order the employer to pay compensation that is just and equitable in all the circumstances up to a maximum of eight weeks' wages.[83] The employee is also protected in the normal way against retaliatory action by the employer for having sought to exercise the right, either by subjecting the employee to a detriment or a dismissal.

When first enacted in 2003, this right to request flexible working was aimed primarily at women returning from maternity leave who sought part-time employment to care for children, although it was extended in 2009 to the care of all school-age children. The right also enabled fathers to seek to adjust their hours of work to help with child-care. Although fathers tend to work longer hours than other male workers, no doubt reflecting a male breadwinner role,

---

[82] ERA 1996, s. 80F; Flexible Working Regulations 2014, SI 2014 No. 1398.

[83] ERA 1996, s. 80I.

nearly all men take advantage of schemes offered by their employers for flexibility in hours; for instance, fathers take up the opportunity to work from home more frequently than other men.[84] But employees' interest in flexible working extends beyond the concerns of child-care: employees may have other responsibilities to care for dependants, or find the costs of commuting on a daily basis excessive or want to perform some other kind of voluntary work, etc. This more general desire for flexible working attracted political support.

From the government's point of view, the extension of flexible working to all employees has many potential benefits: reducing unemployment, decreasing welfare-benefit dependency, reducing child poverty, reducing the gender pay gap, enabling disabled people to work, enabling working people to care for relatives and reducing the cost to the state, helping people as they become elderly to phase their retirement by working fewer hours, encouraging fathers to play a more active role in child-care and home-making, reducing the stress induced by long hours of work and so reducing health care costs and by no means least helping working individuals to participate in the 'Big Society'.[85] More generally, the potential advantage of the right to request flexible working is that it will enable all workers to achieve what for them is a more optimal work/life balance.

Initially, there was considerable resistance from employers to any right to work flexibly. Most employers argue that for reasons of efficiency they need to be able to construct the type of jobs that their businesses require and that often the nature of the job entails that it must be done full time. A breakthrough occurred in the European Part-Time Workers Directive.[86] This Directive was adopted following the 'social dialogue' procedure using a framework agreement between the social partners as the foundation for the text of the Directive. As an agreement between employers and trade unions at the European level, it is strong on general principles and exhortations, but keeps any costly legal obligations for employers to a minimum. Although the employers rejected any entitlement for workers to insist unilaterally on a change in their hours of work, it was agreed that employers should 'give consideration' to requests to transfer into part-time work and vice versa. Although many were sceptical about the effectiveness of a right to request flexible working, fearing that employers would invariably reject requests on one of the permitted grounds, in fact the opposite turned out to be the case. The compulsion placed on employers to consider the request properly seems to have helped to engender a new attitude towards flexible working. The vast majority of such requests are accepted. Surveys report that about 90 per cent

---

[84] L. Biggart and M. O'Brien, *Fathers' Working Hours* (BIS Employment Relations Occasional Paper, November 2009).

[85] BIS, *Consultation on Modern Workplaces* (May 2011).   [86] Directive 96/34.

of employers accept all requests for flexible working, and that about 80 per cent of employees who request changes have them accepted by the employer, albeit after some negotiations over the details.[87] About 80 per cent of employers typically permit requests for part-time working, about 30 per cent permit requests for temporary periods of reduced hours and flexitime and about 14 per cent permit working from home.[88] Despite some concerns about staff shortages, the majority of employers that provide flexible working practices and leave arrangements have found them to be cost effective, with a positive impact on labour turnover, motivation and commitment and employee relations.[89] Flexible job packages widen the available talent pool by attracting highly skilled workers back into the job market. It is also being discovered that many jobs that were assumed to require full-time work turned out to be less rigid in their demands. The UK government reports its own mistake in this respect: research found that in 2008 only 29 per cent of Civil Service vacancies were advertised as available on a part-time or job-share basis. However, when followed up with a phone call, 24 per cent of those advertised as full-time jobs *could* actually also be available on a part-time basis.[90] Although the legislation does not confer a right to work flexibly, in practice it appears to create a presumption in favour of permitting employees to adjust their hours of work in various ways. The remains a question, however, whether a stronger right should be conferred in cases where employees have unavoidable caring responsibilities, in order to place a duty upon the employer to make a reasonable accommodation in favour of the carer.[91]

Types of Flexible Working

- *Part-time*: employees are contracted to work less than normal full-time hours.
- *Flexi-time*: employees work a standard core time, but can vary the start, finish and break times each day within agreed limits.
- *Compressed hours*: employees work their total number of contracted weekly hours in fewer than the usual number of working days each week by working longer individual days.
- *Home-working*: employees work all or part of their contracted hours from home.

---

[87] BIS, *The Fourth Work-Life Employer Survey* (BIS Research Paper No. 184, December 2014), p. 44.
[88] *Ibid.*, p. 32.
[89] BIS, *Costs and Benefits to Business of Adopting Work Life Balance Working Practices: A Literature Review* (June 2014).
[90] Working Families, *We Need to Talk about Hours: Job Advertising in the Civil Service* (2008).
[91] N. Busby, *A Right to care? Unpaid Care Work in European Employment Law* (Oxford University Press, 2011); Victoria, Australia: Equal Opportunity Amendment (Family Responsibility) Act 2008.

- *Annualised hours*: employees average out working time across the year so they work a set number of hours per year rather than per week. Normally, they are split into core hours that are worked each week and unallocated hours that can be used for peaks in demand.
- *Term-time working*: employees' work follows school term patterns. They work as normal during term-time. During school holidays they do not go to work but are still employed.
- *Structured time-off in lieu*: employees work longer hours during busy periods and take an equivalent amount of time off (with pay) at a less busy time. There may be limits on the number of hours individuals can build up and when they can take time off.
- *Job-sharing*: employees work part-time (which could be part-day, part-week or part-year) and share the duties and responsibilities of a full-time position with another worker.
- *Varied-hours working or time banking*: prospective employees advertise which hours they are available to work for the day and employers employ them for short periods of time to manage specific pieces of work, such as covering a telephone help-line. For example, an individual might be employed between 6pm and 9pm on a Tuesday evening.[92]

Discrimination against Part-time Workers

In the UK, in 2017, out of the total workforce of about 32 million (consisting of about 27 million employees and about 5 million self-employed), about 8 million work part-time.[93] About 15 per cent of men work part-time, whereas about 40 per cent of women take part-time jobs. The proportion of the workforce taking part-time jobs has increased over the last half-century, from about 4 per cent in 1951, rising to 25 per cent in 1996 and, having risen during economic recessions, in 2017 is again about 25 per cent. Especially for men, much of this part-time work is involuntary, whereas for women it is often perceived as the optimal way of managing child-care needs. For employers, part-time work can be attractive because it permits numerical flexibility at peak times, as in the case of part-timers working in pubs on popular evenings at the weekend. There may also be savings in the employer's national insurance contributions, if the weekly pay is set below the lower earnings limit for contributions. Although the same exclusion from having to make contributions to national insurance may also benefit part-time workers in the short run, their failure to make regular contributions will disadvantage them in the long term, because it excludes them from 'contributory benefits', such as elements of jobseeker's allowance, the state pension and, as we have seen, statutory maternity pay.

---

[92] BIS, *Consultation on Modern Workplaces* (May 2011).
[93] Office for National Statistics, *Labour Force Survey* (December 2017).

Although women may be attracted to part-time work in order to manage child-care responsibilities, they risk their career prospects and long-term earnings, because often good jobs up the career ladder will be constructed as full time and there will be high expectations of commitment and long hours of work. It is harder to become a partner of a law firm, a hospital consultant, a head teacher of a school when working part time, and a period of part-time work is likely to delay any progress in the career. The consequence will be lower lifetime earnings and perhaps a reluctant decision on the part of the woman not to aim so high.

As well as those career disadvantages, there has been a pattern in the labour market of part-time workers being paid less per hour on average than full-time workers. The part-time pay penalty is illustrated by an estimate in 2011 that, although just over 4 per cent of the workforce are paid at the level of the NMW, 9 per cent of part-time workers are paid at the minimum.[94] This part-time pay penalty is probably attributable to a number of factors:

- occupational segregation and the concentration of part-time workers in the lowest paid occupations within a workplace;
- the exclusion of some groups of part-time workers from the main payment structure;
- fewer part-time opportunities are available in managerial, professional or senior positions;
- exclusion from training opportunities that might lead to promotions and better career opportunities;
- the payment by some employers of a lower basic rate of pay to part-time workers than their full-time counterparts;
- unequal treatment for part-timers in relation to profit sharing and performance pay;
- lack of access of part-time workers to overtime pay and other unsocial hours payments; part-time staff may not be paid overtime rates until their additional hours worked exceed the standard working week;
- part-time workers are more likely than full-time workers to be in employment where no pension scheme is offered, and, even where pension schemes are available, part-time workers are less likely to be a member of the scheme than their full-time colleagues.[95]

It is also evident that women moving from full-time to part-time work often make a downward occupational move, no longer making full use of their skills and experience, particularly if they change employer. It follows that the most effective way to reduce the part-time pay penalty is to strengthen the ability of

---

[94] Low Pay Commission, *Annual Report* (2010), p. 18.

[95] Equal Opportunities Commission, Memorandum to the House of Commons Select Committee on Education and Employment, *Part-Time Working*, Vol. II (Second Report, HC 346-II, 1998–9).

workers to move between full-time and part-time work without losing their current job,[96] as envisaged by the right to ask for flexible working discussed above. The combination of the right to return to work from maternity leave, the right to request flexible working, and the prohibition on discrimination against remuneration for part-time work go a long way in particular towards securing the position of women who wish to work part time after the birth of a child. But the legislation does not grant this right and furthermore there is evidence that at least for career women and professionals the new contractual arrangements are never entirely satisfactory.

Part-timers' Perceived Commitment

The reason that returning mothers have negative work experiences stems from the relationship between professional identity and the social construction of time. Not only are professionals expected to see work as central to their lives ... but they are also expected to demonstrate this centrality by working long hours within the workplace ('face time') and being 'ever available'. Part-time professionals appear to be particularly disadvantaged here. Research that has explored how co-workers and managers respond to the presence of a part-time professional in the work-group, suggests that it is her limited availability that is seen as a problem. Co-workers may complain that they are having to pick up additional work because the part-timer is not as available as full-time staff. Managers, meanwhile, find it difficult to supervise employees who are not working 'normal hours'. They may struggle with deploying such staff to suitable work tasks, especially if these tasks are time-bound and non-substitutable ... When the employee makes the transition to part-time working, she has opted to do so in order to *reduce* her temporal contribution, and the literature suggests that this changes the employee's psychological contract – she *expects* the organisation to understand this change in contribution. The 'problem' for the part-time employee and for the organisation seems to be that while managers and colleagues may well reassess the level of contribution they expect the part-timer to make, this re-evaluation tends to be in substantive as well as temporal terms.[97]

The principal target of the European Directive on part-time work[98] is the part-time pay gap. It prohibits discrimination against part-time workers in comparison with full-time workers with respect to employment-related matters such as pay and benefits, except where the difference in treatment can be justified on other grounds. In addition, workers are not to be penalised

---

[96] A. Manning and B. Petrongolo, 'The Part-Time Pay Penalty' (LSE and Women and Equality Unit, 2004).

[97] P. Dick, 'The Transition to Motherhood and Part-Time Working: Mutuality and Incongruence in the Psychological Contracts Existing Between Managers and Employees' (2010) 24(3) *Work, Employment and Society* 508, at 512–13 (footnotes omitted).

[98] Directive 96/34; M. Jeffrey, 'Not Really Going to Work? Of the Directive on Part-Time Work, "Atypical Work" and Attempts to Regulate It' (1998) 27 *Industrial Law Journal* 193.

in connection with a refusal to transfer from full-time to part-time work or vice versa, except according to law and for reasons which 'arise from the operational requirements of the establishment concerned'. This would cover, for example, reductions in hours to avoid job losses in a redundancy situation. Member States and the social partners are further instructed to 'identify and review' and, where appropriate, eliminate legal and administrative hurdles to part-time work, subject to the principle of non-discrimination, the aims of the Directive and the non-regression rule that the Directive's implementation shall not be valid grounds for a general reduction in the protection of part-time workers. These principles were enacted in the UK by statutory instrument, the Part-Time Workers (Prevention of Less Favourable Treatment) Regulations 2000.[99]

Part-Time Workers (Prevention of Less Favourable Treatment) Regulations 2000, Regulation 5

(1) A part-time worker has the right not to be treated by his employer less favourably than the employer treats a comparable full-time worker –
   (a) as regards the terms of his contract; or
   (b) by being subjected to any other detriment by any act, or deliberate failure to act, of his employer.

(2) The right conferred by paragraph (1) applies only if –
   (a) the treatment is on the ground that the worker is a part-time worker, and
   (b) the treatment is not justified on objective grounds.

(3) In determining whether a part-time worker has been treated less favourably than a comparable full-time worker the pro rata principle shall be applied unless it is inappropriate.

(4) A part-time worker paid at a lower rate for overtime worked by him in a period than a comparable full-time worker is or would be paid for overtime worked by him in the same period shall not, for that reason, be regarded as treated less favourably than the comparable full-time worker where, or to the extent that, the total number of hours worked by the part-time worker in the period, including overtime, does not exceed the number of hours the comparable full-time worker is required to work in the period, disregarding absences from work and overtime.

The accompanying official guidance suggests that equality of treatment should extend to basic hourly rates and (subject to regulation 5(4)) overtime, as well as to contractual sick and maternity pay; access to occupational

---

[99] SI 2000 No. 1551.

pension schemes; selection for redundancy; leave and career breaks (on a pro rata basis where appropriate); reorganisation of hours; and promotion and training, the latter 'to be structured wherever possible to be at the most convenient times for the majority of staff including part-timers'.[100] The less favourable treatment for the part-time worker need not be solely on the ground that the worker is employed for fewer hours, but the part-time status must be part of the reason for the less favourable treatment. For instance, in *Sharma* v. *Manchester City Council*,[101] some, but not all, part-time lecturers in the adult-education service had terms of service that permitted the council to reduce their hours of work, an option not possible for full-time lecturers. This situation fell within the Regulations, even though the part-time work was not the sole reason for the less favourable treatment.

The Regulations apply not only to employees, but also to 'workers' in accordance with the normal statutory UK definition. On the other hand, for the purpose of a comparison between full-time and part-time workers, both must be paid 'wholly or in part by reference to the time he works',[102] which appears to exclude pieceworkers or those paid by commission. With respect to the hours of work, there is no statutory definition of the difference between 'full-time' and 'part-time', but instead the matter is determined by reference to the custom and practice of the employer.[103]

In order to enforce the claim against discrimination, a worker may make a complaint to an ET.[104] If the tribunal finds that a complaint is well founded, it can make a declaration, order the employer to pay compensation and recommend that the employer should take action to obviate the adverse effect. The compensation, although governed by a requirement that it must be just and equitable, is principally directed at the economic loss suffered by the worker as a result of the less favourable treatment. The worker is also protected in the normal way against retaliatory action by the employer for having sought to exercise the right, either by subjecting the employee to a detriment or a dismissal.[105]

The notion of making a comparison between the full-time worker and a part-time worker proves complex. The legislation insists that the comparison must be one of like with like, both in terms of the type of work performed, the

---

[100] Department of Trade and Industry, *Part-Time Workers: The Law and Best Practice, A Detailed Guide for Employers and Part-Timers*. Current guidance can be found on the government information website, www.direct.gov.uk/en/Employment/Employees/Flexibleworking/DG_173304. A broad view of what constitutes pay has been confirmed: Case C-393/10 *O'Brien* v. *Ministry of Justice* [2012] ICR 955; Case C-476/12, *Osterreichischer Gewerkschaftsbund* v. *Verband Osterreichischer Banking and Bankiers* ECJ [2015] ICR D10, ECJ.

[101] [2008] ICR 623 (EAT).

[102] Part-Time Workers (Prevention of Less Favourable Treatment) Regulations 2000, reg. 2.

[103] *Ibid.*   [104] *Ibid.*, reg. 8.   [105] *Ibid.*, reg. 7.

skills of the workers, and the type of contract issued by their common employer.

Part-Time Workers (Prevention of Less Favourable Treatment) Regulations 2000, Regulation 2(4)

A full-time worker is a comparable full-time worker in relation to a part-time worker if, at the time when the treatment that is alleged to be less favourable to the part-time worker takes place –

(a) both workers are –
   (i) employed by the same employer under the same type of contract, and
   (ii) engaged in the same or broadly similar work having regard, where relevant, to whether they have a similar level of qualification, skills and experience; and
(b) the full-time worker works or is based at the same establishment as the part-time worker or, where there is no full-time worker working or based at that establishment who satisfies the requirements of sub-paragraph (a), works or is based at a different establishment and satisfies those requirements.

It is clear that part-time work often involves occupational segregation – dinner-ladies are all part time – so that straightforward comparators are often unavailable in practice, which seriously weakens the possible impact of the legislation. The government's own regulatory impact assessment estimated that the Regulations would benefit only around 7 per cent of the UK's part-time workers, all but 17 per cent being excluded for want of an appropriate comparator. Unlike anti-discrimination laws, it is not possible to overcome that problem by inventing a hypothetical comparator for the purpose of the Regulations.[106] The Directive provides, where no such comparator is available, that 'comparison shall be made by reference to the applicable collective agreement or, where there is no applicable collective agreement, in accordance with national law, collective agreements or practice'. This possible extension is not reflected in the Regulations.

Part-time workers often have different types of contract, which deny career prospects, fringe benefits and indefinite employment; that is the nature of the subtle character of the discrimination against them. Since it would be easy for employers to avoid the application of the legislation by issuing part-time workers with a different type of contract, the Regulations provide a control.

---

[106] *Carl* v. *University of Sheffield* [2009] ICR 1286 (EAT).

Part-Time Workers (Prevention of Less Favourable Treatment) Regulations 2000, Regulation 2(3)

For the purposes of paragraphs (1), (2) and (4), the following shall be regarded as being employed under different types of contract –

(a) employees employed under a contract that is not a contract of apprenticeship;

(b) employees employed under a contract of apprenticeship;

(c) workers who are not employees;

(d) any other description of worker that it is reasonable for the employer to treat differently from other workers on the ground that workers of that description have a different type of contract.

The purpose of this slightly obscure provision has been interpreted to be that it is not possible to make comparisons between workers who fall into the separate categories (a)–(d). For example, if the part-time worker is properly classified as a 'worker' and not an 'employee', no comparison can be made with a full-time employee. The original legislation also included a further category of fixed-term work, but that was eliminated so it should be irrelevant to the question of whether the contracts are of the same type.[107] Paragraph (d) appears to try to place a further control on the manipulation of contractual differences by the employer by setting a test of reasonableness, but it now appears redundant as a result of the decision of the House of Lords in *Matthews* v. *Kent & Medway Towns Fire Authority*.[108] The case concerned a claim brought by 'retained' part-time firefighters for equal treatment *vis-à-vis* full-time firefighters, whose terms and conditions were more favourable in respect of certain matters, including the availability of an occupational pension scheme. An ET ruled that the claimants were not employed on the 'same type of contract' as full-time firefighters for the purposes of regulation 2, taking the view that the full-time firefighters fell within regulation 2(3)(a) and the retained firefighters within regulation 2(3)(d). It also ruled that the retained and full-time firefighters did not do the 'same or broadly similar work' within regulation 2(4)(a)(ii) on the basis that the latter not only responded to emergencies but also engaged in educational, preventive and administrative tasks. The House of Lords held that, in light of the purpose of the underlying Directive, the aim of regulation 3 was to distinguish between different kinds of employment relationship rather than different types of contract. Therefore, the purpose of paragraph (d) was not to enable employers to single out particular types of part-time workers and issue them with different types of contract in

---

[107] Part-Time Workers (Prevention of Less Favourable Treatment) Regulations 2000 (Amendment) Regulations 2002, SI 2002 No. 2035.

[108] [2006] UKHL 8, [2006] ICR 365 (HL).

order to evade the application of the legislation. Indeed, as a result of this decision, it is difficult to imagine a plausible example of a worker who could fall within paragraph (d) and at the same time not be an 'employee' or a 'worker' under paragraph (a) or (c). In this respect, the Regulations may provide broader protection to part-time workers than the Directive, since under the Directive the ECJ has denied the possibility of making a comparison between full-time workers and casual workers under no obligation to accept any work.[109] Since both full-time and retained firefighters were both employed under contracts of employment (and not in the other categories), a comparison could be made in this case. On the second issue of whether or not the work was 'the same or broadly similar' the case was remitted to the tribunal to reassess the facts using the guidance and with the strong hint that it was important to focus on the extent to which the work was exactly the same (fighting fires) and that less weight should be given to the few extra tasks performed by the full-time firefighters.

In a few cases, it is possible to avoid the need for a part-time worker to find a comparator full-time worker. Regulation 3 provides for the case where a full-time worker goes part-time as a result of a new or varied contract. In this case, the part-time worker can make the claim on the basis that he is receiving less than a pro rata reduction in his former pay and benefits. Regulation 4 provides for the similar case where a worker returns after a period of leave, such as maternity leave, within a year, but works part time on her return.

Even if the part-time worker can establish a suitable comparison and demonstrate less favourable treatment with respect to the terms of the contract, taking into account the pro rata principle, it is open to the employer to try to justify the difference 'on objective grounds'. The official guidance which accompanies the Regulations states that differential treatment will be objectively justified for the purposes of the Regulations where 'it is necessary and appropriate to achieve a legitimate business objective', which appears to match the test for justification for indirect discrimination. The guidance suggests that pay differentials might be justified where 'workers are shown to have a different level of performance measured by a fair and consistent appraisal system' and that, while participation in share-option and profit-sharing schemes should, in general, be open to part-timers (benefits to be distributed pro rata), the exclusion of part-timers from the former could be justified 'where the value of the share options was so small that the potential benefit to the part-timer of the options was less than the likely cost of realising them'. The guidance also suggests that, where, as in the case of health insurance, pro-rating is not possible, this might be a ground on which the denial of the benefit to part-timers could be justified. In *Ministry of Justice* v. *O'Brien*,[110] the Supreme Court held that the denial of pensions to part-time judges while

---

[109] Case C-313/02, *Wippel* v. *Peek & Cloppenburg GmbH & Co. KG* [2005] ICR 1604 (ECJ).
[110] *Ministry of Justice* v. *O'Brien* [2013] UKSC 6, [2013] ICR 499.

granting pensions to full-time judges was discrimination against part-time workers that had not been objectively justified by reference to transparent and precise legitimate aims that required this difference in treatment. In particular, the lack of government funds could not justify the failure to award a proportionate pension.

Although the Regulations may do nothing to challenge the major source of disadvantage associated with part-time work arising from occupational segregation, it should be recalled that anti-discrimination laws, including the equal-pay requirement, can be used to insist on equal pay for work of equal value across occupational boundaries. The Regulations do provide some additional protection to a number of part-timers, in particular those who retain the same employer during a move to part-time work. They also provide significant additional protection to male part-time workers, freed as they are from the requirement to prove that they were less favourably treated than a woman part-timer would have been. But they do little to address the real problems associated with part-time work: that it is provided, by and large, in low-paying workplaces and low-paying jobs and that women are frequently being denied the opportunity to continue in their previous roles on transferring to part-time work.

A Vision of the Work/Life Balance

This chapter has examined the legal measures introduced in recent decades that seek to establish a better balance between work and family commitments, an issue that affects everyone, but which has been especially pressing for women. The question remains, however, what is the vision that we should pursue? Should the law simply allow everyone to exercise their own preferences,[111] or should the law seek to impose an approved model of family life? If the latter, how should we choose between a traditional division of labour with a sole male breadwinner and a female partner mostly doing caring at home or, at the other extreme, all adults working outside the home but employing domestic workers to perform child-care or all the possible models in between those poles of a spectrum. Some feminists argue that it is only through performing paid work outside the home that women will be treated as equals, in the same way as men choosing their own projects and forging connected lives.[112] But others say that the crucial problem is rather the devaluing of caring for children and the home, because it is unpaid work or indeed often not regarded as proper work at all. As well as respecting the desire of women to lead fulfilling lives and to enjoy equal respect, we need to take into account the needs of children for stimulating and tender care. We should also

---

[111] C. Hakim, *Work-Lifestyle Choices in the 21st Century: Preference Theory* (Oxford University Press, 2000).

[112] V. Schultz, 'Life's Work' (2000) 100 *Columbia Law Review* 1881.

acknowledge that men find it difficult to escape stereotypes for their role as breadwinner away from the home. Few men so far feel comfortable with informing their employer that they are having a baby and that, after the mother has taken a month of maternity leave, they will take shared parental leave for the rest of the year after birth. In the light of these potentially conflicting considerations, perhaps the best course of action is for the law to offer options to parents, along the lines of the SPL laws and duties placed upon employers to make reasonable adjustments to the terms on which work is performed, without imposing any single model on parents and carers.

In laws governing rights to time off work and to flexibility, since 2000 there has been a marked shift to expand employee's rights to try to negotiate terms and conditions that match their aspirations for a work/life balance. This is a welcome adjustment in the focus of family friendly measures, which hitherto had largely addressed the first year after birth, leaving parents to cope as best they could for the next fifteen years until the children could look after themselves. That expansion of coverage will help to challenge the paradigm used in the employment law of workers who are unencumbered by caring responsibilities.[113] Such negotiations about flexible working are likely to increase as older workers can arrange for their own passage towards retirement rather than complying with the cliff-edge of compulsory retirement arrangements imposed by employers. Despite some opposition from employers, greater flexibility for employees often suits employers because they too want a flexible workforce to meet fluctuating demands.

Much of the discussion about the work/life balance assumes that we can distinguish between the two. But that view is open to question. We need to remember that most people spend a considerable proportion of their time performing work. Ideally, that work should amount to meaningful part of our lives rather than some kind of unfulfilling and objectionable experience. Although this goal will be hard to achieve in practice and may be utopian, we should surely aspire to blending work and life, so that work is not a severable experience but part of a fulfilling and freely chosen life. Technology can help that integration of work and life, by for instance enabling more of us to work from home. Yet technology is also a threat to this vision, for the incessant demands of emails and the social media can turn every waking hour into a frantic attempt to meet the demands of employers, customers, and colleagues as well as friends and family. In France, there is a law that entitles workers to turn off their email and smartphones and therefore create a boundary on working hours. Such measures are necessary to avoid turning all of life into routine work.

---

[113] G. James, 'Family-friendly Employment Law (Re) assessed: The Potential of Care Ethics' (2016) 45 *Industrial Law Journal* 477, at 477–8.

11

Civil Liberties at Work

Contents

Much of the material in this book is concerned with human rights or fundamental rights. These rights include both civil and political rights, such as protection for freedom of association and the right to a fair trial, and also social and economic rights, such as the right to work, the right to fair pay and protection against unjust dismissal. In this chapter we focus on the protection of some of the civil and political rights established in the ECHR, which are enforceable in the UK as a result of the HRA 1998. We focus on the implications of the HRA 1998 for the protection of individual employees in the enjoyment of their civil liberties at work. The Act provides a mechanism by which the ECHR of the Council of Europe may be legally enforceable in national courts. This chapter examines the protection of workers' privacy interests (Article 8), freedom of religion (Article 9) and whistleblowing and other issues relating to freedom of expression (Article 10). Other Convention rights protected under the HRA 1998 that are pertinent to labour law are considered in other chapters. Occasionally, we need to refer as well to the Charter of the Fundamental Rights of the European Union. To the extent that EU legislation protects these rights, under the EU Treaties courts must ensure that their interpretations of the legislation are compatible with the Charter. After the UK has left the EU, although the Charter will cease to be law in the UK, the requirements of those fundamental rights, as developed in the case-law, may influence decisions of UK courts about the meaning of retained EU legislation.[1]

Protecting Human Rights at Work

Before examining the detailed application of Convention rights in labour law, it is important to appreciate how the HRA 1998 may affect the interpretation and application of domestic labour law. Furthermore, it is necessary to note how the ECHR, as an international treaty regarding human rights, itself presents unique challenges with regard to its interpretation and evolution.

Indirect Effect of the Human Rights Act

In the jargon of treaty law, the HRA 1998 creates direct vertical effect, but only indirect horizontal effect. The direct vertical effect occurs by virtue of HRA 1998, section 7, which permits direct actions by individuals against public authorities for breach of their Convention rights. Under this provision, for instance, a public-sector employee might complain that the employing government entity has interfered with a Convention right such as the right to respect for private life. However, section 7 may only apply to claims brought by employees against their employer when their employer's action involves the exercise of a public function rather than a private act such as making a contract.

The indirect horizontal effect of the HRA 1998 concerns the regulation of the contract of employment between individuals and their employer, whether a public or a private entity. The HRA 1998 may influence the interpretation and application of ordinary legal claims brought by an employee against an employer, such as a claim for unfair dismissal. In particular, HRA 1998,

---

[1] European Union (Withdrawal) Act 2018, ss. 5–6.

section 3, imposes upon the courts an obligation to construe domestic legislation in conformity with the Convention rights.[2]

Human Rights Act 1998, Section 3(1)

So far as it is possible to do so, primary legislation and subordinate legislation must be read and given effect in a way which is compatible with the Convention rights.

This provision gives indirect horizontal effect to the Convention rights in ordinary labour relations. The decision of the House of Lords in *Ghaidan v. Godin-Mendoza* made it clear that the interpretive obligation imposed by section 3 is extremely strong:

> The mere fact the language under consideration is inconsistent with a Convention-compliant meaning does not of itself make a Convention-compliant interpretation under section 3 impossible. Section 3 enables language to be interpreted restrictively or expansively. But section 3 goes further than this. It is also apt to require a court to read in words which change the meaning of the enacted legislation, so as to make it Convention-compliant. In other words, the intention of Parliament in enacting section 3 was that, to an extent bounded only by what is 'possible', a court can modify the meaning, and hence the effect, of primary and secondary legislation. Parliament, however, cannot have intended that in the discharge of this extended interpretative function the courts should adopt a meaning inconsistent with a fundamental feature of legislation. That would be to cross the constitutional boundary section 3 seeks to demarcate and preserve.[3]

The strong indirect effect produced by section 3 of the HRA 1998 on statutory labour law was accepted by the Court of Appeal in *X* v. *Y*.[4] The case, which will be considered in greater detail below in connection with Article 8, concerned a claim for unfair dismissal brought against a private-sector employer. The Court of Appeal accepted that a court or tribunal must interpret domestic legislation such as the ERA 1996, which includes the law of unfair dismissal, in a manner that is compliant with the Convention rights, taking into account the interpretation placed on those rights by the ECtHR. It followed that, in making the determination of whether or not a dismissal was unfair, a tribunal should achieve a conception of fairness that complied with Convention rights. Thus, in principle, all employees, both those in the public and those in the private sector, can rely upon the Convention rights contained in the HRA as a

---

[2] HRA 1998, s. 6(5); G. Morris, 'The Human Rights Act and the Public/Private Divide in Employment Law' (1998) 27 *Industrial Law Journal* 293.
[3] [2004] 2 AC 557 (HL), *per* Lord Nicholls.   [4] [2004] ICR 1634 (CA).

source for the interpretation of domestic legislation to ensure its conformity with Convention rights. In general, therefore, a dismissal involving an unjustified interference with an employee's Convention right should be regarded as an unfair dismissal.

The duty to interpret the law so that it complies with the Convention rights also applies to cases where courts and tribunals have to apply the common law. The Convention rights have the potential therefore to influence the interpretation of the common law of the contract of employment, including its implied terms and the rules on wrongful dismissal. The requirement that courts should act compatibly with Convention rights requires them, if possible, to interpret terms of contracts in a manner that respects an employee's rights, including freedom of expression. In *Smith* v. *Trafford Housing Trust*,[5] an employee was demoted for breach of the employer's contractual code of conduct by posting on his personal Facebook page his view that gay marriage in church was 'an equality too far'. Briggs J held that the code of conduct had to be interpreted in the light of Convention rights and that, considering the potential level of interference with freedom of expression, no reasonable person would have understood the employer's code to apply to personal comments posted at weekends to friends. It also seems possible that an employer's violation of an employee's Convention right will be regarded as a breach of the implied term of mutual trust and confidence.[6] But the courts may have to extend the implied terms within the contract of employment to ensure that the common law requires the employer not only to comply with Convention rights in the performance of the contract but also to respect Convention rights of employees in other contexts both inside and outside of the workplace.[7]

The requirement to interpret domestic labour law in a way that complies with Convention rights generally follows a two-stage process. First, courts and tribunals must assess whether the relevant articles of the Convention are applicable to the circumstances. The question is whether or not the alleged conduct of the employer 'engages' a Convention right in the sense that the conduct appears to interfere in a material way with the employee's enjoyment of the right. Next, at a second stage of the enquiry, a court must consider whether any interference with the Convention right can be justified in accordance with a test of proportionality. The test of proportionality requires a court to consider whether the employer's interference was for a legitimate purpose, in accordance with the law, and was necessary and appropriate in the circumstances. The Convention provides some guidance as to the possible kinds of

---

[5] *Smith* v. *Trafford Housing Trust* [2012] EWHC 3221 (Ch), [2013] IRLR 86.
[6] M. Freedland, *The Personal Employment Contract* (Oxford University Press, 2003), p. 162.
[7] H. Collins and V. Mantouvalou, 'Human Rights and the Contract of Employment', in M. Freedland (gen. ed.), *The Contract of Employment* (Oxford University Press, 2016), p. 188.

legitimate purposes. These include national security, the prevention of disorder and crime, the protection of the rights of others and measures necessary to protect a democratic society. In practice, an employer can normally rely on its own business and organisational needs to provide a legitimate reason for the interference. The crucial question then becomes whether the interference with the employee's Convention right for this business purpose was necessary and appropriate in the circumstances. If the conclusion of this enquiry is that the employer did unjustifiably violate an employee's Convention right, a court must try to interpret the relevant law such as the statutory protection against unfair dismissal in a way that ensures that the employee's right is vindicated. The interference must be in accordance with the law, for a legitimate aim and proportionate to the 'pressing social need' pursued. While the scope for justification of such an interference can be broad in the case of private employers, since public-sector bodies are under the duty imposed by HRA 1998 section 6 to act compatibly with Convention rights, their justifications must satisfy the limits of the Convention precisely.[8] It is only if the conduct of the employer both interferes with the employee's enjoyment of the Convention right in a material way and if it cannot be justified under the relevant test of justification for that particular right that the interpretation of domestic law must be adjusted, if necessary and possible in view of its wording, so that the employee's right is effectively protected. In practice, these preconditions for the HRA 1998 to affect the application of domestic labour law are rarely satisfied.

The Influence of the European Court of Human Rights

In carrying out these interpretive obligations, HRA 1998, section 2(1), requires a UK court to take into account any decision of the ECtHR in Strasbourg.[9] Although the UK courts are not bound absolutely to follow the jurisprudence of the ECtHR, they are only likely to depart from its interpretation of Convention rights when its decisions appear obscure or contradictory. A number of features of the approach of the ECtHR to the interpretation of Convention rights should be highlighted at the outset:

- The ECtHR has insisted not only that many Convention rights require a state to refrain from interfering with rights directly, but also that the Convention may place an obligation on the state to prevent individuals from interfering unjustifiably with the rights of others. This effect of the Convention on private parties stems in part from Article 1 of the Convention, which requires states to 'secure to everyone within their jurisdiction the

---

[8] *Hill* v. *Governing Body of Great Tey Primary School* [2013] ICR 691 (EAT).
[9] The same duty applies to the former body, the European Commission on Human Rights, which served to screen applications to the ECtHR for their admissibility.

rights and freedoms' protected by the Convention. This construction of positive obligations upon states to develop their laws so that they provide adequate protection of Convention rights is especially significant in relation to the horizontal effect of the Convention. It imposes a duty upon a government not only to refrain from interfering with a Convention right itself, but also to ensure that laws safeguard the enjoyment of rights in other contexts, including ordinary employment relations.

- The ECtHR has also stressed on many occasions that the Convention is a 'living instrument', which evolves over time and which reflects a consensus of values that underpin the Convention.

- The ECtHR also adopts an integrated approach to the interpretation of the Convention.[10] Under this method, the ECtHR strives to find an interpretation of a Convention right that is compatible with the rights protected in other international conventions. The relevant international conventions in the context of labour law comprise the protection of social and economic rights in the European Social Charter and Conventions of the ILO. The rights of workers protected in those international conventions are not legally enforceable. But under the integrated approach of the ECtHR, these social and economic rights may influence the interpretation of a legally enforceable Convention right. For instance, the ECtHR has interpreted the protection of the right to respect for private life under Article 8 in such a way as to include respect for the right to work, as described in the European Social Charter.[11] This integrated approach has been particularly influential in the interpretation of Article 11 in steering that protection of the freedom of association of trade unions in the direction of protecting the right to collective bargaining and to take industrial action.[12] In *Wilson and National Union of Journalists (NUJ)* v. *United Kingdom*,[13] for instance, the ECtHR paid close attention to the meaning of the right to organise in the European Social Charter and the equivalent and more detailed Conventions of the ILO. It noted that the expert committees under both the Charter and the ILO had expressed the view that UK law was incompatible with the right to organise. The decision illustrates the crucial point that social rights can have indirect legal effect under the integrated approach by influencing the interpretation of legally enforceable Convention rights. Although the courts in the UK have shown little sign of following an integrated approach, the obligation to take into account the decisions of the ECtHR will indirectly push them towards acknowledging the results of this style of interpretation.

---

[10] V. Mantouvalou, 'Labour Rights in the ECHR: An Intellectual Justification for an Integrated Approach to Interpretation' (2013) 13 *Human Rights Law Review* 529.

[11] *Sidabras* v. *Lithuania* [2004] ECHR 395 (ECtHR); V. Mantouvalou, 'Work and Private Life: Sidabras and Dziautas v. Lithuania' (2005) 30 *European Law Review* 573.

[12] See Chapter 12.   [13] [2002] IRLR 568 (ECtHR).

Finally, Article 14 contains a provision against discrimination in the way in which states accord individuals their Convention rights.

European Convention on Human Rights, Article 14

The enjoyment of the rights and freedoms set forth in this Convention shall be secured without discrimination on any ground such as sex, race, colour, language, religion, political or other opinion, national or social origin, association with a national minority, property, birth or other status.

Notice that Article 14 does not limit the grounds of discrimination to established protected grounds such as sex and race, but includes the words 'or other status'; a court may use this phrase to apply Article 14 to any ground for adverse treatment of a group or a class of people that lacks an objective and reasonable justification.[14] The differential treatment of groups will be regarded as lacking such an objective and reasonable justification if it does not pursue a 'legitimate aim' or if there is not a 'reasonable relationship of proportionality between the means employed and the aim sought to be realised'.[15] The ECtHR also insists that it is not necessary to demonstrate an actual breach of a Convention right before invoking Article 14; it suffices to demonstrate that the impugned conduct falls 'within the ambit' of the protected right.[16] If the conduct falls within the ambit of protection, it is unlikely that a government will be able to justify its conduct if it is tainted by invidious or inappropriate grounds of discrimination.

Where national law has not properly implemented an EU Directive, the normal rule is that a claimant cannot rely on the Directive directly unless the claim lies against the state. The claimant's remedy should be to recover losses caused by a failure to implement the Directive against the government.[17] But if the Directive can itself be regarded as an expression of an EU Charter right, as is the case with the WTD, the question arises whether the combination of the Charter right with the Directive may afford a claimant a direct claim against a private employer. Although the courts have rejected that possibility, they have achieved the same result by saying in some instances that national laws that block claims supported by Charter rights should be disapplied.[18]

---

[14] *Cases Relating to Certain Aspects of the Laws on the Use of Languages in Education in Belgium* (1968) 1 EHRR 252 (ECtHR).

[15] *Abdulaziz, Cabales and Balkandali* v. *United Kingdom* (1985) 7 EHRR 471 (ECtHR).

[16] *Ibid.*   [17] C-6/90 and C-9/90 *Francovitch and Bonifaci* v. *Italy* [1992] IRLR 161 (ECJ).

[18] *Benkharbouche* v. *Secretary of State for Foreign and Commonwealth Affairs* [2017] UKSC 62, [2017] 3 WLR 957. Joined cases C-569/16 and C-570/16 *Stadt Wuppertal* v. *Bauer* and *Willmeroth* v. *Brossonn* ECLI:EU:C:2018:871.

Privacy

European Convention on Human Rights, Article 8

(1) Everyone has the right to respect for his private and family life, his home and his correspondence.

(2) There shall be no interference by a public authority with the exercise of this right except such as is in accordance with the law and is necessary in a democratic society in the interests of national security, public safety or the economic well-being of the country, for the prevention of disorder or crime, for the protection of health or morals, or for the protection of the rights and freedoms of others.

The origins of the legal protection of privacy lie in prohibitions against intrusive state interference with our lives, such as techniques of constant surveillance and the attempts of totalitarian governments to control our very thoughts and beliefs. However, other powerful organisations also may interfere with the right to privacy by using economic sanctions. In the particular context of labour law, we can observe how employers may refuse to hire applicants unless they disclose confidential details of their medical history, or fire employees for what they do in their leisure activities. Employers may try to prevent intimate relations between colleagues or discriminate against workers who hold unconventional political or ideological views.

The right to privacy, as Article 8 is commonly described, has evolved a nuanced family of meanings. The starting-point is a notion that the state should not interfere unduly with the way individuals choose to lead their own lives, especially in their own homes. Our freedom to be left alone should include every aspect of ordinary life, from the clothes we wear, to the food we eat and the television shows we enjoy. Privacy also concerns the information that we wish to prevent others, including state officials, from knowing about us without our permission. More deeply, the idea of privacy extends to the freedom to develop our individuality or personality according to our preferences. Facets of our personality include our sexual preferences, our friendships and our intimate relationships.

With regard to the scope of the kinds of privacy interests of workers protected by Article 8(1), the ECtHR has insisted that the notion of 'private life' is not susceptible to exhaustive definition. It protects a right to personal development, whether in terms of personality or personal autonomy. Everyone has the right to live privately, away from unwanted attention. But the right to privacy is not confined to the home; it can operate in a broader space, so that it protects a 'private social life' in which it is possible for an individual to develop his or her social identity through friendships and meeting other people. The notion of private life may include professional activities[19] or activities taking place in a public setting.[20] Crucially, conduct in the workplace can be an aspect of private life. Private personal conversations between individuals in the workplace should fit within this notion of privacy. Files stored on a work computer that are clearly labelled as private and personal are regarded as part of private life are therefore protected from employers opening them save in exceptional circumstances.[21] Restrictions on a person's ability to work or pursue a profession may also fall within Article 8 where they impede the manner in which that person constructs his or her social identity by developing relationships with others,[22] for it is in the workplace that the majority of people develop some of their most significant relationships with others and with the outside world.[23] The concept of 'correspondence' specified in Article 8 is also given a broad meaning to include telephone calls, email and instant messaging, whether or not made from the employer's premises or on the employer's equipment.

Although employers plainly have considerable power to interfere with an individual's privacy, they may have legitimate reasons for doing so. An employer concerned about the health and safety of the workforce may insist upon medical or drug tests. Similarly, an employer concerned about theft or embezzlement may need to use covert surveillance to discover the culprit. The question in many instances of complaints about an employer's invasion of privacy will necessarily involve an assessment of the proportionality of the employer's interference with privacy in the light of the legitimate aim of the employer's actions and the detrimental effect on the employee. Article 8(2) provides a broad range of potential justifications for employers, including the protection of their economic interests and property rights, the protection of the health and safety of the workforce and the public and the protection of moral standards.

Employers sometimes reject any application of the right to privacy to employment relations. It is argued that, by accepting a contract of employment, an employee implicitly consents to any invasion of privacy by the employer. On this view, for instance, as soon as an employee enters the workplace, the employer is entitled to keep every action of the employee under constant surveillance. This implied consent to restrictions on privacy is even said to extend to off-duty activities in leisure time so that, where an employer disapproves of that activity, the employer claims to be entitled to exercise disciplinary powers to discourage or prevent it. The courts have denied that an

---

[19] *Fernández Martínez* v. *Spain*, No. 56030/07, §110, ECHR 2014.

[20] *Von Hannover* v. *Germany (No. 2)*, Nos. 40660/08 and 60641/08, §95, ECHR 2012.

[21] *Libert* v. *France* (App. No. 588/13) 22 February 2018.

[22] *Sidabras and Dziautas* v. *Lithuania* (2004) 42 EHRR 104 (ECtHR).

[23] *Niemitz* v. *Germany* (1992) 16 EHRR 7 (ECtHR); M. Ford, 'Article 8 and the Right to Privacy at the Workplace', in K. D. Ewing (ed.), *Human Rights at Work* (London: Institute of Employment Rights, 2000), p. 31.

employee gives such wide-ranging consent to any intrusion, but certainly the idea that employees have to some extent relinquished their right to privacy by taking the job plays an important role in curtailing the right in the context of employment.

Since the right to privacy has a potentially broad range of applications to the context of employment, it is only possible here to focus on some key issues that frequently arise. These concern electronic surveillance, the misuse of confidential records about intimate details of employees, testing for drugs and alcohol, and discipline for lifestyle activities and sexual orientation outside working hours.

Surveillance

In the past, managers could observe employees at work in the factory or the office, but employees were usually aware of their scrutiny and could find techniques for avoiding their constant inspection. Modern technology makes surveillance possible secretly, constantly and throughout the workplace. Employers can use tiny cameras and microphones to keep the whole premises under constant surveillance and recording. Employers can monitor phone calls, emails and social-networking websites, and examine all the records stored by computer. Using ID cards, employers can record exactly when employees arrive and leave and their precise location in the building. This covert electronic surveillance may be justified by employers on grounds of security for staff, health and safety and the protection of trade secrets, and the need to monitor attendance and work effort. Employers can also argue that an employee has consented to the surveillance by agreement to the relevant terms of the contract of employment. At their extreme, however, these technologies can turn the workplace into a zone where nothing is private any more, not even those personal conversations by the water cooler. Does Article 8 provide the legal basis for challenges to workplace surveillance? First it must be established that the surveillance interferes within the scope of right to respect for private life, and second that the interference was not justifiable under Article 8(2).

On the question of when an employer's interception of communications or other surveillance measures would be regarded as an interference with the right to privacy under Article 8, initially the ECtHR said that the test was whether an employee had a reasonable expectation of privacy with respect to the conduct or activity. In *Halford* v. *United Kingdom*,[24] the applicant, an Assistant Chief Constable of Merseyside, was refused promotion on several occasions. She brought a claim for sex discrimination. Her claim for sex discrimination was settled, but she brought proceedings in Strasbourg for

---

[24] (1997) 24 EHRR 523 (ECtHR).

the violation of her right to privacy, claiming that an office telephone that had been provided for her private use had been tapped in an attempt to obtain information to use against her in the sex-discrimination litigation. Finding the allegation of telephone tapping proven and noting that there was no national legal remedy against an employer tapping an internal-workplace telephone network, the ECtHR upheld the claim for an interference with the right to privacy. Yet the grounds for the decision were extremely narrow. The ECtHR appeared to doubt that employees in general have much expectation of privacy in the workplace. In this case, however, the employer had created a 'reasonable expectation of privacy' by granting the use of the office telephone for private use. In this case, this interference with the right to privacy could not be justified under Article 8(2) as it had not been done in 'accordance with law', as there was no law whatsoever either authorising the tapping of workplace phones or supplying protections for employees against excessive intrusion.

The UK government responded to this lacuna by passing the Regulation of Investigatory Powers Act 2000 and the related Telecommunications (Lawful Business Practice) (Interception of Communications) Regulations 2000.[25] At first sight, the Act, which applies broadly to any form of electronic communication, including internet access, appears to protect the privacy of employees. Section 1(3) provides that it is unlawful for the person with the right to control a private telecommunications system such as an employer to intercept messages of others without lawful authority. The Act governs interceptions of communications not only while they are in the process of transmission, as that phrase is commonly understood, but also when they are stored in email inboxes or as lists of favourite web addresses, etc.[26] Although the Act creates this broad offence, it also grants employers an extensive defence. The crucial question is what counts as 'lawful authority' for the interception. As well as consent by both the sender and the recipient of the communication, further grounds for lawful authority are granted to employers under regulation 3(1)(a) of the Regulations. These grounds include:

- establishing the existence of facts relevant to the business (this might include recording the substance of communications);
- ascertaining compliance with regulatory or self-regulatory practices or procedures relevant to the business;
- ascertaining or demonstrating the standards achieved or which ought to be achieved by persons using the system in the course of their duties (this might include interception and recording for the purposes of quality control);
- protecting national security;

[25] SI 2000 No. 2699.   [26] Regulation of Investigatory Powers Act 2000, s. 2(7) and (8).

- preventing or detecting crime;
- investigating or detecting the unauthorised use of that or any other telecommunication system (this might include checking that employees do not contravene the employer's email or internet policies); and/or
- ensuring the effective operation of the system (this might include checking for viruses).

Interceptions for this broad range of purposes are only permitted where the employer or controller of the system has made all reasonable efforts to inform every person who may use the telecommunication system in question that interceptions will be made.[27] The effect of this broad scope for legal authority to intercept messages seems to be that it permits monitoring and recording of any communication which is not clearly private and has no relevance to the employer's business. Employers will usually have some business reason to conduct surveillance, even if it is just the general need to supervise the performance of work, so the effect of the Act and its Regulations may deprive employees of any significant protection for their privacy with respect to electronic communications on the employer's equipment. Provided that employers warn employees that all telephone calls and email communications may be monitored for the various purposes permitted under the Regulations, the employer will usually be acting lawfully.

It is possible, however, that some aspects of the Regulations may be found overly broad because they permit interferences with the right to privacy that cannot be justified under Article 8(2). The ECtHR has moved away from the test of 'reasonable expectation of privacy', because it recognises that employers can attempt by means of sweeping terms in contracts of employment or by rules set out in the staff handbook to eliminate any privacy in the workplace. In *Bărbulescu* v. *Romania*,[28] the claimant employee was asked by his employer to establish a Yahoo messaging account to communicate with customers of the employer. The employer had established workplace rules that prohibited the personal use of computer equipment, and in addition the employer had notified all employees, including the claimant, that wasting company time on personal messages would be monitored and punished. At about the same time as that notice was sent out, the employer starting recording all the Yahoo messages sent by the employee by somehow circumventing the password. The employee was summoned to a disciplinary meeting where he was charged with misusing the computer equipment for personal messages. When he denied this charge, the employers printed out a transcript of his messages that included personal and intimate messages to his brother and his fiancée. Following dismissal for breach of the company's regulation

---

[27] Telecommunications (Lawful Business Practice) (Interception of Communications) Regulations 2000, SI 2000 No. 2699, reg. 3(2)(c).

[28] *Bărbulescu* v. *Romania* [2017] ECHR 754 (App. no. 61496/08, 5 September 2017).

against personal use of computer equipment, the employee's claim was unsuccessful in the labour courts. Those national courts concluded that the employee was in clear breach of the employer's well-publicised rule against personal use of computers, and that in pursuit of the employer's legitimate interest in supervising performance of work, the monitoring in this case was necessary and appropriate.

The Grand Chamber of the ECtHR disagreed. In accordance with its previous decisions on the scope of Article 8, it first decided that the kind of internet instant-messaging service involved in this case is one of the forms of communication enabling individuals to lead a private social life and that the sending and receiving of such communications is covered by the notion of 'correspondence', even if they are sent from an employer's computer. On the question of whether the employee had a reasonable expectation of any privacy at all in view of the employer's prohibition on personal use, the court first observed that the employer had not made it clear that it would actually read the messages as opposed to merely monitoring the destinations of the messages, but then secondly held that even if the employee had been left with no reasonable expectation of privacy at all,

> an employer's instructions cannot reduce private social life in the workplace to zero. Respect for private life and for the privacy of correspondence continues to exist, even if these may be restricted in so far as necessary.[29]

At the very least, therefore, the reasonable expectation of privacy test is qualified by an insistence that even if the employer's rules and notices purport to eliminate any expectation of privacy in the workplace, Article 8 will nevertheless protect at least some aspects of the privacy of communications such as messages to a family member or a fiancée. To determine the scope of the protection afforded by Article 8 in the context of surveillance in the workplace, drawing on international material and the extensive EU legislation on telecommunications, in accordance with the integrated approach to interpretation, the Grand Chamber sets out a number of principles and considerations that need to be taken into account:

(i) whether the employee has been notified of the possibility that the employer might take measures to monitor correspondence and other communications, and of the implementation of such measures. . . [and] the notification should normally be clear about the nature of the monitoring and be given in advance;

(ii) the extent of the monitoring by the employer and the degree of intrusion into the employee's privacy. . .

(iii) whether the employer has provided legitimate reasons to justify monitoring the communications and accessing their actual content . . .

---

[29] Para. 80.

(iv) whether it would have been possible to establish a monitoring system based on less intrusive methods and measures than directly accessing the content of the employee's communications...

(v) the consequences of the monitoring for the employee subjected to it ...and the use made by the employer of the results of the monitoring operation, in particular whether the results were used to achieve the declared aim of the measure...

(vi) whether the employee had been provided with adequate safeguards, especially when the employer's monitoring operations were of an intrusive nature. Such safeguards should in particular ensure that the employer cannot access the actual content of the communications concerned unless the employee has been notified in advance of that eventuality.[30]

Applying these principles to the case and noting in particular that the employer had not expressly notified the applicant in advance that it would read the content of the messages as part of its general surveillance, the court concluded that there had been interference with the right to privacy.

The Grand Chamber considered finally whether the Romanian labour court had been correct to conclude that dismissal was a proportionate measure in pursuit of a legitimate interest on the part of the employer. It concluded that an employer has a legitimate interest in ensuring the smooth running of the company, and that this can be done by establishing mechanisms for checking that its employees are performing their professional duties adequately and with the necessary diligence. In this case, however, the court held that the national courts had not assessed critically whether the employer had a legitimate purpose for such intrusive surveillance. This case differed from *Kopke* v. *Germany*,[31] where an employer suspected that one of its employees was responsible for theft from the till in a shop. Unable to establish which employee might be guilty, the employer introduced covert video surveillance for two weeks, at the end of which one employee was dismissed for misconduct. In an admissibility decision of a chamber of seven judges, the ECtHR concluded that the covert video surveillance was an interference with the right to privacy under Article 8, but that it was justifiable where the employer had a reasonable suspicion of misconduct and where no other practicable means of establishing the facts was available, for the purpose of protecting the employer's property rights and to ensure the proper conduct of any legal proceedings. While the detection of criminal conduct may sometimes justify covert and intrusive surveillance, there was no suggestion of any such serious wrongdoing in *Bărbulescu* v. *Romania*. The Grand Chamber also noted that in approaching the issue of proportionality or balancing, the national courts had failed to consider whether the employer's aim could have been achieved by less intrusive means and whether some lesser disciplinary sanction as opposed to dismissal would have been a more proportionate

---

[30] Para. 121.   [31] [2010] ECHR 1725.

response to the breach of the company's rule against sending personal messages. Having found that the national courts had failed to prevent or sanction an unjustified interference with the applicant's right to privacy under Article 8, surprisingly the Grand Chamber proceeded to award the applicant no 'just satisfaction' or compensation at all (except some modest legal costs). The court apparently thought that winning the case was reward enough, without the applicant being awarded compensation for his loss of livelihood or injury to feelings.

Notwithstanding that disappointing remedy in the case, the principles set out by the ECtHR in *Bărbulescu* v. *Romania* lay down a challenge to the UK legislation and in particular the broad range of reasons for interceptions and surveillance that are permitted by the Telecommunications (Lawful Business Practice) (Interception of Communications) Regulations 2000. Points where there may be a tension include the requirement of notification, which the ECtHR insists must be precise, transparent and make clear to employees the depth of the surveillance taking place, especially if the employer is reading the content of the communications. The court also examined closely the purported reason for the monitoring, finding the reason of business efficiency vague and not compelling and the degree of interception disproportionate, but the 2000 Regulations do not seem to require such a careful scrutiny of the proportionality of the interference with the right to privacy. We noted that the ECtHR was influenced in developing its principles by the content of the extensive EU regulation of telecommunications and of the protection confidential information. The challenge presented to the 2000 Regulations by EU law may have led to the strange amendment to the Regulations that adds a qualification that interceptions authorised by the Regulations that relate to an employer's conduct of its business are only permitted to the extent that those interceptions are permitted by relevant EU law.[32]

Confidential Records

Employers often hold a considerable amount of confidential and private information about their employees. Employers need to acquire such information in order to carry out their legal duties with respect to health and safety, taxation and occupational pension schemes. Any monitoring and surveillance systems may also be collecting various kinds of personal information – the type of car driven to work, who is friendly with whom or how often an employee goes to the lavatory. Detailed statutory controls, together with codes of practice that are enforced by the Information Comissioner, try to prevent

---

[32] Regulation 3(3), as amended by Privacy and Electronic Communications (EC Directive) Regulations 2003, SI 2003 No. 2426, reg. 34; and Privacy and Electronic Communications (EC Directive) (Amendment) Regulations, SI 2011 No. 1208, reg. 15(b).

the misuse of personal data, including the confidential information held by employers about their employees.

The EU General Data Protection Regulation, SI 2016 No. 679 (GDPR 2016) provides the new general rules governing the processing of data.[33] Following withdrawal of the UK from the EU, it will be re-enacted as domestic law. The Regulation is supplemented by the Data Protection Act 2018, which extends the coverage of the principles to areas outside the scope of EU law and provides detailed enforcement mechanisms for data protection. The preamble to the Regulation stresses the importance in connection with information about individuals of respecting their right to privacy:

> The protection of natural persons in relation to the processing of personal data is a fundamental right. Article 8(1) of the Charter of Fundamental Rights of the European Union (the 'Charter') and Article 16(1) of the Treaty on the Functioning of the European Union (TFEU) provide that everyone has the right to the protection of personal data concerning him or her.[34]

The main aim of the reforms contained in the Regulation is to address issues concerning personal information that arise in the context of the collection of data from consumers browsing on-line, from users of social media, and the need to have uniform rules throughout the EU on the sharing of such personal data. The rules governing the data protection of employees have only been revised to a moderate extent. A detailed study of this complex legislative protection for privacy of personal information is beyond the scope of this work, but some of the key provisions that may affect employees should be highlighted.

The first issue is what kinds of personal information are covered by the legislation. The law tries to distinguish between unorganised or random information about an individual, such as capturing his or her image on a CCTV camera, and more systematic information held or 'processed' about an identified or identifiable individual:

> Mere mention of the data subject in a document held by a data controller does not necessarily amount to his personal data. Whether it does so in any particular instance depends on where it falls in a continuum of relevance or proximity to the data subject as distinct, say, from transactions or matters in which he may have been involved to a greater or lesser degree. It seems to me that there are two notions that may be of assistance. The first is whether the information is biographical in a significant sense, that is, going beyond the recording of the putative data subject's involvement in a matter or an event that has no personal connotations, a life event in respect of which his privacy could not be said to be compromised. The second is one of focus. The information should have the

---

[33] GDPR, SI 2016 No. 679 OJ L119, 4 May 2016, p. 1. These replace the Data Protection Act 1998, based on the European Data Processing Directive 95/46.
[34] GDPR, SI 2016 No. 679, *ibid.*, Preamble para. (1).

putative data subject as its focus rather than some other person with whom he may have been involved or some transaction or event in which he may have figured or have had an interest, for example, as in this case, an investigation into some other person's or body's conduct that he may have instigated. In short, it is information that affects his privacy, whether in his personal or family life, business or professional capacity.[35]

The Regulation extends the protection for the processing of personal data by including systems that are not automated as well as computerised storage of information.[36]

The principal question that is likely to arise with respect to personal data held by the employer is whether it has been processed fairly, lawfully and transparently. The governing data protection principles are set out in the Regulation.[37]

General Data Protection Regulation 2016, Article 5.1

Personal data shall be:

(a) processed lawfully, fairly and in a transparent manner in relation to the data subject ('lawfulness, fairness and transparency');
(b) collected for specified, explicit and legitimate purposes and not further processed in a manner that is incompatible with those purposes; further processing for archiving purposes in the public interest, scientific or historical research purposes or statistical purposes shall, in accordance with Article 89(1), not be considered to be incompatible with the initial purposes ('purpose limitation');
(c) adequate, relevant and limited to what is necessary in relation to the purposes for which they are processed ('data minimisation');
(d) accurate and, where necessary, kept up to date; every reasonable step must be taken to ensure that personal data that are inaccurate, having regard to the purposes for which they are processed, are erased or rectified without delay ('accuracy');
(e) kept in a form which permits identification of data subjects for no longer than is necessary for the purposes for which the personal data are processed; personal data may be stored for longer periods insofar as the personal data will be processed solely for archiving purposes in the public interest, scientific or historical research purposes or statistical purposes in accordance with Article 89(1) subject to implementation of the

---

[35] *Durant* v. *Financial Services Authority* [2003] EWCA Civ 1746, [2004] FSR 28 (CA), *per* Auld LJ.
[36] Reg. 2016/679, Art. 4(2): "'processing' means any operation or set of operations which is performed on personal data or on sets of personal data, whether or not by automated means, such as collection, recording, organisation, structuring, storage, adaptation or alteration, retrieval, consultation, use, disclosure by transmission, dissemination or otherwise making available, alignment or combination, restriction, erasure or destruction'.
[37] The principles are almost identical to those in the Data Protection Act 1998, Sched. 1, Part I.

appropriate technical and organisational measures required by this Regulation in order to safeguard the rights and freedoms of the data subject ('storage limitation');

(f) processed in a manner that ensures appropriate security of the personal data, including protection against unauthorised or unlawful processing and against accidental loss, destruction or damage, using appropriate technical or organisational measures ('integrity and confidentiality').

As before, the Regulation draws a distinction between personal data in general and special categories of data (formerly known as 'sensitive personal data'). This sensitive personal data is defined as information relating to an individual's racial or ethnic origin, political opinions, religious or philosophical beliefs, membership of a trade union, physical or mental health, sexual life or sexual orientation, and the processing of genetic data or biometric data for the purpose of uniquely identifying a natural person.[38] For other kinds of personal data, the employer may lawfully collect the information where the individual concerned has consented to the processing, or where the processing is necessary for the performance of a contract, or for compliance with any non-contractual legal obligation of the employer ('controller') or 'for the purposes of the legitimate interests pursued by the controller or by a third party, except where such interests are overridden by the interests or fundamental rights and freedoms of the data subject [the employee]'.[39] For sensitive personal data, processing of such data is unlawful unless the employer can bring itself within one of the permitted exceptions. These exceptions include 'explicit consent', and where the processing is 'necessary' for the purpose of carrying out the obligations of the employer in connection with employment and social security law, and where the processing is necessary for the establishment, exercise or defence of a legal claim, and finally for the purpose of occupational health.[40]

The GDPR includes rights for individuals against data controllers to be informed about data collection and its purpose and use and a right of access to data held about the individual. An employee also has the right to demand the rectification of any inaccurate personal data,[41] and in a new right granted by the 2016 Regulation, the right to erasure of personal data if it is no longer needed by the employer or the employee has withdrawn consent and there is no other lawful ground for the processing of the data.[42] Employees who believe that their employer is breaching the data-protection principles may make a complaint to the national regulator: the Information Commissioner.[43] The Commissioner should normally investigate the complaint and, if the

---

[38] Reg. 2016/679, Art. 9.   [39] Reg. 2016/679, Art. 6.
[40] Reg. 2016 679 Art. 9.2; Data Protection Act 2018, s. 10.   [41] Reg. 2016/679, Art. 16.
[42] *Ibid.*, Art. 17.   [43] Data Protection Act 2018, Part V, and s. 165.

employer is in breach of the data-protection principles, the Commissioner can issue an enforcement notice[44] and, in grave cases, a penalty notice,[45] as has occurred in relation to blacklisting.[46] Alternatively, an employee can make a written request to the employer to discover whether the employer is processing any personal data and, if so, what the information is, why it is being processed and to whom it may be disclosed. An employer can refuse such a request if the data is being processed for the prevention or detection of crime. Individual employees may seek an order to prevent the employer from processing the information which is likely to cause substantial and unwarranted damage or distress. Furthermore, the employee may claim compensation for damage or distress.

What are the practical implications of these data-protection principles for employment? One important consequence is that, under these principles, employers who collect information for one particular purpose should not in general then use that information for a different purpose without obtaining the consent of the employee first. These rules do not prevent electronic monitoring and surveillance of employees in the workplace, but usually these practices will have to be justified by reference to the employer's need to comply with the law or an employer's legitimate purpose such as the investigation or deterrence of fraud and other criminal offences. The Information Commissioner's office discourages covert surveillance by employers except where necessary for the investigation of crime. It also suggests that the collection of information about the health of workers should not take place unless it is necessary for health and safety in the workplace, compliance with an employer's duties under disability discrimination legislation or if each employee has individually, freely, given their explicit consent, which probably cannot be achieved merely by the insertion of a term in the contract of employment.

In EU courts, the EU Regulation must be interpreted in accordance with the Charter of Fundamental Rights, which includes protection in Article 8 for protection of personal data and Article 9 protection for the right to privacy. This foundation of the legislation in fundamental rights may permit courts to secure strong protection for these civil liberties in the workplace. For instance, the ECJ was asked to advise on the validity of an Austrian law that required all publicly supported organisations to reveal to the government and Parliament the salaries of all their highly paid employees.[47] This disclosure of individuals' salaries was clearly an interference with the right to privacy and contrary to the principles of the Directive unless it could be justified by the public policy of discouraging excessive remuneration in publicly funded bodies. The ECJ instructed the national court to apply a test of proportionality: the measure could only be justified if no other means that reduced the interference with privacy were available to achieve the legitimate goal. Following the UK's exit

---

[44] *Ibid.*, s. 149. [45] *Ibid.*, s. 155. [46] See p. 483.

[47] Case C-465/00, *Rechnungshof* v. *Österrechischer Rundfunk* [2003] ECR I-4989 (ECJ).

from the EU, though the UK courts will not be bound by the Charter, it seems likely that they will align their decisions with EU courts as the protection of personal data and respect for private life are general principles of the law.

Testing for Drugs and Alcohol

Some employers carry out testing of employees for drugs and alcohol. Compulsory blood or urine testing amount to interferences with the right to privacy under Article 8,[48] so an employer will be obliged to justify such practices according to the principle of proportionality. At the same time, these tests are likely to constitute processing of sensitive personal information and therefore will be subject to the controls of the GDPR 2016.

No doubt routine testing for drugs and alcohol may be justified in appropriate cases on health and safety grounds, as in the example of pilots of planes, train drivers and construction workers. As drugs are seldom used by workers in the workplace, the HSE has been unable to find a link between drugs and workplace accidents. Furthermore, unlike testing for alcohol, the methods for testing for residues of drugs in the blood cannot inform the employer whether work performance has actually been adversely affected. On the other hand, testing following an accident at work is likely to be regarded as proportionate as it is less intrusive than random testing of the workforce in general. In the absence of a clear health and safety reason for testing, an employee who is dismissed for refusing to give a sample may succeed in a claim for unfair dismissal. The dismissal may be unfair because the employer's demand was an unjustifiable interference with the right to privacy and therefore outside the range of reasonable responses.

These principles should also be applicable to other kinds of testing. Genetic testing for investigations of an employee's likely future health is so far unreliable, expensive and of dubious predictive value. It is therefore unlikely to satisfy either a test of proportionality or the requirements for fair processing of sensitive personal data. In the United States, both state and federal regulation controls the use of genetic information, but so far these laws have not generated litigation against the collection of intrusive personal information by employers.[49]

Some employers also use various kinds of personality testing for managerial and professional workers with a view to exploring a job applicant's or an employee's motivation.[50] Such tests may involve questions that probe deeply into an employee's private life on the premise that difficult personal

---

[48] *X v. Austria* (1979) 18 DR 75; *Peters v. Netherlands* (1994) 77A DR 75.

[49] P. T. Kim, 'Regulating the Use of Genetic Information: Perspectives from the US Experience' (2010) 31 *Comparative Labour Law and Policy Journal* 693.

[50] B. Kersley, C. Alpin, A. Bryson, H. Bewley, G. Dix and S. Oxenbridge, *Inside the Workplace: Findings from the 2004 Workplace Employment Relations Survey* (London: Routledge, 2006), p. 77.

circumstances may interfere with performance on the job. Do job applicants have any legal remedy if they refuse to take such a personality test and are as a consequence not considered for a position? Apart from anti-discrimination laws, job applicants lack protection under UK law. It is conceivable that a rejected applicant for a public-sector job might be able to make a direct claim under the HRA 1998 against an interference with the right to privacy, interpreted broadly to include the right to work, which would then compel an employer to put forward a justification for its use of personality testing. Employees in post who refuse to take such a personality test may also suffer damage to their potential career but, unless the employer dismisses the employee for refusing to take the test, in which case there may be an unfair dismissal as a result of the test of reasonableness being interpreted in light of Article 8, there does not seem to be any legal remedy available against disciplinary action short of dismissal.

Lifestyle and Sexual Orientation

How far can an employer use its disciplinary powers under the contract of employment to control what employees do outside working hours and outside the workplace? If an employer disapproves of an employee's particular sexual and cultural preferences, can the employer threaten to dismiss the employee unless he or she forgoes these activities in the evenings or at weekends? Can the employer forbid the employee from socialising with certain groups of people, including co-workers, outside of working hours? Do such off-duty activities always constitute private matters, protected by Article 8, so that an employer should not normally be able to dismiss fairly for such reasons?

Prior to the enactment of the HRA 1998, it was clear that employers could dismiss employees fairly for such reasons, provided that they could point to a company rule against such behaviour or articulate concerns such as that the employee's conduct might prove embarrassing to the employer or that customers might not like it. Even in the absence of express conduct rules, interpretations placed on the test of fairness in law of unfair dismissal provided employers with a broad scope for enforcing their prejudices against an employee's choice of lifestyle and activities outside the workplace. The test of reasonableness seemed to permit, for instance, dismissal of employees for being gay where the employer feared an adverse reaction from customers, even if that fear seemed irrational and unwarranted.[51] It was also used to permit fair dismissals of staff for being charged with possession of unlawful drugs such as cannabis outside working hours.[52] An important question that arose on the enactment of the HRA 1998 was whether the Act would confine

---

[51] *Saunders* v. *Scottish National Camps Association Ltd* [1980] IRLR 174 (EAT), [1981] IRLR 277 (Court of Session).

[52] *Mathewson* v. *R. B. Wilson Dental Laboratories* [1988] IRLR 512 (EAT).

this power of employers to control lifestyle choices to instances where the choice seriously interfered with the efficient running of the business or damaged its reputation with customers.

Hopes that employees' sexual and cultural preferences could be protected from employers' disciplinary powers were quickly, although perhaps not irretrievably, dashed by the Court of Appeal in *X* v. *Y*.[53] The claimant had been dismissed from his position with a charity concerned with young offenders after it was discovered that he had been arrested and cautioned for committing a sex offence with another man in a toilet in a café and that his name had been placed on the Sex Offenders' Register. The dismissal was said to be by reason of the applicant's misconduct in (1) having committed a significant criminal offence and (2) having deliberately concealed it from the employer. An ET rejected X's claim for unfair dismissal, and both the EAT and the Court of Appeal dismissed his appeals. According to the Court (Brooke LJ dissenting), Article 8 was not engaged:

> Article 8(1) is not engaged, as the facts found by the employment tribunal do not fall within its ambit ... The applicant's conduct did not take place in his private life nor was it within the scope of application of the right to respect for it. It happened in a place to which the public had, and were permitted to have, access; it was a criminal offence, which is normally a matter of legitimate concern to the public; a criminal offence is not a purely private matter; and it led to a caution for the offence, which was relevant to his employment and should have been disclosed by him to his employer as a matter of legitimate concern to it. The applicant wished to keep the matter private. That does not make it part of his private life or deprive it of its public aspect.

On this reasoning, Article 8 does not apply to any lifestyle choices that are exhibited in public or in places to which the public have access. That interpretation rules out protection by Article 8 for conduct in clubs, bars, on the beach, in the park and at sports events. It confines the scope of Article 8 to conduct in one's own home or some other place that no one else is permitted to enter without permission. Furthermore, this interpretation of the concept of privacy also excludes any criminal offence, even if the commission of the offence was done in a private space, as may be the case with many sexual and drugs offences.

This narrow interpretation of the scope of Article 8 seems contrary to its development by the ECtHR.[54] The ECtHR has applied Article 8 to sexual orientation, sexual activities and the establishment of personal and intimate relationships with others, without confining that protection to the privacy of the home. It was used successfully, for instance, to challenge the ban on gays

---

[53] *X* v. *Y* [2004] ICR 1634 (CA).

[54] V. Mantouvalou, 'Human Rights and Unfair Dismissal: Private Acts in Public Spaces' (2008) 71 *Modern Law Review* 912; M. Freedland, 'Privacy, Employment and the Human Rights Act 1998', in K. Ziegler (ed.), *Human Rights and Private Law* (Oxford: Hart, 2007), p. 141.

and lesbians in the armed services.[55] Furthermore, Article 8 has been applied to conduct in public places, as in the case of celebrities being hounded by photographers as they go about their daily activities such as shopping.[56] The ECtHR has even applied Article 8 to the workplace where an employee objected to a search of his private papers kept in his office on the ground that the forming of private relationships with others should be protected both inside and outside the workplace.[57] Nor is the criminality of the employee's activity outside work necessarily fatal to the employee's attempt to invoke protection from the Convention.[58]

A stronger protection for the protection of an employee's private life was indicated by a chamber of the ECtHR in *Pay* v. *UK*.[59] Following a tip-off from police, the manager of a probation officer discovered that in his leisure time he performed shows in hedonist and fetish clubs and was also a director of a company selling products connected with bondage and sadomasochism on the internet. Photographs of him and semi-naked women and men were on the website, although the faces were obscured by masks. The manager dismissed Mr Pay when he refused to cease these outside activities on the ground that this conduct might embarrass the probation service and that these activities were incompatible with his professional duties, particularly because he sometimes worked with sex offenders. A claim for unfair dismissal was unsuccessful in the UK courts. As in *X* v. *Y*, the right to privacy was held not to be engaged and therefore could not influence the determination of the fairness of the dismissal, because these activities took place in public places such as the internet or places to which the public had access such as clubs. Having exhausted his domestic avenues of redress, Mr Pay applied to the ECtHR. The case was declared to be inadmissible, and therefore a final decision was not issued. Nevertheless, a seven-judge chamber gave a reasoned decision for the rejection of the case. It accepted that there was an arguable case that the right to privacy was engaged. The chamber emphasised that the applicant's performances were in a nightclub likely to be frequented only by a self-selecting group of like-minded people, that the photographs of his stage act which were published on the internet were anonymised and that the applicant claimed that the public-performance aspect of his act was a fundamental part of his sexual expression. Assuming that the right to privacy was engaged,

---

[55] *Smith and Grady* v. *UK*, App. Nos. 33985/96 and 33986/96 (1999) 29 EHRR 493 (ECtHR); *Lustig-Prean and Beckett* v. *UK*, App. Nos. 31417/96 and 32377/96 (1999), 29 EHRR 548 (ECtHR).

[56] *Von Hannover* v. *Germany*, App. No. 59320/00 (ECtHR).

[57] *Niemietz* v. *Germany* (1992) 16 EHRR 7 (ECtHR).

[58] *Dudgeon* v. *UK*, App. No. 7525/76, Judgment of 22 October 1981 (ECtHR); *Thlimmenos* v. *Greece* (2001) 31 EHRR 14 (ECtHR).

[59] App. No. 32792/05 [2009] IRLR 139 (ECtHR); V. Mantouvalou and H. Collins, 'Private Life and Dismissal' (2009) 38 *Industrial Law Journal* 133.

however, the chamber accepted that the interference with the right was probably justifiable in the circumstances on the ground of the legitimate aim of the protection of the reputation of the probation service. The result might have been different if Mr Pay had been prepared to take further measures to reduce the risk that his sex-related activities that had some links with the nature of his job might become known to members of the public or clients of the probation service. Applying this approach to the facts of *X* v. *Y*, it seems that it was incorrect for the Court of Appeal to hold that the right to privacy was not engaged, although the ultimate result of a fair dismissal might have been the same provided the employer had been able to present a legitimate aim as the reason for the dismissal (such as a record on the Sex Offenders' Register) and that dismissal rather than some lesser disciplinary sanction was necessary and appropriate.

The right to respect for private life requires particularly sensitive interpretation in connection with employers who claim that their organisation must uphold particular moral, ethical or religious principles. For instance, should a school that is supported by and professes fidelity to the Roman Catholic church be permitted to dismiss a teacher who breaches the rules of the church by obtaining a divorce, committing adultery or having an abortion? A dismissal in such a case is almost certainly an interference with the Convention right to privacy, but can the employer justify this interference? In *Obst* v. *Germany*,[60] the applicant was dismissed from his position as director of public relations for the Mormon Church for having an extramarital affair. In this case, the dismissal was justifiable because the applicant had been raised as a member of the Mormon Church and was aware that his conduct would be contrary to its beliefs, which he (as a person responsible for its public relations) represented. By signing his contract with the Mormon Church, he had consented to respect marital fidelity as a central tenet of the Church. In contrast, in *Schuth* v. *Germany*,[61] the ECtHR found a breach of Article 8 when the German labour court declined to find that a dismissal was unfair in the circumstance that the organist and choirmaster of a Catholic church was dismissed for having an extramarital affair. The ECtHR held that the dismissal and interference with Article 8 did not satisfy a test of proportionality, because the affair had not been publicised in a way that could harm the image of the Church and because (unlike in *Obst*) it would be hard for the applicant to find another employer given the specialised nature of his work. In these cases, the ECtHR indicates that the special ethical features of the employer can justify an interference with the right to privacy of an employee, but only where the dismissal satisfies a rigorous test of proportionality.

---

[60] *Obst* v. *Germany*, App. No. 425/03, Judgment of 23 September 2010.
[61] *Schuth* v. *Germany*, App. No. 1620/03, Judgment of 23 September 2010.

Freedom of Religion

European Convention on Human Rights, Article 9

(1) Everyone has the right to freedom of thought, conscience and religion; this right includes freedom to change his religion or belief and freedom, either alone or in community with others and in public or private, to manifest his religion or belief, in worship, teaching, practice and observance.

(2) Freedom to manifest one's religion or beliefs shall be subject only to such limitations as are prescribed by law and are necessary in a democratic society in the interests of public safety, for the protection of public order, health or morals, or for the protection of the rights and freedoms of others.

The protection afforded to freedom of religion in the Convention draws a crucial distinction between freedom of belief and freedom to manifest a belief. The former receives absolute protection in Article 9(1), so that no interference with belief can be justified. In contrast, the freedom to manifest a religious belief, protected in Article 9(2), can be justifiably restricted. This distinction in effect denies that for some religions it is absolutely necessary to manifest the belief, not merely to be permitted to hold that belief. In a labour-law context, however, with the exception of religious bodies and churches, most employers are rarely concerned about their employees' personal beliefs. Problems only arise when employees wish to manifest those beliefs by, for example, taking time off work for prayers, or refusing to work on the Sabbath or other religious holidays, or insisting on wearing particular clothes and ornaments as manifestations of faith or refusing to perform certain duties of the job on the ground that those duties are offensive to their religious beliefs. For a long time according to decisions of the ECtHR and its former Commission, employers appeared to enjoy an unfettered discretion to offer terms of employment or impose rules in the staff handbook that interfered with all these aspects of manifestation of religion. This result was justified on the ground that an employee could always take a more congenial job. But that approach has been decisively rejected in connection with employer's dress codes, with the implication that it will also be rejected in other contexts.

Dress as a Manifestation of Religion

Claims that an employer is interfering with the manifestation of religious belief at work are likely to arise either as claims for indirect discrimination on the ground of religion under the EqA 2010, or as claims for unfair dismissal. In either case, the HRA 1998 will require the decision to be compatible with the requirements of Article 9 ECHR. In *Eweida and others*

v. *UK*,[62] the first applicant worked as a member of the check-in staff for British Airways, a private company. The company required her to wear a uniform and had a policy that, apart from a few permitted exceptions such as headscarves in the corporate colours for female Muslim ground staff, religious symbols should always be covered. Ms Eweida, a Coptic Christian, had always worn a cross concealed under clothing, but she decided that she wanted to wear the cross openly as a sign of her faith. She was told by the company to remove or conceal the cross, but on her refusal to do so, she was sent home without pay. Later she was offered administrative work in a back office where she could display a cross, but she refused that offer. Following adverse publicity, eventually British Airways altered its policy and permitted displays of religious and charity symbols, so Ms Eweida was permitted to return to work after about four months. Her claim for compensation for the loss of wages during that period off work on the ground of religious discrimination was unsuccessful in the UK courts on the ground that employer's rule did not disadvantage a particular protected group, and even if it did, it was a proportionate interference, because the employer was pursuing a legitimate aim in projecting a particular corporate image and its measure was appropriate, not least because the claimant had been offered alternative employment.[63]

The ECtHR reversed its prior decisions by saying that:

> Given the importance in a democratic society of freedom of religion, the Court considers that, where an individual complains of a restriction on freedom of religion in the workplace, rather than holding that the possibility of changing job would negate any interference with the right, the better approach would be to weigh that possibility in the overall balance when considering whether or not the restriction was proportionate.

The effect of the decision in *Eweida* v. *UK* is that courts should respect an employee's right to manifest a religion in the workplace. Rules that ban workers from wearing religious symbols will have to be justified according to a test of proportionality. The ECtHR held that in balancing the fundamental right to manifest a religion against the employer's legitimate interest in projecting a certain corporate image, the domestic courts had accorded the employer's interest too much weight, partly because the cross was discreet and did not detract from her professional appearance and partly because other employees had been able to wear religious symbols such as hijabs without adverse effect on the corporate image, a point that had in effect been conceded by the employer's change of policy in its dress code. In other cases, the balance might be struck the other way, as in the case of the second applicant considered by the ECtHR, *Chaplin*, a hospital nurse wearing a necklace cross that the employer had justifiably prohibited for fear that the cross might

---

[62] *Eweida* v. *UK* [2013] ECHR 37, [2013] IRLR 231.
[63] *Eweida* v. *British Airways plc* [2010] EWCA Civ 80.

accidentally harm the health and safety of patients and the nurse herself. UK courts have asserted occasionally that the test of proportionality under the Convention is the same as the test of reasonableness under the law of unfair dismissal.[64] While that proposition may have been true prior to *Eweida* v. *UK*, it now seems to under-estimate the need for a convincing justification for interference by employers with the manifestation of religion.

Hours of Work

Apart from an anomalous specific statutory protection for shop-workers who do not want to work on Sundays,[65] there is no express regulation of hours of work to protect religious observance, so the matter has to be assessed by reference to Article 9 and the law governing the contract of employment. In the past, if the contract specified the hours and days of work, the employer could use those terms to justify interference with the manifestation of religion. Indeed, if for good business reasons an employer needed to vary the hours of work of existing employees, the employer could insist on the change, even though some employees felt unable to comply with the change as the new hours of work clashed with their need to manifest a religion. In *Copsey* v. *WBB Devon Clays Ltd*,[66] the applicant refused on religious grounds to agree to a new contract of employment with a rotating shift system that included some Sunday working. The employer was unable to find alternative suitable work that avoided Sunday working entirely, as the applicant required, so, after failing to reach a compromise agreement, the applicant was dismissed. The ET held that the employee's refusal to agree to a change in his terms of employment provided the employer with a substantial reason for dismissal which in all the circumstances was fair. A majority of the Court of Appeal upheld that decision, concluding that there was no material interference with the right to manifest a religion because the employee could change his job. In the light of *Eweida* v. *UK*, this conclusion now seems incorrect. In accordance with the dissent of Rix LJ, the employer's change of hours of work does amount to an interference with the right to manifest a religion, although it might be justifiable if the employer has a good business reason for the change in hours and there is no reasonable way to accommodate the employee's need for religious observance.

Refusal to Perform Duties on Religious Grounds

A third category of case under Article 9 concerns occasions when an employee refuses to perform some aspect of the job on the ground of religious beliefs.

---

[64] *Copsey* v. *WBB Devon Clays Ltd* [2005] EWCA Civ 932, [2005] ICR 1789, petition refused [2006] ICR 205 (HL); *Turner* v. *East Midland Trains Ltd* [2012] EWCA Civ 1470, [2013] ICR 525.

[65] ERA 1996, s. 101.

[66] [2005] EWCA Civ 932, [2005] ICR 1789, petition refused [2006] ICR 205 (HL).

For instance, a nurse may refuse to assist with certain kinds of work in the hospital such as lawful abortions on the ground of religious conscience. In such a case, *Macfarlane* v. *UK*, the fourth case in the *Eweida* hearing at the ECtHR, the applicant's work concerned relationship counselling for couples who were experiencing difficulties in their relationship. Contrary to the company's stated policy, he refused to perform counselling services for homosexual couples and was dismissed. The ECtHR accepted that this refusal was a manifestation of his religion, but said that this interest was outweighed by a combination of the fact that he knew about the company's policy before he joined it and the consideration that the company's policy at issue was to promote equal opportunities in line with the values of the Convention.

The problem in *Ladelle* v. *UK*, the third case in the *Eweida* hearing in the ECtHR, was slightly different because the applicant, a registrar of marriages working for a local authority, could not have known when she commenced work that the law would be changed and that she would subsequently be required by her employer also to perform the ceremony of civil partnership, which is a similar institution to marriage for homosexual couples, a task that she claimed was contrary to her religious beliefs. Nevertheless, her claim for interference with her Article 9 right to manifest a religion failed on the ground that, in conducting the balancing exercise of proportionality, the local authority was entitled to insist that it should be able to perform its services and duties to the public without discrimination. It should be noted that *Ladelle* had argued that her claim rested on Article 9(1), freedom of conscience, rather than freedom to manifest a religion, for which there can be no justified derogation. Although accepted by a minority of the court, the majority clearly indicated that in these disputes between employees and their employer, the issue would almost invariably require a balancing of the interests of the parties under Article 9(2) and the absolute right in Article 9(1) would not be applicable.

Freedom of Expression

European Convention on Human Rights, Article 10

(1) Everyone has the right to freedom of expression. This right shall include freedom to hold opinions and to receive and impart information and ideas without interference by public authority and regardless of frontiers . . .

(2) The exercise of these freedoms, since it carries with it duties and responsibilities, may be subject to such formalities, conditions, restrictions or penalties as are prescribed by law and are necessary in a democratic society, in the interests of national security, territorial integrity or public safety, for the prevention of disorder or crime, for the protection of

health or morals, for the protection of the reputation or rights of others, for preventing the disclosure of information received in confidence, or for maintaining the authority and impartiality of the judiciary.

Although Article 10 ECHR protects freedom of speech and expression at work, it is qualified by extensive potential justifications for restrictions under Article 10(2). Controls over what people say at work can often be justified as a legitimate protection of the rights of others, including their reputation, and that protection extends in particular to the reputation of the employing undertaking. Employees who insult co-workers, impugn the reputation or integrity of their managers or denigrate the products and services of the firm, may be exercising their right to freedom of expression, but when a court strikes the balance between that freedom and the 'reputation or rights of others' under Article 10(2), freedom of expression in the workplace usually has to give way.[67] Some instances of offensive speech may amount to harassment under the EqA 2010 section 26 if the speech denigrates persons with a protected characteristic such as race or disability.[68] In practice, therefore, employers will lawfully exercise their disciplinary powers over employees if they express themselves in ways at work that are offensive to others or disruptive to the organisation or harm the reputation and interests of others. But the ECtHR has stressed that rude remarks about the employer or managers made in the heat of the moment or under provocation may have to be tolerated under the test of proportionality, at least to the extent of the employer not being permitted to terminate the contract of employment lawfully.[69]

Within that general legal framework set by Article 10, a number of controversial issues arise. First, are the same restrictions on freedom of speech permitted when the words are uttered by trade union activists representing the interests of their members? Second, employers are sometimes drawn to use their disciplinary powers to sanction employees who speak outside the workplace or post messages on social media in ways that the employer believes harms its reputation or creates an undesirable association for the employer. How far does the law protect the job security of workers who criticise their employer to an external audience, such as friends, the media or perhaps even the police? And how far does the law protect the job security of workers who

---

[67] *De Diego Nafria v. Spain* [2002] ECHR 300 (ECtHR); P. Wragg, 'Free Speech Rights at Work: resolving the Differences Between Practice and Liberal Principle' (2015) 44 *Industrial Law Journal* 1.

[68] M. Pearson, 'Offensive Expression and the Workplace' (2014) 43 *Industrial Law Journal* 429.

[69] *Fuentes Bobo v. Spain* (2001) 31 EHRR 50 (ECtHR).

express views and opinions, including political opinions, that an employer strongly dislikes and with which it does not wish to be associated?

Speech of Trade Union Organisers

Should disciplinary action such as dismissal be permitted against trade union officials for defamatory speech while representing the interests of the workforce against an employer? In the heat of industrial conflict, union officials may well criticise employers and managers in harsh and even abusive terms. Should that kind of speech be protected under Article 10 because it is so closely related to the protection for the freedom of association of trade unions in Article 11?

The ECtHR addressed this issue in *Palomo Sánchez v. Spain.*[70] The employees were union activists who had brought legal proceedings against the employer in pursuit of their claim for recognition of their new union. Two other employees had testified against the union in the legal proceedings. The union activists responded by publishing in their newsletter a cartoon of the employer's director of human resources, seated behind a table, under which was drawn an individual on his hands and knees with his back to the viewer, and pictures of the employees who had testified against the union looking at the scene, awaiting their turn to satisfy the director. Inside the bulletin, two articles, worded in crude and vulgar terms, criticised the fact that those two individuals had testified in favour of the company. Following their dismissal for misconduct and their unsuccessful legal claims for unfair dismissal, the unionist applicants argued before the ECtHR that their freedom of expression had been unjustifiably constrained. But the ECtHR disagreed, explaining that, although a trade union and its activists must be able to express themselves freely, Article 10 also carries with it duties and responsibilities. The attacks on the individuals in the bulletin were offensive, intemperate, gratuitous and in no way necessary for the legitimate defence of the applicants' interests. In denying the claims for unfair dismissal, the Spanish courts had correctly balanced the right to freedom of expression against the protection of the rights of others.

As this case demonstrates, although Article 10 is likely to protect serious and substantiated criticisms of co-workers and senior management uttered by union officials, it will not usually protect offensive remarks and unsubstantiated allegations that damage others' reputations. The majority of the court was not prepared to create an exemption from the normal principles applied under Article 10 for speech connected to union representation of the interests of the workforce. A dissenting minority of the court argued that because the intemperate remarks had been made in the course of attempts to achieve recognition of the union, in the light of Article 11 and its protection of the formation of

---

[70] *Palomo Sánchez v. Spain* [2011] ECHR 1319 (ECtHR).

trade unions for the protection of workers' interests, the balance should be struck in favour of protecting the freedom of speech of the union organisers. It could also be argued that even if the cartoon and articles in the bulletin were unprotected speech despite their link to trade union activities, there remains a serious question of whether for an isolated incident of this kind an employer should be permitted to seize the opportunity to rid itself of union activists.

Social Media

Having returned home from a tough day at work, some people let off steam by posting comments on social network sites on the internet. Although they may believe that their intemperate remarks will be visible only to their 'friends', in fact they can be quickly reposted to critics or even posted for all to see on a 'wall'. Similarly employees may tweet their views about work or life more generally, or re-tweet messages that they approve. Some 'friends' or followers may also be colleagues, who may feel it to be their duty to disclose intemperate remarks to the employer. Managers may decide to dismiss an employee for offensive and derogatory comments posted on a social network, especially if they target named individuals or identify the employer and its products by name. The issue of the fairness of the dismissal should engage the employee's rights to privacy and freedom of expression. Courts and tribunals have normally been persuaded to approve the dismissal on such grounds as the posting would be linked to the employer and its content would damage the employer's business, or cause offence to co-workers and customers or bring the employer into disrepute.

For instance, in *Crisp* v. *Apple Retail (UK) Ltd*,[71] a shop assistant in an Apple shop was dismissed for comments made on his 'private' Facebook page in which he denigrated features of his iPhone. The ET held that the dismissal was fair because the employer's clear policy in its rule-book strictly prohibited critical remarks about its products. In interpreting the reasonableness of the dismissal, the tribunal declined to use Article 8 as a protection for private remarks, because 'friends' on the social network site could copy and pass on the comments more widely. The tribunal accepted that Article 10 was engaged by this exercise of freedom of expression, but the employer successfully argued that the restriction was justified and proportionate in view of Apple's need to protect its commercial reputation against potentially damaging posts. In most cases of this kind, however, there is no mention of the HRA 1998, and the tribunals quickly reach the conclusion that dismissal was reasonable because of the risk of damage to the employer's reputation.[72]

Dismissals have been upheld as fair dismissals for remarks that embarrass the employer without being critical of the employer. In *Gibbins* v. *British*

---

[71] ET/1500258/11, 22 November 2011.
[72] E.g. *Weeks* v. *Everything Everywhere Ltd* ET/2503016/2012, 24 October 2012.

Council,[73] the employee made a comment on someone else's vulgar Facebook comments about the monarchy in which, as a republican socialist, she objected to the privilege of the monarchy, and in particular of three-year-old Prince George, to her 'friends'. Following a storm of adverse stories in conservative newspapers based upon misquotations and misattributions of the vulgar comments, the employee wrote a letter of apology to Kensington Palace. Nevertheless, her employer, the British Council, created by a royal charter with the Queen as its patron, dismissed her from her job managing the buildings of the Council in order to avoid further embarrassment and press criticism. The employer decided that by associating herself with unpleasant remarks about the prince, she had recklessly acted in a way that broke their code of practice and brought the Council into disrepute. The ET held that she had been fairly dismissed without considering the relevance of her rights to freedom of expression and privacy. The tribunal also rejected a claim that the employer had discriminated against her on the ground of her republican views. Although these views qualified as a genuine philosophical belief protected under the EqA 2010, section 10(2), the ET rejected a claim for direct discrimination as the reason for dismissal was not those views but the damage to the employer's reputation caused by her association with offensive remarks. A claim for indirect discrimination was rejected on the ground that the code of conduct enforced by the employer was a justifiable interference with the manifestation of philosophical beliefs because it was needed to protect the reputation of the organisation. What is noticeable about this case is the failure by either the employer or the tribunal to take the protection of human rights as a more important principle than the desire of employers to avoid embarrassing stories in the newspapers when their employees, in their personal time and on their personal media sites, express views (or fail to dissociate themselves from views) that some journalists regard as distasteful.

ACAS offers guidance to employers on disciplinary rules and procedures with respect to the content posted on social networks.[74] It is evident from cases such as *Crisp* and *Gibbins* that employers who develop an explicit policy on posting on websites will normally be able to enforce them through disciplinary action, including, in serious cases, a fair dismissal. This power to control employees' use of social media by merely promulgating sweeping rules to that effect may have to be questioned in the light of *Bărbulescu* v. *Romania*,[75] for in that case the ECtHR was not prepared to permit the terms of a contract of employment to remove some essential features of the right to privacy such as the ability to communicate with family during working hours.

In principle, it is acknowledged that there must be cases where the posting is purely private and performed outside working hours with no possible

---

[73] *Gibbins* v. *British Council* ET/2200088/2017, 3 November 2017.
[74] www.acas.org.uk/index.aspx?articleid=3378.
[75] [2017] ECHR 754, App. No. 61496/08, 5 September 2017.

association with the employer, in which case disciplinary action should be unlawful.[76] Yet in practice social media tends to undermine any sharp distinction between work and private life because identities can be inferred, leading to the possibility that an employer will be associated with offensive language used by an employee.[77] That possibility usually suffices for a dismissal to be regarded by a tribunal as fair.[78]

I Lost my Job over a Facebook Post – Was that Fair?

For 21 years, until December 2015, Rachel worked at Park Hall, a residential care home for elderly people and vulnerable adults... She'd been the manager for the last eight years... One of the activities that Rachel organised for the residents at Park Hall was a regular music night, every Friday... One Friday Rachel returned home after music night and decided to share some of the special moments from the evening on-line...

Rachel had done four things wrong. She'd posted the photo on Facebook, she'd identified a Park Hall resident in the photo – a man with Down's syndrome who, eager to be photographed, had jumped into the shot beside her – she had also posted a video of the music night, and she was Facebook friends with a relative of one of the residents. These were all breaches of Surrey County Council policy... Two days later Rachel was suspended from her job. Rachel lost her appeal and was given just two days to decide whether she would accept demotion – with a significant pay cut – or face dismissal. ... She asked for extra time to consider her options, but the council refused... and she was dismissed with immediate effect.

Twenty months later and severely in debt the ET upheld her claim for unfair dismissal. The tribunal accepted that there had been serious misconduct that justified disciplinary action, but there was a procedural flaw because the employer had given her insufficient time to make the choice between demotion and dismissal.[79]

Political Activities

A liberal society must respect the freedom of all citizens to participate in politics. They must be free to form political associations, express their views and vote according to their preferences. The ECHR imposes a positive duty on states to secure both freedom of association and freedom of expression for their citizens. In general, therefore, the law should not permit employers to take disciplinary action against employees on the ground that employees are members of a particular party or support a particular political viewpoint, no matter how much the employer may disapprove. Anti-discrimination laws in

---

[76] *Smith* v. *Trafford Housing Trust* [2012] EWHC 3221 (Ch), [2013] IRLR 86.
[77] *Game Retail Ltd* v. *Laws* UKEAT/0188/14.
[78] V. Mantouvalou, 'I Lost my Job over a Facebook Post: Was that Fair?', UK Labour Law Blog, 21 June 2018, available at https://wordpress.com/view/uklabourlawblog.com.
[79] www.bbc.co.uk/news/stories-41851771, 6 November 2017.

the UK do not protect employees against discrimination on the grounds of political opinion unless it is a philosophical belief.[80] Protection for employees against political discrimination therefore depends on the application of Articles 10 and 11 of the ECHR.

In *Vogt* v. *Germany*,[81] the ECtHR established that Article 10 can protect the freedom to express political opinions. A German schoolteacher was dismissed because she was an active member of the Communist Party. The German government, as the employer, sought to justify its interference with the teacher's freedom of expression on the ground that it was necessary to constrain the freedom of public-sector workers in order to protect a democratic society. Applying a test of proportionality, the ECtHR concluded that the teacher's Convention right had been violated. An employer of a school-teacher would be permitted to impose constraints on freedom of expression to prevent a teacher attempting to indoctrinate pupils in anti-democratic views or to encourage them to be disobedient to the country's constitution, although no such indoctrination had occurred in this case. A complete ban on membership of a lawful political party was, however, disproportionate in view of the damage to the teacher's livelihood and reputation.

Constraints on the activities of some public officials are also justifiable, as in the case of senior civil servants, police[82] and judges, because their neutrality or apparent neutrality is important to the proper functioning of a democratic system and the administration of justice, since without such neutrality public confidence in the ability of elected representatives to implement their political mandate would be undermined. That consideration did not apply to a school-teacher. It does apply, however, to rules that restrict some public-sector workers in local government holding senior positions from standing for election or from giving active support to candidates.[83] Upholding the validity of these rules, the ECtHR stressed that the constraints on political activities were a proportionate interference with freedom of expression, because they only applied to about 2 per cent of local government employees whose duties involved the provision of advice to the elected councillors or press officers dealing with the media.[84]

Article 11 protects freedom of association, including membership of a political party. In *Redfearn* v. *United Kingdom*,[85] the ECtHR held that a dismissal for membership of a political party was an interference with the right to freedom of association. The state should therefore ensure that such a dismissal should be

---

[80] In Northern Ireland, there is a law against political discrimination, the Fair Employment and Treatment (Northern Ireland) Order 1998, SI 1998 No. 3162.

[81] (1996) 21 EHRR 2015 (ECtHR).   [82] *Rekvenyi* v. *Hungary* (1999) 30 EHRR 509 (ECtHR).

[83] Local Government Officers (Political Restrictions) Regulations 1990, SI 1990 No. 851.

[84] *Ahmed* v. *United Kingdom* (1998) 29 EHRR 29 (ECtHR).

[85] *Redfearn* v. *United Kingdom* [2013] IRLR 51, [2012] ECHR 1878 (ECtHR); H. Collins and V. Mantouvalou, 'Redfearn v UK: Political Association and Dismissal' (2013) 76(5) *Modern Law Review* 909.

unlawful unless in the circumstances of the particular case the dismissal was a proportionate measure taken in pursuit of a legitimate aim pursued by an employer. Mr Redfearn's dismissal had resulted from his active membership of the British National Party (BNP), an extreme right-wing political party, which is notorious not only for its anti-immigration and anti-EU positions but also, ironically, for its policy of withdrawal from the ECHR. Although the BNP is a lawful political party because it avoids explicit racist policies, some employers such as the police and the prison service impose a complete ban on membership. What appeared to be a complete list of members of the BNP was once posted on a website, and it was subsequently reported in the press that some employers reacted by dismissing staff who were members, as in the case of a DJ on a radio station.[86] Mr Redfearn had no legal claim available under UK law, because he had not been employed for a sufficient period of time to qualify for a claim for unfair dismissal, and because his claim for race discrimination on the ground that he and all members of the BNP were white was rejected as unfounded.[87] His application to the ECtHR that his right to freedom of association was not sufficiently protected by the law was accepted. As a consequence, the law of unfair dismissal was amended to permit claims where the principal reason for dismissal relates to an employee's political opinions or affiliation to be brought from the commencement of employment.[88]

Although dismissal simply for membership of a political party is almost certainly unfair, an employer may be able to justify the interference with freedom of association as a proportionate response in the circumstances. For instance, Mr Redfearn's employers argued that the dismissal was in response to fears that co-workers and customers of the employer might be provoked into disorder or violent acts against Mr Redfearn which, if true, might have provided a sufficient justification for a fair dismissal. In the particular instance of the BNP, it is worth noting that ECHR Article 17 cautions that 'Nothing in this Convention may be interpreted as implying for any state, group, or person any right to engage in any activity or perform any act aimed at the destruction of any of the rights and freedoms set forth herein or at their limitation to a greater extent than is provided for in the Convention.'

Slightly different principles apply to trade unions. Like other associations that are oriented towards particular values and philosophies, trade unions benefit from the right to freedom of association under Article 11 that includes

---

[86] *Daily Telegraph*, 19 November 2008, available at www.telegraph.co.uk/news/uknews/3484612/Rod-Lucas-dropped-by-TalkSPORT-after-BNP-links-emerge.html.

[87] *Redfearn v. Serco Ltd* [2006] EWCA Civ 659, [2006] ICR 1367 (CA). There was no direct discrimination because the ground or reason for discrimination against Mr Redfearn was not his race but his membership of a political party. Nor was there indirect discrimination, because the correct interpretation of the employer's policy was a rule that led to the dismissal of members of extremist political parties that might damage the employer's reputation, and those employees affected by the policy might be drawn proportionately from all racial groups.

[88] ERA 1996, s. 108(4), as amended by the Enterprise and Regulatory Reform Act 2013, s. 13.

the negative right to exclude people who do not share their views and purposes. ASLEF tried to expel a member of the union who was also a BNP candidate for election. At the time, the domestic law prohibited expulsion of trade union members on the grounds of membership of a political party. ASLEF successfully claimed before the ECtHR that this law against political discrimination unjustifiably interfered with their right to freedom of association. The ECtHR agreed that the law was a disproportionate interference with the union's right to freedom of association, because the union was pursuing a legitimate aim of upholding the principles that it stood for and there was no practical detriment to the particular member who could keep his job and the collectively agreed rate of pay despite not being a member of the union.[89] The UK law was subsequently amended.[90] Perhaps some other employers such as political parties may be able to claim that it is important for all their employees or at least some key employees to share the official values of the organisation, so that they may be able lawfully to dismiss dissenting employees for their political views as an aspect of freedom of association.

Whistleblowing

Whistleblowing occurs when an employee discloses information about the employer's activities or those of fellow workers to a third party such as a public authority, the police or the media, with a view to protecting the public interest. Under the common law, owing to the confidential nature of the information, disclosures to third parties are likely to be regarded as breaches of the implied duty of loyalty owed to the employer under the contract of employment. In the absence in the law of any defence of disclosure in the public interest, an employee's breach of the implied term would often justify summary dismissal. Similarly, with respect to the statutory law of unfair dismissal, unauthorised disclosure of confidential information would be regarded as misconduct that might justify a fair dismissal within the range of reasonable responses. The concept of whistleblowing has been extended to cover instances where employees report suspected misconduct of other employees, typically their own manager, to higher management in the same organisation since these disclosures are also likely to be met with adverse treatment.

Whistleblowing often falls within the protection of Article 10 ECHR. In *Guja v. Moldova*,[91] a press officer in the Prosecutor General's office was dismissed for leaking two letters to the press that strongly suggested improper ministerial interference in criminal proceedings. The ECtHR stressed that

---

[89] *ASLEF* v. *UK* [2007] IRLR 361 (ECtHR); K. Ewing, 'The Implications of the ASLEF Case' (2007) 36 *Industrial Law Journal* 425.

[90] TULRCA 1992, s. 174(2)(d) and (4A)–(4H). See pp. 556–7.

[91] App. No. 14277/04, 12 February 2008.

employees, especially civil servants who have access to sensitive information, normally owe a duty of loyalty, reserve and discretion to their employers. Nevertheless, if there was a strong public interest, disclosure of confidential information should be protected under Article 10, subject to a requirement of proportionality. In the first instance, the employee should disclose concerns about wrongdoing to a superior or other competent authority. Where that course of action was impracticable, the information could, as a last resort, if no other route was possible, be disclosed to the public. Before this was done, the ECtHR emphasised that the employee must verify as far as possible that the information was accurate and reliable. Under the test of proportionality, a court should also consider the motive of the reporting employee and whether the harm suffered as a result of the disclosure outweighed the public interest in knowing the truth. In this case, the dismissal was unjustified. Similarly, in *Heinisch* v. *Germany*,[92] a nurse in a home for the care of the elderly complained on several occasions about shortages of staff that placed the patients at risk as well as putting intolerable pressure on staff. After a year or so and two inspections by a regulator that tended to confirm her complaints, having given the employer notice, she went to the criminal prosecutor to ask it to launch criminal proceedings against her employer. She was dismissed and her dismissal was upheld as lawful in the German courts. Her application to the ECtHR was successful, however, because in applying the test of proportionality the national courts had failed to balance correctly the important public interest in receiving information about the level of care for the elderly in such institutions against the employer's interest in its business reputation. In addition, the ECtHR also noted how the severe sanction of dismissal seemed disproportionate because it could have a chilling effect on all freedom of speech in the public interest by workers.

The principles developed in *Guja* v. *Moldova* are close to those enacted earlier by the Public Interest Disclosure Act 1998. The statute provided much-needed protection for UK employees who sought to disclose other employees' or their employer's wrongdoing by protecting whistleblowers against dismissal and detriment short of dismissal for having made a protected disclosure. The personal scope of the protection extends beyond employees to 'workers', a term that has a unique, exceptionally broad, definition in this context that even creates the possibility for a tribunal to recognise the existence of joint employers.[93] Because the statute protects a Convention right, it has been argued that the personal scope of the statute should not even be limited to an extended definition of worker, but should apply generally to contractors and office-holders. While that view was accepted as possible in a case involving a district

---

[92] *Heinisch* v. *Germany*, App. No. 28274/08 [2011] ECHR 1175, [2011] IRLR 922 (ECtHR).

[93] ERA 1996, s. 43K; *Day* v. *Lewisham & Greenwich NHS Trust and another (Public Concern at Work intervening)* [2017] EWCA Civ 329 [2017] ICR 917.

judge, this interpretation was held to be unnecessary as a public-office-holder should have an adequate remedy under section 7 HRA 1998.[94]

A dismissal for making a protected disclosure is automatically unfair. The employee has to demonstrate that the reason for the dismissal or other disciplinary conduct was the protected disclosure and not some other reason. For instance, a schoolteacher who was worried about the weak security settings on the school's intranet because they might not prevent pupils from gaining access to confidential records, managed to hack into the computer himself, causing considerable disruption for others' access to the computer system. After he had told the head teacher what he had done, he was given a formal warning, which he treated as a constructive dismissal. His dismissal was held not to be a result of the protected disclosure of telling the head teacher about the security problem, but rather because of his misconduct in hacking into the computer system and causing disruption to the service.[95] It was still possible, however, that the dismissal in this case might have been regarded as unfair, because it may have breached the general reasonableness standard of the law of unfair dismissal.

The remedies available for dismissal for making a protected disclosure include interim relief against dismissal and unlimited compensation for dismissal and detriment short of dismissal. Unlike all other claims for unfair dismissal, compensation can include compensation for injury to feelings, which may include an aspect of aggravated damages to represent the particular affront to dignity to someone acting in the public interest.[96] In order to receive this statutory protection, whistleblowers must satisfy two principal conditions: they must be making a 'qualifying disclosure' and they must disclose the information to the appropriate person in the circumstances.

Qualifying Disclosure

Employment Rights Act 1996, Section 43B(1)

In this Part a 'qualifying disclosure' means any disclosure of information which, in the reasonable belief of the worker making the disclosure, is made in the public interest and tends to show one or more of the following –

(a) that a criminal offence has been committed, is being committed or is likely to be committed,

(b) that a person has failed, is failing or is likely to fail to comply with any legal obligation to which he is subject,

---

[94] *Gilham* v. *Ministry of Justice* [2017] EWCA Civ 2220, [2018] ICR 827.

[95] *Bolton School* v. *Evans* [2006] EWCA Civ 1653; [2007] ICR 641 (CA).

[96] *Virgo Fidelis Senior School* v. *Boyle* [2004] ICR 1210 (EAT); *Commissioner of Police of the Metropolis* v. *Shaw* [2011] UKEAT 0125_11_2911 (EAT).

(c) that a miscarriage of justice has occurred, is occurring or is likely to occur,

(d) that the health or safety of any individual has been, is being or is likely to be endangered,

(e) that the environment has been, is being or is likely to be damaged, or

(f) that information tending to show any matter falling within any one of the preceding paragraphs has been, is being or is likely to be deliberately concealed.

Although a disclosure must always be made in 'the public interest', a concept that is not defined in the statute, the list of topics in ERA 1996, section 43B(1) makes clear that issues arising in a particular workplace such as health and safety matters or non-compliance with employment rights might count as a qualifying disclosure in the public interest. The protection should apply, for instance, to a dismissal following a complaint by the employee that the employer was not complying with certain health and safety requirements.[97] Purely personal matters affecting an individual employee may not qualify as issues of public interest, but if a large number of workers are similarly affected, the issue might become a matter of public interest.[98] Although extensive, the list of protected topics of disclosure may be criticised for not including such matters as gross waste or mismanagement of funds and serious misuse or abuse of authority.[99] Notice also that the test is whether the employee has a reasonable belief that the evidence tends to show that a criminal offence (or some other breach of legal duty) has been committed, not proof that one has actually occurred. Provided the employee has reasonable grounds for thinking that criminal acts have occurred or that the impugned actions constitute a criminal offence, a mistake about either of these matters does not prevent the disclosure from being a qualifying disclosure.[100] On the other hand, the employee must disclose what may constitute a legal wrong or a breach of legal obligation, not merely something of which the employee disapproves.[101] The criminal acts concerned need not be those of the employer or its managers. An employer might victimise an employee following disclosure to the police about criminal actions of a customer or client of the employer, and this should also be a protected disclosure.[102]

In the context of complaints to a manager about the conduct of a co-worker or of the manager, the EAT has sought to draw a distinction between, on the

[97] *Parkins* v. *Sodexho Ltd* [2002] IRLR 109 (EAT).

[98] *Chesterton Global Ltd* v. *Numohamed* [2017] EWCA Civ 979, [2018] ICR 731.

[99] Based on US and Australian legislation, recommended in Public Concern and Work, Report on the effectiveness of existing arrangements for workplace whistleblowing in the UK (London, November 2013), p. 17.

[100] *Darnton* v. *University of Surrey* [2003] ICR 615 (EAT); *Babula* v. *Waltham Forest College* [2007] EWCA Civ 175, [2007] ICR 1026 (CA).

[101] *Eiger Securities LLP* v. *Korshunova* [2017] ICR 561 (EAT).

[102] *Hibbins* v. *Hesters Way Neighbourhood Project* [2009] ICR 319 (EAT).

one hand, a protected disclosure of information and, on the other hand, the making of an allegation of wrongdoing, which is said not to fall within the protection for whistleblowing because it is not a 'disclosure'.[103] This confusing distinction will prove hard to draw in practice, for allegations of misconduct will also inevitably involve disclosures of information or suspicions. It should be noted in particular that disclosure of information that is already known to the recipient is nevertheless a disclosure. Moreover, there is a risk that employers may be able to reduce the protection for whistleblowers by excluding from the legal protection a large proportion of instances of whistleblowing that are in practice about employees telling managers about their suspicions of misconduct or wrongdoing.

Appropriate Person

Detailed rules prescribe the appropriate person to whom an employee must disclose the information in order to qualify for the statutory protection for whistleblowing. The broad design of the legislation is to permit disclosure in two ways. The first route is to disclose the information to the employer (ERA 1996, section 43C) or a prescribed regulator of a particular field (ERA 1996, section 43F).[104] In the case of disclosure to a prescribed regulator, the employee must also believe the disclosure to be substantially true rather than merely having a suspicion based on reasonable grounds.

For the second route, the employee can disclose the information more widely, including to the media, but this route is subject to numerous conditions that may prove hard to satisfy. In particular, in accordance with ERA 1996, section 43G, the employee must demonstrate that the disclosure has been made previously either to the employer or to the prescribed regulator. That condition can only be dropped where the relevant failure that is being reported is 'exceptionally serious'.[105]

Employment Rights Act 1996, Section 43G

(1) A qualifying disclosure is made in accordance with this section if - ...
   (b) the worker reasonably believes that the information disclosed, and any allegation contained in it, are substantially true,
   (c) he does not make the disclosure for purposes of personal gain,
   (d) any of the conditions in subsection (2) is met, and
   (e) in all the circumstances of the case, it is reasonable for him to make the disclosure.

---

[103] *Eiger Securities LLP* v. *Korshunova* [2017] ICR 561 (EAT).
[104] Public Interest Disclosure (Prescribed Persons) Order 2014, SI 2014 No. 2418 as amended.
[105] ERA 1996, s. 43H.

(2) The conditions referred to in subsection (1)(d) are –

   (a) that, at the time he makes the disclosure, the worker reasonably believes that he will be subjected to a detriment by his employer if he makes a disclosure to his employer or in accordance with section 43F [to a prescribed regulator],

   (b) that, in a case where no person is prescribed for the purposes of section 43F in relation to the relevant failure, the worker reasonably believes that it is likely that evidence relating to the relevant failure will be concealed or destroyed if he makes a disclosure to his employer, or

   (c) that the worker has previously made a disclosure of substantially the same information –

      (i) to his employer, or

      (ii) in accordance with section 43F.

The requirement of reasonableness permeates this second route. The statute indicates that a tribunal should take into account such matters as the seriousness of the offence, the person to whom the disclosure is made, the employee's duty of confidentiality and the action, if any, that the employer has already taken.[106] A 'gagging clause' in the contract of employment that prohibits any protected disclosure is, however, invalid and will not make the disclosure unreasonable.[107] But a gagging clause that prevents employees from discussing unprotected disclosures, such as statements about the policies of an NHS hospital, would be unaffected. Nor do these rules protect employees against breaches of the Official Secrets Act 1989.

The legislation formerly imposed an additional condition that an employee should act in 'good faith'. This seems to have been an attempt to distinguish between employees who are motivated solely by the public interest and those who act maliciously, from personal antagonism or from a grudge. But this distinction was not easy to draw in most instances because employees usually act from a mixture of motives, both to uphold the law or the public interest and also to ensure that the employer or manager receives the punishment or negative publicity he or she is believed to deserve.[108] Instead of asking whether the employee acted in good faith, now the courts and tribunals must ask whether the disclosure was in the public interest. If there was real substance to the complaint, it seems likely that it will be protected even if the employee was motivated to a considerable extent by having a grudge. Compensation can be reduced by 25 per cent, however, if the tribunal considers that it was not made in good faith.[109]

The practical effect of this legislation is certainly not to provide employees with a right to blow the whistle on wrongdoing as they see it. It would be

---

[106] ERA 1996, s. 43G(3).   [107] ERA 1996, s. 43J.

[108] E.g. *Street* v. *Derbyshire Unemployed Workers' Centre* [2004] ICR 213 (CA).

[109] ERA 1996, ss. 49(6A), 123(6A).

unwise for an employee to do anything before reporting the matter to the person designated by the employer to receive such disclosures. It is possible as an alternative to make a report to a prescribed regulator but, given the complexity of systems of regulation, especially in the public sector, it is easy for the employee to speak to the wrong regulator and risk exclusion from the protective mantle of the legislation.[110] For those whose actions fall outside the protection for disclosures in the public interest, a dismissal for disclosure of confidential information is likely to be regarded as fair unless, perhaps, where the employer is a public authority and the dismissal may be regarded by a tribunal as a disproportionate response that is inconsistent with the standards set by the ECtHR.[111] Ultimately, the main problem with this legislation is that the instinctive reaction of an employer or manager who may be implicated in the wrongdoing is immediately to take disciplinary action including dismissal against the employee. While it is true that the employee should receive protection by way of a generous award of compensation for unfair dismissal, the legislation still leaves the employee with the choice between either keeping the job or doing the right thing. Furthermore, there is much evidence that whistleblowers are likely to be blacklisted or at least tarnished in the eyes of other employers and as a result find it impossible to obtain alternative employment in the same line of work.

Dress Codes

Many employers require employees to conform to a dress and grooming code. They may require employees to wear uniforms or business suits and refrain from wearing certain kinds of jewellery and adornments. An employer may also insist upon short hair and the shaving of facial hair for men. Recently, employers have sought to forbid visible body piercings and tattoos, which are fashionable among younger workers.[112] Sometimes these dress codes are written down, but often they function as unwritten rules and diffuse expect-ations, enforced by peer pressure and pejorative comments. Employers may also exhort their employees to look smart, to be fit and not be overweight and in general conform to a particular conventional or fashionable organisational image. Employers argue that it is an important part of their business to control their corporate image, especially in customer-facing roles. Some employers claim that employees who look and feel smart work harder. A less sanguine interpretation of such rules is offered by Karl Klare:

---

[110] This mistake was made by the employee in *ALM Medical Services Ltd* v. *Bladon* [2002] ICR 1444 (CA).

[111] *Hill* v. *Governing Body of Great Tey Primary School* [2013] ICR 625 (EAT).

[112] V. Nath, S. Bach and G. Lockwood, *Dress Codes and Appearance at Work: Body Supplements, Body Modification and Aesthetic Labour*, ACAS, Research Paper 07/16, 2016.

The primary social function of appearance law is to empower employers, school officials, judges, and other authority figures to enforce the dominant expectations about appearance and to discipline deviance from the approved social norms. Generally speaking, these official appearance standards denigrate cultural and religious diversity and enforce conformity to white, heterosexual, Christian images of beauty and proper grooming. The rules and standards both exploit and repress female sexuality and punish women who depart from (largely) male-created expectations about proper female behaviour and roles. Perhaps the central social function of appearance regulation is to maintain the sexual subordination of women to men. These rules are intolerable and have no place in a democratic society committed (at least in principle) to equality and to cultural and religious diversity.[113]

Some of these dress codes can be challenged by reference to anti-discrimination laws.[114] An employer's prohibition against women wearing trousers at work, for instance, is likely to amount to direct sex discrimination. As we have noted above, prohibitions of religious symbols such as a cross or a headscarf may be challenged, at least in principle, as indirect discrimination on grounds of religion or belief, but the courts have only presented a low threshold for employers to succeed in justifying such rules. Employers may try to justify such rules on a variety of grounds such as efficiency, effectiveness, respect for the views of co-workers and the avoidance of offence to customers. Although customer preferences may not count as a genuine occupational requirement in order to counter a claim of direct discrimination,[115] an employer's concern to present a neutral image to customers is likely to provide a sufficient justification for rules that only have an indirectly discriminatory effect on particular religious groups.[116]

The imposition of a dress code on the workforce may also engage Convention rights. If the rule has effects on the employee outside the workplace, such as a rule requiring men to have short hair and no beard or moustache, it may be regarded as impinging on the right to respect for private life. An extended view of the right to respect for private life, which is not confined to the home or secluded places, understands that a person's identity and sense of personal worth may be affected equally by restrictive rules in the workplace. As Justice Marshall of the US Supreme Court once observed: '[A]n individual's personal appearance may reflect, sustain, and nourish his personality and may well be used as a means of expressing his attitude and lifestyle.'[117] As we have seen,

---

[113] K. E. Klare, 'Power/Dressing: Regulation of Employee Appearance' (1992) 26 *New England Law Review* 1395, at 1398.

[114] See p. 354.

[115] Case C-188/15, *Asma Bougnaoui and ADDH* v. *Micropole* [2017] IRLR 447 (ECJ).

[116] Case C-157/15, *Achbita* v. *G4S Secure Solutions* [2017] IRLR 466; P. Collins, 'Covering up? Client Embarrassment, Neutral Intolerance and Wearing Headscarves at Work' (2018) 134 *Law Quarterly Review* 31.

[117] *Kelley* v. *Johnson*, 425 US 238 (1976).

some clothing and adornments may also have religious significance, so there is a potential interference with the right to manifest a religion. Different styles of dress and some adornments may also be regarded as an aspect of freedom of expression. If an employee is dismissed for failing to comply with some aspect of the employer's dress and grooming code, in principle the issue of the fairness of the dismissal must be assessed in accordance with the HRA 1998 by taking into account any potential interference with a Convention right.

Part IV
Collective Labour Rights

12

Freedom of Association and the Right to Organise

Contents

Introduction

In considering how the law protects (or fails to protect) workers, we have been concerned so far principally with the contract of employment and the regulatory role of legislation (such as the NMWA 2008 and the Working Time Regulations 2008). Also important, however, is the role of trade unions and the process of collective bargaining. By virtue of the latter, trade unions and employers negotiate collective agreements, which regulate the terms and conditions of employment of the workers to whom they apply. These collective agreements may cover both substantive (pay, hours and holidays) and procedural (grievance and disciplinary procedures) issues. Workers covered by a collective agreement will generally be better paid than their counterparts who are not, while workers who are trade union members will be able to call upon their union for support when problems arise at work. But if workers are to enjoy these benefits, they must be free to join trade unions, to take part in their activities, and to use their services. That is to say, they must have the right to organise, a right protecting them from sanctions imposed by the state or from various forms of discrimination by their employer. The right to organise is the first principle of the right to freedom of association, and is considered in this chapter. Following from the right to organise is the right to bargain collectively and the right to strike respectively, both of which are considered in subsequent chapters.

The right to freedom of association is a right of rich subtlety, with at least three dimensions:

- freedom to be in association with others (in the sense that a person may not be restrained or penalised for associating with others);
- freedom in the association of others (in the sense that individuals should be free collectively to decide how their association is to be organised and governed); and
- freedom to act in association with others (in the sense that individuals should be free to act collectively to promote the purposes that brought them together).

Although this chapter is concerned with the first of these dimensions, aspects of the other two are considered in some detail in the chapters that follow. In all three of its dimensions, the right to freedom of association is fully recognised by international law, reflecting the importance of trade unions and collective bargaining in free societies. Key instruments to be encountered later in this chapter include ILO Convention 87 (Freedom of Association and Protection of the Right to Organise Convention, 1948),[1] and ILO Convention 98 (Right to

---

[1] See especially Art. 2 ('Workers and employers, without distinction whatsoever, shall have the right to establish and, subject only to the rules of the organisation concerned, to join organisations of their own choosing without previous authorisation'). See the discussion of the *GCHQ* case below.

Organise and Collective Bargaining Convention, 1949).[2] Also important are the Council of Europe's Social Charter of 1961, Article 5, and the ECHR, Article 11, the latter providing that all workers have the right to form and join trade unions for the protection of their interests.[3]

Refusal of Employment

Legislation to give effect to these measures was a long time coming in the UK, even though it ratified ILO Convention 98 as early as 1950. The first legislation protecting employees from acts of anti-union discrimination was the Industrial Relations Act 1971. The Act was repealed in 1974, but the Trade Union and Labour Relations Act 1974 and the Employment Protection Act 1975 re-introduced protection, although in a different form. It is these latter measures – albeit amended by both Conservative and Labour administrations – which form the basis of the current legislation.[4] In providing protection against detrimental action short of dismissal, and dismissal respectively, initially these provisions did not provide protection against discrimination on trade union grounds at the point of hiring. The provisions relating to the latter were not introduced until 1990.[5] Until then the position was governed only by the common law, which meant that employers were free not to employ someone because of trade union membership.[6]

TULRCA 1992, Section 137

In legislating to close this gap, it is clear that the main aim of the Employment Act 1990 was the pre-entry closed shop whereby workers could be required as a condition of employment to be members of a trade union. Nevertheless, in addressing this latter issue the legislation also applied to the converse situation of someone refused employment (under a contract of employment) because of his or her trade union membership. Thus TULRCA 1992, section 137 provides as follows:

---

[2] See especially Art. 1 ('workers shall enjoy adequate protection against acts of anti-union discrimination in respect of their employment'), and Art. 2 (such protection to apply to 'acts calculated to (a) make employment of the worker subject to the condition that he shall not join a union or shall relinquish trade union membership, or (b) cause the dismissal of or otherwise prejudice a worker by reason of union membership or because of participation in union activities outside working hours or, with the consent of the employer, within working hours').

[3] This has given rise to a number of important complaints from the UK. See *Young, James and Webster* v. *United Kingdom* (1981) 4 EHRR 38, and *Wilson* v. *United Kingdom* [2002] ECHR 552. See also *Palomo Sanchez* v. *Spain* [2011] ECHR 1319, especially para. 58.

[4] TULRCA 1992, ss. 137–67.   [5] Employment Act 1990, s. 1.

[6] See *Allen* v. *Flood* [1898] AC 1, at 172.

Trade Union and Labour Relations (Consolidation) Act 1992, Section 137(1)

It is unlawful to refuse a person employment –

(a) because he is, or is not, a member of a trade union, or

(b) because he is unwilling to accept a requirement –

    (i) to take steps to become or cease to be, or to remain or not to become, a member of a trade union

    . . .

A person who is thus unlawfully refused employment has a right of complaint to an employment tribunal. TULRCA 1992, section 138 applies similar provisions to employment agencies. Remedies (in the form of a declaration and compensation) are dealt with in TULRCA 1992, section 140[7] and awards of compensation may be made against third parties, such as a trade union official trying to enforce a closed shop (section 142).

The substantive provisions of TULRCA 1992, section 137 are, however, narrow in their application insofar as they protect rights relating to trade union membership. They apply only to the refusal of employment because of trade-union membership, not also because of participation in trade union activities. Does this therefore allow the employer to continue lawfully to screen out the trade union activist? This was the issue raised in *Harrison* v. *Kent County Council*,[8] where the appellant had previously been employed by Kent County Council as a social worker. He left in 1991 to work in Nottingham and then had a spell in Greenwich. In 1993 he applied for a job back in Kent, but his application was unsuccessful on the ground that he had 'an unco-operative attitude and an anti-management style'. The industrial tribunal found that he had not been denied employment because of his trade union membership, but because of his trade union activities, for which there was no protection. He appealed successfully to the EAT, which concluded that the 'industrial tribunal's construction of section 137(1) of the Act of 1992 takes a narrower view of the conceptual limits of membership of a trade union than is expressed by the ordinary and natural meaning of the language of the section'.[9]

According to the EAT, 'if a person is refused employment because he was or is a trade union activist or for a reason related to his union activities it is open to the industrial tribunal, under the provisions of section 137(1)(a), to conclude that he is refused employment because he is a member of the union'.[10] It

---

[7] The amount of compensation may not exceed the limit in ERA 1996, s. 124 (which in 2018 was £83,682): TULRCA 1992, s. 140(4). The tribunal may also recommend the employer to take steps to obviate or reduce the adverse effect on the complainant of any conduct to which the complaint relates: TULRCA 1992, s. 140(1)(b).

[8] [1995] ICR 434.   [9] *Ibid.*, 443.   [10] *Ibid.*

will be noted that, in reaching its decision, the EAT relied heavily on the Court of Appeal decision in *Associated British Ports* v. *Palmer*,[11] which was concerned with the meaning of 'trade union membership' for the purposes of TULRCA 1992, section 146.[12] This provides protection for action short of dismissal for employees for reasons related to trade union membership or activities (and now the use of trade union services). In the *Associated British Ports* case, the Court of Appeal adopted a wide construction of 'trade union membership' for the purposes of section 146, and it is on this that the EAT in *Harrison* relied. But the House of Lords in *Palmer* (in a case conjoined with *Associated Newspapers Ltd* v. *Wilson* (see below)) took a very different and a very narrow approach to the construction of TULRCA 1992, section 146. At least some members of the House of Lords in that case took the view that the protection for trade union membership applies only to protection for holding a union card and not much else.

The *Harrison* decision is thus based on an earlier Court of Appeal decision which has been overruled. In *Jet2.Com Ltd* v. *Denby*,[13] however, *Harrison* was adopted in a case where an airline pilot involved in a long dispute with the employer about the recognition of his union was denied re-employment by the company. This was because of his activities as a shop steward during a previous period of employment with the same employer. Having regard to parliamentary material relating to the enactment of TULRCA 1992, section 137 in its original form (Employment Act 1990, section 1), the EAT held that the ET had been entitled to conclude that an 'employer's objection to an applicant's participation in activities incidental to their trade union membership *is* an objection to their status as a trade union member'. So far as *Wilson and Palmer* was concerned, the House of Lords ruling was distinguished and in any event displaced by the subsequent decision of the Strasbourg court in the same case. Bound by the HRA 1998, section 3, to construe TULRCA 1992, section 137 consistently with Convention rights, the EAT concluded also that 'it cannot be right to adopt a narrow construction of section 137(1)(a) if this would lead to a gap in the protection of an employee's article 11 right to join a trade union for the protection of their interests'.[14]

TULRCA 1992, Section 152

So far as access to employment is concerned, the other trick of employers relates to those workers who have evaded pre-employment screening by successfully concealing their history as trade union activists. When the worker's identity becomes known, he or she may be dismissed. But there will

---

[11] [1994] ICR 97.   [12] See pp. 490–6.   [13] [2018] IRLR 417.

[14] This is consistent with an earlier employment tribunal decision relating to blacklisting in which it was held that 'in this context it is not desirable to divorce union activities from union membership': *Dooley* v. *Balfour Beatty Ltd*, Case 2203380/2009, 5 March 2010, para. 6.3.

be no remedy under TULRCA 1992, section 137, because the person in question has not been refused employment. It will be necessary here to rely on TULRCA 1992, section 152, which makes it unfair to dismiss an employee because of trade union membership (section 152(1)(a)) or activities (section 152(1)(b)). (Section 152 is considered more fully below.) The issue here is twofold: if someone conceals his or her employment history for fear of reprisal and is then dismissed, is this dismissal for reasons of trade union membership or activities? And secondly, does the legislation apply where the employee is dismissed not because of trade union activities with his or her current employer, but because of activities with a previous employer?

These issues were considered in *Fitzpatrick* v. *British Railways Board*,[15] where the employee applied for a job with BRB, but concealed in her application form a period of employment with the Ford Motor Company which lasted only nine days before she was dismissed because of bad references. Several months after she started at BRB, an article appeared in the *Evening Standard* indicating that the appellant was a prominent trade union activist and had links with Trotskyist groups, including Socialist Action. She was then dismissed by BRB, for 'untruthfulness and lack of trust'. But although the industrial tribunal concluded that the real reason for the appellant's dismissal was her trade union activities with previous employers, the application nevertheless failed. The industrial tribunal found that the dismissal was not on account of her existing trade union activities but because of her activities with these previous employers. The legislation then in force – Employment Protection (Consolidation) Act 1978, section 58 (now TULRCA 1992, section 152) – was found not to apply.

This decision was upheld by the EAT, but reversed by the Court of Appeal, which emphasised that it was not Fitzpatrick's 'deceit' that led the employer to dismiss her. Nor was she being dismissed to punish her for her trade union activities with a previous employer. Rather, she was dismissed because of her 'previous trade union (and possibly her political) activities, which gave her a reputation for being a disruptive force; and that was the prime reason for her dismissal'.[16] In reversing the ET, the Court of Appeal held that the tribunal had been wrong to rely on the EAT decision in *City of Birmingham District Council* v. *Beyer*.[17] This had led them to conclude that the legislation (now TULRCA 1992, section 152) is applicable only where the employer's conduct has been in response to 'some cogent and identifiable act and not some possible trouble in the future'.[18] According to Lord Woolf, 'the industrial tribunal [was] saying that in order to comply with the provisions of section 58(1)(b) there must have been some activity on the part of the employee to which they took exception, which was not a mere possibility but something which was sufficiently precise to be identifiable in her present employment'.[19]

---

[15] [1992] ICR 221.   [16] *Ibid.*, 224.   [17] [1977] IRLR 211.   [18] *Ibid.*, 227.   [19] *Ibid.*

Lord Woolf continued by saying that:

> The purpose of the subsection, insofar as (b) is concerned, is to protect those who engage in trade union activities and I can see no reason why that should not apply irrespective of whether the precise activities can be identified. If an employer, having learnt of an employee's previous trade union activities, decides that he wishes to dismiss that employee, that is likely to be a situation where almost inevitably the employer is dismissing the employee because he feels that the employee will indulge in industrial activities of a trade union nature in his current employment. There is no reason for a rational and reasonable employer to object to the previous activities of an employee except insofar as they will impinge upon the employee's current employment.[20]

The effect of *Fitzpatrick* is thus to reinforce the protection offered to trade union activists at the point of hiring: refusal of employment following pre-employment screening or dismissal from employment following post-employment screening are both covered. As the following sections reveal, however, the protection is far from adequate.

Blacklisting

On 6 March 2009, the UK data protection watchdog, the ICO, published a report into a previously unknown organisation called the Consulting Association.[21] John McDonnell MP described the findings in the ICO report as 'one of the worst ever cases of organised abuses of human rights in the UK', and called for a full public inquiry.[22] For decades, the Consulting Association had operated a secret blacklisting operation on behalf of forty-four multi-national building contractors. The companies identified by the ICO are all well known and include:

> Amec, Amey, B. Sunley & Sons, Balfour Beatty, Balfour Kilpatrick, Ballast Wiltshire, Bam Construction (HBC Construction), Bam Nuttall (Edmund Nuttall Ltd), CB&I, Cleveland Bridge UK Ltd, Costain UK Ltd, Crown House Technologies, Carillion, Tarmac Construction, Diamond M&E Services, Dudley Bower & Co. Ltd, Emcor (Drake & Scull), Emcor Rail, G. Wimpey Ltd, Haden Young, Kier Ltd, John Mowlem Ltd, Laing O'Rourke, Lovell Construction (UK) Ltd, Miller Construction Ltd, Morgan Ashurst, Morgan Est, Morrison Construction Group, N. G. Bailey, Shepherd Engineering Services, Sias Building Services, Sir Robert McAlpine Ltd, Skanska (Kaverna / Trafalgar House plc), SPIE (Matthew Hall), Taylor Woodrow Construction Ltd, Turriff Construction Ltd,

---

[20] *Ibid.*, 227–8.   [21] ICO Press Release 2009.

[22] *Morning Star*, 25 February 2011. The matter was also pursued in Parliament by Michael Clapham MP, and was considered by the Joint Committee on Human Rights: see HL Paper 5–1, HC 64–1 (2009–10).

Tysons Contractors, Walter Llewellyn & Sons Ltd, Whessoe Oil & Gas, Willmott Dixon, Vinci plc (Norwest Holst Group).[23]

Consulting Association

The ICO investigation discovered a centralised database holding sensitive personal information on 3,213 individuals, with most of the information relating to the trade union membership of workers raising concerns about safety issues. The information was covertly collected by, and shared among, the building firms to prevent the trade union members in question from gaining employment on their projects, the construction firms each paying an annual subscription of £3,000 to the Consulting Association for the service.[24] The constitution of the Consulting Association makes it clear that the body was not merely a company providing facilities to the building industry, but rather an 'unincorporated trade association' owned and controlled by its member companies. Quarterly meetings took place, with representation required from member companies at director level.[25] Consulting Association staff collated the blacklist, relying on data being supplied by senior managers of the major contractors. The latter forwarded information of any employees, workers or sub-contractors regarded as 'troublemakers'.[26] There appear also to have been other means of data collection by means of the covert surveillance of workers,[27] and evidence has emerged of Special Branch infiltration of trade unions, with information obtained 'ultimately appearing on the blacklist'.[28]

Each file entry was dated and accompanied by a reference number denoting the company that supplied the information. File entries included the worker's name, address and national insurance number, and also photographs, work history, press cuttings, medical information, discussion about family relationships, political leanings and sometimes wildly inaccurate malicious gossip.[29] Entries on individual files refer to workers raising concerns about unpaid

---

[23] ICO Press Release 2009.

[24] Department for Business, Innovation and Skills, 'The Blacklisting of Trade Unionists: Revised Draft Regulations' (December 2009), p. 9.

[25] The Consulting Association, Constitution (as agreed and amended after meeting of 7 February 2002).

[26] A good account of how the blacklist worked in practice is provided by the ET in *Willis* v. *CB&I (UK) Ltd*, Case No. 1101269/09, 30 November 2010, where a particular manager was said to have introduced the company to the Consulting Association.

[27] Thus, it appears that on some occasions individuals were followed, and telephone calls were made to their spouses.

[28] BBC News, 23 March 2018. The surveillance of trade unions and trade unionists is part of a wider problem of police surveillance and police undercover operations which led to claims of serious abuse on the part of the police. A judge-led inquiry was established in 2014 (now under Sir John Mitting) to examine these matters, but it has been very slow and is likely to take years to complete. The inquiry is dealing with trade union surveillance among other things, with a number of trade unions as well as the Blacklist Support Group now core participants. More details can be found on the Undercover Policing website.

[29] Some detail of the content of the personal files is provided in K. D. Ewing, *Ruined Lives: Blacklisting in the UK Construction Industry* (London: Institute of Employment Rights, 2009).

wages, or an employer's failure to adhere to nationally negotiated agreements. Safety representatives were identified for speaking to managers about asbestos, near fatal accidents, electrical safety or poor toilet facilities. The credentials of trade union safety representatives were photocopied and appeared in the files, which included entries such as:

> 'Do not employ under any circumstances', 'need to monitor route onto projects via Employment Agencies', and 'would not employ – active in trade union'.

Some of this material is now in the public domain as a result of the ET cases discussed below. While most of the files are only a page or so in length, there are a number that take up many pages. One file – that of Brian Higgins – is forty-nine pages long. Mr Higgins said:

The Blacklist is an economic, social and political prison. I have served a life sentence and other workers continue to be imprisoned. In cases like my own, the Blacklist effectively takes the form of house arrest because of its effect on a person's social life. My wife was also deeply affected and badly scarred. More often than not, she was forced to financially support me, and our two children, on her low wage as a care worker. This has had a devastating effect on our standard of living. To her great credit my wife supported me and our family unstintingly. She held us together when things got really tough – which it did quite often. We kept our dignity intact and just managed to keep our heads above water by almost completely sacrificing our social life. My wife had to take out loans, which we could not afford, since my credit rating was zero due to very long spells of unemployment. All of this is the direct result of the building employers deliberately using the Blacklist, time and again, to deny me the right to work and to earn a living.

The blacklist provided the database for checks to be made by employers on job applicants. Senior managers would provide the Consulting Association with the names of workers applying for employment on their projects. If a name appeared on the database, the company making the check would be informed accordingly, and the worker simply would not be employed (or dismissed if already employed). This was done mainly by telephone to avoid a paper trail, but occasional faxes were retained and supplied as ET evidence. Each name check cost £2.20, and between April 2006 and February 2009 the construction companies jointly paid in total more than £450,000 to use the service. Invoices seized show that, in 2008 alone, one division of Skanska was billed £28,000, equating to thousands of checks on individual workers. Given the simplicity of the process and the scale of the forty-four companies involved, it is hardly surprising that their systematic blacklisting had a devastating impact upon employment prospects. Hundreds of skilled and highly trained workers either

See also D. Smith and P. Chamberlain, *Blacklisted: The Secret War Between Big Business and Union Activists* (2nd edn, Oxford: New Internationalist Publications, 2016).

suffered repeated dismissals and prolonged periods of unemployment or else were forced to leave the industry altogether.[30]

The ICO's raid led to the prosecution of a man called Ian Kerr, who played a prominent part in the activities of the Consulting Association. The action was brought under what was then the Data Protection Act 1998 for processing data without having first registered with the Commissioner as required by the Act.[31] Although Mr Kerr's conviction was applauded, many in the construction industry were surprised by the leniency of the £5,000 fine handed down by the Knutsford Crown Court,[32] to which the case had been committed by the Macclesfield magistrates' court, on the ground that the maximum fine they could impose was 'wholly inadequate'.[33] But what about the multinational construction companies, the household names that had used the blacklist, over many years and on an industrial scale? Here, we encounter the limits of the 1998 Act, with the ICO pointing out on 4 August 2009 that it was 'not a criminal offence to breach the data protection principles, which is why the ICO chose only to prosecute Ian Kerr for failing to notify as a data controller'.[34] Under the Act, the Commissioner could only issue an enforcement notice which effectively means stop doing it, and only if you don't will it be a criminal offence. What is surprising, however, is that enforcement notices were issued against only fourteen companies.[35] The position would now be governed by the GDPR, on which see the discussion in Chapter 11.

Blacklisting Litigation

The action against Kerr and the companies on behalf of which he acted did not of course address the economic losses of the workers who had been blacklisted, and who brought legal proceedings in various forums to recover the losses they sustained. Many of the victims of the blacklist brought ET claims under TULRCA 1992, sections 137 (discriminatory exclusion from employment) or 152 (discriminatory dismissal from employment). But most faced serious

---

[30] These hardships were felt all the more keenly for the fact that the blacklist was operating during a construction boom when skilled workers were in great demand.

[31] Data Protection Act 1998, ss. 17–19. See now Data Protection Act 2018; pp. 445–50 above.

[32] On which, see D. Smith, 'Blacklisting', *Socialist Lawyer*, February 2010, p. 23.

[33] *Construction News*, 23 July 2009.   [34] ICO, Press Release, 4 August 2009.

[35] The companies were told that they must '[r]efrain from using, disclosing or otherwise processing any personal data obtained from Mr Kerr unless the processing is necessary for the purpose of complying with any obligation under the [Data Protection] Act or by law or for obtaining legal advice or for the purpose of, or in connection with, any legal proceedings; [e]nsure that if any personal data relating to recruitment is obtained from a source other than the data subject, the data subject is, insofar as is practicable, provided with the information specified in paragraph 2(3) at Part II of Schedule 1 to the Act in accordance with the First Data Protection Principle; and [e]nsure that if any personal data relating to recruitment is disclosed to a third party for use in connection with the recruitment of workers, the data subject is, insofar as is practicable, provided with the information specified in paragraph 2(3) at Part II of Schedule 1 to the Act in accordance with the First Data Protection Principle'.

problems in doing so. One problem related to time limits, with claims normally to be brought within three months of the event complained of.[36] Many of the complaints related to conduct that took place many years ago, and a misunderstanding about the circumstances whereby the time limits could be extended led to a large number of claims being lost at an early stage in the proceedings.[37] In *Smith* v. *Carillion (JM) Ltd*,[38] however, the complainant was permitted to bring the claims outside the normal limitation periods 'because he had been in ignorance of what had been going on and had taken proceedings within a reasonable period of becoming aware of these activities'.

A second problem related to employment status, relevant to both TULRCA 1992, section 137 and section 152 claims, a difficult issue in the construction industry where the great bulk of the labour force is engaged on a self-employed basis, whether bogus or not.[39] The construction industry is also one in which a large number of workers are supplied to companies by employment agencies, as in *Smith* v. *Carillion (JM) Ltd*, above. There the company accepted that it had penalised the complainant because of his trade union and health and safety activities, but argued that as he was supplied by and paid by an employment agency he was neither an employee nor a worker of the respondents. This was accepted by an ET and upheld by both the EAT and the Court of Appeal, the latter rejecting 'a whole series of matters' which were said arguably to point strongly in favour of an employment contract with the respondents, notably: 'the degree of integration into the business; the fact that he was interviewed and therefore his identity was critical to the business; and that he appeared in every way to be an employee'.

As a result, of the blacklisted workers who applied to ETs, only a handful were able to have a full hearing on the merits of their case. However, it appears that several of those who did so were successful, and were awarded substantial compensation, though whether this addressed the full extent of their losses is unclear. Others settled.

Blacklists Regulations 2010

The government of the day responded quickly to the blacklisting scandal, using powers in the Employment Relations Act 1999,[40] to introduce the Blacklists Regulations 2010.[41] These powers had never been invoked in the mistaken belief that blacklisting was no longer a problem in this country.[42] But although it moved quickly, the government encountered resistance from

---

[36] TULRCA 1992, s. 139(1)(a) (exclusion from employment); ERA 1996, s. 111(2)(a) (dismissal).

[37] On extension, see TULRCA 1992, s. 139(1)(b) (exclusion from employment); ERA 1996, s. 111 (2)(b) (dismissal).

[38] [2015] EWCA Civ 209, [2015] IRLR 467.

[39] In some cases, however, it would have been possible for 'workers' to have brought dismissal claims under TULRCA 1992, s. 146.

[40] Employment Relations Act 1999, s. 2.   [41] SI 2010 No. 493.

[42] For evidence of blacklisting in the past, and the lack of any common-law remedy to stop it, see K. D. Ewing, *Ruined Lives: Blacklisting in the UK Construction Industry* (London: Institute of Employment Rights, 2009). For evidence of workers being removed from their jobs for reasons

employers, which claimed that the 'vetting of prospective employees was necessary to weed out troublemakers, criminal elements or other undesirable people'.[43] In introducing the new regulations, the government thus made it clear that 'it does not wish to deter employers from vetting prospective employees',[44] and that under the new regulations 'virtually all vetting activity, which should *normally* have nothing to do with trade union matters, is left unaffected'.[45] In light of the foregoing, it is perhaps not surprising that allegations of blacklisting should continue to be made, and indeed to surface before the ink on the new Blacklists Regulations 2010 even had an opportunity to dry.[46]

Regulation 3 prohibits the compilation, use, sale or supply of a 'prohibited list',[47] a term defined to mean a list that 'contains details of persons who are or have been members of trade unions or persons who are taking part or have taken part in the activities of trade unions', and is compiled 'with a view to being used by employers or employment agencies for the purposes of discrimination in relation to recruitment or in relation to the treatment of workers'.[48] For these purposes, discrimination means 'treating a person less favourably than another on grounds of trade union membership or trade union activities',[49] and membership of a trade union includes membership of a particular branch or section of a trade union.[50] But there is no definition of trade union activities, a particular concern in this context if it means that the protection applies only to (authorised or official) activities of a trade union, but not also to (unauthorised or unofficial) trade-union-related activities.[51] In this context, however, it must be assumed that industrial action would count as a trade union activity,[52] subject to doubts about unofficial industrial action.[53]

---

related to trade union activities following MI5 intervention, see K. D. Ewing, A. Moretta and J. Mahoney, *Morning Star*, 12 April 2015.

[43] Department for Business, Innovation and Skills, 'The Blacklisting of Trade Unionists: Revised Draft Regulations' (December 2009), p. 9.

[44] *Ibid.*, p. 11.   [45] *Ibid.*, p. 9.

[46] On 14 February 2011, Mr Frank Morris was dismissed from the Olympics Park Media Centre by an electrical firm. It is alleged that the dismissal took place after Mr Morris blew the whistle on the continued use of the blacklist after a number of union activists were removed from the project. It was also alleged that a supervisor later admitted that employees had been dismissed because their names had come up on a list of union activists. Mr Morris's dismissal resulted in numerous protests and an ET application supported by his trade union, RMT. See also on the *Morris* case HC 543 (2013–14), paras. 49–51.

[47] Blacklists Regulations, reg. 3(1).   [48] *Ibid.*, reg. 3(2).   [49] *Ibid.*, reg. 3(3).

[50] *Ibid.*, reg. 3(4).

[51] There is a difference between 'trade union activities' and 'trade-union-related activities': see *Serco Ltd* v. *Dahou* [2015] IRLR 30. And note also the narrow approach of the courts to trade union activities in TULRCA 1992, s. 169, pp. 620–1.

[52] Even though it does not count as a trade union activity for the purposes of TULRCA 1992, ss. 146 and 152.

[53] Such action is treated especially harshly in unfair dismissal law: TULRCA 1992, s. 237. See pp. 793–6.

It is unlawful to refuse to employ someone for a reason related to a prohibited list,[54] unlawful to deny someone employment agency services,[55] unlawful to subject someone to a detriment,[56] and unfair to dismiss an employee for a similar reason.[57] Claims in these cases may be brought before an ET. While it is true that ETs have the power to award reinstatement or re-engagement in unfair dismissal cases, it is also true that this is rarely done in unfair dismissal cases generally, and it seems unlikely that anyone will secure employment by invoking the regulations. In practice it is likely that financial compensation will be the only remedy, assuming that the formidable problems of proof can be overcome.[58] Otherwise, regulation 13 provides that breach of regulation 3 is actionable as a breach of statutory duty in the civil courts. Where a complaint is upheld, 'the court may (without prejudice to any of its other powers) (a) make such order as it considers appropriate for the purpose of restraining or preventing the defendant from contravening regulation 3; and (b) award damages, which may include compensation for injured feelings'.[59]

The regulations came into force on 2 March 2010, with no retrospective or retroactive effect, and no provision to support the existing victims of what was described by one employment tribunal as a 'ghastly' practice.[60] However, following the initiation of a class action by construction workers in 2012 alleging conspiracy to injure, a breach of the Data Protection Act 1998 and the HRA 1998, eight of the construction companies established a compensation fund which was initially welcomed by the House of Commons Scottish Affairs Committee,[61] but subsequently strongly criticised on account of the low levels of compensation and its availability only to those not participating in the class action.[62] The class action was settled in favour of the workers involved, with significantly higher levels of compensation than under the companies' compensation fund, along with an 'agreed joint state-ment made in open court' which: (1) exposed the 'details of the "blacklisting" procedures'; (2) described 'the processes used by the defendant companies and

---

[54] Blacklists Regulations, reg. 5.   [55] *Ibid.*, reg. 6.

[56] *Ibid.*, reg. 9. This could include dismissal in the case of someone who is not an employee and therefore not entitled to bring a claim for unfair dismissal.

[57] *Ibid.*, reg. 12.   [58] As illustrated by *Miller* v. *Interserve Industrial Services Ltd* [2013] ICR 445.

[59] Blacklists Regulations, reg. 13(3). Proceedings generally cannot be brought in the ET and the civil courts in respect of the same conduct: reg. 13(4) and (5).

[60] See the *Dooley* case, p. 481. This compared very unfavourably with the treatment of people sacked in the 1970s for non-membership of a trade union where a closed shop had operated. Then, the Conservative government of Mrs Thatcher introduced a retroactive compensation scheme for the so-called victims: Employment Act 1982, Sched. 1. See K. D. Ewing and W. M. Rees, 'Closed Shop Dismissals 1974–80: A Study of the Retroactive Compensation Scheme' (1983) 12 *Industrial Law Journal* 148.

[61] HC 543 (2013–14).

[62] By falsely suggesting that the scheme had trade union support, the eight companies behind this scheme (and their lawyers) were criticised for being 'callous and manipulative': HC 272 (2014–15), para. 24.

the CA'; and (3) detailed 'how workers were affected by this practice'. The companies also made an unreserved apology.[63]

 ### A Case Study in Successful Labour Rights Campaigning

The campaign for justice by the blacklisted workers following the exposure of the practice in 2009 is a perfect example of how to use the law as a form of leverage against large employers.[64] A blacklist support group was formed, and working with sympathetic lawyers with great energy pursued litigation across a number of fronts, initially with a view ultimately to having the matter resolved by the ECtHR. The litigation was reinforced by exploiting political opportunities designed to put pressure on the companies, and by various forms of protest at high-profile events at which the companies would be present. The companies were exposed constantly as a result to (1) adverse publicity in a number of forums, (2) excoriating and damaging parliamentary criticism,[65] and (3) the risk in some cases of losing lucrative public-sector contracts. It is this pressure that is thought by some to have led to the settlement referred to in the text, which had the effect of avoiding the need for the matter to be considered by the ECtHR. The matter was resolved by litigation in concert with political and protest action. As it is, two complaints were made to the Strasbourg court, including the case of Dave Smith above. However, the application was ruled inadmissible under ECHR, Article 35 (3)(b), mainly on the ground that despite losing in his ET claim, Smith nevertheless secured financial compensation in the High Court class action proceedings.[66] An earlier case was ruled inadmissible on the much less persuasive ground that the applicant had not exhausted his domestic remedies.[67]

Discrimination

Once in employment, the worker (in the case of detriment) and the employee (in the case of detriment and dismissal) will have protection from hostile acts by their employer on the ground of trade union membership, participation in trade union activities, and now for making use of trade union services.[68] The legislation also extends to include protection for workers or employees who suffer detriment or are dismissed because they were not members of a trade union (or refused to make payments to a trade union or a charity in lieu of

---

[63] The details are set out in *Smith* v. *United Kingdom*, App. No. 54357/2015.

[64] For a full account, see D. Smith and P. Chamberlain, *Blacklisted: The Secret War Between Big Business and Union Activists* (2nd edn, Oxford: New Internationalist Publications, 2016). See also F. Kahraman, 'A New Era for Labor Activism? Strategic Mobilisation of Human Rights Against Blacklisting' (2017) 43 *Law and Social Inquiry* 1279.

[65] See esp. HC 1071 (2012–13), HC 453 (2013–14), HC 272 (2014–15) (exhaustive inquiry by the Scottish Affairs Committee).

[66] *Smith* v. *United Kingdom*, App. No. 54357/15, 20 April 2017.

[67] *Brough* v. *United Kingdom* [2013] ECHR 336.

[68] TULRCA 1992, ss. 146–67. Note that, although a 'worker' may not bring an unfair dismissal claim under TULRCA 1992, s. 152, he or she may do so under TULRCA 1992, s. 146.

such membership).[69] This is considered more fully below.[70] In none of these cases – including unfair-dismissal proceedings – is there a qualifying period of employment before an application may be made.[71] The remedy for a worker who suffers a detriment is compensation,[72] with the normal remedies applying in the case of unfair dismissal with some adaptations.[73] The law has been changed on a number of occasions since being introduced in its present form in the mid-1970s, most recently following the *Wilson and Palmer* case, a long-running saga that ended in the ECtHR, the third major case on freedom of association to make its way to Strasbourg from the UK.[74]

The *Wilson and Palmer* Case

The leading case on TULRCA 1992, section 146 is *Wilson* v. *Associated Newspapers Ltd.*[75] That case involved an example not of exclusion or black-listing, but of discrimination arising in circumstances where the employer derecognised a union. It then treated less favourably those workers who – like Mr Wilson – chose to have their employment conditions continue to be governed by a collective agreement, rather than by a personal contract negoti-ated with the employer on a one-to-one basis. As already suggested, this raised important questions about the scope of what is now TULRCA 1992, section 146,[76] and what is meant by trade union membership for this purpose. Does it mean the right to protection simply for holding a union card, or does it mean more to include protection from discrimination for using the services or benefits of trade-union membership?

Mr Wilson complained that his employer, the *Daily Mail*, had derecognised his union, the NUJ, and introduced personal contracts to replace the collect-ively agreed terms. Those employees who were prepared to enter into a personal contract were provided with a financial bonus, which was denied to those employees, like Mr Wilson, who insisted on being paid under the terms of the collective agreements which had been terminated. An industrial tribunal held that Mr Wilson had been discriminated against unlawfully on the ground of his trade union membership. But the employer appealed successfully to the EAT, which held that the discrimination against Mr Wilson had not been on

---

[69] TULRCA 1992, ss. 146(3) and 152(3).   [70] See pp. 510–20.

[71] TULRCA 1992, s. 154, which also disapplies ERA 1996, s. 109(1).

[72] TULRCA 1992, s. 149. Awards may be made against third parties: *ibid.*, s. 150.

[73] Notably, the minimum basic award (TULRCA 1992, s. 156), and interim relief (see pp. 506–9). Awards may be made against third parties: *ibid.*, s. 160.

[74] The other two were *Young, James and Webster* v. *United Kingdom*, discussed at pp. 513–14; and *Council of Civil Service Unions* v. *United Kingdom* (1988) 10 EHRR 269, discussed later in this chapter.

[75] [1995] 2 AC 454.

[76] The legislation in force at the time of the disputed conduct of the employer was the Employment Protection (Consolidation) Act 1978, s. 23.

account of his trade union membership, a view with which the Court of Appeal disagreed following Mr Wilson's appeal.

In this game of ping-pong, the employer then moved the case to the House of Lords, which held that there had been no unlawful discrimination. There were two reasons for the House of Lords decision. The first was that the protection against discriminatory treatment on the ground of trade union membership applied only to action short of dismissal: it did not also apply to omissions. The second reason for the decision was that the conduct of the employer was in any event not for reasons of trade union membership, a term that was narrowly defined to exclude discrimination for making use of the services of a trade union. According to Lord Bridge of Harwich, to equate membership with using the 'essential' services of that union would put 'an unnecessary and imprecise gloss on the statutory language'.[77]

In so holding, the House of Lords appeared to depart from an EAT decision in *Discount Tobacco & Confectioners Ltd* v. *Armitage (Note)*.[78] However, this decision of the House of Lords did not exhaust the legal proceedings, with Mr Wilson making a complaint – this time against the UK government – to the ECtHR. Together with a number of members of the RMT who were involved in similar litigation, which had been conjoined with his in the Court of Appeal and the House of Lords, Mr Wilson alleged that the conduct of his employer violated his Convention rights, for which the UK government was responsible. In light of previous jurisprudence,[79] this was an ambitious claim to be made in a court that had yet to uphold a complaint from a trade unionist that his or her rights to freedom of association as protected by ECHR, Article 11, had been violated. Nevertheless, he was joined by Terry Palmer and a group of RMT members nursing a similar grievance against Associated British Ports.

The Strasbourg Application

The first task of the Court in *Wilson and Palmer* v. *United Kingdom*[80] was to address the fact that the alleged violation had been by an employer and not by the state. Here, the Court acknowledged that 'the essential object of Article 11 is to protect the individual against arbitrary interference by public authorities with the exercise of the rights protected'.[81] But it also contended that there 'may' be 'positive obligations to secure the effective enjoyment of these rights', and concluded that the 'responsibility' of the UK is engaged if the problems encountered by the applicants in this case resulted from a failure on the government's part 'to secure to the applicants under domestic law the rights set forth in Article 11 of the Convention'.[82] The responsibility of the

---

[77] [1995] 2 AC 454, at 478.   [78] [1995] ICR 431.
[79] See M. Forde, 'The European Convention on Human Rights and Labor Law' (1983) 31 *American Journal of Comparative Law* 301.
[80] [2002] ECHR 552.   [81] *Ibid.*, para. 41.   [82] *Ibid.*

state thus engaged, the Court's attention turned to the scope of that responsibility. Here, the Court noted that Article 11 was not a protection of the right to form and join trade unions; but a right to form and join trade unions *for the protection of his interests*. At this point, the Court stressed that the words in italics were not redundant, and that the state must both permit and make possible the freedom of trade unions to protect the occupational interests of trade union members by trade union action.[83] But rehearsing jurisprudence that has since been repudiated,[84] this did not mean that the state was under a duty to require employers to engage in collective bargaining.

Without at this stage departing from the line that Article 11 does not 'secure any particular treatment of trade unions or their members', but leaves each state a free choice of the means to be used to secure the right to be heard,[85] the Court nevertheless made two significant advances. First, it appeared to establish the right of workers to be represented by a trade union, observing in a crucial passage that:

> The Court agrees with the Government that the essence of a voluntary system of collective bargaining is that it must be possible for a trade union which is not recognised by an employer to take steps including, if necessary, organising industrial action, with a view to persuading the employer to enter into collective bargaining with it on those issues which the union believes are important for its members' interests. Furthermore, it is of the essence of the right to join a trade union for the protection of their interests that employees should be free to instruct or permit the union to make representations to their employer or to take action in support of their interests on their behalf. If workers are prevented from so doing, their freedom to belong to a trade union, for the protection of their interests, becomes illusory. It is the role of the State to ensure that trade union members are not prevented or restrained from using their union to represent them in attempts to regulate their relations with their employers.[86]

Secondly, the Court commented adversely on UK law that allowed employers to offer 'employees who acquiesced in the termination of collective bargaining substantial pay rises, which were not provided to those who refused to sign contracts accepting the end of union representation'.[87] The corollary of this, said the Court, was that 'United Kingdom law permitted employers to treat less favourably employees who were not prepared to renounce a freedom that was an essential feature of union membership'.[88] This was said to constitute 'a disincentive or restraint on the use by employees of union membership to protect their interests'.[89] It was also a breach of Article 11:

> Under United Kingdom law at the relevant time it was, therefore, possible for an employer effectively to undermine or frustrate a trade union's ability to strive for

[83] *Ibid.*, para. 42.   [84] *Demir and Baykara* v. *Turkey* [2010] ECHR 1345.
[85] [2002] ECHR 552, para. 42.   [86] *Ibid.*, para. 46.   [87] *Ibid.*, para. 47.   [88] *Ibid.*
[89] *Ibid.*

the protection of its members' interests. The Court notes that this aspect of domestic law has been the subject of criticism by the Social Charter's Committee of Independent Experts and the ILO's Committee on Freedom of Association ... It considers that, by permitting employers to use financial incentives to induce employees to surrender important union rights, the respondent State has failed in its positive obligation to secure the enjoyment of the rights under Article 11 of the Convention. This failure amounted to a violation of Article 11, as regards both the applicant trade unions and the individual applicants.[90]

Apart from establishing another head of liability, this last passage introduces two additional points of note, in a decision already heavily pregnant with interest. The first is the reference to other international treaties and their significance for the construction of Article 11, and the other is that the rights of both the individual applicants *and* the trade unions had been violated by the conduct of the employer. This gave rise to an expectation that the law would be changed not only to protect the individual employee from discriminatory conduct by the employer, but also (and unusually in the UK context) to give the trade union access to legal proceedings to assert its Convention rights. As we shall see, it is not clear that the government implemented this decision to the fullest extent possible, or indeed to the fullest extent required. One final point that may be noted relates to the remedy, the individual workers recovering €7,730 each for injury to feelings, and the unions recovering some of their legal costs incurred in both the domestic legal proceedings and before the Convention organs. Curiously, however, the individual workers were not entitled to recover for loss of earnings, 'namely the loss of the pay increases which were awarded to their co-workers who signed individual contracts'.[91] In rejecting these claims, the Court accepted a government submission that:

> this claim was misconceived, because if domestic law had forbidden employers from offering incentives to employees in exchange for their agreement not to engage in collective bargaining, the obvious inference was that the employers would not have offered financial incentives to any of their employees.[92]

Legislative Responses to *Wilson and Palmer*

Before the *Wilson and Palmer* cases were heard by the Strasbourg court, the newly elected Labour government brought forward amending legislation in 1999.[93] But that legislation dealt with only one of the two grounds of the House of Lords decision, and in any event – not being retrospective – provided

---

[90] *Ibid.*, para. 48.
[91] *Ibid.*, para. 55. This was said to vary from approximately £1,300 to approximately £14,200.
[92] *Ibid.*, para. 56.   [93] Employment Relations Act 1999, s. 2 and Sched. 2.

little comfort to Mr Wilson and his fellow victims. The ERA 1999 made it clear that the protection against discrimination applies to both acts and omissions, but failed to deal with the question of the scope of the protection, that is to say the narrow reading by the House of Lords of what is meant by the term 'membership of an independent trade union'. Even after the 1999 Act, there were still questions about the extent to which TULRCA 1992, sections 146 and 152, offered protection from discrimination for using trade union services (paragraph 46 of the *Wilson and Palmer* judgment), and also about the extent to which it was lawful for an employer to offer financial inducements to a worker to give up trade union representation and collective bargaining rights (paragraph 48 of the *Wilson and Palmer* judgment). Some of these matters were addressed by another round of amendments introduced in the wake of *Wilson and Palmer*.[94]

Trade Union Services and Representation

The 2004 amendments to TULRCA 1992, sections 146 and 152 introduced protection against detriment and dismissal for using the services of a trade union (paragraph 46 of the judgment). Before examining these provisions, however, it is to be pointed out that there was some resistance to the House of Lords decision by the lower courts, and it is hard to believe that the formalism of the latter ruling would have survived intact. In *Specialty Care plc* v. *Pachela*,[95] the applicant care-home workers were dismissed following a dispute about a new shift system. The workers in question were summoned to a disciplinary meeting after which they were dismissed, a tribunal finding that they had been dismissed for having 'joined the trade union and sought to use the trade union as the means of making their protest'. The employer appealed against the finding of unfair dismissal on the ground of trade union membership, but the appeal was dismissed. The EAT took the view that *Wilson and Palmer* was principally about discrimination by way of omission, and that the remarks about trade union membership were *obiter* and inconclusive. Tribunals were advised by the EAT that it was their task in trade union membership cases:

> to find as a fact whether or not the reason or principal reason for dismissal related to the applicant's trade union membership not only by reference to whether he or she had simply joined a union, but also by reference to whether the introduction of union representation into the employment relationship had led the employer to dismiss the employee.[96]

These matters have been addressed by the Employment Relations Act 2004, which amends TULRCA 1992, sections 146 and 152, in the case of section 146 to provide that a worker has the right not to be subjected to any detriment

---

[94] Employment Relations Act 2004, ss. 29–32.   [95] [1996] ICR 633 (EAT).   [96] *Ibid.*, p. 643.

as an individual – by any act or deliberate failure to act – by the employer, if the act or failure to act takes place for 'the sole or main purpose' of 'preventing or deterring the worker in question from making use of the services of a trade union at an appropriate time, or penalizing him [or her] for doing so'.[97] The services of a trade union are defined to mean 'services available to the worker by an independent trade union by virtue of his [or her] membership of the union',[98] while the term 'making use' of trade union services includes the worker 'consenting to the raising of a matter on his [or her] behalf by an independent trade union of which he [or she] is a member'.[99] It is also provided that a worker will be protected where a union raises a matter on behalf of the worker, with or without his or her consent.[100] So trade-union services include being represented by a trade union (for example, in disciplinary or grievance disputes) and having one's concerns being raised by a trade union (although the protection applies only if one is a member).[101]

Links are also made with the second group of amendments introduced by the Employment Relations Act 2004 designed to address *Wilson and Palmer*. These are the provisions of what is now TULRCA 1992, sections 145A and 145B (addressing paragraph 48 of the judgment), considered more fully below.[102] For present purposes, it is enough to note that the latter provisions are designed to discourage employers from offering inducements of various kinds to workers, including inducements to give up trade union membership, trade union activities, or the use of trade union services (TULRCA 1992, section 145A) and/or to give up collective bargaining protection (TULRCA 1992, section 145B). A worker has the right not to suffer a detriment or to be dismissed because of a failure to accept such an inducement. More than that, if the employer makes an inducement and the worker declines, the failure of the employer to pay the benefit offered is to be taken as subjecting the worker to a detriment. So the worker is entitled to the benefit of the inducement, without the terms demanded by the employer.

But although the protection thus appears wide ranging, there are two major limitations. The first relates to the definition of trade union services, with TULRCA 1992, section 145B(4), providing that 'having terms of employment determined by collective agreement shall not be regarded for the purposes of section 145A (or section 146 or 152) as making use of a trade union service'. This is an extraordinary qualification in light of the decision that led to the introduction of TULRCA 1992, section 145B, in the first place, the significance of which will be addressed below. The second limitation is that, while the

---

[97] TULRCA 1992, s. 146(1)(ba). See also TULRCA 1992, s. 152(1)(ba) (unfair dismissal).

[98] TULRCA 1992, s. 146(2A)(a). See also TULRCA 1992, s. 152(2A)(a) (unfair dismissal).

[99] TULRCA 1992, s. 146(2A)(b). See also TULRCA 1992, s. 152(2A)(b) (unfair dismissal).

[100] TULRCA 1992, s. 146(2B). See also TULRCA 1992, s. 152(2B) (unfair dismissal).

[101] TULRCA 1992, s. 146(2A)(a) and (2B). See also TULRCA 1992 (2A)(a) and (2B) (unfair dismissal).

[102] See pp. 497–8.

worker is now protected from detriment and dismissal for using trade union services, there is no obligation on the part of the employer to permit the worker to use these services, in the sense that the right applies only at 'an appropriate time', which – if during working hours – means with the consent of the employer.[103] There are, however, separate provisions in the Employment Relations Act 1999, section 10, that give workers the right to be accompanied in grievance and disciplinary cases. But this is not unqualified, and neither the Employment Relations Act 1999 nor the TULRCA 1992 gives any right to be represented by a union when seeking to renegotiate terms of employment.[104]

Discriminatory Inducements

The second change introduced by the Employment Relations Act 2004 was to address the question of financial inducements to workers to persuade them to give up trade union rights and collective bargaining benefits. This may be done either as part of a process of derecognition of the union (as in *Wilson*) or as part of a process (deliberate or otherwise) to weaken a union. In addressing these matters (following paragraphs 47 and 48 of the *Wilson and Palmer* decision), the government did so in a characteristically clumsy way. By virtue of what is now TULRCA 1992, section 145A, a worker has 'a right not to have an offer made to him by his employer for the sole or main purpose of inducing the worker (a) not to be or seek to become a member of an independent trade union, (b) not to take part, at an appropriate time, in the activities of an independent trade union, (c) not to make use, at an appropriate time, of trade union services, or (d) to be or become a member of any trade union or of a particular trade union or of one of a number of particular trade unions'.[105] An appropriate time is defined as above, as are the terms 'trade union services' and 'making use' of trade union services. So far, so good.

These provisions of TULRCA 1992, section 145A are accompanied by TULRCA 1992, section 145B, which provides that a worker – 'who is a member of an independent trade union which is recognised, or seeking to be recognised, by his employer' – has the right not to have an offer made to him by his employer if '(a) acceptance of the offer, together with other workers' acceptance of offers which the employer also makes to them, would have the prohibited result, and (b) the employer's sole or main purpose in making the offers is to achieve that result'. The prohibited result for these purposes is that the workers' terms of employment, or any of those terms, will

---

[103] TULRCA 1992, s. 146(2). See also TULRCA 1992, s. 152(2) (unfair dismissal).

[104] See Employment Relations Act 1999, ss. 10 and 13(5). The latter provides that '[f]or the purposes of section 10 a grievance hearing is a hearing which concerns the performance of a duty by an employer in relation to a worker'.

[105] TULRCA 1992, s. 145A.

not (or will no longer) be determined by collective agreement negotiated by or on behalf of the union.[106] This was probably designed to apply to the type of situation evident in *Wilson and Palmer*, where inducements to come off collective agreements were part of a process of derecognition. That said, the legislation as drafted would not appear to apply to the facts as they unfolded in the *Wilson* case. Section 145A operates only where the union is recognised or seeking recognition. In *Wilson* in contrast, the union was already derecognised at the time of the inducement. Not so good.

One possible - perhaps unintended - benefit of TULRCA 1992, section 145B was revealed in *Kostal UK Ltd* v. *Dunkley*,[107] where the employer went over the head of a union to offer new terms to employees individually in order to break a deadlock in negotiations. However, the Court of Appeal reversed an EAT decision that section 145B is engaged because in such a situation the workers' terms and conditions on the matter or matters under offer will cease – at least for the time being – to be determined by a collective agreement.

A worker or former worker who has received a prohibited inducement may reject the inducement and seek a declaration and a financial award from an ET.[108] If the complaint is upheld, the worker will be entitled to recover a payment of £4,059 in relation to each breach, with each complaint raising the possibility that more than one term is no longer to be the subject of collective bargaining, as in *Kostal UK Ltd*, where the employer made an offer to individual workers relating to two terms, leading to a financial award of £418,000 in the workers' favour.[109] If, however, the worker accepts the inducement, any agreement made as a result is not enforceable against the worker, while any payment made to him or her as part of the inducement is not recoverable by the employer.[110] A problem arises, however, where the employer makes the inducement only to 'soft targets' within the workforce, and seeks deliberately to isolate activists. In these circumstances, neither the union nor the workers who are not induced have any right to complain, an omission which drew criticism in several rounds of supervision from the European Committee of Social Rights, on the ground of incompatibility with the European Social Charter, Article 6(2). According to the Committee, the union should have standing to vindicate 'its own right to collective bargaining'.[111]

---

[106] TULRCA 1992, s. 145B(2).   [107] [2019] EWCA Civ 1009.   [108] TULRCA 1992, s. 145E.
[109] A worker may also claim to have suffered a detriment under TULRCA 1992, s. 146, if an inducement is scorned by the worker in question but paid to others: 'not conferring a benefit that, if the offer had been accepted by the worker, would have been conferred on him under the resulting agreement shall be taken to be subjecting him to a detriment as an individual (and to be a deliberate failure to act)': TULRCA 1992, s. 146(2D).
[110] TULRCA 1992, s. 145E(4).
[111] European Committee of Social Rights, Conclusions XX-3 (2014) (United Kingdom). The exclusion of a right for the union to complain in this situation is all the more curious for the

But although there are thus concerns about the enforcement regime, the unexpected scope of TULRCA 1992, section 145B has nevertheless caused anxiety on the part of employers, in view of potential financial liability. The risks were revealed shortly after the enactment of TULRCA 1992, section 145B in a dispute between ASDA and the GMB, which represented ASDA staff.[112] In this case, the company offered its workforce a pay rise of 10 per cent to move from collectively agreed terms and conditions to an arrangement in which the employer would deal with each employee individually. Under the company's proposed partnership agreement, the union would continue to be 'recognised' in the sense that it could represent members, its shop stewards would enjoy time-off and other facilities, and the union would enjoy consultation rights under various statutory provisions. These proposals were put to the workforce in a ballot, with 68 per cent voting to reject the company's offer, the union then co-ordinating ET complaints on behalf of 340 workers to whom the offers had been made. In upholding the complaint, the tribunal found that, on the facts, ASDA had made an offer, the sole or main purpose of which was to secure a prohibited result. The 340 applicants were each awarded £2,500, (which was the prescribed statutory sum at the time), the total cost to the company being £850,000.

The GCHQ Case

The protection for trade union membership and activities applies to civil servants as it applies to other workers. There is, however, an exception in TULRCA 1992, section 275, which provides that the application of the Act to Crown employment 'does not apply to employment in respect of which there is in force a certificate issued by or on behalf of a Minister of the Crown certifying that employment of a description specified in the certificate, or the employment of a particular person so specified, is (or, at a time specified in the certificate, was) required to be excepted from that section for the purpose of safeguarding national security'.

That power was exercised in 1984 in relation to staff employed at GCHQ. Steps were also taken under the royal prerogative to alter the terms and conditions of employment of staff at GCHQ, who were no longer to be permitted to remain in membership of trade unions they had been encouraged to join. Those who objected to the arrangements were given the choice of moving to new work in the civil service where they could retain their trade union membership, or be dismissed. A number of workers refused to accept the new terms and refused to be relocated, and so were dismissed, but because of certificates in force under what is now TULRCA 1992, section 275, they were unable to bring claims for unfair dismissal.

---

fact that, in *Wilson and Palmer*, the ECtHR held that the Convention rights of the trade unions had been violated by the employers.

[112] *Davies* v. *ASDA Stores Ltd*, Case No. 2501510/05, 13 February 2006.

Dismissal for trade union membership alone is thought to have been unusual even in the 1980s, and it was more unusual when the employer was the government. The case became a great *cause célèbre*, with a big legal and political campaign waged by the trade unions for the restoration of trade union rights at GCHQ. Judicial review proceedings in the domestic courts to challenge the introduction of the new terms and conditions as being an abuse of power were unsuccessful.[113] So too was an application to Strasbourg, alleging a breach of the ECHR, the European Commission on Human Rights gripping like a limpet to the second sentence of Article 11(2) which provides that 'this article shall not prevent the imposition of lawful restrictions on the exercise of these rights by members of the armed forces, of the police or of the administration of the State'.[114]

The ILO supervisory bodies consistently took a different approach. Both the CFA and the Committee of Experts found that there had been a breach of ILO Convention 87, which (as we saw above) provides by Article 2 that 'workers and employers, without distinction whatso-ever, shall have the right to establish and, subject only to the rules of the organisation concerned, to join organisations of their own choosing without previous authorisation'. However, the then government refused to accept the findings of the ILO supervisory bodies, and, despite repeated requests from the Committee of Experts, the ban remained in place until 1997.[115] It was revoked by the Labour government in what was the early implementa-tion of an election pledge. On 19 May 1997, Robin Cook (Foreign Secretary) announced in the House of Commons that:

[T]he conditions of service of staff at GCHQ have today been changed: they once again have the freedom they previously enjoyed to join any trade union they choose. Talks with the unions will begin as soon as possible to settle future arrangements for staff representation and to secure a collective agreement on no disruption to the work of GCHQ which will ensure that GCHQ's operations are protected from any threat of industrial action.[116]

Victimisation of Workers' Representatives

Apart from exclusion, blacklisting and discrimination, the other threat to trade-union organisation is the victimisation of trade-union activists, includ-ing workplace representatives. Complaints about the growing problem of victimisation have been made in recent years by civil service trade unions,

---

[113] *Council of Civil Service Unions* v. *Minister for the Civil Service* [1985] AC 374.
[114] *Council of Civil Service Unions* v. *United Kingdom* (1988) 10 EHRR 269.
[115] For accounts of the ILO supervisory bodies' response, see K. D. Ewing, *Britain and the ILO* (2nd edn, London: Institute of Employment Rights, 1994); and G. Morris, 'Freedom of Association and the Interests of the State', in K. D. Ewing, C. A. Gearty and B. A. Hepple (eds.), *Human Rights and Labour Law* (London: Mansell, 1994), Ch. 2.
[116] HC Debs., 19 May 1997, cols. 13–14 WA.

by the Unite union (in relation to the bitter dispute with British Airways and elsewhere),[117] and by the RMT in relation to the activists whose cases are considered in the following section. As we have seen, there are supposed to be laws against this, with TULRCA 1992, sections 146, providing protection for a worker against detriment for the sole or main purpose of 'preventing or deterring him from taking part in the activities of an independent trade union at an appropriate time, or penalising him for doing so'. By TULRCA 1992, section 152, there is similar protection in relation to the dismissal of employees.[118] Reading these words carefully but narrowly, however, the Court of Appeal has said that 'it is not enough to show that an employer's action or inaction had the *effect* of causing a detriment to the employee in his trade union activities; it must be shown that this was the purpose or main purpose of the employer's conduct'.[119] Although often arising in the case of naked anti-union activity by an employer, recent cases are a reminder that acts of discrimination sometimes also arise in the context of inter-union rivalry where an established union is seeking to protect its position with an employer.[120]

Nature of the Activity

The protections in TULRCA 1992, sections 146 and 152, apply to participation in the 'activities of an independent trade union', a term that is not defined. However, it has been said by the EAT that the definition applies to activities of a 'wide and varied kind',[121] and the case-law suggests that it would apply to the recruitment of members, the formation of a union branch,[122] as well as 'routine union activities' such as 'participating in ballots, attending meetings,

---

[117] On which, see K. D. Ewing, *Fighting Back: Resisting 'Union-Busting' and 'Strike-Breaking' in the BA Dispute* (London: Institute of Employment Rights, 2011).

[118] On which, see *O'Kelly* v. *Trust House Forte plc* [1984] QB 90. Complaints of dismissal by workers at that time could not be brought under TULRCA 1992, s. 146. See now TULRCA 1992, s. 146(5) and (5A) (dismissal claims by workers who are not employees for the purposes of TULRCA 1992, s. 152).

[119] *Bone* v. *North Essex Partnership NHS Foundation Trust* [2016] EWCA Civ 45, [2016] IRLR 295.

[120] See *Bone* v. *North Essex Partnership NHS Foundation Trust* [2014] EWCA Civ 652, [2014] ICR 1053 and [2016] EWCA Civ 45, [2016] IRLR 295, where the applicant was a member of the Workers of England Trade Union at a workplace where UNISON was the recognised union. UNISON took exception to the Workers Union of England and UNISON representatives expressed hostility to the applicant to which the employer did little to respond, giving rise to a complaint under TULRCA 1992, s. 146. In the first case (2014) the Court of Appeal rejected arguments for the employer that s. 146 did not apply because the Workers of England was not an independent trade union. In the second case (2016) a different Court of Appeal held that the employer subjected Mr Bone to detriment 'by their deliberate failure to act, and did so for the main purpose of preventing him or deterring him from taking part in the activities of the WUE'. This was an unusual case, though see also *Serco Ltd* v. *Dahou* [2015] IRLR 30, [2016] EWCA Civ 832, [2017] IRLR 81 (claimant a member of RMT where Community already recognised).

[121] *Dixon* v. *West Ella Developments Ltd* [1978] ICR 856.

[122] See *Lyon* v. *St James Press* [1976] ICR 413.

arranging or participating in gatherings'.[123] Its application to internal union matters was confirmed by *British Airways Engine Overhaul Ltd* v. *Francis*,[124] which also raises wider questions about employee free speech. Mrs Francis was employed as an aircraft component worker in South Wales. She was also a shop steward for the Amalgamated Union of Engineering Workers (AUEW), representing twenty-seven women workers. The women were involved in a long-standing equal pay dispute, and were concerned that the union was not taking their case seriously. The women met one lunchtime and resolved to secure press publicity for their campaign. A few days later, the *Western Mail* carried a statement by Mrs Francis in which she was critical of the union's failure to carry out its policy of securing equal pay for women. Mrs Francis was thereafter reprimanded by her employer for acting contrary to company regulations by making statements to the 'press or otherwise' about company business.

Thereupon Mrs Francis brought proceedings alleging a breach of the SDA 1975, in the course of which the industrial tribunal referred her to the Employment Protection Act 1975, section 53 (now TULRCA 1992, section 146). The claim for breach of the SDA failed, but the tribunal found a breach of section 53. In upholding the latter decision, the EAT said that 'discussion of matters with which an independent trade union is concerned' is 'quite capable of being an activity of an independent trade union within the meaning of the section'.[125] Noting that 'these women were getting together, as union members, to discuss matters with which the independent trade union was concerned', the EAT also said that:

> it does not seem to us to be conclusive against Mrs Francis's claim that they did not do so at a meeting of some committee or at a formal meeting of the branch. They were a well-defined group of the union, meeting with their shop steward, and even though the criticism which they might be making might not be acceptable to higher branches, or higher officials in the union, it seems to us that they were still engaged in their discussion, their criticism, and in their resolution, in the activities of an independent trade union.[126]

This is not to say that there are no limitations on the scope of the protection. So in *Chant* v. *Aquaboats Ltd*,[127] the applicant organised a petition about health and safety matters, which he had vetted by his local union office before it was presented to the employer. It was held that his dismissal was not because of participation in the activities of an independent trade union: these were the activities of an individual trade unionist.[128] It has also been said that the protection does not apply to 'wholly unreasonable, extraneous or malicious acts done in support of trade union activities'.[129] But it is difficult to find

---

[123] *Serco Ltd* v. *Dahou* [2015] IRLR 30, para. 46.   [124] [1981] ICR 278.   [125] *Ibid.*, p. 284.
[126] *Ibid.*   [127] [1978] ICR 643.   [128] See also *Serco Ltd* v. *Dahou* [2015] IRLR 30.
[129] *Lyon* v. *St James' Press Ltd* [1976] ICR 513. Although industrial action is obviously a trade union activity, it may neverthless be excluded because not undertaken at an 'appropriate time'. See below. As pointed out in *Serco Ltd* v. *Dahou* [2015] IRLR 30, 'Industrial action will rarely (if ever) take place at an appropriate time given the requirement of consent to activities during

examples of cases in which applicants have failed because the tribunals or courts have disapproved of the nature of their trade union activities, and it is certainly not the case that the robust representation of the trade union position would take someone outside the protection. So in *Bass Taverns Ltd* v. *Burgess*,[130] the appellant was a trainer of new managers who resigned after being demoted for what he had said at an induction course, claiming that he had been constructively dismissed on the ground of his trade union activities. Mr Burgess was also a member of the National Association of Licensed House Managers and, during the induction course in question, had made a presentation on behalf of the union, with the consent of the company.

During the course of the presentation, Mr Burgess had some harsh words to say about the physical risks encountered by pub managers: 'You will get threatened and if you get hurt it will be the union who will fight for you, not the company. At the end of the day the company is concerned with profits and this comes before everything else.' The remarks were reported to senior management, leading to the disciplinary action and the resignation. An industrial tribunal found that Mr Burgess had been unfairly dismissed for taking part in trade union activities. The EAT upheld the employer's appeal that, although the dismissal was unfair, it was not for trade union activities. This would affect the amount of compensation which Mr Burgess could recover. The Court of Appeal unanimously restored the finding of the industrial tribunal, with Pill LJ saying that there was

> nothing beyond the rhetoric and hyperbole which might be expected at a recruiting meeting for a trade union or, for that matter, some other organisation or cause. Neither dishonesty nor bad faith are suggested. While harmonious relations between a company and a union are highly desirable, a union recruiting meeting cannot realistically be limited to that object. A consent which at the same time prevents the recruiter from saying anything adverse about the employer is no real consent. Given that there was consent to use the meeting as a forum for recruitment, it cannot be regarded as an 'abuse of privilege' to make remarks to employees which are critical of the company.[131]

Timing of the Activity

As already pointed out, the protection in respect of trade union activities applies only where these activities take place at an 'appropriate time', as defined in TULRCA 1992, sections 146(2) and 152(2). Reflecting the

---

working time and so will rarely constitute an activity within this sub-section'. But referring to *Britool* v. *Roberts* [1993] IRLR 481, the EAT said that on 'the other hand planning and organising industrial action may be done at an appropriate time, and if so, it will be protected' (para. 46).

[130] [1995] IRLR 596.

[131] *Ibid.*, p. 598. For a similarly expansive view relying on Burgess, see *Morris* v. *Metrolink RATP Dev Ltd* [2019] ICR 90 (CA).

provisions of ILO Convention 98, this means that the protection applies only where the activities are undertaken outside working hours, or within working hours with the consent of the employer.[132] The consent of the employer is thus not required where the trade union activities are undertaken on the employer's premises but outside working hours, as for example during meal breaks (even though the employee is being paid by the employer),[133] or before work has started, or after it has finished, provided that the activities are undertaken at a time when the employee is entitled to be on the premises. According to the House of Lords in a case concerning the Post Office, an employee who is a member of a trade union is entitled 'to take part in the activities of his union while he is on his employer's premises but is not actually working'.[134] This would give trade union lay officials the opportunity to distribute leaflets, hold informal meetings, recruit members and collect subscriptions.[135]

The exercise of rights of this kind raises questions about the extent to which the employer has the power to determine the purposes for which his or her private property may be used. But just as it was shown in *Francis* that the legislation takes priority over the employer's contractual rights, so the *Post Office* case also shows that it displaces the employer's property rights. It was pointed out in the latter case that the employer must be prepared to accept that his or her normal property rights will be affected and to put up with what may be a minor inconvenience, although the employer is not expected to 'incur expense or submit to substantial inconvenience'.[136] It is important to emphasise, however, the difference between the law in the books and the operation of the law in practice. It is all very well for the law to say that workers have the right to engage in trade union activities on the employer's property without employer consent. But that may mean very little in practice if the employer is known to be hostile to the actions of the employees concerned, and willing to take steps to prevent them by dismissal if necessary.

The consent of the employer will be required, however, where the activities are to be undertaken during working hours. It will often be given formally and expressly in a 'facilities agreement' to accredited shop stewards.[137] But it can also arise as a matter of custom and practice, although as was pointed out by the Court of Appeal in *Marley Tile Co. Ltd* v. *Shaw*,[138] this can be very difficult

---

[132] 'Working hours' is defined to mean 'any time when, in accordance with his contract of employment, he is required to be at work': TULRCA 1992, ss. 146(2) and 152(2).
[133] *Zucker* v. *Astrid Jewels Ltd* [1978] ICR 1088.
[134] *Post Office* v. *Union of Post Office Workers* [1974] ICR 378.
[135] It is important to emphasise that these rights are not confined to situations where the union is recognised by the employer, but may be used by employees who are representatives of a union which is seeking recognition. This is not to deny that workers in such circumstances will encounter difficulties in trying to build up organisation in this way, as employers may restrict the movement of workers in a building and there may be few opportunities in modern workplaces for a trade union representative to secure access to a workforce as a whole.
[136] *Post Office* v. *Union of Post Office Workers* [1974] ICR 378, at p. 400.
[137] For an example of such a provision, see Chapter 14.   [138] [1980] ICR 72.

to establish. In *Zucker* v. *Astrid Jewels Ltd*,[139] on the other hand, it was suggested that the consent need not be a consent specifically to engage in trade union activities, but may be implied from a consent to engage generally in activities which may include trade union activities:

> For example, if it be the case that the employees while working are permitted to converse upon anything they feel like conversing upon with fellow employees working nearby, there seems to be no reason why they should not, amongst other things, converse upon trade union activities; and if they were to do so, and if such conversation were generally allowed, to the extent that it did not interfere with the proper completion of the work or otherwise cause disruption, there seems no reason why an Industrial Tribunal, in such circumstances, could not come to the conclusion that, although there was no express arrangement or express consent, there was implied consent or implied arrangements.[140]

What happens if the consent is refused? One answer is that, if the union is recognised by the employer for the purposes of collective bargaining, a lay official of the union will be entitled by statute to time-off with pay for trade union duties,[141] these being industrial relations duties with his or her employer, or to undergo training in such duties. These provisions are considered in Chapter 14, but it will be obvious that they provide no assistance where the union is not recognised. Yet it can hardly be said that the union official does not need time off work to attend to his or her trade union duties before the union is recognised: the work of recruitment, organising with a view to recognition, and the servicing of members (even if the union is not recognised), all require the expenditure of time. Questions also arise about the position where consent is withdrawn, a matter considered in *F. W. Farnsworth Ltd* v. *McCoid*,[142] where a shop steward complained that he had been derecognised by the employer because 'the way he conducted himself meant that he was not suited to hold the office of shop steward'. The Court of Appeal rejected the remarkable argument for the employer based on the opening words of TULRCA 1992, section 146(1), then in force, it being contended that 'their effect is that there has to be action short of dismissal taken against the employee as an individual by his employer', the words 'as an individual' being interpreted as meaning 'in his capacity as an employee'.[143] If this argument had been accepted, it would not have been possible for an employee to rely on TULRCA 1992, section 146, where the action was taken against him or her in his or her capacity 'as a shop steward'.

Victimisation and the Problem of Remedies

Although wide-ranging in scope and purposively construed by the tribunals, the protection of workplace representatives is nevertheless seriously flawed in

---

[139] [1978] IRLR 385.   [140] *Ibid.*, p. 387.   [141] TULRCA 1992, s. 168. See Chapter 14.
[142] [1999] ICR 1047.   [143] *Ibid.*, p. 1052.

practice, not least because of the lack of an effective remedy for the enforcement of their rights. When a complaint is made of a breach of TULRCA 1992, section 146, 'it shall be for the employer to show what was the sole or main purpose for which he acted or failed to act', and a similar provision relating to dismissal is to be found in TULRCA 1992, section 98.[144] In *Dahou* v. *Serco Ltd*,[145] however, it was held that a failure on the part of the employer to show a good reason for discriminatory treatment did not necessarily mean that the employee's case would be established as a result (though 'usually no doubt it will'). In the case of dismissal for trade union membership or activity (or services), an employee may make an application to an ET for 'interim relief'.[146] If it appears to the tribunal that it is likely that on determining the complaint it will find that the complainant has been unfairly dismissed, it may ask the employer to reinstate or re-engage the applicant; if the employer refuses, the tribunal may make an order to continue the contract of employment until the determination or settlement of the complaint.[147] But such cases are notoriously difficult to win, and as we explain below legal proceedings may not be enough without industrial muscle to retain someone's job.

The *Lynch* and *Thomas* Cases

The problem of inadequate remedies is highlighted by a high-profile dispute in 2011 between London Underground and the RMT about two separate cases of disciplinary action taken against two workplace representatives of the union, Mr Thomas and Mr Lynch. Mr Thomas was a train operator who had been employed by London Underground for twenty-nine years and had an unblemished disciplinary record. He was a member of the union's executive committee and was assistant branch secretary. On 4 October 2010, Mr Thomas had been engaged in two altercations with other London Underground employees and was dismissed for being 'offensive, abusive, intimidating, bullying, malicious or insulting', while not on duty and while not in uniform. It appears to have been accepted that Mr Thomas's conduct related to 'the activities of an

---

[144] In *Dahou* v. *Serco Ltd* [2016] EWCA Civ 832, [2017] IRLR 81, it was explained that both under s. 146 and s. 152, 'it is for the employee to raise a *prima facie* case. . . If the *prima facie* case is made out, then it is for the employer to show the purpose of his act or the reason for the dismissal, and therefore to prove what were the factors operating on the mind of the decision-maker' (para. 30).

[145] [2016] EWCA Civ 832, [2017] IRLR 81.

[146] TULRCA 1992, s. 161. The application must be brought within seven days of the effective date of dismissal and in some cases must be accompanied by a statement by an official of the union certifying that there are reasonable grounds to believe that the applicant is a victim of anti-union discrimination. The tribunal is required to deal with the matter as soon as practicable after receiving the application, and to this end the employer is entitled to only seven days' notice of the hearing (s. 163).

[147] TULRCA 1992, s. 163. Such an order only requires the employer to pay wages and other benefits. The employer is not required to permit the employee to return to work.

independent trade union', and that it took place at an 'appropriate time', the ET concluding in interim relief proceedings that there was a 'pretty good chance' that a claim under TULRCA 1992, section 152, would be successful.[148] London Underground was not, however, willing to reinstate or re-engage Mr Thomas, leaving the tribunal with the only option of making an order of continuation of the contract of employment.

In a separate development, Mr Lynch was dismissed on 13 October 2010, following an incident with a train he had been driving. In his case, the ET concluded that he too had a 'strong' chance of successfully claiming that he had been dismissed for his trade union activities. Mr Lynch was a health and safety representative, who had developed a reputation of being a 'pain' as far as management was concerned.[149] It appears that he had driven a train in breach of safety procedures, but had done so following (albeit incorrect) instructions and had openly admitted his wrongdoing, while a more severe case involving another employee had been dealt with more leniently. There had also been a failure by London Underground to follow its disciplinary procedures correctly, with Mr Lynch's union/safety roles being referred to during the disciplinary proceedings and being used as an aggravating factor in the disciplinary panel's decision. Here, too, the employer refused to reinstate or re-engage, the tribunal having no option but to make an order for continuation of the contract of employment. An order to this effect was made on 5 November 2010.[150]

Faced with this refusal by the employer to reinstate the workers in question, on 22 November 2010, the union announced that it was balloting its members for industrial action. Two short periods of industrial action on the Bakerloo and Northern Lines took place in December 2010 and January 2011, followed by a fresh ballot in April 2011, in which RMT members voted in favour of further industrial action. With the two men still not reinstated, on 4 May 2011 the union announced six different periods of industrial action, lasting between nine and twenty-four hours each.[151] That was the day an ET ruled that Mr Lynch had been unfairly dismissed.[152] On 10 May 2011, it was announced that the action had been suspended following the re-engagement of Mr Lynch and the agreement of London Underground to hold discussions about Mr Thomas. However, these discussions broke down without an agreement being reached, leading the union on 9 June 2011 to issue fresh threats of industrial action which would begin ten days later. The first bout of industrial action duly went ahead, and it was not until 22 June 2011 that all the action was called off, following the re-engagement of Mr Thomas.[153] Again, this took

---

[148] *Thomas* v. *London Underground Ltd*, Case No. 2358477/2010 (interim relief hearing).

[149] *Lynch* v. *London Underground Ltd*, Case No. 2330511/2010, 2351195/2010, para. 14.

[150] *Lynch* v. *London Underground Ltd*, Case No. 2330511/2010, 2351195/2010 (interim relief hearing).

[151] *Guardian*, 4 May 2011.

[152] *Lynch* v. *London Underground Ltd*, Case No. 2330511/2010, 2351195/2010.

[153] BBC News, 23 June 2011.

place after an ET had found that Mr Thomas had been unfairly dismissed (albeit that he had contributed 50 per cent to his dismissal).[154]

In the *Lynch* case, the clamant was found by the ET to have been unfairly dismissed on a number of grounds: breach of TULRCA 1992, section 152 (trade union activities), ERA 1996, section 100 (health and safety responsibilities) and ERA 1996, section 98 (general unfair dismissal). The unanimous decision of the ET included some sharp comments about London Underground management, expressing concern on a number of occasions about the evidence of a senior manager involved in the decision to dismiss Mr Lynch, highlighting her 'dissembling' as a witness and stating on several occasions that she was 'an unsatisfactory witness'.[155] It is true that the ET found Mr Lynch to be 25 per cent to blame for the dismissal, a finding seized upon with great alacrity by London Underground. It is also true that the legal process was by no means completed by the tribunal decision on the merits, with a remedies hearing having been scheduled for 3 June 2011, in which it is quite possible that the tribunal could have ordered Mr Lynch's reinstatement. But, apart from the fact that that was by no means a guaranteed outcome, it is also the case that, even if reinstatement had been ordered, the employer could not be compelled to reinstate or re-engage an unfairly dismissed employee. It could well have been a rather pyrrhic victory.

Lessons of the *Lynch* and *Thomas* Cases

It is reasonable to speculate that it was the taking of industrial action to reinforce the findings of the employment tribunals that led to the satisfactory resolution of the dispute. For the union, there was an important issue of principle at stake, namely, the duty to protect its workplace representatives, arguably the first duty of any trade union. Following the second tribunal decision in the *Lynch* case, the RMT issued a press release which stated:

> This decision demonstrates beyond any possible doubt that the decision of the RMT to call for industrial action in support of Eamonn Lynch and Arwyn Thomas is wholly reasonable and justifiable. What else could we do?

> Any trade union relies heavily on those members who are prepared to take on the duties of representing their members' interests in addition to their workplace duties. These local officials play a very important role in the union's efforts to improve your working environment and terms and conditions of employment.

> Any member who takes on this role surely should have the support of all fellow trade unionists in the workplace to enable them to carry out their duties without fear of reprisal. This must especially be the case with health and safety representatives in a safety critical industry. Your safety could be compromised if

---

[154] BBC News, 22 June 2011; *Evening Standard*, 22 June 2011.
[155] *Lynch* v. *London Underground Ltd*, Case No. 2330511/2010, 2351195/2010, paras. 67 and 110.

people are increasingly reluctant to come forward to act as health and safety representatives based on what has happened in this case.

What would it say about our trade union or indeed trade unions generally if this wholly unfair treatment of Eamonn Lynch and Arwyn Thomas was to go unanswered?

Perhaps inevitably, the RMT attracted a great deal of criticism for its decision to take industrial action to defend its representatives.[156] It was said that the action was disproportionate, though proportionality is relative. From the point of view of the union, the inconvenience to the travelling public would be greatly outweighed by the need to ensure that its frontline officials were not the easy targets of alleged victimisation, conduct by the employer that threatens if not the existence of the union then certainly its capacity for robust representation. From the point of view of Mr Lynch and Mr Thomas, the inconvenience of the travelling public would be nothing as compared to the consequences for them of losing their job and consequently their livelihood for asserting what is universally acknowledged (at least in legal texts, if not in the *Daily Mail*) as a fundamental human right. There are no other employers of tube drivers. And, while from the point of view of the employer, politicians and the travelling public it may seem disproportionate to take industrial action for the benefit of two individuals, the answer lies not in imposing further controls on the ability of trade unions to take strike action (as some had proposed and have now been implemented),[157] but in having better legal procedures in place to ensure that disputes of the kind on display here can be resolved without the need for industrial action in the first place.

One answer to the problem in this case would be to say that workplace representatives should be better protected. The United Kingdom has ratified ILO Convention 135 (the Workers' Representatives Convention, 1971).

ILO Convention 135, Article 1

Workers' representatives in the undertaking shall enjoy effective protection against any act prejudicial to them, including dismissal, based on their status or activities as a workers' representative or on union membership or participation in union activities, insofar as they act in conformity with existing laws or collective agreements or other jointly agreed arrangements.

---

[156] *Daily Mail*, 5 May 2011.

[157] *Evening Standard*, 9 May 2011 (reporting Boris Johnson's demands for tougher laws). New restrictions were introduced by the Trade Union Act 2016, ss. 2 and 3 in particular, which would directly affect the RMT action in the *Lynch* and *Thomas* cases, on which see Chapter 16.

Workers' representatives for this purpose include 'trade union representatives, namely, representatives designated or elected by trade unions or by members of such unions'.[158] ILO Recommendation 143 (the Workers' Representatives Recommendation, 1971) provides some guidance as to what this protection should mean in practice. It suggests the need for a requirement of consultation with, an advisory opinion from, or agreement of, an independent body, public or private, or a joint body, 'before the dismissal of a workers' representative becomes final'.[159] In other words, there should be no dismissal until the employer has the approval of an appropriate public official or judicial body, placing the onus firmly on the employer to justify in advance the dismissal of any workplace representative.

The principles underpinning ILO Recommendation 143 are reflected in the law and practice of other EU Member States, where it is typically the case that workers' representatives cannot be dismissed without the approval in advance of a labour inspector or a labour court. In Germany, members of the works council may be dismissed only with the prior approval of the works council. If this is not forthcoming, the employer has the right to apply to a labour court to supersede the decision of the works council, the crucial point being that prior approval of the dismissal is required.[160] In France, trade union delegates in the workplace are protected workers who enjoy special protection because of their special vulnerability. This protection takes many forms, but there can be no dismissal without the prior approval of a labour inspector, before whom the worker has a right of audience and from whose decision an appeal lies to the administrative courts.[161] Any dismissal without prior authorisation is void, and the worker has the right to be reinstated in his or her employment, with the right to full pay between the date of dismissal and the date of reinstatement. The worker who does not want to be reinstated is entitled to substantial financial compensation.

Trade Union Security and the Right Not to Join

TULRCA 1992, sections 137, 146 and 152, apply to protection not only on the basis of trade union membership, but on the basis also of non-membership of a trade union. So it is unlawful to refuse employment to someone because he or she is not a member of a trade union (section 137), unlawful for a worker to be subjected to any detriment with a view to compelling him or her to become a member of a trade union, and unfair to dismiss an employee for the same reason (sections 146 and 152). The remedies are as above in relation to

---

[158] ILO Convention 135, Art. 3.   [159] ILO Recommendation 143, Art. 6(b).

[160] M. Weiss and M. Schmidt, 'Germany', in R. Blanpain (ed.), *International Encyclopaedia of Labour Law and Industrial Relations*, vol. 7 (2010), para. 311.

[161] M. Despax and J.-P. Laborde, 'France', in R. Blanpain (ed.), *International Encyclopaedia of Labour Law and Industrial Relations*, vol. 7 (2010), paras. 276–81.

TULRCA 1992, sections 137, 146 and 152. Notably, in all cases an ET may make an award of a compensation against a third party, such as a trade union which has pressurised the employer to act unlawfully.[162] These measures are designed to prohibit or render unenforceable various closed-shop practices whereby employees are required to be members of a trade union as a condition of obtaining employment (the pre-entry closed shop) or to join a trade union within a prescribed number of days of securing employment (the post-entry closed shop). The latter in particular operated openly in the UK either as a matter of custom and practice in a particular workplace, or as a matter of formal agreement between the employer and a trade union.[163] It is important to emphasise that, although the law has moved to recognise a right not to join a trade union, the exercise of this right is likely to have an adverse impact on the substance, quality and effect of the right of those workers who do wish to form and join trade unions, and to act collectively for the protection of their individual interests.

The Closed Shop and Organisational Security

The closed shop was one of the most hotly contested issues of UK labour law in the post-war period. It was strongly defended by trade unions on a number of grounds. The pre-entry closed shop had a labour supply function in the sense that the unions in question could control not only the quality of labour entering the market, but also the supply of that labour. By restricting supply, the union could enhance the wages of its members. But the pre-entry closed shop flourished in only a few industries. The post-entry closed shop was much more common. Although it did not have a 'labour-supply' function, it did have an 'organisational-security' function which it shared with the pre-entry closed shop. This means that collective action could not be undermined by non-union employees, which was particularly important in the case of a strike.

Where there was a closed-shop arrangement in place, those who broke the strike ran the risk of expulsion from the union, and dismissal from their employment as a result. Not unrelated to either the 'labour supply' and 'organisational security' functions, the closed shop also had what some might see as a 'fairness' function. It is sometimes argued that all workers in an enterprise benefit from the activities of the union, such as the negotiation of collective agreements, so that it is only fair that all should contribute to its costs. A close analogy would be motor insurance. We all benefit from the insurance system and we are all required to contribute. A different emphasis was provided by the Royal Commission on Trade Unions and Employers' Associations, which reported in 1968 that:

---

[162] TULRCA 1992, ss. 142, 150 and 160.
[163] The classic study is W. E. J. McCarthy, *The Closed Shop in Britain* (Oxford: Blackwell, 1964). Also, S. Dunn and J. Gennard, *The Closed Shop in British Industry* (London: Macmillan, 1984).

The two most convincing arguments for the closed shop ... depend upon the close link between effective collective bargaining and strong trade unions. The first is that in some industries it is difficult or impossible for a union to establish effective and stable organisation without the help of the closed shop; the second is that even where membership can be recruited and retained without its assistance there are instances where it is needed to deploy the workers' bargaining strength to the full.[164]

But although the 'trade union arguments seem so reasonable and plausible',[165] the closed shop was strongly opposed by some on overlapping grounds relating to individual liberty and economic efficiency. So far as the former is concerned, it is argued that no one should be compelled to join a trade union against his or her wishes. The liberty argument relates not only to the fact that an individual may be required to join a trade union as a condition of employment, but that in doing so the individual may be placed in a position where membership of a trade union compromises conscientious or religious beliefs, or requires the individual to associate with an organisation with political objects with which he or she disagrees. It is also the case that, as a member of a trade union, the individual may be required by the rules of the union to participate in certain activities and support various causes to which he or she objects. Failure to do so could lead to expulsion from the union and ultimately dismissal by the employer. Experience in this and other countries reveals, however, that there are ways of minimising these potential problems by finding a compromise which respects the interests of the majority and the claims of the minority.

The strength of the economic arguments will depend on the nature of the closed-shop arrangement. The pre-entry closed shop is said to give trade unions 'the coercive power to prevent the employment of outsiders',[166] and to be a restrictive practice that enables trade unions artificially to raise wages and consequently prices. But this does not apply with the same cogency in relation to the post-entry closed shop, where the economic argument is based on the much weaker and much more contestable claim that closed-shop practices undermine economic efficiency because they strengthen the power of organised labour, and thereby help trade unions to raise wages in collective bargaining. In this sense the economic attack on the closed shop is as much an attack on collective bargaining as on one of the institutions by which historically it has been sustained. This renders the attack all the more contestable. An equally convincing case can be made from the position of a different economic orthodoxy that strong trade unionism and comprehensive collective bargaining are an essential precondition of rather than a damaging threat to a socially just economy. On this basis, institutions – such as the closed shop – that empower trade unions in collective bargaining are a public good.

---

[164] Cmnd 3623, 1968, para. 592.
[165] C. G. Hanson, *Taming the Trade Unions* (London: Institute of Economic Affairs, 1991).
[166] E. Butler, *Hayek* (Hounslow: Temple Smith, 1983), p. 113.

International Law and the Closed Shop

While the protection from discrimination and dismissal on the ground of trade-union membership and activities is covered by ILO Convention 98, there is no corresponding protection of the right not to belong. The ILO Committee of Experts takes the view that these practices are compatible with the Convention provided 'they are the result of free negotiation between workers' organisations and employers'.[167] However, the Council of Europe bodies take a different view, with the Social Rights Committee surprisingly concluding in very bullish terms that closed-shop practices violate the right to organise in Article 5 of the Social Charter of 18 October 1961.[168] This is surprising because the text of the Social Charter makes it clear that the most likely source of restriction on the closed shop was thought to be not Article 5, but Article 1(2). The latter provides that states undertake to take measures 'to protect effectively the right of the worker to earn his living in an occupation freely entered upon'. Anticipating the problems that this would present for trade union security arrangements, a note in the appendix to the Charter provides that Article 1(2) is 'not [to] be interpreted as prohibiting or authorising any union security clause or practice'.[169]

So far as the ECHR is concerned, the starting-point is *Young, James and Webster* v. *UK*,[170] where the ECtHR read a right not to associate in limited circumstances into Article 11(1). This was a case where British Rail signed a union-membership agreement with a number of trade unions whereby it was a condition of employment that all employees must join one of several specified trade unions. Although at that stage the ECtHR was not ready to say that the right to freedom of association included the corresponding right not to join a trade union, it did say that there were at least circumstances where closed-shop arrangements could constitute a breach: where the obligation to join was imposed on existing as well as new employees; where membership of a trade union would violate other Convention rights of the individual (notably those arising under ECHR, Articles 9 and 10), and where the obligation to join was underpinned by the sanction of dismissal from employment. Although there may be circumstances where closed-shop arrangements could be justified under Article 11(2), this was found not to be one of them.

---

[167] ILO Committee of Experts, *General Survey on Freedom of Association and Collective Bargaining* (1994), para. 102.

[168] See *Confederation of Swedish Enterprise* v. *Sweden*, Complaint No. 12/2002 (European Committee of Social Rights).

[169] Council of Europe Social Charter, 18 October 1961, Appendix, Part II.

[170] (1982) 4 EHRR 38. See generally on the ECHR V. Mantouvalou, 'Is There a Human Right Not to Be a Trade Union Member?', in T. Novitz and C. Fenwick (eds.), *Human Rights at Work: Perspectives on Law and Regulation* (Oxford: Hart, 2010), pp. 439–62.

Young, James and Webster was taken a step further some years later in *Sigurjonnson* v. *Iceland*,[171] a case involving taxi-drivers required to join a taxi-drivers' association, rather than workers required to join a trade union. In that case, it was said by the Court that:

> it should be recalled that the Convention is a living instrument which must be interpreted in the light of present-day conditions. Accordingly, Article 11 must be viewed as encompassing a negative right of association. It is not necessary for the Court to determine in this instance whether this right is to be considered on an equal footing with the positive right.[172]

More recently, the Court has reinforced the view that closed-shop arrangements will be difficult to defend under the Convention, holding in *Sorenson and Rasmussen* v. *Denmark*[173] that pre-entry closed-shop arrangements were a breach of Convention rights. In that case the Court took note of the fact that closed-shop arrangements were now practised in very few Council of Europe Member States, while also making clear that its objections to closed shop arrangements was to both pre-entry and post-entry arrangements.[174] No account is taken of the impact of non-membership on those who do wish to exercise their right to organise, and the security and strength of the organisation in addressing the power of the employer.

Returning to the European Social Charter, as already indicated the provisions in Article 1(2) and the note in the appendix referred to above have been neatly sidestepped by the Social Rights Committee, which takes the view that closed-shop arrangements breach Article 5 (on the right to organise). The fullest treatment of this issue by the Committee is in *Confederation of Swedish Enterprise* v. *Sweden*,[175] which was an initiative by an employers' federation asserting their human rights to challenge pre-entry closed-shop arrangements in the Swedish construction industry. According to the Committee, 'the freedom guaranteed by Article 5 of the Charter implies that the exercise of a worker's right to join a trade union is the result of a choice and that, consequently, it is not to be decided by the worker under the influence of constraints that rule out the exercise of this freedom'.[176] The Committee continued by saying that the clauses of a collective agreement reserving employment for members of a certain union were 'clearly contrary to the freedom guaranteed by Article 5'. This is because they restricted workers' 'free choice' as to whether or not 'to join one or other of the existing trade unions or to set up separate

---

[171] (1993) 16 EHRR 462.   [172] *Ibid.*, p. 479.

[173] Application Nos. 52562/99 and 52620/99, 11 January 2006.

[174] According to the Court, 'the distinction made between pre-entry closed-shop agreements and post-entry closed-shop agreements in terms of the scope of the protection guaranteed by Article 11 is not tenable' (para. 56).

[175] *Confederation of Swedish Enterprise* v. *Sweden*, Complaint No. 12/2002 (European Committee of Social Rights).

[176] *Ibid.*, para. 29.

organisations of this type'. The practice was said by the Committee to strike 'at the very substance of the freedom enshrined in Article 5'.[177] This is even less defensible than the approach of the ECtHR, not only because of the provision in the appendix referred to above but also because the Social Charter creates a 'right to organise' not a 'right to freedom of association'.

Organisational Security and Legal Restriction

In accordance with the traditional UK approach to regulation, there was no formal regulation of closed-shop arrangements by legislation until 1971.[178] Before then, the practice was lawful in both of its forms, and conduct by trade unions to enforce the practice gave rise to a great deal of significant litigation. Much of this was concerned with industrial action, with many of the common-law liabilities of trade unions for organising industrial action being forged on the anvil of the closed shop. Closed-shop disputes and closed-shop-related disputes gave rise to important decisions about liability for conspiracy to injure and intimidation respectively, in cases brought both by employers and by individual workers.[179] The other source of litigation was action by workers who had been denied access to or expelled from the trade union where closed shops operated,[180] claiming that they had been expelled in breach of the rules or in breach of the rules of natural justice, which the courts read into trade union disciplinary proceedings.[181] Disputes of this latter kind rarely reach the courts nowadays, perhaps because the consequences of losing membership of a trade union are much less severe, closed-shop arrangements now being unenforceable.

Statutory Framework

The Industrial Relations Act 1971 – modelled in many respects on the US system of labour law – provided for the first time in UK law that workers had the (legal) right to be or *not to be* trade union members without being penalised by their employers.[182] But the right not to join was qualified in the sense that 'agency-shop' agreements were permitted, as were 'approved-closed-shop' agreements in some cases.[183] By virtue of the former (agency-shop agreements), a worker could be required to pay a fee to a trade union or a charity in lieu of trade union membership – a way of dealing with the free-rider problem which has been found acceptable to the courts in the United

---

[177] *Ibid.*, para. 30.   [178] Industrial Relations Act 1971, s. 5.

[179] *Quinn* v. *Leathem* [1901] AC 495; *Conway* v. *Wade* [1909] AC 506; *Reynolds* v. *Shipping Federation* [1924] 1 Ch 28; and *Rookes* v. *Barnard* [1964] AC 1129.

[180] Notable cases include *Bonsor* v. *Musicians' Union* [1956] AC 104; *Huntley* v. *Thornton* [1957] 1 All ER 234; and *Faramus* v. *Film Artistes' Association* [1964] AC 925.

[181] See pp. 558–61.   [182] Industrial Relations Act 1971, s. 5.

[183] Industrial Relations Act 1971, ss. 11–18.

States and Canada as a reasonable compromise between the interests of the trade union on the one hand and those of the individual on the other.[184] By virtue of the latter (approved closed-shop agreements), stronger arrangements would be permitted if the employer and trade union could persuade a body called the Industrial Court that closed-shop arrangements were necessary for one of four statutory purposes. However, they had first to be supported in a ballot and to allow for the exemption of those workers with conscientious objections to being a member of a trade union.[185]

These arrangements were swept aside by the Trade Union and Labour Relations Act 1974 (as amended in 1976), which permitted trade unions and employers to enter into union membership agreements requiring employees to be members of a specified trade union or one of a number of specified trade unions. An employee dismissed for non-membership of a trade union could not bring a claim for unfair dismissal unless he or she could show genuine religious objections to trade union membership. The exclusion of unfair dismissal protection applied whether or not the employee had wilfully refused to join a trade union or had been expelled from the union. It is easy to forget just how prevalent the closed shop was in the 1970s, with one study estimating that at least 23 per cent of British workers were employed in a situation where a closed shop operated.[186] As some commentators pointed out, closed-shop arrangements flourished because 'bosses loved them'.[187] For the employer, the closed shop eliminated the risk of inter-union competition, enabled it to deal with a single representative of the workforce, and permitted it to rely on the union to ensure that collectively agreed dispute procedures were obeyed.

But not enough bosses loved the closed shop passionately enough, and the present law – as now to be found in TULRCA 1992 – is the culmination of a number of gradual changes introduced since 1980. Under the Employment Acts 1980 and 1982, closed-shop arrangements could be continued or introduced if supported by a ballot of the workers affected. But the ballot threshold was very high (80 per cent of those eligible to vote or 85 per cent of those voting) and even then there were wide exemptions from the duty to belong. The 1982 Act also introduced the higher compensation awards for dismissals on account of trade union membership and activities, or non-membership of a trade union, although it is clear that the latter was the main aim of the legislation. Where the dismissal was caused by pressure from a trade union official, the trade union official could be made to pay all or part of the compensation. This is still the case.[188] The Employment Act 1988 took the logical step of providing that it would be automatically unfair to dismiss

---

[184] See the consideration of this issue and all its complexities by the Supreme Court of Canada in *Lavigne* v. *Ontario Public Service Employees Union* [1991] 2 SCR 211.

[185] Industrial Relations Act 1971, s. 17 and Sched. 1.

[186] S. Dunn and J. Gennard, *The Closed Shop in British Industry* (London: Macmillan, 1984), p. 16.

[187] M. Hart, 'Why Bosses Love the Closed Shop', *New Society*, 15 February 1979.

[188] TULRCA 1992, ss. 142, 150 and 160.

someone because he or she was not a member of a trade union. This was followed by the Employment Act 1990, which included the provisions relating to access to employment now to be found in TULRCA 1992, section 137.

The only significant change which has taken place since has been in the Employment Relations Act 1999, which abolished the special award of compensation for trade union dismissals and dismissals related to non-membership of a trade union.[189] There is now a broad consensus between the political parties, and no likelihood of the current law being changed. In any event, the jurisprudence of the ECtHR makes it impossible even to contemplate turning the clock back as far as the 1970s. But it is important to point out that the right to non-association in Article 11(1) of the ECHR is not unlimited, and that it is qualified by Article 11(2) which may allow some restrictions on the rights of the individual in the interests of the group as a whole. By virtue of Article 11(2), restrictions may be placed on the exercise of Article 11(1) rights where these are 'prescribed by law' and are 'necessary in a democratic society' for 'the protection of the rights and freedoms of others'. It is not clear, for example, why agency shop agreements should be unenforceable, as they are currently by TULRCA 1992, sections 146(3) and 152(3).[190] If permitted, they would not require workers to join a trade union against their will, but only to contribute financially to the costs of running the union, from the activities of which they benefit, whether in the form of higher pay or access to better procedures.

'100 per cent Campaigns' and 'Fair Shares' Agreements

In recent years, at least one trade union has run a campaign designed to increase membership in enterprises where it is already organised. This makes a lot of sense, for workplaces where a union has more members are likely to be workplaces where it has more power. But even in a relatively benign environment, voluntary recruitment of employees into the union is a hard process that in practice requires a big investment of officer time. The other option for the union is thus whether employers can be persuaded to enter into agreements to encourage or require employees to join the union as a condition of employment, or to encourage or require employees to make a contribution to the union or to a charity in lieu of membership of the union. One source of inspiration for this initiative appears to be the United States, as trade unions working closely together across frontiers learn more about each other's practices. In the United States, such practices are sometimes referred to as 'fair shares' or agency-fee agreements. They are agreements between the union and the employer requiring everyone covered by the collective agreement to either (1) join the union as a member, or (2) pay a fee to the union to help defray the costs of union activity.

---

[189] Employment Relations Act 1999, s. 33.   [190] For the text of which, see p. 520.

In a series of Supreme Court decisions beginning in the 1950s, it was held that agency-fee arrangements did not violate the First Amendment's guarantee of freedom of association, provided the employee was not required to contribute to the union's political and ideological causes not germane to collective bargaining. The first of these decisions was made under the Railway Labor Act of 1926,[191] which applied to various categories of transportation workers, but the outcome was extended to cover workers employed in the public sector,[192] as well as workers governed by the National Labor Relations Act of 1935.[193] As a result an employer and a union may agree that all the workers in the bargaining unit must either join the union or pay an agency fee to the union. However, workers who choose the latter option are usually required to pay a fee of about 80 per cent of normal union dues, as they can be required only to pay for the collective bargaining and representational work of the union, but not for its political activities. In a major reversal, however, the Supreme Court controversially held such practices to be unconstitutional when imposed by public-sector employers,[194] who can no longer enforce agency-fee or fair-shares arrangements, even where workers are not required to support the political activities of the trade union.[195]

It is unclear whether such agreements would be consistent with the Council of Europe instruments referred to above.[196] The ECtHR has emphasised that closed-shop agreements (whether pre-entry or post-entry) run contrary to freedom of choice and that states have a limited margin of appreciation.[197] Quite whether the same view would be taken with regard to forms of union security, which do not require membership of the union but a contribution to the union, is far from clear. It may be instructive, however, that in *Confederation of Swedish Enterprise* v. *Sweden* referred to above, the Social Rights Committee of the Council of Europe concluded as follows:

> 39. The Committee observes firstly that the fees deducted from the wages of workers pursuant to a collective agreement concluded between SBWU [the

---

[191] *Railway Employees Department* v. *Hanson*, 351 US 225 (1956).

[192] *Abood* v. *Detroit Board of Education*, 431 US 209 (1977).

[193] *Communications Workers of America* v. *Beck*, 487 US 735 (1988).

[194] *Janus* v. *American Federation of State, County and Municipal Employees, Council 31*, 585 US_ (2018), overruling *Abood* v. *Detroit Board of Education*, 431 US 209 (1977).

[195] In contrast the Supreme Court of Canada held in the *Lavigne* case, note 184, that an agency-fee arrangement is constitutional even where it requires the worker financially to support political causes not directly related to collective bargaining. For several reasons, this was said not to violate freedom of association.

[196] See the discussion in K. Miller, 'Union Exclusivity Arrangements: A Comparative Overview' [2000] *International Journal of Comparative Labour Law and Industrial Relations* 387.

[197] The ECtHR also said that 'In assessing whether a Contracting State has remained within its margin of appreciation in tolerating the existence of closed-shop agreements, particular weight must be attached to the justifications advanced by the authorities for them and, in any given case, the extent to which they impinge on the rights and interests protected by Article 11': *Sorenson and Rasmussen* v. *Denmark* [2006] ECHR 24, para. 58.

Swedish Building Workers' Union] and the Swedish Construction Federation are, according to the collective agreement, for the service of wage monitoring. The Committee considers that the system of wage monitoring may, depending upon national traditions, be assumed either by public authorities, or, on the explicit or implicit authorisation of the legislator, by professional associations or trade unions. In the latter case this could legitimately require the payment of a fee.

40. Consequently, the Committee considers that the payment of a fee to the trade union for financing its activity of wage monitoring cannot be regarded in itself as unjustified. It also considers that it cannot be regarded as an interference with the freedom of a worker to join a trade union as the payment of the fee does not automatically lead to membership of the SBWU and in addition is not required from workers members of trade unions other than SBWU.

41. However, the Committee considers that doubts exist as to the real use of the fees and that, in the present case, if they were to finance activities other than wage monitoring, these fees would, on the grounds indicated in paragraph 29 be deducted, at least for a part, in violation of Article 5.

42. In the present case, the Committee is not in a position to verify the use of the fees and in particular to verify to what extent the fees are proportional to the cost of the service carried out and to the benefits wage monitoring confers on the workers. These are decisive factors in determining a violation of Article 5 with reference to paragraphs 39 and 40 or 41. The Committee considers therefore that it is for the national courts to decide the matter in the light of the principles the Committee has laid down on this subject or, as the case may be, for the legislator to enable the courts to draw the consequences as regards the conformity with the Charter and the legality of the provisions at issue.

43. The Committee reserves the right to supervise the situation in practice through the reporting procedure and, as the case may be, the collective complaints procedure.[198]

The legal basis of fair-shares agreements in the UK was shaken by an ET decision in *Samuel* v. *London Bus Services Ltd*,[199] which may well have nipped in the bud efforts to promote such agreements. In this case, the employer negotiated an agreement with the Transport and General Workers' Union (TGWU) whereby every employee covered by collective bargaining had money deducted weekly from his or her wages, the money being handed over to the union by the employer. Those employees who were members of the union paid an additional sum, which was also deducted by the employer at source. Mr Samuel resigned from the union and objected to this practice, before bringing legal proceedings to recover his fair share, which he claimed had been unlawfully deducted. An ET held that, although the effect of the fair shares agreement was not to compel Mr Samuel to join the union contrary to

---

[198] See also *Gustafsson* v. *Sweden* (1996) 22 EHRR 409 (pressure by industrial action to enter into a collective agreement is not compelled association in breach of Art. 11(1)).

[199] ET Case No. 3202466/2008.

TULRCA 1992, section 146(1), it did nevertheless constitute a breach of TULRCA 1992, section 146(3).

Trade Union and Labour Relations (Consolidation) Act 1992, Section 146(3)

A worker also has the right not to be subjected to any detriment as an individual by any act, or any deliberate failure to act, by his employer if the act or failure takes place for the sole or main purpose of enforcing a requirement (whether or not imposed by a contract of employment or in writing) that, in the event of his not being a member of any trade union or of a particular trade union or of one of a number of particular trade unions, he must make one or more payments.[200]

If, however, such arrangements are permissible under the ECtHR and the European Social Charter, would it be possible to argue the unthinkable? That is to say, that legislation prohibiting such agreements or rendering them unenforceable is a violation of the trade union's right to freedom of association?

Conclusion

An important theme mapped in this chapter has been the growing importance of international labour standards and international human rights law for the protection of workers seeking to assert rights to freedom of association. These standards and instruments are important for three reasons, the first being that they have helped to shape the content of domestic law. This is clear, for example, in the way in which domestic law follows the contours set by ILO Convention 98, and how the law has been adapted (for example, in relation to the use of trade union services, and in relation to the closed shop) to meet these standards and the principles embraced by the ECtHR. Secondly, they provide a reference point by which to assess the nature and quality of the legal protection of trade union freedom in domestic law. Areas where domestic law seemed especially to fall short of international labour standards and human rights obligations are in relation to blacklisting, discrimination and victimisation. Thirdly, they provide a forum for complaints to be made by workers and trade unions where it is alleged that workers or trade unions have been prejudiced because of a failure of domestic law to meet these standards. As

---

[200] TULRCA 1992, s. 146(4), provides that '[f]or the purposes of subsection (3) any deduction made by an employer from the remuneration payable to a worker in respect of his employment shall, if it is attributable to his not being a member of any trade union or of a particular trade union or of one of a number of particular trade unions, be treated as a detriment to which he has been subjected as an individual by an act of his employer taking place for the sole or main purpose of enforcing a requirement of a kind mentioned in that subsection'.

we have seen in this chapter, the ILO supervisory bodies, and the ECtHR have all had occasion to comment on or decide upon major failings of UK law.

It is not unlikely that there will be more developments of this latter kind in this area. In an era of fiscal austerity, Brexit and relative trade union weakness, trade union freedoms may be easy prey for governments and employers seeking to make cuts and to assert more control over their workforces and the terms by which they are employed. But although such litigation is an important way of regaining lost rights, governments retain the power to implement the decisions of international bodies, which is sometimes done with bad grace and in way that seems intended to fall short of obligations. The implementation of *Wilson and Palmer* is a salutary reminder of this, on three fronts: despite what was said by the ECtHR, (i) workers still have no right to be represented by a trade union when they want to renegotiate terms and conditions of employment; (ii) employers retain the right to offer financial inducements to workers if they do it after rather than before the union is derecognised; and (iii) trade unions are still denied the opportunity in domestic law to enforce their Convention rights recognised by the ECtHR. With the decline in their political influence, the legal route to trade-union freedom is about the only route now left. But as *Wilson and Palmer* underlines, hard-won legal victories may be just as hard to implement in a hostile political climate.

13

Freedom of Association and Trade Union Autonomy

Contents

Introduction

As discussed in Chapter 12, the right to freedom of association has several dimensions, including the freedom to be in association with others. It also includes the freedom of the association to govern and administer its own internal affairs, in accordance with the wishes of what are now 6.2 million members in the UK.[1] This is the principle of trade union autonomy, also acknowledged by international law, notably in ILO Convention 87, Article 3.

ILO Convention 87, Article 3

Workers' and employers' organisations shall have the right to draw up their constitutions and rules, to elect their representatives in full freedom, to organise their administration and activities and to formulate their programmes.[2]

The principle of trade union autonomy contained in Article 3 is a recognition that self-government is an important end in itself: it should be for workers and not the state to decide how their organisations are to be organised, structured and administered. But it is also a recognition that intrusive regulation of trade union affairs by the state can be debilitating, and undermine the ability of the trade union to perform the functions for which it was created. This is not to deny that there is a role for the state in supervising the activities of trade unions. But while the ILO supervisory authorities accept that certain restrictions on trade union freedom may be permissible,[3] they also accept that trade unions should not be so burdened by regulation as to be unable most effectively to promote the interests of those they represent.[4]

In this chapter, we consider the way in which the law is used to regulate the government and administration of trade unions.[5] The starting-point is the rule-book, which is enforceable in the courts as a contract between the trade union and individual members.[6] As with other contracts, the express terms of the rule-book may have to be supplemented by implied terms to deal with gaps in its drafting.[7] The rule-book determines the lawful objects of the union,

---

[1] BIS, *Trade Union Membership 2017: Statistical Bulletin* (2018), p. 4.

[2] It is further provided that 'the public authorities shall refrain from any interference which would restrict this right or impede the lawful exercise thereof'. Also important are the European Social Charter of 1961, Art. 5, and the ECHR, Art. 11, both of which are considered below.

[3] ILO, *Compilation of Decisions of the Freedom of Association Committee of the Governing Body* (2018), Chs. 6–9.

[4] *Ibid.*

[5] For a more detailed consideration of some of the issues considered in this chapter, see P. Elias and K. Ewing, *Trade Union Democracy, Members' Rights and the Law* (London: Mansell, 1988).

[6] *Goring* v. *British Actors Equity Association* [1987] IRLR 122.

[7] *AB* v. *CD* [2001] IRLR 808. See also *Unison* v. *Street*, UKEAT/0256/13/LA, and subsequently *Street* v. *Unison*, Decision D/1/15–16 (implied term authorising suspension of rules where branch chaos); *Chapman* v. *Community*, Decision D/1–5/16–17; *Tully* v. *National Crime Officers Association*, Decision D 23–27/17–18 (implied duty of cooperation, though rejection of the duty of mutual trust and confidence); and *Boswell* v. *URTU*, Decision CO/30–32/17–18 (term implied authorising the appointment of a person external to the union to investigate internal disputes). The basis for implying terms varies from custom and practice (*Street*), to business efficacy or the presumed intention of the parties (*Boswell*), to operation of law (*Chapman* and *Tully*).

defines the composition and powers of the different organs of government, and confers rights and duties on the membership. By enforcing the rule-book, the courts are upholding the principle of trade union autonomy, although some may argue that the principle has been undermined by a willingness on the part of the courts in some cases in the past to over-interpret the rules to constrain the operation of internal trade union procedures.[8] A more serious threat to trade autonomy is the comprehensive framework of legislation introduced mainly under Conservative governments between 1980 and 1993, but which survived largely unscathed through the thirteen subsequent years of Labour government. This legislation places a high premium on trade union 'democracy' and 'member protection',[9] dealing mainly with the election of officers and the exclusion and expulsion of members. It also applies to other questions, empowering public authorities to investigate alleged financial irregularities in trade unions.[10] While provisions of the latter kind may in principle be unexceptionable, much of this legislation – reinforced now by the Trade Union Act 2016 – goes beyond the boundaries of international law, however well it may play to a domestic political audience.

The Function of Trade Unions

Although wide ranging, trade union objects clauses nevertheless tend to conceal the fact that trade unions have a number of functions. These are as follows:

- A service function, whereby trade unions provide a range of services to their members. These may vary from traditional 'friendly society' benefits (sickness insurance or death benefits) to the provision of legal advice and assistance.
- A workplace representation function, whereby trade unions represent members in their relations with their employer. This may take the form of individual representation in grievance or disciplinary disputes, or collective representation over pay and other working conditions.
- A regulatory function, whereby trade unions seek to regulate employment conditions. This can be done directly by collective bargaining which determines terms and conditions for a group of workers or indirectly by lobbying for legislation (such as that dealing with the minimum wage or working time).
- A political representation function, whereby trade unions seek to protect and promote the interests of their members in the political arena, whether it be local government, national

---

[8] See *Breen* v. *Amalgamated Engineering Union* [1971] 2 QB 175; and *Esterman* v. *NALGO* [1974] ICR 625.

[9] On which, see H. Morris and P. Fosh, 'Measuring Trade Union Democracy: The Case of the UK Public Services Association' (2000) 38 *British Journal of Industrial Relations* 95.

[10] For a good account of the investigatory powers in relation to alleged financial irregularities, see Certification Officer, *Annual Report 2016–17* (2017), Ch. 3.

government or in Europe. This may require close working relationships with political parties, legislators and governments.

- A public administration function, whereby trade unions may be delegated by government with responsibility for administering or promoting public policy on behalf of the state or various state benefits in a manner which will benefit their members.

The weight and importance attached to these different functions may vary from time to time, and according to circumstances.[11]

Trade Union Definition, Listing and Status

Before we go much further, it is important to address some basic legal questions about trade union form. At the present time these are not matters that give rise to a great deal of concern, although in the past the legal status of trade unions has been hugely controversial and has had far-reaching political consequences. Although superficially such matters may seem now to raise dry conceptual questions, they are of great practical significance. The definition of a trade union will determine which organisations are covered by the statutory requirements discussed later in this chapter (relating to mandatory elections, financial transparency and the discipline and expulsion of members). Similarly, the listing of a trade union will not only provide the union with a protection of its identity but also be a prelude to a certificate of independence which will determine which organisations have access to certain statutory rights discussed in Chapters 14 and 15 (including the right to be recognised by an employer for the purposes of collective bargaining, and subsequently the right to time-off for officials and members and to the disclosure of information). Finally, the legal status of a trade union will help to determine whether a trade union can own property, make contracts and be vicariously liable for the tortious acts of its 'servants and agents'; it may also determine whether a trade union can sue and be sued in its own name.

A trade union is defined principally by reference to its form, personnel and purpose:

- as to form, it must be an 'organisation' (whether temporary or permanent);
- as to personnel, it must consist 'wholly or mainly of workers of one or more descriptions'; and
- as to purpose, its 'principal purposes' must 'include the regulation of relations between workers of that description or those descriptions and employers or employers' associations'.[12]

[11] See K. D. Ewing, 'The Function of Trade Unions' (2005) 34 *Industrial Law Journal* 1.
[12] TULRCA 1992, s. 1(a).

This is fairly straightforward and has not given rise to any serious problems. As indicated by the box on pages 524–5, trade unions can have purposes other than the 'regulation of relations' with employers, and there is no requirement that relations should be regulated in a particular way (for example, by collective bargaining or legislation). However, a trade union is defined also to include federations or confederations of trade unions, such as the TUC, to which many individual trade unions are affiliated. Thus a trade union includes organisations that consist 'wholly or mainly' of (1) constituent or affiliated organisations, which are themselves (a) trade unions or (b) organisations of constituent or affiliated trade unions; or (2) representatives of such constituent or affiliated organisations. In this case, the principal purposes of such bodies must include either 'the regulation of relations between workers and employers or between workers and employers' associations', or 'the regulation of relations between its constituent or affiliated organisations'.[13] This wider definition would include global union federations like the ITF which – unlike most global union federations – is based in London.

There is not now any system of formal registration of trade unions, registration having been controversial during the period of the Industrial Relations Act 1971.[14] Although not prohibited by international law,[15] registration is associated with unacceptable levels of state control over trade union organisation, although it is clear from events since 1971 that registration is by no means an essential precondition of such control, which can operate effectively without it. In 1974, registration gave way to 'listing' with the newly created Certification Officer, which might be seen as registration by another name.[16] An organisation may apply to be on the Certification Officer's list, for entry to which the Certification Officer must be satisfied that the organisation in question is a trade union, that the application has been made in the manner and form prescribed by the Certification Officer, and that the name of the trade union is neither the same as that of another already listed or so similar as to be likely to deceive the public.[17] An appeal lies to the EAT against a refusal by the Certification Officer to enter an organisation on the list,[18] although it is only recently that this power has been used. The fact that an organisation is on the list of trade unions is to be treated as evidence that the organisation in

---

[13] TULRCA 1992, s. 1(b). This would catch the TUC, one of the principal purposes of which is to 'assist in settling disputes between the members of such organisations and their employers or between such organisations and their members or between the organisations themselves': TUC, Rules and Standing Orders (2017), rule 2.

[14] B. Weekes, M. Mellish, L. Dickens and J. Lloyd, *Industrial Relations and the Limits of the Law: The Industrial Effects of the Industrial Relations Act 1971* (Oxford: Blackwell, 1975), Ch. 1.

[15] See ILO, *Compilation of Decisions of the Freedom of Association Committee of the Governing Body* (2018). The ILO CFA is generally hostile to registration as a form of 'previous authorisation', except where 'the registration of trade unions consists solely of a formality where the conditions are not such as to impair the guarantees laid down by the Convention' (*ibid.*, para. 448).

[16] TULRCA 1992, ss. 2–4.   [17] TULRCA 1992, s. 3.   [18] TULRCA 1992, s. 9.

question is a trade union,[19] and full details of the listed trade unions are provided in the Certification Officer's annual report, which is published on the Certification Officer's website.[20]

Returning to the question of legal status, as suggested this has been a controversial question, giving rise to a number of decisions of the House of Lords. The Trade Union Acts 1871–6 were silent on the question of status, and it was contended that trade unions were simply unincorporated associations in the same way as private clubs. This view was rejected by the House of Lords, which held in effect that trade unions had an uncertain legal personality but could be sued in their own name.[21] The 1871–6 Acts were repealed by the short-lived Industrial Relations Act 1971, which provided that trade unions registered under the Act 'shall become a body corporate' on registration.[22] These provisions were, however, repealed in 1974 and replaced with what is now TULRCA 1992, section 10, the side-note to which declares trade unions to have a 'quasi-corporate status'. Thus, although a trade union 'is not a body corporate', it is (a) 'capable of making contracts'; (b) 'capable of suing and being sued in its own name, whether in proceedings relating to property or founded on contract or tort or any other cause of action'; while (c) 'proceedings for an offence alleged to have been committed by it or on its behalf may be brought against it in its own name'.[23] And although trade union property is held in trust, any legal judgments are enforceable 'against any property held in trust for it to the same extent and in the same manner as if it were a body corporate'.[24]

Trade Union Objects

What do trade unions do? To answer this question, a good starting-point is the constitutions of the different trade unions: it is here that they define their

---

[19] TULRCA 1992, s. 2(4). The certificate issued to an organisation that it is a listed trade union is deemed to be evidence that the name of the organisation in question is entered on the list: TULRCA 1992, s. 2(6).

[20] At 31 March 2017, there were 137 listed trade unions. The Certification Officer was aware of thirteen other organisations that fall within the definition of a trade union (and thirty-nine employers' associations) which have not applied to be listed: Certification Officer, *Annual Report 2016–17* (2017), p. 8. Applications for listing are by no means granted automatically. In 2016–17 a decision was taken to reject an application by the Disabled Workers Union on the ground that it did not fall within the statutory definition of a trade union (*ibid.*, p. 10). Various legal obligations applicable to trade unions apply equally to listed and non-listed trade unions.

[21] *Taff Vale Railway Co. Ltd* v. *Amalgamated Society of Railway Servants* [1901] AC 426; *Osborne* v. *Amalgamated Society of Railway Servants* [1910] AC 87; *Bonsor* v. *Musicians' Union* [1956] AC 104.

[22] Industrial Relations Act 1971, s. 74. But this applied only to trade unions registered under the Act, and very few registered. See B. Weekes, M. Mellish, L. Dickens and J. Lloyd, *Industrial Relations and the Limits of the Law: The Industrial Effects of the Industrial Relations Act 1971* (Oxford: Blackwell, 1975), Appendix V.

[23] TULRCA 1992, s. 10(1).   [24] TULRCA 1992, s. 12.

aims and purposes. The objects clauses of trade unions vary to some extent, reflecting the different origins and interests of the different trade union organisations. But most have a basic core of objects, which is perhaps inevitable if each organisation is to fall within the statutory definition of a trade union (which requires the primary purposes of a trade union to be concerned with regulating relations between employers and workers).[25] A good example of trade union objects is provided by Unite, now one of the largest trade unions in the country.

Unite Rule-book

2.1 The objects of the Union shall be:

2.1.1 To organise, recruit and represent workers, and strengthen workplace organisation to achieve real union power for its members.

2.1.2 To defend and improve its members' wages and working conditions including the pursuit of equal pay for work of equal value. To help our members win in the workplace, using the union's resources to assist in that process, and to support our members in struggle including through strike action.

2.1.3 To defend and improve the social and economic well-being of members and their families, both directly and via commensurate policies in relation to society both domestically and abroad.

2.1.4 To have a strong political voice, fighting on behalf of working people's interests, and to influence the political agenda locally, regionally, nationally and internationally, so as to promote a socialist vision for

- a more equal society in which wealth is distributed from the rich to the poor, including by means of progressive taxation and other regulatory measures to restrict excessive wealth

- a collective society in which public services are directly provided on the basis of public need and not private greed, and a fair system of welfare and benefits to support those in need

- public ownership of important areas of economic activity and services, including health, education, water, post, rail and local passenger transport.

2.1.5 To further political objectives including by affiliation to the Labour Party.

2.1.6 To promote equality and fairness for all, including actively opposing prejudice and discrimination on grounds of gender, race, ethnic origin, religion, class, marital status, sexual orientation, gender identity, age, disability or caring responsibilities.

2.1.7 To affiliate to the TUC, ICTU, Welsh and Scottish TUCs and other appropriate trade union cooperation/coordination bodies domestically and internationally.

---

[25] TULRCA 1992, s. 1.

Although fairly bland compared to the more full-bodied objects clauses of other unions,[26] objectives of this kind might nevertheless be unlawful at common law as being in restraint of trade.[27] TULRCA 1992, section 11(1), protects against this continuing risk,[28] by providing that 'the purposes of a trade union are not, by reason only that they are in restraint of trade, unlawful so as (a) to make any member of the trade union liable to criminal proceedings for conspiracy or otherwise, or (b) to make any agreement or trust void or voidable'. TULRCA 1992, section 11(2), provides that 'no rule of a trade union is unlawful or unenforceable by reason only that it is in restraint of trade'.[29]

Objects Clauses

The objects clause does not simply describe what a trade union does: it also defines what it may do and by implication what it may not do. If a trade union engages in activity that is not authorised expressly or impliedly by its objects clause, it may be restrained by a member in the courts. This power of legal restraint is an important form of member protection, ensuring that the union does not engage in unauthorised activities, and that union funds are not used for unauthorised purposes. As with many constitutional documents, however, the scope and extent of the objects clause of a trade union are not always clear, with the result that it may be left to the courts to decide what a union may or may not do in difficult cases. It is here that membership protection may conflict with membership democracy, in the sense that activists may be restrained by the union constitution. If the union wishes to promote objects for which it has no authority under the rules, it may first be necessary to change the rules in order to avoid any unwelcome legal challenge. But it may not be so easy to change the objects of the union as to pass a resolution at conference, if rule changes require a special majority in support.

The importance of the objects clause is illustrated by *Goring* v. *British Actors Equity Association*,[30] where in 1985 the annual general meeting of the association condemned the association's president for working in South Africa, and demanded that the association's council issue an instruction to members not to work there. In March 1986, the council held a referendum of its members in which a majority of those voting resolved that members should be instructed not to work in South Africa. In the following month, the instruction was duly

---

[26] The RMT, for example, is pledged 'to work for the supersession of the capitalist system by a socialistic order of society', while the objects of ASLEF include 'to assist in the furtherance of the Labour Movement generally towards a Socialist Society'. The privatisation of the railways must have been a particular blow to both.

[27] *Hornby* v. *Close* (1867) LR 2 QB 153.

[28] On which, see *Boddington* v. *Lawton* [1994] ICR 478.

[29] These provisions were first introduced as Trade Union Act 1871, ss. 2 and 3, to reverse *Hornby* v. *Close* (1867) LR 2 QB 153.

[30] [1987] IRLR 122.

issued, and under the rules of the association it was binding on the members. Any member who acted in breach of the instruction could be fined, suspended or expelled, which in turn would make it difficult for any individual concerned to secure employment in the entertainment industry in the UK. In this case, the plaintiff sought a declaration that the instruction was *ultra vires* and therefore void. The application succeeded on the ground that the objects of the association provided that it was a non-party-political and non-sectarian organisation, with a duty to acknowledge 'the right of individual members to hold and express their personal political and other beliefs both in their private and professional capacities'.

In determining whether the action of the association was lawful, it was thus necessary to enquire into the purpose for which it was taken. Action with a political aspect could be protected if the main purpose was to promote the professional interests of members. According to Browne-Wilkinson J:

> The language of the 1985 AGM resolution is redolent of sectarian promotion of a boycott for the purpose of putting an end to apartheid: there is no mention of professional interests. Similarly, the Statement For (which, in this regard, I can look at to discover the purposes of those promoting the giving of the instruction) is almost exclusively directed at a general cultural boycott as opposed to the promotion of professional concerns. In the whole statement, the only reference to professional interests is the exhortation to 'support your own Afro-Asian members'. There is no suggestion in the evidence that the Council or anyone else was in favour of the instruction for the narrow, and to my mind rather remote, professional purposes relied on by the defendants in their evidence.[31]

In the absence of any evidence to the contrary, the only purpose of the instruction was thus to promote a general cultural boycott of South Africa, said to be 'a sectarian purpose'.[32] As a result, the instruction was held to be *ultra vires* and void.

The approach adopted in *Goring* is perhaps easy to understand, however much one may applaud the policy which the union introduced. It was still the case at the time the decision was reached that 'the theatrical entertainment industry is a closed shop, membership of the Union being a prerequisite of employment', with the result that 'suspension or expulsion would be a dire penalty for any member'.[33] Consequences of this kind are likely to place a high premium on member protection and strict adherence to the union constitution, in this case the objects clause. This would not be such a compelling consideration today, given that it is now unlawful to refuse someone employment because he or she is not a trade union member.[34] But a commitment to constitutional sovereignty in *Goring* was perhaps all the more compelling given that only 3,320 out of a membership of 32,000 took part in the

---

[31] *Ibid.*, p. 127.   [32] *Ibid.*   [33] *Ibid.*, p. 214.   [34] TULRCA 1992, s. 137.

referendum, and fewer still voted in favour of the disputed policy. Although it might be argued that the courts should develop principles calculated to promote member participation in the affairs of the union, it is likely that such a low turnout would make it difficult to persuade a court of the virtues of membership sovereignty in the event of conflict with the constitution.

Political Objects

It will have been noted that the objects of Unite quoted above include 'to further political objectives including by affiliation to the Labour Party'. This, however, is not a matter over which trade unions have full autonomy, political objects being governed by legislation since the Trade Union Act 1913. The latter was a political compromise to reverse the decision of the House of Lords in *Osborne* v. *Amalgamated Society of Railway Servants*.[35] In that case, it was held that trade unions could not impose a levy on their members in order to support parliamentary representation and other political activities. Such a practice was said to be *ultra vires* the trade union legislation of 1871–6 that had given trade unions legal protection from common law rules relating to restraint of trade.[36] The effect of the decision – which was followed in a number of other cases to restrain political action by a number of other unions – was to threaten the financing and ultimately the future of the Labour Party.[37] Formed in 1900, the latter grew as a direct consequence of another famous House of Lords decision,[38] and by 1905 had twenty-nine members of Parliament. The threat was addressed first by the introduction of a scheme for MPs' salaries in 1911, and secondly by the passing of the 1913 Act, the key requirements of which were threefold:

- a union wishing to adopt political objects had first to seek the approval of its members in a secret ballot;
- if the ballot result was favourable, the union was required to adopt political fund rules whereby political objects were to be financed from a separate political fund, to be financed in turn by a separate contribution by the members; and
- where such a fund was established, every member was to be entitled not to contribute to the fund (by contracting out) and not to suffer disability or disadvantage within the union as a result.

The arrangements for political-fund rules are an unusual example of state intervention in the internal affairs of trade unions, in the sense that trade unions wishing to adopt political objects must also adopt rules prescribed by

---

[35] [1910] AC 87.   [36] See p. 527.
[37] On which, see K. D. Ewing, *Trade Unions, the Labour Party and the Law: A Study of the Trade Union Act 1913* (Edinburgh University Press, 1982), Ch. 2.
[38] *Taff Vale Railway Co. Ltd* v. *Amalgamated Society of Railway Servants* [1901] AC 426.

the state. More recent legislation (such as that requiring ballots before strikes and in the election of executive committees and general secretaries) operates independently of the rules of the unions in question. Model political-fund ballot rules and model political-fund rules to comply with the requirements of the legislation were drafted initially by the Chief Registrar of Friendly Societies, a function now performed by the Certification Officer. The political-fund rules of all trade unions with political objects are thus broadly similar, although there are differences, for example in terms of how much the political contribution is in each union, and in terms of the method of its calculation and collection. Key provisions of the political-fund rules of all trade unions based on the requirements of TULRCA 1992, section 82, include (1) the method of contribution to the fund; (2) the right of non-contributors not to be discriminated against because of their non-contribution; and (3) the right of members to complain to the Certification Officer in the event of any breach of the political fund rules.[39] No complaints were made in the five years between 2012–13 and 2016–17, and before that there was an average of less than one complaint every two years.[40]

Under the 1913 Act, a ballot once held did not have to be renewed: the Trade Union Act 1984 required trade unions to ballot their members every ten years.[41] At a time when support for the Labour Party was thought to be in decline, this was a potentially fatal blow. But with one exception, in what have now been four cycles of political-fund review ballots, no trade union has had to discontinue political objects because of a ballot outcome. The 1984 Act also expanded the definition of political objects, now defined to mean the expenditure of money (i) on contributions to political parties; (ii) on the provision of any service or property for use by or on behalf of any political party; (iii) in connection with the registration of electors, the candidature of any person, the selection of any candidate, or the holding of any ballot by the union in connection with any election to a political office; (iv) on the maintenance of any holder of a political office; and (v) on the holding of any conference or meeting by or on behalf of a political party.[42] But apart from these party-political expenditures, the Act also applies to (vi) expenditure on 'the production, publication or distribution of any literature, document, film, sound recording or advertisement the main purpose of which is to persuade people to vote for a political party or candidate or to persuade them not to vote for a political party or candidate'.[43] The last provision was a particular cause for

---

[39] The jurisdiction of the Certification Officer was extended to allow her also to hear complaints that trade unions have incurred political expenditure without first having adopted political objects: TULRCA 1992, s. 72A.

[40] Most complaints are unsuccessful. An unusually successful complaint is *Bakhsh* v. *Unison (No. 3)*, Decision D/1–6/10, concerning the improper use of branch general funds for political purposes.

[41] See now TULRCA 1992, s. 73.   [42] TULRCA 1992, s. 72(1).

[43] TULRCA 1992, s. 72(1)(f).

concern for those unions not affiliated to the Labour Party, but which engaged in 'independent' electoral activity. Although this activity was not directly identified with any particular political party, it might nevertheless favour one party more than others. In order to continue to engage in this activity, a number of unions were thus required to adopt political objects, having previously met such expenditure from their general funds.[44]

Trade Union Political Funds

There are 137 listed trade unions, but only 25 have political funds, and not all of these are affiliated to the Labour Party. According to the Certification Officer, these 25 trade union political funds raised a total of £24.54 million in the year ending 31 March 2016, and spent £25.59 million, with combined reserves of £31.7 million at the end of the year. The total trade union political fund income of £24.54 million reported in 2015–16 represents only a modest increase in such income in recent years. Nevertheless, political-fund income was only 1.8 per cent of total trade union income of £1.2 billion. Total political-fund income reported from 2000–1 to 2015–16 was over £300 million, although this includes all trade unions with political funds and not only those affiliated to the Labour Party; total political fund income of affiliated trade unions would obviously be less than the total political-fund income of all unions.

According to the Certification Officer's 2016–17 report, the vast bulk of the reported £24.54 million political fund income (to the tune of £21.6 million) was accounted for by five trade unions, namely, the CWU (communication workers) (£1.6 million), GMB (general workers) (£3.3 million), UNISON (public-sector workers) (£6.5 million), Unite (£7.8 million) and USDAW (shop-workers) (£2.1 million). All five unions are affiliated to the Labour Party, and the bulk of this income will be used to pay affiliation fees and make other donations to the Labour Party. The income of non-affiliated unions was thus generally much less, though the position in UNISON is complicated by its two funds, one of which is non-affiliated and is used for a range of political purposes other than affiliations or donations to the Labour Party.

So far as the non-affiliated unions are concerned, the largest were the NUT (teachers) (£441,549), PCS (civil servants) (£331,686) and RMT (£274,000). But it is also the case that most non-affiliated unions have a political fund income of under £100,000 annually, this being true of the prison officers (POA) and tax inspectors (Association of Revenue and Customs), and the unions of professional workers of various kinds (such as Connect). Also, according to the Certification Officer, this £24.54 million was raised from 4.7 million trade unionists, with 622,286 trade unionists (in unions with political funds) not contributing either because of exemption (124,603) or ineligibility under the union's rules. There were 6.8 million members in listed trade unions in total, which means that a political levy was paid by about 69 per cent of the total.[45]

---

[44] See *Paul* v. *NALGO* [1987] IRLR 43, where such expenditure was held to be unlawful following the 1984 amendments.

[45] Source: Certification Officer, *Annual Report 2016–17* (2017) Appendix 9. See also K. D. Ewing, 'The Trade Union Question in British Political Funding', in K. D. Ewing, J. Rowbottom and J.-C. Tham (eds.), *The Funding of Political Parties: Where Now?* (London: Routledge, 2011).

Further changes were introduced by the Trade Union Act 2016. The most important of these is based on the position operating between 1927 and 1946, following the enactment of the Trade Disputes and Trade Unions Act 1927, in direct response to the General Strike of the previous year. The 1927 Act changed the default position so that trade union members had to opt in to the political fund if they wanted to pay the political levy, rather than be obliged to pay the political levy as a condition of membership and opt out if they chose not to contribute. This was repealed in 1946 when opting out was re-introduced.[46] The government's original intention in 2016 was that the 1927 position would be fully restored, but following the intervention of a Select Committee of the House of Lords,[47] a messy compromise was reached so that the change would be phased in by applying only to members recruited after 1 March 2018. Trade unions are thus likely to have three categories of members relating to the political levy: (1) pre-existing members governed by the opting out regime; (2) new members subject to the opting-in regime;[48] and (3) non-contributors (who have opted out under the old regime or failed to opt in under the new regime).[49] If experience of the system between 1927 and 1946 is any guide, it is likely that this change will lead in time to a significant decline in the amount of money in trade union political funds, and ultimately the income of the Labour Party,[50] as no doubt intended.[51]

Trade Union Government

In common with trade union objects, trade union structure and government are also determined initially by the constitution and rules of each union. The structure of trade unions is different, reflecting their diverse origins and perceptions about how best to achieve their goals. But it would be true to say that trade unions are generally organised formally along democratic lines, with constitutional arrangements that provide for some form of representative government of the members. Thus, trade union constitutions will typically

---

[46] Trade Disputes and Trade Unions Act 1946.   [47] HL Paper 106, 2015–16.

[48] Members who opt in may also choose to opt out at any time by giving notice as prescribed in the union rules: TULRCA 1992, s. 84A.

[49] Trade union members must be notified individually on an annual basis of their right to opt out: TULRCA 1992, s. 84A (inserted by the Trade Union Act 2016). The union must send a copy of the notification to the Certification Officer.

[50] K. D. Ewing, *Trade Unions, the Labour Party and the Law: A Study of the Trade Union Act 1913* (Edinburgh University Press, 1983), Ch. 3.

[51] The foregoing provisions deal principally with restraints on trade union income for political purposes, which apply uniquely to trade unions. There are also controversial restraints on expenditure targeted principally on trade unions and NGOs in the Transparency of Lobbying, Non-Party Campaigning and Trade Union Administration Act 2014, Part 2, amending the Political Parties, Elections and Referendums Act 2000. See K. D. Ewing, 'The Importance of Trade Union Political Voice: Labour Law Meets Constitutional Law', in A. Bogg and T. Novitz (eds.), *Voices at Work: Continuity and Change in the Common Law World* (Oxford University Press, 2014), Ch. 13.

provide for an annual conference (though in some cases the conference may be held less frequently), which will be the policy-making forum of the union. Between conferences, the business of the union typically will be conducted by an executive committee or council, directly elected by the members; the executive will generally meet at regular intervals throughout the year. But the executive will not be a full-time body, and its members will normally be employed elsewhere. The day-to-day work of the union will normally be conducted by the officers of the union, the most senior of whom will be the general secretary and the deputy general secretary, who may be accountable to the executive committee for the way in which they discharge their responsibilities for the conduct of the affairs of the union. As full-time officials, the general secretary and his or her deputy have a uniquely powerful position and an opportunity in most cases to be the directing mind and public face of the union.

Rule-book Constraints

The constitution of a trade union may operate to restrain the different organs of government in a number of ways. Although the union may be promoting a lawful object expressly recognised by the objects clause, and although it may be acting in accordance with the wishes of the bulk of its members, it may not have the power under the rules to promote a particular course of action. Depending on the circumstances, trade union powers may be narrowly construed by the courts. Thus, although the union may be empowered to take strike action, the rules may require a particular procedure to be followed before a strike may take place. This was a major issue during the miners' strike of 1984–5. The legality of the strike was tested in *Taylor* v. *National Union of Mineworkers (NUM) (Derbyshire Area) (No. 1)*,[52] which raised questions about the legality of a call to strike by the area executive. This was held to be unlawful on the ground that the area union's rules required a 55 per cent majority in a ballot, and in this case the call to support strike action had the support of only a minority of the members. The action was also said to be a breach of the rules of the national union, which empowered the union to declare a national strike only after a ballot of the members. No national ballot had been held, Nicholls J holding that the call to strike was in effect a declaration of a national strike.

By the same token, although a union may be empowered to pay strike pay to members, this may be conditional on certain formalities being met first.[53] Also arising from the miners' strike of 1984–5 is *Taylor* v. *NUM (Derbyshire Area) (No. 3)*,[54] where the plaintiffs sought an injunction to restrain the union and its senior officers from 'using, procuring or permitting the use of the funds of

---

[52] [1985] IRLR 440.   [53] *Yorkshire Miners' Association* v. *Howden* [1905] AC 256.
[54] [1985] IRLR 99.

the union' for the purposes of the strike, on the ground that the strike was *ultra vires* because of the failure to ballot. They also sought an order requiring the defendants to repay to the union money that had been used to support the strike. The plaintiffs succeeded on the first point, with Vinelott J holding that, if the rules provide for strike pay during an official strike, 'it is impossible to imply consistently with that a power for officers to make a precisely similar allowance to members on "unofficial strike"'.[55] However, Vinelott J was unwilling to make an order that the officers reimburse the union for the £1.7 million incurred by the strike payments already made, although it was accepted in principle that this would be an expected outcome. Although *ultra vires*, the strike enjoyed substantial support among the members, while the officers in question honestly believed that they had the power to make the disputed payments, it also being relevant that the payments were not made for the personal or private benefit of the defendants.

Apart from thus reinforcing the view that it is for the courts to construe the rules and determine the powers of a trade union, *Taylor* v. *NUM (Derbyshire Area) (No. 3)* is also important for reminding us that the courts may not find it appropriate to restrain every constitutional impropriety brought before them. Vinelott J reaffirmed the relevance in a trade union context of the so-called rule in *Foss* v. *Harbottle*,[56] which despite its Dickensian ring is actually intended to discourage prolonged litigation. Explaining the two aspects of the rule, it has been said that:

> First, the proper plaintiff in an action in respect of a wrong alleged to be done to a company or association of persons is *prima facie* the company or the association of persons itself. Secondly, where the alleged wrong is a transaction which might be made binding on the company or association and on all its members by a simple majority of the members, no individual member of the company is allowed to maintain an action in respect of that matter.[57]

The essence of the rule thus seems to be that it would be pointless (and perhaps even contrary to public policy in the administration of justice) if individuals were to be permitted to use the courts to prevent the company or trade union acting irregularly if the decision of the court could subsequently thereafter easily be reversed by a majority of the company or union taking the same decision in a regular manner.

In *Taylor (No. 3)*, it was held as it had been in earlier cases that a majority could not ratify an *ultra vires* act,[58] with the result that the rule in *Foss* v. *Harbottle* had no application in that litigation. There are in fact other exceptions to the rule in *Foss* v. *Harbottle*, set out in *Hodgson* v. *NALGO*

---

[55] *Ibid.*, p. 107.   [56] (1843) 2 Hare 461.

[57] *Edwards* v. *Halliwell* [1950] 2 All ER 1064, at 1066. Vinelott J continued by saying 'for the simple reason that, if a mere majority of the members of the company or association is in favour of what has been done, then [there is no further argument]'.

[58] *Edwards* v. *Halliwell* [1950] 2 All ER 1064.

(discussed below), that operate to override its potential role in blocking members wishing to enforce the constitution. Apart from *ultra vires*, other exceptions apply to decisions that require a special majority (as in *Taylor (No. 1)* (above)). In *Wise* v. *USDAW*,[59] Chadwick J rejected a defence based on the rule in *Foss* v. *Harbottle* in a case about the conduct of an election, holding robustly that the rights which the plaintiffs in that case were seeking to protect were 'rights not to have the constitutional organs of the union, and in particular the composition of a new executive council, the president and the general secretary, imposed upon them save in accordance with the rules of the union'.[60] If union members have a right to ensure that the union is conducted according to the rules, the scope for *Foss* v. *Harbottle* as a bar to enforcing a trade union constitution is likely to be very limited, particularly as there is also another exception applicable to the 'personal and individual rights of membership',[61] as for example where the member is complaining that subscriptions have been increased in breach of the rules.[62]

Constitutional Conflict

There are thus likely to be few obstacles to the member seeking to restrain the unauthorised acts of trade union governing bodies. A slight complication may arise where the dispute is not between a member and an organ of union government, but between two different branches of government within a trade union. The executive committee may, for example, refuse to follow the policy directions given by conference. Or the general secretary may fail to follow instructions given by the executive committee. This is an important question which may lead to the courts being called upon to make a decision – within the constitution of the union – of where power should ultimately reside: in the general secretary and other senior officers, in the executive committee, in the conference or in the membership of the union. That is to say, the courts may have a choice to determine whether on balance a union should pursue a system of executive government, representative government, or membership government. The starting-point of course will be the rules of the union in question. But as on other questions, the rules may not be conclusive (which is probably why the matter is before the court in the first place). Even where there is a clear breach of the rules, there may be other factors to be considered, with common-law principles of construction to be engaged. There is also the

---

[59] [1996] ICR 691.   [60] *Ibid.*, p. 702.   [61] *Edwards* v. *Halliwell* [1950] 2 All ER 1064, at 1067.
[62] But see *Callaghan* v. *ASLEF*, Decision D/21–35/01, where the Certification Officer refers to an unreported decision of Rougier J in relation to the complaints then under consideration, in which *Foss* v. *Harbottle* was applied, the judge reported as saying that it was for the union 'to put its house in order'. So far as the Certification Officer is concerned, he concluded that, although he was unable to 'apply the principles of *Foss* v. *Harbottle* to refuse a declaration under [TULRCA 1992,] s. 108B, [he could] and will have regard to it in determining any remedy in the case of complaints [he upheld]'.

ubiquitous rule in *Foss* v. *Harbottle* to be considered, a rule that seems particularly apt for deployment in matters of internal governance such as those under consideration.

An example of this kind of problem is presented by *Hodgson* v. *NALGO*,[63] concerning a dispute about a conference decision of the union, opposing 'the entry of Britain into the European Economic Community (the Common Market) unless it can be shown to be in the long-term interests of both Britain and the Community'. Shortly thereafter, the union's executive committee instructed the NALGO delegates to the TUC annual conference to support a motion in favour of Britain's joining the Common Market, and to vote against a motion opposing such membership. The plaintiffs in this case, all members of the Leeds branch of the union, sought an order against the union and its TUC delegation to restrain them from acting against the policy of the union as determined by its conference, which under the rules 'directed' its 'general policy'. But, in challenging the instruction to the delegates, the plaintiffs were faced with *Foss* v. *Harbottle* and the fact that none of the admitted exceptions appeared to apply. Thus, it could not be said that the action of the executive committee was *ultra vires* the union. Nor could it be said that 'something in the nature of a proprietary right of [the plaintiffs] is being infringed'.[64] Nor indeed was the case 'one of those in which an exception has been made from the rule on the ground that otherwise the majority might do by some informal machinery what under the rules can only be done with some special formality'.

In a previous case on similar facts, *McNamee* v. *Cooper*,[65] the High Court refused to intervene where union delegates to the TUC voted in favour of the government's prices and incomes policy contrary to a conference resolution of the union. In *Hodgson* v. *NALGO*, however, Goulding J was unwilling to send the plaintiff away empty handed, and effectively created a new exception to the rule in *Foss* v. *Harbottle*, this exception relating to 'the urgency of the matter'. Thus, it would have been impossible after the date of the contested executive committee meeting to have summoned a special conference of the union in order to deal with the matter before the delegates' votes were cast and the damage was done. This meant that 'the practical reasoning that the court should leave matters of internal decision to the proper constitutional machinery of the association really [did] not apply', Goulding J appearing to acknowledge that the court ought not 'to allow the rule in *Foss* v. *Harbottle* to become the possible instrument of an injustice to the majority that the majority could not afterwards correct'. Although unassisted by any relevant authority on the matter, Goulding J nevertheless held that '*Foss* v. *Harbottle* should not be applied if the result may be to deprive the majority of an opportunity of

---

[63] [1972] 1 WLR 130.
[64] *Ibid.*, p. 138: 'as where subscriptions are being altered, or qualifications for office are being altered, or benefits are being altered'.
[65] *The Times*, 8 September 1966.

carrying out their will', as where 'the constitutional machinery of the body cannot operate in time to be of practical effect'. *McNamee* v. *Cooper* was not followed.

The *Hodgson* case reflects a priority attached by the court to the supremacy of conference over the executive, which might be seen as a victory for representative democracy, although it was not formally expressed in these terms. But in some subsequent cases the courts have been presented with conflicts between executive bodies and conferences in circumstances where the former sought to bypass the latter by a direct appeal to the membership in a referendum. In these cases, the courts have tended to favour the executive at the expense of conference, which may be seen as a result to be a victory for direct democracy over representative democracy. In one such case,[66] the NUM agreed a productivity incentive scheme with the National Coal Board in what was said to be a violation of conference resolutions. The union's executive committee decided to put the scheme to a ballot of the members for their approval, although there was no express authority in the rules for such a ballot. An attempt to restrain the executive committee in the courts nevertheless failed. According to Lord Denning:

> The ballot was a sensible and reasonable proposal by the [executive committee] to take the views by the democratic method of a secret ballot of all the workers affected. It was a far more satisfactory and democratic method than leaving it to the delegates of a conference who might not be truly representative in their individual capacities of the views of the various men they represented.[67]

Trade Union Elections

Trade union government has been the subject of detailed legal controls since 1980, controls that became gradually tighter after each general election between 1979 and 1992. The Employment Act 1980 introduced a provision whereby trade unions could claim a reimbursement of the costs of holding postal ballots to a number of designated trade union elections.[68] This carrot was designed to encourage trade unions to change their practices voluntarily,[69] and was quickly followed by the stick of more coercive legislation in the form of the Trade Union Act 1984 requiring trade unions to elect their principal

---

[66] *NUM* v. *Gormley*, *The Times*, 21 October 1977.

[67] A similar preference for direct democracy over representative democracy is to be seen in *British Actors' Equity Association* v. *Goring* [1978] ICR 791 (HL).

[68] See *R* v. *Certification Officer, ex parte Electrical Power Engineers' Association* [1990] ICR 682.

[69] R. Undy and R. Martin, *Ballots and Trade Union Democracy* (Oxford: Blackwell, 1983), Ch. 1.

executive committees at least every five years in a direct election by the members.[70] This meant that trade unions could no longer elect their executive committees or senior officers indirectly through conference or by other means,[71] although as first introduced the ballot could be held either at the workplace or by post. The Employment Act 1988 was more prescriptive in the sense that ballots were now to be held by post, with an additional requirement being introduced whereby a trade union would be obliged to appoint a qualified independent person to act as a scrutineer for the election. Further changes were made by the Trade Union Reform and Employment Rights Act 1993, with only minor liberalising amendments having been made since the election of a Labour government in 1997.

Statutory Procedures

TULRCA 1992, section 46, imposes a duty on trade unions to 'secure' that every person who holds a position in the union to which the Act applies does so 'by virtue of having been elected'. The election must satisfy the requirements of the Act, and no person should hold office for more than five years without being re-elected. The positions to which this provision applies are the executive bodies of the union and the president and general secretary. For these purposes, a 'member of the executive' is defined to include 'any person who, under the rules or practice of the union, may attend and speak at some or all of the meetings of the executive, otherwise than for the purpose of providing the committee with factual information or with technical or professional advice with respect to matters taken into account by the executive in carrying out its functions'.[72] Also for these purposes, elections do not need to be held for the office of president where the position is held for no more than thirteen months and the individual in question is neither a voting member of the executive nor an employee of the union.[73] Nor – provided prescribed statutory criteria are met – need an election be held if the person in question is due to retire within five years of the expiry of his or her term.[74]

TULRCA 1992, section 47, deals with the right to be a candidate in the above-mentioned elections, no member of the trade union to be 'unreasonably excluded from standing as a candidate'.[75] It is expressly provided that no

---

[70] For background, see *Democracy in Trade Unions*, Cmnd 8778 (1983).

[71] See *Petters* v. *Musicians Union*, Decision D/88–90/01; *Gates* v. *BECTU*, Decision D/23–24/00; *Abrahams* v. *URTU*, Decision D/23–25/16/17.

[72] TULRCA 1992, s. 46(3).   [73] TULRCA 1992, s. 46(4A).

[74] TULRCA 1992, s. 58, on which see *Beaumont* v. *Amicus*, Decision D/3/04.

[75] As pointed out in *Staunton* v. *Unison*, Decision D/11–12/08, s. 47 'does not contain any guidance on what constitutes unreasonable exclusion'. It was held in that case that 'the automatic exclusion of someone from standing as a candidate who is merely the subject of a precautionary suspension [from holding office while the subject of a disciplinary investigation] is *prima facie* unreasonable, in the absence of an express rule permitting such exclusion'. In *Williams* v. *Community*, Decision D/56/06, the complainant was not unreasonably excluded from standing as a candidate by virtue

candidate 'shall be required, directly or indirectly, to be a member of a political party', a measure designed to prevent trade unions making membership of the Labour Party a condition of office. It will be noted that trade unions are not prohibited from banning members of certain political parties from standing for office, an omission which seems calculated to continue to permit trade unions to ban members of the Communist Party from holding office. These unions famously included the electricians' union, now part of Unite, where there is now no such rule. It is also provided that a member of a trade union 'shall not be taken to be unreasonably excluded from standing as a candidate if he is excluded on the ground that he belongs to a class of which all the members are excluded by the rules of the union'.[76] So for example, a union may exclude retired or unemployed members, or members in arrears with their subscriptions. However, 'a rule which provides for such a class to be determined by reference to whom the union chooses to exclude shall be disregarded'.[77] This is designed to ensure that a member is not excluded on arbitrary grounds but only on the basis of objective criteria made clear in advance.[78]

The legislation also makes detailed provisions for the issuing of election addresses,[79] and the appointment of an independent scrutineer,[80] and deals with eligibility to vote. Thus, all members of the union are to have an equal right to vote, although certain classes of members may be excluded (such as those who are unemployed or in arrears with their subscriptions).[81] However, restrictions on the right to vote are to be strictly construed, and any rule 'which established a class of members who are to be denied the right to vote should be clearly expressed'.[82] In *Dooley* v. *Union of Construction and Allied Trades and Technicians (UCATT)*,[83] the union accorded entitlement to vote to only 56,867 of its 130,000 or so members in the election for general secretary in 2009, the rest being excluded because they were more than twenty-six weeks in arrears with their subscriptions. In the absence of a clear rule excluding such members, this was held to be unlawful and the election was annulled on this and other grounds, following a complaint to the Certification Officer by an unsuccessful candidate. Initially, the legislation permitted ballots to be conducted at the workplace or by post, but now they must be conducted only on a

---

of the fact that 'he had not personally received from the Union any written notification explaining the nomination process'. Other steps had been taken to bring the procedures to the attention of members. In *Thompson* v. *NUM*, Decision D/10–14/13–14, it was held that it was not unreasonable to restrict eligibility as a candidate to existing members of the National Executive Committee. See also *Henderson* v. *GMB* UKEAT/0294/16/LA.

[76] TULRCA 1992, s. 47(3). The court or the Certification Officer may have to determine whether such a rule in fact exists: *Abrahams* v. *URTU*, Decision D/23–25/16/17 (Certification Officer rejected union submission that union rules prevented full-time officers standing for general secretary).

[77] TULRCA 1992, s. 47(3). See *Thompson* v. *NUM*, Decision D/10–14/13–14.

[78] *Ecclestone* v. *NUJ* [1999] IRLR 166.   [79] TULRCA 1992, s. 48.   [80] TULRCA 1992, s. 49.

[81] TULRCA 1992, s. 50.   [82] *Dooley* v. *UCATT*, Decision D/44–49/10–11, para. 38.   [83] *Ibid*.

fully postal basis at the union's expense.[84] The votes must be counted by an independent scrutineer appointed by the union.[85]

The Act may be enforced in the event of any alleged malpractice by an application either to the Certification Officer under TULRCA 1992, section 55, or to the High Court under TULRCA 1992, section 56. In either case an application may be made by a member of the union (provided that the applicant was also a member at the time of the contested election), or by a candidate in the election (even though he or she may no longer be a member of the union). The Certification Officer is required to make inquiries and to give the parties an opportunity to be heard, and is empowered to make a declaration and an enforcement order.[86] Where a declaration is made, an enforcement order must also be made unless the Certification Officer considers it inappropriate. The enforcement order must impose on the union one or more of the following requirements: (1) secure the holding of an election in accordance with the order; (2) take such other steps to remedy the declared failure as may be specified in the order; (3) abstain from such acts as may be so specified with a view to securing that a failure of the same or a similar kind does not occur in future.[87] An appeal lies from the Certification Officer to the EAT on a point of law 'arising in any proceedings before or arising from any decision' of the Certification Officer.[88]

Rule-book Obligations

The statutory procedures are not the only source of regulation of trade union elections. Trade union constitutions and rules continue to be important in relation to the elections to which the legislation applies, as well as to elections to which the legislation does not apply. Beginning with the former, it is now standard practice for elections in larger unions to be contested. Complaints (usually by defeated candidates) may relate to both an alleged breach of the statutory requirements set out above, as well as alleged breaches of the union's rules. These complaints are now typically made to the Certification Officer in a single application, for although rule-book breaches can be made to the High Court, the Certification Officer has jurisdiction over both types of complaint.[89] Both types of complaint may be made in the same application, and in high-profile cases for the election of General Secretary in UNISON and

---

[84] TULRCA 1992, s. 51.   [85] TULRCA 1992, s. 51A.   [86] TULRCA 1992, s. 55.

[87] TULRCA 1992, s. 55.

[88] TULRCA 1992, s. 56. In *Henderson* v. *GMB* UKEAT/0294/16/LA, the EAT reversed a Certification Officer decision that the appellant had not been unreasonably excluded as a candidate but declined to make an enforcement order because of the passage of time and the likely weakness of the candidature.

[89] TULRCA 1992, s. 108A. The most recent reported High Court challenges for breach of rules in elections governed by statute are now rather dated: *Wise* v. *USDAW* [1996] ICR 691; and *Douglas* v. *Graphical, Print and Media Union* [1995] IRLR 426.

Unite the Union respectively, the complaints have related mainly to rule-book breaches.[90] Although the elections are required and governed by statute, union rules will usually supplement the statutory requirements by dealing with matters such as nomination procedures, the conduct of campaigns, the use of union resources by candidates, and access by the candidates to branch and membership data.

In dealing with these cases, the Certification Officer has adopted an approach to the interpretation of union rules which emphasises that trade union rules 'are not to be construed literally or like a statute, but so to give them a reasonable interpretation which accords with what, in the court's view, they must have been intended to mean, bearing in mind their authorship, their purpose, and the readership to which they are addressed'.[91] Nevertheless in *Burgess* v. *UNISON*,[92] the Assistant Certification Officer held that there had been a breach of the union's rules for the election of general secretary, in what was a sometimes stinging criticism of the union. Many allegations of abuse were made by four candidates who were defeated by an incumbent standing for re-election, although much of the case related to union rules which prohibited (i) union resources being used in support of any of the candidates, and union officials (ii) campaigning for any of the candidates during working time. Although the 'brazenness' of one senior official was said to be 'distasteful', with 'evidence of widespread malpractice throughout the Greater London Region so as to throw doubts on the votes of the whole region', the Assistant Certification Officer nevertheless concluded on a balance of probabilities that the official's conduct was unknown to Mr Prentis, the successful candidate. But the Assistant Certification Officer declined to make an enforcement order to annul the election,[93] on the ground that it would be disproportionate to do so.[94]

As pointed out, the statutory procedures do not apply to all trade union elections, but only to those positions expressly governed by the legislation. But trade unions also elect members to serve at regional, district, branch and workplace level. In these cases, the position will be governed only by the rule-book of the union in question, rather than by a combination of statute and

---

[90] See *Burgess* v. *Unison*, Decision D/5–20/17–18; and *Hicks* v. *Unite the Union*, Decision D/32–39/14–15, *Coyne* v. *Unite the Union*, Decision D/2/18–19 (upheld on appeal).

[91] *Jacques* v. *AUEW (Engineering Section)* [1986] ICR 683. See also *Porter* v. *NUJ* [1980] IRLR 404, and *British Actors Equity* v. *Goring* [1997] ICR 393. In *Burgess* v. *Unison*, Decision D/5–20/17–18, the Certification Officer left open the question whether the rules should always be construed to favour the most democratic manner, an argument she said to be 'controversial' but unnecessary to decide.

[92] Decision D/5–20/17–18.   [93] TULRCA 1992, s. 108B.

[94] On the Certification Officer's discretion, see *Bakhsh* v. *Unison*, Decision D/39/05, and *Burgess* v. *Unison*, Decision D/5–20/17–18. In the latter, the Certification Officer had regard to a range of matters, including cost, and the overall number of votes cast in favour of Mr Prentis in regions where there was a lack of evidence of impropriety. See also *GMB* v. *Stokes*, UKEAT/769/03 – EAT holds that the making of an enforcement order essentially a matter of judgment for the Certification Officer.

rule-book. Although there a number of important cases which in the past have been heard in the High Court and beyond, these cases too are typically heard now by the Certification Officer.[95] Cases of this kind before the Certification Officer are likely to raise questions about (1) the content of the rules;[96] (2) the conduct of the ballot under the rules (in terms of the procedures to be followed and applied);[97] and (3) the removal of an elected member from office before the expiry of his or her term.[98] However, much of the jurisprudence binding the Certification Officer is quite old, it being necessary to go back twenty years or more to determine the governing principles applicable in this field. Indeed, the last Court of Appeal decision of any note was reported in 1971.[99] These cases are referred to by the Certification Officer as appropriate, but they should be treated with caution in what is emerging as a largely autonomous jurisdiction subject to oversight only by the EAT, the decisions of which on trade union internal affairs are generally not reported.

Apart from the costs involved in High Court litigation, the courts typically seemed unwilling to encourage applications dealing with disputes in trade union branches. In *Breen* v. *Amalgamated Engineering Union*,[100] the applicant had been elected as a shop steward but his election was not endorsed by the union's district committee as the rules required. Although the Court of Appeal held that the district committee had to act fairly in deciding whether or not to confirm the election, this did not mean that the committee's decision had to be 'based on reasons which would convince all right-thinking people', provided it arrived at 'an *honest* conclusion' and 'adopted no improper methods in reaching it'. In this case the Court of Appeal held that Breen's practice of paying his subscriptions in arrears and in breach of the rules was sufficient reason to disqualify him: the committee 'were quite entitled to take the view that a shop steward should set a good example and that laxity of this kind should not be tolerated'.[101] Recent Certification Officer decisions suggest that branch and workplace election related complaints are no more likely to be successful before the Certification Officer than they would be before the High Court. Although the Certification Officer could not claim to be deluged by such complaints, there is nevertheless a steady flow of such cases, and although

---

[95] On the jurisdiction of the Certification Officer in such matters, see below.

[96] *Gates* v. *Society of Chiropodists and Podiatrists*, Decision D/7/18–19; *Wilson* v. *Unison*, Decision D/18/15–16.

[97] *Dinsdale* v. *GMB*, Decision D/3–4/18–19; *Penkethman* v. *CWU*, Decision CO/21–22/17–18; *Barton* v. *Unison*, Decision D 52/14–15; and *Knights* v. *NUT*, Decision D/16/14/15.

[98] *Cullen* v. *Unite the Union*, Decision D/1/18–19; *Singh* v. *Unite the Union*, Decision D/54/14–15; *Williams* v. *Musicians' Union*, Decision D/30/13/14.

[99] *Breen* v. *Amalgamated Engineering Union* [1971] 2 QB 175.   [100] [1971] 2 QB 175.

[101] Compare *Shotton* v. *Hammond* (1976) 120 Sol. Jo. 780: a 'rare case' where the elected shop steward was refused ratification because he declined to agree to a district committee condition that he comply with its instructions, whether lawful or not. The applicant succeeded.

no doubt irritating it is probably important that there is some external scrutiny of all levels of trade union government.

Trade Union Members' Rights

Our concern so far has been mainly with the structure of government within trade unions and the powers of the different governing institutions. As we pointed out in the introduction to this chapter, state intervention in this field ought to be consistent with the principles of international law, which give special protection to trade union freedom. Much of what we have discussed relates to the role of the courts in enforcing the constitution of the union, in some cases circumventing rules of their own creation. Intervention of this kind is unlikely to be seen to violate freedom of association, the courts simply enforcing the union's own rules. The other part of the discussion has been concerned with state intervention in the form of legislation to regulate the powers, structure and government of trade unions. But to the extent that this legislation addresses political objects and the mandatory election of union officers and executive bodies, it has been found by the ILO supervisory bodies that the legislation in question does not go beyond the requirements of Convention 87, Article 3, to which we have already referred.[102] The position is different when we turn our attention from the questions of trade union government to member protection, which has been developed by Parliament to give statutory rights to trade unionists beyond those that may be provided by trade union rule-books. Although some of these are unexceptionable, others appear to lose sight of '[t]he essence of a trade union activity' recognised by the High Court, namely, that 'members are bound to act collectively to achieve the objects of the majority'.[103]

Right to Information

An area where intervention is largely unexceptionable relates to access to information, it being the essence of all democratic and accountable organisations that they operate openly and transparently. A right of trade union members to have access to union financial records was first introduced in the Trade Union Act 1871. This was repealed in 1971, it having previously been held that the member could employ skilled agents to inspect the accounts on their behalf.[104] But in some cases the statutory obligation found its way into trade union rule-books, and these rule-book provisions survived the repeal of the 1871 Act. In *Taylor* v. *NUM (Derbyshire Area) (No. 2)*,[105] it was held that

---

[102] See K. D. Ewing, *Britain and the ILO* (2nd edn, London: Institute of Employment Rights, 1994), Ch. 7.
[103] *Goring* v. *British Actors' Equity Association* [1987] IRLR 122, at 125.
[104] *Dodd* v. *Amalgamated Marine Workers' Union* [1924] 1 Ch 116.   [105] [1985] IRLR 65.

the contractual right in the rule-book was to be construed in the same way as the previous statutory right, so that the union could not object to the member inspecting the books in the presence of an accountant. It would of course have been open to the union to provide expressly that the right of inspection in the rule-book was not to be construed as the plaintiffs contended, but this had not been done in this case.

With the repeal of the 1871 Act, trade union members had no greater rights than members of the public to financial information about their union. Under the Trade Union and Labour Relations Act 1974, members of the public were entitled to inspect the annual return which the union was required to submit to the Certification Officer.[106] This gave rise to expressions of concern by the then Conservative government, which in a green paper, *Trade Unions and Their Members*, commented that:

> It is reasonable to assume that a union member has a greater interest in his union's affairs than members of the public. However, in a significant number of major unions, which do not contain provisions on this matter in their rule-books, members may be limited to the information available from the Certification Office or on request from the union. The information required to meet statutory provisions only gives an outline of a union's financial affairs and is usually supplied by the union's head office on behalf of the whole union rather than by individual branches. In addition, because it consists of accounts which have had to be audited, it will not reflect the current state of the union's affairs.[107]

The position is now governed in some detail by TULRCA 1992, containing measures first introduced in the Employment Act 1988.

By virtue of TULRCA 1992, section 28, a trade union is required to keep 'proper accounting records with respect to its transactions and its assets and liabilities', and to 'establish and maintain a satisfactory system of control of its accounting records'. The records must 'give a true and fair view of the state of the affairs of the trade union and to explain its transactions'. By virtue of TULRCA 1992, section 29, these records must be kept available for inspection for a period of six years, and this applies to all records, including those of a branch or section of the union. And by virtue of TULRCA 1992, section 30, a member of a trade union 'has a right to request access to any accounting records of the union which are available for inspection and relate to periods including a time when he was a member of the union'.[108] Where a request for

---

[106] Trade Union and Labour Relations Act 1974, s. 11.   [107] Cm 95 (1987), para. 3.24.

[108] The leading case on TULRCA 1992, s. 30 is *Unite the Union* v. *Mills* UKEAT/0148/16/LA, where it was said that accounting records are 'records which give a true and fair view of the state of affairs of a trade union, its assets and liabilities and those necessary to explain its transactions' (para. 58). In *Mills*, although the EAT disagreed with the Certification Officer as to the definition of accounting records, it agreed that (1) information about payment to branch members were accounting records, and (2) that revealing the identity of the beneficiaries did not breach Convention rights (notably Art. 8).

access is made by a member, the union must make arrangements for access to be provided within twenty-eight days, and must also allow the member to be accompanied by an accountant (provided the accountant accepts a reasonable condition imposed by the union to protect the confidentiality of the records). The member must be allowed to take, or be supplied with, copies of, or of extracts from, the records inspected, but may be charged a fee to meet the reasonable administrative costs of the union.

These provisions are enforceable by way of a complaint to the Certification Officer (and then the EAT) or the High Court. But in addition to these and other measures designed to enhance the accountability of trade unions to their members, the legislation retains a measure of public accountability. Trade unions are required to submit an annual return to the Certification Officer, this to contain the revenue accounts and balance sheet of the union in question, as well as the salary and benefits of senior officers.[109] The annual return must now also include details of industrial action in which the union had been engaged,[110] as well as a detailed breakdown of political expenditure.[111] The financial information must be independently audited.[112] Any person has a right to be supplied with a copy of the annual return (on payment of a reasonable fee) as well as to inspect it at the offices of the Certification Officer.[113] In addition, the union must provide an abbreviated account to its members within eight weeks of the annual return being lodged with the Certification Officer.[114] Failure to comply with the foregoing measures may be an offence,[115] the offence deemed to have been committed not only by the trade union but also by a responsible officer.[116] Summary conviction can lead to a fine or imprisonment.[117]

Right Not to Strike

More controversial than the member's right to be supplied with information about his or her union is the right of the individual member not to strike, in the sense of not being liable to discipline or expulsion for failing to take part in a strike. This is an issue which has caused the courts difficulty from time to time in the past, leading them to thrash around unconvincingly, looking for a way of protecting the member, as in *Esterman* v. *NALGO*[118] discussed below. The issue is also addressed in the green paper, *Trade Unions and Their Members*,[119] where the then-government claimed that 'the right of the

---

[109] TULRCA 1992, s. 32.
[110] TULRCA 1992, s. 32ZA (inserted by Trade Union Act 2016, s. 7).
[111] TULRCA 1992, s. 32ZB (inserted by Trade Union Act 2016, s. 12).
[112] On which, see TULRCA 1992, ss. 33–7.   [113] TULRCA 1992, s. 32(5) and (6).
[114] TULRCA 1992, s. 32A.   [115] TULRCA 1992, s. 45(1).   [116] TULRCA 1992, s. 45(2).
[117] TULRCA 1992, s. 45A.
[118] [1974] ICR 625. See E. McKendrick, 'Trade Unions and Non-Striking Members' (1986) 6 *Legal Studies* 35.
[119] Cm 95 (1987).

individual to choose to go to work despite a call to take industrial action is an essential freedom', and expressed concern that this 'essential freedom' can often be challenged 'by those who take a hard line view of the traditional philosophy of the trade union movement based on the concept of collective strength through solidarity'.[120] Concern was also expressed that a trade union may:

> lead its members into action for which it has legal immunity but for which the members do not. Although it is rare for an employer to sue his workers individually, if they take industrial action they face a real possibility of being dismissed without being able to claim unfair dismissal. A tough choice therefore faces the union member called by his union to take industrial action: either to follow the union down a path which will almost certainly reduce his income and may lead to a loss of job, or to carry on working and face disciplinary action by the union.[121]

These concerns gave rise to what was the Employment Act 1988, section 3,[122] and what are now TULRCA 1992, sections 64 and 65. Section 64 provides that 'an individual who is or has been a member of a trade union has the right not to be unjustifiably disciplined by the union'. For this purpose, discipline means a determination under the rules that the individual should be subject to expulsion; a fine or another financial penalty; the deprivation of benefits, services or facilities; advice given to another trade union not to accept the individual in question as a member; or the imposition of some other detriment. The question whether an individual is 'unjustifiably disciplined' is to be determined in accordance with section 65, which sets out the type of conduct by the individual in relation to which disciplinary penalties may not be imposed.

Trade Union and Labour Relations (Consolidation) Act 1992, Section 65(2)

This section applies to conduct which consists in—

(a) failing to participate in or support a strike or other industrial action (whether by members of the union or by others), or indicating opposition to or a lack of support for such action;

(b) failing to contravene, for a purpose connected with such a strike or other industrial action, a requirement imposed on him by or under a contract of employment;

(c) asserting (whether by bringing proceedings or otherwise) that the union, any official or representative of it or a trustee of its property has contravened, or is proposing to contravene, a requirement which is, or is thought to be, imposed by or under the rules of

---

[120] *Ibid.*, para. 2.10.

[121] *Ibid.*, para. 2.11. Dismissal for participation in protected industrial action may now be unfair. See Chapter 17.

[122] On which, see E. McKendrick, 'The Rights of Trade Union Members: Part I of the Employment Act 1988' (1988) 17 *Industrial Law Journal* 141.

the union or any other agreement or by or under any enactment (whenever passed) or any rule of law;

(d) encouraging or assisting a person—
    (i) to perform an obligation imposed on him by a contract of employment, or
    (ii) to make or attempt to vindicate any such assertion as is mentioned in paragraph (c);

(e) contravening a requirement imposed by or in consequence of a determination which infringes the individual's or another individual's right not to be unjustifiably disciplined;

(f) failing to agree, or withdrawing agreement, to the making from his wages (in accordance with arrangements between his employer and the union) of deductions representing payments to the union in respect of his membership,

(g) resigning or proposing to resign from the union or from another union, becoming or proposing to become a member of another union, refusing to become a member of another union, or being a member of another union,

(h) working with, or proposing to work with, individuals who are not members of the union or who are or are not members of another union,

(i) working for, or proposing to work for, an employer who employs or who has employed individuals who are not members of the union or who are or are not members of another union, or

(j) requiring the union to do an act which the union is, by any provision of this Act, required to do on the requisition of a member.

The foregoing provisions override any disciplinary power the union may otherwise have in its rules. Although they do not apply to all trade union disciplinary decisions,[123] TULRCA 1992, sections 64 and 65 apply to a great deal more than the right not to strike. So in *Kelly* v. *Unison*,[124] four members were unlawfully disciplined by exclusion for office by claiming that their motions to the union's annual conference had not been accepted because the Standing Orders Committee was seeking to stifle debate. This would be covered by TULRCA 1992, section 65(2)(c). Nevertheless, most of the reported cases under TULRCA 1992, sections 64 and 65 have been concerned with strike-breakers who sought to assert their rights not to be disciplined. In *Knowles* v. *Fire Brigades Union*,[125] however, the Court of Appeal cautioned against reading the phrase 'industrial action' too widely for these purposes, holding that what constitutes industrial action is a mixed question of fact and law, in which it will be relevant to take into account the effect of the action being taken on the contracts of employment of those involved. Enforcement of

---

[123] See *Medhurst* v. *NALGO* [1990] ICR 687: TULRCA 1992, ss. 64 and 65 did not apply where the applicant had been suspended from membership for tape-recording the meetings of a local executive committee.

[124] [2012] IRLR 442.   [125] [1997] ICR 595.

TULRCA 1992, section 64, is by way of a complaint to an ET rather than the Certification Officer, with a right of appeal to the EAT and then to the Court of Appeal.[126] In cases of disciplinary decisions where TULRCA 1992, sections 64 and 65 do not apply, other remedies would have to be sought before the Certification Officer or elsewhere, if it can be shown that the decision in question breaches the rules of the union.

It is at this point that we begin seriously to confront questions about the compatibility of domestic law with ILO freedom of association obligations, the ILO Committee of Experts having reported in 1989 in relation to what is now TULRCA 1992, sections 64 and 65, that 'one of the basic rights which is guaranteed by Article 3 of the Convention is the right of organisations of workers and employers to draw up their constitutions and rules free from any interference which would restrict this right or impede the lawful exercise thereof'.[127] The Committee accepted that 'the right of organisations to draw up their constitutions and rules must be subject to the need to respect fundamental human rights and the law of the land (bearing in mind that Article 8(2) of the Convention stipulates that the law of the land shall not be such as to impair the guarantees provided for in the Convention)'.[128] This meant that it would not be inconsistent with the requirements of the Convention to require that union rules must not discriminate against members or potential members on grounds of race or sex. Nor would it be inconsistent with Article 3 to have in place measures such as TULRCA 1992, section 65(2)(c), 'which state that unions may not discipline members who, in good faith, assert that their union has breached its own rules, or the law of the land'.[129] But that was as far as compromise could go, the Committee taking the view that:

> It is clear that provisions which deprive trade unions of the capacity lawfully to give effect to their democratically determined rules are, *prima facie*, not in conformity with this right. Section 3 of the 1988 Act [now TULRCA 1992, sections 64 and 65] clearly has this effect, and on that basis is not in conformity with Article 3 ... It follows that proper respect for the guarantees provided by Article 3 requires that union members should be permitted, when drawing up their constitutions and rules, to determine whether or not it should be possible to discipline members who refuse to participate in lawful strikes and other

---

[126] The remedy is by way of compensation, for which a separate application to an ET must be made (TULRCA 1992, ss. 66 and 67). The amount of compensation is such an amount as the tribunal thinks just and equitable, although it includes injury to feelings (*Massey* v. *UNIFI* [2007] EWCA Civ 800, [2008] ICR 62), and is subject to a statutory minimum of £9,474 at the time of writing (TULRCA 1992, s. 67(8A)).

[127] ILO Committee of Experts, Observation Concerning Convention 87 (United Kingdom) (1989).

[128] *Ibid.* The Convention referred to here is ILO Convention 87.

[129] *Ibid.* See also *Kelly* v. *Unison* [2012] IRLR 442, where it was held that whatever the position with regard to some of the other provisions in TULRCA 1992, ss. 64 and 65, s. 65(2)(c) was not incompatible with the ECHR, Art. 11.

industrial action or who seek to persuade fellow members to refuse to participate in such action. Section 3 of the Act should be amended so as to take account of this view.[130]

A Bill of Rights for Trade Union Members?

UK law now provides a comprehensive Bill of Rights for trade union members, which contrasts sharply with the correspondingly limited rights of trade unions, especially in their dealings with employers. Important rights of trade union members include:

(1) a right of access to information (TULRCA 1992, section 30);

(2) a right to be supplied with information (TULRCA 1992, section 32A);

(3) a right to approve the adoption and renewal of political objects (TULRCA 1992, section 73);

(4) a right to not to pay the political levy, either by opting out, or by not opting in (TULRCA 1992, sections 82, 84);

(5) a right to elect the senior officers and executive body of the union at least every five years (TULRCA 1992, section 46);

(6) a right to stand as a candidate and to vote in such elections (TULRCA 1992, sections 47 and 50);

(7) a right to vote in a ballot before industrial action (TULRCA 1992, section 62);

(8) a right not to be unjustifiably disciplined, including a right not to take part in industrial action (TULRCA 1992, sections 64 and 65);

(9) a right not to be excluded or expelled except for reasons authorised by statute (TULRCA 1992, section 174);

(10) a right not to be denied access to the courts (TULRCA 1992, section 63).

Trade Union Exclusion and Expulsion

In addition to the measures already discussed, there is also specific protection for the trade union member who is expelled from his or her union in order to give effect to the TUC Disputes Principles and Procedures.[131] These are designed in turn to stop one union poaching the members of another, and to stop one union from organising in a workplace where another is already established. Initially adopted at the annual conference of the TUC at Bridlington in 1939 (and known for some time thereafter as the 'Bridlington Principles'), the

---

[130] ILO Committee of Experts, Observation Concerning Convention 87 (United Kingdom) (1989). Similar views have in relation to this issue since been expressed in 1991, 1993, 1995, 1997, 1999, 2001, 2003 and 2005. For the European Social Rights Committee, see European Committee of Social Rights, Conclusions XIX-3 (2010) (United Kingdom), expressing concern that this measure which 'severely restricts the grounds on which a trade union may lawfully discipline members, [represents] unjustified incursions into the autonomy of trade unions' (p. 11).

[131] TUC Disputes Principles and Procedures (2016).

Principles have been revised on a number of occasions since. For present purposes, the most important principle is Principle 2, which provides:

> It is in the interests of all affiliates and the Movement to build trade union membership, and the Movement to develop and maintain stable trade union structures. Members moving from union to union, without agreed regulation and procedure, can undermine collective bargaining structures and may even threaten the existence of trade union organisation within a particular company or group of workers. All affiliates of the TUC accept as a binding commitment to their continued affiliation to the TUC that they will not knowingly and actively seek to take into membership existing or 'recent' members of another union by making recruitment approaches, either directly or indirectly, without the agreement of that organisation.

Notes to Principle 2 require each union to ask prospective members whether they are or have been a member of any other trade union: this is to help avoid any unauthorised transfers of members.

Cheall and its Progeny

The operation of these arrangements has been considered by the courts on a number of occasions, and most recently by the House of Lords in *Cheall* v. *Association of Professional, Executive, Clerical and Computer Staff (APEX)*.[132] The plaintiff in that case had been expelled from the defendant union, after having been accepted into membership in the full knowledge that he was a member of another union, the Association of Cinematograph, Television and Allied Technicians (ACTTS). Under the TUC's Disputes Principles and Procedures, a complaint may be made to the TUC by one union (in this case, the ACTTS) that another (in this case, APEX) has acted in breach of the Principles. If the TUC secretariat is unable to conciliate a settlement, it may appoint a disputes committee from a panel of leading trade unionists to investigate the matter and to make an award.[133] Before 1993, the normal remedy where a complaint was upheld would be an order requiring the offending union to expel from membership those members who had been recruited in breach of the Principles.[134] Most unions had adopted a TUC model rule for this purpose, which enabled them to expel a member with six weeks' notice to give effect to a decision of a disputes committee.[135] It was in

---

[132] [1983] 2 AC 180. See R. C. Simpson. 'The TUC's Bridlington Principles and the Law' (1983) 46 *Modern Law Review* 635.

[133] The procedures, which are expressly stated not to be legally binding, apply only to the unions affiliated to the TUC. These, however, account for the great bulk of trade union members.

[134] TUC affiliated unions typically had adopted a model rule authorising, if necessary, the termination of membership after six weeks' notice of any member, to comply with a decision of the disputes committee.

[135] The courts had refused to imply a power on the part of a union to expel a member to comply with a disputes committee ruling: *Spring* v. *NASDS* [1956] 1 WLR 585.

the exercise of such a rule-book power that Mr Cheall was expelled by APEX, an expulsion which he challenged in the High Court on the ground that he had been expelled in breach of natural justice (no hearing having been offered), under the authority of a rule that was contrary to public policy.

The action failed at first instance before Bingham J, a decision restored by the House of Lords following Mr Cheall's short-lived success in the Court of Appeal. As to the natural-justice point, the House of Lords rejected the claim that the appellant was entitled to be heard either by the TUC disputes committee before it made its decision in the dispute between ACTTS and APEX, or by APEX before it expelled him. As to the former, Cheall had no standing to make representations in a dispute to which he was not a party; and as to the latter, there was no duty to provide a hearing in circumstances 'where nothing he said could affect the outcome'.[136] According to Lord Diplock, 'different considerations might apply if the effect of Cheall's expulsion from APEX were to have put his job in jeopardy, either because of the existence of a closed shop or for some other reason. But this is not the case.'[137] So far as public policy was concerned, this was famously rejected, with Lord Diplock's remark that 'freedom of association can only be mutual; there can be no right of an individual to associate with other individuals who are not willing to associate with him'.[138] He continued:

> I know of no existing rule of public policy that would prevent trade unions from entering into arrangements with one another which they consider to be in the interests of their members in promoting order in industrial relations and enhancing their members' bargaining power with their employers; nor do I think it a permissible exercise of your Lordships' judicial power to create a new rule of public policy to that effect. If this is to be done at all it must be done by Parliament.[139]

The Conservative government duly accepted Lord Diplock's challenge, taking the view that the Bridlington Principles were 'another outdated and undemocratic restriction' on employee 'freedom of choice', 'fundamentally flawed' for making no provision 'for union members to be consulted or for their wishes to be taken into account'.[140] These concerns, which were trailed in the green paper *Industrial Relations in the 1990s*,[141] are reflected in what is now TULRCA 1992, section 174, a measure introduced by the Trade Union Reform and Employment Rights Act 1993, section 14.[142] TULRCA 1992, section 174,

---

[136] [1983] 2 AC 180, at 190.   [137] *Ibid.*, p. 191.

[138] *Ibid.* The European Commission on Human Rights appeared to agree with this analysis, holding that Mr Cheall's Convention rights had not been violated: *Cheall* v. *United Kingdom* (1986) 8 EHRR 74.

[139] [1983] 2 AC 180, at 191.   [140] HC Debs., 17 November 1992, col. 171.

[141] Cm 1602 (1991).

[142] See B. Simpson, 'Individualism Versus Collectivism: An Evaluation of Section 14 of the Trade Union Reform and Employment Rights Act 1993' (1993) 22 *Industrial Law Journal* 181.

provides that an individual may be 'excluded or expelled from a trade union' for one of only four permitted purposes. Essentially, these are related to the fact that the individual:

- is not employed in a trade or occupation in which the union organises;
- is ineligible for membership because the union operates in only another part of the UK;
- is no longer employed by the employer where the purpose of the union 'is the regulation of relations between its members and one particular employer or a number of employers who are associated'; or
- has been excluded for reasons 'wholly attributable to conduct'.

For this last purpose, it was expressly provided that conduct did not include membership of a political party, an apparently innocuous government back-bench amendment that was to cause unanticipated problems for trade unions seeking to deal with infiltration by the BNP.[143]

We return to the BNP problem below.[144] In the meantime, it is to be noted that TULRCA 1992, section 174(5), provides that an excluded or expelled individual may present a claim to an ET, which has an exclusive jurisdiction for this purpose.[145] The tribunal may make a declaration that the complaint is well founded, and the successful applicant may make a subsequent application to the employment tribunal for compensation.[146] Compensation is to be assessed on the basis of what is 'just and equitable' (and may be reduced on the same grounds for contributory fault),[147] although there is a minimum award of compensation payable where the applicant has not been admitted or re-admitted in the union.[148] Following the introduction of what is now section 174, it thus became necessary for the TUC to alter the Disputes Principles and Procedures, particularly in relation to the remedy the disputes committee could award in the event of a breach. Because of the statutory constraints on the expulsion of members, provision is now made for the offending union to compensate the complaining union where complaints are upheld. In practice, however, this does not go to the core of the problem: the Disputes Principles and Procedures are addressed not simply to the loss of revenue, but to the dilution of influence. There has, however, been a decline in the number of TUC Disputes Principles and Procedures cases in recent years, as the number of trade unions continues to decline with a rapid growth of mergers and amalgamations.[149]

---

[143] Nor does it include conduct to which TULRCA 1992, s. 65, applies (now referred to as 'excluded conduct'): TULRCA 1992, s. 174(4).

[144] On which, see J. Hendy and K. D. Ewing, 'Trade Unions, Human Rights and the BNP' (2005) 34 *Industrial Law Journal* 197.

[145] TULRCA 1992, s. 177.   [146] TULRCA 1992, s. 176.

[147] TULRCA 1992, s. 176(4) and (5).

[148] TULRCA 1992, s. 176(6A). At the time of writing, the minimum award is £9,474.

[149] TUC Disputes Committee awards are reported in the TUC's annual report.

ASLEF and its Progeny

As already explained, TULRCA 1992, section 174, as originally enacted, provided that trade unions could exclude or expel someone for a reason 'entirely attributable to his conduct'.[150] But for this purpose, it was expressly provided that conduct did not include being a member of a political party.[151] That is to say, a trade union could not lawfully exclude or expel someone because he or she was a member of a political party (even where this may have been only part of the reason for exclusion or expulsion). Anyone excluded or expelled in this way would have been entitled to recover the minimum award of compensation if the union refused to admit or re-admit. Trade unions are not politically sectarian bodies and typically this restraint would not normally give rise to any problems in practice. They were, however, troubled by the activities of the BNP, and by the perceived infiltration of trade unions by BNP members and activists. BNP policies and activities are contrary to the objects and principles of trade unionism, and some unions had taken express steps to deal with this problem. The rules of UNISON, for example, now provide for the exclusion and expulsion of members of the BNP and the National Front.[152]

This issue came to a head in *Lee* v. *ASLEF*,[153] where proceedings were brought by the applicant train driver. Mr Lee had been expelled from ASLEF, after it was discovered that he had been a BNP candidate in a local election. Further inquiries revealed that he was 'quite a well-known activist in the BNP' and that he had stood before for the party in general elections. It was also alleged that Mr Lee had distributed anti-Islamic leaflets and harassed a member of the Anti-Nazi League. The allegations included taking photographs, making 'throat cut' gestures and following a woman to her home where it is alleged that he 'clocked' her house number. Following his expulsion from the association, Mr Lee brought proceedings in an ET claiming that he had been unlawfully expelled because of his membership of a political party, contrary to TULRCA 1992, section 174. His success in the ET led to a complaint by the union to the ECtHR, alleging that its rights under the ECHR, Article 11, had been violated, this protecting the right to freedom of association. It also led to an amendment to TULRCA 1992, with the Employment Relations Act 2004 providing that, while a trade union could not lawfully exclude or expel someone for membership of a political party (now referred to as 'protected conduct'), it could do so for taking part in the activities of a political party.[154]

---

[150] TULRCA 1992, s. 174(2)(d).   [151] TULRCA 1992, s. 174(4)(a)(iii).

[152] Now UNISON Rules (2017), rule I.3. See p. 558.   [153] EAT/0625/03/RN.

[154] TULRCA 1992, s. 174(4B). The 2004 Act also addressed the situation where the exclusion or expulsion was mainly (as opposed to wholly) on the ground of membership of a political party. In that case, if the other reasons for the exclusion or expulsion were for conduct contrary to the rules or policies of the union, then in some circumstances there would be no right to a minimum award of compensation (TULRCA 1992, s. 176(6B)). This would apply, for example,

After *ASLEF* v. *UK*,[155] however, it was clear that the 2004 amendments did not go far enough to meet Convention obligations. The case raised interesting questions about the substance of Article 11, and whether priority should be given to the individual worker or the trade union he or she wished to join. Does the right to freedom of association mean that the worker has the right to join the trade union of his or her choice? Or does it mean that the trade union has the right to exclude individuals who are hostile to its interests? The ECtHR came down clearly in favour of the latter:

> Article 11 cannot be interpreted as imposing an obligation on associations or organisations to admit whosoever wishes to join. Where associations are formed by people, who, espousing particular values or ideals, intend to pursue common goals, it would run counter to the very effectiveness of the freedom at stake if they had no control over their membership. By way of example, it is uncontroversial that religious bodies and political parties can generally regulate their membership to include only those who share their beliefs and ideals. Similarly, the right to join a union 'for the protection of his interests' cannot be interpreted as conferring a general right to join the union of one's choice irrespective of the rules of the union: in the exercise of their rights under Article 11(1) unions must remain free to decide, in accordance with union rules, questions concerning admission to and expulsion from the union.[156]

This, however, was subject to the permitted restrictions of the Article 11(1) right recognised by Article 11(2), which enables the state to protect the individual against any abuse of a dominant position by trade unions. According to the Court, 'such abuse might occur, for example, where exclusion or expulsion from a trade union was not in accordance with union rules or where the rules were wholly unreasonable or arbitrary or where the consequences of exclusion or expulsion resulted in exceptional hardship'.[157] In this case, there was no evidence of 'any identifiable hardship suffered by Mr Lee or any abusive and unreasonable conduct by the applicant',[158] with the result that the union's claim of a breach of Article 11 succeeded.

The government was thus required to make a second attempt at amending TULRCA 1992, section 174.[159] At the heart of the latest amendments is a power on the part of trade unions to exclude or expel for party membership but only if membership of the party is contrary to a rule or an objective of the

---

where the main reason for exclusion or expulsion was party membership and an ancillary reason was party activities. Where the reason was wholly party membership, this qualification would not apply. Where the reason was wholly party activities, there would be no need for this qualification to apply because the exclusion or expulsion would be lawful.

[155] [2007] ECHR 184. See K. D. Ewing, 'The Implications of the *ASLEF* Case' (2007) 36 *Industrial Law Journal* 425.

[156] [2007] ECHR 184, para. 39.   [157] *Ibid.*, para. 43.   [158] *Ibid.*, para. 52.

[159] Employment Relations Act 2008, s. 19.

union, and provided in the latter case the objective is reasonably ascertainable (in which case it would not be 'protected conduct').[160] But even then, an exclusion or expulsion will not be lawful (1) unless the decision to exclude or expel is taken in accordance with the union's rules; (2) unless the decision to exclude or expel is taken fairly; or (3) if the individual would lose his or her livelihood or suffer other exceptional hardship by reason of not being, or ceasing to be, a member of the union.[161] So far as (2) is concerned, a decision will be unfair if (and only if) the individual is (a) not given notice of the proposal to expel or exclude him or her, or (b) not given a fair opportunity to make representations before the decision is taken.[162] So far as (3) is concerned, a major worry for a union would be that there is no definition of what constitutes exceptional hardship; no one was able to provide any convincing examples during the parliamentary consideration of the new provisions, and it will be impossible to tell at the time the power is exercised whether exclusion or expulsion will cause hardship, or indeed if the hardship will be exceptional.

Trade Union Disciplinary Procedures and Decisions

It is clear from the foregoing that there is now a great deal of statutory regulation of the circumstances in which trade unions may discipline or expel members. But as in the case of the arrangements for trade union elections discussed above, the legislation does not tell the whole story. Most disciplinary action will deal with matters such as the non-payment of subscriptions, or because of the use of racist or sexist language, or because of a failure or refusal to comply with union policy. These are all cases where the individual is being disciplined or expelled for reasons of conduct, a ground for expulsion authorised by TULRCA 1992, section 174. But although expulsion is permitted on these grounds, the union can only discipline or expel to the extent that it has power to do so under its rules, the courts being generally unwilling to imply a power to discipline or expel.[163] In practice, trade unions will normally have wide powers to discipline and expel members expressly provided in the rule-book, as in the case of UNISON, the rules of which are set out below.

---

[160] TULRCA 1992, s. 174(4C), (4D) and (4E).   [161] TULRCA 1992, s. 174(4F) and (4G).

[162] TULRCA 1992, s. 174(4H)(a). The decision will also be unfair if any such representations are not considered fairly (s. 174(4H)(b)).

[163] *Kelly* v. *National Society of Operative Printers* (1915) 31 TLR 632; *Spring* v. *National Amalgamated Stevedores' and Dockers' Society* [1956] 1 WLR 585. But although an implied power to discipline is rare, it is not unknown: *McVitae* v. *Unison* [1996] IRLR 33 (ChD).

UNISON Rules, Rule I, Disciplinary Action

2. Disciplinary action may be taken against any member who:

   2.1 disregards, disobeys or breaks any of the Rules or regulations of the Union applicable to her or him, or any instruction issued in accordance with the Rules;

   2.2 acts in a manner prejudicial or detrimental to the Union, her/his branch, Region or Service Group;

   2.3 commits

     (i) any act of discrimination or harassment on grounds of race, gender, marital status, sexuality, gender identity, disability, age, creed or social class; or

     (ii) any other discriminatory conduct which is prejudicial to the Aims and Objects set out in Rule B.1, B.2 and B.3;

   2.4 misappropriates any money or property belonging to the Union which is under her or his control, or fails properly to account for money which was, is or should be under her or his control or defrauds the Union in any way.

3. The National Executive Committee shall have the power to exclude or expel, as the case may be, from membership of UNISON any individual who gives encouragement to, or participates in the activities of, or is a member of, a political party or organization whose constitution, aims and objectives is/are expressly or impliedly contrary to the equality objectives of UNISON set out in Rules A3 and/or B1.2 and/or B1.3 of the UNISON Rule Book. This specifically includes the British National Party, the National Front and similar parties or organisations as decided from time to time by the National Executive Council.[164]

Disciplinary Procedures

Apart from the need for clear power in the rule-book, a union must also follow the procedures set out in its constitution and rules when taking disciplinary steps against a member. Rule-book procedures vary enormously, although one of the best examples of such procedures (in the sense of being one of the most comprehensive) is provided by UNISON Rules, Schedule D, which are set out on pages 561–3. In addition to UNISON Rule I referred to above, which deals with disciplinary action, Schedule D deals in some detail with disciplinary procedures. A failure to comply with the procedures as laid down in the rules could be enough to render any disciplinary decision invalid and to found the basis for a challenge in the courts or before the Certification Officer. The more detailed the rules, the more likely it is that there will be a procedural lapse, though it is also the case that the courts may be inclined to overlook technical breaches as opposed to breaches of substance.[165] It will be noted that the UNISON procedures make provision for (1) notice to be given to the

---

[164] UNISON Rules (2018).   [165] See *McVitae v. Unison* [1996] IRLR 33, at 44.

respondent; (2) an opportunity for the respondent to be represented; and (3) an opportunity for the respondent to cross-examine the witnesses against him or her. There is also a right of appeal.

Even a superficial review of trade union rule-books will reveal that not all trade union disciplinary procedures are as rigorous and detailed as those of UNISON. In such cases, to adapt a *dictum* well known to administrative lawyers, the common law will supply the omission of the rule-book. This will be done principally by the rules of natural justice, which will be readily applied even if the legal basis for their application in the context of the contract of membership is by no means clear.[166] Thus, they will often be described as implied terms of the contract of membership, though they seem to have a mandatory quality. Natural justice requires a union 'to conduct its disciplinary processes in accordance with the judicially recognised principles of fairness', and there is no suggestion that a union may displace these 'implied duties' by an express term.[167] The rules of natural justice will thus be implied where there are no formal disciplinary procedures in the union rule-book or where there are omissions in the formal disciplinary procedures. The scope of the rules of natural justice varies according to the circumstances of the case, but the standards are becoming gradually more demanding and it is inevitable that their application in this context will be influenced to some extent by developments in other spheres of the law, particularly administrative law and human rights law. So far as trade union cases are concerned, the courts have emphasised the following:

- the need to inform the respondent of the case against him or her: *Anna-munthodo v. Oilfield Workers' Trade Union*;[168] *Stevenson v. United Road Transport Union*;[169]
- the need to provide the respondent with an opportunity to state his or her case: *Radford v. National Society of Operative Printers, Graphical and Media Personnel (NATSOPA)*;[170]
- the right to be tried by a tribunal whose chairman did not appear to have a special reason for bias, conscious or otherwise, against the respondent: *Roebuck v. NUM (Yorkshire Area) (No. 2)*;[171]
- the right to an oral hearing and to cross-examine witnesses, depending upon the nature of the case and the seriousness of the possible sanction: *Payne v. Electrical Trades' Union*;[172]

---

[166] In the case of Unite, 'Disciplinary Hearings shall be organised and conducted under directions issued by the Executive Council. These directions ensure that the process is fair and conducted in accordance with the principles of natural justice' (rule 27.2).

[167] See *Boswell v. URTU*, Decision CO/30–32/17–18, paras. 39–42, where it is acknowledged that implied terms can be displaced by express terms, but where it is also assumed that natural justice must be applied. It is not clear whether natural justice could be excluded even by an express term.

[168] [1961] AC 945.   [169] [1977] ICR 893.   [170] [1972] ICR 484.   [171] [1978] ICR 676.

[172] *The Times*, 14 April 1960.

- the right of the individual to be represented in disciplinary proceedings, including legal representation: *Walker* v. *Amalgamated Union of Engineering and Foundry Workers*.[173]

It is recognised judicially that the third of these principles is difficult to comply with, simply because 'all members of a domestic tribunal where the interests of their own organisation are at stake, have a general inclination to defend the union and its officers against attack from any source'. *Roebuck* v. *NUM (Yorkshire Area) (No. 2)*[174] is nevertheless a textbook example of practice to be avoided. The plaintiffs were members of the union who had given evidence on behalf of the *Sheffield Star* in a libel action brought against the newspaper by Mr Scargill, the president of the union. This led to disciplinary proceedings being taken against the plaintiffs under the union's rules, a step prompted by Mr Scargill who then chaired the disciplinary panel. The plaintiffs were found to have acted in breach of the union's rules and disqualified from holding office in the union for two years. In subsequent legal proceedings, it was found that Mr Scargill had 'a special position' which disqualified him from taking part in the critical meetings of the disciplinary committee. Having 'clearly borne the heat and burden of the libel action', the actions of the plaintiffs must have been 'gall and wormwood to Mr Scargill before, during and after the trial'. Mr Scargill's role as chairman 'undoubtedly gave the impression that the dice were loaded against [the plaintiffs]', so that 'the appearance of bias was inevitable', Templeman J adopting the following *dictum* from *Hannam* v. *Bradford Corporation*:

> If a reasonable person who has knowledge of the matter beyond knowledge of the relationship which subsists between some members of the tribunal and one of the parties would think that there might well be bias, then there is in his opinion a real likelihood of bias. Of course, someone else with inside knowledge of the characters of the members in question, might say: 'Although things don't look very well, in fact there is no real likelihood of bias.' That, however, would be beside the point, because the question is not whether the tribunal will in fact be biased, but whether a reasonable man with no inside knowledge might well think that it might be biased.[175]

The question that now arises is the extent – if any – to which trade union disciplinary proceedings must comply with ECHR, Article 6, following the enactment of the HRA 1998. Article 6 provides that 'everyone is entitled to a fair and public hearing' for 'determination of his civil rights and obligations'. The issue was raised before the Certification Officer in *Foster* v. *Musicians' Union*,[176] where the applicant sought access to information apparently for the purposes of an internal disciplinary hearing, the details of which are unclear. In rejecting Mr Foster's claim that he was entitled to the information sought by virtue of Article 6, the Certification Officer said that:

---

[173] 1969 SLT 150. *Sed quaere?*   [174] [1978] ICR 676.   [175] [1970] 1 WLR 937, at 979.
[176] Decision D/13–17/03.

[T]he Union is not a public authority within the meaning of section 6 of the Human Rights Act 1998. It is an unincorporated association formed by civil contract. Its purpose is to protect the interests of its members. Unions are not creatures of statute. They have no statutory underpinning and their purposes are not of a public nature. The Certification Officer, however, as a public authority within the meaning of the Human Rights Act, is required to act in a way compatible with Convention rights. This requirement is discharged primarily by providing the parties with a means whereby their disputes can be adjudicated in a manner compatible with Article 6.[177]

This would be consistent with the approach of the courts to disciplinary proceedings under the contract of employment.[178] As in these cases, however, there may be cases where expulsion from a trade union will have adverse consequences for a person's livelihood or other substantial interests.[179] It will no doubt be argued that the position in *Foster* will have to be modified in the unlikely event of any such case presenting in the future. In the meantime, however, the view of the Certification Officer in *Foster* was that:

[T]he Union's internal disciplinary process is not analogous to the process which certain professional organisations are required to follow if their disciplinary procedure can result in the removal of a person's qualification to follow his or her profession. I am therefore not persuaded that Article 6 is engaged at all by this disciplinary process, it being a process agreed between two private parties which does not put at risk a person's qualification to remain in professional practice.[180]

UNISON Rules, Schedule D: Disciplinary Procedures

The following procedures shall be adopted for the hearing of any disciplinary charge by a Branch Disciplinary Sub-Committee, a Regional or Service Group Disciplinary Sub-Committee, or the National Executive Council or its Disciplinary Sub-Committee or any other body as decided by the National Executive Council:

1 No later than 21 days before the disciplinary hearing the member shall be sent a written notice of the charge, stating the sub-paragraph(s) of Rule I.2 under which she/he is charged and stating briefly how and when the member is said to have broken the sub-paragraph(s) concerned. At the same time the member shall be sent copies of any written material and correspondence to be considered in relation to the charge, together with the report of any investigation, and shall be told the date, time and place at which the charge against her or him is to be heard.

---

[177] *Ibid.*, para. 40.   [178] See Chapter 18.
[179] *R (G)* v. *Governors of X School* [2011] UKSC 30; [2011] IRLR 750.
[180] *Foster* v. *Musicians' Union*, Decision D/13–17/03, para. 42.

2 The member shall be allowed to submit, not later than 7 days prior to the hearing, any written material in support of her/his case.

3 The member shall be entitled to be represented at the hearing by another person of her/his choice (subject to the approval of the sub-committee, such approval not to be unreasonably refused).

4 The Committee hearing the charge will ensure that the charged member's rights are protected in that the provisions of Rule I and Schedule D.1 been scrupulously applied.

5 In the event that the provisions of Rule I and Schedule D.1 have not been properly applied the charge will be referred back to the body which brought the disciplinary charge.

6 At the hearing, the member shall be asked whether she/he admits or denies the charge. If she/he admits it, the Committee hearing the charge shall then consider whether and to what extent they should exercise any of the disciplinary powers conferred by Rule.

7 If she/he denies the charge, the representative of the Branch, Regional Committee, Service Group Committee, National Executive Council or General Secretary as appropriate (who is called 'Union Representative' in this Schedule) shall state the case against the member in the presence of the member and any representative of the member, and may call witnesses. She/ he will produce any documents which she/he claims support the charge.

8 The member or the member's representative shall have the opportunity to ask questions of the Union Representative and the witnesses.

9 The members of the Committee hearing the charge may ask any questions they think appropriate of the Union Representative and of any witnesses, and may question the member concerned about the charge.

10 The Union Representative shall have the opportunity to re-examine her/his witnesses on any matter about which they have been questioned by the member charged, her/his representative, and by members of the Committee hearing the charge.

11 The member or her/his representative shall put her/his case in the presence of the Union Representative, may call witnesses, and may produce any document she/he wishes that is relevant to the charge.

12 The Union Representative shall have the opportunity to ask questions of the member or the member's representative and witnesses.

13 The members of the Committee hearing the charge shall have the opportunity to ask questions of the member, or her/his representative, and witnesses.

14 The member or the member's representative shall have the opportunity to re-examine her/his witnesses on any matter about which they have been questioned by the Union Representative and/or by members of the Committee hearing the charge.

15 No written material or documents shall be submitted which do not comply with the provisions of existing rule numbers D.1, D.2, D.5 and D.9 of this schedule.

16 No new charge may be raised at the hearing.

17 After all witnesses have been heard and documents produced, the Committee hearing the charge (i) may ask the person presenting the charge to sum up the case; and (whether she/ he does so or not) (ii) must then permit the member charged, or her/his representative, to address them. The member or her/his representative shall have the right to speak last. In summing up no new matters may be introduced.

18 At any time during the procedure set out above, members of the Committee hearing the charge may seek clarification of any statement made, and may enquire of either party as to the evidence that is to be called.

19 The Committee hearing the charge has an absolute discretion to adjourn the hearing to allow either party to produce further evidence, or for any other reason.

20 The Committee hearing the charge shall then consider in private whether the charge is proved to their satisfaction, or not, on the evidence presented before them. All members of the Committee taking part in the discussion must have been present throughout the entirety of the hearing. No new matter can be raised against the member concerned. If any point of uncertainty arises, the Committee may recall both parties to clear the point. In such a case, both parties shall return notwithstanding that only one is concerned with the point giving rise to doubt.

21 If the Committee decides that the charge is not proved, they shall dismiss it.

22 If the Committee decides that the charge is proved, they shall then decide what, if any, action to take. Before determining its decision, the Committee may consider anything that the member wishes to submit in mitigation.

23 The Committee hearing the charge may inform the member of their decision orally, but it shall in any event be confirmed to the member in writing within 14 days of the conclusion of the hearing. Where the charge is found proved, the member shall be notified in writing of (a) her/ his right of appeal, (b) the body to whom the appeal should be directed, and, (c) the date on which the four-week time limit for appealing expires.

24 Any penalty imposed on a member will not take effect until the expiry of the time limit within which the member can submit an appeal or, if an appeal has been submitted, until such time as the appeal has been determined.

25 No person who is a witness, or who has investigated the charge prior to its being brought, shall sit on the Committee hearing the charge or any appeal.

26 If a member intends to appeal, she/he must exercise her/his right to do so by writing to the Secretary of the appropriate Committee within four weeks of her/his being notified in writing of the decision subject to the Appeal.

[There then follows detailed provision for the conduct of appeals, not reproduced here.][181]

---

[181] UNISON Rules (2018).

Disciplinary Decisions

So much then for disciplinary powers and disciplinary procedures. What about the decisions taken under these powers and in accordance with these procedures? Trade union disciplinary rules generally take one of two forms, both of which are to be found in the UNISON disciplinary rules set out above. One category of disciplinary rules is sometimes referred to as specific disciplinary rules (discipline for a specific offence such as non-payment of contributions or sexist or racist behaviour) and the other is sometimes referred to as general disciplinary rules (discipline for unspecified offences contrary to the interests of the union, drafted in subjective terms). The courts typically construe disciplinary rules falling into the first category very narrowly in favour of the member, while the subjective language of the latter will not give the union disciplinary bodies an unlimited discretion, which the language of the rules might otherwise suggest. In the case of both categories of disciplinary rule, the union must construe them in accordance with the law, if they are to 'keep within their jurisdiction'.[182] The final determination of what the rules mean lies not with the disciplinary bodies within the union but with the courts,[183] and it is clear that the courts will on occasion stretch the meaning of the rules, as perhaps most famously in *Esterman* v. *NALGO*.[184]

In that case, the plaintiff was a senior legal assistant employed by Islington London Borough Council. The union had been seeking an increase in the London weighting allowance, and in December 1973 had balloted its members for industrial action. Only 49 per cent had voted in favour of selective strikes on full pay, 48 per cent had voted against and 3 per cent gave no answer. In March 1974, the union reached an agreement with the employer, but this was vetoed by the government under the counter-inflation policy then in force. Thereafter, the Islington branch of the union was instructed to take selective strike action, Islington being chosen because 64 per cent of that branch had indicated a willingness to take such action in the December ballot. Members of the branch were instructed not to volunteer their services in connection with the London borough elections to be held in May 1974, though there was no dispute between NALGO and the returning officers who were responsible for the conduct of the elections. Miss Esterman refused to comply with this instruction and was summoned to a disciplinary hearing, charged under the NALGO rules whereby 'any member who disregards any regulation issued by the branch, or is guilty of conduct which, in the opinion of the executive committee, renders him unfit for membership, shall be liable to expulsion'.

Before the disciplinary meeting was held, Miss Esterman successfully sought an interlocutory injunction to restrain her threatened expulsion until the trial

---

[182] *Lee* v. *Showmen's Guild of Great Britain* [1952] 2 QB 329.
[183] *Radford* v. *NATSOPA* [1972] ICR 484.   [184] [1974] ICR 625.

of the action. Templeman J was satisfied on the evidence then available that it would be 'impossible to convict any member of NALGO of conduct which rendered him unfit to be a member . . . on the ground that the member did not comply with the instructions' not to co-operate with the election. In doing so, he suggested two restraints on the disciplinary decisions available to trade unions under their disciplinary rules. The first was the inference that trade unions may not discipline members for failing to comply with an instruction unless it is clear to the member concerned that the union has the authority to make the decision in the first place. In other words, it is not enough that the member failed to comply with a lawful instruction: the union may take disciplinary action only if the member had no reason to question whether the instruction was lawful. In light of doubts in this case about whether the union's executive committee could 'take the serious step of interfering with the right of a member to volunteer or take work of any description outside his normal employment' (in this case, to assist the returning officer), a member who refused to obey thus 'cannot be found guilty on that account of conduct which renders him unfit to be a member of NALGO'.

The second restraint on trade union disciplinary powers suggested by Templeman J overlaps with but goes beyond the first. This is the possibility that a member could disobey an instruction from the union, even where it was lawful and perhaps also where there was no reason to doubt that it was lawful. Thus, Templeman J referred to the 'special circumstances' in this case, which were such that 'a member could very well come to the conclusion that this was an order to which the national executive council had no right to demand his obedience and it was an order which, as a person – a loyal member of NALGO – acting in its best interests, he felt bound to disobey'. In a subsequent passage, Templeman J referred to the 'extraordinary background of this case', being such that a member could properly say that 'he could not conscientiously accept an order given by the national executive council'. Indeed, Templeman J went further still and suggested that there may be circumstances (as in this case) where the member not only has a right but also a duty to disobey a lawful instruction, if for example he or she were to conclude that the instruction was one that would damage the reputation of the union. Although expressed in the context of a decision about industrial action, these are observations that would apply to a wider range of trade union activity, although their practical significance has since been diminished by TULRCA 1992, sections 64 and 65.

Certification Officer

The final question arising for consideration in this chapter concerns the changing role of the Certification Officer in the conduct of trade union affairs. The office was first created in 1975 and provision is now made in TULRCA 1992, by which the Certification Officer is appointed by the Secretary of State after consultation with ACAS.[185] She does not have the same security of tenure as a judge, though the Trade Union Act 2016 provides that she is not to be subject to ministerial directions in the performance of any of her functions.[186] There are no formal statutory qualifications; in particular there is no requirement that the Certification Officer should be a lawyer. The original role of the Certification Officer was to maintain the list of trade unions, issue certificates of independence (hence the name), receive trade union annual returns required by statute, provide model political fund rules and adjudicate on political fund disputes. Since then the role has been expanded, initially by Conservative governments: (1) in 1984, the Certification Officer was given jurisdiction to deal with complaints about trade union elections;[187] (2) in 1993, the Certification Officer was given investigation powers in relation to alleged financial irregularities in trade unions;[188] and (3) in 2014, the Certification Officer was given greater powers of supervision over trade union membership registers.[189]

However, the Blair government also extended significantly the Certification Officer's adjudicatory role,[190] giving effect to a long-held view that internal trade union affairs should not be administered by the courts, but by a less formal and more expert body.[191] The aim of the then government was to 'enable trade union members to secure their rights more easily and effectively'.[192] Thus, under TULRCA 1992, section 108A, the Certification Officer has a jurisdiction to deal with complaints 'that there has been a breach or threatened breach of the rules of a trade union relating to any of the matters mentioned in subsection (2)'. These matters are '(a) the appointment or election of a person to, or the removal of a person from, any office; (b) disciplinary proceedings by the union (including expulsion);[193] (c) the balloting of members on any issue other than industrial action; (d) the constitution or proceedings of any executive committee or of any decision-making meeting; (e) such other matters as may be specified in an order made by the Secretary of State'. Alongside the extended power to adjudicate the Certification Officer also has the power to make a declaration and an enforcement

---

[185] TULRCA 1992, s. 254.   [186] Trade Union Act 2016, s. 16.   [187] See pp. 539–42.
[188] See now TULRCA 1992, ss. 37A–37E.
[189] Transparency of Lobbying, Non-Party Campaigning and Trade Union Administration Act 2014, Part 3, inserting new TULRCA 1992, ss. 24ZA–24ZK. The duty to maintain a register of members is to be found in TULRCA 1992, s. 24.
[190] TULRCA 1992, s. 108A.
[191] Royal Commission on Trade Unions and Employers' Associations (Chair, Lord Donovan), Cmnd 3623 (1968), para. 176.
[192] Department of Trade and Industry, *Fairness at Work*, Cm 3968 (1998), para. 4.31.
[193] Notable exclusions being disciplinary action for failing to take part in a strike (in relation to which there is a statutory remedy under TULRCA 1992, ss. 64 and 65, though it is to be noted that other disciplinary action prohibited by TULRCA 1992, ss. 64 and 65, could give rise to a complaint to the Certification Officer under TULRCA 1992, s. 108A). Also excluded are matters relating to the discipline under the rules of full-time employees of the union: TULRCA 1992, s. 108A(5).

order where a complaint is upheld, which could include ordering an election to be re-run where it was conducted in breach of the rules.[194] The increasing role of the Certification Officer by no means excludes the courts from this general area, trade union members having a choice of whether to go to the Certification Officer or the courts. Almost all now choose the Certification Officer, the number of rule-book disputes in the courts having declined to a trickle.[195]

It is against this background of increasing supervision that Conservative led governments since 2010 have increased still further the supervisory role of the Certification Officer. Particularly controversial are the new powers in the Trade Union Act 2016,[196] not implemented at the time of writing, which caused the then retiring Certification Officer to reflect that 'the role of the Certification Officer will change from being mainly the adjudicator of members' complaints to become one with more general policing and enforcing responsibilities'.[197] One concern relates to the Certification Officer's proposed new powers of investigation and adjudication, which apply to a range of statutory obligations, including the conduct of elections and the operation of political funds.[198] Here the Certification Officer will be empowered to demand documents if she 'thinks' there is good reason to do so[199] and require an 'explanation' from trade union officials of any of the documents.[200] The Certification Officer may also appoint inspectors where there is 'reasonable grounds to suspect that a trade union has failed to comply with a relevant obligation'.[201] In the course of their investigations, the inspectors will have the power to require: the attendance of trade union officials, the production of documents, and unspecified forms of co-operation ('all assistance').[202] More-over, the Certification Officer will have the additional power to make an order requiring the trade union or other specified person to comply with a Certifi-cation Officer's instruction (sic).[203] Failure to comply with a Certification Officer's instruction is to be enforced as if it were an order of the High Court, presumably giving rise to potential liability for contempt of court.[204]

Related to the foregoing, new powers will enable the Certification Officer to initiate complaints about a range of alleged violations (such as elections and political fund matters) without a complaint having been made by a trade union member, but at the behest of a third party with an axe to grind.[205] As

---

[194] TULRCA 1992, s. 108B. For the comparable procedure in election complaints, see p. 542.

[195] An appeal lies from the Certification Officer to the EAT: TULRCA 1992, s. 108C.

[196] Trade Union Act 2016, Scheds. 1–3, amending TULRCA 1992, various provisions. See S. Cavalier and R. Arthur, 'A Discussion of the Certification Officer Reforms' (2016) 45 *Industrial Law Journal* 363.

[197] Certification Officer, *Annual Report 2015–16* (2016), p. 2.

[198] Trade Union Act 2016, Sched. 1.

[199] *Ibid.*, inserting new TULRCA 1992, Sched. A3, para. 2(1).   [200] *Ibid.*, para. 2(5).

[201] *Ibid.*, para. 3(1).   [202] *Ibid.*, para. 3(2).   [203] *Ibid.*, para. 5(1).   [204] *Ibid.*, para. 5(6).

[205] Trade Union Act 2016, Sched. 2.

the recently retired Certification Officer pointed out, 'trade unions may find themselves subjected to a myriad of references to the Certification Officer by persons and/or organisations seeking to pursue them for industrial, political or other purposes and who have the motivation and money to put any given situation under a microscope'.[206] Even if unions successfully defend all the complaints brought against them, 'at the very least' they 'will have to bear the financial burden of contesting such cases'.[207] This is despite the fact that those bringing complaints to the attention of the Certification Officer may have no legal relationship with the trade union, and would be dismissed in other legal contexts as being 'busybodies, cranks, and other mischief-makers'.[208] But having initiated a complaint (whether or not at the behest of a third party), it will fall to the Certification Officer to process it. In these cases, the Certification Officer will 'in effect be the investigator, prosecutor and adjudicator'. As the retiring Certification Officer pointed out, 'this raises immediate issues of a fair trial, as required by Article 6 of the European Convention on Human Rights and the Human Rights Act 1998'.[209] What it means in practice is that the Certification Officer will have the power to bring a complaint to the Certification Officer (sic); call and examine her own witnesses; make a decision in favour of her own complaint; and impose an order (and by virtue of other new powers impose a financial penalty) on the trade union.[210]

The Role of External Review

Most trade unions now have procedures for dealing with appeals from the decisions of disciplinary bodies within the union. Typically, the members of trade union appeal bodies are drawn from the ranks of the union itself.

In the case of Unite, however, provision is made for an appeals tribunal to deal with some disciplinary appeals, the tribunal to be chaired by an independent person nominated by the chair of ACAS. The Unite rules also provide for the appointment of an independent Election Commissioner to whom complaints may be made by candidates alleging a breach of the union's election rules or any other legal requirement in the election of general secretary and the national executive council.

---

[206] Certification Officer, *Annual Report 2015–16* (2016), p. 2.   [207] *Ibid.*

[208] *R v. Inland Revenue Commissioners, ex parte National Federation of Small and Self-Employed Businesses* [1982] AC 617 (Lord Scarman).

[209] Certification Officer, *Annual Report 2015–16* (2016), p. 2.

[210] It is perhaps unsurprising that the ILO Committee of Experts should have expressed its 'concern that the Act does appear to significantly expand the investigatory and enforcement powers of the Certification Officer, including in cases where no application has been made'. The Committee invited the government 'to review the impact of these provisions with the social partners concerned with a view to ensuring that workers' and employers' organizations can effectively exercise their rights to organize their administration and activities and formulate their programmes without interference from the public authorities': ILO Committee of Experts, Observation Concerning Convention 87 (United Kingdom) (2016).

This is a practice that has benefits for both trade unions and their members, most notably for the fact that it provides a form of supervision that is informal, quick and inexpensive. These are particularly important features of election disputes, which can be resolved before the voting takes place. It also allows for principles of adjudication to develop in a way that is sensitive to the particular circumstances of the union.

External review of this kind does not – and could not – exclude the courts or the Certification Officer, and the decisions of the external reviewer are binding only to the extent that they are accepted by both parties. Thus, it is possible in Unite for a member to eschew the right to complain to the Election Commissioner,[211] though in these cases questions might be asked by the Certification Officer or the courts why domestic remedies had not been exhausted. It would also be possible to bring a rule-book challenge to the Certification Officer or the courts after an Election Commissioner's ruling.[212]

Perhaps the best known example of external review in this country (the Public Review Board of the United Auto Workers is a good example of the phenomenon in North America) was the TUC Independent Review Committee which was established in 1976 to deal with complaints of exclusion or expulsion from a trade union in closed-shop cases. But with the virtual end in practice of the closed shop following severe legal restrictions, the purpose of the Independent Review Committee has disappeared, and it no longer exists.[213]

Conclusion

Since 1980, far-reaching legislation has cut deeply into the principle of freedom of association, by prescribing a high level of regulation not only of the way in which trade unions are governed, but also of the rights and duties of trade union members: more of the former and less of the latter. In this respect, public policy towards the principle of trade union autonomy has comprehensively changed: trade unions are now regulated bodies, to be structured and organised on the basis of a template prescribed by the state, that requires more and more resources to be devoted by trade unions to internal affairs, and which undermines their capacity to command the solidarity of the membership as a whole. The template is one which reflects to some extent the earlier drawings made by the courts, embracing a notion of democracy through membership participation – in the election of the executive committee and other senior offices, and in the requirement for political-fund review ballots and ballots before industrial action. It also embraces a notion of membership whereby the member need not accept the contractual obligations of membership which he or she is free to accept or reject at will. This has been reinforced

---

[211] See *Murray* v. *Unite the Union*, Decision D/20/15–16.

[212] *Coyne* v. *Unite the Union*, Decision D/2/18–19; *Beaumont* v. *Unite the Union (No. 4)*, Decision D/2–6/15–16; *Hicks* v. *Unite the Union*, Decision D/32–39/14–15.

[213] For an account, see K. D. Ewing and W. M. Rees, 'The TUC Independent Review Committee and the Closed Shop' (1981) 10 *Industrial Law Journal* 84.

in relation to the political levy, and has been extended to include industrial action. Indeed, in 1993, trade unions lost the right to exclude members except on prescribed grounds.

This is not to proclaim the virtues of a high level of trade union autonomy, or to disparage a high level of trade union regulation. Public policy is not confined to a choice between the two, with much depending on the social, economic and political problems which the law is addressing and the context in which it is set. But it is to say that the process of trade union regulation in place since 1980 is in some respects paradoxical, in the sense that it has been introduced when trade union power on behalf of workers generally and their members in particular has declined significantly. Trade union membership has fallen sharply in thirty years (with current levels approaching one-half of membership levels of 13 million in 1980), the closed shop which helped sustained trade union power has virtually vanished and industrial action is at its lowest level since the 1870s. The paradox of detailed regulation in these circumstances is all the greater for the fact that much of the regulation extends well beyond the boundaries of international law, in the form of ILO Convention 87, the Council of Europe's Social Charter of 1961 and perhaps also the ECHR. It is thus currently not the case – *pace* ILO Convention 87, Article 3 – that workers' organisations in the UK enjoy 'the right to draw up their constitutions and rules [and] to elect their representatives in full freedom'.

14

The Right to Bargain Collectively

Introduction

Workers join trade unions for a purpose, usually to secure the benefits of higher wages, better conditions of employment, and greater job security, generally gained by a process of collective bargaining. As already explained in Chapter 12, by this process trade unions and employers negotiate a collective agreement to regulate working conditions and to resolve disputes at the workplace. At one time more than two-thirds of the workforce had their terms and conditions of employment regulated in this way, and even today the terms and conditions of 26% of workers are regulated directly by such agreements.[1] Collective bargaining thus continues to be an important process, given that collective agreements are likely also to have an important indirect impact, in the sense that they will influence the terms and conditions of employment of workers beyond those immediately affected by them. In this chapter, we consider the contribution of the law to collective bargaining, the importance of which is recognised in a number of international treaties and by the law and practice of all developed countries.

The role of the state in the collective bargaining process arises in a number of ways. The first relates to the need to establish collective bargaining machinery, the role of law arising where it is not possible for the parties to agree to such machinery being established voluntarily. The second is the duties on the parties in collective bargaining , in terms of the way they conduct themselves and the steps taken to ensure that bargaining takes place in a transparent and informed way. And the third relates to the legal status and effects of collective agreements. Are they legally binding contracts? What is their effect on the contract of employment?[2] In Britain, conventional wisdom is based on Kahn-Freund's ideas of 'legal abstention' and 'collective *laissez faire*', whereby the state was largely removed from the process of collective bargaining, which was left to the self-regulation of labour and capital.[3] But although a profound

---

[1] Department for Business, Energy and Industrial Strategy, *Trade Union Membership Statistical Bulletin 2017* (2018), p. 42. Broken down on a sector basis, collective bargaining density is 15.2% in the private sector and 57.6% in the public sector. Trade union membership density is 23.2%, with 13.5% density in the private sector and 51.8% density in the public sector (*ibid.*, p. 35).

[2] There is also the question of which workers are entitled to enjoy the benefits of a collective agreement. The members of the trade union, or other workers as well, in which case which workers? As we shall see, in some countries collective agreements may be extended by a legal process to employers who are not party to the agreement in question. That is not now possible in the United Kingdom.

[3] O. Kahn-Freund, 'Legal Framework', in A. Flanders and H. Clegg, *The System of Industrial Relations in Great Britain* (Oxford: Basil Blackwell, 1954); and O. Kahn-Freund, 'Labour Law', in M. Ginsberg (ed.), *Law and Opinion in England in the Twentieth Century* (London: Stevens, 1959). See also P. L. Davies and M. R. Freedland, *Labour Legislation and Public Policy* (Oxford University Press, 1993), Chs. 1 and 2; and R. Dukes, 'Constitutionalizing Employment Relations: Sinzheimer, Kahn-Freund and the Role of Labour Law' (2008) 35 *Journal of Law and Society* 341. For valuable reappraisals of Kahn-Freund, see R. Dukes, 'Otto Kahn-Freund and Collective Laissez-Faire: An Edifice without a Keystone?' (2009) 72 *Modern Law Review* 220; and A. Bogg,

insight, 'collective *laissez faire*' is a principle that may tend to under-estimate the active involvement of the state in building and sustaining collective bargaining institutions in the past, and focus too narrowly on particular forms of state intervention.[4]

Collective Bargaining and International Standards

As we saw in Chapter 12, the right to freedom of association has (at least) three dimensions, the first two of which are considered in Chapters 12 and 13. The third dimension is the freedom *to act* in association, to promote the purposes for which people came together in the first place. In the case of trade unions, this essential purpose is collective bargaining. It is true that trade unions perform a number of functions on behalf of workers (and in the public interest generally), some of these functions being laid out also in Chapter 13.[5] But many of these functions could be performed by others, this being especially true of the services trade unions provide to members. What distinguishes trade unions from all other organisations is their unique capacity to engage in collective bargaining, now seen as an essential element of freedom of association. In recognising this link the Supreme Court of Canada also emphasised that collective bargaining was important to promote 'human dignity, equality, liberty, respect for the autonomy of the person and the enhancement of democracy', values which were said to underpin the Canadian Charter of Rights and Freedoms.[6]

International Labour Organization

It is one of the constitutional obligations of the ILO to 'further among the nations of the world programmes which will achieve ... the effective recognition of the right of collective bargaining'.[7] The main ILO instruments dealing

---

The Democratic Aspects of Trade Union Recognition (Oxford: Hart, 2009), Ch. 1. The latter is an excellent and stimulating discussion of collective bargaining and of the law more generally.

[4] It may also under-estimate the role of administrative law rather than 'labour law' as the chosen method of intervention for the best part of the twentieth century. As we shall see, state power was actively used for much of the twentieth century, but for much of the time this was done by means of the administrative rather than the legislative power of the state. But it was no less potent: K. D. Ewing, 'The State and Industrial Relations' (1998) 5 *Historical Studies in Industrial Relations* 1.

[5] See especially pp. 524–5 above.

[6] *Health Services and Support – Facilities Subsector Bargaining Association* v. *British Columbia*, 2007 SCC 27, [2007] 2 SCR 391, para. 81. See subsequently *Ontario (AG)* v. *Fraser*, 2011 SCC 20, and *Mounted Police Association of Ontario* v. *Canada (Attorney General)* [2015] SCC 1, [2015] 1 SCR 3.

[7] ILO, Declaration of Philadelphia (1944), Part III(e). See also ILO Declaration on Fundamental Principles and Rights at Work (1998). See generally B. Gernignon, A. Odero and H. Guido, 'ILO Principles Concerning Collective Bargaining' (2000) 139 *International Labour Review* 33.

with collective bargaining are Conventions 98, 151 and 154.[8] Convention 98 is probably the most important international treaty dealing with collective bargaining, providing that:

ILO Convention 98, Article 4

Measures appropriate to national conditions shall be taken, where necessary, to encourage and promote the full development and utilisation of machinery for voluntary negotiation between employers or employers' organisations and workers' organisations, with a view to the regulation of terms and conditions of employment by means of collective agreements.

ILO Convention 98 does 'not deal with the position of public servants engaged in the administration of the State', though it is not to 'be construed as prejudicing their rights or status in any way'.[9] This exclusion has been narrowly construed by the ILO supervisory bodies, in order to enhance the scope of application of Convention 98.[10]

Convention 98 is complemented by Convention 151, which 'applies to all persons employed by public authorities, to the extent that more favourable provisions in other international labour conventions are not applicable to them'.[11] By Article 7, Convention 151 provides as follows:

ILO Convention 151, Article 7

Measures appropriate to national conditions shall be taken, where necessary, to encourage and promote the full development and utilisation of machinery for negotiation of terms and conditions of employment between the public authorities concerned and public employees' organisations, or of such other methods as will allow representatives of public employees to participate in the determination of these matters.

---

[8] Freedom of Association and Protection of the Right to Organise Convention, 1950 (Convention 87); Right to Organise and Collective Bargaining Convention, 1949 (Convention 98); and Labour Relations (Public Service) Convention, 1978 (Convention 151).

[9] ILO Convention 98, Art. 6.

[10] See B. Gernignon, A. Odero and H. Guido, 'ILO Principles Concerning Collective Bargaining' (2000) 139 *International Labour Review* 33. See also the discussion of this provision in *Demir and Baykara* v. *Turkey* [2008] ECHR 1345, para. 43, making clear that it does not apply to local government staff, but indeed only to employees directly employed in the state administration.

[11] Labour Relations (Public Service) Convention, 1978, Art. 1(1). However, it is also provided by the latter that 'The extent to which the guarantees provided for in this Convention shall apply to high-level employees whose functions are normally considered as policy-making or managerial, or to employees whose duties are of a highly confidential nature, shall be determined by national laws or regulations' (Art. 1(2)). This was an issue in the GCHQ affair (Chapter 12 above), but it was held by the ILO supervisory bodies that the workers in question were protected by the more favourable provisions of ILO Convention 87.

It will be noted that Article 7 of Convention 151 includes a qualification to the general duty to promote collective bargaining which is not to be found in Convention 98, authorising the contracting parties to adopt 'other methods as will allow representatives of public employees to participate in the determination of these matters', which are normally to be dealt with by collective bargaining. This aspect of the Convention is not without passing significance, highlighting that, in the public sector at least, traditional forms of collective bargaining are not the only way by which a state can meet its obligations to the workers covered. Nevertheless, such options are not acknowledged by Convention 98, which imposes a duty exclusively to promote what can only be described as the machinery of collective bargaining.

Further support for the principle of collective bargaining is provided by Convention 154, the preamble to which declares that 'it is desirable to make greater efforts to achieve the objectives of these standards and, particularly, the general principles set out in Article 4 of the Right to Organise and Collective Bargaining Convention, 1949'. Unlike Conventions 98 and 151, Convention 154 attempts to define collective bargaining by providing in Article 2 that:

ILO Convention 154, Article 2

[T]he term *collective bargaining* extends to all negotiations which take place between an employer, a group of employers or one or more employers' organisations, on the one hand, and one or more workers' organisations, on the other, for –

(a) determining working conditions and terms of employment; and/or
(b) regulating relations between employers and workers; and/or
(c) regulating relations between employers or their organisations and a workers' organisation or workers' organisations.

By Article 7, Convention 154 reinforces the obligations in Conventions 98 and 151 by stating again that 'measures adapted to national conditions shall be taken to promote collective bargaining'. It also states specifically, however, that:

- collective bargaining should be made possible for all employers and all groups of workers in the branches of activity covered by this Convention;
- collective bargaining should be progressively extended to all matters covered by subparagraphs (a), (b) and (c) of Article 2 of the Convention;
- the establishment of rules of procedure agreed between employers' and workers' organisations should be encouraged;
- collective bargaining should not be hampered by the absence of rules governing the procedure to be used or by the inadequacy or inappropriateness of such rules;

- bodies and procedures for the settlement of labour disputes should be so conceived as to contribute to the promotion of collective bargaining.[12]

Council of Europe

So far as the Council of Europe is concerned, the right to collective bargaining is recognised by the European Social Charter, on which see the box below. Otherwise, the most interesting Council of Europe development in recent years has been in relation to the ECHR, with Article 11(1) providing that everyone has the right to freedom of association, including specifically the 'right to form and join trade unions for the protection of his interests'. The leading case is *Demir and Baykara* v. *Turkey*,[13] where the applicants were a member and president respectively of a trade union called Tum Bel Sun, which in 1993 negotiated a two-year collective agreement with the Gaziantep Municipal Council in Turkey. The agreement concerned all aspects of the employment relationship, including wages, allowances, and welfare services. When within a few months the local authority failed to comply with the agreement, attempts were made to enforce it in domestic legal proceedings, leading to lengthy litigation. The litigation was concluded when the Court of Cassation held that although trade unions in Turkey were free to exist, they had no legal capacity to enter into collective agreements. As a result, the agreement contested in the case was held invalid *ex tunc*, and, following an audit of the local authority's accounts, those who benefited from it were ordered to repay the benefits secured.

European Social Charter

Article 6: The right to bargain collectively

With a view to ensuring the effective exercise of the right to bargain collectively, the Contracting Parties undertake:

1 to promote joint consultation between workers and employers;
2 to promote, where necessary and appropriate, machinery for voluntary negotiations between employers or employers' organisations and workers' organisations, with a view to the regulation of terms and conditions of employment by means of collective agreements;
3 to promote the establishment and use of appropriate machinery for conciliation and voluntary arbitration for the settlement of labour disputes; and recognise:

---

[12] ILO Convention 154, Art. 5.
[13] [2008] ECHR 1345. For a full consideration, see K. D. Ewing and J. Hendy, 'The Dramatic Implications of *Demir and Baykara*' (2010) 39 *Industrial Law Journal* 2.

4 the right of workers and employers to collective action in cases of conflicts of interest, including the right to strike, subject to obligations that might arise out of collective agreements previously entered into.

The European Court of Human Rights relies on this provision in the construction of the right to freedom of association in ECHR, Article 11.[14] There is also a process of regular supervision by the European Committee of Social Rights to monitor compliance. The United Kingdom has been in breach for many years, despite the legislative changes considered below.[15]

Mrs Demir and Mr Baykara thereupon brought proceedings in the ECtHR, alleging that the invalidation of the collective agreement violated their right to freedom of association, In upholding the complaint, the Grand Chamber relied heavily on a number of other international treaties, including ILO Conventions 98 and 151, both of which Turkey had ratified. But it also referred to the Council of Europe's Social Charter, Article 6(2), which Turkey has not accepted,[16] and the EU Charter of Fundamental Rights,[17] which Turkey is not in a position to ratify, not being a member of the EU. In considering these sources, the Court made clear that it was deferring to the relevant supervisory bodies (the ILO Committee of Experts and the Council of Europe's Social Rights Committee) for their interpretation.[18] The Court concluded that 'having regard to the developments in labour law, both international and national, and to the practice of Contracting States in such matters, the right to bargain collectively with the employer has, in principle, become one of the essential elements of the "right to form and to join trade unions for the protection of [one's] interests" set forth in Article 11 of the Convention, it being understood that states remain free to organise their system so as, if appropriate, to grant special status to representative trade unions'.[19] This led the Court to conclude that:

The absence of the legislation necessary to give effect to the provisions of the international labour conventions already ratified by Turkey, and the Court of Cassation judgment of 6 December 1995 based on that absence, with the resulting *de facto* annulment *ex tunc* of the collective agreement in question,

---

[14] See *Demir and Baykara* v. *Turkey* [2008] ECHR 1345.

[15] European Committee of Social Rights, *Conclusions XX-3* (2014) (United Kingdom).

[16] Under the Social Charter, it is possible to ratify without accepting all of its provisions. The United Kingdom does not accept all of the provisions of the Charter, though it has accepted Art. 6.

[17] The EU Charter provides by Art. 28 that '[w]orkers and employers, or their respective organisations, have, in accordance with Community law and national laws and practices, the right to negotiate and conclude collective agreements at the appropriate levels and, in cases of conflicts of interest, to take collective action to defend their interests, including strike action'.

[18] *Demir and Baykara* v. *Turkey* [2008] ECHR 1345, paras. 43, 50 and 166.   [19] *Ibid.*, para. 154.

constituted interference with the applicants' trade union freedom as protected by Article 11 of the Convention.[20]

Although potentially far reaching, there has been a conspicuous attempt on the part of the Court since to backtrack from this landmark decision. This is to be seen in *Unite the Union* v. *United Kingdom*,[21] which was concerned with the abolition of the Agricultural Wages Board, which was a tripartite body that determined the terms and conditions of employment of agricultural workers.[22] For present purposes it is enough to note that along with its Scottish counterpart the AWB was the only one of several dozen Wages Councils to have survived the abolition of these bodies in 1993, which in their heyday set terms and conditions for about 4 million workers.[23] Although the ECtHR in *Unite the Union* accepted that the AWB was a body involved in collective bargaining, it nevertheless held that the statutory abolition of the Board did not violate the State's duty to promote collective bargaining. Following other cases on related matters, the Court took the view not only that *Demir and Baycara* was concerned with 'a very far-reaching interference with freedom of association', notably 'an interference with the applicants' trade-union freedom as a result of the absence of legislation necessary to give effect to the provisions of international labour conventions ratified by Turkey and a court judgment annulling the voluntary collective agreement entered into by the applicants on account of that absence'.[24]

It is difficult to see how the abolition of the AWB was significantly less serious, the Court acknowledging that it was about 'the abolition of a statutory and mandatory mechanism of collective bargaining'.[25] But in holding that there was no duty to maintain such mechanisms in place, the decision is notable for two reasons, the first being a subtle rowing back on the significance of international treaties to the construction of Article 11. In relation to the European Social Charter for example, it was said that 'States' obligations under Article 6 of the European Social Charter cannot be considered synonymous

---

[20] *Ibid.*, para. 157.

[21] App. No. 65397/13 (3 May 2016). See the powerful critique by K. Arabadjieva, 'Another Disappointment in Strasbourg: Unite the Union v United Kingdom' (2017) 46 *Industrial Law Journal* 289.

[22] The AWB (which applied to England and Wales) was abolished by the Enterprise and Regulatory Reform Act 2013, s. 72. However, a similar body was restored in Wales by the Agricultural Sector (Wales) Act 2014, which gave rise to important constitutional questions about the legislative competence of the Welsh Assembly. The UKSC held that the Bill as it then was fell within the legislative competence of the Assembly: *Agricultural Sector (Wales) Bill – Reference by the Attorney General* [2014] UKSC 43. The Scottish AWB was set up by the Agricultural Wages (Scotland) Act 1949, and is still operating, as an Executive Non-Departmental Body of the Scottish Government.

[23] Trade Union Reform and Employment Rights Act 1993, ss. 12, 13 repealing the Wages Act 1986, Part II. Twenty-six Wages Councils were abolished as a result. The AWB had been set up under a different statutory provision.

[24] *Unite the Union* v. *United Kingdom*, above, paras. 59–60.   [25] *Ibid.*, para. 58.

with the positive obligations which arise under the Convention'.[26] The decision is notable secondly for the formalism and lack of realism of the reasoning. In the absence of the AWB, agricultural workers could fall back on voluntary collective bargaining with individual employers, even though 'voluntary collective bargaining in the agricultural sector is virtually non-existent and impractical'.[27] It nevertheless remained open to the union to 'protect the operational interests of its members by collective action, including collective bargaining, by engaging in negotiations to seek to persuade employers and employees to reach collective agreements and it has the right to be heard'.[28] That is equally implausible.

Collective Bargaining Practice

Apart from being recognised as a right in international law, the right to bargain collectively is also recognised in the constitutional law of a number of countries, with the constitution of Italy providing that:

> Registered trade unions are legal persons. Being represented in proportion to their registered members, they may jointly enter into collective labour contracts which are mandatory for all who belong to the respective industry of these contracts.[29]

Similarly, the Spanish constitution provides that:

> The law shall guarantee the right to collective labour negotiations between the representatives of workers and employers, as well as the binding force of agreements.[30]

As we have seen, in Canada the right to bargain collectively has been implied from the constitutional guarantee of freedom of association.[31] Uniquely, in Ireland the constitutional guarantee of freedom of association has been read to confer a right on companies (as legal persons entitled to constitutional guarantees) not to engage in collective bargaining with a trade union.[32] But although recognised by both international law and constitutional law,

---

[26] *Ibid.*, para. 61.   [27] *Ibid.*, para. 49.

[28] *Ibid.*, para. 65. Compare the approach of the Supreme Court of Canada on a broadly similar question in *Ontario (AG)* v. *Fraser*, above, but on which see F. Faraday, J. Fudge and E. Tucker (eds.), *Constitutional Labour Rights in Canada: Farm Workers and the Fraser Case* (Toronto: Irwin Law, 2012).

[29] Art. 39(4).

[30] Art. 37(1). For a full account, see K. D. Ewing, 'Economic Rights', in M. Rosenfeld and A. Sajó (eds.), *Oxford Handbook of Comparative Constitutional Law* (Oxford University Press, 2012). On the fragility of constitutional guarantees of labour rights, see I. Katsaroumpas, 'De-Constitutionalising Collective Labour Rights: The Case of Greece' (2018) 47 *Industrial Law Journal* 465.

[31] See p. 573 above.   [32] *Ryanair* v. *Labour Court* [2007] IESC 6.

collective bargaining gives rise to a number of problems for labour law, beginning with the different levels at which it takes place.

Bargaining Decentralisation

In the United Kingdom, the role of the state in promoting collective bargaining has changed over the course of the twentieth century.[33] The state has intervened at different times and in different ways, to promote different forms of collective bargaining machinery. A good starting-point is the report of the Whitley Committee in 1917,[34] which recommended that the newly created Ministry of Labour should intervene to seek to establish industry-wide 'joint industrial councils' to conduct collective bargaining between trade unions and employers' associations.[35] Where this proved impossible, it was proposed that a tripartite trade board should be established in the industry or sector in question under statutory authority to set wages and other conditions of employment (the employers and trade unions being represented along with a third party appointed by the Ministry).[36] These recommendations were accepted by the government of the day, with active steps then taken by the new Ministry of Labour to promote joint industrial councils, and with the Trade Boards Act 1918 extending the circumstances in which statutory trade boards could be created.[37] The result was that between 1918 and 1921 an additional 5 million workers were covered either by a collective agreement or a trade board award.[38]

These initiatives were not supported by Conservative governments in the 1920s, with the result that the system established after the First World War declined and in some cases decayed for want of nourishment. In an era of high unemployment, the direction of public policy had changed, and ministers were no longer interested in using administrative powers to promote collective bargaining.[39] But this was not to last. Clear signs of a revival of state support for the institutions of collective bargaining are discernible from about 1934, so

---

[33] See R. Dukes, *The Labour Constitution – The Enduring Idea of Labour Law* (Oxford University Press, 2014). Also K. D. Ewing, 'The State and Industrial Relations' (1998) 5 *Historical Studies in Industrial Relations* 1.

[34] J. H. Whitley, Interim Report on Joint Standing Industrial Councils, Cm 8606 (1917).

[35] The Ministry of Labour (which no longer exists) had been established by the New Ministries and Secretaries Act 1916. See K. D. Ewing, 'The State and Industrial Relations' (1998) 5 *Historical Studies in Industrial Relations* 1; and R. Lowe, *Adjusting to Democracy: The Role of the Ministry of Labour in British Politics, 1916–1939* (Oxford University Press, 1986).

[36] For a fuller discussion, see K. D. Ewing, 'The State and Industrial Relations' (1998) 5 *Historical Studies in Industrial Relations* 1.

[37] Trade Boards had initially been established in four industries to deal with the problem of 'sweating': Trade Boards Act 1909. Their remit was extended by the 1918 Act so that they could now be established in industries where workers' organisation was weak, creating obstacles to the development of bargaining machinery. The threat to create a trade board was used by the Ministry in some cases to coerce employers into participating in joint industrial councils.

[38] See K. D. Ewing, 'The State and Industrial Relations: "Collective Laissez-Faire" Revisited' (1998) 5 *Historical Studies in Industrial Relations* 1, at 19.

[39] *Ibid.*, pp. 21–6.

that by 1946 some 85 per cent of British workers were covered by a collective agreement or a trade board award.[40] Contrary to the 'collective *laissez faire*' school of thought, the state thus played a key role in building collective bargaining institutions:

- a government department was responsible for actively promoting the development of collective bargaining machinery on a multi-employer sectoral basis through NJICs; and
- statutory machinery in the form of trade boards (later renamed Wages Councils) was introduced to establish terms and conditions of employment for sectors where collective bargaining was insufficiently established.

Although collective agreements were not legally enforceable between the parties who made them, campaigns for their 'legalisation' (as the TUC referred to the process) were only partially successful, in the sense that they were not made binding within a sector automatically, but only in relation to specific employers on a case-by-case application by trade unions.[41]

This system of collective bargaining applied to the private as well as the public sector, but it has broken down in relation to both. Nevertheless, it may be possible to argue that the United Kingdom now has a mixed or hybrid system in view of the legacy of pockets of multi-employer bargaining in both private and public sectors, even though the unmistakable drift is in the direction of enterprise-based bargaining:

- In the private sector, multi-employer bargaining arrangements began to break down much earlier – in the 1960s if not before, encouraged by the Royal Commission on Trade Unions and Employers' Associations,[42] and supported for different reasons by both employers (at a time of inward investment) and trade unions (at a time of wage growth). The advantage of enterprise bargaining for trade unions is that they could secure higher wages for members in productive enterprises, with wages otherwise held back by the capacity to pay of the least efficient employer. The disadvantage is that unions lose influence as they are pegged back to enterprises willing to recognize them for the purposes of collective bargaining.
- There have been strong decentralising tendencies in the public sector since the 1980s (notably in the civil service).[43] Moreover, pay determination in much of the public sector (such as teaching) is now done by pay review bodies rather than collective bargaining, while the policy of austerity pursued

---

[40] *Ibid.*, p. 31.

[41] See, for example, Terms and Conditions of Employment Act 1959, s. 8; Employment Protection Act 1975, s. 98, Sched. 11. See generally B. Bercusson, *Fair Wages Resolutions* (London: Mansell, 1978).

[42] Report of the Royal Commission on Trade Unions and Employers' Associations, 1965–1968 (Lord Donovan, Chairman), Cmnd 3623 (1968).

[43] See Civil Service (Management Functions) Act 1992, for a prescient account of which, see M. R. Freedland (1994) 23 *Industrial Law Journal* 32.

by the Treasury since 2010 has seen governments take greater control of pay in the public sector generally, either by freezing pay or by authorising only modest increases. Some senior personnel in the public sector have been able to buck the trend, with improbable market leverage – as in the case of university vice-chancellors – enabling them to use the power of contract to negotiate what have been widely perceived to be wholly unjustified pay deals.

Enterprise-based bargaining is associated with low levels of collective bargaining density, a connection first made by an important OECD study as long ago as 1994, where it was pointed out that 'coverage is always lower in countries characterised by single employer bargaining compared with those where agreements are mainly concluded at the sectoral or economy-wide level'.[44] The first of a number of possible explanations is that this particular model places great emphasis on the need for unions to recruit and organise in company after company, needs which place heavy demands on union resources. Secondly, trade unions often face hostile opposition from employers who in the United States have developed a number of anti-avoidance strategies. In the United States, collective bargaining density in the private sector is said by the OECD to be only about 12 per cent, and indeed in none of the major jurisdictions where a variation of this method prevails is bargaining coverage overall more than about one-third of the workforce.[45] Thirdly, in the past unions might have relied on a strike or other forms of industrial action to force the employer to recognise.[46] Today, however, the legal restrictions on industrial action mean that this is a form of leverage that has lost its potency, as the levels of industrial action have also fallen.

Legacy of Voluntarism

Apart from its decentralised form, a second feature of collective bargaining in Britain is its mainly 'voluntary' nature. It is true that since 1999 provision has been made by statute for the recognition of trade unions by employers for the purposes of collective bargaining (albeit on a limited range of core issues).[47] Under the statutory procedure (considered in detail below), a trade union may seek a declaration of recognition and conclude a procedure agreement for the conduct of collective bargaining. In practice, however, most collective bargaining in Britain takes place without any legal obligation on either side.

---

[44] OECD, *Economic Outlook* (1994), p. 180.

[45] Compare A. Forsyth, J. Howe, P. Gahan and I. Landau, 'Establishing the Right to Bargain Collectively in Australia and the UK: Are Majority Support Determinations under Australia's Fair Work Act a More Effective Form of Union Recognition?' (2017) 46 *Industrial Law Journal* 335, who exaggerate the significance of legislative detail at a time when frustration with the model by Australian trade unions has led to a campaign for radical change of the bargaining model. Notably, the success rate under the Australian variant is broadly comparable to the British.

[46] For an example, see *D. C. Thomson & Co. Ltd.* v. *Deakin* [1952] Ch. 646.

[47] See pp. 587–614 below.

It occurs because employers have agreed voluntarily to recognise a trade union for the purposes of collective bargaining, and to conclude an agreement, that will enable negotiations over working conditions to take place. The overwhelming majority of large employers voluntarily engage in collective bargaining which is seen to have benefits for both the employer and the workers concerned: indeed it was estimated at the time the statutory procedure was introduced that 84 of Britain's top 100 companies recognised trade unions, and did so on the basis of voluntary agreements. This tradition of voluntary recognition strongly infuses the statutory procedure discussed below, the procedure designed to encourage employers and trade unions to conclude voluntary agreements in 'the shadow of the law'.[48]

A written recognition agreement typically will set out a procedure for the parties to meet on a regular basis for the negotiation of working conditions and for the settlement of any differences or disputes that may arise between them. The procedures will vary in their complexity, and in some cases machinery will be provided for dealing with different issues at different levels in the corporate structure. A good example of a recognition agreement is set out in the box on pages 584–6, this agreement being the template used by Unite, one of the largest unions in the United Kingdom. It will be noted that section 8 deals with procedures for 'joint consultation and negotiation' and that the first paragraph of this section makes provision for consultation and negotiation 'on all matters' in which union members have an interest. Also important are the provisions in section 4 relating to the election of workplace representatives, section 5 dealing with the facilities to be provided at the workplace to such representatives, and section 7 dealing with the deduction of trade union contributions by check-off. It will be noted also that paragraph 3.5 of this template provides expressly that '[t]he Company and the Union accept that the terms of the agreement are binding in honour upon them', though unlike earlier iterations does not state that it does 'not constitute a legally enforceable Agreement'.

Like much of the rest of this template, the latter is a fairly standard term of agreements that operate without legal obligation and without legal sanction. An appendix not reproduced here deals with the resolution of disputes. One other point about Unite's template agreement set out in the box is the provision in section 9 for variation or termination, with the former to occur only with mutual consent, and the latter only by either side giving six months' notice. The question that arises, however, is what happens if the agreement is varied or terminated in breach of these provisions, or where an agreement without a termination clause is terminated unilaterally (usually by the employer)? The template agreement would suggest that at least where

---

[48] This is a term associated with the late Professor Brian Bercusson: B. Bercusson, *European Labour Law* (2nd edn, Cambridge University Press, 2010), p. 584.

provisions like paragraph 3.5 are included, there is little the union can do about it, the agreement indicating that it is not legally binding, but binding in 'honour'. In fact, this provision is strictly unnecessary in view of the common law and now statutory presumption against the legal enforceability of *all* collective agreements,[49] which we consider more fully in Chapter 3 above. The only way to overcome that presumption is for the agreement to be in writing, and to contain a provision which, however expressed, states that the parties intend it to be a legally enforceable contract.

UNITE THE UNION

Recognition and Procedural Agreement

This agreement (hereafter called 'the Agreement') is made between INSERT NAME (hereafter called 'the Employer') and UNITE THE UNION (hereafter called 'the Union'). The Employer and the Union are referred to jointly in the Agreement as 'the Parties'.

1. OBJECTIVES

1.1 Industrial relations are a joint responsibility of the Parties and require the meaningful participation of all concerned – Management, Union and individual employees. The Agreement is designed to encourage and assist that co-operation and constructive dialogue.

1.2 The Agreement provides a system of representation and procedures through which the Parties may raise items of common concern, of either individual or collective nature.

1.3 The Parties recognise the importance of ensuring that all management and employee relationships are based on mutual understanding and respect and that employment practices are conducted to the highest possible standards.

1.4 The Parties are committed to developing equal opportunities and anti-harassment procedures for employees or prospective employees. The Parties are further committed to ensure that the treatment of staff will be fair and equitable in all matters of discipline and grievance.

2. SCOPE OF THIS AGREEMENT

The Agreement covers all employees up to and including (INSERT) level and the Employer recognises the Union as the sole union entitled to represent the interests of the employees and negotiate on their behalf.

3. GENERAL PRINCIPLES

3.1 The Employer believes that a union capable of representing its members with authority and responsibility is essential to the maintenance of good industrial relations.

3.2 The Employer recognises the Union's responsibility to represent the interests of its members.

---

[49] See, respectively, *Ford Motor Co. Ltd* v. *AUEFW* [1969] 2 QB 303; TULRCA 1992, ss. 178 and 179. The statutory presumption would apply to voluntary recognition agreements by virtue of TULRCA 1992, s. 178(2)(g).

3.3 The Union recognises the Employer's responsibility to manage its affairs effectively.

3.4 The Employer and the Union recognise that the progress of the Employer is in the interests of the Parties. Both parties declare their common objective to maintain constructive industrial relations.

3.5 The Employer and the Union accept that the terms of the agreement are binding in honour upon them.

4. UNION REPRESENTATION

4.1 The Employer recognises the Union as the *only Trade Union* **(CHECK AND AMEND AS APPROPRIATE)** with which it will consult and negotiate on all matters of interest of the employees.

4.2 The Employer will inform all employees of the Agreement and provide facilities for them to talk to a Union Representative. The Employer will regularly provide the Union with a list of all new employees and provide facilities for them to talk to a Union Representative.

4.3 Union members will elect Union Representatives (for example Shop Stewards and Health and Safety Representatives) in accordance with the rules of the Union to act as their spokespersons and to represent their interests. The Union agrees to inform the Employer of the names of all elected Union Representatives in writing within 5 working days of their election and to inform the Employer in a similar manner of any subsequent changes. Persons whose names have been notified to the Employer shall be the sole representatives of the employees.

4.4 Facilities will be provided by the Employer for elections to be held as required by Union rules.

4.5 Collectively, the elected Union Representatives will be recognised as the Shop Stewards Committee.

4.6 The Shop Stewards Committee may elect a recognised Senior Union Representative from within its ranks.

4.7 The Employer recognises that Union Representatives fulfil an important role and that the discharge of their duties as Union Representatives will, in no way, prejudice their career prospects or employment within the Employer.

5. FACILITIES

5.1 The Employer will provide appropriate time off arrangements and facilities for Union Representatives to carry out their functions effectively.

(Please see separate Union Facilities Agreement)

6. UNION MEETINGS

6.1 The Employer will provide Shop Stewards/Reps and union members with appropriate paid time and facilities to meet collectively with each other, with Shop Stewards/Reps from the Employer's other workplaces, with Officials and with Organisers.

(Please see separate Union Facilities Agreement)

7. CHECK OFF SYSTEM

7.1 It is agreed that a check-off system will operate whereby the Employer will deduct Union subscriptions from the wages/salaries of Union members and pay them to the Union each month with a schedule of payment with no charge to the Union. Individual members will authorise deductions in writing, appropriate forms being provided by Union Representatives.

8.   JOINT CONSULTATION AND NEGOTIATION

8.1 The Employer undertakes to enter into meaningful consultation and negotiation with the Union on all matters in which their members have an interest and will seek to resolve any difference by agreement.

8.2 Formal negotiations will take place between the Parties on an annual basis.

8.3 The anniversary date for negotiations and details of participants of both sides (The Negotiating Committee) will be agreed by the Parties.

8.4 Further arrangements are shown under Procedures for the Avoidance and Resolution of Disputes/Grievance procedures

(Please see Appendix 1 and 2)

9.   VARIATION OR TERMINATION OF AGREEMENT

The Agreement may only be varied by the mutual consent the Parties. In the event of either party wishing to terminate the agreement, the other party will be given six months' notice in writing, during which period the Agreement will remain in force.

Signed on behalf of Unite ....

Date ....

Signed on behalf of (Employer Name) ....

Date ....

Right to be Accompanied

Although a union may not be formally recognised for the purposes of collective bargaining, workers nevertheless may have the right to be accompanied by a trade union official (or by a fellow employee) in their dealings with their employer. The Employment Relations Act 1999, section 10, provides a right to be accompanied in relation to a disciplinary or grievance hearing the worker has been required or invited to attend by his or her employer. While section 10 provides a right to be accompanied rather than a right to representation, the employer must nevertheless permit the companion to address the hearing in order to put the worker's case, sum up that case and respond on the worker's behalf to any view expressed at the hearing. However, the employer is not required to permit the companion to answer questions on behalf of the worker.

A most important qualification to this right is to be found in Employment Relations Act 1999, section 13(4), which defines a disciplinary hearing, and section 13(5), which defines a grievance hearing. So far as disciplinary action is concerned, this is fairly broadly defined: a disciplinary hearing (at which the worker is entitled to be accompanied) is defined to mean a hearing which could result in: '(a) the administration of a formal warning to a worker by his employer, (b) the taking of some other action in respect of a worker by his employer, or (c) the confirmation of a warning issued or some other action taken.' The right to be accompanied is much more narrowly defined in the context of a grievance hearing (assuming that the employer has a grievance procedure). Here, section 13(5) provides that 'a grievance hearing is a hearing which concerns the performance of a duty by an employer in relation to a worker'.

This last provision is thought – in general – to prevent a worker from relying on the right to be accompanied when seeking to renegotiate rather than enforce the terms of his or her contract. It is extremely important because it prevents a trade union from seeking to use the individual's right to be accompanied as a surrogate recognition procedure. This could arise where a number of trade union members made a request for a pay rise in circumstances where the union was not recognised and nominated the union to act on their behalf in their negotiations with the employer. Such a practice would not only enable a trade union to secure *de facto* recognition where it does not have majority membership (as required by the ILO Committee of Experts), but also to secure *de facto* recognition where it does have majority membership though in a way that was much less cumbersome.

The Statutory Recognition Procedure

As we have pointed out, the voluntary recognition procedures are now under-pinned by a statutory procedure, which is designed to enable trade unions to secure recognition where the employer may be unwilling.[50] The Employment Relations Act 1999 inserted a new Schedule A1 into TULRCA 1992, to promote recognition of a trade union where the union can show majority support in the group of workers it wishes to represent.[51] But although the enactment of this procedure was the culmination of a long campaign by trade unions for legal support, it has proved to be a great disappointment.[52] It is true that those drafting the legislation sought to learn lessons from the failure of a similar statutory scheme introduced in 1975 and repealed in 1980,[53] and that they also sought to address some of the problems encountered by US unions in

---

[50] The objectives of the legislation are set out in the important white paper by which it was preceded: Department of Trade and Industry, *Fairness at Work*, Cm 3968 (1998).

[51] For good accounts of the legislation, see R. Dukes, 'The Statutory Recognition Procedure 1999 – No Bias in Favour of Recognition' (2008) 37 *Industrial Law Journal* 236; T. Novitz, 'A Revised Role for Trade Unions as Designed by New Labour' (2002) 29 *Journal of Law and Society* 467; and B. Simpson, 'Trade Union Recognition and the Law: A New Approach' (2000) 29 *Industrial Law Journal* 193. More detailed is T. Novitz and P. Skidmore, *Fairness at Work: A Critical Analysis of the Employment Relations Act 1999 and Its Treatment of Collective Rights* (Oxford: Hart, 2001). A more recent assessment is S. Moore, S. McKay, and S. Veale, *Statutory Regulation and Employment Relations – The Impact of Statutory Trade Union Recognition* (London: Palgrave, 2013).

[52] On the campaign, see K. D. Ewing, 'Trade Union Recognition – A Framework for Discussion' (1990) 19 *Industrial Law Journal* 209; J. O'Hara, *Worker Participation and Collective Bargaining in Britain: The Influence of European Law* (London: Institute of Employment Rights, 1996).

[53] On the scheme introduced by the Employment Protection Act 1975, ss. 11–16, see Lord McCarthy, *Fairness at Work and Trade Union Recognition: Past Comparisons and Future Problems* (London: Institute of Employment Rights, 1999).

the operation of similar legislation.[54] But while important lessons have been learned, it remains the case that Parliament has created a procedure that is much too limited in scope (pay, hours and holidays),[55] and much too cumbersome and long-winded in operation. At the same time, Parliament failed to anticipate the lengths to which hostile employers would go – often with external professional help from lawyers and others – to undermine union recognition campaigns. The procedure has proved to be a game of snakes and ladders, with more snakes than ladders. Here, we concentrate on some of the more contentious features of the procedure.

Applications and Admissibility

The first two statutory obstacles are the obstacles of applicability and admissibility. As to *applicability*, a request for recognition under the Act may be made to an employer only by a trade union that has a certificate of independence.[56] Certificates of independence are issued by the Certification Officer under TULRCA 1992, section 6. An independent trade union is defined in TULRCA 1992, section 5, as meaning a trade union which '(a) is not under the domination or control of an employer or group of employers or of one or more employers' associations', or '(b) is not liable to interference by an employer or any such group or association (arising out of the provision of financial or material support or by any other means whatsoever) tending towards such control'.[57] Otherwise, an application under the Act may be made only to an employer which (together with associated employers) employs twenty-one or more workers.[58] Although the Act uses the more expansive 'worker' rather than the more restrictive 'employee',[59] the threshold of twenty-one is nevertheless a major limitation of its scope. At the time the procedure was introduced, its effect was to exclude as many as 37 per cent of private sector workers, and as many as 90–95 per cent of private sector employers

---

[54] On the US system, see C. Estlund, 'The Ossification of American Labor Law' (2002) 102 *Columbia Law Review* 1527; W. B. Gould, *Agenda for Reform: The Future of Employment Relationships and the Law* (Cambridge, Mass: MIT Press, 1993); and P. C. Weiler, 'Promises to Keep: Securing Workers' Rights: Self-Organisation under the NLRA' (1983) 96 *Harvard Law Review* 1769.

[55] TULRCA 1992, Sched. A1, para. 3. Once recognised a trade union will have access to various other rights, notably time off and disclosure of information rights discussed below, and consultation rights discussed in Chapter 15.

[56] TULRCA 1992, Sched. A1, para. 6.   [57] See pp. 601–4 below.

[58] TULRCA 1992, Sched. A1, para. 7.

[59] On which, see *R (BBC)* v. *CAC* [2003] ICR 1542 (Admin).

from the coverage of the scheme.[60] It is all the more significant an exclusion for the fact that the small business sector is a growing sector of the economy.

Recognition and the Gig Economy

Should workers in the gig economy be entitled to recognition by their employer for the purposes of trade union recognition? This is the issue in the *Deliveroo* case before the CAC where the union argued that their members fell within the definition of worker in TULRCA 1992, section 296. In Chapter 6 we discussed how the definition of worker is now wide enough to cover gig economy workers under the National Minimum Wage Act 1998 and the Working Time Regulations 1998, and that the courts were not prepared to deny to these workers the right to the NMW and holiday pay on the ground that they were genuinely in business on their own account. The definition of worker is slightly different in the 1992 Act, for reasons that are unknown. Nevertheless, the CAC surprisingly held that a substitution clause in the Deliveroo workers' contract allowing them to nominate a substitute rider when they were unavailable was not a sham and that they were not employed as a result personally to provide service to the company.[61] The application was thus inapplicable.

The Secretary of State has power to vary the threshold figure of twenty-one by statutory instrument, so that it could be increased or reduced. This power has never been used.[62] But there is a strong case for saying that the threshold should be reduced or removed altogether in those sectors where there are still national collective agreements, and where the exemption effectively enables small businesses to undercut these agreements by operating union-free operations. A good example of this is printing, where there was a national

---

[60] K. D. Ewing and A. Hock, *The Next Step: Trade Union Recognition in Small Enterprises* (London: Popularis, 2003), pp. 13–14.

[61] *IWGB and RooFoods Ltd T/A Deliveroo*, CAC TUR1/985(2016). An application for judicial review was dismissed: [2019] IRLR 249.

[62] This had been a source of irritation of a number of trade unions which lobbied the government over several years to change the law. In 2005, it was agreed that a research project would be funded from the DTI Partnership Fund, in what was the last project funded by this programme, and the only one to be a partnership between two trade unions (GPMU and KFAT) rather than between a union and an employer. The researchers were asked to find evidence that small businesses did recognise trade unions and to consider what, if any, were the benefits of recognition to the businesses in question. They were also asked to find evidence of abuse of workers by employers, in circumstances where unions had been excluded and where their presence would contribute to a higher level of employment protection. A lengthy report was produced (K. D. Ewing and A. Hock, *Partnership Working Between Trade Unions and Small Businesses* (London: Popularis, 2005)), and it was understood by the authors and by the trade unions that the government would pilot a reduction of the 21 worker threshold in two sectors (printing and clothing) and that this would be done by regulation (TULRCA 1992, Sched. A1, para. 7(6)). However, the report was not published, the regulations were not made, and the government denied all knowledge of this 'understanding', although representatives of the government were present at meetings where it was discussed.

agreement between the British Print Industries Federation (BPIF) and Unite, which small businesses that are not members of the BPIF were not required to apply, but which they would be under strong pressure to apply if the union was able to use the statutory procedure to win bargaining rights in these companies.[63] There is also a strong case for saying that where workers are excluded from the procedure by the twenty-one-worker exemption, there should be some compensating equivalence for the workers concerned. For example, workers employed in small businesses could be entitled to trade union representation on wider grounds than currently provided for in section 10 of the 1999 Act, for example a right to be represented by their trade union on any matter relating to their contract of employment. The need for effective representation at work is not contingent on arbitrary factors such as the happenstance of having twenty rather than nineteen colleagues.

So far as *admissibility* is concerned, there are a number of admissibility conditions built into the scheme. Here, we concentrate on two of these.[64] The first is where 'the CAC [Central Arbitration Committee] is satisfied that there is already in force a collective agreement under which a union is (or unions are) recognised as entitled to conduct collective bargaining on behalf of any workers falling within the relevant bargaining unit'.[65] In principle this is a sensible provision, in the sense that it prevents a trade union from using the procedure to disrupt what may be an already established bargaining relationship between an employer and another trade union. There are, however, problems when the employer recognises a minority union in order to prevent a successful application by a majority union (problems reinforced where the

---

[63] K. D. Ewing and A. Hock, *Partnership Working Between Trade Unions and Small Businesses* (London: Popularis, 2005). There would also be a case for removing or lowering the threshold in agriculture, following the abolition of the Agricultural Wages Board, on which see pp. 578–9 above.

[64] The others are that an application is not made by another union in relation to the same group of workers (TULRCA 1992, Sched. A1, para. 37); and that the application is not made within three years of a previously unsuccessful application in relation to the same group of workers (TULRCA 1992, Sched. A1, paras. 39–41). So far as applications by two unions are concerned, this has not been a problem in practice, being addressed as intended by the TUC through the operation the TUC Disputes Principles and Procedures (2000). We encountered these already in Chapter 13 above (see pp. 551–4 above). For present purposes, it is to be noted that Principle 3 provides that: 'No union shall commence organising activities at any company or undertaking in respect of any group of workers, where another union has the majority of workers employed in membership and/or is recognised to negotiate terms and conditions, unless by arrangement with that union. Neither, in such circumstances, shall a union make approaches to an employer or respond to an employer initiative, which would have the effect of, directly or indirectly, undermining the position of the established union. Where a union considers that another [TUC] affiliate has low levels of membership, and no agreement or a moribund agreement, within any organisation in respect of any group of workers, the union shall consult with the other affiliate, before commencing organising activities (or as soon as it is informed of the interests of another affiliate). If agreement cannot be reached, then either union should refer the matter to the TUC.'

[65] TULRCA 1992, Sched. A1, para. 35(1).

recognised union has only limited bargaining rights). This was the position in the *Racing Post* case where the employer recognised the British Association of Journalists which was said to have only one member, in order to defeat an application by the National Union of Journalists which claimed to have more than half of the relevant employees in membership[66] It is also to be noted that, in some circumstances, the recognition agreement already in force need not be with an independent trade union,[67] as most famously in the case of the recognition agreement concluded by News International with the News International Staff Association. Although the latter is not an independent trade union, the existence of the agreement would be enough to prevent an application by the journalists or printers working for News International.[68]

Even where a union is not blocked by manoeuvres of this kind, an application will be admissible only if the CAC 'decides' that (a) members of the union or unions constitute at least 10 per cent of the workers in the proposed or agreed bargaining unit, and (b) a majority of the workers in the proposed or agreed bargaining unit would be likely to favour recognition of the union or unions making the application.[69] The 10 per cent requirement can be established by a membership check, comparing membership with the number of workers on the payroll. Majority support has been established in a number of ways in the CAC decisions on whether to accept an application: majority membership, petitions, a straw poll, and statements signed by employees indicating support for collective bargaining.[70] But although this appears in principle to be fairly straightforward, in practice it is an increasingly difficult hurdle for trade unions to surmount. Where the bargaining unit cuts across different departments even in the same workplace, there may be physical obstacles preventing trade union representatives in the workplace in question from gaining access to workers in these different departments,

---

[66] *R(NUJ) v. CAC* [2005] EWCA Civ 1309; [2006] ICR 1.

[67] TULRCA 1992, Sched. A1, para. 35(4). See *Prison Officers' Association and Securicor Custodial Services Ltd*, CAC Case No. TUR1/5/00, for an early example. Other examples (News International and Boots the Chemist) follow in the pages below).

[68] So while only an independent trade union may use the procedure, in some circumstances an existing agreement by an employer with a non-independent trade union may operate to block such an application. This matter is considered more fully at pp. 601–4 and 613–14 below.

[69] TULRCA 1992, Sched. A1, para. 36.

[70] In a series of very important early decisions, the CAC resisted employer requests to be supplied with the names of employees who had signed petitions in favour of recognition. Trade unions were concerned that, if this information had to be supplied, the individuals in question could have been the target of unwanted attention by employers in some cases. Had the cases been decided differently, they could well have marked the early death of the procedure. Important cases include *TGWU and Peter Black Healthcare*, CAC Case No. TUR1/78/[2001]; *AEEU and Control Technique Drives*, CAC Case No. TUR1/109/(2001); and *AEEU and GE Caledonian*, CAC Case No. TUR1//120/(2001).

notwithstanding the rights conferred by TULRCA 1992, section 146, with which the statutory procedure needs to be read.[71]

Bargaining Unit

Once it is established that an application is applicable and admissible, a number of opportunities are provided in the Act for the trade union and the employer to deal with the application by agreement, and for the Advisory, Conciliation and Arbitration Service (ACAS) to be involved at the request of the parties. Where this fails, the CAC will be required to consider a number of questions, the first of which concerns the bargaining unit. The trade union is not entitled arbitrarily to choose whom it represents in collective bargaining, but may be entitled to bargaining rights only if it is able to identify a group of workers, within which it has majority support, who constitute a rational unit for the purposes of collective bargaining. This is likely to present the union with some difficulty, for just as bargaining units do not come tailor-made, nor do they necessarily follow pockets of union strength. The union will typically propose a bargaining unit that typically will reflect the concentration of its support (in terms of the occupation and location of the workers in question), while the employer typically will propose a unit that will dilute the union's concentrated support and make it less likely that the union will be able to establish a majority at later stages in the procedure. This latter strategy of employers admittedly could be counterproductive were the union to demonstrate majority support in the larger unit, but it is a risk that some anti-union employers appear confidently to adopt.

TULRCA 1992, Schedule A1, provides, by paragraph 19B(2), that, in determining the bargaining unit, the CAC must take into account:

(a) the need for the unit to be compatible with effective management; [and]
(b) the matters listed in sub-paragraph (3), so far as they do not conflict with that need.

So far as sub-paragraph (3) is concerned, this lists five matters for consideration, as follows:

(a) the views of the employer and of the union (or unions);
(b) existing national and local bargaining arrangements;
(c) the desirability of avoiding small fragmented bargaining units within an undertaking;
(d) the characteristics of workers falling within the proposed bargaining unit and of any other employees of the employer whom the CAC considers relevant;
(e) the location of workers.

---

[71] Particularly important are the remarks in *Post Office* v. *Union of Post Office Workers* [1974] ICR 378, at 400, to the effect that the employer must put up with some inconveniences to his property rights to enable workers to engage in trade union activities at the workplace but outside working time without the consent of the employer. See p. 504 above.

If the employer and the trade union are unable to agree a bargaining unit, the matter will have to be resolved by the CAC in a formal hearing, which may be the second hearing in a dispute still at an early stage in the procedure, as the employer seeks to prevent the union from getting access to the workforce. Bargaining unit disputes are often hotly contested, and for the union it is a potentially long snake: a mistake on the bargaining unit will require the application to be re-validated, which may require the union to withdraw if it is unable to meet the admissibility criteria (10 per cent plus) in relation to the unit decided by the CAC.

The CAC reports that the parties have agreed the bargaining units in 61 per cent of cases referred to it,[72] though as suggested already some of the remaining 39 per cent are vigorously contested by the employer. In *R (Kwik-Fit) v. CAC*,[73] the CAC agreed with the union's proposed unit of all locations within London's M25 orbital motorway, a decision challenged by the employer in judicial review proceedings on the ground that the unit should extend to the company at large, this being the most appropriate bargaining unit. But although accepted by Elias J, the Court of Appeal rejected the employer's claim:

> it should be remembered that the statutory test is set at the comparatively modest level of appropriateness, rather than of the optimum or best possible outcome. Since the CAC has only to find and can only find one bargaining unit, and has only to be satisfied that the unit that it does find is appropriate, I see no escape from the contention that, provided the CAC concludes that the union's unit is appropriate, its inquiry should stop there.[74]

The law was amended by the Employment Relations Act 2004,[75] which introduced a new paragraph 19B(4), that 'in taking an employer's views into account for the purpose of deciding whether the proposed bargaining unit is appropriate, the CAC must take into account any view the employer has about any other bargaining unit that he considers would be appropriate'. This, however, may not swing the pendulum too far in the employer's direction, for according to the CAC subsequently, 'it is required to consider whether the proposed union bargaining unit is compatible with effective management, not whether it is the most effective unit judged by management effectiveness'.[76]

The CAC's latter approach was upheld by the Court of Appeal in *R (Lidl Ltd.) v. CAC*,[77] where it was said that the adoption of 'a broad criterion of "appropriateness", subject to specified considerations to be "taken into account",

---

[72] CAC, *Annual Report 2016–17* (2017), p. 12.   [73] [2002] ICR 1212.

[74] *Ibid.*, p. 1215 (Buxton LJ).   [75] Employment Relations Act 2004, s. 4.

[76] *CWU and Cable & Wireless (No. 2)*, CAC Case No. TUR1/570/2007, para. 36. Judicial review unsuccessful: *R (Cable & Wireless Services UK Ltd) v. CAC* [2008] EWHC 115 (Admin), para. 6 (Collins J). The challenge was based mainly on the CAC's refusal to accept the employer's argument that the union's proposed bargaining unit of 'employees in UK Field Services (except managers)' would cause undue fragmentation.

[77] [2017] EWCA Civ 328, [2017] ICR 1145.

rather than setting hard-edged criteria, reflects an intention on the part of Parliament to allow full range to the expert judgment of the CAC in making decisions about bargaining units'.[78] In that case the issue was about one of the matters to be taken into account, namely '(c) the desirability of avoiding small fragmented bargaining units within an undertaking'. The CAC had accepted a bargaining unit proposed by the GMB for 273 warehouse staff at Lidl's distribution centre at Bridgend, the workers in question representing only 1.2 per cent of the company's total workforce, 1.5 per cent of their 'category 6' employees nationally, and only one of its six distribution centres nationally. The CAC (i) took the view that the proposed unit was compatible with effective management, (ii) rejected the claim that this would lead to fragmented bargaining units within the undertaking, and (iii) rejected the claim about fragmented bargaining units on the ground that the Bridgend unit would be the only Lidl collective bargaining unit. In dismissing an appeal against the High Court's decision to uphold the CAC, Underhill LJ acknowledged that

> the situation which would obtain if the GMB were recognised for the warehouse operatives in Bridgend, but nowhere else, might – though not, I think, very naturally – be described as one where the system for setting the core terms and conditions for Lidl's workforce was 'fragmented', in the sense that in Bridgend such terms were determined by collective bargaining whereas elsewhere they were not; also that the proposed bargaining unit could be described as 'small' when compared with Lidl's overall workforce. It is not difficult to see how, to Lidl at least, that situation could be regarded as undesirable. But that kind of fragmentation is not the mischief referred to by paragraph 19B (3) (c): it does not involve fragmentation *between bargaining units* or fragmented collective bargaining. That does not mean that Lidl's concerns about having a small island of union recognition in a sea of non-recognition are necessarily irrelevant to the issue of whether the proposed unit is appropriate: it only means that they do not come in under paragraph 19B (3) (c). They still fall to be considered under the more general heading of their compatibility with effective management – or indeed, since the considerations itemised in paragraph 19B are not exhaustive, their appropriateness generally. The only difference is that the kind of 'fragmentation' of which Lidl complains is not to be treated as axiomatically undesirable.
>
> It will appear from what I say in the previous paragraph that I do not believe that the issue raised by this ground is of fundamental significance in practice. It has only been so prominent in this case because of the specific misdirection which Lidl alleges. For the future I would strongly discourage legal challenges based on the nice parsing of the constituent parts of paragraph 19B.[79]

---

[78] *Ibid.*, para. 16.

[79] *Ibid.*, paras. 38 and 39. On the last sentence see also *R (Cable & Wireless Services UK Ltd)* v. *CAC* [2008] EWHC 115 (Admin), discussed below, where Collins J also frowns upon reading CAC decisions as if they were statutory texts.

Establishing Majority Support

Once the issue of the bargaining unit is resolved, the next main question under the procedure is the level of union support: it is only if a union has majority support in the bargaining unit that a declaration for recognition may be issued by the CAC. It may be thought that this ought to be a formality, in the sense that the union has initially had to convince the CAC that it has a membership of at least 10 per cent in the proposed bargaining unit and that a majority of the proposed unit is likely to support the union's claim for recognition. Indeed, in light of the difficulties encountered by trade unions at later stages in the procedure, there would be a strong case for saying that a union that satisfies what are currently the admissibility criteria should at that stage be awarded recognition, subject to any challenge by the employer, on whom a heavy onus would lie to show that the proposed bargaining unit is not appropriate or that the union does not have the majority support claimed.[80] But back to reality and the current law, which enables a trade union to establish majority support in one of two ways: by showing that a majority of the workers in the bargaining unit are members of the union, or where the union does not have a majority membership by establishing majority support in a secret ballot in which at least 40 per cent of those eligible to vote do so in favour of recognition.[81]

Forcing a Ballot

The granting of recognition automatically on showing evidence of majority support was something the trade unions saw as a central pillar of the legislation. It rewarded their recruitment efforts, and avoided the problems in the United States of active campaigning by employers, where ballots (or elections) are mandatory in all cases. As might be expected, employers do not like recognition without a ballot, and were able to secure a number of concessions from the government, so that in some cases a ballot may be required even where the union has majority membership. This applies if:

- the CAC is satisfied that a ballot should be held in the interests of good industrial relations (paragraph 22(4)(a));
- the CAC has evidence, which it considers to be credible, from a significant number of the union members within the bargaining unit that they do not want the union (or unions) to conduct collective bargaining on their behalf (paragraph 22(4)(b));
- membership evidence is produced which leads the CAC to conclude that there are doubts whether a significant number of the union members within

---

[80] See also W. B. Gould, *Agenda for Reform: The Future of Employment Relationships and the Law* (Cambridge, Mass: MIT Press, 1993), pp. 162–3, in relation to the US procedure.

[81] TULRCA 1992, Sched. A1, para. 29.

the bargaining unit want the union or unions to conduct collective bargaining on their behalf (paragraph 22(4)(c)).

The last is designed to deal with the concern that trade unions will sign up people on cut-price deals, and the belief apparently held by some that workers join trade unions for cheap holidays, insurance and legal services rather than for the negotiation of the terms and conditions of their employment.

These provisions provide employers with an important opportunity to derail a union campaign. Trade unions often – perhaps usually – face resistance from employers in recognition applications, and employers will often actively campaign against the union. Trade union recognition campaigns sometimes require a great deal of effort on the part of the union, to recruit and retain workers in membership until recognition is secured. The benefit of being entitled to recognition on demonstrating majority membership is that it avoids a ballot which will take place in circumstances usually very favourable to the employer: the ballot will be on the employer's premises, in the employer's time, and in circumstances where workers are held as a 'captive audience'. It thus suits the employer to persuade the CAC that a ballot should be held, even where the union enjoys majority membership, the ballot period giving the employer an opportunity to wage an intensive campaign against the union. A study by Ewing, Moore and Wood of the early years of operation of the statutory scheme revealed that ballots were lost by unions in more than half of the cases where they had started with a majority of workers in the bargaining unit in membership of the union in question.[82]

For the trade union and the workers it represents, it is therefore important that the CAC is not trigger-happy in the exercise of its powers to require a ballot to be held. In an early decision in the life of the procedure, the Court of Session appeared willing to stand back and not require the CAC to make greater use of the power to require a ballot to be held. In that case, a bargaining unit consisted of hourly paid shop-floor workers, of whom 51.3 per cent were members of the union (ISTC). The employer argued that a ballot should be held under paragraph 24(4)(a) as being in the interests of good industrial relations in view of the slender nature of the union's majority. But although 'sensitive' to the employer's argument, it was rejected by the CAC, which held that to require a ballot on that ground without further evidence that a ballot was in the interests of good industrial relations 'would impose, in effect, a threshold for recognition without a ballot higher than that stipulated by the legislators'.[83] In judicial review proceedings,[84] the Court of Session held that there were no grounds for challenging this decision, even if the court 'would have been inclined to

---

[82] K. D. Ewing, S. Moore and S. Wood, *Unfair Labour Practices: Trade Union Recognition and Employer Resistance* (London: Institute of Employment Rights, 2003), p. 36.
[83] *Fullarton Petitioner* [2001] IRLR 752, citing para. 15 of the CAC decision.   [84] *Ibid.*

take the view that a ballot has a stabilising influence and might well improve industrial relations rather than to cause them to deteriorate'.[85]

On the other hand, in *R (Gatwick Express)* v. *CAC*,[86] there was a bargaining unit of thirty-eight workers, of whom twenty were union members. Eight of the union members wrote to the company to say that they did not want the union to be recognised. The letters were in standard form, typed on company-headed notepaper. Seven of the eight letters had been sent to the CAC by the company's human resources department. The letters were addressed to the CAC, which held that none of the three conditions in paragraph 22(4), in particular the one set out in paragraph 22(4)(b), was satisfied. According to the CAC, 'there are difficulties in attesting to the validity of employee opinion when workers are required to indicate their views to their employer either by returning a pre-typed and named letter opposing recognition to the Senior Executive responsible for [human resources], or if they were in favour of recognition, being instructed not to return the letter'. As a result, the CAC 'place[d] no evidential weight on the letters that were produced at the hearing'.[87] The decision was quashed by the High Court, with Wilkie J accepting the argument for the employer that the CAC's reasoning improperly 'imported into paragraph 22(4)(b) a requirement that the CAC has to be informed direct by a worker pursuant to that paragraph and in writing'.[88] Although this decision was effectively reversed by legislation,[89] it does provide a nice example of the kind of tactics that employers employ in order to persuade the CAC to order a ballot, even where there is majority membership.

Conduct of the Ballot

Where a ballot is held, the CAC must appoint a qualified independent person (QIP) to conduct the ballot,[90] the costs to be met equally by the union and the employer.[91] The ballot is to be held within twenty working days of the appointment of the QIP (a period the CAC has a discretion to extend).[92] The ballot is to be held at the workplace, by post, or by a combination of these methods, 'depending on the CAC's preference'.[93] In determining how to exercise its preference, there are a number of considerations to be taken into account by the CAC, including 'costs and practicality'. A mixed ballot is to be

---

[85] *Ibid.*, p. 757.   [86] [2003] EWHC 2035 (Admin).

[87] The eighth letter, in identical terms, had apparently been sent direct to the CAC by the union member. This letter was held not to amount to a significant number so as to satisfy the condition in TULRCA 1992, Sched. A1, para. 22(4)(b).

[88] [2003] EWHC 2035 (Admin), para. 8.

[89] This is the requirement in TULRCA 1992, Sched. A1, para. 22(4)(b), that the evidence received by the CAC must be 'credible', a qualification introduced by the Employment Relations Act 2004.

[90] TULRCA 1992, Sched. A1, para. 25.   [91] TULRCA 1992, Sched. A1, para. 28.

[92] TULRCA 1992, Sched. A1, para. 25.   [93] TULRCA 1992, Sched. A1, para. 25(4).

held, however, only where there are 'special factors', including 'factors arising from the location of workers or the nature of their employment'.[94]

Paragraph 26 (strengthened by the Employment Relations Act 2004) imposes a number of duties on employers in the conduct of the ballot:

- a duty to co-operate with the union and the QIP in the conduct of the ballot;
- a duty to give the union reasonable access to the workers in the bargaining unit, to enable the union to inform the workers of the object of the ballot and to seek their support;
- a duty to give the CAC the names and home addresses of the workers in the bargaining unit, to enable the union to supply campaigning material to the QIP for distribution to the workers concerned;[95]
- a duty not to make an offer to workers designed to induce them not to attend any access meeting held by the union, unless the offer is reasonable in the circumstances; and
- a duty not to take or threaten to take action against a worker for attending or participating (or indicating an intention to do either) in an access meeting with a trade union.

Access arrangements are to be established in accordance with a code of practice approved by Parliament,[96] which encourages the parties to reach an access agreement to enable the union to communicate with the workforce to be balloted. But it also sets out what are in effect minimum conditions in terms of access, and seeks to give the union the opportunity (1) to conduct meetings with the workforce collectively during the balloting period, (2) to communicate with the workforce by posters and other means (including electronic) and (3) where appropriate, to hold surgeries at the workplace which workers would be entitled to attend for up to fifteen minutes during working time. Failure on the part of the employer to comply with any of the foregoing duties is to be dealt with in accordance with paragraph 27. This provides that the union may make a complaint to the CAC, which, if it upholds the complaint, may order the employer to take remedial measures within a time specified in the order. Failure to comply could lead the CAC to order that the union is recognised, though that has never happened, and it seems most unlikely that it ever will.[97]

In addition to steps taken to enable trade unions to contact workers in the bargaining unit, the law also addresses some of the bad practices of employers

---

[94] TULRCA 1992, Sched. A1, para. 25(6).

[95] See also TULRCA 1992, Sched. A1, para. 19B (power to communicate through an independent person with workers in proposed bargaining unit after acceptance of application).

[96] See Department for Business, Innovation and Skills, *Access and Unfair Practices During Recognition and Derecognition Ballots* (2011 edition).

[97] For the use of equivalent powers in the United States, see *National Labor Relations Board v. Gissel Packaging Co. Inc.*, 395 US 575 (1969).

during recognition campaigns.[98] After intense lobbying by the TUC, an amendment was introduced to the statutory procedure in 2004 dealing with unfair practices.[99] The provision is symmetrical in the sense that it applies to unfair practices by both the employer and the trade union, though in practice it is the conduct of the former that has been a problem. So far as the scope or content of unfair practices are concerned, the law applies only to active aggression, such as bribes, threats or the use of undue influence. It does not apply to other more passive aggression, such as the setting up of staff associations as an anti-union strategy. Thus, paragraph 27A provides that during the balloting period both parties must refrain from using an unfair practice, defined to mean any of the following, though only if undertaken with a view to influencing the result of the ballot:

- an offer to pay money or give money's worth to a worker entitled to vote in the ballot in return for the worker's agreement to vote in a particular way or to abstain from voting;
- making an outcome-specific offer to a worker entitled to vote in the ballot;
- coercing or attempting to coerce a worker entitled to vote in the ballot to disclose whether he [or she] intends to vote or to abstain from voting in the ballot, or how he [or she] intends to vote, or how he [or she] has voted, in the ballot;
- dismissing or threatening to dismiss a worker;
- taking or threatening to take disciplinary action against a worker;
- subjecting or threatening to subject a worker to any other detriment; or
- using or attempting to use undue influence on a worker entitled to vote in the ballot.

Some of these unfamiliar terms are defined in the Act: an 'outcome-specific offer' is an offer to pay money or give money's worth which:

(a) is conditional on the issuing by the CAC of a declaration that –
    (i) the union is (or unions are) recognised as entitled to conduct collective bargaining on behalf of the bargaining unit, or
    (ii) the union is (or unions are) not entitled to be so recognised, and
(b) is not conditional on anything which is done or occurs as a result of the declaration in question.[100]

A complaint may be made to the CAC by a trade union or an employer about an unfair practice alleged to have been committed by the other. The applicant must show not only that the respondent used an unfair practice, but also that the unfair practice did or was likely to affect the result.[101] Where these hurdles have been crossed, the CAC may then make orders of a kind which are now familiar: a declaration that the complaint is well founded, followed by an order

---

[98] On which, see K. D. Ewing, S. Moore and S. Wood, *Unfair Labour Practices: Trade Union Recognition and Employer Resistance* (London: Institute of Employment Rights, 2003), Ch. 4.
[99] Employment Relations Act 2004, s. 10(1).   [100] TULRCA 1992, Sched. A1, para. 27A(3).
[101] TULRCA 1992, Sched. A1, para. 27B(4)(b).

that the respondent takes specified action.[102] The CAC may also order a ballot.[103] Where the CAC finds that the unfair practice used consisted of or included (a) the use of violence, or (b) the dismissal of a union official, it is empowered to make a declaration that the union is recognised without any further formality.[104] It is thus an important feature of this procedure that it effectively creates rights which vest in the union and which may be enforced only by the union.[105] So threats or inducements directed to the worker will violate the right not of the worker but of the union,[106] though concerns have been expressed about the substance of these rights in view of their poor drafting and weak enforcement.[107]

The Problem of Employer Resistance

Trade union recognition campaigns are often (though not always) aggressive, adversarial affairs. The fact that the union is using the statutory procedure is an indication that the employer has resisted a request for voluntary recognition. In some cases, this may be because the employer wishes genuinely to test a union claim that it has majority support. In most cases, however, it is likely to be because the employer is hostile to the union. The legislation has in place a number of devices designed to counteract employer resistance, including a right of access,[108] unfair practices,[109] and protection against discrimination and dismissal.[110] There are also strict time limits tailored into the legislation designed to address the problem of delay, which in the United States is a real problem as employers are able to undermine the union by prolonging the process.[111] Employers nevertheless appear able to navigate these devices designed to counteract their resistance to trade unions, with the work of Ewing, Moore and Wood identifying the following responses of some employers in the early years of the operation of the procedure:

[102] TULRCA 1992, Sched. A1, para. 27C(2) and (3)(a).
[103] TULRCA 1992, Sched. A1, para. 27C(3)(b).   [104] TULRCA 1992, Sched. A1, para. 27D.
[105] It is expressly provided that 'The duty imposed by this paragraph does not confer any rights on a worker; but that does not affect any other right which a worker may have' (TULRCA 1992, Sched. A1, para. 27A(4)).
[106] Though of course there may be circumstances where the conduct of the employer may violate rights of the employees or workers existing in other legislation. Apart from those already referred to above, the employer's conduct may also violate the worker or the employee's right under TULRCA 1992, Sched. A1, paras. 156 and 161, which deal with detriment and dismissal in the course of a recognition campaign. Further details of what constitutes an unfair practice is to be found in the Access Code (note 96 above).
[107] See A. Bogg, 'The Mouse That Never Roared: Unfair Practices and Union Recognition' (2009) 38 *Industrial Law Journal* 390. There has not been a single case in which the CAC has found an employer to have used an unfair practice. Apart from the CWU case below, also significant is *Unite the Union and Kettle Foods Ltd*, CAC Case No. TUR1/557/(2007).
[108] See p. 598 above.   [109] See pp. 599–600 above.
[110] TULRCA 1992, Sched. A1, Part VIII.
[111] See W. B. Gould, *Agenda for Reform: The Future of Employment Relationships and the Law* (Cambridge, Mass: MIT Press, 1993), Chs. 5 and 7.

- Pre-emption, where the employer seeks to pre-empt the organising activities of a trade union in one of a number of ways, such as providing other channels for worker representation, or selecting the union to represent the workers so it is in effect imposed upon them.
- Persuasion, coercion and frustration, where the employer responds to the emerging or actual presence of a union with a range of measures designed to frustrate its organising activities or recognition claim. This may involve different forms of active campaigning against the union in the workplace.
- Shaping and using the legal process, where the employer makes full use of the opportunities in the legislation arising from the discretion vested in the statutory agency. This includes helping to shape the bargaining unit, or by persuading the CAC to hold a ballot if the case gets that far.
- Legalism and litigation, whereby the employer sometimes with legal advice will identify and seek to explore legal technicalities, and will use the various opportunities to litigate and contest an application, both before the CAC and in judicial review proceedings.[112]

These different tactics sometimes overlap, and several tactics may be used by the same employer. Here, we provide two examples of how major companies appeared quite lawfully to embrace tactics of these kinds to remain 'union free'.

News International

Employers seeking to discourage trade union membership and trade union recognition may take one of a number of pre-emptive steps. Here, there are three lawful tactics that are currently visible:

- the employer may set up rival forms of organisation such as works councils or employee forums designed ostensibly to give workers a voice;
- the employer may establish its own company union to which it gives negotiating rights on a range of issues; or
- the employer may choose the union with which he or she is prepared to deal, and reach an agreement with a union that may not have the support of the workforce.

The lawful tactic of pre-emption is well known both in this country and overseas, previously acknowledged by Bain in his classic study of white-collar trade unionism.[113] There, he referred to it as the tactic of 'peaceful competition', as one of several obstacles encountered by independent trade unions. There are two problems with alternative forms of worker representation, the first

---

[112] K. D. Ewing, S. Moore and S. Wood, *Unfair Labour Practices: Trade Union Recognition and Employer Resistance* (London: Institute of Employment Rights, 2003).

[113] G. S. Bain, *The Growth of White Collar Unionism* (Oxford University Press, 1970).

being that they may not guarantee adequately resourced or independent representation. In one case encountered by Ewing, Moore and Wood, the body in question was said by a company executive 'to have access to independent legal advice', 'at my discretion'.[114] The second problem is that the imposed form of representation may not reflect the wishes of the workers who may never have been asked about how they wish to be represented in the enterprise, and the voice allowed may not be one permitted to speak loudly or for long.

The leading example of an employer which has adopted this tactic to pre-empt the union is News International, the publisher in the United Kingdom of *The Times*, the *Sunday Times*, the *Sun* and (until its closure) the *News of the World*.[115] The News International Staff Association (NISA) has its origins in the mid-1980s when the company set up a Human Resources Committee at its different plants. It was at this time that the company derecognised the existing trade unions in circumstances that are now well known.[116] The members of the Committee were appointed by the company management, though from 1989 space was provided for elected members. In 1995, the Human Resources Committee was abandoned and replaced with the Employees' Consultative Council, which metamorphosed in turn to become the News International Staff Association. Membership of NISA was granted automatically to every employee of the company, and anyone objecting to membership had to opt out. Those who remained in membership were not required to pay any subscriptions, with the result that the Association was said to be 'dependent on the employer for meeting any costs incurred in the course of [its] activities'.[117] Appropriate administrative assistance was thus provided by the Human Resources Manager of the company, which also undertook to meet all the reasonable costs of the association in taking legal advice, provided the advice was sought from a solicitor approved by the Director of Human Resources.

The NISA Charter was redrafted shortly after the publication of the government's white paper, *Fairness at Work*, in 1998.[118] Under the terms of the Charter, its principal purpose is the 'regulation of relations between workers and News International', which it promotes through collective bargaining with company representatives, thereby falling within the definition of a trade union as provided by TULRCA 1992, section 1.[119] Although all staff association

---

[114] K. D. Ewing, S. Moore and S. Wood, *Unfair Labour Practices: Trade Union Recognition and Employer Resistance* (London: Institute of Employment Rights, 2003), p. 12.

[115] For a fuller account, see K. D. Ewing, 'Trade Union Recognition and Staff Associations – A Breach of International Labour Standards?' (2000) 29 *Industrial Law Journal* 267.

[116] See K. D. Ewing and B. W. Napier, 'The Wapping Dispute and Labour Law' (1986) 45 *Cambridge Law Journal* 285.

[117] *In re NISA*, Decision of Certification Officer, 18 May 2001, para. 24.

[118] Department of Trade and Industry, *Fairness at Work*, Cm 3968 (1998) (the seminal prelude to the Employment Relations Act 1999).

[119] See p. 588 above.

members are elected, NISA is not an independent trade union, having been denied a certificate of independence in May 2001.[120] In concluding that NISA was not independent, the Certification Officer found that recent changes to its constitution and operating practices meant that it was no longer under the domination or control of the employer. Meetings of the executive were no longer co-ordinated, attended and minuted by members of News International's Human Resources Department. But NISA still had some way to go before it could be said not to be 'liable to interference' by the employer. Weighing 'the strength of the employers, the pressures they could bring against the staff association and the facilities they could withdraw' on the one hand, against the membership base, structures and financial resources of NISA on the other, the Certification Officer found that it had not yet reached the stage where it was able to satisfy the statutory definition of independence.[121] Its vulnerability to interference 'cannot be described as insignificant'.[122] Nevertheless, it is currently impossible for an independent trade union to use the recognition procedure against the company.

News International is thus able to take advantage of a curious anomaly in the legislation: while only an independent trade union may bring a claim under the statutory procedure in TULRCA 1992, Schedule A1, the recognition by an employer of a non-independent trade union may in some circumstances block an application by an independent union by virtue of the operation of paragraph 35(4). It will be recalled that paragraph 35(1) provides that an application is 'not admissible if the CAC is satisfied that there is already in force a collective agreement under which a union is (or unions are) recognised as entitled to conduct collective bargaining on behalf of any workers falling within the relevant bargaining unit'. The difficult-to-follow provisions of paragraph 35(4) provide that:

(4) In applying sub-paragraph (1) an agreement for recognition (the agreement in question) must be ignored if –

    (a) the union does not have (or none of the unions has) a certificate under section 6 that it is independent,

    (b) at some time there was an agreement (the old agreement) between the employer and the union under which the union (whether alone or with other unions) was recognised as entitled to conduct collective bargaining on behalf of a group of workers which was the same or substantially the same as the group covered by the agreement in question, and

    (c) the old agreement ceased to have effect in the period of three years ending with the date of the agreement in question.

---

[120] *In re NISA*, Decision of Certification Officer, 18 May 2001.   [121] *Ibid.*, para. 36.
[122] *Ibid.*, para. 29.

In order to take advantage of this loophole (deliberately) tailored into the legislation, it is necessary that the non-independent trade union be given 'bargaining' rather than 'consultation' rights, in order to meet the statutory definition of 'recognition'.[123] However, it is not necessary that the bargaining rights of the non-independent union should relate to pay, hours or holidays, the matters in respect of which the statutory procedure applies.[124] Although it is true that there is a procedure for the derecognition of non-independent unions,[125] the procedure is complex and those thinking of using it may feel disinclined to do so for multiple reasons. The existence of this derecognition procedure was nevertheless enough to insulate paragraph 35(4) from a challenge on Convention grounds in another case where a staff association was recognised by the employer,[126] though questions remain about the extent to which paragraph 35(4) is consistent with ILO Convention 98, Article 2.

ILO Convention 98, Article 2

1. Workers' and employers' organisations shall enjoy adequate protection against any acts of interference by each other or each other's agents or members in their establishment, functioning or administration.
2. In particular, acts which are designed to promote the establishment of workers' organisations under the domination of employers' organisations, or to support workers' organisations by financial or other means, with the object of placing such organisations under the control of employers or employers' organisations, shall be deemed to constitute acts of interference within the meaning of this Article.[127]

Cable & Wireless plc

A second example of union-avoidance tactics being used is provided by the recognition campaign waged by the CWU against Cable & Wireless plc,[128] the union seeking recognition in the employer's Field Services division. The

---

[123] *Ibid.*, para. 3.
[124] *R (Boots Management Services Ltd)* v. *CAC* [2014] EWHC 65 (Admin); and *R (Boots Management Services Ltd)* v. *CAC* [2014] EWHC 2930 (Admin).
[125] TULRCA 1992, Sched. A1, Part VI.
[126] *Pharmacists' Defence Association Union* v. *Secretary of State for Business Innovation and Skills* [2017] EWCA Civ 66, [2017] IRLR 355. For a powerful critique, see A. Bogg and R. Dukes, 'Article 11 ECHR and the Right to Collective Bargaining: Pharmacists' Defence Association Union v Boots Management Services Ltd' (2017) 46 *Industrial Law Journal* 543. But see now *PDAU and Boots Management Services Ltd*, CAC Case No. TUR1/1062/2018, discussed at pp. 613–14 below.
[127] Note also that ILO Convention 98, Art. 3, provides that 'machinery appropriate to national conditions shall be established, where necessary, for the purpose of ensuring respect for the right to organise as defined in the preceding Articles'.
[128] Cable & Wireless no longer exists, and is now part of Vodafone, which had no part to play in the events discussed here, which occurred before the acquisition in 2013.

company had a Business Ethics Policy in which it claimed to be 'obsessional about people', and to 'respect the dignity of the individual and support the Universal Declaration of Human Rights and the ILO Core Conventions'. Not only that, but the company was 'committed to creating a working environment where there is mutual trust, integrity and respect, where everyone is both personally accountable for their actions and responsible for our business performance and reputation'. As we have seen in Chapter 2, the ILO Conventions include the right to freedom of association, which by virtue of ILO Convention 98 and other instruments includes the right to bargain collectively. It is thus curious that in 2007 the company refused a request for recognition by the CWU, and when the union initiated proceedings under the statutory procedure, it responded in a most remarkable manner, which appeared to embrace different aspects of the union-avoidance techniques identified above. In the *News International* case, the employer was able to pre-empt an application under the statutory procedure by preparing well and establishing an organisation with bargaining rights. The *Cable & Wireless* case is very different, the company reacting rather than pre-empting, with allegations that it did so by adopting tactics of a kind identified in the latter three bullet points on page 601 above.

In what reads like a textbook example of such practices, it started with the appointment of 'labour consultants' shortly after the application was lodged. The consultants in question were The Burke Group (TBG), a US-based company whose website states that it has expertise in 'union avoidance', and 'preventive labor relations – union free workplaces',[129] boasting a 96 per cent success rate in the cases in which it has been involved worldwide. Such organisations are sometimes referred to colloquially as 'union busters', though in this case TBG was reported to have been very sensitive to claims made by the CAC in the *Cable & Wireless* case in which '[t]he panel shares the union's concerns about TBG's unfortunate track record, according to union and academic sources'. As revealed by a press report, TBG complained to Sir Michael Burton (Chairman of the CAC) that the panel 'had exceeded its remit and it was "inappropriate" for the arbitrators to accept the union's view without independent validation'. Sir Michael is reported to have 'agreed to make what the committee described as an "exceptional" step of reissuing the judgment . . . with the panel's criticism of the group erased'.[130] The contested passage now reads: 'TBG is alleged by the union to have an unfortunate track record',[131] the Committee being reported as having accepted that 'the original wording could be interpreted by employers as a sign that their use of these consultants would not be looked upon favourably in future disputes coming before the court, which hands down legally binding arbitrations'.[132]

---

[129] See www.tbglabor.com.   [130] *Daily Telegraph*, 4 August 2008.
[131] *CWU and Cable & Wireless (No. 3)*, CAC Case No. TUR1/570/(2007), para. 50.
[132] *Daily Telegraph*, 4 August 2008, where it is also reported that: 'TBG's chairman and chief executive, David Burke, said he was happy with the committee's decision. "It is an exceptional

About the same time as TBG were appointed, the company's Director of Field Services wrote to all employees setting out his concerns about the implications of union recognition, a letter which the union claimed was misleading and inaccurate. Once the application had been accepted by the CAC and the bargaining unit decided in the union's favour, the Director of Field Services wrote again to employees inviting them to write either to him or to the CAC expressing the view that a ballot should be held or that they did not want collective bargaining. According to the CAC, advice was included on how to resign from the union, and the letter was followed up by conference calls to all employees and round-table meetings in six locations. It was also alleged by the union that one-to-one meetings between employees and their managers were held to discuss recognition. The union 'believed that the employer deliberately delayed the process through continually pressurizing the workforce at the instigation of TBG, in an attempt to demoralize union members', the CAC also noting the union's claim that during the delay caused by the lengthy litigation the employer had on the advice of TBG 'attempted to restructure Field Services so as to dilute union influence'.[133] This appears to have been by expanding the size of Field Services, the need for which was doubted by the union other than as a 'deliberate ploy to try to push the union membership below 50% of the bargaining unit'.[134]

So far as the third and fourth bullet points on page 601 are concerned, the company challenged the admissibility of the claim,[135] and it contested the union's proposed bargaining unit before the CAC and then all the way to the Administrative Court,[136] where, in the face of a highly legalistic analysis of the CAC's decision, it was necessary for Collins J to remind the company that decisions of the CAC are 'not to be treated as a statute whose language can be subjected to detailed analysis'.[137] Thereafter, Cable & Wireless successfully contested the union's right to automatic recognition (despite the union having a majority of members in the bargaining unit),[138] persuading the CAC that it would be in accordance with good industrial relations to hold a ballot, in view of the claim that 'exactly three fifths of employees in the bargaining unit' had written to say that they 'did not want automatic union recognition'.[139] The company also successfully resisted a union complaint that it had indulged in

step the CAC has taken and it sets the record straight about us. Our advice, and the work with our clients, complies with the spirit and intent of all current UK legislation and codes of practice", he said.'

[133] CWU and Cable & Wireless (No. 3), CAC Case No. TUR1/570/(2007), para. 12.
[134] Ibid., para. 13.   [135] CWU and Cable & Wireless (No. 1), CAC Case No. TUR1/570/(2007).
[136] CWU and Cable & Wireless (No. 2), CAC Case No. TUR1/570/(2007); R (Cable & Wireless Services UK Ltd) v. CAC [2008] ICR 693.
[137] R (Cable & Wireless Services UK Ltd) v. CAC [2008] ICR 693, para. 14. See also R (Lidl Ltd.) v. CAC [2017] EWCA Civ 328, [2017] ICR 1145, para. 39, discussed above, pp. 593–4.
[138] CWU and Cable & Wireless (No. 3), CAC Case No. TUR1/570/(2007).
[139] Ibid., para. 51. 'While there may have been some allegations of pressure on employees to write letters no substantive evidence has been provided to show that employees were compelled to

an unfair practice,[140] by means of a letter from the CEO of the company to staff during the balloting period 'which mentioned, in the first paragraph, the successful trading year and the size of the consequent bonus payments and then, in the second paragraph drew attention to the union recognition ballot and urged colleagues to vote "No"'.[141] Cable & Wireless thus prevailed, with the union securing seventy-seven votes in the ballot (23 per cent of those voting), despite having 185 members (55.2 per cent) at the start of the balloting period.[142] This was a good result for labour consultants and management-side labour lawyers.

Declaration of Recognition

If a union is able to demonstrate majority membership or majority support in a ballot (representing at least 40 per cent of those eligible to vote), the CAC must make a declaration of recognition.[143] What happens next? International experience suggests that an employer who has lost a bitter campaign for union recognition is unlikely to roll over and extend a warm embrace to union officials. Rather, a successful recognition campaign on the part of a union may simply open a new front of employer resistance, which will require additional legal support to overcome. The aim now is to establish a procedure for negotiating terms and conditions of employment, on the basis of a procedure that the parties have undertaken to follow. Under the current statutory procedure the parties have 30 days (from the date on which they are notified of the CAC's declaration) to agree 'a method of collective bargaining'.[144] If no agreement is reached, either or both of the parties may apply to the CAC for assistance, in which case the CAC (curiously not ACAS) must 'try to help' the parties reach an agreement on a collective bargaining method.[145] If the parties are unable to reach an agreement, 'the CAC must specify to the parties the method by which they are to conduct collective bargaining'.[146] The method to be imposed on the parties is set out in regulations made in 2000, the preamble to which provides expressly that 'the CAC may depart from the specified

---

write in this way against their true beliefs. Even if this were true in some cases the sheer numbers writing cannot be ignored' (*ibid.*).

[140] *CWU and Cable & Wireless (No. 4)*, CAC Case No. TUR1/570/(2007).

[141] *Ibid.*, para. 29. This was not 'undue influence' within the meaning of TULRCA 1992, Sched. A1, para. 27A(2)(g), for the purposes of which there would need to be 'evidence that the employer was threatening or inducing the employees by linking the bonus payment to the outcome of the ballot': *ibid.*

[142] *CWU and Cable & Wireless (No. 5)*, CAC Case No. TUR1/570/(2007).

[143] As we have seen there are other circumstance in which a declaration may be made, notably where the employer is guilty of egregious behaviour during the balloting period, though this has never been done.

[144] TULRCA 1992, Sched. A1, para. 30(1).   [145] TULRCA 1992, Sched. A1, para. 31(2).

[146] TULRCA 1992, Sched. A1, para. 31(3).

method to such extent as it thinks appropriate in the circumstances of individual cases'.[147]

Collective Bargaining Method

The Trade Union Recognition (Method of Collective Bargaining) Order 2000 thus contains a template for use in 'rare cases',[148] 'to specify a method by which the employer and the union conduct collective bargaining concerning the pay, hours and holidays of the workers comprising the bargaining unit'.[149] It is open to the parties voluntarily to extend the collective bargaining matters, though it is also provided that 'the employer shall not grant the right to negotiate pay, hours and holidays to any other union in respect of the workers covered by this method'.[150] The union thus has exclusive bargaining rights in relation to pay, hours and holidays. In terms of procedure, the regulations require the parties to establish a Joint Negotiating Body (JNB) to 'discuss and negotiate the pay, hours and holidays of the workers comprising the bargaining unit',[151] the JNB typically to include three employer representatives and three union representatives.[152] Although there is no duty to bargain in good faith (as there is the United States and Canada), the regulations nevertheless contain equivalent provisions designed to ensure that the employer takes the process seriously. Thus, the employer's representative 'must either be those who take the final decisions within the employer's organisation in respect of the pay, hours and holidays of the workers in the bargaining unit or who are expressly authorised by the employer to make recommendations directly to those who take such final decisions'.[153] Moreover, 'unless it would be unreasonable to do so, the employer shall select as a representative the most senior person responsible for employment relations in the bargaining unit'.[154]

Provision is also made for the administration and organization of the JNB,[155] again placing responsibility on the employer, with the secretary of the Employer Side to act as Secretary to the JNB. As such he or she must 'circulate documentation and agendas in advance of JNB meetings, arrange suitable accommodation for meetings, notify members of meetings and draft the written record of JNB meetings'.[156] In discharging these duties, the Secretary of the Employer Side must work closely with the Secretary of the Union Side, 'disclosing full information about his performance of these tasks'.[157] Otherwise, the regulations deal with the bargaining procedure, prescribing at least one meeting annually to deal with union proposals for adjustments to pay, hours and holidays.[158] The procedure prescribes six steps, in the course of

---

[147] Trade Union Recognition (Method of Collective Bargaining) Order 2000, SI 2000/1300.
[148] *Ibid.*, preamble.   [149] *Ibid.*, para. 2.   [150] *Ibid.*, para. 3.   [151] *Ibid.*, para. 4.
[152] *Ibid.*, para. 5.   [153] *Ibid.*, para. 6.   [154] *Ibid.*   [155] *Ibid.*, paras. 9–13.
[156] *Ibid.*, para. 11.   [157] *Ibid.*   [158] *Ibid.*, paras. 14–18.

which the employer is required to provide the union with information to justify the employer's response, including information 'costing each element of the claim and describing the business consequences, particularly any staffing implications'.[159] However, in 'determining what information is disclosed as relevant, the employer shall be under no greater obligation that he is under the general duty imposed on him by sections 181 and 182 of the 1992 Act to disclose information for the purposes of collective bargaining'.[160] The employer is specifically 'not required to disclose such information for any of the reasons specified in section 182(1) of the 1992 Act'.[161] But although there is a detailed procedure, there is no duty to reach an agreement at the end of it. That said, stage 6 of the procedure does provide the option of a reference to ACAS for conciliation in such circumstances.[162]

These procedures have been strongly criticised. According to Simpson they represent an obligation to do more than meet and talk within a prescribed framework about pay, hours and holidays, 'and little – if anything – else'.[163] We should not, however, under-estimate the provision made for (i) composition of the JNB; (ii) the employer's responsibility for the administration of the JNB; (iii) the procedure set out for the conduct of negotiations; and (iv) the procedure for dispute resolution via ACAS. Nor should we overlook the untested provisions of paragraph 31 that 'the employer and the union shall take all reasonable steps to ensure that this method to conduct collective bargaining is applied efficiently and effectively', which looks very much like a synonym for the duty to bargain in good faith. It is true, nevertheless, that these provisions would be strengthened if there was arbitration as a final option, as was the case with the 1975 Act which as we explain below enabled the CAC unilaterally to vary employment contracts in the event of a failure to agree. A notable but neglected feature of the procedure in this respect is that while the employer is under no duty to agree to any proposal made by a union to improve working conditions in the bargaining unit, the union cannot prevent the employer from imposing any changes that would reduce working conditions. True, an eye-catching provision in paragraph 17 of the procedure states that the 'employer shall not vary the contractual terms affecting the pay, hours or holidays of workers in the bargaining unit, unless he has first discussed his proposals with the union'. But apart from the fact that this applies only to pay, hours and holidays, once the discussions have taken place, the employer is free to proceed.[164]

---

[159] *Ibid.*, para. 15.   [160] *Ibid.* See below, pp. 622–9.   [161] *Ibid.*   [162] *Ibid.*

[163] B. Simpson, 'Trade Union Recognition and the Law, A New Approach – Parts I and II of the Schedule A1 to the Trade Union and Labour Relations (Consolidation) Act 1992' (2000) 29 *Industrial Law Journal* 193.

[164] This of course would be subject to any contractual obligations to the employees concerned individually, or any issues arising under the Information and Consultation of Employees Regulations 2004, SI 2004 No. 3426, or other statutory obligations.

In a major break with the traditions of British industrial relations, it is expressly provided that any such imposed method is to be treated as a legally enforceable contract made by the parties, unless both parties agree otherwise.[165] This thereby reverses the normal statutory presumption, and is a clever way to get the employer to start talking. Specific performance is expressly stated to be the only remedy for enforcing the contract, though as demonstrated by *Balpa* v. *Jet2.Com Ltd*,[166] it may be open to either party to seek a declaration in the High Court as to the meaning of the method. For example, what exactly falls within the scope of pay, hours and holidays? There are in fact very few examples of legally enforceable agreements of this kind imposed by CAC, and given the opportunities to negotiate a voluntary agreement at various stages in the procedure, it is not clear why a rational employer would want to be locked into a legally binding agreement of a continuing nature and indefinite duration from which in principle it would be difficult to escape. The foregoing arrangements depart sharply from the enforcement procedures that had been adopted previously for trade union recognition in the Employment Protection Act 1975, section 16. Under that procedure a union could complain to the CAC, which in effect could vary unilaterally the terms and conditions of employment of the workers in the bargaining unit.[167] Although it did not directly compel the employer to bargain or impose a sanction for his or her failure to do so, the latter procedure did nevertheless provide a compelling incentive for the employer to engage in collective bargaining; otherwise the employer would lose control to a third party (the CAC) over the determination of terms and conditions of employment.

Enterprise Change and Derecognition

An employer who gets locked in by a CAC recognition declaration (whether legally binding or not) has two principal ways to escape from the procedure. The first arises under Part III of Schedule A1 as a result of changes in the enterprise following business restructuring, merger or takeover, or sale or divestment of part of the business. In that situation either party may apply to the CAC if it considers an existing bargaining unit is no longer appropriate. An application will be admissible only if the CAC decides under Schedule A1, paragraph 67(2), that the existing unit is no longer appropriate for any of the following reasons:

---

[165] TULRCA 1992, Sched. A1, para. 31(3), (4).

[166] [2017] EWCA Civ 20, [2017] ICR 547. See also *Jet2.Com Ltd* v. *Denby* [2018] IRLR 417 (p. 481, above).

[167] See B. Doyle, 'A Substitute for Collective Bargaining? – The Central Arbitration Committee's Approach to Section 16 of the Employment Protection Act 1975' (1980) 9 *Industrial Law Journal* 154.

(a) a change in the organisation or structure of the business carried on by the employer;

(b) a change in the activities pursued by the employer in the course of the business carried on by him;

(c) a substantial change in the number of workers employed in the original unit.

If the CAC decides that the bargaining unit is no longer appropriate, it is empowered to decide what unit is appropriate, and having so decided it must then decide whether 'the difference between the original unit and the new unit is such that the support of the union (or unions) within the new unit needs to be assessed'.[168] If the support does not need to be reassessed, the CAC must issue a declaration that the union (or unions) is entitled to conduct collective bargaining on behalf of the new unit.[169] If on the other hand the CAC concludes that the unit needs to be reassessed, a ballot will have to be held.

According to the CAC, there have only ever been four applications under Part III of the statutory procedure,[170] the most recent being *Honda and Unite the Union*,[171] in which the union had been recognised following a CAC declaration in 2001, when an agreement as to collective bargaining method was concluded by the parties. The Bargaining Unit at the time was assessed to apply not only to 'associates' (i.e. employees) of various categories, but also 'coordinators' who had 'first line management roles and as such their job content, pay structure and some terms and conditions differed from those of the Employer's General Associates', these differences having been 'magnified' by recent restructuring activity which affected coordinators in particular. The coordinators appeared to be generally unhappy in any event about being in this bargaining unit which they felt diluted their interests as they represented only about 10 per cent of the unit's total population. The change to the unit was supported by the union which would still have bargaining rights in relation to 2,657 general associates, lead associates and team leaders at the company's site in Swindon, in what nevertheless might be characterised as a partial de-recognition by redefining the bargaining unit. The employer's application to the CAC was upheld as falling within paragraph 67(2)(a) above, and in a separate decision the CAC declared the union recognised in relation to the new bargaining unit. Under the Act this is a declaration the CAC is bound to make where the parties agree a bargaining unit differing from the original,[172] and although the CAC has the power to modify the bargaining method,[173] it was not necessary to do so in this case.

---

[168] TULRCA 1992, Sched. A1, para. 85(1).   [169] TULRCA 1992, Sched. A1, para. 85(2).

[170] CAC, *Annual Report 2016–17* (2017), p. 12.

[171] CAC Case No. TUR/3/4/(2017) (covering two decisions – admissibility and the bargaining method respectively).

[172] TULRCA 1992, Sched. A1, para. 69.   [173] TULRCA 1992, Sched. A1, para. 69(3)(c).

Turning from changes in the bargaining unit to derecognition, this is one of the issues that highlights the folly of the employer who stays in the procedure in the face of clear worker support for recognition of the trade union. If the recognition is voluntary (as a result of an agreement concluded independently of, or at an early stage in, the statutory procedure), the employer is free to derecognise without any formality at any time it seems expedient to do so.[174] This is because like other collective agreements, recognition agreements are not legally binding.[175] It is of course possible for the parties to a voluntary recognition agreement to include a term that will rebut the statutory presumption that the agreement is not a legally binding contract, but this would be very unusual. The general preference on both sides is not to have procedural agreements of this kind to be legally binding, even if it does render the union rather powerless if the employer should decide unilaterally to revoke the agreement. The vulnerability of the union is reinforced by the fact that recognition agreements are unlikely to be apt for incorporation into contracts of employment, and so could not be enforced by employees any more than they can typically be enforced by trade unions.[176] That said, an employer who repudiates a voluntary recognition agreement could now face an application for recognition by the derecognised union under the statutory recognition procedure, if the union has the support to sustain such an application.

In the case of the statutory procedure in contrast, where a declaration of recognition has been made, Parts IV to VI of Schedule A1 provide procedures for dealing with disputes where the employer is seeking to have the union derecognised. These procedures generally do not apply to voluntary agreements, except those voluntary agreements with a non-independent trade union, in which case the derecognition procedure may be initiated by a worker in the bargaining unit.[177] The derecognition procedure applicable to independent trade unions may be initiated by way of application to the CAC. This may be done

- By the employer where the number of workers in the bargaining unit falls below 21.[178] In these cases there is no need for a ballot, the decline in the number of workers employed being sufficient for derecognition.
- By the employer or by a worker or workers in the situation where the applicant believes that the union no longer has the support of a majority of workers in the unit.[179] An application will be admissible only if there is evidence that at least 10 per cent of the workers in the unit favour of an end to recognition, and that this is likely to be supported by a

---

[174] This is subject exceptionally to the provisions of TULRCA 1992, Sched. A1, Part II.
[175] TULRCA 1992, s. 179.
[176] See *Gallacher* v. *Post Office* [1970] 3 All ER 712; and *NUM* v. *NCB* [1986] ICR 736.
[177] TULRCA 1992, Sched. A1, Part VI. See below, pp. 613–14.
[178] TULRCA 1992, Sched. A1, para. 99.
[179] TULRCA 1992, Sched. A1, paras. 105 and 112 respectively.

majority.[180] A deregognition ballot may then be held in which at least a majority of those voting representing at least 40 per cent of those in the bargaining unit must vote in favour of ending the collective bargaining arrangements.[181] If they do, the CAC must issue a declaration that the bargaining arrangements are to cease.[182]

- By the employer where the union was recognised automatically and the employer believes it no longer has majority membership.[183] In these cases a ballot will be required.

The statutory deregognition procedure had never been used in any of these situations, until the *PDAU* case in 2017 where a non-independent union recognised under a voluntary agreement was eventually deregognised.

Derecognition at Boots

The Pharmacists' Defence Association Union (PDAU) applied for recognition at Boots in 2012. However, Boots already had a 'recognition' agreement with Boots Pharmacists' Association (BPA) (an in-house staff association), which had consultation 'rights' on a few marginal topics, the agreement providing that:

the BPA is recognised as having collective bargaining rights for the purpose of negotiation relating to facilities for its officials and the machinery for consultation in respect of the matters upon which we will consult with the BPA (which are those set out in this agreement). This agreement does not provide for collective bargaining rights on any other matters.

Although the PDAU's application appeared to be blocked by TULRCA 1992, Sched. A1, para. 35(4) (on which, see p. 603 above), the application was accepted as admissible by the CAC, greatly influenced by *Demir and Baycara v. Turkey* [2008] ECHR 1345 (on which, see pp. 577–8 above), using the Human Rights Act 1998, section 3 to interpret paragraph 35(4) consistently with Convention rights.[184] After complex litigation, however, this decision was overturned by the High Court,[185] the decision of which in turn was upheld by the Court of Appeal in 2017.[186] The CAC was said to have proceeded on an unwarranted interpretation of

---

[180] TULRCA 1992, Sched. A1, paras. 110 and 114 respectively.
[181] TULRCA 1992, Sched. A1, para. 117.
[182] TULRCA 1992, Sched. A1, para. 121. The proposition to end recognition must be supported by a majority of those voting, representing at least 40% of those eligible to vote.
[183] TULRCA 1992, Sched. A1, Part V.
[184] *Pharmacists' Defence Association Union and Boots Management Services Ltd*, CAC Case No. TUR1/823/2012.
[185] *R (Boots Management Services Ltd) v. CAC* [2014] EWHC 65 (Admin); *R (Boots Management Services Ltd) v. CAC* [2014] EWHC 2930 (Admin).
[186] *Pharmacists' Defence Association Union v. Secretary of State for Business Innovation and Skills* [2017] EWCA Civ 66, [2017] IRLR 355.

paragraph 35(4), which was not incompatible with the Convention rights of the PDAU because of the de-recognition procedure in the statute which provided an opportunity to remove the BPA.

The CAC decision was thus overturned and the PDAU application ruled inadmissible. According to the Court of Appeal the PDAU should have waited for the Boots Pharmacists' Association to be derecognised under Part VI of the statutory procedure before bringing an application for recognition. It was thus necessary for the PDAU to call on its members to trigger a derecognition ballot. This was done in 2017.[187] The ballot led to a majority vote in favour of derecognition of the BPA, the majority vote meeting the required 40% threshold. The BPA was derecognised as a result, and the PDAU made a second application for recognition, which was accepted by the CAC in 2018.[188]

It thus took five years to vindicate the PDAU's right to bargain collectively. It is not difficult to agree with those who argue that this level of complexity should not be required, and that paragraph 35(4) should be repealed.

Rights of Recognised Trade Unions: Facilities for Collective Bargaining

Where a trade union is recognised for the purposes of collective bargaining (whether under the statutory procedure or voluntarily), it will need resources in the workplace to ensure that collective agreements can be negotiated and administered. Once the union is recognised, collective agreements about pay and other terms and conditions of employment will be negotiated by paid full-time officials of the union, responsible for a particular sector, geographical area or workplace. They may otherwise be negotiated by lay representatives of the union employed by the employer to whom the agreement relates, but even where the latter are not directly involved in negotiations, they will have an important part to play in negotiations conducted by paid full-time officials of the union. The Unite the Union template agreement reproduced earlier in this chapter makes provision for union representation and facilities, with paragraph 4.3 providing that union members are to 'elect representatives in accordance with the rules of the Union to act as their spokespersons and to represent their interests'. Crucially, recognised union representatives are to be 'provided appropriate time off arrangements and facilities for Union Representatives to carry out their functions effectively' (paragraph 5.1), with provision also made for a separate facilities agreement to enable trade union representatives to take time off for training relevant to the discharge of their duties. These provisions reflect the fact that collective bargaining can only be

---

[187] *Parker and Boots Pharmacists' Association*, CAC Case No. TUR6/003/2017.
[188] *PDAU and Boots Management Services Ltd*, CAC Case No. TUR1/1062/2018.

effective if workers' representatives have adequate time to discharge their duties and are fully trained.

Legal Framework

Collective agreements such as the template agreement mentioned above are underpinned by both international law and by statute.[189] The legislation relating to time off for *trade union duties* applies only to the officials of recognised trade unions, and applies whether recognition was secured by voluntary or statutory means. First introduced by the Employment Protection Act 1975, the current law was amended by the Employment Act 1989 to narrow the circumstances in which employers are required to permit time off *with pay*. What is now TULRCA 1992, section 168, requires an employer to permit an employee who is 'an official of an independent trade union recognised by the employer to take time off during his working hours for the purpose of carrying out any duties of his, as such an official'. The duties in question must be concerned with collective bargaining with the employer in relation to matters about which the union is recognised, or concerned with related matters (including information and consultation about collective redundancies, or the transfer of the undertaking).[190] TULRCA 1992, section 168, also requires the employer to allow the workplace representative 'to take time off during his working hours for the purpose of undergoing training in aspects of industrial relations',[191] on the ground that 'union officials are more likely to carry out their duties effectively if they possess skills and knowledge relevant to their duties'.[192]

For these purposes, collective bargaining is defined in accordance with TULRCA 1992, section 178, to mean negotiations related to or connected with a list of matters to be found in section 178(2). These include terms and conditions of employment and so on. The leading case is now many years old, the applicants in *London Ambulance Service* v. *Charlton*[193] being members of NUPE who had applied unsuccessfully for paid time off work to attend the meetings of a union joint co-ordinating committee which had been established to monitor negotiations within each division of the negotiating machinery, to develop a common industrial relations approach to the employer, and to examine proposals from and submit proposals to the employer.[194] The

---

[189] The relevant international law instruments include ILO Convention 135 (Workers' Representatives Convention, 1971), ILO Convention 151 (Labour Relations (Public Service) Convention, 1978), and ILO Recommendation 143 (Workers' Representatives Recommendation, 1971).

[190] TULRCA 1992, s. 168(1)(a)–(e).   [191] TULRCA 1992, s. 162(2).

[192] The training must be relevant to the conduct of the duties of the individual in question, and must be approved by the TUC or the trade union of which he or she is an official (s. 162(2)).

[193] [1992] ICR 773.

[194] The application was made under what was then the Employment Protection (Consolidation) Act 1978, s. 27 (now TULRCA 1992, s. 168).

industrial tribunal upheld the employees' claim that the activity fell within the amended statutory purposes for which paid time off should be permitted, a decision upheld by the EAT following an appeal by the employer. The EAT agreed that 'preparatory or coordinating meetings' were covered by the legislation as being connected with collective bargaining where they are called 'for the genuine purpose of officials discussing their approach to forthcoming negotiations or their consideration as a co-ordinating body of negotiations which have or will take place in other bodies'.[195]

So far as the *amount* of time off an individual is to be permitted to take, TULRCA 1992, section 168, provides that this is to be 'reasonable in all the circumstances, having regard to a Code of Practice issued by ACAS'.[196] It will be noticed that the template agreement we saw earlier makes no provision for the amount of time off to be provided for the purposes of trade union duties, though an earlier iteration set a proposed cap of 10 days annually on time off for training in these duties. In practice, the amount of time off permitted will vary enormously, and will depend to some extent on the size of the enterprise. In larger workplaces, there may be workplace representatives who are more or less working full time on trade union duties at the expense of the employer, usually because it is in the employer's interests and because such engagement would be reasonable. Apart from the amount of time off permitted, the 1992 Act also provides that 'the *purposes* for which, the *occasions* on which and any *conditions* subject to which time off may be so taken' are also to be determined on the basis of what is '*reasonable in all the circumstances* having regard to any relevant provisions of a Code of Practice issued by ACAS'.[197] Although there is no right as such to facilities or resources other than time off, the Code of Practice provides that:

> While there is no statutory right for facilities for union representatives, except for representatives engaged in duties related to collective redundancies and the Transfer of Undertakings,[198] employers should, where practical, make available to union representatives the facilities necessary for them to perform their duties efficiently and communicate effectively with their members, colleague union representatives and full-time officers. Where resources permit the facilities should include:
>
> - accommodation for meetings which could include provision for Union Learning Representatives[199] and a union member(s) to meet to discuss relevant training matters
> - access to a telephone and other communication media used or permitted in the workplace such as email, intranet and internet

---

[195] [1992] ICR 773, at 780–1.
[196] As for the ACAS Code of Practice on Time Off for Trade Union Duties and Activities, this was first introduced in 1977, and revised most recently in 2010.
[197] TULRCA 1992, s. 162(3).   [198] On which, see Chapter 15 below.
[199] On which, see pp. 617–18 below.

- the use of notice boards
- where the volume of the union representative's work justifies it, the use of dedicated office space
- confidential space where an employee involved in a grievance or disciplinary matter can meet their representative or to discuss other confidential matters
- access to members who work at a different location
- access to e-learning tools where computer facilities are available.[200]

It is important to emphasise that the right to time off under TULRCA 1992, section 168, is to time off with pay.[201] A major weakness of these provisions is the enforcement regime that leaves to employees the responsibility to bring claims in an employment tribunal that they have been denied the time off to which they believe they are entitled, or that time off has been subject to unreasonable conditions or limitations.[202] This is a weakness because individual employees may be reluctant to take action against their own employer to enforce what is in reality a right of the union to have an adequate workplace resource for the purposes of collective bargaining. It would be more appropriate if the right to enforce these rights was made available to the union as well as the employee. This simply reflects a more general problem of the vulnerability of trade union representatives to hostile conduct of the employer, which recognition agreements will typically seek to address. So in paragraph 4.7 of the template agreement, the employer's attention is directed to the need not to take steps that will prejudice the career prospects or employment of workplace representatives. Such provisions are underpinned by the statutory right of workers' representatives to take part in trade union activities at an appropriate time, which include activities undertaken with the consent of the employer.[203] However, one problem in this context lies not so much in the overt discrimination against trade union activists as in the fact that, by taking themselves away from the workplace, trade union activists may suffer disadvantage when it comes to matters such as career development and promotion.[204]

Union Learning Representatives

The provisions relating to time off for trade union duties and activities have been in place in one form or another since 1975. An important addition to their ranks is the right to time off (*with pay*) introduced for union learning representatives in 2002, as an amendment to TULRCA 1992.

Union learning representatives play a part in identifying and developing the learning and skills needs of trade union members. The needs may vary greatly – from reading and writing, to letter writing, to foreign language training, to computer and IT skills. Many employers

---

[200] ACAS Code of Practice on Time Off for Trade Union Duties and Activities (2010), para. 46.
[201] TULRCA 1992, s. 169.   [202] TULRCA 1992, s. 168(4).   [203] See pp. 500–5 above.
[204] See *Department of Transport* v. *Gallacher* [1994] ICR 697.

welcome this input from trade unions, as they too will benefit from a better skilled and more thoughtful workforce. Nevertheless, the right of union learning representatives to time off work applies only where the union is recognised, the government having baulked at the prospect of giving unions representational entitlements where their membership and organisational basis is ostensibly under-developed. It is also to be noted that the rights of union learning representatives apply only in relation to union members: there is no right to time off to attend to the needs of non-members.

By virtue of what is now TULRCA 1992, section 168A, union learning representatives are entitled to time off for the following purposes: (i) analysing learning or training needs of union members, (ii) providing information and advice about learning or training matters, (iii) arranging learning or training, and (iv) promoting the value of learning or training. The union learning representative is also entitled to time off to consult the employer about carrying on any of his or her activities, to prepare for these activities, and to undergo training. Again, the amount of time off, as well as the purposes for which, the occasions on which and any conditions subject to which time off may be so taken, are those that are reasonable in all the circumstances having regard to the ACAS *Code of Practice on Time Off for Trade Union Duties and Activities* (2010).

Trade Union Facilities under Attack

It was pointed out above that the right to facilities is based on international treaties, of which ILO Conventions 135 and 151 are the most important, both having been ratified by the United Kingdom (paradoxically for reasons that will be explained) by Conservative governments in 1973 and 1980, respectively. So far as Convention 135 is concerned, this provides that:

ILO Convention 135, Article 2

Such facilities in the undertaking shall be afforded to workers' representatives as may be appropriate in order to enable them to carry out their functions promptly and efficiently.

Similarly, the more narrowly worded Convention 151 (which deals with the public sector) provides that:

ILO Convention 151, Article 6

Such facilities shall be afforded to the representatives of recognised public employees' organisations as may be appropriate in order to enable them to carry out their functions promptly and efficiently, both during and outside their hours of work.

In addition to these treaties, there is the accompanying ILO Recommendation 143. This provides specifically that the facilities in question should include the right to paid time off for workplace representatives 'in order to enable them to carry out their functions promptly and efficiently'. Provision is also made for time off for training in these functions, as well as 'material facilities' necessary for the performance of their functions.[205]

The significance of these treaties has been enhanced by a decision of the European Court of Human Rights, in which a Spanish workers' representative complained that hostile action taken against him by his employer for publishing offensive remarks violated his rights under Article 10 of the ECHR.[206] Although the claim was a weak one which was not surprisingly rejected on its facts by the Grand Chamber, the decision is significant for the fact that the Court relied in part on ILO Convention 135 and ILO Recommendation 143 to inform its decision, noting that the conduct in question was of such a nature that it would likely have been beyond the scope of the ILO instruments.[207] All this is important in light of the vigorous campaign since 2010 by right-leaning think tanks (such as the so-called Taxpayers' Alliance) to diminish trade union facility time in the public sector,[208] on the tendentious ground that the taxpayer is being used to subsidise trade unions, tendentious because these attacks fail to take into account the purpose for which paid time off and other facilities are provided, and fails to assess the possible costs to the taxpayer in the form of protracted disputes and their related costs if the time off and the facilities were to be withdrawn. This campaign struck a bulls-eye when, in October 2011, the minister responsible announced at the Conservative party conference that the government was planning to make savings by cutting back on trade union facility arrangements.[209]

The attack on trade union facilities was spearheaded by the Cabinet Office and applied first to the civil service unions, along with an attack on the provision of check-off facilities for trade unions (on which see the box on page 621).[210] New procedures for the civil service restricted the amount of time any lay official could spend on paid trade union duties, so that only exceptionally would anyone be permitted to spend more than 50 per cent of working time on such matters, and that where these exceptional circumstances arose no one would be permitted to occupy such a position for more than three years. It is difficult to see how such an arbitrary cap can be justified by

---

[205] ILO Recommendation 143, Arts. 9–11.   [206] *Palomo Sanchez* v. *Spain* [2011] ECHR 1319.

[207] Ibid., paras. 21, 56 and 67.

[208] According to the Taxpayers' Alliance in 2011, the taxpayer was subsidising trade unions in the public sector to the tune of £113 million annually through direct grants and paid time off for union representatives. They are still at it, see Taxpayers' Alliance, *Local Authority Facility Time* (2017).

[209] *Daily Telegraph*, 2 October 2011.

[210] See A. Bogg and K. D. Ewing, *The Political Attack on Workplace Representation – A Legal Response* (London: Institute of Employment Rights, 2012).

the language of the legislation relating to time off, if the circumstances are such that it would be reasonable to provide more time off than that now prescribed. In some workplaces in the private sector there may well be workplace representatives with 100 per cent time off for trade union duties paid for by the employer. These latter restrictions were nevertheless reinforced by the Trade Union Act 2016, which authorises regulations to be made requiring designated public sector employers to publish *inter alia*

- how many of an employer's employees are relevant union officials, or relevant union officials within specified categories;
- the total amount spent by an employer in a specified period on paying relevant union officials for paid facility time, or for specified categories of facility time;
- the percentage of an employer's total pay bill for a specified period spent on paying relevant union officials for facility time, or for specified categories of facility time.[211]

The Trade Union Act 2016 also contains reserve powers authorising the responsible minister by regulations to cap paid facility time by designated public sector employers.[212] All this may mean that workplace organisation is diminished and that workplace representation will be more heavily reliant on TULRCA 1992, section 169, rather than section 168. Section 169 provides a parallel right of employees to time off work for the purpose of *trade union activities* rather than *trade union duties*. On this occasion, the time off is without pay, but again the amount that may be taken and the purposes, occasions and restrictions are those that are reasonable in all the circumstances, having regard to the ACAS Code of Practice. There is no statutory definition of a trade union activity for these purposes, though the term is narrowly defined in the ACAS Code of Practice, which refers to matters such as time off work to attend workplace meetings to discuss and vote on the outcome of negotiations and meeting full-time officials to discuss issues relevant to the workplace.[213] Similarly, the EAT has said that, although the phrase trade union activities 'should not be understood too restrictively', nevertheless, 'it cannot have been the intention of Parliament to have included any activity of whatever nature'.[214] According to the EAT, '[t]he whole context of the phrase is within the ambit of the employment relationship between that employee and that employer and that trade union'. As a result, a local

---

[211] Trade Union Act 2006, s. 13. See Trade Union (Facility Time Publication Requirements) Regulations 2017: SI 2017, No. 328. By the Trade Union (Wales) Act 2017, this provision does not apply in Wales.

[212] Trade Union Act 2006, s. 14. By the Trade Union (Wales) Act 2017, this provision does not apply in Wales.

[213] ACAS Code of Practice on Time Off for Trade Union Duties and Activities (2010), paras. 37–8.

[214] *Luce* v. *Bexley London Borough Council* [1990] ICR 591.

authority was not required to permit six teachers from Bexley to attend a lobby of Parliament organised by the TUC in connection with proposed legislation affecting the teaching profession.

The Check-Off

Apart from time off, the other major benefit a trade union might seek from an employer is the collection of trade union subscriptions by way of deduction from the wages of employees. Sometimes referred to as the check-off, money deducted in this way will then be passed onto the union, the employer perhaps making a small administration charge. But a union has no right to insist on a check-off arrangement, even when it is recognised. Such arrangements are nevertheless common, as an efficient way for trade unions to collect their subscriptions, though more unions are attempting to introduce collection by direct debit from members' bank accounts. An example of such an arrangement is to be found in the Unite the Union template agreement above (para 7.1).

Direct debit where it is possible combines efficient collection with protection against the threat of withdrawal of check-off facilities: the threat of withdrawal is a potent bargaining chip for employers. It is also the case that the check-off enables the employer to know the identity of union members as well as the levels of union membership in the workplace. Yet although there is no formal legal support for the collection of subscriptions by employers, the practice has not escaped attention of policy-makers. Conservative governments in particular have been anxious to ensure that those who were covered by arrangements of this kind consented to have their subscriptions deducted from their wages, and renewed their consent on a regular basis.

The Employment Rights Act 1996 permits employers to deduct money from a worker's wages and pay it over to a third party (which could include a trade union), provided the worker has agreed or consented in writing (ERA 1996, section 14(4)). TULRCA 1992 provides further that subscriptions can be deducted from wages only if the worker has authorised the deduction in writing (TULRCA 1992, section 68). The requirement that the authorisation must be renewed every three years introduced by the Trade Union Reform and Employment Rights Act 1993 has been repealed. This means that deductions can be made until such time as the worker revokes the authorisation: there is no need for periodic renewal of the authorisation.[215]

Governments since 2010 have, however, continued to attack check-off arrangements as part of their attack on trade union facilities generally. This was done initially by unilaterally

---

[215] Provision is also made for the situation where the check-off operates in the case of a union with a political fund. If a trade union member notifies his or her employer that he or she is not a contributor to the political fund the employer 'shall ensure that no amount representing a contribution to the political fund is deducted by him from the emoluments payable to the member' (TULRCA 1992, s. 86(1)). This means that the employer may have to deduct different amounts from different employees. The employer cannot refuse to operate the check-off for exempt members where he or she continues to operate it for other members of the union.

revoking check-off arrangements in some central government departments, leading to litigation by civil servants who successfully claimed that check-off arrangements were incorporated into their contracts of employment.[216] Subsequent litigation established that as contractual terms, these arrangements could not be revoked without the consent of the employees concerned, and more notably conceptually that the union could sue under the Contracts (Rights of Third Parties) Act 1999 as a beneficiary of these contracts to enforce them.[217]

The effect may be to permit the union to bring proceedings to enforce the terms of collective agreements to which it was a party, provided the term in question is incorporated into contracts of employment.[218] It was not established in *Cavanagh* that the source of the check-off was a collective agreement, though it is likely to have been. If it was a collective agreement, it is not clear why the union's claim could succeed in the light of TULRCA 1992, section 179 (collective agreements presumed not to be legally binding unless expressly rebutted), having regard to the Contracts (Rights of Third Parties) Act 1999, section 1(2) (no third party right where evidence of intention that the parties did not intend the term to be enforceable by a third party).

Since then, the Trade Union Act 2016, section 15 (inserting a new TULRCA 1992, section 116B) includes provisions authorising the making of regulations to prohibit designated public sector employers from operating check-off facilities without charging the unions in question for the cost of doing so.[219] By the Trade Union (Wales) Act 2017, this provision does not apply in Wales. The government abandoned plans to abolish check-off arrangements throughout the public sector.

Rights of Recognised Trade Unions: Information for Collective Bargaining

Trade unions recognised for the purposes of collective bargaining are entitled to information held by the employer which may be relevant to collective bargaining. Again, this applies where the union is recognised voluntarily or by statute. These provisions are an acknowledgement that collective bargaining can take place effectively only if the trade union has adequate information about the economic position of the employer with whom it is dealing, if the union is to engage in an informed and measured way, and if it is to be able realistically to assess the bargaining position of the employer. There ought not to be anything

---

[216] *Hickey* v. *Secretary of State for Communities and Local Government*, 3 September 2013. For a very valuable account, see A. James, *Check-Off Arrangements – The Law* (Thompsons Trade Union Service, 17 March 2014).

[217] *Cavanagh* v. *Secretary of State for Work and Pensions* [2016] EWHC 1136 (QB).

[218] This is rather convoluted. A union cannot enforce a collective agreement to which it is a party. But employees can enforce the terms of the agreement if the terms in question have been incorporated into their contracts of employment (Chapter 3 above). But where the latter confer benefits on a third party – the union which negotiated them in the first place – the third party can enforce the contract of which it was a principal author.

[219] See Trade Union (Deduction of Trade Union Subscriptions from Wages in the Public Sector) Regulations 2017, SI 2017 No. 9780.

controversial about employers being required to disclose information to trade unions (which may obtain access in other ways – under obligations imposed by company law and local government law, depending on the nature of the employer). Employers have been required to disclose information to recognised trade unions since the Industrial Relations Act 1971 (under a statutory formula very similar to that currently in force).[220] In other countries such as the United States and Canada, the disclosure of information has long been seen as part and parcel of the employer's duty to bargain in good faith.[221] In the United Kingdom, the duty of the employer to disclose information to the representatives of a recognised trade union is in addition to the more recently enacted Information and Consultation of Employees Regulations 2004,[222] with which there is some overlap, but which are equally under-utilised.

Statutory Obligation

The current duty of employers to disclose information to the representatives of recognised trade unions was introduced by the Employment Protection Act 1975, sections 17–21, though, as we have seen, the substance of the obligation has a longer pedigree. Indeed, a duty to disclose was recommended by the Donovan Royal Commission in 1968,[223] and included in the Labour government's ill-fated white paper, *In Place of Strife*, in the following year.[224] The 1975 legislation survives in its original form, its entire operation from 1980 to 1999 depending upon the voluntary recognition of the trade union by the employer. By virtue of TULRCA 1992, section 181(1), 'an employer who recognises an independent trade union shall, for the purposes of all stages of collective bargaining about matters, and in relation to descriptions of workers, in respect of which the union is recognised by him, disclose to representatives of the union, on request, the information required by this section'. It is then provided by section 181(2) that:

> the information to be disclosed is all information relating to the employer's undertaking which is in his possession, or that of an associated employer, and is information –
>
> (a) without which the trade union representatives would be to a material extent impeded in carrying on collective bargaining with him, and

---

[220] Industrial Relations Act 1971, s. 56.

[221] See *National Labor Relations Board* v. *Truitt Mfg Co.*, 351 US 149 (1956): '[g]ood faith bargaining necessarily requires that claims made by either bargainer should be honest claims, and if such claim is important enough to present in the give and take of bargaining, it is important enough to require some sort of proof of its accuracy' (pp. 152–3).

[222] SI 2004 No. 3426. See Chapter 15 below.

[223] Report of the Royal Commission on Trade Unions and Employers' Associations, 1965–1968 (Lord Donovan, Chairman), Cmnd 3623 (1968), para. 184.

[224] Department of Employment and Productivity, *In Place of Strife*, Cmnd 3888 (1969), paras. 47–8.

(b) which it would be in accordance with good industrial relations practice that he should disclose to them for the purposes of collective bargaining.

The employer may require any such request to be made in writing,[225] while regard must be had to any ACAS Code of Practice to determine 'what would be in accordance with good industrial relations practice' for the purposes of section 188(2).[226]

The ACAS Code of Practice acknowledges that collective bargaining within an undertaking can 'range from negotiations on specific matters arising daily at the workplace affecting particular sections of the workforce, to extensive periodic negotiations on terms and conditions of employment affecting the whole workforce in multi-plant companies'.[227] As a result, 'it is not possible to compile a list of items that should be disclosed in all circumstances'.[228] Nevertheless, the following examples are given of information relating to the undertaking 'which could be relevant in certain collective bargaining situations'. These are as follows:

(i) Pay and benefits: principles and structure of payment systems; job evaluation systems and grading criteria; earnings and hours analysed according to workgroup, grade, plant, sex, out-workers and home-workers, department or division, giving, where appropriate, distributions and make-up of pay showing any additions to basic rate or salary; total pay bill; details of fringe benefits and non-wage labour costs.

(ii) Conditions of service: policies on recruitment, redeployment, redundancy, training, equal opportunity, and promotion; appraisal systems; health, welfare and safety matters.

(iii) Manpower: numbers employed analysed according to grade, department, location, age and sex; labour turnover; absenteeism; overtime and short-time; manning standards; planned changes in work methods, materials, equipment or organisation; available manpower plans; investment plans.

(iv) Performance: productivity and efficiency data; savings from increased productivity and output, return on capital invested; sales and state of order book.

(v) Financial: cost structures; gross and net profits; sources of earnings; assets; liabilities; allocation of profits; details of government financial assistance; transfer prices; loans to parent or subsidiary companies and interest charged.[229]

It is expressly provided that the foregoing examples are 'not intended to represent a check list of information that should be provided for all negotiations. Nor are they meant to be an exhaustive list of types of information as other items may be relevant in particular negotiations'.[230]

---

[225] TULRCA 1992, s. 188(3).   [226] TULRCA 1992, s. 188(4).

[227] ACAS Code of Practice on Disclosure of Information (2003 edition), para. 11.   [228] *Ibid.*

[229] *Ibid.* See *R v. CAC, ex parte BTP Tioxide Ltd* [1981] ICR 843; *Unite the Union, UCU and Unison and University College, London*, CAC Case No. DI/4/(2007).

[230] *Ibid.*, para. 12.

A good lawyer representing the interests of the employer will find a number of contestable questions here:

- Is the union recognised?[231]
- If so, is it recognised for the purposes for which the information is sought?[232]
- Does the information sought relate to the employer's undertaking?[233]
- Does the union need the information for the purposes of collective bargaining?[234]
- Would it be in accordance with good industrial relations practice to disclose the information?

Before considering some of the implications of these questions, it is important to note also that there are important qualifications to the duty to disclose, with TULRCA 1992, section 182(1), excluding information

(a) the disclosure of which would be against the interests of national security, or
(b) which [the employer] could not disclose without contravening a prohibition imposed by or under an enactment, or
(c) which has been communicated to the employer in confidence, or which he has otherwise obtained in consequence of the confidence reposed in him by another person, or
(d) which relates specifically to an individual (unless that individual has consented to its being disclosed), or
(e) the disclosure of which would cause substantial injury to [the employer's] undertaking for reasons other than its effect on collective bargaining, or
(f) obtained by [the employer] for the purpose of bringing, prosecuting or defending any legal proceedings.

Again, there is scope here for vigorous challenge around many of these terms,[235] which are neither defined nor fully explained in the ACAS Code of Practice, where it is said that:

> 14. Some examples of information which if disclosed in particular circumstances might cause substantial injury are: cost information on individual products; detailed analysis of proposed investment, marketing or pricing policies; and price quotas or the make-up of tender prices. Information which has to be made

---

[231] *GMB and Kuehne +Nagel*, CAC Case No. DI/10/(2014).

[232] *Unite the Union and Fujitsu Services Ltd*, CAC Case No. DI/04/2017.

[233] See *Unite the Union and Fujitsu Services Ltd*, CAC Case No. DI/7/(2014). The term 'undertaking' is to be read widely to mean the employer's business, to include information about subsidiary companies, even though these might be said in other contexts to be separate undertakings.

[234] *Unite the Union and Fujitsu Services Ltd*, CAC Case No. DI/04/2017.

[235] See *CSU v. CAC* [1980] IRLR 274 (on material supplied to the employer in confidence).

available publicly, for example under the Companies Acts, would not fall into this category.

15. Substantial injury may occur if, for example, certain customers would be lost to competitors, or suppliers would refuse to supply necessary materials, or the ability to raise funds to finance the company would be seriously impaired as a result of disclosing certain information. The burden of establishing a claim that disclosure of certain information would cause substantial injury lies with the employer.

Unlike the time-off provisions (which are enforced by an individual employee in the employment tribunal), the disclosure of information provisions are enforced by the trade union before the CAC.[236] Following the lodging of a complaint, the matter may be referred by the CAC to ACAS for conciliation, and if this is successful the complaint will be withdrawn.[237] If the matter proceeds to a hearing before the CAC, the latter is empowered to make a declaration if the complaint is wholly or partially well-founded, the declaration to specify the information in respect of which the complaint is upheld, and the period within which the information should be provided.[238] Where the employer continues to fail to disclose the information, the trade union may make a further complaint to the CAC,[239] and on making that complaint the union may also present a claim that the CAC should vary the terms and conditions of employment of employees specified in the claim.[240] The sanction for failure to provide the information following a CAC declaration is thus not an order that the information should be disclosed, but the threat that the terms and conditions of employment of the employees concerned will be varied unilaterally without the consent of the employer. In the event of such an order being made, the new terms can be varied only by a subsequent CAC order, a collective agreement, or an agreement between the employer and employees individually.[241] This is not, however, a widely used power.

Law in Practice

These provisions enable trade unions to require employers to provide information necessary for the purposes of collective bargaining, notably in cases where the information was sought to enable the union to make a realistic pay claim.[242] In one case where the Lloyds Banking Group was engaged in a process of harmonising terms and conditions of employment following the acquisition of Halifax Bank of Scotland (HBOS),[243] the union obtained a declaration that the employer should disclose the following information:

---

[236] TULRCA 1992, s. 183.   [237] TULRCA 1992, s. 183(2).   [238] TULRCA 1992, s. 183(5).
[239] TULRCA 1992, s. 184.   [240] TULRCA 1992, s. 185.   [241] *Ibid.*, s. 185(6).
[242] See *PCS and HP Enterprises Ltd*, CAC Case No. DI/3/(2011).
[243] *Lloyds Trade Union and Lloyds Banking Group*, CAC Case No. DI/2/(2011).

The number of staff who signed the new contracts of employment broken down by business unit, grade, sex, full time, part time, ethnicity and disability.

The number of staff who refused to sign the new contracts of employment broken down by business unit, grade, sex, full time, part time, ethnicity and disability.

Of those staff that chose not to sign the new contracts of employment how many are below the minimum of the new salary scales? Can we have that information broken down by business unit, grade, sex, full time, part time, ethnicity and disability?

The total number of staff in each grade broken down by business unit, sex, grade, full time, part time, ethnicity and disability.

The total numbers of staff in each pay zone, broken down by business unit, sex, grade, full time, part time, ethnicity and disability.

Current salary positions in 2.5% ranges for each business unit broken down by grade, sex, full time, part time, ethnicity and disability.

In respect of out of cycle pay reviews in 2010, can we have details of the number of staff receiving such awards broken down by business unit, grade, sex, full time, part time, ethnicity and disability.

Details of time in role, broken down by years for example less than 1 year, less then 2 years etc., for all staff covered by our negotiations broken down by business unit, grade, sex, full time, part time, ethnicity and disability.

Average staff salaries for each business unit covered by our negotiations broken down by grade, sex, full time, part time, ethnicity and disability as at the 1st April 2010?

Average staff salaries for each business unit covered by our negotiations broken down by grade, sex, full time, part time, ethnicity and disability as at the 1st October 2010?

The average Group bonuses paid in 2010 broken down by business unit, grade, sex, full time and part time and ethnicity.

What, if any, exceptions are there to the Group's Pay Policy? Where there are exceptions who is responsible for setting pay in that office/area/department/business unit?

The 2009 performance ratings broken down by business unit, grade, sex, full time, part time, ethnicity and disability?

The 2010 half-yearly performance ratings broken down by business unit, grade, sex, full time, part time, ethnicity and disability?

Market movement data for each grade covered by our Recognition Agreement.[244]

---

[244] The items in italics were requested but not subject to the order, the union agreeing that the former was not a matter covered by collective bargaining and satisfied that the employer had disclosed the latter already.

Applying the statutory criteria, the CAC accepted in this case that the union would be impeded to a material extent by the employer's failure to provide the information requested, on the ground that 'it would not be possible to make an informed response to harmonisation proposals without an understanding of the implications for its members'.[245] Nor, said the CAC, 'would it be possible to enter meaningful discussions'. Also applying TULRCA 1992, section 181, it was said that, in the Committee's experience, 'it would accord with good industrial relations practice for the Company to disclose the requested information' with 'all the items of information requested [being] unexceptional and routinely requested and provided in mature collective bargaining relationships'.[246] In coming to these conclusions, the CAC referred to the ACAS Code of Practice (as it is required to by statute), and noted that the information requested was of a kind that ACAS thought should be disclosed if it was relevant, the CAC holding that it was indeed relevant. Disclosure of the information requested was found not to be excused by any of the permitted grounds in TULRCA 1992, section 182; nor could it be said that the compilation or assembly of the information requested imposed a disproportionate burden on the employer.

Despite the significance of the disclosure of information procedure for collective bargaining, its use is notably limited. The CAC website reveals that, between 2014 and mid 2018, there were eleven (2014), nine (2015), five (2016), twelve (2017) and six (2018) applications, that is to say, an average of just over only eight a year. This is consistent with the figures for earlier years set out in the last edition of this book. The great bulk of these forty-three complaints were withdrawn, settled or disposed of without a hearing, with only five proceeding to a full hearing. It is not known why so many cases were withdrawn, but one plausible explanation is that the union was able to secure the information from the employer without the need to go to a CAC hearing and that initiating the statutory procedure is enough to persuade the employer to provide the information it previously denied to the union. So far as the cases that did go to a hearing are concerned, the union was successful in only two of these cases, the last successful disputed case at the time of writing being in 2014. The other three cases failed on the following grounds:

- the information was sought for purposes which did not fall within the scope of the union's recognition arrangements,[247]
- the union request related to a future pay claim rather than a current pay claim, that had concluded,[248] and
- the union would not be to a material extent impeded in collective bargaining without the information.[249]

---

[245] *Lloyds Trade Union and Lloyds Banking Group*, CAC Case No. DI/2/(2011), para. 52.
[246] *Ibid.*, para. 53.   [247] *Unite the Union and Fujitsu Services Ltd*, CAC Case No. DI/04/2017.
[248] *Ibid.*
[249] *BECTU and Rio Centre (Dalston) Ltd*, CAC Case No. DI/1/2017; *Unite the Union and John N Group Ltd*, CAC Case No. DI/4/2016.

Gospel and Lockwood have highlighted a number of problems with the law, including (1) the fact that 'information need only be provided for the purposes of collective bargaining as defined by the Act and disclosure is limited to matters for which the union is recognised';[250] (2) the vagueness of the test of 'good industrial relations' practice in section 181(2) and 'the weak consensus as to current practice';[251] while (3) the 'second test, of material impediment, is an even bigger obstacle to a union seeking to pursue a complaint where it has managed without such information in the past';[252] and (4) the enforcement mechanism contained in TULRCA 1992, section 185, 'does not force disclosure of the information or provide for a punitive element to be included in the award'.[253] One other concern identified by Gospel and Lockwood is that 'the CAC may only adjudicate upon a past failure to disclose and may not declare what information the employer should disclose in the future, even though the disclosure might help avoid a subsequent dispute between the parties'.[254] It is to be noted that in the *Lloyd's Banking Group* case discussed above, the CAC said in relation to the last item of information requested that 'the duty [to disclose] exists for the purposes of all stages of collective bargaining still outstanding'. However, the Committee acknowledged the suggestion by the union that 'the information was needed in anticipation of the 2011 pay negotiations but also for more general matters such as equal opportunities and that it could be used for the formulation of future proposals'.[255]

Conclusion

There is a gradual shift in the nature and purpose of collective bargaining in the United Kingdom. At one time it could be said to have performed a regulatory role, being conducted at industry level, effectively setting terms on a sector-wide basis. In many cases now it can be said to perform a largely representative role in which trade unions act effectively as a bargaining agent for a group of workers, usually in a single enterprise.[256] There is a clear public policy preference for collective bargaining at enterprise rather than sector

---

[250] H. Gospel and G. Lockwood, 'Disclosure of Information for Collective Bargaining: The CAC Approach Revisited' (1999) 28 *Industrial Law Journal* 233, at 243.

[251] *Ibid.*, 244.   [252] *Ibid.*

[253] *Ibid.*, 245. To which we might add (i) the breadth of the exclusions in TULRCA 1992, s. 182; (ii) the self-restraint of the CAC, especially in the earlier cases; and (iii) the uncertain impact of judicial review. As to the last, see *CSU* v. *CAC* [1980] IRLR 274; and *R* v. *CAC, ex parte BTP Tioxide Ltd* [1981] ICR 843.

[254] H. Gospel and G. Lockwood, 'Disclosure of Information for Collective Bargaining: The CAC Approach Revisited' (1999) 28 *Industrial Law Journal* 233, at 245. See *Unite the Union and Fujitsu Services Ltd*, CAC Case No. DI/04/2017.

[255] *Lloyds Trade Union and Lloyds Banking Group*, CAC Case No. DI/2/(2011), para. 50.

[256] That at least is the conventional wisdom, though the truth is probably that we continue to operate a mixed system, albeit one with great decentralising pressures.

level, and this policy of decentralisation will not easily be reversed. What we now have in this country is what may be referred to as a *trade union recognition strategy*, which enables workers to have their union recognised if this is the wish of a majority. But what we do not now have is a *collective bargaining strategy*, as we had in the 1930s when government took the initiative to use various levers of state power to establish collective bargaining machinery on a large scale.[257] It is true that the existing recognition scheme led to a flurry of new, mainly voluntary, recognition agreements shortly before and shortly after it was introduced.[258] But while it may be premature to write the obituary of the current recognition procedure, it has been claimed plausibly that it is being left to wither on the vine.[259] Paradoxically, the number of CAC applications is very low despite the fact that the level of collective bargaining density continues to fall, indicating perhaps the extent to which employers have managed to gain control of the statutory procedure.

Table CAC Recognition Applications 2014–18

Year	Number of Applications
2016–17	51
2015–16	48
2014–15	38
2013–14	30
2012–13	54

Source: CAC Annual Reports

The CAC Annual Report for 2016–17 reveals further that there had been only 1,006 applications since the scheme was introduced in 2000, this representing an average of only 60 or so annually, barely one a week. Of these 1006 applications,

- 587 were accepted, 128 not accepted, and 278 withdrawn (for reasons unknown but which may include the voluntary recognition by the employer);[260]
- the union claimed majority membership in 179 (with the CAC declaring recognition in 144, or 76.5% of cases where majority membership was claimed);

---

[257] The last Labour government declined a number of opportunities that would help to promote collective bargaining more actively. These included union proposals for 'sector forums' to kickstart sectoral regulatory activity, and proposals to use the *Laval* decision (see Chapter 2) as an opportunity to provide for the registration of remaining sector-wide agreements (such as the National Agreement for the Engineering Construction Industry) so that they became universally applicable.

[258] See TUC, *Focus on Recognition* (2002).

[259] A. Bogg, 'The Death of Statutory Recognition' (2012) 54 *Journal of Industrial Relations* 409.

[260] Decisions on a number of other applications were pending.

- The overall success rate in ballots is only 63%, which is very low considering the threshold questions for admissibility.

The low ballot success rates may reflect the importance of the campaign and the influence of employer resistance. In total, since the recognition procedure was introduced, a union had been formally recognised in only 293 cases, which represents 29.1% of applications, 49.9% of accepted cases, an average of about 18 cases annually. It should be pointed out, however, that 110 of the 587 cases accepted were withdrawn after acceptance, which may well be because the parties had negotiated a voluntary agreement in the shadow of the law. Otherwise, it is notable that where a union is declared to be recognised, the parties agree a collective bargaining method in the 'overwhelming majority of cases', though the figures reveal that the method was agreed in 258 cases and decided by the CAC in 27 cases.[261]

These figures from the hand of the CAC reinforce the view that the statutory recognition procedure is no panacea for the declining levels of collective bargaining coverage, and that fairly radical action is required. That could begin with changes that would at least bring existing law into line with international human rights obligations, notably ILO Convention 98.[262] This would mean addressing the small business exemption; the blocking of applications under the procedure by employers making agreements with non-independent staff associations; and the limited scope of the unfair practice provisions which apply only during the balloting period.[263] There is also concern that a trade union which does not have majority support is denied bargaining rights on behalf of its members,[264] the ILO supervisory bodies having developed an interesting line of jurisprudence to the effect that in such cases a union must be permitted to bargain at least for those it directly represents:

> The Committee [of Experts] takes note of the TUC's statement that the statutory procedure for union recognition requires a union to have a majority of the workers in the bargaining unit as members, or a majority vote in a ballot in which at least 40 per cent of the bargaining unit must vote in favour of union recognition. In this respect, the Committee recalls that problems of conformity with the Convention may arise when the law stipulates that a trade union must receive the support of 50 per cent of the members of a bargaining unit to be recognized as a bargaining agent, as a majority union which fails to secure this

---

[261] CAC, *Annual Report 2016–17* (2017).

[262] See further K. D. Ewing and J. Hendy, 'The Dramatic Implications of *Demir and Baykara*' (2010) 39 *Industrial Law Journal* 2.

[263] ILO Committee of Experts, Observation Concerning Convention 98 (United Kingdom) (2007), (2009). For discussion, see R. Dukes, 'The Statutory Recognition Procedure 1999 – No Bias in Favour of Recognition' (2008) 37 *Industrial Law Journal* 236.

[264] This is referred to in the United States as 'members-only bargaining', and is equally not encouraged under the National Labor Relations Act, though it has the support of progressive labour lawyers (C. W. Summers, 'Unions Without Majority – A Black Hole?' (1990) 66 *Chicago-Kent Law Review* 351).

absolute majority is thus denied the possibility of bargaining. The Committee considers that, under such a system, if no union covers more than 50 per cent of the workers, collective bargaining rights should be granted to all the unions in this unit, at least on behalf of their own members (see General Survey of 1994 on Freedom of Association and Collective Bargaining, paragraph 241). The Committee requests the Government to indicate the measures taken or envisaged to ensure that, in cases where no union has been able to obtain the required majority for bargaining, the organizations concerned should at least be able to conclude a collective agreement on behalf of their own members.[265]

But in truth reforms of this kind are unlikely to make much difference in practice: the problem is the model not the trim. It is now more widely understood that if steps are to be taken to address the collective bargaining deficit, this will need to address the nature of collective bargaining (regulatory or representational) and the level at which it is conducted (sector or enterprise). It is only by sharpening the focus on regulatory bargaining conducted at sectoral level that there is any prospect of returning to the high levels of collective bargaining coverage that were a feature of life until the Thatcher counter-revolution from the 1980s onwards. That would require legislation establishing sectoral bargaining machinery leading to collective agreements which applied to everyone in the sector in question – employers even though they were not a party to the agreement, and workers even though they were not union members. This does not exclude a role for enterprise bargaining, which would continue to operate to implement and build upon the sectoral agreement, as well as cover items not dealt with at sectoral level.[266] This would be an ambitious project, though one to which the Labour Party was committed in its general election manifesto in 2017.[267] It is all the more ambitious for the fact that the European Commission is moving by stealth to dismantle sectoral bargaining structures throughout much of the European Union.[268]

---

[265] ILO Committee of Experts, Observation Concerning Convention 98 (United Kingdom) (2007). It is of course open to employers voluntarily to recognise trade unions that do not have majority support. Where a union has members but not majority support and is unable to secure recognition, it is denied also the right collectively to represent its members in pay negotiations. See Employment Relations Act 1999, ss. 10, 13, which has been drafted in such a way to assuage business concerns that it could be used as a surrogate recognition procedure for workers and trade unions where there is not majority support. See especially ERA 2009, s. 13(5).

[266] See K. D. Ewing and J. Hendy QC, *A Manifesto for Collective Bargaining* (London: Institute of Employment Rights, 2013), and K. D. Ewing, J. Hendy QC and C. Jones (eds.), *A Manifesto for Labour Law* (London: Institute of Employment Rights, 2016). See also K. D. Ewing and J. Hendy QC, 'New Perspectives on Collective Labour Law: Trade Union Recognition and Collective Bargaining' (2017) 46 *Industrial Law Journal* 43.

[267] Labour Party, *For the Many Not the Few* (2017), p 47.

[268] See K. D. Ewing, 'The Death of Social Europe?' (2015) 26 *King's Law Journal* 76, Also, A. Bogg and K. D. Ewing, 'A Tale of Two Documents: The Eclipse of the Social Democratic Constitution', in E. Nanopoulos and F. Vergis (eds.), *The Crisis Behind the Euro-Crisis: The Euro-Crisis as a Multi-Dimensional Systematic Crisis of the EU* (forthcoming).

15

The Right to be Informed and Consulted

Contents

Introduction

In addition to the long-established practice of collective bargaining over pay and related matters, European law has introduced the practice of mandatory information and consultation to the UK. These information and consultation rights have grown since first introduced to deal with collective redundancies, and now apply to an extensive range of decisions by employers. Attempts have been made to encourage not only *ad hoc* consultations on specific events, but also the creation of standing and permanent procedures for the exchange of information and consultation on a wide and indeterminate range of issues. Indeed, information and consultation rights not only apply in respect of decisions taken by employers at the national level, but also extend to information and consultation at the transnational level through the medium of European works councils (EWCs).

These information and consultation rights generally apply to all workplaces over a certain size (which varies according to the matter in question). In practice, however, they are most likely to arise in workplaces where there is a recognised trade union. This is because, in some cases, the trade union enjoys priority status in the sense that, if there is a recognised trade union, it is the union that the employer must inform and consult. This would be true, for example, of the redundancy consultation procedures. In other cases, although the rights in question may be neutral between trade union and non-trade union based arrangements, the role of the trade union will be crucial in providing the initiative to get the procedures established and to ensure that representatives are properly trained and supported. This would be true, for example, of the EWCs.

In practice, these procedures may thus be said to develop the trade union collective bargaining agenda at the enterprise level (although, as we shall see, there are workplaces where non-union-based information and consultation procedures exist). Apart from the trade union priority and the need for a trade union institutional capacity, the consultation that takes place is usually consultation with a view to reaching an agreement, which places the obligation closer to negotiation rather than consultation in the classical and weaker sense understood by English administrative law.[1] Indeed, it has been recognised by the ECJ that the Collective Redundancies Directive 'imposes an obligation to negotiate'.[2] For trade unions, these procedures also provide an opportunity to organise the creation of information and consultation structures in the workplace, which could be used to whet the appetite of workers for more fully developed systems of workplace representation.

In practice, however, this system of information and consultation has proved to be ill suited to the British system of workplace representation. It is common practice in the mainland EU15 for works councils to operate at enterprise level to represent the interests of workers, and for collective

---

[1] See *Rollo* v. *Minister of Town and Country Planning* [1948] 1 All ER 13.
[2] Case C-188/03, *Junk Irmtraud* v. *Wolfgang Kühnel* [2005] ECR I-885, para. 43.

bargaining to operate at sector level in what is a complementary process. In the UK, by contrast, the dual channel of representation is sometimes seen by trade unions as competitive, with non-union forms of workplace procedures being viewed as a threat to trade union organisation rather than something trade unions should embrace. This helps to explain the low take-up and relative failure of the Information and Consultation of Employees (ICE) Regulations 2004,[3] which we consider below.

Consultation Rights and European Law

Consultation rights are not well developed in international law. This may reflect the reluctance on the part of trade unions to support such initiatives, as well as the inability of the ILO to adapt quickly to new forms of workplace representation. Although there is acknowledgement of their importance in ILO Convention 158,[4] and in the Council of Europe's Revised Social Charter,[5] it is the EU that has made most of the running on questions relating to information and consultation procedures, with the Community Charter on the Fundamental Rights of Workers of 1989 provisions in Articles 17 and 18.

Charter on the Fundamental Rights of Workers 1989, Articles 17 and 18

17. Information, consultation and participation for workers must be developed along appropriate lines, taking account of the practices in force in the various Member States.

This shall apply especially in companies or groups of companies having establishments or companies in several Member States of the European Community.

---

[3] SI 2004 No. 3426.

[4] Termination of Employment Convention, 1982 (not ratified by the UK). By Art. 13, where an employer contemplates 'terminations for reasons of an economic, technological, structural or similar nature', he or she shall inform and consult workers' representatives, 'recognised as such by national law or practice, in conformity with the Workers' Representatives Convention, 1971'. This bears the heavy imprint of Council Directive 75/129/EEC. See pp. 636–41. See also ILO Convention 155 (Occupational Safety and Health Convention, 1981), Art. 19 (information and consultation at level of the undertaking on health and safety matters) (again, not ratified by the UK).

[5] See Council of Europe, Revised Social Charter 1996, Art. 21: 'With a view to ensuring the effective exercise of the right of workers to be informed and consulted within the undertaking, the Parties undertake to adopt or encourage measures enabling workers or their representatives, in accordance with national legislation and practice: (a) to be informed regularly or at the appropriate time and in a comprehensible way about the economic and financial situation of the undertaking employing them, on the understanding that the disclosure of certain information which could be prejudicial to the undertaking may be refused or subject to confidentiality; and (b) to be consulted in good time on proposed decisions which could substantially affect the interests of workers, particularly on those decisions which could have an important impact on the employment situation in the undertaking.' The Revised Social Charter has been signed but not ratified by the UK. This measure anticipates the provisions of Council Directive 2002/14/EC.

18. Such information, consultation and participation must be implemented in due time, particularly in the following cases:

- when technological changes which, from the point of view of working conditions and work organisation, have major implications for the workforce are introduced into undertakings;
- in connection with restructuring operations in undertakings or in cases of mergers having an impact on the employment of workers;
- in cases of collective redundancy procedures;
- when transfrontier workers in particular are affected by employment policies pursued by the undertaking where they are employed.

Also important is the EU Charter of Fundamental Rights of 2000.

EU Charter of Fundamental Rights 2000, Article 27

Workers or their representatives must, at the appropriate levels, be guaranteed information and consultation in good time in the cases and under the conditions provided for by Community law and national laws and practices.

It will be noted, however, that, while the former is a part of a programme for action, the latter is a declaration of progress, recognising the existence of the right but only to the extent already provided by EU law.

From Specific Duties …

EU law obligations on information and consultation arose in the first instance as a right to be informed and consulted in specific circumstances in relation to specific events. Measures of this kind were introduced in 1975 with the Collective Redundancies Directive, followed shortly thereafter by the Acquired Rights Directive of 1977.[6] Both of these provisions have since been amended, although in both cases the core obligation to consult with employee representatives remains intact. As the title of the former suggests, the duty to inform and consult arises where the employer is 'contemplating collective redundancies', whereas the latter applies where the employer is proposing to transfer the business to a new owner, in which case there may be information and consultation duties on the part of both the transferor and the transferee.

The obligations in the Collective Redundancies Directive apply widely, redundancy dismissals being defined as 'dismissals effected by an employer

---

[6] For background, see B. A. Hepple, 'The Crisis in EEC Labour Law' (1977) 6 *Industrial Law Journal* 77.

for one or more reasons not related to the individual workers concerned'.[7] According to the ECJ in a case from Portugal, this aspect of the Directive must be given an 'autonomous and uniform interpretation'.[8] Specifically, the Court held that the Directive 'has to be interpreted as including any termination of [a] contract of employment not sought by the worker, and therefore without his consent'.[9] It was thus not necessary that 'the underlying reasons [for the dismissals] should reflect the will of the employer'.[10] Where – as in some countries – the employer has the statutory power unilaterally to vary the contract of employment for economic reasons, the CJEU has held that the Directive is invoked and that consultations must take place before the power is used, in cases where refusal by employees to accept the changes will lead to the termination of the employment relationship.[11]

The duty to consult does not apply to all redundancies, but, as the title of the Directive makes clear, only to collective redundancies, which is to say redundancies of at least ten or twenty employees, depending on the method of transposition chosen. For this purpose, the Directive provides Member States with an option, in the sense that it applies where the number of redundancies is:

(i) either, over a period of thirty days:
  - at least 10 in establishments normally employing more than 20 and fewer than 100 workers,
  - at least 10 per cent of the number of workers in establishments normally employing at least 100 but fewer than 300 workers,
  - at least thirty in establishments normally employing 300 workers or more,

(ii) or, over a period of ninety days, at least twenty, whatever the number of workers normally employed in the establishments in question.

In those circumstances where it applies, the Directive imposes two duties on employers. The first is to inform and consult worker representatives, with consultations to begin 'in good time with a view to reaching an agreement'.[12]

---

[7] Council Directive 75/129/EEC of 17 February 1975 and Council Directive 77/187/EEC of 14 February 1977, respectively. Now Council Directive 98/59/EC of 20 July 1998 and Council Directive 2001/23/EC of 12 March 2001. For parallel obligations relating to takeovers and mergers, see Panel on Takeovers and Mergers, *The Takeover Code* (12th edn, 2016). See also HC 871 (2011) (select committee investigation of the Kraft takeover of Cadbury).

[8] Case C-55/02, *Commission* v. *Portugal* [2004] ECR I-9387, para. 45.   [9] *Ibid.*, para. 50.

[10] *Ibid.* This meant that the Court rejected the Portuguese government's claim that the Directive did not apply in the case of dismissals taking place for reasons of compulsory liquidation, compulsory purchase, fire or other cases of *force majeure*. To limit the scope of the Directive in this way would mean that its objectives would be only partially obtained (para. 53).

[11] Case C-422/14, *Pujante Rivera* v. *Gestora Clubs Dir SL* [2016] IRLR 56; and Case C-149/16, *Socha* v. *Szpital Specjalistyczny im. A. Falkiewicza we Wrocławiu* [2018] IRLR 72. For a vivid example of this issue in the UK context, see *Kelly* v. *Hesley Group Ltd* [2013] IRLR 514.

[12] Council Directive 98/59/EC, Art. 2.

The second is to notify the public authorities about the projected redundancies,[13] an important duty which must be performed at least thirty days before the 'projected redundancies'. In an important decision of the ECJ, it was held that the employer cannot terminate contracts of employment before having complied with these obligations.[14] The other point to note at this stage is that the Directive anticipates the situation of redundancies within corporate groups, where redundancies may arise as a result of a decision taken by the controlling undertaking, which is then implemented by the undertaking at the place where the workers concerned are employed. It is specifically provided that the Directive is to apply 'irrespective of whether the decision regarding collective redundancies is being taken by the employer or by an undertaking controlling the employer'.[15]

Resisting Employer Avoidance

The ECJ has been presented with a number of attempts to restrict the scope of the Directive, with employers and governments seeking to avoid its application in national law. An early attempt was made by US multinational, Goodyear, which sought to exploit the uncertain meaning of 'redundancy' by enlisting the constitutional right of its Greek subsidiary to economic and financial freedom. Based on this apparent constitutional right, it was argued that the Directive did not apply where an employer closed its business of its own volition without a judicial decision requiring the closure. According to the ECJ, no basis could be found for such an interpretation, either in the wording of the Directive, in the objective pursued by it, or in the jurisprudence of the Court itself.[16] This is the opposite situation from the Portuguese case, where it was argued (also unsuccessfully) that the Directive had no application *except* in cases of redundancy arising from the employer's volition.

A second argument presented by employers has related to the meaning of 'establishment', it being recalled that the Directive applies only where a minimum number of workers are to be dismissed for redundancy in establishments normally employing a prescribed number of workers. In *Rockfon*, another case involving a multinational company, Rockwool,[17] one of the companies in the group, planned to make twenty-four or twenty-five employees redundant, but claimed that, because it had 5,300 workers worldwide and 1,435 workers in Denmark, the Directive (as transposed in Danish law) did not apply. This was an argument that clearly troubled the Court, which

---

[13] *Ibid.*, Art. 3.

[14] Case C-188/03, *Junk Irmtraud v. Wolfgang Kühnel* [2005] ECR I-885, para. 41. See p. 663.

[15] Council Directive 98/59/EC, Art. 2(4). It is no defence that the necessary information had not been provided to the employer by the undertaking which took the decision leading to collective redundancies.

[16] Joined Cases C-187/05–190/05, *Agorastoudis v. Goodyear Hellas* [2006] ECR I-7775.

[17] Case C-449/93, *Rockfon A/S v. Specialarbejderforbundet i Danmark* [1995] ECR I-4291.

acknowledged that there was no definition of establishment in the Directive, but which also expressed concern about this term being manipulated to allow companies like Rockwool to avoid responsibilities under the Directive. Holding that what was important in an employment relationship was the link between the employee and the part of the undertaking where he or she is engaged, the Court held that:

> [t]he term 'establishment' appearing in Article 1(1)(a) of the Directive must therefore be interpreted as designating, depending on the circumstances, the unit to which the workers made redundant are assigned to carry out their duties. It is not essential, in order for there to be an 'establishment', for the unit in question to be endowed with a management which can independently effect collective redundancies.[18]

A third area of vulnerability which multinationals have sought to exploit also relates to the position where the redundancies are to be made in one part of a group of undertakings, where the decision is made by a parent company at some remote location elsewhere. Here, the question is not whether there is a duty to inform and consult, but what the consultations should be about and when they should begin. In one leading case, the Dutch giant Fujitsu Siemens Computers (Holding) BV (the parent company) owned a subsidiary called Fujitsu Siemens Computers, which had production plants in Finland and Germany. On 14 December 1999, the board of directors of the parent company decided to support a proposal to close the Finnish factory of the subsidiary. But although no formal decision was taken, the subsidiary nevertheless started consultations, which took place between 20 December 1999 and 31 January 2000, with the decision to close being taken on 1 February 2000, implemented one week later. The ECJ appeared to reject the argument that the real decision had been taken on 14 December 1999 and that following *Junk*, the consultations should have been concluded in advance of that date. According to the Court:

> It must therefore be held that, in circumstances such as those of the case in the main proceedings, the consultation procedure must be started by the employer once a strategic or commercial decision compelling him to contemplate or to plan for collective redundancies has been taken.[19]

The *Fujitsu Siemens* case is important for establishing the boundaries of the Directive and its focus on the employer rather than the controlling

---

[18] *Ibid.*, para. 32. The qualification 'depending on the circumstances' is important.
[19] Case C-44/08, *Akavan Erityisalojen Keskusliitto AEK ry* v. *Fujitsu Siemens Computers Oy* [2009] ECR I-8163; [2009] IRLR 944, para. 48. This is a formulation not without difficulty, leading to a reference from the UK seeking clarification of its meaning. See *USA* v. *Nolan* [2010] EWCA Civ 1223, [2011] IRLR 40. See pp. 656–7. At the time of writing the uncertainty remains unresolved.

undertaking.[20] It is to be noted that, in reaching its decision, the ECJ referred to an intervention by the UK government which had warned against 'a premature triggering of the obligation to hold consultations', concerned that this 'could lead to results contrary to the purpose of Directive 98/59, such as restricting the flexibility available to undertakings when restructuring, creating heavier administrative burdens and causing unnecessary uncertainty for workers about the safety of their jobs'.[21] It is thus not only companies that are seeking to minimise the impact of the Directive, with other ECJ cases involving enforcement proceedings by the European Commission against countries such as the UK, which argued unsuccessfully that the duty to consult could be restricted to employers that recognised a trade union,[22] and France which argued, equally unsuccessfully, that workers under the age of twenty-six need not be taken into account in calculating the size of the workforce to determine whether the Directive applied.[23]

The EU Charter: Whose Rights?

AGET Iraklis (owned by French multinational group Lafarge), produced cement at three plants in Greece. It proposed a number of redundancies but was unable to secure union agreement. Under Greek law, the company then had to secure the consent of the Ministry of Labour, which could veto a decision taking into account the conditions in the labour market (sic), the situation of the undertaking, and the interests of the national economy. The minister refused to authorise the decision and the company challenged the minister's decision on a number of grounds, including the breach of the TFEU, Article 49 (freedom of establishment), and also the EU Charter of Fundamental Rights. Although the latter contains a number of rights of workers, Article 16 provides that 'the freedom to conduct a business in accordance with Community law and national laws and practices is recognised'. The matter was referred to the CJEU.[24]

In this case a multinational corporation was thus invoking its freedom of establishment and its right to conduct a business to defeat legislation designed to protect workers' jobs. The claim succeeded on both grounds before the CJEU. Responding to the Article 16 claim, the Court said that it could not be contested that 'the establishment of a regime imposing a framework for collective redundancies such as the regime at issue in the main proceedings constitutes an interference in the exercise of the freedom to conduct a business and, in

---

[20] Thus, it was also held that, 'in the case of a group of undertakings consisting of a parent company and one or more subsidiaries, the obligation to hold consultations with the workers' representatives falls on the subsidiary which has the status of employer only once that subsidiary, within which collective redundancies may be made, has been identified'. *Ibid.*, para. 65.

[21] *Ibid.*, para. 45.   [22] Case C-383/92, *Commission* v. *United Kingdom* [1994] ECR I-2479.

[23] Case C-385/05, *Confédération Générale du Travail (CGT)* v. *Premier Ministre and Ministre de l'Emploi, de la Cohésion Sociale et du Logement* [2007] 2 CMLR 6.

[24] Case C-201/15, *Anonymi Geniki Etairia Tsimenton Iraklis (AGET Iraklis)* v. *Ypourgos Ergasias, Koinonikis Asfalisis kai Koinonikis Allilengyis*, 21 December 2016.

particular, the freedom of contract which undertakings in principle have, inter alia in respect of the workers which they employ, since it is not in dispute that under that regime the national authority's opposition to certain plans for collective redundancies may result in the employer being prevented from putting those plans into effect'.

The question then was whether the restrictions on the employer's freedom and right respectively could be justified. In the case of TFEU, Article 49, 'a restriction on freedom of establishment is permissible only if it is justified by overriding reasons in the public interest', and 'further necessary, in such a case, that the restriction should be appropriate for ensuring the attainment of the objective in question and not go beyond what is necessary to attain that objective'. In the case of the EU Charter, Article 16, a restriction can be justified 'in accordance with the principle of proportionality, [if it is] necessary and genuinely [meets] objectives of general interest recognised by the European Union or the need to protect the rights and freedoms of others'. In both cases, however, it was held that while in principle a regime of ministerial approval may be permissible, in this case the legal requirements were excessive.

... to General Obligations

In addition to these duties to inform and consult in circumstances affecting job security, there has also been a move to introduce more wide-ranging duties to inform and consult. The Information and Consultation Directive makes provision for a second level of obligation, building on the earlier *ad hoc* initiatives of specific obligation with procedures of a more general nature.[25] The different objectives of the Directive are made clear by recital 6, where it is recorded that 'the existence of legal frameworks at national and Community level intended to ensure that employees are involved in the affairs of the undertaking employing them and in decisions which affect them has not always prevented serious decisions affecting employees from being taken and made public without adequate procedures having been implemented beforehand to inform and consult them'. Apart from also recording that there is a need to strengthen dialogue and promote mutual trust within undertakings, it was claimed in recital 8 that:

> There is a need, in particular, to promote and enhance information and consultation on the situation and likely development of employment within the undertaking and, where the employer's evaluation suggests that employment within the undertaking may be under threat, the possible anticipatory measures envisaged, in particular in terms of employee training and skill development, with a view to offsetting the negative developments or their consequences and increasing the employability and adaptability of the employees likely to be affected.

---

[25] Directive 2002/14/EC of 11 March 2002 (establishing a general framework for informing and consulting employees in the European Community).

According to Article 1, the purpose of the Directive is 'to establish a general framework setting out minimum requirements for the right to information and consultation of employees in undertakings or establishments within the Community'. For this purpose, 'consultation' is defined to mean 'the exchange of views and establishment of dialogue between the employees' representatives and the employer'.[26] This strongly suggests an intention to establish a standing procedure unlike the *ad hoc* provisions relating to redundancy and other matters. However, there is no universal right to be informed and consulted, the application of the Directive applying only to '(a) undertakings employing at least 50 employees in any one Member State, or (b) establishments employing at least 20 employees in any one Member State'.[27] It is left to each Member State to choose whether to apply the Directive to undertakings or establishments, the latter probably leading to a wider application of its provisions.[28] For these purposes, an undertaking 'means a public or private undertaking carrying out an economic activity, whether or not operating for gain',[29] while an establishment means 'a unit of business defined in accordance with national law and practice' where 'an economic activity is carried out on an ongoing basis with human and material resources'.[30]

It is also left to Member States to 'determine the practical arrangements for exercising the right to information and consultation'.[31] However, the information and consultation 'shall cover':

(a) information on the recent and probable development of the undertaking's or the establishment's activities and economic situation;

(b) information and consultation on the situation, structure and probable development of employment within the undertaking or establishment and on any anticipatory measures envisaged, in particular where there is a threat to employment;

(c) information and consultation on decisions likely to lead to substantial changes in work organisation or in contractual relations, including those covered by the Community provisions referred to in Article 9(1).[32]

The information must be given at such time, in such fashion and with such content as are appropriate to enable, in particular, employees' representatives to conduct an adequate study and, where necessary, prepare for consultation. Also important in terms of the obligation to consult is Article 4(4)(e), which provides that the consultation must take place 'with a view to reaching an agreement on decisions within the scope of the employer's powers referred to

---

[26] *Ibid.*, Art. 2(g).   [27] *Ibid.*, Art. 3(1).   [28] *Ibid.*   [29] *Ibid.*, Art. 2(a).

[30] *Ibid.*, Art. 2(b). It will be noted that the definition of establishment here coincides with that in the *Rockfon* case above, though the implications of this for a UK audience are limited, in view of the fact that the UK government restricted the application of the Directive in domestic law to 'undertakings'.

[31] *Ibid.*, Art. 4(1). See also Art. 1(1).

[32] *Ibid.*, Art. 4(2). Art. 9(1) deals with collective redundancies and the transfer of undertakings.

in paragraph 2(c)'. Again, consultation in this context is a synonym for negotiation, which means that Articles 2(g) and 4(4)(e) combined suggest the need for a standing procedure in which workers' representatives have negotiating rights in relation to workplace changes. As we will see, however, there is many a slip b'twixt law on the page and law in practice.

Although the Directive already gives a good deal of flexibility to Member States in implementation, yet more flexibility is to be found in Article 7, which provides that:

> Member States may entrust management and labour at the appropriate level, including at undertaking or establishment level, with defining freely and at any time through negotiated agreement the practical arrangements for informing and consulting employees. These agreements, and agreements existing on the date laid down in Article 11, as well as any subsequent renewals of such agreements, may establish, while respecting the principles set out in Article 1 and subject to conditions and limitations laid down by the Member States, provisions which are different from those referred to in Article 4.

This is a remarkable provision which reduces the EU principle of subsidiarity to a new level, in the sense that it allows for agreements to be concluded at the level of the enterprise (or even the workplace) to derogate from the minimum standards set down in the Directive. As will be seen when we move to consider the domestic transposition of this instrument, it is important to note that there are two types of agreement anticipated here: the first are those negotiated at any time (before or after implementation), and the second are those existing on the date of implementation (23 March 2005).[33] The important point is that, in the case of both types of agreement, it is necessary that the agreements in question must respect the principles set out in Article 1. Having regard to the definitions in Article 2 of terms used in Article 1, this would seem to imply as a minimum not only the 'exchange of views' but also the 'establishment of a dialogue'.

Limited Impact

It is important to note that the Directive establishes a general framework setting out minimum standards to be applied throughout the EU on a subject where practice varies greatly between Member States. There is thus no attempt to harmonise the law or to set a uniform standard. As it is, the requirements of the Directive fall well below the law operating in a number of Member States at the time it was made, and well beyond the law operating in a number of other Member States. In several respects, the text reflects the contradictory positions of the governments which drafted it, contradictions perhaps no more clearly exposed than in recital 22. This provides that '[a] Community

---

[33] This is the date in Art. 11 referred to in Art. 7.

framework for informing and consulting employees should keep to a minimum the burden on undertakings or establishments while ensuring the effective exercise of the rights granted'. Other doubts about a full commitment to the principle of information and consultation through collective mechanisms are to be seen in recital 16. This provides that the Directive is 'without prejudice to those systems which provide for the direct involvement of employees, as long as they are always free to exercise the right to be informed and consulted through their representatives'.

The Information and Consultation Directive appears thus to have been introduced without the universal enthusiasm of Member States for the principles it embraces. The lack of enthusiasm is reflected also in the fact that, by the date of transposition, implementing legislation had been introduced in only eight Member States. In a valuable comparative study, Carley and Hall report that it was thus necessary for enforcement proceedings by the Commission to be commenced against no fewer than nine Member States.[34] The proceedings against Estonia, Ireland, Malta and Poland were dropped following the introduction of transposition legislation. The proceedings against Belgium, Greece, Italy, Luxembourg and Spain, however, led to decisions of the CJEU in separate proceedings that the Member States were in breach of their obligations relating to the Directive.[35] There is little of interest in the jurisprudence, the cases holding simply that there had been a failure to introduce domestic legislation by the implementation date of 23 March 2005, without any consideration of any alleged shortcoming of domestic law. It has since been held in complaints against France (1) that workers under the age of twenty-six;[36] and (2) workers on what were referred to as 'assisted contracts',[37] cannot be excluded in calculating the size of the workforce to determine whether the Directive applies.

Limits of the EU Charter

In Case C-176/12, *Association de Médiation Sociale* v. *Hichem Laboubi*,[38] it was held that the exclusion of certain categories of workers from calculating whether the employer employed more than fifty employees was a breach of the Directive. However, it was held that although the Directive had direct effect, it did not have horizontal direct effect, and it was also held that domestic law could not be construed consistently with the Directive. The question then was whether the EU Charter, Article 27 could be relied upon to displace the offending national law,

---

[34] M. Carley and M. Hall, 'Impact of the Information and Consultation Directive on Industrial Relations', European Industrial Relations Observatory Online, 9 March 2009.
[35] *Ibid.*
[36] Case C-385/05, *Confédération Générale du Travail (CGT)* v. *Premier Ministre and. Ministre de l'Emploi, de la Cohésion Sociale et du Logement* [2007] 2 CMLR 6.
[37] Case C-176/12, *Association de Médiation Sociale* v. *Hichem Laboubi*, 15 January 2014.
[38] *Ibid.*

in line with 'settled case-law that the fundamental rights guaranteed in the legal order of the European Union are applicable in all situations governed by European Union law'. In this case, however, it was held that Article 27 was not expressed with sufficient clarity to confer on individuals a right that could be relied on in this case. The Court thus held that the Charter could not be invoked in a dispute between private parties to disapply a national law incompatible with Directive 2002/14. The only remedy was thus to bring a claim against the Member State under the *Francovich* principles for failure to implement the Directive.

Apart from this lack of enthusiasm in some Member States, Carley and Hall also point out that the Directive has had a varying impact. One group of countries with highly developed systems of information and consultation (through works councils or related bodies) found it unnecessary to make any changes or to make only minor changes to their existing law, these countries including Austria, France, Germany and the Netherlands. A second group of countries were required to make 'minor' changes, these countries including Finland, Greece and Hungary. The changes are said to relate to matters such as 'the issues subject to information and consultation, the definitions of information and consultation, confidentiality and the role of collective agreements in this area'.[39] A third group of countries have had to make major changes, including not only the UK but also Bulgaria, Cyprus, Poland and Romania. In the case of the UK, legislation had to be introduced from scratch due to the single channel of workplace representation that had developed in the British system of industrial relations, in which there has traditionally been no space for any form of representation other than that provided by a recognised trade union.

Information and consultation procedures thus vary greatly between Member States, with Carley and Hall highlighting differences in five areas where Member States have discretion under the Directive.[40] These are: (1) whether the law applies at establishment or undertaking level; (2) the identity of the employee representatives; (3) whether information and consultation is mandatory or depends on employee initiative; (4) the subjects of information and consultation; and (5) the enforcement procedures. There is no consistent position on any of this, but best practice would provide for information and consultation at (1) the level of the establishment with a threshold of five employees (Austria), conducted with (2) trade unions or works councils (several countries), in circumstances where (3) information and consultation procedures are mandatory and not dependent on the initiative of employees to establish them (the majority of Member States), (4) on subjects which may go

---

[39] M. Carley and M. Hall, 'Impact of the Information and Consultation Directive on Industrial Relations', European Industrial Relations Observatory Online, 9 March 2009.
[40] *Ibid.*

beyond but not below the minimum requirements of the Directive (Austria, Spain, France, Netherlands and Sweden), with (5) failure on the part of the employer to comply leading to fines of varying size, and in the case of Ireland to the improbable possibility of up to three years' imprisonment. There does not appear to be any provision for status quo orders pending compliance with the duty to inform and consult under the Directive.

European Works Councils

The information and consultation procedures to be established at national level complement an earlier initiative to establish EWCs, introduced in 1994.[41] There are thus now three levels of obligation relating to information and consultation: for *ad hoc* matters affecting establishments; for more wide-ranging matters affecting undertakings at national level; and for wider-ranging matters still at transnational level.[42] The purpose of the EWC Directive 94/45 is set out clearly in the recitals, where it is noted that the functioning of the internal market involved a concentration of undertakings and a growing 'transnationalisation' of business. There was a concern that this process would be resisted unless workers had a voice in the processes by which they were affected. And while it is true that procedures for informing and consulting employees were to be found at the time in the legislation of several Member States, this legislation was often 'not geared to the transnational structure of the entity which takes the decisions', and that this could lead to 'the unequal treatment of employees affected by decisions within one and the same undertaking or group of undertakings'. It was proposed that these obligations would apply not only to companies based in EU Member States, but also to foreign-owned companies which traded in two or more Member States.[43]

---

[41] Council Directive 94/45/EC. See B. Bercusson, *European Works Councils: Extending the Trade Union Role* (London: Institute of Employment Rights, 1997); B. Bercusson, *European Labour Law* (Cambridge University Press, 2010), pp. 619–23. See also C. McGlynn, 'European Works Councils: Towards Industrial Democracy?' (1995) 24 *Industrial Law Journal* 78.

[42] The EWC Directive has its origins in earlier attempts to make such provision which foundered on the UK veto. However, provision was made for the establishment of information and consultation procedures in the Community Charter of the Fundamental Rights of Workers of 1989, and the provisions of the Maastricht protocol empowered the then eleven Member States to legislate on this matter by qualified majority voting. Council Directive 94/45 was made under this procedure, and thus did not apply in the first instance to the UK. It was not until the election of the Labour government in 1997 that the UK ended its opt-out from the Maastricht procedures (which have now been fully integrated into the TFEU). See Council Directive 97/74/EC of 15 December 1997 (extending the EWC Directive to the UK). But although the UK may have been exempt from the obligations arising under the Directive, British employees of companies based elsewhere in the EU in practice enjoyed the benefits of the Directive.

[43] In this way, many US multinationals would be caught by the obligations of the Directive, compelled to adopt procedures and practices they would not entertain in their home jurisdiction.

Although the proposal for EWCs was audacious, the ambitions of at least some of the advocates were dashed by what was a mouse of a measure. The process to establish an EWC or an information and consultation procedure may be initiated either (1) by the central management of a Community-scale undertaking or a Community-scale group of undertakings, or (2) at the request of at least a hundred employees or their representatives in at least two undertakings or establishments in at least two Member States.[44] A special negotiating body (SNB) is then established to determine with the central management 'the scope, composition, functions and term of office of the EWC or the information and consultation procedure', the SNB to include representatives from the different territories in which the Community-scale undertaking operates.[45] The two sides must negotiate in a spirit of co-operation (or – as they might say in other jurisdictions – in good faith), 'with a view to reaching an agreement on the detailed arrangements for implementing the information and consultation of employees' in accordance with the Directive.[46] In the course of their negotiations, the parties are required to determine a number of matters, including the undertakings covered by the agreement, the composition of the EWC, the procedure for informing and consulting the EWC, the frequency of meetings, the financial and material resources to be allocated to the EWC, and the duration of the agreement and the procedure for its renegotiation.[47]

As an alternative to an EWC, Article 6 provides that the parties may agree to establish an information and consultation procedure, in which case the agreement must specify the method by which employee representatives are to have the right to meet to discuss information conveyed to them. Provision is also made for the situation where the employer seeks to frustrate negotiations about establishing an EWC, with provision made in Article 7 for minimum fallback standards to apply. These so-called 'subsidiary requirements' apply where the management refuses to commence negotiations within six months of a request being made under Article 5(1), or where the SNB and central management have been unable to reach an agreement within three years of the request being made. Set out in an Annex to the Directive, the subsidiary requirements may also apply if the parties decide that this is the procedure they wish to adopt, these requirements dealing with both the composition and the competence of EWCs. The problem that arises here is that, while the provisions dealing with composition are fairly innocuous, those dealing with competence are very limited, with paragraph 2 of the Directive's Annex providing that the EWC shall have the right to an annual meeting with the central management, 'to be informed and consulted, on the basis of a report drawn up by the central management'. Paragraph 2 also provides that the purpose of that meeting shall relate in particular to:

---

[44] Council Directive 94/45/EC, Art. 5.   [45] *Ibid.*, Art. 5(2) and (3).   [46] *Ibid.*, Art. 6(1).
[47] *Ibid.*, Art. 6(2).

the structure, economic and financial situation, the probable development of the business and of production and sales, the situation and probable trend of employment, investments, and substantial changes concerning organisation, introduction of new working methods or production processes, transfers of production, mergers, cut-backs or closures of undertakings, establishments or important parts thereof, and collective redundancies.

In addition to the annual meeting, the subsidiary requirements make provision for 'exceptional circumstances affecting the employees' interests to a considerable extent, particularly in the event of relocations, the closure of establishments or undertakings or collective redundancies'.[48] In these cases, the EWC has the right to be informed, and the right to meet any layer of management with decision-making authority. The purpose of any such meeting is for the EWC to be 'informed and consulted on measures significantly affecting employees' interests'. It is expressly provided, however, that any such meeting 'shall not affect the prerogatives of the central management',[49] which suggests that decisions cannot be challenged on the ground that information has not been provided or that consultation has not taken place. Otherwise, the subsidiary requirements provide that the operating expenses of EWCs are to be borne by central management, which must also provide EWC members with financial and material resources to enable them to perform their duties in an appropriate manner. This includes the cost of organising meetings and travelling expenses, although Member States may impose financial limits for these purposes. In particular, while EWCs are entitled to seek the assistance of experts of their choice, where the subsidiary requirements apply Member States may limit the employer's duty to pay for the cost of one expert only.

The 'Recast Directive'

The EWC Directive 94/45 is clearly an important attempt by law to address the power of transnational companies. It is a pioneering initiative, there being no equivalent measure in any other major labour law system of which we are aware. Although limited in scope to questions of information and consultation, the reach of the Directive is nevertheless extensive, including companies based in the USA and other third countries as well as the EU.[50] By 2008, it was claimed that, of the estimated 2,264 companies potentially covered by the Directive, some 828 (34 per cent) had EWCs in operation.[51] By 2015, the latter

---

[48] *Ibid.*, Sched., para. 3.　　[49] *Ibid.*

[50] According to S. de Spiegelaere and R. Jagodzinski, *European Works Councils and SE Works Councils in 2015* (Brussels: ETUI, 2015), 23 per cent of EWCs are based in companies with headquarters outside the EU.

[51] ETUC, *European Works Councils*, 5 May 2008. By 2016, there were thought to be about 2,400 companies potentially covered: European Commission, *Evaluation Study on the Implementation of Directive 2009/38/EC on the Establishment of a European Works Council, Final Report* (2016).

had risen to 1,071, the rate of growth being slow but steady, after the initial implementation. A leading study has found that EWCs are more likely to be found in larger multinationals, with the ETUC claiming that 61 per cent of companies employing more than 10,000 workers had an EWC (compared to only 23 per cent of companies with less than 5,000 workers). Overall, it was thought that by 2008, EWCs covered 64 per cent of all workers eligible to be represented in this way.[52]

Nevertheless, trade unions had a number of concerns about the limited effectiveness of EWCs,[53] and lobbied to have the Directive strengthened. An opportunity for revision was provided by Directive 94/45 itself, with Article 15 providing for a review of its operation no later than 22 September 1999, the review to look at the 'workforce size thresholds' in particular. Although proposing a lower threshold to include companies with fewer than a thousand workers, trade unions also had other concerns, including a clearer definition of information and consultation, a reduction in the period allowed for negotiating agreements from three years to one year, a right to training for EWC members, better access to expert advice and the right to hold preparatory and follow-up meetings. A particular concern was the need for a better framework of sanctions for companies that failed to comply with information and consultation obligations, with a number of high-profile incidents occurring in which it was claimed that the companies in question had carried out major restructuring in breach of the spirit of the Directive. These included Renault in Belgium and Nokia in Finland, the ETUC proposing that provision should be made for 'proportionate and dissuasive sanctions', and more optimistically, that:

> If companies take decisions that have a substantial impact on workers, without supplying information or taking part in consultation, they would be legally invalid, or the employer would have to make special compensation.[54]

Directive 2009/38 makes a number of amendments to Directive 94/45, though the changes had only lukewarm support from the UK government,[55] and do not go as far as the trade unions had proposed.[56] Nevertheless, the ETUC identified a number of improvements in the new Directive, which were said to include the following:

---

[52] De Spiegelaere and Jagodzinski, above, according to whom 39 per cent of EWCs are 'pre-Directive'.

[53] See D. Redfern, 'An Analysis of the Role of European Works Councils in British Workplaces' (2007) 29 *Employee Relations* 292.

[54] ETUC, *European Works Councils*, 5 May 2008.

[55] HC 16-xxxii (2007–8) (European Scrutiny Committee, 32nd Report), paras. 1.1–1.7.

[56] For a critique, see S. Laulom, 'The Flawed Review of the European Works Council Directive' (2010) 39 *Industrial Law Journal* 202.

- Trade unions have been granted a more prominent role in implementing the EWC Directive.
- There are new regulations on the composition of the SNB.
- Work in the EWC should become more effective due to a number of innovations, including:
  o the setting up of a select committee in the EWC as standard;
  o a broadening of skills and know-how by means of EWC members' right to training;
- The provisions on information and consultation are formulated more precisely.
- The EWC is granted the right [of] re-negotiation [of the agreement] in the event of structural changes at the enterprise.

Other changes were also highlighted by the UK government, including the bringing of the definitions of 'information' and 'consultation' into line with those in Article 4 of the Information and Consultation Directive, as well as requiring the management of an undertaking to provide employees and their representatives with the information necessary to open negotiations on whether an EWC should be set up.

It is clear, however, that core trade union concerns were not met in the revised Directive. From the trade union point of view, the Directive continues to exclude too many companies because of the high thresholds, which remain unchanged. There is concern that the negotiating period for the establishment of an EWC is too long, still enabling the employer to stall for up to at least three years before the subsidiary requirements apply. And there is concern too about the uncertain competence of EWCs, it being argued that the 'redefinition of transnationality does not clarify matters unambiguously', with the ETUC concerned that 'a narrow reading of this definition could unduly restrict EWC activities in cases where a decision affecting the whole company is in practice implemented in different stages, affecting one country after the other'.[57] Otherwise, questions have been raised about the lack of substance in the procedures, in the sense that provision continues to be made for a minimum of only one mandatory meeting a year (though the parties are of course free to agree to more). Questions continue to be raised about enforcement and sanctions, with the exhortations in recital 36 to the new Directive that sanctions in the case of violation must be 'effective, dissuasive and proportionate' being unmatched by the weak provisions of the Directive requiring Member States to 'provide appropriate measures in the event of failure to comply with this Directive'.[58]

---

[57] ETUC, *The New European Works Council Directive (Recast)* (Brussels: ETUC, 2011).

[58] Art. 11(2). See R. Jagodzinski, 'Implementation of enforcement provisions of the European Works Councils Recast Directive: are sanctions really "effective, proportionate and dissuasive?"' (Brussels: ETUI, 2014) – concern also expressed about the absence of any power to annul a decision taken in breach of an EWC agreement. For concerns at an official level, see European

Redundancy Consultation

The Collective Redundancies Directive[59] provides, by Article 2(1), that 'where an employer is contemplating collective redundancies, he shall begin consultations with the workers' representatives in good time with a view to reaching an agreement'. Article 2(2) provides in turn that the consultations must cover at least 'ways and means of avoiding collective redundancies or reducing the number of workers affected, and of mitigating the consequences by recourse to accompanying social measures aimed, *inter alia*, at aid for redeploying or retraining workers made redundant'.[60] Implementing legislation is to be found in TULRCA 1992, section 188(1), which now provides that:

> Where an employer is proposing to dismiss as redundant 20 or more employees at one establishment within a period of 90 days or less, the employer shall consult about the dismissals all the persons who are appropriate representatives of any of the employees who may be affected by the proposed dismissals or may be affected by measures taken in connection with those dismissals.

Redundancy for this purpose is defined in TULRCA 1992, section 195, to mean 'dismissal for a reason not related to the individual concerned or for a number of reasons all of which are not so related'.[61] According to the UK Supreme Court (UKSC):

> A reason relates to the individual if it is something to do with him such as something he is or something he has done. It is to be distinguished from a reason relating to the employer, such as his (or in the case of insolvency, his creditors') need to effect business change in some respect.[62]

Collective Redundancies and Convention Rights

In *Vining* v. *Wandsworth LBC*,[63] the dispute concerned the narrow question of the statutory exclusion of the police service from the right to be consulted about collective redundancies. Insofar as this general exclusion applied to parks police, was it compatible with the ECHR, Article 11, particularly in light of the decision in *Demir and Baykara* v. *Turkey*,[64] discussed above?

Commission, *Evaluation Study on the Implementation of Directive 2009/38/EC on the Establishment of a European Works Council, Final Report* (2016).

[59] Council Directive 98/59/EC of 20 July 1998.

[60] Member States may provide that the workers' representatives may call on the services of experts in accordance with national legislation and/or practice.

[61] This is wider than the definition applicable to the law relating to unfair dismissal and redundancy payments discussed in Chapter 20.

[62] *UCU* v. *Stirling University* [2015] UKSC 26: the expiry and non-renewal of a limited-term contract was for a reason unrelated to the indvidual concerned (e.g. because the research project or the course on which he or she was engaged as a teacher had come to an end). See also *Kelly* v. *Hesley Group Ltd* [2013] IRLR 514.

[63] [2017] EWCA Civ 1092.   [64] [2008] ECHR 1345.

Although concerned with a narrow point, the Court of Appeal nevertheless reflected in general terms about the nature of the duty to consult, holding that 'whether or not the consultation rights afforded to a recognised trade union by sections 188-192 constitute "collective bargaining" in the sense that the Grand Chamber used that term in *Demir*, they are so closely analogous to the rights there recognised that they are plainly to be treated as "essential elements" of the rights protected by article 11'.[65]

Neither the employer nor the government provided any justification of the exclusion of the parks police from the duty to consult, and applying the HRA, section 3 it was held that the legislation was to be read in such a way as to render the exclusion inoperative. Such a construction would not go against the grain of the statutory exclusion, the main aim having been to exclude 'traditional' police forces.

Collective Redundancy

The question whether there is a collective redundancy thus depends not only on the nature of the employment relationship, but also on the organisation and structure of the enterprise. Beginning with the nature of the employment relationship, it is necessary in the first instance to identify the employer, the problems in this context highlighted by *E. Green & Son (Castings) Ltd v. ASTMS*,[66] where there were three employers, namely E. Green & Son (Castings) Ltd, E. Green & Son Ltd, and E. Green & Son (Site Services) Ltd. All three operated from the same premises and were subsidiaries of the same holding company, Green's Economisers Group plc. They all shared services such as accounting services, while the personnel director of the holding company was responsible for all the subsidiaries and the managing director of the holding company was responsible for a decision to make redundancies in each of these companies. It was proposed that there should be ninety-seven redundancies in Castings, thirty-six in Green & Son and twenty-four in Site Services. The question was whether more than a hundred people were to be dismissed by the same employer at one establishment, a crucial question which would affect the length of the minimum consultation period. Although there was only one establishment, the EAT held that there were three employers and resisted arguments that it should 'pierce the corporate veil' to look at the reality underneath the formal legal position.[67] As a matter of law, there may have been three employers, but as a matter of common sense there was only one.

Closely related to the identity of the employer is the legal identity of the workers. The obligation arises only in respect of employees and not workers, although it applies to employees who may not qualify for a redundancy

---

[65] [2017] EWCA Civ 1092, para. 63. It is notable that in coming to this conclusion, the Court of Appeal referred to ILO Conventions 98, 151 and 154.

[66] [1984] ICR 352.   [67] Compare *NALGO* v. *National Travel (Midlands) Ltd* [1978] ICR 598.

payment, for example because they have insufficient service. Nevertheless, the effect is to exclude many atypical workers whose dismissal will not count in determining whether twenty or a hundred people are to be made redundant, and in respect of whom consultations will not have to take place. In addition, it is expressly provided that the redundancy consultation procedures do not apply to employees on fixed-term contracts unless the dismissal takes place before the expiry of the fixed term.[68] This change made in 2013 reverses the effect of the subsequent decision of the UKSC in *UCU* v. *Stirling University*,[69] which was being litigated at the time the change was made. In that case the UKSC held that workers on fixed-term contracts were covered by the procedure if the expiry took place during the consultation period. So an employer proposing to reduce numbers by, say, twenty may do so by dismissing nineteen full-time permanent staff members and by not renewing a fixed-term contract that has expired. The same could be done by dismissing, say, nineteen full-time permanent staff and one agency staff member, who is likely to be either treated as self-employed or an employee of the agency.[70] In these circumstances there will be no duty to consult, because fewer than twenty employees are to be dismissed.

Moving to the organisation and structure of the enterprise, the issue here relates to the decentralisation of activity, and to the fact that, although employed by the same employer, workers to be made redundant may not be employed in the same place. As we have seen, it may not be enough under TULRCA 1992, section 188, that twenty or more redundancies are being contemplated by the same employer, if those to be made redundant work at a number of different establishments. 'Establishment' and 'employer' are not synonyms in this context. Curiously, the term 'establishment' is not defined, and it is left to the tribunals to determine on the facts of each particular case what is an establishment for these purposes. As we have seen, in *Rockfon*,[71] the ECJ held that the term must be understood as meaning, 'depending on the circumstances', the unit to which the workers made redundant are assigned to carry out their duties.[72] Applying this finding in *MSF* v. *Refuge Assurance plc*,[73] the EAT suggested that it 'would effectively disapply section 188' in some – perhaps many – cases 'by reason of the smallness of the branches concerned and the thin spread of redundancies over a large number of them'.[74] However, it is important to emphasise and not to overlook the phrase 'depending on the circumstances', as used in *Rockfon*. For example, a supermarket chain might decide that it must make a hundred redundancies and that the best way to achieve this would be to dismiss one person in each of its

---

[68] TULRCA 1992, s. 282, as amended by SI 2013 No. 763.   [69] [2015] UKSC 26.

[70] The position is not addressed by the Agency Workers Regulations 2010, SI 2010 No. 93, which by Sched. 2 amend TULRCA 1992, s. 188(4), only to the extent that in the consultation process the employer must provide information about the number of agency workers engaged, in what part of the enterprise they are engaged, and the nature of the work in which they are engaged.

[71] [1995] ECR I-04291.   [72] *Ibid.*, para. 32.   [73] [2002] IRLR 324.   [74] *Ibid.*, p. 331.

hundred stores throughout the country.[75] Although an extreme example of the problem, on the above analysis there would be no duty on the part of the employer to inform and consult. This is because only one person is being dismissed at each establishment.

It was argued in the previous edition of this book that the foregoing construction of section 188 was not consistent with the Directive. Thus, TULRCA 1992, section 188, defines a collective redundancy as being the dismissal by an employer of twenty or more employees at one establishment. The corresponding provisions of the Directive refer to 'dismissals effected by an employer', where the number of redundancies is 'over a period of 90 days, at least 20, whatever the number of workers normally employed in the establishments in question' (Article 1(a)(ii)). The problem is the gratuitous inclusion of the words 'one establishment' in section 188, which make it difficult to construe section 188 consistently with the text or the social purpose of the Directive. A literal reading of the Directive would apply Article 1(a)(i) where there were 10 per cent or more redundancies at a decentralised work unit (an establishment) (as in *Rockfon*), and Article 1(a)(ii) where there were twenty or more redundancies at the different decentralised work units of the employer (establishments). So, while in the former case establishments are to be disaggregated to ensure compliance with the Directive, in the latter case they are to be aggregated for the same purpose. This approach or a variation thereon was nevertheless rejected by the CJEU, with arbitrary and unjust consequences.

The Wonder of Woolies: Case C-80/14, *USDAW* v. *WW Realisation 1 Ltd*[76]

The Woolworths collapse is a classic example of the problems caused by TULRCA 1992, section 188 discussed above. The collapse of the company led to several thousand employees being dismissed, and to claims for a protective award being made by USDAW on their behalf on the ground of the employer's failure to consult. The claims were successful in relation to some employees but not those who were employed at stores with less than 20 employees. On appeal by the union, the EAT held that all Woolworths' employees were employed at one establishment and all were entitled to recover. On a further appeal by the Secretary of State for Business, the Court of Appeal referred to the CJEU the question of what is meant by the term establishments in Directive 98/59, Article 1(1)(a)(ii), and in particular whether the phrase 'at least 20' referred 'to the number of dismissals across all of the employer's

---

[75] The same issue would arise in relation to schools where an education authority was proposing to dismiss twenty or more in several rather than one school (*Renfrewshire Council* v. *EIS* [2013] ICR 172), or building sites where a construction company is proposing to dismiss twenty or more at several rather than one construction site (*Barratt Developments (Bradford) Ltd* v. *UCATT* [1978] ICR 319).

[76] [2015] IRLR 577.

establishments in which dismissals are effected within a 90 day period, or does it refer to the number of dismissals in each individual establishment'.

The CJEU took the view that the word establishments was to be construed in Article 1(1)(a)(ii) in the same way as in Article 1(1)(a)(i). According to the Court, the *Rockfon* and subsequent decisions on this point were to apply in this case, despite the fact that the mischief to which these cases were addressed was radically different from the mischief to which the Woolworths' case was addressed. Nevertheless, the Court argued that there was 'nothing in the wording of Article 1(1)(a) of Directive 98/59 to suggest that a different meaning is to be given to the terms "establishment" or "establishments" in the same subparagraph of that provision', and that to construe the two provisions differently 'would be contrary to the need to promote the approximation of the laws of the Member States relating to collective redundancies'. And although the position contended by the union 'would, admittedly, significantly increase the number of workers eligible for protection under Directive 98/59', it would nevertheless 'be contrary to the objective of ensuring comparable protection for workers' rights in all Member States'.

This was very unconvincing, and a triumph of legal formalism. It is precisely in order to ensure that there would be comparable protection of workers that the different interpretations of establishment was called for. Similarly, such a construction would better advance the need to avoid the 'very different costs for the undertakings that have to satisfy the information and consultation obligations', in order to render 'comparable the burden of those costs in all Member States'. The Court was no more persuasive when concluding that its approach was supported by the provisions of Directive 2002/14/EC (the information and consultation directive), which by Article 2(a) and (b) 'also establishes a clear distinction between the term "undertaking" and the term "establishment"'. The wording and purpose of Directive 98/59/EC are clear: the obligation to consult arises where the employer proposes to dismiss 'at least 20, whatever the number of workers normally employed in the *establishments* in question' [emphasis added]. TULRCA 1992, section 188 is not a faithful implementation.

'Proposing' to Dismiss

It is important to note that the duty to consult arises only where the employer is 'proposing' to dismiss as redundant. As explained by the EAT in *Securicor Omega Express Ltd* v. *GMB*,[77] it is thus a duty to consult 'in relation to the consequences of the closures, with a view to reducing, possibly even avoiding entirely, but certainly reducing, the redundancies which were consequential upon it'.[78] The question has arisen, however, about whether there is a duty to consult about the closure itself, it being suggested that TULRCA 1992, section 188, does not meet the requirements of EU law, with Glidewell LJ pointing out that:

in the Directive consultation is to begin as soon as an employer contemplates redundancies, whereas under the Act of 1992 it only needs to begin when he

---

[77] [2004] IRLR 9.   [78] *Ibid.*, p. 15.

proposes to dismiss as redundant an employee. The verb 'proposes' in its ordinary usage relates to a state of mind which is much more certain and further along the decision-making process than the verb 'contemplate'; in other words, the Directive envisages consultation at an early stage when the employer is first envisaging the possibility that he may have to make employees redundant. Section 188 applies when he has decided that, whether because he has to close a plant or for some other reason, it is his intention, however reluctant, to make employees redundant.[79]

These concerns were subsequently addressed in *MSF* v. *Refuge Assurance plc*,[80] where it was later held that it is not possible to construe section 188 consistently with the Directive 'without distorting the meaning of the domestic legislation'.[81]

The matter was revisited in *UK Coal Mining Ltd* v. *NUM (Northumberland Area)*,[82] where it was pointed out that the law had been changed since *Vardy* so that consultations must now take place about ways of avoiding the dismissals, whereas previously the consultation need only be about the consequences of the dismissals. Although the EAT in *UK Coal* accepted that it was not possible to read 'proposed' as if it meant 'contemplated', this did not prevent 'the consultation obligation extending to consultations over closures leading to redundancies'. In an important passage, the EAT said that:

> in a closure context where it is recognised that dismissals will inevitably, or almost inevitably, result from the closure, dismissals are proposed at the point when the closure is proposed. The difference between proposed and contemplated will still impact on the point at which the duty to consult arises – it will not be when the closure is mooted as a possibility but only when it is fixed as a clear, albeit provisional, intention.[83]

The effect of this decision is nicely illustrated by *Ivor Hughes Educational Foundation* v. *Morris*,[84] where a school decided on 27 February 2013 that it would close unless student numbers increased. When it was clear that numbers had not gone up, the school decided on 25 April 2013 that it would close in the following August. Applying *UK Coal*, it was held that consultations should have started on 27 February, on the ground that at that point closure was a 'fixed, clear, albeit provisional intention'.[85]

UK Coal has not, however, resolved the problem of when the duty to consult arises, the matter falling to be considered by the Court of Appeal for the first time in *USA* v. *Nolan*.[86] Here, the US army closed down one of its military bases in the UK and made 200 civilian staff redundant. The evidence suggests that the decision had been taken at a senior level within the US army by 13 March 2006, and that it had begun to leak into the press, being the subject of a BBC news

---

[79] *R* v. *British Coal Corporation, ex parte Vardy* [1993] ICR 720, at 753.
[80] [2002] IRLR 324 (EAT).   [81] *Ibid.*, p. 330.   [82] [2008] ICR 163 (EAT).
[83] *Ibid.*, para. 86.   [84] [2015] IRLR 696.   [85] *Ibid.*, para. 22.
[86] [2010] EWCA Civ 1223, [2011] IRLR 40 (CA).

report on 21 April 2006. On 24 April 2006, an announcement was made to the staff to inform them of the decision, and on 9 May 2006 the US army informed the UK government of its plans to vacate the site by 30 September 2006, shortly thereafter also holding informal discussions with the workers' representatives at the base. A memorandum was prepared in early June making clear that redundancy notices would be issued to all staff on 30 June, with contracts to terminate by 29 September 2006. Formal consultations began on 5 June 2006, leading the employment tribunal to conclude that there had been a breach of TULRCA 1992, section 188, noting that there was:

> no evidence as to why there was delay in commencing consultation either from a date prior to 13th March 2006 or from 24th April 2006 or from a public announcement of 9th May 2006 until 5th June 2006 when the formal consultation began.[87]

In reaching this decision (which was upheld by the EAT), the employment tribunal relied on the decision in *UK Coal* above. Since that decision, however, the ECJ had delivered its decision in the *Fujitsu* case above,[88] which was thought by the Court of Appeal to call into question the approach taken in *UK Coal* (although notably in *Ivor Hughes Educational Foundation* above, the EAT thought the outcome would be same whether *UK Coal* or *Fujitsu* were applied).[89] According to the Court of Appeal it was now unclear whether:

> the consultation obligation arises (i) when the employer is proposing, but has not yet made, a strategic business or operational decision that will foreseeably or inevitably lead to collective redundancies; or (ii) only when that decision has actually been made and he is then proposing consequential redundancies.[90]

If the answer is (i), then *UK Coal* will have been correctly decided; but if the answer is (ii), then *UK Coal* will have been incorrectly decided.[91] As a result, a reference was made to the CJEU for further clarification of the law.[92] However, the CJEU declined to rule on the matter on the ground that a redundancy at a military establishment was outside the scope of the Directive.[93] The matter was thus returned to the Court of Appeal to decide the *Fujitsu* point, but its power to do so was challenged in subsequent litigation by the US government,

---

[87] *Ibid.*, para. 25.
[88] Case C-44/08, *Akavan Erityisalojen Keskusliitto Alek ry* v. *Fujitsu Siemens Computers Oy* [2009] ECR I-8163, [2009] IRLR 944.
[89] See also the earlier attempt at reconciliation in *Kelly* v. *Hesley Group Ltd* [2013] IRLR 514.
[90] [2010] EWCA Civ 1223, [2011] IRLR 40 (CA), para. 57.
[91] *Ivor Hughes Educational Foundation* v. *Morris* [2015] IRLR 696.
[92] The issue appears to be whether consultations should have begun at the end of March (ninety days before the dismissal notices were issued on 30 June 2006) after the strategic decision had been taken, but before the date had been announced and the decisions to dismiss had been settled. The alternative would be that consultations should have begun on 9 May 2006 when the decision to vacate the premises was announced, when surely redundancies were both contemplated and proposed.
[93] Case C-583/10, *USA* v. *Nolan* [2013] ICR 193.

which argued that TULRCA 1992, section 188 should be construed to have no application to employment at US bases in the UK. This argument was rejected by the UKSC (4:1), which confirmed the Court of Appeal's power to deal with the matter on 21 October 2015.[94] There has been no decision since.[95]

Employee Representatives

When first introduced in 1975, the duty to consult was a duty to consult only with the representatives of a recognised trade union. This meant that, if there was no recognised union, there was no duty to consult, a position found by the ECJ to be inconsistent with the requirements of the Directive.[96] The legislation thus had to be changed to bring it into line with obligations under the Directive, and the employer's duty to consult is now a universal duty, which applies even where there is no recognised trade union. Where there is a recognised trade union, the union enjoys a priority status in the sense that it is with the union that redundancy consultations must take place.[97] For this purpose, recognition means recognition for the purposes of collective bargaining.[98] Where there is no recognised trade union, the employer must consult with 'whichever of the following employee representatives the employer chooses':

    (i) employee representatives appointed or elected by the affected employees otherwise than for the purposes of this section, who (having regard to the purposes for and the method by which they were appointed or elected) have authority from those employees to receive information and to be consulted about the proposed dismissals on their behalf; [or]

    (ii) employee representatives elected by the affected employees, for the purposes of this section, in an election satisfying the requirements of section 188A(1).[99]

It is these latter categories that are the most novel in the UK context.[100] As already suggested, the Directive fits in nicely with the standard collective bargaining arrangements operating in much of the EU, in the sense that in many (though not all) countries there are dual channels of worker representation. In simple terms, this leads to workers being represented by trade unions in collective bargaining at sector level on economic questions, and by works councils in the enterprise on social questions. In the UK, however, there is a system of single-channel representation, which means that for different

---

[94] *USA* v. *Nolan* [2015] UKSC 63, [2015] ICR 1347.

[95] The employment tribunals must soldier on in the meantime. See *Kelly* v. *Hesley Group Ltd* [2013] IRLR 514, and *Ivor Hughes Educational Foundation* v. *Morris* [2015] IRLR 696.

[96] Case C-383/92, *Commission* v. *United Kingdom* [1994] ECR 1–2479.

[97] TULRCA 1992, s. 188(1B)(a).   [98] TULRCA 1992, s. 179.

[99] See *USA* v. *Nolan* [2010] EWCA Civ 1223, [2011] IRLR 40, and *Kelly* v. *Hesley Group Ltd* [2013] IRLR 514.

[100] For the impact of non-union forms of redundancy consultation, see M. Hall and P. Edwards, 'Reforming the Redundancy Consultation Procedure' (1999) 28 *Industrial Law Journal* 299.

reasons there are unlikely to be non-union channels of representation that would satisfy the requirements of paragraph (i) above. Indeed the perils of consulting with a pre-existing 'advisory body [set up] to communicate the views of staff to management and vice versa' were exposed in *Kelly v. Hesley Group Ltd*.[101] The EAT appeared to look unfavourably on the adequacy of the body in question, described as 'akin to the passive transferee of information and views rather than a participative body, attempting not merely to inform and discuss but to agree, to which the description "negotiation" is addressed'. As a result, where there is not a trade union recognised for the purposes of collective bargaining, redundancy consultation might be better to take place through the medium of representatives elected in accordance with paragraph (ii), which means representatives elected specifically for the purpose of a redundancy consultation exercise.

Where the latter provisions apply, the employer must invite the affected employees to elect employee representatives,[102] the invitation to be issued 'long enough before the time when the consultation is required by subsection (1A)(a) or (b) to begin to allow them to elect representatives by that time'.[103] So far as the election process is concerned, this is very much in the control of the employer, who must 'make such arrangements as are reasonably practical to ensure that the election is fair'.[104] But it is for the employer to 'determine the number of representatives to be elected', as well as whether employees are to be represented by 'representatives of all the affected employees' or by 'representatives of particular classes of those employees'.[105] It is also for the employer to ensure that all the candidates are affected employees; that no affected employee is unreasonably excluded from standing for election; that all affected employees on the date of the election are entitled to vote; and that the election is conducted so as to secure a secret ballot in which the votes are accurately counted.[106] There is no public agency such as the CAC with responsibilities here,[107] and there is no obligation for independent scrutineers as in the case of trade union internal elections.[108] Similar provisions apply in the case of consultation for the purpose of business transfers under the Transfer of Undertakings (Protection of Employment) (TUPE) Regulations 2006.[109]

So far as the facilities available to employee representatives are concerned, TULRCA 1992, section 188(5A), provides simply that employee representatives for the purposes of redundancy consultation are to be allowed by the employer 'access to the affected employees', and 'such accommodation and

---

[101] [2013] IRLR 514.
[102] But what happens if the number of candidates equals the number of positions to be filled? See *Phillips v. Xtera Communications Ltd* [2011] IRLR 724.
[103] TULRCA 1992, s. 188(7A).   [104] TULRCA 1992, s. 188A(1)(a).
[105] TULRCA 1992, s. 188A(1)(b) and (c).   [106] TULRCA 1992, s. 188A(1)(d)–(i).
[107] See Chapter 14 in relation to trade union recognition ballots.   [108] See p. 541.
[109] SI 2006 No. 246, regs. 13–16.

other facilities as may be appropriate'. Similar provision is made in the amended TUPE Regulations 2006.[110] Provision is made for time-off to carry out the functions of a candidate for the post of representative, as well as the functions of the representative itself, and now to undergo training to perform these duties.[111] There is also statutory protection against both action short of dismissal and dismissal for carrying out the functions of a candidate or the responsibilities of office.[112] One point to note is that the protection applies both to acts and to omissions, unlike the protection for trade union membership until the changes introduced by the Employment Relations Act 1999. If, after the employer has invited affected employees to elect representatives, the affected employees fail to do so within a reasonable time, the employer must give to each affected employee the information set out in TULRCA 1992, section 188(4), on which see below.[113]

Process of Consultation

Having established that there is a duty to consult and with whom, the question arises as to timing. Here, the legislation provides that the consultation shall begin 'in good time', and in any event (1) where the employer is proposing to dismiss a hundred or more employees at least forty-five days,[114] and (2) otherwise, at least thirty days, before the first of the dismissals takes effect.[115] This appears to conflate the Directive's definition of collective redundancies (Article 1(1))[116] with its duty to consult 'in good time' (Article 2). The Directive does not impose any minimum period within which information should be provided and consultation should take place with employee representatives, though it does impose a duty on the part of employers in some cases to give at least thirty days' notice to the public authorities (Article 4).[117] It will be noted that there is no equivalent minimum period for consultation in TUPE 2006, where information must be provided 'long enough before a relevant transfer to enable the employer to consult the appropriate representatives of any affected employees'.[118] In the context of collective redundancies consultation, the forty-five-day or thirty-day minimum consultation period

---

[110] *Ibid.*, reg. 13(8).   [111] ERA 1996, s. 61.   [112] ERA 1996, ss. 47 and 103.

[113] TULRCA 1992, s. 188(7B).

[114] Until 2013, the minimum consultation period where a hundred or more employees were to be dismissed over a period of ninety days was ninety not forty-five days. The law was changed by SI 2013 No. 763.

[115] TULRCA 1992, s. 188(1A).   [116] See pp. 636–7.

[117] The corresponding provisions of domestic law are to be found in TULRCA 1992, ss. 193 and 194. Section 193 was amended following Case C-188/03, *Junk Irmtraud* v. *Wolfgang Kühnel* [2005] ECR I-885, so that the notification must take place 'before giving notice to terminate an employee's contract of employment in respect of any of those dismissals' (TULRCA 1992, s. 193(1)(a)).

[118] SI 2006 No. 246, reg. 13.

has the virtue of certainty and has no doubt helped to avoid unnecessary litigation of what constitutes 'in good time'. But it may be rather arbitrary and arguably there may be cases where more than thirty or forty-five days is required.

The question also arises as to the purpose of consultation. By virtue of TULRCA 1992, section 188(2), the consultation should be about ways of (a) avoiding the dismissals, (b) reducing the numbers of employees to be dismissed and (c) mitigating the consequences of the dismissals.[119] It should also be 'undertaken by the employer with a view to reaching agreement with the appropriate representatives',[120] the EAT emphasising on a number of occasions that 'consultation must be genuine and meaningful',[121] or 'fair and meaningful'.[122] Referring to TULRCA 1992, section 188(2), in *Middlesbrough Borough Council* v. *TGWU*,[123] the EAT said that it viewed paragraphs (a) to (c) above disjunctively, and continued by saying that:

> an employer may genuinely consult with the unions about ways of reducing the numbers of employees to be dismissed and mitigating the consequences of the dismissals, without genuinely consulting as to the principle of whether or not to declare redundancies at all . . . The duties under the section are mandatory. It is not open to an employer, for this purpose, to argue, as would be open to him in defending a complaint of unfair dismissal by the individual employee, that consultation would, in the circumstances, be futile or utterly useless.[124]

In that case, it was held that there had been a breach of TULRCA 1992, section 188, where the local authority consulted the union about 150 redundancies, but failed to do so in a way designed to reduce the numbers to be made redundant.

Consultation is not just about timing and purpose. It is also about manner and form. By virtue of TULRCA 1992, section 188(4), for the purposes of the consultation the employer must disclose in writing to the appropriate representatives:

(a) the reasons for his proposals,
(b) the numbers and descriptions of employees whom it is proposed to dismiss as redundant,
(c) the total number of employees of any such description employed by the employer at the establishment in question,
(d) the proposed method of selecting the employees who may be dismissed,

---

[119] It is the responsibility of the employer to ensure that these mandatory matters are raised and discussed, and not good enough that an opportunity is provided for employee representatives to raise them: *Kelly* v. *Hesley Group Ltd* [2013] IRLR 514, citing *Susie Radin Ltd* v. *GMB* [2004] ICR 893 (CA). This is more likely to be an issue in the case of non-union-based consultation with inexperienced representatives.

[120] SI 2006 No. 246, reg. 13. There is no corresponding duty on the part of the representatives.

[121] *Middlesbrough Borough Council* v. *TGWU* [2002] IRLR 333 (EAT).

[122] *Securicor Omega Express Ltd* v. *GMB* [2004] IRLR 9, at 13 (EAT).

[123] [2002] IRLR 333 (EAT).   [124] *Ibid.*, p. 338.

(e) the proposed method of carrying out the dismissals, with due regard to any agreed procedure, including the period over which the dismissals are to take effect, and

(f) the proposed method of calculating the amount of any redundancy payments to be made (otherwise than in compliance with an obligation imposed by or by virtue of any enactment) to employees who may be dismissed.[125]

It has been held that it is not enough for the employer to give the union information in the section 188(4) notice about the total number of redundancies and their broad job category, but not the divisions of the company which would be affected.[126] But it has also been held that the employer is not required to provide the union with a section 188(4) notice before consultations begin, and that a minute of a meeting at which section 188(4) issues were discussed would be enough.[127] But this seems to be of doubtful authority.

A final question relates to the conclusion of the consultations. This brings us back to the question of timing, and to the requirement that consultation must take place before the dismissals take effect. The minimum periods in which consultation must take place are to be calculated by working back from the date any notice of dismissal expires, rather than the date on which it is issued.[128] This does not mean that consultation could begin after the employer had issued dismissal notices, even though the notice period to end the contract exceeded the minimum consultation period laid down in the statute.[129] But it does appear to mean that the employer could issue notices to terminate the contract before the consultations were concluded,[130] a practice said to 'jeopardise' the objectives of the Directive if 'the consultation of workers' representatives were to be subsequent to the employer's decision'.[131] According to the then Department for Business, Innovation and Skills, however, 'the 30 day [or 45 day] period continues to be counted back from the date when the first of the dismissals takes effect, not from the date when redundancy notices are issued'.[132] For this purpose, a dismissal takes effect when the individual in question leaves the service of the employer following the expiry of the notice.

---

[125] Member States may provide that the workers' representatives may call on the services of experts in accordance with national legislation and/or practice.

[126] *MSF* v. *GEC Ferranti (Defence Systems) Ltd (No. 2)* [1994] IRLR 113 (EAT). On the importance of fully and formally complying with s. 188(4), see *Kelly* v. *Hesley Group Ltd* [2013] IRLR 514, again citing *Susie Radin Ltd* v. *GMB* [2004] ICR 893 (CA) to emphasise the 'mandatory' and 'absolute' nature of the duty to address each of the matters listed.

[127] *Securicor Omega Express Ltd* v. *GMB* [2004] IRLR 9 (EAT).

[128] *Middlesbrough Borough Council* v. *TGWU* [2002] IRLR 333 (EAT).

[129] *E. Green & Son (Castings) Ltd* v. *ASTMS* [1984] ICR 382.

[130] *Middlesbrough Borough Council* v. *TGWU* [2002] IRLR 333 (EAT).

[131] Case C-188/03, *Junk Irmtraud* v. *Wolfgang Kühnel* [2005] ECR I-885, para. 38.

[132] BIS, *Redundancy Consultation and Notification: Guidance* (2006), p. 7. This is the position reflected in the form HR1 which informs employers that they must notify the government 'at least 30/45 days before the first dismissal and before you issue any individual notices of dismissal'. See also *Leicestershire County Council* v. *Unison* [2005] IRLR 920 (EAT), para. 33.

An Additional Duty of the Employer

In addition to the employer's duty to inform and consult employee representatives, there is a duty on the part of the employer also to inform BEIS. This latter obligation applies only to those collective redundancies to which the duty to inform and consult employees' representatives applies. Failure of the employer to comply with this obligation is a criminal offence. Following the *Junk* decision of the ECJ, the legislation imposing this duty on employers was amended. TULRCA 1992, section 193, now provides that the employer must inform BEIS (a) 'before giving notice to terminate an employee's contract of employment in respect of any of those dismissals', and (b) 'at least 45 [or 30] days before the first of those dismissals takes effect'. As in the case of TULRCA, section 188, the section 193 obligation was previously ninety rather than forty-five days, the law changed for both in 2013.[133]

Although the government thought it necessary to amend TULRCA 1992, section 193 in the light of *Junk*, it was not thought necessary at the time to amend TULRCA 1992, section 188. However, the subsequent reduction from ninety to forty-five days of the duty to consult employee representatives and inform the government may be another consequence of the costs associated with the latter decision, albeit not acknowledged in public statements by the government. The government has no power to veto a collective redundancy, though it would be possible for such powers to be taken consistently with the Directive. In *AGET Iraklis,* it was held that it was possible in principle to enable the public authorities to veto a decision on grounds relating to the protection of workers. But the same case also revealed the difficulties in introducing such powers compatibly with TFEU, Article 49, and the EU Charter of Fundamental Rights, Article 16.[134]

Special Circumstances

By virtue of TULRCA 1992, section 188(7), it is a defence that 'there are special circumstances which render it not reasonably practicable for the employer to comply with a requirement of subsection (1A), (2) or (4) [of section 188]', provided he or she took 'all such steps towards compliance as are reasonably practicable in those circumstances'. The question of what are 'special circumstances' for these purposes was considered by the Court of Appeal at an early stage in the life of this provision. In *Clark's of Hove* v. *Bakers' Union*,[135] the employer terminated the employment of nearly all the workforce of 380 people, and ceased trading on the same day (26 October 1976). The company had been in financial difficulties since midsummer, and had been trying to raise capital to deal with these difficulties. When it became clear that a possible source of capital was not interested in investing in the

---

[133] SI 2013 No. 763.

[134] Case C-201/15, *Anonymi Geniki Etairia Tsimenton Iraklis (AGET Iraklis)* v. *Ypourgos Ergasias, Koinonikis Asfalisis kai Koinonikis Allilengyis,* 21 December 2016, pp. 640–41 above.

[135] [1978] ICR 1076 (CA).

company, 'it dawned upon the directors of the company that the shutters would have to be put up', and it was at that moment that a notice was posted dismissing the staff. The union complained that the company had been in breach of what was then the Employment Protection Act 1975, section 99. The employer argued that the circumstances were covered by section 99(8) (now TULRCA 1992, section 188(7)). The Court of Appeal upheld an industrial tribunal decision that the circumstances were not special.

As pointed out by Geoffrey Lane LJ, where an employer has failed to give the requisite notice (in this case, ninety days), 'the burden is clearly imposed upon them, by the statute, to show that there were special circumstances which made it not reasonably practicable for them to comply with the provisions of the Act, and also that they took steps towards compliance with the requirements, such steps as were reasonably practicable in the circumstances'.[136] As also pointed out by Geoffrey Lane LJ, there are three stages in discharging this burden: '(1) Were there special circumstances? If so, (2) did they render compliance with section 99 not reasonably practicable? And, if so, (3) did the employers take all such steps towards compliance with section 99 as were reasonably practicable in the circumstances?'[137] The crux of the question, however, is the meaning of 'special circumstances', a question to which (predictably) neither the Directive nor the statute gives any answers, with Geoffrey Lane LJ turning to cases under the Road Traffic Acts to find that:

> A 'special reason' is one ... special to the facts of the particular case ... special to the facts which constitute the offence ... A circumstance peculiar to the offender as distinguished from the offence is not a 'special reason'.[138]

Applying these principles to the context of redundancy consultation, the Court of Appeal held that 'insolvency is, on its own, neither here nor there. It may be a special circumstance, it may not be a special circumstance.'[139] According to the Court, 'it will depend entirely on the cause of the insolvency whether the circumstances can be described as special or not. If, for example, sudden disaster strikes a company, making it necessary to close the concern, then plainly that would be a matter which was capable of being a special circumstance; and that is so whether the disaster is physical or financial.'[140] On the other hand, if the insolvency were merely due to a gradual run-down of the company, 'as it was in this case', then it is possible to conclude that the circumstances may not be special. It was held that:

> the industrial tribunal approached the matter in precisely the correct way. They distilled the problem which they had to decide down to its essence, and they asked themselves this question: do these circumstances, which undoubtedly caused the summary dismissal and the failure to consult the union as required by [the Employment Protection Act 1975, section 99], amount to special

---

[136] *Ibid.*, p. 1084.   [137] *Ibid.*   [138] *Ibid.*, p. 1085.   [139] *Ibid.*   [140] *Ibid.*

circumstances; and they went on, again correctly, as it seems to me, to point out that insolvency *simpliciter* is neutral, it is not on its own a special circumstance.[141]

Clark's of Hove was in some ways a very straightforward case, even if very distressing for all those involved. The changing nature of business ownership means that in other cases the position may not be so straightforward. Thus, in some cases, the employer of the redundant employees may not be the person who made the decision to close or reduce staffing levels. That decision may have been made some distance away by the managers of a parent company of which the UK-based company in peril is a wholly owned subsidiary. The problem in these cases is that there may be no advance notice by the parent company and no consultation before the announcement of closure and redundancy. In this situation, the second sentence in TULRCA 1992, section 188(7) provides that the failure of the parent company to provide information to the subsidiary cannot be excused as a special circumstance for the purposes of the first sentence of the subsection. According to the EAT in *GMB* v. *Beloit Walmsley Ltd*,[142] '[i]t is delay in communicating that decision that is the mischief at which the special circumstances defence in TULRCA 1992 section 188(7) is aimed'. Other cases have stressed that a decision about special circumstances will depend on the facts of the case.[143]

Enforcement of Duty to Consult

The final question for consideration here relates to the enforcement of the duty to consult. What happens if the employer fails to consult, or fails to consult within the prescribed minimum times, or fails to consult in the manner prescribed by the Act? By Article 6, the Collective Redundancies Directive provides that 'Member States shall ensure that judicial and/or administrative procedures for the enforcement of obligations under this Directive are available to the workers' representatives and/or workers'. In implementing this obligation, TULRCA 1992 has adopted a most convoluted procedure, whereby an application may be made to an ET for a 'protective award', which has the effect of requiring the employer to continue to pay remuneration to the staff to be made redundant for a protected period.[144] The period, which may not exceed ninety days, is 'of such length as the tribunal determines to be just and equitable in all the circumstances having regard to

---

[141] *Ibid.*, pp. 1085–6. Geoffrey Lane LJ continued by saying that 'whether it is or is not will depend upon the causes of the insolvency. They define "special" as being something out of the ordinary run of events, such as, for example, a general trading boycott . . . Here, again, I think they were right.' *Ibid.*, p. 1086.

[142] [2004] IRLR 18 (EAT).

[143] *Ivor Hughes Educational Foundation* v. *Morris* [2015] IRLR 696 (risk of leakage of sensitive information not a special circumstance in this case, although it might be in others).

[144] TULRCA 1992, s. 189.

the seriousness of the employer's default'.[145] If the employer fails to make the payment, the individual employees in respect of whom the award was made may then bring a claim for recovery to an ET.[146] Enforcement of the employer's duty is thus in the hands of the trade union or other employee representatives in the first instance.

The question arose in *Northgate HR Ltd* v. *Mercy*[147] whether an application for a protective award could be made by an individual employee. By virtue of TULRCA 1992, section 189(1), a complaint may be made to an ET:

(a) in the case of a failure relating to the election of employee representatives, by any of the affected employees or by any of the employees who have been dismissed as redundant;

(b) in the case of any other failure relating to employee representatives, by any of the employee representatives to whom the failure related;

(c) in the case of failure relating to representatives of a trade union, by the trade union; and

(d) in any other case, by any of the affected employees or by any of the employees who have been dismissed as redundant.

In this case, there was an Employee Consultation Council in place, composed of elected and appointed members. It was held by the EAT that, because there were employee representatives, an application by Mr Mercy (permissible under TULRCA 1992, section 189(1)(d)) was barred by TULRCA 1992, section 189(1)(b). The Court of Appeal agreed, holding that the Act was to be construed literally, so that individual claims could be brought only where there were no employee representatives, which was not the case here. According to the Court of Appeal, 'the statute deals with the complaint as a collective rather than an individual matter and limits standing, no doubt so as to prevent the possibility of numerous individual challenges which are not supported by appropriate representatives'.[148]

A failure on the part of the employer to inform and consult in the context of a redundancy which leads to dismissal may give the employees in question a right to claim for unfair dismissal, and to be compensated as a result.[149] The

---

[145] TULRCA 1992, s. 189.   [146] TULRCA 1992, s. 192.

[147] [2007] EWCA Civ 1304, [2008] ICR 410 (CA).

[148] *Ibid.*, para. 15. The Court continued by saying that 'If Mr Mercy had understood this at the appropriate time, he could have raised his concerns with his representatives on the [Employee Consultation Council] and, in the absence of their being able to obtain a satisfactory response from the employer, they could have commenced proceedings under section 189(1)(b). In these circumstances, there is no protection gap in the legislation which results from according the statutory language its obvious and natural meaning': *ibid.* But what would happen if the Employee Consultation Council refused to apply for a protective award? On the collective nature of the right in this context, see also Case C-12/08 *Mono Car Styling SA* v. *Dervis Odemis* [2009] ECR I-06653.

[149] See Chapter 20.

provisions relating to a protective award are quite separate,[150] and a protective award may be made to those employees who do not qualify for either a redundancy payment or unfair dismissal.[151] Unlike the latter, the protective award is not designed to be compensatory but punitive, with the Court of Appeal holding in *Susie Radin Ltd* v. *GMB* that:

> [t]he purpose of the award was to provide a sanction for breach by the employer of the obligations in section 188: it was not to compensate the employees for loss which they had suffered in consequence of the breach.[152]

In terms of assessing the amount of the protective award, further guidance was given in *Susie Radin Ltd*, where it was said that 'a proper approach in a case where there has been no consultation is to start with the maximum period [of ninety days] and reduce it only if there are mitigating circumstances justifying a reduction to an extent which the [tribunal] consider appropriate'.[153] Otherwise, the tribunal has 'a wide discretion to do what is just and equitable in all the circumstances, but the focus should be on the seriousness of the employer's default'.[154] It is immaterial that the employees did not suffer loss as a result of the employer's default.[155]

Whether this is the most appropriate remedy for dealing with collective redundancies is open to question.[156] Compensation may be welcome and it may be very costly where hundreds of workers have been fired, but it does not restore the right to be consulted. In *ex parte Vardy*,[157] the High Court quashed a decision by British Coal to close collieries where there was a failure to consult on the ground that the union had a legitimate expectation under public law to be consulted before redundancies were made. The court then granted a declaration effectively requiring consultations to take place, giving rise to questions as to why remedies of this kind should not be available under the 1992 Act with contracts of employment continuing until consultations required by law have been held. The

---

[150] Breach of TULRCA 1992, s. 188, does not in itself make a dismissal unfair: TULRCA 1992, s. 188(8).

[151] In addition, a protective award may be recoverable for a failure to consult, even though the dismissals are not procedurally unfair.

[152] [2004] EWCA Civ 80; [2004] ICR 893 (CA), para. 45.   [153] *Ibid.*

[154] *Ibid.* See also *Unison* v. *Leicestershire County Council* [2006] EWCA Civ 825, [2006] IRLR 810 (CA).

[155] *Ivor Hughes Educational Foundation* v. *Morris* [2015] IRLR 696: ninety-day protective award made.

[156] Following a number of high-profile collective redundancies thought by some to flout the legislation, a study by the House of Commons Trade and Industry Committee in 2000 heard that 'the remedy currently available under United Kingdom law to enforce [the Collective Redundancies] Directive is extremely weak, if not non-existent': HC Commons Trade and Industry Committee, 8th Report, *BMW and Longbridge* (HC 383, 1999–2000), Minutes of Evidence, para. 142. The Committee concluded that BMW's 'disgraceful failure to consult or even inform the workforce' may have constituted a breach of the 1975 Directive, and emphasised the importance of ensuring that the existing structure for multinational companies 'which would seem to have proved wholly ineffective on this occasion', provides real rights for workforce representatives. *Ibid.*, para. 26.

[157] *R* v. *British Coal Corporation, ex parte Vardy* [1993] ICR 720.

granting of such a remedy would, however, require a forum other than the ET and could be expensive to operate. Another option is suggested by the ICE Regulations,[158] which are considered fully in the following section. It is to be noted, however, that complaint of a failure to inform and consult under negotiated agreements or the standard provisions of the ICE Regulations may be made to the CAC. The CAC is then empowered to 'make a declaration to that effect and may make an order requiring the employer to take such steps as are necessary to comply with the terms of the negotiated agreement or, as the case may be, the standard information and consultation provisions'.[159]

Variation of Contractual Terms

TULRCA 1992 was introduced to give additional protection to workers in the event of dismissal for redundancy: it provided a procedure that enabled employees to be involved in a process that would help to reduce the number of redundancies and to ameliorate the impact of unavoidable redundancies.

In recent years, however, the TULRCA 1992, section 188, procedure has been caught up in controversy, used by employers to impose changes to the contractual relationship rather than reduce the number of employees engaged. In other words, it is being used as a means to vary rather than terminate contracts of employment.[160]

The problem has arisen mainly in the public sector as local authority employers seek to adapt to budget cuts imposed by central government in the age of austerity. The issue first came to light during a dispute in the London fire service, but, as the industrial relations scholar, Gregor Gall, explains:

> By late November [2010], Rhondda Cynon Taf (10,000 employees), Sheffield city council (8,500), Birmingham city council (26,000), Walsall (8,400), Croydon (4,000), London fire service (700) and Northumberland county council (14,780) had all begun the process of dismissing their workforces in order to then re-engage them on poorer terms and conditions of employment. The main focus of the imposed deterioration here was pay, because it gives a more immediate saving on labour costs.[161]

In many of these and other cases it is thought that the employer issued a section 188 notice. This is despite the fact that there was probably no desire to make anyone redundant in the traditional sense, but a desire only to vary terms and conditions as a result of government-imposed budget cuts.

As we have seen, the CJEU has since held that the Directive applies where the employer is imposing changes which if not accepted will lead to termination.[162] It might be argued that

---

[158] SI 2004 No. 3426.   [159] *Ibid.*, reg. 22(4).

[160] See *Kelly* v. *Hesley Group Ltd* [2013] IRLR 514, an important case.

[161] Gregor Gall, *Guardian CiF*, 7 July 2011.

[162] C-422/14, *Pujante Rivera* v. *Gestora Clubs Dir SL* [2016] IRLR 51; and C-149/16, *Socha* v. *Szpital Specjalistyczny im. A. Falkiewicza we Wrocławiu* [2018] IRLR 72. See p. 637 above.

section 188 thus provides additional protection for employees where there is an imposed change as well as unwanted terminations.

In practice, however, there is a concern that consultation in these circumstances is a rather forlorn process, and what section 188 does is to provide an employer with a convenient vehicle to impose changes in an orderly manner under the cover of a statutory procedure that was initially designed for another purpose.

Information and Consultation Procedures

The provisions of the Information and Consultation Directive 2002 proved to be extremely controversial with British employers,[163] and it appears that the Labour government lobbied extensively to block the Directive. Indeed, it has been claimed that:

> the ETUC, the European [Trade] Union [Confederation] which represents European trade unions in Brussels ... was startled to find that the Directive had a strong and determined enemy in the new British government. 'Britain went to war to block the Directive', is how John Monks [then general secretary of the British TUC] puts it.[164]

Having failed to block the Directive, the UK government managed successfully to dilute its impact. The weaknesses of the Directive are now fully exposed by the Information and Consultation of Employees Regulations,[165] weaknesses reflected in the apparently limited use of the procedures they contain, even though these procedures would appear to be especially relevant in an age of austerity and the erosion of workers' rights. There are in fact a number of problems with the ICE Regulations, including the need for workers to trigger the formation of an information and consultation procedure, the encouragement to set up a voluntary 'pre-existing agreement' that need not meet the Directive's standard provisions, and (notwithstanding the comments above) the absence of a sensible enforcement regime even where a statutory procedure has been triggered.

---

[163] Directive 2002/14/EC of 11 March 2002 establishing a general framework for informing and consulting employees in the European Community.

[164] F. Beckett and D. Hencke, *The Blairs and Their Court* (London: Aurum Press, 2004), p. 201.

[165] SI 2004 No. 3426. See G. M. Truter, *Implementing the Information and Consultation Directive in the UK: Lessons from Germany* (London: Institute of Employment Rights, 2003); K. D. Ewing and G. M. Truter, 'The Information and Consultation of Employees Regulations: Voluntarism's Bitter Legacy' (2005) 68 *Modern Law Review* 626; M. Hall, 'Assessing the Information and Consultation of Employees Regulations' (2005) 34 *Industrial Law Journal* 103; and M. Hall, 'A Cool Response to the ICE Regulations? Employer and Trade Union Approaches to the New Legal Framework for Information and Consultation' (2006) 37 *Industrial Relations Journal* 456.

Questions of Scope

The ICE Regulations apply only to undertakings employing more than fifty employees (not workers). The government thus chose to adopt the most conservative option when implementing the Directive – preferring a threshold of fifty employees in an undertaking rather than twenty employees in an establishment.[166] An 'undertaking' is defined to mean 'a public or private undertaking carrying out an economic activity, whether or not operating for gain'.[167] While this appears to be wide in scope, it is thought to exclude the activities of central government departments, though the government has introduced a Code of Practice to apply the substance of the Directive to the civil service.[168] So far as an 'economic activity' is concerned, this is not a phrase which is known to British labour law, and the government seems content to leave the matter to the courts to sort out. In holding that ACAS was engaged in economic activity for the purposes of the Regulations, the CAC read the term widely and rejected the argument that the phrase should be equated with 'commercial activity'. According to the CAC, an employer (in this case ACAS) could be carrying out economic activity even though funded 90 per cent by government grants and 10 per cent by charging for services.[169]

The significance of limiting the application of the Directive to undertakings employing more than fifty rather than establishments employing more than twenty is demonstrated clearly in *Pye and Partnerships in Care Ltd*,[170] where thirty-one employees submitted a request to the company for the establishment of information and consultation arrangements, claiming that the request had been made by over 10 per cent of the employees at Redford Lodge Hospital. The applicant argued that Redford Lodge was an autonomous unit within Partnerships in Care Ltd and that letters sent to staff were routinely headed Redford Lodge rather than Partnerships in Care Ltd. It was also argued that operational practices were governed by management at Redford Lodge and that the company had described Redford Lodge as a local employment unit during ET proceedings. Nevertheless, the CAC accepted the respondent's argument that 'Redford Lodge is but one of its establishments and that the undertaking is Partnerships in Care Ltd', which was 'a company employing some 2,700 staff across several locations', there being 'no evidence that the Company comprises a number of separate undertakings'.

---

[166] ICE Regulations, reg. 3.   [167] ICE Regulations, reg. 2.

[168] Cabinet Office, Code of Practice on Informing and Consulting Employees in the Civil Service, available at www.civilservice.gov.uk.

[169] *Public Services Union and ACAS*, CAC Case No. IC/54/16. See now *ACAS* v. *PCS* [2018] ICR 1793 (CAC upheld).

[170] *Pye and Partnerships in Care Ltd*, CAC Case IC/11/2007.

Meaning of Undertaking

A variation of this issue arose in *Moyer-Lee* v. *Cofely Workplace Ltd*,[171] where the employer employed 210 employees under a service contract with the University of London. However, the employer also had many other contracts with other organisations and had a total workforce of 9,200 employees working at 600 different sites. In this case twenty-eight employees at the University of London combined to make a request under the regulations, representing 13 per cent of the staff on the University of London contract but 0.3 per cent of the respondent's total workforce. In upholding the CAC's decision that the employees engaged on the University of London service contract were not engaged in a separate undertaking, the EAT held that 'there is no principled basis' for suggesting an undertaking should be construed 'as merely a division or department' of a single employer.[172]

The effect of the high threshold of fifty employees is that about one-third of the UK workforce will not be covered by the ICE Regulations, which apply to only a small minority of employers. At the time of transposition of the Directive, there were thought to be roughly 24 million employees in the UK, of whom some 17 million were thought to work for employers employing fifty or more employees: this means that some 7 million workers would be denied coverage. There were also thought to be some 1.2 million employers in the UK, of whom only 36,500 employed fifty or more employees. But even then, not all employers of more than fifty people would be covered. This is because an employer can choose not to count certain part-time employees as whole employees. By virtue of regulation 4(2)(b), an employee working for 75 hours or fewer a month may be treated as a half employee. This latter provision appears to be particularly controversial, not only because there is no provision for it in the Directive, but also because it appears to cut across initiatives such as the Part-Time Workers Directive which were designed to address discrimination against part-time workers.[173]

The uncertain legal basis for this discriminatory treatment is highlighted by the *CGT* case (discussed above) in relation to the Collective Redundancies

---

[171] [2015] IRLR 879.

[172] Although it is not possible to claim that a 'division or department' within a company is a separate undertaking, on the other hand a separate company within the same corporate group is nevertheless a separate undertaking. So in *Coombs and Holder and G E Aviation Systems Ltd*, CAC Case IC/43/(2012), it was held that each separate legal entity of a wholly owned global enterprise was a separate undertaking, and the contention that 'the 4 separate UK companies within the GE Aviation division, should be treated as a single undertaking was contrary not only to the legal requirements of the Regulations, but to the structure of the business' (*ibid.*). In that case the decision was not unhelpful to the applicant, the employer arguing unsuccessfully that there was a single rather than multiple undertakings.

[173] Directive 97/81/EC. See A. Davies, '"Half a Person": A Legal Perspective on Organizing and Representing "Non-Standard" Workers', in A. Bogg and T. Novitz (eds.), *Voice at Work: Continuity and Change in the Common Law World* (Oxford University Press, 2014), Ch. 6.

Directive.[174] In the same proceedings, however, the ECJ was asked to consider whether it would be permissible to exclude employees under the age of twenty-six from the Information and Consultation Directive. Here, the Court responded by noting that, under Article 2(d) of the latter Directive, an 'employee' means any person who, in the Member State concerned, is 'protected as an employee under national employment law and in accordance with national practice'.[175] Since employees under the age of twenty-six were protected by national employment legislation, they were therefore to be treated as employees for the purposes of the Directive. But although this might be thought to call into question the discriminatory treatment of part-time workers in the British regulations, the Court also acknowledged Article 3(1), which provides that Member States are to determine the method for calculating the thresholds of employees employed. Although the Directive 'does not prescribe the manner in which the Member States are to take account of employees falling within its scope',[176] it seems most unlikely that this would permit discrimination against what is otherwise a protected group of workers.

Pre-existing Agreements

An employer *may* take the initiative to establish an information and consultation procedure, though there is no obligation on the part of the employer to do so.[177] In the absence of such an initiative, by virtue of regulation 7, a request may be made by at least 2 per cent of the employees in the undertaking to negotiate an information and consultation procedure.[178] An employee (or an employee's representative) may request data from the employer in order to determine the number of people employed by the employer.[179] If the employer refuses to comply, a complaint may be made to the CAC.[180] The requirement

---

[174] Case C-385/05, *Confédération Générale du Travail (CGT)* v. *Premier Ministre and Ministre de l'Emploi, de la Cohésion Sociale et du Logement* [2007] 2 CMLR 6. See also Case C-176/12, *Association de Médiation Sociale* v. *Hichem Laboubi* [2014] ICR 411

[175] *Ibid.*, para. 31.　　[176] *Ibid.*, para. 34.

[177] ICE Regulations, reg. 11. Indeed, a major weakness of the Regulations is that (unlike the redundancy consultation procedures where the duty to inform and consult is obligatory), the establishment of an information and consultation procedure is not mandatory.

[178] Until 2019, the request had to be made by at least 10 per cent of the employees in the undertaking. See below, p. 683. In practice, the request may be made by a trade union on behalf of a group of workers: see *Amicus and Macmillan Publishers Ltd*, CAC Cases IC/04/2005 and IC/08/2006; *Unite the Union and Newsquest (Worcester) Ltd*, CAC Case IC/12/2007. But see *Nixon and Freightliner Ltd*, CAC Case IC/32/2010, where it is suggested that there must be some evidence (such as a letter of authority) that the union (in this case a non-recognised union) is acting on behalf of employees.

[179] ICE Regulations, reg. 5.

[180] ICE Regulations, reg. 6. See *Amicus and Macmillan Publishers Ltd*, CAC Case IC/04/2005 (and subsequently *Amicus* v. *Macmillan Publishers Ltd* [2007] IRLR 885 (EAT)); *Darnton and Bournemouth University*, CAC Case IC/14/2007; *Nixon and Freightliner Ltd*, CAC Case IC/32/2010.

of 2 per cent may, however, be misleading in some cases in view of the fact that the request must be made by a minimum of fifteen employees.[181] This means that, in smaller undertakings, the threshold requirement is in fact much higher, and indeed may be as high as 30 per cent in the case of an undertaking which employs fifty people. Conversely, in the case of very large undertakings, if the 2 per cent requirement would lead to more than 2,500 having to request the establishment of an information and consultation procedure, the limit is fixed at 2,500.[182] In practice, however, the fact that the creation of an information and consultation procedure will normally have to rely on triggering by employees means that it is less likely to happen.

Apart from the fact that the employer is not obliged to initiate a procedure, another concern is that it is possible to have what is referred to as a 'pre-existing agreement' in place of a statutory information and consultation procedure. A pre-existing agreement does not mean an agreement in place before the ICE Regulations came into force as might be assumed (and as is the case in relation to EWCs).[183] Rather, it means an agreement in force before an application is made by employees under regulation 7 to set up an information and consultation procedure under the ICE Regulations. By virtue of regulation 8(1), to be valid a pre-existing agreement must be in writing, it must cover all the employees in the undertaking, it must be approved by all the employees[184] and it must 'set out how the employer is to give information to the employees or their representatives and to seek their views on such information'. The reason why a pre-existing agreement may be a problem is that such agreements may make less favourable provision than those arrangements governed by the ICE Regulations. A pre-existing agreement simply requires the employer to 'seek [the] views' of employees or their representatives, without so much as a duty to respond.[185]

Although pre-existing agreements may be used to limit the scope of the ICE Regulations, they may also be used by employers and trade unions to preserve existing arrangements for employee representation, through the single channel of collective bargaining. It is open to the employer and the trade union to conclude a collective agreement that purports to meet the requirements of regulation 8, which may then make it difficult for non-union employees to

---

[181] ICE Regulations, reg. 7(3).

[182] For the purposes of regs. 7 and 8, a part-time worker becomes a whole person once again.

[183] See pp. 687–8.

[184] But as the EAT pointed out in *Moray Council* v. *Stewart* [2006] ICR 1253, para. 37, the Regulations do not prescribe any particular way by which employee approval is to be demonstrated. The EAT also noted that the position in relation to pre-existing agreements under reg. 8 contrasted sharply with the position relating to negotiated agreements under reg. 16 (on which, see below).

[185] ICE Regulations, reg. 8(1)(d). In contrast, consultation for negotiated agreements governed by the statutory procedures means 'the exchange of views' and the 'establishment of a dialogue' (reg. 2), while consultation that takes place under the standard procedure must do so 'with a view to reaching an agreement'.

establish a second channel of employee representation in the form of an information and consultation procedure. True, where a pre-existing agreement is in place, it is still open to 10 per cent of the employees to request that a statutory information and consultation procedure is established. But unless 40 per cent of the employees make the request, the employer is required to agree only after a ballot (held by the employer),[186] in which a majority of those voting support the establishment of such a procedure, with the majority of those voting representing at least 40 per cent of those eligible to vote.[187] But while this is a formidable procedure, we should not under-estimate the difficulties in practice of squeezing collective agreements into the regulation 8(1) definition of a pre-existing agreement. If the collective agreement does not meet the requirements of regulation 8, a request by 10 per cent of the employees will be enough to trigger an information and consultation procedure, to operate alongside the collective bargaining procedures.

The issue arose in *Moray Council* v. *Stewart*,[188] where over 500 employees made a request for a procedure to be established. The employer argued that there was no need to begin steps to initiate an information and consultation procedure, for although the request was made by more than 10 per cent of the employees (as the law then required), there were pre-existing agreements in force and the 500 or so employees did not represent 40 per cent. In these circumstances, the employer was not prepared to initiate a procedure without a ballot in which at least 40 per cent of those eligible to vote would have to vote in favour of establishing a procedure. The applicants argued, however, that there was no valid pre-existing agreement, on the ground that the agreements in question did not fall within the definition of a pre-existing agreement in regulation 8(1). The disputed pre-existing agreements were collective agreements between the employer and a number of trade unions, which appeared to cover the bulk of the workforce and applied to union members and non-members alike, as is the standard practice in the UK. It was held by both the CAC and (on appeal) the EAT that the agreements met the second and third of the regulation 8(1) requirements for a pre-existing agreement, but not the fourth in the sense that one of them (relating to schoolteachers) failed to set out how the employer gave information to employees or their representatives and sought their views on the information.[189]

---

[186] The employer must notify the employees within one month of the request being made under reg. 7 of its intention to hold a ballot; otherwise, the employer must proceed to negotiate an agreement under the Regulations: see *Unite the Union and Newsquest (Worcester) Ltd*, CAC Case IC/12/2007.

[187] ICE Regulations, reg. 8(6). Complaints about ballot irregularities may be made by an employee or an employee's representative to the CAC (*ibid.*, reg. 10).

[188] [2006] IRLR 598. For discussion of *Stewart*, see R. Dukes, 'The ICE Regulations: Pre-Existing Agreements and Standard Provisions: A Warning to Employers' (2007) 36 *Industrial Law Journal* 329.

[189] There being no pre-existing agreement, the employer would thus be required to enter into negotiations to set up an information and consultation procedure, the collective agreements in

Establishing a Procedure

Where a valid request has been made under regulations 7 or 8, the employer must make arrangements for the election or appointment of negotiating representatives and invite these representatives to enter into negotiations to reach a negotiated agreement.[190] By regulation 14(2), the procedures for appointing or electing negotiating representatives must ensure that all employees are entitled to take part in the appointment or election process. The procedures must also be arranged in such a way as to ensure that all employees are represented in the proceedings.[191]

Complying with ICE Regulation 14(2)

In *Morrissey* v. *University of London*,[192] a group of employees made a request to establish an information and consultation procedure. The employer already recognised two trade unions but only about 25 per cent of the workforce was in membership of either. Thereafter the employer agreed with the unions to revise existing procedures to accommodate the requirements of the Regulations but made 'no attempt to invite non-union members to put forward candidates for appointment or election, nor to put across a clear message that the union representatives would also represent non-members'. While accepting that regulation 14 gave the employer a significant element of flexibility when establishing information and consultation procedures, the EAT agreed with the CAC that the employer had failed to comply with regulation 14(2), which called for participation of 'a meaningful kind by the employees in the process of election or appointment', which required in turn 'the engagement of all of the employees so far as can be achieved'. According to the EAT, 'the Regulations seek to achieve is demonstrably not that placemen acceptable to the employer, but only to a minority of the workforce, should be representatives, however much that might fall within the wording of the Regulation if narrowly approached'.

The parties have nine months from the date of the employee request to conclude an agreement, failing which the standard procedure outlined below

---

that case not being regarded as pre-existing agreements for the purposes of the Regulations. Although the second and third requirements of reg. 8 were satisfied in this case by an agreement made by collective bargaining, it might be a mistake to think that employers and trade unions could inevitably address *Stewart* with the simple expedient of clearer provisions in collective agreements to deal with the fourth requirement of reg. 8. It may thus be that a collective agreement with a recognised trade union will not necessarily meet the requirements of a pre-existing agreement, and that employees excluded from its scope could then bring a claim under reg. 7, assuming they could command what is now 2 per cent of all employees.

[190] ICE Regulations, reg. 14.

[191] ICE Regulations, reg. 14(2). Complaints about the appointment or election of negotiating representatives may be made to the CAC (*ibid.*, reg. 15), as may complaints about the conduct of the ballot under reg. 16 (*ibid.*, reg. 17). For the corresponding provisions of the TICE Regulations (which are considered in more detail), see below.

[192] [2016] ICR 893.

applies. So far as negotiated agreements are concerned, the ICE Regulations provide that they must cover all employees of the undertaking and may consist either of a single agreement or 'of different parts ... which, taken together, cover all the employees of the undertaking'.[193] The agreement (or each part of it) must set out the circumstances in which the employer must inform and consult the employees to which it relates, and these employees must approve the agreement, in a manner prescribed by regulation 16(3).[194] The information that must be provided need not necessarily satisfy the requirements of the standard procedure outlined below. And although there is a duty to consult within the definition of consultation in regulation 2, there is no duty to do so with a view to reaching an agreement.

Apart from pre-existing agreements and negotiated agreements, a third type of arrangement for which provision is thus made are those arrangements based on the standard procedure set out in regulation 20. The latter will apply either where the parties agree that it should, or where they are unable otherwise to agree an alternative procedure. Regulation 19 provides that, where the standard provisions apply, the employer must make arrangements for the holding of a ballot of its employees to elect information and consultation representatives. There should be one elected representative for every fifty employees, with a minimum of two and a maximum of twenty-five representatives. The ballot procedures are laid out in Schedule 2 to the ICE Regulations and make provision for eligibility to be a candidate and to vote. It is for the employer to decide whether there should be a single constituency or a series of constituencies to 'better reflect the interests of the employees as a whole'. Thereafter, the employer must appoint an independent person to supervise the conduct of the ballot, to ensure that those voting are able to do so in secret and that the votes given in the ballot are fairly and accurately counted. It is also for the employer to meet the costs of the ballot (including the costs of the ballot supervisor). Complaints about the failure to hold a ballot or about the conduct of the ballot may be made to the CAC.

In terms of the substance of the duty to inform and consult, regulation 20 essentially writes into domestic law Article 4 of the Directive. Regulation 20 (1) provides that:

> (1) ... the employer must provide the information and consultation representatives with information on –
> > (a) the recent and probable development of the undertaking's activities and economic situation;
> > (b) the situation, structure and probable development of employment within the undertaking and on any anticipatory measures envisaged,

---

[193] ICE Regulations, reg. 16(1).
[194] This means that the agreement must be signed by all the negotiating representatives. If signed by only a majority of them, the agreement must then be approved by the employees, in some cases by a ballot.

in particular, where there is a threat to employment within the undertaking; and

(c) subject to paragraph (5), decisions likely to lead to substantial changes in work organisation or in contractual relations . . .

The information referred to in paragraph (1) must be 'given at such time, in such fashion and with such content as are appropriate to enable, in particular, the information and consultation representatives to conduct an adequate study and, where necessary, to prepare for consultation'.[195] Consultation must take place on the matters referred to in paragraph (1)(b) and (c), and the employer must ensure that the consultation is conducted:

(a) in such a way as to ensure that the timing, method and content of the consultation are appropriate;

(b) on the basis of the information supplied by the employer to the information and consultation representatives and of any opinion which those representatives express to the employer;

(c) in such a way as to enable the information and consultation representatives to meet the employer at the relevant level of management depending on the subject under discussion and to obtain a reasoned response from the employer to any such opinion; and

(d) in relation to matters falling within paragraph (1)(c), with a view to reaching agreement on decisions within the scope of the employer's powers.[196]

There are two points to note about regulation 20. The first is that – as already indicated – it includes a higher standard in terms of information to be provided and the consultation to be undertaken than either pre-existing agreements or negotiated agreements. Consultation is defined as meaning the establishment of a dialogue, which must be undertaken with a view to reaching an agreement.[197] There are thus in fact three ways in which the term consultation is used in the regulations, from the weakest form in relation to pre-existing agreements, through negotiated agreements, to the highest form in relation to the standard procedure. The other point to note is that regulation 20 deals with the interface between the ICE Regulations and the redundancy and transfer of undertaking consultation procedures. By virtue of regulation 20(5), the former cease to apply when the latter become applicable. The latter have a different regime in the event of non-compliance. As we have seen, however, there is uncertainty about when the duty to consult arises in a redundancy situation: does it arise at the time of a strategic decision, making redundancies inevitable or at a later date? If the CJEU decides in favour of the latter,[198] it seems likely that the employer would continue to have a duty to

---

[195] ICE Regulations, reg. 20(2).   [196] ICE Regulations, reg. 20(4).
[197] ICE Regulations, regs. 2 and 20(4)(d), respectively.   [198] See pp. 656–8.

inform and consult about the former under the ICE Regulations if not under the collective redundancy procedure.[199]

Decisions Likely to Lead to Substantial Changes in Work Organisation or in Contractual Relations

Regulation 20(1)(c) is perhaps the most important substantive provision in the Directive. Although there have been very few cases disputing its meaning, all have been unsuccessful. The CAC has tended to emphasise the need for the change to be substantial in relation to the employer concerned. So the planned dismissal of people representing less than 1 per cent of the workforce was not 'substantial', nor was a change to a new office layout, even though in the former case it would be substantial to the individuals concerned.[200]

In the former case, the CAC pointed out that 'once the number of redundancies proposed exceeds 19 in any period of 90 days [TULRCA 1992, section 188] requires employers to consult with a view to reaching agreement with the representatives of any recognised trade union or, if none exists, employee representatives, which category includes representatives elected under the standard provisions. Thus, the Regulations under consideration in this case do not carry the whole burden of providing consultation in respect of proposed redundancies.'[201]

While Regulation 20(1)(c) clearly has a role to play in redundancy preparation, it is important to emphasise that it is about more than redundancy. In *Wright and Rolls Royce plc*,[202] the question was whether a change to travel policy fell within the paragraph's scope, the CAC holding that the arrangements in question were neither contractual nor related to work organisation. Despite its potential importance, this is a provision that is yet to take off.

Enforcing the Employer's Obligation

What happens if the employer fails to provide information or to consult as required by an information and consultation procedure? Exceptionally, the employer may withhold information the disclosure of which would 'according to objective criteria' 'seriously harm the functioning of, or would be prejudicial to, the undertaking'.[203] Otherwise, however, Article 8 of the Directive provides that:

---

[199] In that case, however, the extent of the duty will depend on workers having taken the initiative to establish an information and consultation procedure that complies fully with the standard provisions. They would be foolish not to do so.

[200] *Gale and Bournemouth University*, CAC Case IC/28/2009; and *Darnton and Bournemouth University*, CAC Case IC/25/2009, respectively.

[201] *Gale and Bournemouth University*, CAC Case IC/28/2009, para. 35.

[202] CAC Case IC/46/(2013).

[203] ICE Regulations, reg. 26. A complaint may be made to the CAC to contest the withholding of information on this ground, and the CAC may order disclosure if it takes the view that disclosure would not be seriously harmful or prejudicial. By virtue of ICE Regulations, reg. 25, it is a breach of statutory duty for an employee representative to disclose information provided in confidence. For the corresponding provisions of the Transnational Information and Consultation of Employees Regulations 1999 (TICE Regulations), see p. 699.

1. Member States shall provide for appropriate measures in the event of non-compliance with this Directive by the employer or the employees' representatives. In particular, they shall ensure that adequate administrative or judicial procedures are available to enable the obligations deriving from this Directive to be enforced.

2. Member States shall provide for adequate sanctions to be applicable in the event of infringement of this Directive by the employer or the employees' representatives. These sanctions must be effective, proportionate and dissuasive.

It is important to note here that the Directive provides a framework of enforcement and sanctions against a recalcitrant employer, but does not make provision for remedies by way of compensation for employees prejudiced by the employer's failure. It is also important to note that no provision is made for mandatory status quo orders, whereby the employer is required to refrain from taking action until he or she has complied with obligations stemming from the Directive. But nor does the Directive appear to prohibit such orders.

In implementing the enforcement provisions of the Directive, the ICE Regulations provide that a complaint may be made to the CAC by appropriate employee representatives, but only where there is a negotiated agreement, or if the standard provisions apply.[204] If the CAC finds the complaint well founded, it must make a declaration to that effect, and may 'make an order requiring the employer to take such steps as are necessary to comply with the terms of the negotiated agreement or, as the case may be, the standard information and consultation provisions'.[205] The foregoing order must specify the steps the employer is required to take, and the period within which the order must be complied with. However, it is important to note the limitations of any such order, with regulation 22(9) providing that:

> No order of the CAC under this regulation shall have the effect of suspending or altering the effect of any act done or of any agreement made by the employer or of preventing or delaying any act or agreement which the employer proposes to do or to make.

This means in effect that, although an employer can be ordered to inform and consult about, say, changes to working practices (and to do so with a view to reaching an agreement), the same employer ultimately cannot be compelled to do so and cannot be restrained from taking decisions even where these decisions are in breach of duties under the ICE Regulations.

What happens if the employer fails to comply with the CAC order? Here we encounter another unusual procedure, in the sense that the matter may be referred by the original applicant in the CAC proceedings to the EAT for a penalty notice

---

[204] There is no way of enforcing a pre-existing agreement under the ICE Regulations, although conceivably the agreement itself may make provision for breach. There is also the question whether such agreements would be caught by the common-law and statutory presumptions against the legal enforceability of collective agreements, on which see pp. 128–9; 583–4.

[205] ICE Regulations, reg. 22(4).

to be issued.[206] This will require the employer to pay a sum to the Secretary of State in respect of the failure unless the EAT is satisfied that there is a reasonable excuse for the failure.[207] The amount of the penalty must not exceed £75,000, the amount to depend on the gravity of the failure, the period of time over which the failure occurred, the reason for the failure, the number of employees affected by the failure and the number of employees employed by the undertaking.[208] The only case so far in which this procedure was invoked involved a failure by the employer to comply with an order to set up election procedures for information and consultation representatives, rather than a failure to provide information or engage in consultations.[209] In that case, the EAT thought it necessary to impose a penalty that would 'deter others from adopting what can only be described as the wholly cavalier attitude to their obligations that has been demonstrated by the respondent'. While accepting that this was not 'the most serious breach of these obligations which might be envisaged', the EAT held that it was 'nonetheless a very grave breach', and a penalty of £55,000 was imposed.

The foregoing provisions are designed to provide an exclusive remedy for infringement of the rights conferred by the ICE Regulations.[210] It is not clear, however, whether they meet the requirements of the Directive that the sanction should be 'effective, proportionate and dissuasive'.[211] The imposition of a sanction for failure to comply with the duty to inform and consult (where it exists) ultimately depends on the willingness of a trade union (as the employees' representative) to pursue the employer through the CAC and on to the EAT for the imposition of a financial penalty. But there may be little incentive for the union to incur the expense of pursuing at least the latter claim, given that any penalty imposed would be paid to the government rather than to the union or the employees who have been affected by the failure to consult. The union is unable even to recover its costs in these proceedings (whether internal staff costs or external legal costs). Some may see this as a cynical way of undermining a weak enforcement regime, the state outsourcing what ought to be a public responsibility, and doing so without paying for the service outsourced. Apart from anything else, quite how employee representatives in a non-union company are expected to seek a sanction in the EAT, against their own employer and at their own expense, has never been explained.

Protection of Employee Representatives

The final issue to consider relates to the protection of employee representatives. The Directive provides, by Article 7, that:

---

[206]   ICE Regulations, reg. 22(6).   [207]   ICE Regulations, reg. 22(7).
[208]   ICE Regulations, reg. 23(1) and (2).
[209]   *Amicus* v. *Macmillan Publishers Ltd* [2007] IRLR 885.   [210]   ICE Regulations, reg. 24.
[211]   See further K. D. Ewing and G. M. Truter, 'The Information and Consultation of Employees Regulations: Voluntarism's Bitter Legacy' (2005) 68 *Modern Law Review* 626.

Member States shall ensure that employees' representatives, when carrying out their functions, enjoy adequate protection and guarantees to enable them to perform properly the duties which have been assigned to them.

The ICE Regulations provide:

- A right to paid time off for negotiating representatives and information and consultation representatives. The representatives in question are entitled to 'reasonable time off' during working hours 'in order to perform [their] functions as such a representative'.[212] Complaints about refusal of time off or failure to pay for the time off are to be made to an ET.[213]
- Protection from detriment or dismissal for an employee who is (a) an employees' representative, (b) a negotiating representative, (c) an information and consultation representative, or (d) a candidate in an election for any of these positions. The employee is protected in relation to the performance of any function or activities as a representative or candidate.[214]

It might be said that this is a very minimalist interpretation of the Directive's requirements, which requires 'adequate protection and guarantees' to enable representatives to 'perform properly' the duties of office. With this in mind, a number of points are to be noted:

- The negotiating representatives and the information and consultation representatives are entitled to time-off only to enable them to perform their duties as representatives. This contrasts with ERA 1996, section 61, which deals with the right to time-off of employee representatives appointed or elected for the purposes of consultation about redundancies or the transfer of an undertaking. As well as time off to perform their duties as an employee representative, ERA 1996, section 61, also allows time-off for candidates. It is not clear why the same provision could not also apply to the ICE Regulations, particularly as candidates are expressly protected from detriment and dismissal by regulations 32 and 30 respectively. It is all the more surprising that candidates should be denied the right to time-off (with pay) when candidates enjoy such a right under the TICE Regulations 1999.[215]
- The right to time-off for information and consultation representatives compares very unfavourably with the provisions in TULRCA 1992, section 168.[216] This deals with the right of trade union officials to time-off for trade union duties, defined to mean duties relating to collective bargaining. There is a difference between the two in the sense that the meaning of trade union duties is to be determined by reference to the ACAS Code of Practice 3 on Time Off for Trade Union Duties and Activities. This makes it clear that trade union duties include not only negotiations with the employer, but also,

---

[212] ICE Regulations, reg. 27.   [213] ICE Regulations, reg. 29.
[214] ICE Regulations, regs. 30 and 32.   [215] SI 1999 No. 3323, regs. 25 and 26.
[216] See pp. 615–18.

for example, preparation for negotiations, informing members of progress and explaining outcomes to members. There is no similar guidance for ICE representatives, who may also need time off to consult external advisers off site and to report on these consultations to the workforce. Additionally, they may need time off to meet with other representatives in the company.

In addition, there are concerns about the lack of facilities to be made available to the information and consultation representatives. In particular, there is no time-off for training, and there is no provision for other facilities being made available. This contrasts unfavourably with the provisions relating to trade union officials in respect of whom provision is made in the ACAS Code of Practice. The Code refers to accommodation for meetings, access to a telephone and email, the use of notice boards, the use of dedicated office space and access to members employed at different locations.[217] It also contrasts unfavourably with the rights of employee representatives in redundancy and transfer of undertaking cases, in relation to which the employer 'shall allow the appropriate representatives access to the affected employees and shall afford to those representatives such accommodation and other facilities as may be appropriate'.[218] There is also the question of financial resources being made available to information and consultation representatives. The silence of the ICE Regulations compares with the TICE Regulations, the schedule to which provides that management 'shall provide the members of the European Works Council with such financial and material resources as enable them to perform their duties in an appropriate manner'.[219]

Implementing the Directive

As suggested above, it is widely thought that the ICE Regulations have had a limited impact, with a low take-up by employees. Some evidence to support this view is to be found in the number of complaints to the CAC under the ICE Regulations. By the end of the year 2016–17, there had been only fifty-seven applications to the CAC in the first eleven years of the scheme's operation, albeit raising a wide range of issues. Indeed, in recent years there has been a significant reduction in activity, with only fourteen applications between 2012 and 2017, leading to only seven CAC decisions under this jurisdiction

---

[217] ACAS, Code of Practice on Time Off for Trade Union Duties and Activities (2010), p. 21.
[218] See TULRCA 1992, s. 188(5A).
[219] TICE Regulations, Schedule, para. 9(6). It is further provided there that 'the cost of organising meetings and arranging for interpretation facilities and the accommodation and travelling expenses of members of the European Works Council and its select committee shall be met by the central management unless the central management and European Works Council, or select committee, otherwise agree'.

in that period,[220] two of which were contested by way of appeal to the EAT. Given some of the problems referred to above, the limited use of the procedure is perhaps not surprising, particularly in non-union workplaces. The difficulties in organising workforce support without any resources, in circumstances where the employer may regard the employee's conduct to be provocative, are not to be under-estimated. But although the law was changed following the recommendation of a government-appointed inquiry that the 10 per cent threshold should be reduced to 2 per cent,[221] this may serve little purpose unless the regulations were to apply to establishments rather than undertakings. The problems exposed by *Pye* and *Moyer-Lee*, above, will not easily be overcome without a significant change in the law that permits workers to trigger information and consultation procedures at their place of work.[222]

What is perhaps more surprising is the failure of trade unions to engage more fully with the information and consultation procedures, particularly at a time when their members' terms and conditions of employment are under threat by changes taking place in workplaces the length and breadth of the country. It is true that the ICE Regulations differ significantly from other information and consultation procedures transposed by domestic legislation from EU law. The normal practice hitherto has been to consolidate the position of a recognised trade union by requiring the employer to inform and consult the union, and elected representatives only in the absence of a recognised union.[223] In this way, a single channel of representation is preserved, with consultation rights being an additional benefit of recognition. In the case of the ICE Regulations (and specifically the duty to inform and consult about changes) in contrast, the recognised trade union has no priority status, and indeed the ICE Regulations can be used in principle by non-members to dilute the role of the union by requiring the establishment of two separate channels of representation in the same workplace.[224] This possibility seems to be reinforced by the decision in the *Moray Council* v. *Stewart* case (discussed above), where the local authority with what appeared to be comprehensive coverage of collective agreements was ordered by the CAC to initiate an information and consultation procedure in proceedings brought by an employee who was not a union member.

But although recognised trade unions have no priority under the ICE Regulations, it remains the case that they are likely to be the key to the successful operation of the information and consultation procedures, and that

---

[220] These are all referred to above except for *Demming and Coin Street Community Builders*, CAC Case IC/41/(2012) and *Hayward and Sita UK*, CAC No. IC/44/(2012).

[221] M. Taylor, *Good Work: The Taylor Review of Modern Working Practices* (2017), p. 53.

[222] See also K. Bates, A. Bogg and T. Novitz, '"Voice" and "Choice" in Modern Working Practices: Problems with the Taylor Review' (2018) 47 *Industrial Law Journal* 46.

[223] See pp. 658–60.

[224] See also *Nixon and Freightliner Ltd*, CAC Case IC/32/2010 (use of reg. 5 by non-recognised union to obtain information).

the most likely consequence of the Regulations is that they will expand the scope of collective bargaining rather than the scope of worker representation. Partly this is because the Regulations require workers to take the initiative to establish an information and consultation procedure, something more likely to happen in a unionised workforce where there are already representative structures in place. And partly this is because it is possible for an employer to enter into a 'pre-existing agreement' with a union for the purposes of information and consultation. There are strong incentives for an employer to reach such an agreement, the most important of which is that the statutory enforcement procedures do not apply. But even where there is no pre-existing agreement and steps are taken to invoke the statutory procedures, it is likely that it will be a trade union in a recognised workplace that co-ordinates such an initiative and that it will be a recognised trade union that will be behind any attempts to conclude a 'negotiated agreement' under the ICE Regulations.[225]

It is true that the establishment of a statutory information and consultation procedure may require a union to share a table with non-union representatives. But that would be a small price to pay for creating a process that the union would ultimately dominate. It is also a process that allows non-recognised unions to establish themselves in a company and for recognised unions to broaden their bargaining agenda (to the extent that regulation 20 requires negotiation about change). Moreover, this is a process that allows these things to be done under the supervision of the CAC in relation to agreements negotiated with trade unions as the *de facto* principal party. Indeed, the ICE Regulations (along with the TICE Regulations 1999) offer an unusual opportunity that enables trade unions to take a complaint to a public body which has the power to order the employer to negotiate with the union (though this has not yet been done in any of the decisions at the time of writing). In order to enjoy the benefit of these opportunities, however, trade unions need not only to engage with the procedure, but also to do so in a way that eschews unenforceable 'pre-existing agreements', and insists on the application of the legally enforceable standard provisions. The latter should be the floor rarely touched rather than the ceiling never reached. It is an extraordinary lapse on the part of the trade union movement that it has not made better use of this machinery.

European Works Councils

The TICE Regulations 1999[226] are designed to implement the EWC Directive. As we have seen, this provides for the establishment of EWCs, or agreed information and consultation procedures as an alternative. The TICE

---

[225] See *Morrissey* v. *University of London* [2016] IRLR 893.

[226] SI 1999 No. 3323. See M. Carley and M. Hall, 'The Implementation of the European Works Council Directive' (2000) 29 *Industrial Law Journal* 103.

Regulations were amended in 2010,[227] to give effect to the requirements of the so-called Recast Directive of 2009. It has been said that

> The purpose of the Directive and the Regulations is to provide employees in large Community-wide multinational companies with the right to be informed and consulted about transnational issues that affect them through an EWC or some tailor-made form of transnational information and consultation procedure.[228]

Although there are concerns that the TICE Regulations may not go as far as the Directive requires, it remains the case nevertheless that at the time of its implementation an estimated 265 UK-based companies were covered by the Directive, and that 113 UK-based companies had an EWC.[229] It is unlikely that trade unions will be recognised for the purposes of collective bargaining in all of these companies, though EWCs are most likely to operate effectively where there is a trade union presence. Indeed, under the amending Recast Directive, trade unions have acquired rights in the operation of EWCs. The Directive has thus enabled trade unions to take their bargaining concerns to a new level.

Questions of Scope

The TICE Regulations apply principally to UK-based transnational companies, which carry on significant activities in at least one other Member State. More precisely, they apply to 'Community-scale undertakings' (undertakings which employ at least 1,000 employees within the Member States, with at least 150 in at least two Member States).[230] They also apply to 'Community-scale groups of undertakings' (groups of undertakings operating in different Member States with at least 1,000 employees within the Member States; and at least two group undertakings in different Member States; and with two group undertakings in different Member States employing at least 150

---

[227] TICE (Amendment) Regulations 2010, SI 2010 No. 1088. The amendments came into force on 5 June 2011 and 1 October 2011. References to the TICE Regulations in this chapter are to the TICE Regulations as amended.

[228] *Lean and Manpower Group*, CAC Case No. EWC/15/2017, para. 68.

[229] Department for Business, Innovation and Skills, *Implementation of the Recast European Works Council Directive* (2010). These figures were said to imply 'a current take-up rate of 43 per cent, which compares with the EEA average of 36 per cent'. It was also pointed out that '60 per cent were created under Article 13 of the Directive, which allows companies to continue with agreements arranged before the Directive came into force, with the remaining 40 per cent having established newly formed council agreements under Article 6, which entails a specific procedure as set out by the Directive'. There are also many companies based in other Member States trading in the UK that will have EWCs on which there are British representatives.

[230] This is wide enough to include bodies such as the British Council, 'an executive non-departmental public body, a public corporation and a registered charity': *Haines and British Council*, CAC Case No. EWC/7/2012.

employees).[231] For these purposes, a 'group of undertakings' means a 'controlling undertaking and its controlled undertakings', terms extensively defined by regulation 3(1). The latter provides that a 'controlling undertaking' means 'an undertaking which can exercise a dominant influence over another undertaking by virtue, for example, of ownership, financial participation or the rules which govern it', while a controlled undertaking is an undertaking over which such a dominant influence can be exercised. A dominant influence is to be presumed where directly or indirectly one undertaking can appoint more than half of the members of the other's administrative, management or supervisory board, controls a majority of the shareholding, or holds a majority of the shares.

Where this threshold is met, the 'central management' is responsible for creating the conditions necessary for an EWC or an information and consultation procedure.[232] The question at this stage is who is the 'central management' for this purpose, given the transnational nature of the enterprises to which the TICE Regulations apply. Regulation 2 defines 'central management' in a rather circular fashion, to mean the central management of a Community-scale undertaking, or the central management of a controlling undertaking in the case of a Community-scale group of undertakings. Although not shining any further light on the definition of 'central management', regulation 5 nevertheless provides that the responsibility created by that regulation applies where the central management is situated in the UK, or a representative agent of the central management is situated in the UK (where the central management is situated elsewhere), or where more employees of the undertaking or group of undertakings are employed in the UK than in any other Member State (where neither the central management nor a representative agent is situated in the UK). By these means, the TICE Regulations apply not only to UK-based companies operating in the UK, and not only to EU-based companies operating in the UK, but also to companies based in any other country (most likely the USA) trading in the UK and at least one other Member State (assuming they meet the threshold number of employees).[233]

EWCs will thus be established in UK-based companies (as just described), in which case the TICE Regulations will of course apply. But EWCs will also be established in other EU Member States in which central management is based, in companies which also operate in the United Kingdom. In these cases, regulation 5 will not apply: responsibility will lie with the central management located in another Member State. UK-based workers of the undertaking or the group of undertakings may nevertheless be entitled to be represented on the

---

[231] TICE Regulations, reg. 4 (the definitions are to be found in reg. 2).

[232] *Ibid.*, reg. 5. There is no corresponding obligation in the ICE Regulations.

[233] See *CEMEX Investments Ltd and Federation Nationale des Salaries de la Construction CGT*, CAC Case EWC/3/2006 (company based in Mexico), and *Emerson Electric European Works Council and Emerson Electric Europe*, CAC Case No. EWC/13/2015 (company based in USA).

EWC and to take part in its activities.[234] Consequently, some of the provisions of the TICE Regulations apply to EWCs established in other Member States:

- regulations 7 and 8, dealing with the right of employees or employees' representatives to information to determine whether their employer is part of a Community-scale undertaking or group of undertakings;[235]
- regulations 13–15, dealing with elections to the SNB;
- regulation 18, the subsidiary requirements, so far as they deal with UK representation;
- regulation 23, dealing with the duty of confidentiality of EWC members;
- regulations 25–33, time-off for EWC members and protection from detriment and dismissal;
- regulations 34–9, dealing with the jurisdiction of the CAC and the EAT; and
- regulations 40 and 41, dealing with restrictions on contracting out.

Where the EWC is based in another Member State, the provisions of the TICE Regulations relating to its operation are otherwise not applicable, and any failure to comply with the duty to inform and consult would have to be pursued through the courts of the jurisdiction in which the EWC was established.

One final point that may be made here is that employers may avoid obligations under the TICE Regulations where there are 'pre-existing agreements' in force (though this is a term defined more narrowly than in the case of the ICE Regulations).[236] Thus the TICE Regulations excluding the operation of the legislation apply to agreements concluded by UK-based companies before 16 December 1999 (the date when the original Directive was first applicable in the UK) (so called Article 6 agreements),[237] and by non-UK-based companies before 23 September 1996 (when the original Directive came into force elsewhere in the EU) (so called Article 13 agreements).[238] In order to be exempt from the TICE Regulations, an agreement in force must cover the entire body of workers in the different Member States and provide for their transnational information and consultation.[239] There is no additional formality or minimum

---

[234] See *Morgan and Safron Group*, CAC Case No. EWC/8/2013 (French based company).

[235] On the corresponding provisions of the ICE Regulations, see p. 672.

[236] On which, pp. 672–74 above.   [237] See Directive 97/74/EC and Directive 2009/38/EC.

[238] On which, see *CEMEX Investments Ltd and Federation Nationale des Salaries de la Construction CGT*, CAC Case EWC/3/2006. In this important case, it was held that an Art. 13 agreement was not invalidated by the expansion of the business into new Member States. Although the requirement that the agreement should cover the entire workforce did not appear to be met, the CAC accepted that 'an agreement can be amended to take account of a shifting business landscape' (para. 62). It follows from this that an agreement does not cease to be an Art. 13 agreement because it has been amended or modified after 23 September 1996, the agreement in the *CEMEX* case containing an amendment clause. It is to be noted that regs. 44 and 45 now allow for the TICE Regulations to apply to both Art. 6 and Art. 13 agreements where there is no provision for the continuation of the EWC agreement or information and consultation procedure when there is a significant change in the structure of the undertaking.

[239] TICE Regulations, regs. 44 and 45.

standard that must be met.[240] In addition, provision is made to exempt from the obligations arising under the new Recast Directive existing agreements made under the umbrella of the original Directive. This applies to new agreements signed for the first time or to established agreements revised in some way, in both cases between 5 June 2009 and 5 June 2011.[241] The latter exemption derives from a provision in the Recast Directive that had been agreed between the ETUC and BUSINESSEUROPE, said by the ETUC to have been necessary in order to secure an agreement with BUSINESSEUROPE.

Special Negotiating Body

By regulation 7, an employee may request information from an employer to determine whether 'it is part of a Community-scale undertaking or Community-scale group of undertakings'. This may require the employer to provide information about 'the name and address of the unit or entity to which the Employer's employees and agency workers are assigned to carry out their duties', in order to enable the employee to obtain access to these employees to 'find out if others would like to join in his request to negotiate an agreement for a EWC'.[242] An EWC or an information and consultation procedure may be initiated by a request by at least a hundred employees or their representatives in at least two undertakings, in at least two Member States.[243] The constitution of the EWC or the information and consultation procedure is to be determined by a Special Negotiating Body (SNB).[244] The composition of the SNB was changed by the amendments to the TICE Regulations in 2010. The position now is that there should be balanced representation on the SNB from each of the Member States in which the undertaking operates. There should be one representative appointed or elected from each Member State for every 10 per cent (or fraction thereof) of the total number of employees of the undertaking in question.[245]

- To take a simple example, if the undertaking has 2,000 employees in total, of whom 1,000 are employed in the UK and 1,000 are employed in France, each would have five members. Where employees employed in a Member State constitute less than 10 per cent, they too must have a place.
- To take another simple example, if the undertaking has 2,000 employees of whom 1,000 are employed in the UK, 950 are employed in France and 50 in Luxembourg there would be eleven members: ten each from the UK and France, and one from Luxembourg.[246]

---

[240] See *CEMEX Investments Ltd and Federation Nationale des Salaries de la Construction CGT*, CAC Case EWC/3/2006.
[241] TICE Regulations, reg. 45A.
[242] *Agyemang-Prempah and Facilicom Services Group*, CAC Case No. EWC/14/2016.
[243] TICE Regulations, reg. 9.   [244] *Ibid.*, reg. 11.   [245] *Ibid.*, reg. 12(2).
[246] Once elected or appointed, the SNB must inform the central management, local managements and the 'European social partner organisations' of its composition and of the date it proposes to start negotiations: *ibid.*, reg. 12(4). The 'European social partner organisations' are not

The UK members of the SNB are to be nominated by a consultative committee where one exists,[247] failing which by a ballot of the UK employees.[248] It is unclear how far the definition of a consultative committee would enable a recognised trade union or trade unions to perform the role of the consultative committee.[249] It is true that (1) their normal functions would include carrying out an information and consultation function, (2) which is done without interference from management, and (3) in which the committee represents all the UK employees. The problem, however, is (d), that is to say, whether such a committee consists wholly of persons who were elected by a ballot (or a series of ballots) in which all the UK employees were entitled to vote. We saw above in *Moray Council* v. *Stewart* that, for the purposes of a 'pre-existing agreement' in the ICE Regulations, the CAC (and the EAT) were prepared to accept that a collective agreement could be said to cover 'all the employees' in the undertaking, and to 'have been approved by the employees' when signed or accepted by trade union officials.[250] However, it may be a stretch too far to say that a trade union committee would meet the requirements of the TICE Regulations that it is a committee 'wholly' of persons elected by a ballot (or a series of ballots) 'in which all the UK employees were entitled to vote'.[251]

So far as the ballots are concerned, it is the responsibility of management to make the necessary arrangements.[252] For this purpose, the election must comply with the requirements of regulation 13(3). This deals with (1) the constituencies, (2) the right to vote and (3) the right to stand as a candidate. So far as (1) is concerned, the distribution of constituencies is a management decision, with the employer to decide whether there should be a single UK constituency or a number of constituencies 'to better reflect the interests of UK employees as a whole'.[253] So far as (2) is concerned, eligibility to vote is extended to all employees on the day the ballot takes place or on the first of those days where the ballot runs over several days. And, so far as (3) is concerned, any employee or employees' representative may stand as a candidate. For this purpose, an employees' representative is defined to include a trade union official in cases where the union is recognised, and the official in question 'normally takes part as [a negotiator] in the collective bargaining process'.[254] The employer must also appoint an 'independent' ballot supervisor to supervise the conduct of the ballot,[255] and, so far as possible, must

---

defined. The Directive refers to 'the competent European workers' and employers' organisations' (Art. 5(2)(c)).

[247] *Ibid.*, reg. 15.   [248] *Ibid.*, reg. 13.   [249] *Ibid.*, reg. 15(4).

[250] *Moray Council* v. *Stewart* [2006] ICR 1253.

[251] At best, they would be elected in a ballot, in which all members of the union would be entitled to vote. See also *Morrissey* v. *University of London* [2016] ICR 893.

[252] TICE Regulations, reg. 13. For the corresponding provisions of the ICE Regulations, see p. 675.

[253] *Ibid.*, reg. 13(3)(ii).   [254] *Ibid.*, reg. 2(1).

[255] 'A person is an independent ballot supervisor only if the UK management reasonably believes that he or she will carry out his or her duties competently, *and* it has no reasonable grounds for believing that his or her independence in relation to the ballot might reasonably be called into question': TICE Regulations, reg. 13(7).

consult with UK employee representatives about the ballot proposals before publishing the final arrangements.[256] In practice, that means consulting with the representatives of a recognised trade union (who may themselves be candidates in the election), it being unlikely that there will be employee representatives otherwise.

Claims that the ballot arrangements are defective (including claims about a failure to consult employee representatives) may be made by either an employee or an employees' representative to the CAC.[257] If the complaint is upheld, the latter has the power to order the employer to modify the arrangements or to consult employees' representatives as required by regulation 13(3)(e).[258] The employer has additional responsibilities to ensure that the ballot supervisor carries out his or her duties, and does so without any interference from management.[259] The employer must also comply with all reasonable requests from the ballot supervisor for the purposes of carrying out his or her functions.[260] The ballot supervisor in turn has a number of duties. First, he or she must ensure that the employer has complied with his or her duty under regulation 13(3)(e) to consult with employee representatives about the ballot arrangements.[261] Indeed, the ballot may not take place until the ballot supervisor is satisfied that this duty has been discharged, nor may the ballot take place until after twenty-one days from the publishing of the final arrangements for the ballot, or before the determination of any complaint.[262] Finally, the ballot supervisor must conduct the ballot to secure that those entitled to vote are given an opportunity to do so, that those entitled to stand as candidates are given an opportunity to do so, and that voting takes place in secret.[263]

Negotiating an Agreement

As we have seen, once elections or appointments have taken place in the different Member States, the SNB must notify management of the composition of the SNB and of when it would like to start negotiations.[264] Regulation 12(4) also requires the SNB to inform the 'European social partner organisations' of its composition. It then becomes the responsibility of central management to convene a meeting with the SNB and to inform local managements that it is doing so.[265] An amendment to the TICE Regulations now permits the SNB to meet privately before and after any meeting with management, presumably to enable it to formulate a joint position and to consider outcomes.[266] The SNB may proceed on the basis of majority voting (with each member to have one vote), and provision is made for the SNB to be assisted by experts of its choice. These experts may include representatives of European trade union

---

[256] See *Unite the Union and Easyjet*, CAC Case EWC/4/2008.
[257] TICE Regulations, reg. 13(4).   [258] *Ibid.*, reg. 13(5).   [259] *Ibid.*, reg. 14.
[260] *Ibid.*, reg. 14(1)(b).   [261] *Ibid.*, reg. 14(2)(b).   [262] *Ibid.*   [263] *Ibid.*, reg. 14(2)(c).
[264] *Ibid.*, reg. 12(4).   [265] *Ibid.*, reg. 16(1).   [266] *Ibid.*, reg. 16(1A).

organisations, and they may attend in an advisory capacity any SNB meeting with management.[267] Central management must meet the reasonable expenses relating to the negotiations that are 'necessary to enable the SNB to carry out is functions in a reasonable manner', including the cost of assistance provided by one expert.[268]

In seeking to negotiate an agreement, the parties are under a duty to negotiate in a spirit of co-operation, with a view to reaching a written agreement on the detailed arrangements for the information and consultation of employees.[269] The parties may agree to establish an EWC, or an information and consultation procedure.[270] In the case of the former, the agreement must cover the following matters:

(a) the undertakings of the Community-scale group of undertakings or the establishments of the Community-scale undertaking which are covered by the agreement;

(b) the composition of the European Works Council, the number of members, the allocation of seats and the term of office of the members;

(c) the functions and the procedure for information and consultation of the European Works Council and arrangements to link information and consultation of the European Works Council with information and consultation of national employee representation bodies;

(d) the venue, frequency and duration of meetings of the European Works Council;

(dd) where the parties decide that it is necessary to establish a select committee, the composition of the select committee, the procedure for appointing its members, the functions and the procedural rules;

(e) the financial and material resources to be allocated to the European Works Council; and

(f) the date of entry into force of the agreement and its duration, the arrangements for amending or terminating the agreement, the circumstances in which the agreement is to be re-negotiated including where the structure of the Community-scale undertaking or Community-scale group of undertakings changes and the procedure for renegotiation of the agreement.[271]

Although the content of any EWC agreement (or any information and consultation agreement) is a matter for the autonomy of the parties, the 2010 amendments to the TICE Regulations set down minimum standards in

---

[267] *Ibid.*, reg. 16(5).   [268] *Ibid.*, reg. 16(6).   [269] *Ibid.*, reg. 17.

[270] *Ibid.*, reg. 17(3). Where the parties negotiate an 'information and consultation procedure' instead of an EWC, their agreement should specify a method by which the information and consultation representatives are to enjoy a right to meet and discuss the information conveyed to them (*ibid.*, reg. 17(5)).

[271] *Ibid.*, reg. 17(4). However, where there are significant changes in the structure of the undertaking or Community-scale group of undertakings, it may be necessary to renegotiate an EWC or an information and consultation procedure. Provision is made for this to be done in reg. 19F. Similar provision is made in the case of pre-existing agreements in regs. 44 and 45. See note 238.

terms of the employer's duty to provide information. By virtue of regulation 18A, 'the content of the information, the time when and manner in which it is given' must be such as to enable employee representatives to be able to make good use of it. The idea here is that it should not be provided at the last minute, but should be given 'in such a way as will enable the representatives to acquaint themselves with it, undertake a detailed assessment of its possible impact, and where appropriate, prepare for consultations'.[272] In the same way, by regulation 18A(5) the timing and manner of any consultation must be such as to enable the EWC or the information and consultation representatives to express an opinion on the basis of the information provided to them.[273] It is a major limitation of the TICE Regulations, however, that even if the EWC's opinion (or that of the information and consultation representatives) is provided within a reasonable time, there is no obligation on the part of management to take it into account. Rather disarmingly, regulation 18A(6) states simply that, 'having regard to the responsibilities of management to take decisions effectively', the opinion of the EWC 'may be taken into account by the central management or any more appropriate level of management'.[274]

The other point to arise here relates to regulation 18A(7), which provides that for the purposes of an EWC (or an information and consultation agreement), the information and consultation 'shall be limited to transnational matters'. This is a term that has given rise to some uncertainty, not defined in the Directive but referred to in recital 16 as follows:

> The transnational character of a matter should be determined by taking account of both the scope of its potential effects, and the level of management and representation that it involves. For this purpose, matters which concern the entire undertaking or group or at least two Member States are considered to be transnational. These include matters which, regardless of the number of Member States involved, are of importance for the European workforce in terms of the scope of their potential effects or which involve transfers of activities between Member States.

The TICE Regulations provide that, for the purposes of regulation 18A (and otherwise), matters are transnational where they concern (1) the Community-scale undertaking or Community-scale group of undertakings as a whole, or (2) at least two undertakings or establishments of the Community-scale undertaking or Community-scale group of undertakings situated in two

---

[272] TICE Regulations, reg. 18A(3). Contrast *Emerson Electric European Works Council and Emerson Electric Europe*, CAC Case No. EWC/13/2015 (p. 693), and *Oracle EWC and Oracle Corporation Ltd*, CAC Case No. EWC/17/2017 (p. 701), the former taking a much narrower view about the timing of information provision than the latter. It is not clear that the cases can be distinguished on the ground that the former is dealing with the construction of an agreement and the latter the construction of the regulations.

[273] On the meaning of consultation, see *Oracle EWC and Oracle Corporation Ltd*, CAC Case No. EWC/17/2017 (p. 701) – questions about whether it can be done virtually.

[274] See *Oracle EWC and Oracle Corporation Ltd*, CAC Case No. EWC/17/2017 (p. 701).

different Member States.[275] The government explained that the foregoing 'very closely reflects the wording of the Directive', but that 'there is no legal obligation on the UK to transpose the recitals of the Directive and it is our policy not to do so generally'.[276] It has been held by the CAC that a matter is not transnational if it relates to only one country, but that it is transnational if it is global and not simply EU/EEA in impact.[277]

The Legal Enforceability of EWC Agreements

Current controversies and complexities around the application of the EWC Directive and the TICER, and the construction of EWC agreements, are highlighted by the complaint about the breach of an agreement in *Emerson Electric EWC [EEEWC] and Emerson Electric Europe*.[278] This is an insight into a world which the British system of industrial relations has hitherto avoided, but is one to which we would have to become accustomed were the ICE and TICE Regulations to lead to more applications for the construction of agreements negotiated under either which are capable of adjudication before the CAC. There were three categories of complaint in the *Emerson Electric* case:

1 The head of the US-based company announced major restructuring plans without consulting the EWC. In a complaint by the EWC, the CAC rejected the employer's claim that the agreement did not apply because the plans were global and not European. According to the CAC, 'matters which otherwise fall within the EEEWC's jurisdiction are [not] excluded purely because they may affect, in addition, employees in countries beyond that jurisdiction'. It was held that there had been a breach of the agreement, though the CAC refrained from making an order because the employer undertook to hold a meeting.

2 At the annual meeting between the EWC and management, the employer had failed to provide any information before the meeting, at which a number of management presentations were made. According to the CAC, however, there was nothing in the agreement that said the information had to be given before the meeting, holding that 'a three-day annual meeting facilitates the opportunity for effective dialogue and, if appropriately organised, allows the EEEWC, with the help of experts, to consider, question and give feedback to management on the information given'. This is despite 'evidence at the hearing that the volume of information and the speed with which it had been delivered at the annual meeting had been overwhelming and had made it impossible to form a judgment on what was being presented'.

[275] TICE Regulations, reg. 2(4A).
[276] BIS, *Implementation of the Recast European Works Council Directive* (2010).
[277] See *Haines and British Council*, CAC Case No. EWC/7/2012, and *Emerson Electric European Works Council and Emerson Electric Europe*, CAC Case No. EWC/13/2015 respectively.
[278] CAC Case No. EWC/13/2015.

3 Issues were raised about the employer's responsibility for the costs of the EWC's experts and in particular the legal fees involved in the CAC claim. The agreement provided that the 'EWC and Select Committee will be provided with the means required to apply their rights arising from this agreement'. The employer argued, however, that this did not apply to legal fees on the ground that 'the payment of legal costs for employee representatives taking action against the employer may exist in other jurisdictions within the EU but that it had never been part of UK industrial relations practice for employers to be required to fund these costs upfront'. The CAC agreed, on the ground that the CAC is not a body where lawyers are required, and the CAC takes steps to ensure that an 'unrepresented party is not disadvantaged'.

Subsidiary Requirements

Where after three years the parties are unable to agree an EWC or an information and consultation procedure, the SNB may apply to the CAC for an order that the fallback provisions (referred to as the 'subsidiary requirements') will apply.[279] The subsidiary requirements are important in the sense that they provide a floor below which an EWC should not fall, though as in the case of the ICE Regulations it is still possible to negotiate for something less, whether in the form of a pre-existing agreement or a negotiated agreement.[280] As in the case of the ICE Regulations, however, trade unions would be extremely foolish to agree to anything less then the subsidiary requirements, which provide a statutory framework and a statutory procedure for enforcing the obligations included in that procedure. The subsidiary requirements applicable in the case of the TICE Regulations are much more detailed than the equivalent provisions of the ICE Regulations,[281] and address three questions: (i) the composition of the EWC; (ii) the competence of the EWC; and (iii) the rights of the EWC in terms of the frequency of meetings with management.

So far as (1) the composition of the EWC is concerned, the subsidiary requirements provide that there should be balanced representation from the Member States, with each Member State to have one EWC member for every 10 per cent (or a fraction thereof) of the total number of employees employed by the undertaking (or group of undertakings) in the Member State in question. In the case of UK members of the EWC, the EWC representatives must be UK employees. They may be appointed or elected by the representatives of an independent trade union recognised by the employer, provided the

---

[279] TICE Regulations, regs. 18, 20. See *Lean and Manpower Group*, CAC Case EWC/15/2017 (application can be brought *only* by the SNB, which may delay making the application).

[280] See *Morgan and Safron Group*, CAC Case EWC/8/2013, though it is to be noted that any negotiated EWC or information and consultation agreement would have to meet the requirements of reg. 18A on the meaning of information and consultation, which would appear to impose minimum standards below which the parties may not fall.

[281] On which, see pp. 676–7.

existing mandate of the trade union or trade unions covers all the UK employees. For this purpose, it makes no difference that some of the employees in question are not members of the union and therefore had no say in electing the representative who may now decide who is to sit on the EWC.[282] This is an important provision that gives the recognised trade union a priority position in the composition of the EWC, though it is provided (rather cryptically) that, where not all employees are covered in this way, the EWC representatives must be elected by a ballot. A ballot procedure similar to that relating to negotiating representatives is to be found in paragraphs 4 and 5 of the Schedule to the TICE Regulations.[283]

So far as (2) the competence of the EWC is concerned, this is limited generally by the TICE Regulations to 'the matters which concern the Community-scale undertaking or Community-scale group of undertakings as a whole or at least two of its establishments or group undertakings situated in different Member States'. This thus excludes matters relating to the under-taking outside the EU. The EWC is entitled to at least one annual meeting with central management, and for this purpose to be provided with information relating to 'the structure, economic and financial situation, the probable development of the business and of production and sales of the Community-scale undertaking or group of undertakings'.[284] It is further provided that the annual information and consultation meeting:

> shall relate in particular to the situation and probable trend of employment, investments, and substantial changes concerning organisation, introduction of new working methods or production processes, transfers of production, mergers, cut-backs or closures of undertakings, establishments or important parts of such undertakings or establishments, and collective redundancies.[285]

In addition to the foregoing, there is a right to additional meetings where there are 'exceptional circumstances affecting the employees' interests to a considerable extent, particularly in the event of relocations, the closure of establishments or undertakings or collective redundancies'.[286] Information supplied under these provisions of the TICE Regulations must include information about agency workers.

Turning to (3) the procedures for information and consultation, the EWC or the select committee (where one exists) are free to meet before a consultation meeting, without central management being present. So far as the process of consultation is concerned, paragraph 9(7) of the Schedule to the

---

[282] See also *Moray Council* v. *Stewart* [2006] ICR 1253, discussed above.

[283] An amendment introduced in 2010 also requires each EWC to 'elect from among its members a select committee comprising no more than five members who are to act on behalf of the European Works Council'. This is done to 'ensure that it can co-ordinate its activities' (Sched. 9, para. 2(4)).

[284] TICE Regulations, Schedule, para. 7(3).   [285] *Ibid.*, Schedule, para. 7(4).

[286] On which see *Oracle EWC and Oracle Corporation Ltd*, CAC Case No. EWC/17/2017 (p. 701).

TICE Regulations provides that the EWC should be able to meet with central management and to receive a reasoned response for any opinions they express in relation to reports provided by central management. The provisions of regulation 18A above (relating to the way in which information and consultation should be conducted) apply to EWCs established under the subsidiary provisions, though unlike the ICE Regulations there is no obligation on the part of the employer to consult with a view to reaching an agreement:[287] this is consultation in the strict sense, not negotiation. After any of these meetings has taken place, EWC representatives must report back to other employee representatives in the company or group of companies about the content and outcome of the meeting. Otherwise, it is to be noted that the EWC may be assisted in its work by experts, with central management under a duty to pay for the cost of at least one of these experts.[288] In addition:

> The central management shall provide the members of the European Works Council and its select committee with such financial and material resources as enable them to perform their duties in an appropriate manner. In particular, the cost of organising meetings and arranging for interpretation facilities and the accommodation and travelling expenses of members of the European Works Council and its select committee shall be met by the central management unless the central management and European Works Council, or select committee, otherwise agree.

Rights and Duties of Workers' Representatives

As with the redundancy consultation procedures and the ICE Regulations, the TICE Regulations make provision for the rights of EWC members, apart from rights in relation to elections and rights in relation to information and consultation. The position is not, however, straightforward, with regulation 19A providing that central management must provide EWC members with the 'means required to fulfil their duty to represent collectively the interests of the employees' of the Community-scale undertaking or Community-scale group of undertakings. Although clumsily expressed in the TICE Regulations, this uncertain duty to provide the 'means required' appears to be in addition to three other rights expressly referred to in regulation 19A and provided for elsewhere in the TICE Regulations. These are, first, the right to time-off with pay to perform the functions of a representative;[289] secondly, to be provided by central management with the means required to undergo training 'to the extent necessary for the exercise of the employee's representative duties';[290] and, thirdly, the right to time-off during working hours to undertake that

---

[287] *Oracle EWC and Oracle Corporation Ltd*, CAC Case No. EWC/17/2017 (p. 701).

[288] For discussion on the number and role of experts, see *Emerson Electric European Works Council and Emerson Electric Europe*, CAC Case No. EWC/13/2015.

[289] TICE Regulations, regs. 25 and 26.   [290] *Ibid.*, reg. 19B.

training.[291] The open-ended obligation to provide the 'means required' is a matter that ought to be tested by EWCs before the CAC to extend as far as possible the facilities to be made available by the employer, to complement the provisions of the subsidiary requirements referred to above.[292]

So far as the three specific rights are concerned, the right to time-off for workers' representatives remains unchanged following the 2010 amendments. This means that the right to time-off with pay applies not only to members of a SNB, to members of an EWC and to information and consultation representatives, but also (as already mentioned) to candidates for election to any of the foregoing positions.[293] The second of the rights referred to in the foregoing paragraph is new, and is clearly the most opaque of the three rights referred to. It may be read, however, as imposing a duty on the employer to provide training for EWC and SNB members (but not to information and consultation representatives). It may also impose a duty on the employer to provide training or to pay for external training to the extent that in-house company training is not likely to prepare employee representatives 'to the extent necessary for the exercise of [their] representative duties'. The third of these rights is also new, and applies to both the members of the SNB and the members of the EWC (but not information and consultation representatives). Here, there is a right to reasonable time-off to undertake training to the extent necessary for the employee's representative duties. As with the right to time-off for candidates and representatives for the discharge of their duties, the right to time-off for training is to time-off with pay, although in both cases subject to the statutory limit of a week's pay.[294]

Unlike the other information and consultation provisions discussed above, EWC members have a duty to communicate with those they represent. By regulation 19C, the EWC must inform employees' representatives in each of the undertaking's establishments of the 'content and outcome of the information and consultation procedure'. If there are no such representatives in any establishment, the information should be provided to employees individually. Failure to comply with this duty could lead to legal proceedings against the EWC itself, following a complaint brought by either an employee or an employee's representative. The complaint may be made to the CAC, and, if the complaint is upheld, the CAC may order the EWC to disclose the relevant information to the complainant. However, a complaint is not to be upheld if the EWC's failure resulted from 'a failure by the central management to provide the members of the EWC with the means required to fulfil their duty to represent collectively the interests of the employees' of the EWC.[295] Note

---

[291] Ibid., reg. 25(1A).

[292] The early jurisprudence is not propitious: *Emerson Electric European Works Council and Emerson Electric Europe*, CAC Case No. EWC/13/2015 (does not include legal costs for bring claims to the CAC). See pp. 693–4.

[293] TICE Regulations, reg. 25(1).   [294] Ibid., reg. 26.   [295] Ibid., reg. 19D(3).

that what is in effect a defence in proceedings brought against the EWC is not that the information was withheld by the central management, but that the latter failed to provide the means to enable the EWC's duty to be discharged. This suggests that the means required under regulation 19A requires providing the means to establish some kind of administrative infrastructure for the EWC, which may include financial resources for various purposes.[296]

In addition to the above, provision is made for the protection of representatives and candidates from detriment and dismissal on account of their performance of their duties.[297] But save in exceptional circumstances (relating to 'protected disclosures'),[298] there is no protection against detriment or dismissal where the representative discloses information in breach of regulation 23.[299] The latter imposes a duty on anyone who is or has been a member of an SNB or EWC not to disclose information that was entrusted to him or her by central management in confidence. This is an obligation – which applies also to information and consultation representatives and EWC experts – owed to central management, with breach of the obligation being actionable as a breach of statutory duty.[300] Where an undertaking of confidentiality is imposed by the central management, the recipient may refer the matter to the CAC (at least in cases where the central management is based in the UK).[301] The latter is empowered to determine whether it was reasonable to impose a condition of confidentiality, having regard to 'prejudice' or 'serious harm' to the undertaking. If the CAC declares that such a condition was not reasonable, the obligation of confidentiality is waived, and would be unenforceable at the suit of the employer.[302]

Enforcement

The TICE Regulations create a fascinating procedure for the legal enforcement of what often are in effect likely to be collective agreements. Although they are

---

[296] It is to be noted that the TICE Regulations are silent on who pays for any legal advice sought by the EWC in relation to reg. 19D proceedings, on the cost of representing the EWC before the CAC in such proceedings, or on the other costs (travel and accommodation) that may be associated with such proceedings. In *Emerson Electric European Works Council and Emerson Electric Europe*, CAC Case No. EWC/13/2015 (pp. 693–4), it was held that the 'means required' for the purposes of reg. 19A did not cover the costs of legal representation. But this does not necessarily apply to other legal expenses. It is not clear if the EWC members are jointly and severally liable for any debts incurred by the EWC (which has no legal personality) that are not recoverable from the employer.

[297] TICE Regulations, regs. 28–32.

[298] A protected disclosure refers to a disclosure under the whistleblowing legislation: see pp. 466–72 above.

[299] TICE Regulations, regs. 28(4) and 31(4).

[300] *Ibid.*, reg. 23. On the corresponding provisions of the ICE Regulations, see p. 678.

[301] TICE Regulations, reg. 23(6).

[302] *Ibid.*, reg. 23(7). See *Oracle EWC and Oracle Corporation Ltd*, CAC Case No. EWC/17/2017, in relation to the imposition of a confidentiality obligation on information widely known.

not described as such, most EWC agreements will be negotiated between trade unions and employers, and they may indeed fall within the statutory definition of a collective agreement in TULRCA 1992, section 178. And although the ICE Regulations potentially created a similar and more immediate procedure, there is a major difference between the ICE and TICE Regulations for this purpose. It is true that in both cases pre-existing agreements may operate to take the procedure outside the statutory framework. In the case of the TICE Regulations, however, a pre-existing agreement is an agreement made before the TICE Regulations came into force,[303] whereas in the case of the ICE Regulations a pre-existing agreement is one made before the ICE Regulations are invoked.[304] As a result, there are likely to be more agreements negotiated within the statutory framework in relation to the former than in relation to the latter. These agreements are enforceable by the CAC, even if this potentially fascinating laboratory will require a larger body of complaints than hitherto has been the case if it is to yield any meaningful results.[305]

Where there is a failure on the part of central management to establish an EWC or an information and consultation procedure in accordance with an agreement under regulation 17, a complaint may be made to the CAC (which in 2011 inherited this jurisdiction previously exercised by the EAT). By virtue of regulation 20, the application may be made by a 'relevant applicant', which means an SNB (in its own name, although it would appear to have no legal status) where such a body exists, failing which an application may be made by an employee, an employee's representative or a former member of an SNB which no longer exists. The same may occur where the regulation 18 subsidiary requirements apply and the central management is sleeping on its obligations.[306] Where the CAC upholds the complaint, it may make an order requiring the central management to establish an EWC as agreed, an information and consultation procedure, or establish an EWC under the subsidiary requirements. As in the case of the ICE Regulations, the relevant applicant may apply to the EAT for a penalty order where the CAC's order is not complied with. In this case, the penalty order must not exceed £100,000, and, as in the case of the ICE Regulations, the penalty is paid to the UK government and not the applicant or those he or she represents.

Provision is also made for cases where an EWC or an information and consultation procedure has been established, or where the subsidiary provisions of the Schedule apply. In these cases, a 'relevant applicant' may bring a claim

---

[303] See p. 687.

[304] The legal status of pre-existing agreements will depend on the wishes of the parties, and they are unenforceable under the statutory procedure. If they are collective agreements, they will fall within the scope of TULRCA 1992, ss. 178 and 179.

[305] For cases so far, see *Haines and British Council*, CAC Case No. EWC/7/2012, *Morgan and Safron Group*, CAC Case No. EWC/8/2013 and *Emerson Electric European Works Council and Emerson Electric Europe*, CAC Case No. EWC/13/2015 (pp. 693–4).

[306] TICE Regulations, regs. 20 and 21.

under regulation 21 that there has been a failure to comply with any of the foregoing, or that there has been a breach of regulation 18A (either because the information has not been provided, or because it is false or incomplete).[307] Here, a 'relevant applicant' means the EWC in the case of a complaint relating to such a body, or an information and consultation representative where there is an information and consultation procedure instead. It is to be contemplated that the EWC or information and consultation representatives could also be in breach of an EWC or an information and consultation agreement, in which case a complaint may be initiated by central management. In practice, however, it is difficult to see how cases in the latter category could arise, especially where the subsidiary requirements apply. The procedure for dealing with regulation 21 cases is the same as the procedure for dealing with regulation 20 cases, though it is only in the case of a default by central management that the second stage of the procedure (the application to the CAC for a penalty notice) can be invoked.[308] Additional provision of a similar nature is made in regulation 21A for enforcing – among other things – the new regulations 19A and 19B.[309]

The provisions relating to penalties have been strongly criticised, and questions have been asked about whether they go far enough to meet the provisions of the Directive that require Member States to ensure that 'adequate administrative or judicial procedures are available' to enable the obligations deriving from the Directive to be enforced. A civil penalty of up to £100,000 in the case of the most serious violation has been said to be of limited utility as a means of persuading compliance by what will often be large transnational corporations.[310] Although recital 36 refers to 'sanctions that are effective, dissuasive and proportionate', the exclusive focus of the text of the Directive is with 'enforcement'. It is thus greatly to be regretted that TICE Regulations 20(10), 21(9) and 21A(9) should say that 'No order of the CAC under this regulation shall have the effect of suspending or altering the effect of any act done or any agreement made by the central management or the local management.' Perhaps what is needed above all is a power on the part of a judicial body – here and in relation to the equivalent problem under the ICE Regulations – to grant an order imposing the status quo until the information and consultation obligations have been met. It is to be noted that the subsidiary provisions in the TICE Regulations also provide that the 'exceptional information and consultation meeting referred to in the Schedule 'does not affect the prerogatives of central management',[311] reinforcing the view that the freedom of companies to make decisions is not affected by the failure to inform and consult.[312]

---

[307] On reg. 18A, see p. 692.   [308] *Ibid.*, reg. 21(6).   [309] On regs. 19A and 19B, see p. 697.
[310] TICE Regulations, reg. 22.   [311] *Ibid.*, Sched., para. 8(4).
[312] See *Oracle EWC and Oracle Corporation Ltd*, CAC Case No. EWC/17/2017. One other question of enforcement relates to a failure by an employer to comply with a substantive agreement that has been made with an EWC. Can this be enforced under the Regulations? An example would be a Global Framework Agreement concluded between a multinational and its

The Limits of the EWC Legislation Laid Bare

The weaknesses and limitations of the EWC Directive and the TICE Regulations are laid bare by the CAC decision in *Oracle EWC and Oracle Corporation Ltd*,[313] where 'the EWC was informed by Central Management by way of a conference call of its intention to relocate activities currently located in various Member States to an Oracle location in a different Member State with up to 380 jobs at risk'.[314]

The EWC made a number of complaints, relating to (1) the procedure (conference call), (2) that it had been denied financial data without which it could not make a detailed assessment of the employer's proposed changes, and (3) the timing of the consultation, in the sense that redundancies had already started at national level before the European-level consultations had taken place. According to the EWC, consultation could only be meaningful if no decisions were taken until it was concluded.

As to (1) procedure, the CAC held that although virtual meetings may be acceptable depending on the circumstances of the case, the process in this case did not comply with the duty to inform and consult, which were separate processes that should not be wrapped up in one event. According to the CAC, 'information and consultation are seen as distinct, albeit interrelated, and that consultation takes place following provision of at least some substantive information'.[315]

So far as (2) access to the information is concerned, the CAC made no determination, but in the course of its decision it did say that while 'information provision needs [only] to relate to employees affected to a considerable extent by management's decision',[316] this is not limited to the workers made redundant: 'restructuring decisions also may affect to a considerable extent the interests of retained employees'.[317] Less positive was the CAC's observation in relation to some of the information sought that it is 'not the role of the EWC to seek to reverse management decision or any action taken'.[318]

The EWC was thus to keep in mind:

a distinction between on the one hand seeking financial detail of the business case for reorganisation in order to challenge or seek to reverse managerial decision and, on the other hand, seeking information necessary to understand the rationale or thinking behind a proposed action in order to represent the interests of those employees affected by it and provide an opinion which 'will be useful in the decision-making process'.[319]

But as to (3) timing, the CAC rejected the claim that national decisions cannot be taken until transnational consultation has taken place:

EWC (and perhaps also international trade union organisations) committing the company to respect ILO standards in all of its global operations (applicable perhaps also to its suppliers). What is the status of such an agreement, which will apply to matters outside the Member States? For a discussion, see K. D. Ewing, 'International Regulation of the Global Economy: The Role of Trade Unions', in B. Bercusson and C. Estlund (eds.), *Regulating Labour in the Wake of Globalisation* (Oxford: Hart, 2008), Ch. 10.

[313] CAC Case No. EWC/17/2017.   [314] *Ibid.*, para. 4.   [315] *Ibid.*, para. 66.
[316] *Ibid.*, para. 82.   [317] *Ibid.*   [318] *Ibid.*, para. 83.   [319] *Ibid.*, para. 84.

Management's 'right to manage' is protected (e.g. Recital 37 and 14; para. 8(4)). In return it appears the Directive requires management do all it can in terms of arrangements for information and consultation to facilitate the EWC being able to give an opinion in a timely fashion which 'will be useful to the decision-making process' (Recital 23 definition of consultation) and obtain a reasoned response (para. 9(7)(b)).[320]

According to the CAC, 'transnational consultation is intended to add value to managerial decision making. However the Regulations do not stipulate that management cannot implement its decision until an opinion has been given by the EWC'.[321] Along with the CAC's earlier remarks in this decision about the role and purpose of the EWC (not to challenge but only to represent), that is a crushing assessment. The contradiction here of course is that the consultation will be completely useless to the decision-making process, if the decision has already been taken before the consultations have started.

Conclusion

The foregoing by no means exhausts the duty of employers to inform and consult employee representatives, duties that are associated with developments at EU level. Among the other obligations to which reference may be made are the duties to inform and consult employee representatives in the context of occupational health and safety (in this case, duties that pre-dated EU obligations). The Safety Representatives and Safety Committees Regulations 1977 provide that a recognised trade union may appoint a safety representative.[322] The Regulations impose a duty on the employer to consult safety representatives on a range of issues, and empower representatives to conduct inspections at the workplace. Safety representatives may also initiate a safety committee at the workplace. In cases where there is no recognised trade union, provision for consultation is made by the Health and Safety (Consultation with Employees) Regulations 1996.[323] It will be noted that the latter allow for consultation directly with employees individually or with their representatives.

These different provisions for information and consultation are important for a number of reasons. In the first place, they give workers an opportunity for an organised voice on general questions affecting their employment, and an opportunity to use legal procedures to influence specific decisions that affect their employment security. The legal framework also provides an opportunity to slow down the process of change and to require employers to justify and account for their actions in a public forum. It is true that the law may help employers too – especially in cases where the aim is to impose changes to working conditions rather than reduce the number of employees. But on balance, the main beneficiaries of these procedures are probably the employees, given that employers would push through their changes anyway in

---

[320] *Ibid.*, para. 91.   [321] *Ibid.*   [322] SI 1977 No. 500, reg. 3.   [323] SI 1996 No. 1513.

the absence of a duty to consult (and negotiate with) trade union or other employee representatives.

It is in relation to the missed opportunities that the foregoing procedures have even greater significance. In terms of developing a strategy for trade union recognition, it was proposed many years ago that trade unions need three rights: a right to represent members who have disciplinary or grievance problems, a right now largely won;[324] a right to be consulted by the employer where the union can show a sufficient level of support (10–20 per cent) of the workforce, a right now largely won; and a right to negotiate a collective agreement with the employer, where the union can demonstrate majority support, a right now largely won. In this way, the union can always have a foot in the enterprise, even though there are serious flaws in the legislation, which need badly to be addressed. If it is unable to demonstrate majority support, the union should always be able to fall back to consultation rights; and, if it has insufficient strength for consultation purposes, it should always be able to fall back to representation rights.[325]

Given, however, that the foregoing information and consultation obligations almost exclusively are EU-sourced initiatives, questions arise about their survival post-Brexit. Although the government has indicated on several occasions that EU-sourced employment rights will be retained, it is difficult to see how the arrangements for EWCs can continue in their present form in the absence of an agreement with the European Commission. A number of questions will need to be dealt with urgently:

- Will some companies no longer be required to retain EWCs now in existence because the thresholds for establishing an EWC are no longer met?
- Will EWCs in companies headquartered in the UK be required to rehouse the EWC in another Member State?
- Will companies based outside the EU continue to be able to establish their EWC under UK law, or be required to relocate them elsewhere?
- Will British representatives of EU-based companies continue as entitled to be represented on EWCs?

The UK government has acknowledged that the position relating to EWCs 'cannot stay the same'. However, no answer has been provided to these questions, the draft regulations on the continued operation of EU-sourced

---

[324] Employment Relations Act 1999, ss. 10–13, though a major defect of this procedure is that the right to be accompanied in the context of grievance hearings applies only where the grievance relates to existing contractual obligations and cannot be invoked by an employee seeking to change terms and conditions of employment. See pp. 586–7.

[325] See K. D. Ewing, 'Trade Union Recognition: A Framework for Discussion' (1990) 9 *Industrial Law Journal* 209; T. Novitz, 'A Revised Role for Trade Unions as Designed by New Labour: The Representation Pyramid and "Partnership"' (2002) 29 *Journal of Law and Society* 487; and P. Davies and C. Kilpatrick, 'UK Worker Representation after Single Channel' (2004) 33 *Industrial Law Journal* 121.

employment rights being published with a blank space in the part dealing with EWCs. According to the government, 'the future of EWCs may be subject to discussions with the EU and any required amendments to *TICE* will be inserted before the SI is laid in Parliament'.[326] The outcome of these discussions will have been eagerly awaited.

---

[326] BEIS, Note on the draft Statutory Instruments: The Employment Rights (Amendment) (EU Exit) Regulations 2018; and The Employment Rights (Amendment) (EU Exit) (No. 2) Regulations 2018.

16

Collective Action and the Right to Strike

Contents

Introduction

In this chapter, we consider the legal responses to workplace disputes that lead to strikes or other forms of industrial action. A strike is a withdrawal of labour by a group of workers who are in dispute with their own employer, or sometimes with another employer. The dispute may lead to forms of action other than (or as well as) a strike, such as an overtime ban, working to rule or refusing to carry out certain tasks – all designed to put pressure on the employer. There are many reasons why workers may feel compelled to act in these ways, sometimes seeking to improve their terms and conditions of employment, with negotiations between the employer and their trade union having failed. At other times, the employer may be seeking to change existing terms and conditions of employment, with the workers fighting to hold on to what they have. In an era of economic austerity and public-sector cuts, defensive action of this latter kind is much more common than in the immediate past. But whatever the reason for taking industrial action, the right to strike is often justified as being 'an essential element in the principle of collective bargaining',[1] with the importance of the right to strike in the context of collective bargaining being recognised by the European Social Charter. Being the first international treaty expressly to recognise the right to strike, the Social Charter does so 'with a view to ensuring the effective exercise of the right to bargain collectively'.[2] If workers were unable to strike, they would have no means of pressing their demands or of resisting the pressure of the employer.

Although predominantly a weapon in collective bargaining, the strike may have a wider function as an instrument of political protest.[3] Indeed, the strike may be said to have two important political dimensions. In the first place, it is a way of enabling the citizen as worker to carry his or her concerns as a citizen into the workplace: the dockers who in 1919 refused to load the *Jolly George* then being supplied with armaments to help the Polish government in its campaign against Soviet Russia; the musicians in the 1950s who refused to perform in establishments which operated a colour bar;[4] and the broadcasting technicians in 1977 who refused to broadcast the FA Cup Final to South Africa.[5] Not all of these protests related to collective bargaining, and it is unrealistic to expect workers to leave their concerns as citizens at the entrance to the workplace. Secondly, and perhaps more fundamentally, the strike is a way of enabling people to protest about government conduct: a way of enabling the worker as citizen to express concerns about oppressive laws in

---

[1] *Crofter Hand Woven Harris Tweed* v. *Veitch* [1942] AC 435, at 463, *per* Lord Wright: '[T]he right to strike is an essential element in the principle of collective bargaining.'
[2] European Social Charter, Art. 6.
[3] See H. J. Laski, *Liberty in the Modern State* (Harmondsworth: Penguin, 1937), pp. 128–31.
[4] *Scala Ballroom (Wolverhampton) Ltd* v. *Ratcliffe* [1958] 1 WLR 1057.
[5] *BBC* v. *Hearn* [1977] ICR 686.

the workplace or the impact of government policy on living standards.[6] This does not imply a right of veto of the policies of a democratically elected government: but there is a chasm that separates the activities of those who would protest and those who would obstruct. As in the General Strike in 1926, however, it is easy for governments wrongly to characterise industrial action to protest against government policy or to express sympathy with other workers as being a challenge to the authority of the government and a threat to democracy itself.[7]

Right to Strike and International Standards

The right to strike is now fully recognised in international human rights treaties,[8] although its recognition is matched only by the failure of many countries to meet the full extent of their obligations. These treaties include the International Covenant on Economic, Social and Cultural Rights of 1966, where, by Article 8, states parties undertake to ensure 'the right to strike, provided that it is exercised in conformity with the laws of the particular country'.[9] By the same article, it is also provided that:

> Nothing in this article shall authorize States Parties to the International Labour Organization Convention of 1948 concerning Freedom of Association and Protection of the Right to Organize to take legislative measures which would prejudice, or apply the law in such a manner as would prejudice, the guarantees provided for in that Convention.[10]

This rather assumes that the right to strike is protected by ILO Convention 87, a matter we address below. In the meantime, the recognition of the right to strike as a human right has implications for the scope and content of the right. For example, it is difficult to see how a human rights perspective could entertain a situation in which the right to strike could be exercised only in the context of collective bargaining. It also raises important questions about possible limits and constraints on the exercise of the right to strike. For example, if it is a right vested in individuals (albeit that it can be exercised only by individuals acting collectively), can the exercise of the right be constrained by a collective agreement negotiated by a trade union (as is the legal position in some countries), and can the exercise of the right be made

---

[6] See K. D. Ewing and J. Hendy, *Days of Action: The Legality of Protest Strikes against Government Cuts* (London: Institute of Employment Rights, 2011).

[7] On the general strike, see *NSFU* v. *Reed* [1926] Ch 536.

[8] The classic work is T. Novitz, *International and European Protection of the Right to Strike* (Oxford University Press, 2003).

[9] See also ICCPR, Art. 22, where the right is implied: See K. D. Ewing and J. Hendy, *Days of Action: The Legality of Protest Strikes against Government Cuts* (London: Institute of Employment Rights, 2011).

[10] Art. 8(3). See also ICCPR, Art. 22(3).

conditional on the wishes of a majority voting in a ballot?[11] Can the exercise of a fundamental right be made conditional on the consent of third parties?

The International Labour Organization

Returning to the ILO, it is curious to reflect that there is no express recognition of the right to strike in ILO Convention 87, or in any other international labour convention for that matter. In a valuable study of ILO principles concerning the right to strike, Gernigon, Odero and Guido point out that the right to strike has been read into Convention 87 separately by the two supervisory bodies of the ILO, namely, the Committee of Experts (a body of independent jurists appointed by the ILO Governing Body), and the CFA (a tripartite body also appointed by the Governing Body).[12] In both cases, it has been possible to develop a right to strike from the provisions of Articles 3 and 10 of Convention 87. As we are reminded by Gernigon, Odero and Guido, the former establishes the right of workers' and employers' organisations to 'organise their administration and activities and to formulate their programmes', while the latter refers to the aims of such organisations as 'furthering and defending the interests of workers or of employers'.[13] From such unlikely a source has sprung a very fully developed recognition of the right to strike, fashioned by regular supervision of national law and practice by the ILO Committee of Experts, as well as what have now been several thousand cases of the ILO CFA, which may receive complaints from trade unions even in countries which have not ratified Convention 87.

Through this process of supervision, the ILO authorities have adopted a wide approach to the scope of the right to strike. Indeed, this would seem inevitably to follow from the location of the right to strike in Convention 87 (the freedom of association and right to organise convention), rather than its conjoined twin, Convention 98 (the right to organise and collective bargaining convention). According to Gernigon, Odero and Guido, the supervisory bodies have made it clear that the right to strike is a right of both trade unions and workers, and also that it is not a right the exercise of which is confined to collective bargaining. Although strikes that are 'purely political in character do not fall within the scope of freedom of association',[14] strikes to protest against government policy with a direct bearing on the economic and social interests of workers are protected. Indeed, the CFA has expressed the view that 'a declaration of the illegality of a national strike protesting against the social and labour consequences of the government's economic policy and the

---

[11] For further discussion of these questions, see K. D. Ewing, 'Laws Against Strikes Revisited', in C. Barnard, S. Deakin and G. Morris (eds.), *The Future of Labour Law* (Oxford: Hart, 2004), Ch. 2.

[12] B. Gernigon, A. Odero and H. Guido, 'ILO Principles Concerning the Right to Strike' (1998) 137 *International Labour Review* 441.

[13] *Ibid.*, 442.   [14] *Ibid.*, 445.

banning of the strike constitute a serious violation of freedom of association'.[15] The distinction seems to be that strikes that are used as a weapon to bring down a government are not protected (which is sensible in liberal democracies, although perhaps less so in other regimes), but strikes used as a weapon of protest against government policy are protected.

Gernigon, Odero and Guido record that the supervisory bodies have gradually 'reduced the number of categories of workers who may be deprived of [the] right [to strike], as well as the legal restrictions on its exercise, which should not be excessive'.[16] So while restraints may be imposed on senior civil servants,[17] this does not justify restrictions on all public servants. And while restrictions on strikes in essential services may be imposed, this means only those services 'the interruption of which would endanger the life, personal safety or health of the whole or part of the population'.[18] In both cases, however, where a restriction is imposed, it must be accompanied by an alternative form of dispute resolution, such as independent review or arbitration, the outcome of which is binding.[19] In the case of some public services that are not essential services, it may be possible for the government to require a minimum service to be provided during the strike. But this should be done in accordance with procedures in place before the strike starts, in the application of which any disputes are resolved by a body independent of government.[20] In practice, such arrangements seem likely to collapse in a well-supported strike, simply because no one can be required to turn up for work, no matter what the law may say. Also important in terms of the scope of industrial action is the ILO position that solidarity action must be permitted. According to the Committee of Experts with reference to the UK, in what is now a well-rehearsed line:

> [W]here a boycott relates directly to the social and economic interests of the workers involved in either or both of the original dispute and the secondary action, and where the original dispute and the secondary action are not unlawful in themselves, then that boycott should be regarded as a legitimate exercise of the right to strike.[21]

But although there are thus few permitted substantive restraints (in the sense that political, public service and sympathy strikes are protected), there are permissible temporal restraints that are important. In particular, it is accepted that employers and trade unions may agree a 'no-strikes clause' during the

---

[15] *Ibid.*, p. 446. See also K. D. Ewing and J. Hendy, *Days of Action: The Legality of Protest Strikes against Government Cuts* (London: Institute of Employment Rights, 2011), Ch. 3.

[16] B. Gernigon, A. Odero and H. Guido, 'ILO Principles Concerning the Right to Strike' (1998) 137 *International Labour Review* 441, at 444.

[17] *Ibid.*, 448–9.   [18] *Ibid.*, 450.

[19] On which, see *Prison Officers' Association* v. *Ministry of Justice* [2008] IRLR 380.

[20] B. Gernigon, A. Odero and H. Guido, 'ILO Principles Concerning the Right to Strike' (1998) 137 *International Labour Review* 441, at 458–9.

[21] ILO Committee of Experts, Observation Concerning Convention 87 (United Kingdom) (1989).

lifetime of a collective agreement, which has important implications for the frequency with which strikes may take place.[22] It is difficult to see how the waiving of the right to strike by contract in this way is consistent with the right to strike being a human right, especially as the waiver will be made not by the worker himself or herself, but by a trade union purporting to act on his or her behalf. The ILO supervisory bodies also permit procedural restraints on the right to strike, with both mandatory pre-strike ballots and mandatory pre-strike notice being permissible. The Committee of Experts has made it clear, however, that 'the ballot method, the quorum, and the majority required should not be such that the exercise of the right to strike becomes very difficult, or even impossible in practice'.[23] These permitted restrictions notwithstanding, a bitter dispute at the ILO in 2012 saw the Employers' Group contest the claim that the right to strike was protected by ILO Convention 87, and challenge the authority of the Committee of Experts to construe Convention 87 as widely as it had. The dispute was resolved (but not settled) by an agreement in 2014 in which the Employers' Group and the Workers' Group accepted that:

> The right to take industrial action by workers and employers in support of their legitimate industrial interests is recognised by the constituents of the International Labour Organisation.[24]

Council of Europe

Moving from international to regional instruments, the right to strike is recognised by both Council of Europe and EU instruments. So far as the former are concerned, it has already been pointed out that the European Social Charter was the first international or regional instrument expressly to recognise the right to strike. And although the Social Charter refers to the right to strike in the context of collective bargaining, in practice the European Committee of Social Rights has read it much more widely. This, of course, has important implications for the other relevant Council of Europe instrument, namely, the ECHR, which, as we have seen in other chapters, protects the right to freedom of association, 'including the right to form and join trade unions for the protection of [one's] interests'. The right to strike is not expressly referred to here, any more than any other specific trade union right. But the right to strike is now recognised by the ECtHR following the landmark decision in *Demir and Baykara* v. *Turkey*.[25] It is true that this case was concerned with collective bargaining rather than collective action. But it is also true that the arguments presented by the Court for recognising the right

---

[22] B. Gernigon, A. Odero and H. Guido, 'ILO Principles Concerning the Right to Strike' (1998) 137 *International Labour Review* 441, at 460–1.

[23] *Ibid.*, 457.

[24] See pp. 93–4 above. There is a huge literature on this dispute. See p. 94, note 195.

[25] [2008] ECHR 1345.

to bargain collectively under the umbrella of Article 11 apply with just as equal force to the right to collective action.

Sure enough, in *Enerji Yapi-Yol Sen* v. *Turkey*,[26] the ECtHR applied the principles in *Demir and Baykara* to a circular published by the Prime Minister's Public Service Policy Directorate banning public-sector workers from taking part in a one-day strike organised by the public-service trade union confederation. The strike was designed to secure a collective agreement and, despite the circular, a number of trade union members took part in the action, for which they were disciplined by their employer. In upholding the complaint by the union, the ECtHR is said to have acknowledged that:

> The right to strike was not absolute and could be subject to certain conditions and restrictions. However, while certain categories of civil servants could be prohibited from taking strike action, the ban did not extend to all public servants or to employees of State-run commercial or industrial concerns. In this particular case the circular had been drafted in general terms, completely depriving all public servants of the right to take strike action.[27]

It is also reported that, by joining the action, the members of the applicant trade union had simply been making use of its Article 11(1) freedom, the effect of the disciplinary action being to discourage trade union members and others from exercising their 'legitimate right to take part in such one-day strikes or other actions aimed at defending their members' interests'.[28] So far as Article 11(2) is concerned, the Turkish government had failed to justify the need for the impugned restriction in a democratic society. According to the Court, the ban did not answer a 'pressing social need', and there had been a disproportionate interference with the union's rights.

The decision in *Enerji Yapi-Yol Sen* that the right to strike is protected by Article 11 has been reinforced by a growing number of subsequent decisions from a range of other countries, notably Turkey, Russia, Ukraine and Croatia.[29] These have raised a series of different questions about (1) the nature of the right to strike, (2) the scope of the right to strike, and (3) the type of restrictions that would constitute a violation of the right to strike. On all of these questions the Court has generally taken a wide and generous approach to the complaint. *RMT* v. *United Kingdom* was, however, something of a retreat, the Court addressing two questions relating to conditions and restrictions on the right to strike operating in British law.[30] The first related to the trade union's duty to give notice to the employer of its intention to conduct an

---

[26] App. No. 68959/01, 21 April 2009.   [27] *Ibid.*   [28] *Ibid.*

[29] See *Saime Ozcan* v. *Turkey*, App. No. 22943/04, *Karacay* v. *Turkey*, App. No. 6615/03, *Kaya and Seyhan* v. *Turkey*, App. No. 30946/04, *Danilenkov* v. *Russia*, App. No. 7336/01, *Tymoshenko* v. *Ukraine* [2013] ECHR 468; and *Hrvatski Lijecnicki Sindikat* v. *Croatia* [2014] ECHR 1417. But see now *Association of Academics* v. *Iceland*, App. No. 2451/16, 27 June 2018.

[30] *RMT* v. *United Kingdom* [2014] ECHR 366. See A. Bogg and K. D. Ewing, 'The Implications of the *RMT* Case' (2014) 43 *Industrial Law Journal* 221.

industrial action ballot. The union had been restrained by an injunction for failing to comply with the statutory procedures, but was able eventually to take industrial action by ensuring that the more detailed demands of the employer were met. In holding that the case was inadmissible, the Court failed to do justice to the complaint, the essence of which was that the detailed notice requirements were incompatible with the Convention, whether or not they were complied with.

The second issue was whether the total ban on secondary action in the UK was compatible with Convention rights. Here the Court held that while the right to take secondary industrial action was protected by the Convention and that the total ban on secondary action was a breach of Article 11(1), a hitherto unknown distinction was to be drawn between 'core' trade union activity and 'accessory' trade union activity. Previous post *Demir and Baycara* cases – in which the right to strike by public-sector workers was held to be protected by Article 11 – were evidently different from the secondary action in dispute in *RMT*. The Court appeared to take the view that prohibitions and restrictions on conduct dubbed 'accessory' could more easily be justified under Article 11 (2) as being necessary in a democratic society for the protection of the rights and freedoms of others. In such cases, the respondent state was to be permitted a wide margin of appreciation, the Court influenced here by the fact that there was a consensus between the major political parties in the UK in favour of the prohibition of what was said to be 'accessory', even though no other Council of Europe state had such a wide ban on secondary industrial action. This unusual step backwards by the Court in what had been fast-flowing jurisprudence gave rise to speculation about the Court's motives.[31]

Common-law Liability and Statutory Protection

Under English law, the right to strike is not generally characterised as a fundamental right. As Maurice Kay LJ rather disarmingly put it in 2009:

> In this country, the right to strike has never been much more than a slogan or a legal metaphor. Such a right has not been bestowed by statute. What has happened is that, since the Trade Disputes Act 1906, legislation has provided limited immunities from liability in tort. At times the immunities have been widened, at other times they have been narrowed. Outside the scope of the immunities, the rigour of the common law applies in the form of breach of contract on the part of the strikers and the economic torts as regards the organisers and their union.

> Indeed, even now the conventional analysis at common law is that by going on strike employees commit repudiatory breaches of their contracts of employment ... No statutory immunity attaches to such individual breaches,

---

[31] K. D. Ewing and J. Hendy QC, 'Article 11(3) of the European Convention on Human Rights' (2017) EHRLR 356.

although those who induce them are protected and, since 1999, the dismissal of those taking part in official, but not unofficial, industrial action will in defined circumstances constitute unfair dismissal ... It helps to keep this history and conceptual framework in mind when construing and applying the detailed provisions of the statute.[32]

This, however, is a contested and dynamic area. Although formally the foregoing represents the law, a differently constituted Court of Appeal has since openly acknowledged that the ECtHR has recognised a right to strike, and that this recognition of the right to strike must have a bearing on how the domestic courts view industrial action cases, a matter to which we return more fully below.[33] More recently still the High Court has acknowledged that 'the law of this country gives effect to the fundamental right to take industrial action which workers enjoy under international labour law. That is a right which they also enjoy, as is now confirmed by the jurisprudence of the European Court of Human Rights, by virtue of the right to freedom of association in Article 11 of the Convention on Human Rights'.[34]

Common-law Liability

It is nevertheless important to emphasise that English law starts from the presumption that a strike is unlawful as a breach of the contract of employment of each of the workers taking part. At common law, almost all forms of industrial action are likely to constitute a breach of contract by the employee.[35] Also at common law, it is tortious to induce someone to break his or her contract of employment, a principle established in 1853, albeit not in the context of industrial action by a trade union.[36] This means that, if a union calls on its members to strike, it will be inducing them to break their contracts of employment. The application of this principle of tort liability to trade unions was developed in the late nineteenth century and confirmed in three seminal

---

[32] *Metrobus Ltd* v. *Unite the Union* [2009] IRLR 851, para. 118. See R. Dukes, 'The Right to Strike under UK Law: Not Much More Than a Slogan?' (2010) 39 *Industrial Law Journal* 82.

[33] *RMT* v. *Serco Ltd/ASLEF* v. *London and Birmingham Railway Ltd* [2011] EWCA Civ 226, [2011] ICR 848.

[34] *ISS Mediclean Ltd* v. *GMB* [2014] EWHC 4208 (QB), [2015] IRLR 96, para. 6 (Singh J). See also *Govia Gtr Railway Ltd* v. *ASLEF* [2016] EWCA Civ 1309, [2017] ICR 497.

[35] *RMT* v. *Serco Ltd/ASLEF* v. *London and Birmingham Railway Ltd* [2011] EWCA Civ 226, [2011] ICR 848, para. 2; 'Workers who take strike action will be usually acting in breach of their contract of employment': Elias LJ. But compare P. Elias, 'The Strike and Breach of Contract: A Reassessment', in K. D. Ewing, C. A. Gearty and B. A. Hepple (eds.), *Human Rights and Labour Law* (London: Mansell, 1994), Ch. 11.

[36] *Lumley* v. *Gye* (1853) 2 E&B 216. See D. Howarth, 'Against *Lumley* v. *Gye*' (2005) 68 *Modern Law Review* 195. For a modern restatement, see *OBG Ltd* v. *Allan* [2007] UKHL 21; [2008] 1 AC 1, on which see S. Deakin and J. Randall, 'Rethinking the Economic Torts' (2009) 72 *Modern Law Review* 519.

decisions of the House of Lords in the early years of the twentieth century.[37] In *Taff Vale Railway Co. Ltd* v. *ASRS*,[38] the House of Lords also held that trade unions could be vicariously liable for the torts of their servants and agents when organising industrial action. Confirming the existence of liability for inducing breach of contracts of employment later in the same year, in *Quinn* v. *Leathem*[39] the House of Lords held further that there was liability separately for conspiracy to injure, in a case where there was insufficient evidence that contracts had been broken. And in *South Wales Miners' Federation* v. *Glamorgan Coal Co.* a few years later, the House of Lords held further still that it was no defence to an action for inducing breach of a contract of employment that the conduct of the defendants was dictated by an honest desire to promote the interests of trade union members and not to injure the employer.[40]

These developments were to make it impossible for trade unionists to provide a lawful excuse or justification for their actions: they stood naked and unprotected at the altar of the common law. It was thus left to Parliament to respond with the Trade Disputes Act 1906, passed as one of the first measures of the newly elected landslide Liberal government, and only six years after the foundation of the Labour Party,[41] support for which among trade unions had grown as a result of the *Taff Vale* case. The Act created protection against existing torts in the context of trade disputes, with section 1 addressing civil liability for conspiracy.

Trade Disputes Act 1906, section 1

An act done in pursuance of an agreement or combination by two or more persons shall, if done in contemplation or furtherance of a trade dispute, not be actionable unless the act, if done without any such agreement or combination, would be actionable . . .

---

[37] On the historic struggle between the judges and the trade unions, see Lord Wedderburn, *The Worker and the Law* (3rd edn, Harmondsworth: Penguin, 1986), Ch. 1; and Lord Wedderburn, 'Industrial Relations and the Courts' (1980) 9 *Industrial Law Journal* 65.

[38] [1901] AC 426. See G. Lockwood, 'Taff Vale and the Trade Disputes Act 1906', in K. D. Ewing and J. Hendy (eds.), *The Right to Strike: From the Trade Disputes Act 1906 to a Trade Union Freedom Bill 2006* (London: Institute of Employment Rights, 2007), Ch. 2.

[39] [1901] AC 495. See J. McIlroy, 'The Belfast Butchers: *Quinn* v. *Leathem* After a Hundred Years', in K. D. Ewing and J. Hendy (eds.), *The Right to Strike: From the Trade Disputes Act 1906 to a Trade Union Freedom Bill 2006* (London: Institute of Employment Rights, 2007), Ch. 3.

[40] [1905] AC 239. See generally on justification, H. Carty, *An Analysis of the Economic Torts* (2nd edn, Oxford University Press, 2010), pp. 63–70.

[41] See J. Saville, 'The Trade Disputes Act of 1906', in K. D. Ewing and J. Hendy (eds.), *The Right to Strike: From the Trade Disputes Act 1906 to a Trade Union Freedom Bill 2006* (London: Institute of Employment Rights, 2007), Ch. 4.

The same Act also addressed liability for inducing breach of contract and interference with business in section 3.

Trade Disputes Act 1906, section 3

An act done by a person in contemplation or furtherance of a trade dispute shall not be actionable on the ground only that it induces some other person to break a contract of employment or that it is an interference with the trade, business, or employment of some other person, or with the right of some other person to dispose of his capital or his labour as he wills.

The 1906 Act further provided, by section 4, an almost complete protection for trade union funds from liability in tort, subject to a number of limited exceptions, thereby effectively overruling the *Taff Vale* decision. Although the liability of *trade unions* in tort was thus largely removed, it would still be possible to sue a *trade union official* personally for tortious acts outside the scope of the protections in sections 1–3 of the 1906 Act.[42]

The 1906 Act was to prove a largely effective basis for the protection of trade union freedom until after the end of the Second World War. But matters were to change radically thereafter. The period from 1952 to 1969 in particular saw the emergence of new grounds of tortious liability in a period of industrial turbulence as inventive plaintiffs sought to 'get round' the protections in the 1906 Act, in order to restrain what was often secondary action or action to enforce the closed shop.[43] With the demise of conspiracy to injure in a major House of Lords decision in 1942,[44] new causes of action would have to be found to deal with the persistence of this type of conduct. Sure enough, the common law in this period was to advance along two quite different fronts, with developments coming to a spectacular climax in two House of Lords decisions in the mid 1960s. In the first, *Rookes* v. *Barnard*,[45] the question was whether there could be liability (unprotected by the 1906 Act) where the union officials did not induce their members to take strike action, but threatened the

---

[42] Trade union liability was restored in 1982 (see chapter 17). Between 1906 and 1982 (subject to the brief period of the Industrial Relations Act 1971 (from 1971 to 1974)), legal proceedings for unprotected torts committed in the course of industrial action would typically be brought against the union official directly responsible for giving the instruction to strike.

[43] See generally B. Simpson, 'The 1906 Act: The Second Fifty Years', in K. D. Ewing and J. Hendy (eds.), *The Right to Strike: From the Trade Disputes Act 1906 to a Trade Union Freedom Bill 2006* (London: Institute of Employment Rights, 2007), Ch. 8.

[44] *Crofter Hand Woven Harris Tweed* v. *Veitch* [1942] AC 435. See D. Brodie, 'The Scottish Case : *Crofter Hand Woven Harris Tweed* v. *Veitch*', in K. D. Ewing and J. Hendy (eds.), *The Right to Strike: From the Trade Disputes Act 1906 to a Trade Union Freedom Bill 2006* (London: Institute of Employment Rights, 2007), Ch. 6.

[45] [1964] AC 1129. See K. W. Wedderburn (1964) 27 *Modern Law Review* 257; L. Hoffmann (1965) 81 *Law Quarterly Review* 116.

employer that they would do so unless it dismissed an employee who was not a member of the union. The House of Lords held that there was liability in such a case, not to the employer, but to the individual employee who was the target of the union's action, even though the contract of employment of the latter had been lawfully terminated in response to the union's threat. This was the tort of intimidation.

Rookes v. *Barnard* was a significant landmark in the development of labour law and in defining the relationship between the courts and the trade union movement. The second decision of the House of Lords, *J. & T. Stratford & Son* v. *Lindley*,[46] raised a rather different series of questions. What was the position if, in inducing breach of a contract of employment, the defendants also intentionally procured the breach of a commercial contract – as say between the employer involved in the strike and one or more of its customers or suppliers? The possibility of liability to the employer (the intended target of the action) in such circumstances had already been accepted in principle in an important Court of Appeal decision in *D. C. Thomson & Co. Ltd* v. *Deakin*.[47] But, on the facts, the ingredients of the tort were not made out in that case. In *J. & T. Stratford & Son* v. *Lindley*, however, liability was established in a case where the union had placed an embargo on the plaintiff company, which had a controlling interest in a company with which the union was in dispute about recognition. If *Rookes* v. *Barnard* would have important implications for closed-shop disputes, *J. & T. Stratford & Son* v. *Lindley* would have equally important implications for the use of secondary action as a way of putting commercial pressure on employers in dispute. The position was made even more difficult by the subsequent decisions of the Court of Appeal diluting further the essential ingredients of tort liability.[48]

Statutory Protection

The 1906 Act was thus being undermined by the development of new heads of tortious liability for which there was no protection. A quick patch-up job after *Rookes* v. *Barnard* took care of intimidation,[49] but it was not until the election of a Labour government in 1974 that steps were taken to widen the scope of the protection. The wider protection introduced by the Trade Union and Labour Relations Act 1974 has, however, been cut back sharply, following a number of amendments introduced by the Conservative government in 1982. The law is now to be found in TULRCA 1992, section 219, which, as already pointed out, has been said judicially to be the 'legal mechanism' through which 'the law of this country gives effect to the fundamental right to take industrial action which workers enjoy under

---

[46] [1965] AC 269. See K. W. Wedderburn (1965) 28 *Modern Law Review* 205.
[47] [1952] Ch 646.   [48] [1969] 2 Ch 106.
[49] Trade Disputes Act 1965. See K. W. Wedderburn (1966) 29 *Modern Law Review* 53.

international labour law'.[50] Section 219 thus determines the scope of the protection for industrial action: if the action falls within section 219, it will be protected; if it falls outside, it will not be protected. Indeed action which falls outside, the scope of section 219 will almost certainly be tortious and vulnerable to legal challenge. Although there are cases in the past where trade unions defended actions against them on the ground that the action complained of was not tortious,[51] it is now rare for questions of tortious liability to be contested.[52] It is more likely that the parties will contest whether or not there is a trade dispute, or whether the union has met the conditions of legal protection discussed below.

Trade Union and Labour Relations (Consolidation) Act 1992, Section 219

(1) An act done by a person in contemplation or furtherance of a trade dispute is not actionable in tort on the ground only –

   (a) that it induces another person to break a contract or interferes or induces another person to interfere with its performance, or

   (b) that it consists in his threatening that a contract (whether one to which he is a party or not) will be broken or its performance interfered with, or that he will induce another person to break a contract or interfere with its performance.

(2) An agreement or combination by two or more persons to do or procure the doing of an act in contemplation or furtherance of a trade dispute is not actionable in tort if the act is one which if done without any such agreement or combination would not be actionable in tort.

The foregoing provision is designed to take a number of torts out of active service, notably inducing breach of contract (section 219(1)(a)), intimidation (section 219(1)(b)) and conspiracy (section 219(2)). But what is the position relating to procuring the breach of a commercial contract by unlawful means? This had been expressly protected by Trade Union and Labour Relations Act 1974, section 13(3), until the latter was repealed in 1982. But although important, the impact of this change has not yet been significant, with the effect of Trade Union and Labour Relations Act 1974, section 13(3), always unclear, the courts apparently prepared (for now) to accept that conduct covered by the protection cannot form the basis of liability for a tort which is not protected.[53] In any event, secondary action – the main target of the

---

[50] *ISS Mediclean Ltd* v. *GMB* [2014] EWHC 4208 (QB), [2015] IRLR 96, para. 6.

[51] Including the great cases of *Crofter Hand Woven Harris Tweed* v. *Veitch* [1942] AC 435; *D. C. Thomson & Co. Ltd* v. *Deakin* [1952] Ch 646; and *Rookes* v. *Barnard* [1964] AC 1129.

[52] Though for an unusual example, see *Govia Thameslink Railway Ltd* v. *ASLEF (No. 2)* [2016] EWHC 1320 (QB), [2016] IRLR 686.

[53] *Camellia Tanker SA* v. *ITF* [1976] ICR 274. See K. W. Wedderburn (1976) 39 *Modern Law Review* 715.

tort – is now expressly excluded from protection.[54] It is thus perhaps a greater concern that TULRCA 1992, section 219, has not been revised to take account of the evolving common law, and in particular the continuing development of new species of liability since 1979. This is one of the weaknesses of the current method of protection for the freedom to strike: protection can be provided only for those torts known to exist at the time the protection is enacted. History has shown that, in an evolving and dynamic area of law, the protection can quickly be outflanked by the emergence of new grounds of liability for which there is no cover. This has been less of a problem in recent years in view of the tight statutory regulation of industrial action which, as explained below, has provided employers with more straightforward ways to challenge the legality of action taken against them.

That said, one area of potential unprotected liability relates to inducing or procuring breach of a statutory duty. Liability for inducing breach of a statutory duty was confirmed by the Court of Appeal in *Associated British Ports* v. *TGWU*,[55] where it was said that such inducement is 'akin' to the inducement of a breach of contract, with both species of tort being 'classed as torts which involve the interference with a person's legal rights'.[56] But it was also held that 'a breach of statutory duty cannot be relied on as unlawful means for the purposes of this tort unless it is actionable',[57] that is to say, unless the plaintiff would have a right of action in tort for breach of statutory duty against the party who is not complying with a statutory duty. Tort lawyers will be aware that not all breaches of statutory duty give rise to liability: the duty must be one that is owed by the defendant to the applicant.[58] In the *Associated British Ports* case, however, the House of Lords held that the statutory duty broken in that case – in the Dock Workers (Regulation of Employment) Order 1947 (as amended) – was essentially a contractual obligation. As a result, it was 'no more than a case of inducing other persons to break their contracts'.[59] Liability for inducing or procuring breach of a statutory duty is nevertheless a potentially important source of restraint, and there may well be circumstances where a wrongful act is committed for which there is no protection.

This was revealed most recently in a case involving BALPA, in dispute with British Airways about the moving of part of the latter's operations to Paris. Following the ECJ ruling in *Viking*,[60] British Airways argued that proposed industrial action by the union would violate its rights under EC Treaty, Article 43 (now TFEU, Article 49), for which there was no protection in English law (and indeed for which there could be no protection in English law because of the direct effect of EU law). Although the action of the union appeared to be

---

[54] TULRCA 1992, s. 224. See pp. 746–9.   [55] [1989] ICR 557.   [56] *Ibid.*, 570 (Neill LJ).
[57] *Ibid.*, 573 (Neill LJ).
[58] For a discussion of this issue, see P. Elias and K. D. Ewing, 'Economic Torts: Old Principles and New Liabilities' (1982) 41 *Cambridge Law Journal* 321.
[59] [1989] ICR 557, at 599.
[60] See Chapter 3. For a full account of the BALPA dispute, see pp. 777–8.

otherwise lawful under TULRCA 1992, the employer threatened the union with legal action if it went ahead with industrial action, apparently claiming also that its losses would amount to £100 million per day.[61] The union faced the prospect of either (1) taking industrial action and risking its own financial destruction which would result from a successful damages claim, or (2) pre-empting such a claim by taking the unusual and disarming step of seeking a declaration in the High Court that its proposed action was lawful. BALPA chose the latter course, but discontinued the legal proceedings after only a few days: even if it eventually won assurances from the highest courts that strike action could lawfully be taken, it would be too late: the bargaining agenda would have moved on and the right to hold a strike on an issue that was no longer relevant would be pointless. The threat of legal action in such circumstances thus remains open, with no legal protection for a tort-based claim for interfering with horizontally applicable Treaty rights or for the losses suffered as a result of such action.[62]

Limiting the Dangers of EU Law

The dangers of EU law for the right to strike were revealed in *Govia Gtr Railway Ltd v. ASLEF*,[63] where the union was involved in a dispute about driver only operated trains. This led to strike action which would disrupt the transport of passengers to Gatwick Airport. It was argued that the action was an unlawful interference with the right of establishment under TFEU, Article 49, and the right to provide and receive services under TFEU, Article 56. The former was based on the argument that the company was 35 per cent owned by a French company, and the latter on the argument that flights would be disrupted. Both claims were dismissed by the Court of Appeal as revealing no serious issue to be tried.

As to the first, it was held that 'it is the object or purpose of the industrial action and not the damage caused by the action itself which renders it potentially subject to the freedom of movement provisions'. It was not the purpose of the action in this case to frustrate the company's freedom of establishment. According to Elias LJ: 'article 49 does not protect companies from having to deal with strong or even bloody minded trade unions. The true analogy with this case would be if *Viking*, once operating in Estonia, was faced with threatened industrial action over terms and conditions of employment from an Estonian trade union. Nothing in *Viking* begins to support the proposition that such action would constitute a prima facie interference with the right of establishment.'[64]

---

[61] K. D. Ewing and J. Hendy (eds.), *The Right to Strike: From the Trade Disputes Act 1906 to a Trade Union Freedom Bill 2006* (London: Institute of Employment Rights, 2007).

[62] This issue is considered in greater detail at pp. 777–8.

[63] [2016] EWCA Civ 1309, [2017] ICR 497.

[64] *Viking* is a reference to Case C-438/05, *International Transport Workers' Federation* v. *Viking Line ABP* [2007] ECR I-10779, [2008] IRLR 143, pp. 88–9.

So far as the Article 59 point was concerned, the Court was uneasy on a number of grounds about the company riding in the slipstream of airline passengers, but also held that:

> it is not possible in this case to say, in advance of the action being taken, with respect to any individual passenger, that his or her ability to travel to or from the EU will be interfered with. Moreover, it would undermine the right to strike in a most fundamental way if all passengers potentially and indirectly affected by the strike could claim that it was interfering with their rights to provide and receive services. Subject to a defence of justification, the union's liability would be open ended. That would be an extraordinary consequence of this argument succeeding.

In this way the Court of Appeal appears to have contained the dangers of the CJEU's *Viking* and *Laval* decisions for industrial action that does not have a cross-border object or purpose,[65] the Court noting that 'it would hardly be compatible with the freedom of association or the protection of the right to strike as a fundamental right effectively to put the legality of industrial action in every strike with cross-border impact into the hands of the courts, with the onus on the union to persuade them that the action was not disproportionate'. There was no reference to the ILO jurisprudence that followed the *BALPA* case in particular, in which the Committee of Experts raised serious concerns about the impact of the *Viking* decision on the right to strike.[66]

Narrow Scope of Protected Action

To recap: the right to strike may serve a number of purposes. On the one hand, it may be seen principally as a fundamental human right, recognised as such by international treaties and the constitutions of many nation states.[67] On the other hand, it may be seen principally as a weapon in collective bargaining, as a sanction that may be used when the parties reach an impasse in negotiations for a new agreement, or when the employer fails to comply with the terms of an existing agreement. The perspective adopted varies from country to country, although it can be said confidently that Germany, the United States and the UK are at the industrial relations end of the spectrum, and that France, Italy and Portugal are at the fundamental human rights end of the spectrum. It

---

[65] *Laval* is a reference to Case C-341/05, *Laval un Partneri Ltd* v. *Svenska Byggnadsarbetareförbundet* [2007] ECR I-11767, [2008] IRLR 160, pp. 66–7.

[66] ILO Committee of Experts, Observation Concerning Convention 87 (United Kingdom) (2010, 2011). See further, pp. 777–8.

[67] For example, the right to strike is recognised expressly in the constitutions of Italy, France, Greece, Portugal, Spain and Sweden, and by implication in the constitutions of Finland, Germany and the Netherlands. For a fuller discussion, see K. D. Ewing, 'Economic Rights', in M. Rosenfeld and A. Sajó (eds.), *The Oxford Handbook of Comparative Constitutional Law* (Oxford University Press, 2012), Ch. 50. On the fragility of such constitutional guarantees in times of crisis, see I. Katsaroumpas, 'De-Constitutionalising Collective Labour Rights: The Case of Greece' (2018) 47 *Industrial Law Journal* 465.

is instructive, however, that the ILO sees the right to strike as a human right which can be used for purposes other than collective bargaining, and that the right to strike has its international law roots in ILO Convention 87 (dealing with freedom of association and the right to organise) rather than Convention 98 (dealing with the right to organise and to bargain collectively). The perspective from which the right to strike emerges greatly informs the nature and scope of its protection.

'Trade' Disputes, not 'Political' Disputes

With this in mind, the protection in TULRCA 1992, section 219, applies only to conduct 'in contemplation or furtherance of a trade dispute'. The term 'trade dispute' is defined in TULRCA 1992, section 244, so that, to enjoy legal protection, the dispute must be 'between workers and their employer', and relate 'wholly or mainly to one or more' of the items listed in section 244(1) (a)–(g). These include matters such as: (a) the terms and conditions of employment; (b) engagement or non-engagement, or termination or suspension of employment, or the duties of employment, of one or more workers; (c) allocation of work or the duties of employment between workers or groups of workers; and (d) matters of discipline. The protection is thus limited according to the parties to the dispute and according to its subject matter.[68] In addition to the matters discussed below, the question of subject matter has been an issue in several fairly contentious cases. So, although it was held that industrial action by schoolteachers about an unruly pupil was protected,[69] there was no protection when UNISON sought by industrial action to persuade UCL Hospital Trust to promise that staff would be employed under existing collectively agreed terms and conditions if transferred to a private employer.[70]

The existing restraints thus make it difficult if not impossible for a British trade union to organise industrial action for a political purpose. This is an issue of particular significance in the context of protest action against government policy, an area where there is a sharp divergence between international standards and domestic law. The leading authority illustrating the limitations of British law is *Express Newspapers Ltd* v. *Keys*,[71] where a number of unions called out their members to join a one-day national strike as part of a TUC 'Day of Action' to protest about the Employment Bill 1980, variously described

---

[68] See R. C. Simpson, 'Trade Dispute and Industrial Dispute in British Labour Law' (1977) 40 *Modern Law Review* 16.

[69] *P* v. *NAS/UWT* [2003] ICR 386.

[70] *UCL Hospitals NHS Trust* v. *Unison* [1999] ICR 204. See also *Unison* v. *United Kingdom* [2002] IRLR 497 (no breach of ECHR, Art. 11). Applying TULRCA 1992, s. 244(1) and (5), the Court of Appeal was unable to see how it was possible to apply the language of the Act 'in a way which covers the terms and conditions of employment of employees of a third party who have never been employed by the employer who is to be the subject of the strike action'.

[71] [1980] IRLR 247.

as part of 'the anti-working class policies of this Government' and an example of 'the present reactionary attacks on the hard-won rights of the British trade union movement'. The proceedings arose when members of SOGAT were 'directed' to stop work on 14 May 1980. NATSOPA members were 'urged' to do the same, NGA members were to 'ensure' that they did not report for work, and NUJ members were 'encouraged' to withdraw their labour and to do everything they could to bring about maximum NUJ involvement. Injunctions were granted on the ground that 'there is no trade dispute in this case. This is not a call to withdraw labour arising out of an industrial dispute, it is an avowed political strike, and none of the defendants has sought to argue that they are entitled to the protection conferred by [what was then Trade Union and Labour Relations Act 1974], section 13'.[72]

It does not follow of course that action against the government will always be unprotected. There may be cases where the government is the employer and where the dispute relates to the pay of its own employees. Where the government is acting *qua* employer the normal rules apply. Similarly, there may be cases where the dispute about pay or other working conditions is not with the direct employer but with the government as the provider of funds to the employer. In these latter circumstances action may be protected by virtue of TULRCA 1992, section 244(2), which provides that:

> A dispute between a Minister of the Crown and any workers shall, notwithstanding that he is not the employer of those workers, be treated as a dispute between those workers and their employer if the dispute relates to matters which –
>
> (a) have been referred for consideration by a joint body on which, by virtue of provision made by or under any enactment, he is represented, or
> (b) cannot be settled without him exercising a power conferred on him by or under an enactment.

Secretary of State for Education v. *NUT* is a rare example of this provision being relied on, the union having organised a one-day strike of college teaching staff to secure higher funding for the further education sector.[73] It was held on the facts that the dispute was one between the union and the minister which was aimed mainly at enhancing teachers' working conditions and job protection. It was also held that the dispute could not be settled without the minister exercising powers under the Education Act 2002 to increase funding for the colleges.

However, it is not only strikes aimed in protest at the government that may be banned. So too may strikes with a political dimension albeit arising out of disputes between workers and their employer, as illustrated by the decision in

---

[72] *Ibid.*, p. 249.
[73] See *Secretary of State for Education* v. *NUT* [2016] EWHC 812 (QB), [2016] IRLR 512.

Mercury Communications v. *Scott-Garner.*[74] The dispute was a consequence of POEU opposition to the 'liberalisation' of what was then a monopoly telecommunications system run by what was then the publicly owned British Telecommunications, albeit on the threshold of privatisation. In 1982, Mercury, a private-sector telecommunications company, was granted a licence by the government to run a telecommunications system, and an agreement was subsequently struck between BT and Mercury to enable each to interconnect with the other's systems. However, when BT employees were instructed to secure a connection between BT and Mercury, they refused to obey, in furtherance of a union decision not to co-operate with Mercury. The latter thereupon sought an injunction to restrain the defendants from interfering by unlawful means with its contractual relations with BT. The application failed before Mervyn Davies J, but was successful on appeal, on the ground that the dispute did not relate 'wholly or mainly' to a 'trade' matter within what is now TULRCA 1992, section 244. According to the Court of Appeal, the dispute was 'mainly' about the union's political opposition to the liberalisation and privatisation of the telephone network, rather than its concern with the protection of its members' job security.[75]

Narrow Scope of 'Trade' Disputes

These restrictions on the scope of protected action are a clear violation of the principles developed by the ILO supervisory bodies in relation to ILO Convention 87. But, if restricting the scope of protection to 'trade disputes' is too narrow, so too is the scope of protected 'trade' disputes, a matter which has also generated criticism from the ILO supervisory bodies.[76] Of some concern recently has been the requirement that, in order to be protected, a dispute must be between workers and 'their' employer, a limitation all the more restrictive as a result of the growing complexity of corporate forms. The difficulties – which do not arise only in the context of trade disputes[77] – were highlighted by the House of Lords in *Dimbleby and Sons Ltd* v. *NUJ*,[78] a case with complex facts. Because of a dispute with the NGA, the plaintiff company sent its newspapers for printing to a company called TBF, which was an associated company of T. Bailey Forman Ltd, the two companies being controlled by the same third company. The NUJ was in dispute with T. Bailey Forman Ltd, which was also the publisher of the *Nottingham Evening*

---

[74] [1984] ICR 74.

[75] But compare *Secretary of State for Education* v. *NUT* [2016] EWHC 812 (QB), [2016] IRLR 512: 'It does not follow that the predominant purpose of the NUT and its members is outside the scope of a trade dispute merely because the demand is for increased funding for sixth (sic) colleges' (para. 63).

[76] See pp. 756–77.

[77] See *E. Green & Son (Castings) Ltd* v. *ASTMS* [1984] ICR 352 (redundancy consultation).

[78] [1984] 1 WLR 427.

Post. On learning of the arrangement between Dimbleby and TBF, the NUJ instructed its members at Dimbleby not to supply copy for printing by TBF, an instruction with which the members complied.

One of several important issues in this case was whether the NUJ's instruction to members at Dimbleby was in contemplation of furtherance of the trade dispute with T. Bailey Forman Ltd. The House of Lords held that it was not, with Lord Diplock rejecting the view that 'TBF, although a separate entity from T. Bailey Forman Ltd, was nevertheless a party to the trade dispute between the NUJ and the latter company'.[79] Here, the union had come up against the rule of British company law that each company is a distinct legal person with its own legal personality, whatever reality may be disguised by that legal form. It is true that Lord Diplock conceded that there may be circumstances where:

> even in the absence of express words stating that in specified circumstances one company, although separately incorporated, is to be treated as sharing the same legal personality of another, a purposive construction of the statute may lead inexorably to the conclusion that such must have been the intention of Parliament.[80]

This, however, was not one such case, although it is difficult to imagine circumstances where it would be more appropriate to treat two companies as sharing the same legal personality. In fact, there are no known examples before or since in which the courts have been prepared to 'lift the corporate veil' where an employer is seeking to take advantage of a complex legal structure to defeat a trade union's freedom to take what otherwise would be protected action.

A more recent example of this problem occurred in 2010, in another case involving the NUJ, which had balloted its members employed in Johnston Press, which owned a number of regional newspapers. The dispute was concerned with a number of issues, including the resourcing of newsrooms as well as health and safety matters. According to the union, the 550 workers who had been balloted had voted 'overwhelmingly' for industrial action. Johnston Press claimed that it was not an employer, and therefore could not be a party to a protected trade dispute. According to the union:

> Johnston Press produced a 600-page court submission purporting to show that the group 'employs no journalists' – despite the JP stamp on the pay slips of staff working on their titles; the JP company handbook issued to all staff; the Johnston Press plc intranet that publishes company-wide procedures including policies on grievance, disciplinary procedure and health and safety; despite the group's claims in the annual report, in company bulletins and external publications that it employs 1,900 journalists and more than 7,000 employees. Johnston

---

[79] *Ibid.*, p. 435.   [80] *Ibid.*

Press made the claim although there were group-wide decisions on the recent pay freeze, pensions, and employment terms and conditions.[81]

Nevertheless, as already explained, under British law a trade union may take industrial action only in contemplation or furtherance of a trade dispute. A trade dispute means a dispute between an employer and his or her workers.

If a holding company owns a number of subsidiary companies (each responsible for employing staff), each subsidiary company is a separate employer and action directed at the holding company will not be protected action (even though it is the holding company that makes the decisions which are the subject of the dispute). Presented with the Johnston Press claim, the NUJ was forced to call off its action, 'given the threat of injunctions, legal costs, the loss by individual members of their protection against unfair dismissal and punitive damages being imposed'.[82] In so doing, the union explained further that:

> Johnston Press plc closed the group-wide pension scheme. Johnston Press plc imposed the group-wide pay freeze. Johnston Press plc imposed the group-wide introduction of the ATEX content management system. Yet Johnston Press plc has worked hard to ensure that under the anti-trade union laws, we are forced to have a dispute not with it, but with each and every one of its wholly owned subsidiaries. It is patently unfair and the law is an ass.[83]

An injunction was in fact granted against the union and, although the application was unopposed, the union was nevertheless liable to pay the employer's not inconsiderable legal costs. Although the case is unreported, it is nevertheless important for illustrating the excessive formalism of British law, and for highlighting the failure of successive governments to address ILO concerns that workers should be free to take industrial action against their 'real' employer.[84]

Before the Ballot

The scope of protected industrial action is thus highly restricted. Yet even within this narrowly defined protected area, industrial action may be banned if it does not follow statutorily prescribed procedures which require the union to (a) give notice to the employer of its intention to hold an industrial action ballot; (b) hold a ballot of its members in accordance with a highly prescribed statutory procedure; and (c) give notice to the employer of its intention to take industrial action. These provisions were first introduced in 1984 (balloting)

---

[81] See Journalism.co.uk, 'NUJ-Johnston press blocks staff strike with legal action', 18 May 2010.
[82] *Ibid.*
[83] D. Ponsford, 'Johnston Press Legal Challenge Blocks Group Wide Strike', *Press Gazette*, 18 May 2010.
[84] ILO Committee of Experts, Observation Concerning Convention 87 (United Kingdom) (1989).

and 1993 (notice requirements), and were retained with slight modifications (in 1999 and 2004) by the subsequent Labour governments. In recent years, the notice and ballot requirements have been the hotly contested battlegrounds chosen by employers seeking court orders to ban industrial action. Additional restraints introduced by the Trade Union Act 2016 are considered below.

Notice of Intention to Ballot

By virtue of TULRCA 1992, section 226, a trade union must give notice to the employer of its intention to hold a ballot about industrial action, and this must be done at least seven days before the ballot takes place.[85] The union must provide not only a list of the categories of employee to which those who are to be balloted belong; but also a list of the workplaces at which the affected employees work; as well as the total number of employees concerned and the total number in each category and at each workplace.[86] The information supplied 'must be as accurate as is reasonably practicable in the light of the information in the possession of the union at the time when it complies with [this] obligation'.[87] Trade unions complain that the legislation imposes demands that are often impossible in practice to comply with because of the problems they face in maintaining accurate up-to-date records in circumstances when (1) membership turnover is high, and (2) members fail to notify the union of changed circumstances (such as who they work for and where they work). This was a problem highlighted in *Network Rail Infrastructure* v. *RMT*,[88] where there was evidence of 'job changes, constant movement and also disappearances of workplaces'.[89] The problems faced by trade unions are highlighted by two leading cases.

In *EDF Energy Powerlink Ltd* v. *RMT*,[90] a pay dispute between the RMT and EDF Energy Powerlink Ltd involved a relatively small number of employees at three electricity stations. The union arranged for a ballot to be held, and gave notice to the employer of its intention to conduct a ballot under TULRCA 1992, notifying the employer that it proposed to ballot 'engineers/technicians', of whom it had fifty-two members. The employer categorised workers in other terms – 'fitters, jointers, test room inspectors, day testers, shift testers and OLBI fitters', and claimed that the information provided by the union was inadequate. Although the union did not have the information required by the employer in its possession, the High Court nevertheless took the view that this 'highly material' consideration was not 'decisive'. According to Blake J, the union was under 'a duty to do [its] reasonable best to address the essential

---

[85] TULRCA 1992, s. 226A(1)(a). There is a separate duty to give the employer a copy of the ballot paper 'not later than the third day before the opening day of the ballot': TULRCA 1992, s. 226A (1)(b).

[86] TULRCA 1992, s. 226A(2A) and (2B).   [87] TULRCA 1992, s. 226A(2D).

[88] *Network Rail Infrastructure* v. *RMT* [2010] EWHC 1084 (QB).   [89] *Ibid.*, para. 47.

[90] [2009] EWHC 2852 (QB).

criteria and to explain as far as [it] can how [it] got to the information that it supplies'.[91] In this case, the court took the view that the union could have obtained the additional information by asking its shop stewards, and that 'the employer would be entitled to know who was being balloted in respect of those trades and who might be called out pursuant to ballot in an industrial dispute'.[92]

In *British Airways plc* v. *Unite the Union*,[93] the union balloted its members for industrial action; 10,288 votes were cast (representing an 80 per cent turnout), 9,514 of which were in favour of strike action. The employer objected to the fact that the ballot notice had included a number of people likely to take voluntary redundancy before the strike started, the legislation providing that the information in the ballot notice must identify only those employees the union reasonably believed would be entitled to vote in the ballot.[94] Entitlement to vote is restricted to those 'it is reasonable at the time of the ballot for the union to believe will be induced by the union to take part . . . in the industrial action in question, and to no others'.[95] Rejecting arguments from the union that 'it was neither practicable nor reasonable for the union to discover who amongst its members was to be made redundant and when',[96] the High Court granted the injunction to the employer on the ground that the union was required to 'enquire of its membership' (in a ballot of some 11,000 people) which of them were leaving before the start of the strike. Although the union was required by law only to provide information in its possession, it was held that 'the union cannot just sit on its hands, say no more than that it does not have the necessary information, and make no effort to obtain information which is relevant to that which they have to provide'.[97]

It was a striking feature of both of these cases that the union was put on notice that it was under an obligation to obtain and create the information prescribed by the legislation. The same was true in the *Network Rail* case,[98] where it was also held that it was not acceptable for the union to identify twenty-nine members as having unknown workplaces, and that it was under a duty to obtain the information it was required to provide about these workplaces. Some relief for trade unions was subsequently provided in *RMT*

---

[91] *Ibid.*, para. 18.

[92] *Ibid.* The union subsequently 'set about gathering the precise job descriptions of the workers concerned and included these in a fresh notice of a strike ballot, the result of which supported industrial action'. This led in turn to industrial action and an improved offer from the employer. A complaint that the union's Convention rights were nevertheless violated was ruled inadmissible by the ECtHR on the ground that the union only suffered delay in conducting industrial action and that it was not prohibited altogether. According to the Court, 'It would be artificial for the Court to consider the issuing of the injunction against the RMT in isolation from subsequent events': *RMT* v. *United Kingdom* [2014] EHRR 366. See A. Bogg and K. D. Ewing, 'The Implications of the *RMT* Case' (2014) 43 *Industrial Law Journal* 221.

[93] [2009] EWHC 3541 (QB).   [94] TULRCA 1992, s. 226A(2H).   [95] TULRCA 1992, s. 227.

[96] [2009] EWHC 3541 (QB), para. 43.   [97] *Ibid.*, para. 63.   [98] [2010] EWHC 1084 (QB).

v. *Serco Ltd* and *ASLEF* v. *London and Birmingham Railway Ltd*,[99] where the employer was clearly pushing its luck one step too far, seeking to restrain action where the union had mistakenly informed the employer that fifty-four rather than fifty-two workers would be taking part in the ballot. In upholding the union's appeal against yet another injunction, the Court of Appeal emphasised the need to read all the words of the statute, and in particular the provisions of TULRCA 1992, section 226A, that the union is required only to provide the employer with information which must be as accurate as is reasonably practicable in the light of the information in the possession of the union.[100] These words were said to be 'important limiting words',[101] which it seems had largely been ignored in the previous cases.[102]

Duty to Provide Explanation to Employer

In addition to the duty under TULRCA 1992, section 226A, to provide the lists and the figures referred to above, the ballot notice must also include an explanation of how these figures were arrived at.[103] That is to say, the figures relating to (a) the total number of employees concerned, (b) the number of the employees concerned in each of the categories of employee to which the employees concerned belong, and (c) the number of the employees concerned who work at each workplace in the workplaces at which the employees concerned work. Where the union members have their union subscriptions deducted at source by the employer (a system known as the check-off or DOCAS (Deduction of Contributions at Source)), the union may provide the lists and figures in the foregoing manner. Alternatively, it may otherwise provide such information as will enable the employer (a) readily to deduce the total number of employees concerned, (b) the categories of employee to which the employees concerned belong and the number of the employees concerned in each of those categories, and (c) the workplaces at which the employees concerned work and the number of them who work at each of those workplaces.[104]

Where DOCAS is in operation, it is enough for the union to provide an explanation to the employer by reference to DOCAS in the manner indicated immediately below. Particular problems arise, however, where the industrial action involves both (a) members who pay their subscriptions by check-off, and (b) members who do not. These difficulties were fully ventilated in *Metrobus Ltd* v. *Unite the Union*,[105] where this duty to provide an explanation was used to derail industrial action by bus workers in a dispute with Metrobus about terms and conditions of employment. The union gave notice to the employer of an intention to conduct a ballot, in the following form:

---

[99] [2011] EWCA Civ 226.   [100] TULRCA 1992, s. 226A(2D).
[101] [2011] EWCA Civ 226, para. 70.
[102] *Ibid.* According to Elias LJ, 'if the intention of Parliament had been to create a duty to create records not otherwise available to the union, it would have said so unambiguously' (*ibid.*).
[103] TULRCA 1992, s. 226A(2)(c)(i).   [104] TULRCA 1992, s. 226A(2)(c)(ii).
[105] [2009] EWCA Civ 829.

This letter is to give you notice that this union intends to hold a ballot for industrial action. The ballot will open on 18 August 2008. Your employees who will be entitled to vote will be those who are members of the T&G Section of Unite the Union employed by you at Crawley, Croydon and Orpington depots in the following category, Operating Staff (drivers). Those members in any of the above category who pay union subscriptions through check-off are known to you, including their individual categories and workplaces, and I believe that they number 776. A number of, I believe 69 members pay union subscriptions by means other than check-off. The attached matrix provides such information as the union possesses about the numbers in particular categories of the non check-off members. I believe that the total number of your employees who will be entitled to vote in the ballot (both check-off and non check-off) is therefore 845. The information set out in this notice is as accurate as possible in the light of the information in the possession of the union at the date this notice is given.[106]

No objection was taken to this notice at the time it was issued and, after conducting a ballot which produced a majority in favour of strike action, the union gave notice of intention to strike. A two-day strike then took place. When the union announced its intention to hold a second strike, the employer sought and obtained an injunction to restrain the action on a number of grounds, including the claim that the union in its notice above had failed to comply with the particular duty to explain how the figures in its ballot notice had been arrived at in relation to the non-check-off members involved in the dispute.[107] The injunction on this ground was upheld on appeal by a majority, it being said in the Court of Appeal that 'the union cannot avoid the obligation to provide an explanation of how the figures were arrived at' in relation to non-check-off members.[108] This is despite the small numbers of non-check-off employees involved in this case, 'and the absence of suggestion that the figures supplied in respect of non check-off employees were materially inaccurate'.[109] One member of the Court of Appeal dissented at this point, observing in so doing that, 'having regard to the detailed and complicated way in which strike action is procedurally circumscribed by the ballot provisions', the position of the majority was 'too strict',[110] with the legislation perfectly capable of being read in such a way that allowed the union to do as it had done in this case. Acknowledging that the employer 'was denied "an explanation" in relation to the non-check-off employees', it was also acknowledged by the judge in the minority that 'such an explanation is often permissibly formulaic or anodyne'.[111]

---

[106] As reproduced at *ibid.*, para. 52.
[107] *Metrobus Ltd* v. *Unite the Union* [2009] EWCA Civ 829.   [108] *Ibid.*, para. 94.
[109] *Ibid.*, para. 128.   [110] *Ibid.*, para. 124.
[111] *Ibid.* The explanation subsequently given by Unite in its dispute with British Airways provided as follows: 'The explanation of how we arrived at this information with regard to non-check-off members is that it is derived from information in our possession relating to the numbers, category or workplace of such members which is held in any document, including any

Subsequent developments were to suggest, however, that the explanation was not quite so 'formulaic or anodyne' as Maurice Kay LJ suggested, with employers turning their attentions from the duty to provide an explanation to its content. This was one of several issues in the *Network Rail* case, where Sharp J was persuaded that the explanation provided by the union was a 'conclusion' rather than an 'explanation', for reasons which (ironically) were not clearly explained.[112] Nevertheless, this too looked as if it might be a fertile seam for employers in litigation to have strikes stopped, and it was one which the employer tried to deep-mine in *RMT* v. *Serco Ltd* and *ASLEF* v. *London and Birmingham Railway Ltd*.[113] The details of this case are considered more fully below, it being sufficient for present purposes to note that the Court of Appeal drew back, and held in the spirit of Maurice Kay LJ that the duty on the union to provide an explanation is 'not an onerous one'.[114] It is enough that the union has complied with the government's Code of Practice on Industrial Action Ballots and Notice to Employers accompanying the legislation, which provides that:

> When providing the explanation of how the figures in the written notice were arrived at, unions should consider describing the sources of the data used (for example, the membership lists held centrally or information held at regional offices, or data collected from surveys or other sources). It is not reasonable to expect union records to be perfectly accurate and to contain detailed information on all members. Where the union's data are known to be incomplete or to contain other inaccuracies, it is a desirable practice for unions to describe in the notices the main deficiencies. In some cases, the figures will be estimates based on assumptions and the notice should therefore describe the main assumptions used when making the estimates.[115]

The Ballot

Mandatory strike ballots were first introduced in 1984. At first sight, intervention by the state in the internal government of trade unions may be thought to violate the right to freedom of association and in particular the right of trade unions to 'draw up their constitutions and rules', as required by ILO Convention 87. However, the ILO supervisory bodies have taken the view that mandatory ballots imposed by the state do not breach Convention 87, provided the law does not impose unduly onerous obligations. It is at this point that the TULRCA 1992 is open to strong criticism, the complexity of the legislation having been a source of considerable difficulty for trade unions in trying to

---

document in electronic form, which is in the possession of any union officer or employee': [2009] EWHC 3541 (QB), para. 37.

[112] *Network Rail Infrastructure* v. *RMT* [2010] EWHC 1084 (QB).

[113] [2011] EWCA Civ 226, [2011] ICR 848.   [114] *Ibid.*, para. 95.

[115] BIS, Code of Practice on Industrial Action Ballots and Notice to Employers, para. 16. A revised version of the Code is now issued by BEIS, following the Trade Union Act 2016.

organise industrial action in accordance with the law. Ballots under the legislation are also very expensive to administer, not only because of the balloting costs themselves but also because of the need for expensive legal advice, which seems to be required by unions trying to navigate the dangerous statutory currents. In addition, the balloting procedures are long and protracted, and take at least a month to complete, removing any possibility of surprise on the part of the union and giving the employer a long time to prepare. Altogether, the complexity, the compliance costs and the delays create burdens which are wholly disproportionate, the blunt edge of the legislation applying whether or not the union is planning a short one-day protest or a long, indefinite strike. The statutory burden was nevertheless controversially increased by changes introduced by the Trade Union Act 2016, to some of which we now turn.

The Statutory Duty

The statutory duty to hold a ballot is also set out in TULRCA 1992, section 226. This provides that '[a]n act done by a trade union to induce a person to take part, or continue to take part, in industrial action' is 'not protected unless the industrial action has the support of a ballot'. Like the pre-ballot notice provisions discussed in the previous section, the duty to hold a ballot was thus tied to the statutory protection, which means in effect that the duty is one owed by the union to the employer rather than to its members. It is true that in 1988 the law was changed so that trade union members could also bring legal proceedings against the union to ban industrial action called without the support of a ballot, or not conducted in accordance with the statutory requirements relating thereto.[116] But while there are many cases of action having been taken by employers to restrain industrial action for not having been conducted in accordance with the ballot rules, there is no reported case in which a disgruntled trade union member was the applicant.

Until the Trade Union Act 2016, it was enough that a majority of those voting did so in favour of industrial action.[117] However, the 2016 Act introduced two new requirements:

- at least 50 per cent of those eligible to vote must do so, which means that at least 25 per cent + 1 of those eligible to vote must do so in favour of the action. This was in response to claims that industrial action was often authorised following ballots in which there were low participation levels;
- in addition, for industrial action by those normally engaged in the provision of 'important public services', the industrial action must be supported by at least 40 per cent of those eligible to vote (who must also constitute a majority of those actually voting).

[116] TULRCA 1992, s. 62.   [117] TULRCA 1992, s. 228.

For this latter purpose, the Act allows the minister by regulations to define what is an important public service, which must be restricted to six specified services: health services; education of those aged under seventeen; fire services; transport services; decommissioning of nuclear installations and management of radio-active waste and spent fuel; and border security. These powers have been used to specify workers in each of the six services mentioned, in some cases extending beyond those workers directly providing the services in question.[118]

Apart from these thresholds, there are separate provisions to regulate the voting constituencies, so that the position is even more complicated than it ought to be. First introduced in 1988, these provisions were said to be necessary, for otherwise:

> it would be possible to construct an artificial constituency, the effect of which would be to ensure that one group of voters for that purpose would swamp another. In other words, one would artificially create a constituency so that if one wanted to get a certain result one could manipulate it in that way.[119]

So where the strike or industrial action in furtherance of a trade dispute with a particular employer spreads across more than one workplace, a separate ballot must be held in each workplace.[120] A strike or industrial action may be called only at those workplaces where a majority of those voting do so in favour, with entitlement to vote in each workplace being restricted to those actually employed there.[121] This of course begs the question of what is a workplace for these purposes, the Act defining it to mean the premises from which a person works rather than any sub-division within the premises.[122] This in turn begs other questions: are several buildings at one site (such as a university or hospital) one set of premises or several premises? Special provision is made for those who do not work from a single workplace (in which case, their work-place is the one with which they have the closest connection).[123]

Picky litigation around the meaning of a workplace for these purposes appears to have been contained largely as a result of the wide exceptions, which allow for single and aggregate ballots in some circumstances, a point which indeed the minister was at pains to point out at some length in Standing Committee in 1988.[124] But the legislation is extremely complex, despite amendments in 1999 designed to simplify the position.[125] The effect of the exceptions in TULRCA 1992, section 228A thus appear so far largely to

---

[118] See SI 2017 Nos. 132–6, dealing respectively with health, education, fire, transport and border security.

[119] Official Report, Standing Committee F, 14 January 1988, col. 473.

[120] TULRCA 1992, s. 228.   [121] TULRCA 1992, s. 228(3).   [122] TULRCA 1992, s. 228(4)(a).

[123] TULRCA 1992, s. 228(4)(b). See *Inter-City West Coast Ltd* v. *RMT* [1996] IRLR 583, highlighting problems of train crew, leading to amendments in 2009.

[124] Official Report, Standing Committee F, 14 January 1988, col. 473.

[125] TULRCA 1992, s. 228A. See *Govia Thameslink Railway Ltd* v. *ASLEF (No 2)* [2016] EWHC 1320 (QB), [2016] IRLR 686.

swallow the rule requiring separate workplace ballots. As a result, TULRCA 1992, section 228, simply prevents the union from extending the ballot to include people who have little interest in the dispute, but who in the mind of the minister above might be drawn in to ensure majority support. This limited purpose of TULRCA 1992, section 228, is revealed most clearly in TULRCA 1992, section 228A(4), whereby a union can hold a single ballot covering all workplaces if the vote is 'accorded to, and limited to, all the members of the union who are employed by a particular employer, or by any of a number of particular employers, with whom the union is in dispute'.[126] In that case, it does not matter if some workplaces vote in favour and some against: the union is entitled to call the industrial action at all the workplaces, even though the majority of workplaces vote against, with the outcome swung by the weight of votes at a particular workplace.

Conduct of the Ballot

For the ballot to be valid, 'entitlement to vote' must be 'accorded equally to all members of the trade union who it is reasonable at the time of the ballot for the union to believe will be induced to take part, or as the case may be, to continue to take part in the industrial action in question, and to no others'.[127] Industrial action is not regarded as being supported by a ballot if (i) any person who was a member of the trade union at the time the ballot was held, (ii) has been denied entitlement to vote in the ballot, and (iii) is induced by the union to take part or, as the case may be, to continue to take part in the industrial action.[128] This has the effect indirectly of protecting the union that calls out members who may have joined after the industrial action started, and who as a result may not have been balloted.[129] Express provision is also made for some 'small accidental failures' to be disregarded where these are 'unlikely to affect the result of the ballot'.[130] TULRCA 1992, section 229, provides that the 'method of voting must be by the marking of a voting paper by the person voting'. So no hand

---

[126] For other exceptions, see TULRCA 1992, s. 228A(2) and (3). However, these provisions must be strictly complied with. See *Govia Thameslink Railway Ltd* v. *ASLEF (No. 2)* [2016] EWHC 1320 (QB), [2016] IRLR 686, where it was held that the requirements of s. 228A are not met 'if the union reasonably, though mistakenly, believed' that at least one worker was directly affected at various workplaces balloted (para. 75). The laxity shown in the *Serco* case above to failings in relation to the notice procedures were expressly said not to apply here.

[127] TULRCA 1992, s. 227(1). This does not mean that a union must call out all those balloted to take part in all the industrial action in the course of the dispute: *London Underground Ltd* v. *ASLEF* [2011] EWHC 3506 (QB).

[128] TULRCA 1992, s. 232A.

[129] *London Underground Ltd* v. *National Union of Railwaymen (NUR)* [1996] ICR 170.

[130] TULRCA 1992, s. 232B. This was an issue that also arose in the *Serco* case above, where the union inadvertently extended the vote to two members who were not entitled to it, the Court of Appeal being required by the employer in that case to engage in a detailed consideration of the word 'accidental': *RMT* v. *Serco Ltd/ASLEF* v. *London and Birmingham Railway Ltd* [2011] EWCA Civ 226, [2011] ICR 848, paras. 47–57.

counts and no proxies. The voting paper must contain at least one of the following questions:

- a question (however framed) which requires the person answering it to say, by answering 'Yes' or 'No', whether he or she is prepared to take part or, as the case may be, to continue to take part in a strike;
- a question (however framed) which requires the person answering it to say, by answering 'Yes' or 'No', whether he or she is prepared to take part or, as the case may be, to continue to take part in industrial action short of a strike.[131]

The voting paper must specify who is authorised in the event of a vote in favour, and must contain the following statement:

> If you take part in a strike or other industrial action, you may be in breach of your contract of employment. However, if you are dismissed for taking part in strike or other industrial action which is called officially and is otherwise lawful, the dismissal will be unfair if it takes place fewer than twelve weeks after you started taking part in the action, and depending on the circumstances may be unfair if it takes place later.[132]

Since the Trade Union Act 2016, the following additional information must also be included on the voting paper:

- a summary of the matter or matters in issue in the trade dispute to which the proposed industrial action relates;
- where there is a question about taking part in industrial action short of a strike, the type or types of industrial action must be specified; and
- an indication of the period or periods within which the industrial action or, as the case may be, each type of industrial action is expected to take place.[133]

Ballots are to be conducted in secret, by post.[134] Although those voting must be allowed to do so without interference or constraint from the union, and

---

[131] The Employment Relations Act 1999 reversed *Connex South Eastern Ltd* v. *RMT* [1999] IRLR 249 in the sense that overtime and call-out bans are to be treated as action short of a strike for these purposes: TULRCA 1992, s. 229(2A). A 'strike' is otherwise defined to mean 'any concerted stoppage of work': *ibid.*, s. 246.

[132] The second sentence was added in 1999 (and amended in 2004), to reflect changes in unfair dismissal law introduced in 1999. See pp. 785–91.

[133] In *Thomas Cook Airlines Ltd* v. *BALPA* [2017] EWHC 2252 (QB), it was held that for this last purpose it was enough to state that 'It is proposed to take discontinuous industrial action in the form of strike action on dates to be announced over the period from 8th September 2017 to 18th February 2018'.

[134] TULRCA 1992, s. 230. Provision is made in the Trade Union Act 2016 for piloting electronic voting in industrial action ballots. This is something for which trade unions have lobbied actively, although it is difficult not to be sceptical. A review of e-balloting conducted for the government by Sir Kenneth Knight in 2017 fell short of providing an enthusiastic endorsement and highlighted a number of practical problems that would have to be overcome. If ballot turnout is a concern, the issue is not how balloting is conducted, but where it takes place. Workplace ballots (as under the trade union recognition legislation) would make more sense.

without incurring any cost, the union may, nevertheless, campaign in favour of a 'Yes' vote.[135] A state scheme to help with the costs of a wide range of ballots (including strike ballots) was introduced in 1980; but this was gradually phased out in the 1990s. The cost of the ballot must now be borne by the union alone and, given that all ballots must be fully postal, these costs must be very significant, particularly when the associated costs of officer time and legal advice are taken into account. In addition to the foregoing, the union must meet the costs of an independent scrutineer, who must make a report to the union on the conduct of the ballot, and 'take such steps as appear to him to be appropriate for the purpose of enabling him to make [that] report'.[136] The scrutineer's report must address a number of statutory requirements, and must state whether the scrutineer is satisfied that there were no reasonable grounds to believe that there was any contravention of any legal obligation relating to the ballot.[137] Where the scrutineer is not so satisfied, the report must give 'particulars of his reasons for not being satisfied'.[138]

The important role of the scrutineer was highlighted in the British Airways cabin crew dispute between 2009 and 2011. Following a third ballot in favour of industrial action, on 8 February 2011, the company moved against the independent scrutineer (a company called ERS) in an unusual but effective way to have the industrial action stopped without the need for an injunction.[139] Although the circumstances surrounding the intervention are unclear, Unite issued a press statement in which it claimed that the conduct of the company:

> doubtless reflects BA's decision to place its chief legal officer in charge of employee relations. While not addressing the union directly, BA advised the ERS that the ballot was unlawful and that any industrial action taken on the basis of it would be unprotected. This is merely an assertion by BA – however, the ERS decided, on the basis of protecting its own legal position, to issue a qualification in its official report on the industrial action ballot. UNITE therefore cannot call industrial action based on this ballot, since such a move would expose our members to sanctions by a bullying employer.[140]

Although the precise reason for the challenge was never formally published, the independent scrutineer is said to have 'accepted there were grounds for believing the union had given inaccurate information about the numbers of

---

[135] *London Borough of Newham* v. *NALGO* [1993] IRLR 83.   [136] TULRCA 1992, s. 226B(1).
[137] TULRCA 1992, s. 231B(1)(a).   [138] TULRCA 1992, s. 231B(1).
[139] In a slightly different move, in a dispute between Virgin Atlantic and BALPA in 2011, the company challenged the independence of the scrutineer.
[140] Unite the Union, Statement on British Airways Ballot, 8 February 2011. According to the *Daily Mail*, 3 February 2011, 'It is understood BA is challenging the latest strike ballot by the giant Unite union on a number of grounds, including the validity of names on the ballot papers, as well as the reasons given for the proposed cabin crew strike action. A spokesman for BA confirmed to the *Daily Mail*: "We wrote to Unite and the Electoral Reform Services during the ballot process to draw attention to a number of concerns."'

employees to be balloted'.[141] So, although paid for by the union, this affair is a reminder that the scrutineer will himself or herself be closely scrutinised by the employer, and may add further to the costs by alerting scrutineers to the need for their own legal guidance through the balloting maze.

After the Ballot

After the ballot has been held, the union must inform those entitled to vote of the result,[142] as well as the employer.[143] As already pointed out, the scrutineer must state whether or not he or she is satisfied with the way the ballot has been conducted.[144] The action must be called by a specified person, and must not be called before the ballot takes place.[145] The mandate provided by the ballot is no longer of unlimited duration and expires after six months, although it may be extended to nine with the agreement of the employer.[146] If a union wishes to prolong a dispute beyond the six-month limit, it will need the authority of a fresh ballot. At least fourteen days before the industrial action starts,[147] the union must give notice to the employer of the proposed action, the requirement in TULRCA 1992, section 234A largely reflecting the provisions of section 226A, 'in relation to the provision of information to an employer as to the numbers, categories and workplaces of employees', and the accompanying explanation. For these purposes, 'the total number of affected employees' is defined to mean those employees of the employer 'the union reasonably believes will be induced by the union or have been so induced to take part or continue to take part in the industrial action'.[148] A similar provision to TULRCA 1992, section 226A(2D), provides that the information supplied by the union must be as accurate as is reasonably practicable in light of the information in the possession of the union.[149] As we will see below, these additional obligations provide fresh opportunities for employers to use legal means to restrain industrial action.[150] There have been two areas of contention

---

[141] *Financial Times*, 8 February 2011.   [142] TULRCA 1992, s. 231.

[143] TULRCA 1992, s. 231A.   [144] TULRCA 1992, s. 231B.

[145] TULRCA 1992, s. 233. See *Govia Thameslink Railway Ltd* v. *ASLEF (No. 1)* [2016] EWHC 1320 (QB).

[146] TULRCA 1992, s. 234(1), as amended.

[147] The period of fourteen days may be reduced to seven if the employer agrees: TULRCA 1992, s. 234A(4)(b).

[148] TULRCA 1992, s. 234A(5C).   [149] TULRCA 1992, s. 234A(3D).

[150] In explaining the reason for this additional obligation, the responsible minister said in Standing Committee: 'Employers and the public should be protected against the damage that can be caused if unions proceed to organise industrial action without prior warning, and as soon as a ballot has been concluded. The concept of providing strike notice, albeit in the context of different institutional and legal arrangements, is familiar enough in other countries.' Official Report, Standing Committee F, 15 December 1992, col. 258. But as a rationale this is slightly disingenuous: in view of the obligation to give notice to the employer of the ballot result, there is no one who can be taken by surprise by a strike or other industrial action.

in relation to these various provisions: the notice of the ballot result and the notice of proposed industrial action.

Notice of Ballot Result

One of the foregoing obligations on trade unions is the duty to inform both union members and the employer about the ballot outcome, in both cases 'as soon as reasonably practicable' after the holding of the ballot. Until the 2016 amendments, the duty was simply to provide information about the ballot result. Now there is a duty to tell union members entitled to vote and relevant employers the following:

(a) the number of individuals who were entitled to vote in the ballot;

(b) the number of votes cast in the ballot;

(c) the number of individuals answering 'Yes' to the question, or as the case may be, to each question;

(d) the number of individuals answering 'No' to the question, or as the case may be, to each question;

(e) the number of spoiled or otherwise invalid voting papers returned;

(f) whether or not the number of votes cast in the ballot is at least 50 per cent of the number of individuals who were entitled to vote in the ballot; and

(g) where section 226(2B) applies, whether or not the number of individuals answering 'Yes' to the question (or each question) is at least 40 per cent of the number of individuals who were entitled to vote in the ballot.

Even before the 2016 amendments, the duty to give notice to members gave rise to a surprising amount of litigation. In the *Network Rail* case,[151] it was held to be insufficient for the purposes of the Act for the union to notify its members by sending them an SMS text message which referred to 'a solid vote for industrial action', and then giving a link to the union's website for the full result.

The same issue arose in *British Airways plc* v. *Unite the Union (No. 2)*, where following an injunction the union held a second ballot, this again producing an overwhelming majority on a high turnout. The employer complained this time that the union had not given adequate notice of the result to its members. Again, the union had notified its members by text message, while a press release giving details of the result was put out on all the union's websites and emailed to members. By these means, however, the union did not convey all the information required by TULRCA 1992, section 231, and the employer complained that the union had not fulfilled its obligations under the Act. Nevertheless, the injunction was discharged on appeal, with one of the appeal judges saying that 'the Union is not required to prove that literally

---

[151] [2010] EWHC 1084 (QB).

every eligible member was personally sent his or her own individual report of the full results. A test of such strictness would be unrealistic.'[152] But although welcome, it is to be noted that this was a majority decision (in which the Master of the Rolls dissented); and, although the approach in the *Network Rail* case was disapproved on the ground that 'universally applied, it represents a gloss on the statutory requirements',[153] there continues to be considerable uncertainty about what a trade union must do to meet its obligations under TULRCA 1992, section 231. All will depend on the facts of each case: in *British Airways plc* v. *Unite the Union (No. 2)*, it was permissible to direct the members to a website because they were highly computer literate. But what is the situation in other cases?

The union's duty to notify the employer of the ballot result was another of the legal issues in the dispute between Metrobus and Unite considered above.[154] One of the other grounds for granting the injunction was the union's alleged failure to comply with TULRCA 1992, section 231A, said by the Court of Appeal to be 'a hard temporal burden' for the union,[155] it being said also to be significant that the legislation requires the information to be given 'as soon as reasonably practicable', rather than 'within a reasonable time'.[156] In this case, the ballot closed at noon on 1 September but the independent scrutineer had failed to notify the union until 3.15 pm on the following day (2 September), with the union notifying the employer at 11.15 am on 3 September. The delay was the natural consequence of communication from the scrutineer to a local office of the union and from there to the general secretary whose authorisation was necessary before industrial action could proceed. This was said not to be 'as soon as reasonably practicable', and the union's failure was one reason for the granting of the injunction, even though no industrial action could take place without the union giving the employer at least before the action could begin strike notice. According to the High Court judge (in a passage approved on appeal by the Court of Appeal), 'The defendant was not entitled ... to delay informing the employer of the result, even by one day, while it determined whether to give notice of industrial action based upon that result.'[157]

In upholding the injunction on this ground, the Court of Appeal took a very robust view of the union's obligations. First, the union must inform the employer of the result, even though it has not yet decided to take industrial action on the basis of a vote supporting such action: 'section 231A imposes a free-standing obligation on the union, which must be performed even if the union does not initiate industrial action, and which is independent in its timing.'[158] Secondly, it was no defence that the union had not received a prompt report from the independent scrutineer: it would not have been 'anything other than proper and reasonable, in the absence of prior communication of the result, for Unite to have asked ERS about progress before the end of the

---

[152] *Ibid.*, para. 31.   [153] *Ibid.*, para. 30.   [154] [2009] EWCA Civ 829.   [155] *Ibid.*, para. 122.
[156] *Ibid.*   [157] *Ibid.*, para. 71.   [158] *Ibid.*, para. 73.

afternoon of 1 September'.[159] Thirdly, even if the union 'came under no obligation to pass the information on until it actually received it from ERS',[160] it failed
to convey the information to the employer 'as soon as reasonably practicable'.
The result should have been sent to the employer on 2 September at 3.30 pm,
the time by when it was received by an officer of the union: the fact that the
officer concerned had no authority to communicate this information 'is not a
reason which the union can rely on for withholding the information from the
employer'.[161] By requiring the union in this way to subvert its own rules and
procedures for informing the employer, the Court of Appeal appears to compound the injustice of its decision by completely eliding the right of the union
'to organise its administration and activities' without state interference.[162]

Notice of Industrial Action

The other area of contestation at this stage of disputes relates to the industrial
action notice. In addition to the duty to specify details of the workers to be
induced to take part in industrial action and the places at which they are
employed, at this stage the union must now also state whether the industrial
action is intended to be continuous or discontinuous. If it is continuous, the
notice must state the intended date of the commencement of the action, and if
it is discontinuous it must state the intended dates of the proposed action.[163]
Action is discontinuous for these purposes where it is to take place 'only on
some days on which there is an opportunity to take the action'.[164] The duty to
give notice of the nature of the action was considered in *Milford Haven Ports
Authority v. Unite the Union*,[165] where there was a dispute about pensions, in
the course of which the union balloted for industrial action and issued the
following notice to the employer:

> This action will be continuous and discontinuous. The continuous action will
> consist of an overtime ban, work to rule, not providing a call out service, not
> covering absenteeism and withdrawal of goodwill will commence on February
> 18th 2010 at 6 am. In addition, our members concerned will not handle any
> ships of more than 65,000 gross tonnes from 6 am on the 20th February 2010.
> The discontinuous action will consist of a 48 hour stoppage commencing 6 am
> on February 18th 2010, concluding 6 am on February 20th 2010.[166]

The employer took two exceptions to this notice, arguing first that it was not
sufficient to give the notice of discontinuous action and continuous action in the
same notice, and that the notice was thus irregular because it should have been
given on two separate pieces of paper rather than one. It is a matter of some
concern that an injunction was granted on this flimsy ground, it being argued by

---

[159] *Ibid.*, para. 80.   [160] *Ibid.*, para. 82.   [161] *Ibid.*   [162] ILO Convention 87, Art. 3.
[163] TULRCA 1992, s. 234A(3)(b).   [164] TULRCA 1992, s. 234A(6)(a).
[165] [2010] EWCA Civ 400.   [166] *Ibid.*, para. 11.

the union on appeal that 'it is simply untenable to require two notices to be put in the same envelope or to deny the union protection simply because the relevant officer failed to take a pair of scissors and cut between the relevant paragraphs to create two notices'.[167] This then led to a consideration in the Court of Appeal about whether TULRCA 1992, section 234A(3)(b), is 'disjunctive' or not (surely an inappropriate level of questioning for legislation restricting a fundamental right),[168] before it was accepted that 'one notice was sufficient for both continuous and discontinuous action, providing, of course, that the notice otherwise satisfied the requirements of the legislation'.[169] But although the Court of Appeal thus accepted the validity of the notice, it was of little consolation to the union which (1) ought not to have been placed in a position of having to appeal on a matter of such banal inconsequence, and (2) had in any event taken the precaution to issue fresh notices before the appeal was heard.

The Court of Appeal left unresolved the other ground on which the High Court granted the injunction. Thus, referring to the notice reproduced above, it was seriously argued by the employer that it was 'unclear as to what action the union's members intended to take and would take between these times and dates', and the employer was thus unclear 'as to how best to try to cover for the industrial action which is going to take place'. This was because:

> according to the notice, from 6 am on 18 February 2010 to 6 am on 20 February 2010, the union's members will refuse to perform some of the usual requirements of their role: an overtime ban, work to rule, not providing a callout service, not covering absenteeism and withdrawal of goodwill, which presumes that they will perform all other elements of their work during that time. However, at the same time the notice states that the members will not work at all, so that two forms of inconsistent action are specified as the same period.[170]

In what was perhaps the low point in a gradual decline to absurdity, this in turn led to a discussion as to whether it was possible to carry out continuous and discontinuous action simultaneously, although (whatever the answer to this question), as the union pointed out, 'it was self-evident from the fact that there was to be an all-out strike on 18 and 19 February that [continuous] action could not occur on these dates'.[171]

Apparently unsatisfied, the Court of Appeal considered the further question whether the notice could be read in such a way that the union had reserved itself the choice of going for an all-out strike on 18 and 19 February or going for only the less grave but still very serious continuous action from 6 am on 18 February. The question then was whether it was 'perfectly proper' as the union argued 'to give such notice, thereby leaving open to the union the subsequent decision as to which action to take'.[172] The matter was left open and may have to be resolved by another court on another day. It was left open because, as

---

[167] *Ibid.*, para. 13.　　[168] *Ibid.*　　[169] *Ibid.*, para. 14.　　[170] *Ibid.*, para. 15.
[171] *Ibid.*, para. 16.　　[172] *Ibid.*, para. 18.

already explained, the union had issued fresh notices to the employer, after having resolved to go through the balloting process again, in what was admittedly a dispute involving only a small number of workers. The fresh notices indicated that the workers concerned would take discontinuous strike action between 6 am and 6 pm on 23 February 2010, and continuous action commencing at 7 pm on 23 February 2010. It cannot be assumed, however, that the previous notice was lawful, with Laws LJ explaining that:

> whether notice can be given at the same time on what may turn out to be an alternative basis of continuous or discontinuous action, or for that matter of more than one kind of either continuous or discontinuous action, is a point with potentially wider importance which, before it is decided, merits fuller consideration and debate than has been possible on this appeal.[173]

Trade Union Statutory Notice Obligations

In order to retain statutory protection from common law liability, a trade union must give to the employer:

- notice of its intention to conduct an industrial action ballot, at least seven days before the ballot opens (TULRCA 1992, section 226A(1)(a));
- a sample copy of the ballot paper, at least three days before the ballot opens (TULRCA 1992, section 226A(1)(b));
- information about the ballot, as soon as reasonably practicable after the holding of the ballot (TULRCA 1992, section 231A);
- notice of its intention to take industrial action, at least 14 days before the action begins (TULRCA 1992, section 234A).

The union must also inform those taking part in the ballot of the ballot result, again as soon as reasonably practicable after the holding of the ballot (TULRCA 1992, section 231).

Can the Notice and Ballot Rules be Justified in their Present Form?

The balloting rules have been in operation for about thirty-five years now, and have confounded the wisdom of those who thought that they would not work. It is true that there were some early teething troubles. But the presence of the contempt of court jurisdiction (on which see Chapter 17) seemed enough to convince trade union leaders (said to be more cautious and risk averse than in the past) of the virtues of complying with the new law.

It has been said judicially that:

---

[173] *Ibid.*, para. 20.

Parliament's object in introducing the democratic requirement of a secret ballot is not to make life more difficult for trade unions by putting further obstacles in their way before they can call for industrial action with impunity, but to ensure that such action should have the genuine support of the members who are called upon to take part. The requirement has not been imposed for the protection of the employer or the public, but for the protection of the union's own members. Those who are members at the date of the ballot, and whom the union intends to call on to take industrial action, are entitled to be properly consulted without pressure or intimidation.[174]

If the purpose of the ballot is to ensure that industrial action has the support of the trade union members, it is not clear why the obligation to ballot should be tied to legal obligations owed by the union to the employer. If unballoted members do not wish to take proceedings against their union or are satisfied that a technical breach of the ballot rules has not affected the outcome, why should an employer be permitted to bring proceedings 'on their behalf' and in 'their' interests?

Quite apart from who should enforce the ballot rules, there is also the question of their content, and the need for a much more simplified procedure allowing ballots to be held at the workplace in the same way that recognition ballots are held at the workplace. This would help to reduce the cost of the procedure and the quite unjustifiable delay that a fully postal ballot causes. Workplace ballots would also help to increase turnout and the legitimacy of ballot results.

So far as the notice obligations are concerned, these too have been a serious impediment to trade union freedom. While the principle of strike notice may be unexceptionable, nevertheless some of the provisions of the existing law are such that they have led to some head-scratching on the bench:

> What I do, however, question is whether as a matter of principle it can be appropriate that even a complete failure to inform the Union members – not the employers – of the fact that an infinitesimal proportion of spoilt ballots were returned which could have had no possible bearing on the outcome of the ballot could leave the Union liable in tort for calling a strike which had the support of the vast preponderance of its members. At the risk of repetition, it does indeed seem curious to me that the employers can rely on a provision designed to protect the interests of members of the Union in order to circumvent their wishes.[175]

This is really the same point as arises in relation to the ballot obligation. If the purpose of the legislation is to protect the union members, why does the employer have the right to sue to enforce an obligation where the members are content that substantial compliance is enough? More generally, it is not clear why all the various notices required of trade unions are really necessary, and why so much detailed information needs to be provided to the employer.

---

[174] *London Underground Ltd* v. *NUR* [1996] ICR 170, *per* Millett LJ.
[175] *British Airways plc* v. *Unite the Union (No. 2)* [2010] EWCA Civ 669, para. 62, *per* Lord Chief Justice.

If the purpose is to let the employer know that action is about to take place, this could be done by means of a very simple procedure. Not all (if any) strikes are acts of aggression designed to beat an employer into submission and designed in the process to cause massive public disruption. In truth, a strike may be a purely defensive response by a workforce that is being badly treated, in which case it is unclear why the law should be used to give so much procedural ammunition to employers.

If legislation is to delay the right to resort to self-help remedies, there is a heavy responsibility on those who draft such legislation to ensure that there are in place effective alternative means to ensure the quick and effective restraint on employers acting unreasonably or unlawfully. This is something that British labour law historically has failed to provide. In the present climate, however, there is little prospect of such provision being made.

Prohibitions and Restrictions

Problems with the right to strike in British law are not confined to the narrow scope of the protection and the tight procedural restrictions relating thereto. A third problem relates to restrictions on the steps that might be taken by a trade union to put pressure on an employer during the course of a dispute. In taking industrial action, a trade union might hope to bring the enterprise to a halt, thereby forcing the employer to the bargaining table. But this may not always happen, and the employer may be able to continue in production, with the result that the union may seek to persuade other workers to join them by picketing the strike-hit workplace, and seek to persuade customers and suppliers of the employer in dispute not to deal with him or her. In the latter case, in the past this might involve instructing union members at the customer or supplier not to handle goods destined for or received from the employer in the dispute; or it may involve asking workers at the customer or supplier who are members of a different union not to handle the said materials. In these different ways, the union in dispute could potentially put a great deal of pressure on the employer in dispute, and perhaps principally for that reason pressure by both picketing and secondary action are either tightly constrained or banned altogether.

Picketing

Picketing is a common feature of many trade disputes. A group of workers will assemble outside a workplace, usually for two purposes: first to let people know that there is a dispute taking place; and secondly to seek support from other workers. To this end, the pickets will seek to persuade fellow workers not to cross the picket line and to abstain from working. They may also seek to persuade workers employed by other employers (such as drivers of lorries delivering supplies) not to cross the picket line and to abstain from working. These steps will be taken in order to increase the pressure on the employer: by depriving the employer of workers and supplies, it may be compelled to yield to the strikers' demands. But of course, other workers may not want to stop or to abstain from working: they may disagree with the pickets' case; they may be indifferent to it; or they may be unwilling to lose pay by joining the action. They may indeed support the strike's objectives but plan to work through the strike and enjoy the benefits of any settlement afterwards. The picket line can thus quickly become a source of conflict as tensions rise and incomes (of the pickets) fall, aggravated in some cases still further by the presence of replacement workers doing the jobs once done by the strikers.[176]

Protection for peaceful picketing was included in the Trade Disputes Act 1906, in direct response to the decision of the Court of Appeal in *J. Lyons & Sons* v. *Wilkins*[177] that even peaceful picketing could constitute an offence under the Conspiracy and Protection of Property Act 1875, section 7.[178] This provided – among other things – that it was an offence 'wrongfully and without legal authority' to 'watch and beset' the 'house or other place where [a] person resides, works, carries on business or happens to be'. In addressing this matter, section 2 of the 1906 Act provided that it was 'lawful' – in contemplation or furtherance of a trade dispute – 'to attend at or near a house or place where a person resides or works or carries on business or happens to be, if [the pickets] so attend merely for the purpose of peacefully obtaining or communicating information, or of peacefully persuading any person to work or abstain from working'. It will be noted that there were no restrictions here as to the numbers or location of the picketing, the only limits being those relating to purpose (peaceful communication or peaceful persuasion) and circumstances (it must be in contemplation or furtherance of a trade dispute). Designed principally to provide protection from the over-enthusiastic use of the Conspiracy and Protection of Property Act 1875, section 7 (which is still with us in the form of TULRCA 1992, section 241), the 1906 Act, section 2, would also provide protection from liability other than unlawful watching and besetting, such as obstruction of the highway under the Highways Act 1980, section 137,[179] and nuisance at common law.[180]

---

[176] See P. Kahn, N. Lewis, R. Livock and P. Wiles, *Picketing: Industrial Disputes, Tactics and the Law* (London: Routledge, 1983). See also P. Wallington, 'Policing the Miners' Strike' (1985) 14 *Industrial Law Journal* 145; and D. Lyddon and P. Smith, 'The 1906 Act: The First Fifty Years – Industrial Relations, Picketing and the Employers' Challenge', in K. D. Ewing and J. Hendy (eds.), *The Right to Strike: From the Trade Disputes Act 1906 to a Trade Union Freedom Bill 2006* (London: Institute of Employment Rights, 2007), Ch. 7.

[177] [1896] 1 Ch 811, [1899] 1 Ch 255.

[178] Compare *Ward Lock & Co.* v. *OPAS* (1906) 22 TLR 327, *Hubbard* v. *Pitt* [1976] 1 QB 142 (especially Lord Denning's dissent) and *Middlebrook Mushrooms Ltd* v. *TGWU* [1993] ICR 612.

[179] On liability under the Highways Act 1980, see *Tynan* v. *Balmer* [1967] 1 QB 91; *Broome* v. *DPP* [1974] AC 587; and *Kavanagh* v. *Hiscock* [1974] 1 QB 600. See more recently, *DPP* v. *Jones* [1999] 2 AC 240.

[180] But not trespass: *British Airports Authority* v. *Ashton* [1983] IRLR 287.

The provisions of the Trade Disputes Act 1906, section 2, were substantially re-enacted in the Trade Union and Labour Relations Act 1974, section 15, but substantially revised by the Employment Act 1980. The latter was designed to confine protection for picketing to picketing outside one's own place of work.[181] Now to be found in TULRCA 1992, section 220, the current law thus restricts the purpose for which picketing may occur (peaceful communication and persuasion),[182] *and* the location at which it may take place. By virtue of a Code of Practice on Picketing to which the courts attach great importance,[183] there is also a limit as to numbers, it being recommended that there should be no more than six at any one entrance.[184] A larger number (or fewer if the police so decide) will provide evidence that the pickets had a purpose other than peaceful communication or persuasion.[185] Where large numbers attend to picket or protest against a particular employer the practice of the courts – informed by Convention rights and the practice adopted in protests about other issues – is not to ban the protest but to require the protestors to relocate to a place some distance from the workplace while permitting a limited number to attend at or near the workplace. The courts may be particularly concerned where the protests 'tip into public disorder, harassment, intimidation, and other interferences with the rights of others which it is necessary and proportionate to prevent'. In these cases a geographical restriction or exclusion zone for protest may be imposed. In *Thames Cleaning and Support Services Ltd* v. *United Voices of the World*,[186] it was said that

> Such an order sets no limit on the kinds of speech that may be used by those involved in a protest. It defines where protest may take place. It is possible to frame an order of this kind which sets clear boundaries, without destroying the essence of the right to protest, which does not depend on location, and without interfering disproportionately with Article 10 and 11 rights: see *Appleby* v. *United Kingdom* (2003) 37 EHRR 38 [47], and *Manchester Ship Canal Developments Ltd* v. *Persons Unknown* [2014] EWHC 645 (Ch) [37], where the court was concerned with a protest camp in the vicinity of a fracking site.

It is important to emphasise that the protection offered by TULRCA 1992, section 220, is quite limited. It does not allow pickets to stop vehicles,[187] nor does it provide any protection from public order offences that may be committed on a picket line (such as obstructing a police officer in the execution of

---

[181] On which, see *Rayware Ltd* v. *TGWU* [1989] ICR 457 (workplace on a private trading estate to which no right of access).

[182] On which, see *Mersey Docks and Harbour Co.* v. *Verrinder* [1982] IRLR 152.

[183] See *Thomas* v. *NUM (South Wales Area)* [1985] ICR 887.

[184] BEIS, Code of Practice on Picketing (2017), para. 56: 'frequently a smaller number will be appropriate'.

[185] *Tynan* v. *Balmer* [1967] 1 QB 91.

[186] [2016] EWHC 1310 (QB). See also *Gate Gourmet London Ltd* v. *TGWU* [2005] EWHC 1889 (QB), [2005] IRLR 881 (QB).

[187] *Broome* v. *DPP* [1974] AC 587.

his duty).[188] Nor is it the source of protection from liability for the tort which in the past was most likely to be committed in the course of picketing, namely, inducing breach of contracts of employment or procuring breach of a commercial contract by unlawful means. However, protection for inducing breach of contract or indeed the other torts mentioned in TULRCA 1992, section 219, will arise only when committed in the course of picketing if the picketing is within the scope of TULRCA 1992, section 220. Any economic torts committed by picketing outside TULRCA 1992, section 220, have no section 219 protection.[189] A new TULRCA 1992, section 220A introduced by the Trade Union Act 2016 requires trade unions to appoint a picket supervisor, who is either an official or member of the union who must be familiar with the Code of Practice on Picketing.[190] The union must take reasonable steps to notify the police of the identity of the picket supervisor, and supply the supervisor with a letter of approval. The latter must be shown to the employer on request, in what is designed to enhance trade union responsibility for picketing. Protection under TULRCA 1992, sections 219 (so far as it relates to picketing) and 220 is now conditional on complying with TULRCA 1992, section 220A, which also requires the picket supervisor to wear something (such as an armband or vest) that 'readily identifies' him or her as such.[191]

Secondary Action

One of the fundamental features of trade unionism is solidarity and the willingness to help other workers in distress. This may take many forms, both financial and practical. Help of the latter kind may involve various forms of industrial action by workers of the same union employed by another employer, or by workers of another union employed by another employer. Throughout the twentieth century, secondary action of this kind by trade unions has been a matter of great political controversy. The target of the secondary action will be a third party not directly involved in the dispute

---

[188] Police Act 1996, s. 89(2). See *Piddington* v. *Bates* [1961] 1 WLR 162; *Moss* v. *McLachlan* [1985] IRLR 76; and now *R (Laporte)* v. *Chief Constable of Gloucestershire* [2006] UKHL 55, [2007] 2 AC 207.

[189] See TULRCA 1992, s. 219(3). One other point that may be noted here is that picketing outside one's own place of work may nevertheless constitute secondary action as defined by TULRCA 1992, s. 224, on which see below. This is because it may have the effect of inducing an employee of an employer other than the employer in the dispute (such as a delivery driver) to break his or her contract of employment, if he or she refuses to cross the picket line. TULRCA 1992, s. 224, provides expressly that secondary action occurring in such circumstances is exempt from the ban on secondary action otherwise contained in that section.

[190] BEIS, Code of Practice on Picketing (2017).

[191] For background to the picketing changes and valuable discussions of the Trade Union Act 2016 more generally, see A. Bogg, 'Beyond Neo-Liberalism: The Trade Union Act 2016 and the Authoritarian State' (2016) 45 *Industrial Law Journal* 299, and R. Dukes and N. Kountouris, 'Pre-Strike Ballots, Picketing and Protest: Banning Industrial Action by the Back Door?' (2016) 45 *Industrial Law Journal* 337.

between the trade union and the employer – usually a supplier or customer of the employer involved in the dispute. The purpose of the action will normally be to put economic pressure on the employer, in order to encourage him or her to settle on the union's terms. Good examples of secondary action include *Quinn* v. *Leathem*,[192] where the union sought to put pressure on the plaintiff by means of his customer, Munce, by calling on its members at the latter to take supportive action; and *D. C. Thomson & Co. Ltd* v. *Deakin*,[193] where the print union NATSOPA sought to put pressure on the non-union plaintiff by disrupting its supply of paper by enlisting the support of TGWU drivers. Indeed, it is a feature of many of the cases involving the development of tortious liability that they have involved secondary action of one form or another, reflecting a degree of judicial hostility to such trade union conduct, hostility which is not always thinly disguised.[194]

This is not to say that secondary action has always been condemned by the courts. After all, the landmark *Crofter Hand Woven Harris Tweed* v. *Veitch*[195] was a case about secondary action: a union in dispute with the independent producers of Harris tweed calling upon dockers not to handle the supplies or finished products of these producers. Indeed in that case, Lord Thankerton provided what is perhaps the strongest (and perhaps the only) judicial endorsement of secondary action when he said:

> In the present case the pressure was applied by means of action by the dockers, who were in no sense employees in, or directly connected with, the trade in Harris tweed; but employees in this trade were members of the same union, and the interest of the dockers and the trade employees in the union and its welfare were mutual, and I can see no ground for holding that it was not legitimate for the union to avail itself of the services of its docker members to promote the interests of the union. On the other hand, I doubt if it would be legitimate for a union to use a means of pressure with which it had no connection except that which was constituted by a money payment, for instance.[196]

Even here there are limits: secondary action is legitimate provided that it is taken by members of the same union as the workers in the dispute. What is not clear is whether the action by the dockers would have been as sympathetically received if it had been in support of the members of another union (as say in *D. C. Thomson & Co. Ltd* v. *Deakin*).[197] But in a sense it does not really matter: following *J. & T. Stratford & Son* v. *Lindley*[198] and *Torquay Hotel Co. Ltd* v. *Cousins*,[199] the foundations of liability for secondary action were to shift on to territory (procuring breach of a commercial contract by unlawful means)

---

[192] [1901] AC 495.   [193] [1952] Ch 646.

[194] See *J. & T. Stratford & Son* v. *Lindley* [1965] AC 269; *Torquay Hotel Co. Ltd* v. *Cousins* [1969] 2 Ch 106. See also *Merkur Island Shipping Corporation* v. *Laughton* [1983] 2 AC 570. But note now *OBG Ltd* v. *Allan* [2007] UKHL 21, [2008] 1 AC 1.

[195] [1942] AC 435.   [196] *Ibid.*, p. 460.   [197] [1952] Ch 646.   [198] [1965] AC 269.

[199] [1969] 2 Ch 106.

from which there was no escape on the basis of legitimate self-interest.[200] It is at this point that secondary action would be protected only if it was covered by the protection in the 1906 Act and its progeny, a matter which was to prove extremely controversial.

How then would secondary action in principle be protected? There would not normally be a dispute between the trade union and the target of the secondary action (the customer or supplier). Traditionally, however, torts committed in the course of the secondary action would be protected as being 'in furtherance of' the trade dispute between the trade union and the employer. The point was established in *Conway* v. *Wade*,[201] where Lord Loreburn said:

> I come now to the meaning of the words 'an act done in contemplation or furtherance of a trade dispute'. These words are not new in an Act of Parliament; they appear in the Conspiracy and Protection of Property Act 1875. I think they mean that either a dispute is imminent and the act is done in expectation of and with a view to it, or that the dispute is already existing and the act is done in support of one side to it. In either case the act must be genuinely done as described, and the dispute must be a real thing imminent or existing. I agree with the Master of the Rolls that the section cannot fairly be confined to an act done by party to the dispute. I do not believe that was intended. A dispute may have arisen, for example, in a single colliery, of which the subject is so important to the whole industry that either employers or workmen may think a general lock-out or a general strike is necessary to gain their point. Few are parties to, but all are interested in, the dispute.[202]

In practice, however, the courts were reluctant to conclude that secondary action could enjoy statutory protection in this way. A good example of this reluctance was *J. & T. Stratford & Son* v. *Lindley*,[203] where the union took action against the plaintiff's customers in response to a decision of an associated company to recognise a rival union. Another is the *Torquay Hotel* case, where the union organised a boycott on the supply of oil to a hotel with which it was in dispute. In these cases, the courts restrained the secondary action on the ground that there was no trade dispute. As a result, the protection was cut away: the secondary action could not be said to have been done in contemplation or furtherance of a trade dispute if no such trade dispute existed.

Following the expansion of the statutory protection in 1974 and 1976 – and the wider definition of a trade dispute – a new approach was adopted by some courts. There might be a trade dispute, but could the secondary action be said to be in 'furtherance' of it? Here, the courts began to introduce a number of qualifications and restrictions, which would restrain the circumstances in which secondary action might be taken within the boundaries of the protection. These qualifications and restrictions are considered by Lord Diplock in

---

[200] But see H. Carty, *An Analysis of the Economic Torts* (2nd edn, Oxford University Press, 2010), pp. 63–70. And see p. 714.
[201] [1909] AC 506.   [202] *Ibid.*, p. 512.   [203] [1965] AC 269.

Express Newspapers Ltd v. *McShane*,[204] where he viewed critically a number of Court of Appeal decisions where limits had been imposed because the secondary action had no practical effect in putting pressure on the employer engaged in the dispute,[205] or was too remote from the primary dispute.[206] But although the newly elected Conservative government intervened with legislation in 1980, it did not ban all forms of secondary action, accepting that 'in some cases, secondary action is the only means by which pressure can be brought on an employer in dispute, for example where the employer has sacked all his unionised employees', and that to impose a total ban 'could tilt the balance of power unacceptably to the benefit of employers'.[207] A different approach was adopted ten years later, with the Employment Act 1990 removing protection from all forms of secondary action. The government now claimed that 'there is no good reason why any threats of this kind, or the organisation of action of this kind, should enjoy [protection]'.[208] As discussed above, the prohibition was upheld by the ECtHR in *RMT* v. *United Kingdom*.[209]

The Human Rights Act 1998

Between the *Metrobus* decision on 31 July 2009 and the High Court decision in *Serco* on 19 January 2010, unions were restrained by the High Court from taking industrial action in at least eight cases.[210] In five of these cases, it was necessary for the unions to appeal to the Court of Appeal,[211] and in four of these cases, the union was successful,[212] as the Court of Appeal gradually wearied of the technical grounds on which injunctions were granted by trigger-happy High Court judges to restrain the exercise of a fundamental

---

[204] [1980] ICR 42.   [205] *Express Newspapers Ltd* v. *McShane* [1979] ICR 210.

[206] *Associated Newspapers Group* v. *Wade* [1979] ICR 664. Other important Court of Appeal cases at this time are gathered up in K. D. Ewing, 'The Golden Formula: Some Recent Developments' (1979) 8 *Industrial Law Journal* 133.

[207] Department of Employment, *Trade Union Immunities*, Cmnd 8128 (1981), para. 149.

[208] Department of Employment, *Removing Barriers to Employment*, Cm 655 (1989), para. 3.10. The then Opposition spokesman, Tony Blair, claimed at the time that '[t]he abolition of sympathy action is unreasonable, unjustified and way out of line with anything that happens anywhere else': Official Report, Standing Committee D, 22 February 1990, cols. 171–8. But he did nothing to remove the restraints on such action – now to be found in TULRCA 1992, section 224 – during the ten years he served as prime minister.

[209] *RMT* v. *United Kingdom* [2014] ECHR 366, pp. 711–12 above.

[210] *EDF Energy, Network Rail Infrastructure, British Airways plc, British Airways plc (No. 2), Milford Haven Port Authority, Johnston Press, Serco Ltd*, and *London and Birmingham Railway*, all discussed above. Not all employer applications were successful. Sometimes the slot machine jammed: *London Underground Ltd* v. *ASLEF* [2011] EWHC 7 (QB).

[211] *EDF Energy, British Airways (No. 2), Milford Haven Port Authority, Serco Ltd*, and *London and Birmingham Railway*, all discussed above.

[212] *British Airways (No. 2), Milford Haven Port Authority, Serco Ltd*, and *London and Birmingham Railway*, all discussed above.

human right.[213] But although the Court of Appeal has in these ways stopped some of the more fanciful arguments by employers' legal teams, it has not stopped them all. Nor does it mean that trade unions do not suffer adverse consequences, even in those cases where they win. In the *Milford Haven* case, for example, the union re-balloted rather than wait for the forensic lottery to run its course.[214] More to the point, however, why was this even happening? After all, this is the era of the HRA 1998, in which there is now judicial recognition of the 'fundamental right to take industrial action which workers enjoy under international labour law', a 'right which they also enjoy, as is now confirmed by the jurisprudence of the European Court of Human Rights, by virtue of the right to freedom of association in Article 11 of the Convention on Human Rights'.[215]

Stalling in the Court of Appeal

The answer lies partly in the blow delivered to trade union rights by the Court of Appeal in *Metrobus* and maintained by the Court of Appeal in all but one of its subsequent decisions.[216] In the *Metrobus* case, it had been argued that the restrictive British trade union law must now be read consistently with Convention rights, the court's attention being drawn not only to *Demir and Baykara* v. *Turkey*,[217] but also to *Enerji Yapi-Yol Sen*,[218] where it was held that the right to freedom of association includes the right to take collective action as well as to engage in collective bargaining. It is true that Lloyd LJ accepted that the latter was 'a decision to the effect that action to prevent participation in a strike, or to impose sanctions for such participation is an interference with the right to freedom of association under Article 11, for which justification has to be shown in accordance with Article 11(2)'.[219] But pouring cold water on the idea that the right to strike might thereby be protected in English law, Lloyd LJ continued by saying that:

> The contrast between the full and explicit judgment of the Grand Chamber in *Demir and Baykara* on the one hand, and the more summary discussion of the point in *Enerji Yapi-Yol Sen* on the other hand is quite noticeable. It does not seem to me that it would be prudent to proceed on the basis that the less fully articulated judgment in the later case has developed the Court's case law by the

---

[213] For a more sensitive approach in the High Court post-*Serco Ltd* and *London and Birmingham Railway*, see *London Underground Ltd* v. *ASLEF* [2011] EWHC 3506 (QB). But for an equally insensitive approach, see *Govia Thameslink Railway Ltd* v. *ASLEF (No 2)* [2016] EWHC 1320 (QB), [2016] IRLR 686.

[214] *Milford Haven Port Authority* v. *Unite* [2010] EWCA Civ 400.

[215] *ISS Mediclean Ltd* v. *GMB* [2014] EWHC 4208 (QB), [2015] IRLR 96, para 6. See also pp. 713, 716 above.

[216] *Metrobus Ltd* v. *Unite the Union* [2009] EWCA Civ 829, [2009] IRLR 851.

[217] [2008] ECHR 1345.   [218] *Enerji Yapi-Yol Sen* v. *Turkey*, App. No. 68959/01, 21 April 2009.

[219] *Metrobus Ltd* v. *Unite the Union* [2009] EWCA Civ 829, para. 35.

discrete further stage of recognising a right to take industrial action as an essential element in the rights afforded by article 11.[220]

The attention of the Court of Appeal was also directed to ILO Conventions in which the right to strike is recognised (notably, ILO Convention 87), as well as to the Council of Europe's Social Charter of 1961. It is true that these instruments have not been incorporated into English law and that, as international treaties, they cannot be enforced in the domestic courts. The point here, however, is that this material (including the jurisprudence of the supervisory bodies of the ILO and the Council of Europe) was relied upon by the ECtHR not only to justify reading the right to freedom of association widely to include the right to bargain and the right to strike, but also to inform the substance and content of these rights. But according to Lloyd LJ:

> [I]nteresting as this material is, it does not, for the purposes of this appeal, affect the substance of the points arising under the ECHR itself. To the extent that material from these and similar sources informed the decision of the Court in *Demir and Baykara*, it provides part of the context for that decision. I do not regard it as relevant in any more direct way to the present appeal. The ILO general survey confirms what one might expect, namely that member States have a widely differing variety of legislative provision on these points. The binding effect of article 11 of the ECHR does not restrict the scope for a wide variety of different legislative approaches, other than in a rather general way, at the extremes. Such variety is to be expected and is permitted by the margin of appreciation permitted to member States as regards conformity with the Convention.[221]

The effect of this blinkered reasoning was that developments under the HRA stalled while employers were racing to the High Court for their injunctions to stop strike action, sometimes for the most feeble and trivial reasons. The impact of *Metrobus* was soon to be seen in *EDF Energy Powerlink Ltd v. RMT*, where Convention rights were considered at first instance but dismissed by Blake J.[222] The latter was bound by *Metrobus*, dismissing arguments based on Convention rights simply on the ground that:

> In *Metrobus* the court concluded that the requirements as to pre-strike notification and ballots were not onerous or oppressive and did not unduly restrict the exercise of the right to strike. I would accept for present purposes Mr Hendy's submission that locating the interpretation of the legislation within the context of an important right could be a pointer to construction in a debatable case and could be a guide to avoid unreasonable requirements being imposed upon the union that might otherwise be said to interfere with the right. It may also in appropriate cases be relevant to discretion whether any failure by the Defendant is merely a technical one and has no material impact upon the employer's ability

---

[220] *Ibid.*   [221] *Ibid.*, para. 50.   [222] [2009] EWHC 2852 (QB), para. 4.

to make use of the information. But for reasons that follow, in my judgment, neither consideration requires further exploration on the facts of this case.[223]

Convention rights were raised before Cox J in the first *British Airways* case,[224] but she too was bound by *Metrobus* to conclude that 'the statutory requirements relating to ballots and strike notification in Part V of the 1992 Act do not unduly restrict the exercise of the right to strike; that the legislation has been carefully adapted over many years, in order to balance the interests of employers, unions and members of the public; and that its provisions are proportionate'.[225] Similar noises were made in *Network Rail*, where Sharp J thought it important to note that '*Metrobus* establishes [that] these requirements are proportionate and compliant with the European Convention on Human Rights'.[226]

While Convention rights were thus being ignored by the High Court (as they were bound to be in the light of Court of Appeal authority), the *EDF Energy* case provided an opportunity to revisit this question and for a differently constituted Court of Appeal to do better second time around. Again, the court fluffed its lines. John Hendy QC, representing the union, invited the court to reopen the matter, on the ground that 'the *Metrobus* decision, very recent decision as it is, has not had the opportunity of fully taking into account a small number of further Strasbourg decisions'.[227] But in rejecting this opportunity to revisit the matter, Rix LJ said that 'none of those decisions in any way shows that *Metrobus* is clearly to be set aside on the basis of Strasbourg jurisprudence', while he was also to have regard to House of Lords jurisprudence that 'precedent must be given effect even in the context of ECHR disputes'.[228] So what about the possibility of referring this to the Supreme Court to test Mr Hendy's 'bald submission' that '*Metrobus* was wrongly decided'?[229] No chance of that either, in view of the fact that the dispute 'has now happily been settled' so that the matter was now 'academic'.[230] There the matter lay until March 2011, not being revisited in either *Milford Haven Port Authority* or *British Airways plc* v. *Unite the Union (No. 2)*,[231] since the injunctions were lifted in both these cases without the need to rely on Convention rights.

Into First Gear on Convention Rights

If the High Court in the *Milford Haven Port Authority* case plumbed new depths in the historic conflict between workers, trade unions and the courts, the decision of the Court of Appeal in *RMT* v. *Serco Ltd* and *ASLEF* v. *London*

---

[223] *Ibid.*   [224] [2009] EWHC 3541 (QB).   [225] *Ibid.*, para. 27.
[226] [2010] EWHC 1084 (QB), para. 16.   [227] [2010] EWCA Civ 173, para. 13.   [228] *Ibid.*
[229] *Ibid.*   [230] *Ibid.*, para. 15.
[231] *Milford Haven Port Authority* v. *Unite* [2010] EWCA Civ 400; and *British Airways plc* v. *Unite the Union (No. 2)* [2010] EWCA Civ 669.

and Birmingham Railway Ltd scaled new heights.[232] The latter is a historic decision in which the Court of Appeal finally recognised not only the defects of English common law which 'confers no right to strike in this country',[233] but also the importance of 'various international instruments' in which these rights are openly acknowledged.[234] Not only that, but the Court of Appeal has at long last further acknowledged that the ECtHR 'has in a number of cases confirmed that the right to strike is an element of the right to freedom of association' as 'conferred by Article 11(1) of the European Convention on Human Rights'.[235] This recognition of a right to strike means that the laws restricting trade union freedom are not to be strictly applied against trade unions, the courts no longer to start from the presumption that Parliament intended that the interests of employers will always hold sway.[236]

This new approach was immediately put into practice in *ASLEF* v. *London and Birmingham Railway Ltd*, where – as we have seen – an injunction had been granted against ASLEF, first, because the union had inadvertently included in the ballot two members who were not entitled to vote. This was a genuine mistake, openly acknowledged by the union; but it did not affect the result of the ballot. As reported by the Court of Appeal, ballot papers had been sent to 605 drivers. Of the 472 who voted (a turnout of 78 per cent), 410 (87 per cent of those voting) voted in favour of industrial action. The accidental inclusion of the two members not entitled to vote was said by the Court of Appeal to be trivial and therefore excusable. As we have also seen, a second ground for the injunction was that the union had provided inaccurate information in the notice of its intention to hold a strike ballot. The High Court took the view that the notice was inaccurate for including the two disputed members. As pointed out above, however, the Court of Appeal took a robustly realistic view of the situation, reminding employers everywhere that the duty on the unions under the legislation is simply to provide a notice that is accurate in relation to the information actually held by the union. In other words, the union is not under a duty to go looking for information to satisfy the convenience or whim of the employer, the Court of Appeal's decision in this respect calling into question the validity of the injunctions granted against RMT in earlier cases involving EDF Energy and Network Rail respectively.[237]

A third ground for the injunction was that the union had failed properly to explain to the employer how it had arrived at the information contained in the ballot notice. The union had said that the information was based on union membership records, which had been updated and audited to ensure accuracy. Not good enough, said counsel for London Midland. In his view, the union

---

[232] [2011] EWCA Civ 226, [2011] ICR 848. See R. Dukes, 'The Right to Strike under UK Law: Something More than a Slogan?' (2011) 40 *Industrial Law Journal* 302.

[233] *Ibid.*, para. 2 (Elias LJ).   [234] *Ibid.*, para. 8.   [235] *Ibid.*   [236] *Ibid.*, para. 9.

[237] *EDF Energy Powerlink Ltd* v. *RMT* [2009] EWHC 2852 (QB); *Network Rail Infrastructure* v. *RMT* [2010] EWHC 1084 (QB).

should have disclosed precisely who did what and when, as well as when the records were last updated. Not only that. According to Mr Bear, the notice was fatally flawed for being a 'conclusion' rather than an 'explanation',[238] a distinction he had previously persuaded the High Court to accept in the *Network Rail* case, and a good example of the kind of problems that the RMT in particular has had to endure in a number of cases. But as we also saw above, the Court of Appeal was having none of it, taking the view that 'nothing is to be achieved by stating which particular officer obtained the information, or on which particular day, or whether contacts with local officers were by email or phone'.[239] Nor was the court having any of the employer's argument that the union had given an inaccurate explanation by claiming that it had audited its records before giving the information to the employer. In a withering rebuttal of the arguments presented by the employers' legal team, Elias LJ said that:

> In assessing the accuracy of the explanation, it must be borne in mind that the union officials providing it are not drafting a statute, and nor are they required to use undue precision or accuracy in their use of language. In my view the courts should not take the draconian step of invalidating the ballot, thereby rendering the strike unlawful, simply because the term used to describe a particular process is infelicitous. In my judgment the description of the process undertaken would have to be positively and materially misleading before the explanation could be said to fall short of the statutory requirement.[240]

Having discharged the injunction against ASLEF, the Court of Appeal also discharged the injunction against RMT, and did so for similar reasons. In this comprehensive victory for ASLEF and the RMT, the Court of Appeal stressed that the freedom to take industrial action was not to be constrained by ridiculous arguments invented by lawyers. Nor was it the role of the court to 'set traps and hurdles for the union which have no legitimate purpose or function'.[241] The effect has been largely to put an end to litigation about notices and ballots, with only a few reported cases on such matters in the years since.[242] This may of course reflect the fact that unions are now more experienced and skilful in handling the demands of the statutory procedures, although it may also reflect the fact that there are many fewer strikes, with industrial action having fallen in recent years to historic low levels. For the time being, however, it is hard to avoid the conclusion that some judges are more sensitive to the right to strike as a human right, which is now openly acknowledged judicially at a time when it is the subject of even more swingeing restrictions by Parliament. This was particularly notable in the *Govia Gtr*

---

[238] [2011] EWCA Civ 226, [2011] ICR 848, paras. 41 and 96.   [239] *Ibid.*, para. 94.
[240] *Ibid.*, para. 103.   [241] *Ibid.*, para. 94.
[242] *ISS Mediclean Ltd* v. *GMB* [2014] EWHC 4208 (QB), [2015] IRLR 96; *Govia Thameslink Railway Ltd* v. *ASLEF (No. 2)* [2016] EWHC 1320 (QB), [2016] IRLR 686; *Thomas Cook Airlines Ltd* v. *BALPA* [2017] EWHC 2252 (QB),

Railway Ltd case,[243] where the Court of Appeal moved to close down any possible damaging consequences of the *Viking* and *Laval* cases for industrial action with a mainly domestic purpose.[244] In this way the Court of Appeal is using human rights not only narrowly to construe the statutory limits but also to restrain the development of new causes of action against trade union.

Conclusion

RMT v. *Serco Ltd* and *ASLEF* v. *London and Birmingham Railway Ltd*[245] represent an important shift in British law, and mean that trade union action will not be quite so easily restrained in the future. Returning to Maurice Kay LJ, no longer can it be said that in British law the right to strike is no more than a metaphor or a slogan.[246] On the contrary, 'the [ECtHR] has in a number of cases confirmed that the right to strike is conferred as the right to freedom of association conferred by Article 11(1) of the European Convention on Human Rights which in turn is given effect by the Human Rights Act'.[247] As Elias LJ pointed out, however, 'the right is not unlimited and may be justifiably restricted under Article 11(2)'.[248] In *Metrobus*, the current statutory restrictions in their full glory were found not to constitute a breach of Article 11, having regard to Article 11(2). Although the point was made in the two most recent Court of Appeal cases by John Hendy QC for the unions that 'the detailed complexity of the balloting provisions, and their unnecessary intrusion into the union's processes, involves a disproportionate interference with the Article 11(1) right',[249] it was not pressed on the ground that, so far as the Court of Appeal was concerned, the questions had been answered by *Metrobus*.

But although the decision of the Court of Appeal in *RMT* v. *Serco Ltd* has (1) acknowledged a right to strike from Convention rights via the Human Rights Act 1998, (2) instructed the High Court that it must not start from the presumption in injunction proceedings that the law has to be construed against trade unions, and (3) probably removed some of the 'traps and hurdles' set by the courts beyond those erected by Parliament, it has yet (4) to succeed in removing any of the major obstacles to the right to strike built up in legislation in the years since 1980. In the absence of a government willing to respect its international legal obligations, that is a battle that will have to be fought in the Supreme Court, or in the ECtHR. But as we saw in the *RMT* case, expressions of optimism in the first edition of this

---

[243] [2016] EWCA Civ 1309, [2017] ICR 497.

[244] As the Court of Appeal pointed out in *Govia Gtr Railway Ltd*, 'it would undermine the right to strike in a most fundamental way if all passengers potentially and indirectly affected by the strike could claim that it was interfering with their rights to provide and receive services. Subject to a defence of justification, the union's liability would be open ended' (para. 60). Compare *Falconer* v. *NUR* [1996] IRLR 331, the prelude to TULRCA 1992, s. 235A.

[245] [2011] EWCA Civ 226.   [246] *Metrobus Ltd* v. *Unite the Union* [2009] IRLR 851, para. 118.

[247] [2011] EWCA Civ 226, para. 8.   [248] *Ibid.*   [249] *Ibid.*

book that the Strasbourg court would provide the necessary leverage for change proved to be misplaced, the Court still reluctant to challenge either substantive or procedural restrictions on the right to strike in British law, despite a host of decisions upholding the right to strike in complaints from other countries. The matter will doubtless be revisited at some time in the future, but for the time being we are stuck in first gear – the Strasbourg Court providing a wide margin of appreciation in which the British government and its supporters were prepared to live, when defending the additional restrictions introduced by the Trade Union Act 2016.[250]

UK Law and ILO Convention 87

As pointed out by Cox J in *Unite the Union (No. 1)*,[251] it is inevitable that at some stage there will be a day of reckoning in which common-law liabilities and inadequate statutory protections confront the full measure of inconsistency with international standards and human rights obligations. As we saw in the second section of this chapter, the ILO supervisory agencies have for many years now recognised that the right to strike is part and parcel of ILO Convention 87. This is an instrument that has been ratified by the UK, and which gives rise to obligations under international law. On a regular basis since 1989, the ILO Committee of Experts has reminded UK governments of these obligations and has indicated in the strongest terms that the UK imposes 'excessive limitations on the right to strike, for a host of reasons'.[252]

These include the following:

- the restriction of the protection to disputes between workers and their own employer, which 'could make it impossible for unions to take effective action in situations where the "real" employer with whom they were in dispute was able to take refuge behind one or more subsidiary companies';
- the lack of protection for action with a political dimension, particularly in view of changes made in 1982 requiring action to relate wholly or mainly to listed matters, said to deny protection where unions have mixed motives, as where they are pursuing industrial, political and social objectives;
- the restrictions on solidarity and secondary action (including picketing), which prompted the Committee to conclude that their effect is 'to make it virtually impossible for workers and employers lawfully to engage in any form of boycott activity, or sympathetic action against parties not directly involved in a given dispute'.[253]

---

[250] Official Report, Public Bill Committee – Trade Union Bill, 15 October 2015, Q348.
[251] *British Airways plc* v. *Unite the Union* [2009] EWHC 3541 (QB).
[252] For full details, see K. D. Ewing, *Britain and the ILO* (2nd edn, London: Institute of Employment Rights, 2004); and W. B. Creighton, 'The ILO and Protection of Freedom of Association in the United Kingdom', in K. D. Ewing, C. A. Gearty and B. A. Hepple (eds.), *Human Rights and Labour Law* (London: Mansell, 1994), Ch. 1.
[253] ILO Committee of Experts, Observation Concerning Convention 87 (United Kingdom) (1989).

The Trade Union Act 2016 prompted fresh criticism, especially with regard to the requirement that in important public services, at least 40 per cent of those balloted must vote in favour of industrial action as a condition of its protection. This obligation was found to breach ILO Convention 87, at least insofar as it applied to education and transport.[254] However, the ILO Committee of Experts has not yet commented adversely on the notice and ballot provisions detailed above, although it took the view that the much less detailed regime as introduced in 1984 did not constitute a breach of Convention 87. But it has opened a fresh line of criticism of the UK in the wake of the *BALPA* case referred to above. Not only did the Committee reserve its strongest criticism yet for the UK, but in its 2011 report it was wholly unimpressed by the UK government's argument that the *BALPA* case was a direct result of a decision of the CJEU over which it has no control.[255] It is because of an Act of the UK Parliament that EU law has direct effect in the UK: the government cannot shirk its responsibilities under treaties that predated membership of the EU.

UK Law and the European Social Charter

As already pointed out, the European Social Charter protects the right to strike (Article 6(4)), subject to various permitted restrictions (Article 31). In January 2015 the European Committee of Social Rights repeated a number of concerns about the UK's compliance with Article 6(4)), including the pre-ballot notice obligation. According to the Committee, the situation in the UK is not in conformity with the Charter on the following grounds:

• the possibilities for workers to defend their interests through lawful collective action is excessively circumscribed;
• the requirement to give notice to an employer of a ballot on industrial action is excessive;
• the protection of workers against dismissal when taking industrial action is insufficient.[256]

These concerns have been expressed by the Social Rights Committee over several cycles of supervision, and were not allayed by the *Serco* decision in the Court of Appeal, to which reference was made.[257]

---

[254] ILO Committee of Experts, Observations Concerning Convention 87 (United Kingdom) (2016).
[255] On the *BALPA* case, see pp. 777–8.
[256] European Committee of Social Rights, Conclusions XX-3 (United Kingdom) (2015), p. 24.
[257] *RMT* v. *Serco Ltd* and *ASLEF* v. *London and Birmingham Railway Ltd* [2011] EWCA Civ 226. The Committee also favourably referred to *Balfour Beatty Engineering Services Ltd* v. *Unite the Union* [2012] EWHC 267 (QB), which is discussed in Chapter 17.

17

Liability for Collective Action

Contents

Introduction

There is probably a manual in a law firm somewhere that provides guidance to employers who want to break a union. The early pages of the manual will be devoted to tactics to be used to keep the union out. But there will also be pages of the manual that deal with the situation where a union has become established. Some of these pages will guide the employer on how to break a strike. The aim of the employer will usually be to keep production or the delivery of services going during the strike, and to minimise its impact in various ways. In the first instance, the employer may be advised to prevent or stop the action by seeking a remedy in the courts to restrain the union by way of injunction on the ground that the tortious conduct of the union is actionable. Alternatively – or if this fails – the employer may seek to enlist third-party support to maintain production or the delivery of services. In the British Airways cabin crew dispute of 2009–11, this involved contracting with other airlines to provide aircraft and crew to carry BA passengers, and to encourage other employees to train for cabin-crew duties so that BA could continue to operate at least some of its own fleet.[1] On other occasions, employers have recruited new staff or recruited temporary staff, sometimes from an employment agency, though as we shall see this is a practice that is now unlawful.[2]

A harsher part of that section of the manual dealing with strike-breaking may advise the employer to take action against the strikers themselves. This may take the form of intimidatory measures designed to spread fear among the workforce, and to weaken the resolve of the strikers. Such intimidation – which may also be designed to crush the union – may lead to the withholding of benefits from individual workers or the withdrawal of facilities from their organisation. It may also lead to dismissals of key activists, and in extreme cases the employer may want to dismiss and replace a striking workforce, although in the latter case the employer's options may be constrained not only by law but also by the absence of a readily available tailor-made body of replacements.[3] Apart from sanctions against individuals, a strike-bound employer may seek to recover losses from the union and indeed may use the dispute to weaken or crush the union as well as to resist its demands. Litigation may thus have the dual purpose of restraining the action or (exceptionally) obtaining damages for losses suffered, but also of burdening the union with substantial legal costs. Most employers, however, will want to settle the dispute, and if unable to do so by their own efforts may be directed by a thoughtful lawyer's manual to a different kind of third-party support, in the

---

[1] See K. D. Ewing, *Fighting Back: Resisting Union-Busting and Strike-Breaking in the BA Dispute* (London: Institute of Employment Rights, 2011).

[2] See p. 785.

[3] But see K. D. Ewing and B. W. Napier, 'The Wapping Dispute and Labour Law' (1986) 45 *Cambridge Law Journal* 285.

form of the advice, conciliation and arbitration provided by ACAS, the statutory body which exists for these very purposes.[4]

Chapter 16 provided an account of the legal framework within which these pages of the manual will be developed. As we saw, there are tight legal controls on the purposes for which strike action may be taken, on the procedures that must be followed by trade unions and on the practices that may be engaged in and the tactics that may be deployed.[5] Although many of these controls appear to be inconsistent with international human-rights obligations, there seems to be little doubt about the controls and attendant empowerment of employers to constrain industrial action, the incidence of which is now very low by historical standards. It is true that the restrictive legislation is not the only explanation for the decline in levels of strike activity. Other factors have played a part, not the least being the changing economic and political environment since the 1970s in particular, as well as the not unrelated decline in the number of trade unionists from 13 million in 1979 to around 6.2 million in 2017.[6] Nor should we overlook the work of ACAS in bringing the majority of disputes to a negotiated settlement.[7] But while there is no single factor that helps to explain the staggering decline in the levels of strike activity in recent years, it is unlikely that anyone would deny that the law has played a part, even if there may be some debate on the nature and extent of that part.

Labour Injunctions

The first aim of the employer in a dispute may be to prevent industrial action from taking place, and for this purpose an injunction may be sought. A party who feels that he or she is the victim of a legal wrong being committed by another may apply for interim relief to have the action restrained until the trial of the action. In an industrial dispute, the employer will seek an injunction on the ground that the action of the union is tortious. It is true that the union will enjoy certain legal protections for acts done in contemplation or furtherance of a trade dispute.[8] But the employer will argue that the action is not protected by the legislation, perhaps because there is no trade dispute or because the action is not supported by the notice and ballot procedures required by law.[9] In seeking an injunction, the employer will encounter a procedure stacked very much in its favour: the application can be made at the last minute, the union may be given only limited notice of an application that the employer may have been preparing for weeks, and it is not a requirement of the granting of an injunction that the employer can say unequivocally that its legal rights have been violated. Nor is the employer required to act

---

[4] See TULRCA 1992, ss. 209–18.   [5] See Chapter 16.
[6] BEIS, *Trade Union Membership 2017. Statistical Bulletin* (2018), p. 4.   [7] See pp. 803–8.
[8] See Chapter 16.   [9] See Chapter 16.

timeously: the employer may sleep on its rights and invoke them when tactically expedient to do so.[10]

Interim Injunctions

An application for an interim injunction is governed by the Civil Procedure Rules.[11] The application must normally be supported by evidence, and the respondent must normally be given at least three days' notice of the application.[12] So far as granting an application for interim relief is concerned, the landmark case is *American Cyanamid Co.* v. *Ethicon Ltd*,[13] where Lord Diplock said that, in determining whether interim relief should be granted, it is not necessary for the applicant to show a '*prima facie* case' or a 'strong *prima facie* case', but simply that 'there is a serious issue to be tried'. He continued by saying that, 'unless the material available to the court at the hearing of the application for an [interim] injunction fails to disclose that the plaintiff has any real prospect of succeeding in his claim for a permanent injunction at the trial, the court should go on to consider whether the balance of convenience lies in favour of granting or refusing the interlocutory relief that is sought'.[14] Lord Diplock continued:

> It would be unwise to attempt even to list all the various matters which may need to be taken into consideration in deciding where the balance lies, let alone to suggest the relative weight to be attached to them. These will vary from case to case. Where other factors appear to be evenly balanced it is a counsel of prudence to take such measures as are calculated to preserve the *status quo*. If the defendant is enjoined temporarily from doing something that he has not done before, the only effect of the interlocutory injunction in the event of his succeeding at the trial is to postpone the date at which he is able to embark upon a course of action which he has not previously found it necessary to undertake; whereas to interrupt him in the conduct of an established enterprise would cause much greater inconvenience to him since he would have to start again to establish it in the event of his succeeding at the trial.[15]

This is a very low threshold for issuing an interim injunction, which presents problems in the context of industrial action. At the time of the decision in *American Cyanamid Co.* v. *Ethicon Ltd*, trade unions were not vicariously liable in damages for tortious acts committed in the course of a trade dispute.[16]

---

[10] For example, the employer may challenge a known defect of a notice to conduct industrial action after the union has held a ballot, given notice to strike and embarked upon industrial action: *Metrobus Ltd* v. *Unite the Union* [2009] EWCA Civ 829, [2010] ICR 173 (CA).

[11] Civil Procedure Rules, Part 25.

[12] *Ibid.* See also Practice Direction 25A (Interim Injunctions). See also TULRCA 1992, s. 221(1) (requirement of notice to the respondent in trade dispute cases).

[13] [1975] AC 396 (HL).   [14] *Ibid.*, p. 408.   [15] *Ibid.*

[16] Trade Union and Labour Relations Act 1974, s. 14. This protection of trade unions had previously been found in the Trade Disputes Act 1906, s. 4.

Any application for an injunction would therefore have to be brought against the trade union official who called the action. Were the interim injunction to be refused, there would be no question of an employer being compensated in damages for losses suffered during a strike, should the application ultimately succeed at the full trial. (Indeed, even if damages were recoverable from the union, it is difficult to contemplate in many cases – such as large-scale national strikes – how damages would compensate.) This made it more likely that an interim injunction would be granted to restrain industrial action until the trial of the action. The difficulty, however, is that the interim injunction would effectively dispose of the matter: once stopped, a strike or other industrial action would be very difficult to revive.[17] Even if the trial were to take place, it could be months or even years later, by which time the dispute will have moved on, as indeed may have many of the workers who were involved in the first place.[18]

So it was necessary to ensure that employers were not able to obtain interim relief if their application was without substance on legal grounds, and if they were unlikely to succeed on legal grounds were the matter to come to trial. Otherwise, Parliament's intention of giving trade unions the freedom to take industrial action could in practice be frustrated by procedural law, in a manner that would undermine any simple notion of the rule of law: industrial action would be restrained not because it was unlawful, but because there was a possibility that it might be held unlawful in legal proceedings which were likely never to take place. Measures originally introduced in the Trade Union and Labour Relations Act 1974 and the Employment Protection Act 1975 are now to be found in TULRCA 1992, section 221. This seeks not only to discourage the granting of *ex parte* injunctions in trade dispute cases,[19] but also to raise the standard for the granting of interim injunctions in such cases to a level beyond *American Cyanamid*. Thus, TULRCA 1992, section 221(2), provides that where

> the party against whom it is sought claims that he acted in contemplation or furtherance of a trade dispute, the court shall, in exercising its discretion whether or not to grant the injunction, have regard to the likelihood of that party's succeeding at the trial of the action in establishing any matter which would afford a defence to the action under section 219 (protection from certain tort liabilities) or section 220 (peaceful picketing).

---

[17] As explained in *NWL Ltd* v. *Woods* [1979] ICR 867 (HL); and *Serco Ltd* v. *RMT* [2011] EWCA Civ 226, [2011] ICR 848 (CA).

[18] The classic study of these problems from a US perspective is F. Frankfurter and N. Greene, *The Labor Injunction* (University of Chicago Press, 1930). The classic UK study is S. Anderman and P. L. Davies, 'Injunction Procedure in Labour Disputes' (1973) 2 *Industrial Law Journal* 213 and (1974) 3 *Industrial Law Journal* 30.

[19] TULRCA 1992, s. 221(1).

The meaning of what is now TULRCA 1992, section 221(2), was considered in a number of cases in the 1970s. There was a feeling in some quarters that the Court of Appeal in particular was doing less than justice to the underlying purpose of the measure, or indeed to its literal provisions.[20] The matter was addressed by the House of Lords in *NWL Ltd* v. *Woods*,[21] where the ITF had a policy of 'blacking' ships flying a flag of convenience. The purpose of the policy was to compel the owners of the ships in question to employ crew on terms approved by the ITF, or to transfer the vessels' registration to the countries of domicile of their beneficial owners. In this case, an injunction was granted by Donaldson J to prevent the defendants from issuing instructions and/or persuading stevedores, tug operators and pilots to break their contracts of employment to prevent the free passage of a ship called the *Nawala*, which was docked at Redcar. The Court of Appeal discharged the injunction, and upheld another decision of Donaldson J not to grant an injunction against other defendants. The House of Lords upheld the Court of Appeal in both cases, and, in the course of doing so, Lord Diplock said, in relation to injunctive relief:

> Judges would, I think, be respecting the intention of Parliament in making this change in the law in 1975, if in the normal way the injunction were refused in cases where the defendant had shown that it was more likely than not that he would succeed in his defence of statutory immunity; but this does not mean that there may not be cases where the consequences to the employer or to third parties or the public and perhaps the nation itself, may be so disastrous that the injunction ought to be refused, unless there is a high degree of probability that the defence will succeed.[22]

Evolution of the Law

These remarks notwithstanding, an important feature of the *Woods* case was the additional observation of Lord Diplock in which he appeared to suggest that what is now TULRCA 1992, section 221(2), was unnecessary. This is because *American Cyanamid* had not been 'properly understood', in the sense that it was never intended to apply to cases where the interlocutory proceedings would have the effect of resolving the dispute between the parties, on the ground that the matter was of such a nature that it was never likely to go to full trial.[23] Trade disputes would most obviously fall into this category, and in such cases the judge in interlocutory proceedings ought to give 'full weight to all the practical realities of the situation in which the injunction will apply'.[24] According to Lord Diplock, where:

---

[20] For an account of these cases, see K. D. Ewing, 'The Golden Formula: Some Recent Developments' (1979) 8 *Industrial Law Journal* 133.
[21] [1979] ICR 867 (HL).   [22] *Ibid.*, p. 881.   [23] *Ibid.*, pp. 879–81.   [24] *Ibid.*, p. 880.

the grant or refusal of the interlocutory injunction will have the practical effect of putting an end to the action because the harm that will have been already caused to the losing party by its grant or its refusal is complete and of a kind for which money cannot constitute any worthwhile recompense, the degree of likelihood that the plaintiff would have succeeded in establishing his right to an injunction if the action had gone to trial, is a factor to be brought into the balance by the judge in weighing the risks that injustice may result from his deciding the application one way rather than the other.[25]

However, a largely overlooked reconsideration of the foregoing guidelines took place in *Dimbleby & Sons Ltd* v. *NUJ*,[26] where Lord Diplock (again) noted that the circumstances had changed since the *Woods* case. Legislation in 1980 and 1982 had restricted the scope of the protection: by virtue of the Employment Act 1980, section 17, protection was withdrawn from certain forms of secondary action (widened in 1990 to withdraw protection from all secondary action);[27] and, by virtue of the Employment Act 1982, trade unions could now be liable in damages for industrial action which fell outside the scope of the protection.[28] So how should the courts proceed in the future with applications for interim injunctions? Here, Lord Diplock said that what is now TULRCA 1992, section 221(2), is the test to be applied not only where the defendant is relying on the statutory protection, but also where 'any issue' arises 'between the plaintiff and the defendant as to whether the acts complained of were excluded from the protection of [what is now section 219] of the Act of [1992] by the provisions of section 17 of the Act of 1980'.[29]

Regarding all other issues raised by way of defence (such as a claim that the defendant's conduct was not tortious),[30] according to Lord Diplock 'the criterion to be applied in order to make recourse to the balance of convenience necessary is the ordinary criterion laid down in *American Cyanamid Co.* v. *Ethicon Ltd*: "Is there a serious question to be tried?"'[31] This lowering of the bar set in *Woods* was explained as being caused principally by the change in the law in 1982 so that trade unions could now be sued in their own names and could be liable in damages for losses caused in the course of unprotected action. According to the House of Lords, this meant that it could no longer be assumed that cases would not go to trial or that the interlocutory injunction would finally dispose of the matter. But although it is clearly the case that the law has been changed greatly since 1979, it is not clear that there has been any change to the underlying realities that led Lord Diplock in *Woods* to address the 'misunderstandings' of *American Cyanamid*. The employer is still likely to suffer considerable financial loss during a strike and will want the action

---

[25] *Ibid.*, p. 881.   [26] [1984] ICR 386 (HL).   [27] See pp. 746–9.   [28] See pp. 777–9.
[29] [1984] ICR 386 (HL), p. 406.
[30] On this, see also *NWL Ltd* v. *Woods* [1979] ICR 867 (HL), p. 880 (Lord Diplock).
[31] [1984] ICR 386 (HL), p. 406.

stopped. For its part, the trade union will still incur expense and inconvenience if the action is stopped, while it is very rare for cases to go to full trial[32] and rarer still for damages to be sought in these cases.

It is true – as Lord Diplock pointed out in *Dimbleby* – that trade unions are now liable in damages and can now be sued for the losses they cause. As already pointed out, there was no trade union liability before the law was changed in 1982 so that any injunction had to be obtained against the union official who gave the instruction to strike. As also already pointed out, there was no prospect of damages being recovered in such cases, even if the employer was so minded to seek recovery. In practice, however, the change to the law has made little difference to these particular realities either, and provides no justification for departing from the approach in *Woods*. Partly this is because employers in practice have no desire to recover damages, and partly because the damages are capped in such a way that the employer would be unable to recover its losses even if he or she were minded to do so. As we shall see, the size of the cap depends on the size of the trade union (not the losses incurred by the employer), the cap not having been increased since it was introduced in 1982.[33] The fact that damages are available subject to limited liability ought thus not to affect the general principle that *American Cyanamid* should not be applied in its undiluted form in cases where the injunction is likely finally to dispose of the legal proceedings between the parties.[34]

Labour Injunctions in Practice

From time to time there are periods in which a spate of labour injunctions is granted on what appear to be flimsy and controversial grounds. The spate is subsequently reduced to a trickle by a key intervention, which has a decisive impact, and will persist until the floodgates are reopened at some future date. The years 2008–11 were one such period.[35] *Serco Ltd* v. *RMT* may be one such

---

[32] But see *Ministry of Justice* v. *POA* [2017] EWHC 621 (QB), [2017] IRLR 621; and subsequently [2017] EWHC 1839 (QB), [2018] ICR 181.

[33] See pp. 777–9.

[34] *Dimbleby* thus appeared to create a distinction in trade disputes between cases where the TULRCA 1992, s. 219 defence was to be considered and cases dealing with all other issues. In the latter, *American Cyanamid* was to apply, without the qualification in *Woods*. So far unresolved is the question of what issue falls into which category. In *Dimbleby*, Lord Diplock suggested that the former would apply to any question about the meaning of the protection as well as any exclusion of protection because the conduct complained of constituted secondary action from which protection had been withdrawn. But there have been many other restrictions on the scope of the protection, both substantive but mainly procedural since 1980. In these cases, are the restrictions to be treated (1) in the same way as the now repealed provisions of the Employment Act 1980 (in which case, the defendant's likelihood of success at full trial must be taken into account), or (2) in the same way as 'all other issues' (in which case, the ordinary criterion is to apply)?

[35] Others would include the periods 1901–6, 1964–9 and 1977–80.

intervention.[36] Not that anything dramatic was said in the latter case, simply that an injunction should normally be refused if the court finds it more likely than not that the union will succeed at the (imaginary) trial in showing that the statutory protections will apply.[37] Although it does not follow 'as a matter of law' that the interim injunction 'has to be refused' in such circumstances, 'it will have to be a very exceptional case indeed' for the injunction to be refused.[38] This is a welcome restatement of orthodoxy which will clearly make the employer's task in interim proceedings more difficult,[39] although we should not be complacent about the willingness of the courts in finely balanced cases to give disproportionate effect to the interests of the employer. Nor should we be complacent about the risk in exceptional circumstances of attention being directed to 'public interest' considerations as trumps in interim injunction applications.

The Employer's Interest

So far as disproportionate attention to the interests of the employer is concerned, the point is illustrated well by *BT plc* v. *CWU*,[40] where the employer contested an alleged failure of the union to provide it with adequate information in its industrial action ballot notices under TULRCA 1992, sections 226A and 234A, respectively. The union had given notice that it would ballot 'all CWU engineering members employed in BT Customer Services Field Operations and in BT Northern Ireland'. Although this amounted to 90 per cent of the workforce, BT nevertheless complained that the information did not enable it to identify the employees who would be taking part in the ballot and subsequently the industrial action. This is despite the fact that 'probably most and perhaps the very great majority' of union members would be known to BT by virtue of the fact that the company checked off their union dues for the CWU.[41] Nevertheless, the notices were said by BT not to be enough to enable it to 'make plans', although they were unable to say what plans they would make, a failure thought to be 'surprising', but excused by the judge because of the speed with which the proceedings had been brought.[42]

---

[36] [2011] EWCA Civ 226, [2011] ICR 848 (CA). For cases of similar significance restraining an earlier spate of injunctions, see *NWL Ltd* v. *Woods* [1979] ICR 867 (HL); *Express Newspapers Ltd* v. *McShane* [1980] ICR 42 (HL); and *Duport Steels Ltd* v. *Sirs* [1980] ICR 161 (HL).

[37] [2011] EWCA Civ 226, [2011] ICR 848 (CA), para. 13.

[38] *Ibid*. See also *Balfour Beatty Engineering Services Ltd* v. *Unite the Union* [2012] EWHC 267 (QB), para. 4.

[39] As already revealed by *Balfour Beatty Engineering Services Ltd* v. *Unite the Union* [2012] EWHC 267 (QB); and *London Underground Ltd* v. *ASLEF* [2011] EWHC 3506 (QB).

[40] [2004] IRLR 58 (QB).   [41] *Ibid*., p. 61.

[42] The statutory provisions then in force stated that the ballot and industrial action notices must contain 'such information in the union's possession as would help the employer to make plans and bring information to the attention of those of his employees': TULRCA 1992, ss. 226A(2)(c) and 234A(3)(a). These provisions were repealed in 2004.

In deciding whether to grant the injunction, Stanley Burnton J said that 'the Act requires the court to take into account the likelihood of the defendants succeeding at the trial of the action in establishing any matter which would afford a defence to the action brought by BT', that is to say, in effect, 'the likelihood, on the basis of the findings I have made, of the notice of ballot and of strike action that have been given being held to have been insufficient for the purpose of the statute'.[43] But he continued by saying that while this was 'an important consideration, it is not the only consideration', with the balance of convenience requiring 'a consideration of the losses which would be incurred on either side'.[44] Once the debate is deflected away from law on to extraneous matters of this kind, the union's arguments are never likely to prevail, and seem calculated always to yield to the superior claims of the employer. In this case, it was a straightforward choice between 'the financial losses on the part of BT' on the one hand, and 'the relatively small cost of arranging a second ballot complying with the requirements of the statute'.[45] No contest it might be thought, given that it was unlikely that BT's losses 'would be recovered in due course from the union if BT establish that the strike was unlawful but no injunction is granted'.[46]

In an unusually thorough examination of competing considerations, Stanley Burnton J acknowledged that there were considerations other than financial ones to be weighed in the balance of convenience. However, these were given short shrift. Thus, if there was a fresh ballot, the likelihood was that the result would be the same, and that 'BT [would] suffer the loss now indicated in any event'.[47] But although he held in the circumstances that he should assume that it was likely that the membership would vote in favour of a strike if re-balloted, he also held that he 'cannot take that as being a foregone conclusion'.[48] There is also the point of realism recognised by Lord Diplock in the *Woods* case that 'it is the nature of industrial action that it can be promoted effectively only so long as it is possible to strike while the iron is still hot; once postponed it is unlikely that it can be revived'.[49] But although Stanley Burnton J claimed to understand – *pace* Lord Diplock – that the union wanted to strike while the 'iron is hot', that was 'a minor consideration, in the scheme of things, compared with the very large sums which would be lost on the part of BT'.[50]

Having thus diminished the trade union's arguments by holding that immediate losses trump both the level of support and the disadvantage to the union caused by further delay (bearing in mind too the time it takes to hold a ballot and give the various notices to the employer), we are back to the question of just how much the employer has to show that the balance of legality is in its favour. Just how 'important' a 'consideration' is law in a process that is likely to be a final determination of the issues between the parties? In this case, it was enough that there was a 'significant prospect' of BT

---

[43] [2004] IRLR 58 (QB), p. 62.   [44] *Ibid.*   [45] *Ibid.*   [46] *Ibid.*   [47] *Ibid.*
[48] *Ibid.*, p. 63.   [49] [1979] ICR 867 (HL), 879.   [50] [2004] IRLR 58 (QB), p. 63.

successfully arguing that the notices provided insufficient information to enable it to 'make plans', Stanley Burnton J saying expressly that he '[did] not put the prospect any higher'.[51] What 'significant prospect' means in this context is not clear: a good chance? More likely than not? A real likelihood? Did the union also have a 'significant' chance of successfully resisting the employer's argument? Or did the 'significant' chance of the employer rule out that possibility? We will never know.[52] But we might have been more convinced if the employer had been able to say – even in interim proceedings – which plans it had been unable to make because of alleged omissions in the union's notices.[53]

The Public Interest

Writing in 1989, Wedderburn argued that the willingness of the courts to grant interim injunctions was undermining the sovereignty of Parliament.[54] There is a strong sense of these concerns in *Duport Steel* v. *Sirs*, where Lord Diplock said that:

> The British constitution, though largely unwritten, is firmly based upon the separation of powers; Parliament makes the laws, the judiciary interpret them.[55]

As already suggested, however, there is another constitutional principle in danger of being traduced in this area, namely, the rule of law.[56] The latter is usually taken to mean that people are free to do that which is lawful and to mean that they may be restrained only for doing that which is unlawful. Some sensitivity to such concerns appears to be implicit in *Woods*, and the acknowledgement that special rules are required for interim proceedings where the decision of the court is likely to be conclusive of the dispute between the parties. But although sensitive to these concerns, the sensitivity is not complete, in light of observations in cases such as *BT* that, while legal rights are an 'important consideration', there are 'other considerations'.[57]

---

[51] *Ibid.*

[52] For similar problems under the Human Rights Act 1998, s. 12(3), see *Cream Holdings Ltd* v. *Banerjee* [2004] UKHL 44, [2005] 1 AC 253 (HL). Note also the reference to HRA 1998, s. 12(3) in *Balfour Beatty Engineering Services Ltd* v. *Unite the Union* [2012] EWHC 267 (QB).

[53] The employer's case would have been more persuasive still if it had acted in a timely fashion. If the ballot notice prevented the employer from making plans, why did the employer wait until the eve of the strike to complain?

[54] Lord Wedderburn, 'The Injunction and the Sovereignty of Parliament' (1989) 23 *Law Teacher* 4.

[55] [1980] ICR 161 (HL), p. 177.

[56] Lord Diplock also raised rule of law concerns, albeit of a slightly different nature, relating to the effect of the injunctions in the lower courts in defiance of Parliament's will on the 'continued public confidence in the political impartiality of the judiciary': *ibid.*, p. 178.

[57] *BT plc* v. *CWU* [2004] IRLR 58 (QB), p. 63. This does not necessarily cease to be the case after *Serco* and its progeny. In *Balfour Beatty Engineering Services Ltd* v. *Unite the Union* [2012] EWHC 267 (QB), Eady J said that it is now clear that 'no applicant in this claimant's position can expect to succeed in obtaining interlocutory relief merely by showing (i) that there is a

These concerns are compounded by recent cases where the courts have not only granted injunctions on what some perceive to be flimsy grounds, but have done so by having regard to a range of issues wider than simply the immediate economic losses of the employer. In the three House of Lords cases in the 1980s where the modern law and practice relating to interim relief in trade disputes was fully developed,[58] it appeared to be accepted that there might be circumstances in which injunctions could be granted in the public interest, with such considerations being a paramount consideration. Thus, although injunctions should not normally be granted where the weight of the law lies with the defendant, as we saw above this was qualified by Lord Diplock as follows:

> this does not mean that there may not be cases where the consequences to the employer or to third parties or the public and perhaps the nation itself, may be so disastrous that the injunction ought to be refused, unless there is a high degree of probability that the defence will succeed.[59]

Similar remarks were to be found in the speeches of other senior judges at the time, including Lord Scarman, who said that, 'in a case where action alleged to be in contemplation or furtherance of a trade dispute endangers the nation or puts at risk such fundamental rights as the right of the public to be informed and the freedom of the press, it could well be a proper exercise of the court's discretion to restrain industrial action pending trial of the action'.[60]

This thread was gathered by Mrs Justice Cox in the BA cabin-crew dispute already referred to in this chapter,[61] when, in granting an injunction to restrain strike action following the first ballot, she said that she 'can and should have regard to the wider public interest in considering whether or not to grant the relief sought'.[62] This enabled her to acknowledge that:

> A strike of this kind taking place now, over twelve days of the Christmas period, is in my view fundamentally more damaging to BA, and indeed to the wider public, than a strike taking place at almost any other time of year.[63]

The injunction was granted, as it was in the subsequent decision of Mrs Justice Sharp in *Network Rail Infrastructure Ltd v. RMT*,[64] where she said that:

---

serious issue to be tried, (ii) that the balance of convenience lies in its favour and (iii) that it is likely otherwise to suffer harm which cannot be adequately compensated for in damages' (para. 3). But that still leaves a penumbra of uncertainty, particularly in cases where it 'is not always easy to form a judgment about the outcome of a case at an early stage and, in particular, when the court is confined to only partial or inchoate evidence' (*ibid.*).

[58] *NWL Ltd v. Woods* [1979] ICR 867 (HL); *Express Newspapers Ltd v. McShane* [1980] ICR 42 (HL); and *Duport Steels Ltd v. Sirs* [1980] ICR 161 (HL). See Lord Wedderburn, 'Industrial Relations and the Courts' (1980) 9 *Industrial Law Journal* 65.

[59] *NWL Ltd v. Woods* [1979] ICR 867 (HL), pp. 881–2.

[60] *Express Newspapers Ltd v. McShane* [1980] ICR 42 (HL), 65. This is the top of a slippery slope.

[61] *British Airways plc v. Unite the Union* [2009] EWHC 3541 (QB), [2010] IRLR 423 (QB).

[62] *Ibid.*, para. 81.   [63] *Ibid.*, para. 83.   [64] [2010] EWHC 1084 (QB).

Mr Bear [for the employer] has invited me in addition to conclude, even if I could not form a view as to the likely outcome of the trial, that Network Rail has a seriously arguable case under normal *American Cyanamid* principles. Therefore, he submits, the court will still be justified in the circumstances in granting an injunction having regard to the level of damage which a strike would cause to Network Rail and nationally. That matter has not been argued before me by Mr Reynold [representing the union]. But I am satisfied having regard to the significant damage which is identified, and will obviously result if the strike goes ahead (I refer in this context to what is said by Mr MacFarlane [a witness for the employer] in paragraphs 104–108 of his first witness statement) that the consequences of the strike are likely to be particularly severe, and that as the case is clearly arguable it would be appropriate in any event for an interim injunction to be granted. Any harm to the Union in having to await a speedy trial in my view would be clearly outweighed by the disproportionate damage done to others as Mr Bear submits, by holding a strike which is arguably unlawful.[65]

It remains standard practice to justify injunctions in rail disputes by reference to the public interest (or specifically the interests of the travelling public).[66]

This potential dilution of legality in the interests of a range of competing concerns raises questions about the extent to which the injunction procedure is compatible with Article 6 of the ECHR, concerns all the more urgent for the fact that the defendant is being prevented from exercising a substantive human right (the right to strike) which the Convention purports to protect.[67] Article 6 provides that everyone has a right to a fair trial in the determination of his or her civil rights and obligations. According to Countouris and Freedland, in 'the Grand Chamber's judgment in *Micallef* v. *Malta*,[68] the Strasbourg Court's jurisprudence on this fundamental aspect of the right to fair trial has gone through a dramatic evolution, with the Court asserting that "whenever an interim measure can be considered effectively to determine the civil right or obligation at stake ... Article 6 will be applicable."[69] If it is the case – as Countouris and Freedland suggest – that Article 6 is engaged by the interim injunction procedure, it is for consideration whether it is compatible with the right to a fair trial for the determination of one's rights and obligations that questions of law – and the freedom to exercise a human right – can be displaced not only by (1) extraneous economic considerations, but also by (2) the presumed concerns of third parties who are not directly involved in the

---

[65] *Ibid.*, para. 73.

[66] *Govia Thameslink Railway Ltd* v. *ASLEF* [2016] EWHC 985 (QB), and subsequently [2016] EWHC 1320 (QB).

[67] See Chapter 16.   [68] [2009] ECHR 1571, (2009) 50 EHRR 37.

[69] N. Countouris and M. Freedland, 'Injunctions, *Cyanamid*, and the Corrosion of the Right to Strike in the UK' (2010) 1 *European Labour Law Journal* 489. The authors also argue that, under the Human Rights Act 1998, the courts 'should abandon the traditional, *American Cyanamid*-based, test typically used in awarding interlocutory injunctions in industrial action cases, in favour of the more human rights-attuned "proportionality test"'.

litigation, (3) in circumstances where these third parties (the 'public') have not given evidence one way or another.

Injunctions Granted on Flimsy Grounds?

A major concern of trade unions is that injunctions have been granted routinely on flimsy grounds of alleged petty procedural lapses. These cases are discussed in Chapter 15. But to recap, injunctions have been granted because:

- The union notified the employer of its plans to ballot 'engineers/technicians', the employer demanding to know which 'fitters, jointers, test room inspectors, day testers, shift testers and OLBI fitters' would be involved.[70]
- The union gave notice of an intention to ballot and balloted members who because of redundancy would not be taking part in the action, in circumstances where their participation did not affect the result.[71]
- The union did not explain how numbers and categories of a minority of workers in the ballot and strike notices were arrived at, in circumstances where the genuine uncertainty of the law was recognised by the court.[72]
- The union delayed by a few days (as a result of an administrative oversight, for which in part the union was not at fault) in informing the employer of the ballot result.[73]
- The union informed its members of the ballot result by text, referring the members to the union's website for full details and failed to notify members of spoiled ballots, though in this case the injunction was lifted on appeal.[74]
- The union gave notice of continuous and discontinuous industrial action on one rather than two pieces of paper, in a decision that perhaps plumbs the depths of a legal system in which form has replaced substance.[75]

It is true that in the last case the High Court was also overturned on appeal.[76] Nevertheless, the union was thus prevented by an injunction issued on the most petty grounds from taking industrial action on the original date proposed. Fresh notices had to be issued for the action to begin five days later than planned. The fact that the union won on appeal in relation to one of the grounds on which the injunction was granted is of little consolation: the decision of the Court of Appeal did not restore the right to take the action at the time proposed, nor did it resolve the other question in relation to which the union was restrained and subsequently appealed.

---

[70] *EDF Energy Powerlink Ltd* v. *RMT* [2009] EWHC 2852 (QB), [2010] IRLR 14, [2010] EWCA Civ 173 (CA). See subsequently *RMT* v. *United Kingdom* [2014] ECHR 366.

[71] *British Airways plc* v. *Unite the Union* [2009] EWHC 3541 (QB), [2010] IRLR 423 (QB).

[72] *Metrobus Ltd* v. *Unite the Union* [2009] EWCA Civ 829, [2010] ICR 173 (CA).   [73] *Ibid.*

[74] *British Airways plc* v. *Unite the Union (No. 2)* [2010] EWCA Civ 669, [2010] ICR 1316.

[75] *Milford Haven Port Authority* v. *Unite the Union* [2010] EWCA Civ 400 (CA).   [76] *Ibid.*

Trade Union Liability

It is one thing to have a right and a remedy, but another to have a party against which the right can be claimed and the remedy sought. In the famous *Taff Vale* case, the House of Lords held that trade unions could be liable for the torts of their servants and agents, which meant that they could be restrained by injunction and sued for damages. There was great hostility towards trade unions in some quarters at the time, reflected by the remarks of Farwell J at first instance in *Taff Vale*, where he said that trade unions were 'irresponsible bodies with such wide capacity for evil'.[77] In reversing the *Taff Vale* decision, the Trade Disputes Act 1906 by section 4 gave trade unions an almost complete protection from liability in tort. Justified by the newly elected Liberal government as being necessary to protect trade unions from the courts, this measure was condemned in equal measure as being inconsistent with the rule of law, with Farwell LJ (as he now was) lamenting that 'the legislature cannot make evil good, but it can make it not actionable'.[78] Nevertheless, from 1906 until 1982 it was thus not possible for injunctions to be obtained against trade unions (with the exception of a short period between 1971 and 1974). By the same token, it was generally not possible to obtain damages against a trade union for losses incurred in the course of a strike (though there were exceptions), even where the union's action was not done in contemplation or furtherance of a trade dispute.

Injunctions against Trade Unions

As we have seen, by the Employment Act 1982 all this was to change radically, with the protection from liability inherited from the Trade Disputes Act 1906 having been repealed.[79] Although it is never likely to be reinstated, much of the hyperventilation that this protection induced was wholly unnecessary. The protection of the trade union did not stop litigation by employers seeking to stop strikes, and indeed a great deal of jurisprudence developing the scope and content of the economic torts discussed in Chapter 16 was forged in the course of that litigation. In these cases, however, the action was brought against the union official (often the general secretary) who gave the instruction to take the action, and not the union on behalf of whom he was acting.[80] So although there was constant grumbling about the trade union protection and exaggerated claims about it being inconsistent with the rule of law, it is unlikely that anyone wronged by a union would have been denied a legal

---

[77] *Taff Vale Railway Co. Ltd* v. *ASRS* [1901] AC 426 (HL), p. 431.

[78] *Conway* v. *Wade* [1908] 2 KB 844 (CA), p. 856.

[79] By then to be found in the Trade Union and Labour Relations Act 1974, s. 14.

[80] See *D. C. Thomson & Co. Ltd* v. *Deakin* [1952] Ch 646 (CA); *Torquay Hotel Co. Ltd* v. *Cousins* [1969] 2 Ch 106 (CA). In both cases, the defendants were high-profile general secretaries of the TGWU.

remedy. True, a party seeking damages for loss caused by a union for action that was not a protected tort, or for action that was not in contemplation or furtherance of a trade dispute, would be unlikely to sue a hapless union official for losses caused by the union. But it is also true that there were few situations where Parliament in 1906 can have expected liability to arise; where it did, it would be open to the employer to avoid the need for damages by seeking an injunction to prevent the loss in the first place.

Trade union liability (by way of injunction and damages) is now governed by TULRCA 1992, sections 20 and 21. In some cases (such as conspiracy to injure, inducing breach of contract, and intimidation), the trade union will be liable only if the action in question 'is to be taken to have been authorised or endorsed by the trade union'.[81] For these purposes, 'an act shall be taken to have been authorised or endorsed by a trade union if it was done, or was authorised or endorsed' by:

- any person empowered by the rules to do, authorise or endorse acts of the kind in question; or
- the principal executive committee, or the president or general secretary; or
- any other committee of the union or any other official of the union (whether employed by it or not).[82]

It is then provided that, for the purposes of the third of these bullet points (TULRCA 1992, section 20(2)(c)), 'any group of persons constituted in accordance with the rules of the union is a committee of the union'.[83] Moreover, 'an act shall be taken to have been done, authorised or endorsed by an official if it was done, authorised or endorsed by, or by any member of, any group of persons of which he was at the material time a member, the purposes of which included organising or co-ordinating industrial action'.[84] This latter provision has been read by at least one employer to mean that a trade union could be made liable by the actions of a member of a strike committee which includes at least one official of the union.[85]

These provisions are extremely wide in scope and override any union rules to the contrary. For the trade union there is something of a dilemma. Either it must face the risk of liability caused by conduct which it has not formally approved or take steps to repudiate the action, which will be unpopular with the activists who may be discouraged by such a response, which they may also construe as a betrayal. Nevertheless, the scope of liability is illustrated by *Gate Gourmet* v. *TGWU*,[86] where the union members rejected a pay deal negotiated by the union and engaged in a spontaneous walk-out, setting up a picket line and a protest at a site close to the workplace. An injunction was sought by the

---

[81] TULRCA 1992, s. 20(1).   [82] TULRCA 1992, s. 20(2).   [83] TULRCA 1992, s. 20(3)(a).
[84] TULRCA 1992, s. 20(3)(b).
[85] *Gate Gourmet London Ltd* v. *TGWU* [2005] EWHC 1889 (QB), [2005] IRLR 881 (QB), para. 19.
[86] *Ibid.*

employer to restrain the picketing at the different sites, the respondents being the union, a large number of union members who were participating in the picketing, and 'persons unknown'. Eight union officials (none of them senior national officials) attended the picket (in the case of two full-time paid officials on one day only). According to Fulford J, in relation to the union:

> [O]n the evidence at this stage, between them the various officials named above have been present at the pickets on sufficient days to mean there is a clear arguable case that the union over the relevant period has fully appreciated and understood the types of unlawful activity which were being routinely perpetrated, particularly, at, or close to, site B, but also on occasion at, or close to, site A.[87]

Along with the alleged conduct of one of the officials, this was said to demonstrate that there was 'a good arguable case that unlawful and tortious acts' had occurred, 'which have been authorised or endorsed by the union'.[88] It was thus arguable on what was no more than their 'probable level of knowledge as to what was occurring' that 'specific officials can be said to have authorised these unlawful and tortious activities', and that by their attendance at the site the officials in question 'have, in reality, constituted a group who are organising or coordinating industrial action'.[89] In the absence of repudiation of the conduct by the union, an injunction was granted. So far as repudiation is concerned, as Fulford J pointed out, there is a formal statutory procedure that must be complied with if the repudiation is to have effect. The procedure requires repudiation to be by senior officials. Moreover, 'the union must without delay give written notice of repudiation to the official or committee whose act is being repudiated', while 'it must also "do its best" to give an individual written notice "without delay" to every member of the union whom it has reason to believe is participating or might participate in the relevant industrial action'.[90] By virtue of TULRCA 1992, section 21(3), the latter must include the following warning:

> Your union has repudiated the call (or calls) for industrial action to which this notice relates and will give no support to unofficial action taken in response to it (or them). If you are dismissed whilst taking unofficial industrial action, you will have no right to complain of unfair dismissal.

Enforcing the Injunction

Since 1982, legal action by employers against trade unions has become commonplace. Not only could legal action now be brought against trade unions rather than their officials, but with the other changes in the law such actions could be brought in a wide range of circumstances: because there was no trade dispute; because the trade union was involved in unlawful secondary action; or

---

[87] *Ibid.*, para. 23.   [88] *Ibid.*, para. 24.   [89] *Ibid.*   [90] *Ibid.*, para. 20.

because the action did not have the support of a ballot; and so on. A question that soon arose after the introduction of the new liabilities was what would happen when an injunction was granted against a trade union, which then refused to comply with the order. Could the unions successfully defy the law, as they had done under the Industrial Relations Act 1971,[91] which for a brief period had also exposed trade unions to liability? They were soon to find out that failure to comply with an injunction is a contempt of court and that the arm of the law has a long reach.

An initial belief by trade unions that the law could be ignored or casually applied led to contempt proceedings being brought by employers.[92] In most of these cases, modest fines were imposed, although in *Austin Rover* no penalty was imposed because the court was persuaded of the union's lack of culpability. On the other hand, in *Richard Read (Transport) Ltd* v. *NUM (South Wales Area)*[93] a more substantial penalty was imposed in a case where union officials narrowly avoided imprisonment for contempt. The plaintiffs were hauliers, who during the miners' strike of 1984–5 had been contracted to carry coke from Port Talbot to a number of locations. Pickets prevented the drivers from delivering their loads, and the plaintiff company had obtained an interim injunction against the defendant union – as well as three named officials – to restrain the pickets. But the picketing continued and there was no evidence from which an inference could be drawn that the union had revoked its instructions to its members to interfere with the plaintiff's vehicles. It was argued for the union that the conduct of the employer made it impossible for the respondents to comply with the injunction. This was because the employer's vehicles were travelling in convoy with the vehicles of other employers, it being claimed in correspondence from the union to the employer's lawyers that:

> The convoy travels at speed, the vehicles of the various companies are bunched close together, and in these circumstances it is impossible or impractical for any person on the picket line to identify the lorries which belong to your clients and distinguish them from the remainder of the vehicles in the convoy. If your clients' vehicles were travelling in a group of their own either ahead or at the rear of the convoy and our clients were so advised of the arrangement, the position would be different as they would be clearly recognizable.[94]

It was claimed in these circumstances that the respondents could not be said knowingly to be in breach of the injunction. This is a claim that drew a frosty response from Park J, who understood the foregoing letter to 'suggest that the

---

[91] On which, see B. Weekes, M. Mellish, L. Dickens and J. Lloyd, *Industrial Relations and the Limits of Law* (Oxford: Basil Blackwell, 1975).

[92] *Messenger Newspapers Group Ltd* v. *NGA (1982)* [1984] IRLR 397 (QB); *Richard Read (Transport) Ltd* v. *NUM (South Wales Area)* [1985] IRLR 67 (QB); *Austin Rover* v. *AUEW (TASS)* [1985] IRLR 162 (QB); *Express and Star Ltd* v. *NGA* [1986] IRLR 222 (CA); and *Kent Free Press* v. *NGA* [1987] IRLR 267 (QB).

[93] [1985] IRLR 67 (QB).   [94] *Ibid.*, p. 70.

officials have in fact ceased to instruct or encourage the pickets to interfere with the plaintiff companies' vehicles and to abuse their drivers but that, owing to the failure of the companies in some way to distinguish their vehicles from the vehicles of other hauliers, any breaches of the injunction have been unknowingly committed. It would have been interesting to know what instructions, if any, were given to pickets in relation to the plaintiffs' vehicles.'[95] Park J said that this was an 'unacceptable explanation',[96] before adopting a *dictum* of Sir John Donaldson in *Howitt Transport Ltd* v. *TGWU*,[97] where he said that 'orders of any court must be complied with strictly in accordance with their terms', and that 'it is not sufficient, by way of an answer to an allegation that a court order has not been complied with, for the person concerned to say that he "did his best"'.[98] It is clear that Park J saw this as a serious contempt, and resisted the temptation of jailing the officials only with 'some hesitation', and only because he was not pressed to do so by the employer. He continued by saying that:

> the imposition of fines is in the present circumstances the proper method of dealing with both contempts. But having regard to the manner in which the defendant union has deliberately defied the court orders, the fines have to be substantial. For the contempt in each case I fine the defendant union £25,000. The total of the fine will be £50,000 to be paid within 48 hours.[99]

But what if defiance means non-payment of the fine? Here, the stakes are raised much higher, with non-payment leading to the likely sequestration of the assets of the union. This is a risk about which the union will be warned at the time the injunction is granted, with a penal notice attached to the injunction stating that if it does not comply with the order, the union may be in contempt of court and its officers imprisoned or fined, and its assets seized.[100] The procedure is governed by the Civil Procedure Rules,[101] although there is no recent experience of trade union funds being sequestrated, for although there have been dozens of injunctions issued to employers, these have been generally complied with. Sequestration is a potent weapon of employers: union officials lose control of the assets of the union, while sequestrators run up considerable costs to be met from union funds. The appointment of sequestrators is thus not something that in normal circumstances a court would do lightly: in the *Richard Read* case, Park J drew attention to a newspaper report indicating that the union might be seeking to avoid the payment of any fines by transferring its funds into the private bank accounts of its leaders. So he gave the plaintiffs leave to issue

---

[95] *Ibid.*   [96] *Ibid.*   [97] [1973] IRLR 25 (NIRC).   [98] *Ibid.*, p. 26.

[99] *Richard Read (Transport) Ltd* v. *NUM (South Wales Area)* [1985] IRLR 67 (QB), p. 71. For a full account of this dimension to the miners' strike of 1984–5, see R. Benedictus, 'The Use of the Law of Tort in the Miners' Dispute' (1985) 14 *Industrial Law Journal* 176.

[100] Civil Procedure Rules, Rule 81.9. See *Ministry of Justice* v. *POA* [2017] EWHC 1839, [2018] ICR 181.

[101] Civil Procedure Rules, Part 81.

writs of sequestration, but also gave the union officials time to reflect on their position, the writs 'to lie in the office' for forty-eight hours.[102]

Damages

As we saw earlier in this chapter, for much of the twentieth century trade unions enjoyed protection from suit.[103] However, liability was restored by the Employment Act 1982, which means that employers may proceed against a trade union for both injunctive relief and damages. The amount of damages that may be recovered is subject to a statutory ceiling, the maximum liability in respect of any applicant being £250,000 for trade unions with 100,000 or more members; £125,000 for trade unions with 25,000 or more but fewer than 100,000 members; £50,000 for trade unions with 5,000 or more but fewer than 25,000 members; and £10,000 for trade unions with fewer than 5,000 members.[104] The ceiling applies to each plaintiff in an action and not to the proceedings as a whole, so, in a case where there are multiple applicants,[105] the liability potentially could be extensive (though this has not been an issue in modern times). Perhaps more importantly, the ceiling does not apply to legal costs, unions often being left to bear both their own as well as those of the employer. Nor does the ceiling apply to liability in tort that is unrelated to industrial action, such as (1) proceedings for personal injury as a result of negligence, nuisance or breach of duty; (2) proceedings for breach of duty in connection with the ownership, occupation, possession, control or use of property; and (3) proceedings brought by virtue of Part I of the Consumer Protection Act 1987 (product liability).[106]

There have been very few reported cases where employers have sought damages against trade unions, although there may be unknown circumstances where a trade union has settled in favour of an employer. For the most part, it seems that employers are content that an injunction can be obtained against a union to restrain industrial action, in the knowledge that the contempt laws will give the unions little option but fully to comply. Nevertheless, liability for losses caused by industrial action will arise if the action is unprotected by the legislation for whatever reason (an unprotected tort, not in contemplation or furtherance of a trade dispute, or protection withdrawn because it constitutes secondary action, or because the balloting and notice provisions have not been complied with). In one case involving secondary picketing and other forms of secondary action to enforce the closed shop, it was held that both exemplary and aggravated damages were recoverable.[107] Although there could be no aggravated damages for the injury to the feelings of a corporate applicant, and although aggravated damages were 'compensatory', an award under this head was appropriate against a trade union 'where the injury to the plaintiff has been aggravated by malice or by the manner of doing the injury; that is, the insolence or arrogance by which it is

---

[102]   For an account of these procedures in the context of a particularly bitter dispute between News International and the print unions, see K. D. Ewing and B. W. Napier, 'The Wapping Dispute and Labour Law' (1986) 45 *Cambridge Law Journal* 285.

[103]   Trade Disputes Act 1906, s. 4.   [104]   TULRCA 1992, s. 22(2).

[105]   As in *Glamorgan Coal Co.* v. *South Wales Miners' Federation* [1905] AC 239 (HL).

[106]   TULRCA 1992, s. 22(1).   [107]   *Messenger Group Ltd* v. *NGA* [1984] IRLR 397 (QB).

accompanied'.[108] In a second case, Saville J held that the limit on damages did not fetter the discretion of the court to award interest on the damages.[109]

A matter of concern has arisen following the *Viking* and *Laval* decisions of the ECJ,[110] in which it was held that industrial action could constitute a breach of the freedom of movement and freedom to provide services under EC Treaty, Articles 43 and 49 (now TFEU, Articles 49 and 56). Shortly after these decisions were published in December 2007, the UK airline pilots' union, BALPA, was in dispute about British Airways' plan to run flights to the United States from France. It had been suggested that BA's losses could amount to up to £100 million a day. In order to pre-empt a possible threat of action for damages by the company on the ground that the action would violate its rights under EU law, BALPA sought a declaration that the proposed action was lawful. It might have been thought that any claim for damages by BA would be subject to the statutory cap in TULRCA 1992, section 22. However, BA argued first that such a claim was not a claim in tort (thought by BALPA to have been a weak argument), and secondly that the cap on damages was in any event incompatible with EU law requiring effective remedies for breach of EU obligations. The union discontinued the action before the court could consider these matters, and the issues raised now await full examination.[111] In the meantime, trade unions have been placed on notice that industrial action that violates the EU Treaty rights of businesses could lead to litigation with the potential of financial ruin.[112]

This issue has since been considered by the ILO Freedom of Association Committee in response to a complaint by BALPA. BALPA complained that the possible exposure of a trade union to unlimited damages in the light of *Viking* and *Laval* violated the right to freedom of association as protected by ILO Convention 87. In 2010 the Committee observed with serious concern the practical limitations on the effective exercise of the right to strike of the BALPA members in this case. The Committee took the view that 'the omnipresent threat of an action for damages that could bankrupt the union, possible now in the light of the *Viking* and *Laval* judgments, creates a situation where the rights under the Convention cannot be exercised'. While taking due note of the government statement that it was premature at this stage to presume what the impact would have been had the court been able to render its judgment given that BALPA withdrew its application, the Committee continued by saying that there was 'a real threat to the union's existence and that the request for the injunction and the delays that would

---

[108] *Ibid.*, 406–7.

[109] *Boxfoldia Ltd* v. *NGA (1982)* [1988] IRLR 383 (QB). So, in addition to damages of £250,000, interest of £90,000 was awarded against the union. More recently, the sum of £130,000 was awarded against a union where the action was unprotected because of notice and ballot irregularities: *Willerby Holiday Homes Ltd* v. *UCATT* [2003] EWHC 2608 (IDS Brief 749, January 2004).

[110] Case C-438/05, *International Transport Workers' Federation (ITF) and Finnish Seamen's Union (FSU)* v. *Viking Line* [2007] ECR I-10779; Case 341/05, *Laval un Partneri Ltd* v. *Svenska Byggnadsarbetareförbundet et al.* [2007] ECR I-5751.

[111] See K.D. Ewing and J. Hendy, 'The Dramatic Implications of *Demir and Baykara*' (2010) 39 *Industrial Law Journal* 2, for a discussion of this affair.

[112] On the unresolved damages point, see K. Apps, 'Damages Claims against Trade Unions after *Viking* and *Laval*' (2009) 34 *European Law Review* 141.

necessarily ensue throughout the legal process would probably render the action irrelevant and meaningless'.

Resisting a number of arguments presented by the government, the Committee requested the government to 'review the TULRCA and consider appropriate measures for the protection of workers and their organizations to engage in industrial action and to indicate the steps taken in this regard'.[113]

Discipline and Dismissal

International labour standards are said to support the general principle that 'no person shall be prejudiced in his employment by reason of his trade union membership or legitimate trade union activities'.[114] This general principle has led the ILO Freedom of Association Committee to maintain that 'no one should be penalized for carrying out or attempting to carry out a legitimate strike'.[115] By the same token, the ILO Committee of Experts 'has also affirmed the protection of workers and union officials against acts of anti-union discrimination and has confirmed that most national legislation contains general or detailed provisions which protect workers against such acts of discrimination, although the level of protection may vary'.[116] As the Committee pointed out, however, 'sanctions or redress measures are frequently inadequate when strikers are singled out' by means of 'disciplinary action, transfer, demotion, dismissal', the problem being said to be 'particularly serious' in the case of dismissal 'if workers may only obtain damages and not their reinstatement'.[117] This is a passage that might well have been written with the UK specifically in mind, the provisions relating to protection from discrimination and dismissal for trade union membership and activities in British law being inapplicable to discrimination and dismissal for taking part in industrial action.[118] For these latter purposes, dedicated – but inadequate – legislative protection has been enacted separately.[119]

---

[113] ILO Committee of Experts, Observation Concerning Convention 87 (United Kingdom) (2010). In the following year, the Committee repeated its concerns and called for 'effective limitations on actions for damages so that unions are not faced with threats of bankruptcy for carrying out legitimate industrial action': ILO Committee of Experts, Observation Concerning Convention 87 (United Kingdom) (2011). See now limiting the potential damage, *Govia Gtr Railway Ltd* v. *ASLEF* [2016] EWCA Civ 1309, [2017] ICR 497, pp. 719–20 above.

[114] B. Gernigon, A. Odero and H. Guido, 'ILO Principles Concerning the Right to Strike' (1998) 137 *International Labour Review* 441, at 463.

[115] *Ibid.*, 464.   [116] *Ibid.*   [117] *Ibid.*

[118] This follows from the fact that TULRCA 1992, ss. 146 and 152, provide protection from discrimination and dismissal for trade union activities, but only where these take place either outside working hours or during working hours with the employer's consent. This is subject to the possibility that matters such as the preparation of industrial action might be undertaken at an appropriate time: *Serco Ltd* v. *Dahou* 2015 IRLR 30 (EAT).

[119] See pp. 785–96.

Action Short of Dismissal

As we have seen, by calling on its members to take industrial action, a trade union will invariably be calling on its members to take action in breach of their contracts of employment. According to Lord Templeman in *Miles* v. *Wakefield Metropolitan Borough Council*,[120] '[a]ny form of industrial action by a worker is a breach of contract',[121] though this is a view which has been disputed, Sir Patrick Elias writing before his elevation to the bench that:

> employees may be able to take strike action in response to a repudiatory breach by the employer in one of two ways. Either they may be able to withhold their labour until the employer is willing to perform his part of the contract; or they may be able to give notice to terminate their contracts in response to the repudiatory breach.[122]

However, this view has never been endorsed by (or to our knowledge in recent times argued before) a court, and indeed Sir Patrick has since expressed the view that 'workers who take strike action will usually be acting in breach of their contracts of employment'.[123] One consequence of this is that it is unlikely that those taking part in such action will be entitled to be paid by the employer; at best they will be entitled to be paid only for work actually done where the action takes a form other than a strike. Even here, however, the employer has the option to decide whether or not to accept partial performance in lieu of full performance.[124] Although international labour standards create no objection to 'wage deductions for days of strikes',[125] the scope of the current common law rules are controversial. Thus, if the employer decides that partial performance is unacceptable, the workers in question may find that they are not entitled to be paid at all, even for work which has been done and accepted by the employer, and even where the work done amounts to performance of the great bulk of the employee's obligations under the contract.[126]

But although an employer may be permitted to make a deduction for days of industrial action, questions arise as to how much the employer can deduct for each day of industrial action. In some cases, the position will be expressly governed by contract, but in others it may be left to the discretion of the

---

[120] [1987] AC 539 (HL).   [121] *Ibid.*, p. 559.

[122] P. Elias, 'The Strike and Breach of Contract: A Reassessment', in K. D. Ewing, C. A. Gearty and B. A. Hepple (eds.), *Human Rights and Labour Law* (London: Mansell, 1994), Ch. 11.
 Although such a review of the contractual liability of strikers is to be welcomed, it is not to be overlooked that the view expressed extra-judicially by Sir Patrick would have implications for the law of tort as well as the law of contract. Thus, if the industrial action is not a breach of contract, there can be no liability for inducing breach of contract, and no need for the action to be supported by a ballot.

[123] *RMT* v. *Serco Ltd* [2011] EWCA Civ 226, [2011] ICR 848 (CA), para. 2.

[124] *Ticehurst* v. *British Telecommunications* [1992] ICR 383 (CA).

[125] B. Gernigon, A. Odero and H. Guido, 'ILO Principles Concerning the Right to Strike' (1998) 137 *International Labour Review* 441, at 471.

[126] *Wiluszynski* v. *Tower Hamlets London Borough Council* [1989] ICR 493 (CA).

employer. In *Hartley* v. *King Edward VI College*,[127] it was held that a deduction could be made of only 1/365th of the annual salary for each day of strike action, the UKSC rejecting the employer's argument that it could make a deduction at the rate of 1/260th of annual salary. The employer's claim was based on the total number of weekdays in the calendar year, but the Court preferred the argument that the matter was governed by the Apportionment Act 1870 which provides that salaries accrue from day to day, 'in cases where the contracts provide for an annual salary paid monthly'. As suggested by the Court, however, this will not always be the applicable rule. Even in the absence of express terms to the contrary, the rate of any permitted deduction 'would no doubt be different if the contracts were not annual contracts'.[128] Where wages have been improperly withheld, the claim must be brought in the county court. The procedure in the Employment Rights Act 1996, section 13 for the recovery of unauthorised deductions in the ET does not apply to deductions made for having taken part in a strike or other industrial action.[129]

In addition to 'wage reductions for days of strikes', participants in industrial action may find themselves on the receiving end of other sanctions or penalties imposed by the employer, including the cancellation or withholding of benefits. A good example is provided by the British Airways cabin crew dispute, when allegations were made by the trade union that the employer had taken punitive steps against strikers, some of whom it was claimed were also victimised for their strike-related activities. A major concern of the union was the withdrawal by the company of various travel concessions, a step taken after three days of industrial action. Although these were reinstated with the settlement of the dispute, benefits accrued between April and October 2010 were not restored. If these were contractual benefits, it might be possible to sue to recover them on the ground that the employer's conduct amounted to a unilateral variation of the employment contracts of the individuals in question. Here, however, the employer argued that the benefits in question were *ex gratia* rather than contractual, notwithstanding their considerable value to the individuals concerned. In the absence of any statutory equivalent to TULRCA 1992, section 146 for taking part in industrial action,[130] there was no way by which these benefits could be recovered in legal proceedings. The

---

[127] [2017] UKSC 39.   [128] *Ibid.*, para. 48.

[129] ERA 1996, s. 14(5). See *Norris* v. *London Fire and Emergency Planning Authority* [2013] ICR 819. A refusal by employee to carry out a task which he or she believes to be under no contractual obligation to perform is not industrial action 'in the absence of any other element'. According to the EAT, it would be 'very undesirable if the law were that a mere refusal to perform a non-contractual task constituted industrial action, because if an employee were dismissed for such a refusal – which on the face of it would normally be unfair – the effect of section 238 of the 1992 Act would (absent special circumstances) be that he would be unable to claim for unfair dismissal'.

[130] This provides protection from detrimental action short of dismissal for trade union membership and some trade union activities: see Chapter 12.

absence of a remedy for workers penalised for taking part in lawful industrial action is a notable lacuna in British labour law.[131]

The other major risk facing workers in a dispute is the risk of disciplinary action, a risk that may be felt more acutely by those who hold office as shop stewards or branch representatives. In the same BA cabin crew dispute, the BBC reported that ninety-three cabin crew were sacked or disciplined for conduct relating to the dispute,[132] while the *Observer* reported that the union had 'appealed for cabin crew to volunteer as shop stewards' because of the loss of 'key members to sackings and suspensions, including the official in charge of representing staff in disciplinary hearings'.[133] Those dismissed for taking part in a dispute may have a remedy for unfair dismissal, which is discussed later. But those who suffer disciplinary action short of dismissal may find it more difficult to complain, depending on the nature of the disciplinary sanction. It is true that someone who suffers a financial penalty may be able to contest the penalty in legal proceedings as being a breach of contract, most likely in the county court. But although there is no guarantee of success, this is an opportunity unlikely to be available to a worker who is issued with a disciplinary warning, even where the warning includes a final warning. The only obvious redress for a worker who claims to have been unfairly singled out for such treatment would be to resign and claim that he or she had been constructively dismissed and that the dismissal was unfair.[134] But this is not a solution that any responsible legal adviser is likely to recommend, unless the employee has had enough and is already determined to leave.

Dismissal and Replacement

Perhaps a more serious concern for workers involved in a dispute is the risk of dismissal. At common law, a worker who takes part in a strike or other industrial action will normally be liable to dismissal without notice. In view of the fact that the striker will be failing to perform a fundamental term of the contract, it is unlikely that a remedy will be available for wrongful dismissal (not that this would in any event provide much security).[135] As suggested above, however, international labour standards require national governments to provide adequate protection for workers, in the sense that participating in a lawful strike should be regarded as suspending rather than terminating the contract of employment, and in the sense also that those who take part in such

---

[131] An attempt to close the gap was made in *Roffey* v. *United Kingdom*, App. No. 1278/11 (21 May 2013), in which the withholding of travel benefits was challenged as violating Convention rights. The application was ruled inadmissible on the ground that it was out of time.
[132] BBC News, 12 May 2011.   [133] *Observer*, 5 September 2010.   [134] See pp. 866–9.
[135] On wrongful dismissal, see Chapter 18.

action should be protected from dismissal with a right to reinstatement at the end of the dispute.[136] According to the ILO Committee of Experts:

> [I]t is inconsistent with the right to strike as guaranteed by [ILO Convention 87] for an employer to be permitted to refuse to reinstate some or all of its employees at the conclusion of a strike, lock-out or other industrial action without those employees having the right to challenge the fairness of that dismissal before an independent court or tribunal.[137]

As in the case of action short of dismissal, British law relating to the dismissal of strikers does not meet minimum international requirements. This is despite the introduction of the statutory right to unfair dismissal in 1971. When the unfair dismissal law was reintroduced by the then Labour government in 1974, an employee dismissed for taking part in a strike or other industrial action (or in the course of a lock-out) had no right to bring a claim for unfair dismissal, unless it could be shown that the employee in question had been selectively dismissed or that the dismissed employee could show that other dismissed employees had been selectively re-engaged.[138] In other words, the legislation provided the employer with an immunity from legal proceedings, although it was an immunity contingent upon dismissing all and not re-engaging any of those who were on strike and who had been on strike.[139] But even if the immunity from litigation was lost by the employer selectively dismissing a striking employee, the dismissal would not necessarily be unfair. The discriminatory treatment of strikers, or the participants in other industrial action would simply open the door to the tribunal, where the application would have to be contested on the usual grounds: was the applicant an employee, did the employer have a reason for the dismissal, and if so did the employer act fairly (within the band of reasonable responses) in dismissing the employees? There are few reported cases which address the fairness or otherwise of such industrial action dismissals.

The employer's immunity was extended in a number of ways by the Employment Act 1982, section 9, providing most notably that an employer could selectively re-engage dismissed employees after three months: it was no longer necessary never to re-engage as a condition of retaining the immunity. Still further changes introduced by the Employment Act 1990 provided that an employee dismissed while engaged in unofficial action could not bring

---

[136] B. Gernigon, A. Odero and H. Guido, 'ILO Principles Concerning the Right to Strike' (1998) 137 *International Labour Review* 441, pp. 461–5.

[137] ILO Committee of Experts, Observation Concerning Convention 87 (United Kingdom) (1989).

[138] Trade Union and Labour Relations Act 1974, Sched. 1, para. 8; Employment Protection (Consolidation) Act 1978, s. 62. The former provided that a dismissal would 'not be regarded as unfair' in the absence of victimisation; the latter provided that an industrial tribunal 'shall not determine whether a dismissal was fair or unfair'.

[139] *Stock v. Frank Jones (Tipton) Ltd* [1978] 1 WLR 231 (HL).

proceedings for unfair dismissal (even though the employee had been select-ively dismissed). The law nevertheless continued to offer some protection for striking workers, in the sense that an employer was immune from legal proceedings (except in the case of unofficial action) only if it dismissed all those involved in the industrial action. But although mass dismissal might not always be possible, in truth this was a feeble form of protection. Employers in the 1980s were to take full advantage of the weaknesses of this particular approach and some appeared to feel no constraint in dismissing an entire workforce. The watershed event was probably the News International dispute at Wapping in 1985–6, when the company dismissed some 5,500 striking print workers and replaced them with a ready-made alternative workforce recruited, with the help of a 'renegade' trade union and bussed in to the Wapping plant from Southampton on a daily basis.[140] If an employer could take such steps in relation to a skilled workforce of this size, what price other workers faced with imposed changes to working conditions?[141]

Wapping and other events exposed the defects of a system of protection for striking workers that had been introduced by a Labour government in 1974–5. These defects would not have been addressed simply by repealing the relevant amendments of 1982 and 1990, the trade unions now calling for the law to be reformed to provide better protection for workers. The position appeared all the more unfair for the fact that employees could be dismissed for taking part in a strike even where the increasingly complex conditions of trade union protection were complied with: the action could be in furtherance of a trade dispute, supported by a ballot, with proper notice given to the employer. Yet those taking part in the action could still be dismissed. The claims of those who sought to reform the law were supported by the growing realisation that in other European countries workers were protected from dismissal for taking part in lawful strikes, and by the conclusions of international supervisory bodies (such as the Social Rights Committee of the Council of Europe, as well as the CFA and the Committee of Experts of the ILO) that British law was in breach of international labour standards – notably the Council of Europe's Social Charter and ILO Convention 87. The law was changed by the Employ-ment Relations Act 1999, and now offers some protection against unfair dismissal. But, as already suggested, it remains deeply flawed and out of line with minimum international standards.[142]

---

[140] The Electrical Electronic Telecommunications and Plumbing Union (EEPTU) was expelled from the TUC as a result. It is now part of Unite the Union, as a result of a number of mergers.

[141] For full details, see K. D. Ewing and B. W. Napier, 'The Wapping Dispute and Labour Law' (1986) 45 *Cambridge Law Journal* 285.

[142] See T. Novitz, 'International Promises and Domestic Pragmatism: To What Extent Will the Employment Relations Act 1999 Implement International Labour Standards Relating to Freedom of Association?' (2000) 63 *Modern Law Review* 379.

Recruitment of Replacement Workers

Faced with industrial action, the employer may try to hire temporary replacements to take the place of those on strike. There are no legal obstacles to the hiring of temporary replacements, provided that this is not done through an employment business. Under the Conduct of Employment Agencies and Employment Businesses Regulations 2003,[143] an employment business may not supply a workseeker to an employer to perform 'duties normally performed by a worker who is taking part in a strike or other industrial action'. It is a criminal offence to violate this obligation, which applies also to prohibit businesses from supplying workers to perform the work of employees who have been moved to perform the work of people on strike. The restrictions do not apply to unofficial industrial action.

Although it is sometimes complained that these provisions are not as rigorously enforced as they should be, it is to be noted that during the 'Day of Action' on 30 November 2011, Richmond-upon-Thames London Borough Council advised schools that:

> they are not able to cover striking staff with Agency staff. To do so would breach Regulation 7 of the Conduct of Employment Agencies and Employment Businesses Regulations 2003 [which do] not allow temporary workers to perform the duties normally performed by a permanent worker who is taking part in a strike or other industrial action. An agency supplying workers in these circumstances will be committing a criminal offence, and the employer could be found to be aiding and abetting that offence.[144]

In 2015 the then government published proposals to revoke regulation 7, as part of its commitment to 'tackling the disproportionate impact of strikes in important public services', citing two sectors – education and postal services – where the right of employers to use replacements supplied by employment businesses would be particularly valuable. More generally, the government claimed that 'removing Regulation 7 from the Conduct Regulations will give the recruitment sector the opportunity to help employers to limit the impact to the wider economy and society of strike action, by ensuring that businesses can continue to operate to some extent'.[145] At the time of writing, however, these proposals have not been implemented, it being unclear whether they enjoy the support of the recruitment industry.

Protected Industrial Action

The election of the Labour government in 1997 led to a new statutory approach to the treatment of strikers dismissed for taking part in industrial action. The position of the new government was set out in the white paper, *Fairness at Work*, in the following terms:

---

[143] SI 2003 No. 3319.
[144] Richmond-upon-Thames London Borough Council, 'Information on the Strike Action – 30 November 2011' (2011).
[145] BIS, *Hiring Agency Staff During Strike Action: Reforming Regulation* (2015).

The Government has no plans to change the position in relation to those dismissed for taking unofficial action. However, in relation to employees dismissed for taking part in lawfully organised official industrial action, the Government believes that the current regime is unsatisfactory and illogical. The Government believes that in general employees dismissed for taking part in lawfully organised official industrial action should have the right to complain of unfair dismissal to a tribunal. In any particular case the tribunal would not get involved in looking at the merits of the dispute; its role would be to decide whether the employer had acted fairly and reasonably taking into account all the circumstances of the case.[146]

The outcome is a new section introduced into the 1992 Act by the Employment Relations Act 1999 (subsequently amended by the Employment Relations Act 2004),[147] which provides in certain circumstances not that a tribunal may hear a case of unfair dismissal, but that it is automatically unfair to dismiss an employee for taking part in a strike or other industrial action.

Statutory Protection

The right not to be unfairly dismissed applies specifically in the context of 'protected industrial action'.[148] This is defined by TULRCA 1992, section 238A, to be 'an act which, or a series of acts each of which; [the individual] is induced to commit by an act which by virtue of [TULRCA 1992] section 219 is not actionable in tort'.[149] The new protection introduces an important symmetry between the liability of the trade union and the protection of the individual worker. Where the trade union is protected from liability in tort, the worker is protected from dismissal (subject to temporal limits discussed below). But there are nevertheless a number of interesting (not to say bizarre) consequences that flow from this, the first being that the protection of the employee applies only where the industrial action is not actionable in tort by virtue of TULRCA 1992, section 219. This is likely to cover the large majority of – if not all – cases. But it is possible nevertheless that there may be cases where the industrial action is not actionable for reasons unconnected with TULRCA 1992, section 219: for example, it may not be actionable because the industrial action is not tortious, a possible example being *Power Packing Casemakers* v. *Faust*,[150] which concerned a ban on non-contractual overtime. The Court of Appeal held that conduct may constitute industrial action even though it is not a breach of contract. If it is not a breach of contract, there is unlikely to be a tort.[151]

We could thus have the paradoxical spectacle (which to our knowledge has not yet arisen) of an employer arguing in an ET that the employees have no

---

[146] DTI, *Fairness at Work*, Cm 3968 (1998), para. 4.22.
[147] Employment Relations Act 1999, s. 16, introducing TULRCA 1992, s. 238A.
[148] TULRCA 1992, s. 238A(1).   [149] *Ibid.*   [150] [1983] ICR 292 (CA).
[151] *OBG Ltd* v. *Allan* [2007] UKHL 21, [2008] 1 AC 1 (HL).

protection against unfair dismissal because the conduct of their officials was not tortious, with the employees arguing otherwise on the ground that they will have to establish tortious liability of the union as a necessary condition in an application for unfair dismissal. Apart from the possibility that the industrial action may not be tortious, the protection in TULRCA 1992, section 238A, may be defeated on the additional or alternative ground that, although the action is tortious, it is nevertheless unprotected. This might be argued where the industrial action involves the commission of a tort for which there is no TULRCA 1992, section 219, protection (as in the *BALPA* case),[152] or where it involves the commission of a tort for which there is statutory protection in TULRCA 1992, section 219, but where the action in question falls outside the scope of the protection (because, for example, it was not in contemplation or furtherance of a trade dispute). In these cases, it will now be in the employer's interest to argue that there is a tort, but one which is unprotected, and on this occasion for the employees to argue the converse. But whatever the circumstances, one unavoidable consequence is that ETs could be drawn into the darker corners of tort law. If as a result the industrial action is unprotected, it would fall to be covered by TULRCA 1992, section 238, some of the aspects of which are considered below.[153]

There is, however, one additional limitation to the unfair dismissal protection in TULRCA 1992, section 238A. Thus, apart from the need to show that the action is protected action, it is also necessary to show that it falls within the protected period in TULRCA 1992, section 238A(3)–(5). As a general principle, this means that the protection from dismissal applies in relation to protected action taken for up to 12 weeks.[154] If the action exceeds 12 weeks, the protection will continue to apply if the claimant discontinued participating in the action before the 12 week period expired.[155] Otherwise, a dismissal that takes place after the expiry of the protected period will be unfair only if the employer had failed to take reasonable procedural steps to bring an end to the dispute to which the protected industrial action relates.[156] For this latter purpose, the Act directs attention to a number of considerations, including whether the employer (or union) had complied with procedures in an applicable collective agreement, whether the employer (or union) had offered or agreed to begin or resume negotiations after the start of the protected industrial action, and whether the employer (or union) had – after the commencement of the protected industrial action – unreasonably refused a request that conciliation or mediation services be used.[157]

---

[152] See pp. 778–9.   [153] See pp. 791–3.   [154] TULRCA 1992, s. 238A(3) and (7B).
[155] TULRCA 1992, s. 238A(4).   [156] TULRCA 1992, s. 238A(5).
[157] TULRCA 1992, s. 238A(6).

Additional provision is made where there is an agreement to use concili-ation or mediation services, to ensure that both parties enter into the process in good faith.[158] The employer cannot defeat a claim for unfair dismissal after the expiry of the protected period by agreeing to a union's proposal to concili-ate or mediate, and then stonewall once in the process. Thus, in determining whether the employer has taken reasonable procedural steps to resolve the dispute, the tribunal must consider whether the employer (and the union) was represented by an appropriate person, defined to mean someone with author-ity to settle the matter or to make a recommendation to someone with such authority.[159] Otherwise, the tribunal must consider whether the parties have, so far as requested to do so, co-operated in the making of arrangements for meetings to be held with the conciliator or mediator, whether the employer or the union have fulfilled any commitments made during the conciliation or mediation process, and whether the employer (or the union) answered any reasonable questions put to it during the course of the conciliation or medi-ation.[160] Where these matters are to be taken into account by an ET, any notes taken by the conciliator or mediator are not to be admissible in legal proceed-ings, and the conciliator or mediator must refuse to give evidence if, in his or her opinion, this would involve the making of a 'damaging disclosure', which includes information that would be commercially sensitive.[161]

Limits of Statutory Protection

An important feature of the foregoing protection against unfair dismissal is that it applies without the need to satisfy the normal qualifying conditions for bringing an unfair-dismissal claim: in other words, it is not necessary to have worked for two years. As in the case of the protection from dismissal on the ground of trade union membership and activities, the protection thus applies from 'day one'.[162] This is important not only as a tacit acknowledgement of the right to strike as a fundamental social right, but also because it removes an otherwise possible opportunity for employers to discriminate between workers engaged in a common cause. Also significant for these reasons was the removal of the upper age limit from such dismissals.[163] There is nevertheless one important category of workers excluded, namely, those who are employed under a contract for services, an exclusion of great significance in sectors such as construction, where a large number of people are engaged on a self-employed basis. The statutory protection (unlike the protection from dismissal on grounds of trade union membership or activities) applies only to employees (even though the title to Schedule 5 to the 1999 Act refers to 'Unfair Dismissal

---

[158] TULRCA 1992, s. 238B.   [159] TULRCA 1992, s. 238B(2).
[160] TULRCA 1992, s. 238B(3)–(5).   [161] TULRCA 1992, s. 238B(8)–(9).
[162] TULRCA 1992, s. 239(1).   [163] *Ibid.*

of Striking Workers').[164] It is true that it would be open to the government to extend the law relating to unfair dismissal to workers other than employees. But this has not been done.

Apart from these questions of eligibility and coverage, there are other major concerns with the protection. It is true that, as already explained, the protected period was extended in 2004 from eight weeks to twelve weeks, and that the protection may extend beyond the twelve-week protected period if the employer is not seriously engaged in trying to bring the dispute to an end. Nevertheless, it is not clear how extending the time limit for automatic protection in this way addresses the claim that the legislation as enacted fails to meet the requirements of the international labour standards by which it was inspired.[165] Indeed, it is clear that it does not, with the ILO Committee of Experts repeating in 2011 that it:

> considers that restricting the right to maintain the employment relationship to industrial action of twelve weeks or less places an arbitrary limit on the effective protection of the right to strike in a manner contrary to the Convention. The Committee therefore once again requests the Government to review the TULRCA, in full consultation with workers' and employers' organizations concerned, with a view to strengthening the protection available to workers who stage official and lawfully organized industrial action and to provide information on the steps taken in this regard.[166]

A similar approach was taken by the European Committee on Social Rights which has concluded that the twelve-week protected period is 'arbitrary', and not in conformity with the requirements of the Social Charter, Article 6(4). In so concluding, the Committee dismissed the government's defence that 96.5 per cent of all industrial action lasts for less than twelve weeks.[167]

Although it is thus unlikely that many disputes will exceed twelve weeks, there are examples of those which do, including the British Airways cabin-crew dispute to which we have referred on several occasions: this started in 2009 and was not settled until 2011. Indeed, that dispute revealed a curious anomaly with the current statutory protection, in the sense that the twelve-week protection period is the twelve weeks 'beginning with the first day of protected industrial action'.[168] This does not necessarily mean the first twelve weeks of industrial action. Thus, although it may be true that most disputes do not last for longer than twelve weeks, it is also true that the nature of industrial

---

[164] TULRCA 1992, s. 238A, is more restrained, referring to 'Participation in Official Industrial Action'.

[165] See T. Novitz, 'International Promises and Domestic Pragmatism: To What Extent Will the Employment Relations Act 1999 Implement International Labour Standards Relating to Freedom of Association?' (2000) 63 *Modern Law Review* 379.

[166] ILO Committee of Experts, Individual Observation Concerning Convention 87 (United Kingdom) (2011).

[167] European Committee of Social Rights, Conclusions XIX-3 (2010) (United Kingdom).

[168] TULRCA 1992, s. 238A(7B).

action has changed, with a growing focus on discontinuous rather than continuous action. In the BA cabin-crew dispute, the workers took twenty-two days of industrial action in total, these twenty-two days being the seven days in March 2010, followed by a further three periods of five days each in May and June later that year.[169] It is unlikely that the last period of industrial action was still within the protected period, while it is clear that any further industrial action would have been well outside it. There were suggestions that, in order to overcome this problem, the union would have had to hold a fresh ballot in order to trigger a fresh period of twelve-week protection. But it is not certain whether this would overcome any problem. When TULRCA 1992, section 228A(7), refers to '12 weeks beginning with the first day of protected industrial action', is the first day the first day since the first ballot, or the first day since the most recent ballot? It is not clear.[170]

Apart from problems of scope (employees not workers), and length of protection (twelve weeks, subject to tortuous rules whereby the twelve weeks can be extended), there is also a problem with remedies. The ILO position is clear:

> [F]or the right to strike to be effectively guaranteed, the workers who stage a lawful strike should be able to return to their posts after the end of the industrial action. Making the return to work conditional on time limits and on the employer's consent constituted, in the Committee's view, obstacles to the effective exercise of this right, which constitutes an essential means for workers to promote and defend the interests of their members.[171]

Even in the case of protected industrial action, however, British workers who are unfairly dismissed are not entitled to be reinstated against the wishes of the employer, the only remedy lying in compensation.[172] Although the sums recoverable by way of compensation may be substantial, this limitation seems to suggest that the 1999 reforms (as amended in 2004) offer a rather hollow protection of the right to strike, if it still means that those who strike lose their job. This concern is reinforced by the experience of workers employed by Friction Dynamics, who were dismissed for taking part in a lawful strike in 2003. True, eighty-six workers succeeded in proceedings for unfair dismissal after having been dismissed during the protected period (which at that time was eight weeks).[173] But although they were awarded compensation, the employees in question were nevertheless unable to recover the money awarded

---

[169] See K. D. Ewing, *Fighting Back: Resisting Union-Busting and Strike-Breaking in the BA Dispute* (London: Institute of Employment Rights, 2011).

[170] Although the union did hold a third ballot (and a fourth after the third was challenged), there were no further strike days before settlement of the dispute.

[171] ILO Committee of Experts, Observation Concerning Convention 87 (United Kingdom) (2011).

[172] On unfair dismissal remedies, see pp. 893–911.

[173] See A. Chamberlain, 'The Role of the "Eight-Week Rule" in the Friction Dynamics Dispute', *The Lawyer*, 3 November 2003, for an account of this extraordinary episode.

to them by the ET: in one of the most notorious examples of corporate avoidance of legal liabilities, Friction Dynamics went into liquidation, only to rise Phoenix-like shortly thereafter as Dynamex Friction.[174]

Unprotected and Unofficial Industrial Action

The question which now arises is this: what happens if the industrial action falls outside the scope of TULRCA 1992, section 238A? As we have seen, there are a number of reasons why industrial action may be unprotected. In these circumstances, we fall back on the law in force before the Employment Relations Act 1999, with the relevant provisions now to be found in TULRCA 1992, sections 237 and 238. The effect of the latter is to exclude unfair dismissal claims from the jurisdiction of the ETs where the employer has dismissed all those taking part in the strike at the date of the claimant's dismissal. It is only if the employer has selectively dismissed or subsequently selectively re-engaged striking employees that an unfair dismissal claim may be brought. The effect of TULRCA 1992, section 237, on the other hand, is that an employee has no right to complain of unfair dismissal at all if at the time of the dismissal he or she was taking part in an unofficial strike or unofficial industrial action, even if he or she has been selectively dismissed or others have been selectively re-engaged. Action is unofficial if it is not authorised or endorsed by a trade union in accordance with TULRCA 1992, sections 20–2, the contents of which are considered above.[175]

Unprotected Action

More specifically, TULRCA 1992, section 238, applies 'in relation to an employee who has a right to complain of unfair dismissal (the "complainant") and who claims to have been unfairly dismissed, where at the date of the dismissal (a) the employer was conducting or instituting a lock-out, or (b) the complainant was taking part in a strike or other industrial action'.[176] In such cases, an ET has no jurisdiction to consider the fairness of the dismissal, unless it is shown (1) that one or more relevant employees of the same employer has not been dismissed, or (2) that a relevant employee has before the expiry of the period of three months beginning with the date of his dismissal been offered re-engagement and that the complainant has not been offered re-engagement. It is to be emphasised that this immunity of the employer from unfair dismissal liability applies also where the dismissals take place while the

---

[174] See also *Dynamex Friction Ltd* v. *Amicus* [2008] EWCA Civ 381, [2009] ICR 511 (CA), where the conduct of the employer attracted some ripe criticism from the Court of Appeal.

[175] See pp. 777–9.

[176] A 'strike' is defined for this purpose to mean 'any concerted stoppage of work': TULRCA 1992, s. 246.

employer was conducting a lock-out. Here, however, the position is much more difficult for the employer, for in order to retain immunity it is necessary to dismiss not only those locked out, but also those with a direct interest in the dispute in which the lock-out occurs, a potentially wide and unpredictable group of employees.[177]

TULRCA 1992, section 238, in effect confers a conditional immunity on employers. The immunity is extremely wide in scope, and applies (1) regardless of whether the employer is at fault in provoking the strike;[178] (2) regardless of whether the strike is caused by the unlawful or unreasonable conduct of the employer;[179] and (3) regardless of whether the conduct of the employees in taking industrial action involves a breach of contract on their part, as made clear in *Power Packing Casemakers Ltd* v. *Faust*.[180] In that case, a group of employees were in dispute with the respondent company about wages, as a result of which the employees in question refused to work overtime. Overtime working was voluntary and in this case the company had asked employees to agree to overtime to help meet an urgent deadline. When threatened with dismissal unless they complied with the company's request, all but three of the company's employees agreed to the request. The three who refused were dismissed, and the Court of Appeal held that they had been dismissed while taking part in industrial action, even though not contractually obliged to work overtime. In rejecting the employees' argument that a breach of contract was a necessary feature of industrial action, Stephenson LJ said that where an employee:

> refuses because he and others who refuse with him hope to extract an increase of wages out of his employers because their business will be disrupted if they do not grant it, that continued application of pressure is industrial action in the common sense of the words.[181]

A second major challenge for the courts under these provisions relates to the requirement that, in order to retain immunity, the employer must dismiss all the 'relevant employees' and not re-engage within three months a 'relevant employee' who has been dismissed. As we have seen, when these measures were first introduced (as the only protection for employees in a trade dispute), the employer's immunity was conditional on dismissing not only all those on strike at the date of the dismissals, but also those who had been on strike but had returned to work. TULRCA 1992, section 238(3), now defines a relevant employee to mean, in the case of a lock-out, those employees 'who were directly interested in the dispute in contemplation or furtherance of which

---

[177] See *Fisher* v. *York Trailer Co. Ltd* [1979] IRLR 385 (EAT).
[178] *Thompson* v. *Eatons Ltd* [1976] ICR 336 (EAT).
[179] *Wilkins* v. *Cantrell and Cochrane (GB) Ltd* [1978] IRLR 483 (EAT).
[180] [1983] ICR 292 (CA). But see *Norris* v. *London Fire and Emergency Planning Authority* [2013] ICR 819, on the meaning of 'industrial action' for the purposes of ERA 1996, s. 13(5).
[181] [1983] ICR 292 (CA).

the lock-out occurred'; and in the case of a strike or other industrial action 'those employees at the establishment of the employer at or from which the complainant works who at the date of the dismissal were taking part in the action'.[182] Although it is thus no longer necessary to dismiss those who have returned to work by the time of the dismissals (perhaps after a threat by the employer to return or be fired), what this does not address is the point at which the relevant employee must be dismissed in order to enable the employer to retain its immunity.

This is an issue which gave rise to one of the issues before the Court of Appeal in *P&O European Ferries (Dover) Ltd* v. *Byrne*,[183] where the respondent was one of 1,024 employees dismissed for taking part in a strike against the company about new working conditions which the company wished to introduce. The application for unfair dismissal was brought because the company had allegedly, and it seems inadvertently, not dismissed all the employees who had taken part in the strike. There were two issues for the Court of Appeal: one was whether the employer could dismiss the employee on learning of his or her identity at this late stage and still retain his or her immunity from unfair dismissal proceedings; and the other was whether and if so when the applicant was required to reveal to the employer the identity of the relevant employee who had not been dismissed. In a remarkable decision, the Court responded to the first question by holding that what is now TULRCA 1992, section 228(2)(a), enables the employer to dismiss the relevant employee at any time 'immediately before the hearing begins'.[184] As to the second question, Neill LJ said that:

> it is necessary and proper in this case that these particulars should be given to enable the employer to prepare for trial, even though the particulars may also have the effect that the employer will be able to take action which will in the result frustrate the claims which the employees make. That is a matter with which we have been much concerned in the course of this hearing, but in the light of the plain words of section [238](2), it seems to me that that is the inevitable result of the legislation as it is presently enacted.[185]

Unofficial Action

As already pointed out, there is generally no protection for workers who are dismissed while taking part in unofficial industrial action. There are, however, a number of exceptions, so that employers cannot use the cover of unofficial

---

[182] TULRCA 1992, s. 238(3).   [183] [1989] ICR 779 (CA).

[184] According to May LJ, 'the material point in time is when the industrial tribunal either determines the substantive hearing which involves determining the jurisdiction point as well, or alternatively determines the jurisdiction point on a preliminary hearing prior to going on, or not going on, as the case may be, with the substantive hearing for compensation'. *Ibid.*, p. 786.

[185] *Ibid.*, p. 789. The dismissal of the P&O seafarers was considered in 1988 by the ILO CFA, which concluded that there had been a breach of ILO Convention 87.

industrial action to victimise employees who have asserted certain prescribed statutory rights.[186] Although the employer is thus generally free to victimise unofficial strikers by dismissing people on a discriminatory basis, unfair dismissal protection is not withdrawn where the reason or principal reason for the dismissal during unofficial action was for any of the following reasons: jury service; family considerations (pregnancy, childbirth or maternity); health and safety (in the sense that (1) the employee was dismissed for activities as a safety representative, or (2) not being a safety representative for raising concerns about health and safety issues in workplaces where there was no such representative, or (3) walking off the job in the face of serious and imminent danger); refusing to work in breach of the Working Time Regulations or refusing to agree to opt out of the maximum forty-eight-hour requirement; being an employee representative for the purposes of collective redundancies or TUPE; whistleblowing; or making use of the flexible working procedures. While the list continues to expand, the protection is by no means complete, and this rather haphazard body of exceptions relates mainly to obligations tied to EU law.

One particularly notable exception is that there is no protection from the list of impermissible grounds for victimisation relating to trade union membership and activities. Unofficial action provides the employer with a nice opportunity to decapitate a union in the workplace by removing its key activists who have no remedy in unfair dismissal, even if it is the employer's purpose self-evidently and publicly to decapitate the union. Although ordinarily such conduct would be unlawful, it is important to recall that TULRCA 1992, section 237(1), empowers the employer to dismiss not because the employee is taking part in unofficial action, but '*if* the employee was taking part in such action at the time of dismissal'. This power of the employer generally to dismiss during unofficial action is a violation of the European Social Charter, Article 6(4), in relation to which the Social Rights Committee has said that:

> Article 6(4) of the Charter provided for the right of all workers to participate in collective action, whether supported by a trade union or not and that limiting protection against dismissal to official action was therefore contrary to the Charter.[187]

This mischief would almost certainly be compounded where the unaccountable power of dismissal during unofficial action was being abused, in the sense that it was being used as a cover for anti-union activity not immediately related to the unofficial action.[188] It would surely also give rise to questions about the compatibility of this power with the ECHR, Article 11.

---

[186] TULRCA 1992, s. 237(1A).

[187] European Committee of Social Rights, Conclusions XVIII-1 (United Kingdom) (2006).

[188] The Committee further noted that, by virtue of TULRCA 1992, s. 223, 'it was not lawful for a trade union to take industrial action in support of workers dismissed in such circumstances'.

In light of the foregoing, it is important to establish what unofficial action means for these purposes. Curiously, the Act presumes all industrial action to be unofficial in relation to an employee unless the employee in question:

- is a member of a trade union and the action is authorised or endorsed by that union; or
- is not a member of a trade union but there are among those taking part in the industrial action members of a trade union by which the action has been authorised or endorsed.[189]

This means that, if a group of workers (trade union members and non-members) walk off the job to protest about the conduct of the employer (for example, a pay cut or the dismissal of a colleague), or refuse (as in *Faust*) to take on additional (non-contractual) responsibilities, all or some of them could be dismissed. In principle, it might be possible for the union to cover them with a shroud of protection by endorsing the action. But if the union does so, it will almost certainly expose itself to the risk of legal liability – whether in the form of an injunction or damages – for so doing. This is because the unofficial action is certain – given the nature of the action – not to have complied with the statutory notice and ballot provisions that are a precondition of protection for a trade union that has authorised or endorsed industrial action.[190]

An unofficial strike is thus one which is not authorised or endorsed by the union, which could lead to the dismissal of both union members and non-members alike, provided of course that those dismissed were participating in the action. But what happens if none of those taking part is a member of a trade union? Although in such cases the action is unlikely to have been authorised or endorsed by a trade union, the legislation provides expressly that such action is not unofficial, provided that 'none of those taking part in it are members of a trade union'.[191] Spontaneous action will be dubbed official and the workers will be protected, even though it has not been balloted (and does not fall within the definition of a trade dispute), giving rise to nice questions about statutorily authorised discrimination against trade unionists. If spontaneous unballoted action by non-members can be protected, why cannot spontaneous unballoted action by members of a trade union equally be protected? And how can we justify a rule that says that the non-members will lose their protection if, unknown to them, there is an inactive trade

---

This the Committee held to be 'a serious restriction on the right to strike', and to be an additional reason for non-conformity with the Social Charter.

[189] TULRCA 1992, s. 237(2).

[190] TULRCA 1992, s. 237(3): 'The provisions of sections 20(2) apply for the purpose of determining whether industrial action is to be taken to have been authorised or endorsed by a trade union.'

[191] TULRCA 1992, s. 237(2).

unionist lurking among them in a workplace otherwise closed to trade union activity? This latter fatal impact on the protection of a non-union workforce can be countered only where the membership of a trade union is for purposes unconnected with the employment in question (whatever that may mean), in which case – and only in such a case – it 'shall be disregarded'.[192]

The 'Public Interest'

Industrial action typically involves a dispute between two parties, the employer and the trade union, though there may be a third party in the background informing the employer's position, perhaps as a funder or a contractor. But although a dispute between two parties, industrial action may have wider implications for the community as a whole or sections of the community. This will be particularly the case in relation to disputes in public services, which will have implications for those who rely on these public services. Although the public interest has always been a feature of public policy in dealing with industrial action, it has become a noticeably more prominent feature in recent years. Notions of the public interest may be used to justify or help to explain:

- Exceptional requirements to be met before industrial action is permitted by certain categories of worker, as in the case of those engaged in important public services, required to show the support of at least 40 per cent of those eligible to vote in the ballot.
- Exceptional prohibitions or conditions on particular groups of workers, or emergency powers on the part of the state to deal with the consequences of industrial action which is otherwise lawful.

The first of these matters is dealt with in Chapter 16, and we deal with the second below. It is also important to recall, however, that public interest considerations may now be taken into account in the granting of a remedy.[193] They may also shape the law in terms of who may apply for a remedy. A nod in this direction is also to be found in the provisions of TULRCA 1992, section 235A, which allows applications for injunctions in certain circumstances by the users of the services the provision of which has been or is likely to be disrupted by 'unlawful' industrial action.[194]

---

[192] TULRCA 1992, s. 237(6). However, 'an employee who was a member of a trade union when he began to take part in industrial action shall continue to be treated as a member for the purpose of determining whether that action is unofficial in relation to him or another notwithstanding that he may in fact have ceased to be a member' (*ibid.*).

[193] *British Airways plc* v. *Unite the Union* [2009] EWHC 3541, [2010] IRLR 423 (QB), para. 83. See pp. 768–71.

[194] See also the quite separate development in *Secretary of State for Education* v. *NUT* [2016] EWHC 812 (QB), [2016] IRLR 512. See pp. 802–3.

Prohibited Industrial Action

There may be circumstances where the 'public interest' in preventing industrial action is such that the right to strike is denied to a particular group of
workers altogether. It is common practice to deny the right to strike to
members of the armed forces, the police, and the senior civil service. ILO
Convention 87, Article 6, allows for exemptions from the right to freedom of
association for the first of these two groups of workers, but makes no such
exemption for the third.[195] It is true that the ILO supervisory bodies allow the
right to strike to be withdrawn from some but not all civil servants, provided
they are working in the most senior offices of state and that there is an
alternative system of dispute resolution binding on the government.[196] However, although industrial action by the armed forces and the police (but not
police civilian staff) is prohibited,[197] there are no restrictions in the UK on
industrial action by civil servants. Indeed, it was reported that senior civil
servants voted overwhelmingly to support the TUC 'Day of Action' against the
government's spending cuts on 30 November 2011.[198] When in 1984 industrial
action by a group of civil servants at the GCHQ was causing particular
concern to the government on the ground of national security, it was met
with the disproportionate response of a ban on trade union membership
rather than a restriction on the right of the workers in question from taking
industrial action.[199] While the step taken was a clear breach of ILO Convention 87, it is unlikely that a more proportionate response would have been so
regarded.

British law thus does not generally distinguish between different groups of
workers for the purposes of industrial action law, subject to the normal
exceptions of the police and the armed forces, though there is also a long-
standing anomaly in relation to merchant seamen, which has been regularly
commented upon adversely by the European Social Rights Committee.[200]

---

[195] Compare ILO Convention 98, Art. 6, which in contrast does allow for exceptions (in relation
to collective bargaining).

[196] See B. Gernigon, A. Odero and H. Guido, 'ILO Principles Concerning the Right to Strike'
(1998) 137 *International Labour Review* 441, at 448–9.

[197] See Police Act 1996, s. 91.   [198] *Guardian*, 14 November 2011.

[199] For a full account of this episode, see W. B. Creighton, 'The ILO and Freedom of Association
in the UK', in K. D. Ewing, C. A. Gearty and B. A. Hepple (eds.), *Human Rights and Labour
Law: Essays for Paul O'Higgins* (London: Mansell, 1994), Ch. 1. See also K. D. Ewing, *Britain
and the ILO* (2nd edn, London: Institute of Employment Rights, 2004).

[200] The Merchant Shipping Act 1995, s. 59, exposes seamen on strike to the risk of criminal
sanctions for disobeying a lawful command or disrupting a voyage. The European Committee
of Social Rights had for a long time taken the view that this was a breach of the Social Charter,
Art. 1(2), which deals with the right to work. More recently, however, the Committee 'decided
to deal with this issue under Article 6(4) of the Charter', which deals with the right to strike. In
2010, the Committee reported the government's view that the Merchant Shipping Act 1995,
s. 59, 'must be read so as to be in conformity with the Human Rights Act 1998 which
incorporates the European Convention on Human Rights into UK law and which takes
precedence over all other legislation. Therefore, according to the report a sanction could not be

A more recent and controversial exception to this rule relates to prison officers who were prohibited from taking industrial action by the Criminal Justice and Public Order Act 1994.[201] This makes it unlawful to induce a prison officer to take or continue to take any industrial action, or to commit a breach of discipline, whether under the prison rules or any applicable code of discipline. The obligation not to breach this provision is a duty owed to the Home Secretary (or, in Scotland, the Scottish ministers), who might enforce the duty by injunction or interdict, and may also seek to recover any loss or damage sustained as a result of the unlawful inducement. The foregoing provisions of the Criminal Justice and Public Order Act 1994 were disapplied for a short period by the last Labour government, but were reinstated with modifications in 2008.[202] The restrictions have been widely construed and apply to industrial action even though the action in question does not constitute a breach of contract by the prison officers involved.[203] Nevertheless the ECtHR rejected as inadmissible a challenge by the POA that the legislation violated ECHR, Article 11(1), on the ground that the substance of the complaint had already been ventilated before the ILO CFA.[204]

As already indicated, it is permissible under ILO Convention 87 for Member States to impose restrictions on strikes in essential services, though there are two preconditions. The first is that the services in question must be essential in the 'strict sense of the term', defined to mean those 'the interruption of which would endanger the life, personal safety or health of the whole or part of the population'.[205] The second is that a prohibition on strikes must be 'accompanied by adequate, impartial and speedy conciliation and arbitration proceedings in which the parties concerned can take part at every stage and in which awards, once made, are fully and properly implemented'.[206] Although it is likely that a ban on strikes by prison officers would meet the first of these requirements, the difficulty in the UK relates to the second requirement. When the ban on industrial action was introduced by the Criminal Justice and Public Order Act 1994, the same Act also provided that the Home Secretary may by regulations 'provide for the establishment, maintenance and operation of procedures', for the determination of pay, allowances and working conditions of prison officers.[207] However, the government did not regard itself as bound by the outcome of the statutory pay review process,

---

imposed on a striking seaman unless such action endangered the life of persons etc.' The Committee 'reserve[d] its position on this point:' European Committee of Social Rights, Conclusions XIX-3 (2010) (United Kingdom) (2010). This was repeated in 2014: European Committee of Social Rights, Conclusions XIX-3 (2010) (United Kingdom) (2014).

[201] Criminal Justice and Public Order Act 1994, s. 127.

[202] See Criminal Justice and Immigration Act 2008, ss. 138 and 139.

[203] *Ministry of Justice* v. *POA* [2017] EWHC 1839 (QB), [2018] ICR 181.

[204] *POA* v. *United Kingdom* [2013] ECHR 600.

[205] B. Gernigon, A. Odero and H. Guido, 'ILO Principles Concerning the Right to Strike' (1998) 137 *International Labour Review* 441, at 450.

[206] *Ibid.*, 453.   [207] Criminal Justice and Public Order Act 1994, s. 128.

leading the ILO Committee of Experts to conclude in 2005 that the process does not comply with ILO Convention 87, and recommending that the government:

> initiate consultations with the complainant and the prison service with a view to improving the current mechanism for the determination of prison officers' pay in England, Wales and Northern Ireland. In particular, the Committee requests the Government to continue to ensure that: (i) the awards of the Prison Service Pay Review Body are binding on the parties and may be departed from only in exceptional circumstances; and (ii) the members of the Prison Service Pay Review Body are independent and impartial, are appointed on the basis of specific guidance or criteria and have the confidence of all parties concerned.[208]

In 2007, in the immediate aftermath of the CFA ruling, the government failed to implement the recommendations of the pay review body, which was to be phased in over two years for reasons of affordability. Industrial action taken as a result was restrained by injunction in *Ministry of Justice* v. *Prison Officers' Association*,[209] which was an unusual case in the sense that the injunction was granted to restrain the breach of a no strike provision in a legally binding collective agreement which had been put in place while the Criminal Justice and Public Order Act 1994, section 127 had been temporarily suspended.Perhaps predictably, the court was unpersuaded by equitable arguments that the injunction should not be granted while the government was in breach of ILO obligations. Controversy was reignited when in 2018 the government again failed to implement the recommendations of the pay-review body,ostensibly in order to maintain a consistent pay policy across the public sector. This did not appear to impress the Chair of the review body who wrote to the Lord Chancellor claiming that at the time of the complaint referred to above, the 'Government gave a clear and unequivocal undertaking to the ILO that it would accept the recommendations of the [pay review body], in its role as a compensatory mechanism for the loss of the right to strike, and "they would only be departed from in exceptional circumstances". That pledge has never been rescinded, and successive Governments have abided by it.' This is not now the case, if indeed it ever was the case.

Industrial Action in Essential Services

Although international law permits restrictions on strikes in essential services, the UK has generally avoided bans and restrictions, preferring instead a policy that encourages work to continue and services to be provided. Thus, steps are taken to ensure that those who want to work during a strike are not prevented from doing so. This now takes two forms, the first being the removal of any

---

[208] ILO, CFA, Case No. 2383, Report No. 336 (United Kingdom): Complaint against the Government of United Kingdom presented by the Prison Officers' Association (POA).

[209] [2008] EWHC 239, [2008] ICR 702 (QB).

possible liabilities from those who do work. So a member of a trade union who is unhappy with the call to arms is free to resign from the union without any threat to his or her job. As we saw in Chapter 12, it is now unfair to dismiss someone because he or she is not a member of a trade union.[210] A trade union or trade union official may be liable to pay some of the compensation if found to have put pressure on the employer to dismiss the individual in question.[211] And, as we saw in Chapter 13, a member of a trade union who works during a strike may not be disciplined or expelled by the union for doing so.[212] This prohibition applies even where the strike has been supported by a ballot in which the individual may have participated, despite the fact that the individual may be acting in breach of a contractual obligation to the union in behaving in this way, and despite the fact that a restriction of this kind is contrary to ILO Convention 87 as well as the Council of Europe's Social Charter of 1961.[213]

Related to this is the co-ordinated use of the police where necessary to ensure that workplaces are kept open, to allow access not only by workers but also by suppliers and customers. This is an issue that was particularly important in the context of large national disputes of a kind that have not really been seen since the miners' strike in 1984–5 when the police adopted a number of strategies to 'preserve both order and freedom of access to and from the premises picketed'.[214] These strategies were said to include not only 'tactics of containment and if necessary dispersal of pickets to preserve order and access', but also the 'extensive use' of the police's 'common law preventive powers to keep pickets and their supporters away from potential trouble-spots'.[215] The Code of Practice on Picketing issued by the government now makes special provision for picketing in essential services, it being provided that 'care should be taken to ensure that the movement of essential goods and supplies, the carrying out of essential maintenance of plant and equipment, and the provision of services essential to the life of the community are not impeded, still less prevented'.[216] For this purpose, 'essential supplies, services and operations' are very widely defined and are said to include:

- the production, packaging, marketing and/or distribution of medical and pharmaceutical products;
- the provision of supplies and services essential to health and welfare institutions, e.g. hospitals, old people's homes;
- the provision of heating fuel for schools, residential institutions, medical institutions and private residential accommodation;
- the production and provision of other supplies for which there is a crucial need during a crisis in the interests of public health and safety (e.g. chlorine,

---

[210] TULRCA 1992, s. 152. See pp. 510–11.　　[211] TULRCA 1992, s. 160.
[212] TULRCA 1992, ss. 64–7. See pp. 547–51.　　[213] See pp. 550–1.
[214] P. Wallington, 'Policing the Miners' Strike' (1985) 14 *Industrial Law Journal* 145, at 153.
[215] *Ibid.*　　[216] BEIS, Code of Practice on Picketing (2017), para. 66.

lime and other agents for water purification; industrial and medical gases; sand and salt for road-gritting purposes);

- activities necessary to the maintenance of plant and machinery;
- the proper care of livestock;
- necessary safety procedures (including such procedures as are necessary to maintain plant and machinery);
- the production, packaging, marketing and/or distribution of food and animal feeding stuffs;
- the operation of essential services, such as police, fire, ambulance, medical and nursing services, air safety, coastguard and air sea rescue services, and services provided by voluntary bodies (e.g. Red Cross and St John's ambulances, meals on wheels, hospital car service), and mortuaries, burial and cremation services.[217]

But the state intervenes not only to protect access to the workplace and with it the continuity of production. Also important are the steps taken to prevent the disruption in the supply of goods and services to the public. Formal powers for dealing with the consequences of disputes were introduced by the Emergency Powers Act 1920, introduced to deal with the consequences of large-scale industrial action organised on a national basis by coal miners and transport workers in particular. Current emergency powers are now to be found in the Civil Contingencies Act 2004, which applies to a much wider range of potential emergencies than those anticipated in 1920. However, modern governments have learned to live without invoking emergency powers, and indeed the Emergency Powers Act 1920 had not been used since 1973.[218] The fact that it was not necessary to declare a state of emergency during the miners' strike of 1984–5 or the national fire strike in 2002–3 is an indication perhaps that emergency powers are now largely redundant in the context of industrial action, even if the 1920 Act was invoked on twelve occasions in total from 1920 to 1973. Should such powers ever be invoked, the Civil Contingencies Act 2004 provides that emergency regulations may not 'prohibit or enable the prohibition of participation in, or any activity in connection with, a strike or other industrial action'.[219] The government also has the power to use the armed forces for 'urgent work of national importance' without the need to make emergency regulations.[220]

---

[217] *Ibid.*, para. 67.

[218] See G. Morris, *Strikes in Essential Services* (London: Mansell, 1986), p. 51.

[219] Civil Contingencies Act 2004, s. 23(3)(b). This was a late amendment to the 2004 Act. The government thought it necessary to point out that TULRCA 1992, s. 240, was still in force. This makes it an offence wilfully and maliciously to break a contract of service, knowing or having reasonable cause to believe that it will endanger human life or cause serious bodily injury, or expose valuable property to the risk of serious injury.

[220] Emergency Powers Act 1964, s. 2. This is a power which has been used during strikes, and is now perhaps more significant than formal emergency powers such as those now contained in the Civil Contingencies Act 2004.

In some countries, special provision is made for strikes that may not be in essential services as strictly defined, but which may nevertheless cause significant public inconvenience, as for example in the case of transport strikes. Although a ban on such strikes may not be consistent with international labour standards, the ILO supervisory bodies have permitted restrictions whereby strikes may take place provided minimum service arrangements are agreed between the union and the employer. However, there are a number of requirements that must be met before such procedures will be acceptable, such as a need to agree the level of service before the dispute begins and the resolution of disputes about the agreement by an independent agency.[221] No such provision is made in British law, though the government's Code of Practice on Picketing provides that:

> Arrangements to ensure these safeguards for essential supplies, services and operations should be agreed in advance between the pickets, or anyone organising the picket, and the employer, or employers, concerned.[222]

On the occasion of the 'Day of Action' in 2011, one trade union (PCS) rejected a government request to provide a minimum service in the Border Agency to minimise disruption at passport control. On the other hand, although health service staff took part in the 'Day of Action' leading to the cancellation of medical appointments, various agreements were concluded between management and trade unions to ensure emergency cover arrangements (for example, in the ambulance service). This was based on consent rather than obligation.

A New Public Interest Guardian?

An important but neglected development is the application for an interim declaration by the Secretary of State for Education in *Secretary of State for Education* v. *NUT*.[223] Apart from the novelty of the remedy, this appears to be the first reported case in which a minister has applied for a remedy in a dispute in which he or she was not a direct party. The application was sought on the day before the union was due to take strike action in a number of further education colleges. It was argued for the union that 'the court should not entertain the claim for an interim declaration because the Secretary of State asserts no cause of action in tort and has no standing to claim relief in respect of torts against third party employers who have not brought any claim and whose point of view is not represented before the court'. This argument was, however, rejected by Kerr J who said that 'there is a real dispute between the present parties over whether tomorrow's strike is lawful'. He continued: 'The Secretary of State is invested with statutory responsibility for education in England, including that provided

---

[221] B. Gernigon, A. Odero and H. Guido, 'ILO Principles Concerning the Right to Strike' (1998) 137 *International Labour Review* 441, at 452–3.

[222] BEIS, Code of Practice on Picketing (2017), para. 67.

[223] *Secretary of State for Education* v. *NUT* [2016] EWHC 812 (QB), [2016] IRLR 512.

at sixth form colleges. That responsibility is exercised on behalf of the public.' The action failed on the ground that the union was acting in contemplation or furtherance of a trade dispute, but it is nevertheless important if it signals a desire on the part of government to intervene by litigation on public-interest grounds in disputes to which it is not a party. It is all the more important for the fact that the court in this case gave it permission to do so, in the exercise of the court's power 'to entertain and determine the Secretary of State's application for a declaration, including an interim declaration, if the court decides that it is appropriate to do so'.

Alternatives to Litigation

The state has a number of different roles in regulating industrial conflict. In the first place, it must establish the boundaries of lawful conduct and determine the sanctions which may be imposed on those who step beyond these boundaries. But although it has a role in permitting such action, the state paradoxically also has a role in restraining it. Since the late nineteenth century, the state has been an active player in trade disputes, using its administrative and legislative power to prevent industrial disputes and resolve industrial conflict on the one hand, and to coerce workers back to work on the other. The modern law relating to the intervention of the state with a view to resolving industrial disputes has its origins in the Conciliation Act 1896 and the Industrial Courts Act 1919. The system is based on the idea that the parties should seek to resolve their own differences in accordance with their own agreements, and that the state should assist where appropriate. But intervention by the state should not involve any compulsion, the 1896 Act being based on the principle of voluntary conciliation, and the 1919 Act on the principle of voluntary arbitration by an independent arbiter. The 1896 and 1919 Acts remained in force until 1971 when they were repealed by the Industrial Relations Act 1971.

Conciliation

So far as the role of the state and state institutions is concerned, the parties to a trade dispute are more likely to meet an ACAS conciliator than a lawyer or a judge. The work of ACAS is drawn to public attention during particularly newsworthy or controversial disputes. These include the cabin-crew dispute at British Airways where an ACAS conciliation meeting was the subject of a highly publicised disruption by the Socialist Workers Party.[224] For the most part, however, ACAS intervention is much lower-key, operating quietly and efficiently to help parties to 're-establish a direct dialogue' in some cases, and

---

[224] *Guardian*, 23 May 2010.

in others helping to settle the immediate dispute.[225] ACAS is involved in a surprisingly large number of cases, though the numbers are nevertheless in decline. Nevertheless in 2017–18 alone, the organisation dealt with 794 disputes for conciliation, of which only 57 were 'unsuccessfully completed'. Most of the disputes dealt with relate to pay and terms and conditions of employment, though changing working practices, redundancy and recognition accounted for others.[226]

The statutory power for ACAS to conciliate in a dispute is now to be found in TULRCA 1992, section 210. This provides that 'where a trade dispute exists or is apprehended', ACAS may, 'at the request of one or more parties to the dispute or otherwise', offer the parties to the dispute its assistance with a view to bringing about a settlement. This assistance may be by way of conciliation 'or by other means', and 'may include the appointment of a person other than an officer or servant of ACAS to offer assistance to the parties to the dispute with a view to bringing about a settlement'.[227] In exercising these powers, ACAS must 'have regard to the desirability of encouraging the parties to a dispute to use any appropriate agreed procedures for negotiation or the settlement of disputes'.[228] So although these latter procedures may not be legally binding,[229] the parties may nevertheless invoke the legal powers of ACAS to encourage the full use of their own agreements. Nevertheless, it is important to emphasise that ACAS has no power to compel compliance with these procedures, nor any power to impose a sanction where the procedures are not followed.

It may also be noted that the definition of a trade dispute for the purposes of TULRCA 1992, section 210, is now wider than the definition of a trade dispute for the purposes of protection from tortious liability for acts done in contemplation or furtherance of a trade dispute. So, by virtue of TULRCA 1992, section 218, the procedures for conciliation apply to trade disputes in relation to which there is no protection by virtue of the narrower definition of 'trade dispute' in TULRCA 1992, section 244. In practice, however, it is likely that most disputes in which ACAS is involved will fall within the latter definition as well as within the wider definition in TULRCA 1992, section 218. It remains the case nevertheless that the powers of ACAS apply to disputes between employers and workers and between workers and workers, rather than solely between employers and their own workers. It also means that a dispute need only be 'connected with' rather than relate 'wholly or mainly' to one or more of the statutory matters, while ACAS intervention is not constrained by the fact that a ballot has not been held, or that inadequate ballot or strike notice has been given to the employer. ACAS also has the power to intervene in

---

[225] ACAS, *Annual Report 2010–2011* (2011), p. 13.
[226] ACAS, *Annual Report 2017–2018* (2018), pp. 19–20.   [227] TULRCA 1992, s. 210(2).
[228] TULRCA 1992, s. 210(3).   [229] TULRCA 1992, ss. 178 and 179. See pp. 128–9.

unofficial disputes. Although the power is not unlimited, there is no known example of ACAS being restrained by judicial review from offering its services.

The value of the ACAS conciliation role was acknowledged by the Court of Appeal in *Milford Haven Port Authority* v. *Unite*,[230] where there was a dispute about pensions, in which the union was challenged in the courts by the employer, on the ground that it had given inadequate notice of its intention to take industrial action.[231] An injunction was granted at first instance, but was discharged on appeal, the union in the meantime having in any event conducted a fresh ballot. In addressing some of the wider issues of the dispute (as well as some extremely narrow legal points), Leveson LJ acknowledged that 'both sides have powerful arguments',[232] and said that:

> The authority needs to address the deficits in its final salary scheme. All those who work at the port, and in particular the pilots whose job is absolutely critical to the safe navigation of enormous vessels through the very difficult haven, have legitimate rights to the contractual terms under which they are employed.[233]

According to Leveson LJ, 'the continued and successful development of the operation of the authority at the Haven sits above these interests'. But in a refreshingly realistic reflection of the relative merits of adjudication and conciliation, he continued by saying that he 'would therefore encourage all parties to continue to engage with ACAS and seek to resolve these issues through negotiation rather than action with the potential serious adverse consequences that might follow'.[234] In fact, ACAS was well aware of the importance of the dispute, which, although 'involving relatively few people', nevertheless had the potential 'to disrupt the nation's supplies of liquid gas and oil'.[235] Following ACAS intervention, 'detailed and intensive conciliation talks' produced 'an agreement that was acceptable to both sides'.[236]

Arbitration and Other Powers

Although conciliation is the main ACAS role in the settlement of disputes, the service does have other powers, including powers to arbitrate. The definition of a trade dispute for the purposes of the arbitration power is the same as the definition for the purposes of conciliation.[237] So, 'where a trade dispute exists or is apprehended', ACAS may, 'at the request of one or more of the parties to the dispute and with the consent of all the parties to the dispute', refer all or any of the matters to which the dispute relates for settlement by arbitration.[238] For these purposes, the arbitrator may be a person appointed *ad hoc* by ACAS, or it may be the CAC. As a form of dispute resolution, arbitration is a step

---

[230] [2010] EWCA Civ 400 (CA).   [231] For a discussion of this case, see pp. 739–41.
[232] [2010] EWCA Civ 400 (CA), para. 19.   [233] *Ibid.*   [234] *Ibid.*
[235] ACAS, *Annual Report 2009–2010* (2010), p. 14.   [236] *Ibid.*   [237] TULRCA 1992, s. 218.
[238] TULRCA 1992, s. 212(1).

beyond conciliation: it is a process that will lead to an award by an arbitrator or a panel of arbitrators as a basis for resolution, rather than a process that will encourage the parties to reach their own solution. The legislation reflects a preference for conciliation over arbitration, recognising that a long-lasting solution to a dispute is more likely if the parties agree than if it is imposed (whether formally or informally by an arbitrator's award, or formally by a judge's injunction). So in deciding whether or not to refer a matter for arbitration, ACAS must first consider 'the likelihood of the dispute being settled by conciliation'.[239]

A second feature of the arbitration power is the importance attached to collectively agreed procedures, which we also see in relation to the conciliation power. Thus, arbitration must not be used until the collectively agreed procedures of the parties to the dispute have been exhausted, unless 'there is in ACAS's opinion, a special reason which justifies arbitration'.[240] Like conciliation, state power is thus not to be used to undermine voluntary procedures. A third, very important feature of the arbitration power is that it is voluntary. While one party may refer a dispute to ACAS for arbitration, arbitration may be authorised only with the consent of both parties. Thus, there can be no compulsory arbitration of trade disputes, even in cases such as the Milford Haven dispute referred to above, where a strike involving relatively few people had the potential 'to disrupt the nation's supplies of liquid gas and oil'.[241] Intentionally or otherwise, the general principle of no compulsory arbitration reflects the position under international labour law, whereby compulsory arbitration is said by the ILO supervisory bodies to violate the right to freedom of association, except in limited circumstances involving certain categories of public servants and workers involved in what are genuinely essential services, in which case arbitration awards should be binding.[242] It is to be noted that, consistently with the voluntary nature of ACAS arbitration, the awards are not binding (although in practice likely to be followed), and there is no legal sanction available in the event of a refusal to accept the arbitrator's award.[243]

There is nevertheless much less arbitration of trade disputes being conducted by ACAS or by the CAC than in the past. While a small number of cases are dealt with by ACAS annually,[244] the CAC reported again in 2016–17 that its provision of voluntary arbitration in collective disputes 'has not been

---

[239] TULRCA 1992, s. 212(2).   [240] TULRCA 1992, s. 212(3).

[241] ACAS, *Annual Report 2009–2010* (2010), p. 14.

[242] See B. Gernigon, A. Odero and H. Guido, 'ILO Principles Concerning the Right to Strike' (1998) 137 *International Labour Review* 441, at 450–3.

[243] Part I of the Arbitration Act 1996 (general provisions as to arbitration) does not apply to an arbitration under TULRCA 1992, s. 212. See TULRCA 1992, s. 212(5). The Arbitration Act 1996, s. 58 provides that, 'unless otherwise agreed by the parties, an award made by the tribunal pursuant to an arbitration agreement is final and binding both on the parties and on any persons claiming through or under them'.

[244] Only thirteen cases were referred to ACAS for collective arbitration in 2017–18: ACAS, *Annual Report 2017–2018* (2018), p. 21.

used for some years'.[245] It is not altogether clear why this should be so, although it is possible to speculate about some of the more obvious explanations, not the least of which is that there are fewer trade union members and fewer trade disputes today than at any time since the Second World War. Another likely explanation is that at the political level the state has chosen to intervene in the industrial-relations arena by the use of different tools, based on techniques of legal restraint and coercion. New powers for employers to have action stopped by adjudication may have replaced other forms of dispute resolution by conciliation and arbitration, and altered the dynamic within which conciliation and arbitration powers now operate. It is thus the case that the other powers of ACAS and the CAC are also used less frequently than in the past. For example, TULRCA 1992 formally empowers the Secretary of State, 'where a trade dispute exists or is apprehended', to enquire into the causes and circumstances of the dispute, and if he thinks fit appoint a court of inquiry.[246] There has been no court of inquiry since 1977.

Less frequent use does not mean less effective use. In addition to its conciliation and arbitration functions, if it 'thinks fit' ACAS may 'inquire into any question relating to industrial relations generally or to industrial relations in any particular industry or in any particular undertaking or part of an undertaking'.[247] In one difficult high-profile and politically charged dispute at East Lindsey oil refinery in 2009, ACAS was requested by the Secretary of State for Business, Enterprise and Regulatory Reform (as it then was) to conduct an inquiry into the dispute. Various allegations had been made about the employment of Portuguese and Italian workers by a sub-contractor (IREM), which was widely believed to be observing terms and conditions of employment inferior to those provided by the National Agreement for the Electrical Contracting Industry (NAECI).[248] This was an unusual exercise of power in unusual circumstances, ACAS taking the precaution of agreeing terms of reference with several parties, which were simply to 'determine the facts surrounding the IREM contracting arrangements at Lindsey Refinery and publish a report including the current legal context of contracting practices'.[249] ACAS intervention secured a return-to-work agreement, while the subsequent ACAS inquiry report recommended 'an enhanced role for the NAECI independent auditor'.[250] According to ACAS, their intervention 'helped the parties to reach an agreement on a process which provides for greater transparency'.[251] The different powers of ACAS may thus be exercised simultaneously as part of its role in supporting employers and trade unions to resolve their

---

[245] CAC, *Annual Report 2016–2017* (2017), p. 16.   [246] TULRCA 1992, s. 215.

[247] TULRCA 1992, s. 214.   [248] For further consideration of this dispute, see p. 65 above.

[249] ACAS, *Report of an Inquiry into the Circumstances Surrounding the Lindsey Oil Refinery Dispute* (2009). See also, p. 65 above.

[250] *Ibid.*, p. 10.   [251] ACAS, *Annual Report 2009–2010* (2010), p. 11.

disputes. ACAS employs extremely skilful personnel, whose contribution to industrial relations is quite remarkable.

Conclusion

As we saw in Chapter 16, the right to strike is recognised in international law as a human right. As we have seen in this chapter, however, it is a right that can very easily yield to the claims of the employer, with employers having developed a number of tactics to break strikes. In the most extreme cases, these may involve:

- the use of the courts to prevent or stop a strike by means of an injunction;
- the use of third-party support, by outsourcing of work or by the use of replacement workers, whether transferred internally or recruited externally;
- the 'decapitation' of the union in the workplace by the victimisation of its officials and the removal of its facilities;
- the spreading of fear among the workforce by the withdrawal of benefits and the use of disciplinary sanctions;
- the dismissal of employees, in some cases with the permanent replacement of the strikers.

It is also to be noted that employees who are not trade union members can be encouraged to continue working during a dispute, while those employees who are members of trade unions cannot be disciplined or expelled by the union for refusing to take part in the action.[252]

The other problem workers will encounter is the problem of income. Striking workers will of course not be paid by their employer, and it is unlikely that their trade union will be able to sustain them with strike pay, if only because unions generally are not sufficiently well-funded to sustain expenditure of this kind. In addition, striking workers will encounter penal social security rules, purporting to represent a policy of 'state neutrality' towards strikes, being disqualified from both jobseeker's allowance and income support.[253] Jobseeker's allowance is both a contribution-based benefit for unemployed claimants for up to twenty-six weeks who have paid sufficient national insurance contributions, and a means-tested benefit for those who do not have sufficient contributions or who have been claiming for more than twenty-six weeks. In both cases, a claimant will be disqualified from benefit if he or she falls within the scope of the trade dispute disqualification, which applies where there is a stoppage of work that causes a person to be unemployed because of a

---

[252] For the operation of some of these tactics, see K. D. Ewing, *Fighting Back: Resisting Union-Busting and Strike-Breaking in the BA Dispute* (Institute of Employment Rights, 2011).

[253] For a full consideration of this issue, see K. D. Ewing, *The Right to Strike* (Oxford University Press, 1991), Chs. 5 and 6.

trade dispute at his or her place of work.[254] The claimant can escape disqualification only by showing that he or she is not directly interested in the dispute, or that he or she has been *bona fide* employed elsewhere, dismissed for redundancy, or had resumed employment with the employer and was subsequently dismissed for reasons unrelated to the dispute.

Although the scope of the disqualification has been narrowed – particularly as a result of changes introduced by the Employment Protection Act 1975 – it remains extremely far-reaching. It applies regardless of the merits of the dispute, and regardless of whether the claimant is on strike or locked out: it makes no difference that the dispute was caused by an employer's attempts to reduce pay or diminish working conditions, or that the strike or industrial action is lawful.[255] The disqualification applies even though the claimant is not taking part but has a direct interest in the dispute, and even though the claimant has no control over the circumstances of the lay-off, and regardless of the nature of the interest: the claimant may be opposed to the action and may be prejudiced by its outcome, yet still be disqualified for having a direct interest. In the leading case *Presho* v. *Department of Health and Social Security*,[256] it was held that, where production workers were laid off because of a strike by engineering workers, the production workers had a direct interest in the dispute where its outcome would automatically lead to an increase in their wages as well as the wages of the strikers.[257] The disqualification applies for as long as the dispute lasts, although it was once a maximum of only six weeks, which at the time seemed long enough. Penal rules – which can be traced back to the poor law – also apply to other benefits.[258]

It is not clear whether financial pressure on members has induced trade unions to organise strikes for a few days at a time over a number of weeks and months, though this may have to change as a result of the six-month time limit on ballot mandates introduced by the Trade Union Act 2016.[259] Such tactics may reduce the effectiveness of industrial action, but they do at least ensure

---

[254] Jobseekers Act 1995, s. 14. A trade dispute for this purpose is widely defined, and is different from the definitions in TULRCA 1992, ss. 218 and 244. By virtue of Jobseekers Act 1995, s. 35, a trade dispute is defined to mean 'any dispute between employers and employees, or between employees and employees, which is connected with the employment or non-employment or the terms of employment or the conditions of employment of any persons, whether employees in the employment of the employer with whom the dispute arises, or not'. This is based on the definition in place when the trade dispute disqualification was first introduced for unemployment benefit in the National Insurance Act 1911, which in turn was based on the definition of a trade dispute in the Trade Disputes Act 1906. It had been the practice to use the same definition in relation to both the trade dispute protection from tortious liability and the trade dispute disqualification.

[255] See K. D. Ewing, *The Right to Strike* (Oxford University Press, 1991), pp. 78–80.

[256] [1984] AC 310 (HL).

[257] 'Automatically' for this purpose was widely defined to mean 'automatically in practice'.

[258] *Attorney-General* v. *Merthyr Tydfil Union* [1900] 1 Ch 516.

[259] See G. Gall, 'The Tory Trade Union Act 2016: What Has Been Its Impact So Far?', *Huffington Post*, 20 June 2017.

that workers are paid (by their employer) for part of the weeks on which they are on strike (though it is unlikely that the employer can be required to accept such partial performance of the contract by his or her employees).[260] But although the nature of industrial action may be changing, it is unlikely ever to cease so long as people continue to work for a living in the service of employers, and so long as they have aspirations to bargain collectively. In a free-enterprise economy, in which employers and trade unions are ultimately serving different interests (owners and workers respectively), strikes and other forms of industrial action are inevitable if workers are not to be wholly submissive. Such action is all the more inevitable in a legal system that ultimately fails to provide effective means to prevent an employer from unilaterally changing working conditions. In the good times workers will strike for better pay and conditions, and in the bad times to ensure they are not required to carry a disproportionate share of the burden.

---

[260] *Ticehurst v. British Telecommunications* [1992] ICR 383 (CA).

Part V
Termination of Employment

18

Wrongful Dismissal

Contents

The Right to Protection against Unjustified Dismissal

The law of dismissal plays a pivotal role in labour law. The legal rules governing the employer's power to terminate the employment relationship indirectly control the whole of employer's disciplinary power. In order to co-ordinate production and to discourage actions that impede the objectives of the business, an employer needs the authority to discipline the workforce. The greatest civil sanction in support of this necessary disciplinary power is the ability to dismiss employees in circumstances where their continued employment threatens the economic success of the enterprise. Although the threat of dismissal may be carried out infrequently, its presence in the background provides employers with the necessary power to issue instructions that will normally be obeyed. In view of these efficiency considerations, the legal question that arises is not whether the employer should have the authority to dismiss employees, but rather what should be the legal constraints on the procedures and substantive grounds for dismissal.

Owing to the grave consequences of dismissal, employees require protections and safeguards. When an employee terminates the contract by resigning from the job, the employer usually incurs some costs and inconvenience. The task of finding a replacement imposes search and recruitment costs upon the employer. Training costs for the replacement employee may also be incurred. When the employer terminates the contract, however, the employee loses his or her main source of income and may forfeit long-term opportunities to augment income through work experience, seniority and promotion. In addition, insofar as work provides an opportunity to create social relations, bonds of friendship and to establish a position of status in the community, the loss of a job can inflict psychic damage on the employee. The stakes on termination of employment are therefore usually uneven between the parties: the employer needs to incur the costs of finding and training a replacement; an employee is threatened with loss of income and risks social exclusion.

The interests of employers and employees with respect to the termination of contracts of employment are not completely opposed. Employees have a long-term interest in the efficient management of the business, so that a disciplinary power exercised in order to exclude incompetent, absent or disruptive employees serves the interests of employees as well as the owners of the business. Equally, employers share an interest with employees that the power to dismiss employees should be exercised for its proper purposes and not abused, for the dismissal of competent and reliable workers imposes costs on the business. These costs include unnecessary recruitment and training expenses, but more significantly, the misuse of disciplinary power may undermine the confidence of employees that the employer will treat them with respect, which in turn may lead to a withdrawal of co-operation and high labour turnover. An employer has an interest in earning a reputation for fair treatment, in order to encourage commitment and co-operation on the part of employees.

Nevertheless, the exercise of disciplinary power does provoke a conflict of interest. Because employees have more at stake in relation to dismissals, they would prefer the employer to adopt more elaborate and costly procedures that are designed to investigate the facts carefully and to weigh the appropriate disciplinary sanction. Employees also prefer stricter and less discretionary requirements for an employer to justify a dismissal. For instance, employees may desire that dismissal should only occur for 'gross misconduct' or breach of clear rules laid down in advance, and should only be permitted following a rigorous enquiry into all the circumstances of the matter. Furthermore, employees may want to insist upon a stricter requirement of proportionality than the employer, for the employer may wish to enhance the general deterrent effect of disciplinary measures by dismissing workers for even trivial offences, whereas the employee will be concerned to emphasise the merits and gravity of the particular case. In the development and interpretation of the relevant legal standards, therefore, the legal system has to determine where the balance between these conflicting interests should lie.

As well as being a vital aspect of the disciplinary power of the employer, the right to terminate the contract of employment is an important dimension of the employer's ability to adjust labour supply and costs in the light of changing business conditions. More than a million people lose their jobs involuntarily each year, but typically about 80 per cent of these dismissals, depending on the health of the economy, will be for economic rather than disciplinary reasons.[1] The reduction of the size of the workforce in response to reduced demand for the product or service permits employers to preserve the solvency or enhance the profitability of the company. In many instances, therefore, reductions in the size of the workforce will be a necessary measure to protect the economic interests of the remaining employees and the investors in the company. Although the action of termination of employment by the employer remains the same in these instances of economic dismissals as in those concerning disciplinary dismissals, the potential justifications for legal intervention are quite different. In economic dismissals the issues concern, first, the extent to which the law may seek to place brakes on reductions in the workforce by either mandatory procedures or substantive criteria and, secondly, the extent to which the employer may be required to pay financial compensation to the employees or the social security system, in order to reduce the costs of the dismissals to the employees or the taxpayer. We consider the legal regulation of economic dismissals or redundancies in Chapter 20. This and Chapter 19 examine the legal regulation of disciplinary dismissals.

The need for legal regulation of the employer's power of dismissal has been a cornerstone of international conventions regarding employment.

European Social Charter 1961, Article 4(4)

to recognise the right of all workers to a reasonable period of notice for termination of employment

The UK has fully accepted this right and is subject to the determinations of the expert committee with respect to compliance.

---

[1] DTI estimate based on the Labour Force Surveys in *The Unfair Dismissal and Statement of Reasons for Dismissal Order 1999: Regulatory Impact Statement*, para. 41.

Article 30 of the Charter of Fundamental Rights of the European Union 2007

Every worker has the right to protection against unjustified dismissal, in accordance with Community law and national laws and practices.

Even within the EU, this Charter is not directly enforceable by individual employees, but it may influence the interpretation of European law.

ILO Convention 158 concerning Termination of Employment at the Initiative of the Employer (1985)

Article 4

The employment of a worker shall not be terminated unless there is a valid reason for such termination connected with the capacity or conduct of the worker or based on the operational requirements of the undertakings, establishment or service.

Article 7

The employment of a worker shall not be terminated for reasons related to the worker's conduct or performance before he is provided an opportunity to defend himself against the allegations made, unless the employer cannot reasonably be expected to provide this opportunity.

Article 8

1. A worker who considers that his employment has been unjustifiably terminated shall be entitled to appeal against that termination to an impartial body, such as a court, labour tribunal, arbitration committee or arbitrator.

As a Convention which has been signed but not ratified by the UK, it does not even have the force of a standard by which national law may be criticised in the expert bodies of the ILO. Nevertheless, the three rights listed there – the right to a reason for a dismissal, the right to a fair procedure prior to dismissal, and the right to appeal to an impartial body – have certainly influenced the content of national legislation.

European Social Charter (1996), Article 24

With a view to ensuring the effective exercise of the right of workers to protection in cases of termination of employment, the Parties undertake to recognise –

(1) the right of all workers not to have their employment terminated without valid reasons for such termination connected with their capacity or conduct or based on the operational requirements of the undertaking, establishment or service.

(2) the right of workers whose employment is terminated without a valid reason to adequate compensation or other appropriate relief.

To this end the parties undertake to ensure that a worker who considers that his employment has been terminated without a valid reason shall have the right to appeal to an impartial body.

Again, this Convention has been signed but not ratified by the UK. Its legal effect is likely to be restricted to its influence on the interpretation of legally enforceable rights in the ECHR.

Indeed, the European Court of Human Rights has taken significant steps towards recognising that many unjust dismissals amount to an unjustified interference with the right to respect for private life in Article 8 of the Convention. The damage to private life may occur as a result of substantial financial loss to the family income,[2] the effective exclusion from a chosen career, trade or profession,[3] serious injury to an employee's reputation and self-esteem,[4] or the effect of social exclusion by the deprivation to an employee of an intimate circle of friends and family.[5] Provided that the employee suffers serious disadvantage to these interests, the ECtHR requires national laws to compel employers to justify such dismissals in accordance with a test of proportionality, which includes a requirement that the employer should have followed a fair procedure.[6] The Grand Chamber confirmed these principles in *Denisov* v. *Ukraine*,[7] a case concerning the dismissal of a judge from his position as the president of the Kyiv Administrative Court of Appeal (though he remained an ordinary judge) for alleged 'significant shortcomings' by the High Council of Justice while he was away on holiday. As well as a violation of Article 6 ECHR for the failure to ensure an independent and impartial examination of the applicant's case against the dismissal by judges in Ukraine, the Grand Chamber considered the application of Article 8, in particular the damage to the judge's reputation, loss of income, and loss of career, but

---

[2] *Denisov* v. *Ukraine*, App. No. 73369/11, [2018] ECHR 1061.

[3] *Oleksandr Volkov* v. *Ukraine*, App. No. 21722/11, [2013] ECHR 32, §§ 65–71, ECHR 2013; *Özpinar* v. *Turkey*, App. No. 20999/04, 19 October 2010.

[4] *Erményi* v. *Hungary*, App. No. 22254/14, 22 November 2016; *Boyraz* v. *Turkey*, App. No. 61960/08, [2014] ECHR 1344.

[5] *Fernandez Martinez* v. *Spain*, App. No. 56030/07, [2014] ECHR 615.

[6] *Özpinar* v. *Turkey*, App. No. 20999/04, 19 October 2010.

[7] *Denisov* v. *Ukraine*, App. No. 76639/11, [2018] ECHR 1061.

eventually concluded that the negative effects were insufficiently serious to amount to an interference with Article 8.

Many interesting questions of principle and legal technique emerge in the consideration of disciplinary dismissals.

Key Issues in Disciplinary Dismissals

- Does the law strike a fair balance between the interests of employers and employees in determining the justice of disciplinary dismissals? This question can be divided into an examination of the fairness of the required procedure and the adequacy of the substantive grounds that may justify a disciplinary dismissal.
- To what extent should the parties be permitted to set their own standards of justice for disciplinary dismissals through their contractual arrangements?
- How can legal regulation establish workable standards and yet prove sensitive to the variety of contexts in which disciplinary dismissals occur?
- How can legal regulation be effective in ensuring compliance with its standards?
- In general, when is a dismissal fair or unfair? When is there justice in dismissal?

Common Law and Statute

In the UK, there are two systems of legal regulation to be considered:

(1) **Wrongful dismissal**: the common law rules, made by judges and derived from the general law of contract, that govern the termination of contracts of employment, breach of which gives may give rise to a claim for damages, commonly known as a claim for wrongful dismissal.
(2) **Unfair dismissal**: a statutory right conferred on employees to claim compensation or reinstatement for an unreasonable or unfair dismissal by the employer.

During the nineteenth century, English courts began to apply the ordinary private law of contract to the termination of an employment relation. This scheme of legal regulation emphasised the importance of the terms of the contract in setting the standards governing disciplinary dismissals. In principle, the parties were free to regulate the conditions under which dismissal could take place, and breach of those conditions would result in an award of damages for breach of contract. In practice, of course, for most workers these terms afforded no protection at all against the employer's misuse of disciplinary power. A casual oral agreement at the time of hiring would be supplemented by implied terms based upon the customs of the workshop and the default rules provided by the common law. Under these terms, the employer enjoyed a general power to terminate the contract for disciplinary reasons, because any kind of misconduct or incompetence was likely to amount to a breach of the implied terms, in particular the implied term of obedience to lawful orders.

There were no implied terms that required the employer to act fairly or to have a good reason for dismissal. In the words of Lord Reid in 1971:

> At common law a master is not bound to hear his servant before he dismisses him. He can act unreasonably or capriciously if he so chooses but the dismissal is valid. The servant has no remedy unless the dismissal is in breach of contract and then the servant's only remedy is damages for breach of contract.[8]

Under the common law, an employer could dismiss a worker for a good reason, a bad reason or no reason at all.

Nevertheless, in the UK, while there was no general duty placed upon the employer not to terminate the contract of employment unfairly, the common law could enforce respect for any terms agreed explicitly or implicitly between the parties. Such terms might place limits upon the employer's power to dismiss a worker at will for any reason at all. In the nineteenth century, during the growth of industrialisation, the courts tended to assume that no such protection from the terms of the contracts was applicable to contracts for day labourers or workers hired by the hour. But for more skilled workers, and including managers and clerical workers, more protective terms might be recognised. One common term, either express or implied, required the employer to give a period of reasonable notice or warning prior to the termination of the contract. This potential of the common law to enforce contractual agreements became important in the second half of the twentieth century when, as a result of the increasing effectiveness of collective bargaining to determine the terms of contracts of employment, the extensive self-regulation of employment issues by public authorities, and the increasing formalisation of the contract of employment in the private sector, the terms of the contract of employment began to contain both procedural and substantive restrictions on the power of the employer to terminate the contract for disciplinary reasons. Under the ordinary law of contract, the courts were bound to enforce these restrictions on the disciplinary power of the employer, thereby protecting employees against disciplinary dismissals in breach of the binding terms of the contract.

But this enforcement of express terms of the contract never extended in the common law to the creation of either compulsory or implied terms that might require an employer to act fairly. In other countries, the courts developed the ordinary law to provide some protections against unjust dismissal. In the USA, for instance, although the general rule permits employers to dismiss employees at will without even giving notice, many states have recognised an implied term not to terminate a contract in bad faith, a principle of commercial contracts that has been extended to dismissals from a job. Another principle recognised by many states in the USA is that an employer may commit a tort by dismissing someone for reasons contrary to public policy, such as absence

---

[8] *Malloch* v. *Aberdeen Corporation* [1971] 1 WLR 1578 (HL), at 1581.

due to jury service.[9] In Canada, the courts have recognised a duty of honest performance of contracts or good faith, which applies to performance of the contract of employment and dismissal.[10] In civil-law jurisdictions as well, it is possible to use a similar good faith principle found in the general law of contract and also to ask a court to prevent an 'abuse of rights', such as the arbitrary or opportunist use of the legal right to dismiss an employee.[11] But the English common law never developed such a general restraint on the power of the employer to terminate contracts of employment, and the prospects for the evolution of such a principle remain bleak.

Given that the most that the English courts were prepared to do to control dismissal was to enforce the terms of the contract, a further question became what remedies might be afforded to employees in order to protect their contractual rights. For most breaches of contract, the ordinary remedy offered by the courts is an award of damages. One question is how such compensation for breach of contract should be calculated? If employees could obtain substantial compensation for damage to their career or reputation, the benefits afforded by the terms of the contract would become serious constraints upon the employer's disciplinary power. That prospect was firmly and apparently permanently rejected by the House of Lords in *Addis* v. *Gramophone Co Ltd*.[12] While in this case the employee was entitled to claim the amount of his salary during his express contractual entitlement to six months' notice, any greater sum representing injury to his feelings, to his reputation or to his future career prospects was rejected. Given the meagre levels of compensation for wrongful dismissal at common law, a second crucial question became whether employees might be able to obtain an order forbidding the employer from breaching the terms of the contract with the ultimate threat of contempt of court for ignoring an injunction. Such a remedy would greatly enhance the benefits promised by the terms of the contract, for in effect it would prevent employers from breaching the contract whenever it seemed efficient to do so.

When the statutory right to claim unfair dismissal was introduced in 1971,[13] as illustrated in Lord Reid's pithy summary of the position, it was widely believed that the common law of wrongful dismissal offered scant protection

---

[9] G. Pitt, 'Dismissal at Common Law: The Relevance in Britain of American Developments' (1989) 52 *Modern Law Review* 22; C. W. Summers, 'Employment at Will in the United States: The Divine Right of Employers' (2000–2001) 3 *U. Pa. Journal of Employment and Labor Law* 65.

[10] E.g. *Potter* v. *New Brunswick Legal Aid Services Commission*, 2015 SCC 10; C. Mummé, 'A Comparative Reflection from Canada: A Good Faith Perspective', in M. Freedland *et al.* (eds.), *The Contract of Employment* (Oxford University Press, 2016), p. 295.

[11] M. Plascencia, 'Employment at Will: The French Experience as a Basis for Reform' (1988) 9 *Comparative Labor Law Journal* 294.

[12] [1909] AC 488 (HL); A. Bogg and M. Freedland, 'The Wrongful Termination of the Contract of Employment', in M. Freedland *et al.* (eds.), *The Contract of Employment* (Oxford University Press, 2016), p. 537.

[13] Industrial Relations Act 1971.

for employees against unjust disciplinary action. It was assumed, first, that employers would continue to set the terms of employment, so that they would grant few protective rights to employees against dismissal. A second assumption was that the measure of compensatory damages afforded by the common law was too meagre to provide any substantial deterrent to an employer's dismissal in breach of contract. Thirdly, it was believed that injunctive relief was unavailable to enforce the terms of contracts of employment and to prevent a dismissal. With hindsight, we have learned that none of these assumptions was wholly accurate. Under certain conditions the common law may offer employees some safeguards that may even prove superior to the statutory regime.

The statutory rules of unfair dismissal had as their principal aim to establish principles, in line with the international conventions, to require an employer to have a just reason for dismissal, to follow a fair procedure and to ensure that the decision was made impartiality. These principles therefore filled a crucial gap in the common law and made a substantial contribution to the job security of employees. Although these principles can be founded in fundamental rights contained in international law, unfortunately few British employers welcome the constraint that the law places upon the exercise of disciplinary powers. Even if some employers are prepared to pay dismissed employees a sum of money to provide them with moderate compensation for the loss of a job, all employers tend to resist public investigations of the fairness of the disciplinary decision on the grounds that such controls interfere too greatly in the efficient management of the business and that, in the last resort, taking into account the need for mutual trust and confidence, the question of whether a particular employee should keep his or her job should be the employer's private decision. Given this view of many employers, not only is the precise content of the legislation on unfair dismissal often a fierce political battleground but also any litigation involved in the vindication of the right not to be unfairly dismissed is likely to be contested harshly and vindictively. Even after losing a case, few, if any, employers admit that their decision to dismiss an employee was unfair.

As a consequence of the law of unfair dismissal being so controversial, from its inception the legislation never granted a universal right to all employees. Many workers were excluded because the right was restricted to employees, narrowly construed, and the legislation specified a qualifying period of continuous employment with a particular employer before the right accrued. Furthermore, the remedies for unfair dismissal were sharply restricted. In practice, few unfairly dismissed employees could ever get their jobs back using the legislation. More significantly, the amount of compensation available was always restricted by narrow interpretations of what might be compensated and the imposition of an upper limit in the amount. The details of all these limitations on the right to claim unfair dismissal will be examined in Chapter 19. It is important to mention them here, however, in order to provide the background to the recent, unprincipled, development of the common law of wrongful dismissal by the courts.

When the UK Parliament enacted the statutory law of unfair dismissal, it did not abolish the common law of wrongful dismissal. The legislation was completely silent about the remaining position of the common law, presumably because most legislators believed that it would cease to be significant in practice in view of the superior rights provided by the statute. It subsequently became clear, however, that for some employees the common law might in fact offer a superior remedy. The common law might prove superior to the statutory remedy in a number of circumstances: where the employee lacked the necessary qualifying period of employment to bring the statutory claim; where the employee sought a sum in compensation for dismissal in excess of the upper limit fixed for claims for unfair dismissal; and where the express terms of the contract placed procedural or substantive constraints on the employer's contractual powers to take disciplinary action.

The first attempt to achieve superior results from the common law in fact took place in public law. Employees in the public sector sought to use judicial review to challenge the validity of their dismissals. The potential prize for this line of argument would be a judicial declaration that the purported dismissal had been void on such grounds as breach of 'natural justice' or *ultra vires*, thereby awarding the employee his job back with full arrears of pay. Building on the decision in *Ridge* v. *Baldwin*,[14] which emphasised the importance of following the correct legal procedure in government decisions,[15] some employees succeeded in using judicial review to protect their job security. This use of public law was, however, effectively blocked for most of the public sector by the decision in *R* v. *East Berkshire Health Authority, ex parte Walsh*.[16] The Court of Appeal held that most employees in the public sector, such as the senior nurse in this instance, were engaged under a contract of employment governed by private law and they were required, as a matter of civil procedure, to use the ordinary private-law remedies for wrongful dismissal or the statutory claim for unfair dismissal. Exceptions, where judicial review might be available, were limited to instances where the dismissal resulted from a broader policy decision whose legality could be challenged on grounds of illegality or irrationality,[17] or where the particular position or office was one created by statute, rather

---

[14] [1964] AC 40 (HL).

[15] M. Freedland, 'Status and Contract in the Law of Public Employment' (1991) 20 *Industrial Law Journal* 72.

[16] [1984] ICR 743 (CA).

[17] *R* v. *Hertfordshire County Council, ex parte NUPE* [1985] IRLR 258 (CA); *R* v. *Liverpool City Council, ex parte Ferguson, The Times*, 20 November 1985, noted G. S. Morris (1986) 15 ILJ 194; *R* v. *Secretary of State for Employment, ex parte Equal Opportunities Commission* [1994] IRLR 176 (HL); *R* v. *Secretary of State for Foreign and Commonwealth Affairs ex parte The Council of Civil Service Union* [1985] IRLR 28 (HL).

than contract, so that any dismissal had to be conducted according to the rules laid down by the statutory underpinning.[18] Public law claims for judicial review against dismissal are still occasionally possible, even on these narrow grounds. In *R (Shoesmith)* v. *OFSTED* (Office for Standards in Education, Children's Services and Skills),[19] a Director of Children's Services in Haringey successfully claimed a declaration that her dismissal had been unlawful on the ground that it was contrary to natural justice, when the minister, under pressure from a petition organised by the *Sun* newspaper regarding the tragic death of a baby in Haringey, ordered her dismissal without affording her any opportunity to respond to the charges made against her.

Having stymied the device of using judicial review in public law to circumvent the limitations of the statutory claim for unfair dismissal, the courts were then confronted with more direct challenges using the ordinary private law of contract. Dismissed employees sought to bring claims against their employer for substantial damages for breach of contract or in the tort of negligence for personal injury. In particular, the claims that promised generous awards of compensatory damages included (1) breach of the implied term of mutual trust and confidence; (2) breach of an employer's duty of care resulting in psychiatric illness; and (3) breach of express terms in the contract that laid down disciplinary procedures and rules that the employer had to follow prior to making a lawful dismissal. As we shall see in the course of the discussion in this chapter, the courts have sought to block such claims, even though they are apparently perfectly valid claims under the ordinary principles of the common law, wherever the court views such a claim as a technique for avoiding the statutory limitations placed on the claim for unfair dismissal. In effect, the courts have added a provision to the statute on unfair dismissal which appears to state that the statute pre-empts the common law wherever the latter provides claims regarding the fairness of dismissal. The justification advanced by the judges for this pre-emption is the pragmatic one of preserving the balance set by Parliament between the interests of employers and employees under the statutory framework. But this aim, whatever its merits from the point of view of policy and constitutional propriety,[20] leads to unprincipled and opaque restrictions on the application of the ordinary principles of the common law of contract.

---

[18] *Malloch* v. *Aberdeen Corporation* [1971] WLR 1578 (HL).

[19] *R (Shoesmith)* v. *OFSTED* [2011] EWCA Civ 642, [2011] ICR 1195 (CA).

[20] A. Bogg and H. Collins, 'Lord Hoffmann and the Law of Employment: The Notorious Episode of Johnson v Unisys Ltd', in P. S. Davies and J. Pila (eds.), *The Jurisprudence of Lord Hoffmann* (Oxford: Hart, 2015), p. 185; A. Bogg and M. Freedland, 'The Wrongful Termination of the Contract of Employment', in M. Freedland *et al.* (eds.), *The Contract of Employment* (Oxford University Press, 2016) p. 537.

Breach of the Duty to Give Notice

Implied Term of Reasonable Notice

Contracts of employment may have a fixed or indefinite duration. Under contracts for an indefinite duration, either the express terms of the contract fix a period of notice or warning that must be given prior to termination of the contract, or the common law implies a term of reasonable notice. It is common these days for contracts to determine explicitly the required period of notice. In the absence of an express term, however, since the late nineteenth century the courts have implied a term requiring both parties to give reasonable notice. This implied procedural term permits notice of termination for any substantive reason or no reason at all, but it does require an employer to give reasonable notice of dismissal or to pay damages for breach of that obligation. In the common law there is no further implied procedural requirement such as the opportunity for an employee to respond to allegations of misconduct.

At the time of its inception, this implied term of reasonable notice prior to termination probably served the interests of both employers and employees: the employer wanted to be able to adjust labour costs more rapidly than was possible under the old agricultural practice of year-long hiring of labourers; and employees wanted to be able to leave lawfully at short notice while avoiding the criminal penalties imposed for 'leaving work without permission' under the Master and Servant Act 1824. In the United States the rule that was adopted was that either party could terminate the contract at will (without any notice),[21] but in the English common law a presumption applicable to commercial contracts was applied to contracts of employment so that, subject always to the express terms of the contract, a contract of employment of indefinite duration contained an implied term that it could be terminated by either party only on giving reasonable notice.

The determination of the period of reasonable notice granted under the common law depends upon all the circumstances of the case. If any clear custom can be established, that customary implied term determines the period of notice. Otherwise two factors predominate in the common law's determination of a period of reasonable notice. The period between payment of wages under the contract provides a starting-point,[22] so that a employee who is paid by the week in arrears will be entitled by implication to a week's notice. Secondly, this period is likely to be extended by the courts for high-status employees such as managers and professionals. Although an employer remains free to dismiss employees for any substantive reason, the dismissal can normally occur lawfully under the common law only after an employer

---

[21] J. Feinman, 'The Development of the Employment at Will Rule' (1976) 20 *American Journal of Legal History* 118.

[22] *Nokes* v. *Doncaster Collieries Ltd* [1940] AC 1014 (HL).

follows the procedure of giving warning or notice. The employer is not usually required to continue to permit the employee to perform work, but may instead pay wages for the period of notice in lieu. The effect of the presumption of a requirement of notice is to create a thin measure of job security at common law. This protection was considerably enhanced by statute.

Statutory Minimum Notice Period

The idea that notice periods provide a degree of security of employment was used by the Contracts of Employment Act 1963 to enhance the protection by introducing mandatory notice periods. The current form of the legislation contained in section 86 ERA 1996 provides employees with a minimum period of notice based upon periods of service. After a qualifying period of continuous employment for a month, an employee is entitled to a minimum of one week's notice. After two years of employment, there is an entitlement to a second week of notice, which increases for each year of service up to a maximum entitlement of twelve weeks. Breach of these minimum notice requirements entitles an employee to claim compensation for breach of contract for the wages that would have been due for the period of notice.

The effect of this legislation was to increase substantially the minimum notice period for low-status employees paid on a weekly basis who had several years of continuous service for a particular employer, for whom otherwise the common law was likely to imply a period of reasonable notice of one week. The statutory right to a minimum period of notice also prevents employers from inserting extremely short periods of notice such as an hour into the terms of the contract or from relying on an hourly payment mechanism as setting the period of reasonable notice. The statute does not prevent an employer from terminating a contract with immediate effect, but it does give the employee a right to compensation at common law for breach of the minimum-notice provision. Although these minimum entitlements cannot be excluded by contrary agreement, on termination of the contract of employment by the employer, the employee may agree to relinquish the statutory right to notice with or without compensation. An employee rarely has any incentive either to waive the right to notice or to relinquish compensation for breach of that right, so courts should be suspicious of assertions of such agreements. An alleged waiver was upheld in *Baldwin* v. *British Coal Corporation*,[23] however, because by agreeing to waive the right to receive £3,000 for a notice entitlement of twelve weeks, the employee qualified for a government payment of £5,000 conferred by a special statutory scheme to compensate miners for redundancies.

The statutory right to a minimum period of notice on the basis of continuous employment of one month or more applies equally to contracts for the

---

[23] [1995] IRLR 139 (QB).

performance of a particular task or contracts for a fixed term. At common law, it was difficult to assert that a fixed-term contract could be terminated on reasonable notice under an implied term when the contract expressly specified a fixed duration such as three months or a year. Yet it is possible to have both a fixed-term contract and an express provision that permits an employer to give notice of termination prior to the expiration of the contract. ERA 1996, section 86(4) prevents exclusion of the statutory entitlement to notice by the technique of a succession of one month (or shorter) fixed-term contracts. For example, in *Brown* v. *Chief Adjudication Officer*,[24] a care worker was employed on a daily basis every week for about nine months. It was held that she was entitled to the statutory right to a week's notice, even though at common law her contract terminated at the end of each day as a fixed-term contract.

Wrongful Dismissal without Notice

An employer may decide to breach these contractual and statutory notice provisions by summarily dismissing the employee. An employer breaches the notice requirement by dismissing the employee peremptorily, or on shorter notice than required under the statute or by the contractual terms, or by failing to pay the employee all or part of the wages due during the greater of the statutory or contractual notice periods. If the contract is frustrated, however, as where an employee is imprisoned, there is no requirement to give notice.[25]

From a technical point of view, a summary dismissal represents a repudiatory breach of contract by the employer. In theory, the employee then has the choice under the general principles of contract law either to accept the repudiation, thereby bringing the contract to an end, or to affirm the contract and insist on its continuation.[26] That latter option of the employee trying to keep his job is, of course, rarely practicable if the employer excludes the employee from the workplace. Furthermore, as soon as an employee acts in ways that are inconsistent with the continuation of the contract, such as commencing an action for damages for wrongful dismissal or taking another job, the employee may be deemed to have accepted the employer's repudiation of the contract. Nor can the employee purport to affirm the contract and claim wages indefinitely.[27] Wages are only due if work has been performed, which is normally impossible without the co-operation of the employer. Even if wages could be claimed, subject to any express terms of the contract, they would be limited to the notice period to which the employee was entitled, since the courts will assume that the summary dismissal, even if ineffective to terminate the

---

[24] [1997] ICR 266 (CA).
[25] *Notcutt* v. *Universal Equipment Co (London) Ltd* [1986] ICR 414 (CA); see Chapter 19.
[26] *Geys* v. *Société Générale, London Branch* [2012] UKSC 63, [2013] 1 AC 523, [2013] ICR 117.
[27] A spectre invented by Sir John Donaldson in *Saunders* v. *Earnest Neale Ltd* [1974] ICR 565 (NIRC).

contract, will constitute notice of dismissal. The question whether a summary dismissal or repudiatory breach has terminated the contract therefore rarely arises in practice. It may be relevant if an employee seeks an injunction against dismissal, because to obtain such an injunction, among the many conditions that the employee has to satisfy is one that the contract of employment continues to subsist. The issue also arose in *Geys* v. *Société Générale, London Branch*,[28] because the amount of a payment due under the express terms of the contract depended on the precise date on which the contract had been terminated. The Supreme Court concluded that since the employee had not accepted the repudiation, the contract of employment subsisted until the bank had validly exercised its express right under the contract to terminate the contract by making the payment and notifying the employee that the payment had been made.

In response to a summary dismissal or a dismissal that fails to comply with the notice provisions in the contract, normally an employee can only bring a claim for damages for breach of contract. This claim is commonly known as the claim for damages for wrongful dismissal. The available damages are usually fairly meagre.

Claim for Loss of Wages

The quantification of damages for breach of the notice provision commences with the upper limit of the wages and other types of remuneration that might be claimed under the contract during the required notice period. It is then assumed that the employer will take advantage of any contractual provision that permits an abatement of wages by, for example, declining to award a discretionary bonus. The statute provides detailed rules on the calculation of the wages due during the minimum notice period, although these rules do not apply if the notice due under the contract exceeds by one week or more the statutory minimum.[29] The general rule for the calculation of wages due during the statutory-notice period is that the employee is entitled to wages for 'normal working hours' provided the employee is ready and willing to work (or is taking a holiday entitlement).[30] Where the employee is unable to work through sickness or pregnancy, the statute requires the employer to pay wages for the notice period as if the employee were at work.[31] In the absence of 'normal working hours', as in the case of piecework or casual workers, a week's pay is calculated by reference to the average hours and average hourly pay over a twelve-week reference period.[32]

This upper limit of the wages due during the notice period is then subject to numerous reductions designed to ensure that the employee is no better off than if he or she had worked out the notice period. The gross wages are

---

[28] [2012] UKSC 63, [2013] 1 AC 523, [2013] ICR 117.   [29] ERA 1996, s. 87(4).
[30] ERA 1996, s. 88(1).   [31] ERA 1996, s. 88 (1).   [32] ERA 1996, ss. 89, 221–4, 226, 234.

reduced by the amount of normal deductions such as tax.[33] The compensation is also reduced by any social security benefits received by the employee as a result of being made unemployed. The employee also falls under the normal duty to mitigate loss, so that compensation will be reduced if the court believes that by taking reasonable steps the employee could have obtained fresh employment to reduce any losses resulting from dismissal. Although these reductions of compensation apply to the normal common-law method for awarding the net loss as compensatory damages for breach of contract, the effect can be in many instances to remove much of the support for job security intended by the provisions for statutory minimum periods of notice. Because the claim for wages during a notice period that has not been worked is not regarded as an action for debt but merely one for damages, if an employee obtains another job immediately (or should reasonably have done so in mitigation), the employer may not have to pay any compensation for breach of the statutory right to a minimum period of notice.

Compensation for Fringe Benefits

Termination of the contract may deprive the employee not only of wages but also remove many fringe benefits, such as occupational pension rights, holiday pay, other deferred payments such as bonuses, personal loans, private health-care insurance, share options and a company car. In principle, the employee is entitled to compensation for the loss of these additional benefits resulting from termination of employment in breach of contract. Insofar as the compensatory damages are taxable, the amount of compensation will be increased so that the net amount after tax will represent the employee's actual loss flowing from wrongful dismissal.[34] Claims for the loss of these types of additional benefits often encounter two obstacles.

The first obstacle concerns the discretionary nature of some additional benefits. The contract may provide that the employer has the unfettered discretion to give or to withhold the benefit such as a bonus or a share option. An employer can object to the award of compensation for such a discretionary fringe benefit on the ground that the benefit was not an entitlement and the employer had or would have exercised its discretion not to award it, so the employee had in fact suffered no loss. The employee must counter this objection by asserting that the employer's discretion to award the benefit was limited by express or implied terms in the contract, so that the discretion should not have been exercised to deny the benefit to the employee. High-profile cases addressing these issues have concerned compensation for the loss of bonuses by city workers for investment banks, as in *Horkulak* v. *Cantor Fitzgerald International*.[35] The claimant, a dealer trading in interest rate

---

[33] *British Transport Commission* v. *Gourley* [1956] AC 185 (HL).
[34] *Shove* v. *Downs Surgical plc* [1984] ICR 532 (QB).
[35] [2004] EWCA Civ 1287, [2005] ICR 402 (CA).

derivatives, was appointed under a three-year fixed-term contract, with a basic annual salary of £250,000, together with some guaranteed bonuses and an 'annual discretionary bonus', either to be fixed by mutual agreement, or by a 'final decision' at the 'sole discretion' of the president of the company. In the face of bullying and abusive behaviour, the claimant resigned and succeeded in a claim for wrongful dismissal and was awarded about £900,000 in damages, most of which sum represented loss under the discretionary bonus scheme. The employer appealed against any award of compensation for losses under the discretionary bonus scheme. The Court of Appeal upheld this aspect of the award, although it reduced it slightly on the ground of the claimant's failure to mitigate her loss. The Court held that the discretion conferred by the contract must not only be exercised honestly and in good faith but, having regard to the provision of the contract by which it is conferred, it must not be exercised arbitrarily, capriciously or unreasonably. This implied term was necessary to give genuine value, rather than nominal force, to the obligation of the party required or empowered to exercise discretion. The implied term represents a presumption that it is the reasonable expectation and the common intention of the parties that there should be a genuine and rational exercise of the discretion. Damages should be awarded on the basis of what bonus would have been awarded, if the employment had continued and if the employer had honestly and in good faith exercised its discretion according to its customary criteria (such as performance and loyalty). The broad principle that a defendant is not liable for that which he is not contractually bound to do is not applicable in a case where there is a contractual obligation to exercise a discretion rationally.

A second common obstacle to claims for compensation for loss of additional benefits is that contractual rights to fringe benefits will usually be limited in time or other conditions, which places a cap on the possible measure of compensation. For some fringe benefits, the entitlement may only arise when the employee is actually performing work, as in the case of free meals or luncheon vouchers.[36] In most other instances, fringe benefits such as healthcare insurance and share options terminate expressly with the expiration of the contract of employment. A claim for compensation for such benefits will therefore be limited to the date when the contract has been terminated by notice or by acceptance of repudiatory breach. The value of the claim can therefore turn crucially on the moment when the employer has succeeded in bringing the contract to an end.[37] For occupational pensions, however, the scheme should make express provision either for the vesting of rights, which may be claimed on the employee reaching retirement age or, in the case of short-service employees, for the refund of contributions. It may be possible to argue that the employer commits a breach of an implied term such as performance in good faith or mutual trust and confidence, if the employer

---

[36] *Mcgrath* v. *de Soissons* (1962) 112 LJ 60.
[37] *Brompton* v. *AOC International Ltd* [1997] IRLR 639 (CA).

uses the power to terminate the contract for the purpose of avoiding liabilities to pay fringe benefits.[38] But this argument must overcome the problem that a court usually regards behaviour that merely exercises powers under the contract to reduce liabilities as reasonable and fair.

In the case of some fringe benefits, it may be possible to argue that the withdrawal of the benefit or the failure to supply it should give rise to compensation not only for the loss of economic value but also for the loss of expected comfort and pleasure. Although damages for breach of contract do not usually include compensation for vexation and disappointment, where the purpose of a contractual promise was to guarantee comfort or enjoyment a court may award compensation for breach of that undertaking. If, for example, an employee was promised rent-free accommodation in a luxury home in order to induce him to accept a relocation of his employment to a foreign country, and on arrival he discovered that the house did not exist or was squalid, the employee might claim compensation not only for the loss of the value of the promised accommodation but also for the deprivation of comfort.

In summary, damages for wrongful dismissal in breach of the implied notice provision will therefore not usually afford an employee a substantial measure of compensation. The rules on statutory minimum periods of notice have also been criticised as failing to conform to the European Social Charter 1961 Article 4(4) (above) by not providing sufficient notice of termination of employment for workers with less than three years' service.[39] It is only when the required notice period of a highly paid employee extends over many months and the employee cannot reasonably mitigate his or her loss that the measure of compensation may function to deter dismissal and protect job security.

Justified Summary Dismissal

Employers may defend themselves against a claim for damages for wrongful dismissal in breach of any notice requirement by arguing that the summary dismissal was justified in the circumstances. If the defence succeeds, the employee is not entitled to any compensation for breach of the notice provision. To establish the defence of justification, the employer must either prove a serious breach of contract by the employee or point to a term of the contract that authorises summary dismissal in specified circumstances such as 'gross misconduct'.

Employers used to be able to justify summary dismissal by pointing to the breach of any fundamental terms of the contract. More recently the courts have preferred to ask whether the employee intended to repudiate the contract of employment and no longer be bound by it. The shift in approach was

---

[38] *Adin v. Seco Forex International Resources Ltd* [1997] IRLR 280 (Ct Sess, Outer House).
[39] Council of Europe, Committee of Experts, Conclusions XIV-2, vol. 2 (1998), p. 774.

illustrated by *Laws v. London Chronicle (Indicator Newspapers) Ltd*,[40] where an isolated breach of contract by the employee, even if serious, did not reveal such an intention to repudiate the contract of employment. The employee disobeyed the managing director's order not to leave the room and was dismissed without notice. She had left the room because a fierce argument had developed between her immediate superior and the managing director of the company. In leaving the room, she had followed the instruction of her immediate superior and had ignored the contradictory order of the managing director. The action of disobedience to a lawful instruction given by the managing director was certainly a breach of one of the fundamental implied terms of the contract of employment. Yet it was also plain on the facts that the employee had no intention of repudiating the contract of employment. She made a mistake about the implicit hierarchy of the organisation, but did not mean by her conduct to signify an unwillingness to be bound by her contract of employment. The Court of Appeal held that a summary dismissal was not justified, even though there had been a serious breach of contract, because there was no intention on the part of the employee to be no longer bound by the contract. Lord Evershed MR observed:

> It is, no doubt, therefore, generally true that wilful disobedience of an order will justify summary dismissal, since wilful disobedience of a lawful and reasonable order shows a disregard – a complete disregard – of a condition essential to the contract of service, namely, the condition that the servant must obey the proper orders of the master, and that unless he does so the relationship is, so to speak, struck at fundamentally ... One act of disobedience or misconduct can justify dismissal only if it is of a nature which goes to show (in effect) that the servant is repudiating the contract, or one of its essential conditions; and for that reason, therefore, I think that you find in the passages I have read that the disobedience must at least have the quality that it is 'wilful': it does (in other words) connote a deliberate flouting of the essential contractual conditions ...

Thus an employee's breach of a fundamental term of the contract does not warrant summary dismissal unless in the circumstances of the case the breach can be construed as conduct that is calculated to destroy the employment relation. An employee's absence from work or failure to comply with an instruction therefore does not justify termination without notice unless these breaches of contract evidence a repudiation of the contractual relation in its entirety. The difficult question becomes what interpretation to place upon an employee's serious breach of contract.

The dominant approach in the modern cases asks whether in all the circumstances of the case the breach of contract reasonably destroyed the employer's trust and confidence in the employee. The facts of each case have to be examined carefully to ascertain all the circumstances, including the gravity of

---

[40] [1959] 1 WLR 698 (CA).

the offence and any mitigating factors. Depending on the gravity of the employee's misconduct, an isolated breach may therefore constitute repudiatory conduct. For example, summary dismissal for a single offence was justified in *Denco Ltd* v. *Joinson*,[41] where an unauthorised employee used a password in order to obtain computer access to confidential information. In *Adesokan* v. *Sainsbury's Supermarkets Ltd*,[42] an omission to correct a significant breach of the employer's policies committed by a subordinate employee was regarded as gross misconduct sufficient to justify summary dismissal. In *Wilson* v. *Racher*,[43] the plaintiff was summarily dismissed from his position as head gardener after the defendant employer had made numerous complaints which resulted in an altercation and the use of obscene language. The court found that the employer's complaints were either unjustified or extremely trivial. Eventually, after having tried to leave, in the face of further unjustified criticism and provocation, the gardener lost his temper and said to his employer 'Get stuffed', and 'Go and shit yourself'. The Court of Appeal upheld the decision that the summary dismissal was unjustified, holding that although normally the use of such bad language towards a superior would justify summary dismissal, in this case it was insufficient in view of the employer's provocation and the absence of evidence that the gardener had resolved to follow a line of conduct that made the continuation of the employment relationship impossible.

One oddity in relation to the claim for damages for wrongful dismissal is the decision in *Boston Deep Sea Fishing and Ice Company* v. *Ansell*,[44] when the Court of Appeal permitted an employer to rely upon a serious breach of contract by the employee that only came to light after termination of contract, in order to provide a defence to a claim for damages for loss of wages during the notice period. This decision provides an incentive for employers to try to discover misconduct of an employee retrospectively after the contract has been terminated by summary dismissal. The same incentive applies where the employer initially decides to pay wages due in lieu of notice under the contract. In *Williams* v. *Leeds United Football Club*,[45] for instance, the club succeeded in defending itself against a claim under the contract for wages for a lengthy period of contractual notice brought by an assistant manager on the ground that some investigators they had hired after the dismissal for this purpose had discovered that five years previously the manager had forwarded an email to colleagues in the club and friends outside that contained pornographic images. Perhaps hoping to prevent any expansion of this device that permits employers to avoid a claim for damages for breach of the term requiring notice by retrospectively discovering misconduct, the Court of Appeal has decided that where the promised payment becomes a fixed debt that the employer has agreed to pay, as in the case of settlement agreement, it

---

[41] [1991] IRLR 63.   [42] [2017] EWCA Civ 22, [2017] ICR 590.   [43] [1974] ICR 428 (CA).
[44] *Boston Deep Sea Fishing and Ice Company* v. *Ansell* (1888) 39 Ch D 339.
[45] *Williams* v. *Leeds United Football Club* [2015] EWHC 376, [2015] IRLR 383.

is no longer possible for the employer to refuse to pay damages in lieu of wages for breach of the notice period.[46] The rule in the *Boston Deep Sea Fishing* case therefore seems to be confined to instances where the employer is resisting a claim for damages for breach of a notice provision on the ground that the dismissal was justified (albeit only with the benefit of hindsight).

Implied Term of Mutual Trust and Confidence

The entire framework of the common law regarding termination of employment is based on the default rule that the employer should be entitled to terminate a contract of employment on giving reasonable (or contractual) notice for any reason or no reason at all. The common law recognised no implied constraint on the manner or reasons for dismissal. The question that arose in recent decades was whether or not that default rule was valid any longer. Could the absence of control over the fairness of dismissals at common law be rectified by either express terms of the contract or implied terms? Two important implied terms imposed on employers are the duty to take reasonable care of the health and safety of employees and the duty not to act in a manner calculated to destroy mutual trust and confidence. The question to be considered next is whether or not these implied terms may provide grounds for compensation in the context of dismissal.

There is undoubtedly a tension between the common law's default rule that permits dismissal for any reason or no reason at all and the implied term of mutual trust and confidence. If an employer dismisses an employee for no good reason, this conduct certainly qualifies as the sort of behaviour that the implied term of mutual trust and confidence forbids. But if the implied term of mutual trust and confidence were to apply in such circumstances, it would override the default rule regarding dismissal that the employer can terminate the contract for any reason or no reason at all. That default rule is certainly out of tune with contemporary attitudes. It reflects the values of the nineteenth century, when a master enjoyed almost absolute powers to run his business as he wished. Today such arbitrary power is curtailed by statute and by the development of implied terms, in particular the implied term of mutual trust and confidence. A strong case could be made for saying that the implied term of mutual trust should displace the old default rule that permitted dismissal at will, subject only to a requirement of a short period of notice.

When this crucial issue came before the House of Lords in *Johnson* v. *Unisys Ltd*,[47] however, it rejected the application of the implied term of mutual trust and confidence to the manner or grounds of dismissal. Mr Johnson had been summarily dismissed from his job in a multinational software service company. He won a statutory claim for unfair dismissal on the ground that the

---

[46] *Cavenagh* v. *William Evans Ltd* [2012] EWCA Civ 697 [2012] ICR 1231.
[47] [2001] UKHL 13, [2001] ICR 480 (HL).

company had not given him a fair opportunity to defend himself and had not complied with its disciplinary procedure. The tribunal awarded £11,691 in compensation for unfair dismissal, which was the statutory maximum at that time. Mr Johnson then commenced a claim for £400,000 at common law for breach of contract and in tort. He alleged that as a result of the fact of his dismissal and the manner of his dismissal, he had suffered a mental break-down, which had prevented him from working again. The House of Lords, Lord Steyn dissenting, struck out this claim. The disciplinary procedure in the employer's handbook was not an express term of the contract, and so could not provide the basis for a claim for damages. Nor was there an implied term that the employer would conduct a fair disciplinary procedure. The Judicial Committee recognised that the common law, as a body of law that evolves, may have reached the point that it would not be wrong in principle to accept that the old default rule of the master and servant relationship was inappropriate in the context of contemporary relations of employment and that it should be replaced by an implied term of the kind represented by mutual trust and confidence or a good-faith standard that might place limits on an employer's discretion to dismiss employees for any reason without a fair procedure. Nevertheless, the court concluded that Parliament had already addressed the problem with the statutory law of unfair dismissal and that this legislative innovation removed the need to modify the common law. An employee's remedy for unfairness in the manner or grounds for dismissal should lie exclusively with the statute, with its carefully constructed and democratically endorsed balancing of the interests of employers and employees. The invention of such an implied term would circumvent the limits imposed by Parliament on remedies for unfair dismissal. For the same reason, the claim in tort based upon a duty of care was also rejected. It is evident that the dominant consideration that influenced the court was a concern not to circumvent the limits placed on the measure of compensation by the statutory law of unfair dismissal. This decision appears to block any possibility of the common law in the UK developing further implied terms with respect to the procedure or manner of dismissal. It was followed in *Reda* v. *Flag Ltd*,[48] where the Privy Council rejected an argument that an express contractual power to dismiss summarily without cause could be circumscribed by an implied term either with respect to procedure, such as reasonable notice, or substance, such as good faith or mutual trust and confidence.

Johnson Exclusion Zone

The full implications of *Johnson* v. *Unisys Ltd* are still emerging. We consider below the consequences of the decision for express terms of the contract that

---

[48] [2002] IRLR 747 (PC).

apparently limit the disciplinary powers of the employer. Here we concentrate on the implications of the decision with regard to other claims for breach of the implied term of mutual trust and confidence or of the duty to take reasonable care of the health and safety of an employee. Such claims are mostly brought after the employment has been terminated either by the employer or the employee. Are all such claims prevented by the ruling in *Johnson* v. *Unisys Ltd*?

This issue was addressed by the House of Lords in *Eastwood* v. *Magnox Electric plc* and *McCabe* v. *Cornwall County Council*.[49] In the *Eastwood* case, the assumed facts were that a supervisor harboured a grudge against Mr Eastwood and used his position to bring false allegations of misconduct against him. When Mr Eastwood brought an internal appeal against a finding of misconduct, another manager demanded that a fellow employee, Mr Williams, should provide a false statement against Mr Eastwood. When Mr Williams refused to do so, he was threatened with a trumped up investigation of misconduct. Mr Eastwood's internal appeal was successful, but then the managers encouraged another worker to revive and 'beef up' earlier allegations of sexual harassment against Mr Eastwood and to extend those allegations to Mr Williams as well. After the internal disciplinary appeal, during which no witnesses were found to support the charges, both employees were dismissed. Subsequently, both employees accepted a financial settlement of their statutory claims for unfair dismissal, but they continued with their claims at common law for personal injuries in the form of psychiatric illness caused by the managers' deliberate abuse of the disciplinary process. In the *McCabe* case, the employee schoolteacher won a claim for unfair dismissal on the ground that serious allegations of inappropriate behaviour towards certain female pupils had not been properly investigated prior to the dismissal. Mr McCabe then brought an action at common law for compensation for psychiatric illness caused by the employer's failure to investigate the allegations properly. In both cases the central legal issue was whether the decision in *Johnson* v. *Unisys Ltd* barred such common-law claims. Differently constituted Courts of Appeal had excluded the claims by Mr Eastwood and Mr Williams, but had permitted the claim brought by Mr McCabe to proceed.

The House of Lords held that all three claims should be permitted to proceed as the assumed facts constituted causes of action which had accrued before the dismissal. The crucial distinction drawn by the court was between causes of action, whether breaches of implied terms or of a tortious duty of care, which concerned conduct prior to the dismissal and other claims regarding implied terms and torts concerning the manner of dismissal. The question is whether the cause of action at common law precedes and is independent of the dismissal process, or whether it flows directly from the employer's failure to act fairly when taking steps leading to dismissal. The

---

[49] [2004] UKHL 35, [2004] ICR 1064 (HL).

latter claims were precluded by *Johnson* v. *Unisys Ltd*, since the remedy for the employee in such cases should be governed by the statutory claim for unfair dismissal. These precluded claims are described as falling within the '*Johnson* exclusion zone'.

Although this distinction appears clear in theory, in practice it proves hard to apply to the facts of particular cases. If an employer follows an unfair procedure for dismissal, such as a summary dismissal without giving the employee a chance to put forward a defence, the unfair conduct falls within the *Johnson* exclusion zone. But the unfair conduct by the employer may continue over a period of time, through unsatisfactory disciplinary processes and false allegations, culminating perhaps only months later in a dismissal. Here a claim for breach of the implied term of mutual trust and confidence or for a breach of the employer's duty of care should be permitted, as happened in *Eastwood* and *McCabe*.

As recognised by the court, this artificial dividing line creates some unfortunate practical implications.[50] Instead of carrying out a prolonged though unfair disciplinary procedure, an employer would be better advised to dismiss an employee summarily without any procedure or suspension pending an investigation, for then any psychiatric damage caused by the mistreatment in the manner of dismissal would have to be dealt with in the statutory claim for unfair dismissal, including the application of its limitations on the amount of compensation. Employees who are subject to harsh treatment that they feel may be likely to cause them psychiatric illness should be advised not to resign immediately and claim wrongful dismissal for fear that their claim might fall within the *Johnson* exclusion zone. It would be difficult in such cases to chop up the facts into events that occurred prior to the resignation and those associated with the resignation itself: in truth, all those events will be the same harsh conduct by the employer that culminates in the employee feeling forced to quit. For the purpose of the *Johnson* exclusion zone, however, it is necessary for the employee to establish that any psychiatric illness or other loss was caused by the employer's conduct prior to the events that triggered the resignation. The more outrageous the employer's conduct, the less likely that the employee will feel able to remain in the job; yet an immediate resignation would bring any cause of action based on the employer's intolerable conduct within the *Johnson* exclusion zone and beyond the possibility of a claim for damages for breach of an implied term of the contract of employment.

Economic Loss

In those cases that avoid the *Johnson* exclusion zone and succeed in a claim for a breach of an express or an implied term during performance of the contract,

---

[50] L. Barmes, 'The Continuing Conceptual Crisis in the Common Law of the Contract of Employment' (2004) 67(3) *Modern Law Review* 435, at 451.

the question becomes how will the courts assess the measure of damages? Technically, of course, none of these cases has anything to do with dismissal, and so should not be considered here but rather in the earlier chapters concerning breach of contract. But the artificiality of the *Johnson* exclusion zone should not disguise the reality of the situation that in nearly all these cases an employee is claiming compensation under the common law following a dismissal or a repudiatory breach by the employer. Unlike an ordinary claim for wrongful dismissal, where the measure of damages is typically confined to the loss of wages during the notice period, the assessment of compensation for breach of an express or an implied term during performance of the contract should attempt to quantify the losses caused by that breach.

The courts have decided that in general any economic losses caused by the employer's breach of contract during performance of the contract should be recoverable in a claim for damages. In principle, each breach of a term of the contract should give rise to liability for the losses attributable to that breach.[51] In *Mahmoud* v. *Bank of Credit and Commerce International SA*,[52] the leading decision on the implied term of trust and confidence, the final issue was whether employees could be awarded compensation for the financial loss they had suffered by being unable to obtain employment after their employer's bank had collapsed amid allegations of mismanagement and corruption. The House of Lords approved in principle an award of 'stigma damages' or compensation for damage to reputation causing economic loss in the form that the employees could not obtain employment owing to their linkage to the fraudulent bank. Similarly, if in breach of contract an employer negligently writes an inaccurate and damaging reference for an employee, which harms his job prospects, it was decided in *Spring* v. *Guardian Assurance plc* that in principle the employee should be able to recover compensation for the economic losses caused by the damage to reputation.[53] This claim for the economic loss resulting from damage to reputation faces great obstacles in practice, however, because the employee will have to prove the causal link between the stigma and the failure to obtain employment. In effect, the employee will have to bring evidence from prospective employers that his or her job application was rejected owing to the cloud of suspicion caused by the employer's misconduct or negligent reference, and that this cause of rejection was weightier than other considerations such as qualifications and experience.[54] Although an employer does not have to give a reason for dismissal under the common law, if it deliberately gives a false reason, that may amount to a breach of the implied term of mutual trust and confidence prior to the

---

[51] K. D. Ewing, 'Remedies for Breach of the Contract of Employment' (1993) 52 *Cambridge Law Journal* 405.

[52] [1998] AC 20 (HL).   [53] [1994] ICR 596 (HL).

[54] E.g. *Bank of Credit and Commerce International SA* v. *Ali* [1999] IRLR 508 (ChD).

dismissal and which therefore may result in recoverable economic losses by the dismissed employee.[55]

In contrast to the broad acceptance of claims for economic loss resulting from the employer's breach of terms of the contract, claims for compensation for anxiety, frustration and disappointment have been rejected. This exclusion of claims other than for economic loss derives from *Addis* v. *Gramophone Co Ltd*.[56] The plaintiff was summarily dismissed from his position as manager in a way that damaged his reputation in his local business community in Calcutta. His claim for damages for loss of salary and commissions during his contractual entitlement to six months' notice was successful, but the House of Lords denied that any other claim for compensation was possible in the context of wrongful dismissal. That decision has been distinguished, as we have seen, in claims for stigma damages for economic loss resulting from damage to reputation and employability caused by a breach of the implied terms of mutual trust and confidence during performance of the contract. But the decision in *Addis* still precludes claims regarding psychological injury, anxiety, frustration and disappointment caused by the manner of the dismissal or the fact of dismissal.[57]

Psychiatric Illness

Although the rule in *Addis* v. *Gramophone Co Ltd* prevents claims for compensation for distress and anxiety caused by the employer's breach of implied terms, it is possible to seek compensation for the economic losses resulting from a recognised psychiatric illness caused by an employer's breach of its duty of care with respect to the health and safety of employees. Confusingly and perhaps unsatisfactorily, it seems that a claim for compensation for psychiatric illness resulting in economic loss can also be advanced through an allegation of breach of the implied term of mutual trust and confidence. In *Gogay* v. *Hertfordshire County Council*,[58] the employee successfully claimed that an unjustified suspension from work amounted to a breach of the implied term of trust and confidence. The court approved a claim for general damages for an identifiable psychiatric illness that resulted from the unwarranted suspension. It might be clearer if all such claims for economic loss arising from psychiatric illness were channelled through either a claim in tort or the almost identical claim of a breach of the term that imposes a duty on employers to take reasonable care of the health and safety of employees.

To establish such a claim in tort, it is necessary to prove that the employer has failed to perform its duty of care, that this breach of duty caused the psychiatric illness of the employee and that the psychiatric illness was a reasonably foreseeable result and not too remote a loss. In principle, it is

---

[55] *Rawlinson* v. *Brightside Group Ltd* UKEAT/142/17, [2018] ICR 621.
[56] [1909] AC 488 (HL).   [57] *French* v. *Barclays Bank plc* [1998] IRLR 652 (CA).
[58] [2000] IRLR 703 (CA).

possible that a grievously unfair misuse of a disciplinary procedure to make unfounded charges and impose disciplinary sanctions might amount to a breach of the employer's duty of care, but the Court of Appeal has generally rejected such claims on the ground that employees can be expected to be more robust and not become seriously depressed by such treatment, so the injury is not reasonably foreseeable.[59] A failure to perform the duty of care may be the result of an omission by an employer to take appropriate action. In *Waters* v. *Commissioner of Police for the Metropolis*,[60] a woman police officer alleged that she had been sexually assaulted by a male police officer when they were off duty. After enquiries, no action was taken against the man. The woman further alleged that after she had made her complaint, she had been harassed, treated unfairly and victimised by other police officers, to such an extent that she had suffered mental illness. The House of Lords held that a claim in tort for breach of the employer's personal duty of care should not be struck out as disclosing no cause of action in these circumstances. The employer might be in breach of its duty of care either if the employer knew that employees were committing acts against another employee that might cause her physical or mental harm, or if the employer could foresee that such acts might happen, and if the employer failed to take reasonable steps to protect her against such victimisation or harassment.

Work-related Stress

Some pressure at work can give people a 'buzz' and help to motivate them, but excessive pressures and demands placed on employees can damage their mental health by provoking anxiety and depression and other psychiatric illnesses. Based upon the National Labour Force Survey, the HSE calculates that the total number of cases of work-related stress, depression or anxiety in 2015/16 was 488,000 cases, a prevalence rate of 1,510 per 100,000 workers. The total number of working days lost due to this condition in 2015/16 was 11.7 million days. Stress accounted for 37 per cent of all work related ill health cases and 45 per cent of all working days lost due to ill health.The main work factors cited by respondents as causing work related stress, depression or anxiety were workload pressures, including tight deadlines and too much responsibility and a lack of managerial support.[61] Job insecurity can also lead to stress.

An employer owes a duty of care under the law of negligence in tort and section 2 of the Health and Safety at Work Act 1974 to take reasonable steps to avoid foreseeable harm to the health of workers, including the possibility of damage to their mental health. To fulfil this duty with respect to stress, an employer would normally need to make an assessment of the risk of stress arising from excessive demands from the job, and if the degree of resulting stress would foreseeably cause injury to the mental health of an employee with normal fortitude,

---

[59] *Croft* v. *Broadstairs & St Peter's Town Council* [2003] EWCA Civ 676; *Yapp* v. *Foreign and Commonwealth Office* [2014] EWCA Civ 1512.
[60] [2000] IRLR 720 (HL).   [61] www.hse.gov.uk/statistics/causdis/stress/index.htm.

the employer is required to take reasonable steps to reduce the level of stress. Employers may be held liable in tort for substantial loss of earnings by employees who become unable to work as a result of depression and other psychiatric orders provoked by stress at work. Breach of the duty of care may arise from a failure to recognise that a job foreseeably involves excessive demands, or, if the problem is noticed by the employer, a failure to do anything about it (*Dickins* v. *O2 plc* [2008] EWCA Civ 1144), or a failure to implement measures agreed with the employee that were intended to reduce the level of stress (*Young* v. *The Post Office* [2002] EWCA Civ 661). If, however, an employee simply puts up with the pressure without complaint, thereby failing to alert the employer to the risk, an employer's duty to take reduce the stressful workplace conditions may not be triggered. As Hale LJ explained in *Hatton* v. *Sutherland*,[62] in general an employer is usually entitled to assume that an employee can withstand the normal pressures of the job, and that a duty to take additional steps will generally only be triggered when the indications of impending harm to health arising from stress at work are plain enough for any reasonable employer to realise that he should do something about it. The employer must then take reasonable steps, bearing in mind the probability of harm, its likely magnitude and the costs and practicability of preventing it. An employer who offers a confidential advice service with appropriate treatment services is likely to fulfil the duty of care. It is not sufficient for the employee to demonstrate that stress at work caused the psychiatric harm; it is essential to demonstrate that it was the employer's breach of duty in failing to address the problem adequately which materially contributed to the harm suffered.

The House of Lords approved this general guidance in *Barber* v. *Somerset County Council*.[63] Mr Barber was a mathematics teacher in a school. As a consequence of cuts in resources, he had to take on additional work in order to maintain his salary, and he was working up to seventy hours per week, including sometimes at weekends. During a summer term he was off work for three weeks with a medical note explaining that he was suffering from stress and depression. On his return to school, the head teacher and deputies were not sympathetic and no steps were taken to remedy the situation. At the beginning of the next term, his workload had further increased and he went to see his doctor; but before the doctor took action, Mr Barber had a breakdown at work and never returned to work. The House of Lords allowed the claimant's appeal, and restored the original judgment for damages for £72,547. The employer had broken the duty of care by failing to take any steps after the employee had been off work for three weeks for anxiety and depression in the summer term. The duty to take reasonable steps was a continuing one, which existed in the autumn term as well, when the managers of the school should have enquired into the claimant's mental health and when they could have taken steps to reduce his workload.

These claims for economic loss resulting from psychiatric illness caused by an employer are similarly affected by the *Johnson* exclusion zone. The *Johnson*

[62] [2002] EWCA Civ 76, [2002] ICR 613 (CA).   [63] [2004] UKHL 13, [2004] ICR 457 (HL).

decision rules out claims for compensation at common law for breach of either an implied term such as good faith or mutual trust and confidence or for a duty of care in connection with a dismissal and the manner of the dismissal, but it seems likely that in many cases such as *Eastwood* v. *Magnox Electric plc* and *McCabe* v. *Cornwall County Council*,[64] that the employer's conduct prior to the dismissal may provide the grounds for similar claims and so fall outside the exclusion zone. The courts will award compensation for economic loss attributable to breaches of contract or the duty of care in the employer's performance of the contract. Although the courts will not award compensation for stress, anxiety and distress caused by the employer's breach of contract, if the employee suffers an identifiable psychiatric illness resulting from a breach of the employer's duty of care, this can form the basis for a substantial claim for general damages in tort. In effect, the scope of the *Johnson* exclusion zone has been narrowly confined to claims regarding the manner of dismissal, thereby allowing the common law once again to develop according to basic principles in relation to performance of the contract prior to any dismissal.

Disciplinary Procedure

A contract of employment may incorporate a disciplinary or grievance procedure in its express terms. This procedure may be created by the employer or by a collective agreement. As part of an employer's duty to provide written statement of particulars of employment, ERA 1996 section 3(1) (aa) provides that the statement shall include a note:

> specifying any procedure applicable to the taking of disciplinary decisions relating to the employee, or to a decision to dismiss the employee, or referring the employee to the provisions of a document specifying such a procedure which is reasonably accessible to employees.

The disciplinary procedure may be described as forming part of the terms of the contract or it may be presented as merely a section of the employer's rule-book.

If the disciplinary procedure is only part of the rule-book, it will probably not create a binding contractual obligation,[65] although compliance with the disciplinary rules is likely to be highly pertinent to the question of the fairness of a dismissal under the statutory claim for unfair dismissal.[66]

---

[64] [2004] UKHL 35, [2004] ICR 1064 (HL).   [65] Chapter 4.

[66] *West Midlands Co-operative Society* v. *Tipton* [1986] ICR 192 (HL); *Skidmore* v. *Dartford and Gravesham NHS Trust* [2003] UKHL 27, [2003] ICR 721 (HL).

Right to Representation

During the disciplinary procedure, by virtue of the Employment Relations Act 1999 section 10, an employee has a statutory right to be accompanied and represented by a trade union official or a co-worker.[67] Within those two categories, the employee's choice of companion is unfettered, so the employer cannot object to the selection of a particular representative.[68] The terms of the contract of employment or the rules of the employer's disciplinary procedure may supplement these two categories of representative, as in the case of an NHS doctor permitted to bring either his spouse or a legally qualified representative retained by a defence organisation.[69] A refusal to permit an employee to bring a companion at all or to bring someone with appropriate expertise may also constitute a breach of the implied term of mutual trust and confidence.[70]

A more troublesome question is whether an employee is entitled to representation by a lawyer in the absence of express permission in the rules of the disciplinary procedure.[71] In order to establish the legal right to legal representation at disciplinary hearings, employees have sought to rely on the HRA 1998 and Article 6 of the ECHR.

European Convention of Human Rights, Article 6

1. In the determination of his civil rights and obligations or of any criminal charge against him, everyone is entitled to a fair and public hearing within a reasonable time by an independent and impartial tribunal established by law.

In general, an employer's disciplinary procedure does not 'determine civil rights'. A public court or tribunal subsequently performs that function when an employee brings a claim for wrongful or unfair dismissal. For Article 6 to apply to an employer's internal disciplinary procedure, the consequences of the procedure must be more serious than loss of a particular job. If, however, Article 6 applies to a disciplinary procedure, its requirements of a fair and public hearing would probably include the right to legal representation.

Occasionally, the outcome of an employer's disciplinary procedure may in effect determine the civil rights of an employee in this technical sense. In the case of a junior doctor facing serious charges, which, if upheld by a disciplinary hearing, would effectively render the doctor unemployable and prevent him

---

[67] Employment Relations Act 1999, s. 10. See p. 586.

[68] *Roberts* v. *GB Oils Ltd* UKEAT/177/13, [2014] ICR 462.

[69] *Kulkarni* v. *Milton Keynes Hospital NHS Trust* [2009] EWCA Civ 789, [2010] ICR 101 (CA).

[70] *The Leeds Dental Team Ltd* v. *Rose* UKEAT/16/13, [2014] ICR 94; *Stevens* v. *University of Birmingham* [2015] EWHC 2300, [2017] ICR 96 (QB).

[71] A. Sanders, 'A "Right" to Legal Representation (in the Workplace) during Disciplinary Proceedings?' (2010) 39 *Industrial Law Journal* 166.

from qualifying as a doctor in the UK, the Court of Appeal suggested that Article 6 would be engaged because the hearing would be dispositive of his right to work in his chosen field.[72] Although the right to work is not explicitly protected in the ECHR, it has been described as being an aspect of the right to respect for private life in Article 8.[73] Any determination that in effect blocks people from pursuing their chosen occupation or right to work will be regarded as a determination of a civil right and therefore one that engages Article 6.[74] In the normal run of contractual disciplinary procedures, the employer's decision to dismiss an employee will not prevent the pursuit of a vocation with another employer. But in some cases, especially those in regulated professions, if the employee is placed on a register that prevents future work in that profession as a result of a disciplinary decision, the employee's right to work is at stake and it will be necessary to comply with Article 6.

R(G) v. Governors of X School,[75] concerned the difficult question of assessing when an employer's disciplinary procedure should comply with Article 6 because, although it did not determine the right to pursue a chosen occupation, an adverse decision for the employee would be likely to lead to that result as a consequence of a further determination within an official regulatory process. The claimant was employed as a teaching assistant at a state-funded primary school. Disciplinary proceedings were commenced following an allegation that he had formed an inappropriate relationship by kissing a fifteen-year-old boy undergoing work experience at the school. The school governors refused to permit the claimant to have legal representation before the disciplinary committee or the internal appeal body. Although the police decided not to prosecute, the claimant was summarily dismissed for gross misconduct and the school referred the matter to the Secretary of State who had the power to prohibit a person from working with children in educational establishments. The claimant sought judicial review of the decision of the school to refuse to permit him legal representation on the ground that this public body had denied him his right to a fair trial in compliance with Article 6. The Supreme Court held that Article 6 would only be applicable to an employer's disciplinary proceedings if those proceedings would have a substantial influence or effect on the second set of proceedings conducted by the regulatory authority. In this case, however, the regulatory authority, which advised the Secretary of State, would carry out its own investigation and bring its own independent judgement to bear as to the seriousness and significance of the allegations before deciding to bar the claimant from the teaching profession, although it would not actually conduct its own hearing. The majority of the Supreme Court (disagreeing with the Court of Appeal) held that the regulatory process

---

[72] *Kulkarni* v. *Milton Keynes Hospital NHS Trust* [2009] EWCA Civ 789, [2010] ICR 101 (CA).
[73] *Sidabras and Dziautas* v. *Lithuania* (2004) 42 EHRR 104 (ECtHR).
[74] *R (Wright)* v. *Secretary of State for Health* [2009] UKHL 3, [2009] AC 739 (HL).
[75] [2011] UKSC 30, [2011] ICR 1033 (SC).

was sufficiently independent. It followed that there had been no interference with Article 6 and the claimant was not entitled to legal representation at the school's disciplinary procedure. The underlying policy of the decision to keep lawyers out of employers' disciplinary procedures was candidly explained by Lord Hope, when he identified the 'serious risk' presented by requiring legal representation in disciplinary proceedings that:

> [D]isciplinary proceedings in the public sector would be turned into a process of litigation, with all the consequences as to expense and delay that that would involve. The burden that this would impose on employers, and its chilling effect on resort to the procedure for fear of its consequences, is not hard to imagine. A good indication that it was Parliament's wish to avoid this is to be found in section 10 of the Employment Relations Act 1999 which provides that the employee has the right to be accompanied by an official of a trade union, not by a lawyer.[76]

Contractual Disciplinary Procedure

In *Johnson* v. *Unisys Ltd*,[77] the court held that the employer's disciplinary procedure in that case was only part of the rule-book, not a term of the contract. Lord Hoffmann pointed out that the main reason why employers adopt disciplinary procedures is to reduce the risk of successful claims for unfair dismissal. Given this purpose, Lord Hoffmann argued that it was unlikely that the parties would intend the rules of a disciplinary procedure to give rise to contractual duties which were independently actionable in damages.[78] Nevertheless, it is not impossible for the parties to agree a disciplinary procedure that is an express, enforceable term of the contract.

In *Gunton* v. *Richmond-upon-Thames London Borough Council*,[79] the plaintiff had been dismissed summarily with payment in lieu of notice. Although the contract permitted the employer to give one month's notice, it specified that if the dismissal was on disciplinary grounds, it was necessary to follow a disciplinary procedure. Even though the dismissal in this case was on disciplinary grounds, the employer had failed to follow this disciplinary procedure in its entirety. The Court of Appeal awarded additional compensation by reference to the net wages payable during the period when the employee, according to the terms of the contract, should have been suspended on full pay pending the outcome of the disciplinary procedure. Estimating that the proper procedure would have taken about four weeks to complete, the plaintiff was awarded damages equivalent to a further four weeks of salary in addition to the period of notice. This decision can be interpreted as one where an express contractual disciplinary procedure provides the basis for an additional claim for damages

---

[76] Para. 95.   [77] *Johnson* v. *Unisys Ltd* [2001] UKHL 13, [2001] ICR 480, HL.
[78] *Ibid.*, para. 66.
[79] [1980] ICR 755 (CA); followed in *Boyo* v. *London Borough of Lambeth* [1995] IRLR 50 (CA).

on top of damages for failure to give the required period of notice.[80] The case may be interpreted restrictively by reference to its particular facts as only permitting additional compensation where the employee is entitled to receive remuneration until the outcome has been determined. Alternatively, it can be interpreted even more narrowly as a decision that did not award damages for breach of the contractual disciplinary procedure, but rather awarded compensation for the failure to give reasonable notice, which in this case was calculated as eight weeks, comprising the normal time taken by the disciplinary procedure plus the express contractual requirement of four weeks.[81]

The question whether a contractually binding disciplinary procedure was enforceable by an additional claim for damages was addressed by an unusually large Supreme Court of seven judges in the combined cases of *Edwards* v. *Chesterfield Royal Hospital NHS Foundation Trust; Botham* v. *Ministry of Defence.*[82] In *Edwards* v. *Chesterfield Royal Hospital Trust,*[83] the Court of Appeal had concluded that a breach of a contractual disciplinary procedure, like the breach of any term of a contract, could provide the basis for a claim for damages that was separate from and in addition to a claim for damages for the employer's failure to give the required period of notice. A consultant surgeon employed by the defendant NHS trust was summarily dismissed for gross professional and personal misconduct. He claimed that the defendant had not followed the correct contractual disciplinary procedure, as determined by a collective agreement, and that if the employer had followed the correct procedure, he would not have been found guilty and would not have been dismissed from his position. He claimed compensation in the sum of £4.3 million for loss of income until the age of retirement, plus an additional sum for loss of an occupational pension, on the basis that this amount represented his loss of earnings for the remainder of his career, because the dismissal would prevent him from ever obtaining a permanent consultant position in the NHS again. The Court of Appeal only considered a preliminary question raised by the defendant hospital, which was that, whatever the merits of the claim, at a maximum, following *Gunton*, the measure of compensation payable to the claimant would be limited to the contractual notice period of three months' salary plus wages due during an additional period during which he would have remained employed while the correct disciplinary procedure had been followed. The Court of Appeal disagreed with that contention: on the assumption that an incorrect procedure had been followed and on the further assumption that had the correct procedure been followed it would have resulted in a finding of no misconduct, the claimant was entitled to recover damages for the loss of the opportunity to hold another full-time appointment with the NHS as

---

[80] *Saeed* v. *Royal Wolverhampton Hospitals NHS Trust* [2001] ICR 903 (CA).

[81] Lords Dyson and Walker, *Edwards* v. *Chesterfield Royal Hospital NHS Foundation Trust* [2011] UKSC 58 (SC) paras. 47–8.

[82] [2011] UKSC 58 (SC).   [83] [2010] EWCA Civ 571, [2010] ICR 1181 (CA).

a consultant surgeon for the remainder of his career. In *Botham* v. *Ministry of Defence*, an ET had found that the employer had dismissed the employee unfairly and in breach of a contractual disciplinary procedure. The award of compensation reached the upper limit permitted under the statutory claim for unfair dismissal. Mr Botham then sought additional compensation for breach of contract based upon the employer's breach of the contractual disciplinary procedure. This claim was rejected by the High Court,[84] on the ground it fell within the 'Johnson exclusion zone'. If that view was correct, it was arguable that the claim in *Edwards* should also have been rejected on the same ground.

The Supreme Court was sharply divided in its opinions on these cases. Although giving different reasons, a bare majority decided that neither claim for additional compensation for breach of the contractual disciplinary procedure would be permitted. Three justices of the Court (Lords Dyson, Mance and Walker) applied the *Johnson* exclusion zone to the claims. In brief, they held that, although a contractual disciplinary procedure might have some legal effects, a breach of that procedure could not provide the basis for a claim for compensation for damage to reputation resulting in economic loss, because such a claim under the common law would circumvent the carefully circumscribed limits established by Parliament for claims for unfair dismissal. Three justices of the Court (Lady Hale and Lords Kerr and Wilson) declined to extend the *Johnson* exclusion zone to cover breaches of express terms (as opposed to the implied term of mutual trust and confidence) that had been broken by the employer during the performance of the contract. On this approach, they were willing to permit the claim in *Edwards* for breach of contract with respect to the employer having used the wrong disciplinary procedure. On the assumed facts, the damage to his reputation was caused by this breach of contract during performance of the contract. In the case of *Botham*, however, only Lady Hale would have permitted the claim to proceed, the others taking the view that any damage to his reputation arose from the dismissal itself rather than defects in the contractual disciplinary process, so that it fell within the *Johnson* exclusion zone. Lady Hale held that breaches of express terms in the contract were always outside the *Johnson* exclusion zone. The remaining justice, Lord Phillips, President of the Court, although agreeing with the result favoured by the first group of justices, doubted whether it was possible to deprive a contractual disciplinary term of legal effect by reference to the presumed intention of Parliament to exclude its enforcement or of the parties to the contract of employment. Instead, he held that *Addis* v. *Gramophone Co. Ltd*[85] had decided that a claim for damage to reputation (stigma damages), which results from the manner of dismissal or the fact of dismissal, was not recoverable, and that the same rule should be applicable to breach of contractual disciplinary procedures leading up to a dismissal.

---

[84] [2010] EWHC 646 (QB).   [85] [1909] AC 488 (HL).

What guidance can be gleaned from this divided court? All members of the Supreme Court appear to accept that a contractual disciplinary procedure may be a binding legal agreement. Everyone also appears to accept that the employees in these cases might have been able to obtain an injunction to prevent the employer from using the wrong disciplinary procedure or from failing to use a procedure at all.[86] With the possible exception of Lady Hale, no one challenges the existence of a *Johnson* exclusion zone with respect to claims for damages regarding the manner of dismissal or the fact of dismissal causing distress and harm to reputation. Compensation in such cases must be sought exclusively within the jurisdiction of the statutory claim for unfair dismissal. The Court was principally divided rather on how to describe the scope of the *Johnson* exclusion zone. The division highlights the difficulty identified in *Eastwood* v. *Magnox Electric plc*,[87] in distinguishing between claims concerning the manner of dismissal and claims regarding breaches of terms of the contract during its performance. The simple truth is that an employer's abuse of a disciplinary procedure or breach of a contractual disciplinary procedure that ends in a dismissal is both a breach of contract during the performance of the contract and a decision that affects the manner of the dismissal. This will always make it hard and perhaps impossible to draw an intelligible distinction that describes the boundary of the *Johnson* exclusion zone.

Interaction between Common Law and Statute

There is a close but uneasy relationship between the common law and statutes in labour law. Often statutes can only be understood by reference to the concepts developed by the common law.[88] But unless the courts are careful, those common-law concepts such as the very idea of the contract of employment may tend to frustrate the purpose of the statute. More deeply, the question arises whether statutes should be regarded in some instances as excluding or supplanting the common law entirely. For instance, the principal argument accepted by the courts in favour of restricting the development of the common law of wrongful dismissal to provide remedies for unjust dismissals has been the view that, by passing the legislation on unfair dismissal, Parliament has pre-empted this field by establishing detailed rules that should not be undermined or circumvented by the development of the common law.

Judges often justify their restricted development of the common law by claiming that this stance supports the intention of Parliament.[89] On most occasions, however, Parliament has not expressed any view about the common law. In the case of unfair dismissal, Parliament

---

[86] See p. 851.   [87] [2004] UKHL 35, [2005] AC 503 (HL).

[88] S. Anderman, 'The Interpretation of Protective Employment Statutes and Contracts of Employment' (2000) 29 *Industrial Law Journal* 223.

[89] A. Bogg and H. Collins, 'Lord Hoffmann and the Law of Employment: The Notorious Episode of Johnson v Unisys Ltd', in P. S. Davies and J. Pila (eds.), *The Jurisprudence of Lord Hoffmann* (Oxford: Hart, 2015), p. 185.

only said that the statutory law of unfair dismissal was required because the common law of wrongful dismissal provided inadequate rules and remedies for ordinary working people. Parliament did not say that it was pre-empting or abolishing the common law; it simply regarded it as largely irrelevant, though it must have been aware of a few rare instances of the enforcement of contractual disciplinary procedures.[90] Showing how speculative these claims about parliamentary intent can be, it is worth remembering that the courts took the opposite view of the Workmen's Compensation Act 1897: the legislation provided a simplified procedure for workers to claim compensation for personal injuries at work, but the courts simultaneously maintained and developed the application of the common law of claims for negligently caused personal injuries.

An alternative argument in favour of restricting the development of the common law in the light of parallel legislation concerns a desire to maintain or improve the coherence of the law.[91] Sometime coherence might require restricting the common law, but in other instances, such as *Barber* v. *RJB Mining (UK) Ltd,*[92] it may require development of the common law to fill a gap in the statute. But how should we judge coherence? In the *Johnson* case itself, the problem of inconsistency was believed to be readily apparent: the statutory remedy for the unfair dismissal imposed a severe limit on the compensatory remedy, whereas the common law has no artificial restrictions on the measure of damages, although the quantum can be limited by such standard rules as mitigation and remoteness. Yet, contrary to that point, it might be argued that there is nothing incoherent in permitting claims in tort, including claims for psychiatric injury, to survive beside the statutory claim for unfair dismissal, since the claim for personal injury is quite different from a claim for economic loss caused by an unfair dismissal. We might further ask why it would be incoherent, as seems to have been thought by three justices in *Edwards*, for the common law to permit claims for breach of contractual disciplinary procedures under the general law of contract while providing a remedy under the law of unfair dismissal for unfairness in non-contractual disciplinary procedures. It might seem more coherent to permit the claim in *Edwards*, *especially when one appreciates that the denial of a remedy creates the anomaly and incoherence in the common law that there is no claim for damages, but only for an injunction, for breach of this particular kind of contractual term.*

It is certainly important that the courts should be mindful of their constitutional position as subservient to a democratic legislature that acts within its powers, but that should not lead to the unprincipled and unpredictable development or restriction of the common law, since the judges also have a duty to develop the common law in a coherent way.

---

[90] *Barber* v. *Manchester Regional Hospital Board* [1958] 1 WLR 181 (QB); K. Costello, '*Edwards v Chesterfield Royal Hospital*: Parliamentary Intention and Damages Caused by Maladminstration of a Contractual Disciplinary Procedure' (2013) 76(1) *Modern Law Review* 134.

[91] M. Freedland and N. Kountouris, *The Legal Construction of Personal Work Relations* (Oxford University Press, 2012), pp. 222–45; A. C. L. Davies, 'The Relationship between the Contract of Employment and Statute', in M. Freedland *et al.* (eds.) *The Contract of Employment* (Oxford University Press, 2016), p. 73.

[92] [1999] ICR 679; see p. 333.

Terms Restricting Grounds of Dismissal

Instead of an employer enjoying the normal right at common law to terminate the contract for any reason, the express terms of the contract may restrict the power to dismiss by reference to specific grounds such as 'good cause', 'gross misconduct', or 'redundancy'. For example, in *Jones* v. *Gwent County Council*,[93] the contract of employment of a college lecturer specified that dismissal without the normal contractual requirement of two months' notice given prior to the end of the spring or autumn term could only be made on the ground of 'misconduct or other urgent cause' and could only occur after a detailed allegation had been considered at a hearing with the employee and upheld by the college's disciplinary committee. Although the disciplinary committee rejected the main allegations of misconduct, the employer eventually dismissed the lecturer. The High Court issued a declaration that, as the disciplinary committee had rejected the allegation, the dismissal could not constitute an exercise of the contractual power of dismissal for misconduct conferred by the contract. The employer was therefore in breach of contract because it had not been terminated on grounds permitted by the express terms.

Most of the legal difficulties in these instances of substantive limits on dismissal concern the interpretation of the express terms of the contract of employment. For instance, where a contract restricted the power of the employer to dismiss except for 'good cause shown', the court implied a term that there should, before any dismissal, be a prior hearing and investigation, fairly conducted.[94] Whether proven misconduct should be described as 'gross misconduct' or whether carelessness can be classified as 'gross negligence' can be tested in court as a matter of the interpretation of the contract, but a court is unlikely to disagree with the employer's stance unless it seems wholly unreasonable in the circumstances.[95]

Furthermore the courts appear reluctant to accept an interpretation of the contract that substantially deprives an employer of its power to terminate a contract. Ambiguities and internal contradictions in the terms of the contract are likely to be resolved in favour of minimal restrictions on the employer's normal power to terminate the contract on giving reasonable notice. For instance, though the contract in *Taylor* v. *Secretary of State for Scotland*[96] stated expressly that there should be no age discrimination, the court awarded greater weight to another term that permitted the employer to make employees over the age of fifty-five redundant. Nevertheless, provided the contract is sufficiently explicit and precise, the express terms can confer a kind of tenure upon employees by excluding the ordinary implied terms regarding dismissal.

[93] [1992] IRLR 521 (Ch).
[94] *King* v. *University Court of the University of St Andrews* [2002] IRLR 252.
[95] *Chhabra* v. *West London Mental Health NHS Trust* [2013] UKSC 80, [2014] ICR 194.
[96] [2000] ICR 595 (HL).

In *McClelland* v. *Northern Ireland General Health Services*,[97] upon her marriage, a clerk was dismissed with six months' notice from her permanent position. This dismissal followed the highly discriminatory social convention of the time that married women should give up employment and stay at home, a convention that was expressed in a rule of the employers that 'Female officers will on marriage be required to tender their resignations to the board.' Her terms of employment provided in condition 12 that: 'The board may dismiss any officer for gross misconduct and may dismiss any officer who is proved to their satisfaction to be inefficient and unfit to merit continued employment.' By a majority of 3:2, the House of Lords upheld the employee's appeal. The construction placed by the majority on the terms and conditions was that the express powers to dismiss contained in condition 12 were exhaustive and excluded any implied power to dismiss without reason on giving reasonable notice. The minority opinion was that the terms were insufficiently explicit to exclude the normal presumption that every contract of employment is terminable for any reason on reasonable notice. The minority view probably represents the normal approach to the construction of express substantive conditions that restrict an employer's right to terminate a contract of employment.

Assuming that the employer has dismissed an employee in breach of an express substantive condition in the contract such as a requirement of good cause, the question becomes what measure of compensation should be granted. The employer cannot rely upon the ordinary rule that limits compensation to the wages payable during the period of notice, because the contract has excluded the normal right of the employer to terminate the contract on giving notice. For example, if the contract states that the employee can only be dismissed for 'gross misconduct' and will otherwise be entitled to remain in employment until a contractual retirement age, should the employee be entitled to recover damages representing the loss of income until retirement age? If a court were minded to award such a substantial amount, no doubt it could be reduced on the basis of the ordinary principles for the calculation of damages in order to take into account such possibilities as the premature death of the employee, the winding up or closure of the employer or that the employee might be guilty of misconduct justifying dismissal on some future occasion.[98] A further major reduction in the measure of compensation could be imposed to reflect the employee's duty to mitigate loss by finding another job.[99] This approach seems to accord with the general approach of the common law towards the calculation of compensatory damages, and was condoned *obiter* by Lord Mance in *Edwards*:

---

[97] [1957] 1 WLR 594 (HL).

[98] *Gregory* v. *Philip Morris Ltd* (1988) 80 ALR 455; K. D. Ewing, 'Job Security and the Contract of Employment' (1989) 18 *Industrial Law Journal* 217.

[99] *Wheeler* v. *Philip Morris Ltd* (1989) 97 ALR 282.

The case of an employee with an express contractual right not to be dismissed save for cause is not before us, and gives rise to different issue to those which are. Damages for wrongful dismissal in breach of such a contract would on the face of it be measured on the basis that the contract would have continued unless and until the employee left, retired or gave cause for dismissal (in the relation to the prospects of all of which an assessment would have to be made), but questions would no doubt also arise as to whether the employee had accepted or had to accept the dismissal and/or had to mitigate or had mitigated his or her loss.[100]

The question remains whether any claim in damages might be excluded by reference to the *Johnson* exclusion zone. If a contract states that the employee may only be dismissed for gross misconduct and the employer nevertheless dismisses the employee for some other reason, would a claim be blocked, following *Edwards*, on the ground that it plainly concerned a claim for compensation for dismissal, which Parliament has allocated to the statutory jurisdiction for unfair dismissal? One way of approaching this question is to ask whether the statutory claim for unfair dismissal provides a remedial framework for such claims for protection of contractually enhanced job security. As we shall see below, the statutory question of whether or not a dismissal was fair is not determined by reference to the terms of the contract, so that a dismissal in breach of contract but for a substantial reason can in principle be held to be unfair. If so, we might conclude that the statute does not protect the contractual entitlement to job security, and so the common-law claim should be permitted.

The uncertainty of this reasoning really only serves to highlight the paradox of the *Johnson* exclusion zone: if a claim, right or remedy or head of loss can be met by the statutory law of unfair dismissal, the exclusion zone applies to rule out the claim at common law. Yet, at the same time, if a claim or loss cannot be met by the statutory claim, it may be inferred that Parliament does not want such a claim to exist, so that common-law claim too should fall within the *Johnson* exclusion zone.[101]

Injunctions

Express terms that fetter an employer's disciplinary powers create the opportunity for an employee to seek an injunction against a dismissal or some other breach of contract. At the time of the enactment of the statutory right to claim unfair dismissal, it was doubted that any claim for an injunction against dismissal might be successful except perhaps in the special case of public officials holding an office under statute. Yet this view immediately turned out to be a misconception of the capacity of private law to respond to claims to

---

[100] *Edwards* v. *Chesterfield Royal Hospital NHS Foundation Trust* [2011] UKSC 58 (SC), para. 105.
[101] H. Collins, 'Compensation for Dismissal: In Search of Principle' (2012) 41 *Industrial Law Journal* 208.

job security based upon express terms of the contract. In *Hill* v. *CA Parsons & Co Ltd*,[102] the Court of Appeal issued an injunction against dismissal in the unusual circumstance (now effectively prohibited by statute)[103] where the employer had reluctantly given the employee notice because a trade union insisted, contrary to the wishes of the employee, that he should join that particular union or be dismissed.

In applications for injunctions against a dismissal, the employee must establish that the contract of employment has not already been terminated by dismissal or some other mechanism, for otherwise there remains no contract for the court to enforce. As a practical matter, therefore, the employee needs to act swiftly before the contract has been terminated by notice by making an application for an interim or pre-trial injunction pending a full trial. In the case of summary dismissal, the employee must not act in any way that might be construed as an acceptance of the employer's repudiatory breach of contract. A court will then issue such an interim injunction if it finds that there is:

- a serious issue to be tried;
- the normal conditions for the award of an injunction are satisfied; and
- the balance of convenience favours an order.

There cannot be a serious issue to be tried unless the employee has some prospect of success. For this purpose, the employee must be able to point to an arguable breach of the express terms of the contract. In *Hill* v. *CA Parsons & Co Ltd*, there was no term requiring the employee to join any union, so the employers were unilaterally imposing a variation without the employee's consent. In many cases the express term that is broken specifies a disciplinary procedure that must be followed prior to a dismissal. The use of an injunction to enforce a contractual disciplinary procedure was unanimously approved in *Edwards* v. *Chesterfield Royal Hospital NHS Foundation Trust*,[104] although, as in *Johnson* v. *Unisysis Ltd*,[105] it was thought that normally a disciplinary procedure in the employer's rule-book would not be intended to have contractual force. Nevertheless, some irregularities in the operation of the disciplinary procedure applicable to doctors in the NHS, including an allegation of 'gross misconduct' that seemed overstated in the circumstances of a careless disclosure of confidential information, were sufficient for the Supreme Court to grant a declaration and injunction to prevent the further use of the disciplinary procedure unless the whole process was recommenced properly in accordance with the rules.[106]

A normal condition for the award of an interim injunction is that, if the claim were successful at trial, a remedy in damages would be inadequate. This

---

[102] [1972] Ch. 305 (CA).　　[103] p. 511.　　[104] [2011] UKSC 58, [2012] 2 AC 22.
[105] [2001] UKHL 13, [2003] 1 AC 518 (HL).
[106] *Chhabra* v. *West London Mental Health NHS Trust* [2013] UKSC 80, [2014] ICR 194.

condition seems to be relatively easy to satisfy in the context of employment, where courts can be persuaded that the prevention of the dismissal with the consequence that the employee retains the job will be rather more valuable to the employee than a successful claim for the meagre damages awarded for wrongful dismissal. This argument will be strengthened if the employee has no reasonable prospect of obtaining another job,[107] or a job of equal status and remuneration.[108] In *Robb* v. *London Borough of Hammersmith and Fulham*,[109] damages were held to be an inadequate remedy because they would not compensate the plaintiff for the manner of his dismissal and his deprivation of the opportunity to ventilate his case and justify himself under the contractual disciplinary procedure. Following views expressed in *Edwards* v. *Chesterfield Royal Hospital*, such a claim for damages may be unavailable because it falls within the *Johnson* exclusion zone, which should make the case of issuing an interim injunction even more compelling.[110]

A further condition applied to an award of injunctions in cases of employment is the requirement that an injunction would not compel the employer to continue to employ a person in whom the employer had lost trust and confidence. In *Hill* v. *CA Parsons & Co Ltd*, of course, the employer had full confidence in the employee; it was the trade union that objected to his continued employment. In *Powell* v. *Brent London Borough Council*,[111] where an injunction was awarded, the dismissal was instituted not because of any criticism of the employee, but because the council believed that the appointment had not been made in accordance with its policy of equal opportunities, so that there was no absence of mutual trust and confidence. It can also be argued with respect to larger organisations that, even though the personal relationship between the employee and his or her immediate manager may have broken down, that fact does not entail the conclusion that the employing organisation as a whole has lost trust and confidence in the employee.[112] It may also be doubted whether this condition is pertinent to claims that require an employer to carry out a contractual disciplinary procedure: barring truly exceptional cases, the employer's trust in the employee seems irrelevant to the issue of whether or not the contractual disciplinary procedure should be followed.

Finally, the courts consider whether the balance of convenience favours the order of an injunction. The employee needs to show that his legal position will be harmed without the injunction and that the proposed order does not impose a serious disadvantage on the employer. The adverse effect on the

---

[107] *Hill* v. *CA Parsons & Co Ltd* [1972] Ch. 305 (CA).

[108] *Irani* v. *Southampton and South West Hampshire Health Authority* [1985] ICR 590 (ChD).

[109] [1991] IRLR 72 (QB).

[110] D. Cabrelli, 'Liability and Remedies for Breach of the Contract of Employment' (2016) 45 *Industrial Law Journal* 207.

[111] [1988] ICR 176 (CA).

[112] *Irani* v. *Southampton and South West Hampshire Health Authority* [1985] ICR 590 (ChD).

employee focuses on the possible deprivation of employment by the employer's termination of the contract. The potential disadvantage to the employer concerns the continuing presence of the employee at the workplace, which might cause disruption to working arrangements. This last problem can usually be avoided by drafting the terms of the order so that the employee does not attend work or agrees to comply with the employer's instructions.

Irani v. *Southampton and South West Hampshire Health Authority*[113] illustrates the modern use of interim injunctions in relation to dismissal.[114] The claimant, Mr Irani, a part-time ophthalmologist, was dismissed by the employer following a quarrel with a full-time senior colleague. The employer decided that the differences between the employees were such that they could no longer work together and, in the absence of alternative employment, the junior part-timer would have to go. Mr Irani brought an action for a declaration that the employer had failed to follow the disciplinary procedure incorporated into his contract of employment and for an injunction restraining the defendants from implementing their decision to terminate the employment with notice without following the contractual procedure. The claimant then successfully sought an injunction pending trial, giving an undertaking not to attend the relevant hospitals pending the outcome of the disciplinary procedure. The court considered that the employer, viewed as the health authority as a whole, had not lost trust and confidence in the claimant. It recognised further that losing a job in the NHS by dismissal would seriously damage the employee's prospects in obtaining a job elsewhere in this nearly monopoly employer of health services. Finally, in view of the undertaking given by Mr Irani, the order was practicable and imposed no unfair burden on the employer.

These decisions indicate that employees have a good chance of success in obtaining interim injunctions against dismissals in breach of express contractual disciplinary procedures, provided that the employee makes suitable undertakings to avoid any deleterious effects to the employer's operations. If the employee can demonstrate a serious question to be tried that the employer has broken the contractual disciplinary procedure, the balance of convenience usually favours the interim injunction. Beyond the application to disciplinary procedures, however, the employee usually faces severe hurdles. Not only does the employee have to make the claim swiftly, before the contract has been terminated, but also the employee must show that on the balance of convenience the injunction will not cause substantial detriment to the employer. Forcing an employer to take back an employee who has been dismissed is normally regarded by the courts as impracticable and therefore against the balance of convenience.

---

[113] [1985] ICR 590 (ChD).

[114] See also: L. Barmes, 'Remedying Workplace Harassment' (2002) 55 *Current Legal Problems* 347, at 354–64.

Reform

Despite frequent calls from the senior judiciary for Parliament to step in to sort out the law of wrongful dismissal, there are no signs of impending reform. Nevertheless, it is clear that judge-made laws on wrongful dismissal from the nineteenth century are unsuitable for contemporary society. Parliament did successfully revise the law on the requirement of reasonable notice, although the period remains comparatively short. What is most urgently needed now is legislation that will permit the parties to a contract of employment to agree legally binding disciplinary procedures. Although most employers probably follow their own disciplinary procedures, the sanctions for not doing so are unpredictable and weak. Unless an employee has the opportunity and resources to obtain an injunction in the ordinary courts, any breach of procedure by the employer may be overlooked in a statutory claim for unfair dismissal if there is a strong substantive case for dismissal. But the law should encourage contractually binding disciplinary procedures, not only because they may achieve fairer outcomes for employees but also because they are likely to encourage internal dispute settlement without recourse to the courts and tribunals. Part of that reform would require a specification of the measure of damages for breach of the legally binding procedure. Admittedly the value of the loss of the chance of a fair hearing under the contractual procedure is speculative, but certainly the employee should receive compensation for that loss rather than being turned away with no redress at all.

19

Unfair Dismissal

Contents

The statutory claim for unfair dismissal was introduced in 1971.[1] Although some important details have altered since then, the general aim, structure and core principles of the law have remained constant. The aim of the legislation is to fill the major gap in the common law of wrongful dismissal by providing

---

[1] Industrial Relations Act 1971.

employees with a substantial remedy for unfairness and arbitrariness in the manner and reasons for dismissal. A claim must be brought by an employee before an ET. The applicable standards of fairness are mandatory and in principle cannot be excluded or modified by contractual agreement. An ET must determine whether or not the employer's reason for dismissal was unfair and, if so, order a remedy of reinstatement or compensation.

The law of unfair dismissal has a crucial role to play in any labour law system. It represents the principal control afforded by the law over the misuse of managerial contractual and discretionary powers to discipline the workforce. It reduces, though never abolishes, the degree of subordination of employers to their employing organisation. More than that, the law of unfair dismissal provides a principal vehicle for workers to assert other labour rights, such as the right to be a member of a trade union and the right to enjoy civil liberties without unjustifiable interference by their employer. These labour rights and civil liberties can often only be vindicated retrospectively by the employee bringing a claim for unfair dismissal.

Our analysis of the legal framework of unfair dismissal divides the topic into four main issues. The first concerns the justifications for the qualifying conditions that an employee has to satisfy in order to bring a claim. The second concerns the judicial application of the requirement for a claimant to prove that he or she has been dismissed by the defendant employer. The third issue examines the test of fairness applied by the tribunals and considers whether the standard adequately protects employees against arbitrary and unreasonable managerial behaviour. The final topic concerns an assessment of whether the remedies of compensation and reinstatement that may be awarded by a tribunal are adequate to achieve satisfactory levels of compliance with the standards of fairness required by the law.

Qualifying Conditions

Contract of Employment

The statutory provisions commence with a ringing declaration of the right.

Employment Rights Act 1996, Section 94

(1) An employee has the right not to be unfairly dismissed by his employer.

Yet this statement already contains within it a vital limitation: the right is only available to employees working under a contract of employment. This restriction on the ambit of protection implicitly adopts the common law's traditional distinction between contracts of employment and contracts for services provided by independent contractors. We have suggested that the formula adopted in other employment rights legislation of extending protection to all 'workers', that is individuals who perform work personally under a contract except where they are conducting a profession or a business undertaking, might be a preferable definition of the scope for most rights in the ERA 1996, including unfair dismissal and redundancy.[2] Such a broader scope for protection from dismissal would obstruct employers from avoiding the law of unfair dismissal by trying to reclassify employees as self-employed independent contractors. At present, workers whose contracts designate them as self-employed and place many risks of the business on their shoulders can only hope for statutory protection against dismissal by persuading a court that the terms of the contract are a sham and that the true agreement between the parties places the worker in the category of employee.

Qualifying Period of Continuous Service

Ever since the inception of the right to claim unfair dismissal, the right has been limited to workers with a qualifying period of continuous service,[3] although the length of the period has varied.[4] The current requirement of a qualifying period of two years excludes both employees during their first two years of service under a contract of indefinite duration and temporary workers hired for a period of less than two years if the contract is not renewed.

More than twenty-five exceptions to this qualifying period of one year are contained in ERA 1996, section 108(3). The purpose of these exceptions that grant protection from the first day of employment is to provide immediate guarantees for other vital labour rights. Dismissals involving breach of these 'day one rights' such as dismissals for membership of a trade union, dismissals on prohibited grounds of discrimination or for pregnancy, are often also specified to be automatically unfair dismissals.[5] Employees who lack the requisite qualifying period for a claim for unfair dismissal often try to fit the facts of their cases into these categories of day one rights. Outside those exceptions, the statutory qualifying period creates a space of two years for employers to exercise their disciplinary power of dismissal unfettered by statutory regulation and oversight.

Given the difficulty of acquiring adequate information in advance about the employee's capability and motivation, employers inevitably find that some hires have been mistaken, and for this reason often insist upon a probationary period during which the employer has an explicit contractual right to terminate the contract. The presence of a qualifying period in the legislation is justified primarily by the employer's need to have such a probationary period in order to 'weed out mistakes'. It is true that if the employee is indeed

---

[2] Chapter 6.
[3] The concept of 'continuity of employment' in ERA 1996, ss. 210–19, is explained in Chapter 5.
[4] ERA 1996, s. 108(1).   [5] P. 876.

unsuitable for the job, the employer should have no difficulty in defending a claim for unfair dismissal. However, the qualifying period saves the employer the management time and expense of having to justify the dismissal, costs that are often estimated to amount to in excess of £5,000.[6] It is also argued that without a qualifying period, employers would be more reluctant to hire new workers, thereby causing higher levels of employment, although there is no empirical evidence to support that hypothesis. It seems be more likely, however, that, in the absence of a qualifying period, employers would engage in more intensive screening of applicants, a practice that might diminish the job prospects of workers with poor records of employment. Another concern voiced about the abolition of any qualifying period is that employers would respond by offering unattractive jobs on such short fixed-term contracts and as temporary work wherever possible.[7] It is unclear, however, why employers would respond in those ways, because the termination of such contracts in the absence of a qualifying period would trigger an employee's right to claim unfair dismissal. The principal argument against any qualifying period is to prevent the risk of unfairness and injury to the dignity of workers by an employer's misuse of unfettered disciplinary powers.

Assuming that some kind of qualifying period is appropriate, however, there is much political disagreement regarding its length. The selection of a qualifying period of one year in 1999 (replacing the former two-year period and extending coverage by about 2.8 million employees)[8] was justified by the Labour government on the ground that it achieved the optimal balance between fairness, security and flexibility. The Coalition government of 2010 returned to a two-year qualifying period even though it acknowledged that the measure would eliminate the coverage of the statutory protection against unfair dismissal from about 2.9 million employees, about 10 per cent of the nation's workforce.[9] As well as the arguments discussed above regarding the beneficial employment effects of a lengthy qualifying period on the unproven theory that employers would be more likely to hire workers, the government stressed the need to reduce the costs of litigation before tribunals both to employers and to governments. Extension of the qualifying period does reduce the number of claims before tribunals and saves employers the costs of defending them, but it has been demonstrated that the savings to employers from avoiding the likely number of about a hundred successful

---

[6] B. Hayward, M. Peters, N. Rousseau, and K. Seeds, *Findings from the Survey of Employment Tribunal Applications 2003*, Employment Relations Research Series No. 33 (London: DTI, 2004), p. 117.

[7] DTI, *The Unfair Dismissal and Statement of Reasons for Dismissal (variation of qualifying period) Order 1999: Regulatory Impact Assessment*, para. 8.

[8] C. Kilpatrick, 'Has New Labour Reconfigured Employment Legislation?' (2003) 32 *Industrial Law Journal* 135.

[9] BIS, *Resolving Workplace Disputes: A consultation* (London: BIS, 2011), pp. 50–2.

claims in total each year are small.[10] The prior consultation document concluded: 'We do not see this as a charter for businesses to sack workers unfairly', although it is hard to see what other impact it might have on the 10 per cent of the nation's workforce affected.

Surveys of employers cast considerable doubt on whether the statutory qualifying period has much influence on their attitudes to probationary periods.[11] Very few employers adopt an open recruitment policy and subsequently 'weed out' unsatisfactory employees after a short period of time. If the employee requires any training, this sort of hire-and-fire policy is usually inefficient. Most employers do have probation periods, but they are fixed at much less than the statutory level and have not been affected by legislative changes to the period from one year to two years and back to one. The most common period for probation is about ten to twelve weeks, although with longer periods for jobs requiring higher skills and in larger firms. The length of the probation period used by employers is determined by a variety of factors concerning the ability of management to evaluate fully the type of employee concerned. The type and complexity of the employee's skills are very significant to this decision; but the need for management to signal an employee's formal inclusion into the firm's establishment is a factor which acts to reduce the overall level of probationary period lengths. Changes in the statutory qualifying period seem hardly to influence the employers' use of probationary periods. In a proposed EU Directive, there will be a mandatory limit of six months on probationary periods,[12] but it is unclear whether this limit merely applies to terms of the contract of employment or whether it may have some effect on the statutory qualifying period as well.

Since the statutory qualifying period does not seem to play a significant role in the practice of a HRM, it is worth considering what might happen if it were abolished or drastically shortened. One possible effect is that employers would have to become clearer about what they mean by a 'probationary employee'. They could no longer treat probationary employees as short fixed-term employees who can be dismissed with impunity. Instead employers would have to give probationary employees adequate supervision, training and support, so that if the employee still proved inadequate in performing the job, the employer would be able to defend itself successfully against any possible claim for unfair dismissal.[13] Another possible effect of the abolition of the qualifying period might be that employees would be more willing to risk changing their employer. This increase in flexibility in labour markets should be attractive to

[10] K. D. Ewing and J. Hendy, 'Unfair Dismissal Changes – Unfair?' (2012) 41 *Industrial Law Journal* 115.

[11] S. Evans, J. Goodman, and L. Hargreave, *Unfair Dismissal Law and Employment Practice in the 1980s* (London: Department of Employment, Research Paper No. 53, 1985).

[12] Art. 7, Proposal for a Directive on transparent and predictable working conditions in the European Union, Brussels, 21 December 2017, COM(2017) 797 final.

[13] E.g. *Post Office* v. *Mughal* [1977] ICR 763 (EAT).

governments, because by changing jobs employees can acquire new skills, establish wider networks and improve their employability, thereby contributing more generally to competitiveness in the economy.

A qualifying period of one year or two years thus apparently has few benefits for either employers or employees, and it may create some rigidity in labour markets, although all its effects may be only marginal. The exceptions granted for claims based upon discrimination and other fundamental rights reveal that behind the qualifying period lurks the view that the right to claim unfair dismissal is not as important a social right as many others. That view may have reflected public attitudes in the past, but it may be out of date today in view of the inclusion of the right to claim unfair dismissal in many international declarations of social rights.

Three-month Limitation Period

A claim for unfair dismissal must normally be presented to an ET within three months of the dismissal.[14] The tribunal is permitted to grant an extension of such further period as it regards as reasonable in a case where it is satisfied that it was not reasonably practicable for the complaint to be presented before the end of that period of three months. The time limit is extended where the applicant is obliged to contact ACAS for the purpose of facilitation of conciliation until a certificate of compliance with the conciliation requirement is received.[15]

Effective Date of Termination

It is necessary to determine exactly when the contract of employment ended for the purpose of calculating whether or not the employee satisfied the qualifying period of continuous employment, for determining whether or not the claim was brought within the three-month limitation period, and for the calculation of the amount of compensation payable for a basic award (which is based on length of service).[16] To determine the precise moment of the dismissal for these purposes, the statute creates the concept of an 'effective date of termination' (sometimes called EDT). Section 97(1) ERA 1996 defines the EDT as either the expiration of the notice of termination of the contract given by the employer or employee, or the expiration of a limited-term contract or, if no notice is given, the date 'on which termination takes effect'. This statutory provision is surprisingly unhelpful. Having created the special statutory concept of the effective date of termination, it fails to define the concept except in the two straightforward cases of the expiry of notice and

---

[14] ERA 1996, s. 111(2).

[15] ERA 1996 s. 207B, referring to the conciliation obligation in Employment Tribunals Act 1996, s. 18A.

[16] ERA 1996, s. 119.

the completion of a fixed term. As a result, the question when the termination 'takes effect' has generated considerable litigation, particularly where employers believe that they have dismissed employees just before the end of the qualifying period.

The courts have provided further specificity to the statutory concept. In the case of summary dismissal, without notice, the EDT is regarded as the day of the summary dismissal, whether or not that dismissal was justified.[17] With respect to the EDT, there is no requirement for the employee to 'accept the repudiation'. The summary dismissal may be effected implicitly by conduct in fundamental breach of contract such as a refusal to pay wages.[18] If the employer gives shorter notice than is required under the contract, the EDT is the expiration of the short notice.[19] Both of these rules are subject, however, to ERA 1996, section 97(2), which extends the effective date of termination to the expiration of the statutory minimum notice period. In both cases of summary dismissal and dismissal on short notice, the effective date of termination cannot be earlier than the date on which dismissal is communicated to the employee,[20] which, in the case of communication by letter, normally means when the employee reads the letter or at least has a reasonable opportunity to read the letter.[21] Nor can the effective date of termination be antedated by agreement between the parties.[22] When a contractual right to a disciplinary and appeal procedure applies, the EDT depends on the terms of that procedure. If under the procedure the employee is suspended until the final outcome is known, the EDT is fixed by the communication of the final approval of the decision to dismiss.[23] If the procedure provides instead that the dismissal is effective, though the employee may be reinstated by a domestic appeal, following an unsuccessful appeal the EDT is set by the initial dismissal.[24] If, on the other hand, the appeal is successful, the employee may be reinstated or the earlier decision varied, at which point, if the employer nevertheless decides to dismiss the employee, the EDT will be governed by the second dismissal.[25] What renders these cases hard for the tribunals to decide is the frequent vagueness of the contractual procedures with respect to legal implications of dismissal with a right to an appeal.

Under these rules, therefore, an employer who wishes to dismiss before the deadline of the qualifying period must either give due notice that expires

---

[17] *Dedman v. British Building & Engineering Appliances Ltd* [1974] ICR 53; *Stapp v. Shaftesbury Society* [1982] IRLR 326 (CA).

[18] *Kirklees Metropolitan Council v. Radecki* [2009] EWCA Civ 298, [2009] ICR 1244 (CA).

[19] *TBA Industrial Products v. Morland* [1982] IRLR 331 (EAT).

[20] *McMaster v. Manchester Airport plc* [1998] IRLR 112 (EAT).

[21] *Gisda Cyf v. Barratt* [2010] UKSC 41, [2010] ICR 1475 (SC).

[22] *Fitzgerald v. University of Kent at Canterbury* [2004] EWCA Civ 143, [2004] IRLR 300 (CA).

[23] *Drage v. Governors of Greenford High School* [2000] IRLR 314 (CA).

[24] *J Sainsbury Ltd v. Savage* [1980] IRLR 109 (CA).

[25] *Salmon v. Castlebeck Care (Teesdale) Ltd and another* [2015] ICR 735 (EAT); *Hawes & Curtis Ltd v. Arfan* [2012] ICR 1244 (EAT).

before the completion of the qualifying period or summarily dismiss the employee more than a week before the end of the qualifying period to avoid the application of the minimum statutory notice period. A summary dismissal, however, leaves the employer vulnerable to a claim for wrongful dismissal at common law. Damages might be successfully claimed for wages during the correct notice period, but the courts have decided that those damages do not include compensation for the loss of the chance to claim unfair dismissal by completing the qualifying period, even where a contractual notice period, which is longer than the statutory minimum notice, would have completed the necessary qualifying period.[26] In cases where an employee hopes that some kind of settlement can be negotiated, to safeguard the position with regard to a claim for unfair dismissal it is necessary to launch a legal claim before the tribunal within the three-month period, unless the contract or other arrangements with the employer provide clearly that the employee is temporarily suspended on full pay pending the outcome of the negotiations.

Statutory Concept of Dismissal

For the purpose of bringing a statutory claim for unfair dismissal or redundancy, the employee must demonstrate that a dismissal has occurred. This concept of dismissal has a statutory definition in the Employment Rights Act 1996, section 95(1).

Employment Rights Act 1996, Section 95(1)

For the purposes of this Part an employee is dismissed by his employer if (and, subject to subsection (2) and section 96, only if)—

(a) the contract under which he is employed is terminated by the employer (whether with or without notice),

(b) he is employed under a limited-term contract and that contract terminates by virtue of the limiting event without being renewed under the same contract, or

(c) the employee terminates the contract under which he is employed (with or without notice) in circumstances in which he is entitled to terminate it without notice by reason of the employer's conduct.

The three instances of dismissal may be described more briefly as (a) termination by the employer; (b) expiration of a fixed-term contract; and (c) constructive dismissal. Categories (a) and (c) appear to replicate the common law's conception of dismissal, but category (b) is significantly different.

---

[26] *Harper* v. *Virgin Net Ltd* [2004] EWCA Civ 271, [2004] IRLR 390 (CA).

A limited-term contract is one not intended to be permanent and provision is made in the contract for it to terminate at the expiration of a period of time (a fixed-term contract) or on the completion of the performance of a specific task or on the occurrence of an event when that event happens.[27] A contract may be a fixed-term contract even if it also makes provision for earlier dismissal on notice.[28] This statutory concept of dismissal in relation to the expiration of fixed-term contract is broader than the concept of dismissal in the common law. It is needed to block possible attempts by the employer to avoid the legislation. If the expiry of fixed-term contracts did not count as dismissals, employers could place all employees on short fixed-term contracts and simply permit the contracts to expire without renewal. This expiry of the contract would not be regarded as a dismissal in the common law. Without a dismissal, the employer would not be required to justify the fairness of the dismissal. Similarly, if constructive dismissal were not included within the statutory definition, employers could avoid a statutory claim by refraining from outright dismissal and instead making the employment relation intolerable through actions such as reducing wages, increasing hours and augmenting responsibilities, thereby compelling the employee to resign.

The main purpose of the statutory requirement for the employee to establish a dismissal is to exclude from the coverage of the legislation cases where the employee willingly resigns from a job. While the aim of excluding cases where an employee has voluntarily resigned from a job makes sense, the legal requirement for the employee to establish a dismissal has created considerable opportunities for employers to contest claims. If the employer persuades a tribunal that for some reason no dismissal has taken place, the tribunal has no jurisdiction to consider the matter further. Although in most cases it is a straightforward question of fact whether or not the employer terminated the contract, sometimes the tribunals need to evaluate the circumstances closely. Particularly in cases of constructive dismissal, but also in other cases of confusion surrounding an apparent resignation, the question is not so much who terminated the contract but whose fault was it that the contract came to an end. We focus here on those difficult cases of evaluation of the circumstances together with a judicial addition to the legislation through the application of the common law doctrine of frustration of contracts.

Dismissal or Resignation?

The statute defines the principal example of dismissal to include termination of the contract initiated by the employer either with notice or summarily. This definition departs from the elective approach to termination at common

---

[27] ERA 1996, s. 235(2A)(2B), amended to conform to EC Directive 99/70 on fixed-term work (Annex cl. 3).

[28] *Dixon v. BBC* [1979] ICR 281 (CA).

law,[29] for it holds that for the purpose of the statutory concept of dismissal the contract may be terminated unilaterally by summary dismissal, whether or not the summary dismissal was justified or the repudiatory breach accepted. The crucial question under this first limb of the statutory definition is whether the employer initiated the dismissal or whether the employee in fact resigned.

On its face, the statute poses a question of fact and causation. The issue is whose actions initiated the termination of the contract, or simply 'Who really terminated the contract of employment?'[30] Although the courts have emphasised that this issue is primarily a question of fact for the tribunal, this stance is misleading. The issue slides into broader issues of attribution of responsibility, which ask who should be held responsible for termination.

This broadening of the enquiry occurs for three reasons. First, there are no formalities which require dismissals or resignations to be carried out in a particular way such as in writing. An employee can request a written statement of the employer's reasons for dismissal,[31] and the employer's failure to comply can result in an award of compensation equal to two weeks' pay.[32] But no formality is required to effect the dismissal itself. Under the common law of termination of contracts, termination can be initiated by both express statements and conduct which is held to evince an intention no longer to be bound by the contract. The interpretation of this evidence provides the opportunity for tribunals to expand the scope of the enquiry towards the dimension of responsibility. The approach applies an objective test to words and conduct, having regard to all the circumstances, so that the employee's actual intention is not decisive. The test is 'whether a reasonable employer or employee might have understood the words to be tantamount to dismissal or resignation'.[33] Once given, a notice of resignation or dismissal has effect according to the ordinary interpretation of its terms and cannot be withdrawn except by consent.[34]

Secondly, the ordinary law of contract looks for a precise moment for the initiation of the termination, a repudiatory breach of contract, but in the repetitive contact required by the employment relation there is rarely a single moment at which it is absolutely clear that one party has initiated termination. Instead, we discover a progressive breakdown of relations over a period of time and ambiguous statements indicating that the employment relation is likely to end. Indeed, careful and considerate personnel management, when confronted with a disciplinary issue, is likely to produce initially cautious statements such as: 'It may be in your best interests to resign rather than face a disciplinary enquiry.'[35] There have been suggestions that unambiguous statements of dismissal or resignation should be always interpreted as initiating termination

---

[29] *Geys* v. *Société Générale, London Branch* [2012] UKSC 63, [2013] 1 AC 523.

[30] *Martin* v. *MBS Fastenings (Glynwed) Distribution Ltd* [1983] IRLR 198, 201 (CA).

[31] ERA 1996, s. 92.   [32] ERA 1996, s. 93.

[33] *J & J Stern* v. *Simpson* [1983] IRLR 52, 53 (CA).

[34] *Willoughby* v. *CF Capital plc* [2011] EWCA Civ 1115, [2012] ICR 1038.

[35] *Martin* v. *MBS Fastenings (Glynwed) Distribution Ltd* [1983] IRLR 198 (CA).

of employment, but in fact tribunals must always consider the context of the statements in order to judge their intended meaning, their reception and whether it would be reasonable for the other party to act on them. Even apparently clear statements, such as 'I am resigning',[36] must be viewed in context in order to comprehend whether they should be regarded as an assumption of responsibility for commencing the termination of the contract.

Thirdly, the personal relations often involved in employment relations sometimes cause dismissals and resignations to take place in the context of heated disagreements and abusive language. The language may be explicit on such occasions, such as 'Go, get out, get out',[37] but whether this statement really amounts to a dismissal may have to be established by reference to subsequent conduct and the general context of the statement. Tribunals are reluctant to conclude that statements uttered in the heat of the moment should be treated at face value, even though in a commercial context such statements would inevitably indicate repudiation of the contract. Where resignations are expressed in temper or in the heat of the moment, the employer should not accept them forthwith, but rather to allow a reasonable time, at most a day or two, to elapse to see if resignation was really intended.[38] Resignations declared in anger in response to misconduct by the employer may in fact be instances of constructive dismissal.

Constructive Dismissal

The way in which the interpretation and application of the statutory concept of dismissal becomes embroiled in issues of responsibility becomes even more apparent in the context of constructive dismissal under the third limb of the statutory definition. On the facts of these cases of constructive dismissal, it is plain that the employee initiated the termination of employment by resignation. The question before the tribunal is whether in the circumstances of the case the employee was entitled to resign in response to the employer's conduct, with the consequence that the resignation can be deemed to have been a dismissal for the purposes of a statutory claim under ERA 1996, section 95(1)(c).

In *Western Excavating (ECC) Ltd* v. *Sharp*,[39] the Court of Appeal ruled that an employee is only entitled to resign in response to the employer's conduct if the employer has committed a fundamental breach of contract. Using the language of the common law of discharge by breach of contract Lord Denning MR expressed the test in these terms:

> If the employer is guilty of conduct which is a significant breach going to the root of the contract of employment, or which shows that the employer no longer

---

[36] *Sothern* v. *Franks Charlesly & Co* [1981] IRLR 278 (CA).
[37] *J & J Stern* v. *Simpson* [1983] IRLR 52 (CA).
[38] *Kwik-Fit (GB) Ltd* v. *Lineham* [1992] ICR 183 (EAT).   [39] [1978] ICR 221 (CA).

intends to be bound by one or more of the essential terms of the contract, then the employee is entitled to treat himself as discharged from any further performance. If he does so, then he terminates the contract by reason of the employer's conduct. He is constructively dismissed. The employee is entitled in those circumstances to leave at the instant without giving any notice at all or, alternatively, he may give notice and say he is leaving at the end of the notice. But the conduct must in either case be sufficiently serious to entitle him to leave at once. Moreover, he must make up his mind soon after the conduct of which he complains: for, if he continues for any length of time without leaving, he will lose his right to treat himself as discharged. He will be regarded as having elected to affirm the contract.

Lord Denning argued that this approach, based on the ordinary law of contract, would produce more predictable and fewer whimsical results than an alternative test of reasonableness that had been favoured by the tribunals. This alternative formulation stated: if the employer conducts himself or his affairs so unreasonably that the employee cannot fairly be expected to put up with it any longer, the employee is justified in leaving.[40] The difference was crucial in this particular case: the employer had not broken any term of the contract, but merely failed to assist the employee who was suffering from financial hardship as a result of his suspension without pay for five days for absence without permission. In the absence of any breach of contract by the employer, the decision of the tribunal in favour of constructive dismissal was reversed.

As an interpretation of the wording of the statute, Lord Denning's contractual definition of constructive dismissal is persuasive. The statute refers to an employee's 'entitlement' to terminate the contract 'without notice', which suggests some kind of legal entitlement that could only arise by the application of the law of contract. The wording appears to signal the obverse situation to an employer's justified summary dismissal. On the other hand, it is not difficult to imagine conduct by an employer that falls short of amounting to a fundamental breach of contract, but which the employee feels is intolerable and leaves no option but to resign. An employer may behave unpleasantly, harshly or in some way harass an employee, but in the absence of a fundamental breach of contract, the employee will not be permitted to resign and claim constructive dismissal.

A good example of such a situation occurred in *Woods* v. *WM Car Services (Peterborough) Ltd.*[41] The employer had purchased a garage business and retained the existing staff, including the appellant, who was described as 'Chief Secretary and Accounts Clerk'. The new owners thought that she was paid too much. They tried to persuade her to accept less money or to work longer hours, but withdrew the suggestion when she objected strongly and went to solicitors. As part of a general reorganisation of the business, the new owners then suggested further changes to her duties and job title. The employee

---

[40] E.g. *Turner* v. *London Transport Executive* [1977] ICR 952 (CA).   [41] [1982] ICR 693 (CA).

rejected all these changes. Realising that the employers were going to insist upon changes, on advice from her solicitor she resigned and claimed constructive dismissal. Work relations had become extremely acrimonious and as Lord Denning MR observed, 'All trust and confidence was lost on both sides.'[42] The tribunal decided, however, that there had not been a constructive dismissal. The Court of Appeal rejected the appeal because there had been no error of law, since the employer had not (yet) committed a fundamental breach of contract.

In this context it is also worth considering the situation in *Western Excavating* v. *Sharp* again. While one can appreciate the reasons for the employer's reluctance to provide the employee with some kind of advance of pay, because that would undermine the effect in the short run of the employer's disciplinary sanction of a deduction from pay, the employee seems to have been left without any money at all and seems to have taken the view that a good and considerate employer, in accordance with the relational expectations of mutual trust and confidence, would help him out of his financial difficulty.

The main criticism of the contractual test of constructive dismissal is that it does not fit exactly the purpose of this provision. The concept of constructive dismissal provides a principal rule governing the limits of managerial disciplinary power. Faced with intolerable managerial conduct, the main legal weapon available to employees is to resign and claim substantial compensation for unfair dismissal. In a sense, the law of constructive dismissal is the means by which employees discipline their managers. The alternative 'reasonableness test' understood this purpose well and tried to express it by reference to the idea of behaviour that was so intolerable that the employee should no longer be expected to put up with it. That situation may well have been reached in *Woods* v. *WM Car Services (Peterborough) Ltd*, but the application of the contract test disentitled Mrs Woods from using her only sanction against the oppressive conduct, which was to resign and claim compensation for constructive unfair dismissal. This flaw in the contract test has, however, been substantially although not completely remedied by the development of the implied term of mutual trust and confidence.

Under the contract test of constructive dismissal, tribunals must establish whether the employer was in breach of a fundamental term of the contract, either express or implied. For express terms, the term must represent a fundamental or basic obligation established by the contract, such as the obligation to pay contractually agreed wages or to employ the employee in a particular job. For implied terms as well, the obligation must be one which is regarded as essential to the contract. Serious breaches of health and safety standards or a failure to pay the NMW are likely to be regarded as such essential implied terms.[43] In this context, however, the implied term that the

---

[42] At 696.   [43] *Mruke* v. *Khan* [2018] EWCA Civ 280, [2018] ICR 1146.

employer will not, without reasonable and proper cause, conduct himself in a manner calculated or likely to destroy or seriously damage the relationship of confidence and trust between employer and employees became the key implied obligation that governs the boundaries of constructive dismissal. It is assumed that the term of mutual trust and confidence is fundamental, so that breach of it will invariably satisfy the contract test of constructive dismissal. Importantly in the context of constructive dismissal, a breach of this term may be constituted either by a single event or a series of relatively minor instances of harsh or unfair treatment.[44]

Once the enquiry is framed by the question whether or not the employer breached the implied term of trust and confidence, it broadens again to something approaching the disapproved test of reasonableness.[45] Questions about degrees of fault, responsibility for what has gone wrong and how intolerable the situation of the employee has become are relevant factors to the question of the breach of the implied term. The re-introduction of these factors brings back considerations of reasonableness and inevitably reduces the predictability of the test of constructive dismissal, one of the alleged advantages of the contract test.

Frustration

In the common law of long-term commercial contracts, an event which renders performance of the contract impossible or unlawful, for which the contract makes no provision, may be held to have frustrated the contract. Frustration terminates the contract without the choice or consent of the parties. In order to avoid a finding of dismissal, employers have sometimes argued that an event such as the illness or imprisonment of the employee has frustrated the contract of employment. If the tribunal agrees that the contract of employment has been frustrated, the apparent dismissal by the employer will be of no effect, since the contract will have been terminated by the frustrating event without any action by either party. As a consequence, the employer is under no duty to give notice or compensation for lack of notice, and nor can the employee bring any claim for unfair dismissal or a redundancy payment. The use of the doctrine of frustration is therefore plainly an instrumental gambit used by employers to avoid having to justify the decision to dismiss the employee. Although the courts have frequently applied the doctrine of frustration to the contract of employment, these decisions may be criticised on the grounds both that they fail to conform to the common-law principles, and that they represent an unsatisfactory gloss of the statutory concept of dismissal.

---

[44] *Lewis* v. *Motorworld Garages Ltd* [1986] ICR 157 (CA).

[45] A. L. Bogg, '*Bournemouth University Higher Education Corporation* v. *Buckland*: Re-establishing Orthodoxy at the Expense of Coherence?' (2010) 39 *Industrial Law Journal* 408.

With regard to the principles of the common law, the doctrine of frustration can apply only where the parties have failed to make any provision for the event in the contract. In contracts of employment, however, the parties have almost invariably made suitable provision by creating the unilateral power to terminate the contract on giving reasonable notice. For this reason, in principle, the doctrine of frustration should apply to contracts of employment only when they are for a fixed term, with a substantial period of time yet to expire, and do not contain either expressly or by implication a power to terminate by giving notice. As Bristow J observed in a case of long-term sickness where the contract was terminable on one week's notice:

> In the employment field the concept of discharge by operation of law, that is frustration, is normally only in play where the contract of employment is for a long term which cannot be determined by notice. Where the contract is terminable by notice, there is really no need to consider the question of frustration and if it were the law that, in circumstances such as are before us in this case, an employer was in a position to say 'this contract has been frustrated', then that would be a very convenient way in which to avoid the provisions of the [ERA 1996].[46]

The application of the doctrine of frustration to the contract of employment also represents an unsatisfactory interpretation of the statutory concept of dismissal. The purpose of this statutory requirement is to exclude claims when the employee has resigned without cause. In none of the cases involving frustration has the employee resigned, but instead the employer has plainly initiated the termination, albeit claiming subsequently that these actions were of no significance due to the prior frustrating event. The employer's objective is to avoid scrutiny of the fairness of the decision to dismiss the employee by a tribunal. In *Harman* v. *Flexible Lamps Ltd*, for instance, the employer's advisers were probably concerned that the tribunal might find the dismissal unfair because the employer had not fully investigated the reasons for absence and had dismissed the employee precipitately without prior warning. In the end these concerns proved unwarranted, and the EAT was not prepared to find the tribunal's decision that the dismissal was fair perverse. An event which might be regarded as frustrating the contract is therefore likely to provide a substantial ground for a fair dismissal, but it obstructs the purpose of the unfair dismissal legislation to prevent a tribunal from considering the substantive merits of the case by treating the employee's absence from work as equivalent to a resignation.

Despite these criticisms of the application of the doctrine of frustration to claims for unfair dismissal, the Court of Appeal has insisted that the doctrine of frustration can apply to a contract of employment terminable on notice. It used the doctrine of frustration in *Notcutt* v. *Universal Equipment Co*

---

[46] *Harman* v. *Flexible Lamps Ltd* [1980] IRLR 418 (EAT).

(London) Ltd[47] to prevent an employee from claiming wages in lieu of the statutory minimum period of notice.[48] In that case, the employee had suffered a heart attack and a subsequent doctor's report concluded that it was unlikely that the employee would ever work again. Once those facts were characterised as a frustrating event on the ground that performance of the contract had become impossible, there was no need for the employers to have given any notice of dismissal, let alone pay wages or sick pay in lieu. Dillon LJ observed:

> I can see no reason in principle why such a periodic contract of employment should not, in appropriate circumstances, be held to have been terminated without notice by frustration according to the accepted and long established doctrine of frustration in our law of contract. The mere fact that the contract can be terminated by the employer by relatively short notice cannot of itself render the doctrine of frustration inevitably inapplicable. Accordingly the words of Bristow J [above] must be taken as no more than a warning that the court must look carefully at any submission that a periodic contract of employment has been discharged by frustration if that submission is put forward to avoid the provisions of the Act.

The Court of Appeal has also applied the doctrine of frustration to cases where the employee has been sentenced to prison for more than a short time.[49]

These decisions of the Court of Appeal reaffirm the application of the doctrine of frustration to contracts of employment and place little weight on the criticism that its use permits employers to avoid their statutory obligations with respect to giving notice and avoiding unfair dismissals. In cases of long-term illness, however, although the doctrine of frustration applied in *Notcutt* denied a man struck down by a coronary even his entitlement to wages during the minimum statutory notice period, today an employer will have to be able to demonstrate that it has complied with the law of disability discrimination, which imposes a duty on employers to make reasonable adjustments that might include the offer of a less physically demanding job.[50]

Agreed Termination and Settlements

Under the general law of contract, a contract may always be terminated by the agreement of the parties. Such an agreed termination does not fit into the statutory concept of dismissal. It is not a termination by the employer but by both parties jointly. Termination by the employer by giving notice or wages in lieu of notice as agreed in the contract is a form of agreed termination that is included in the statutory concept of dismissal. In some instances, an agreed termination might be described as the expiry of a fixed-term contract or

---

[47] [1986] ICR 414 (CA).   [48] ERA 1996, s. 89(3): see Chapter 18.

[49] *FC Shepherd & Co Ltd* v. *Jerrom* [1986] IRLR 358; *Hare* v. *Murphy Brothers Ltd* [1974] ICR 603 (CA).

[50] *Warner* v. *Armfield Retail & Leisure Ltd* [2014] ICR 239 (EAT).

contracts that expire with the occurrence of a particular event such as the completion of a project, although such instances are included within the statutory concept of dismissal.[51] In the absence of those statutory exceptions, an agreed termination may disqualify an employee from bringing a claim for unfair dismissal because the statutory concept of dismissal cannot be satisfied.

Yet employees may well have been induced to agree to termination of employment by a proposed financial settlement or the fear that they may be dismissed and then experience great difficulty in obtaining compensation and another job. The danger presented by such agreements is that employees will in effect be contracting out of their statutory rights on dismissal, but there are no safeguards to alert them to the possible loss of their legal entitlements. The courts have sometimes been sensitive to this risk: 'the tribunal and the court should not find an agreement unless it is proved that he really did agree with full knowledge of the implications which it held for him'.[52] But agreed terminations have been upheld as effective to exclude a dismissal even when the consequences have not been fully disclosed to the employee. For instance, in *Birch* v. *University of Liverpool*,[53] faced by cuts in government funding, the employer invited staff to take advantage of an early retirement scheme which was intended to reduce the workforce by 300 posts. The employee applied for early retirement. The university chose between the applicants and the claimant's application was approved. The university then formally requested the claimant's retirement on a particular date. The employee subsequently claimed a redundancy payment, but was defeated on the preliminary point that he had not been dismissed. The fact that the employer had reserved the power to determine who should be permitted to take early retirement did not prevent the case from being one of agreed termination. Nor was the employer's failure to disclose to the employee that he would lose his redundancy payment fatal to the employer's defence.

Some instances of agreed termination may be attacked indirectly as attempts to contract out of the mandatory regulation contrary to ERA 1996, section 203(1).

Employment Rights Act 1996, Section 203(1)

Any provision in an agreement (whether a contract of employment or not) is void in so far as it purports –

(a) to exclude or limit the operation of any provision of this Act, or
(b) to preclude a person from bringing any proceedings under this Act before an employment tribunal.

---

[51] ERA 1996, s. 95(b).
[52] Lord Denning MR, *Lees* v. *Arthur Greaves (Lees) Ltd* [1974] ICR 501 (CA), at 505.
[53] [1985] ICR 470 (CA).

This provision does not, however, prevent either settlements of legal proceedings under the supervision of an ACAS conciliation officer,[54] or written settlement agreements that satisfy various conditions set out in ERA 1996, section 203(3), including that the employee received independent legal advice regarding its effect on his ability to pursue his rights before an ET.[55] Even if a settlement satisfies those conditions, it may be set aside on the normal grounds for the invalidity of contracts such as misrepresentation and duress.[56] Nor does ERA 1996, section 203 prevent binding agreements to refrain from legal proceedings where the matter is being conciliated by a conciliation officer.[57]

In the light of those statutory procedural protections for employees when entering settlements of their possible claims, it seems likely that courts will treat informal settlements as creating binding agreements for payment of sums of money such as wages during a notice period,[58] but not permit such informal agreements indirectly to exclude the possibility of statutory claims for dismissal by applying ERA 1996, section 203(1). This approach was adopted in *Igbo v. Johnson, Matthey Chemicals Ltd*,[59] where the applicant had asked for three extra days of holiday to be tacked on to her regular entitlement. This request had been granted, but she had been asked to sign a document which stated that if she failed to return on the agreed date 'your contract of employment will automatically terminate on that date'. Owing to illness, the employee failed to return to work, but informed the manager and sent in a medical certificate. The employer nevertheless informed her that her contract of employment was terminated in accordance with the document that she had signed. The Court of Appeal insisted, however, that this provision for automatic termination was equivalent to a term that purported to exclude the applicant's right to claim unfair dismissal and was therefore void. This approach seems correct, for otherwise the more covert the employer's technique for exclusion of statutory rights on dismissal by means of an agreed termination or settlement, the less protection would be afforded to the employee.

The Test of Fairness

The standard of fairness at the heart of the statutory right to claim unfair dismissal regulates the employer's exercise of disciplinary power. In determining the content of this standard, the law decides how closely managerial decisions will be scrutinised by tribunals, and determines how and when the

---

[54] ERA 1996, s. 203(2)(e).

[55] Under s. 203(3A) an independent adviser may be a lawyer, a member of a trade union who is certified by the union as competent and authorised to give advice, or someone who works at an advice centre who is similarly competent and authorised.

[56] *Horizon Recruitment Ltd* v. *Vincent* [2010] ICR 491 (EAT).   [57] ERA 1996, s. 203(2)(f).

[58] *Cavenagh* v. *William Evans Ltd* [2012] EWCA Civ 697, [2012] ICR 1231.

[59] [1986] ICR 505 (CA).

disciplinary power of dismissal can be exercised justifiably. Section 98 ERA 1996 provides a framework to guide this enquiry. It defines three steps for the fairness enquiry to follow:

(1) The employer has to give the reason or principal reason for the dismissal.
(2) The employer has to show that the reason relied on for dismissal was a substantial reason, such as incapability or misconduct, which might justify a dismissal.
(3) The tribunal has to consider whether dismissal for that reason was reasonable or unreasonable in accordance with equity and the substantial merits of the case.

The principal purpose of this framework is to compel the employer to fix the reason for dismissal, so that the tribunal can assess its merits. Out of the frequently muddled allegations and suspicions that characterise the breakdown of many employment relations, the law requires the construction of what may be a rather artificial rational basis for the decision to dismiss, so that the tribunal can assess its fairness by reference to the open-textured standard of reasonableness.

Principal Reason for Dismissal

The first step in this structure requires the employer to give the main reason for dismissal. This requirement prevents the employer from shifting the ground for dismissal as the case proceeds. In particular, the reason for the dismissal must be one that the employer relied upon at the time of dismissal and cannot be a reason based upon facts discovered subsequent to termination of employment. In *W. Devis & Sons Ltd* v. *Atkins*,[60] for instance, the employer was not permitted to justify the dismissal by reference to dishonest conduct of the employee that was discovered only after the date of the dismissal. For this purpose, the time of the dismissal appears to be the same as the statutory concept of the effective date of termination; in the case of summary dismissal the reason is fixed immediately;[61] but in cases of termination by notice, the reason may be affected by events during the notice period.[62]

In addition, the requirement to fix the reason for dismissal prevents the employer from leaving the reason obscure or indeterminate, for then the tribunal will decide that the employer has failed to provide a reason at all and that therefore the dismissal must be unfair. In *Smith* v. *Glasgow City District Council*,[63] the employee was dismissed for unsatisfactory performance relating to three separate complaints. An industrial tribunal found that the second complaint was unfounded, but held the dismissal to be fair on the other

---

[60] [1977] ICR 672 (HL).
[61] *West Midlands Co-operative Society Ltd* v. *Tipton* [1986] ICR 192 (HL).
[62] *Alboni* v. *Ind Coope Retail Ltd* [1998] IRLR 131 (CA).   [63] [1987] ICR 796 (HL).

grounds. On appeal, the House of Lords held that dismissal was unfair because either (1) the employer had failed to establish the principal reason for dismissal by not distinguishing between the three complaints against the employee, or (2) the employer had relied upon the second complaint as part of the principal reason for dismissal, and this reason had been found by the tribunal to be neither established in fact nor believed to be true on reasonable grounds.

The ambition of fixing the reason for the dismissal at a particular time implicitly emphasises the importance of the rationality of the decision to dismiss: the dismissal must be for a clear reason based on facts and beliefs held at the time. This model of rationality fits uneasily on the common factual pattern of dismissals, where the employer has a mixture of reasons, not all of which may be mentioned at the time of dismissal. The courts therefore permit the employer to reformulate the real reason for the dismissal as one other than the reason given to the employee at the time of the dismissal if it was probably the real reason for dismissal.[64] The ambition to fix the reason for dismissal has an extraordinary air of unreality about it in cases of constructive dismissal. How can the employer provide a reason for dismissal when the employer has not decided to dismiss the employee at all? The approach adopted by the courts is to require the employer to show the reasons for his conduct that entitled the employee to terminate the contract.[65]

Substantial Reason

The second step in the structure of the fairness enquiry demands that the employer's reason for dismissal should have been a substantial reason. In practice, this requirement places little constraint upon the types of reasons for dismissal that an employer may put forward. The statute illustrates the notion of substantial reasons with the examples of capability, qualifications and misconduct, but a substantial reason does not have to be a reason of the same kind or nature as those reasons.[66] The idea of 'capability' is further defined to include capability assessed by reference to skill, aptitude, health or any other physical or mental quality. 'Qualifications' is defined as any degree, diploma or other academic, technical or professional qualification relevant to the position held by the employee. The type of reason presented under the category of a substantial reason need not be confined to allegations of fault or breach of contract by the employee, but can refer to general business considerations, such as the need to reduce staff or to respond to pressure from a major customer.

[64] *Abernethy v. Mott, Hay and Anderson* [1974] ICR 323 (CA).
[65] *Delabole Slate Ltd v. Berriman* [1985] ICR 546 (CA).
[66] *RS Components Ltd v. Irwin* [1973] ICR 535 (NIRC).

If an economic or business reason for dismissal is put forward, the case may be considered as one of redundancy or some other substantial reason. The boundary between the concepts of redundancy and other substantial reasons is considered below.[67] The mere expiry of a fixed-term contract is not, however, in itself regarded as a substantial reason: the employer must provide a reason for failure to renew the contract, such as the completion of the temporary work or project.[68]

Automatically Unfair Dismissal

At the third stage of the framework for dismissals, the tribunal has to assess the fairness of the dismissal for the substantial reason given by the employer. In some instances, however, the legislation specifies that certain types of reason for dismissal are automatically unfair reasons and therefore the dismissal must be unfair. The automatic unfairness of the dismissal serves as a signal to employers that they should not consider dismissal on such grounds. The automatic unfairness of dismissals applies to three broad categories of cases: to protect an employee's individual civil liberties and social rights, to provide guarantees for workers who take on representative roles on behalf of the workforce and to protect workers against victimisation if they assert their legal rights against their employer. Some grounds for dismissal are, perhaps surprisingly, not included expressly in this category of automatic unfairness, such as dismissal on grounds prohibited by anti-discrimination legislation, though undoubtedly once such reasons are established a tribunal will immediately conclude that such an unlawful dismissal was also unfair. Most of these special provisions are considered in more detail elsewhere. Three broader points are worth making here.

First, the selection of categories of automatic unfairness reveals decisions about which interests of employees or workers are regarded as inalienable social rights. This pattern of thinking has not been traditional in English law, so it is not surprising that historically the reason these particular instances have been selected as categories of automatic unfairness has often been in response to decisions of the ECtHR or the CJEU.

The second general observation is that the method of enforcement of employment rights selected in the UK has been to grant individuals claims for compensation. In Chapter 1 we noted that this is a relatively ineffective method for securing labour standards. One fundamental defect is of course that most employees will be reluctant to launch a legal action against their employer. The victimisation provisions, which protect the employee's right to pursue individual employment rights, are a weak and probably ineffectual

---

[67] Chapter 20.   [68] *North Yorkshire County Council* v. *Fay* [1985] IRLR 247 (CA).

attempt to remove one powerful reason why employees might not wish to enforce their rights. A general principle is emerging that whatever legal rights are granted to an employee, there is a parallel protection against victimisation for the enforcement of those rights, although the principle has not yet been applied to all individual employment rights. One must doubt, however, whether the certain success of a claim for unfair dismissal, if the victimisation occurs and the employee can prove it, provides adequate reassurance for employees who are contemplating taking legal action against their employer.

The third general observation is that automatic unfairness does not necessarily augment the amount of compensation payable to the employee. The sanction against the employer for violating basic social rights or interfering with their enforcement is normally no greater than an ordinary unfair dismissal for poorly justified disciplinary reasons. It is perhaps surprising that there is no room for a general principle permitting an award of aggravated damages here, though such awards are permitted in discrimination claims.

Examples of the Three Kinds of Automatically Unfair Dismissals

Social and Labour Rights

- Dismissal for the reason that the employee is taking leave for family reasons including pregnancy, maternity, adoption, parental, paternity, and emergency leave: ERA 1996, section 99.
- Dismissal of certain shop-workers and betting workers for refusing Sunday work: ERA 1996, section 101.
- Dismissal in connection with trade union membership and activities, including in relation to blacklists of trade union members: TULRCA 1992, sections 152, 153; ERA 1996, section 104F.
- Dismissal in connection with recognition claims: TULRCA 1992, Schedule A1, paragraphs 161, 162.
- Dismissal in connection with a transfer of an undertaking: Transfer of Undertakings (Protection of Employment) Regulations 2006.
- Dismissal for refusals to work under conditions of serious and imminent danger: ERA 1996, section 100(1)(d)(e).
- Dismissal for refusing to work in breach of the Working Time Regulations 1998: ERA 1996, section 101A.
- Dismissal for making a protected disclosure: ERA 1996, section 103A.
- Dismissal for taking protected industrial action: TULRCA 1992, section 238A.

Protection of Worker Representatives

- Dismissal in connection with representation on health and safety issues: ERA 1996, section 100.
- Dismissal for performing functions as trustee of occupational pension scheme: ERA 1996, section 102.

- Dismissal for performing functions of representing workers in connection with redundancies or transfers of undertakings: ERA 1996, section 103.
- Dismissal for performing function of representative for the purposes of the Working Time Regulations 1998, Schedule 1: ERA 1996, section 101A (1)(d).
- Dismissal for performing function of representative in an EWC: TICE Regulations 1999 SI 3323, reg. 28, or for performing the function of a representative for the purpose of information and consultation: ICE Regulations 2004, reg. 30.

Victimisation

- Dismissal for assertion of statutory rights enforceable in employment tribunals, including the right to a minimum wage, a working tax credit, the right to ask for flexible working, and working time rights: ERA 1996, sections 104, 104A, 104B, 104C, 101A.
- Selection for redundancy on the above victimisation grounds: ERA 1996, section 105.
- Dismissal for assertion of the right of a part-time worker not to be treated less favourably: Part-time Workers (Prevention of Less Favourable Treatment) Regulations 2000, reg. 7
- Dismissal for assertion of the right of fixed-term employees not to be subjected to less favourable treatment: Fixed-Term Employees (Prevention of Less Favourable Treatment) Regulations 2002, reg. 6.

The Range of Reasonable Responses Test

In the absence of specific regulations regarding the unfairness of dismissals, the tribunals must apply the general default test of reasonableness.

Employment Rights Act 1996, Section 98(4)

... the determination of the question whether the dismissal is fair or unfair (having regard to the reason shown by the employer)—

(a) depends on whether in the circumstances (including the size and administrative resources of the employer's undertaking) the employer acted reasonably or unreasonably in treating it as a sufficient reason for dismissing the employee, and

(b) shall be determined in accordance with equity and the substantial merits of the case.

Using this statutory test, how far do tribunals supervise management's disciplinary practices? The legislation empowers the tribunal to determine whether the employer's reason for the dismissal was fair or unfair. The question a tribunal must ask is whether the employer acted reasonably. Yet the tribunals have refrained from the imposition of detailed standards upon employers. Instead, tribunals have respected the autonomy of managerial disciplinary decisions by recognising a discretion within which the employer can act without detailed supervision. Important guidance to the tribunals was given by Browne-Wilkinson J in *Iceland Frozen Foods Ltd* v. *Jones:*[69]

> We consider that the authorities establish that in law the correct approach for the industrial tribunal to adopt in answer the question posed by [ERA, section 98(4)] is as follows: (1) the starting point should always be the words of section [98(4)] themselves; (2) in applying the section an industrial tribunal must consider the reasonableness of the employer's conduct, not simply whether they (the members of the industrial tribunal) consider the dismissal to be fair; (3) in judging the reasonableness of the employer's conduct an industrial tribunal must not substitute its decision as to what was the right course to adopt for that of the employer; (4) in many, though not all, cases there is a band of reasonable responses to the employee's conduct within which one employer might reasonably take one view, another quite reasonably take another; (5) the function of the industrial tribunal, as an industrial jury, is to determine whether in the particular circumstances of each case the decision to dismiss the employee fell within the band of reasonable responses which a reasonable employer might have adopted. If the dismissal falls within the band the dismissal is fair: if the dismissal falls outside the band it is unfair.

This gloss on the statute that refers to a band or range of reasonable responses has been approved many times by the Court of Appeal.[70] For instance, in *British Leyland UK Ltd* v. *Swift*,[71] after eighteen years' service, an employee was dismissed when a car's tax disc belonging to the employer was discovered on the employee's personal vehicle. He was subsequently convicted of a criminal offence. The tribunal held that the employer had abundant evidence to support the view that the applicant had been guilty of gross misconduct, but it found the dismissal unfair on the ground that the dismissal was too severe a penalty for a relatively minor offence after many years of satisfactory service. The Court of Appeal allowed the employer's appeal. Lord Denning MR insisted:

> The correct test is: Was it reasonable for the employers to dismiss him? If no reasonable employer would have dismissed him, then the dismissal was unfair. But if a reasonable employer might reasonably have dismissed him, then the dismissal was fair. It must be remembered that in all these cases there is a band of reasonableness, within which one employer might reasonably take one view: another quite reasonably take a different view. One would quite reasonably dismiss the man. The other would quite reasonably keep him on. Both views may be quite reasonable. If it was quite reasonable to dismiss him, then the dismissal must be upheld as fair, even though some other employers may not have dismissed him.

Lord Denning MR concludes that as a reasonable employer might well have dismissed the employee in the circumstances of the theft, even if others might

---

[69] [1983] ICR 17 (EAT).

[70] E.g. recently in *Orr* v. *Milton Keynes Council* [2011] EWCA Civ 62, [2011] ICR 704; *Turner* v. *East Midlands Trains Ltd* [2012] EWCA Civ 1470, [2013] ICR 525; *Newbound* v. *Thames Water Utilities Ltd* [2015] EWCA Civ 677, [2015] IRLR 734.

[71] [1981] IRLR 91 (CA).

not, the dismissal must have been fair. The tribunal had plainly thought that dismissal was too harsh a punishment, but by imposing its own view it had committed an error of law in not applying the range of reasonable responses test.

The range or band of reasonable responses test, sometimes abbreviated to RORR, suggests that tribunals must respect management's disciplinary decisions provided that the dismissal was within the scope of a reasonable exercise of discretion. Tribunals must therefore refrain from acting like an appeal body against every decision to dismiss an employee. They do not declare a dismissal to have been unfair simply because none of the members of the tribunal would have dismissed the employee in the circumstances. They must not substitute their own views. Their intervention is limited to instances of patent abuse of managerial power. This interpretation of ERA 1996, section 98(4) limits the degree of judicial supervision of managerial discretion. Tribunals respect the autonomy of management's power to govern the business by setting boundaries for the justifiable exercise of power, but not exercising that power themselves. It is worth identifying some of the practical implications of the range of RORR test.

Proportionality of Punishment

One effect of the RORR test is that it discourages a tribunal's assessment of the proportionality of the disciplinary punishment. Dismissal is the harshest sanction available to an employer. Other sanctions may include a deduction from pay, a demotion, a formal warning that dismissal would follow a repeat offence. The RORR impedes an assessment of proportionality because the tribunal's impression that the sanction was unduly harsh in the circumstances is irrelevant if the tribunal also thinks that some reasonable employers might have used the toughest sanction. That interpretation was confirmed in *British Leyland* v. *Swift*. Although it must be correct that if tribunals are not to substitute their own judgments as to the fairness of a dismissal, they must refrain from precise calibrations of the proportionality of the punishment, Lord Denning's interpretation of the RORR test effectively denies any test of proportionality at all. The tribunal had taken the view that under the conventions of good industrial relations practice, the employee's lengthy period of satisfactory service should have reduced the sanction imposed by the employer. But the Court of Appeal decided that the tribunal committed an error of law: the RORR test does not permit the enforcement of the tribunal's interpretation of the convention; the employer can act upon its own interpretation provided the tribunal accepts that other employers share that view of the convention. The Court has also subsequently made it clear that in determining the reasonableness of the severity of the sanction the employer can look beyond the facts of the particular case in order to use a severe disciplinary sanction as a deterrent to others.[72]

---

[72] *British Railways Board* v. *Jackson* [1994] IRLR 235 (CA).

Compliance with Rule-book

Another effect of the RORR test is that employers can usually rely upon their own rule-book to set the required standards of behaviour for employees. If the rule-book states, for instance, that lateness for work on two occasions will be met with dismissal, a tribunal is likely to find that a dismissal for breach of that rule was reasonable. A tribunal can be persuaded fairly easily that if an employer lays down a clear disciplinary code and follows it, this conduct falls within the RORR. A tribunal is reluctant to suggest that the disciplinary code was itself unduly harsh, because that intervention appears to amount to the substitution of the tribunal's opinion for that of the employer. In *Hadjioannou v. Coral Casinos Ltd*,[73] the applicant was suspended and then dismissed from his position as a blackjack inspector at the employer's gambling clubs for breach of a rule that stated: 'Staff are not permitted to socialise with any members of the clubs or their guests on the premises and should not do so off the premises without the knowledge and consent of the management.' The tribunal held that the employer had been reasonable in dismissing the applicant for an admitted breach of this rule, because the employer regarded breaches of this rule as particularly grave. The tribunal did not ask itself whether other employers in the gambling sector enforced a similar tough rule or whether the rule really was needed by the employer.

On the other hand, if the employer's rule-book limits the grounds on which dismissals can be made, those rules should influence what a reasonable employer would regard as substantial reason for dismissal. In the case of a university lecturer who had not disclosed a sexual relationship with a student he supervised, the Council of the university had promulgated a statute that listed possible grounds for dismissal including 'conduct of an immoral scandalous or disgraceful nature incompatible with the duties of the office or employment'. An ET must consider under ERA 1996, section 98(4) whether the employer acted reasonably having regard to its own permitted grounds for dismissal.[74]

The claimant in *Hadjioannou v. Coral Casinos Ltd* also pointed out that he had suffered from disparate treatment, because another employee guilty of the same offence had not been dismissed. It has been said that the word 'equity' in the phrase 'having regard to equity and the substantial merits of the case' in ERA 1996, section 98(4) comprehends the concept that employees who behave in much the same way should have meted out to them much the same punishment.[75] But disparate treatment does not make the dismissal necessarily unfair if, as in this case, the tribunal accepts that the dismissal was within the RORR in the particular circumstances of the case. When a tribunal considers evidence of inconsistent management application of the disciplinary rule, there is strong deference to management's appreciation of

[73] [1981] IRLR 352 (EAT).   [74] *Dronsfield v. University of Reading* [2016] ICR 1107 (EAT).
[75] *Post Office v. Fennell* [1981] IRLR 221 (CA).

the differences between particular cases and respect for the employer's exercise of discretion whether or not to use the ultimate sanction of dismissal. It may be possible sometimes to challenge an employer's consistent application of a harsh disciplinary rule, but only where the employee's breach of the rule was venial and the employer had given an impression that the rule might be relaxed.[76] This endorsement of employers' disciplinary rules, marked by deference to the employer's view of the convention governing good industrial practice at the particular workplace, reveals how the RORR standard is unlikely to require disapproval of dismissal decisions in many instances.

Belief of the Employer in Facts

Another important implication of the RORR test is that the tribunal must concentrate on the facts as they were perceived by the employer at the time of dismissal, not on the true facts of the matter as they subsequently emerged at the tribunal. The test is not whether the dismissal was fair or reasonable in the light of all the circumstances, but in view of the facts known to the employer at the time, whether it was within the RORR for the employer to dismiss the employee. This emphasis on the facts known to and believed by the employer at the time of dismissal often becomes crucial in the context of dismissals for misconduct, because the employer may not have overwhelming proof of dishonesty or be aware of all extenuating circumstances.

The approach that the tribunals must follow in such circumstances is to apply a three-stage test developed in *British Home Stores Ltd* v. *Burchell*:[77]

> the tribunal has to consider whether there was a genuine belief on the part of the employer that the employee was guilty of the alleged misconduct, whether that belief was reasonably founded as a result of the employer carrying out a reasonable investigation, and whether a reasonable employer would have dismissed the employee for that misconduct.

For example, if an employer makes a decision to dismiss on the basis of belief that there have been two instances of serious misconduct, a tribunal cannot substitute its own view that there was only one instance of serious misconduct and that as a result the dismissal was unreasonable. The tribunal must instead assess whether the dismissal was unreasonable on the assumption that there had been two instances of serious misconduct, because that was the basis on which the employer reached the decision. On a precise interpretation, the three-stage test in *Burchell* only determines whether the employer had a substantial reason for dismissal,[78] but the courts have permitted tribunals to use it to address the additional question of whether the dismissal was within the RORR.[79]

---

[76] *Ladbroke Racing Ltd* v. *Arnott* [1983] IRLR 154 (Ct. Sess.).
[77] (Note) [1980] ICR 303 (EAT).
[78] *Reilly* v. *Sandwell Metropolitan Borough Council* [2018] UKSC 16 [21].
[79] E.g. *Post Office* v. *Foley; HSBC* v. *Madden* [2000] ICR 1283, 1287 (CA).

Harsh but Fair

The main reason for this abstention from interfering with managerial decisions to make disciplinary dismissals may lie in the courts' fear of encouraging dismissed employees to flood the tribunals with claims against every dismissal in the hope that the ET might take a different view of the merits of the case. Another explanation of the use of the RORR test may also lie in reluctance on the part of the tribunals and courts to become too involved in detailed managerial decisions, where the adjudicators may lack adequate information and expertise to make better decisions. The approach may also reflect a perception of the proper division between public and private power: the state, as represented by the tribunals, should not intervene in private market relations except for compelling reasons of public interest. This view implicitly downgrades the public interest in the fairness of disciplinary decisions. This abstention is also reminiscent of the stance of the common law of wrongful dismissal. The common law refused to judge the substantive grounds for dismissal unless there was a breach of the terms of the contract. The RORR test establishes a similar abnegation, although with the new exception of the obscure boundary of unreasonableness.

Whatever the explanation of this interpretation of the statute, there can be no doubt that the RORR test draws the sharpest teeth from the legislation. A dismissal can be 'harsh but fair'. As a consequence, the RORR test has been subjected to a considerable amount of criticism.[80] In particular, it is questioned whether the test is coherent and a faithful gloss on the words of the statute.

'Harsh but Fair' Dismissal

During his lunch break, Mr Mathewson left his place of work, where he had been employed for five and half years to polish metal dentures, to go to the bank to cash his pay cheque. By chance he met a friend waiting at a bus stop, from whom he purchased a small quantity of cannabis. He decided to take his stash home, but on the way he bumped into a friend in the park, so he stopped for a chat. Two police officers then approached and with apparent clairvoyance arrested him on suspicion of being in possession of drugs. He was taken to the police station and charged. Eventually he returned to work an hour late. When asked for an explanation, Mr Mathewson told the truth about what had happened. Having discussed the

---

[80] H. Collins, 'Capitalist Discipline and Corporatist Law' (1982) 11 *Industrial Law Journal* 78; P. Davies and M. Freedland, *Labour Law: text and materials* (2nd edn, London: Weidenfeld and Nicholson, 1984), pp. 467–93; H. Collins, *Justice in Dismissal* (Oxford University Press, 1992); A. Freer, 'The Range of Reasonable Responses Test: From Guidelines to Statute' (1998) 27 *Industrial Law Journal* 335; M. Freedland and H. Collins, 'Finding the Right Direction for the "Industrial Jury"' (2000) 29 *Industrial Law Journal* 288; H. Collins, *Nine Proposals for the Reform of the Law on Unfair Dismissal* (London: Institute of Employment Rights, 2004), Ch. 5.

matter with another senior manager, his boss then summarily dismissed him. In assessing his claim for unfair dismissal, the tribunal noted that the employer had given Mr Mathewson no chance to explain himself or point to any mitigating matters in his favour. Nor had the employer given him the company rule-book, which stated that an employee would be dismissed 'should he or she be convicted by a court of an offence such as theft, indecent behaviour or assault, which, though not connected with the company, gives reasonable doubt as to the individual suitability for employment in our type of business'. Nor was there any evidence either at the time of the dismissal or at the hearing to suggest that the employee had ever used or been in possession of drugs at work. Nevertheless, a majority of the tribunal (the legally qualified chairman dissenting) decided that the dismissal was fair. They concluded that it could not be said, on the information before the employers at the time of the dismissal, that their reaction in dismissing the employee summarily, although harsh, was outwith the band of reasonable responses, and so the dismissal was fair. Harsh but fair.[81]

Is the Range of Reasonable Responses Test Coherent?

Under the RORR test, the tribunals set outer limits to the exercise of management's disciplinary power. How do the tribunals fix the limits of reasonableness, without doing what they are forbidden to do, namely to impose their own opinion of the merits of the decision in this particular case? The answer in *Iceland Frozen Foods Ltd* v. *Jones* is rather uninformative: the limits of the band of reasonableness are fixed by reference to the standards of a reasonable employer. But how does a tribunal ascertain the content of those standards? There is plainly a danger that the tribunal may assume that all employers act reasonably. If so, the standard of reasonableness will merely reflect the practices of employers, no matter how harsh they may appear to be. To escape this problem of a 'standard-reflecting' approach to fixing the boundaries of reasonableness, the tribunals need to impose their own standards. Although the tribunals are not permitted to impose their own opinions of what would have been fair in a particular case, they are required to insist that every employer should conform to the standards of a reasonable employer.

These standards of the reasonable employer are often described as 'objective', but where do these standards originate if not the subjective opinions of the members of the tribunal? Browne-Wilkinson J further suggested that the ET, using its expertise in the conventions and practices of industrial relations, could ascertain objective standards.[82] The standards adopted by tribunals are described as objective, because they are supposed to exist already in the conventional practices of HRM. Such standards are not necessarily written down, but may be common knowledge among persons experienced in industrial relations. These conventions are presumably the result of explicit and implicit negotiations between employers and employees over a long period of

---

[81] *Mathewson* v. *R B Wilson Dental Laboratories* [1988] IRLR 512 (EAT).
[82] *Williams* v. *Compair Maxam Ltd* [1982] ICR 156 (EAT).

time. In exercising disciplinary powers, the employer is reluctant to incite resentment or anger on the part of the workforce, for such reactions are likely to damage the co-operation on which efficient production depends. The employer therefore confines the exercise of disciplinary power to those instances when the employer believes dismissal will accrue, on balance, to the efficiency of the business by deterring misconduct and poor work, without damaging good working relations. This point of balance represents the product of an implicit negotiation between the employer and the employees, marking the limits to which disciplinary power can be exercised without inducing disruptive reactions from the employees. The conventions which evolve from this implicit negotiation seem to provide the objective standard for the tribunal's decision.

Yet this conventional standard is not necessarily endorsed by the tribunal as the standard of the reasonable employer. The objective standard is held up as 'good' industrial practice. It is not every custom or convention that may satisfy this standard. The tribunals must reflect upon those conventions and adopt only those which they regard as representing good industrial practice. In this way, the reliance upon conventional standards is not merely standard reflecting, but entails the imposition of some normative standards devised by the tribunal itself. The idea of good industrial practice requires an interpretation and assessment of customs and conventions.[83] But if the tribunal has to decide in its own opinion what amounts to good industrial practice in a context such as that in the case before it, does this not involve the substitution of its own opinion to that of management?

The conundrum for tribunals of setting an objective standard of fairness while at the same time not substituting their own views about the fairness of the dismissal for those taken by the employer is well illustrated by a decision of the Court of Appeal that reaffirmed the RORR test in two expedited appeals: *Post Office* v. *Foley*; *HSBC* v. *Madden*.[84] In *HSBC* v. *Madden*, an ET had determined that the dismissal of a bank employee for suspected dishonesty had been unfair. The tribunal criticised the employer for not carrying out a sufficient investigation of the fraudulent use of debit cards. The bank's investigation strongly suggested that it must have been a bank employee who had appropriated the debit cards because the bank's computer had also been used to examine the status of the customers' accounts. Furthermore, Mr Madden had had the opportunity to take the cards and was perhaps the only employee who had had access to the relevant computer terminals. At the instigation of the bank, Mr Madden was arrested and his home searched by the police, although nothing was discovered and all charges were dropped. The bank did not carry out any further investigation of other employees. Despite Mr Madden's protests of his innocence, his long record of good service, the

---

[83] H. Collins, *Justice in Dismissal* (Oxford University Press, 1992), p. 78.
[84] *Post Office* v. *Foley*; *HSBC* v. *Madden* [2000] ICR 1283 (CA).

absence of any obvious motive for him to acquire the goods purchased fraudulently with the cards and the absence of tangible proof of guilt, the bank dismissed him summarily on the ground that the bank had a reasonable belief that he had been involved in the misappropriation of the debit cards which had been used fraudulently and that trust had irretrievably broken down. The ET decided that the dismissal was unfair because more enquiries and investigations should have been made and that the decision to dismiss was not taken on reasonable grounds and was therefore unfair. The Court of Appeal held that the tribunal had misapplied the law by substituting its own views of the fairness of the bank's investigation rather than applying the RORR test. As Mummery LJ said:

> Instead of determining whether the Bank had made reasonable investigations into the matter and whether it had acted within the range of responses of a reasonable employer, the tribunal in effect decided that, had it been the employer, it would not have been satisfied by the evidence that Mr Madden was involved in the misappropriation of the debit cards or their fraudulent use and would not have dismissed him. The tribunal focused on the insufficiency of the evidence to prove to its satisfaction that Mr Madden was guilty of misconduct rather than on whether the Bank's investigation into his alleged misconduct was a reasonable investigation.

The tribunal had therefore committed an error of law by substituting its own judgement for that of the employer rather than applying the RORR test.

It is certainly correct that the tribunal formed the view that the employer's investigation was inadequate in the circumstances and that as a result it was unreasonable to dismiss on the basis of suspicion rather than more substantial evidence of guilt. It was this use of judgement, that is, the exercise of the power of the industrial jury to set standards, which the Court of Appeal castigates for misapplying the statutory test of reasonableness. But surely the same criticism could be directed at the Court of Appeal? It also formed a view about what procedures should have been followed, although one that regarded the bank's investigation as reasonable in the circumstances. Is not the Court of Appeal also substituting its own judgement, though, as it happens, it is an opinion about reasonableness that endorses the employer's conduct?

Is the Range of Reasonable Responses Test a Faithful Interpretation of the Statute?

The statute requires a tribunal to ask whether an employer acted reasonably or unreasonably. But the RORR seems to require the tribunal to ask a different question: was the decision to dismiss the employee a decision that no reasonable employer would have made because it was outside the RORR? Instead of asking whether the dismissal was reasonable, the question becomes: was the dismissal so unreasonable that no reasonable employer would have acted in that way? The test of RORR seems to create a conflict with the first principle articulated in *Iceland Frozen Foods* v. *Jones* described above that a tribunal should apply the words of the statute, for if a tribunal applies the statute literally and asks itself whether the employer acted reasonably, it will be held to have committed an error of law by substituting its own view of reasonableness.

The ostensible purpose of the statement of principles in *Iceland Frozen Foods Ltd* v. *Jones* was to prevent the tribunals from using of a test of perversity or extreme unreasonableness, which would confine cases of unfair dismissal to instances where the employer had acted irrationally or capriciously. That interpretation of substituting the idea of irrationality for reasonableness was also thought to comprise an error of law. Yet in practice it is hard to discern how the RORR test of fairness differs from the minimal protection afforded to job security by a requirement that the employer should not have acted irrationally or capriciously.

It is important to note that there is a difference between asking what decision was reasonable in the circumstances and asking whether the decision was one that no reasonable employer would have made. Drawing an analogy with the test of reasonableness used in medical negligence, the difference lies between a test that asks whether a doctor conformed to standard good medical practice (and therefore acted reasonably) and a test which asks whether the doctor acted in a way that no qualified doctor would have done in the circumstances. The latter test provides the doctor with more leeway to provide treatment that is barely adequate. Similarly, the RORR test permits employers to operate a harsh disciplinary policy and they will not be required to meet the best or even normal standards of HRM. For instance, by giving considerable latitude to the employer in *HSBC* v. *Madden* to determine what amounted to a reasonable investigation prior to dismissal, the Court of Appeal appears to come close to limiting its intervention to instances of perversity or disciplinary action that no reasonable employer would have carried out.

As the Court of Appeal has subsequently stressed, however, the RORR test, while rejecting the legality of a tribunal substituting its own view for that of the employer, does require a tribunal to reach a decision whether or not the employer's conduct fell within the RORR. There are instances where the tribunal has determined that a dismissal was unfair because it was outside the RORR and that decision has been upheld by the Court of Appeal despite the EAT viewing it as an illegitimate instance of the tribunal substituting its own views. In *Bowater* v. *NW London Hospitals NHS Trust*,[85] a female nurse helped a team trying to subdue a male patient having an epileptic fit. In the ensuing tussle, she unexpectedly ended up sitting astride the naked patient. Perhaps to cover her embarrassment, she said 'It's been a few months since I have been in this position with a man underneath me.' Following a disciplinary hearing, she was summarily dismissed for gross misconduct. The ET

---

[85] [2011] EWCA Civ 63, [2011] IRLR 331.

found that the dismissal for a humorous remark that was not heard by any patient or relative was outside the RORR. The EAT allowed an appeal on the ground that the ET had substituted its own opinion, but the Court of Appeal reinstated the decision of the ET. Stanley Burnton LJ said:

> It is right that the ET, the EAT and this court should respect the opinions of the experienced professionals who decided that summary dismissal was appropriate. However, having done so, it was for the ET to decide whether their views represented a reasonable response to the appellant's conduct. It did so. In agreement with the majority of the ET, I consider that summary dismissal was wholly unreasonable in the circumstances of this case.

Longmore LJ reminded tribunals of the purpose of the law of unfair dismissal: 'the employer cannot be the final arbiter of its own conduct in dismissing an employee'. Similarly, where an ET had found an unfair dismissal of a sewage worker who had been dismissed for not following new safety procedures in which he had not been trained, the Court of Appeal overturned the successful appeal of the employer to the EAT by criticising its decision as 'an attempt to stretch the band of reasonable responses to an infinite width'.[86]

Despite these problems with the test of RORR that it appears to deviate from the meaning of the statute and tends to prevent any challenges to employers' disciplinary decisions unless they are irrational or perverse, it must be acknowledged that it is hard to formulate a test of fairness that avoids the weakness of a test of perversity or irrationality without encouraging tribunals to function as an appeal court against every decision to dismiss an employee, no matter how slender the chances of success. As Mummery LJ once cautioned:

> It is all too easy, even for an experienced ET, to slip into the substitution mindset. In conduct cases the claimant often comes to the ET with more evidence and with an understandable determination to clear his name and to prove to the ET that he is innocent of the charges made against him by his employer. He has lost his job in circumstances that may make it difficult for him to get another job. He may well gain the sympathy of the ET so that it is carried along the acquittal route and away from the real question – whether the employer acted fairly and reasonably in all the circumstances at the time of the dismissal.[87]

What is required is a test that establishes a balance between the interests of employees in job security and the protection of their reputation and the need of employers to enhance efficiency and deter misconduct without their

---

[86] Bean LJ, *Newbound* v. *Thames Water Utilities Ltd* [2015] EWCA Civ 677, [2015] IRLR 734, [77]. C. Wynn-Evans, 'Harsh But Fair: The "Range of Reasonable Responses" Test and the "Substitution Mindset" Revisited: Newbound v Thames Water Utilities Ltd' (2015) 44 *Industrial Law Journal* 566.

[87] *London Ambulance Service NHS Trust* v. *Small* [2009] IRLR 563, [2009] EWCA Civ 220, [43].

decisions being constantly questioned before tribunals. One alternative to the RORR test is to adopt the approach used in public law and anti-discrimination law, which applies a test of proportionality to determine the legality of decisions made under a discretionary power. A test of proportionality investigates whether the decision-maker is pursuing a legitimate objective and, if so, asks whether the means that were adopted were necessary and proportionate to achieving that objective. Under this test, a court scrutinises closely the means chosen in order to ensure that they did not unnecessarily or disproportionately interfere with the rights of an individual. In the context of dismissal, we could apply this approach by analogy so that the question for the tribunals would be first whether the employer was exercising the disciplinary power for a legitimate purpose such as ensuring the efficiency of production or deterring misconduct, and secondly whether the disciplinary sanction of dismissal was a necessary and proportionate means for achieving that goal in the circumstances of the case.

Procedural Fairness

Despite the courts' evident reluctance to supervise disciplinary dismissals closely, in one respect they have been remarkably assertive in setting normative standards of conduct for employers. Courts and tribunals have insisted in their interpretation of ERA 1996, section 98(4) and as part of the conventions of 'good industrial practice' that employers should follow reasonable procedural steps prior to making a dismissal. These required procedural steps have not been formulated as precise rules, but according to the circumstances of the case the tribunal may insist that standards of fairness require, for example, the employer to give the opportunity to explain alleged misconduct, or to improve performance, before any dismissal takes place. In the case of allegations of misconduct, the employer must carry out as much investigation into the matter as was reasonable in the circumstances.[88] The relevant circumstances include the gravity of the charge and its potential effect on the employee's reputation or ability to work in his or her chosen field.[89] A claim that an employer operated an unfair procedure prior to dismissal is by far the most likely ground for a successful application for unfair dismissal.

This willingness of tribunals and judges to impose procedural standards may have several explanations. Procedural requirements may be perceived by the courts as posing a lesser degree of interference with managerial discretion than substantive standards. A fair procedure can be presented as a necessary ingredient of any rational personnel policy, because it ensures both that dismissals occur only when dismissal lies in the employer's economic interest, and that potential damage to co-operation from the remaining workforce

---

[88] *British Home Stores Ltd* v. *Burchell (Note)* [1980] ICR 303 (EAT).
[89] *Salford Royal NHS Foundation Trust* v. *Roldan* [2010] EWCA Civ 522, [2010] ICR 1457 (CA).

owing to resentment against harsh discipline is minimised. Another explanation may simply be that in addressing questions of procedural fairness the courts are dealing with familiar principles of 'natural justice' or 'due process', which can be applied by analogy to public-law standards.

The courts' readiness to set procedural standards was reinforced by the promulgation of a detailed Code of Practice by ACAS.[90] The Code articulates standards of good industrial practice with respect to disciplinary procedures. Tribunals are expected to take into account the advice from ACAS on best practice with respect to disciplinary procedures in determining whether or not the employer acted reasonably, although non-compliance with the Code does not necessarily lead to a finding of unfairness.[91] The Code recognises that its provisions may be adapted according to the size and resources of the employer and other circumstances of the case. The principal requirements for a fair procedure outlined in the Code are set out in the box.

ACAS Code of Practice, Principal Requirements for a Fair Procedure

- An investigation to establish the facts of the case.
- Written notice to the employee of the allegation.
- A meeting or hearing between employer and employee.
- The employee is entitled to be accompanied at the meeting by a colleague or a trained trade union official,[92] though not a lawyer.[93]
- If the employer decides that disciplinary action is appropriate, unless it is a case of gross misconduct justifying summary dismissal, it is normal in the case of a first offence to give a formal warning that any repeat may result in dismissal, and in the case of a second offence a final warning.
- Provide employees with the opportunity to appeal to more senior managers against the formal warning or the dismissal.

An employer's breach of fair procedural standards may therefore render a dismissal unfair in itself under ERA 1996 section 98(4). But this principle is heavily qualified by two further considerations. First, although the dismissal may be found to have been unfair as a result of the employer's failure to follow a fair procedure, if in fact the employer had a good substantive reason for dismissal, the tribunal will reduce the measure of compensation on the ground of contributory fault.[94] Sometimes the tribunal reduces the compensatory award to zero.[95] Second, the requirement for the employer to follow a fair

---

[90] ACAS Code of Practice 1, *Code of Practice on Disciplinary and Grievance Procedures* (2015), issued under TULRCA 1992, s. 199.

[91] TULRCA 1992, s. 207.   [92] Employment Relations Act 1999, s. 10.

[93] *R (on the application of G)* v. *Governors of X School* [2011] UKSC 30 (SC).   [94] Below.

[95] *Earl* v. *Slater Wheeler (Airlyne) Ltd* [1973] 1 WLR 51 (NIRC).

procedure must be understood to comprise one strand in the broad RORR test of fairness. According to the circumstances of the case, therefore, a tribunal may determine that a reasonable employer could have dispensed with all or part of the normal requirements for a fair disciplinary procedure.

The leading decision of the House of Lords, *Polkey* v. *A.E. Dayton Services Ltd*,[96] confirms and illustrates these principles governing procedural fairness in dismissals. After four years of employment as a van driver, the appellant was summoned to the manager's office and told out of the blue that he was dismissed immediately for redundancy. The tribunal described the employer's conduct as a 'heartless disregard of the provisions of the code of practice'. Nevertheless, the tribunal held that the dismissal had been fair because it had been inevitable owing to the employer's urgent business need to make redundancies. The House of Lords allowed Mr Polkey's appeal and remitted the case to be heard again by another tribunal. It is worth examining carefully the relevant principles of procedural fairness as set out by Lord Bridge:

> Employers contesting a claim of unfair dismissal will commonly advance as their reason for dismissal one of the reasons specifically recognised as valid by [ERA 1996 section 98(2)(a)(b)(c)]. These, put shortly, are: (a) that the employee could not do his job properly; (b) that he had been guilty of misconduct; (c) that he was redundant. But an employer having prima facie grounds to dismiss for one of these reasons will in the great majority of cases not act reasonably in treating the reason as a sufficient reason for dismissal unless and until he has taken the steps, conveniently classified in most of the authorities as 'procedural,' which are necessary in the circumstances of the case to justify that course of action. Thus, in the case of incapacity, the employer will normally not act reasonably unless he gives the employee fair warning and an opportunity to mend his ways and show that he can do the job; in the case of misconduct, the employer will normally not act reasonably unless he investigates the complaint of misconduct fully and fairly and hears whatever the employee wishes to say in his defence or in explanation or mitigation; in the case of redundancy, the employer will normally not act reasonably unless he warns and consults any employees affected or their representative, adopts a fair basis on which to select for redundancy and takes such steps as may be reasonable to avoid or minimise redundancy by redeployment within his own organisation. If an employer has failed to take the appropriate procedural steps in any particular case, the one question the industrial tribunal is not permitted to ask in applying the test of reasonableness posed by section [98(4)] is the hypothetical question whether it would have made any difference to the outcome if the appropriate procedural steps had been taken. On the true construction of section [98(4)] this question is simply irrelevant. It is quite a different matter if the tribunal is able to conclude that the employer himself, at the time of dismissal, acted reasonably in taking the view that, in the exceptional circumstances of the particular case, the procedural steps normally appropriate would have been futile, could not have

---

[96] [1988] ICR 142 (HL).

altered the decision to dismiss and therefore could be dispensed with. In such a case the test of reasonableness under section [98(4)] may be satisfied . . .

If it is held that taking the appropriate steps which the employer failed to take before dismissing the employee would not have affected the outcome, this will often lead to the result that the employee, though unfairly dismissed, will recover no compensation or, in the case of redundancy, no compensation in excess of his redundancy payment.

The mistake that the tribunal had made in this case was to conclude that the dismissal was fair because it was inevitable owing to the dire financial straits of the employer. The correct question is, however, whether in the circumstances a reasonable employer would have dispensed with all procedural steps such as a discussion of the situation and an explanation of the need for redundancy.

It is important to notice that the standards of procedural fairness are influenced by the requirements of substantive fairness, so that when the employer has a compelling ground for dismissal, such as grave misconduct or an urgent need to make redundancies, the employer may act within the RORR in relaxing or ignoring procedural standards of fairness. If an employee is caught red handed committing a major act of misconduct, a tribunal may conclude that a summary dismissal on the spot was fair despite the absence of any investigation or hearing. It follows that where an employer fails to comply with a contractual disciplinary procedure, this will not necessarily result in a finding of unfairness under section 98(4) ERA 1996. Although normally the employer's failure to comply with its own disciplinary code, by for example denying the employee a right of appeal, will result in a finding of unfair dismissal for a failure to follow a fair procedure,[97] the employer may be able to persuade the tribunal that in the circumstances, such as grave misconduct, the breach of a contractual disciplinary procedure was within the RORR. Assuming that most reasonable employers would at least have a personal interview and consultation with an employee before making the employee redundant, no matter how difficult the financial situation of the business, the perfunctory dismissal of Mr Polkey was almost certainly outside of the RORR and therefore unfair.

The insistence by the courts and tribunals on a requirement for employers to follow a fair disciplinary procedure induced all medium and large employers to introduce formal disciplinary procedures into the workplace. The procedures are usually set out in staff handbooks and works rules. Sometimes they may be included as terms of the contract of employment. These formal procedures are modelled on the guidance from the ACAS Code of Practice. By following such procedures, employers greatly reduce the risk that a tribunal might determine that a dismissal has been unfair. Indeed tribunals sometimes fall into the trap of thinking that, having determined that the procedure

---

[97] *West Midlands Co-operative Society* v. *Tipton* [1986] ICR 192 (HL).

leading up to the dismissal was fair, that the dismissal must have been fair, whereas of course there remains the further question whether it was reasonable for the employer to dismiss for that substantive reason. A mistake of this kind appears to have occurred in the EAT in *Bowater* v. *Northwest London Hospitals Hospital Trust*,[98] where the employer's procedure was impeccable, but even so the Court of Appeal confirmed the view of the ET that the dismissal for a humorous and embarrassed remark was outside the RORR.

Despite the strong support accorded to the requirement of a fair procedure, studies of applications to tribunals reveal that most cases still involve a failure on the part of an employer to follow a fair procedure. Small employers tend to dismiss their employees summarily without any formal process of an investigation and a hearing or meeting with the employee. In the hope of reducing the number of applications to tribunals by curbing the number of instances of perfunctory and unfair disciplinary procedures, legislation introduced a mandatory requirement for all employers to follow a specified minimum standard of a disciplinary procedure that normally included a meeting prior to dismissal, and the failure to comply with the procedure would lead to an automatic finding of unfair dismissal and a higher level of compensation.[99] No sooner was the ink dry on the legislation, however, than employers' organisations objected that it was unworkable and imposed unnecessary costs. Employers were aggrieved that they had lost the chance to win against a claim for unfair dismissal on the ground that, notwithstanding the perfunctory quality of the disciplinary procedure followed, in the circumstances the summary dismissal was within the RORR. Following a brief enquiry and report, the legislation was abolished. In its place, new provisions require tribunals to increase the amount of the compensatory award for a failure to follow the ACAS Code of Practice.[100] Where an employer has failed to follow the Code of Practice and a tribunal decides that the failure was unreasonable, the tribunal may, if it considers it just and equitable in all the circumstances to do so, increase the compensatory award by no more than 25 per cent.

Remedies for Unfair Dismissal

Compliance and Corrective Justice

The sanctions for unfair dismissal may have two principal aims. One objective is to try to ensure that employers generally comply with the standard of fairness established by the legislation. In other words, the legislation should deter or prevent unfair dismissals. The other objective should be that an employee who has been subjected to an unfair dismissal should be properly

---

[98] [2011] EWCA Civ 63, [2011] IRLR 331.
[99] Employment Act 2002; Employment Act 2002 (Dispute Resolution) Regulations 2004.
[100] TULRCA 1992, s. 207A and ERA 1996, s. 124A, introduced by Employment Act 2008.

compensated. The simultaneous pursuit of these two aims may not always prove compatible, and the pursuit of both may have to be qualified by the costs involved.

What happens to a claim for unfair dismissal once it has been lodged with a tribunal? On the basis of the most recent official statistics that provide a detailed breakdown,[101] of the approximately 50,000 claims for unfair dismissal that were filed in 2009–10, 25 per cent were withdrawn either because the employee gave up or some settlement was achieved; 41 per cent were successfully conciliated by ACAS; 11 per cent were struck out before any hearing on some technical ground; 3 per cent were struck out at a preliminary hearing before the tribunal; 10 per cent of the claims failed at the hearing; which leaves about 8 per cent of the initial claims successful at tribunal (about 4,200 cases with a further 2 per cent where the employer failed to respond). The normal outcome of a successful claim for dismissal is the award of a modest amount of compensation to the employee. Of those 4,200 successful cases, 2,600 employees were awarded compensation, 1,400 received no award at all, and for most of the remainder the parties agreed a settlement, leaving only 8 dismissed employees winning reinstatement. The median award of compensation was £4,591; 28 per cent received less than £2,000 in compensation; about 5 per cent received more than £30,000.

It is worth remembering in this context that an award by a tribunal does not necessarily entail that the employer actually pays up. Unless the employer does so voluntarily, the employee has to take further, expensive legal proceedings before a county court to enforce the tribunal's judgment. In a survey of 448 successful claimants for an award of compensation,[102] it was reported that 57 per cent had been paid in full, 8 per cent paid in part and 35 per cent were not paid at all. Small employers were less likely to pay up, especially if the sum exceeded a few hundred pounds. Many small employers had disappeared or closed down to avoid payment.

This normal result of successful claims of an award of compensation of less than £5,000 serves neither proposed aim of the remedies very satisfactorily. The sum of money provides only a minor deterrent to the employer against breach of standards, so that in many cases employers, especially larger employers, may conclude that it will be cheaper and more convenient to dismiss the employee and pay compensation than to comply with the law. The cost to the employer is further reduced because the expenses of dealing with a claim may be deducted from taxable profits as a business expense. Nor does the award of compensation appear to reflect all the employee's losses, especially once these include intangible expectations of security and enhanced

---

[101] Ministry of Justice, Courts and Tribunals Service, *Employment Tribunals and EAT Statistics 2010–2011* (1 September 2011).

[102] L. Adams, A. Moore, K. Gore and J. Browne, *Research into Enforcement of Employment Tribunal Awards in England and Wales*, Ministry of Justice Research Series 9/09 (May 2009).

income through long service and promotion. An enhanced measure of compensation would redress these faults. It would supply the necessary incentive for compliance and provide full compensation for the employee. But it may be objected that heavy financial penalties for dismissal would deter employers from making even justified or fair dismissals, because the standard is too vague to provide a reliable guide for employers to use in a practical way.

Reinstatement provides a potential solution to this dilemma. A reinstatement reverses the dismissal, thereby ensuring compliance with the standard of fairness, without imposing major costs upon the employer. At the same time it prevents the employee's long-term losses from arising. But this remedy frequently appears unattractive to the parties concerned: the dismissal and its surrounding events will probably have led to a loss of trust and confidence on both sides, to such an extent that neither party wishes to continue the relationship. Reinstatement therefore appears to be a solution that usually no one wants.

Reinstatement

The primacy of the remedy of reinstatement or re-engagement is emphasised in the legislation. Reinstatement requires the employer to take back the employee on his previous job with full back pay in all respects as if he had not been dismissed.[103] Re-engagement is an order for the employee to be re-employed on such terms as the tribunal may decide in a job that is comparable to that from which he was dismissed or other suitable employment.[104] The ET is required to explain to a successful complainant that it may make an order of reinstatement or re-engagement and ask if he or she wants such an order.[105] If the complainant replies affirmatively, the ET has a discretion whether or not to make an order. In exercising this discretion, the tribunal must consider whether it is 'practicable' for the employer to comply with an order and, where the complainant caused or contributed to the dismissal, whether it would be just to order his reinstatement or re-engagement.[106]

These criteria for the exercise of discretion severely limit the scope for orders of reinstatement and re-engagement. The tribunal is required to take into account the wishes of the employee, which in most cases may be opposed to reinstatement because, by the time the case reaches the tribunal, it is likely that either the employee will have found another job or that the relations between the parties will have become so acerbic that the employee believes that the breakdown of trust and confidence will prevent a workable and satisfactory restoration of the employment relation. In one survey, at the commencement

---

[103] ERA 1996, s. 114. The job may be conceived as the work previously being done as opposed to the formal contractual requirements: *McBride* v. *Scottish Police Authority* [2016] UKSC 27, [2016] ICR 788.

[104] ERA 1996, s. 115.   [105] ERA 1996, ss. 112 and 113.   [106] ERA 1996 s. 116.

of proceedings, 75 per cent of claimants wanted reinstatement, but only 20 per cent continued to desire it after the hearing and winning the case.[107] Later surveys suggest that now a smaller percentage of employees put reinstatement as their preferred remedy on their original claim form.[108] Since in most instances of disciplinary dismissals the employee is not wholly blameless, the second criterion for the exercise of discretion that justifies a denial of reinstatement on the ground of contributory fault has the potential to rule out an order in the majority of cases. The third criterion for the exercise of discretion asks whether reinstatement is practicable. Practicable means more than merely possible but 'capable of being carried into effect with success'.[109] This criterion runs the risk that in effect it will give employers a veto over reinstatement. Employers can argue that owing to a breakdown of trust and confidence, if not before the dismissal then certainly afterwards during acrimonious legal proceedings, it is not practicable to expect the necessary degree of co-operation for the employment relation to be restored properly. Although the courts are sensitive to this danger of giving the employer a veto over reinstatement, given their view that the employment relation depends upon co-operation, which relies on mutual trust and confidence, the employer's assertion that there has been a breakdown of trust and confidence does strongly point to the conclusion that reinstatement is impracticable. The most that a tribunal is permitted to do is to test whether the employer's view of the breakdown of trust and confidence was genuine and founded on a rational basis.[110]

In the unusual case where the tribunal orders reinstatement (recall that in the statistics it was only in 8 cases out of 4,200 successful claims)[111] the employer must comply or face a claim for compensation by the employee in addition to the normal compensation for unfair dismissal. This sanction is a type of punitive damages known as the additional award.[112] This additional award may not present a strong measure of deterrence against disobedience to the order for reinstatement for two reasons. First, the level set for this additional award is not less than twenty-six and not more than fifty-two weeks' pay.[113] For low-paid employees this sum of money may not suffice to induce employers to comply with the order for reinstatement. Unlike the common-law power of holding an employer to be in contempt of court and subject to unlimited fines for breach of an injunction, the employer can decide whether it prefers to comply with the order or pay the limited additional measure of compensation instead. Second, the employer can avoid any

---

[107] P. Lewis, 'An Analysis of Why Legislation has Failed to Provide Employment Protection for Unfairly Dismissed Workers' (1981) 19 *British Journal of Industrial Relations* 316.

[108] L. Dickens *et al.*, *Dismissed* (Oxford: Blackwell, 1985), p. 116.

[109] *Coleman* v. *Magnet Joinery Ltd* [1975] ICR 46, 52 (Stephenson LJ) (CA).

[110] *United Lincolnshire Hospitals NHS Foundation Trust* v. *Farren* [2017] ICR 513.

[111] It should be noted, however, that a small percentage of the cases resolved through ACAS may have resulted in re-engagement as well.

[112] ERA 1996, s. 117.   [113] ERA 1996, s. 117(3).

sanction for disobedience to the order if the employer satisfies the tribunal that it was not practicable to comply with the order.[114] This second insertion of the requirement that reinstatement should be practicable again presents the danger that the employer has an effective veto over the remedy. In determining this question, the statute merely provides the guidance that the fact that the employer has engaged a permanent replacement should be regarded as irrelevant, unless the employer shows that it was not practicable to arrange for the work to be done without engaging a permanent replacement.[115]

The way in which the employer has two bites at the cherry to resist an order of reinstatement is illustrated in *Port of London Authority* v. *Payne*.[116] The case also raises the question of whether the employer's business decision that it would not be efficient to reinstate the employee in effect determines the outcome of the case. The employers had derecognised the union, changed terms of employment and made a large number of dock-workers redundant. Among those dismissed, seventeen shop stewards succeeded in claims for (automatically) unfair dismissal because they had been selected for redundancy on the ground of their trade union activities. The industrial tribunal ordered re-engagement for twelve claimants, making a finding at this first stage that re-engagement was practicable, but the employers failed to comply with the orders. In defence to a claim for an additional award, the employers argued again that compliance with the order was not practicable on the grounds that there were no vacancies and that it would be too disruptive and expensive to ask the remaining workforce if any wished to take voluntary redundancy in order to create suitable vacancies, and any such enquiry would probably only produce a handful of vacancies. The industrial tribunal rejected the employer's defence at this second stage. On appeal to the Court of Appeal, the court upheld the tribunal's initial decision to order reinstatement, but permitted the employer's defence to the claim for an additional award. Neil LJ explained:

> the test is practicability not possibility. The Industrial Tribunal, though it should carefully scrutinise the reasons advanced by the employer, should give due weight to the commercial judgment of the management unless of course the witnesses are to be disbelieved. The standard must not be set too high. The employer cannot be expected to explore every possible avenue which ingenuity might suggest. The employer does not have to show that reinstatement or re-engagement was impossible. It is a matter of what is practicable in the circumstances of the employer's business at the relevant time.

This decision is important for revealing that the test of practicability seems to be little more than a question of the degree of inconvenience for the employer. It is also significant because it demonstrates how an employer that is determined to exclude a union can selectively dismiss the leading union activists. Although the

---

[114] ERA 1996, s. 117(4)(a).   [115] ERA 1996, s. 117(7).   [116] [1994] IRLR 9 (CA).

employer has to pay ordinary compensation for unfair dismissal, it can resist orders for reinstatement and evade any kind of punitive damages such as the additional award for this calculated act of anti-union discrimination.

Despite the emphasis in the legislation upon reinstatement or re-engagement being the primary remedy for unfair dismissal, the remedy is rarely effective. There is a tendency to blame the tribunals for a failure to apply the remedies of reinstatement and re-engagement. Yet the statute lays down guidelines for the exercise of discretion that prevent tribunals from making such orders. The tribunal must comply with the employee's wishes, and by the end of the tribunal hearing few employees still seek reinstatement. In the remaining instances, the test of whether the order was practicable emphasises the employer's business judgement rather than whether it might be fair or just to the employee to order reinstatement. The effect of that emphasis upon business judgement, as we saw in *Payne*, is that the employer's strong opposition can justify a refusal to make an order.

Can the legal procedures be reformed to increase the incidence of reinstatement? In order to overcome the problem that by the end of the hearing most employees no longer seek reinstatement, a tribunal might be empowered to order reinstatement as a form of interim relief. The tribunals have this power in cases where it appears to the tribunal that applicant is likely to succeed in his claim that the reason for dismissal is one which relates to trade union membership or activities, or relates to the employee's position as a health and safety representative or a trustee of the pension fund, that is some of the grounds for automatically unfair dismissals.[117] But the employer can prevent reinstatement and merely continue to pay the employee's wages until the full hearing.[118] This power to order interim relief might be extended to all cases of unfair dismissal with a view to increasing the chances of a final reinstatement order, but it seems unlikely that employers would comply if they had the option of merely paying wages, and most employers would object to any payment at all, if they believed that the dismissal was justified. The procedure would also place a heavy and perhaps impracticable task on the tribunal to estimate the likelihood of success of a case before it had properly heard the evidence. Arbitration has also been presented as a possible procedure for enhancing the opportunity for reinstatement. But the technique of arbitration will not overcome the problem that at the time of the hearing most employees no longer seek reinstatement unless it occurs extremely quickly and avoids the antagonism of litigation. In any case, the delays associated with legal proceedings are only one factor in the absence of reinstatement as the normal remedy for unfair dismissal. Even where a settlement is achieved quickly through conciliation, it is clear that compensation is usually preferred by both parties as a solution to the dispute. The employer prefers to pay cash rather than

---

[117] ERA 1996, ss. 128–9.   [118] ERA 1996, ss. 129(9), 130.

reverse the disciplinary decision, and employees usually believe that their best interests in the long term lie in seeking alternative employment.

Despite the primacy accorded to reinstatement in the procedures of the tribunals, the legislation in fact does not provide significant support for the remedy. It carefully avoids forcing employers to take back employees. As Lord Donaldson MR once observed, an order for reinstatement is 'wholly unenforceable'.[119] It may therefore be a mistake to regard the objective of the legislation as one of protecting job security in the sense of protecting the employee's position in holding on to his job. The regulatory aim of the legislation may be rather one of improving the fairness of employer's disciplinary practices. For this purpose, a financial remedy suffices, provided that it is set sufficiently high that it becomes cost effective for employers to alter their disciplinary practices in order to avoid the financial penalty. Indeed, a remedy of reinstatement may have much less impact upon employer's disciplinary practices, because reinstatement is usually cheap for employers, so that they can afford to ignore the regulation. Substantial financial compensation as the remedy for unfair dismissal should therefore be a much better regulatory strategy for enhancing job security. The level of compensation has, however, been kept rather low, so that the remedy has not provided sufficient incentive to comply with the objectives of the legislation.

Against these arguments for suggesting that substantial compensation may increase compliance, it must be recognised that it is hard for tribunals to provide compensation for all the expectations arising in an employment relation. The employee may have expectations of promotions and wage increases arising from seniority, or the employee may enjoy this particular kind of work and be unable to find a similar satisfying vocation with another employer. A remedy of reinstatement can protect an employee against these losses completely, whereas an award of compensation will not capture these losses except to the extent that the employee can demonstrate that a wage increase was imminent,[120] or that the wages in a subsequent job are lower because the employee cannot use his or her particular skills and experience. It should also be recognised that a dismissed employee is likely to find it harder to obtain work than one who is currently in employment. Although tribunals can award 'stigma damages' as part of the compensation for unfair dismissal, if the manner of dismissal impedes the employee from obtaining fresh employment, reinstatement may be a more effective remedy for damage to reputation.

Compensation

The normal remedy for unfair dismissal comprises financial compensation in two parts: the basic award and the compensatory award.

---

[119] *O'Laire v. Jackal International Ltd* [1990] IRLR 70, 73 (CA).
[120] *York Trailer Ltd v. Sparkes* [1973] ICR 518 (NIRC).

Basic Award

The basic award (which is the same as a redundancy payment) is calculated mathematically according to three main variables: age, years of service and level of pay. In a simple case, an employee receives compensation amounting to a week's pay (or one and a half weeks' pay for years over forty years old) for each year of service, up to a maximum of twenty years.[121] There is an upper limit on a week's pay fixed at £508.[122] The exact purpose of the basic award remains puzzling. It looks backwards rather than forwards, compensating the employee for seniority rather than future economic loss. Loss of particular seniority rights, such as loss of accrued statutory rights by the elimination of a qualifying period in the new job, will be compensated by the compensatory award. Thus the basic award compensates a broader notion of seniority, the idea of job security based upon length of service. In so doing, however, it introduces elements of indirect age discrimination (by increasing the award for older employees), and almost certainly indirect sex discrimination, since women employees will not on average acquire similar lengths of service in one job owing to interruptions in paid work for family reasons. Nevertheless, the basic award may be justified as an attempt to provide compensation for the employee's expectations from employment that are hard to measure in financial terms, such as the wasted investment in firm-specific skills, job satisfaction and the psychological distress caused by dismissal.

Compensatory Award

The compensatory award is, in contrast, left to the discretion of the tribunal.

Employment Rights Act 1996, Section 123(1)

...the amount of the compensatory award shall be such amount as the tribunal considers just and equitable in all the circumstances, having regard to the loss sustained by the complainant in consequence of the dismissal in so far as that loss is attributable to action taken by the employer.

Although the statute apparently confers on tribunals a broad discretion to award just and equitable compensation to unfairly dismissed employees, the courts moved swiftly to control the exercise of discretion by the tribunals. In *Norton Tool Co. Ltd* v. *Tewson*,[123] the court insisted that the compensatory award should be calculated according to identifiable items of economic loss rather than a general award in the round. The objective should be to

---

[121] ERA 1996, s. 119.

[122] ERA 1996, s. 227. This upper limit is periodically raised by statutory instrument.

[123] [1972] ICR 501 (NIRC).

compensate the employee fully but not to award the employee a bonus or any kind of punitive damages. The court also ruled that although the measure of the compensatory award was not governed at all by the common law of wrongful dismissal, like the common law it did not include awards of aggravated damages to reflect any psychological suffering by the employee caused by the manner of dismissal, because the word 'loss', in its natural meaning according to the court, does not include injury to pride or feelings.

A typical compensatory award therefore includes the following items of economic loss suffered by the employee as a result of the unfair dismissal:

- Wages (after tax) owing as a result of the employer's failure to give sufficient notice in accordance with the statutory minimum or contractual undertaking. Unlike the common law, however, this item should not in general be reduced if the employee obtains another job or receives a social security benefit during the appropriate notice period.[124] That protection of compensation for wages during the notice period does not apply to instances of constructive dismissal on the ground that the employer did not make the choice not to give proper notice of dismissal.[125]

- Compensation for the actual or likely period of unemployment before the employee obtains another job, taking due account of the employee's duty to take reasonable steps to mitigate loss. This item represents the major improvement of compensation for unfair dismissal in comparison with the common law of wrongful dismissal. If a new job obtained by the dismissed employee prior to the tribunal hearing has better remuneration than the job that was lost as a result of the unfair dismissal, compensation is normally restricted for losses that arose until the new job commenced.[126] If, in contrast, the tribunal finds that there is permanent damage to a person's career and that future employment is likely to be much less well remunerated, it is possible to reflect this career loss in the award.[127]

- Compensation for the reduction in job security in any new job. This item reflects the point that the employee will no longer satisfy the qualifying period of employment for statutory rights such as unfair dismissal. Furthermore, the new job may appear less secure where, for example, the employer is a small business or the work appears to be only temporary.

- Stigma damages or compensation for damage to employability caused by the fact of dismissal and the damage to the employee's reputation resulting from it.

---

[124] *Addison* v. *Babcock FATA Ltd* [1987] ICR 805 (CA); *Langley* v. *Burlo* [2006] EWCA Civ 1778, [2007] ICR 390 (CA).

[125] *Stuart Peters Ltd* v. *Bell* [2009] EWCA Civ 938, [2009] ICR 1556 (CA).

[126] *Dench* v. *Flynn and Partners* [1998] IRLR 653 (CA); *Aegon UK Corporate Services Ltd* v. *Roberts* [2009] EWCA Civ 932, [2010] ICR 596 (CA).

[127] *Wardle* v. *Crédit Agricole Corporate and Investment Bank* [2011] EWCA Civ 545, [2011] ICR 1290 (CA).

- Compensation for the loss of fringe benefits such as a company car, medical insurance, share options and an employer's occupational pension scheme.

In this list, the major item of financial compensation in most claims for unfair dismissal is the loss of income for the period of unemployment following dismissal. The applicant is placed under a duty to mitigate loss, which requires reasonable efforts to secure alternative employment. If, despite such efforts, the applicant fails to obtain another job, the tribunal will award compensation for the period it regards as likely to elapse before employment may be found. The tribunal has considerable discretion to make such an estimate, and these judgements may reflect the broader merits of the case. In exercising this discretion, the tribunals draw upon their knowledge of the local labour market and the characteristics of the complainant. In theory the amount of compensation awarded under this heading should on average increase during periods of high unemployment, but the difference appears to be no more than two or three extra weeks of pay, which suggests a significant degree of under-compensation in periods of high unemployment.[128]

By framing the compensatory award around the question of the economic loss suffered by the employee, the degree of fault of the employer is excluded from consideration. No matter how arbitrarily or harshly the employer acted, in principle the measure of compensation will remain the same, because 'the purpose of assessing compensation is not to express disapproval of industrial relations policy. It is to compensate for financial loss.'[129] It is entirely possible that, if an employee obtains another job immediately, there will be no compensatory award at all, although in these circumstances unfairly dismissed employees should receive the basic award. We noted earlier, however, that in cases of alleged misconduct, where the unfairness of the dismissal consists in the employer's failure to follow a disciplinary procedure consistent with the ACAS Code of Practice, as in the case of an unwarranted summary dismissal without a hearing, tribunals have the power to increase the compensatory award.[130] To that extent, if it is just and equitable to do so, the employer's fault with regard to the disciplinary procedure can be reflected in a compensatory award. It should be noted, however, that an uplift of 25 per cent on a compensatory award is only significant if the compensatory award is substantial. At the same time, the compensation may be reduced if the employee fails to comply with the ACAS Code of Practice by, for instance, failing to attend a scheduled meeting without excuse.

---

[128] L. Dickens *et al.*, *Dismissed* (Oxford: Blackwell, 1985), p. 124.
[129] *Per* Sir John Donaldson, *Clarkson International Tools Ltd* v. *Short* [1973] ICR 191, 196 (NIRC).
[130] ERA 1996, s. 124A; TULRCA 1992, s. 207A.

Contributory Fault

In sharp contrast, the tribunal is encouraged to ensure that the amount of compensation reflects the fault of the employee. There are three mechanisms by which a tribunal can reduce compensation in order to reflect its assessment of the fault or responsibility of the employee for the termination of his employment.

In the first place, the legislation empowers the tribunal to reduce both the basic award and the compensatory award on the ground that the complainant caused or contributed to the dismissal.[131] Some forms of alleged misconduct cannot be regarded as contributory fault. An employee's refusal to join a trade union or not to join a trade union, and a refusal to desist from taking part in trade union activities, cannot count as contributory fault.[132] Participation in industrial action in itself also cannot be regarded as contributory fault in those cases where a tribunal has jurisdiction due to the premature or selective nature of the dismissals.[133] Aside from those limitations, however, the meaning of contributory fault in this context is broad enough to encompass not merely breach of contract but also unreasonable or foolish behaviour by the employee.

For instance, in *Nelson* v. *British Broadcasting Corporation (No. 2)*,[134] the employee's job was abolished but he was offered another position, subject to a report after three months on his performance in the new job. The employee refused the job and won a claim for unfair dismissal, but his compensation was reduced by 60 per cent. Approving that outcome, Brandon LJ in the Court of Appeal described the type of conduct that merited a reduction of compensation for contributory fault:

> The concept does not, in my view, necessarily involve any conduct of the complainant amounting to a breach of contract or a tort. It includes, no doubt, conduct of that kind. But it also includes conduct which, while not amounting to a breach of contract or a tort, is nevertheless perverse or foolish, or, if I may use the colloquialism, bloody-minded. It may also include action which, though not meriting any of those more pejorative epithets, is nevertheless unreasonable in all the circumstances. I should not, however, go so far as to say that all unreasonable conduct is necessarily culpable or blameworthy; it must depend on the degree of unreasonableness involved.

This expansive interpretation of the notion of contributory fault contrasts unfavourably with the requirement of fundamental breach of contract in the law of wrongful dismissal as a disentitlement to compensation, and seems to give employers a second bite at the cherry: reasons for dismissal that were found inadequate to justify the dismissal are resurrected to avoid paying full compensation.

---

[131] ERA 1996, ss. 122(2), 123(6).   [132] TULRCA 1992, s. 155.
[133] *Crossville Wales Ltd* v. *Tracey (No. 2)* [1997] IRLR 691 (HL).   [134] [1980] ICR 110 (CA).

Polkey Deduction

The decision of the House of Lords in *Polkey* v. *A.E. Dayton Services Ltd*,[135] endorses the view that where the misconduct of the employee was grave, but the dismissal was unfair as a result of the employer's failure to follow a fair procedure, it may be appropriate to reduce the measure of compensation to zero on the ground of contributory fault.[136] More controversially, the House of Lords extended this reasoning to cases of redundancy, where the employee is not at fault at all, but the financial business position of the employer entailed that the dismissal was inevitable in the circumstances. This extension to redundancy and economic dismissals where consultation would have been futile is known as the '*Polkey* deduction'.[137] In a case of failure to consult properly prior to a dismissal for redundancy, the compensation will be reduced to reflect the likelihood that the dismissal would have occurred in a short period of time in any event,[138] so that either no compensation for unfair dismissal will be payable where dismissals resulting from plant closure were immediate and inevitable[139] or compensation will be reduced according to the tribunal's assessment of the risk of redundancy of this applicant.[140] This result is justified by the courts on the ground that while the dismissal was unfair for procedural reasons, in fact the employee suffered no loss as a result of the unfair procedure, since the dismissal would have occurred in any event. The problem with that reasoning is, however, that it permits an employer to forgo a fair procedure with financial impunity where the particular employee was bound to have been dismissed.

More troublingly still, this reasoning has been extended to instances of disciplinary dismissals, where the employer argues that compensation should be reduced because it is likely that the employee would have been dismissed fairly shortly thereafter for other reasons. Reasons of this kind that have been advanced have included the antagonistic and intransigent attitude of the employee towards management[141] or the probable refusal of the employee of new terms and conditions even after a proper period of consultation.[142] In *Thornett* v. *Scope*,[143] for instance, the breakdown of relations between the dismissed employee and a co-worker as a result of allegations of bullying and harassment led the tribunal to predict that the employment would have only continued for six months in any event. Although the Court of Appeal remitted the case to the tribunal to examine more carefully the evidence, it agreed that in principle that the tribunal should make such a determination. This case was unfortunately confused because the employers made an additional argument

---

[135] [1988] ICR 142 (HL).   [136] *Earl* v. *Slater & Wheeler (Airlyne) Ltd* [1972] ICR 508 (NIRC).
[137] Chapter 20.   [138] *British United Shoe Machinery Co. Ltd* v. *Clarke* [1978] ICR 70 (EAT).
[139] *James W Cook & Co. (Wivenhoe) Ltd* v. *Tipper* [1990] IRLR 386 (CA).
[140] *Contract Bottling Ltd* v. *Cave* [2015] ICR 146 (EAT).
[141] *O'Donogue* v. *Redcar and Cleveland Borough Council* [2001] IRLR 615 (CA).
[142] *Gover* v. *Propertycare Ltd* [2006] EWCA Civ 286, [2006] ICR 1073 (CA).
[143] *Thornett* v. *Scope* [2006] EWCA Civ 1600, [2007] ICR 236 (CA).

that the employee would have been made redundant at some point, so that it resembled to some extent a *Polkey* deduction', but the exact ground of the tribunal's decision that was reviewed on appeal consisted in speculation about future disciplinary grounds for dismissal. These decisions invite tribunals to make predictions about what would have happened if the employers had acted reasonably and if there had been no dismissal initially. The tribunals are instructed to have regard to any material and reliable evidence and use their judgement to make such tentative predictions, even though, unlike the cases concerning redundancy, such predictions must be no more than a guess about future behaviour and management's response to it. This extension of the *Polkey* deduction' to disciplinary dismissals is regrettable not only for the degree of conjecture or guesswork it invites, but also for the way in which it undermines the protection of fair procedures. Where an employee is to an extent the author of his or her own misfortune owing to misconduct or unreasonable behaviour, the compensatory award for unfair dismissal can be reduced on the ground of contributory fault. These decisions impose an additional penalty on the employee by reducing compensation further on the speculative ground that in the future the employer might have had a good reason for dismissal and would have conducted the disciplinary procedure fairly. Surely tribunals should be unwilling to accept such an argument from an employer who has already demonstrated a disposition to dismiss an employee unfairly? Furthermore, it is unclear why this estimation of risk is even relevant to the question of the proper amount of compensation: the question is what loss the employee has suffered as a result of the unfair dismissal, and the guiding principle should refer to the likely period of unemployment before another job is obtained.

Just and Equitable Amount

As a third technique for reducing compensation to reflect the fault of the employee, when applying the compensatory award under ERA 1996, section 123, the courts have decided that the notion of 'just and equitable' must include an assessment of the actual fault of the employee. In *Devis & Sons Ltd* v. *Atkins*,[144] the employer had unfairly dismissed the employee, but subsequent to the dismissal the employer discovered evidence of misconduct that would have justified the dismissal. The House of Lords confirmed that the dismissal was unfair, because the reasonableness of the employer's conduct must be judged according to the facts known to the employer at the time. Nevertheless, when the issue of the assessment of the compensatory award arose, a tribunal should reflect the true state of the facts in making a just and equitable award. 'No compensation should be awarded when in fact the employee has suffered no injustice by being dismissed.'[145] The emphasis of

---

[144] [1977] ICR 662 (HL).   [145] Viscount Dilhorne, [1977] ICR 662, 679 (HL).

the compensatory award is thus upon the employee's economic loss and fault, not the fault of the employer. As a result, the employer has little incentive to minimise deviation from standards of good industrial relations practice, and may be lucky enough to have to pay minimal compensation if the employee suffers no financial loss by obtaining another job.

Compensation for the Manner of Dismissal

We have noted above that the courts have decided that while the compensatory award must fully reflect any fault attributable to the employee, the gravity of the employer's misconduct in making an unfair dismissal should not affect the measure of compensation. Is there a contradiction here in the interpretation of the just and equitable compensatory award in ERA 1996, section 123? How can the courts' interpretation of what compensation is just and equitable take full account of the employee's conduct, including fairly minor acts of behaving unreasonably, yet maintain the position that the amount of compensation will not be increased to reflect the extent of the fault of the employer (except insofar as it consists of procedural unfairness that a tribunal uses as the basis for an uplift to the just and equitable award under the special powers conferred by statute)? The problem, as perceived by the courts, was that to award compensation for the sheer arbitrariness, capriciousness or harshness of the employer's conduct would amount to compensation for the manner of dismissal. It would involve compensation for non-economic loss such as distress and humiliation.

Such compensation was unavailable under the common law of wrongful dismissal and, as we have seen, when the new statutory claim for unfair dismissal arrived, the courts again insisted that there could be no compensation for the manner of dismissal because the term 'loss' in the statute referred only to economic loss. In *Johnson* v. *Unysis Ltd*,[146] however, while the House of Lords rejected the possibility of a claim for the manner of dismissal under the common law based upon breach of the implied term of mutual trust and confidence, Lord Hoffmann observed in a passage that was strictly speaking *obiter*, but was nevertheless part of his reasoning, that the common law should not be developed to avoid the statutory regime: 'The emphasis is upon the tribunal awarding such compensation as it thinks just and equitable. So I see no reason why in an appropriate case it should not include compensation for distress, humiliation, damage to reputation in the community or to family life.' In other words, one of the major reasons for the restriction of the remedy under the common law was said to be that compensation for such injuries of distress and humiliation were available under the statutory claim for unfair dismissal.

---

[146] [2001] UKHL 13, [2001] ICR 480 (HL).

Shortly afterwards, however, the House of Lords rejected such a claim for injuries arising from the manner of dismissal in a claim for unfair dismissal. In *Dunnachie* v. *Kingston-upon-Hull City Council*,[147] the employee had worked for the Council in the field of environmental health for fifteen years, when he resigned in response to bullying and harassment by his manager and the failure of more senior managers to respond to his plight. The tribunal accepted that there had been a constructive dismissal as a result of a breach of the implied term of mutual trust and confidence. The tribunal awarded compensation for unfair dismissal up to the maximum for the compensatory award at that time of £51,700, and included in that award £10,000 for injury to feelings. The EAT disallowed that aspect of the award, but the Court of Appeal by a majority (Sedley LJ, Evans-Lombe J; Brooke LJ dissenting) restored it. Evans-Lombe J thought that the word 'loss' could include non-economic loss. Sedley LJ accepted that the more natural meaning of the word loss only referred to pecuniary loss, but he argued that the correct interpretation of ERA 1996, section 123 required the tribunal to assess what was just and equitable in all the circumstances. The statute also instructed the tribunal to have regard to the economic loss, but it did not say that they were prohibited from compensating non-economic loss: 'in section 123(1) loss is not the defining category but a subset of the larger category of just and equitable compensation'.[148] This interpretation reflected similar scholarly commentary:

> The correct interpretation of subsection 123(1) is as simple as – well – one, two, three. Rule one, the dominant principle, is to provide compensation that is just and equitable in all the circumstances. Rule two is that in assessing compensation a tribunal must include the economic loss caused to the employee. Rule three limits any assessment of compensation by the ordinary principle of causation (for breach of contract): any item of compensation must be attributable to the dismissal.[149]

Sedley LJ stressed, however, that not every dismissed employee could bring a claim for the manner of dismissal; it was only available to an employee who could demonstrate a 'real injury to his or her self-respect'.[150]

Yet the House of Lords in *Dunnachie* v. *Kingston-upon-Hull City Council* finally and firmly rejected the award for injury to feelings. Almost certainly the underlying motives were to avoid both unpredictability in the calculation of the compensatory award and the risk for employers that the awards would be greatly increased in response to harsh treatment. The reasons given by Lord Steyn, speaking for a unanimous House, which perhaps surprisingly included Lord Hoffmann, were, first, that nobody could seriously suggest that

---

[147] [2004] UKHL 36, [2004] ICR 1052 (HL).

[148] *Dunnachie* v. *Kingston-upon-Hull City Council* [2004] IRLR 287 (CA), paras. 32–3.

[149] H. Collins, 'Compensation for the Manner of Dismissal' (2004) 33(2) *Industrial Law Journal* 152, 154; on the problem of bullying, see: Lizzie Barmes, *Bullying and Behavioural Conflict at Work* (Oxford University Press, 2016).

[150] *Dunnachie* v. *Kingston-upon-Hull City Council* [2004] IRLR 287 (CA), para. 48.

Parliament had intended to make it possible for tribunals to make awards of aggravated or exemplary compensation in order to punish the employer. If Parliament had so intended to introduce 'palm-tree justice', it was argued, it would have said so in clearer terms. The natural meaning of the word 'loss' was confined to economic loss. Secondly, the decision in *W. Devis & Sons* v. *Atkins*,[151] was distinguished on the ground that it merely authorised a reduction of compensation for the employee's fault; it did not authorise compensation for non-economic loss. This argument misses the point that *W. Devis & Sons* v. *Atkins* had encouraged a broad, moral interpretation of the concept of just and equitable compensation for the purpose of limiting the employer's liability. The question is why the phrase is suddenly confined in its scope when it comes to augmenting the level of compensation to reflect the fault of the employer. Third, Lord Steyn argued that the purpose of the phrase 'just and equitable' was not to grant the tribunals a broad discretion with respect to the kinds of loss but rather to permit them to adopt a broad-brush approach to the calculation of economic loss, taking into account some of the uncertainties such as the employee's likely period of unemployment resulting from the dismissal.

This decision in *Dunnachie* v. *Kingston-upon-Hull City Council* confirms the earlier case-law that the compensatory award is confined to the employee's economic losses, broadly construed, caused by the dismissal. Tribunals are not permitted to award compensation for injury to feelings, affronts to dignity, distress in personal life caused by the manner or fact of dismissal, unless the employee can demonstrate that the manner of the dismissal caused additional economic loss by, for example, damage to reputation. If the manner of the dismissal causes the employee to suffer from a recognised psychiatric illness such as severe depression, in a claim for unfair dismissal the tribunal cannot award compensation for that personal injury in itself, but can increase its estimate of the economic losses flowing from the dismissal in order to take into account the probable length of time before the employee can resume paid work. The problem with such a claim is that it is unlikely that the dismissal itself caused that reduced earning capacity, but rather the cause of the illness such as depression was almost certainly the employer's prior conduct. Accordingly, the reduced ability to earn an income resulting from psychiatric illness cannot be attributed to the dismissal and cannot be compensated under ERA 1996, section 123.[152] A claim for psychiatric illness caused by the conduct of the employer during the performance of the contract can be brought under the common law,[153] but it should be remembered that *Johnson* v. *Unisys Ltd* ruled out the possibility of such a claim at common law arising from the manner or the fact of dismissal itself. For the type of claim for constructive unfair

---

[151] [1977] ICR 662 (HL).
[152] *GAB Robins (UK) Ltd* v. *Triggs* [2008] EWCA Civ 17, [2008] ICR 529.
[153] *Eastwood* v. *Magnox* [2004] UKHL 35, [2004] ICR 1064.

dismissal advanced in *Dunnachie*, although there would be a common law action for breach during the performance of the contract of the implied term of trust and confidence and also a claim for negligence causing personal injury, it is not possible to use a claim for unfair dismissal to recover such losses.

Thus the courts have blocked any claim, whether at common law or under statute, where the gist is to penalise the employer for harsh treatment, bullying, harassment and affronts to dignity, in the manner of dismissal. Nevertheless, deterrence may be provided by the Employment Tribunals Act, section 12A, which empowers tribunals to order the employer to pay a penalty to the Secretary of State if the breach of an employment right has 'aggravating features', normally calculated as 50 per cent of the compensatory award up to a maximum of £20,000.

Social Security Benefits and Disciplinary Dismissals

Following dismissal, an employee may seek to claim social security benefits in the form of either a jobseeker's allowance or income support (a means-tested assistance for those whose personal circumstances are such that they are not required to seek work as a condition of receiving the benefit). Without a job the dismissed worker may have no other means of support. Assuming that the claimant satisfies the conditions for the jobseeker's allowance, such as contributions of national insurance payment for a year and is actively seeking work, the claimant may still be denied the benefit or disqualified temporarily if the loss of employment was caused by misconduct or if the employee gave up his employment without just cause.

Jobseekers Act 1995, Section 19

(1) Even though the conditions for entitlement to a jobseeker's allowance are satisfied with respect to a person, the allowance shall not be payable in any of the circumstances mentioned in subsection . . . (6) . . .
(2) If the circumstances are any of those mentioned in subsection (6), the period for which the allowance is not to be payable shall be such period (of at least one week but not more than 26 weeks) as may be determined by the Secretary of State . . .
(3) The circumstances referred to in subsections (1) and (3) are that the claimant—
    (a) has lost his employment as an employed earner through misconduct;
    (b) has voluntarily left such employment without just cause . . .

These standards, which have applied to claims for contributory unemployment benefits since their inception in 1911, do not necessarily coincide with the principles of the law of unfair dismissal in determinations of whether it was fair for the employer to dismiss the employee for misconduct or for the employee to regard himself as having been constructively dismissed. The disqualifying misconduct may not be sufficiently grave to justify dismissal, and the employer's serious breach of contract may not amount to a just cause for leaving a job and claiming the allowance. It is therefore possible to be a successful claimant for unfair dismissal, but a lawfully disqualified claimant for jobseeker's allowance. The reason given for this strange result is that the law of unfair dismissal is concerned with the justice of the dismissal between employer and employee, whereas the social security system has to look at wider distributive considerations including the minimisation of the social costs of dismissal. In accordance with that policy, if the benefit is paid and the employee eventually wins a claim for compensation through the law of unfair dismissal, the Secretary of State can recoup the expenditure from the employer prior to the employer paying compensation to the employee to the extent that the award of compensation consists of amounts calculated as lost wages.[154] But it should be observed as well that the absence of jobseeker's allowance on dismissal for misconduct adds significantly to an employer's disciplinary power, because the disqualification from compulsory social insurance benefits at a time when they are likely to be needed most urgently augments the implicit sanction of economic disadvantage that provides the principal source of the employer's power over the workforce. It is also questionable whether workers, if their opinion was sought, would accept these terms of their compulsory insurance policy, instead of agreeing with Winston Churchill: 'In my judgment if a man has paid to the fund for six months he should have his benefit in all circumstances, including dismissal for personal fault even of the gravest character; two securities being the low scale of benefits, and the solid, rigid qualifying period.'[155]

Upper Limit on Compensation

Unlike the common law, the statutory claim for unfair dismissal has always been restricted by an upper limit on the amount of compensation payable. The compensatory award has a upper limit in ERA 1996, section 124 of the lower of £83,682 or fifty-two times the actual week's pay of the applicant. The upper limit only operates if the total sum of the compensatory award minus deductions for such matters as contributory fault exceeds the limit.[156] The main effect of this upper limit is to deprive highly paid employees of most of their possible compensation, thereby creating the incentive to resort to a claim for wrongful dismissal. The original justification put forward by the Donovan Commission[157] for an upper limit (of two years' salary) was to enable employers to take out liability insurance, although the desirability of facilitating the avoidance of the deterrent element of the law of unfair dismissal by liability

---

[154] Employment Protection (Recoupment of Jobseeker's Allowance and Income Support) Regulations 1996, SI 1996 No. 2349.

[155] D. Lewis, 'Losing Benefits Through Misconduct: Time to Stop Punishing the Unemployed?' [1985] *Journal of Social Welfare Law* 145, at 149.

[156] *Leonard* v. *Strathclyde Buses Ltd* [1998] IRLR 693 (Ct of Sess., Inner House).

[157] Cmnd 3623, para. 554.

insurance must be doubted. A more cynical explanation of the upper limit, especially as it was eroded by inflation in the 1980s and early 1990s, is that the limit ensures that it will never be prohibitively expensive for employers to make a dismissal.

A proposal to abolish the upper limit on compensation entirely was dropped in the face of pressure from employers, which argued that the proposal would lead to an avalanche of new claims and would discourage settlements. These arguments seem unconvincing. The removal of an upper limit would surely make employers more cautious before dismissing highly paid employees, thereby reducing the number of dismissals and consequent claims. It is true that the upper limit assists settlements for highly paid employees, because the upper limit in effect determines the amount of compensation. But this fixed solution applies perhaps only to a hundred or so of the highest paid employees who commence an application for unfair dismissal in any given year; for the remaining thousands of settlements, the upper limit is in practice irrelevant. Even so, for those employees who are denied full compensation for their losses, which is most likely to happen when a reinstatement order has be rejected by the employer and the employee seeks arrears of wages as well as compensation for a future period of unemployment, the upper limit provides a disincentive to employers to comply with the standards of the law. 'There is a degree of arbitrariness in such a cap, and anyone against whom it operates is bound to see it as unfair.'[158]

Effectiveness

Many employers assert that the law of unfair dismissal makes it nearly impossible to dismiss employees. They lobby governments to restrict the impact of claims for unfair dismissal by various devices such as extending the qualifying period, creating procedural and financial obstacles for making tribunal claims, and placing an upper limit on the amount of compensation that may be awarded. Operating under the belief that the law of unfair dismissal makes it extremely inadvisable to dismiss anyone, within larger firms, the human resources departments are usually extremely risk averse, avoiding if at all possible dismissing anyone for misconduct or incompetence, and always requiring elaborate procedures prior to dismissal.

As we have seen in this chapter, however, the law is very different from the myths told about it in management circles. It is true that the law requires a fair procedure in most cases, but summary dismissal is certainly permitted in egregious cases of misconduct. With regard to substantive fairness, the RORR test grants employers a broad discretion to impose disciplinary action. In particular, if employers promulgate and communicate rules about misconduct

---

[158] *Per* Maurice Kay LJ, *Parry v. National Westminster Bank plc* [2004] EWCA Civ 1563, [2005] ICR 396, 401 (CA).

and competence and then follow those rules, it is most unlikely that a tribunal will find a dismissal to have been unfair. The upper limit on compensation has varied over the years, but even the relatively generous upper limit of a year's wages that applies at present should not deter dismissals in most instances if the employer has a strong reason for dismissal, and in any case the upper limit is only reached in a handful of awards by tribunals each year.

What may be most evident about this gap between management myth and legal reality is the persistent refusal by employers to accept protection against unjust dismissal as part of the culture of the organisation. With respect to discrimination law, most employers genuinely try to have an equal opportunities policy (though of course they may fall short of those aspirations), but with regard to the law of unfair dismissal, employers have not accepted the idea that they should only dismiss their employees fairly. Instead, employers still prefer to retain the unbridled discretion that they enjoyed under the common law to be able to dismiss an employee at any time, for any reason or no reason at all, on giving notice period wages. The idea that respect for the dignity of workers requires fairness in the exercise of disciplinary powers has not been accepted by many employers.

To make the law of unfair dismissal more effective by raising levels of voluntary compliance by employers therefore probably requires a different regulatory strategy. The standards of fairness need to become part of the employer's normal operational procedures. For this purpose, the standards need to become more specific, established by codes of practice and similar normative guides. The employer probably needs to be given an incentive to adopt those standards by gaining protection against claims for compensation or reinstatement, provided that the employer has genuinely complied with the detailed standards. The major difficulty with this 'safe harbour' regulatory strategy is, of course, to agree a set of standards applicable to the wide range of different kinds of undertakings. A possible model is that each employer should be required to agree a detailed disciplinary code with a recognised trade union, a workplace council or a labour inspector.

20

Economic Dismissal

Contents

This chapter examines the legal protections afforded to workers in the event of managerial decisions that require major changes in the business. The employer may become insolvent or the business may be sold to a new owner. Changing market conditions and technologies may force the employer to seek to reduce the number of employees, to alter their contractual terms or to recruit new staff with different skills. Most restructuring exercises aim to improve, at least in the short term, the profits and the value of shares in solvent and successful companies. Whatever the cause of the restructuring, it is likely to have a significant adverse impact on the number of jobs or the terms and conditions of employment. In Chapter 5 we considered the law governing changes in the terms of employment and the content of the job. Here we focus on dismissals for business or economic reasons. What legal rights do employees have in respect of these decisions, and are these rights adequate to protect their interests?

Competing Policies

Legal regulation in this sphere has been shaped by four dominant policy considerations. These policies push in different directions and are hard to reconcile. Having described these policies briefly, we will consider evidence about whether the law in fact has much of an impact in this field of economic dismissals.

Facilitating efficient use of capital: for the general purpose of increasing the wealth of the country, the first policy respects the importance of permitting the managers of businesses to make decisions to improve the profitability of the business or to minimise costs and losses. The law launches this policy through its general endorsement of freedom of contract. More specifically corporate law imposes a duty upon directors of companies to act in the best interests of the company, which is understood to mean usually the best interests of the shareholders or capital investors. Unless those interests are fully respected, investors will take their capital elsewhere. The capital market disciplines the management of a company to maximise the profits of the company and the law is reluctant to impede this process of wealth generation and inward investment. This policy points the law away from any restriction on management decisions about restructuring the business, because legal rights that protect workers' interests, including the opportunity to have a say in such decisions, might prevent or obstruct such wealth-maximising decisions.

From this perspective, economic dismissals are to be encouraged insofar as they represent necessary adjustments to changing technologies, product markets and competitive conditions which will enable firms to survive and to increase their competitiveness and profits. Although economic dismissals may be popularly regarded as a sign of economic decline and recession, they occur in large numbers even in periods of economic growth as part of competitive pressures and displacement of workers from one industrial sector to another. In 2018, when there were low levels of unemployment, there were about 400,000 redundancies each year, though during the financial crises and recession of 2008–9 the number reached about one million.[1]

Employment and job security: the second policy recognises, however, that employees have certain interests deserving protection. As well as enforcing contractual entitlements, workers claim protection for a broader range of interests. These interests include advance notification to employees about changes in the business, the opportunity to be consulted about the proposed changes, the protection of contractual rights if the business is sold to a new owner and the protection of an employee's interest in employment and economic security. Dismissals for redundancy dash any expectations of the employees for job security and threaten financial hardship and social exclusion. Workers' fears about these adverse effects no doubt lead to the pervasive use of euphemisms for economic dismissals among managers, such as downsizing, de-recruiting, de-layering, resizing and right-sizing. Employers may not always welcome economic dismissals either, not least because they damage the employer's credibility in offering good jobs, and will provoke among the retained workforce damaging reactions such as less commitment and heightened resistance to change. Nevertheless, managers and shareholders usually regard economic dismissals in the face of technological change and competitive pressures as inevitable and desirable in terms of efficiency and productivity in the long run.

Social costs: there is a public interest in reducing the social costs of business restructuring. These social costs include the costs to the government and taxpayers of providing economic support to the unemployed, the expense of retraining workers so that they can gain alternative employment and all kinds of hidden and indirect costs of plant closures such as health care and criminal justice that typically correlate to regions of high unemployment. There appears to be a correlation between economic dismissal and marital breakdowns and divorces. A government will also be concerned about the effects of social exclusion on displaced workers and the expense of reintegrating the long-term unemployed into society.

Regulatory competition: at the European level, there is an additional concern about competition between the Member States. Regulation of economic dismissals may discourage inward investment into an economy, for investors will be concerned that the regulation may impose costs on the business and make it hard to move capital elsewhere. To attract inward investment, Member States may be tempted to minimise their national regulation of economic dismissals. In turn, this deregulation may provoke a 'race to the bottom' in the sense that each state will compete by deregulating business further. To avoid the potential damage to workers from such regulatory

---

[1] Office for National Statistics, LFS: ILO redundancy level (thousands): UK.

competition and to help to reduce social costs, the EU has tried to establish a level playing field between Member States by requiring the harmonisation of laws about economic dismissal at or above some minimum standards.

It should be apparent that these policy considerations may conflict sharply in particular instances. If the shareholders of a company agree with a management proposal that their best interests lie in closing a plant (with a view perhaps to relocating the production abroad), the first policy supports this decision and rejects the need for any legal intervention. But the second policy expresses the concern that the interests of the workforce in stable jobs and in having a voice in decisions about the long-term fate of the business are being utterly ignored. And with regard to the third policy, the social costs of the shareholders' decision are almost certainly treated as externalities by the company; these are costs that can be safely ignored when making the decision to relocate the plant because they will not fall on the company and its shareholders. The resulting costs to the community of unemployment, social alienation and social exclusion may, however, be far higher than the marginal benefits to the wealth of the shareholders. If this calculation applies, the case for regulatory intervention to compel businesses to take into account externalities becomes powerful. If the proposed relocation of the plant were to be in another EU country because of its minimal rules on business restructuring, the facilitation of the export of jobs would no doubt make the EU unpopular with workers and discourage further economic integration.

Nevertheless, it should be acknowledged from the outset that it is dubious whether regulation designed to protect the interests of employees in the event of changes in the business has a significant impact on the conduct of employers, the economic position of workers or indeed the competitive advantage of nations. Many attempts have been made by economists to determine whether legal regulation has an impact on labour markets. A straightforward hypothesis is that the higher the levels of compensation that employers have to pay for dismissals made in the course of restructuring, the lower the levels of employment in the economy, for these severance payments represent an additional labour cost that should depress employers' demand for labour. Although there is some statistical support for this hypothesis,[2] the same statistics reveal that lengthy notice requirements, which are surely an equivalent cost, probably have the opposite effect.[3] In comparative studies between countries in order to test the effect of differences in legal regulation, another puzzling result emerges. Even though Germany has a much more elaborate system of employment protection than the United States, the two countries appear to adjust in similar ways and at similar speeds to business cycles. The

[2] E. P. Lazear, 'Job Security Provisions and Employment' (1990) 105 *Quarterly Journal of Economics* 699.

[3] J. T. Addison and J.-L. Grosso, 'Job Security Provisions and Employment: Revised Estimates' (1996) 35 *Industrial Relations* 585.

UK, with legal protections somewhere in the middle between Germany and the United States, exhibits stronger elasticities in levels of employment and hours (i.e. numbers employed and hours worked vary more significantly during business cycles), but these changes occur relatively slowly.[4]

These economic studies, although fascinating, share two weaknesses. First, it is difficult to generalise about legal systems in a comparative way, in order to determine whether or not they afford the workers high levels of protection. A simple comparison of statutory rules does not reveal how they may be interpreted in practice or the extent to which they are actually enforced. In addition, many aspects of labour law may impinge on managerial decisions to restructure the business; without considering the totality of regulation, one cannot grasp its possible impact. For example, in the United States, the social security system penalises employers who make economic dismissals by raising their contribution requirements, whereas this device is not used in the UK. Although the United States may figure in these comparative assessments as a jurisdiction that lacks regulation of economic dismissals, this additional tax burden may be far more influential than any regulation directed towards requiring severance payments. A second general weakness of these econometric studies is that, although they demonstrate that regulation may not be as important as might be commonly supposed, they do not reveal what factors are significant. We may surmise that complex institutional factors relating to managerial techniques play an important role, but the studies do not help to establish the validity of this idea. For example, in some countries such as Japan, it may be a central aspect of managerial technique to create a co-operative workforce by engaging in extensive consultation and by making a commitment to protect employment security. Variations in labour costs may be achieved, as in Japan, by making a large part of the salary bill dependent upon profit sharing, so that in the event of a downturn in business, there is a reduction in wages, but no dismissals or reductions in hours. The decision by management to approach changes in the business in such a way may reflect some aspect of the regulatory environment such as taxation. It may, alternatively, embody a conventional wisdom about successful methods of management. In any case, even if legal regulation of economic dismissals does have adverse employment effects, there may be offsetting benefits in other respects such as more rapid earnings growth, greater equality of earnings and the reduction of other social costs such as health care and crime.[5] With that important reservation about the impact of regulation in this field we now examine the principal types of legal regulation of managerial decisions involving changes in the business that adversely affect the interests of employees.

---

[4] C. F. Buechtemann, 'Introduction', in C. F. Buechtemann (ed.), *Employment Security and Labour Market Behaviour* (Ithaca, NY: ILR Press, 1993).

[5] R. Buchele and J. Christiansen, 'Do Employment and Income Security Cause Unemployment? A Comparative Study of the US and the E-4' (1998) 22 *Cambridge Journal of Economics* 117.

Dismissal for Redundancy

In the event of the employer planning economically motivated dismissals, two kinds of legal obligations will be triggered. The first concerns a duty to consult the workforce collectively, which arises from TULRCA 1992, sections 188–98, which implement Directive 98/59 on the approximation of the laws relating to collective redundancies. The scope and application of that duty is considered above.[6] The second legal duty placed upon employers is to give a dismissed employee a redundancy payment or, in some cases, compensation for unfair dismissal. This chapter is concerned primarily with the rights of individual employees in the event of economic dismissals.

Redundancy and Unfair Dismissal

An economic dismissal may permit a claim for a redundancy payment or compensation for unfair dismissal or both. From the employee's perspective, it is desirable to obtain the higher level of compensation for unfair dismissal, if possible, but there is a risk in pursuing a claim for unfair dismissal that the employee will end up with no compensation at all.

The first question to consider is whether the reason for the dismissal falls within the statutory concept of redundancy (to be considered shortly). If the reason does qualify as redundancy, the employee is entitled to a redundancy payment. In addition, however, the employee may claim that the dismissal was also unfair. Although redundancy counts as a substantial reason for dismissal, the employer's decision to make the dismissal may be regarded as unreasonable under ERA 1996, section 98(4). The claim that the dismissal for redundancy was unreasonable will usually be based either on the ground that the employer failed to follow a fair procedure of consultation prior to the dismissal or that the employee was unfairly selected for dismissal in comparison with other employees who were not dismissed.

If the economic dismissal does not qualify for a redundancy payment under the statutory concept of redundancy, the employer must seek to justify it on the ground that the dismissal was for 'some other substantial reason' and that it was reasonable to dismiss the employee for that reason. We have already considered some cases of that kind in connection with the variation of the terms of the contract of employment.[7] If the employer succeeds in demonstrating that the dismissal was fair for some other substantial reason, no compensation whatsoever will be due from the employer.

Many of the cases that we shall consider, although in form a claim for unfair dismissal against an employer, involve a conflict of interest within the workforce about which workers should be selected for redundancy. Those who are selected for dismissal may express this claim in two ways. One is to admit that

---

[6] See Chapter 15.   [7] See Chapter 5.

the dismissal was for redundancy, but to argue that the dismissal was nevertheless unfair owing to the employer's use of unfair procedures or selection criteria. The other route is to challenge whether the employee was redundant at all, and to argue instead that the employee was still required by the employer, although other workers, who have not been dismissed, may have been redundant. If successful, this second argument may lead to the conclusion that the employer has not established a substantial reason for dismissal, so the dismissal was unfair. This second way of challenging selection for redundancy poses difficult questions for the courts on the meaning of the statutory concept of redundancy.

Aim of Redundancy Payments

Legal regulation of economic dismissals reveals the competing and sometimes ambiguous policy goals of governments. The legislation, introduced originally as the Redundancy Payments Act 1965 and now contained in ERA 1996, Part XI, provides employees with the right to claim compensation for economic dismissals. The redundancy payment, which is normally the same as the basic award for unfair dismissal,[8] is calculated under a formula by reference to the statutory concept of the weekly wage, years of service (with an upper limit of twenty) and the age of the worker:

(a) one-and-a-half weeks' pay for each year of employment in which the employee was not below the age of forty-one;

(b) one week's pay for each year of employment (not within paragraph (a)) in which he was not below the age of twenty-two; and

(c) half a week's pay for each year of employment not within paragraph (a) or (b).[9]

The right to this severance payment was presented by some of its proponents as a protection of the employee's expectation of job security by deterring employers from making workforce reductions and compensating employees for the loss of their jobs. Yet in the original legislation, the government provided employers with a subsidy when making redundancy payments. The subsidy reduced the deterrent effect of the legislation against workforce reductions, because the government did not wish to discourage employers from making efficient adjustments to the workforce. The government believed that, by compelling employers to adopt the practice of making severance payments, the practice of making redundancies would become more acceptable to both

---

[8] See Chapter 19. The statutory concept of week's pay is defined in ERA 1996, ss. 220–6. The maximum amount of a week's pay in ERA 1996, s. 227 applies to redundancy payments. In the context of lay-offs and short-time working, special rules determine the date of assessment of the weekly wage: ERA 1996, s. 226(4) and (6).

[9] ERA 1996, s. 162(2).

sides of industry, thus enabling businesses to become more competitive by the reduction of over-manning and the introduction of new technology. An early survey of employers and trade unions confirmed that three-quarters of employers believed that the legislation had made it easier to dismiss employees for redundancy.[10] The subsidy to employers was gradually withdrawn in the 1980s, however, as the policy objective became increasingly one of discouraging economic dismissals, owing to the mounting social costs of high levels of unemployment.

The tensions in the policy behind the regulation of economic dismissals run through judicial interpretations of the legislation. Often it is unclear whether it is to the advantage of an employer or an employee to seek a broad or a narrow interpretation of the application of the redundancy payments legislation. A court that is sympathetic to the managerial objective of saving the business or improving efficiency might wish to minimise the employer's liability to make severance payments by a restrictive interpretation of the statutory concept of redundancy. Yet a court with the same motivation might equally take the opposite stance: to award redundancy payments wherever possible, in order to encourage workers to accept the need for a workforce reduction and, in the past, to enable the employer to obtain a subsidy. After 1971 (and especially after the introduction of the basic award for unfair dismissal in 1975), with the advent of the greater potential compensation for unfair dismissal, a court with the same motivation would be even keener to make the employer liable to pay a redundancy payment, in order to help the employer to avoid the greater liability for compensation for unfair dismissal. It is often the employee who contests that he or she is redundant in the hope of obtaining the superior level of compensation for unfair dismissal.

Qualifying Conditions for Redundancy Payments

The right to claim a redundancy payment for an economic dismissal is subject to various statutory conditions. Like other statutory claims for dismissal, the right is confined to employees.[11] It does not apply therefore to the kind of dependent contractors such as consultants and freelancers who might fall within the statutory definition of a 'worker'. As the highlighted extract from a newspaper makes clear, one of the main advantages to employers of using agency workers is that they avoid any of the legal obligations triggered by economic dismissals. The qualifying period for the right to a redundancy payment is two years.[12]

---

[10] S. R. Parker, C. G. Thomas, N. D. Ellis and W. E. J. McCarthy, *Effects of the Redundancy Payments Act* (London: HMSO, 1971).

[11] Although there is power to make exceptions by regulation: ERA 1996, s. 171.

[12] ERA 1996, s. 155.

The right to a redundancy payment is, of course, inapplicable when the principal reason for dismissal concerned factors personal to the employee, such as misconduct. Where this misconduct is strike action in response to a notice of dismissal for redundancy, however, the claim for a redundancy payment is usually preserved.[13]

The right to claim a redundancy payment is normally conditional on an employee establishing the fact of a dismissal by the employer. For this purpose, the statutory concept of dismissal discussed in Chapter 19 in connection with the law of unfair dismissal applies. In particular, it should be noted that calls for volunteers for redundancy or 'early retirement' amount to a request for an agreed termination of the contract, which falls outside the statutory concept of dismissal, so that employees taking early retirement may relinquish any claim to a statutory redundancy payment.[14] It is also worth remembering that the expiration of a fixed-term contract counts as a dismissal. It follows that a researcher on a fixed-term contract (for two or more years) that expires when the funding for research ends may claim a redundancy payment.[15] As an exception to the statutory concept of dismissal, however, an employee may bring a claim for a redundancy payment under detailed statutory rules if he or she terminates the contract of employment, after having given notice, in response to prolonged lay-offs or periods of short-time working during which the employee is not paid or receives less than half pay.[16] In a further special provision applicable to redundancies, if the employer gives notice of dismissal for redundancy, an employee may decide to leave early in order to take up another job. The legislation tries to balance the interests of the employee in looking for a new job and the interests of the employer in carrying out the planned reduction of the workforce: if the employee leaves early, the employer can withdraw the redundancy payment, but the employee has a right to claim all or part of the redundancy payment on the ground that in the circumstances it would be 'just and equitable'.[17]

Uproar in Cowley as BMW Confirms 850 job cuts at Mini Factory

Weekend working to end from 2 March
Agency workers given just one hour's notice of redundancies

There was anger today as BMW confirmed that 850 jobs were being cut by ending weekend working at its Mini car plant near Oxford. The cuts will mostly affect agency workers when they come into force from 2 March when the plant begins operating five days a week,

---

[13] ERA 1996, s. 140(2).   [14] *Birch* v. *Liverpool University* [1985] ICR 470 (CA).
[15] However, the statutory duty to consult does not arise on the expiration of a fixed-term contract: TULRCA 1992, s. 282.
[16] ERA 1996, ss. 147–54.   [17] ERA 1996, s. 142.

instead of the current seven. Union sources said workers booed and threw apples and oranges at managers after being told they were losing their jobs.

Agency workers leaving Cowley this morning expressed their fury at being given just one hour's notice of the redundancies. 'It's a disgrace. I feel as though I've been used', said one worker. 'We should have been given one month's notice, not one hour.' Axed agency staff were given the grim news in meetings at the factory following weekend speculation that hundreds of jobs were to go.

Almost a third of the Cowley workforce are agency staff and some complained today they would not receive any redundancy pay. The contract staff, who have few employment rights, were brought in to work alongside full-time employees on the production lines, which built 230,000 vehicles last year.

Tony Woodley, the joint leader of the Unite union, said: 'The manner in which these cuts were announced today was disgraceful. It is tough enough for workers in those car companies who have seen their market collapse in recent months, but BMW makes a top-selling product in the Mini and owed it to staff to treat them better. Sacking an entire shift like this, and targeting agency workers who have no rights to redundancy pay, is blatant opportunism on BMW's part and nothing short of scandalous. BMW's parent company couldn't attempt this in Germany because it would be illegal to do so. It is a disgrace, therefore, that workers in this country can be so casually thrown to the dole.'[18]

Statutory Concept of Redundancy

The statutory concept of redundancy is presented in ERA 1996, section 139(1).

Employment Rights Act 1996, Section 139(1)

For the purposes of this Act an employee who is dismissed will be taken to be dismissed by reason of redundancy if the dismissal is wholly or mainly attributable to –

(a) the fact that his employer has ceased or intends to cease –
  (i) to carry on the business for the purposes of which the employee was employed by him, or
  (ii) to carry on that business in the place where the employee was so employed, or
(b) the fact that the requirements of that business –
  (i) for employees to carry out work of a particular kind, or
  (ii) for employees to carry out work of a particular kind in the place where the employee was employed by the employer

have ceased or diminished or are expected to cease or diminish.

---

[18] T. Macalister and H. Pidd, www.guardian.co.uk, Monday 16 February 2009.

This definition of the concept of redundancy is surprisingly complicated. It does not apply generally to dismissals for business or economic reasons, or for reasons unconnected with the personal conduct or circumstances of the dismissed employee. Such a broader definition of redundancy or economic dismissals is used, however, in the context of the duty to consult workforce representatives about economic dismissals under TULRCA 1992, section 195(1).

Trade Union and Labour Relations (Consolidation) Act 1992, section 195(1)

In this chapter references to dismissal as redundant are references to dismissal for a reason not related to the individual concerned or for a number of reasons all of which are not so related.

Since that broader test seeks to implement EU law,[19] it must conform to the EU concept of redundancy, as developed by the CJEU, which encompasses any dismissals that are not related to the individual concerned, including cases of constructive dismissal where an employee resigns in the face of unilateral changes to the contract of employment to the significant detriment of the employee.[20]

Instead of this broad test, the national statutory definition of redundancy used for the purpose of claiming individual compensation introduces some further conditions: either a diminution in requirements 'for employees to carry out work of a particular kind' or a similar diminution in the 'place where the employee was so employed'. The latter condition provokes questions about where the employee worked. The former condition provokes disagreements about what kind of work the employee was required to perform, and whether the employer has a reduced demand for that kind of work. These questions are avoided by the broader definition of redundancy used for the purpose of triggering the employer's obligation to consult. In particular, it is clear that an employer's decision to alter the terms of employment of a group of workers unilaterally (a constructive dismissal) will fall within the broad concept of redundancy for the purpose of consultation, even though the employer has no intention of reducing the number of workers and therefore will probably not be liable to pay redundancy payments.[21]

---

[19] Directive 98/59 on the approximation of the law of the Member States relating to collective redundancies 20 July 1998.

[20] Case C-422/14, *Pujante Rivera* v. *Gestora Clubs Dir SL* EU:C:2015:743, [2016] ICR 227; Case C-429/16, *Ciupa* v. *Szpital Ginekologiczno-Położniczy im dr L Rydygiera sp z oo w Lodzi* EU:C:2017:711, [2018] ICR 249.

[21] *GMB* v. *Man Truck & Bus UK Ltd* [2000] IRLR 636 (EAT).

In both statutory definitions of the concept of redundancy, however, it is clear that the tribunal is not required to decide whether the managerial decision was sensible, necessary or justifiable. A tribunal is not permitted to assess whether in the circumstances the management strategy of making employees redundant furthered the business goals of the employers. The law requires courts and tribunals to respect the managerial decision to engage in restructuring; the only question is whether and how much compensation should be payable to individual workers who lose their jobs.

Although we shall focus on some of the complexities surrounding the statutory definition of redundancy in ERA 1996, section 139, at the margins, we should recognise that most economic dismissals will be covered, and so the employer will be required to pay a redundancy payment. Typical instances of redundancy include plant closures, the reduction of the size of the workforce in order to reduce labour costs, the reduction of the workforce as a result of the introduction of new technology or capital equipment, the elimination of some jobs on the ground that there is overstaffing,[22] the elimination of a job and the introduction of a new job requiring different skills[23] and the insolvency of the business leading to its closure. Here, we examine three particularly contested topics related to the boundaries of the statutory concept of redundancy.

Perhaps the underlying source of this complexity in the application of the statutory concept of redundancy can best be understood by referring to the contrast between 'employment security' and 'job security'. Protection for employment security suggests that compensation should be awarded only if the employee has been dismissed, not when the particular job performed or the terms and conditions have been varied although there is still work for the employee, perhaps involving different skills. Protection for job security would in contrast provide compensation whenever the employee's particular job was no longer required, even though the employee might have been offered alternative employment by the same employer. The phrase, 'work of a particular kind', in the statute is susceptible to the interpretation that it requires compensation for job security, not just employment security. It therefore implies that a redundancy payment should be awarded where a particular job disappears, even though the employer immediately offers another job to the dismissed employee. This aim of protecting job security could be plausibly attributed to the legislation as a device to encourage employees to be flexible in the sense of giving up rigid job demarcations in return for compensation. But in general the courts have been reluctant to accept this interpretation and have instead preferred the view that redundancy payments should only be made when the employer is actually reducing the number of employees as opposed

---

[22] *Carry All Motors Ltd* v. *Pennington* [1980] IRLR 455 (EAT); *Robinson* v. *British Island Airways Ltd* [1977] IRLR 477 (EAT).

[23] *Murphy* v. *Epsom College* [1985] ICR 80 (CA).

to reorganising the workforce. Furthermore, the view that the concept of redundancy protects job security is hard to square with the provisions considered below, under which the employer can avoid paying compensation by making an offer of suitable alternative employment.

Reorganisation Involving New Job Specifications

We have noted already that the most common response of employers to changing business conditions is to seek to vary the terms of employment. These variations may involve minor reductions of hours or the elimination of overtime, or they may encompass a more fundamental restructuring of the business. In the 1990s, a common managerial response to competitive pressures involved 'de-layering', which involves the elimination of many middle-management positions and the redesignation of some existing jobs to lower positions of responsibility in the hierarchy of the organisation. These business reorganisations often involve dismissals, either because the employer dismisses employees and invites them to apply for the new jobs, or because the employees refuse to agree to the variations in the terms of the contract of employment so that there is a constructive dismissal. It was established in early cases that variations in the terms of employment for reasons of efficiency did not necessarily amount to cases of redundancy. For example, a change in the hours of work without a reduction in the amount of work to be performed,[24] or the withdrawal of a free bus service to enable employees to reach the workplace,[25] were not instances of redundancy. In *Lesney Products & Co. v. Nolan*,[26] as sales of the factory's product fell, the employers introduced a new shift system. The night shift was eliminated by dismissals, and the day work was divided into two shifts. The amount of production and the number of workers required during the day remained the same, but the employers reduced costs by eliminating overtime payments through the new shift system. Several employees refused to work the new day-shift system, no doubt because it reduced their wages by about one-third owing to the loss of overtime payments, and were dismissed. Their claims for redundancy payments were upheld by an industrial tribunal, but the Court of Appeal allowed the employer's appeal. The dismissals were not for redundancy, because there was no drop in the amount of work required during the day. Lord Denning MR viewed the claims for redundancy payments as a potential interference with restructuring for efficiency:

---

[24] *Johnson* v. *Nottinghamshire Combined Police Authority* [1974] ICR 170 (CA); reductions in hours of work corresponding to a reduction in the employer's needs for work to be performed is a redundancy: *Packman* v. *Fauchon* [2012] ICR 1362 (EAT).
[25] *Chapman* v. *Goonvean and Rostowrack China Clay Co. Ltd* [1973] ICR 310 (CA).
[26] [1977] ICR 235 (CA).

> [I]t is important that nothing should be done to impair the ability of employers to reorganise their work force and their times and conditions of work so as to improve efficiency. They may reorganise it so as to reduce overtime and thus to save themselves money, but that does not give the man a right to redundancy payment. Overtime might be reduced, for instance, by taking on more men: but that would not give the existing staff a right to redundancy payments. Also when overtime is reduced by a reorganisation or working hours, that does not give rise to a right to a redundancy payment, so long as the work to be done is the same.

This decision left open the possibility that major changes in the terms of employment, such as the creation of a completely new job specification, might amount to a redundancy. The old job would be eliminated and replaced by the new one, with a different title and varied duties and remuneration. The legal question was whether the elimination of the old job and its replacement with a new position meant that the employer's requirements for employees to perform work of a particular kind had diminished. One answer, sometimes described as the 'job-function' approach, examines the work actually done by different employees, and concludes that the redundant employees are those whose 'jobs have gone' in the sense that the tasks are no longer required. A different answer is to look at the terms of the contracts of employment in order to decide which employees are no longer required. The continuing presence or the replacement of job titles and packages of terms indicate whether employees are no longer required. The Court of Appeal in *Lesney Products & Co. v. Nolan* appeared to suggest that the effect of contractual variation should be determined by reference to the work performed, that is, a job-function approach: if the employees were performing much the same work, albeit under different terms of employment, their dismissal for rejecting the new terms would not be a redundancy dismissal. In other decisions, however, courts appeared to place greater weight on the terms of the contract: if the terms remained the same, though the duties varied as a result of the reorganisation, the employee would not be redundant. A workshop manager of car repairs for a garage was dismissed after thirty years of service because he could not cope with new working methods required by the new owners of the business, which included increased paperwork and the provision of estimates in advance to customers, but according to the court he was not redundant because the garage still required a manager, albeit one with different skills.[27]

In more recent cases, however, with the approval of the House of Lords in *Murray v. Foyle Meats Ltd*,[28] the approach to business reorganisations involving variations in the contract or the job has rejected both the job-function and the contract-package tests. The issue is said simply to be whether there has been a reduction of the workforce as a result of a business reorganisation, and whether the dismissal under consideration was connected to that reduction.

---

[27] *North Riding Garages v. Butterwick* [1967] 2 QB 56 (QB).   [28] [1999] ICR 827 (HL).

The terms of the contract or the actual job performed by an employee may be relevant to the question of causation, in the sense that the employee will not have been dismissed for redundancy if the need for dismissals occurs in another part of the business in which the employee has not worked and could not be required to work under the terms of the contract. This approach seems to attribute little significance to the phrase in the statute 'work of a particular kind'.

A leading and difficult example of this interpretation of the concept of redundancy is the decision of the EAT in *Safeway Stores plc* v. *Burrell*.[29] The employer engaged in a major restructuring of its supermarket business involving 'de-layering' of middle management and the reorganisation of departments. The applicant was employed as petrol-station manager at the filling station located at the site of one of the supermarkets. The reorganisation plan involved the disappearance of the post of petrol-station manager and its replacement by the grade of petrol-station controller at a lower rate of pay. Much of the work required under the new job description remained the same as under the former position. Furthermore, although the former job description carried additional managerial responsibilities, in practice the employee had not performed them. So the job remained much the same in practice, but the new contractual package differed substantially. The employee decided not to apply for the new post on the ground that his pay would be reduced, and he was given a redundancy payment. Subsequently, he claimed unfair dismissal. By a majority, the ET decided that the employers had not demonstrated that the employee was redundant, because the new job involved much the same work as the employee had performed formerly in practice, so there was no diminution in the employer's requirement for 'work of a particular kind'. On appeal against the finding of unfair dismissal, the EAT held that the tribunal had adopted the wrong test of redundancy and remitted the case for a rehearing. The correct test was to ask, first, whether there was a diminution of the employer's requirement for employees and, secondly, whether the dismissal was caused by that diminution. According to the EAT, the terms of the contract of employment or the actual work performed were not relevant to those questions. Presumably, in this case, the tribunal would have concluded that the de-layering exercise did necessarily produce dismissals and that this dismissal was caused by that exercise.

What does this decision imply about the application of the statutory concept of redundancy to business reorganisations? If the employer reduces the number of employees overall, provided that the dismissal of any individual is attributable to this workforce reduction rather than some other reason or motive, the dismissal should be regarded as a case of redundancy. A reduction of the number of employees may occur if the employer requires fewer hours

---

[29] [1997] ICR 523 (EAT).

from the same number of employees.[30] In the case of *Safeway Stores plc* v. *Burrell*, the issue was whether the supermarket had reduced its number of employees or merely reorganised the same number of employees. As the de-layering did involve the reduction of managerial employees across the organisation, on this reasoning the applicant was dismissed for redundancy if the dismissal was part of that reorganisation. The terms of the contract of employment are relevant only to this question of causation: the employers were dismissing only middle managers and the terms of Mr Burrell's employment placed him in that category. If the employer continues to require the same number of employees, albeit on different terms and conditions or performing different tasks, in general the conclusion should be that any dismissal is not on the ground of redundancy. The unilateral variation of terms of employment, including new designations of jobs, new job descriptions and alterations in hours and wages, does not in itself create a redundancy situation.

Yet there does come a point when the variation of the job description becomes so great that a court will conclude that, even though the number of employees remains constant, the new job description is so different that in effect the old job has disappeared and a completely new one has been created. This is the explanation of *Murphy* v. *Epsom College*,[31] where the applicant was one of two plumbers employed by a school. His work consisted mainly of general plumbing work. The employers decided to employ a heating technician to maintain their improved heating system. They then decided to dismiss one of the two plumbers and selected the employee for dismissal. The Court of Appeal upheld the majority view of the industrial tribunal that the reason for dismissal was redundancy. The employer originally had two plumbers; now it only required one (plus a heating engineer). The employee was dismissed by reason of redundancy. In order to reach the determination that one job has disappeared altogether, it seems to be necessary to examine and compare the terms of employment of the two jobs. The effort in *Safeway Stores plc* v. *Burrell* to exclude consideration of the terms of the contract cannot therefore be followed entirely. The terms can be relevant both to the question of causation and also to the prior question whether the workforce has been reduced.

If this continuing relevance of the terms of employment is correct, however, it throws in doubt the straightforward disposal of the claim in *Safeway Stores plc* v. *Burrell*. Although the store reduced its number of managers in general, with respect to the petrol-station operation, it still required someone to perform much the same job as that performed by Mr Burrell, albeit with a different job title and lower wages. To say that there is a redundancy in such a case requires the tribunal both to ignore the terms of employment and to rely on them. The terms must be ignored for the purpose of lumping together all

---

[30] *Packman* v. *Fauchon* [2012] ICR 1362 (EAT).   [31] [1985] ICR 80 (CA).

the middle managers in order to demonstrate a workforce reduction. But then, paradoxically, the tribunal must rely upon the terms of the contract to demonstrate that, despite the fact that Mr Burrell's job still needed to be done by someone, it no longer existed because the precise job title, although not the job function, had disappeared in the reorganisation. The reluctance of the EAT to examine either the job function or the terms of employment seems to mark a strong rejection of the idea that redundancy payments should protect job security. Instead, the emphasis on the issue of whether there was a dismissal linked to a reduction in the workforce suggests that the court regards the protection of employment security as the principal objective of the redundancy payments scheme.

Flexibility Clauses

As we have noted in an earlier chapter,[32] many employers insert a flexibility clause into contracts of employment. This term permits the employer to direct employees to perform a wide range of tasks, even though in practice each employee is primarily employed to work on a particular job. If the employer decides to reduce the workforce, perhaps in response to a drop in product demand or to improve efficiency, the question arises of which employees are redundant. Since, in theory, under the flexibility clause, all or most employees are interchangeable, there is no apparent ground for determining which employees are redundant. Under the 'contractual approach', it is arguable that the insertion of a flexibility clause into the contracts of employment of the workforce means that no particular employee can be singled out as no longer required; all employees working under a broad flexibility clause are equally vulnerable to job loss because they all perform the same work of a particular kind. According to this approach, the employer must therefore adopt a policy that ensures a fair selection from the whole workforce, not just the employees who normally work on the jobs that are being lost.

The House of Lords rejected this interpretation of the concept of redundancy in *Murray* v. *Foyle Meats Ltd.*[33] The employer ran a slaughterhouse business. In response to a decline in the market, the employer decided to eliminate one production line in the slaughter hall. After consultation with the union on the criteria of selection, the employer dismissed thirty-five 'meat plant operatives' who worked in the slaughter hall as redundant. The employees of the company were all employed on similar contractual terms and were subject to flexibility clauses, so that they could (and sometimes did) work in other departments such as the boning hall or the loading bay. The dismissed employees argued that it was wrong for the company to select for redundancy solely those who normally worked in the slaughter hall, because all employees

---

[32] See Chapter 5.   [33] [1999] ICR 827 (HL).

could be instructed to work there under the flexibility clause. Approving the decision in *Safeway Stores plc* v. *Burrell*, Lord Irvine rejected this argument on the ground that for a finding of redundancy all that is required was a reduction in the size of the workforce and a causal link to the dismissal because it was attributable wholly or mainly to that diminution in the workforce:

> My Lords, the language of [Employment Rights Act 1996, section 139(1)(b)] is in my view simplicity itself. It asks two questions of fact. The first is whether one or other of various states of economic affairs exists. In this case, the relevant one is whether the requirements of the business for employees to carry out work of a particular kind have diminished. The second question is whether the dismissal is attributable, wholly or mainly, to that state of affairs. This is a question of causation. In the present case, the Tribunal found as a fact that the requirements of the business for employees to work in the slaughter hall had diminished. Secondly, they found that that state of affairs had led to the appellants being dismissed. That, in my opinion, is the end of the matter.

Once the employer had decided to discontinue one production line, whichever employees lost their jobs as a consequence, they would have been redundant. The effect of the decision in *Murray* v. *Foyle Meats Ltd* is to prevent employees working under a broad flexibility clause from challenging their selection for economic dismissal on the ground that they were not redundant, or no more redundant than many other employees or even the whole workforce. In this context, the court attributes little or no meaning at all to the phrase 'work of a particular kind'. The question is simply whether the employer has a reduced demand for workers. If such a workforce reduction is required, then the second question is simply whether or not that business requirement caused the dismissal.

Place of Work and Mobility Clauses

The application of the concept of redundancy to plant closures is usually straightforward. But where an employer carries on business at several sites and the reduction in the workforce applies at only one site, the issue can arise of whether the dismissed employees are redundant. If the employer is transferring a business from one site to another, with no reduction of the workforce overall, the issue of redundancy turns on whether or not the place of work of the dismissed employees was at only one site. The presence of a mobility clause in the contract that permits the employer to direct an employee to work at any site might suggest that the place of work extends to all the sites of the business. But the courts have disapproved such reliance on mobility clauses and have looked primarily at the actual performance of the work in order to determine the place of work. The place where the employee was employed 'is to be established by a factual inquiry, taking into account the employee's fixed or changing place or places of work and any contractual terms which go to evidence or define the place of employment and its extent, but not those (if any) which make provision for the employee to be transferred to another'.[34] 'If an employee has worked in only one location under his contract of employment for the purposes of the employer's business, it defies common sense to widen the extent of the place where he was so employed merely because of the existence of a mobility clause.'[35]

There appears to be a common theme in these decisions concerning the statutory concept of redundancy. Courts insist that the tribunals should avoid technicalities and detailed reference to the terms of employment in order to decide whether the statutory concept of redundancy has been satisfied. These technical points are often raised by employees who feel aggrieved at their treatment and selection for redundancy. In order to claim the superior measure of compensation for unfair dismissal, employees seek to persuade the tribunal that they were not dismissed for redundancy. By insisting that a reduction in the number of employees suffices to support a finding of redundancy, and by asserting that flexibility and mobility clauses in the contract of employment are irrelevant to the statutory concept, the courts have in recent years placed considerable obstacles in the way of such technical arguments. Whether or not these interpretations ultimately disadvantage employees in their quest for higher levels of compensation is doubtful.

Claims for Unfair Dismissal

Some other Substantial Reason for Dismissal

As we noted in Chapter 5, if the dismissal is not for reasons of redundancy, an economic dismissal will be classified as 'some other substantial reason for dismissal'. The question then becomes whether it was reasonable to dismiss the employee for that reason under the general test of fairness contained in ERA 1996, section 98(4). If a tribunal concludes that it was reasonable for the employer to dismiss for that business reason, the employee will fail to obtain any compensation for loss of a job. Many claims for economic dismissal will therefore receive no compensation, as in cases considered above: *Hollister* v. *National Farmers' Union*[36] and *Richmond Precision Engineering Ltd* v. *Pearce*.[37] The strategy adopted by some employees (such as Mr Burrell in *Safeway Stores plc* v. *Burrell*) of denying that they are redundant in the hope of obtaining higher compensation for unfair dismissal is therefore a risky one, because employees may end up with no compensation at all. The employer could rely on the de-layering policy and Mr Burrell's refusal to accept the new

[34] *Bass Leisure Ltd* v. *Thomas* [1994] IRLR 104 (EAT).
[35] *High Table Ltd* v. *Horst* [1998] ICR 409 (CA), *per* Peter Gibson LJ.
[36] [1979] ICR 542 (CA).   [37] [1985] IRLR 179 (EAT).

contract as a substantial reason for dismissal, and successfully insist that it was reasonable to dismiss Mr Burrell for that reason.

Fairness of Selection for Redundancy

In practice, it seems that the only way in which an employee who loses his or her job for economic reasons can obtain the higher level of compensation provided by a claim for unfair dismissal is to allege either unfair selection for redundancy or the failure to follow a fair procedure. The tribunals must apply the general test of unfairness for unfair dismissal in order to determine whether or not it was reasonable in the circumstances to dismiss the employee for redundancy. The tribunal may find that the dismissal was unfair in view of the absence of a fair procedure such as individual consultation with the employee or because it was unreasonable to select this particular employee for redundancy in comparison with another who was not laid off.

The legal principles applicable to unfair dismissal claims in the context of redundancy were first fully articulated by Browne-Wilkinson J in *Williams* v. *Compair Maxam Ltd.*[38] In that case, following a dramatic fall in orders from customers, the employer decided to reorganise the business and reduce labour costs. The works manager asked departmental managers to 'pick a team' for the department, so that the business could remain viable if those staff members were retained. The departmental managers chose employees to retain on the basis of personal preference and what was in the best interests of the company. The union was not consulted on the principles of selection. Other employees were dismissed for redundancy and they were given notice payments and further payments considerably in excess of their statutory entitlements. Five dismissed workers claimed unfair dismissal, but the industrial tribunal, by a majority, dismissed their claims, holding that it was reasonable for the employer to decide to retain those employees whom the managers regarded as being those who would keep the company viable in the long run. The EAT held that the tribunal had committed an error of law by reaching a decision that was perverse; the dismissals were unfair because they had been carried out in blatant contravention of the standards of fair treatment generally accepted by fair employers. In connection with dismissals for redundancy, the RORR test of fairness in the law of unfair dismissal required employers to adopt the principles of procedure and selection that, in current industrial practice, a reasonable employer would be expected to adopt. Although the fair conduct of redundancy dismissals must depend on the circumstances of each case, the following principles apply where the employees are represented by an independent trade union recognised by the employer:

---

[38] [1982] ICR 156 (EAT).

(1) The employer will seek to give as much warning as possible of impending redundancies so as to enable the union and employees who may be affected to take early steps to inform themselves of the relevant facts, consider possible alternative solutions and, if necessary, find alternative employment in the undertaking or elsewhere.

(2) The employer will consult the union as to the best means by which the desired management result can be achieved fairly and with as little hardship to the employees as possible. In particular, the employer will seek to agree with the union the criteria to be applied in selecting the employees to be made redundant. When a selection has been made, the employer will consider with the union whether the selection has been made in accordance with those criteria.

(3) Whether or not an agreement as to the criteria to be adopted has been agreed with the union, the employer will seek to establish criteria for selection which so far as possible do not depend solely upon the opinion of the person making the selection but can be objectively checked against such things as attendance record, efficiency at the job, experience, or length of service.

(4) The employer will seek to ensure that the selection is made fairly in accordance with these criteria and will consider any representations the union may make as to such selection.

(5) The employer will seek to see whether instead of dismissing an employee he could offer him alternative employment.[39]

These principles were generally endorsed by the House of Lords in *Polkey v. A. E. Dayton Services Ltd*,[40] where Lord Bridge stated:

> [I]n the case of redundancy, the employer will normally not act reasonably unless he warns and consults any employees affected or their representative, adopts a fair basis on which to select for redundancy and takes such steps as may be reasonable to avoid or minimise redundancy by redeployment within his own organisation.

It is important to recall, however, that, even if a tribunal concludes that an employer should have consulted the individual employee or a representative trade union prior to a dismissal for redundancy, the tribunal still has the discretion not to award compensation if it believes that the consultation would not have affected the outcome. This limitation on the compensatory award, already encountered and known as the '*Polkey* deduction',[41] subverts the procedural protection provided by the law of unfair dismissal dramatically, because the employer can usually argue extremely plausibly that workforce reductions were inevitable, so that consultation would have made no difference to the final outcome. If that argument is accepted, although the employee who

---

[39] *Ibid., per* Browne-Wilkinson J.   [40] [1988] ICR 142 (HL).   [41] See Chapter 19.

has been dismissed for redundancy has not been treated fairly, the additional compensation for unfair dismissal may be nil or merely reflect a short period of employment during which consultation should have taken place..

With regard to the issue of unfair selection for redundancy, the crucial phrases in the principles set out in *Williams* v. *Compair Maxam Ltd* are that the criteria for selection should be 'objective' and that the criteria should be followed. The fairness standard does not endorse any particular criteria for selection, such as seniority (last in first out). The employer can choose the relevant criteria, preferably following consultation with any recognised union, provided those criteria are transparent and verifiable. Those criteria are likely to include a mixture of rewarding long service and good conduct, on the one hand, and on the other ensuring that the employer has the requisite mix of skills and experience to help the business prosper in the future.

This requirement of objectivity establishes a measure of judicial scrutiny of fairness in the context of selection for redundancy. Provided the employer declares what standards it is using, however, it is hard to challenge the content of those standards unless they really represent a concealed test based upon personal preferences of managers or amount to indirect discrimination against a protected group. Furthermore, it is difficult to question the application of those standards to particular cases, because the employer is not usually required to justify the detailed application of the selection criteria. In *British Aerospace plc* v. *Green and Others*,[42] the employers needed to reduce the workforce of 7,000 at one plant by 530 employees. The employers divided the workforce into twenty-one categories, determined how many workers in each category needed to be dismissed, and then carried out an individual assessment of the capabilities and experience of each of the 7,000 employees. Those employees who were awarded the lowest number of points under this system of assessment were chosen for dismissal. About 235 of the employees contested the fairness of the dismissals. The employer disclosed the points assessment forms of each employee who claimed unfair dismissal, but refused to disclose the forms of all employees or all employees in the relevant group of the twenty-one categories of workers. A number of sample or test cases were brought before the tribunal for rulings on procedural issues. The industrial tribunal ordered the employer to disclose the forms of retained employees, but the Court of Appeal allowed the employer's appeal against that procedural ruling. Disclosure of the assessments of retained employees would be ordered only where they became necessary in order to deal with a specific issue that had been raised, such as the allegation that the employer had unfairly applied the criteria of assessment to a particular employee. The policy behind this decision was said to be the protection of respect for this process of points assessment and the avoidance of protracted tribunal hearings.

[42] [1995] ICR 1006 (CA).

In the *British Aerospace* case itself, it seems that the employer had done exactly what the law requires and that the employees were trying to fish for evidence of mistakes or misapplication of the points-assessment system. It seems clear that the employer must disclose to dismissed employees what points they were awarded, if only to permit them to respond and question why they were awarded fewer points during the consultation process[43] or some other kind of appeal process.[44] But the case left open the crucial question of when, if at all, a dismissed employee can obtain information about the points awarded to other retained employees. What sort of evidence does the claimant for unfair dismissal have to produce in order to obtain disclosure of assessments of retained employees? Does the claimant have to be able to point to some apparent bias in the application of the assessment criteria, or is it sufficient merely to argue that such a possibility exists (which, presumably, it always does)? However, the whole tenor of the decision of the Court of Appeal in the *British Aerospace* case is a warning to tribunals not to investigate the fairness of dismissals in connection with selection for redundancy, if the employer has apparently adopted a satisfactory objective system of selection. In short, employers can probably avoid the risk of challenges to the fairness of selection for redundancy by the precaution of incurring the expense of conducting an elaborate procedure of assessment.

Redeployment

Within larger businesses, the need to make redundancies may be limited to one aspect of the business, or one organisational division or one company in a group of companies. In such cases, the employer may be able to offer alternative employment to a dismissed worker. It appears to be in the interests of both employer and employee to consider redeployment in every case, and the chance of avoiding the social cost of an economic dismissal must also render redeployment an attractive possibility for governments. The law provides some incentives for employers to redeploy workers, but does not clearly impose a legal duty to do so. We need to consider separately the legal position both where the employer does offer another job, that is, redeployment, and where the employer fails to consider this possibility.

Offer of Alternative Employment

An employer can avoid liability to make a redundancy payment if the employer offers the dismissed worker another job, either on the same or on suitable alternative terms, and the employee unreasonably refuses the offer.[45]

[43] *Alexander* v. *Brigden Enterprises Ltd* [2006] ICR 1277 (EAT); *Pinewood Repro Ltd* v. *Page* [2011] ICR 508 (EAT).
[44] *John Brown Engineering Ltd* v. *Brown* [1997] IRLR 90 (EAT).   [45] ERA 1996, s. 141.

This job offer can be made by the employer or an 'associated employer' such as another company in the group.[46] The requirement that a different job must be a suitable job has been interpreted to mean that the job should be substantially equivalent in terms of status, wages and types of duties.[47] It is more difficult to determine when it is unreasonable for the employee to reject the job offer. It was held to be reasonable for the employee to reject the offer of re-engagement when the offer was made only on the day before his dismissal took effect and he had, during the six weeks' notice period, entered into a contract for a new job.[48] The EAT also suggested in that case that it was reasonable for the employee to take into account the risk that the new job might not last very long. It also seems likely that it would be reasonable for an employee to reject a job that turned out in practice to be unsuitable with regard to its status and duties.

If the employee takes up an offer of re-engagement, the employee enjoys a statutory four-week 'trial period' in the new job. The period may be extended by agreement for the purpose of training. During the trial period, the employee can opt to terminate the contract and still claim that a dismissal for redundancy has occurred.[49] The right to a redundancy payment is lost, however, if a tribunal decides that the employee acted unreasonably in terminating the new contract.[50] Again, it seems likely that the employee will have to demonstrate that the new job was unsuitable in certain respects in order to convince a tribunal that it was reasonable to terminate the contract.

In some cases, it has been suggested that, in addition to the statutory trial period, under the common law of contract there is also a trial period which may be longer than the statutory period.[51] Although the legal basis for this common law period is unclear, the suggestion seems to be that, if an employer unilaterally alters the terms of a contract of employment, which in effect the employer does by offering another job, the employee is entitled to a period of time to decide whether or not to accept the employer's repudiatory breach, thereby ending the contract by constructive dismissal, and that during that period the employee can continue to work under the new job under protest. Another possible explanation of the legal position is that the old contract has not yet been terminated by dismissal, but the employee consents to work at other duties temporarily. It is certainly correct, however, that the parties themselves can agree explicitly an arrangement of this kind with a longer trial period than the statutory four-week period, so that the contract continues on a temporary basis that allows the employee to try the new job. But the parties must agree to such an arrangement or at least reach some kind of contractual understanding that is different from the statutory four-week trial

---

[46] ERA 1996, s. 146.   [47] *Taylor* v. *Kent County Council* [1969] 2 QB 560 (QB).
[48] *Thomas Wragg & Sons Ltd* v. *Wood* [1976] ICR 313 (EAT).   [49] ERA 1996, s. 138.
[50] ERA 1996, s. 141(4).
[51] *Turvey* v. *C. W. Cheney & Son Ltd* [1979] ICR 341 (EAT); *Air Canada* v. *Lee* [1978] ICR 1202 (EAT).

period.[52] It remains puzzling, however, that in these cases the tribunals still permit a claim for a redundancy payment, for if the employee has been working at a new job still required by the employer, there is no redundancy situation because there is no dismissal. These decisions regarding extended trial periods may be explained as deliberate and sensible attempts to circumvent both the short time limit of the statutory trial period and also the risk of the employee losing the entitlement to a redundancy payment because the tribunal may regard the employee's decision to leave during the trial period as unreasonable.

Failure to Consider Redeployment

There is no express statutory duty placed upon employers to search for alternative employment for a redundant employee within the organisation or to offer dismissed workers any alternative employment that might be available. But failure to do so might provide an employee with grounds to challenge the fairness of selection for redundancy. This is the fifth principle stated by Browne-Wilkinson J in *Williams* v. *Compair Maxam Ltd* (above). It was also endorsed by Lord Bridge in *Polkey* v. *A. E. Dayton Services Ltd*,[53] who indicated that one aspect of fairness in making dismissals for redundancy was that the employer should take 'such steps as may be reasonable to avoid or minimise redundancy by redeployment within his own organisation'. It has become a standard interpretation of the requirement of fairness in relation to redundancy dismissals that, as well as consideration of the issues of consultation and unfair selection, a tribunal should also consider whether the dismissal was unfair due to a failure by the employer to seek alternative employment for the employee.[54]

A complementary legal duty that would assist redeployment in large organisations might be a requirement placed upon employers to notify the workforce of vacancies and opportunities for retraining. This duty is already envisaged for employees under fixed-term contracts. Under the Fixed-Term Employees (Prevention of Less Favourable Treatment) Regulations 2002, regulation 3(2) requires the employer not to treat a fixed-term employee less favourably than the employer treats a comparable permanent employee with respect to the opportunity to receive training and to secure a permanent position. Furthermore, regulation 3(6) provides that the fixed-term employee has the right to be informed by his employer of available vacancies in the establishment. Although no such general legal duty to notify the workforce of vacancies applies to all employees, in practice larger employers do circulate such notices in order to assist compliance with the principle of equality of opportunity.

---

[52] *Optical Express Ltd* v. *Williams* [2008] ICR 1 (EAT).   [53] [1988] ICR 142 (HL).
[54] *Thomas & Betts Manufacturing Ltd* v. *Harding* [1980] IRLR 255 (CA); *Langston* v. *Cranfield University* [1998] IRLR 172 (EAT).

Insolvency

When a business can no longer pay its debts, the investors in and lenders to a company can initiate proceedings leading to the liquidation of the company and a distribution of its assets among creditors. A similar procedure of distribution of assets applies to an individual's bankruptcy. Because not all creditors can be paid out of the limited funds available, a crucial issue is which creditors can obtain priority over the others in the division of the assets. Employees occupy a special ranking order among creditors during insolvency proceedings in respect of the protection of the payment of their outstanding wages. Employees also benefit uniquely from guarantees of wage payments that are provided by the social security system. These principles conform to the ILO Convention 173, Protection of Workers' Claims (Employer's Insolvency) 1992. A contentious issue in this area of the law is whether employees are awarded too little or too much priority as between different groups of creditors.[55]

As well as simply liquidating the assets of an insolvent company into cash in order to pay creditors, in recent years legal structures for insolvency proceedings have emphasised the possibility of keeping the business going, in order to reduce losses and perhaps even to avoid losses to creditors altogether. If such a 'corporate rescue' can be mounted, employees may both keep their jobs and receive any outstanding pay. The Enterprise Act 2002 introduced substantial reforms to the law of corporate insolvency with a view to increasing the opportunities for corporate rescue.[56] To some extent, the interests of creditors in maximising the value of the pool of assets to be divided, the interests of workers in retaining their jobs and the interests of government in minimising the social costs of changes in business coincide in the promotion of corporate rescues. But some conflicts of interest persist, and the issue becomes how the decision to mount a rescue should be reached.

Although this topic lies on the fringes of the interests of labour lawyers, in periods of recession it can have great practical importance. The topic also poses some profound theoretical questions central to the concerns of labour law. In order to justify a strengthening of employees' rights on insolvency, proponents often switch their terminology from that of the employee as 'unsecured creditor' who, owing to lack of bargaining power, needs assistance in achieving a fair distributive outcome, to that of employee as 'stakeholder'. The implicit suggestion of the 'stakeholder' rhetoric is that, by virtue of their contribution to the assets of the company, employees should be entitled to a share in those assets. Their position is implicitly contrasted with that of other unsecured creditors, such as contractors with the company, who have a claim

---

[55] C. Villiers, 'Employees as Creditors: A Challenge for Justice in Insolvency Law' (1999) 20 *Company Lawyer* 222.

[56] V. Finch, 'Re-invigorating Corporate Rescue' [2003] *Journal of Business Law* 527.

for compensation for contractual debts, but not a type of proprietary claim or special claim for priority in the consideration granted to their interests:

> [T]he company's stakeholders are not simply the 'affected parties', but those whose cooperation is required for innovation and productivity within the firm – those whose relations to the enterprise cannot be completely contracted for, but upon whose cooperation and creativity it depends for its survival and prosperity.[57]
>
> [T]he employees' proprietary interest arises when they contribute firm-specific human capital. Firm-specific human capital ... refers to the time, skill and knowledge invested by employees in the firm.[58]

The language of stakeholding has many other applications in issues of corporate governance, but in the area of insolvency it enjoys a particular cutting edge, because it may influence views on the appropriate division of the company's assets between the different creditors.

Protection of Wages

The protection of employees with respect to unpaid wages is achieved by two mechanisms. Employees are treated under general insolvency law as 'preferential creditors', so that some claims for wages have to be met before other creditors are paid. In addition, the state provides a limited guarantee of wages, so that, if the employer's assets cannot meet the wage bill, the social security system will pay workers some compensation.

Preferential Creditors

As a claim for 'preferential debt', an employee's claim for outstanding wages obtains a particular position in the priorities between creditors, as revised by the Enterprise Act 2002. Although preferential creditors rank behind secured creditors with fixed charges over the assets of the company and the expenses of the liquidator of the company, their claims rank ahead of other creditors such as holders of floating charges, unsecured creditors, the tax authorities and shareholders. The list of preferential claims has been extended in the Insolvency Act 1986, Schedule 6, to include, as well as wages, many other items such as unpaid contributions to occupational pension schemes, accrued holiday pay, guarantee pay, payments for time-off for trade union duties and protective award payments. The claim for wages as a preferential debt is limited to a period of four months with an upper limit of the total that can

---

[57] S. Deakin and G. Slinger, 'Company Law: An Instrument for Inclusion: Regulating Stakeholder Relations in Takeover Situations', in P. Askonas and A. Stewart (eds.), *Social Inclusion: Possibilities and Tensions* (London: Macmillan, 2000).

[58] W. Njoya, 'Employee Ownership and Efficiency: An Evolutionary Perspective' (2004) 33 *Industrial Law Journal* 211, at 229.

be claimed of £800.[59] One explanation of this meagre upper limit is that it prevents highly paid managers, who may have been responsible for the collapse of the business, from obtaining priority over other creditors for their inflated wages and bonuses.

Social Security Guarantee

Unlike other creditors, an employee (but not a 'worker' or some other category of personal work contract) also has recourse to the social security system to claim certain payments that have not been met by an insolvent employer. One set of regulations permits employees to recover any redundancy payments owed by the insolvent company.[60] A slightly different set of rules permits employees to recover a wide range of payments due to them from their insolvent employer.[61] These payments include up to eight weeks' wages, holiday pay and statutory guarantee pay, but not occupational pension contributions. A special regime applies to occupational pensions, which are protected against insolvency by a different guarantee mechanism enacted by the Pensions Act 2004. It is also possible for employees to recover some payments due on dismissal including compensation for lost wages during the notice period, the basic award for unfair dismissal and the protective award for failure to consult with representatives of the workforce. An important exclusion from this list is the compensatory award for unfair dismissal, which usually represents the largest component of awards of compensation for dismissal.

Employees may bring a claim for these guaranteed payments against the Secretary of State before an ET. For such a claim to arise, the employer must either have been adjudged bankrupt, or, if the employer is a company, there must have been a winding-up order, the appointment of a receiver, an administration order or a voluntary arrangement under Part 1 of the Insolvency Act 1986.[62] There is an upper limit placed on recovery of payments referable to a period of a week of £489. If the Secretary of State makes any payments to employees, the right to claim compensation against the insolvent employer is subrogated to the Secretary of State. On this ground, the Secretary of State may effectively pursue the employee's claims for a redundancy payment and other preferential debts in the insolvency proceedings against the assets of the employer.

This legislation mostly preceded, but is required in part by, the European Directive on the protection of employees in the event of the insolvency of the employer.[63] Although the Directive is narrower in scope than the UK legislation in some respects, employees can rely on the Directive as a guide to the

---

[59] Insolvency Proceedings (Monetary Limits) Order 1986, Art. 4, SI 1986 No. 1996.
[60] ERA 1996, ss. 166–70.   [61] ERA 1996, ss. 182–90.   [62] ERA 1996, ss. 166 and 183.
[63] Directive 2008/94, on the protection of employees in the event of the insolvency of their employer, consolidating earlier Directives; M. Sargeant, 'Protecting Employees with Insolvent Employers' (2003) 32 *Industrial Law Journal* 53.

legal interpretation of national legislation. The ECJ has stressed the importance of the general principle of guaranteeing wages, and that derogations
permitted by the Directive must be construed narrowly.[64] This principle of
giving the principle of guarantee great weight and interpreting exceptions
narrowly was accepted, for instance, in *Mann* v. *Secretary of State for Employment*.[65] In that case, it was observed that employees should be able to choose
the particular eight weeks in respect of which they were claiming arrears of pay
against the guarantee institution, thus choosing eight weeks in which they had
not been paid at all instead of the last eight weeks when they might have
received some payments. Article 4(3) of the Directive permits national governments to set ceilings on the payments made by the guarantee institutions,
but also states that: 'These ceilings must not fall below a level which is socially
compatible with the social objective of this Directive.' The question posed for
UK law is whether the ceiling of £489 per week for claims for outstanding
wages satisfies the test of being 'socially compatible with the social objective' of
the Directive.

The above patchwork of provisions represents an uneasy and perhaps not
entirely coherent compromise of principles about the claims of employees in
the event of insolvency. One principle suggests that employees, as both the
group most likely to be seriously harmed by the employer's liquidation
(because the risk of insolvency cannot be diversified) and the group least able
to protect itself through proprietary security rights, should be awarded the
highest priority (or 'super-priority') in the distribution of assets. A competing
principle suggests that employees should be treated in the same way as other
unsecured creditors on the ground that the only fair way to spread the loss
between employees and small business creditors is absolutely equally (*pari
passu*, as insolvency lawyers say). A third principle holds that the state should
provide a guarantee of wages and other sums due to employees out of general
taxation as a type of social insurance, thereby removing employees from the
contest in insolvency. The current insolvency rules satisfy none of those
principles in their entirety. Employees are given a degree of priority, but not
absolute priority, and at the same time the state guarantees some, but not all,
payments due and benefits owed to the workforce by the insolvent employer.

Corporate Rescue

The possibility of a corporate rescue is generally regarded favourably by the
workforce. Employees have a chance of keeping their jobs, at least for the time
being. Nevertheless a successful rescue may entail some adverse consequences
such as wage cuts and a reduction of the workforce. It is usually hard, however,

[64] Case C-125/97, *Regeling* v. *Bestur van de Bedrijfsvereniging voor de Metaalnijverheid* [1999]
IRLR 379 (ECJ).
[65] [1999] IRLR 566 (HL).

for the workforce to calculate where its best interests lie, because it is rarely given access to the relevant information about the company's prospects. For similar reasons, the policy of reducing social costs usually points towards the exploration of the possibility of corporate rescue. But other creditors, especially secured creditors, may share little sympathy with these objectives. They may want to retrieve their money as soon as possible, rather than wait for what might prove a better dividend at some uncertain future date. To promote corporate rescues requires subtle regulation that produces the intended advantage to the workforce and society as a whole without harming the interests of creditors so much that they might become reluctant to assume that risk.

The Enterprise Act 2002 tries to promote corporate rescues by preventing banks in most cases from simply appointing a receiver to seize assets to the value of the floating charge they hold over the assets of the company, and instead requiring all creditors (other than holders of fixed charges) to follow an administration procedure under the supervision of a court. By an appointment by the floating charge holder or a court on the request of creditors of a company, an administrator takes over the management of the business of an insolvent company. The administrator is instructed to perform his functions with the following objectives in order of priority of:

(a) rescuing the company or as much of its business as possible as a going concern, if reasonably practicable, or
(b) achieving a better result for the company's creditors as a whole than would be likely if the company were wound up, or
(c) realising property to make a distribution to secured or preferential creditors.[66]

While the insolvent company is in administration, which can last for a year, there is a moratorium so that none of the creditors can pursue its claims in the courts, though the administrator has the power to make interim payments to secured and preferred creditors. During this period of a year, the administrator may discover ways in which to preserve the viability of all or part of the company in business as a going concern. These routes to corporate rescue may, however, affect adversely a large part of the workforce by including detrimental variations of terms of employment, plant closures, workforce reductions and sales of parts of the business.

The first step to assist a corporate rescue is to induce the retained workforce to continue to work. Employees will be reluctant to help, however, unless they receive a better assurance that they will receive their wages than a promise from an insolvent company. The crucial question therefore becomes: who is their employer or, more crudely, who will pay their wages and any compensation for any subsequent dismissal? Under an administration order, the

---

[66] Insolvency Act 1986, Sched. B1, para. 3, as amended by the Enterprise Act 2002.

Insolvency Act 1986[67] ranks any claims against the assets of the company by giving first priority to any claims based upon contracts entered into by the administrator and claims under contracts of employment 'adopted' by the administrator for wages and salary. The administrator is given a period of fourteen days during which to decide whether to 'adopt' contracts of employment with the existing workforce. Having reviewed the prospects for the company for two weeks, an administrator who decides to mount a rescue or at least keep part of the business going with a view to a sale will rehire the relevant employees, acting as agent for the company. Employees have the assurance that their claims for payment, once their contracts have been adopted, will have priority over all other creditors, including the administrator, except others with whom the administrator contracts for the purpose of the rescue. The extent to which employees enjoy this 'super-priority' over other creditors, including the administrator, applies to wages, contributions to occupational pension schemes, holiday pay and sick pay.[68] Employees are therefore given a strong inducement to carry on working for the insolvent company in administration, for their wages are fairly assured by their super-priority. But this super-priority does not apply to claims for compensation for dismissal[69] or for protective awards,[70] for which retained employees are in no better and no worse position than they were before the administrator took control; they are ranked as unsecured creditors of the company, but have the entitlement to the social security guarantee for wages during the notice period and a redundancy payment (or basic award for unfair dismissal). The legislature and the courts are anxious not to impose substantial indeterminate liabilities upon administrators towards employees lest they might decide not to attempt a corporate rescue.[71]

The reforms in insolvency law introduced by the Enterprise Act 2002 may help to encourage corporate rescues, but they do not significantly improve the position of employees compared to the former rules governing receiverships. The government has not taken powers to force a corporate rescue to be attempted, and nor has it extended the social security guarantee to cover all wages, including those above the ceiling, falling due during the rescue attempt. But the assurance of first priority of wages once the administrator has adopted the contracts of employment should generally suffice to induce the workforce to assist with the corporate rescue. At the second stage of the rescue, however, it is likely that the administrator will try to sell all or part of the business as a going concern in order to realise its assets for creditors. At this point, the

---

[67] *Ibid.*, para. 99(5) (as amended).   [68] *Ibid.*, para. 99(6).
[69] *Re Allders Department Stores Ltd* [2005] 2 All ER 122.
[70] *Re Huddersfield Fine Worsteds Ltd* [2005] BCC 915 (CA).
[71] V. Finch, *Corporate Insolvency Law: Perspectives and Principles* (2nd edn, Cambridge University Press, 2009), p. 759.

employees may face a fresh round of dismissals and variations in their terms of employment in connection with the transfer of the undertaking.

Transfers of Undertakings

A change in ownership of a business often creates a period of uncertainty for employees. The new owners may wish to reorganise the business, vary terms of employment, close down some parts and make economic dismissals. We have already noted that the sale may take place in the context of insolvency, forming part of a corporate rescue or the realisation of assets by a liquidator, administrator or a receiver. As part of the process of capital flight to economies with low wages, some sales may be organised by a parent company between a UK subsidiary and another foreign subsidiary. This section is concerned with special protections provided for employees on sales of the business in addition to the other rules concerning workforce reductions and variations of contract. It also concerns reorganisations in the public sector where parts of government administration are transferred either to another public employer entity or into the private sector through privatisation.

Under the common law, the legal position of employees depends on the method by which the sale of a business is achieved. If the sale of the business is achieved by the sale of shares in a company, the employer in the form of a company retains the same identity, so that all the contracts of employment and other legal obligations of the employer and employee remain the same. If the sale of the business is achieved by any other transaction, however, the ownership of the business is transferred to a new legal entity or person. The content of the transaction may include the sale of physical assets such as premises and machinery and the assignment of a lease and other rights. Often the most valuable element is the 'goodwill', which refers to the reputation of the business and its existing customer base. On general legal principles of the law of contract, the new owner or employer is not bound by the legal and contractual obligations of the previous owner of the business except insofar as it expressly agrees to assume those obligations by entering new contracts (novation). The new owner of the business may decide to employ all or part of the existing workforce, being attracted towards their skills, training and experience, but under the common law these contracts would be new contracts of employment.

Acquired Rights Directive

The Acquired Rights Directive[72] applies two principles to a sale of a business that are designed to ensure that the legal position of employees in the event of

---

[72] Directive 2001/23; formerly Directive 77/187.

a sale of a business duplicates the legal position when the transfer is effected by a sale of shares in the company. The principal objective of the Directive is to ensure that employees are not adversely affected in any way by the fact that the sale of the business or administrative reorganisation in the public sector involves a change in the identity of the employer of the employees concerned:

- The first principle is that on the sale of a business or transfer of an administrative unit the workforce is automatically transferred to the new owner on their existing terms of employment.[73] Subject to the consent of the employee, there is an automatic novation of the contract of employment, placing the employee in the position as if the contract had been originally made by the transferee employer. This principle also extends to any applicable collective agreement and the rights of a recognised trade union.
- The second principle of the Directive is that, if either the seller or the purchaser of the business dismisses any of the workforce in order to avoid the application of the first principle, those dismissals should be ineffective to achieve that result.[74]

In addition, both employers (the transferor and the transferee) are placed under a legal obligation to consult the workforce about the proposed transfer,[75] and there is potential liability in tort for negligent misstatements issued by employers that use inaccurate statements to persuade the workforce to support the transfer of the business.[76] The Directive is implemented by the Transfer of Undertakings (Protection of Employment) Regulations 2006,[77] usually known as TUPE. The questions of the precise meaning and application of these principles in the Directive, and whether TUPE implements the Directive properly, have been the subject of considerable controversy and litigation.

The main source of this controversy is not hard to find. The value of a business put up for sale must depend on its existing debts and potential future revenues. To maximise the value of the business, the seller (or transferor) should protect the purchaser (or transferee) against debts arising from labour costs such as outstanding claims for pay and compensation for dismissal, and should hand over to the purchaser the business as a going concern with only those employees that the transferee needs. By protecting the financial claims of all employees and their job security, the Directive and TUPE place considerable obstacles in the way of this business approach to sales of a business. Many employers have sought loopholes in TUPE, usually without ultimate success.

TUPE also has a potential application to measures of privatisation by public authorities, such as the transfer of public services to a private-sector company

---

[73] Art. 3.   [74] Art. 4.   [75] See Chapter 15.
[76] *Hagen* v. *ICI Chemicals and Polymers Ltd* [2002] IRLR 31 (QB).
[77] SI 2006 No. 246, replacing the Transfer of Undertakings (Protection of Employment) Regulations 1981 (SI 1981 No. 1794).

or the outsourcing of some public sector operations to private contractors. TUPE applies broadly to a transfer of an 'undertaking' or 'part of an undertaking'.[78] The concept of an 'undertaking' is defined in TUPE, following decisions of the ECJ, as an economic entity that consists of an organised grouping of resources which has the objective of pursuing an economic activity, whether or not that activity is central or ancillary. A transfer of an undertaking within the meaning of TUPE occurs whenever there is a transfer of an economic entity that retains its identity, except of course for the fact that the employer is a different person or legal entity. This definition could apply, for instance, to the outsourcing to a private contractor of cleaning for an NHS hospital or a local authority school. In this context, TUPE may reduce the savings to be obtained from using the private sector and in other ways restrict the ability of private sector employers to introduce efficiencies in the delivery of the service. Public-sector employees may be able to use TUPE to resist disadvantageous changes to their terms of employment proposed by their new private sector employer. Our examination of this topic focuses on some of the standard problems that arise in connection with TUPE.

Dismissals before the Sale or Transfer

In order to improve the value of the business to be sold, a transferor may decide to reduce the size of the workforce or even to make the whole workforce redundant. Prior to TUPE, such dismissals would have left the purchaser free to decide which employees to rehire, leaving the cost of compensating employees for their dismissals to be met by the transferor. If the transferor was insolvent, those costs might well be met in part by the state. TUPE changes the legal position, so that it becomes doubtful whether there is any advantage to the transferor to dismiss employees before a sale.

Transfer of Undertakings (Protection of Employment) Regulations 2006, Regulation 7

(1) Where either before or after a relevant transfer, any employee of the transferor or transferee is dismissed, that employee shall be treated for the purposes of Part X of the 1996 Act (unfair dismissal) as unfairly dismissed if the sole or principal reason for his dismissal is the transfer.

(2) This paragraph applies where the sole or principal reason for the dismissal is an economic technical or organizational reason entailing changes in the workforce of either the transferor or the transferee.

---

[78] Reg. 3(1).

This wording of regulation 7 derives from an amendment in 2014.[79] The revised wording narrowed the scope of the protection afforded by regulation 7(1) by limiting it to cases where the transfer was the sole or principal reason for the dismissal, whereas previously the regulation also applied when the dismissal was for a reason 'connected with the transfer'. Many cases decided before this amendment would now be regarded differently: although the dismissals might have been connected in some way to the transfer or the expectation of a transfer, their immediate purpose might have been different, such as an immediate saving on wage costs for financial reasons. Regulation 7 has four major effects.

First, prior to the Regulations, a dismissal connected with the sale would probably have been regarded as a dismissal for redundancy, for the business would no longer have a requirement for any employees. Regulation 7(1) creates a presumption that an employee may obtain the higher level of compensation for unfair dismissal that includes the compensatory award under ERA 1996, section 123, where the reason for the dismissal was the transfer of the business to a new proprietor. It remains possible, of course, that dismissals prior to a sale of the business were not in fact for the purpose of the transfer, but were rather the result of some independent process of making savings through redundancies or disciplinary dismissals, in which case regulation 7(1) does not apply. The right to bring the statutory claim for unfair dismissal is subject to the normal conditions for claims for unfair dismissal; in particular, the qualifying period of two years of continuous employment applies.

Secondly, regulation 7(1) declares that, if the reason for the dismissal is the transfer, the dismissal is automatically unfair. Dismissals that occur shortly before a sale of a business will almost certainly fall within the category of dismissals for a reason connected to a transfer. Since TUPE is largely derived from the EU Acquired Rights Directive, national courts must ensure that their interpretation conforms to the purpose and principles of the Directive and also conforms to interpretations placed on the Directive by the ECJ. For instance, if the dismissals of the workforce take place well before the sale of the business is completed, a court or tribunal must nevertheless try to assess whether the underlying reason for the dismissals was to effect the transfer, in which case TUPE regulation 7(1) applies, because, in accordance with the Directive, those dismissals should never have occurred since they violated the principle of the automatic transfer of contracts of employment on a transfer of an undertaking.[80]

---

[79] Collective Redundancies and Transfer of Undertakings (Protection of Employment) (Amendment) Regulations 2014, SI 2014 No. 16.

[80] *Litster* v. *Forth Dry Dock & Engineering Co. Ltd* [1989] ICR 341 (HL), following Case C-101/87, *P. Bork International A/S* v. *Foreningen af Arbejdsledere I Danmark* [1989] IRLR 41 (ECJ).

The third effect is that where regulation 7(2) applies because the employer can establish there was an 'economic, technical or organisational reason' (ETOR) for the dismissal, and that the reason for the dismissal was not the transfer itself, the automatic unfairness of the dismissal is replaced by a finding that the dismissal was for redundancy or perhaps for a substantial reason. If so, the employee should normally receive instead a redundancy payment rather than full compensation for unfair dismissal. The dismissal for redundancy or a substantial reason may still be found to be unfair, but only in accordance with the provisions for unfair procedures or unfair selection described earlier in this chapter.[81] The general aim of regulation 7(2) is to ensure that an employee is not in a better position than would have been the case in the absence of a transfer. It follows that, if the reason for dismissal either before or after the transfer was that the employee was redundant, the dismissal should be compensated by a redundancy payment rather than a finding of an automatically unfair dismissal. The principal reason for the dismissal might be categorised as an ETOR if the transferor dismisses employees because it cannot afford their wages any longer,[82] or if the transferor seeks to reduce its workforce in the face of declining demand for its product, or if it seeks to reduce costs by concentrating production in one location and dismissing employees at other locations.

Fourthly, and this effect of regulation 7(1) is perhaps the most important, any dismissal by the seller for the purpose of the transfer is deemed also to have been a dismissal by the purchaser of the business. Thus employees can claim their compensation for unfair dismissal against the purchaser or transferee, even though they may have been dismissed prior to the sale. This effect of making the transferee liable for claims for unfair dismissal results from the automatic transfer of contracts of employment, together with all outstanding rights and liabilities, from the seller to the transferee. Regulation 4(2)(a) specifies, in relation to contracts of employment in existence 'immediately before' the transfer,[83] that, on the completion of the relevant transfer of the business or undertaking, 'all the transferor's rights, powers, duties and liabilities under or in connection with any such contract shall be transferred by virtue of this regulation to the transferee'. The effect of regulation 4 is that the transferee acquires all the outstanding obligations of the transferor with respect to the employees of the transferor, including contractual obligations (except occupational pensions under regulation 10),[84] liabilities to preferential creditors, compensation due for unfair dismissal and any other form of liability (except criminal liability) such as tort claims for personal injuries

---

[81] P. 932.   [82] *Kavanagh v. Crystal Palace FC Ltd* [2013] EWCA Civ 1410, [2014 ICR 251.

[83] TUPE, reg. 4(3).

[84] B. Hepple and K. Mumgaard, 'Pension Rights in Business Transfers' (1998) 27 *Industrial Law Journal* 309. Early-retirement benefits paid in the event of dismissal prior to the normal pensionable age are automatically transferred: Case C-4/01, *Martin v. South Bank University* [2004] IRLR 74 (ECJ).

arising in connection with the contract of employment. This measure there-fore greatly reduces the incentive to follow the old practice regarding what lawyers call 'acquisitions' of requiring the seller to dismiss all the workforce prior to the sale of the business in order to minimise the transfer of existing liabilities. On the contrary, the purchaser of the business may best be advised to retain the workforce and, at a later date, implement a reorganisation involving a workforce reduction. Such a reorganisation might be seen as not related to the transfer but rather as dismissals for an ETOR.

If the dismissals carried out by a transferor prior to a transfer of an undertaking are classified as dismissals for an ETOR, does the liability to pay compensation for those dismissals (usually redundancy payments) also transfer to the transferee? This is a more difficult question: if the transferor has dismissed employees genuinely for an ETOR reason prior to the transfer, the dismissals should be effective to terminate the contracts of employment. In *Wilson v. St Helens Borough Council*,[85] the House of Lords held that dismissals before a transfer were effective in law to terminate the contracts of employ-ment, though if they were automatically unfair dismissals (under regulation 7(1)), it might be possible for the dismissed employees to seek the remedy of reinstatement or re-engagement against the transferee.[86] Therefore, employees dismissed prior to a transfer for an ETOR would probably not have been employed 'immediately before' the transfer, and so the liability to pay the redundancy payment might remain solely with the transferor.

Dismissals before the sale of a business will often be carried out by an administrator in control over a company that has become insolvent. The administrator may be seeking to make the business attractive for a purchaser by reducing current wage costs or separating the profitable parts of the business from the remainder that will be closed. There is a risk that if all the existing liabilities of the transferor pass to the transferee on the completion of the sale, the purchase price may be reduced to the detriment of creditors of the transferor. In effect, if the transferee might be faced with payment of all outstanding liabilities towards the workforce, the employees would indirectly gain super-priority over other creditors of the insolvent company by having all their claims met in full by the solvent purchaser. To prevent this possible discouragement of purchases and corporate rescues, the Directive was amended, and regulation 8 of TUPE 2006 now provides that, in the case of a corporate rescue of a company undergoing insolvency proceedings,[87] the transferee will not be liable to the employees (or the Secretary of State) for compensation for the amounts owed by the transferor that are guaranteed by

---

[85]   *Wilson v. St Helens Borough Council* [1992] 2 AC 52 (HL).

[86]   E.g. *Hazel v. The Manchester College* [2014] EWCA Civ 72, [2014] ICR 989.

[87]   The date of the institution of proceedings depends on the type of proceeding, but in any event there must be the formal appointment of an insolvency practitioner to manage the company: *Secretary of State for Trade and Industry v. Slater* [2008] ICR 54 (EAT).

the social security fund. Employees must claim those amounts, which include redundancy payments, from the insolvent transferor or the Secretary of State. For payments and compensation owed by the insolvent transferor that do not fall within the guarantee provisions, however, employees will be permitted to claim their compensation from the transferee. For example, an employee who is dismissed by the insolvent company immediately before a transfer may claim a basic award or redundancy payment from the transferor or the Secretary of State but, if the dismissal is an unfair dismissal, as will be the case if it is for the purpose of the transfer or there has been an unfair procedure or unfair grounds for selection for redundancy, the compensatory award for unfair dismissal may still be claimed against the solvent transferee. Similarly, outstanding wages of employees who are transferred as part of the corporate rescue can be claimed against the transferor and the social security system, but only up to the limits fixed by legislation. For sums owing above those limits, the employees can still claim the excess from the transferee.

The likely effect of this regulation on corporate rescues is uncertain, because there is no clear evidence as to whether in the past the automatic transfer of the costs of dismissal has impeded corporate rescues. The transfer of such costs may not discourage rescues, but merely reduce the sum available to the secured creditor on insolvency by reducing the price of the sale. The reduced price for the sale of a going concern may still have been superior to the alternative sum realised by a simple asset sale. Yet where the potential costs are indeterminate, as will be the case with respect to compensatory awards for unfair dismissal, the possibility of greater-than-expected liabilities probably has a chilling effect on rescues. Regulation 8 permits the transferee to avoid many of the debts owed to employees, leaving the social security system to pick up the bill, thereby increasing the value of the business on sale to the potential advantage of secured creditors. Since that option is only available in the case of corporate rescues of insolvent companies, or more precisely is unavailable under regulation 8(6) when there is a mere liquidation of the assets of the transferor,[88] it may encourage creditors and administrators to view corporate rescues comparatively favourably. But the transferee still may encounter unforeseen substantial costs in the form of wages owed and compensatory awards for unfair dismissal, which may discourage corporate rescues. In an attempt to counter that problem of indeterminate liability for unfair dismissal, regulations 11 and 12 require the transferor to notify the transferee of outstanding liabilities towards employees. Failure to provide this information may result in the award of compensation payable to the transferee by the transferor in an amount that is 'just and equitable' though with a normal minimum amount of not less than £500 per employee in respect of

---

[88] In the case of liquidation of all the assets of a company, reg. 8(7) prevents the automatic transfer of employment or claims for dismissal, although it seems unlikely in such a case that there would be a transfer of an undertaking at all.

whom the transferor has failed to comply with the duty to provide information about liabilities. The availability of such a remedy against the transferor to counter unexpected liabilities may not be especially reassuring to the transferee in the case of corporate rescues where the transferor that is incurring this liability is insolvent.

Dismissals after the Transfer

If the purchaser of the business takes on all or most of the transferor's employees, but then decides to reduce the size of the workforce in order to achieve efficiencies, TUPE regulation 7 will also apply. TUPE also applies to existing employees of the transferee who may be selected for dismissal as part of the restructuring.[89] Under the amended wording of regulation 7(1), however, most restructuring in this context will avoid claims for automatic unfair dismissals. Previously, a dismissal after the transfer only had to be connected with the transfer to trigger regulation 7(1), so a link might be made between dismissals and the transfer for many months after the deal had gone through. The purchaser had to wait a significant period of time before reducing the numbers of employees or changing their terms and conditions. Under the current wording, however, it seems unlikely that the transfer itself, rather than an ETOR, will be regarded as the reason for the restructuring. This broad scope of the ETOR defence can be justified because it places dismissed employees in the same position as if there had been no transfer at all. These dismissed employees may therefore bring a claim for a redundancy payment or, if their situation falls outside the concept of redundancy, a claim for unfair dismissal in which the employer is likely to advance 'some other substantial reason' as the ground for dismissal.[90] The normal requirements with respect to the employer following a fair procedure and using fair criteria for selection for dismissal will also apply. Insofar as the financial entitlements of dismissed workers depend on their length of continuous service, the period should be calculated by combining service with the transferor and the transferee.[91]

Variation of Terms by Transferee

A frequent problem encountered in the application of TUPE concerns the case where the new owner of the business proposes to vary the terms of the contracts of employment of the employees formerly employed by the transferor. Such variations may be unwelcome to employees, who may seek either to insist upon their previous terms or to resign and claim compensation for constructive unfair dismissal.[92] In principle such variations should be

---

[89] Reg. 7(4).   [90] Reg. 7(3).

[91] Case C-336/15, *Unionen* v. *Almega Tjänsteförbunden*, EU C:2017:276 [2017] ICR 909.

[92] Proposed variations that are to the 'material detriment' of a transferred employee are deemed to amount to a constructive dismissal: reg. 4(9).

ineffective due to the automatic novation of contracts of employment established by regulation 4. If an employee is transferred to the new owner, regulation 4 deems the employment relation to be the same as if the new owner had been the original employer. If the employer attempts to alter the contract of employment in any respect, therefore, this must be regarded as an attempt to vary the contract unilaterally, which in principle should have no legal effect without the consent of the employee. But if the employee consents to a new contract, is the variation effective?

The normal restrictions on contracting out of statutory rights to claim unfair dismissal and redundancy payments apply in this context.[93] Furthermore, regulation 4(4) provides that any purported variation of the contract of employment shall be void if the principal reason for the variation is the transfer or a reason connected with the transfer that is not an ETOR. However, regulation 4(5) provides that an agreed variation of the contract of employment will be valid if the reason for the variation counts as an ETOR or the reason is unconnected with the transfer. This provision may enable the transferee employer to propose changes in terms and conditions to the transferred workforce. In many instances, the transferee will be seeking to harmonise the terms of the employment of the new staff with the existing employees of the workforce. This purpose may fall within the scope of an ETOR because it may be regarded as an organisational reason. Faced with the proposed variation, the workforce may either accept it or reject it and try to resist a unilateral imposition of the variation.[94] It is unclear, however, that the ETOR exception applies where there are merely variations of contracts and no dismissals, because then the variations may not satisfy the further requirement that the ETOR entails 'changes in the workforce'.[95] The phrase 'changes in the workforce' seems to require changes in the numbers of employees, alterations in their duties, requirements for new skills, or (as a result of change in the regulations) a change in the location of the workplace.[96] It does not seem to include a simple wage cut. Alternatively, the transferee employer may opt to wait for a period of time until the proposed variation will no longer be perceived to be connected to the transfer at all. An earlier version of these rules was applied in *Wilson* v. *St Helens Borough Council*[97] to a reorganisation of a school system during which teachers at a school were dismissed for redundancy by their old employer, the county council, but immediately afterwards most were offered employment on different terms by the new school authority, the borough council. The teachers subsequently complained that their wages were lower in their new jobs and sought to recover the shortfall in pay as an

---

[93] Reg. 18.   [94] See Chapter 5.   [95] *Berriman* v. *Delabole Slate Ltd* [1985] ICR 546 (CA).

[96] TUPE 2006, reg. 7(3A); *RR Donnelley Global Document Solutions Group Ltd* v. *Besagni* [2014] ICR 1008 (EAT).

[97] [1998] ICR 1141 (HL).

unauthorised deduction. The House of Lords upheld the tribunal's decision that the transfer had not been the reason for the variation, so the new terms that had been agreed were legally binding. It was possible also that the variations fell within the ETOR exception, as the employer needed to reduce labour costs at the school through both reductions in the number of staff and pay cuts. Alternatively, as the tribunal had held, the variations were not connected to the transfer at all because, even if the transfer had not taken place, similar economies would have been necessary. This decision, though strictly speaking *obiter* in that case, supports a broad reading of the circumstances when the transferee employer can seek to introduce agreed variations of the terms of contracts of employment.

If an employee refuses to accept the variation and is dismissed or resigns in protest, it remains possible that the dismissal or constructive dismissal will be regarded as automatically unfair as a dismissal for the purpose of the transfer. In the past, such constructive dismissals arising from refusals to accept variations in terms could be classified as automatically unfair dismissals because they were connected to the transfer and there was no ETOR because the employer did not require a diminution in the size of the workforce.[98] Now it seems unlikely that the variation will be regarded as motivated by the transfer, as required by regulation 7(1), so there should be no possibility of a claim for automatic unfair dismissal. It is more likely that the constructive dismissal will be classified as one for a substantial reason and that it will be regarded as fair if the tribunal accepts that it was reasonable for the employer to insist upon the variation of the terms of the contract.

In order to facilitate sales of a business in the context of a corporate rescue, regulation 9 creates an alternative permitted route to the variation of contracts of employment following a transfer from an insolvent employer. The transferee can make a collective agreement with a recognised trade union or a workforce agreement with elected representatives of the workforce that introduces variations in the contracts of employment. These variations will be binding on the transferred employees provided that they are designed to safeguard employment opportunities by ensuring the survival of the transferred undertaking.

The prohibition on variation of the terms of contracts of employment in connection with the transfer of an undertaking also applies to a term that incorporates provisions set by a collective agreement.[99] The collectively negotiated terms should normally apply until the expiration of the collective agreement, but the Directive permits TUPE to set a maximum limit of one year.[100] If the terms of the contract of employment are fixed by reference to a collective agreement prior to the transfer, those terms will survive even though

---

[98] *Berriman* v. *Delabole Slate Ltd* [1985] ICR 546 (CA); *Hazel* v. *The Manchester College* [2014] EWCA Civ 72, [2014] ICR 989.
[99] Directive 2001/23, Art. 3(3).   [100] TUPE, reg. 4(5B).

the collective agreement has been abandoned or rescinded following the transfer, for once those terms have been applied to the individual contract of employment they are binding until the parties agree a variation.[101] Since the Directive permits Member States to improve on its minimum standards,[102] it was argued that national law could prohibit the variation of a suitably drafted term of the contract of employment incorporating the relevant collective agreement indefinitely. In *Alemo-Herron* v. *Parkwood Leisure Ltd*,[103] the running of a leisure centre was transferred from a public authority to a private business. A term of the contracts of employment of the staff provided that their terms and conditions would be set periodically in accordance with the public sector collective agreements. Following the transfer to the private business, the employer declared that a subsequent public sector collective agreement, to which it could not be a party, was not binding on it and so refused to grant the collectively negotiated pay increase. On a reference to the CJEU, the Court decided that the Directive should be interpreted in a way that complied with Article 16 of the Charter of the Fundamental Rights of the EU, which provides for the fundamental freedom to conduct a business. Interpreting that 'fundamental right' to include 'freedom of contract', the ECJ concluded that the transferee must be able to protect its interests in negotiating its contracts of employment, which was not possible if the public sector collective agreement continued to be binding after the transfer. The practical effect of this case is that terms of the contract that incorporate changing collectively agreed terms indefinitely will not be binding following a transfer, unless the transferee employer is a party to the collective agreement. The most striking feature of this decision is the way in which the fundamental right to freedom of contract that is said to be part of the Charter freedom to conduct a business is used to rewrite the Directive in a way that, instead of protecting the interests of employees, it becomes an instrument for depriving them of the benefit of an apparently applicable collective agreement.[104]

Outsourcing

One of the most contested questions regarding TUPE has been whether or not any 'transfer of an undertaking' has taken place at all. It is sometimes thought that the Directive and TUPE apply only where the purchaser takes over the business in every aspect, including its plant, machinery, goodwill and at least part of its workforce. But this view is misconceived. The Directive applies

---

[101] Case C-328/13, *Osterreichischer Gewerkschaftsbund* v. *Wirtschaftskammer Osterreich-Fachverband Autobus-, Luftfahrt und Schifffahrtsunternehmungen* [2001] ICR 1152.
[102] Directive 2001/23, Art. 8.
[103] Case C-426/11, *Alemo Herron* v. *Parkwood Leisure Ltd* [2013] ICR 1116.
[104] J. Prassl, 'Freedom of Contract as a General Principle of EU Law? Transfer of Undertakings and the Protection of Employer Rights in EU Labour Law' (2013) 42 *Industrial Law Journal* 434.

broadly to most sales. For instance, in *Kerry Foods Ltd* v. *Creber*,[105] TUPE was applied to a sale merely of goodwill, stock and existing contracts, without any transfer of premises, plant, machinery or the continuation of the workforce. The breadth of the factors to be considered has been stressed by the ECJ in *Spijkers* v. *Gebroeders Benedik Abattoir CV*.[106] In that case, the ECJ said that the question whether or not there has been a transfer turns mainly on:

> whether, having regard to all the facts characterising the transaction, the business was disposed of as a going concern, as would be indicated *inter alia* by the fact that its operation was actually continuing or resumed by the new employer, with the same or similar activities. In order to determine whether these conditions are met, it is necessary to consider all the facts characterising the transaction in question, including the type of undertaking or business, whether or not the business's tangible assets, such as buildings and moveable property, are transferred, the value of its intangible assets at the time of the transfer, whether or not the majority of its employees are taken over by the new employer, whether or not its customers are transferred and the degree of similarity between the activities carried on before and after the transfer and the period, if any, for which those activities were suspended.[107]

The most contentious applications of the concept of 'transfer of undertaking' have involved outsourcing. An employer may decide to contract out the work of part of its business to another employer. Cleaning and catering services are often provided by external contractors, but the technique of outsourcing can be applied to any type of work. The use of external contractors may reduce costs for a number of reasons, including the better management skills of the contractor, economies of scale for the contractor and the lower wage costs of the contractor. These savings in wages occur typically because the contractor is not governed by the rules of the core employer's internal labour market or relevant collective agreements. Since the 1980s, the UK government has promoted the use of outsourcing in the public sector, especially in the services provided by local authorities and the health service. Most of the savings from outsourcing can be achieved only if the employees accept new terms and conditions of employment. In many instances of outsourcing, the same workers continue at their jobs, although on adverse terms of employment such as longer hours and lower rates of pay. A crucial question for the management strategy of outsourcing and the government policy of contracting out public services to private contractors was whether the Acquired Rights Directive applied to outsourcing. If the Directive applied, the new employer would have to pay the same rates of pay and continue any collective bargaining arrangements or face claims for unfair dismissal. During the 1980s, the UK government denied that the Directive had any application to contracting out

---

[105] [2000] IRLR 10 (EAT).
[106] Case 24/85 *Spijkers* v. *Gebroeders Benedik Abattoir CV* [1986] ECR 1119 (ECJ).   [107] *Ibid.*

public services but eventually, as a result of a series of decisions of the ECJ, it had to be conceded that outsourcing might be covered in some instances by the Directive.[108] As a result of the application of TUPE to outsourcing, it becomes a much less attractive managerial strategy, for, if the employees are entitled to keep their jobs, their wages and their recognised trade union, the transferee has little room to make savings on costs and provide a significantly cheaper service.

The central legal question under the Directive in relation to outsourcing is whether there has been a transfer of an undertaking or part of one. The ECJ declared that the answer to this question depended upon whether the 'entity' retained its 'identity' after the transfer. The task for a tribunal, which is now set out in the Directive,[109] is, first, to identify an 'entity', which is defined as an organised grouping of persons and of tangible and intangible assets that facilitates the performance of an economic activity or particular business purpose. Having found such an entity, the question is whether the entity has survived the transfer by retaining its identity, excepting of course the fact that ownership and the identity of the employer has changed. The meaning of these phrases has been explained in numerous decisions of the ECJ, including *Süzen* v. *Zehnacker Gebäudereinigung GmbH Krankenhausservice*.[110] The defendant employer had a contract to clean a private school. When the school terminated that contract and gave the work to another contractor, the defendant dismissed the cleaners, including the claimant. The German labour court made a reference to the ECJ to ask the question whether there could be a transfer of an undertaking even though there had been no sale of tangible or intangible assets. The ECJ held that the correct question was whether the entity, that is, an organised grouping of persons and assets pursuing an economic objective, had retained its identity. The mere fact that the new contractor provided the same service was insufficient. On the other hand, in labour-intensive industries such as cleaning, it is not necessary for a transfer to involve the sale of tangible or intangible assets such as 'goodwill'; it is sufficient if the new employer carries out the same activity by taking over a structured group of employees that supply similar manpower in terms of their numbers and skills to those that formerly worked on that activity.[111] It was therefore possible to apply the Directive to such an instance of successive contractors, provided that there was a business entity, such as an organised group of workers, which remained much the same after the business was taken over by the new contractor. This decision made it clear that, where the business amounted to little more than a group of workers who provided a service, there might be a

---

[108] A. Kerr and M. Radford, 'Acquiring Rights – Losing Power: A Case Study in Ministerial Resistance to the Impact of European Community Law' (1997) 60 *Modern Law Review* 55.
[109] Directive 2001/23, Art. 1(1)(b).   [110] Case C-13/95, [1997] ICR 662 (ECJ).
[111] Case C-108/10, *Scattolon v. Ministero dell'Istuzione, dell'Universita e della Ricerca* [2012] ICR 740.

transfer even though no physical assets or goodwill was transferred to the new contractor. On the other hand, where the business did involve the use of tangible assets, such as the buses to run a public transport service, the mere transfer of the workers, in this case the drivers, without the buses and other tangible assets, would not be a transfer of an undertaking.[112]

Further guidance in *Süzen* and subsequent cases[113] suggests that, in labour-intensive industries without substantial tangible assets, the absence of transfer of the workforce almost certainly will exclude a finding of a transfer of an undertaking, even if the contract for services won by the employer was exactly the same. British employers sometimes tried to avoid the application of TUPE by declining to take on any of the existing workforce at all. If the employees are not retained, what is left in a labour-intensive business service to give the entity its continuing identity? Of course, such an interpretation creates an opportunity for employers to avoid TUPE and thereby to increase social costs by causing economic dismissals. The Court of Appeal has insisted, however, that *Süzen* does not mean that the absence of the transfer of any of the workforce necessarily excludes the possibility of a transfer of an undertaking, because under *Spijkers* it remains important to consider all the circumstances of the case. In a series of decisions concerning putative transfers from one contractor to another, the Court of Appeal has found that the tribunal did not err in concluding that there was a transfer of an undertaking even though the new contractor did not take on any of the existing workforce at all.[114] These results are striking, for in effect the court discovers a transfer of an undertaking, even though no equipment and no staff were taken over by the transferee. Nor was it clear that such decisions were consistent with the principles stated by the ECJ, because, in the absence of a transfer of staff or assets, it was hard to see what the business entity was that had retained its identity.

To avoid this legal difficulty and to ensure the protection of the job security of employees during the transfer from one contractor to another, TUPE now goes further than is required by the Directive. TUPE applies not only to a transfer of undertaking, as defined by EU law, but also to a 'service provision change'.[115] Such a service provision change may occur in the original outsourcing by the core business or client to a contractor, between a succession of contractors, and when the core business or client takes back the work in-house. A relevant service provision change occurs when there is an organised grouping of employees, which has as its principal purpose the carrying out of the activities concerned on behalf of the client, and the client intends that

---

[112] Case C-172/99, *Oy Liikenne AB* v. *Liskojarvie and Juntunen* [2001] IRLR 171 (ECJ).

[113] Eg Case C200/16, *Securitas-Serviços e Tecnologia de Seguranca SA* v. *ICTS Portugual-Consultadoria de Aviação Comercial SA* EU:C2017:780, [2018] ICR 525.

[114] *ECM (Vehicle Delivery Service) Ltd* v. *Cox* [1999] ICR 1162 (CA); *ADI (UK) Ltd* v. *Willer* [2001] IRLR 542 (CA); *RCO Support Services Ltd* v. *Unison* [2002] EWCA Civ 464; [2002] ICR 751 (CA).

[115] TUPE 2006, reg. 3(1).

the activities will, following the service provision change, be carried out by the transferee contractor, other than in connection with a single specific event or task of short-term duration; and the activities concerned do not consist wholly or mainly of the procurement or supply of goods for the client's use. This definition of the scope of TUPE in its application to outsourcing focuses on the question whether the activities of the contractor (performed by an organised grouping of employees) are 'fundamentally the same' as those activities performed by the subsequent contractor.[116] TUPE does not require the transfer of any employees for a transfer of a service contract to qualify as a service provision change. It also follows that, where the activity is divided between two or more subsequent contractors, there will be a qualifying service provision change, with the allocation of employees to the new contractor that is performing that part of the activity in which those employees were involved.[117] A service provision change requires the continuity of the same client for whom the service has been provided,[118] a condition that is not satisfied where a client company goes into administration because the administrators represent a new client.[119] It is insufficient to establish that a service was supplied to a client by the transferor, for it is necessary to identify an organised grouping of employees or organisational unit who performed the service for that client, who would then be transferred by the service provision change as a unit.[120] Nevertheless, it is possible that the organised grouping providing the service to a client might consist of a solitary employee.[121]

Controlling Capital

A fundamental problem addressed by the legal regulation considered in this chapter and earlier chapters has been the extent to which significant changes in businesses should be controlled.[122] In the past, the common law recognised the right of management to direct the workforce, to determine the size of the workforce, and to act in any way which management believed would best serve the interests of shareholders. The sole constraint on this power lay in the contracts of workers, which placed few limits on managerial discretion, and could in any case usually be terminated on short notice. The common law thus accorded priority to the policy of leaving management alone in the hope and belief that in the long run market incentives would maximise the aggregate wealth of society. Modern regulation qualifies to some extent that traditional

---

[116] YUPE 2006b, reg. 3(2)(A).
[117] *Kimberley Group Housing Ltd* v. *Hambley* [2008] ICR 1031 (EAT).
[118] *Hunter* v. *McCarrick* [2012] EWCA Civ 1399, [2013] ICR 235.
[119] *SNR Denton UK LLP* v. *Kirwan* [2013] ICR 101.
[120] *Eddie Stobart Ltd* v. *Moreman* [2012] ICR 919 (EAT).
[121] *Ryanda (UK) ltd* v. *Rhijnsburger* [2015] EWCA Civ 75, [2015] ICR 1300.
[122] S. Leader, 'Three Faces of Justice and the Management of Change' (2000) 63 *Modern Law Review* 55.

policy. But how far does the law control employers' decisions with respect to restructuring and for what purposes?

With respect to constraints on how management might direct the workforce to perform new jobs and adapt to new technologies and working methods, any control exercised by legal regulation has surely proved slight.[123] The advent of protection against dismissal, especially the possibility of claiming constructive unfair dismissal for the employer's unilateral variation of terms of the contract of employment, suggested a measure of control over how far employers might impose new working conditions. But in the end, these restrictions appear largely illusory. The employer can remove the legal controls by insisting upon flexibility clauses in contracts of employment and by reserving a broad managerial discretion. If the employer is entitled under the contract to direct the workforce to perform different jobs, there is no breach of contract or constructive dismissal. To put the seal on the preservation of the employer's power to vary jobs, the courts have concluded that an employee's refusal to accept new terms and conditions of employment could amount to justification for a fair dismissal for 'some other substantial reason'. In effect, any control over managerial discretion to vary working methods depends more or less, as it always did, on the bargaining power of the employee, not on any legal protection.

Nor was the redundancy payments legislation any more forceful in restricting the power of employers to carry out economic dismissals. Indeed, it must be doubted whether control fell within the original purpose of the legislation, which was surely intended to legitimate and subsidise workforce reductions for reasons of efficiency rather than to question the employer's decision.[124] At no time have employers been required to justify the need to make redundancies or to demonstrate that economic dismissals were a proportionate response to the need for the business to reduce labour costs. Such a demand might have been warranted by the legitimate concern of governments to minimise the social costs associated with plant closures and mass unemployment. But in the UK, legislation never attempted to provide a legal mechanism for that purpose. Regulation was limited to insisting that a fair procedure was followed at the individual level, and even then the so-called *Polkey* deduction normally avoids any sanctions where economic dismissals were inevitable.

In contrast, EU law has developed some tentative regulation that places some controls over managerial decisions. The requirement for consultation with the workforce before mass economic dismissals and sales of the business entwines two justifications for regulation. In part, consultation is designed to minimise social costs by encouraging the parties to find ways to avoid economic dismissals. At the same time, this regulation also signals acceptance of a requirement for worker participation in major decisions that affect

---

[123] See Chapter 5 above.
[124] R. H. Fryer, 'The Myths of the Redundancy Payments Act' (1973) 2 *Industrial Law Journal* 1.

employment security. These foreign ideas about procedures for reaching such decisions with the workforce as 'stakeholders' fit uneasily with the traditional autonomy granted to employers in making business decisions in the UK.

The deepest shock to the traditional respect paid by UK law to employers' decisions arrived with the Acquired Rights Directive and its progeny TUPE. Governments, employers and insolvency practitioners simply could not believe that legislation could attempt both to prevent employers from carrying out dismissals in order to effect a sale and to prevent the purchaser from reorganising the business as it wished. They were astounded that, for the sake of protecting the contractual expectations of the workforce, legal controls might prevent employers from achieving the maximum value from the sales of businesses, prevent acquirers from introducing efficient reorganisations involving alterations in the terms of employment and might block the use of outsourcing of parts of the business in order to take advantage of lower labour costs in the secondary labour market. Initially, the courts shared this disbelief, but before long, they accorded respect to the decisions of the ECJ which laid bare the purposes of the Directive. The strange result of TUPE is that, having been designed to equalise the position of workers whose business was sold compared to those whose companies were taken over by a share acquisition, the TUPE rules now protect the former group with the most intense regulation over employers' decisions with respect to changes in the business, and leave the latter group at the mercy of the new owners of the shares. Even more unexpected is the outcome that, while the Directive was intended to harmonise the national laws by improving the protections afforded to employees to the minimum levels set in Germany and France, in the UK in some respects, such as outsourcing, the protections contained in TUPE now far exceed those granted in other Member States.[125]

Although the pressures arising from global capital movements may discourage or render ineffectual legal interventions to control employers' decisions with respect to changes in the business, it is surely possible to justify some regulation even if only on the narrow grounds of promoting allocative efficiency or the reduction of social cost. Severance payments, if modest, can legitimise workforce reductions, encourage employers to check that reductions will improve the efficient use of capital and help to reduce social cost by compelling the employer to internalise some of the social costs of economic support for the workforce. The requirement to consult with the workforce may produce better proposals for the efficient use of capital that also serve to enhance employment security. These justifications fit into the policy of promoting the efficient use of capital. In addition, it is important to remember that economic analysis of the effects of regulation indicates that predictions about the inefficient use of capital caused by restrictions have been exaggerated.

---

[125] P. L. Davies, 'Preliminary Remarks', in S. Sciarra (ed.), *Labour Law in the Courts* (Oxford: Hart, 2001), pp. 131–44.

One can also argue, however, that some controls over employers' decisions ought to be imposed for the sake of broader notions of social justice, not just allocative efficiency. The participation of the workforce in such decisions can embody respect for the principle that the ideal of democracy should not only be confined to the public sphere but should also apply to other powerful private institutions in society. The cushioning of dismissed workers against the vicissitudes of the circulation of capital can be justified as part of a strategy to establish economic security, as opposed to job security, for all citizens. Active manpower policies that assist displaced workers to find jobs can also form part of a strategy to tackle social exclusion. One of the fundamental purposes of labour law has always been to help to establish social cohesion in the face of the disintegrative tendencies of market economies. Business restructuring presents labour law with a fundamental challenge to social cohesion or social solidarity, because as well as the loss of jobs it can involve the destruction of local communities and ways of life. The law in the UK has so far been relatively timid in tackling this form of challenge to social cohesion in comparison to our European neighbours. The result of this abstention may have been a competitive advantage in attracting inward capital investment, but the price may have been a subtle process of disintegration of social solidarity and civility.

Index